Legends of t...

אגדות היהודים

by Louis Ginzberg

Legends of the Jews

Volume 1

Chapter 1

THE FIRST THINGS CREATED

In the beginning, two thousand years before the heaven and the earth, seven things were created: the Torah written with black fire on white fire, and lying in the lap of God; the Divine Throne, erected in the heaven which later was over the heads of the Hayyot; Paradise on the right side of God, Hell on the left side; the Celestial Sanctuary directly in front of God, having a jewel on its altar graven with the Name of the Messiah, and a Voice that cries aloud, "Return, ye children of men."

When God resolved upon the creation of the world, He took counsel with the Torah. Her advice was this: "O Lord, a king without an army and without courtiers and attendants hardly deserves the name of king, for none is nigh to express the homage due to him." The answer pleased God exceedingly. Thus did He teach all earthly kings, by His Divine example, to undertake naught without first consulting advisers.

The advice of the Torah was given with some reservations. She was skeptical about the value of an earthly world, on account of the sinfulness of men, who would be sure to disregard her precepts. But God dispelled her doubts. He told her, that repentance had been created long before, and sinners would have the opportunity of mending their ways. Besides, the Temple service would be invested with atoning power, and Paradise and hell were intended to do duty as reward and punishment. Finally, the Messiah was appointed to bring salvation, which would put an end to all sinfulness.

Nor is this world inhabited by man the first of things earthly created by God. He made several worlds before ours, but He destroyed them all, because He was pleased with none until He created ours. But even this last world would have had no permanence, if God had executed His original plan of ruling it according to the principle of strict justice. It was only when He saw that justice by itself would undermine the world that He associated mercy with justice, and made them to rule jointly. Thus, from the beginning of all things prevailed Divine goodness, without which nothing could have continued to exist. If not for it, the myriads of evil spirits had soon put an end to the generations of men. But the goodness of God has ordained, that in every Nisan, at the time of the spring equinox, the seraphim shall approach the world of spirits, and intimidate them so that they fear to do harm to men. Again, if God in His goodness had not given protection to the weak, the tame animals would have been extirpated long ago by the wild animals. In Tammuz, at the time of the summer solstice, when the strength of behemot is at its height, he roars so loud that all the animals hear it, and for a whole year they are affrighted and timid, and their acts become less ferocious than their nature is. Again, in Tishri, at the time of the autumnal equinox, the great bird ziz flaps his wings and utters his cry, so that the birds of prey, the eagles and the vultures, blench, and they fear to swoop down upon the others and annihilate them in their greed. And, again, were it not for the goodness of God, the vast number of big fish had quickly put an end to the little ones. But at the time of the winter solstice, in the month of Tebet, the sea grows restless, for then leviathan spouts up water, and the big fish become uneasy. They restrain their appetite, and the little ones escape their rapacity.

Finally, the goodness of God manifests itself in the preservation of His people Israel. It could not have survived the enmity of the Gentiles, if God had not appointed protectors for it, the archangels Michael and Gabriel. Whenever Israel disobeys God, and is accused of misdemeanors by the angels of the other nations, he is defended by his designated guardians, with such good result that the other angels conceive fear of them. Once the angels of the other nations are terrified, the nations themselves venture not to carry out their wicked designs against Israel.

That the goodness of God may rule on earth as in heaven, the Angels of Destruction are assigned a place at the far end of the heavens, from which they may never stir, while the Angels of Mercy encircle the Throne of God, at His behest.

THE ALPHABET

When God was about to create the world by His word, the twenty-two letters of the alphabet descended from the terrible and august crown of God whereon they were engraved with a pen of flaming fire. They stood round about God, and one after the other spake and entreated, "Create the world through me! The first to step forward was the letter Taw. It said: "O Lord of the world! May it be Thy will to create Thy world through me, seeing that it is through me that Thou wilt give the Torah to Israel by the hand of Moses, as it is written, 'Moses commanded us the Torah.' " The Holy One, blessed be He, made reply, and said, "No!" Taw asked, "Why not?" and God answered: "Because in days to come I shall place thee as a sign of death upon the foreheads of men." As soon as Taw heard these words issue from the mouth of the Holy One, blessed be He, it retired from His presence disappointed.

The Shin then stepped forward, and pleaded: "O Lord of the world, create Thy world through me: seeing that Thine own name Shaddai begins with me." Unfortunately, it is also the first letter of Shaw, lie, and of Sheker, falsehood, and that incapacitated it. Resh had no better luck. It was pointed out that it was the initial letter of Ra', wicked, and Rasha' evil, and after that the distinction it enjoys of being the first letter in the Name of God, Rahum, the Merciful, counted for naught. The Kof was rejected, because Kelalah, curse, outweighs the advantage of being the first in Kadosh, the Holy One. In vain did Zadde call attention to Zaddik, the Righteous One; there was Zarot, the misfortunes of Israel, to testify against it. Pe had Podeh, redeemer, to its credit, but Pesha: transgression, reflected dishonor upon it. 'Ain was declared unfit, because, though it begins 'Anawah, humility, it performs the same service for 'Erwah, immorality. Samek said: "O Lord, may it be Thy will to begin the creation with me, for Thou art called Samek, after me, the Upholder of all that fall." But God said: "Thou art needed in the place in which thou art; thou must continue to uphold all that fall." Nun introduces Ner, "the lamp of the Lord," which is "the spirit of men," but it also introduces Ner, "the lamp of the wicked," which will be put out by God. Mem starts Melek, king, one of the titles of God. As it is the first letter of Mehumah, confusion, as well, it had no chance of accomplishing its desire. The claim of Lamed bore its refutation within itself. It advanced the argument that it was the first letter of Luhot, the celestial tables for the Ten Commandments; it forgot that the tables were shivered in pieces by Moses. Kaf was sure of victory Kisseh, the throne of God, Kabod, His honor, and Keter, His crown, all begin with it. God had to remind it that He would smite together His hands, Kaf, in despair over the misfortunes of Israel. Yod at first sight seemed the appropriate letter for the beginning of creation, on account of its association with Yah, God, if only Yezer ha-Ra' the evil inclination, had not happened to begin with it, too. Tet is identified with Tob, the good. However, the truly good is not in this world; it belongs to the world to come. Het is the first letter of Hanun, the Gracious One; but this advantage is offset by its place in the word for sin, Hattat. Zain suggests Zakor, remembrance, but it is itself the word for weapon, the doer of mischief. Waw and He compose the Ineffable Name of God; they are therefore too exalted to be pressed into the service of the mundane world. If Dalet Wad stood only for Dabar, the Divine Word, it would have been used, but it stands also for Din, justice, and under the rule of law without love the world would have fallen to ruin. Finally, in spite of reminding one of Gadol, great, Gimel would not do, because Gemul, retribution, starts with it.

After the claims of all these letters had been disposed of, Bet stepped before the Holy One, blessed be He, and pleaded before Him: "O Lord of the world! May it be Thy will to create Thy world through me, seeing that all the dwellers in the world give praise daily unto Thee through me, as it is said, 'Blessed be the Lord forever. Amen, and Amen.' " The Holy One, blessed be He, at once granted the petition of Bet. He said, "Blessed be he that cometh in the name of the Lord." And He created His world through Bet, as it is said, "Bereshit God created the heaven and the earth." The only letter that had refrained from urging its claims was the modest Alef, and God rewarded it later for its humility by giving it the first place in the Decalogue.

THE FIRST DAY

On the first day of creation God produced ten things: the heavens and the earth, Tohu and Bohu, light and darkness, wind and water, the duration of the day and the duration of the night.

Though the heavens and the earth consist of entirely different elements, they were yet created as a unit, "like the pot and its cover." The heavens were fashioned from the light of God's garment, and the earth from the snow under the Divine Throne. Tohu is a green band which encompasses the whole world, and dispenses darkness, and Bohu consists of stones in the abyss, the producers of the waters. The light created at the very beginning is not the same as the light emitted by the sun, the moon, and the stars, which appeared only on the fourth day. The light of the first day was of a sort that would have enabled man to see the world at a glance from one end to the other. Anticipating the wickedness of the sinful generations of the deluge and the Tower of Babel, who were unworthy to enjoy the blessing of such light, God concealed it, but in the world to come it will appear to the pious in all its pristine glory.

Several heavens were created, seven in fact, each to serve a purpose of its own. The first, the one visible to man, has no function except that of covering up the light during the night time; therefore it disappears every morning. The planets are fastened to the second of the heavens; in the third the manna is made for the pious in the hereafter; the fourth contains the celestial Jerusalem together with the Temple, in which Michael ministers as high priest, and offers the souls of the pious as sacrifices. In the fifth heaven, the angel hosts reside, and sing the praise of God, though only during the night, for by day it is the task of Israel on earth to give glory to God on high. The sixth heaven is an uncanny spot; there originate most of the trials and visitations ordained for the earth and its inhabitants. Snow lies heaped up there and hail; there are lofts full of noxious dew, magazines stocked with storms, and cellars holding reserves of smoke. Doors of fire separate these celestial chambers, which are under the supervision of the archangel Metatron. Their pernicious contents defiled the heavens until David's time. The pious king prayed God to purge His exalted dwelling of whatever was pregnant with evil; it was not becoming that such things should exist near the Merciful One. Only then they were removed to the earth.

The seventh heaven, on the other hand, contains naught but what is good and beautiful: right, justice, and mercy, the storehouses of life, peace, and blessing, the souls of the pious, the souls and spirits of unborn generations, the dew with which God will revive the dead on the resurrection day, and, above all, the Divine Throne, surrounded by the seraphim, the ofanim, the holy Hayyot, and the ministering angels.

Corresponding to the seven heavens, God created seven earths, each separated from the next by five layers. Over the lowest earth, the seventh, called Erez, lie in succession the abyss, the Tohu, the Bohu, a sea, and waters. Then the sixth earth is reached, the Adamah, the scene of the magnificence of God. In the same way the Adamah is separated from the fifth earth, the Arka, which contains Gehenna, and Sha're Mawet, and Sha're Zalmawet, and Beer Shahat, and Tit ha-Yawen, and Abaddon, and Sheol, and there the souls of the wicked are guarded by the Angels of Destruction. In the same way Arka is followed by Harabah, the dry, the place of brooks and streams in spite of its name, as the next, called Yabbashah, the mainland, contains the rivers and the springs. Tebel, the second earth, is the first mainland inhabited by living creatures, three hundred and sixty-five species, all essentially different from those of our own earth. Some have human heads set on the body of a lion, or a serpent, or an ox; others have human bodies topped by the head of one of these animals. Besides, Tebel is inhabited by human beings with two heads and four hands and feet, in fact with all their organs doubled excepting only the trunk. It happens sometimes that the parts of these double persons quarrel with each other, especially while eating and drinking, when each claims the best and largest portions for himself. This species of mankind is distinguished for great piety, another difference between it and the inhabitants of our earth.

Our own earth is called Heled, and, like the others, it is separated from the Tebel by an abyss, the Tohu, the Bohu, a sea, and waters.

Thus one earth rises above the other, from the first to the seventh, and over the seventh earth the heavens are vaulted, from the first to the seventh, the last of them attached to the arm of God. The seven heavens form a unity, the seven kinds of earth form a unity, and the heavens and the earth together also form a unity.

When God made our present heavens and our present earth, "the new heavens and the new earth" were also brought forth, yea, and the hundred and ninety-six thousand worlds which God created unto His Own glory.

It takes five hundred years to walk from the earth to the heavens, and from one end of a heaven to the other, and also from one heaven to the next, and it takes the same length of time to travel from the east to the west, or from the south to the north. Of all this vast world only one-third is inhabited, the other two-thirds being equally divided between water and waste desert land.

Beyond the inhabited parts to the east is Paradise with its seven divisions, each assigned to the pious of a certain degree. The ocean is situated to the west, and it is dotted with islands upon islands, inhabited by many different peoples. Beyond it, in turn, are the boundless steppes full of serpents and scorpions, and destitute of every sort of vegetation, whether herbs or trees. To the north are the supplies of hell-fire, of snow, hail, smoke, ice, darkness, and windstorms, and in that vicinity sojourn all sorts of devils, demons, and malign spirits. Their dwelling-place is a great stretch of land, it would take five hundred years to traverse it. Beyond lies hell. To the south is the chamber containing reserves of fire, the cave of smoke, and the forge of blasts and hurricanes. Thus it comes that the wind blowing from the south brings heat and sultriness to the earth. Were it not for the angel Ben Nez, the Winged, who keeps the south wind back with his pinions, the world would be consumed. Besides, the fury of its blast is tempered by the north wind, which always appears as moderator, whatever other wind may be blowing.

In the east, the west, and the south, heaven and earth touch each other, but the north God left unfinished, that any man who announced himself as a god might be set the task of supplying the deficiency, and stand convicted as a pretender.

The construction of the earth was begun at the centre, with the foundation stone of the Temple, the Eben Shetiyah, for the Holy Land is at the central point of the surface of the earth, Jerusalem is at the central point of Palestine, and the Temple is situated at the centre of the Holy City. In the sanctuary itself the Hekal is the centre, and the holy Ark occupies the centre of the Hekal, built on the foundation stone, which thus is at the centre of the earth. Thence issued the first ray of light, piercing to the Holy Land, and from there illuminating the whole earth. The creation of the world, however, could not take place until God had banished the ruler of the dark. "Retire," God said to him, "for I desire to create the world by means of light." Only after the light had been fashioned, darkness arose, the light ruling in the sky, the darkness on the earth. The power of God displayed itself not only in the creation of the world of things, but equally in the limitations which He imposed upon each. The heavens and the earth stretched themselves out in length and breadth as though they aspired to infinitude, and it required the word of God to call a halt to their encroachments.

THE SECOND DAY

On the second day God brought forth four creations, the firmament, hell, fire, and the angels. The firmament is not the same as the heavens of the first day. It is the crystal stretched forth over the heads of the Hayyot, from which the heavens derive their light, as the earth derives its light from the sun. This firmament saves the earth from being engulfed by the waters of the heavens; it forms the partition between the waters above and the waters below. It was made to crystallize into the solid it is by the heavenly fire, which broke its bounds, and condensed the surface of the firmament. Thus fire made a division between the celestial and the terrestrial at the time of creation, as it did at the revelation on Mount Sinai. The firmament is not more than three fingers thick, nevertheless it divides two such heavy bodies as the waters below, which are the foundations for the nether world, and the waters above, which are the foundations for the seven heavens, the Divine Throne, and the abode of the angels.

The separation of the waters into upper and lower waters was the only act of the sort done by God in connection with the work of creation. All other acts were unifying. It therefore caused some difficulties. When God commanded, "Let the waters be gathered together, unto one place, and let the dry land appear," certain parts refused to obey. They embraced each other all the more closely. In His wrath at the waters, God determined to let the whole of creation resolve itself into chaos again. He summoned the Angel of the Face, and ordered him to destroy the world. The angel opened his eyes wide, and scorching fires and thick clouds rolled forth from them, while he cried out, "He who divides the Red Sea in sunder!"--and the rebellious waters stood. The all, however, was still in danger of destruction. Then began the singer of God's praises: "O Lord of the world, in days to come Thy creatures will sing praises without end to Thee, they will bless Thee boundlessly, and they will glorify Thee without measure. Thou wilt set Abraham apart from all mankind as Thine own; one of his sons Thou wilt call 'My first-born'; and his descendants will take the yoke of Thy kingdom upon themselves. In holiness and purity Thou wilt bestow Thy Torah upon them, with the words, 'I am the Lord your God,' whereunto they will make answer, 'All that God hath spoken we will do.' And now I beseech Thee, have pity upon Thy world, destroy it not, for if Thou destroyest it, who will fulfil Thy will?" God was pacified; He withdrew the command ordaining the destruction of the world, but the waters He put under the mountains, to remain there forever. The objection of the lower waters to division and Separation was not their only reason for rebelling. The waters had been the first to give praise to God, and when their separation into upper and lower was decreed, the waters above rejoiced, saying, "Blessed are we who are privileged to abide near our Creator and near His Holy Throne." Jubilating thus, they flew upward, and uttered song and praise to the Creator of the world. Sadness fell upon the waters below. They lamented: "Woe unto us, we have not been found worthy to dwell in the presence of God, and praise Him together with our companions." Therefore they attempted to rise upward, until God repulsed them, and pressed them under the earth. Yet they were not left unrewarded for their loyalty. Whenever the waters above desire to give praise to God, they must first seek permission from the waters below.

The second day of creation was an untoward day in more than the one respect that it introduced a breach where before there had been nothing but unity; for it was the day that saw also the creation of hell. Therefore God could not say of this day as of the others, that He "saw that it was good." A division may be necessary, but it cannot be called good, and hell surely does not deserve the attribute of good. Hell has seven divisions, one beneath the other. They are called Sheol, Abaddon, Beer Shahat, Tit ha-Yawen, Sha'are Mawet, Sha'are Zalmawet: and Gehenna. It requires three hundred years to traverse the height, or the width, or the depth of each division, and it would take six thousand three hundred years to go over a tract of land equal in extent to the seven divisions.

Each of the seven divisions in turn has seven subdivisions, and in each compartment there are seven rivers of fire and seven of hail. The width of each is one thousand ells, its depth one thousand, and its length three hundred, and they flow one from the other, and are supervised by ninety thousand Angels of Destruction. There are, besides, in every compartment seven thousand caves, in every cave there are seven thousand crevices, and in every crevice seven thousand scorpions. Every scorpion has three hundred rings, and in every ring seven thousand pouches of venom, from which flow seven rivers of deadly poison. If a man handles it, he immediately bursts, every limb is torn from his body, his bowels are cleft asunder, and he falls upon his face. There are also five different kinds of fire in hell. One devours and absorbs, another devours and does not absorb, while the third absorbs and does not devour, and there is still another fire, which neither devours nor absorbs, and furthermore a fire which devours fire. There are coals big as mountains, and coals big as hills, and coals as large as the Dead Sea, and coals like huge stones, and there are rivers of pitch and sulphur flowing and seething like live coals.

The third creation of the second day was the angel hosts, both the ministering angels and the angels of praise. The reason they had not been called into being on the first day was, lest men believe that the angels assisted God in the creation of the heavens and the earth. The angels that are fashioned from fire have forms of fire, but only so long as they remain in heaven. When they descend to earth, to do the bidding of God here below, either they are changed into wind, or they assume the guise of men. There are ten ranks or degrees among the angels.

The most exalted in rank are those surrounding the Divine Throne on all sides, to the right, to the left, in front, and behind, under the leadership of the archangels Michael, Gabriel, Uriel, and Raphael.

All the celestial beings praise God with the words, "Holy, holy, holy, is the Lord of hosts," but men take precedence of the angels herein. They may not begin their song of praise until the earthly beings have brought their homage to God. Especially Israel is preferred to the angels. When they encircle the Divine Throne in the form of fiery mountains and flaming hills, and attempt to raise their voices in adoration of the Creator, God silences them with the words, "Keep quiet until I have heard the songs, praises, prayers, and sweet melodies of Israel." Accordingly, the ministering angels and all the other celestial hosts wait until the last tones of Israel's doxologies rising aloft from earth have died away, and then they proclaim in a loud voice, "Holy, holy, holy, is the Lord of hosts." When the hour for the glorification of God by the angels draws nigh, the august Divine herald, the angel Sham'iel, steps to the windows of the lowest heaven to hearken to the songs, prayers, and praises that ascend from the synagogues and the houses of learning, and when they are finished, he announces the end to the angels in all the heavens. The ministering angels, those who come in contact with the sublunary world, now repair to their chambers to take their purification bath. They dive into a stream of fire and flame seven times, and three hundred and sixty-five times they examine themselves carefully, to make sure that no taint clings to their bodies. Only then they feel privileged to mount the fiery ladder and join the angels of the seventh heaven, and surround the throne of God with Hashmal and all the holy Hayyot. Adorned with millions of fiery crowns, arrayed in fiery garments, all the angels in unison, in the same words, and with the same melody, intone songs of praise to God.

THE THIRD DAY

Up to this time the earth was a plain, and wholly covered with water. Scarcely had the words of God, "Let the waters be gathered together," made themselves heard, when mountains appeared all over and hills, and the water collected in the deep-lying basins. But the water was recalcitrant, it resisted the order to occupy the lowly spots, and threatened to overflow the earth, until God forced it back into the sea, and encircled the sea with sand. Now, whenever the water is tempted to transgress its bounds, it beholds the sand, and recoils.

The waters did but imitate their chief Rahab, the Angel of the Sea, who rebelled at the creation of the world. God had commanded Rahab to take in the water. But he refused, saying, "I have enough." The punishment for his disobedience was death. His body rests in the depths of the sea, the water dispelling the foul odor that emanates from it.

The main creation of the third day was the realm of plants, the terrestrial plants as well as the plants of Paradise. First of all the cedars of Lebanon and the other great trees were made. In their pride at having been put first, they shot up high in the air. They considered themselves the favored among plants. Then God spake, "I hate arrogance and pride, for I alone am exalted, and none beside," and He created the iron on the same day, the substance with which trees are felled down. The trees began to weep, and when God asked the reason of their tears, they said: "We cry because Thou hast created the iron to uproot us therewith. All the while we had thought ourselves the highest of the earth, and now the iron, our destroyer, has been called into existence." God replied: "You yourselves will furnish the axe with a handle. Without your assistance the iron will not be able to do aught against you."

The command to bear seed after their kind was given to the trees alone. But the various sorts of grass reasoned, that if God had not desired divisions according to classes, He would not have instructed the trees to bear fruit after their kind with the seed thereof in it, especially as trees are inclined of their own accord to divide themselves into species. The grasses therefore reproduced themselves also after their kinds. This prompted the exclamation of the Prince of the World, "Let the glory of the Lord endure forever; let the Lord rejoice in His works."

The most important work done on the third day was the creation of Paradise. Two gates of carbuncle form the entrance to Paradise, and sixty myriads of ministering angels keep watch over them. Each of these angels shines with the lustre of the heavens. When the just man appears before the gates, the clothes in which he was buried are taken off him, and the angels array him in seven garments of clouds of glory, and place upon his head two crowns, one of precious stones and pearls, the other of gold of Parvaim, and they put eight myrtles in his hand, and they utter praises before him and say to him, "Go thy way, and eat thy bread with joy." And they lead him to a place full of rivers, surrounded by eight hundred kinds of roses and myrtles. Each one has a canopy according to his merits, and under it flow four rivers, one of milk, the other of balsam, the third of wine, and the fourth of honey. Every canopy is overgrown by a vine of gold, and thirty pearls hang from it, each of them shining like Venus. Under each canopy there is a table of precious stones and pearls, and sixty angels stand at the head of every just man, saying unto him: "Go and eat with joy of the honey, for thou hast busied thyself with the Torah, and she is sweeter than honey, and drink of the wine preserved in the grape since the six days of creation, for thou hast busied thyself with the Torah, and she is compared to wine." The least fair of the just is beautiful as Joseph and Rabbi Johanan, and as the grains of a silver pomegranate upon which fall the rays of the sun. There is no light, "for the light of the righteous is the shining light." And they undergo four transformations every day, passing through four states. In the first the righteous is changed into a child. He enters the division for children, and tastes the joys of childhood. Then he is changed into a youth, and enters the division for the youths, with whom he enjoys the delights of youth. Next he becomes an adult, in the prime of life, and he enters the division of men, and enjoys the pleasures of manhood. Finally, he is changed into an old man. He enters the division for the old, and enjoys the pleasures of age.

There are eighty myriads of trees in every corner of Paradise, the meanest among them choicer than all the spice trees. In every corner there are sixty myriads of angels singing with sweet voices, and the tree of life stands in the middle and shades the whole of Paradise. It has fifteen thousand tastes, each different from the other, and the perfumes thereof vary likewise. Over it hang seven clouds of glory, and winds blow upon it from all four sides, so that its odor is wafted from one end of the world to the other. Underneath sit the scholars and explain the Torah. Over each of them two canopies are spread, one of stars, the other of sun and moon, and a curtain of clouds of glory separates the one canopy from the other. Beyond Paradise begins Eden, containing three hundred and ten worlds and seven compartments for seven different classes of the pious. In the first are "the martyr victims of the government," like Rabbi Akiba and his colleagues; in the second those who were drowned; in the third Rabbi Johanan ben Zakkai and his disciples; in the fourth those who were carried off in the cloud of glory; in the fifth the penitents, who occupy a place which even a perfectly pious man cannot obtain; in the sixth are the youths who have not tasted of sin in their lives; in the seventh are those poor who studied Bible and Mishnah, and led a life of self-respecting decency. And God sits in the midst of them and expounds the Torah to them.

As for the seven divisions of Paradise, each of them is twelve myriads of miles in width and twelve myriads of miles in length. In the first division dwell the proselytes who embraced Judaism of their own free will, not from compulsion. The walls are of glass and the wainscoting of cedar. The prophet Obadiah, himself a proselyte, is the overseer of this first division. The second division is built of silver, and the wainscoting thereof is of cedar. Here dwell those who have repented, and Manasseh, the penitent son of Hezekiah, presides over them. The third division is built of silver and gold. Here dwell Abraham, Isaac, and Jacob, and all the Israelites who came out of Egypt, and the whole generation that lived in the desert. Also David is there, together with all his sons except Absalom, one of them, Chileab, still alive. And all the kings of Judah are there, with the exception of Manasseh, the son of Hezekiah, who presides in the second division, over the penitents. Moses and Aaron preside over the third division. Here are precious vessels of silver and gold and jewels and canopies and beds and thrones and lamps, of gold, of precious stones, and of pearls, the best of everything there is in heaven. The fourth division is built of beautiful rubies, and its wainscoting is of olive wood. Here dwell the perfect and the steadfast in faith, and their wainscoting is of olive wood, because their lives were bitter as olives to them. The fifth division is built of silver and gold and refined gold, and the finest of gold and glass and bdellium, and through the midst of it flows the river Gihon. The wainscoting is of silver and gold, and a perfume breathes through it more exquisite than the perfume of Lebanon. The coverings of the silver and gold beds are made of purple and blue, woven by Eve, and of scarlet and the hair of goats, woven by angels. Here dwells the Messiah on a palanquin made of the wood of Lebanon, "the pillars thereof of silver, the bottom of gold, the seat of it purple." With him is Elijah. He takes the head of Messiah, and places it in his bosom, and says to him, "Be quiet, for the end draweth nigh." On every Monday and Thursday and on Sabbaths and holidays, the Patriarchs come to him, and the twelve sons of Jacob, and Moses, Aaron, David, Solomon, and all the kings of Israel and of Judah, and they weep with him and comfort him, and say unto him, "Be quiet and put trust in thy Creator, for the end draweth nigh. "Also Korah and his company, and Dathan, Abiram, and Absalom come to him on every Wednesday, and ask him: "How long before the end comes full of wonders? When wilt thou bring us life again, and from the abysses of the earth lift us?" The Messiah answers them, "Go to your fathers and ask them"; and when they hear this, they are ashamed, and do not ask their fathers.

In the sixth division dwell those who died in performing a pious act, and in the seventh division those who died from illness inflicted as an expiation for the sins of Israel.

THE FOURTH DAY

The fourth day of creation produced the sun, the moon, and the stars. These heavenly spheres were not actually fashioned on this day; they were created on the first day, and merely were assigned their places in the heavens on the fourth. At first the sun and the moon enjoyed equal powers and prerogatives. The moon spoke to God, and said: "O Lord, why didst Thou create the world with the letter Bet?" God replied: "That it might be made known unto My creatures that there are two worlds." The moon: "O Lord: which of the two worlds is the larger, this world or the world to come?" God: "The world to come is the larger." The moon: "O Lord, Thou didst create two worlds, a greater and a lesser world; Thou didst create the heaven and the earth, the heaven exceeding the earth; Thou didst create fire and water, the water stronger than the fire, because it can quench the fire; and now Thou hast created the sun and the moon, and it is becoming that one of them should be greater than the other." Then spake God to the moon: "I know well, thou wouldst have me make Thee greater than the sun. As a punishment I decree that thou mayest keep but one-sixtieth of thy light." The moon made supplication: "Shall I be punished so severely for having spoken a single word?" God relented: "In the future world I will restore thy light, so that thy light may again be as the light of the sun." The moon was not yet satisfied. "O Lord," she said, "and the light of the sun, how great will it be in that day?" Then the wrath of God was once more enkindled: "What, thou still plottest against the sun? As thou livest, in the world to come his light shall be sevenfold the light he now sheds." The Sun runs his course like a bridegroom. He sits upon a throne with a garland on his head. Ninety-six angels accompany him on his daily journey, in relays of eight every hour, two to the left of him, and two to the right, two before Him, and two behind. Strong as he is, he could complete his course from south to north in a single instant, but three hundred and sixty-five angels restrain him by means of as many grappling-irons. Every day one looses his hold, and the sun must thus spend three hundred and sixty-five days on his course. The progress of the sun in his circuit is an uninterrupted song of praise to God. And this song alone makes his motion possible. Therefore, when Joshua wanted to bid the sun stand still, he had to command him to be silent. His song of praise hushed, the sun stood still.

The sun is double-faced; one face, of fire, is directed toward the earth, and one of hail, toward heaven, to cool off the prodigious heat that streams from the other face, else the earth would catch afire. In winter the sun turns his fiery face upward, and thus the cold is produced. When the sun descends in the west in the evening, he dips down into the ocean and takes a bath, his fire is extinguished, and therefore he dispenses neither light nor warmth during the night. But as soon as he reaches the east in the morning, he laves himself in a stream of flame, which imparts warmth and light to him, and these he sheds over the earth. In the same way the moon and the stars take a bath in a stream of hail before they enter upon their service for the night.

When the sun and the moon are ready to start upon their round of duties, they appear before God, and beseech him to relieve them of their task, so that they may be spared the sight of sinning mankind. Only upon compulsion they proceed with their daily course. Coming from the presence of God, they are blinded by the radiance in the heavens, and they cannot find their way. God, therefore, shoots off arrows, by the glittering light of which they are guided. It is on account of the sinfulness of man, which the sun is forced to contemplate on his rounds, that he grows weaker as the time of his going down approaches, for sins have a defiling and enfeebling effect, and he drops from the horizon as a sphere of blood, for blood is the sign of corruption. As the sun sets forth on his course in the morning, his wings touch the leaves on the trees of Paradise, and their vibration is communicated to the angels and the holy Hayyot, to the other plants, and also to the trees and plants on earth, and to all the beings on earth and in heaven. It is the signal for them all to cast their eyes upward. As soon as they see the Ineffable Name, which is engraved in the sun, they raise their voices in songs of praise to God. At the same moment a heavenly voice is heard to say, "Woe to the sons of men that consider not the honor of God like unto these creatures whose voices now rise aloft in adoration." These words, naturally, are not heard by men; as little as they perceive the grating of the sun against the wheel to which all the celestial bodies are attached, although the noise it makes is extraordinarily loud. This friction of the sun and the wheel produces the motes dancing about in the sunbeams. They are the carriers of healing to the sick, the only health-giving creations of the fourth day, on the whole an unfortunate day, especially for children, afflicting them with disease. When God punished the envious moon by diminishing her light and splendor, so that she ceased to be the equal of the sun as she had been originally, she fell, and tiny threads were loosed from her body. These are the stars.

THE FIFTH DAY

On the fifth day of creation God took fire and water, and out of these two elements He made the fishes of the sea. The animals in the water are much more numerous than those on land. For every species on land, excepting only the weasel, there is a corresponding species in the water, and, besides, there are many found only in the water.

The ruler over the sea-animals is leviathan. With all the other fishes he was made on the fifth day. Originally he was created male and female like all the other animals. But when it appeared that a pair of these monsters might annihilate the whole earth with their united strength, God killed the female. So enormous is leviathan that to quench his thirst he needs all the water that flows from the Jordan into the sea. His food consists of the fish which go between his jaws of their own accord. When he is hungry, a hot breath blows from his nostrils, and it makes the waters of the great sea seething hot. Formidable though behemot, the other monster, is, he feels insecure until he is certain that leviathan has satisfied his thirst. The only thing that can keep him in check is the stickleback, a little fish which was created for the purpose, and of which he stands in great awe. But leviathan is more than merely large and strong; he is wonderfully made besides. His fins radiate brilliant light, the very sun is obscured by it, and also his eyes shed such splendor that frequently the sea is illuminated suddenly by it. No wonder that this marvellous beast is the plaything of God, in whom He takes His pastime.

There is but one thing that makes leviathan repulsive, his foul smell: which is so strong that if it penetrated thither, it would render Paradise itself an impossible abode.

The real purpose of leviathan is to be served up as a dainty to the pious in the world to come. The female was put into brine as soon as she was killed, to be preserved against the time when her flesh will be needed. The male is destined to offer a delectable sight to all beholders before he is consumed. When his last hour arrives, God will summon the angels to enter into combat with the monster. But no sooner will leviathan cast his glance at them than they will flee in fear and dismay from the field of battle. They will return to the charge with swords, but in vain, for his scales can turn back steel like straw. They will be equally unsuccessful when they attempt to kill him by throwing darts and slinging stones; such missiles will rebound without leaving the least impression on his body. Disheartened, the angels will give up the combat, and God will command leviathan and behemot to enter into a duel with each other. The issue will be that both will drop dead, behemot slaughtered by a blow of leviathan's fins, and leviathan killed by a lash of behemot's tail. From the skin of leviathan God will construct tents to shelter companies of the pious while they enjoy the dishes made of his flesh. The amount assigned to each of the pious will be in proportion to his deserts, and none will envy or begrudge the other his better share. What is left of leviathan's skin will be stretched out over Jerusalem as a canopy, and the light streaming from it will illumine the whole world, and what is left of his flesh after the pious have appeased their appetite, will be distributed among the rest of men, to carry on traffic therewith.

On the same day with the fishes, the birds were created, for these two kinds of animals are closely related to each other. Fish are fashioned out of water, and birds out of marshy ground saturated with water.

As leviathan is the king of fishes, so the ziz is appointed to rule over the birds. His name comes from the variety of tastes his flesh has; it tastes like this, zeh, and like that, zeh. The ziz is as monstrous of size as leviathan himself. His ankles rest on the earth, and his head reaches to the very sky.

It once happened that travellers on a vessel noticed a bird. As he stood in the water, it merely covered his feet, and his head knocked against the sky. The onlookers thought the water could not have any depth at that point, and they prepared to take a bath there. A heavenly voice warned them: "Alight not here! Once a carpenter's axe slipped from his hand at this spot, and it took it seven years to touch bottom." The bird the travellers saw was none other than the ziz. His wings are so huge that unfurled they darken the sun. They protect the earth against the storms of the south; without their aid the earth would not be able to resist the winds blowing thence. Once an egg of the ziz fell to the ground and broke. The fluid from it flooded sixty cities, and the shock crushed three hundred cedars. Fortunately such accidents do not occur frequently. As a rule the bird lets her eggs slide gently into her nest. This one mishap was due to the fact that the egg was rotten, and the bird cast it away carelessly. The ziz has another name, Renanin, because he is the celestial singer. On account of his relation to the heavenly regions he is also called Sekwi, the seer, and, besides, he is called "son of the nest," because his fledgling birds break away from the shell without being hatched by the mother bird; they spring directly from the nest, as it were. Like leviathan, so ziz is a delicacy to be served to the pious at the end of time, to compensate them for the privations which abstaining from the unclean fowls imposed upon them.

THE SIXTH DAY

As the fish were formed out of water, and the birds out of boggy earth well mixed with water, so the mammals were formed out of solid earth, and as leviathan is the most notable representative of the fish kind, and ziz of the bird kind, so behemot is the most notable representative of the mammal kind. Behemot matches leviathan in strength, and he had to be prevented, like leviathan, from multiplying and increasing, else the world could not have continued to exist; after God had created him male and female, He at once deprived him of the desire to propagate his kind. He is so monstrous that he requires the produce of a thousand mountains for his daily food. All the water that flows through the bed of the Jordan in a year suffices him exactly for one gulp. It therefore was necessary to give him one stream entirely for his own use, a stream flowing forth from Paradise, called Yubal. Behemot, too, is destined to be served to the pious as an appetizing dainty, but before they enjoy his flesh, they will be permitted to view the mortal combat between leviathan and behemot, as a reward for having denied themselves the pleasures of the circus and its gladiatorial contests.

Leviathan, ziz, and behemot are not the only monsters; there are many others, and marvellous ones, like the reem, a giant animal, of which only one couple, male and female, is in existence. Had there been more, the world could hardly have maintained itself against them. The act of copulation occurs but once in seventy years between them, for God has so ordered it that the male and female reem are at opposite ends of the earth, the one in the east, the other in the west. The act of copulation results in the death of the male. He is bitten by the female and dies of the bite. The female becomes pregnant and remains in this state for no less than twelve years. At the end of this long period she gives birth to twins, a male and a female. The year preceding her delivery she is not able to move. She would die of hunger, were it not that her own spittle flowing copiously from her mouth waters and fructifies the earth near her, and causes it to bring forth enough for her maintenance. For a whole year the animal can but roll from side to side, until finally her belly bursts, and the twins issue forth. Their appearance is thus the signal for the death of the mother reem. She makes room for the new generation, which in turn is destined to suffer the same fate as the generation that went before. Immediately after birth, the one goes eastward and the other westward, to meet only after the lapse of seventy years, propagate themselves, and perish. A traveller who once saw a reem one day old described its height to be four parasangs, and the length of its head one parasang and a half. Its horns measure one hundred ells, and their height is a great deal more.

One of the most remarkable creatures is the "man of the mountain," Adne Sadeh, or, briefly, Adam. His form is exactly that of a human being, but he is fastened to the ground by means of a navel-string, upon which his life depends. The cord once snapped, he dies. This animal keeps himself alive with what is produced by the soil around about him as far as his tether permits him to crawl. No creature may venture to approach within the radius of his cord, for he seizes and demolishes whatever comes in his reach. To kill him, one may not go near to him, the navel-string must be severed from a distance by means of a dart, and then he dies amid groans and moans. Once upon a time a traveller happened in the region where this animal is found. He overheard his host consult his wife as to what to do to honor their guest, and resolve to serve "our man," as he said. Thinking he had fallen among cannibals, the stranger ran as fast as his feet could carry him from his entertainer, who sought vainly to restrain him. Afterward, he found out that there had been no intention of regaling him with human flesh, but only with the flesh of the strange animal called "man." As the "man of the mountain" is fixed to the ground by his navel-string, so the barnacle-goose is grown to a tree by its bill. It is hard to say whether it is an animal and must be slaughtered to be fit for food, or whether it is a plant and no ritual ceremony is necessary before eating it.

Among the birds the phoenix is the most wonderful. When Eve gave all the animals some of the fruit of the tree of knowledge, the phoenix was the only bird that refused to eat thereof, and he was rewarded with eternal life. When he has lived a thousand years, his body shrinks, and the feathers drop from it, until he is as small as an egg. This is the nucleus of the new bird.

The phoenix is also called "the guardian of the terrestrial sphere." He runs with the sun on his circuit, and he spreads out his wings and catches up the fiery rays of the sun. If he were not there to intercept them, neither man nor any other animate being would keep alive. On his right wing the following words are inscribed in huge letters, about four thousand stadia high: "Neither the earth produces me, nor the heavens, but only the wings of fire." His food consists of the manna of heaven and the dew of the earth. His excrement is a worm, whose excrement in turn is the cinnamon used by kings and princes. Enoch, who saw the phoenix birds when he was translated, describes them as flying creatures, wonderful and strange in appearance, with the feet and tails of lions, and the heads of crocodiles; their appearance is of a purple color like the rainbow; their size nine hundred measures. Their wings are like those of angels, each having twelve, and they attend the chariot of the sun and go with him, bringing heat and dew as they are ordered by God. In the morning when the sun starts on his daily course, the phoenixes and the chalkidri sing, and every bird flaps its wings, rejoicing the Giver of light, and they sing a song at the command of the Lord. Among reptiles the salamander and the shamir are the most marvellous. The salamander originates from a fire of myrtle wood which has been kept burning for seven years steadily by means of magic arts. Not bigger than a mouse, it yet is invested with peculiar properties. One who smears himself with its blood is invulnerable, and the web woven by it is a talisman against fire. The people who lived at the deluge boasted that, were a fire flood to come, they would protect themselves with the blood of the salamander.

King Hezekiah owes his life to the salamander. His wicked father, King Ahaz, had delivered him to the fires of Moloch, and he would have been burnt, had his mother not painted him with the blood of the salamander, so that the fire could do him no harm.

The shamir was made at twilight on the sixth day of creation together with other extraordinary things. It is about as large as a barley corn, and it possesses the remarkable property of cutting the hardest of diamonds. For this reason it was used for the stones in the breastplate worn by the high priest. First the names of the twelve tribes were traced with ink on the stones to be set into the breastplate, then the shamir was passed over the lines, and thus they were graven. The wonderful circumstance was that the friction wore no particles from the stones. The shamir was also used for hewing into shape the stones from which the Temple was built, because the law prohibited iron tools to be used for the work in the Temple. The shamir may not be put in an iron vessel for safe-keeping, nor in any metal vessel, it would burst such a receptacle asunder. It is kept wrapped up in a woollen cloth, and this in turn is placed in a lead basket filled with barley bran. The shamir was guarded in Paradise until Solomon needed it. He sent the eagle thither to fetch the worm. With the destruction of the Temple the shamir vanished. A similar fate overtook the tahash, which had been created only that its skin might be used for the Tabernacle. Once the Tabernacle was completed, the tahash disappeared. It had a horn on its forehead, was gaily colored like the turkey-cock, and belonged to the class of clean animals. Among the fishes there are also wonderful creatures, the sea-goats and the dolphins, not to mention leviathan. A sea-faring man once saw a sea-goat on whose horns the words were inscribed: "I am a little sea-animal, yet I traversed three hundred parasangs to offer myself as food to the leviathan." The dolphins are half man and half fish; they even have sexual intercourse with human beings; therefore they are called also "sons of the sea," for in a sense they represent the human kind in the waters.

Though every species in the animal world was created during the last two days of the six of creation, yet many characteristics of certain animals appeared later. Cats and mice, foes now, were friends originally. Their later enmity had a distinct cause. On one occasion the mouse appeared before God and spoke: "I and the cat are partners, but now we have nothing to eat." The Lord answered: "Thou art intriguing against thy companion, only that thou mayest devour her. As a punishment, she shall devour thee." Thereupon the mouse: "O Lord of the world, wherein have I done wrong?" God replied: "O thou unclean reptile, thou shouldst have been warned by the example of the moon, who lost a part of her light, because she spake ill of the sun, and what she lost was given to her opponent. The evil intentions thou didst harbor against thy companion shall be punished in the same way. Instead of thy devouring her, she shall devour thee." The mouse: "O Lord of the world! Shall my whole kind be destroyed?" God: "I will take care that a remnant of thee is spared." In her rage the mouse bit the cat, and the cat in turn threw herself upon the mouse, and hacked into her with her teeth until she lay dead. Since that moment the mouse stands in such awe of the cat that she does not even attempt to defend herself against her enemy's attacks, and always keeps herself in hiding. Similarly dogs and cats maintained a friendly relation to each other, and only later on became enemies. A dog and a cat were partners, and they shared with each other whatever they had. It once happened that neither could find anything to eat for three days. Thereupon the dog proposed that they dissolve their partnership. The cat should go to Adam, in whose house there would surely be enough for her to eat, while the dog should seek his fortune elsewhere. Before they separated, they took an oath never to go to the same master. The cat took up her abode with Adam, and she found sufficient mice in his house to satisfy her appetite. Seeing how useful she was in driving away and extirpating mice, Adam treated her most kindly. The dog, on the other hand, saw bad times. The first night after their separation he spent in the cave of the wolf, who had granted him a night's lodging. At night the dog caught the sound of steps, and he reported it to his host, who bade him repulse the intruders. They were wild animals. Little lacked and the dog would have lost his life. Dismayed, the dog fled from the house of the wolf, and took refuge with the monkey. But he would not grant him even a single night's lodging; and the fugitive was forced to appeal to the hospitality of the sheep. Again the dog heard steps in the middle of the night. Obeying the bidding of his host, he arose to chase away the marauders, who turned out to be wolves. The barking of the dog apprised the wolves of the presence of sheep, so that the dog innocently caused the sheep's death. Now he had lost his last friend. Night after night he begged for shelter, without ever finding a home. Finally, he decided to repair to the house of Adam, who also granted him refuge for one night. When wild animals approached the house under cover of darkness, the dog began to bark, Adam awoke, and with his bow and arrow he drove them away. Recognizing the dog's usefulness, he bade him remain with him always. But as soon as the cat espied the dog in Adam's house, she began to quarrel with him, and reproach him with having broken his oath to her. Adam did his best to pacify the cat. He told her he had himself invited the dog to make his home there, and he assured her she would in no wise be the loser by the dog's presence; he wanted both to stay with him. But it was impossible to appease the cat. The dog promised her not to touch anything intended for her. She insisted that she could not live in one and the same house with a thief like the dog. Bickerings between the dog and the cat became the order of the day. Finally the dog could stand it no longer, and he left Adam's house, and betook himself to Seth's. By Seth he was welcomed kindly, and from Seth's house, he continued to make efforts at reconciliation with the cat. In vain. Yes, the enmity between the first dog and the first cat was transmitted to all their descendants until this very day.

Even the physical peculiarities of certain animals were not original features with them, but owed their existence to something that occurred subsequent to the days of creation. The mouse at first had quite a different mouth from its present mouth. In Noah's ark, in which all animals, to ensure the preservation of every kind, lived together peaceably, the pair of mice were once sitting next to the cat. Suddenly the latter remembered that her father was in the habit of devouring mice, and thinking there was no harm in following his example, she jumped at the mouse, who vainly looked for a hole into which to slip out of sight. Then a miracle happened; a hole appeared where none had been before, and the mouse sought refuge in it. The cat pursued the mouse, and though she could not follow her into the hole, she could insert her paw and try to pull the mouse out of her covert. Quickly the mouse opened her mouth in the hope that the paw would go into it, and the cat would be prevented from fastening her claws in her flesh. But as the cavity of the mouth was not big enough, the cat succeeded in clawing the cheeks of the mouse. Not that this helped her much, it merely widened the mouth of the mouse, and her prey after all escaped the cat. After her happy escape, the mouse betook herself to Noah and said to him, "O pious man, be good enough to sew up my cheek where my enemy, the cat, has torn a rent in it." Noah bade her fetch a hair out of the tail of the swine, and with this he repaired the damage. Thence the little seam-like line next to the mouth of every mouse to this very day.

The raven is another animal that changed its appearance during its sojourn in the ark. When Noah desired to send him forth to find out about the state of the waters, he hid under the wings of the eagle. Noah found him, however, and said to him, "Go and see whether the waters have diminished." The raven pleaded: "Hast thou none other among all the birds to send on this errand?" Noah: "My power extends no further than over thee and the dove." But the raven was not satisfied. He said to Noah with great insolence: "Thou sendest me forth only that I may meet my death, and thou wishest my death that my wife may be at thy service." Thereupon Noah cursed the raven thus: "May thy mouth, which has spoken evil against me, be accursed, and thy intercourse with thy wife be only through it." All the animals in the ark said Amen. And this is the reason why a mass of spittle runs from the mouth of the male raven into the mouth of the female during the act of copulation, and only thus the female is impregnated. Altogether the raven is an unattractive animal. He is unkind toward his own young so long as their bodies are not covered with black feathers, though as a rule ravens love one another. God therefore takes the young ravens under His special protection. From their own excrement maggots come forth, which serve as their food during the three days that elapse after their birth, until their white feathers turn black and their parents recognize them as their offspring and care for them.

The raven has himself to blame also for the awkward hop in his gait. He observed the graceful step of the dove, and envious of her tried to enmulate it. The outcome was that he almost broke his bones without in the least succeeding in making himself resemble the dove, not to mention that he brought the scorn of the other animals down upon himself. His failure excited their ridicule. Then he decided to return to his own original gait, but in the interval he had unlearnt it, and he could walk neither the one way nor the other properly. His step had become a hop betwixt and between. Thus we see how true it is, that he who is dissatisfied with his small portion loses the little he has in striving for more and better things.

The steer is also one of the animals that have suffered a change in the course of time. Originally his face was entirely overgrown with hair, but now there is none on his nose, and that is because Joshua kissed him on his nose during the siege of Jericho. Joshua was an exceedingly heavy man. Horses, donkeys, and mules, none could bear him, they all broke down under his weight. What they could not do, the steer accomplished. On his back Joshua rode to the siege of Jericho, and in gratitude he bestowed a kiss upon his nose.

The serpent, too, is other than it was at first. Before the fall of man it was the cleverest of all animals created, and in form it resembled man closely. It stood upright, and was of extraordinary size. Afterward, it lost the mental advantages it had possessed as compared with other animals, and it degenerated physically, too; it was deprived of its feet, so that it could not pursue other animals and kill them. The mole and the frog had to be made harmless in similar ways; the former has no eyes, else it were irresistible, and the frog has no teeth, else no animal in the water were sure of its life.

While the cunning of the serpent wrought its own undoing, the cunning of the fox stood him in good stead in many an embarrassing situation. After Adam had committed the sin of disobedience, God delivered the whole of the animal world into the power of the Angel of Death, and He ordered him to cast one pair of each kind into the water. He and leviathan together thus have dominion over all that has life. When the Angel of Death was in the act of executing the Divine command upon the fox, he began to weep bitterly. The Angel of Death asked him the reason of his tears, and the fox replied that he was mourning the sad fate of his friend. At the same time he pointed to the figure of a fox in the sea, which was nothing but his own reflection. The Angel of Death, persuaded that a representative of the fox family had been cast into the water, let him go free. The fox told his trick to the cat, and she in turn played it on the Angel of Death. So it happened that neither cats nor foxes are represented in the water, while all other animals are.

When leviathan passed the animals in review, and missing the fox was informed of the sly way in which he had eluded his authority, he dispatched great and powerful fish on the errand of enticing the truant into the water. The fox walking along the shore espied the large number of fish, and he exclaimed, "How happy he who may always satisfy his hunger with the flesh of such as these." The fish told him, if he would but follow them, his appetite could easily be appeased. At the same time they informed him that a great honor awaited him. Leviathan, they said, was at death's door, and he had commissioned them to install the fox as his successor. They were ready to carry him on their backs, so that he had no need to fear the water, and thus they would convey him to the throne, which stood upon a huge rock. The fox yielded to these persuasions, and descended into the water. Presently an uncomfortable feeling took possession of him. He began to suspect that the tables were turned; he was being made game of instead of making game of others as usual. He urged the fish to tell him the truth, and they admitted that they had been sent out to secure his person for leviathan, who wanted his heart, that he might become as knowing as the fox, whose wisdom he had heard many extol. The fox said reproachfully: "Why did you not tell me the truth at once? Then I could have brought my heart along with me for King Leviathan, who would have showered honors upon me. As it is, you will surely suffer punishment for bringing me without my heart. The foxes, you see," he continued, "do not carry their hearts around with them. They keep them in a safe place, and when they have need of them, they fetch them thence." The fish quickly swam to shore, and landed the fox, so that he might go for his heart. No sooner did he feel dry land under his feet than he began to jump and shout, and when they urged him to go in search of his heart, and follow them, he said: "O ye fools, could I have followed you into the water, if I had not had my heart with me? Or exists there a creature able to go abroad without his heart?" The fish replied: "Come, come, thou art fooling us." Whereupon the fox: "O ye fools, if I could play a trick on the Angel of Death, how much easier was it to make game of you?" So they had to return, their errand undone, and leviathan could not but confirm the taunting judgment of the fox: "In very truth, the fox is wise of heart, and ye are fools."

ALL THINGS PRAISE THE LORD

"Whatever God created has value." Even the animals and the insects that seem useless and noxious at first sight have a vocation to fulfil. The snail trailing a moist streak after it as it crawls, and so using up its vitality, serves as a remedy for boils. The sting of a hornet is healed by the house-fly crushed and applied to the wound. The gnat, feeble creature, taking in food but never secreting it, is a specific against the poison of a viper, and this venomous reptile itself cures eruptions, while the lizard is the antidote to the scorpion. Not only do all creatures serve man, and contribute to his comfort, but also God "teacheth us through the beasts of the earth, and maketh us wise through the fowls of heaven." He endowed many animals with admirable moral qualities as a pattern for man. If the Torah had not been revealed to us, we might have learnt regard for the decencies of life from the cat, who covers her excrement with earth; regard for the property of others from the ants, who never encroach upon one another's stores; and regard for decorous conduct from the cock, who, when he desires to unite with the hen, promises to buy her a cloak long enough to reach to the ground, and when the hen reminds him of his promise, he shakes his comb and says, "May I be deprived of my comb, if I do not buy it when I have the means." The grasshopper also has a lesson to teach to man. All the summer through it sings, until its belly bursts, and death claims it. Though it knows the fate that awaits it, yet it sings on. So man should do his duty toward God, no matter what the consequences. The stork should be taken as a model in two respects. He guards the purity of his family life zealously, and toward his fellows he is compassionate and merciful. Even the frog can be the teacher of man. By the side of the water there lives a species of animals which subsist off aquatic creatures alone. When the frog notices that one of them is hungry, he goes to it of his own accord, and offers himself as food, thus fulfilling the injunction, "If thine enemy be hungry, give him bread to eat; and if he be thirsty, give him water to drink."

The whole of creation was called into existence by God unto His glory, and each creature has its own hymn of praise wherewith to extol the Creator. Heaven and earth, Paradise and hell, desert and field, rivers and seas-- all have their own way of paying homage to God. The hymn of the earth is, "From the uttermost part of the earth have we heard songs, glory to the Righteous." The sea exclaims, "Above the voices of many waters, the mighty breakers of the sea, the Lord on high is mighty."

Also the celestial bodies and the elements proclaim the praise of their Creator--the sun, moon, and stars, the clouds and the winds, lightning and dew. The sun says, "The sun and moon stood still in their habitation, at the light of Thine arrows as they went, at the shining of Thy glittering spear"; and the stars sing, "Thou art the Lord, even Thou alone; Thou hast made heaven, the heaven of heavens, with all their host, the earth and all things that are thereon, the seas and all that is in them, and Thou preservest them all; and the host of heaven worshippeth Thee."

Every plant, furthermore, has a song of praise. The fruitful tree sings, "Then shall all the trees of the wood sing for joy, before the Lord, for He cometh; for He cometh to judge the earth"; and the ears of grain on the field sing, "The pastures are covered with flocks; the valleys also are covered over with corn; they shout for joy, they also sing."

Great among singers of praise are the birds, and greatest among them is the cock. When God at midnight goes to the pious in Paradise, all the trees therein break out into adoration, and their songs awaken the cock, who begins in turn to praise God. Seven times he crows, each time reciting a verse. The first verse is: "Lift up your heads, O ye gates; and be ye lift up, ye everlasting doors, and the King of glory shall come in. Who is the King of glory? The Lord strong and mighty, the Lord mighty in battle." The second verse: "Lift up your heads, O ye gates; yea, lift them up, ye everlasting doors, and the King of glory shall come in. Who is this King of glory? The Lord of hosts, He is the King of glory." The third: "Arise, ye righteous, and occupy yourselves with the Torah, that your reward may be abundant in the world hereafter." The fourth: "I have waited for Thy salvation, O Lord!" The fifth: "How long wilt thou sleep, O sluggard? When wilt thou arise out of thy sleep?" The sixth: "Love not sleep, lest thou come to poverty; open thine eyes, and thou shalt be satisfied with bread." And the seventh verse sung by the cock runs: "It is time to work for the Lord, for they have made void Thy law."

The song of the vulture is: "I will hiss for them, and gather them; for I have redeemed them, and they shall increase as they have increased"--the same verse with which the bird will in time to come announce the advent of the Messiah, the only difference being, that when he heralds the Messiah he will sit upon the ground and sing his verse, while at all other times he is seated elsewhere when he sings it.

Nor do the other animals praise God less than the birds. Even the beasts of prey give forth adoration. The lion says: "The Lord shall go forth as a mighty man; He shall stir up jealousy like a man of war; He shall cry, yea, He shall shout aloud; He shall do mightily against his enemies." And the fox exhorts unto justice with the words: "Woe unto him that buildeth his house by unrighteousness, and his chambers by injustice; that useth his neighbor's service without wages, and giveth him not his hire."

Yea, the dumb fishes know how to proclaim the praise of their Lord. "The voice of the Lord is upon the waters," they say, "the God of glory thundereth, even the Lord upon many waters"; while the frog exclaims, "Blessed be the name of the glory of His kingdom forever and ever."

Contemptible though they are, even the reptiles give praise unto their Creator. The mouse extols God with the words: "Howbeit Thou art just in all that is come upon me; for Thou hast dealt truly, but I have done wickedly." And the cat sings: "Let everything that hath breath praise the Lord. Praise ye the Lord."

Chapter 2

ADAM--MAN AND THE WORLD

With ten Sayings God created the world, although a single Saying would have sufficed. God desired to make known how severe is the punishment to be meted out to the wicked, who destroy a world created with as many as ten Sayings, and how goodly the reward destined for the righteous, who preserve a world created with as many as ten Sayings.

The world was made for man, though he was the last-comer among its creatures. This was design. He was to find all things ready for him. God was the host who prepared dainty dishes, set the table, and then led His guest to his seat. At the same time man's late appearance on earth is to convey an admonition to humility. Let him beware of being proud, lest he invite the retort that the gnat is older than he.

The superiority of man to the other creatures is apparent in the very manner of his creation, altogether different from theirs. He is the only one who was created by the hand of God. The rest sprang from the word of God. The body of man is a microcosm, the whole world in miniature, and the world in turn is a reflex of man. The hair upon his head corresponds to the woods of the earth, his tears to a river, his mouth to the ocean. Also, the world resembles the ball of his eye: the ocean that encircles the earth is like unto the white of the eye, the dry land is the iris, Jerusalem the pupil, and the Temple the image mirrored in the pupil of the eye. But man is more than a mere image of this world. He unites both heavenly and earthly qualities within himself. In four he resembles the angels, in four the beasts. His power of speech, his discriminating intellect, his upright walk, the glance of his eye--they all make an angel of him. But, on the other hand, he eats and drinks, secretes the waste matter in his body, propagates his kind, and dies, like the beast of the field. Therefore God said before the creation of man: "The celestials are not propagated, but they are immortal; the beings on earth are propagated, but they die. I will create man to be the union of the two, so that when he sins, when he behaves like a beast, death shall overtake him; but if he refrains from sin, he shall live forever." God now bade all beings in heaven and on earth contribute to the creation of man, and He Himself took part in it. Thus they all will love man, and if he should sin, they will be interested in his preservation.

The whole world naturally was created for the pious, the God-fearing man, whom Israel produces with the helpful guidance of the law of God revealed to him. It was, therefore, Israel who was taken into special consideration at the time man was made. All other creatures were instructed to change their nature, if Israel should ever need their help in the course of his history. The sea was ordered to divide before Moses, and the heavens to give ear to the words of the leader; the sun and the moon were bidden to stand still before Joshua, the ravens to feed Elijah, the fire to spare the three youths in the furnace, the lion to do no harm to Daniel, the fish to spew forth Jonah, and the heavens to open before Ezekiel.

In His modesty, God took counsel with the angels, before the creation of the world, regarding His intention of making man. He said: "For the sake of Israel, I will create the world. As I shall make a division between light and darkness, so I will in time to come do for Israel in Egypt--thick darkness shall be over the land, and the children of Israel shall have light in their dwellings; as I shall make a separation between the waters under the firmament and the waters above the firmament, so I will do for Israel--I will divide the waters for him when he crosses the Red Sea; as on the third day I shall create plants, so I will do for Israel--I will bring forth manna for him in the wilderness; as I shall create luminaries to divide day from night, so I will do for Israel--I will go before him by day in a pillar of cloud and by night in a pillar of fire; as I shall create the fowl of the air and the fishes of the sea, so I will do for Israel--I will bring quails for him from the sea; and as I shall breathe the breath of life into the nostrils of man, so I will do for Israel--I will give the Torah unto him, the tree of life." The angels marvelled that so much love should be lavished upon this people of Israel, and God told them: "On the first day of creation, I shall make the heavens and stretch them out; so will Israel raise up the Tabernacle as the dwelling-place of My glory. On the second day, I shall put a division between the terrestrial waters and the heavenly waters; so will he hang up a veil in the Tabernacle to divide the Holy Place and the Most Holy. On the third day, I shall make the earth put forth grass and herb; so will he, in obedience to My commands, eat herbs on the first night of the Passover, and prepare showbread for Me. On the fourth day, I shall make the luminaries; so will he make a golden candlestick for Me. On the fifth day, I shall create the birds; so will he fashion the cherubim with outstretched wings. On the sixth day, I shall create man; so will Israel set aside a man of the sons of Aaron as high priest for My service."

Accordingly, the whole of creation was conditional. God said to the things He made on the first six days: "If Israel accepts the Torah, you will continue and endure; otherwise, I shall turn everything back into chaos again." The whole world was thus kept in suspense and dread until the day of the revelation on Sinai, when Israel received and accepted the Torah, and so fulfilled the condition made by God at the time when He created the universe.

THE ANGELS AND THE CREATION OF MAN

God in His wisdom having resolved to create man, He asked counsel of all around Him before He proceeded to execute His purpose--an example to man, be he never so great and distinguished, not to scorn the advice of the humble and lowly. First God called upon heaven and earth, then upon all other things He had created, and last upon the angels.

The angels were not all of one opinion. The Angel of Love favored the creation of man, because he would be affectionate and loving; but the Angel of Truth opposed it, because he would be full of lies. And while the Angel of Justice favored it, because he would practice justice, the Angel of Peace opposed it, because he would be quarrelsome.

To invalidate his protest, God cast the Angel of Truth down from heaven to earth, and when the others cried out against such contemptuous treatment of their companion, He said, "Truth will spring back out of the earth."

The objections of the angels would have been much stronger, had they known the whole truth about man. God had told them only about the pious, and had concealed from them that there would be reprobates among mankind, too. And yet, though they knew but half the truth, the angels were nevertheless prompted to cry out: "What is man, that Thou art mindful of him? And the son of man, that Thou visitest him?" God replied: "The fowl of the air and the fish of the sea, what were they created for? Of what avail a larder full of appetizing dainties, and no guest to enjoy them?" And the angels could not but exclaim: "O Lord, our Lord, how excellent is Thy name in all the earth! Do as is pleasing in Thy sight."

For not a few of the angels their opposition bore fatal consequences. When God summoned the band under the archangel Michael, and asked their opinion on the creation of man, they answered scornfully: "What is man, that Thou art mindful of him? And the son of man, that Thou visitest him?" God thereupon stretched forth His little finger, and all were consumed by fire except their chief Michael. And the same fate befell the band under the leadership of the archangel Gabriel; he alone of all was saved from destruction.

The third band consulted was commanded by the archangel Labbiel. Taught by the horrible fate of his predecessors, he warned his troop: "You have seen what misfortune overtook the angels who said 'What is man, that Thou art mindful of him?' Let us have a care not to do likewise, lest we suffer the same dire punishment. For God will not refrain from doing in the end what He has planned. Therefore it is advisable for us to yield to His wishes." Thus warned, the angels spoke: "Lord of the world, it is well that Thou hast thought of creating man. Do Thou create him according to Thy will. And as for us, we will be his attendants and his ministers, and reveal unto him all our secrets." Thereupon God changed Labbiel's name to Raphael, the Rescuer, because his host of angels had been rescued by his sage advice. He was appointed the Angel of Healing, who has in his safe-keeping all the celestial remedies, the types of the medical remedies used on earth.

THE CREATION OF ADAM

When at last the assent of the angels to the creation of man was given, God said to Gabriel: "Go and fetch Me dust from the four corners of the earth, and I will create man therewith." Gabriel went forth to do the bidding of the Lord, but the earth drove him away, and refused to let him gather up dust from it. Gabriel remonstrated: "Why, O Earth, dost thou not hearken unto the voice of the Lord, who founded thee upon the waters without props or pillars?" The earth replied, and said: "I am destined to become a curse, and to be cursed through man, and if God Himself does not take the dust from me, no one else shall ever do it." When God heard this, He stretched out His hand, took of the dust of the ground, and created the first man therewith. Of set purpose the dust was taken from all four corners of the earth, so that if a man from the east should happen to die in the west, or a man from the west in the east, the earth should not dare refuse to receive the dead, and tell him to go whence he was taken. Wherever a man chances to die, and wheresoever he is buried, there will he return to the earth from which he sprang. Also, the dust was of various colors--red, black, white, and green--red for the blood, black for the bowels, white for the bones and veins, and green for the pale skin.

At this early moment the Torah interfered. She addressed herself to God: "O Lord of the world! The world is Thine, Thou canst do with it as seemeth good in Thine eyes. But the man Thou art now creating will be few of days and full of trouble and sin. If it be not Thy purpose to have forbearance and patience with him, it were better not to call him into being." God replied, "Is it for naught I am called long-suffering and merciful?"

The grace and lovingkindness of God revealed themselves particularly in His taking one spoonful of dust from the spot where in time to come the altar would stand, saying, "I shall take man from the place of atonement, that he may endure."

THE SOUL OF MAN

The care which God exercised in fashioning every detail of the body of man is as naught in comparison with His solicitude for the human soul. The soul of man was created on the first day, for it is the spirit of God moving upon the face of the waters. Thus, instead of being the last, man is really the first work of creation.

This spirit, or, to call it by its usual name, the soul of man, possesses five different powers. By means of one of them she escapes from the body every night, rises up to heaven, and fetches new life thence for man.

With the soul of Adam the souls of all the generations of men were created. They are stored up in a promptuary, in the seventh of the heavens, whence they are drawn as they are needed for human body after human body.

The soul and body of man are united in this way: When a woman has conceived, the Angel of the Night, Lailah, carries the sperm before God, and God decrees what manner of human being shall become of it-- whether it shall be male or female, strong or weak, rich or poor, beautiful or ugly, long or short, fat or thin, and what all its other qualities shall be. Piety and wickedness alone are left to the determination of man himself. Then God makes a sign to the angel appointed over the souls, saying, "Bring Me the soul so-and-so, which is hidden in Paradise, whose name is so-and-so, and whose form is so-and-so." The angel brings the designated soul, and she bows down when she appears in the presence of God, and prostrates herself before Him. At that moment, God issues the command, "Enter this sperm." The soul opens her mouth, and pleads: "O Lord of the world! I am well pleased with the world in which I have been living since the day on which Thou didst call me into being. Why dost Thou now desire to have me enter this impure sperm, I who am holy and pure, and a part of Thy glory?" God consoles her: "The world which I shall cause thee to enter is better than the world in which thou hast lived hitherto, and when I created thee, it was only for this purpose." The soul is then forced to enter the sperm against her will, and the angel carries her back to the womb of the mother. Two angels are detailed to watch that she shall not leave it, nor drop out of it, and a light is set above her, whereby the soul can see from one end of the world to the other. In the morning an angel carries her to Paradise, and shows her the righteous, who sit there in their glory, with crowns upon their heads. The angel then says to the soul, "Dost thou know who these are?" She replies in the negative, and the angel goes on: "These whom thou beholdest here were formed, like unto thee, in the womb of their mother. When they came into the world, they observed God's Torah and His commandments. Therefore they became the partakers of this bliss which thou seest them enjoy. Know, also thou wilt one day depart from the world below, and if thou wilt observe God's Torah, then wilt thou be found worthy of sitting with these pious ones. But if not, thou wilt be doomed to the other place."

In the evening, the angel takes the soul to hell, and there points out the sinners whom the Angels of Destruction are smiting with fiery scourges, the sinners all the while crying out Woe! Woe! but no mercy is shown unto them. The angel then questions the soul as before, "Dost thou know who these are?" and as before the reply is negative. The angel continues: "These who are consumed with fire were created like unto thee. When they were put into the world, they did not observe God's Torah and His commandments. Therefore have they come to this disgrace which thou seest them suffer. Know, thy destiny is also to depart from the world. Be just, therefore, and not wicked, that thou mayest gain the future world."

Between morning and evening the angel carries the soul around, and shows her where she will live and where she will die, and the place where she will buried, and he takes her through the whole world, and points out the just and the sinners and all things. In the evening, he replaces her in the womb of the mother, and there she remains for nine months.

When the time arrives for her to emerge from the womb into the open world, the same angel addresses the soul, "The time has come for thee to go abroad into the open world." The soul demurs, "Why dost thou want to make me go forth into the open world?" The angel replies: "Know that as thou wert formed against thy will, so now thou wilt be born against thy will, and against thy will thou shalt die, and against thy will thou shalt give account of thyself before the King of kings, the Holy One, blessed be He." But the soul is reluctant to leave her place. Then the angel fillips the babe on the nose, extinguishes the light at his head, and brings him forth into the world against his will. Immediately the child forgets all his soul has seen and learnt, and he comes into the world crying, for he loses a place of shelter and security and rest.

When the time arrives for man to quit this world, the same angel appears and asks him, "Dost thou recognize me?" And man replies, "Yes; but why dost thou come to me to-day, and thou didst come on no other day?" The angel says, "To take thee away from the world, for the time of thy departure has arrived." Then man falls to weeping, and his voice penetrates to all ends of the world, yet no creature hears his voice, except the cock alone. Man remonstrates with the angel, "From two worlds thou didst take me, and into this world thou didst bring me." But the angel reminds him: "Did I not tell thee that thou wert formed against thy will, and thou wouldst be born against thy will, and against thy will thou wouldst die? And against thy will thou wilt have to give account and reckoning of thyself before the Holy One, blessed be He."

THE IDEAL MAN

Like all creatures formed on the six days of creation, Adam came from the hands of the Creator fully and completely developed. He was not like a child, but like a man of twenty years of age. The dimensions of his body were gigantic, reaching from heaven to earth, or, what amounts to the same, from east to west. Among later generations of men, there were but few who in a measure resembled Adam in his extraordinary size and physical perfections. Samson possessed his strength, Saul his neck, Absalom his hair, Asahel his fleetness of foot, Uzziah his forehead, Josiah his nostrils, Zedekiah his eyes, and Zerubbabel his voice. History shows that these physical excellencies were no blessings to many of their possessors; they invited the ruin of almost all. Samson's extraordinary strength caused his death; Saul killed himself by cutting his neck with his own sword; while speeding swiftly, Asahel was pierced by Abner's spear; Absalom was caught up by his hair in an oak, and thus suspended met his death; Uzziah was smitten with leprosy upon his forehead; the darts that killed Josiah entered through his nostrils, and Zedekiah's eyes were blinded.

The generality of men inherited as little of the beauty as of the portentous size of their first father. The fairest women compared with Sarah are as apes compared with a human being. Sarah's relation to Eve is the same, and, again, Eve was but as an ape compared with Adam. His person was so handsome that the very sole of his foot obscured the splendor of the sun.

His spiritual qualities kept pace with his personal charm, for God had fashioned his soul with particular care. She is the image of God, and as God fills the world, so the soul fills the human body; as God sees all things, and is seen by none, so the soul sees, but cannot be seen; as God guides the world, so the soul guides the body; as God in His holiness is pure, so is the soul; and as God dwells in secret, so doth the soul.

When God was about to put a soul into Adam's clod-like body, He said: "At which point shall I breathe the soul into him? Into the mouth? Nay, for he will use it to speak ill of his fellow-man. Into the eyes? With them he will wink lustfully. Into the ears? They will hearken to slander and blasphemy. I will breathe her into his nostrils; as they discern the unclean and reject it, and take in the fragrant, so the pious will shun sin, and will cleave to the words of the Torah"

The perfections of Adam's soul showed themselves as soon as he received her, indeed, while he was still without life. In the hour that intervened between breathing a soul into the first man and his becoming alive, God revealed the whole history of mankind to him. He showed him each generation and its leaders; each generation and its prophets; each generation and its teachers; each generation and its scholars; each generation and its statesmen; each generation and its judges; each generation and its pious members; each generation and its average, commonplace members; and each generation and its impious members. The tale of their years, the number of their days, the reckoning of their hours, and the measure of their steps, all were made known unto him.

Of his own free will Adam relinquished seventy of his allotted years. His appointed span was to be a thousand years, one of the Lord's days. But he saw that only a single minute of life was apportioned to the great soul of David, and he made a gift of seventy years to her, reducing his own years to nine hundred and thirty.'

The wisdom of Adam displayed itself to greatest advantage when he gave names to the animals. Then it appeared that God, in combating the arguments of the angels that opposed the creation of man, had spoken well, when He insisted that man would possess more wisdom than they themselves. When Adam was barely an hour old, God assembled the whole world of animals before him and the angels. The latter were called upon to name the different kinds, but they were not equal to the task. Adam, however, spoke without hesitation: "O Lord of the world! The proper name for this animal is ox, for this one horse, for this one lion, for this one camel." And so he called all in turn by name, suiting the name to the peculiarity of the animal. Then God asked him what his name was to be, and he said Adam, because he had been created out of Adamah, dust of the earth. Again, God asked him His own name, and he said: "Adonai, Lord, because Thou art Lord over all creatures"--the very name God had given unto Himself, the name by which the angels call Him, the name that will remain immutable evermore. But without the gift of the holy spirit, Adam could not have found names for all; he was in very truth a prophet, and his wisdom a prophetic quality.

The names of the animals were not the only inheritance handed down by Adam to the generations after him, for mankind owes all crafts to him, especially the art of writing, and he was the inventor of all the seventy languages. And still another task he accomplished for his descendants. God showed Adam the whole earth, and Adam designated what places were to be settled later by men, and what places were to remain waste.

THE FALL OF SATAN

The extraordinary qualities with which Adam was blessed, physical and spiritual as well, aroused the envy of the angels. They attempted to consume him with fire, and he would have perished, had not the protecting hand of God rested upon him, and established peace between him and the heavenly host. In particular, Satan was jealous of the first man, and his evil thoughts finally led to his fall. After Adam had been endowed with a soul, God invited all the angels to come and pay him reverence and homage. Satan, the greatest of the angels in heaven, with twelve wings, instead of six like all the others, refused to pay heed to the behest of God, saying, "Thou didst create us angels from the splendor of the Shekinah, and now Thou dost command us to cast ourselves down before the creature which Thou didst fashion out of the dust of the ground!" God answered, "Yet this dust of the ground has more wisdom and understanding than thou." Satan demanded a trial of wit with Adam, and God assented thereto, saying: "I have created beasts, birds, and reptiles, I shall have them all come before thee and before Adam. If thou art able to give them names, I shall command Adam to show honor unto thee, and thou shalt rest next to the Shekinah of My glory. But if not, and Adam calls them by the names I have assigned to them, then thou wilt be subject to Adam, and he shall have a place in My garden, and cultivate it." Thus spake God, and He betook Himself to Paradise, Satan following Him. When Adam beheld God, he said to his wife, "O come, let us worship and bow down; let us kneel before the Lord our Maker." Now Satan attempted to assign names to the animals. He failed with the first two that presented themselves, the ox and the cow. God led two others before him, the camel and the donkey, with the same result. Then God turned to Adam, and questioned him regarding the names of the same animals, framing His questions in such wise that the first letter of the first word was the same as the first letter of the name of the animal standing before him. Thus Adam divined the proper name, and Satan was forced to acknowledge the superiority of the first man. Nevertheless he broke out in wild outcries that reached the heavens, and he refused to do homage unto Adam as he had been bidden. The host of angels led by him did likewise, in spite of the urgent representations of Michael, who was the first to prostrate himself before Adam in order to show a good example to the other angels. Michael addressed Satan: "Give adoration to the image of God! But if thou doest it not, then the Lord God will break out in wrath against thee." Satan replied: "If He breaks out in wrath against me, I will exalt my throne above the stars of God, I will be like the Most High! "At once God flung Satan and his host out of heaven, down to the earth, and from that moment dates the enmity between Satan and man.'

WOMAN

When Adam opened his eyes the first time, and beheld the world about him, he broke into praise of God, "How great are Thy works, O Lord!" But his admiration for the world surrounding him did not exceed the admiration all creatures conceived for Adam. They took him to be their creator, and they all came to offer him adoration. But he spoke: "Why do you come to worship me? Nay, you and I together will acknowledge the majesty and the might of Him who hath created us all. 'The Lord reigneth,' " he continued, " 'He is apparelled with majesty.' "

And not alone the creatures on earth, even the angels thought Adam the lord of all, and they were about to salute him with "Holy, holy, holy, is the Lord of hosts," when God caused sleep to fall upon him, and then the angels knew that he was but a human being.

The purpose of the sleep that enfolded Adam was to give him a wife, so that the human race might develop, and all creatures recognize the difference between God and man. When the earth heard what God had resolved to do, it began to tremble and quake. "I have not the strength," it said, "to provide food for the herd of Adam's descendants. "But God pacified it with the words, "I and thou together, we will find food for the herd." Accordingly, time was divided between God and the earth; God took the night, and the earth took the day. Refreshing sleep nourishes and strengthens man, it affords him life and rest, while the earth brings forth produce with the help of God, who waters it. Yet man must work the earth to earn his food.

The Divine resolution to bestow a companion on Adam met the wishes of man, who had been overcome by a feeling of isolation when the animals came to him in pairs to be named. To banish his loneliness, Lilith was first given to Adam as wife. Like him she had been created out of the dust of the ground. But she remained with him only a short time, because she insisted upon enjoying full equality with her husband. She derived her rights from their identical origin. With the help of the Ineffable Name, which she pronounced, Lilith flew away from Adam, and vanished in the air. Adam complained before God that the wife He had given him had deserted him, and God sent forth three angels to capture her. They found her in the Red Sea, and they sought to make her go back with the threat that, unless she went, she would lose a hundred of her demon children daily by death. But Lilith preferred this punishment to living with Adam. She takes her revenge by injuring babes--baby boys during the first night of their life, while baby girls are exposed to her wicked designs until they are twenty. days old The only way to ward off the evil is to attach an amulet bearing the names of her three angel captors to the children, for such had been the agreement between them.

The woman destined to become the true companion of man was taken from Adam's body, for "only when like is joined unto like the union is indissoluble." The creation of woman from man was possible because Adam originally had two faces, which were separated at the birth of Eve.

When God was on the point of making Eve, He said: "I will not make her from the head of man, lest she carry her head high in arrogant pride; not from the eye, lest she be wanton-eyed; not from the ear, lest she be an eavesdropper; not from the neck, lest she be insolent; not from the mouth, lest she be a tattler; not from the heart, lest she be inclined to envy; not from the hand, lest she be a meddler; not from the foot, lest she be a gadabout. I will form her from a chaste portion of the body," and to every limb and organ as He formed it, God said, "Be chaste! Be chaste! "Nevertheless, in spite of the great caution used, woman has all the faults God tried to obviate. The daughters of Zion were haughty and walked with stretched forth necks and wanton eyes; Sarah was an eavesdropper in her own tent, when the angel spoke with Abraham; Miriam was a talebearer, accusing Moses; Rachel was envious of her sister Leah; Eve put out her hand to take the forbidden fruit, and Dinah was a gadabout.

The physical formation of woman is far more complicated than that of man, as it must be for the function of child-bearing, and likewise the intelligence of woman matures more quickly than the intelligence of man. Many of the physical and psychical differences between the two sexes must be attributed to the fact that man was formed from the ground and woman from bone. Women need perfumes, while men do not; dust of the ground remains the same no matter how long it is kept; flesh, however, requires salt to keep it in good condition. The voice of women is shrill, not so the voice of men; when soft viands are cooked, no sound is heard, but let a bone be put in a pot, and at once it crackles. A man is easily placated, not so a woman; a few drops of water suffice to soften a clod of earth; a bone stays hard, and if it were to soak in water for days. The man must ask the woman to be his wife, and not the woman the man to be her husband, because it is man who has sustained the loss of his rib, and he sallies forth to make good his loss again. The very differences between the sexes in garb and social forms go back to the origin of man and woman for their reasons. Woman covers her hair in token of Eve's having brought sin into the world; she tries to hide her shame; and women precede men in a funeral cortege, because it was woman who brought death into the world. And the religious commands addressed to women alone are connected with the history of Eve. Adam was the heave offering of the world, and Eve defiled it. As expiation, all women are commanded to separate a heave offering from the dough. And because woman extinguished the light of man's soul, she is bidden to kindle the Sabbath light.

Adam was first made to fall into a deep sleep before the rib for Eve was taken from his side. For, had he watched her creation, she would not have awakened love in him. To this day it is true that men do not appreciate the charms of women whom they have known and observed from childhood up. Indeed, God had created a wife for Adam before Eve, but he would not have her, because she had been made in his presence. Knowing well all the details of her formation, he was repelled by her. But when he roused himself from his profound sleep, and saw Eve before him in all her surprising beauty and grace, he exclaimed, "This is she who caused my heart to throb many a night!" Yet he discerned at once what the nature of woman was. She would, he knew, seek to carry her point with man either by entreaties and tears, or flattery and caresses. He said, therefore, "This is my never-silent bell!"

The wedding of the first couple was celebrated with pomp never repeated in the whole course of history since. God Himself, before presenting her to Adam, attired and adorned Eve as a bride. Yea, He appealed to the angels, saying: "Come, let us perform services of friendship for Adam and his helpmate, for the world rests upon friendly services, and they are more pleasing in My sight than the sacrifices Israel will offer upon the altar." The angels accordingly surrounded the marriage canopy, and God pronounced the blessings upon the bridal couple, as the Hazan does under the Huppah. The angels then danced and played upon musical instruments before Adam and Eve in their ten bridal chambers of gold, pearls, and precious stones, which God had prepared for them.

Adam called his wife Ishah, and himself he called Ish, abandoning the name Adam, which he had borne before the creation of Eve, for the reason that God added His own name Yah to the names of the man and the woman--Yod to Ish and He to Ishah--to indicate that as long as they walked in the ways of God and observed His commandments, His name would shield them against all harm. But if they went astray, His name would be withdrawn, and instead of Ish there would remain Esh, fire, a fire issuing from each and consuming the other.

ADAM AND EVE IN PARADISE

The Garden of Eden was the abode of the first man and woman, and the souls of all men must pass through it after death, before they reach their final destination. For the souls of the departed must go through seven portals before they arrive in the heaven 'Arabot. There the souls of the pious are transformed into angels, and there they remain forever, praising God and feasting their sight upon the glory of the Shekinah. The first portal is the Cave of Machpelah, in the vicinity of Paradise, which is under the care and supervision of Adam. If the soul that presents herself at the portal is worthy, he calls out, "Make room! Thou art welcome!" The soul then proceeds until she arrives at the gate of Paradise guarded by the cherubim and the flaming sword. If she is not found worthy, she is consumed by the sword; otherwise she receives a pass-bill, which admits her to the terrestrial Paradise. Therein is a pillar of smoke and light extending from Paradise to the gate of heaven, and it depends upon the character of the soul whether she can climb upward on it and reach heaven. The third portal, Zebul, is at the entrance of heaven. If the soul is worthy, the guard opens the portal and admits her 'to the heavenly Temple. Michael presents her to God, and conducts her to the seventh portal, 'Arabot, within which the souls of the pious, changed to angels, praise the Lord, and feed on the glory of the Shekinah.

In Paradise stand the tree of life and the tree of knowledge, the latter forming a hedge about the former. Only he who has cleared a path for himself through the tree of knowledge can come close to the tree of life, which is so huge that it would take a man five hundred years to traverse a distance equal to the diameter of the trunk, and no less vast is the space shaded by its crown of branches. From beneath it flows forth the water that irrigates the whole earth, parting thence into four streams, the Ganges, the Nile, the Tigris, and the Euphrates. But it was only during the days of creation that the realm of plants looked to the waters of the earth for nourishment. Later on God made the plants dependent upon the rain, the upper waters. The clouds rise from earth to heaven, where water is poured into them as from a conduit. The plants began to feel the effect of the water only after Adam was created. Although they had been brought forth on the third day, God did not permit them to sprout and appear above the surface of the earth, until Adam prayed to Him to give food unto them, for God longs for the prayers of the pious.

Paradise being such as it was, it was, naturally, not necessary for Adam to work the land. True, the Lord God put the man into the Garden of Eden to dress it and to keep it, but that only means he is to study the Torah there and fulfil the commandments of God. There were especially six commandments which every human being is expected to heed: man should not worship idols; nor blaspheme God; nor commit murder, nor incest, nor theft and robbery; and all generations have the duty of instituting measures of law and order. One more such command there was, but it was a temporary injunction. Adam was to eat only the green things of the field. But the prohibition against the use of animals for food was revoked in Noah's time, after the deluge. Nevertheless, Adam was not cut off from the enjoyment of meat dishes. Though he was not permitted to slaughter animals for the appeasing of his appetite, the angels brought him meat and wine, serving him like attendants. And as the angels ministered to his wants, so also the animals. They were wholly under his dominion, and their food they took out of his hand and out of Eve's. In all respects, the animal world had a different relation to Adam from their relation to his descendants. Not only did they know the language of man, but they respected the image of God, and they feared the first human couple, all of which changed into the opposite after the fall of man.

THE FALL OF MAN

Among the animals the serpent was notable. Of all of them he had the most excellent qualities, in some of which he resembled man. Like man he stood upright upon two feet, and in height he was equal to the camel. Had it not been for the fall of man, which brought misfortune to them, too, one pair of serpents would have sufficed to perform all the work man has to do, and, besides, they would have supplied him with silver, gold, gems, and pearls. As a matter of fact, it was the very ability of the serpent that led to the ruin of man and his own ruin. His superior mental gifts caused him to become an infidel. It likewise explains his envy of man, especially of his conjugal relations. Envy made him meditate ways and means of bringing about the death of Adam. He was too well acquainted with the character of the man to attempt to exercise tricks of persuasion upon him, and he approached the woman, knowing that women are beguiled easily. The conversation with Eve was cunningly planned, she could not but be caught in a trap. The serpent began, "Is it true that God hath said, Ye shall not eat of every tree in the garden?" "We may," rejoined Eve, "eat of the fruit of all the trees in the garden, except that which is in the midst of the garden, and that we may not even touch, lest we be stricken with death." She spoke thus, because in his zeal to guard her against the transgressing of the Divine command, Adam had forbidden Eve to touch the tree, though God had mentioned only the eating of the fruit. It remains a truth, what the proverb says, "Better a wall ten hands high that stands, than a wall a hundred ells high that cannot stand." It was Adam's exaggeration that afforded the serpent the possibility of persuading Eve to taste of the forbidden fruit. The serpent pushed Eve against the tree, and said: "Thou seest that touching the tree has not caused thy death. As little will it hurt thee to eat the fruit of the tree. Naught but malevolence has prompted the prohibition, for as soon as ye eat thereof, ye shall be as God. As He creates and destroys worlds, so will ye have the power to create and destroy. As He doth slay and revive, so will ye have the power to slay and revive. He Himself ate first of the fruit of the tree, and then He created the world. Therefore doth He forbid you to eat thereof, lest you create other worlds. Everyone knows that 'artisans of the same guild hate one another.' Furthermore, have ye not observed that every creature hath dominion over the creature fashioned before itself? The heavens were made on the first day, and they are kept in place by the firmament made on the second day. The firmament, in turn, is ruled by the plants, the creation of the third day, for they take up all the water of the firmament. The sun and the other celestial bodies, which were created on the fourth day, have power over the world of plants. They can ripen their fruits and flourish only through their influence. The creation of the fifth day, the animal world, rules over the celestial spheres. Witness the ziz, which can darken the sun with its pinions. But ye are masters of the whole of creation, because ye were the last to be created. Hasten now and eat of the fruit of the tree in the midst of the garden, and become independent of God, lest He bring forth still other creatures to bear rule over you."

To give due weight to these words, the serpent began to shake the tree violently and bring down its fruit. He ate thereof, saying: "As I do not die of eating the fruit, so wilt thou not die." Now Eve could not but say to herself, "All that my master"--so she called Adam--"commanded me is but lies," and she determined to follow the advice of the serpent. Yet she could not bring herself to disobey the command of God utterly. She made a compromise with her conscience. First she ate only the outside skin of the fruit, and then, seeing that death did not fell her, she ate the fruit itself. Scarce had she finished, when she saw the Angel of Death before her. Expecting her end to come immediately, she resolved to make Adam eat of the forbidden fruit, too, lest he espouse another wife after her death. It required tears and lamentations on her part to prevail upon Adam to take the baleful step. Not yet satisfied, she gave of the fruit to all other living beings, that they, too, might be subject to death. All ate, and they all are mortal, with the exception of the bird malham, who refused the fruit, with the words: "Is it not enough that ye have sinned against God, and have brought death to others? Must ye still come to me and seek to persuade me into disobeying God's command, that I may eat and die thereof? I will not do your bidding." A heavenly voice was heard then to say to Adam and Eve: "To you was the command given. Ye did not heed it; ye did transgress it, and ye did seek to persuade the bird malham. He was steadfast, and he feared Me, although I gave him no command. Therefore he shall never taste of death, neither he nor his descendants--they all shall live forever in Paradise."

Adam spoke to Eve: "Didst thou give me of the tree of which I forbade thee to eat? Thou didst give me thereof, for my eyes are opened, and the teeth in my mouth are set on edge." Eve made answer, "As my teeth were set on edge, so may the teeth of all living beings be set on edge." The first result was that Adam and Eve became naked. Before, their bodies had been overlaid with a horny skin, and enveloped with the cloud of glory. No sooner had they violated the command given them than the cloud of glory and the horny skin dropped from them, and they stood there in their nakedness, and ashamed. Adam tried to gather leaves from the trees to cover part of their bodies, but he heard one tree after the other say: "There is the thief that deceived his Creator. Nay, the foot of pride shall not come against me, nor the hand of the wicked touch me. Hence, and take no leaves from me!" Only the fig-tree granted him permission to take of its leaves. That was because the fig was the forbidden fruit itself. Adam had the same experience as that prince who seduced one of the maid-ser vants in the palace. When the king, his father, chased him out, he vainly sought a refuge with the other maid-servants, but only she who had caused his disgrace would grant him assistance.

THE PUNISHMENT

As long as Adam stood naked, casting about for means of escape from his embarrassment, God did not appear unto him, for one should not "strive to see a man in the hour of his disgrace." He waited until Adam and Eve had covered themselves with fig leaves. But even before God spoke to him, Adam knew what was impending. He heard the angels announce, "God betaketh Himself unto those that dwell in Paradise." He heard more, too. He heard what the angels were saying to one another about his fall, and what they were saying to God. In astonishment the angels exclaimed: "What! He still walks about in Paradise? He is not yet dead?" Whereupon God: "I said to him, 'In the day that thou eatest thereof, thou shalt surely die!' Now, ye know not what manner of day I meant--one of My days of a thousand years, or one of your days. I will give him one of My days. He shall have nine hundred and thirty years to live, and seventy to leave to his descendants."

When Adam and Eve heard God approaching, they hid among the trees--which would not have been possible before the fall. Before he committed his trespass, Adam's height was from the heavens to the earth, but afterward it was reduced to one hundred ells. Another consequence of his sin was the fear Adam felt when he heard the voice of God: before his fall it had not disquieted him in the least. Hence it was that when Adam said, "I heard Thy voice in the garden, and I was afraid," God replied, "Aforetime thou wert not afraid, and now thou art afraid?"

God refrained from reproaches at first. Standing at the gate of Paradise, He but asked, "Where art thou, Adam?" Thus did God desire to teach man a rule of polite behavior, never to enter the house of another without announcing himself. It cannot be denied, the words "Where art thou?" were pregnant with meaning. They were intended to bring home to Adam the vast difference between his latter and his former state-- between his supernatural size then and his shrunken size now; between the lordship of God over him then and the lordship of the serpent over him now. At the same time, God wanted to give Adam the opportunity of repenting of his sin, and he would have received Divine forgiveness for it. But so far from repenting of it,

Adam slandered God, and uttered blasphemies against Him. When God asked him, "Hast thou eaten of the tree whereof I commanded thee thou shouldst not eat?" he did not confess his sin, but excused himself with the words: "O Lord of the world! As long as I was alone, I did not fall into sin, but as soon as this woman came to me, she tempted me." God replied: "I gave her unto thee as a help, and thou art ungrateful when thou accusest her, saying, 'She gave me of the tree.' Thou shouldst not have obeyed her, for thou art the head, and not she." God, who knows all things, had foreseen exactly this, and He had not created Eve until Adam had asked Him for a helpmate, so that he might not have apparently good reason for reproaching God with having created woman.

As Adam tried to shift the blame for his misdeed from himself, so also Eve. She, like her husband, did not confess her transgression and pray for pardon, which would have been granted to her. Gracious as God is, He did not pronounce the doom upon Adam and Eve until they showed themselves stiff-necked. Not so with the serpent. God inflicted the curse upon the serpent without hearing his defense; for the serpent is a villain, and the wicked are good debaters. If God had questioned him, the serpent would have answered: "Thou didst give them a command, and I did contradict it. Why did they obey me, and not Thee?" Therefore God did not enter into an argument with the serpent, but straightway decreed the following ten punishments: The mouth of the serpent was closed, and his power of speech taken away; his hands and feet were hacked off; the earth was given him as food; he must suffer great pain in sloughing his skin; enmity is to exist between him and man; if he eats the choicest viands, or drinks the sweetest beverages, they all change into dust in his mouth; the pregnancy of the female serpent lasts seven years; men shall seek to kill him as soon as they catch sight of him; even in the future world, where all beings will be blessed, he will not escape the punishment decreed for him; he will vanish from out of the Holy Land if Israel walks in the ways of God.

Furthermore, God spake to the serpent: "I created thee to be king over all animals, cattle and the beasts of the field alike; but thou wast not satisfied. Therefore thou shalt be cursed above all cattle and above every beast of the field. I created thee of upright posture; but thou wast not satisfied. Therefore thou shalt go upon thy belly. I created thee to eat the same food as man; but thou wast not satisfied. Therefore thou shalt eat dust all the days of thy life. Thou didst seek to cause the death of Adam in order to espouse his wife. Therefore I will put enmity between thee and the woman." How true it is--he who lusts after what is not his due, not only does he not attain his desire, but he also loses what he has!

As angels had been present when the doom was pronounced upon the serpent--for God had convoked a Sanhedrin of seventy-one angels when He sat in judgment upon him--so the execution of the decree against him was entrusted to angels. They descended from heaven, and chopped off his hands and feet. His suffering was so great that his agonized cries could be heard from one end of the world to the other.

The verdict against Eve also consisted of ten curses, the effect of which is noticeable to this day in the physical, spiritual, and social state of woman. It was not God Himself who announced her fate to Eve. The only woman with whom God ever spoke was Sarah. In the case of Eve, He made use of the services of an interpreter.

Finally, also the punishment of Adam was tenfold: he lost his celestial clothing--God stripped it off him; in sorrow he was to earn his daily bread; the food he ate was to be turned from good into bad; his children were to wander from land to land; his body was to exude sweat; he was to have an evil inclination; in death his body was to be a prey of the worms; animals were to have power over him, in that they could slay him; his days were to be few and full of trouble; in the end he was to render account of all his doings on earth."

These three sinners were not the only ones to have punishment dealt out to them. The earth fared no better, for it had been guilty of various misdemeanors. In the first place, it had not entirely heeded the command of God given on the third day, to bring forth "tree of fruit." What God had desired was a tree the wood of which was to be as pleasant to the taste as the fruit thereof. The earth, however, produced a tree bearing fruit, the tree itself not being edible. Again, the earth did not do its whole duty in connection with the sin of Adam. God had appointed the sun and the earth witnesses to testify against Adam in case he committed a trespass. The sun, accordingly, had grown dark the instant Adam became guilty of disobedience, but the earth, not knowing how to take notice of Adam's fall, disregarded it altogether. The earth also had to suffer a tenfold punishment: independent before, she was hereafter to wait to be watered by the rain from above; sometimes the fruits of the earth fail; the grain she brings forth is stricken with blasting and mildew; she must produce all sorts of noxious vermin; thenceforth she was to be divided into valleys and mountains; she must grow barren trees, bearing no fruit; thorns and thistles sprout from her; much is sown in the earth, but little is harvested; in time to come the earth will have to disclose her blood, and shall no more cover her slain; and, finally, she shall, one day, "wax old like a garment."

When Adam heard the words, "Thorns and thistles shall it bring forth," concerning the ground, a sweat broke out on his face, and he said: "What! Shall I and my cattle eat from the same manger?" The Lord had mercy upon him, and spoke, "In view of the sweat of thy face, thou shalt eat bread."

The earth is not the only thing created that was made to suffer through the sin of Adam. The same fate overtook the moon. When the serpent seduced Adam and Eve, and exposed their nakedness, they wept bitterly, and with them wept the heavens, and the sun and the stars, and all created beings and things up to the throne of God. The very angels and the celestial beings were grieved by the trans gression of Adam. The moon alone laughed, wherefore God grew wroth, and obscured her light. Instead of shining steadily like the sun, all the length of the day, she grows old quickly, and must be born and reborn, again and again. The callous conduct of the moon offended God, not only by way of contrast with the compassion of all other creatures, but because He Himself was full of pity for Adam and his wife. He made clothes for them out of the skin stripped from the serpent. He would have done even more. He would have permitted them to remain in Paradise, if only they had been penitent. But they refused to repent, and they had to leave, lest their godlike understanding urge them to ravage the tree of life, and they learn to live forever. As it was, when God dismissed them from Paradise, He did not allow the Divine quality of justice to prevail entirely. He associated mercy with it. As they left, He said: "O what a pity that Adam was not able to observe the command laid upon him for even a brief span of time!

To guard the entrance to Paradise, God appointed the cherubim, called also the ever-turning sword of flames, because angels can turn themselves from one shape into another at need. Instead of the tree of life, God gave Adam the Torah, which likewise is a tree of life to them that lay hold upon her, and he was permitted to take up his abode in the vicinity of Paradise in the east.

Sentence pronounced upon Adam and Eve and the serpent, the Lord commanded the angels to turn the man and the woman out of Paradise. They began to weep and supplicate bitterly, and the angels took pity upon them and left the Divine command unfulfilled, until they could petition God to mitigate His severe verdict. But the Lord was inexorable, saying, "Was it I that committed a trespass, or did I pronounce a false judgment?" Also Adam's prayer, to be given of the fruit of the tree of life, was turned aside, with the promise, however, that if he would lead a pious life, he would be given of the fruit on the day of resurrection, and he would then live forever.

Seeing that God had resolved unalterably, Adam began to weep again and implore the angels to grant him at least permission to take sweet-scented spices with him out of Paradise, that outside, too, he might be able to bring offerings unto God, and his prayers be accepted before the Lord. Thereupon the angels came before God, and spake: "King unto everlasting, command Thou us to give Adam sweetscented spices of Paradise," and God heard their prayer. Thus Adam gathered saffron, nard, calamus, and cinnamon, and all sorts of seeds besides for his sustenance. Laden with these, Adam and Eve left Paradise, and came upon earth. They had enjoyed the splendors of Paradise but a brief span of time--but a few hours. It was in the first hour of the sixth day of creation that God conceived the idea of creating man; in the second hour, He took counsel with the angels; in the third, He gathered the dust for the body of man; in the fourth, He formed Adam; in the fifth, He clothed him with skin; in the sixth, the soulless shape was complete, so that it could stand upright; in the seventh, a soul was breathed into it; in the eighth, man was led into Paradise; in the ninth, the Divine command prohibiting the fruit of the tree in the midst of the garden was issued to him; in the tenth, he transgressed the command; in the eleventh, he was judged; and in the twelfth hour of the day, he was cast out of Paradise, in atonement for his sin.

This eventful day was the first of the month of Tishri. Therefore God spoke to Adam: "Thou shalt be the prototype of thy children. As thou hast been judged by Me on this day and absolved, so thy children Israel shall be judged by Me on this New Year's Day, and they shall be absolved."

Each day of creation brought forth three things: the first, heaven, earth, and light; the second, the firmament, Gehenna, and the angels; the third, trees, herbs, and Paradise; the fourth, sun, moon, and stars; and the fifth, fishes, birds, and leviathan. As God intended to rest on the seventh day, the Sabbath, the sixth day had to do double duty. It brought forth six creations: Adam, Eve, cattle, reptiles, the beasts of the field, and demons. The demons were made shortly before the Sabbath came in, and they are, therefore, incorporeal spirits--the Lord had no time to create bodies for them.

In the twilight, between the sixth day and the Sabbath, ten creations were, brought forth: the rainbow, invisible until Noah's time; the manna; watersprings, whence Israel drew water for his thirst in the desert; the writing upon the two tables of stone given at Sinai; the pen with which the writing was written; the two tables themselves; the mouth of Balaam's she-ass; the grave of Moses; the cave in which Moses and Elijah dwelt; and the rod of Aaron, with its blossoms and its ripe almonds.

SABBATH IN HEAVEN

Before the world was created, there was none to praise God and know Him. Therefore He created the angels and the holy Hayyot, the heavens and their host, and Adam as well. They all were to praise and glorify their Creator. During the week of creation, however, there was no suitable time to proclaim the splendor and praise of the Lord. Only on the Sabbath, when all creation rested, the beings on earth and in heaven, all together, broke into song and adoration when God ascended His throne and sate upon it. It was the Throne of Joy upon which He sate, and He had all the angels pass before Him--the angel of the water, the angel of the rivers, the angel of the mountains, the angel of the hills, the angel of the abysses, the angel of the deserts, the angel of the sun, the angel of the moon, the angel of the Pleiades, the angel of Orion, the angel of the herbs, the angel of Paradise, the angel of Gehenna, the angel of the trees, the angel of the reptiles, the angel of the wild beasts, the angel of the domestic animals, the angel of the fishes, the angel of the locusts, the angel of the birds, the chief angel of the angels, the angel of each heaven, the chief angel of each division of the heavenly hosts, the chief angel of the holy Hayyot, the chief angel of the cherubim, the chief angel of the ofanim, and all the other splendid, terrible, and mighty angel chiefs. They all appeared before God with great joy, laved in a stream of joy, and they rejoiced and danced and sang, and extolled the Lord with many praises and many instruments. The ministering angels began, "Let the glory of the Lord endure forever!" And the rest of the angels took up the song with the words, "Let the Lord rejoice in His works!" 'Arabot, the seventh heaven, was filled with joy and glory, splendor and strength, power and might and pride and magnificence and grandeur, praise and jubilation, song and gladness, steadfastness and righteousness, honor and adoration.

Then God bade the Angel of the Sabbath seat himself upon a throne of glory, and He brought before him the chiefs of the angels of all the heavens and all the abysses, and bade them dance and rejoice, saying, "Sabbath it is unto the Lord!" and the exalted princes of the heavens responded, "Unto the Lord it is Sabbath!" Even Adam was permitted to ascend to the highest heaven, to take part in the rejoicing over the Sabbath.

By bestowing Sabbath joy upon all beings, not excepting Adam, thus did the Lord dedicate His creation. Seeing the majesty of the Sabbath, its honor and greatness, and the joy it conferred upon all, being the fount of all joy, Adam intoned a song of praise for the Sabbath day. Then God said to him, "Thou singest a song of praise to the Sabbath day, and singest none to Me, the God of the Sabbath?" Thereupon the Sabbath rose from his seat, and prostrated himself before God, saying, "It is a good thing to give thanks unto the Lord," and the whole of creation added, "And to sing praises unto Thy Name, O Most High!"

This was the first Sabbath, and this its celebration in heaven by God and the angels. The angels were informed at the same time that in days to come Israel would hallow the day in similar manner. God told them: "I will set aside for Myself a people from among all the peoples. This people will observe the Sabbath, and I will sanctify it to be My people, and I will be God unto it. From all that I have seen, I have chosen the seed of Israel wholly, and I have inscribed him as My first-born son, and I sanctified him unto Myself unto all eternity, him and the Sabbath, that he keep the Sabbath and hallow it from all work."

For Adam the Sabbath had a peculiar significance. When he was made to depart out of Paradise in the twilight of the Sabbath eve, the angels called after him, "Adam did not abide in his glory overnight!" Then the Sabbath appeared before God as Adam's defender, and he spoke: "O Lord of the world! During the six working days no creature was slain. If Thou wilt begin now by slaying Adam, what will become of the sanctity and the blessing of the Sabbath?" In this way Adam was rescued from the fires of hell, the meet punishment for his sins, and in gratitude he composed a psalm in honor of the Sabbath, which David later embodied in his Psalter.

Still another opportunity was given to Adam to learn and appreciate the value of the Sabbath. The celestial light, whereby Adam could survey the world from end to end, should properly have been made to disappear immediately after his sin. But out of consideration for the Sabbath, God had let this light continue to shine, and the angels, at sundown on the sixth day, intoned a song of praise and thanksgiving to God, for the radiant light shining through the night. Only with the going out of the Sabbath day the celestial light ceased, to the consternation of Adam, who feared that the serpent would attack him in the dark. But God illumined his understanding, and he learned to rub two stones against each other and produce light for his needs.

The celestial light was but one of the seven precious gifts enjoyed by Adam before the fall and to be granted to man again only in the Messianic time. The others are the resplendence of his countenance; life eternal; his tall stature; the fruits of the soil; the fruits of the tree; and the luminaries of the sky, the sun and the moon, for in the world to come the light of the moon shall be as the light of the sun, and the light of the sun shall be sevenfold.

ADAM'S REPENTANCE

Cast out of Paradise, Adam and Eve built a hut for themselves, and for seven days they sat in it in great distress, mourning and lamenting. At the end of the seven days, tormented by hunger, they came forth and sought food. For seven other days, Adam journeyed up and down in the land, looking for such dainties as he had enjoyed in Paradise. In vain; he found nothing. Then Eve spoke to her husband: "My lord, if it please thee, slay me. Mayhap God will then take thee back into Paradise, for the Lord God became wroth with thee only on account of me." But Adam rejected her plan with abhorrence, and both went forth again on the search for food. Nine days passed, and still they found naught resembling what they had had in Paradise. They saw only food fit for cattle and beasts. Then Adam proposed: "Let us do penance, mayhap the Lord God will forgive us and have pity on us, and give us something to sustain our life." Knowing that Eve was not vigorous enough to undergo the mortification of the flesh which he purposed to inflict upon himself, he prescribed a penance for her different from his own. He said to her: "Arise, and go to the Tigris, take a stone and stand upon it in the deepest part of the river, where the water will reach as high as thy neck. And let no speech issue forth from thy mouth, for we are unworthy to supplicate God, our lips are unclean by reason of the forbidden fruit of the tree. Remain in the water for thirty-seven days."

For himself Adam ordained forty days of fasting, while he stood in the river Jordan in the same way as Eve was to take up her stand in the waters of the Tigris. After he had adjusted the stone in the middle of the Jordan, and mounted it, with the waters surging up to his neck, he said: "I adjure thee, O thou water of the Jordan! Afflict thyself with me, and gather unto me all swimming creatures that live in thee. Let them surround me and sorrow with me, and let them not beat their own breasts with grief, but let them beat me. Not they have sinned, only I alone!" Very soon they all came, the dwellers in the Jordan, and they encompassed him, and from that moment the water of the Jordan stood still and ceased from flowing.

The penance which Adam and Eve laid upon themselves awakened misgivings in Satan. He feared God might forgive their sin, and therefore essayed to hinder Eve in her purpose. After a lapse of eighteen days he appeared unto her in the guise of an angel. As though in distress on account of her, he began to cry, saying: "Step up out of the river, and weep no longer. The Lord God hath heard your mourning, and your penitence hath been accepted by Him. All the angels supplicated the Lord in your behalf, and He hath sent me to fetch you out of the water and give you the sustenance that you enjoyed in Paradise, and for which you have been mourning." Enfeebled as she was by her penances and mortifications, Eve yielded to the solicitations of Satan, and he led her to where her husband was. Adam recognized him at once, and amid tears he cried out: "O Eve, Eve, where now is thy penitence? How couldst thou let our adversary seduce thee again--him who robbed us of our sojourn in Paradise and all spiritual joy?" Thereupon Eve, too, began to weep and cry out: "Woe unto thee, O Satan! Why strivest thou against us without any reason? What have we done unto thee that thou shouldst pursue us so craftily?" With a deep-fetched sigh, Satan told them how that Adam, of whom he had been jealous, had been the real reason of his fall. Having lost his glory through him, he had intrigued to have him driven from Paradise.

When Adam heard the confession of Satan, he prayed to God: "O Lord my God! In Thy hands is my life. Remove from me this adversary, who seeks to deliver my soul to destruction, and grant me the glory he has forfeited." Satan disappeared forthwith, but Adam continued his penance, standing in the waters of the Jordan for forty days.

While Adam stood in the river, he noticed that the days were growing shorter, and he feared the world might be darkened on account of his sin, and go under soon. To avert the doom, be spent eight days in prayer and fasting. But after the winter solstice, when he saw that the days grew longer again, he spent eight days in rejoicing, and in the following year he celebrated both periods, the one before and the one after the solstice. This is why the heathen celebrate the calends and the saturnalia in honor of their gods, though Adam had consecrated those days to the honor of God.

The first time Adam witnessed the sinking of the sun he was also seized with anxious fears. It happened at the conclusion of the Sabbath, and Adam said, "Woe is me! For my sake, because I sinned, the world is darkened, and it will again become void and without form. Thus will be executed the punishment of death which God has pronounced against me!" All the night he spent in tears, and Eve, too, wept as she sat opposite to him. When day began to dawn, he understood that what he had deplored was but the course of nature, and be brought an offering unto God, a unicorn whose horn was created before his hoofs, and he sacrificed it on the spot on which later the altar was to stand in Jerusalem.

THE BOOK OF RAZIEL

After Adam's expulsion from Paradise, he prayed to God in these words: "O God, Lord of the world! Thou didst create the whole world unto the honor and glory of the Mighty One, and Thou didst as was pleasing unto Thee. Thy kingdom is unto all eternity, and Thy reign unto all generations. Naught is hidden from Thee, and naught is concealed from Thine eyes. Thou didst create me as Thy handiwork, and didst make me the ruler over Thy creatures, that I might be the chief of Thy works. But the cunning, accursed serpent seduced me with the tree of desire and lusts, yea, he seduced the wife of my bosom. But Thou didst not make known unto me what shall befall my children and the generations after me. I know well that no human being can be righteous in Thine eyes, and what is my strength that I should step before Thee with an impudent face? I have no mouth wherewith to speak and no eye wherewith to see, for I did sin and commit a trespass, and, by reason of my sins, I was driven forth from Paradise. I must plough the earth whence I was taken, and the other inhabitants of the earth, the beasts, no longer, as once, stand in awe and fear of me. From the time I ate of the tree of knowledge of good and evil, wisdom departed from me, and I am a fool that knoweth naught, an ignorant man that understandeth not. Now, O merciful and gracious God, I pray to Thee to turn again Thy compassion to the head of Thy works, to the spirit which Thou didst instil into him, and the soul Thou didst breathe into him. Meet me with Thy grace, for Thou art gracious, slow to anger, and full of love. O that my prayer would reach unto the throne of Thy glory, and my supplication unto the throne of Thy mercy, and Thou wouldst incline to me with lovingkindness. May the words of my mouth be acceptable, that Thou turn not away from my petition. Thou wert from everlasting, and Thou wilt be unto everlasting; Thou wert king, and Thou wilt ever be king. Now, have Thou mercy upon the work of Thy hands. Grant me knowledge and understanding, that I may know what shall befall me, and my posterity, and all the generations that come after me, and what shall befall me on every day and in every month, and mayest Thou not withhold from me the help of Thy servants and of Thy angels."

On the third day after he had offered up this prayer, while he was sitting on the banks of the river that flows forth out of Paradise, there appeared to him, in the heat of the day, the angel Raziel, bearing a book in his hand. The angel addressed Adam thus: "O Adam, why art thou so fainthearted? Why art thou distressed and anxious? Thy words were heard at the moment when thou didst utter thy supplication and entreaties, and I have received the charge to teach thee pure words and deep understanding, to make thee wise through the contents of the sacred book in my hand, to know what will happen to thee until the day of thy death. And all thy descendants and all the later generations, if they will but read this book in purity, with a devout heart and an humble mind, and obey its precepts, will become like unto thee. They, too, will foreknow what things shall happen, and in what month and on what day or in what night. All will be manifest to them--they will know and understand whether a calamity will come, a famine or wild beasts, floods or drought; whether there will be abundance of grain or dearth; whether the wicked will rule the world; whether locusts will devastate the land; whether the fruits will drop from the trees unripe; whether boils will afflict men; whether wars will prevail, or diseases or plagues among men and cattle; whether good is resolved upon in heaven, or evil; whether blood will flow, and the death-rattle of the slain be heard in the city. And now, Adam, come and give heed unto what I shall tell thee regarding the manner of this book and its holiness."

Raziel, the angel, then read from the book, and when Adam heard the words of the holy volume as they issued from the mouth of the angel, he fell down affrighted. But the angel encouraged him. "Arise, Adam," he said, "be of good courage, be not afraid, take the book from me and keep it, for thou wilt draw knowledge from it thyself and become wise, and thou wilt also teach its contents to all those who shall be found worthy of knowing what it contains."

In the moment when Adam took the book, a flame of fire shot up from near the river, and the angel rose heavenward with it. Then Adam knew that he who had spoken to him was an angel of God, and it was from the Holy King Himself that the book had come, and he used it in holiness and purity. It is the book out of which all things worth knowing can be learnt, and all mysteries, and it teaches also how to call upon the angels and make them appear before men, and answer all their questions. But not all alike can use the book, only he who is wise and God-fearing, and resorts to it in holiness. Such an one is secure against all wicked counsels, his life is serene, and when death takes him from this world, he finds repose in a place where there are neither demons nor evil spirits, and out of the hands of the wicked he is quickly rescued.

THE SICKNESS OF ADAM

When Adam had lived to be nine hundred and thirty years old, a sickness seized him, and he felt that his days were drawing to an end. He summoned all his descendants, and assembled them before the door of the house of worship in which he had always offered his prayers to God, to give them his last blessing. His family were astonished to find him stretched out on the bed of sickness, for they did not know what pain and suffering were. They thought he was overcome with longing after the fruits of Paradise, and for lack of them was depressed. Seth announced his willingness to go to the gates of Paradise and beg God to let one of His angels give him of its fruits. But Adam explained to them what sickness and pain are, and that God had inflicted them upon him as a punishment for his sin. Adam suffered violently; tears and groans were wrung from him. Eve sobbed, and said, "Adam, my lord, give me the half of thy sickness, I will gladly bear it. Is it not on account of me that this hath come upon thee? On account of me thou undergoest pain and anguish."

Adam bade Eve go with Seth to the gates of Paradise and entreat God to have mercy upon him, and send His angel to catch up some of the oil of life flowing from the tree of His mercy and give it to his messengers. The ointment would bring him rest, and banish the pain consuming him. On his way to Paradise, Seth was attacked by a wild beast. Eve called out to the assailant, "How durst thou lay hand on the image of God?" The ready answer came: "It is thine own fault. Hadst thou not opened thy mouth to eat of the forbidden fruit, my mouth would not be opened now to destroy a human being." But Seth remonstrated: "Hold thy tongue! Desist from the image of God until the day of judgment." And the beast gave way, saying, "See, I refrain myself from the image of God," and it slunk away to its covert.

Arrived at the gates of Paradise, Eve and Seth began to cry bitterly, and they besought God with many lamentations to give them oil from the tree of His mercy. For hours they prayed thus. At last the archangel

Michael appeared, and informed them that he came as the messenger of God to tell them that their petition could not be granted. Adam would die in a few days, and as he was subject to death, so would be all his descendants. Only at the time of the resurrection, and then only to the pious, the oil of life would be dispensed, together with all the bliss and all the delights of Paradise. Returned to Adam, they reported what had happened, and he said to Eve: "What misfortune didst thou bring upon us when thou didst arouse great wrath! See, death is the portion of all our race! Call hither our children and our children's children, and tell them the manner of our sinning." And while Adam lay prostrate upon the bed of pain, Eve told them the story of their fall.

EVE'S STORY OF THE FALL

After I was created, God divided Paradise and all the animals therein between Adam and me. The east and the north were assigned to Adam, together with the male animals. I was mistress of the west and the south and all the female animals. Satan, smarting under the disgrace of having been dismissed from the heavenly host," resolved to bring about our ruin and avenge himself upon the cause of his discomfiture. He won the serpent over to his side, and pointed out to him that before the creation of Adam the animals could enjoy all that grew in Paradise, and now they were restricted to the weeds. To drive Adam from Paradise would therefore be for the good of all. The serpent demurred, for he stood in awe of the wrath of God. But Satan calmed his fears, and said, "Do thou but become my vessel, and I shall speak a word through thy mouth wherewith thou wilt succeed in seducing man."

The serpent thereupon suspended himself from the wall surrounding Paradise, to carry on his conversation with me from without. And this happened at the very moment when my two guardian angels had betaken themselves to heaven to supplicate the Lord. I was quite alone therefore, and when Satan assumed the appearance of an angel, bent over the wall of Paradise, and intoned seraphic songs of praise, I was deceived, and thought him an angel. A conversation was held between us, Satan speaking through the mouth of the serpent:

"Art thou Eve?"

"Yes, it is I."

"What art thou doing in Paradise?"

"The Lord has put us here to cultivate it and eat of its fruits."

"That is good. Yet you eat not of all the trees."

That we do, excepting a single one, the tree that stands in the midst of Paradise. Concerning it alone, God has forbidden us to eat of it, else, the Lord said, ye will die."

The serpent made every effort to persuade me that I had naught to fear--that God knew that in the day that Adam and I ate of the fruit of the tree, we should be as He Himself. It was jealousy that had made Him say, "Ye shall not eat of it." In spite of all his urging, I remained steadfast and refused to touch the tree. Then the serpent engaged to pluck the fruit for me. Thereupon I opened the gate of Paradise, and he slipped in. Scarcely was he within, when he said to me, "I repent of my words, I would rather not give thee of the fruit of the forbidden tree." It was but a cunning device to tempt me more. He consented to give me of the fruit only after I swore to make my husband eat of it, too. This is the oath he made me take: "By the throne of God, by the cherubim, and by the tree of life, I shall give my husband of this fruit, that he may eat, too." Thereupon the serpent ascended the tree and injected his poison, the poison of the evil inclination, into the fruit, and bent the branch on which it grew to the ground. I took hold of it, but I knew at once that I was stripped of the righteousness in which I had been clothed. I began to weep, because of it and because of the oath the serpent had forced from me.

The serpent disappeared from the tree, while I sought leaves wherewith to cover my nakedness, but all the trees within my reach had cast off their leaves at the moment when I ate of the forbidden fruit. There was only one that retained its leaves, the fig-tree, the very tree the fruit of which had been forbidden to me. I summoned Adam, and by means of blasphemous words I prevailed upon him to eat of the fruit. As soon as it had passed his lips, he knew his true condition, and he exclaimed against me: "Thou wicked woman, what hast thou brought down upon me? Thou hast removed me from the glory of God."

At the same time Adam and I heard the archangel Michael blow his trumpet, and all the angels cried out: "Thus saith the Lord, Come ye with Me to Paradise and hearken unto the sentence which I will pronounce upon Adam."

We hid ourselves because we feared the judgment of God. Sitting in his chariot drawn by cherubim, the Lord, accompanied by angels uttering His praise, appeared in Paradise. At His coming the bare trees again put forth leaves. His throne was erected by the tree of life, and God addressed Adam: "Adam, where dost thou keep thyself in hiding? Thinkest thou I cannot find thee? Can a house conceal itself from its architect?"

Adam tried to put the blame on me, who had promised to hold him harmless before God. And I in turn accused the serpent. But God dealt out justice to all three of us. To Adam He said: "Because thou didst not obey My commands, but didst hearken unto the voice of thy wife, cursed is the ground in spite of thy work. When thou dost cultivate it, it will not yield thee its strength. Thorns and thistles shall it bring forth to thee, and in the sweat of thy face shalt thou eat bread. Thou wilt suffer many a hardship, thou wilt grow weary, and yet find no rest. Bitterly oppressed, thou shalt never taste of any sweetness. Thou shalt be scourged by heat, and yet pinched by cold. Thou shalt toil greatly, and yet not gain wealth. Thou shalt grow fat, and yet cease to live. And the animals over which thou art the master will rise up against thee, because thou didst not keep my command."

Upon me God pronounced this sentence: "Thou shalt suffer anguish in childbirth and grievous torture. In sorrow shalt thou bring forth children, and in the hour of travail, when thou art near to lose thy life, thou wilt confess and cry, 'Lord, Lord, save me this time, and I will never again indulge in carnal pleasure,' and yet thy desire shall ever and ever be unto thy husband."

At the same time all sorts of diseases were decreed upon us. God said to Adam: "Because thou didst turn aside from My covenant, I will inflict seventy plagues upon thy flesh. The pain of the first plague shall lay hold on thy eyes; the pain of the second plague upon thy hearing, and one after the other all the plagues shall come upon thee." The serpent God addressed thus: "Because thou becamest the vessel of the Evil One, deceiving the innocent, cursed art thou above all cattle and above every beast of the field. Thou shalt be robbed of the food thou wast wont to eat, and dust shalt thou eat all the days of thy life. Upon thy breast and thy belly shalt thou go, and of thy hands and thy feet thou shalt be deprived. Thou shalt not remain in possession of thy ears, nor of thy wings, nor of any of thy limbs wherewith thou didst seduce the woman and her husband, bringing them to such a pass that they must be driven forth from Paradise. And I will put enmity between thee and the seed of man. It shall bruise thy head, and, thou shalt bruise his heel until the day of judgment."

THE DEATH OF ADAM

On the last day of Adam's life, Eve said to him, "Why should I go on living, when thou art no more? How long shall I have to linger on after thy death? Tell me this!" Adam assured her she would not tarry long. They would die together, and be buried together in the same place. He commanded her not to touch his corpse until an angel from God had made provision regarding it, and she was to begin at once to pray to God until his soul escaped from his body.

While Eve was on her knees in prayer, an angel came, and bade her rise. "Eve, arise from thy penance," he commanded. "Behold, thy husband hath left his mortal coil. Arise, and see his spirit go up to his Creator, to appear before Him." And, lo, she beheld a chariot of light, drawn by four shining eagles, and preceded by angels. In this chariot lay the soul of Adam, which the angels were taking to heaven. Arrived there, they burnt incense until the clouds of smoke enveloped the heavens. Then they prayed to God to have mercy upon His image and the work of His holy hands. In her awe and fright, Eve summoned Seth, and she bade him look upon the vision and explain the celestial sights beyond her understanding. She asked, "Who may the two Ethiopians be, who are adding their prayers to thy father's?" Seth told her, they were the sun and the moon, turned so black because they could not shine in the face of the Father of light. Scarcely had he spoken, when an angel blew a trumpet, and all the angels cried out with awful voices, "Blessed be the glory of the Lord by His creatures, for He has shown mercy unto Adam, the work of His hands!" A seraph then seized Adam, and carried him off to the river Acheron, washed him three times, and brought him before the presence of God, who sat upon His throne, and, stretching out His hand, lifted Adam up and gave him over to the archangel Michael, with the words, "Raise him to the Paradise of the third heaven, and there thou shalt leave him until the great and fearful day ordained by Me." Michael executed the Divine behest, and all the angels sang a song of praise, extolling God for the pardon He had accorded Adam.

Michael now entreated God to let him attend to the preparation of Adam's body for the grave. Permission being given, Michael repaired to earth, accompanied by all the angels. When they entered the terrestrial Paradise, all the trees blossomed forth, and the perfume wafted thence lulled all men into slumber except Seth alone. Then God said to Adam, as his body lay on the ground: "If thou hadst kept My commandment, they would not rejoice who brought thee hither. But I tell thee, I will turn the joy of Satan and his consorts into sorrow, and thy sorrow shall be turned into joy. I will restore thee to thy dominion, and thou shalt sit upon the throne of thy seducer, while he shall be damned, with those who hearken unto him."

Thereupon, at the bidding of God, the three great archangels covered the body of Adam with linen, and poured sweet-smelling oil upon it. With it they interred also the body of Abel, which had lain unburied since Cain had slain him, for all the murderer's efforts to hide it had been in vain. The corpse again and again sprang forth from the earth, and a voice issued thence, proclaiming, "No creature shall rest in the earth until the first one of all has returned the dust to me of which it was formed." The angels carried the two bodies to Paradise, Adam's and Abel's--the latter had all this time been lying on a stone on which angels had placed it-- and they buried them both on the spot whence God had taken the dust wherewith to make Adam.

God called unto the body of Adam, "Adam! Adam!" and it answered, "Lord, here am I!" Then God said: "I told thee once, Dust thou art, and unto dust shalt thou return. Now I promise thee resurrection. I will awaken thee on the day of judgment, when all the generations of men that spring from thy loins, shall arise from the grave." God then sealed up the grave, that none might do him harm during the six days to elapse until his rib should be restored to him through the death of Eve.

THE DEATH OF EVE

The interval between Adam's death and her own Eve spent in weeping. She was distressed in particular that she knew not what had become of Adam's body, for none except Seth had been awake while the angel interred it. When the hour of her death drew nigh, Eve supplicated to be buried in the selfsame spot in which the remains of her husband rested. She prayed to God: "Lord of all powers! Remove not Thy maid-servant from the body of Adam, from which Thou didst take me, from whose limbs Thou didst form me. Permit me, who am an unworthy and sinning woman, to enter into his habitation. As we were together in Paradise, neither separated from the other; as together we were tempted to transgress Thy law, neither separated from the other, so, O Lord, separate us not now." To the end of her prayer she added the petition, raising her eyes heavenward, "Lord of the world! Receive my spirit!" and she gave up her soul to God.

The archangel Michael came and taught Seth how to prepare Eve for burial, and three angels descended and interred her body in the grave with Adam and Abel. Then Michael spoke to Seth, "Thus shalt thou bury all men that die until the resurrection day." And again, having given him this command, he spoke: "Longer than six days ye shall not mourn. The repose of the seventh day is the token of the resurrection in the latter day, for on the seventh day the Lord rested from all the work which He had created and made."

Though death was brought into the world through Adam, yet he cannot be held responsible for the death of men. Once on a time he said to God: "I am not concerned about the death of the wicked, but I should not like the pious to reproach me and lay the blame for their death upon me. I pray Thee, make no mention of my guilt." And God promised to fulfil his wish. Therefore, when a man is about to die, God appears to him, and bids him set down in writing all he has done during his life, for, He tells him, "Thou art dying by reason of thy evil deeds." The record finished, God orders him to seal it with his seal. This is the writing God will bring out on the judgment day, and to each will be made known his deeds. As soon as life is extinct in a man, he is presented to Adam, whom be accuses of having caused his death. But Adam repudiates the charge: "I committed but one trespass. Is there any among you, and be he the most pious, who has not been guilty of more than one?"

Chapter 3

THE BIRTH OF CAIN - There were ten generations from Adam to Noah, to show how long-suffering is the Lord, for all the generations provoked Him unto wrath, until He brought the deluge upon them. By reason of their impiousness God changed His plan of calling one thousand generations into being between the creation of the world and the revelation of the law at Mount Sinai; nine hundred and seventy-four He suppressed before the flood. Wickedness came into the world with the first being born of woman, Cain, the oldest son of Adam. When God bestowed Paradise upon the first pair of mankind, He warned them particularly against carnal intercourse with each other. But after the fall of Eve, Satan, in the guise of the serpent, approached her, and the fruit of their union was Cain, the ancestor of all the impious generations that were rebellious toward God, and rose up against Him. Cain's descent from Satan, who is the angel Samael, was revealed in his seraphic appearance. At his birth, the exclamation was wrung from Eve, "I have gotten a man through an angel of the Lord." Adam was not in the company of Eve during the time of her pregnancy with Cain. After she had succumbed a second time to the temptations of Satan, and permitted herself to be interrupted in her penance, she left her husband and journeyed westward, because she feared her presence might continue to bring him misery. Adam remained in the east. When the days of Eve to be delivered were fulfilled, and she began to feel the pangs of travailing, she prayed to God for help. But He hearkened not unto her supplications. "Who will carry the report to my lord Adam?" she asked herself. "Ye luminaries in the sky, I beg you, tell it to my master Adam when ye return to the east!" In that self same hour, Adam cried out: "The lamentation of Eve has pierced to my ear! Mayhap the serpent has again assaulted her," and he hastened to his wife. Finding her in grievous pain, he besought God in her behalf, and twelve angels appeared, together with two heavenly powers. All these took up their post to right of her and to left of her, while Michael, also standing on her right side, passed his hand over her, from her face downward to her breast, and said to her, "Be thou blessed, Eve, for the sake of Adam. Because of his solicitations and his prayers I was sent to grant thee our assistance. Make ready to give birth to thy child!" Immediately her son was born, a radiant figure. A little while and the babe stood upon his feet, ran off, and returned holding in his hands a stalk of straw, which he gave to his mother. For this reason he was named Cain, the Hebrew word for stalk of straw. Now Adam took Eve and the boy to his home in the east. God sent him various kinds of seeds by the hand of the angel Michael, and he was taught how to cultivate the ground and make it yield produce and fruits, to sustain himself and his family and his posterity. After a while, Eve bore her second son, whom she named Hebel, because, she said, he was born but to die.

FRATRICIDE - The slaying of Abel by Cain did not come as a wholly unexpected event to his parents. In a dream Eve had seen the blood of Abel flow into the mouth of Cain, who drank it with avidity, though his brother entreated him not to take all. When she told her dream to Adam, he said, lamenting, "O that this may not portend the death of Abel at the hand of Cain!" He separated the two lads, assigning to each an abode of his own, and to each he taught a different occupation. Cain became a tiller of the ground, and Abel a keeper of sheep. It was all in vain. In spite of these precautions, Cain slew his brother. His hostility toward Abel had more than one reason. It began when God had respect unto the offering of Abel, and accepted it by sending heavenly fire down to consume it, while the offering of Cain was rejected. They brought their sacrifices on the fourteenth day of Nisan, at the instance of their father, who had spoken thus to his sons: "This is the day on which, in times to come, Israel will offer sacrifices. Therefore, do ye, too, bring sacrifices to your Creator on this day, that He may take pleasure in you." The place of offering which they chose was the spot whereon the altar of the Temple at Jerusalem stood later. Abel selected the best of his flocks for his sacrifice, but Cain ate his meal first, and after he had satisfied his appetite, he offered unto God what was left over, a few grains of flax seed. As though his offense had not been great enough in offering unto God fruit of the ground which had been cursed by God! What wonder that his sacrifice was not received with favor! Besides, a chastisement was inflicted upon him. His face turned black as smoke. Nevertheless, his disposition underwent no change, even when God spoke to him thus: "If thou wilt amend thy ways, thy guilt will be forgiven thee; if not, thou wilt be delivered into the power of the evil inclination. It coucheth at the door of thy heart, yet it depends upon thee whether thou shalt be master over it, or it shall be master over thee." Cain thought he had been wronged, and a dispute followed between him and Abel. "I believed," he said, "that the world was created through goodness, but I see that good deeds bear no fruit. God rules the world with arbitrary power, else why had He respect unto thy offering, and not unto mine also?" Abel opposed him; he maintained that God rewards good deeds, without having respect unto persons. If his sacrifice had been accepted graciously by God, and Cain's not, it was because his deeds were good, and his brother's wicked. But this was not the only cause of Cain's hatred toward Abel. Partly love for a woman brought about the crime. To ensure the propagation of the human race, a girl, destined to be his wife, was born together with each of the sons of Adam. Abel's twin sister was of exquisite beauty, and Cain desired her. Therefore he was constantly brooding over ways and means of ridding himself of his brother. The opportunity presented itself ere long. One day a sheep belonging to Abel tramped over a field that had been planted by Cain. In a rage, the latter called out, "What right hast thou to live upon my land and let thy sheep pasture yonder?" Abel retorted: "What right hast thou to use the products of my sheep, to make garments for thyself from their wool? If thou wilt take off the wool of my sheep wherein thou art arrayed, and wilt pay me for the flesh of the flocks which thou hast eaten, then I will quit thy land as thou desirest, and fly into the air, if I can do it." Cain thereupon said, "And if I were to kill thee, who is there to demand thy blood of me?" Abel replied: "God, who brought us into the world, will avenge me. He will require my blood at thine hand, if thou shouldst slay me. God is the Judge, who will visit their wicked deeds upon the wicked, and their evil deeds upon the evil. Shouldst thou slay me, God will know thy secret, and He will deal out punishment unto thee." These words but added to the anger of Cain, and he threw himself upon his brother. Abel was stronger than he, and he would have got the worst of it, but at the last moment he begged for mercy, and the gentle Abel released his hold upon him. Scarcely did he feel himself free, when he turned against Abel once more, and slew him. So true is the saying, "Do the evil no good, lest evil fall upon thee."

THE PUNISHMENT OF CAIN - The manner of Abel's death was the most cruel conceivable. Not knowing what injury was fatal, Cain pelted all parts of his body with stones, until one struck him on the neck and inflicted death. After committing the murder, Cain resolved to flee, saying, "My parents will demand account of me concerning Abel, for there is no other human being on earth." This thought had but passed through his mind when God appeared unto him, and addressed him in these words: "Before thy parents thou canst flee, but canst thou go out from My presence, too? 'Can any hide himself in secret places that I shall not see him?' Alas for Abel that he showed thee mercy, and refrained from killing thee, when he had thee in his power! Alas that he granted thee the opportunity of slaying him!" Questioned by God, "Where is Abel thy brother?" Cain answered: "Am I my brother's keeper? Thou art He who holdest watch over all creatures, and yet Thou demandest account of me! True, I slew him, but Thou didst create the evil inclination in me. Thou guardest all things; why, then, didst Thou permit me to slay him? Thou didst Thyself slay him, for hadst Thou looked with a favorable countenance toward my offering as toward his, I had had no reason for envying him, and I had not slain him." But God said, "The voice of thy brother's blood issuing from his many wounds crieth out against thee, and likewise the blood of all the pious who might have sprung from the loins of Abel." Also the soul of Abel denounced the murderer, for she could find rest nowhere. She could neither soar heavenward, nor abide in the grave with her body, for no human soul had done either before. But Cain still refused to confess his guilt. He insisted that he had never seen a man killed, and how was he to suppose that the stones which he threw at Abel would take his life? Then, on account of Cain, God cursed the ground, that it might not yield fruit unto him. With a single punishment both Cain and the earth were chastised, the earth because it retained the corpse of Abel, and did not cast it above ground. In the obduracy of his heart, Cain spake: "O Lord of the world! Are there informers who denounce men before Thee? My parents are the only living human beings, and they know naught of my deed. Thou abidest in the heavens, and how shouldst Thou know what things happen on earth?" God said in reply: "Thou fool! I carry the whole world. I have made it, and I will bear it"--a reply that gave Cain the opportunity of feigning repentance. "Thou bearest the whole world," he said, "and my sin Thou canst not bear? Verily, mine iniquity is too great to be borne! Yet, yesterday Thou didst banish my father from Thy presence, to-day Thou dost banish me. In sooth, it will be said, it is Thy way to banish." Although this was but dissimulation, and not true repentance, yet God granted Cain pardon, and removed the half of his chastisement from him. Originally, the decree had condemned him to be a fugitive and a wanderer on the earth. Now he was no longer to roam about forever, but a fugitive he was to remain. And so much was hard enough to have to suffer, for the earth quaked under Cain, and all the animals, the wild and the tame, among them the accursed serpent, gathered together and essayed to devour him in order to avenge the innocent blood of Abel. Finally Cain could bear it no longer, and, breaking out in tears, he cried: "Whither shall I go from Thy spirit? Or whither shall I flee from Thy presence?" To protect him from the onslaught of the beasts, God inscribed one letter of His Holy Name upon his forehead," and furthermore He addressed the animals: "Cain's punishment shall not be like unto the punishment of future murderers. He has shed blood, but there was none to give him instruction. Henceforth, however, he who slays another shall himself be slain." Then God gave him the dog as a protection against the wild beasts, and to mark him as a sinner, He afflicted him with leprosy. Cain's repentance, insincere though it was, bore a good result. When Adam met him, and inquired what doom had been decreed against him, Cain told how his repentance had propitiated God, and Adam exclaimed, "So potent is repentance, and I knew it not!" Thereupon he composed a hymn of praise to God, beginning with the words, "It is a good thing to confess thy sins unto the Lord!" The crime committed by Cain had baneful consequences, not for himself alone, but for the whole of nature also. Before, the fruits which the earth bore unto him when he tilled the ground had tasted like the fruits of Paradise. Now his labor produced naught but thorns and thistles. The ground changed and deteriorated at the very moment of Abel's violent end. The trees and the plants in the part of the earth whereon the victim lived refused to yield their fruits, on account of their grief over him, and only at the birth of Seth those that grew in the portion belonging to Abel began to flourish and bear again. But never did they resume their former powers. While, before, the vine had borne nine hundred and twenty-six different varieties of fruit, it now brought forth but one kind. And so it was with all other species. They will regain their pristine powers only in the world to come. Nature was modified also by the burial of the corpse of Abel. For a long time it lay there exposed, above ground, because Adam and Eve knew not what to do with it. They sat beside it and wept, while the faithful dog of Abel kept guard that birds and beasts did it no harm. On a sudden, the mourning parents observed how a raven scratched the earth away in one spot, and then hid a dead bird of his own kind in the ground. Adam, following the example of the raven, buried the body of Abel, and the raven was rewarded by God. His young are born with white feathers, wherefore the old birds desert them, not recognizing them as their offspring. They take them for serpents. God feeds them until their plumage turns black, and the parent birds return to them. As an additional reward, God grants their petition when the ravens pray for rain.

THE INHABITANTS OF THE SEVEN EARTHS - When Adam was cast out of Paradise, he first reached the lowest of the seven earths, the Erez, which is dark, without a ray of light, and utterly void. Adam was terrified, particularly by the flames of the ever-turning sword, which is on this earth. After he had done penance, God led him to the second earth, the Adamah, where there is light reflected from its own sky and from its phantom-like stars and constellations. Here dwell the phantom-like beings that issued from the union of Adam with the spirits." They are always sad; the emotion of joy is not known to them. They leave their own earth and repair to the one inhabited by men, where they are changed into evil spirits. Then they return to their abode for good, repent of their wicked deeds, and till the ground, which, however, bears neither wheat nor any other of the seven species. In this Adamah, Cain, Abel, and Seth were born. After the murder of Abel, Cain was sent back to the Erez, where he was frightened into repentance by its darkness and by the flames of the ever-turning sword. Accepting his penitence, God permitted him to ascend to the third earth, the Arka, which receives some light from the sun. The Arka was surrendered to the Cainites forever, as their perpetual domain. They till the ground, and plant trees, but they have neither wheat nor any other of the seven species. Some of the Cainites are giants, some of them are dwarfs. They have two heads, wherefore they can never arrive at a decision; they are always at loggerheads with themselves. It may happen that they are pious now, only to be inclined to do evil the next moment. In the Ge, the fourth earth, live the generation of the Tower of Babel and their descendants. God banished them thither because the fourth earth is not far from Gehenna, and therefore close to the flaming fire. The inhabitants of the Ge are skilful in all arts, and accomplished in all departments of science and knowledge, and their abode overflows with wealth. When an inhabitant of our earth visits them, they give him the most precious thing in their possession, but then they lead him to the Neshiah, the fifth earth, where he becomes oblivious of his origin and his home. The Neshiah is inhabited by dwarfs without noses; they breathe through two holes instead. They have no memory; once a thing has happened, they forget it completely, whence their earth is called Neshiah, "forgetting." The fourth and fifth earths are like the Arka; they have trees, but neither wheat nor any other of the seven species. The sixth earth, the Ziah, is inhabited by handsome men, who are the owners of abundant wealth, and live in palatial residences, but they lack water, as the name of their territory, Ziah, "drought," indicates. Hence vegetation is sparse with them, and their tree culture meets with indifferent success. They hasten to any waterspring that is discovered, and sometimes they succeed in slipping through it up to our earth, where they satisfy their sharp appetite for the food eaten by the inhabitants of our earth. For the rest, they are men of steadfast faith, more than any other class of mankind. Adam remained in the Adamah until after the birth of Seth. Then, passing the third earth, the Arka, the abiding place of the Cainites, and the next three earths as well, the Ge, the Neshiah, and the Ziah, God transported him to the Tebel, the seventh earth, the earth inhabited by men.

THE DESCENDANTS OF CAIN - Cain knew only too well that his blood-guiltiness would be visited upon him in the seventh generation. Thus had God decreed against him. He endeavored, therefore, to immortalize his name by means of monuments, and he became a builder of cities. The first of them he called Enoch, after his son, because it was at the birth of Enoch that he began to enjoy a measure of rest and peace. Besides, he founded six other cities. This building of cities was a godless deed, for he surrounded them with a wall, forcing his family to remain within. All his other doings were equally impious. The punishment God had ordained for him did not effect any improvement. He sinned in order to secure his own pleasure, though his neighbors suffered injury thereby. He augmented his household substance by rapine and violence; he excited his acquaintances to procure pleasures and spoils by robbery, and he became a great leader of men into wicked courses. He also introduced a change in the ways of simplicity wherein men had lived before, and he was the author of measures and weights. And whereas men lived innocently and generously while they knew nothing of such arts, he changed the world into cunning craftiness. Like unto Cain were all his descendants, impious and godless, wherefore God resolved to destroy them. The end of Cain overtook him in the seventh generation of men, and it was inflicted upon him by the hand of his great-grandson Lamech. This Lamech was blind, and when he went a-hunting, he was led by his young son, who would apprise his father when game came in sight, and Lamech would then shoot at it with his bow and arrow. Once upon a time he and his son went on the chase, and the lad discerned something horned in the distance. He naturally took it to be a beast of one kind or another, and he told the blind Lamech to let his arrow fly. The aim was good, and the quarry dropped to the ground. When they came close to the victim, the lad exclaimed: "Father, thou hast killed something that resembles a human being in all respects, except it carries a horn on its forehead!" Lamech knew at once what had happened--he had killed his ancestor Cain, who had been marked by God with a horn. In despair he smote his hands together, inadvertently killing his son as he clasped them. Misfortune still followed upon misfortune. The earth opened her mouth and swallowed up the four generations sprung from Cain--Enoch, Irad, Mehujael, and Methushael. Lamech, sightless as he was, could not go home; he had to remain by the side of Cain's corpse and his son's. Toward evening, his wives, seeking him, found him there. When they heard what he had done, they wanted to separate from him, all the more as they knew that whoever was descended from Cain was doomed to annihilation. But Lamech argued, "If Cain, who committed murder of malice aforethought, was punished only in the seventh generation, then I, who had no intention of killing a human being, may hope that retribution will be averted for seventy and seven generations." With his wives, Lamech repaired to Adam, who heard both parties, and decided the case in favor of Lamech. The corruptness of the times, and especially the depravity of Cain's stock, appears in the fact that Lamech, as well as all the men in the generation of the deluge, married two wives, one with the purpose of rearing children, the other in order to pursue carnal indulgences, for which reason the latter was rendered sterile by artificial means. As the men of the time were intent upon pleasure rather than desirous of doing their duty to the human race, they gave all their love and attention to the barren women, while their other wives spent their days like widows, joyless and in gloom. The two wives of Lamech, Adah and Zillah, bore him each two children, Adah two sons, Jabal and Jubal, and Zillah a son, Tubal-cain, and a daughter, Naamah. Jabal was the first among men to erect temples to idols, and Jubal invented the music sung and played therein. Tubal-cain was rightly named, for he completed the work of his ancestor Cain. Cain committed murder, and Tubal-cain, the first who knew how to sharpen iron and copper, furnished the instruments used in wars and combats. Naamah, "the lovely," earned her name from the sweet sounds which she drew from her cymbals when she called the worshippers to pay homage to idols.

THE DESCENDANTS OF ADAM AND LILITH - When the wives of Lamech heard the decision of Adam, that they were to continue to live with their husband, they turned upon him, saying, "O physician, heal thine own lameness!" They were alluding to the fact that he himself had been living apart from his wife since the death of Abel, for he had said, "Why should I beget children, if it is but to expose them to death?" Though he avoided intercourse with Eve, he was visited in his sleep by female spirits, and from his union with them sprang shades and demons of various kinds, and they were endowed with peculiar gifts. Once upon a time there lived in Palestine a very rich and pious man, who had a son named Rabbi Hanina. He knew the whole of the Torah by heart. When he was at the point of death, he sent for his son, Rabbi Hanina, and bade him, as his last request, to study the Torah day and night, fulfil the commands of the law, and be a faithful friend to the poor. He also told him that he and his wife, the mother of Rabbi Hanina, would die on the selfsame day, and the seven days of mourning for the two would end on the eve of the Passover. He enjoined him not to grieve excessively, but to go to market on that day, and buy the first article offered to him, no matter how costly it might be. If it happened to be an edible, he was to prepare it and serve it with much ceremony. His expense and trouble would receive their recompense. All happened as foretold: the man and his wife died upon the same day, and the end of the week of mourning coincided with the eve of the Passover. The son in turn carried out his father's behest: he repaired to market, and there he met an old man who offered a silver dish for sale. Although the price asked was exorbitant, yet he bought it, as his father had bidden. The dish was set upon the Seder table, and when Rabbi Hanina opened it, he found a second dish within, and inside of this a live frog, jumping and hopping around gleefully. He gave the frog food and drink, and by the end of the festival he was grown so big that Rabbi Hanina made a cabinet for him, in which he ate and lived. In the course of time, the cabinet became too small, and the Rabbi built a chamber, put the frog within, and gave him abundant food and drink. All this he did that he might not violate his father's last wish. But the frog waxed and grew; he consumed all his host owned, until, finally, Rabbi Hanina was stripped bare of all his possessions. Then the frog opened his mouth and began to speak. "My dear Rabbi Hanina," he said, "do not worry! Seeing thou didst raise me and care for me, thou mayest ask of me whatever thy heart desireth, and it shall be granted thee." Rabbi Hanina made reply, "I desire naught but that thou shouldst teach me the whole of the Torah." The frog assented, and he did, indeed, teach him the whole of the Torah, and the seventy languages of men besides. His method was to write a few words upon a scrap of paper, which he had his pupil swallow. Thus he acquired not alone the Torah and the seventy tongues, but also the language of beasts and birds. Thereupon the frog spoke to the wife of Rabbi Hanina: "Thou didst tend me well, and I have given thee no recompense. But thy reward will be paid thee before I depart from you, only you must both accompany me to the woods. There you shall see what I shall do for you." Accordingly, they went to the woods with him. Arrived there, the frog began to cry aloud, and at the sound all sorts of beasts and birds assembled. These he commanded to produce precious stones, as many as they could carry. Also they were to bring herbs and roots for the wife of Rabbi Hanina, and he taught her how to use them as remedies for all varieties of disease. All this they were bidden to take home with them. When they were about to return, the frog addressed them thus: "May the Holy One, blessed be He, have mercy upon you, and requite you for all the trouble you took on my account, without so much as inquiring who I am. Now I shall make my origin known to you. I am the son of Adam, a son whom he begot during the hundred and thirty years of his separation from Eve. God has endowed me with the power of assuming any form or guise I desire." Rabbi Hanina and his wife departed for their home, and they became very rich, and enjoyed the respect and confidence of the king.

SETH AND HIS DESCENDANTS - The exhortations of the wives of Lamech took effect upon Adam. After a separation of one hundred and thirty years, he returned to Eve, and the love he now bore her was stronger by far than in the former time. She was in his thoughts even when she was not present to him bodily. The fruit of their reunion was Seth, who was destined to be the ancestor of the Messiah. Seth was so formed from birth that the rite of circumcision could be dispensed with. He was thus one of the thirteen men born perfect in a way. Adam begot him in his likeness and image, different from Cain, who had not been in his likeness and image. Thus Seth became, in a genuine sense, the father of the human race, especially the father of the pious, while the depraved and godless are descended from Cain. Even during the lifetime of Adam the descendants of Cain became exceedingly wicked, dying successively, one after another, each more wicked than the former. They were intolerable in war, and vehement in robberies, and if any one were slow to murder people, yet was he bold in his profligate behavior in acting unjustly and doing injury for gain. Now as to Seth. When he was brought up, and came to those years in which he could discern what was good, he became a virtuous man, and as he was himself of excellent character, so he left children behind him who imitated his virtues. All these proved to be of good disposition. They also inhabited one and the same country without dissensions, and in a happy condition, without any misfortune's falling upon them, until they died. They also were the inventors of that peculiar sort of wisdom which is concerned with the heavenly bodies and their order. And that their inventions might not be lost before they were sufficiently known, they made two pillars, upon Adam's prediction that the world was to be destroyed at one time by the force of fire and at another time by the violence and quantity of water. The one was of brick, the other of stone, and they inscribed their discoveries on both, that in case the pillar of brick should be destroyed by the flood, the pillar of stone might remain, and exhibit these discoveries to mankind, and also inform them that there was another pillar, of brick, erected by them.

ENOSH - Enosh was asked who his father was, and he named Seth. The questioners, the people of his time, continued: "Who was the father of Seth?" Enosh: "Adam."--"And who was the father of Adam?"--"He had neither father nor mother, God formed him from the dust of the earth."--"But man has not the appearance of dust!"--"After death man returns to dust, as God said, 'And man shall turn again unto dust;' but on the day of his creation, man was made in the image of God."--"How was the woman created?"- "Male and female He created them."--"But how?"--"God took water and earth, and moulded them together in the form of man."--"But how?" pursued the questioners. Enosh took six clods of earth, mixed them, and moulded them, and formed an image of dust and clay. "But," said the people, "this image does not walk, nor does it possess any breath of life." He then essayed to show them how God breathed the breath of life into the nostrils of Adam, but when he began to blow his breath into the image he had formed, Satan entered it, and the figure walked, and the people of his time who had been inquiring these matters of Enosh went astray after it, saying, "What is the difference between bowing down before this image and paying homage to a man?" The generation of Enosh were thus the first idol worshippers, and the punishment for their folly was not delayed long. God caused the sea to transgress its bounds, and a portion of the earth was flooded. This was the time also when the mountains became rocks, and the dead bodies of men began to decay. And still another consequence of the sin of idolatry was that the countenances of the men of the following generations were no longer in the likeness and image of God, as the countenances of Adam, Seth, and Enosh had been. They resembled centaurs and apes, and the demons lost their fear of men. But there was a still more serious consequence from the idolatrous practices introduced in the time of Enosh. When God drove Adam forth from Paradise, the Shekinah remained behind, enthroned above a cherub under the tree of life. The angels descended from heaven and repaired thither in hosts, to receive their instructions, and Adam and his descendants sat by the gate to bask in the splendor of the Shekinah, sixty-five thousand times more radiant than the splendor of the sun. This brightness of the Shekinah makes all upon whom it falls exempt from disease, and neither insects nor demons can come nigh unto them to do them harm. Thus it was until the time of Enosh, when men began to gather gold, silver, gems, and pearls from all parts of the earth, and made idols thereof a thousand parasangs high. What was worse, by means of the magic arts taught them by the angels Uzza and Azzael, they set themselves as masters over the heavenly spheres, and forced the sun, the moon, and the stars to be subservient to themselves instead of the Lord. This impelled the angels to ask God: " 'What is man, that Thou art mindful of him?' Why didst Thou abandon the highest of the heavens, the seat of Thy glory and Thy exalted Throne in 'Arabot, and descend to men, who pay worship to idols, putting Thee upon a level with them?" The Shekinah was induced to leave the earth and ascend to heaven, amid the blare and flourish of the trumpets of the myriads of angel hosts.

THE FALL OF THE ANGELS - The depravity of mankind, which began to show itself in the time of Enosh, had increased monstrously in the time of his grandson Jared, by reason of the fallen angels. When the angels saw the beautiful, attractive daughters of men, they lusted after them, and spoke: "We will choose wives for ourselves only from among the daughters of men, and beget children with them." Their chief Shemhazai said, "I fear me, ye will not put this plan of yours into execution, and I alone shall have to suffer the consequences of a great sin." Then they answered him, and said: "We will all swear an oath, and we will bind ourselves, separately and together, not to abandon the plan, but to carry it through to the end." Two hundred angels descended to the summit of Mount Hermon, which owes its name to this very occurrence, because they bound themselves there to fulfil their purpose, on the penalty of Herem, anathema. Under the leadership of twenty captains they defiled themselves with the daughters of men, unto whom they taught charms, conjuring formulas, how to cut roots, and the efficacy of plants. The issue from these mixed marriages was a race of giants, three thousand ells tall, who consumed the possessions of men. When all had vanished, and they could obtain nothing more from them, the giants turned against men and devoured many of them, and the remnant of men began to trespass against the birds, beasts, reptiles, and fishes, eating their flesh and drinking their blood. Then the earth complained about the impious evil-doers. But the fallen angels continued to corrupt mankind. Azazel taught men how to make slaughtering knives, arms, shields, and coats of mail. He showed them metals and how to work them, and armlets and all sorts of trinkets, and the use of rouge for the eyes, and how to beautify the eyelids, and how to ornament themselves with the rarest and most precious jewels and all sorts of paints. The chief of the fallen angels, Shemhazai, instructed them in exorcisms and how to cut roots; Armaros taught them how to raise spells; Barakel, divination from the stars; Kawkabel, astrology; Ezekeel, augury from the clouds; Arakiel, the signs of the earth; Samsaweel, the signs of the sun; and Seriel, the signs of the moon. While all these abominations defiled the earth, the pious Enoch lived in a secret place. None among men knew his abode, or what had become of him, for he was sojourning with the angel watchers and holy ones. Once he heard the call addressed to him: "Enoch, thou scribe of justice, go unto the watchers of the heavens, who have left the high heavens, the eternal place of holiness, defiling themselves with women, doing as men do, taking wives unto themselves, and casting themselves into the arms of destruction upon earth. Go and proclaim unto them that they shall find neither peace nor pardon. For every time they take joy in their offspring, they shall see the violent death of their sons, and sigh over the ruin of their children. They will pray and supplicate evermore, but never shall they attain to mercy or peace." Enoch repaired to Azazel and the other fallen angels, to announce the doom uttered against them. They all were filled with fear. Trembling seized upon them, and they implored Enoch to set up a petition for them and read it to the Lord of heaven, for they could not speak with God as aforetime, nor even raise their eyes heavenward, for shame on account of their sins. Enoch granted their request, and in a vision he was vouchsafed the answer which he was to carry back to the angels. It appeared to Enoch that he was wafted into heaven upon clouds, and was set down before the throne of God. God spake: "Go forth and say to the watchers of heaven who have sent thee hither to intercede for them: Verily, it is you who ought to plead in behalf of men, not men in behalf of you I Why did ye forsake the high, holy, and eternal heavens, to pollute yourselves with the daughters of men, taking wives unto yourselves, doing like the races of the earth, and begetting giant sons? Giants begotten by flesh and spirits will be called evil spirits on earth, and on the earth will be their dwelling-place. Evil spirits proceed from their bodies, because they are created from above, and from the holy watchers is their beginning and primal origin; they will be evil spirits on earth, and evil spirits they will be named. And the spirits of heaven have their dwelling in heaven, but the spirits of the earth, which were born upon the earth, have their dwelling on the earth. And the spirits of the giants will devour, oppress, destroy, attack, do battle, and cause destruction on the earth, and work affliction. They will take no kind of food, nor will they thirst, and they will be invisible. And these spirits will rise up against the children of men and against the women, because they have proceeded from them. Since the days of murder and destruction and the death of the giants, when the spirits went forth from the soul of their flesh, in order to destroy without incurring judgment--thus will they destroy until the day when the great consummation of the great world be consummated. And now as to the watchers who have sent thee to intercede for them, who had been aforetime in heaven, say to them: You have been in heaven, and though the hidden things had not yet been revealed to you, you know worthless mysteries, and in the hardness of your hearts you have recounted these to the women, and through these mysteries women and men work much evil on earth. Say to them therefore: You have no peace!"

ENOCH, RULER AND TEACHER - After Enoch had lived a long time secluded from men, he once heard the voice of an angel calling to him: "Enoch, Enoch, make thyself ready and leave the house and the secret place wherein thou hast kept thyself hidden, and assume dominion over men, to teach them the ways in which they shall walk, and the deeds which they shall do, in order that they may walk in the ways of God." Enoch left his retreat and betook himself to the haunts of men. He gathered them about him, and instructed them in the conduct pleasing to God. He sent messengers all over to announce, "Ye who desire to know the ways of God and righteous conduct, come ye to Enoch!" Thereupon a vast concourse of people thronged about him, to hear the wisdom he would teach and learn from his mouth what is good and right. Even kings and princes, no less than one hundred and thirty in number, assembled about him, and submitted themselves to his dominion, to be taught and guided by him, as he taught and guided all the others. Peace reigned thus over the whole world all the two hundred and forty-three years during which the influence of Enoch prevailed. At the expiration of this period, in the year in which Adam died, and was buried with great honors by Seth, Enosh, Enoch, and Methuselah, Enoch resolved to retire again from intercourse with men, and devote himself wholly to the service of God. But he withdrew gradually. First he would spend three days in prayer and praise of God, and on the fourth day he would return to his disciples and grant them instruction. Many years passed thus, then he appeared among them but once a week, later, once a month, and, finally, once a year. The kings, princes, and all others who were desirous of seeing Enoch and hearkening to his words did not venture to come close to him during the times of his retirement. Such awful majesty sat upon his countenance, they feared for their very life if they but looked at him. They therefore resolved that all men should prefer their requests before Enoch on the day he showed himself unto them. The impression made by the teachings of Enoch upon all who heard them was powerful. They prostrated themselves before him, and cried "Long live the king! Long live the king!" On a certain day, while Enoch was giving audience to his followers, an angel appeared and made known unto him that God had resolved to install him as king over the angels in heaven, as until then he had reigned over men. He called together all the inhabitants of the earth, and addressed them thus: "I have been summoned to ascend into heaven, and I know not on what day I shall go thither. Therefore I will teach you wisdom and righteousness before I go hence." A few days yet Enoch spent among men, and all the time left to him he gave instruction in wisdom, knowledge, God-fearing conduct, and piety, and established law and order, for the regulation of the affairs of men. Then those gathered near him saw a gigantic steed descend from the skies, and they told Enoch of it, who said, "The steed is for me, for the time has come and the day when I leave you, never to be seen again." So it was. The steed approached Enoch, and he mounted upon its back, all the time instructing the people, exhorting them, enjoining them to serve God and walk in His ways. Eight hundred thousand of the people followed a day's journey after him. But on the second day Enoch urged his retinue to turn back: "Go ye home, lest death overtake you, if you follow me farther." Most of them heeded his words and went back, but a number remained with him for six days, though he admonished them daily to return and not bring death down upon themselves. On the sixth day of the journey, he said to those still accompanying him, "Go ye home, for on the morrow I shall ascend to heaven, and whoever will then be near me, he will die." Nevertheless, some of his companions remained with him, saying: "Whithersoever thou goest, we will go. By the living God, death alone shall part us." On the seventh day Enoch was carried into the heavens in a fiery chariot drawn by fiery chargers. The day thereafter, the kings who had turned back in good time sent messengers to inquire into the fate of the men who had refused to separate themselves from Enoch, for they had noted the number of them. They found snow and great hailstones upon the spot whence Enoch had risen, and, when they searched beneath, they discovered the bodies of all who had remained behind with Enoch. He alone was not among them; he was on high in heaven.

THE ASCENSION OF ENOCH - This was not the first time Enoch had been in heaven. Once before, while he sojourned among men, he had been permitted to see all there is on earth and in the heavens. On a time when he was sleeping, a great grief came upon his heart, and he wept in his dream, not knowing what the grief meant, nor what would happen to him. And there appeared to him two men, very tall. Their faces shone like the sun, and their eyes were like burning lamps, and fire came forth from their lips; their wings were brighter than gold, their hands whiter than snow. They stood at the head of Enoch's bed, and called him by his name. He awoke from his sleep, and hastened and made obeisance to them, and was terrified. And these men said to him: "Be of good cheer, Enoch, be not afraid; the everlasting God hath sent us to thee, and lo! to-day thou shalt ascend with us into heaven. And tell thy sons and thy servants, and let none seek thee, till the Lord bring thee back to them." Enoch did as he was told, and after he had spoken to his sons, and instructed them not to turn aside from God, and to keep His judgment, these two men summoned him, and took him on their wings, and placed him on the clouds, which moved higher and higher, till they set him down in the first heaven. Here they showed him the two hundred angels who rule the stars, and their heavenly service. Here he saw also the treasuries of snow and ice, of clouds and dew. From there they took him to the second heaven, where he saw the fallen angels imprisoned, they who obeyed not the commandments of God, and took counsel of their own will. The fallen angels said to Enoch, "O man of God! Pray for us to the Lord," and he answered: "Who am I, a mortal man, that I should pray for angels? Who knows whither I go, or what awaits me?" They took him from thence to the third heaven, where they showed him Paradise, with all the trees of beautiful colors, and their fruits, ripe and luscious, and all kinds of food which they produced, springing up with delightful fragrance. In the midst of Paradise he saw the tree of life, in that place in which God rests when He comes into Paradise. This tree cannot be described for its excellence and sweet fragrance, and it is beautiful, more than any created thing, and on all its sides it is like gold and crimson in appearance, and transparent as fire, and it covers everything. From its root in the garden there go forth four streams, which pour out honey, milk, oil, and wine, and they go down to the Paradise of Eden, that lies on the confines between the earthly region of corruptibility and the heavenly region of incorruptibility, and thence they go along the earth. He also saw the three hundred angels who keep the garden, and with never-ceasing voices and blessed singing they serve the Lord every day. The angels leading Enoch explained to him that this place is prepared for the righteous, while the terrible place prepared for the sinners is in the northern regions of the third heaven. He saw there all sorts of tortures, and impenetrable gloom, and there is no light there, but a gloomy fire is always burning. And all that place has fire on all sides, and on all sides cold and ice, thus it burns and freezes. And the angels, terrible and without pity, carry savage weapons, and their torture is unmerciful. The angels took him then to the fourth heaven, and showed him all the comings in and goings forth, and all the rays of the light of the sun and the moon. He saw the fifteen myriads of angels who go out with the sun, and attend him during the day, and the thousand angels who attend him by night. Each angel has six wings, and they go before the chariot of the sun, while one hundred angels keep the sun warm, and light it up. He saw also the wonderful and strange creatures named phoenixes and chalkidri, who attend the chariot of the sun, and go with him, bringing heat and dew. They showed him also the six gates in the east of the fourth heaven, by which the sun goes forth, and the six gates in the west where he sets, and also the gates by which the moon goes out, and those by which she enters. In the middle of the fourth heaven he saw an armed host, serving the Lord with cymbals and organs and unceasing voices. In the fifth heaven he saw many hosts of the angels called Grigori. Their appearance was like men, and their size was greater than the size of the giants, their countenances were withered, and their lips silent. On his question who they were, the angels leading him answered, "These are the Grigori, who with their prince Salamiel rejected the holy Lord." Enoch then said to the Grigori, "Why wait ye, brethren, and serve ye not before the face of the Lord, and why perform ye not your duties before the face of the Lord, and anger not your Lord to the end?" The Grigori listened to the rebuke, and when the trumpets resounded together with a loud call, they also began to sing with one voice, and their voices went forth before the Lord with sadness and tenderness. In the seventh heaven he saw the seven bands of archangels who arrange and study the revolutions of the stars and the changes of the moon and the revolution of the sun, and superintend the good or evil conditions of the world. And they arrange teachings and instructions and sweet speaking and singing and all kinds of glorious praise. They hold in subjection all living things, both in heaven and on earth. In the midst of them are seven phoenixes, and seven cherubim, and seven six-winged creatures, singing with one voice. When Enoch reached the seventh heaven, and saw all the fiery hosts of great archangels and incorporeal powers and lordships and principalities and powers, he was afraid and trembled with a great terror. Those leading him took hold of him, and brought him into the midst of them, and said to him, "Be of good cheer, Enoch, be not afraid," and they showed him the Lord from afar, sitting on His lofty throne, while all the heavenly hosts, divided in ten classes, having approached, stood on the ten steps according to their rank, and made obeisance to the Lord. And so they proceeded to their places in joy and mirth and boundless light, singing songs with low and gentle voices, and gloriously serving Him. They leave not nor depart day or night, standing before the face of the Lord, working His will, cherubim and seraphim, standing around His throne. And the six-winged creatures overshadow all His throne, singing with a soft voice before the face of the Lord,

"Holy, holy, holy, is the Lord of hosts; heaven and earth are full of His glory." When he had seen all these, the angels leading him said to him, "Enoch, up to this time we were ordered to accompany thee." They departed, and he saw them no more. Enoch remained at the extremity of the seventh heaven, in great terror, saying to himself, "Woe is me! What has come upon me!" But then Gabriel came and said unto him, "Enoch, be not afraid, stand up and come with me, and stand up before the face of the Lord forever." And Enoch answered: "O my lord, my spirit has departed from me with fear and trembling. Call the men to me who have brought me to the place! Upon them I have relied, and with them I would go before the face of the Lord." And Gabriel hurried him away like a leaf carried off by the wind, and set him before the face of the Lord. Enoch fell down and worshipped the Lord, who said to him: "Enoch, be not afraid! Rise up and stand before My face forever." And Michael lifted him up, and at the command of the Lord took his earthly robe from him, and anointed him with the holy oil, and clothed him, and when he gazed upon himself, he looked like one of God's glorious ones, and fear and trembling departed from him. God called then one of His archangels who was more wise than all the others, and wrote down all the doings of the Lord, and He said to him, "Bring forth the books from My store-place, and give a reed to Enoch, and interpret the books to him." The angel did as he was commanded, and he instructed Enoch thirty days and thirty nights, and his lips never ceased speaking, while Enoch was writing down all the things about heaven and earth, angels and men, and all that is suitable to be instructed in. He also wrote down all about the souls of men, those of them which are not born, and the places prepared for them forever. He copied all accurately, and he wrote three hundred and sixty-six books. After he had received all the instructions from the archangel, God revealed unto him great secrets, which even the angels do not know. He told him how, out of the lowest darkness, the visible and the invisible were created, how He formed heaven, light, water, and earth, and also the fall of Satan and the creation and sin of Adam He narrated to him, and further revealed to him that the duration of the world will be seven thousand years, and the eighth millennium will be a time when there is no computation, no end, neither years, nor months, nor weeks, nor days, nor hours. The Lord finished this revelation to Enoch with the words: "And now I give thee Samuil and Raguil, who brought thee to Me. Go with them upon the earth, and tell thy sons what things I have said to thee, and what thou hast seen from the lowest heaven up to My throne. Give them the works written out by thee, and they shall read them, and shall distribute the books to their children's children and from generation to generation and from nation to nation. And I will give thee My messenger Michael for thy writings and for the writings of thy fathers, Adam, Seth, Enosh, Kenan, Mahalalel, and Jared thy father. And I shall not require them till the last age, for I have instructed My two angels, Ariuk and Mariuk, whom I have put upon the earth as their guardians, and I have ordered them in time to guard them, that the account of what I shall do in thy family may not be lost in the deluge to come. For on account of the wickedness and iniquity of men, I will bring a deluge upon the earth, and I will destroy all, but I will leave a righteous man of thy race with all his house, who shall act according to My will. From their seed will be raised up a numerous generation, and on the extinction of that family, I will show them the books of thy writings and of thy father, and the guardians of them on earth will show them to the men who are true and please Me. And they shall tell to another generation, and they, having read them, shall be glorified at last more than before." Enoch was then sent to earth to remain there for thirty days to instruct his sons, but before he left heaven, God sent an angel to him whose appearance was like snow, and his hands were like ice. Enoch looked at him, and his face was chilled, that men might be able to endure the sight of him. The angels who took him to heaven put him upon his bed, in the place where his son Methuselah was expecting him by day and by night. Enoch assembled his sons and all his household, and instructed them faithfully about all things he had seen, heard, and written down, and he gave his books to his sons, to keep them and read them, admonishing them not to conceal the books, but tell them to all desiring to know. When the thirty days had been completed, the Lord sent darkness upon the earth, and there was gloom, and it hid the men standing with Enoch. And the angels hasted and took Enoch, and carried him to the highest heaven, where the Lord received him and set him before His face, and the darkness departed from the earth, and there was light. And the people saw, and did not understand how Enoch was taken, and they glorified God. Enoch was born on the sixth day of the month of Siwan, and he was taken to heaven in the same month, Siwan, on the same day and in the same hour when he was born. And Methuselah hasted and all his brethren, the sons of Enoch, and built an altar in the place called Achuzan, whence Enoch was taken up to heaven. The elders and all the people came to the festivity and brought their gifts to the sons of Enoch, and made a great festivity, rejoicing and being merry for three days, praising God, who had given such a sign by means of Enoch, who had found favor with them.

THE TRANSLATION OF ENOCH - The sinfulness of men was the reason why Enoch was translated to heaven. Thus Enoch himself told Rabbi Ishmael. When the generation of the deluge transgressed, and spoke to God, saying, "Depart from us, for we do not desire to know Thy ways," Enoch was carried to heaven, to serve there as a witness that God was not a cruel God in spite of the destruction decreed upon all living beings on earth. When Enoch, under the guidance of the angel 'Anpiel, was carried from earth to heaven, the holy beings, the ofanim, the seraphim, the cherubim, all those who move the throne of God, and the ministering spirits whose substance is of consuming fire, they all, at a distance of six hundred and fifty million and three hundred parasangs, noticed the presence of a human being, and they exclaimed: "Whence the odor of one born of woman? How comes he into the highest heaven of the fire-coruscating angels?" But God replied: "O My servants and hosts, ye, My cherubim, ofanim, and seraphim, let this not be an offense unto you, for all the children of men denied Me and My mighty dominion, and they paid homage to the idols, so that I transferred the Shekinah from earth to heaven. But this man Enoch is the elect of men. He has more faith, justice, and righteousness than all the rest, and he is the only reward I have derived from the terrestrial world." Before Enoch could be admitted to service near the Divine throne, the gates of wisdom were opened unto him, and the gates of understanding, and of discernment, of life, peace, and the Shekinah, of strength and power, of might, loveliness, and grace, of humility and fear of sin. Equipped by God with extraordinary wisdom, sagacity, judgment, knowledge, learning, compassionateness, love, kindness, grace, humility, strength, power, might, splendor, beauty, shapeliness, and all other excellent qualities, beyond the endowment of any of the celestial beings, Enoch received, besides, many thousand blessings from God, and his height and his breadth became equal to the height and the breadth of the world, and thirty-six wings were attached to his body, to the right and to the left, each as large as the world, and three hundred and sixty-five thousand eyes were bestowed upon him, each brilliant as the sun. A magnificent throne was erected for him beside the gates of the seventh celestial palace, and a herald proclaimed throughout the heavens concerning him, who was henceforth to be called Metatron in the celestial regions: "I have appointed My servant Metatron as prince and chief over all the princes in My realm, with the exception only of the eight august and exalted princes that bear My name. Whatever angel has a request to prefer to Me, shall appear before Metatron, and what he will command at My bidding, ye must observe and do, for the prince of wisdom and the prince of understanding are at his service, and they will reveal unto him the sciences of the celestials and the terrestrials, the knowledge of the present order of the world and the knowledge of the future order of the world. Furthermore, I have made him the guardian of the treasures of the palaces in the heaven 'Arabot, and of the treasures of life that are in the highest heaven." Out of the love He bore Enoch, God arrayed him in a magnificent garment, to which every kind of luminary in existence was attached, and a crown gleaming with forty-nine jewels, the splendor of which pierced to all parts of the seven heavens and to the four corners of the earth. In the presence of the heavenly family, He set this crown upon the head of Enoch, and called him "the little Lord." It bears also the letters by means of which heaven and earth were created, and seas and rivers, mountains and valleys, planets and constellations, lightning and thunder, snow and hail, storm and whirlwind--these and also all things needed in the world, and the mysteries of creation. Even the princes of the heavens, when they see Metatron, tremble before him, and prostrate themselves; his magnificence and majesty, the splendor and beauty radiating from him overwhelm them, even the wicked Samael, the greatest of them, even Gabriel the angel of the fire, Bardiel the angel of the hail, Ruhiel the angel of the wind, Barkiel the angel of the lightning, Za'miel the angel of the hurricane, Zakkiel the angel of the storm, Sui'el the angel of the earthquake, Za'fiel the angel of the showers, Ra'miel the angel of the thunder, Ra'shiel the angel of the whirlwind, Shalgiel the angel of the snow, Matriel the angel of the rain, Shamshiel the angel of the day, Leliel the angel of the night, Galgliel the angel of the solar system, Ofaniel the angel of the wheel of the moon, Kokabiel the angel of the stars, and Rahtiel the angel of the constellations. When Enoch was transformed into Metatron, his body was turned into celestial fire--his flesh became flame, his veins fire, his bones glimmering coals, the light of his eyes heavenly brightness, his eyeballs torches of fire, his hair a flaring blaze, all his limbs and organs burning sparks, and his frame a consuming fire. To right of him sparkled flames of fire, to left of him burnt torches of fire, and on all sides he was engirdled by storm and whirlwind, hurricane and thundering.

METHUSELAH - After the translation of Enoch, Methuselah was proclaimed ruler of the earth by all the kings. He walked in the footsteps of his father, teaching truth, knowledge, and fear of God to the children of men all his life, and deviating from the path of rectitude neither to the right nor the left. He delivered the world from thousands of demons, the posterity of Adam which he had begotten with Lilith, that she-devil of she-devils. These demons and evil spirits, as often as they encountered a man, had sought to injure and even slay him, until Methuselah appeared, and supplicated the mercy of God. He spent three days in fasting, and then God gave him permission to write the Ineffable Name upon his sword, wherewith he slew ninety-four myriads of the demons in a minute, until Agrimus, the first-born of them, came to him and entreated him to desist, at the same time handing the names of the demons and imps over to him. And so Methuselah placed their kings in iron fetters, while the remainder fled away and hid themselves in the innermost chambers and recesses of the ocean. And it is on account of the wonderful sword by means of which the demons were killed that he was called Methuselah. He was so pious a man that he composed two hundred and thirty parables in praise of God for every word he uttered. When he died, the people heard a great commotion in the heavens, and they saw nine hundred rows of mourners corresponding to the nine hundred orders of the Mishnah which he had studied, and tears flowed from the eyes of the holy beings down upon the spot where he died. Seeing the grief of the celestials, the people on earth also mourned over the demise of Methuselah, and God rewarded them therefor. He added seven days to the time of grace which He had ordained before bringing destruction upon the earth by a flood of waters.

Chapter 4

NOAH--THE BIRTH OF NOAH

Methuselah took a wife for his son Lamech, and she bore him a man child. The body of the babe was white as snow and red as a blooming rose, and the hair of his head and his long locks were white as wool, and his eyes like the rays of the sun. When he opened his eyes, he lighted up the whole house, like the sun, and the whole house was very full of light. And when he was taken from the hand of the midwife, he opened his mouth and praised the Lord of righteousness. His father Lamech was afraid of him, and fled, and came to his own father Methuselah. And he said to him: "I have begotten a strange son; he is not like a human being, but resembles the children of the angels of heaven, and his nature is different, and he is not like us, and his eyes are as the rays of the sun, and his countenance is glorious. And it seems to me that he is not sprung from me, but from the angels, and I fear that in his days a wonder may be wrought on the earth. And now, my father, I am here to petition thee and implore thee, that thou mayest go to Enoch, our father, and learn from him the truth, for his dwelling place is among the angels."

And when Methuselah heard the words of his son, he went to Enoch, to the ends of the earth, and he cried aloud, and Enoch heard his voice, and appeared before him, and asked him the reason of his coming. Methuselah told him the cause of his anxiety, and requested him to make the truth known to him. Enoch answered, and said: "The Lord will do a new thing in the earth. There will come a great destruction on the earth, and a deluge for one year. This son who is born unto thee will be left on the earth, and his three children will be saved with him, when all mankind that are on the earth shall die. And there will be a great punishment on the earth, and the earth will be cleansed from all impurity. And now make known to thy son Lamech that he who was born is in truth his son, and call his name Noah, for he will be left to you, and he and his children will be saved from the destruction which will come upon the earth." When Methuselah had heard the words of his father, who showed him all the secret things, he returned home, and he called the child Noah, for he would cause the earth to rejoice in compensation for all destruction.

By the name Noah he was called only by his grandfather Methuselah; his father and all others called him Menahem. His generation was addicted to sorcery, and Methuselah apprehended that his grandson might be bewitched if his true name were known, wherefore he kept it a secret. Menahem, Comforter, suited him as well as Noah; it indicated that he would be a consoler, if but the evil-doers of his time would repent of their misdeeds. At his very birth it was felt that he would bring consolation and deliverance. When the Lord said to

Adam, "Cursed is the ground for thy sake," he asked, "For how long a time?" and the answer made by God was, "Until a man child shall be born whose conformation is such that the rite of circumcision need not be practiced upon him." This was fulfilled in Noah, he was circumcised from his mother's womb.

Noah had scarcely come into the world when a marked change was noticeable. Since the curse brought upon the earth by the sin of Adam, it happened that wheat being sown, yet oats would sprout and grow. This ceased with the appearance of Noah: the earth bore the products planted in it. And it was Noah who, when he was grown to manhood, invented the plough, the scythe, the hoe, and other implements for cultivating the ground. Before him men had worked the land with their bare hands.

There was another token to indicate that the child born unto Lamech was appointed for an extraordinary destiny. When God created Adam, He gave him dominion over all things: the cow obeyed the ploughman, and the furrow was willing to be drawn. But after the fall of Adam all things rebelled against him: the cow refused obedience to the ploughman, and also the furrow was refractory. Noah was born, and all returned to its state preceding the fall of man.

Before the birth of Noah, the sea was in the habit of transgressing its bounds twice daily, morning and evening, and flooding the land up to the graves. After his birth it kept within its confines. And the famine that afflicted the world in the time of Lamech, the second of the ten great famines appointed to come upon it, ceased its ravages with the birth of Noah.

THE PUNISHMENT OF THE FALLEN ANGELS

Grown to manhood, Noah followed in the ways of his grandfather Methuselah, while all other men of the time rose up against this pious king. So far from observing his precepts, they pursued the evil inclination of their hearts, and perpetrated all sorts of abominable deeds. Chiefly the fallen angels and their giant posterity caused the depravity of mankind. The blood spilled by the giants cried unto heaven from the ground, and the four archangels accused the fallen angels and their sons before God, whereupon He gave the following orders to them: Uriel was sent to Noah to announce to him that the earth would be destroyed by a flood, and to teach him how to save his own life. Raphael was told to put the fallen angel Azazel into chains, cast him into a pit of sharp and pointed stones in the desert Dudael, and cover him with darkness, and so was he to remain until the great day of judgment, when he would be thrown into the fiery pit of hell, and the earth would be healed of the corruption he had contrived upon it. Gabriel was charged to proceed against the bastards and the reprobates, the sons of the angels begotten with the daughters of men, and plunge them into deadly conflicts with one another. Shemhazai's ilk were handed over to Michael, who first caused them to witness the death of their children in their bloody combat with each other, and then he bound them and pinned them under the hills of the earth, where they will remain for seventy generations, until the day of judgment, to be carried thence to the fiery pit of hell.

The fall of Azazel and Shemhazai came about in this way. When the generation of the deluge began to practice idolatry, God was deeply grieved. The two angels Shemhazai and Azazel arose, and said: "O Lord of the world! It has happened, that which we foretold at the creation of the world and of man, saying, 'What is man, that Thou art mindful of him?' " And God said, "And what will become of the world now without man?" Whereupon the angels: "We will occupy ourselves with it." Then said God: "I am well aware of it, and I know that if you inhabit the earth, the evil inclination will overpower you, and you will be more iniquitous than ever men." The angels pleaded, "Grant us but permission to dwell among men, and Thou shalt see how we will sanctify Thy Name." God yielded to their wish, saying, "Descend and sojourn among men!"

When the angels came to earth, and beheld the daughters of men in all their grace and beauty, they could not restrain their passion. Shemhazai saw a maiden named Istehar, and he lost his heart to her. She promised to surrender herself to him, if first he taught her the Ineffable Name, by means of which he raised himself to heaven. He assented to her condition. But once she knew it, she pronounced the Name, and herself ascended to heaven, without fulfilling her promise to the angel. God said, "Because she kept herself aloof from sin, we will place her among the seven stars, that men may never forget her," and she was put in the constellation of the Pleiades.

Shemhazai and Azazel, however, were not deterred from entering into alliances with the daughters of men, and to the first two sons were born. Azazel began to devise the finery and the ornaments by means of which women allure men. Thereupon God sent Metatron to tell Shemhazai that He had resolved to destroy the world and bring on a deluge. The fallen angel began to weep and grieve over the fate of the world and the fate of his two sons. If the world went under, what would they have to eat, they who needed daily a thousand camels, a thousand horses, and a thousand steers?

These two sons of Shemhazai, Hiwwa and Hiyya by name, dreamed dreams. The one saw a great stone which covered the earth, and the earth was marked all over with lines upon lines of writing. An angel came, and with a knife obliterated all the lines, leaving but four letters upon the stone. The other son saw a large pleasure grove planted with all sorts of trees. But angels approached bearing axes, and they felled the trees, sparing a single one with three of its branches.

When Hiwwa and Hiyya awoke, they repaired to their father, who interpreted the dreams for them, saying, "God will bring a deluge, and none will escape with his life, excepting only Noah and his sons." When they heard this, the two began to cry and scream, but their father consoled them: "Soft, soft! Do not grieve. As often as men cut or haul stones, or launch vessels, they shall invoke your names, Hiwwa! Hiyya!" This prophecy soothed them.

Shemhazai then did penance. He suspended himself between heaven and earth, and in this position of a penitent sinner he hangs to this day. But Azazel persisted obdurately in his sin of leading mankind astray by means of sensual allurements. For this reason two he-goats were sacrificed in the Temple on the Day of Atonement, the one for God, that He pardon the sins of Israel, the other for Azazel, that he bear the sins of Israel.

Unlike Istehar, the pious maiden, Naamah, the lovely sister of Tubal-cain, led the angels astray with her beauty, and from her union with Shamdon sprang the devil Asmodeus. She was as shameless as all the other descendants of Cain, and as prone to bestial indulgences. Cainite women and Cainite men alike were in the habit of walking abroad naked, and they gave themselves up to every conceivable manner of lewd practices. Of such were the women whose beauty and sensual charms tempted the angels from the path of virtue. The angels, on the other hand, no sooner had they rebelled against God and descended to earth than they lost their transcendental qualities, and were invested with sublunary bodies, so that a union with the daughters of men became possible. The offspring of these alliances between the angels and the Cainite women were the giants, known for their strength and their sinfulness; as their very name, the Emim, indicates, they inspired fear. They have many other names. Sometimes they go by the name Rephaim, because one glance at them made one's heart grow weak; or by the name Gibborim, simply giants, because their size was so enormous that their thigh measured eighteen ells; or by the name Zamzummim, because they were great masters in war; or by the name Anakim, because they touched the sun with their neck; or by the name Ivvim, because, like the snake, they could judge of the qualities of the soil; or finally, by the name Nephilim, because, bringing the world to its fall, they themselves fell.

THE GENERATION OF THE DELUGE

While the descendants of Cain resembled their father in his sinfulness and depravity, the descendants of Seth led a pious, well-regulated life, and the difference between the conduct of the two stocks was reflected in their habitations. The family of Seth was settled upon the mountains in the vicinity of Paradise, while the family of Cain resided in the field of Damascus, the spot whereon Abel was slain by Cain.

Unfortunately, at the time of Methuselah, following the death of Adam, the family of Seth became corrupted after the manner of the Cainites. The two strains united with each other to execute all kinds of iniquitous deeds. The result of the marriages between them were the Nephilim, whose sins brought the deluge upon the world. In their arrogance they claimed the same pedigree as the posterity of Seth, and they compared themselves with princes and men of noble descent.

The wantonness of this generation was in a measure due to the ideal conditions under which mankind lived before the flood. They knew neither toil nor care, and as a consequence of their extraordinary prosperity they grew insolent. In their arrogance they rose up against God. A single sowing bore a harvest sufficient for the needs of forty years, and by means of magic arts they could compel the very sun and moon to stand ready to do their service. The raising of children gave them no trouble. They were born after a few days' pregnancy, and immediately after birth they could walk and talk; they themselves aided the mother in severing the navel string. Not even demons could do them harm. Once a new-born babe, running to fetch a light whereby his mother might cut the navel string, met the chief of the demons, and a combat ensued between the two. Suddenly the crowing of a cock was heard, and the demon made off, crying out to the child, "Go and report unto thy mother, if it had not been for the crowing of the cock, I had killed thee!" Whereupon the child retorted, "Go and report unto thy mother, if it had not been for my uncut navel string, I had killed thee!"

It was their care-free life that gave them space and leisure for their infamies. For a time God, in His long-suffering kindness, passed by the iniquities of men, but His forbearance ceased when once they began to lead unchaste lives, for "God is patient with all sins save only an immoral life."

The other sin that hastened the end of the iniquitous generation was their rapacity. So cunningly were their depredations planned that the law could not touch them. If a countryman brought a basket of vegetables to market, they would edge up to it, one after the other, and abstract a bit, each in itself of petty value, but in a little while the dealer would have none left to sell.

Even after God had resolved upon the destruction of the sinners, He still permitted His mercy to prevail, in that He sent Noah unto them, who exhorted them for one hundred and twenty years to amend their ways, always holding the flood over them as a threat. As for them, they but derided him. When they saw him occupying himself with the building of the ark, they asked, "Wherefore this ark?"

Noah: "God will bring a flood upon you."

The sinners: "What sort of flood? If He sends a fire flood, against that we know how to protect ourselves. If it is a flood of waters, then, if the waters bubble up from the earth, we will cover them with iron rods, and if they descend from above, we know a remedy against that, too."

Noah: "The waters will ooze out from under your feet, and you will not be able to ward them off."

Partly they persisted in their obduracy of heart because Noah had made known to them that the flood would not descend so long as the pious Methuselah sojourned among them. The period of one hundred and twenty years which God had appointed as the term of their probation having expired, Methuselah died, but out of regard for the memory of this pious man God gave them another week's respite, the week of mourning for him. During this time of grace, the laws of nature were suspended, the sun rose in the west and set in the east. To the sinners God gave the dainties that await man in the future world, for the purpose of showing them what they were forfeiting. But all this proved unavailing, and, Methuselah and the other pious men of the generation having departed this life, God brought the deluge upon the earth.

THE HOLY BOOK

Great wisdom was needed for building the ark, which was to have space for all beings on earth, even the spirits. Only the fishes did not have to be provided for. Noah acquired the necessary wisdom from the book given to Adam by the angel Raziel, in which all celestial and all earthly knowledge is recorded.

While the first human pair were still in Paradise, it once happened that Samael, accompanied by a lad, approached Eve and requested her to keep a watchful eye upon his little son until he should return. Eve gave him the promise. When Adam came back from a walk in Paradise, he found a howling, screaming child with Eve, who, in reply to his question, told him it was Samael's. Adam was annoyed, and his annoyance grew as the boy cried and screamed more and more violently. In his vexation he dealt the little one a blow that killed him. But the corpse did not cease to wail and weep, nor did it cease when Adam cut it up into bits. To rid himself of the plague, Adam cooked the remains, and he and Eve ate them. Scarcely had they finished, when Samael appeared and demanded his son. The two malefactors tried to deny everything; they pretended they had no knowledge of his son. But Samael said to them: "What! You dare tell lies, and God in times to come will give Israel the Torah in which it is said, 'Keep thee far from a false word'?"

While they were speaking thus, suddenly the voice of the slain lad was heard proceeding from the heart of Adam and Eve, and it addressed these words to Samael: "Go hence! I have penetrated to the heart of Adam and the heart of Eve, and never again shall I quit their hearts, nor the hearts of their children, or their children's children, unto the end of all generations."

Samael departed, but Adam was sore grieved, and he put on sackcloth and ashes, and he fasted many, many days, until God appeared unto him, and said: "My son, have no fear of Samael. I will give thee a remedy that will help thee against him, for it was at My instance that he went to thee." Adam asked, "And what is this remedy?" God: "The Torah." Adam: "And where is the Torah?" God then gave him the book of the angel Raziel, which he studied day and night. After some time had passed, the angels visited Adam, and, envious of the wisdom he had drawn from the book, they sought to destroy him cunningly by calling him a god and prostrating themselves before him, in spite of his remonstrance, "Do not prostrate yourselves before me, but magnify the Lord with me, and let us exalt His Name together." However, the envy of the angels was so great that they stole the book God had given Adam from him, and threw it in the sea. Adam searched for it everywhere in vain, and the loss distressed him sorely. Again he fasted many days, until God appeared unto him, and said: "Fear not! I will give the book back to thee," and He called Rahab, the Angel of the Sea, and ordered him to recover the book from the sea and restore it to Adam. And so he did.

Upon the death of Adam, the holy book disappeared, but later the cave in which it was hidden was revealed to Enoch in a dream. It was from this book that Enoch drew his knowledge of nature, of the earth and of the heavens, and he became so wise through it that his wisdom exceeded the wisdom of Adam. Once he had committed it to memory, Enoch hid the book again.

Now, when God resolved upon bringing the flood on the earth, He sent the archangel Raphael to Noah, as the bearer of the following message: "I give thee herewith the holy book, that all the secrets and mysteries written therein may be made manifest unto thee, and that thou mayest know how to fulfil its injunction in holiness, purity, modesty, and humbleness. Thou wilt learn from it how to build an ark of the wood of the gopher tree, wherein thou, and thy sons, and thy wife shall find protection."

Noah took the book, and when he studied it, the holy spirit came upon him, and he knew all things needful for the building of the ark and the gathering together of the animals. The book, which was made of sapphires, he took with him into the ark, having first enclosed it in a golden casket. All the time he spent in the ark it served him as a time-piece, to distinguish night from day. Before his death, he entrusted it to Shem, and he in turn to Abraham. From Abraham it descended through Jacob, Levi, Moses, and Joshua to Solomon, who learnt all his wisdom from it, and his skill in the healing art, and also his mastery over the demons.

THE INMATES OF THE ARK

The ark was completed according to the instructions laid down in the Book of Raziel. Noah's next task was gathering in the animals. No less than thirty-two species of birds and three hundred and sixty-five of reptiles he had to take along with him. But God ordered the animals to repair to the ark, and they trooped thither, and Noah did not have to do so much as stretch out a finger. Indeed, more appeared than were required to come, and God instructed him to sit at the door of the ark and note which of the animals lay down as they reached the entrance and which stood. The former belonged in the ark, but not the latter. Taking up his post as he had been commanded, Noah observed a lioness with her two cubs. All three beasts crouched. But the two young ones began to struggle with the mother, and she arose and stood up next to them. Then Noah led the two cubs into the ark. The wild beasts, and the cattle, and the birds which were not accepted remained standing about the ark all of seven days, for the assembling of the animals happened one week before the flood began to descend. On the day whereon they came to the ark, the sun was darkened, and the foundations of the earth trembled, and lightning flashed, and the thunder boomed, as never before. And yet the sinners remained impenitent. In naught did they change their wicked doings during those last seven days.

When finally the flood broke loose, seven hundred thousand of the children of men gathered around the ark, and implored Noah to grant them protection. With a loud voice he replied, and said: "Are ye not those who were rebellious toward God, saying, 'There is no God'? Therefore He has brought ruin upon you, to annihilate you and destroy you from the face of the earth. Have I not been prophesying this unto you these hundred and twenty years, and you would not give heed unto the voice of God? Yet now you desire to be kept alive!" Then the sinners cried out: "So be it! We all are ready now to turn back to God, if only thou wilt open the door of thy ark to receive us, that we may live and not die." Noah made answer, and said: "That ye do now, when your need presses hard upon you. Why did you not turn to God during all the hundred and twenty years which the Lord appointed unto you as the term of repentance? Now do ye come, and ye speak thus, because distress besets your lives. Therefore God will not hearken unto you and give you ear; naught will you accomplish!"

The crowd of sinners tried to take the entrance to the ark by storm, but the wild beasts keeping watch around the ark set upon them, and many were slain, while the rest escaped, only to meet death in the waters of the flood. The water alone could not have made an end of them, for they were giants in stature and strength. When Noah threatened them with the scourge of God, they would make reply: "If the waters of the flood come from above, they will never reach up to our necks; and if they come from below, the soles of our feet are large enough to dam up the springs." But God bade each drop pass through Gehenna before it fell to earth, and the hot rain scalded the skin of the sinners. The punishment that overtook them was befitting their crime. As their sensual desires had made them hot, and inflamed them to immoral excesses, so they were chastised by means of heated water.

Not even in the hour of the death struggle could the sinners suppress their vile instincts. When the water began to stream up out of the springs, they threw their little children into them, to choke the flood.

It was by the grace of God, not on account of his merits, that Noah found shelter in the ark before the overwhelming force of the waters. Although he was better than his contemporaries, he was yet not worthy of having wonders done for his sake. He had so little faith that he did not enter the ark until the waters had risen to his knees. With him his pious wife Naamah, the daughter of Enosh, escaped the peril, and his three sons, and the wives of his three sons."

Noah had not married until he was four hundred and ninety-eight years old. Then the Lord had bidden him to take a wife unto himself. He had not desired to bring children into the world, seeing that they would all have to perish in the flood, and he had only three sons, born unto him shortly before the deluge came. God had given him so small a number of offspring that he might be spared the necessity of building the ark on an overlarge scale in case they turned out to be pious. And if not, if they, too, were depraved like the rest of their generation, sorrow over their destruction would but be increased in proportion to their number.

As Noah and his family were the only ones not to have a share in the corruptness of the age, so the animals received into the ark were such as had led a natural life. For the animals of the time were as immoral as the men: the dog united with the wolf, the cock with the pea-fowl, and many others paid no heed to sexual purity. Those that were saved were such as had kept themselves untainted.

Before the flood the number of unclean animals had been greater than the number of the clean. Afterward the ratio was reversed, because while seven pairs of clean animals were preserved in the ark, but two pairs of the unclean were preserved.

One animal, the reem, Noah could not take into the ark. On account of its huge size it could not find room therein. Noah therefore tied it to the ark, and it ran on behind. Also, he could not make space for the giant Og, the king of Bashan. He sat on top of the ark securely, and in this way escaped the flood of waters. Noah doled out his food to him daily, through a hole, because Og had promised that he and his descendants would serve him as slaves in perpetuity.

Two creatures of a most peculiar kind also found refuge in the ark. Among the beings that came to Noah there was Falsehood asking for shelter. He was denied admission, because he had no companion, and Noah was taking in the animals only by pairs. Falsehood went off to seek a partner, and he met Misfortune, whom he associated with himself on the condition that she might appropriate what Falsehood earned. The pair were then accepted in the ark. When they left it, Falsehood noticed that whatever he gathered together disappeared at once, and he betook himself to his companion to seek an explanation, which she gave him in the following words, "Did we not agree to the condition that I might take what you earn?" and Falsehood had to depart empty-handed."

THE FLOOD

The assembling of the animals in the ark was but the smaller part of the task imposed upon Noah. His chief difficulty was to provide food for a year and accommodations for them. Long afterward Shem, the son of Noah, related to Eliezer, the servant of Abraham, the tale of their experiences with the animals in the ark. This is what he said: "We had sore troubles in the ark. The day animals had to be fed by day, and the night animals by night. My father knew not what food to give to the little zikta. Once he cut a pomegranate in half, and a worm dropped out of the fruit, and was devoured by the zikta. Thenceforth my father would knead bran, and let it stand until it bred worms, which were fed to the animal. The lion suffered with a fever all the time, and therefore he did not annoy the others, because he did not relish dry food. The animal urshana my father found sleeping in a corner of the vessel, and he asked him whether he needed nothing to eat. He answered, and said: 'I saw thou wast very busy, and I did not wish to add to thy cares.' Whereupon my father said, 'May it be the will of the Lord to keep thee alive forever,' and the blessing was realized."

The difficulties were increased when the flood began to toss the ark from side to side. All inside of it were shaken up like lentils in a pot. The lions began to roar, the oxen lowed, the wolves howled, and all the animals gave vent to their agony, each through the sounds it had the power to utter.

Also Noah and his sons, thinking that death was nigh, broke into tears. Noah prayed to God: "O Lord, help us, for we are not able to bear the evil that encompasses us. The billows surge about us, the streams of destruction make us afraid, and death stares us in the face. O hear our prayer, deliver us, incline Thyself unto us, and be gracious unto us! Redeem us and save us!"

The flood was produced by a union of the male waters, which are above the firmament, and the female waters issuing from the earth. The upper waters rushed through the space left when God removed two stars out of the constellation Pleiades. Afterward, to put a stop to the flood, God had to transfer two stars from the constellation of the Bear to the constellation of the Pleiades. That is why the Bear runs after the Pleiades. She wants her two children back, but they will be restored to her only in the future world.

There were other changes among the celestial spheres during the year of the flood. All the time it lasted, the sun and the moon shed no light, whence Noah was called by his name, "the resting one," for in his life the sun and the moon rested. The ark was illuminated by a precious stone, the light of which was more brilliant by night than by day, so enabling Noah to distinguish between day and night.

The duration of the flood was a whole year. It began on the seventeenth day of Heshwan, and the rain continued for forty days, until the twenty-seventh of Kislew. The punishment corresponded to the crime of the sinful generation. They had led immoral lives, and begotten bastard children, whose embryonic state lasts forty days. From the twenty seventh of Kislew until the first of Siwan, a period of one hundred and fifty days, the water stood at one and the same height, fifteen ells above the earth. During that time all the wicked were destroyed, each one receiving the punishment due to him. Cain was among those that perished, and thus the death of Abel was avenged. So powerful were the waters in working havoc that the corpse of Adam was not spared in its grave.

On the first of Siwan the waters began to abate, a quarter of an ell a day, and at the end of sixty days, on the tenth day of Ab, the summits of the mountains showed themselves. But many days before, on the tenth of Tammuz, Noah had sent forth the raven, and a week later the dove, on the first of her three sallies, repeated at intervals of a week. It took from the first of Ab until the first of Tishri for the waters to subside wholly from the face of the earth. Even then the soil was so miry that the dwellers in the ark had to remain within until the twenty-seventh day of Heshwan, completing a full sun year, consisting of twelve moons and eleven days.

Noah had experienced difficulty all along in ascertaining the state of the waters. When he desired to dispatch the raven, the bird said: "The Lord, thy Master, hates me, and thou dost hate me, too. Thy Master hates me, for He bade thee take seven pairs of the clean animals into the ark, and but two pairs of the unclean animals, to which I belong. Thou hatest me, for thou dost not choose, as a messenger, a bird of one of the kinds of which there are seven pairs in the ark, but thou sendest me, and of my kind there is but one pair. Suppose, now, I should perish by reason of heat or cold, would not the world be the poorer by a whole species of animals? Or can it be that thou hast cast a lustful eye upon my mate, and desirest to rid thyself of me?" Where unto Noah made answer, and said: "Wretch! I must live apart from my own wife in the ark. How much less would such thoughts occur to my mind as thou imputest to me!"

The raven's errand had no success, for when he saw the body of a dead man, he set to work to devour it, and did not execute the orders given to him by Noah. Thereupon the dove was sent out. Toward evening she returned with an olive leaf in her bill, plucked upon the Mount of Olives at Jerusalem, for the Holy Land had not been ravaged by the deluge. As she plucked it, she said to God: "O Lord of the world, let my food be as bitter as the olive, but do Thou give it to me from Thy hand, rather than it should be sweet, and I be delivered into the power of men."

NOAH LEAVES THE ARK

Though the earth assumed its old form at the end of the year of punishment, Noah did not abandon the ark until he received the command of God to leave it. He said to himself, "As I entered the ark at the bidding of God, so I will leave it only at His bidding." Yet, when God bade Noah go out of the ark, he refused, because he feared that after he had lived upon the dry land for some time, and begotten children, God would bring another flood. He therefore would not leave the ark until God swore He would never visit the earth with a flood again.

When he stepped out from the ark into the open, he began to weep bitterly at sight of the enormous ravages wrought by the flood, and he said to God: "O Lord of the world! Thou art called the Merciful, and Thou shouldst have had mercy upon Thy creatures." God answered, and said: "O thou foolish shepherd, now thou speakest to Me. Thou didst not so when I addressed kind words to thee, saying: 'I saw thee as a righteous man and perfect in thy generation, and I will bring the flood upon the earth to destroy all flesh. Make an ark for thyself of gopher wood.' Thus spake I to thee, telling thee all these circumstances, that thou mightest entreat mercy for the earth. But thou, as soon as thou didst hear that thou wouldst be rescued in the ark, thou didst not concern thyself about the ruin that would strike the earth. Thou didst but build an ark for thyself, in which thou wast saved. Now that the earth is wasted, thou openest thy mouth to supplicate and pray."

Noah realized that he had been guilty of folly. To propitiate God and acknowledge his sin, he brought a sacrifice. God accepted the offering with favor, whence he is called by his name Noah. The sacrifice was not offered by Noah with his own hands; the priestly services connected with it were performed by his son Shem. There was a reason for this. One day in the ark Noah forgot to give his ration to the lion, and the hungry beast struck him so violent a blow with his paw that he was lame forever after, and, having a bodily defect, he was not permitted to do the offices of a priest.

The sacrifices consisted of an ox, a sheep, a goat, two turtle doves, and two young pigeons. Noah had chosen these kinds because he supposed they were appointed for sacrifices, seeing that God had commanded him to take seven pairs of them into the ark with him. The altar was erected in the same place on which Adam and Cain and Abel had brought their sacrifices, and on which later the altar was to be in the sanctuary at Jerusalem.

After the sacrifice was completed, God blessed Noah and his sons. He made them to be rulers of the world as Adam had been, and He gave them a command, saying, "Be fruitful and multiply upon the earth," for during their sojourn in the ark, the two sexes, of men and animals alike, had lived apart from each other, because while a public calamity rages continence is becoming even to those who are left unscathed. This law of conduct had been violated by none in the ark except by Ham, by the dog, and by the raven. They all received a punishment. Ham's was that his descendants were men of dark-hued skin.

As a token that He would destroy the earth no more, God set His bow in the cloud. Even if men should be steeped in sin again, the bow proclaims to them that their sins will cause no harm to the world. Times came in the course of the ages when men were pious enough not to have to live in dread of punishment. In such times the bow was not visible.

God accorded permission to Noah and his descendants to use the flesh of animals for food, which had been forbidden from the time of Adam until then. But they were to abstain from the use of blood. He ordained the seven Noachian laws, the observance of which is incumbent upon all men, not upon Israel alone. God enjoined particularly the command against the shedding of human blood. Whoso would shed man's blood, his blood would be shed. Even if human judges let the guilty man go free, his punishment would overtake him. He would die an unnatural death, such as he had inflicted upon his fellow-man. Yea, even beasts that slew men, even of them would the life of men be required.

THE CURSE OF DRUNKENNESS

Noah lost his epithet "the pious" when he began to occupy himself with the growing of the vine. He became a "man of the ground," and this first attempt to produce wine at the same time produced the first to drink to excess, the first to utter curses upon his associates, and the first to introduce slavery. This is the way it all came about. Noah found the vine which Adam had taken with him from Paradise, when he was driven forth. He tasted the grapes upon it, and, finding them palatable, he resolved to plant the vine and tend it. On the selfsame day on which he planted it, it bore fruit, he put it in the wine-press, drew off the juice, drank it, became drunken, and was dishonored--all on one day. His assistant in the work of cultivating the vine was Satan, who had happened along at the very moment when he was engaged in planting the slip he had found. Satan asked him: "What is it thou art planting here?"

Noah: "A vineyard."

Satan: "And what may be the qualities of what it produces?"

Noah: "The fruit it bears is sweet, be it dry or moist. It yields wine that rejoiceth the heart of man."

Satan: "Let us go into partnership in this business of planting a vineyard."

Noah: "Agreed!"

Satan thereupon slaughtered a lamb, and then, in succession, a lion, a pig, and a monkey. The blood of each as it was killed he made to flow under the vine. Thus he conveyed to Noah what the qualities of wine are: before man drinks of it, he is innocent as a lamb; if he drinks of it moderately, he feels as strong as a lion; if he drinks more of it than he can bear, he resembles the pig; and if he drinks to the point of intoxication, then he behaves like a monkey, he dances around, sings, talks obscenely, and knows not what he is doing.

This deterred Noah no more than did the example of Adam, whose fall had also been due to wine, for the forbidden fruit had been the grape, with which he had made himself drunk.

In his drunken condition Noah betook himself to the tent of his wife. His son Ham saw him there, and he told his brothers what he had noticed, and said: "The first man had but two sons, and one slew the other; this man Noah has three sons, yet he desires to beget a fourth besides." Nor did Ham rest satisfied with these disrespectful words against his father. He added to this sin of irreverence the still greater outrage of attempting to perform an operation upon his father designed to prevent procreation.

When Noah awoke from his wine and became sober, he pronounced a curse upon Ham in the person of his youngest son Canaan. To Ham himself he could do no harm, for God had conferred a blessing upon Noah and his three sons as they departed from the ark. Therefore he put the curse upon the last-born son of the son that had prevented him from begetting a younger son than the three he had." The descendants of Ham through Canaan therefore have red eyes, because Ham looked upon the nakedness of his father; they have misshapen lips, because Ham spoke with his lips to his brothers about the unseemly condition of his father; they have twisted curly hair, because Ham turned and twisted his head round to see the nakedness of his father; and they go about naked, because Ham did not cover the nakedness of his father. Thus he was requited, for it is the way of God to mete out punishment measure for measure.

Canaan had to suffer vicariously for his father's sin. Yet some of the punishment was inflicted upon him on his own account, for it had been Canaan who had drawn the attention of Ham to Noah's revolting condition. Ham, it appears, was but the worthy father of such a son. The last will and testament of Canaan addressed to his children read as follows: "Speak not the truth; hold not yourselves aloof from theft; lead a dissolute life; hate your master with an exceeding great hate; and love one another."

As Ham was made to suffer requital for his irreverence, so Shem and Japheth received a reward for the filial, deferential way in which they took a garment and laid it upon both their shoulders, and walking backward, with averted faces, covered the nakedness of their father. Naked the descendants of Ham, the Egyptians and Ethiopians, were led away captive and into exile by the king of Assyria, while the descendants of Shem, the Assyrians, even when the angel of the Lord burnt them in the camp, were not exposed, their garments remained upon their corpses unsinged. And in time to come, when Gog shall suffer his defeat, God will provide both shrouds and a place of burial for him and all his multitude, the posterity of Japheth.

Though Shem and Japheth both showed themselves to be dutiful and deferential, yet it was Shem who deserved the larger meed of praise. He was the first to set about covering his father. Japheth joined him after the good deed had been begun. Therefore the descendants of Shem received as their special reward the tallit, the garment worn by them, while the Japhethites have only the toga. A further distinction accorded to Shem was the mention of his name in connection with God's in the blessing of Noah. "Blessed be the Lord, the God of Shem," he said, though as a rule the name of God is not joined to the name of a living person, only to the name of one who has departed this life.

The relation of Shem to Japheth was expressed in the blessing their father pronounced upon them: God will grant a land of beauty to Japheth, and his sons will be proselytes dwelling in the academies of Shem. At the same time Noah conveyed by his words that the Shekinah would dwell only in the first Temple, erected by Solomon, a son of Shem, and not in the second Temple, the builder of which would be Cyrus, a descendant of Japheth.

NOAH'S DESCENDANTS SPREAD ABROAD

When it became known to Ham that his father had cursed him, he fled ashamed, and with his family he settled in the city built by him, and named Neelatamauk for his wife. Jealous of his brother, Japheth followed his example. He likewise built a city which he named for his wife, Adataneses. Shem was the only one of the sons of Noah who did not abandon him. In the vicinity of his father's home, by the mountain, he built his city, to which he also gave his wife's name, Zedeketelbab. The three cities are all near Mount Lubar, the eminence upon which the ark rested. The first lies to the south of it, the second to the west, and the third to the east.

Noah endeavored to inculcate the ordinances and the commands known to him upon his children and his children's children. In particular he admonished them against the fornication, the uncleanness, and all the iniquity which had brought the flood down upon the earth. He reproached them with living apart from one another, and with their jealousies, for he feared that, after his death, they might go so far as to shed human blood. Against this he warned them impressively, that they be not annihilated from the earth like those that went before. Another law which he enjoined upon them, to observe it, was the law ordaining that the fruit of a tree shall not be used the first three years it bears, and even in the fourth year it shall be the portion of the priests alone, after a part thereof has been offered upon the altar of God. And having made an end of giving his teachings and injunctions, Noah said: "For thus did Enoch, your ancestor, exhort his son Methuselah, and Methuselah his son Lamech, and Lamech delivered all unto me as his father had bidden him, and now I do exhort you, my children, as Enoch exhorted his son. When he lived, in his generation, which was the seventh generation of man, he commanded it and testified it unto his children and his children's children, until the day of his death."

In the year 1569 after the creation of the world, Noah divided the earth by lot among his three sons, in the presence of an angel. Each one stretched forth his hand and took a slip from the bosom of Noah. Shem's slip was inscribed with the middle of the earth, and this portion became the inheritance of his descendants unto all eternity. Noah rejoiced that the lot had assigned it to Shem. Thus was fulfilled his blessing upon him, "And God in the habitation of Shem," for three holy places fell within his precincts--the Holy of Holies in the Temple, Mount Sinai, the middle point of the desert, and Mount Zion, the middle point of the navel of the earth.

The south fell to the lot of Ham, and the north became the inheritance of Japheth. The land of Ham is hot, Japheth's cold, but Shem's is neither hot nor cold, its temperature is hot and cold mixed.

This division of the earth took place toward the end of the life of Peleg, the name given to him by his father Eber, who, being a prophet, knew that the division of the earth would take place in the time of his son. The brother of Peleg was called Joktan, because the duration of the life of man was shortened in his time.

In turn, the three sons of Noah, while they were still standing in the presence of their father, divided each his portion among his children, Noah threatening with his curse any who should stretch out his hand to take a portion not assigned to him by lot. And they all cried, "So be it! So be it!"

Thus were divided one hundred and four lands and ninety-nine islands among seventy-two nations, each with a language of its own, using sixteen different sets of characters for writing. To Japheth were allotted forty-four lands, thirty-three islands, twenty-two languages, and five kinds of writing; Ham received thirty-four lands, thirty-three islands, twenty-four languages, and five kinds of writing; and Shem twenty-six lands, thirty-three islands, twenty-six languages, and six kinds of writing--one set of written characters more to Shem than to either of his brothers, the extra set being the Hebrew.

The land appointed as the inheritance of the twelve sons of Jacob was provisionally granted to Canaan, Zidon, Heth, the Jebusites, the Amorites, the Girgashites, the Hivites, the Arkites, the Sinites, the Arvadites, the Zemarites, and the Hamathites. It was the duty of these nations to take care of the land until the rightful owners should come.

No sooner had the children of Noah and their children's children taken possession of the habitations apportioned to them, than the unclean spirits began to seduce men and torment them with pain and all sorts of suffering leading to spiritual and physical death. Upon the entreaties of Noah God sent down the angel Raphael, who banished nine-tenths of the unclean spirits from the earth, leaving but one-tenth for Mastema, to punish sinners through them. Raphael, supported by the chief of the unclean spirits, at that time revealed to Noah all the remedies residing in plants, that he might resort to them at need. Noah recorded them in a book, which he transmitted to his son Shem. This is the source to which go back all the medical books whence the wise men of India, Aram, Macedonia, and Egypt draw their knowledge. The sages of India devoted themselves particularly to the study of curative trees and spices; the Arameans were well versed in the knowledge of the properties of grains and seeds, and they translated the old medical books into their language. The wise men of Macedonia were the first to apply medical knowledge practically, while the Egyptians sought to effect cures by means of magic arts and by means of astrology, and they taught the Midrash of the Chaldees, composed by Kangar, the son of Ur, the son of Kesed. Medical skill spread further and further until the time of aesculapius. This Macedonian sage, accompanied by forty learned magicians, journeyed from country to country, until they came to the land beyond India, in the direction of Paradise. They hoped there to find some wood of the tree of life, and thus spread their fame abroad over the whole world. Their hope was frustrated. When they arrived at the spot, they found healing trees and wood of the tree of life, but when they were in the act of stretching forth their hands to gather what they desired, lightning darted out of the ever-turning sword, smote them to the ground, and they were all burnt. With them disappeared all knowledge of medicine, and it did not revive until the time of the first Artaxerxes, under the Macedonian sage Hippocrates, Dioscorides of Baala, Galen of Caphtor, and the Hebrew Asaph.

THE DEPRAVITY OF MANKIND

With the spread of mankind corruption increased. While Noah was still alive, the descendants of Shem, Ham, and Japheth appointed princes over each of the three groups- Nimrod for the descendants of Ham, Joktan for the descendants of Shem, and Phenech for the descendants of Japheth. Ten years before Noah's death, the number of those subject to the three princes amounted to millions. When this great concourse of men came to Babylonia upon their journeyings, they said to one another: "Behold, the time is coming when, at the end of days, neighbor will be separated from neighbor, and brother from brother, and one will carry on war against the other. Go to, let us build us a city, and a tower, whose top may reach unto heaven, and let us make us a great name upon the earth. And now let us make bricks, and each one write his name upon his brick." All agreed to this proposal, with the exception of twelve pious men, Abraham among them. They refused to join the others. They were seized by the people, and brought before the three princes, to whom they gave the following reason for their refusal: "We will not make bricks, nor remain with you, for we know but one God, and Him we serve; even if you burn us in the fire together with the bricks, we will not walk in your ways." Nimrod and Phenech flew into such a passion over the twelve men that they resolved to throw them into the fire. Joktan, however, besides being a God-fearing man, was of close kin to the men on trial, and he essayed to save them. He proposed to his two colleagues to grant them a seven days' respite. His plan was accepted, such deference being paid him as the primate among the three. The twelve were incarcerated in the house of Joktan. In the night he charged fifty of his attendants to mount the prisoners upon mules and take them to the mountains. Thus they would escape the threatened punishment. Joktan provided them with food for a month. He was sure that in the meantime either a change of sentiment would come about, and the people desist from their purpose, or God would help the fugitives. Eleven of the prisoners assented to the plan with gratitude. Abraham alone rejected it, saying: "Behold, to-day we flee to the mountains to escape from the fire, but if wild beasts rush out from the mountains and devour us, or if food is lacking, so that we die by famine, we shall be found fleeing before the people of the land and dying in our sins. Now, as the Lord liveth, in whom I trust, I will not depart from this place wherein they have imprisoned me, and if I am to die through my sins, then will I die by the will of God, according to His desire."

In vain Joktan endeavored to persuade Abraham to flee. He persisted in his refusal. He remained behind alone in the prison house, while the other eleven made their escape. At the expiration of the set term, when the people returned and demanded the death of the twelve captives, Joktan could produce only Abraham. His excuse was that the rest had broken loose during the night. The people were about to throw themselves upon Abraham and cast him into the lime kiln. Suddenly an earthquake was felt, the fire darted from the furnace, and all who were standing round about, eighty four thousand of the people, were consumed, while Abraham remained untouched. Thereupon he repaired to his eleven friends in the mountains, and told them of the miracle that had befallen for his sake. They all returned with him, and, unmolested by the people, they gave praise and thanks to God.

NIMROD

The first among the leaders of the corrupt men was Nimrod. His father Cush had married his mother at an advanced age, and Nimrod, the offspring of this belated union, was particularly dear to him as the son of his old age. He gave him the clothes made of skins with which God had furnished Adam and Eve at the time of their leaving Paradise. Cush himself had gained possession of them through Ham. From Adam and Eve they had descended to Enoch, and from him to Methuselah, and to Noah, and the last had taken them with him into the ark. When the inmates of the ark were about to leave their refuge, Ham stole the garments and kept them concealed, finally passing them on to his first-born son Cush. Cush in turn hid them for many years. When his son Nimrod reached his twentieth year, he gave them to him. These garments had a wonderful property. He who wore them was both invincible and irresistible. The beasts and birds of the woods fell down before Nimrod as soon as they caught sight of him arrayed in them, and he was equally victorious in his combats with men. The source of his unconquerable strength was not known to them. They attributed it to his personal prowess, and therefore they appointed him king over themselves. This was done after a conflict between the descendants of Cush and the descendants of Japheth, from which Nimrod emerged triumphant, having routed the enemy utterly with the assistance of a handful of warriors. He chose Shinar as his capital. Thence he extended his dominion farther and farther, until he rose by cunning and force to be the sole ruler of the whole world. the first mortal to hold universal sway, as the ninth ruler to possess the same power will be the Messiah.

His impiousness kept pace with his growing power. Since the flood there had been no such sinner as Nimrod. He fashioned idols of wood and stone, and paid worship to them. But not satisfied to lead a godless life himself, he did all he could to tempt his subjects into evil ways, wherein he was aided and abetted by his son Mardon. This son of his outstripped his father in iniquity. It was their time and their life that gave rise to the proverb, "Out of the wicked cometh forth wickedness."

The great success that attended all of Nimrod's undertakings produced a sinister effect. Men no longer trusted in God, but rather in their own prowess and ability, an attitude to which Nimrod tried to convert the whole world. Therefore people said, "Since the creation of the world there has been none like Nimrod, a mighty hunter of men and beasts, and a sinner before God."

And not all this sufficed unto Nimrod's evil desire. Not enough that he turned men away from God, he did all he could to make them pay Divine honors unto himself. He set himself up as a god, and made a seat for himself in imitation of the seat of God. It was a tower built out of a round rock, and on it he placed a throne of cedar wood, upon which arose, one above the other, four thrones, of iron, copper, silver, and gold. Crowning all, upon the golden throne, lay a precious stone, round in shape and gigantic in size. This served him as a seat, and as he sate upon it, all nations came and paid him Divine homage.

THE TOWER OF BABEL

The iniquity and godlessness of Nimrod reached their climax in the building of the Tower of Babel. His counsellors had proposed the plan of erecting such a tower, Nimrod had agreed to it, and it was executed in Shinar by a mob of six hundred thousand men. The enterprise was neither more nor less than rebellion against God, and there were three sorts of rebels among the builders. The first party spoke, Let us ascend into the heavens and wage warfare with Him; the second party spoke, Let us ascend into the heavens, set up our idols, and pay worship unto them there; and the third party spoke, Let us ascend into the heavens, and ruin them with our bows and spears.

Many, many years were passed in building the tower. It reached so great a height that it took a year to mount to the top. A brick was, therefore, more precious in the sight of the builders than a human being. If a man fell down, and met his death, none took notice of it, but if a brick dropped, they wept, because it would take a year to replace it. So intent were they upon accomplishing their purpose that they would not permit a woman to interrupt herself in her work of brick-making when the hour of travail came upon her. Moulding bricks she gave birth to her child, and, tying it round her body in a sheet, she went on moulding bricks.

They never slackened in their work, and from their dizzy height they constantly shot arrows toward heaven, which, returning, were seen to be covered with blood. They were thus fortified in their delusion, and they cried, "We have slain all who are in heaven." Thereupon God turned to the seventy angels who encompass His throne, and He spake: "Go to, let us go down, and there confound their language, that they may not understand one another's speech." Thus it happened. Thenceforth none knew what the other spoke. One would ask for the mortar, and the other handed him a brick; in a rage, he would throw the brick at his partner and kill him. Many perished in this manner, and the rest were punished according to the nature of their rebellious conduct. Those who had spoken, "Let us ascend into the heavens, set up our idols, and pay worship unto them there," God transformed into apes and phantoms; those who had proposed to assault the heavens with their arms, God set against each other so that they fell in the combat; and those who had resolved to carry on a combat with God in heaven were scattered broadcast over the earth. As for the unfinished tower, a part sank into the earth, and another part was consumed by fire; only one-third of it remained standing. The place of the tower has never lost its peculiar quality. Whoever passes it forgets all he knows.

The punishment inflicted upon the sinful generation of the tower is comparatively lenient. On account of rapine the generation of the flood were utterly destroyed, while the generation of the tower were preserved in spite of their blasphemies and all their other acts offensive to God. The reason is that God sets a high value upon peace and harmony. Therefore the generation of the deluge, who gave themselves up to depredation, and bore hatred to one another, were extirpated, root and branch, while the generation of the Tower of Babel dwelling amicably together, and loving one another, were spared alive, at least a remnant of them.

Beside the chastisement of sin and sinners by the confounding of speech, another notable circumstance was connected with the descent of God upon earth--one of only ten such descents to occur between the creation of the world and the day of judgment. It was on this occasion that God and the seventy angels that surround His throne cast lots concerning the various nations. Each angel received a nation, and Israel fell to the lot of God. To every nation a peculiar language was assigned, Hebrew being reserved for Israel--the language made use of by God at the creation of the world.

Chapter 5

ABRAHAM--THE WICKED GENERATIONS

Ten generations there were from Noah to Abraham, to show how great is the clemency of God, for all the generations provoked His wrath, until Abraham our father came and received the reward of all of them. For the sake of Abraham God had shown himself long-suffering and patient during the lives of these ten generations. Yea, more, the world itself had been created for the sake of his merits. His advent had been made manifest to his ancestor Reu, who uttered the following prophecy at the birth of his son Serug: "From this child he shall be born in the fourth generation that shall set his dwelling over the highest, and he shall be called perfect and spotless, and shall be the father of nations, and his covenant shall not be dissolved, and his seed shall be multiplied forever."

It was, indeed, high time that the "friend of God" should make his appearance upon earth. The descendants of Noah were sinking from depravity to lower and lower depths of depravity. They were beginning to quarrel and slay, eat blood, build fortified cities and walls and towers, and set one man over the whole nation as king, and wage wars, people against people, and nations against nations, and cities against cities, and do all manner of evil, and acquire weapons, and teach warfare unto their children. And they began also to take captives and sell them as slaves. And they made unto themselves molten images, which they worshipped, each one the idol he had molten for himself, for the evil spirits under their leader Mastema led them astray into sin and uncleanness. For this reason Reu called his son Serug, because all mankind had turned aside unto sin and transgression. When he grew to manhood, the name was seen to have been chosen fittingly, for he, too, worshipped idols, and when he himself had a son, Nahor by name, he taught him the arts of the Chaldees, how to be a soothsayer and practice magic according to signs in the heavens. When, in time, a son was born to Nahor, Mastema sent ravens and other birds to despoil the earth and rob men of the proceeds of their work. As soon as they had dropped the seed in the furrows, and before they could cover it over with earth, the birds picked it up from the surface of the ground, and Nahor called his son Terah, because the ravens and the other birds plagued men, devoured their seed, and reduced them to destitution.

THE BIRTH OF ABRAHAM

Terah married Emtelai, the daughter of Karnabo, and the offspring of their union was Abraham. His birth had been read in the stars by Nimrod, for this impious king was a cunning astrologer, and it was manifest to him that a man would be born in his day who would rise up against him and triumphantly give the lie to his religion. In his terror at the fate foretold him in the stars, he sent for his princes and governors, and asked them to advise him in the matter. They answered, and said: "Our unanimous advice is that thou shouldst build a great house, station a guard at the entrance thereof, and make known in the whole of thy realm that all pregnant women shall repair thither together with their midwives, who are to remain with them when they are delivered. When the days of a woman to be delivered are fulfilled, and the child is born, it shall be the duty of the midwife to kill it, if it be a boy. But if the child be a girl, it shall be kept alive, and the mother shall receive gifts and costly garments, and a herald shall proclaim, 'Thus is done unto the woman who bears a daughter!' "

The king was pleased with this counsel, and he had a proclamation published throughout his whole kingdom, summoning all the architects to build a great house for him, sixty ells high and eighty wide. After it was completed, he issued a second proclamation, summoning all pregnant women thither, and there they were to remain until their confinement. Officers were appointed to take the women to the house, and guards were stationed in it and about it, to prevent the women from escaping thence. He furthermore sent midwives to the house, and commanded them to slay the men children at their mothers' breasts. But if a woman bore a girl, she was to be arrayed in byssus, silk, and embroidered garments, and led forth from the house of detention amid great honors. No less than seventy thousand children were slaughtered thus. Then the angels appeared before God, and spoke, "Seest Thou not what he doth, yon sinner and blasphemer, Nimrod son of Canaarl, who slays so many innocent babes that have done no harm?" God answered, and said: "Ye holy angels, I know it and I see it, for I neither slumber nor sleep. I behold and I know the secret things and the things that are revealed, and ye shall witness what I will do unto this sinner and blasphemer, for I will turn My hand against him to chastise him."

It was about this time that Terah espoused the mother of Abraham, and she was with child. When her body grew large at the end of three months of pregnancy, and her countenance became pale, Terah said unto her, "What ails thee, my wife, that thy countenance is so pale and thy body so swollen?" She answered, and said, "Every year I suffer with this malady." But Terah would not be put off thus. He insisted: "Show me thy body. It seems to me thou art big with child. If that be so, it behooves us not to violate the command of our god Nimrod." When he passed his hand over her body, there happened a miracle. The child rose until it lay beneath her breasts, and Terah could feel nothing with his hands. He said to his wife, "Thou didst speak truly," and naught became visible until the day of her delivery.

When her time approached, she left the city in great terror and wandered toward the desert, walking along the edge of a valley, until she happened across a cave. She entered this refuge, and on the next day she was seized with throes, and she gave birth to a son. The whole cave was filled with the light of the child's countenance as with the splendor of the sun, and the mother rejoiced exceedingly. The babe she bore was our father Abraham.

His mother lamented, and said to her son: "Alas that I bore thee at a time when Nimrod is king. For thy sake seventy thousand men children were slaughtered, and I am seized with terror on account of thee, that he hear of thy existence, and slay thee. Better thou shouldst perish here in this cave than my eye should behold thee dead at my breast." She took the garment in which she was clothed, and wrapped it about the boy. Then she abandoned him in the cave, saying, "May the Lord be with thee, may He not fail thee nor forsake thee."

THE BABE PROCLAIMS GOD

Thus Abraham was deserted in the cave, without a nurse, and he began to wail. God sent Gabriel down to give him milk to drink, and the angel made it to flow from the little finger of the baby's right hand, and he sucked at it until he was ten days old. Then he arose and walked about, and he left the cave, and went along the edge of the valley. When the sun sank, and the stars came forth, he said, "These are the gods!" But the dawn came, and the stars could be seen no longer, and then he said, "I will not pay worship to these, for they are no gods." Thereupon the sun came forth, and he spoke, "This is my god, him will I extol." But again the sun set, and he said, "He is no god," and beholding the moon, he called her his god to whom he would pay Divine homage. Then the moon was obscured, and he cried out: "This, too, is no god! There is One who sets them all in motion."

He was still communing with himself when the angel Gabriel approached him and met him with the greeting, "Peace be with thee," and Abraham returned, "With thee be peace," and asked, "Who art thou?" And Gabriel answered, and said, "I am the angel Gabriel, the messenger of God," and he led Abraham to a spring of water near by, and Abraham washed his face and his hands and feet, and he prayed to God, bowing down and prostrating himself.

Meantime the mother of Abraham thought of him in sorrow and tears, and she went forth from the city to seek him in the cave in which she had abandoned him. Not finding her son, she wept bitterly, and said, "Woe unto me that I bore thee but to become a prey of wild beasts, the bears and the lions and the wolves!" She went to the edge of the valley, and there she found her son. But she did not recognize him, for he had grown very large. She addressed the lad, "Peace be with thee!" and he returned, "With thee be peace!" and he continued, "Unto what purpose didst thou come to the desert?" She replied, "I went forth from the city to seek my son." Abraham questioned further, "Who brought thy son hither?" and the mother replied thereto: "I had become pregnant from my husband Terah, and when the days of my delivery were fulfilled, I was in anxiety about my son in my womb, lest our king come, the son of Canaan, and slay him as he had slain the seventy thousand other men children. Scarcely had I reached the cave in this valley when the throes of travailing seized me, and I bore a son, whom I left behind in the cave, and I went home again. Now am I come to seek him, but I find him not."

Abraham then spoke, "As to this child thou tellest of, how old was it?"

The mother: "It was about twenty days old."

Abraham: "Is there a woman in the world who would forsake her new-born son in the desert, and come to seek him after twenty days?"

The mother: "Peradventure God will show Himself a merciful God!"

Abraham: "I am the son whom thou hast come to seek in this valley!"

The mother: "My son, how thou art grown! But twenty days old, and thou canst already walk, and talk with thy mouth!"

Abraham: "So it is, and thus, O my mother, it is made known unto thee that there is in the world a great, terrible, living, and ever-existing God, who doth see, but who cannot be seen. He is in the heavens above, and the whole earth is full of His glory."

The mother: "My son, is there a God beside Nimrod?"

Abraham: "Yes, mother, the God of the heavens and the God of the earth, He is also the God of Nimrod son of Canaan. Go, therefore, and carry this message unto Nimrod."

The mother of Abraham returned to the city and told her husband Terah how she had found their son. Terah, who was a prince and a magnate in the house of the king, betook himself to the royal palace, and cast himself down before the king upon his face. It was the rule that one who prostrated himself before the king was not permitted to lift up his head until the king bade him lift it up. Nimrod gave permission to Terah to rise and state his request. Thereupon Terah related all that had happened with his wife and his son. When Nimrod heard his tale, abject fear seized upon him, and he asked his counsellors and princes what to do with the lad. They answered, and said: "Our king and our god! Wherefore art thou in fear by reason of a little child? There are myriads upon myriads of princes in thy realm, rulers of thousands, rulers of hundreds, rulers of fifties, and rulers of tens, and overseers without number. Let the pettiest of the princes go and fetch the boy and put him in prison." But the king interposed, "Have ye ever seen a baby of twenty days walking with his feet, speaking with his mouth, and proclaiming with his tongue that there is a God in heaven, who is One, and none beside Him, who sees and is not seen?" All the assembled princes were horror struck at these words.

At this time Satan in human form appeared, clad in black silk garb, and he cast himself down before the king. Nimrod said, "Raise thy head and state thy request." Satan asked the king: "Why art thou terrified, and why are ye all in fear on account of a little lad? I will counsel thee what thou shalt do: Open thy arsenal and give weapons unto all the princes, chiefs, and governors, and unto all the warriors, and send them to fetch him unto thy service and to be under thy dominion."

This advice given by Satan the king accepted and followed. He sent a great armed host to bring Abraham to him. When the boy saw the army approach him, he was sore afraid, and amid tears he implored God for help. In answer to his prayer, God sent the angel Gabriel to him, and he said: "Be not afraid and disquieted, for God is with thee. He will rescue thee out of the hands of all thine adversaries." God commanded Gabriel to put thick, dark clouds between Abraham and his assailants. Dismayed by the heavy clouds, they fled, returning to Nimrod, their king, and they said to him, "Let us depart and leave this realm," and the king gave money unto all his princes and his servants, and together with the king they departed and journeyed to Babylon.

ABRAHAM'S FIRST APPEARANCE IN PUBLIC

Now Abraham, at the command of God, was ordered by the angel Gabriel to follow Nimrod to Babylon. He objected that he was in no wise equipped to undertake a campaign against the king, but Gabriel calmed him with the words: "Thou needest no provision for the way, no horse to ride upon, no warriors to carry on war with Nimrod, no chariots, nor riders. Do thou but sit thyself upon my shoulder, and I shall bear thee to Babylon."

Abraham did as he was bidden, and in the twinkling of an eye he found himself before the gates of the city of Babylon. At the behest of the angel, he entered the city, and he called unto the dwellers therein with a loud voice: "The Eternal, He is the One Only God, and there is none beside. He is the God of the heavens, and the God of the gods, and the God of Nimrod. Acknowledge this as the truth, all ye men, women, and children. Acknowledge also that I am Abraham His servant, the trusted steward of His house."

Abraham met his parents in Babylon, and also he saw the angel Gabriel, who bade him proclaim the true faith to his father and his mother. Therefore Abraham spake to them, and said: "Ye serve a man of your own kind, and you pay worship to an image of Nimrod. Know ye not that it has a mouth, but it speaks not; an eye, but it sees not; an ear, but it hears not; nor does it walk upon its feet, and there is no profit in it, either unto itself or unto others?"

When Terah heard these words, he persuaded Abraham to follow him into the house, where his son told him all that had happened--how in one day he had completed a forty days' journey. Terah thereupon went to Nimrod and reported to him that his son Abraham had suddenly appeared in Babylon. The king sent for Abraham, and he came before him with his father. Abraham passed the magnates and the dignitaries until he reached the royal throne, upon which he seized hold, shaking it and crying out with a loud voice: "O Nimrod, thou contemptible wretch, that deniest the essence of faith, that deniest the living and immutable God, and Abraham His servant, the trusted steward of His house. Acknowledge Him, and repeat after me the words: The Eternal is God, the Only One, and there is none beside; He is incorporeal, living, ever-existing; He slumbers not and sleeps not, who hath created the world that men might believe in Him. And confess also concerning me, and say that I am the servant of God and the trusted steward of His house."

While Abraham proclaimed this with a loud voice, the idols fell upon their faces, and with them also King Nimrod. For a space of two hours and a half the king lay lifeless, and when his soul returned upon him, he spoke and said, "Is it thy voice, O Abraham, or the voice of thy God?" And Abraham answered, and said, "This voice is the voice of the least of all creatures called into existence by God." Thereupon Nimrod said, "Verily, the God of Abraham is a great and powerful God, the King of all kings," and he commanded Terah to take his son and remove him, and return again unto his own city, and father and son did as the king had ordered.

THE PREACHER OF THE TRUE FAITH

When Abraham attained the age of twenty years, his father Terah fell ill. He spoke as follows to his sons Haran and Abraham, "I adjure you by your lives, my sons, sell these two idols for me, for I have not enough money to meet our expenses." Haran executed the wish of his father, but if any one accosted Abraham, to buy an idol from him, and asked him the price, he would answer, "Three manehs," and then question in turn,

"How old art thou?" "Thirty years," the reply would be. "Thou art thirty years of age, and yet thou wouldst worship this idol which I made but to-day?" The man would depart and go his way, and another would approach Abraham, and ask, "How much is this idol?" and "Five manehs" would be the reply, and again Abraham would put the question, "How old art thou?"--"Fifty years."--"And dost thou who art fifty years of age bow down before this idol which was made but to-day?" Thereupon the man would depart and go his way. Abraham then took two idols, put a rope about their necks, and, with their faces turned downward, he dragged them along the ground, crying aloud all the time: "Who will buy an idol wherein there is no profit, either unto itself or unto him that buys it in order to worship it? It has a mouth, but it speaketh not; eyes, but it seeth not; feet, but it walketh not; ears, but it heareth not."

The people who heard Abraham were amazed exceedingly at his words. As he went through the streets, he met an old woman who approached him with the purpose of buying an idol, good and big, to be worshipped and loved. "Old woman, old woman," said Abraham, "I know no profit therein, either in the big ones or in the little ones, either unto themselves or unto others. And," he continued to speak to her, "what has become of the big image thou didst buy from my brother Haran, to worship it?" "Thieves," she replied, "came in the night and stole it, while I was still at the bath." "If it be thus," Abraham went on questioning her, "how canst thou pay homage to an idol that cannot save itself from thieves, let alone save others, like thyself, thou silly old woman, out of misfortune? How is it possible for thee to say that the image thou worshippest is a god? If it be a god, why did it not save itself out of the hands of those thieves? Nay, in the idol there is no profit, either unto itself or unto him that adores it."

The old woman rejoined, "If what thou sayest be true, whom shall I serve?" "Serve the God of all gods," returned Abraham, "the Lord of lords, who hath created heaven and earth, the sea and all therein--the God of Nimrod and the God of Terah, the God of the east, the west, the south, and the north. Who is Nimrod, the dog, who calleth himself a god, that worship be offered unto him?"

Abraham succeeded in opening the eyes of the old woman, and she became a zealous missionary for the true God. When she discovered the thieves who had carried off her idol, and they restored it to her, she broke it in pieces with a stone, and as she wended her way through the streets, she cried aloud, "Who would save his soul from destruction, and be prosperous in all his doings, let him serve the God of Abraham." Thus she converted many men and women to the true belief.

Rumors of the words and deeds of the old woman reached the king, and he sent for her. When she appeared before him, he rebuked her harshly, asking her how she dared serve any god but himself. The old woman replied: "Thou art a liar, thou deniest the essence of faith, the One Only God, beside whom there is no other god. Thou livest upon His bounty, but thou payest worship to another, and thou dost repudiate Him, and His teachings, and Abraham His servant."

The old woman had to pay for her zeal for the faith with her life. Nevertheless great fear and terror took possession of Nimrod, because the people became more and more attached to the teachings of Abraham, and he knew not how to deal with the man who was undermining the old faith. At the advice of his princes, he arranged a seven days' festival, at which all the people were bidden to appear in their robes of state, their gold and silver apparel. By such display of wealth and power he expected to intimidate Abraham and bring him back to the faith of the king. Through his father Terah, Nimrod invited Abraham to come before him, that he might have the opportunity of seeing his greatness and wealth, and the glory of his dominion, and the multitude of his princes and attendants. But Abraham refused to appear before the king. On the other hand, he granted his father's request that in his absence he sit by his idols and the king's, and take care of them.

Alone with the idols, and while he repeated the words, "The Eternal He is God, the Eternal He is God!" he struck the king's idols from their thrones, and began to belabor them with an axe. With the biggest he started, and with the smallest he ended. He hacked off the feet of one, and the other he beheaded. This one had his eyes struck out, the other had his hands crushed. After all were mutilated, he went away, having first put the axe into the hand of the largest idol.

The feast ended, the king returned, and when he saw all his idols shivered in pieces, he inquired who had perpetrated the mischief. Abraham was named as the one who had been guilty of the outrage, and the king summoned him and questioned him as to his motive for the deed. Abraham replied: "I did not do it; it was the largest of the idols who shattered all the rest. Seest thou not that he still has the axe in his hand? And if thou wilt not believe my words, ask him and he will tell thee."

IN THE FIERY FURNACE

Now the king was exceedingly wroth at Abraham, and ordered him to be cast into prison, where he commanded the warden not to give him bread or water. But God hearkened unto the prayer of Abraham, and sent Gabriel to him in his dungeon. For a year the angel dwelt with him, and provided him with all sorts of food, and a spring of fresh water welled up before him, and he drank of it. At the end of a year, the magnates of the realm presented themselves before the king, and advised him to cast Abraham into the fire, that the people might believe in Nimrod forever. Thereupon the king issued a decree that all the subjects of the king in all his provinces, men and women, young and old, should bring wood within forty days, and he caused it to be thrown into a great furnace and set afire. The flames shot up to the skies, and the people were sore afraid of the fire. Now the warden of the prison was ordered to bring Abraham forth and cast him in the flames. The warden reminded the king that Abraham had not had food or drink a whole year, and therefore must be dead, but Nimrod nevertheless desired him to step in front of the prison and call his name. If he made reply, he was to be hauled out to the pyre. If he had perished, his remains were to receive burial, and his memory was to be wiped out henceforth.

Greatly amazed the warden was when his cry, "Abraham, art thou alive?" was answered with "I am living." He questioned further, "Who has been bringing thee food and drink all these many days?" and Abraham replied: "Food and drink have been bestowed upon me by Him who is over all things, the God of all gods and the Lord of all lords, who alone doeth wonders, He who is the God of Nimrod and the God of Terah and the God of the whole world. He dispenseth food and drink unto all beings. He sees, but He cannot be seen, He is in the heavens above, and He is present in all places, for He Himself superviseth all things and provideth for all."

The miraculous rescue of Abraham from death by starvation and thirst convinced the prison-keeper of the truth of God and His prophet Abraham, and he acknowledged his belief in both publicly. The king's threat of death unless he recanted could not turn him away from his new and true faith. When the hangman raised his sword and set it at his throat to kill him, he exclaimed, "The Eternal He is God, the God of the whole world as well as of the blasphemer Nimrod." But the sword could not cut his flesh. The harder it was pressed against his throat, the more it broke into pieces.

Nimrod, however, was not to be turned aside from his purpose, to make Abraham suffer death by fire. One of the princes was dispatched to fetch him forth. But scarcely did the messenger set about the task of throwing him into the fire, when the flame leapt forth from the furnace and consumed him. Many more attempts were made to cast Abraham into the furnace, but always with the same success- whoever seized him to pitch him in was himself burnt, and a large number lost their lives. Satan appeared in human shape, and advised the king to place Abraham in a catapult and sling him into the fire. Thus no one would be required to come near the flame. Satan himself constructed the catapult. Having proved it fit three times by means of stones put in the machine, they bound Abraham, hand and foot, and were about to consign him to the flames. At that moment Satan, still disguised in human shape, approached Abraham, and said, "If thou desirest to deliver thyself from the fire of Nimrod, bow down before him and believe in him." But Abraham rejected the tempter with the words, "May the Eternal rebuke thee, thou vile, contemptible, accursed blasphemer!" and Satan departed from him.

Then the mother of Abraham came to him and implored him to pay homage to Nimrod and escape the impending misfortune. But he said to her: "O mother, water can extinguish Nimrod's fire, but the fire of God will not die out for evermore. Water cannot quench it." When his mother heard these words, she spake, "May the God whom thou servest rescue thee from the fire of Nimrod!"

Abraham was finally placed in the catapult, and he raised his eyes heavenward, and spoke, "O Lord my God, Thou seest what this sinner purposes to do unto me!" His confidence in God was unshakable. When the angels received the Divine permission to save him, and Gabriel approached him, and asked, "Abraham, shall I save thee from the fire?" he replied, "God in whom I trust, the God of heaven and earth, will rescue me," and God, seeing the submissive spirit of Abraham, commanded the fire, "Cool off and bring tranquillity to my servant Abraham."

No water was needed to extinguish the fire. The logs burst into buds, and all the different kinds of wood put forth fruit, each tree bearing its own kind. The furnace was transformed into a royal pleasance, and the angels sat therein with Abraham. When the king saw the miracle, he said: "Great witchcraft! Thou makest it known that fire hath no power over thee, and at the same time thou showest thyself unto the people sitting in a pleasure garden." But the princes of Nimrod interposed all with one voice, "Nay, our lord, this is not witchcraft, it is the power of the great God, the God of Abraham, beside whom there is no other god, and we acknowledge that He is God, and Abraham is His servant." All the princes and all the people believed in God at this hour, in the Eternal, the God of Abraham, and they all cried out, "The Lord He is God in heaven above and upon the earth beneath; there is none else."

Abraham was the superior, not only of the impious king Nimrod and his attendants, but also of the pious men of his time, Noah, Shem, Eber, and Asshur. Noah gave himself no concern whatsoever in the matter of spreading the pure faith in God. He took an interest in planting his vineyard, and was immersed in material pleasures. Shem and Eber kept in hiding, and as for Asshur, he said, "How can I live among such sinners?" and departed out of the land. The only one who remained unshaken was Abraham. "I will not forsake God," he said, and therefore God did not forsake him, who had hearkened neither unto his father nor unto his mother.

The miraculous deliverance of Abraham from the fiery furnace, together with his later fortunes, was the fulfilment and explanation of what his father Terah had read in the stars. He had seen the star of Haran consumed by fire, and at the same time fill and rule the whole world. The meaning was plain now. Haran was irresolute in his faith, he could not decide whether to adhere to Abraham or the idolaters. When it befell that those who would not serve idols were cast into the fiery furnace, Haran reasoned in this manner: "Abraham, being my elder, will be called upon before me. If he comes forth out of the fiery trial triumphant, I will declare my allegiance to him; otherwise I will take sides against him." After God Himself had rescued Abraham from death, and Haran's turn came to make his confession of faith, he announced his adherence to Abraham. But scarcely had he come near the furnace, when he was seized by the flames and consumed, because he was lacking in firm faith in God. Terah had read the stars well, it now appeared: Haran was burnt, and his daughter Sarah became the wife of Abraham, whose descendants fill the earth. In another way the death of Haran was noteworthy. It was the first instance, since the creation of the world, of a son's dying while his father was still alive.

The king, the princes, and all the people, who had been witnesses of the wonders done for Abraham, came to him, and prostrated themselves before him. But Abraham said: "Do not bow down before me, but before God, the Master of the universe, who hath created you. Serve Him and walk in His ways, for He it was who delivered me from the flames, and He it is who hath created the soul and the spirit of every human being, who formeth man in the womb of his mother, and bringeth him into the world. He saveth from all sickness those who put their trust in Him."

The king then dismissed Abraham, after loading him down with an abundance of precious gifts, among them two slaves who had been raised in the royal palace. 'Ogi was the name of the one, Eliezer the name of the other. The princes followed the example of the king, and they gave him silver, and gold, and gems. But all these gifts did not rejoice the heart of Abraham so much as the three hundred followers that joined him and became adherents of his religion.

ABRAHAM EMIGRATES TO HARAN

For a period of two years Abraham could devote himself undisturbed to his chosen task of turning the hearts of men to God and His teachings. In his pious undertaking he was aided by his wife Sarah, whom he had married in the meantime. While he exhorted the men and sought to convert them, Sarah addressed herself to the women. She was a helpmeet worthy of Abraham. Indeed, in prophetical powers she ranked higher than her husband. She was sometimes called Iscah, "the seer," on that account.

At the expiration of two years it happened that Nimrod dreamed a dream. In his dream he found himself with his army near the fiery furnace in the valley into which Abraham had been cast. A man resembling Abraham stepped out of the furnace, and he ran after the king with drawn sword, the king fleeing before him in terror. While running, the pursuer threw an egg at Nimrod's head, and a mighty stream issued therefrom, wherein the king's whole host was drowned. The king alone survived, with three men. When Nimrod examined his companions, he observed that they wore royal attire, and in form and stature they resembled himself. The stream changed back into an egg again, and a little chick broke forth from it, and it flew up, settled upon the head of the king, and put out one of his eyes.

The king was confounded in his sleep, and when he awoke, his heart beat like a trip-hammer, and his fear was exceeding great. In the morning, when he arose, he sent and called for his wise men and his magicians, and told them his dream. One of his wise men, Anoko by name, stood up, and said: "Know, O king, this dream points to the misfortune which Abraham and his descendants will bring upon thee. A time will come when he and his followers will make war upon thy army, and they will annihilate it. Thou and the three kings, thy allies, will be the only ones to escape death. But later thou wilt lose thy life at the hands of one of the descendants of Abraham. Consider, O king, that thy wise men read this fate of thine in the stars, fifty-two years ago, at the birth of Abraham. As long as Abraham liveth upon the ground, thou shalt not be stablished, nor thy kingdom." Nimrod took Anoko's words to heart, and dispatched some of his servants to seize Abraham and kill him. It happened that Eliezer, the slave whom Abraham had received as a present from Nimrod, was at that time at the royal court. With great haste he sped to Abraham to induce him to flee before the king's bailiffs. His master accepted his advice, and took refuge in the house of Noah and Shem, where he lay in hiding a whole month. The king's officers reported that despite zealous efforts Abraham was nowhere to be found. Thenceforth the king did not concern himself about Abraham.

When Terah visited his son in his hiding-place, Abraham proposed that they leave the land and take up their abode in Canaan, in order to escape the pursuit of Nimrod. He said: "Consider that it was not for thy sake that Nimrod overloaded thee with honors, but for his own profit. Though he continue to confer the greatest of benefactions upon thee, what are they but earthly vanity? for riches and possessions profit not in the day of wrath and fury. Hearken unto my voice, O my father, let us depart for the land of Canaan, and serve the God that hath created thee, that it may be well with thee."

Noah and Shem aided and abetted the efforts of Abraham to persuade Terah, whereupon Terah consented to leave his country, and he, and Abraham, and Lot, the son of Haran, departed for Haran with their households. They found the land pleasant, and also the inhabitants thereof, who readily yielded to the influence of Abraham's humane spirit and his piety. Many of them obeyed his precepts and became God-fearing and good.

Terah's resolve to quit his native land for the sake of Abraham and take up his abode in strange parts, and his impulse to do it before even the Divine call visited Abraham himself--this the Lord accounted a great merit unto Terah, and he was permitted to see his son Abraham rule as king over the whole world. For when the miracle happened, and Isaac was born unto his aged parents, the whole world repaired to Abraham and Sarah, and demanded to know what they had done that so great a thing should be accomplished for them. Abraham told them all that had happened between Nimrod and himself, how he had been ready to be burnt for the glory of God, and how the Lord had rescued him from the flames. In token of their admiration for Abraham and his teachings, they appointed him to be their king, and in commemoration of Isaac's wondrous birth, the money coined by Abraham bore the figures of an aged husband and wife on the obverse side, and of a young man and his wife on the reverse side, for Abraham and Sarah both were rejuvenated at the birth of Isaac, Abraham's white hair turned black, and the lines in Sarah's face were smoothed out.

For many years Terah continued to live a witness of his son's glory, for his death did not occur until Isaac was a youth of thirty-five. And a still greater reward waited upon his good deed. God accepted his repentance, and when he departed this life, he entered into Paradise, and not into hell, though he had passed the larger number of his days in sin. Indeed, it had been his fault that Abraham came near losing his life at the hands of Nimrod.

THE STAR IN THE EAST

Terah had been a high official at the court of Nimrod, and he was held in great consideration by the king and his suite. A son was born unto him whom he called Abram, because the king had raised him to an exalted place. In the night of Abraham's birth, the astrologers and the wise men of Nimrod came to the house of Terah, and ate and drank, and rejoiced with him that night. When they left the house, they lifted up their eyes toward heaven to look at the stars, and they saw, and, behold, one great star came from the east and ran athwart the heavens and swallowed up the four stars at the four corners. They all were astonished at the sight, but they understood this matter, and knew its import. They said to one another: "This only betokens that the child that hath been born unto Terah this night will grow up and be fruitful, and he will multiply and possess all the earth, he and his children forever, and he and his seed will slay great kings and inherit their lands."

They went home that night, and in the morning they rose up early, and assembled in their meeting-house. They spake, and said to one another: "Lo, the sight that we saw last night is hidden from the king, it has not been made known to him, and should this thing become known to him in the latter days, he will say to us, Why did you conceal this matter from me? and then we shall all suffer death. Now, let us go and tell the king the sight which we saw, and the interpretation thereof, and we shall be clear from this thing." And they went to the king and told him the sight they had seen, and their interpretation thereof, and they added the advice that he pay the value of the child to Terah, and slay the babe.

Accordingly, the king sent for Terah, and when he came, he spake to him: "It hath been told unto me that a son was born to thee yesternight, and a wondrous sign was observed in the heavens at his birth. Now give me the boy, that we may slay him before evil comes upon us from him, and I will give thee thy house full of silver and gold in exchange for him." Terah answered: "This thing which thou promisest unto me is like the words which a man spoke to a mule, saying, 'I will give thee a great heap of barley, a houseful thereof, on condition that I cut off thy head!' The mule replied, 'Of what use will all the barley be to me, if thou cuttest off my head? Who will eat it when thou givest it to me?' Thus also do I say: What shall I do with silver and gold after the death of my son? Who shall inherit me?" But when Terah saw how the king's anger burned within him at these words, he added, "Whatever the king desireth to do unto his servant, that let him do, even my son is at the king's disposal, without value or exchange, he and his two older brethren."

The king spake, however, saying, "I will purchase thy youngest son for a price." And Terah made answer, "Let my king give me three days' time to consider the matter and consult about it with my family." The king agreed to this condition, and on the third day he sent to Terah, saying, "Give me thy son for a price, as I spoke unto thee, and if thou wilt not do this, I will send and slay all thou hast in thy house, there shall not be a dog left unto thee."

Then Terah took a child which his handmaid had borne unto him that day, and he brought the babe to the king, and received value for him, and the king took the child and dashed his head against the ground, for he thought it was Abraham. But Terah took his son Abraham, together with the child's mother and his nurse, and concealed them in a cave, and thither he carried provisions to them once a month, and the Lord was with Abraham in the cave, and he grew up, but the king and all his servants thought that Abraham was dead.

And when Abraham was ten years old, he and his mother and his nurse went out from the cave, for the king and his servants had forgotten the affair of Abraham.

In that time all the inhabitants of the earth, with the exception of Noah and his household, transgressed against the Lord, and they made unto themselves every man his god, gods of wood and stone, which could neither speak, nor hear, nor deliver from distress. The king and all his servants, and Terah with his household, were the first to worship images of wood and stone. Terah made twelve gods of large size, of wood and of stone, corresponding to the twelve months of the year, and he paid homage to them monthly in turn.

THE TRUE BELIEVER

Once Abraham went into the temple of the idols in his father's house, to bring sacrifices to them, and he found one of them, Marumath by name, hewn out of stone, lying prostrate on his face before the iron god of Nahor. The idol was too heavy for him to raise it alone, and he called his father to help him put Marumath back in his place. While they were handling the image, its head dropped off, and Terah took a stone, and chiselled another Marumath, setting the head of the first upon the new body. Then Terah continued and made five more gods, and all these he delivered to Abraham, and bade him sell them in the streets of the city.

Abraham saddled his mule, and went to the inn where merchants from Fandana in Syria put up on their way to Egypt. He hoped to dispose of his wares there. When he reached the inn, one of the camels belonging to the merchants belched, and the sound frightened his mule so that it ran off pell-mell and broke three of the idols. The merchants not only bought the two sound idols from him, they also gave him the price of the broken ones, for Abraham had told them how distressed he was to appear before his father with less money than he had expected to receive for his handiwork.

This incident made Abraham reflect upon the worthlessness of idols, and he said to himself: "What are these evil things done by my father? Is not he the god of his gods, for do they not come into being by reason of his carving and chiselling and contriving? Were it not more seemly that they should pay worship to him than he to them, seeing they are the work of his hands?" Meditating thus, he reached his father's house, and he entered and handed his father the money for the five images, and Terah rejoiced, and said, "Blessed art thou unto my gods, because thou didst bring me the price of the idols, and my labor was not in vain." But Abraham made reply: "Hear, my father Terah, blessed are thy gods through thee, for thou art their god, since thou didst fashion them, and their blessing is destruction and their help is vanity. They that help not themselves, how can they help thee or bless me?"

Terah grew very wrathful at Abraham, that he uttered such speech against his gods, and Abraham, thinking upon his father's anger, left him and went from the house. But Terah called him back, and said, "Gather together the chips of the oak wood from which I made images before thou didst return, and prepare my dinner for me." Abraham made ready to do his father's bidding, and as he took up the chips he found a little god among them, whose forehead bore the inscription "God Barisat." He threw the chips upon the fire, and set Barisat up next to it, saying: "Attention! Take care, Barisat, that the fire go not out until I come back. If it burns low, blow into it, and make it flame up again." Speaking thus, he went out. When he came in again, he found Barisat lying prone upon his back, badly burnt. Smiling, he said to himself, "In truth, Barisat, thou canst keep the fire alive and prepare food," and while he spoke, the idol was consumed to ashes. Then he took the dishes to his father, and he ate and drank and was glad and blessed his god Marumath. But Abraham said to his father, "Bless not thy god Marumath, but rather thy god Barisat, for he it was who, out of his great love for thee, threw himself into the fire that thy meal might be cooked." "Where is he now?" exclaimed Terah, and Abraham answered, "He hath become ashes in the fierceness of the fire." Terah said, "Great is the power of Barisat! I will make me another this day, and to-morrow he will prepare my food for me."

These words of his father made Abraham laugh in his mind, but his soul was grieved at his obduracy, and he proceeded to make clear his views upon the idols, saying: "Father, no matter which of the two idols thou blessest, thy behavior is senseless, for the images that stand in the holy temple are more to be worshipped than thine. Zucheus, the god of my brother Nahor, is more venerable than Marumath, because he is made cunningly of gold, and when he grows old, he will be worked over again. But when thy Marumath becomes dim, or is shivered in pieces, he will not be renewed, for he is of stone. And the god Joauv, who stands above the other gods with Zucheus, is more venerable than Barisat, made of wood, because he is hammered out of silver, and ornamented by men, to show his magnificence. But thy Barisat, before thou didst fashion him into a god with thy axe, was rooted in the earth, standing there great and wonderful, with the glory of branches and blossoms. Now he is dry, and gone is his sap. From his height he has fallen to the earth, from grandeur he came to pettiness, and the appearance of his face has paled away, and he himself was burnt in the fire, and he was consumed unto ashes, and he is no more. And thou didst then say, 'I will make me another this day, and to-morrow he will prepare my food for me.' Father," Abraham continued, and said, "the fire is more to be worshipped than thy gods of gold and silver and wood and stone, because it consumes them. But also the fire I call not god, because it is subject to the water, which quenches it. But also the water I call not god, because it is sucked up by the earth, and I call the earth more venerable, because it conquers the water. But also the earth I call not god, because it is dried out by the sun, and I call the sun more venerable than the earth, because he illumines the whole world with his rays. But also the sun I call not god, because his light is obscured when darkness cometh up. Nor do I call the moon and the stars gods, because their light, too, is extinguished when their time to shine is past. But hearken unto this, my father Terah, which I will declare unto thee, The God who hath created all things, He is the true God, He hath empurpled the heavens, and gilded the sun, and given radiance to the moon and also the stars, and He drieth out the earth in the midst of many waters, and also thee hath He put upon the earth, and me hath He sought out in the confusion of my thoughts."

THE ICONOCLAST

But Terah could not be convinced, and in reply to Abraham's question, who the God was that had created heaven and earth and the children of men, he took him to the hall wherein stood twelve great idols and a large number of little idols, and pointing to them he said, "Here are they who have made all thou seest on earth, they who have created also me and thee and all men on the earth," and he bowed down before his gods, and left the hall with his son.

Abraham went thence to his mother, and he spoke to her, saying: "Behold, my father has shown those unto me who made heaven and earth and all the sons of men. Now, therefore, hasten and fetch a kid from the flock, and make of it savory meat, that I may bring it to my father's gods, perhaps I may thereby become acceptable to them." His mother did according to his request, but when Abraham brought the offering to the gods, he saw that they had no voice, no hearing, no motion, and not one of them stretched forth his hand to eat. Abraham mocked them, and said, "Surely, the savory meat that I prepared doth not please you, or perhaps it is too little for you! Therefore I will prepare fresh savory meat to-morrow, better and more plentiful than this, that I may see what cometh therefrom." But the gods remained mute and without motion before the second offering of excellent savory meat as before the first offering, and the spirit of God came over Abraham, and he cried out, and said: "Woe unto my father and his wicked generation, whose hearts are all inclined to vanity, who serve these idols of wood and stone, which cannot eat, nor smell, nor hear, nor speak, which have mouths without speech, eyes without sight, ears without hearing, hands without feeling, and legs without motion!"

Abraham then took a hatchet in his hand, and broke all his father's gods, and when he had done breaking them he placed the hatchet in the hand of the biggest god among them all, and he went out. Terah, having heard the crash of the hatchet on the stone, ran to the room of the idols, and he reached it at the moment when Abraham was leaving it, and when he saw what had happened, he hastened after Abraham, and he said to him, "What is this mischief thou hast done to my gods?" Abraham answered: "I set savory meat before them, and when I came nigh unto them, that they might eat, they all stretched out their hands to take of the meat, before the big one had put forth his hand to eat. This one, enraged against them on account of their behavior, took the hatchet and broke them all, and, behold, the hatchet is yet in his hands, as thou mayest see."

Then Terah turned in wrath upon Abraham, and he said: "Thou speakest lies unto me! Is there spirit, soul, or power in these gods to do all thou hast told me? Are they not wood and stone? and have I not myself made them? It is thou that didst place the hatchet in the hand of the big god, and thou sayest he smote them all." Abraham answered his father, and said: "How, then, canst thou serve these idols in whom there is no power to do anything? Can these idols in which thou trustest deliver thee? Can they hear thy prayers when thou callest upon them?" After having spoken these and similar words, admonishing his father to mend his ways and refrain from worshipping idols, he leapt up before Terah, took the hatchet from the big idol, broke it therewith, and ran away.

Terah hastened to Nimrod, bowed down before him, and besought him to hear his story, about his son who had been born to him fifty years back, and how he had done to his gods, and how he had spoken. "Now, therefore, my lord and king," he said, "send for him that he may come before thee, and do thou judge him according to the law, that we may be delivered from his evil." When Abraham was brought before the king, he told him the same story as he had told Terah, about the big god who broke the smaller ones, but the king replied, "Idols do neither speak, nor eat, nor move." Then Abraham reproached him for worshipping gods that can do nothing, and admonished him to serve the God of the universe. His last words were, "If thy wicked heart will not hearken to my words, to cause thee to forsake thy evil ways and serve the Eternal God, then wilt thou die in shame in the latter days, thou, thy people, and all that are connected with thee, who hear thy words, and walk in thy evil ways."

The king ordered Abraham to be put into prison, and at the end of ten days he caused all the princes and great men of the realm to appear before him, and to them he put the case of Abraham. Their verdict was that he should be burnt, and, accordingly, the king had a fire prepared for three days and three nights, in his furnace at Kasdim, and Abraham was to be carried thither from prison to be burnt.

All the inhabitants of the land, about nine hundred thousand men, and the women and the children besides, came to see what would be done with Abraham. And when he was brought forth, the astrologers recognized him, and they said to the king, "Surely, this is the man whom we knew as a child, at whose birth the great star swallowed the four stars. Behold, his father did transgress thy command, and he made a mockery of thee, for he did bring thee another child, and him didst thou kill."

Terah was greatly terrified, for he was afraid of the king's wrath, and he admitted that he had deceived the king, and when the king said, "Tell me who advised thee to do this. Hide naught, and thou shalt not die," he falsely accused Haran, who had been thirty-two years old at the time of Abraham's birth, of having advised him to deceive the king. At the command of the king, Abraham and Haran, stripped of all their clothes except their hosen, and their hands and feet bound with linen cords, were cast into the furnace. Haran, because his heart was not perfect with the Lord, perished in the fire, and also the men who cast them into the furnace were burnt by the flames which leapt out over them, and Abraham alone was saved by the Lord, and he was not burnt, though the cords with which he was bound were consumed. For three days and three nights Abraham walked in the midst of the fire, and all the servants of the king came and told him, "Behold, we have seen Abraham walking about in the midst of the fire."

At first the king would not believe them, but when some of his faithful princes corroborated the words of his servants, he rose up and went to see for himself. He then commanded his servants to take Abraham from the fire, but they could not, because the flames leapt toward them from the furnace, and when they tried again, at the king's command, to approach the furnace, the flames shot out and burnt their faces, so that eight of their number died. The king then called unto Abraham, and said: "O servant of the God who is in heaven, go forth from the midst of the fire, and come hither and stand before me," and Abraham came and stood before the king. And the king spoke to Abraham, and said, "How cometh it that thou wast not burnt in the fire?" And Abraham made answer, "The God of heaven and earth in whom I trust, and who hath all things in His power, He did deliver me from the fire into which thou didst cast me."

ABRAHAM IN CANAAN

With ten temptations Abraham was tempted, and he withstood them all, showing how great was the love of Abraham. The first test to which he was subjected was the departure from his native land. The hardships were many and severe which he encountered, and he was loth to leave his home, besides. He spoke to God, and said, "Will not the people talk about me, and say, 'He is endeavoring to bring the nations under the wings of the Shekinah, yet he leaves his old father in Haran, and he goes away.' " But God answered him, and said: "Dismiss all care concerning thy father and thy kinsmen from thy thoughts. Though they speak words of kindness to thee, yet are they all of one mind, to ruin thee."

Then Abraham forsook his father in Haran, and journeyed to Canaan, accompanied by the blessing of God, who said unto him, "I will make of thee a great nation, and I will bless thee, and make thy name great." These three blessings were to counteract the evil consequences which, he feared, would follow emigration, for travelling from place to place interferes with the growth of the family, it lessens one's substance, and it diminishes the consideration one enjoys. The greatest of all blessings, however, was the word of God, "And be thou a blessing." The meaning of this was that whoever came in contact with Abraham was blessed. Even the mariners on the sea were indebted to him for prosperous voyages. Besides, God held out the promise to him that in time to come his name would be mentioned in the Benedictions, God would be praised as the Shield of Abraham, a distinction accorded to no other mortal except David. But the words, "And be thou a blessing," will be fulfilled only in the future world, when the seed of Abraham shall be known among the nations and his offspring among the peoples as "the seed which the Lord hath blessed."

When Abraham first was bidden to leave his home, he was not told to what land he was to journey--all the greater would be his reward for executing the command of God. And Abraham showed his trust in God, for he said, "I am ready to go whithersoever Thou sendest me." The Lord then bade him go to a land wherein He would reveal Himself, and when he went to Canaan later, God appeared to him, and he knew that it was the promised land.

On entering Canaan, Abraham did not yet know that it was the land appointed as his inheritance. Nevertheless he rejoiced when he reached it. In Mesopotamia and in Aramnaharaim, the inhabitants of which he had seen eating, drinking, and acting wantonly, he had always wished, "O that my portion may not be in this land," but when he came to Canaan, he observed that the people devoted themselves industriously to the cultivation of the land, and he said, "O that my portion may be in this land!" God then spoke to him, and said, "Unto thy seed will I give this land." Happy in these joyous tidings, Abraham erected an altar to the Lord to give thanks unto Him for the promise, and then he journeyed on, southward, in the direction of the spot whereon the Temple was once to stand. In Hebron he again erected an altar, thus taking possession of the land in a measure. And likewise he raised an altar in Ai, because he foresaw that a misfortune would befall his offspring there, at the conquest of the land under Joshua. The altar, he hoped, would obviate the evil results that might follow.

Each altar raised by him was a centre for his activities as a missionary. As soon as he came to a place in which he desired to sojourn, he would stretch a tent first for Sarah, and next for himself, and then he would proceed at once to make proselytes and bring them under the wings of the Shekinah. Thus he accomplished his purpose of inducing all men to proclaim the Name of God.

For the present Abraham was but a stranger in his promised land. After the partition of the earth among the sons of Noah, when all had gone to their allotted portions, it happened that Canaan son of Ham saw that the land extending from the Lebanon to the River of Egypt was fair to look upon, and he refused to go to his own allotment, westward by the sea. He settled in the land upon Lebanon, eastward and westward from the border of the Jordan and the border of the sea. And Ham, his father, and his brothers Cush and Mizraim spoke to him, and said: "Thou livest in a land that is not thine, for it was not assigned unto us when the lots were drawn. Do not thus! But if thou persistest, ye, thou and thy children, will fall, accursed, in the land, in a rebellion. Thy settling here was rebellion, and through rebellion thy children will be felled down, and thy seed will be destroyed unto all eternity. Sojourn not in the land of Shem, for unto Shem and unto the children of Shem was it apportioned by lot. Accursed art thou, and accursed wilt thou be before all the children of Noah on account of the curse, for we took an oath before the holy Judge and before our father Noah."

But Canaan hearkened not unto the words of his father and his brothers. He dwelt in the land of the Lebanon from Hamath even unto the entrance of Egypt, he and his sons. Though the Canaanites had taken unlawful possession of the land, yet Abraham respected their rights; he provided his camels with muzzles, to prevent them from pasturing upon the property of others.

HIS SOJOURN IN EGYPT

Scarcely had Abraham established himself in Canaan, when a devastating famine broke out--one of the ten God appointed famines for the chastisement of men. The first of them came in the time of Adam, when God cursed the ground for his sake; the second was this one in the time of Abraham; the third compelled Isaac to take up his abode among the Philistines; the ravages of the fourth drove the sons of Jacob into Egypt to buy grain for food; the fifth came in the time of the Judges, when Elimelech and his family had to seek refuge in the land of Moab; the sixth occurred during the reign of David, and it lasted three years; the seventh happened in the day of Elijah, who had sworn that neither rain nor dew should fall upon the earth; the eighth was the one in the time of Elisha, when an ass's head was sold for fourscore pieces of silver; the ninth is the famine that comes upon men piecemeal, from time to time; and the tenth will scourge men before the advent of Messiah, and this last will be "not a famine of bread, nor a thirst for water, but of hearing the words of the Lord."

The famine in the time of Abraham prevailed only in Canaan, and it had been inflicted upon the land in order to test his faith. He stood this second temptation as he had the first. He murmured not, and he showed no sign of impatience toward God, who had bidden him shortly before to abandon his native land for a land of starvation. The famine compelled him to leave Canaan for a time, and he repaired to Egypt, to become acquainted there with the wisdom of the priests and, if necessary, give them instruction in the truth.

On this journey from Canaan to Egypt, Abraham first observed the beauty of Sarah. Chaste as he was, he had never before looked at her, but now, when they were wading through a stream, he saw the reflection of her beauty in the water like the brilliance of the sun. Wherefore he spoke to her thus, "The Egyptians are very sensual, and I will put thee in a casket that no harm befall me on account of thee." At the Egyptian boundary, the tax collectors asked him about the contents of the casket, and Abraham told them he had barley in it. "No," they said, "it contains wheat." "Very well," replied Abraham, "I am prepared to pay the tax on wheat." The officers then hazarded the guess, "It contains pepper!" Abraham agreed to pay the tax on pepper, and when they charged him with concealing gold in the casket, he did not refuse to pay the tax on gold, and finally on precious stones. Seeing that he demurred to no charge, however high, the tax collectors, made thoroughly suspicious, insisted upon his unfastening the casket and letting them examine the contents. When it was forced open, the whole of Egypt was resplendent with the beauty of Sarah. In comparison with her, all other beauties were like apes compared with men. She excelled Eve herself. The servants of Pharaoh outbid one another in seeking to obtain possession of her, though they were of opinion that so radiant a beauty ought not to remain the property of a private individual. They reported the matter to the king, and Pharaoh sent a powerful armed force to bring Sarah to the palace, and so bewitched was he by her charms that those who had brought him the news of her coming into Egypt were loaded down with bountiful gifts.

Amid tears, Abraham offered up a prayer. He entreated God in these words: "Is this the reward for my confidence in Thee? For the sake of Thy grace and Thy lovingkindness, let not my hope be put to shame." Sarah also implored God, saying: "O God, Thou didst bid my lord Abraham leave his home, the land of his fathers, and journey to Canaan, and Thou didst promise him to do good unto him if he fulfilled Thy commands. And now we have done as Thou didst command us to do. We left our country and our kindred, and we journeyed to a strange land, unto a people which we knew not heretofore. We came hither to save our people from starvation, and now hath this terrible misfortune befallen. O Lord, help me and save me from the hand of this enemy, and for the sake of Thy grace show me good."

An angel appeared unto Sarah while she was in the presence of the king, to whom he was not visible, and he bade her take courage, saying, "Fear naught, Sarah, for God hath heard thy prayer." The king questioned Sarah as to the man in the company of whom she had come to Egypt, and Sarah called Abraham her brother. Pharaoh pledged himself to make Abraham great and powerful, to do for him whatever she wished. He sent much gold and silver to Abraham, and diamonds and pearls, sheep and oxen, and men slaves and women slaves, and he assigned a residence to him within the precincts of the royal palace. In the love he bore Sarah, he wrote out a marriage contract, deeding to her all he owned in the way of gold and silver, and men slaves and women slaves, and the province of Goshen besides, the province occupied in later days by the descendants of Sarah, because it was their property. Most remarkable of all, he gave her his own daughter Hagar as slave, for he preferred to see his daughter the servant of Sarah to reigning as mistress in another harem.

His free-handed generosity availed naught. During the night, when he was about to approach Sarah, an angel appeared armed with a stick, and if Pharaoh but touched Sarah's shoe to remove it from her foot, the angel planted a blow upon his hand, and when he grasped her dress, a second blow followed. At each blow he was about to deal, the angel asked Sarah whether he was to let it descend, and if she bade him give Pharaoh a moment to recover himself, he waited and did as she desired. And another great miracle came to pass. Pharaoh, and his nobles, and his servants, the very walls of his house and his bed were afflicted with leprosy, and he could not indulge his carnal desires. This night in which Pharaoh and his court suffered their well deserved punishment was the night of the fifteenth of Nisan, the same night wherein God visited the Egyptians in a later time in order to redeem Israel, the descendants of Sarah.

Horrified by the plague sent upon him, Pharaoh inquired how he could rid himself thereof. He applied to the priests, from whom he found out the true cause of his affliction, which was corroborated by Sarah. He then sent for Abraham and returned his wife to him, pure and untouched, and excused himself for what had happened, saying that he had had the intention of connecting himself in marriage with him, whom he had thought to be the brother of Sarah. He bestowed rich gifts upon the husband and the wife, and they departed for Canaan, after a three months' sojourn in Egypt.

Arrived in Canaan they sought the same night-shelters at which they had rested before, in order to pay their accounts, and also to teach by their example that it is not proper to seek new quarters unless one is forced to it.

Abraham's sojourn in Egypt was of great service to the inhabitants of the country, because he demonstrated to the wise men of the land how empty and vain their views were, and also he taught them astronomy and astrology, unknown in Egypt before his time.

THE FIRST PHARAOH

The Egyptian ruler, whose meeting with Abraham had proved so untoward an event, was the first to bear the name Pharaoh. The succeeding kings were named thus after him. The origin of the name is connected with the life and adventures of Rakyon, Have-naught, a man wise, handsome, and poor, who lived in the land of Shinar. Finding himself unable to support himself in Shinar, he resolved to depart for Egypt, where he expected to display his wisdom before the king, Ashwerosh, the son of 'Anam. Perhaps he would find grace in the eyes of the king, who would give Rakyon the opportunity of supporting himself and rising to be a great man. When he reached Egypt, he learnt that it was the custom of the country for the king to remain in retirement in his palace, removed from the sight of the people. Only on one day of the year he showed himself in public, and received all who had a petition to submit to him. Richer by a disappointment, Rakyon knew not how he was to earn a livelihood in the strange country. He was forced to spend the night in a ruin, hungry as he was. The next day he decided to try to earn something by selling vegetables. By a lucky chance he fell in with some dealers in vegetables, but as he did not know the customs of the country, his new undertaking was not favored with good fortune. Ruffians assaulted him, snatched his wares from him, and made a laughing-stock of him. The second night, which he was compelled to spend in the ruin again, a sly plan ripened in his mind. He arose and gathered together a crew of thirty lusty fellows. He took them to the graveyard, and bade them, in the name of the king, charge two hundred pieces of silver for every body they buried. Otherwise interment was to be prevented. In this way he succeeded in amassing great wealth within eight months. Not only did he acquire silver, gold, and precious gems, but also he attached a considerable force, armed and mounted, to his person.

On the day on which the king appeared among the people, they began to complain of this tax upon the dead. They said: "What is this thou art inflicting upon thy servants- permitting none to be buried unless they pay thee silver and gold! Has a thing like this come to pass in the world since the days of Adam, that the dead should not be interred unless money be paid therefor! We know well that it is the privilege of the king to take an annual tax from the living. But thou takest tribute from the dead, too, and thou exactest it day by day. O king, we cannot endure this any longer, for the whole of the city is ruined thereby."

The king, who had had no suspicion of Rakyon's doings, fell into a great rage when the people gave him information about them. He ordered him and his armed force to appear before him. Rakyon did not come empty-handed. He was preceded by a thousand youths and maidens, mounted upon steeds and arrayed in state apparel. These were a present to the king. When he himself stepped before the king, he delivered gold, silver, and diamonds to him in great abundance, and a magnificent charger. These gifts and the display of splendor did not fail of taking effect upon the king, and when Rakyon, in well-considered words and with a pliant tongue, described the undertaking, he won not only the king to his side, but also the whole court, and the king said to him, "No longer shalt thou be called Rakyon, Have-naught, but Pharaoh, Paymaster, for thou didst collect taxes from the dead."

So profound was the impression made by Rakyon that the king, the grandees, and the people, all together resolved to put the guidance of the realm in the hands of Pharaoh. Under the suzerainty of Ashwerosh he administered law and justice throughout the year; only on the one day when he showed himself to the people did the king himself give judgment and decide cases. Through the power thus conferred upon him and through cunning practices, Pharaoh succeeded in usurping royal authority, and he collected taxes from all the inhabitants of Egypt. Nevertheless he was beloved of the people, and it was decreed that every ruler of Egypt should thenceforth bear the name Pharaoh.

THE WAR OF THE KINGS

On his return from Egypt Abraham's relations to his own family were disturbed by annoying circumstances. Strife developed between the herdmen of his cattle and the herdmen of Lot's cattle. Abraham furnished his herds with muzzles, but Lot made no such provision, and when the shepherds that pastured Abraham's flocks took Lot's shepherds to task on account of the omission, the latter replied: "It is known of a surety that God said unto Abraham, 'To thy seed will I give the land.' But Abraham is a sterile mule. Never will he have children. On the morrow he will die, and Lot will be his heir. Thus the flocks of Lot are but consuming what belongs to them or their master." But God spoke: "Verily, I said unto Abraham I would give the land unto his seed, but only after the seven nations shall have been destroyed from out of the land. To-day the Canaanites are therein, and the Perizzites. They still have the right of habitation."

Now, when the strife extended from the servants to the masters, and Abraham vainly called his nephew Lot to account for his unbecoming behavior, Abraham decided he would have to part from his kinsman, though he should have to compel Lot thereto by force. Lot thereupon separated himself not from Abraham alone, but from the God of Abraham also, and he betook himself to a district in which immorality and sin reigned supreme, wherefore punishment overtook him, for his own flesh seduced him later unto sin.

God was displeased with Abraham for not living in peace and harmony with his own kindred, as he lived with all the world beside. On the other hand, God also took it in ill part that Abraham was accepting Lot tacitly as his heir, though He had promised him, in clear, unmistakable words, "To thy seed will I give the land." After Abraham had separated himself from Lot, he received the assurance again that Canaan should once belong to his seed, which God would multiply as the sand which is upon the sea-shore. As the sand fills the whole earth, so the offspring of Abraham would be scattered over the whole earth, from end to end; and as the earth is blessed only when it is moistened with water, so his offspring would be blessed through the Torah, which is likened unto water; and as the earth endures longer than metal, so his offspring would endure forever, while the heathen would vanish; and as the earth is trodden upon, so his offspring would be trodden upon by the four kingdoms.

The departure of Lot had a serious consequence, for the war waged by Abraham against the four kings is intimately connected with it. Lot desired to settle in the well-watered circle of the Jordan, but the only city of the plain that would receive him was Sodom, the king of which admitted the nephew of Abraham out of consideration for the latter. The five impious kings planned first to make war upon Sodom on account of Lot and then advance upon Abraham. For one of the five, Amraphel, was none other than Nimrod, Abraham's enemy from of old. The immediate occasion for the war was this: Chedorlaomer, one of Nimrod's generals, rebelled against him after the builders of the tower were dispersed, and he set himself up as king of Elam. Then he subjugated the Hamitic tribes living in the five cities of the plain of the Jordan, and made them tributary. For twelve years they were faithful to their sovereign ruler Chedorlaomer, but then they refused to pay the tribute, and they persisted in their insubordination for thirteen years. Making the most of Chedorlaomer's embarrassment, Nimrod led a host of seven thousand warriors against his former general. In the battle fought between Elam and Shinar, Nimrod suffered a disastrous defeat, he lost six hundred of his army, and among the slain was the king's son Mardon. Humiliated and abased, he returned to his country, and he was forced to acknowledge the suzerainty of Chedorlaomer, who now proceeded to form an alliance with Arioch king of Ellasar, and Tidal, the king of several nations, the purpose of which was to crush the cities of the circle of the Jordan. The united forces of these kings, numbering eight hundred thousand, marched upon the five cities, subduing whatever they encountered in their course, and annihilating the descendants of the giants. Fortified places, unwalled cities, and flat, open country, all fell in their hands. They pushed on through the desert as far as the spring issuing from the rock at Kadesh, the spot appointed by God as the place of pronouncing judgment against Moses and Aaron on account of the waters of strife. Thence they turned toward the central portion of Palestine, the country of dates, where they encountered the five godless kings, Bera, the villain, king of Sodom; Birsha, the sinner, king of Gomorrah; Shinab, the father-hater, king of Admah; Shemeber, the voluptuary, king of Zeboiim; and the king of Bela, the city that devours its inhabitants. The five were routed in the fruitful Vale of Siddim, the canals of which later formed the Dead Sea. They that remained of the rank and file fled to the mountains, but the kings fell into the slime pits and stuck there. Only the king of Sodom was rescued, miraculously, for the purpose that he might convert those heathen to faith in God that had not believed in the wonderful deliverance of Abraham from the fiery furnace.

The victors despoiled Sodom of all its goods and victuals, and took Lot, boasting, "We have taken the son of Abraham's brother captive," so betraying the real object of their undertaking; their innermost desire was to strike at Abraham.

It was on the first evening of the Passover, and Abraham was eating of the unleavened bread, when the archangel Michael brought him the report of Lot's captivity. This angel bears another name besides, Palit, the escaped, because when God threw Samael and his host from their holy place in heaven, the rebellious leader held on to Michael and tried to drag him along downward, and Michael escaped falling from heaven only through the help of God.

When the report of his nephew's evil state reached Abraham, he straightway dismissed all thought of his dissensions with Lot from his mind, and only considered ways and means of deliverance. He convoked his disciples to whom he had taught the true faith, and who all called themselves by the name Abraham. He gave them gold and silver, saying at the same time: "Know that we go to war for the purpose of saving human lives. Therefore, do ye not direct your eyes upon money, here lie gold and silver before you." Furthermore he admonished them in these words: "We are preparing to go to war. Let none join us who hath committed a trespass, and fears that Divine punishment will descend upon him." Alarmed by his warning, not one would obey his call to arms, they were fearful on account of their sins. Eliezer alone remained with him, wherefore God spake, and said: "All forsook thee save only Eliezer. Verily, I shall invest him with the strength of the three hundred and eighteen men whose aid thou didst seek in vain."

The battle fought with the mighty hosts of the kings, from which Abraham emerged victorious, happened on the fifteenth of Nisan, the night appointed for miraculous deeds. The arrows and stones hurled at him effected naught, but the dust of the ground, the chaff, and the stubble which he threw at the enemy were transformed into death-dealing javelins and swords. Abraham, as tall as seventy men set on end, and requiring as much food and drink as seventy men, marched forward with giant strides, each of his steps measuring four miles, until he overtook the kings, and annihilated their troops. Further he could not go, for he had reached Dan, where Jeroboam would once raise the golden calves, and on this ominous spot Abraham's strength diminished.

His victory was possible only because the celestial powers espoused his side. The planet Jupiter made the night bright for him, and an angel, Lailah by name, fought for him. In a true sense, it was a victory of God. All the nations acknowledged his more than human achievement, and they fashioned a throne for Abraham, and erected it on the field of battle. When they attempted to seat him upon it, amid exclamations of "Thou art our king! Thou art our prince! Thou art our god!" Abraham warded them off, and said, "The universe has its King, and it has its God!" He declined all honors, and returned his property unto each man. Only the little children he kept by himself. He reared them in the knowledge of God, and later they atoned for the disgrace of their parents.

Somewhat arrogantly the king of Sodom set out to meet Abraham. He was proud that a great miracle, his rescue from the slime pit, had been performed for him, too. He made Abraham the proposition that he keep the despoiled goods for himself. But Abraham refused them, and said: "I have lift up mine hand unto the Lord, God Most High, who hath created the world for the sake of the pious, that I will not take a thread nor a shoe-latchet nor aught that is thine. I have no right upon any goods taken as spoils, save only that which the young men have eaten, and the portion of the men who tarried by the stuff, though they went not down to the battle itself." The example of Abraham in giving a share in the spoils even unto the men not concerned directly in the battle, was followed later by David, who heeded not the protest of the wicked men and the base fellows with him, that the watchers who staid by the stuff were not entitled to share alike with the warriors that had gone down to the battle.

In spite of his great success, Abraham nevertheless was concerned about the issue of the war. He feared that the prohibition against shedding the blood of man had been transgressed, and he also dreaded the resentment of Shem, whose descendants had perished in the encounter. But God reassured him, and said: "Be not afraid! Thou hast but extirpated the thorns, and as to Shem, he will bless thee rather than curse thee." So it was. When Abraham returned from the war, Shem, or, as he is sometimes called, Melchizedek, the king of righteousness, priest of God Most High, and king of Jerusalem, came forth to meet him with bread and wine. And this high priest instructed Abraham in the laws of the priesthood and in the Torah, and to prove his friendship for him he blessed him, and called him the partner of God in the possession of the world, seeing that through him the Name of God had first been made known among men. But Melchizedek arranged the words of his blessing in an unseemly way. He named Abraham first and then God. As a punishment, he was deposed by God from the priestly dignity, and instead it was passed over to Abraham, with whose descendants it remained forever.

As a reward for the sanctification of the Holy Name, which Abraham had brought about when he refused to keep aught of the goods taken in battle, his descendants received two commands, the command of the threads in the borders of their garments, and the command of the latchets to be bound upon their hands and to be used as frontlets between their eyes. Thus they commemorate that their ancestor refused to take so much as a thread or a latchet. And because he would not touch a shoe-latchet of the spoils, his descendants cast their shoe upon Edom.

THE COVENANT OF THE PIECES

Shortly after the war, God revealed Himself unto Abraham, to soothe his conscience as to the spilling of innocent blood, for it was a scruple that gave him much anguish of spirit. God assured him at the same time that He would cause pious men to arise among his descendants, who, like himself, would be a shield unto their generation. As a further distinction, God gave him leave to ask what he would have, rare grace accorded to none beside, except Jacob, Solomon, Ahaz, and the Messiah. Abraham spoke, and said: "O Lord of the world, if in time to come my descendants should provoke Thy wrath, it were better I remained childless. Lot, for the sake of whom I journeyed as far as Damascus, where God was my protection, would be well pleased to be my heir. Moreover, I have read in the stars, 'Abraham, thou wilt beget no children.' " Thereupon God raised Abraham above the vault of the skies, and He said, "Thou art a prophet, not an astrologer!" Now Abraham demanded no sign that he would be blessed with offspring. Without losing another word, he believed in the Lord, and he was rewarded for his simple faith by a share in this world and a share in the world to come as well, and, besides, the redemption of Israel from the exile will take place as a recompense for his firm trust.

But though he believed the promise made him with a full and abiding faith, he yet desired to know by what merit of theirs his descendants would maintain themselves. Therefore God bade him bring Him a sacrifice of three heifers, three she-goats, three rams, a turtle dove, and a young pigeon, thus indicating to Abraham the various sacrifices that should once be brought in the Temple, to atone for the sins of Israel and further his welfare. "But what will become of my descendants," asked Abraham, "after the Temple is destroyed?" God replied, and said, "If they read the order of sacrifices as they will be set down in the Scriptures, I will account it unto them as though they had offered the sacrifices, and I will forgive all their sins." And God continued and revealed to Abraham the course of Israel's history and the history of the whole world: The heifer of three years indicates the dominion of Babylon, the she-goat of three years stands for the empire of the Greeks, the ram of three years for the Medo-Persian power, the rule of Ishmael is represented by the ram, and Israel is the innocent dove.

Abraham took him these animals and divided them in the midst. Had he not done so, Israel would not have been able to resist the power of the four kingdoms. But the birds he divided not, to indicate that Israel will remain whole. And the birds of prey came down upon the carcasses, and Abraham drove them away. Thus was announced the advent of the Messiah, who will cut the heathen in pieces, but Abraham bade Messiah wait until the time appointed unto him. And as the Messianic time was made known unto Abraham, so also the time of the resurrection of the dead. When he laid the halves of the pieces over against each other, the animals became alive again, as the bird flew over them.

While he was preparing these sacrifices, a vision of great import was granted to Abraham. The sun sank, and a deep sleep fell upon him, and he beheld a smoking furnace, Gehenna, the furnace that God prepares for the sinner; and he beheld a flaming torch, the revelation on Sinai, where all the people saw flaming torches; and he beheld the sacrifices to be brought by Israel; and an horror of great darkness fell upon him, the dominion of the four kingdoms. And God spake to him: "Abraham, as long as thy children fulfil the two duties of studying the Torah and performing the service in the Temple, the two visitations, Gehenna and alien rule, will be spared them. But if they neglect the two duties, they will have to suffer the two chastisements; only thou mayest choose whether they shall be punished by means of Gehenna or by means of the dominion of the stranger." All the day long Abraham wavered, until God called unto him: "How long wilt thou halt between two opinions? Decide for one of the two, and let it be for the dominion of the stranger!" Then God made known to him the four hundred years' bondage of Israel in Egypt, reckoning from the birth of Isaac, for unto Abraham himself was the promise given that he should go to his fathers in peace, and feel naught of the arrogance of the stranger oppressor. At the same time, it was made known to Abraham that his father Terah would have a share in the world to come, for he had done penance for his sinful deeds. Furthermore it was revealed to him that his son Ishmael would turn into the path of righteousness while yet his father was alive, and his grandson Esau would not begin his impious way of life until he himself had passed away. And as he received the promise of their deliverance together with the announcement of the slavery of his seed, in a land not theirs, so it was made known to him that God would judge the four kingdoms and destroy them.

THE BIRTH OF ISHMAEL

The covenant of the pieces, whereby the fortunes of his descendants were revealed to Abraham, was made at a time when he was still childless. As long as Abraham and Sarah dwelt outside of the Holy Land, they looked upon their childlessness as a punishment for not abiding within it. But when a ten years' sojourn in Palestine found her barren as before, Sarah perceived that the fault lay with her. Without a trace of jealousy she was ready to give her slave Hagar to Abraham as wife, first making her a freed woman. For Hagar was Sarah's property, not her husband's. She had received her from Pharaoh, the father of Hagar. Taught and bred by Sarah, she walked in the same path of righteousness as her mistress, and thus was a suitable companion for Abraham, and, instructed by the holy spirit, he acceded to Sarah's proposal.

No sooner had Hagar's union with Abraham been consummated, and she felt that she was with child, than she began to treat her former mistress contemptuously, though Sarah was particularly tender toward her in the state in which she was. When noble matrons came to see Sarah, she was in the habit of urging them to pay a visit to "poor Hagar," too. The dames would comply with her suggestion, but Hagar would use the opportunity to disparage Sarah. "My lady Sarah," she would say, "is not inwardly what she appears to be outwardly. She makes the impression of a righteous, pious woman, but she is not, for if she were, how could her childlessness be explained after so many years of marriage, while I became pregnant at once?"

Sarah scorned to bicker with her slave, yet the rage she felt found vent in these words to Abraham: "It is thou who art doing me wrong. Thou hearest the words of Hagar, and thou sayest naught to oppose them, and I hoped that thou wouldst take my part. For thy sake did I leave my native land and the house of my father, and I followed thee into a strange land with trust in God. In Egypt I pretended to be thy sister, that no harm might befall thee. When I saw that I should bear no children, I took the Egyptian woman, my slave Hagar, and gave her unto thee for wife, contenting myself with the thought that I would rear the children she would bear. Now she treats me disdainfully in thy presence. O that God might look upon the injustice which hath been done unto me, to judge between thee and me, and have mercy upon us, restore peace to our home, and grant us offspring, that we have no need of children from Hagar, the Egyptian bondwoman of the generation of the heathen that cast thee in the fiery furnace!"

Abraham, modest and unassuming as he was, was ready to do justice to Sarah, and he conferred full power upon her to dispose of Hagar according to her pleasure. He added but one caution, "Having once made her a mistress, we cannot again reduce her to the state of a bondwoman." Unmindful of this warning, Sarah exacted the services of a slave from Hagar. Not alone this, she tormented her, and finally she cast an evil eye upon her, so that the unborn child dropped from her, and she ran away. On her flight she was met by several angels, and they bade her return, at the same time making known to her that she would bear a son who should be called Ishmael--one of the six men who have been given a name by God before their birth, the others being Isaac, Moses, Solomon, Josiah, and the Messiah.

Thirteen years after the birth of Ishmael the command was issued to Abraham that he put the sign of the covenant upon his body and upon the bodies of the male members of his household. Abraham was reluctant at first to do the bidding of God, for he feared that the circumcision of his flesh would raise a barrier between himself and the rest of mankind. But God said unto him, "Let it suffice thee that I am thy God and thy Lord, as it sufficeth the world that I am its God and its Lord."

Abraham then consulted with his three true friends, Aner, Eshcol, and Mamre, regarding the command of the circumcision. The first one spoke, and said, "Thou art nigh unto a hundred years old, and thou considerest inflicting such pain upon thyself?" The advice of the second was also against it. "What," said Eshcol, "thou choosest to mark thyself so that thy enemies may recognize thee without fail?" Mamre, the third, was the only one to advise obedience to the command of God. "God succored thee from the fiery furnace," he said, "He helped thee in the combat with the kings, He provided for thee during the famine, and thou dost hesitate to execute His behest concerning the circumcision? Accordingly, Abraham did as God had commanded, in bright daylight, bidding defiance to all, that none might say, "Had we seen him attempt it, we should have prevented him."

The circumcision was performed on the tenth day of Tishri, the Day of Atonement, and upon the spot on which the altar was later to be erected in the Temple, for the act of Abraham remains a never-ceasing atonement for Israel.

THE VISIT OF THE ANGELS

On the third day after his circumcision, when Abraham was suffering dire pain, God spoke to the angels, saying, "Go to, let us pay a visit to the sick." The angels refused, and said: "What is man, that Thou art mindful of him? And the son of man, that Thou visitest him? And Thou desirest to betake Thyself to a place of uncleanness, a place of blood and filth?" But God replied unto them, "Thus do ye speak. As ye live, the savor of this blood is sweeter to me than myrrh and incense, and if you do not desire to visit Abraham, I will go alone."

The day whereon God visited him was exceedingly hot, for He had bored a hole in hell, so that its heat might reach as far as the earth, and no wayfarer venture abroad on the highways, and Abraham be left undisturbed in his pain. But the absence of strangers caused Abraham great vexation, and he sent his servant Eliezer forth to keep a lookout for travellers. When the servant returned from his fruitless search, Abraham himself, in spite of his illness and the scorching heat, prepared to go forth on the highway and see whether he would not succeed where failure had attended Eliezer, whom he did not wholly trust at any rate, bearing in mind the well-known saying, "No truth among slaves." At this moment God appeared to him, surrounded by the angels. Quickly Abraham attempted to rise from his seat, but God checked every demonstration of respect, and when Abraham protested that it was unbecoming to sit in the presence of the Lord, God said, "As thou livest, thy descendants at the age of four and five will sit in days to come in the schools and in the synagogues while I reside therein."

Meantime Abraham beheld three men. They were the angels Michael, Gabriel, and Raphael. They had assumed the form of human beings to fulfil his wish for guests toward whom to exercise hospitality. Each of them had been charged by God with a special mission, besides, to be executed on earth. Raphael was to heal the wound of Abraham, Michael was to bring Sarah the glad tidings that she would bear a son, and Gabriel was to deal destruction to Sodom and Gomorrah. Arrived at the tent of Abraham, the three angels noticed that he was occupied in nursing himself, and they withdrew. Abraham, however, hastened after them through another door of the tent, which had wide open entrances on all sides. He considered the duty of hospitality more important than the duty of receiving the Shekinah. Turning to God, he said, "O Lord, may it please Thee not to leave Thy servant while he provides for the entertainment of his guests." Then he addressed himself to the stranger walking in the middle between the other two, whom by this token he considered the most distinguished,- it was the archangel Michael--and he bade him and his companions turn aside into his tent. The manner of his guests, who treated one another politely, made a good impression upon Abraham. He was assured that they were men of worth whom he was entertaining. But as they appeared outwardly like Arabs, and the people worshipped the dust of their feet, he bade them first wash their feet, that they might not defile his tent.

He did not depend upon his own judgment in reading the character of his guests. By his tent a tree was planted, which spread its branches out over all who believed in God, and afforded them shade. But if idolaters went under the tree, the branches turned upward, and cast no shade upon the ground. Whenever Abraham saw this sign, he would at once set about the task of converting the worshippers of the false gods. And as the tree made a distinction between the pious and the impious, so also between the clean and the unclean. Its shade was denied them as long as they refrained from taking the prescribed ritual bath in the spring that flowed out from its roots, the waters of which rose at once for those whose uncleanness was of a venial character and could be removed forthwith, while others had to wait seven days for the water to come up. Accordingly, Abraham bade the three men lean against the trunk of the tree. Thus he would soon learn their worth or their unworthiness.

Being of the truly pious, "who promise little, but perform much," Abraham said only: "I will fetch a morsel of bread, and comfort ye your heart, seeing that ye chanced to pass my tent at dinner time. Then, after ye have given thanks to God, ye may pass on." But when the meal was served to the guests, it was a royal banquet, exceeding Solomon's at the time of his most splendid magnificence. Abraham himself ran unto the herd, to fetch cattle for meat. He slaughtered three calves, that he might be able to set a "tongue with mustard" before each of his guests. In order to accustom Ishmael to God-pleasing deeds, he had him dress the calves, and he bade Sarah bake the bread. But as he knew that women are apt to treat guests niggardly, he was explicit in his request to her. He said, "Make ready quickly three measures of meal, yea, fine meal." As it happened, the bread was not brought to the table, because it had accidentally become unclean, and our father Abraham was accustomed to eat his daily bread only in a clean state. Abraham himself served his guests, and it appeared to him that the three men ate. But this was an illusion. In reality the angels did not eat, only Abraham, his three friends, Aner, Eshcol, and Mamre, and his son Ishmael partook of the banquet, and the portions set before the angels were devoured by a heavenly fire.

Although the angels remained angels even in their human disguise, nevertheless the personality of Abraham was so exalted that in his presence the archangels felt insignificant.

After the meal the angels asked after Sarah, though they knew that she was in retirement in her tent, but it was proper for them to pay their respects to the lady of the house and send her the cup of wine over which the blessing had been said. Michael, the greatest of the angels, thereupon announced the birth of Isaac. He drew a line upon the wall, saying, "When the sun crosses this point, Sarah will be with child, and when he crosses the next point, she will give birth to a child." This communication, which was intended for Sarah and not for Abraham, to whom the promise had been revealed long before, the angels made at the entrance to her tent, but Ishmael stood between the angel and Sarah, for it would not have been seemly to deliver the message in secret, with none other by. Yet, so radiant was the beauty of Sarah that a beam of it struck the angel, and made him look up. In the act of turning toward her, he heard her laugh within herself: "Is it possible that these bowels can yet bring forth a child, these shrivelled breasts give suck? And though I should be able to bear, yet is not my lord Abraham old?

And the Lord said unto Abraham: "Am I too old to do wonders? And wherefore doth Sarah laugh, saying, Shall I of a surety bear a child, which am old?" The reproach made by God was directed against Abraham as well as against Sarah, for he, too, had showed himself of little faith when he was told that a son would be born unto him. But God mentioned only Sarah's incredulity, leaving Abraham to become conscious of his defect himself.

Regardful of the peace of their family life, God had not repeated Sarah's words accurately to Abraham. Abraham might have taken amiss what his wife had said about his advanced years, and so precious is the peace between hus band and wife that even the Holy One, blessed be He, preserved it at the expense of truth.

After Abraham had entertained his guests, he went with them to bring them on their way, for, important as the duty of hospitality is, the duty of speeding the parting guest is even more important. Their way lay in the direction of Sodom, whither two of the angels were going, the one to destroy it, and the second to save Lot, while the third, his errand to Abraham fulfilled, returned to heaven.

THE CITIES OF SIN

The inhabitants of Sodom and Gomorrah and the three other cities of the plain were sinful and godless. In their country there was an extensive vale, where they foregathered annually with their wives and their children and all belonging to them, to celebrate a feast lasting several days and consisting of the most revolting orgies. If a stranger merchant passed through their territory, he was besieged by them all, big and little alike, and robbed of whatever he possessed. Each one appropriated a bagatelle, until the traveller was stripped bare. If the victim ventured to remonstrate with one or another, he would show him that he had taken a mere trifle, not worth talking about. And the end was that they hounded him from the city.

Once upon a time it happened that a man journeying from Elam arrived in Sodom toward evening. No one could be found to grant him shelter for the night. Finally a sly fox named Hedor invited him cordially to follow him to his house. The Sodomite had been attracted by a rarely magnificent carpet, strapped to the stranger's ass by means of a rope. He meant to secure it for himself. The friendly persuasions of Hedor induced the stranger to remain with him two days, though he had expected to stay only overnight. When the time came for him to continue on his journey, he asked his host for the carpet and the rope. Hedor said: "Thou hast dreamed a dream, and this is the interpretation of thy dream: the rope signifies that thou wilt have a long life, as long as a rope; the varicolored carpet indicates that thou wilt own an orchard wherein thou wilt plant all sorts of fruit trees." The stranger insisted that his carpet was a reality, not a dream fancy, and he continued to demand its return. Not only did Hedor deny having taken anything from his guest, he even insisted upon pay for having interpreted his dream to him. His usual price for such services, he said, was four silver pieces, but in view of the fact that he was his guest, he would, as a favor to him, content himself with three pieces of silver.

After much wrangling, they put their case before one of the judges of Sodom, Sherek by name, and he said to the plaintiff, "Hedor is known in this city as a trustworthy interpreter of dreams, and what he tells thee is true." The stranger declared himself not satisfied with the verdict, and continued to urge his side of the case. Then Sherek drove both the plaintiff and the defendant from the court room. Seeing this, the inhabitants gathered together and chased the stranger from the city, and lamenting the loss of his carpet, he had to pursue his way.

As Sodom had a judge worthy of itself, so also had the other cities--Sharkar in Gomorrah, Zabnak in Admah, and Manon in Zeboiim. Eliezer, the bondman of Abraham, made slight changes in the names of these judges, in accordance with the nature of what they did: the first he called Shakkara, Liar; the second Shakrura, Arch-deceiver; the third Kazban, Falsifier; and the fourth, Mazle-Din, Perverter of Judgment. At the suggestion of these judges, the cities set up beds on their commons. When a stranger arrived, three men seized him by his head, and three by his feet, and they forced him upon one of the beds. If he was too short to fit into it exactly, his six attendants pulled and wrenched his limbs until he filled it out; if he was too long for; it, they tried to jam him in with all their combined strength, until the victim was on the verge of death. Hit outcrles were met with the words, "Thus will be done to any man that comes into our land."

After a while travellers avoided these cities, but if some poor devil was betrayed occasionally into entering them, they would give him gold and silver, but never any bread, so that he was bound to die of starvation. Once he was dead, the residents of the city came and took back the marked gold and silver which they had given him, and they would quarrel about the distribution of his clothes, for they would bury him naked.

Once Eliezer, the bondman of Abraham, went to Sodom, at the bidding of Sarah, to inquire after the welfare of Lot. He happened to enter the city at the moment when the people were robbing a stranger of his garments. Eliezer espoused the cause of the poor wretch, and the Sodomites turned against him; one threw a stone at his forehead and caused considerable loss of blood. Instantly, the assailant, seeing the blood gush forth, demanded payment for having performed the operation of cupping. Eliezer refused to pay for the infliction of a wound upon him, and he was haled before the judge Shakkara. The decision went against him, for the law of the land gave the assailant the right to demand payment. Eliezer quickly picked up a stone and threw it at the judge's forehead. When he saw that the blood was flowing profusely, he said to the judge, "Pay my debt to the man and give me the balance."

The cause of their cruelty was their exceeding great wealth. Their soil was gold, and in their miserliness and their greed for more and more gold, they wanted to prevent strangers from enjoying aught of their riches. Accordingly, they flooded the highways with streams of water, so that the roads to their city were obliterated, and none could find the way thither. They were as heartless toward beasts as toward men. They begrudged the birds what they ate, and therefore extirpated them. They behaved impiously toward one another, too, not shrinking back from murder to gain possession of more gold. If they observed that a man owned great riches, two of them would conspire against him. They would beguile him to the vicinity of ruins, and while the one kept him on the spot by pleasant converse, the other would undermine the wall near which he stood, until it suddenly crashed down upon him and killed him. Then the two plotters would divide his wealth between them.

Another method of enriching themselves with the property of others was in vogue among them. They were adroit thieves. When they made up their minds to commit theft, they would first ask their victim to take care of a sum of money for them, which they smeared with strongly scented oil before handing it over to him. The following night they would break into his house, and rob him of his secret treasures, led to the place of concealment by the smell of the oil.

Their laws were calculated to do injury to the poor. The richer a man, the more was he favored before the law. The owner of two oxen was obliged to render one day's shepherd service, but if he had but one ox, he had to give two days' service. A poor orphan, who was thus forced to tend the flocks a longer time than those who were blessed with large herds, killed all the cattle entrusted to him in order to take revenge upon his oppressors, and he insisted, when the skins were assigned, that the owner of two head of cattle should have but one skin, but the owner of one head should receive two skins, in correspondence to the method pursued in assigning the work. For the use of the ferry, a traveller had to pay four zuz, but if he waded through the water, he had to pay eight zuz.

The cruelty of the Sodomites went still further. Lot had a daughter, Paltit, so named because she had been born to him shortly after he escaped captivity through the help of Abraham. Paltit lived in Sodom, where she had married. Once a beggar came to town, and the court issued a proclamation that none should give him anything to eat, in order that he might die of starvation. But Paltit had pity upon the unfortunate wretch, and every day when she went to the well to draw water, she supplied him with a piece of bread, which she hid in her water pitcher. The inhabitants of the two sinful cities, Sodom and Gomorrah, could not understand why the beggar did not perish, and they suspected that some one was giving him food in secret. Three men concealed themselves near the beggar, and caught Paltit in the act of giving him something to eat. She had to pay for her humanity with death; she was burnt upon a pyre.

The people of Admah were no better than those of Sodom. Once a stranger came to Admah, intending to stay overnight and continue his journey the next morning. The daughter of a rich man met the stranger, and gave him water to drink and bread to eat at his request. When the people of Admah heard of this infraction of the law of the land, they seized the girl and arraigned her before the judge, who condemned her to death. The people smeared her with honey from top to toe, and exposed her where bees would be attracted to her. The insects stung her to death, and the callous people paid no heed to her heartrending cries. Then it was that God resolved upon the destruction of these sinners.

ABRAHAM PLEADS FOR THE SINNERS

When God saw that there was no righteous man among the inhabitants of the sinful cities, and there would be none among their descendants, for the sake of whose merits the rest might be treated with lenient consideration, He resolved to annihilate them one and all. But before judgment was executed, the Lord made known unto Abraham what He would do to Sodom, Gomorrah, and the other cities of the plain, for they formed a part of Canaan, the land promised unto Abraham, and therefore did God say, "I will not destroy them without the consent of Abraham."

Like a compassionate father, Abraham importuned the grace of God in behalf of the sinners. He spoke to God, and said: "Thou didst take an oath that no more should all flesh be cut off by the waters of a flood. Is it meet that Thou shouldst evade Thy oath and destroy cities by fire? Shall the Judge of all the earth not do right Himself? Verily, if Thou desirest to maintain the world, Thou must give up the strict line of justice. If Thou insistest upon the right alone, there can be no world." Whereupon God said to Abraham: "Thou takest delight in defending My creatures, and thou wouldst not call them guilty. Therefore I spoke with none but thee during the ten generations since Noah." Abraham ventured to use still stronger words in order to secure the safety of the godless. "That be far from Thee," he said, "to slay the righteous with the wicked, that the dwellers on the earth say not, 'It is His trade to destroy the generations of men in a cruel manner; for He destroyed the generation of Enosh, then the generation of the flood, and then He sent the confusion of tongues. He sticks ever to His trade.' "

God made reply: "I will let all the generations I have destroyed pass before thee, that thou mayest see they have not suffered the extreme punishment they deserved. But if thou thinkest that I did not act justly, then instruct thou Me in what I must do, and I will endeavor to act in accordance with thy words." And Abraham had to admit that God had not diminished in aught the justice due to every creature in this world or the other world. Nevertheless he continued to speak, and he said: "Wilt Thou consume the cities, if there be ten righteous men in each?" And God said, "No, if I find fifty righteous therein, I will not destroy the cities."

Abraham: "I have taken upon me to speak unto the Lord, I who would have been turned long since into dust of the ground by Amraphel and into ashes by Nimrod, had it not been for Thy grace. Peradventure there shall lack five of the fifty righteous for Zoar, the smallest of the five cities. Wilt Thou destroy all the city for lack of five?"

God: "I will not destroy it, if I find there forty and five."

Abraham: "Peradventure there be ten pious in each of the four cities, then forgive Zoar in Thy grace, for its sins are not so great in number as the sins of the others."

God granted his petition, yet Abraham continued to plead, and he asked whether God would not be satisfied if there were but thirty righteous, ten in each of the three larger cities, and would pardon the two smaller ones, even though there were no righteous therein, whose merits would intercede for them. This, too, the Lord granted, and furthermore He promised not to destroy the cities if but twenty righteous were found therein; yes, God conceded that He would preserve the five cities for the sake of ten righteous therein. More than this Abraham did not ask, for he knew that eight righteous ones, Noah and his wife, and his three sons and their wives, had not sufficed to avert the doom of the generation of the flood, and furthermore he hoped that Lot, his wife, and their four daughters, together with the husbands of their daughters, would make up the number ten. What he did not know was that even the righteous in these sin-laden cities, though better than the rest, were far from good.

Abraham did not cease to pray for the deliverance of the sinners even after the Shekinah had removed from him. But his supplications and his intercessions were in vain. For fifty-two years God had warned the godless; He had made mountains to quake and tremble. But they hearkened not unto the voice of admonition. They persisted in their sins, and their well-merited punishment overtook them. God forgives all sins, only not an immoral life. And as all these sinners led a life of debauchery, they were burnt with fire.

THE DESTRUCTION OF THE SINFUL CITIES

The angels left Abraham at noon time, and they reached Sodom at the approach of evening. As a rule, angels proclaim their errand with the swiftness of lightning, but these were angels of mercy, and they hesitated to execute their work of destruction, ever hoping that the evil would be turned aside from Sodom. With nightfall, the fate of Sodom was sealed irrevocably, and the angels arrived there.

Bred in the house of Abraham, Lot had learnt from him the beautiful custom of extending hospitality, and when he saw the angels before him in human form, thinking they were wayfarers, he bade them turn aside and tarry all night in his house. But as the entertainment of strangers was forbidden in Sodom on penalty of death, he dared invite them only under cover of the darkness of night, and even then he had to use every manner of precaution, bidding the angels to follow him by devious ways.

The angels, who had accepted Abraham's hospitality without delay, first refused to comply with Lot's request, for it is a rule of good breeding to show reluctance when an ordinary man invites one, but to accept the invitation of a great man at once. Lot, however, was insistent, and carried them into his house by main force. At home he had to overcome the opposition of his wife, for she said, "If the inhabitants of Sodom hear of this, they will slay thee."

Lot divided his dwelling in two parts, one for himself and his guests, the other for his wife, so that, if aught happened, his wife would be spared. Nevertheless it was she who betrayed him. She went to a neighbor and borrowed some salt, and to the question, whether she could not have supplied herself with salt during daylight hours, she replied, "We had enough salt, until some guests came to us; for them we needed more." In this way the presence of strangers was bruited abroad in the city.

In the beginning the angels were inclined to hearken to the petition of Lot in behalf of the sinners, but when all the people of the city, big and little, crowded around the house of Lot with the purpose of committing a monstrous crime, the angels warded off his prayers, saying, "Hitherto thou couldst intercede for them, but now no longer." It was not the first time that the inhabitants of Sodom wanted to perpetrate a crime of this sort. They had made a law some time before that all strangers were to be treated in this horrible way. Lot, who was appointed chief judge on the very day of the angels' coming, tried to induce the people to desist from their purpose, saying to them, "My brethren, the generation of the deluge was extirpated in consequence of such sins as you desire to commit, and you would revert to them?" But they replied: "Back! And though Abraham himself came hither, we should have no consideration for him. Is it possible that thou wouldst set aside a law which thy predecessors administered?"

Even Lot's moral sense was no better than it should have been. It is the duty of a man to venture his life for the honor of his wife and his daughters, but Lot was ready to sacrifice the honor of his daughters, wherefor he was punished severely later on.

The angels told Lot who they were, and what the mission that had brought them to Sodom, and they charged him to flee from the city with his wife and his four daughters, two of them married, and two betrothed. Lot communicated their bidding to his sons-in-law, and they mocked at him, and said: "O thou fool! Violins, cymbals, and flutes resound in the city, and thou sayest Sodom will be destroyed!" Such scoffing but hastened the execution of the doom of Sodom. The angel Michael laid hold upon the hand of Lot, and his wife and his daughters, while with his little finger the angel Gabriel touched the rock whereon the sinful cities were built, and overturned them. At the same time the rain that was streaming down upon the two cities was changed into brimstone.

When the angels had brought forth Lot and his family and set them without the city, he bade them run for their lives, and not look behind, lest they behold the Shekinah, which had descended to work the destruction of the cities. The wife of Lot could not control herself. Her mother love made her look behind to see if her married daughters were following. She beheld the Shekinah, and she became a pillar of salt. This pillar exists unto this day. The cattle lick it all day long, and in the evening it seems to have disappeared, but when morning comes it stands there as large as before.

The savior angel had urged Lot himself to take refuge with Abraham. But he refused, and said: "As long as I dwelt apart from Abraham, God compared my deeds with the deeds of my fellow-citizens, and among them I appeared as a righteous man. If I should return to Abraham, God will see that his good deeds outweigh mine by far." The angel then granted his plea that Zoar be left undestroyed. This city had been founded a year later than the other four; it was only fifty-one years old, and therefore the measure of its sins was not so full as the measure of the sins of the neighboring cities.

The destruction of the cities of the plain took place at dawn of the sixteenth day of Nisan, for the reason that there were moon and sun worshippers among the inhabitants. God said: "If I destroy them by day, the moon worshippers will say, Were the moon here, she would prove herself our savior; and if I destroy them by night, the sun worshippers will say, Were the sun here, he would prove himself our savior. I will therefore let their chastisement overtake them on the sixteenth day of Nisan at an hour at which the moon and the sun are both in the skies."

The sinful inhabitants of the cities of the plain not only lost their life in this world, but also their share in the future world. As for the cities themselves, however, they will be restored in the Messianic time.

The destruction of Sodom happened at the time at which Abraham was performing his morning devotions, and for his sake it was established as the proper hour for the morning prayer unto all times. When he turned his eyes toward Sodom and beheld the rising smoke, he prayed for the deliverance of Lot, and God granted his petition--the fourth time that Lot became deeply indebted to Abraham. Abraham had taken him with him to Palestine, he had made him rich in flocks, herds, and tents, he had rescued him from captivity, and by his prayer he saved him from the destruction of Sodom. The descendants of Lot, the Ammonites and the Moabites, instead of showing gratitude to the Israelites, the posterity of Abraham, committed four acts of hostility against them. They sought to compass the destruction of Israel by means of Balaam's curses, they waged open war against him at the time of Jephthah, and also at the time of Jehoshaphat, and finally they manifested their hatred against Israel at the destruction of the Temple. Hence it is that God appointed four prophets, Isaiah, Jeremiah, Ezekiel, and Zephaniah, to proclaim punishment unto the descendants of Lot, and four times their sin is recorded in Holy Writ.

Though Lot owed his deliverance to the petition of Abraham, yet it was at the same time his reward for not having betrayed Abraham in Egypt, when he pretended to be the brother of Sarah. But a greater reward still awaits him. The Messiah will be a descendant of his, for the Moabitess Ruth is the great-grandmother of David, and the Ammonitess Naamah is the mother of Rehoboam, and the Messiah is of the line of these two kings.

AMONG THE PHILISTINES

The destruction of Sodom induced Abraham to journey to Gerar. Accustomed to extend hospitality to travellers and wayfarers, he no longer felt comfortable in a district in which all traffic had ceased by reason of the ruined cities. There was another reason for Abraham's leaving his place; the people spoke too much about the ugly incident with Lot's daughters.

Arrived in the land of the Philistines, he again, as aforetime in Egypt, came to an understanding with Sarah, that she was to call herself his sister. When the report of her beauty reached the king, he ordered her to be brought before him, and he asked her who her companion was, and she told him that Abraham was her brother. Entranced by her beauty, Abimelech the king took Sarah to wife, and heaped marks of honor upon Abraham in accordance with the just claims of a brother of the queen. Toward evening, before retiring, while he was still seated upon his throne, Abimelech fell into a sleep, and he slept until the morning, and in the dream he dreamed he saw an angel of the Lord raising his sword to deal him a death blow. Sore frightened, he asked the cause, and the angel replied, and said: "Thou wilt die on account of the woman thou didst take into thy house this day, for she is the wife of Abraham, the man whom thou didst cite before thee. Return his wife unto him! But if thou restore her not, thou shalt surely die, thou and all that are thine."

In that night the voice of a great crying was heard in the whole land of the Philistines, for they saw the figure of a man walking about, with sword in hand, slaying all that came in his way. At the same time it happened that in men and beasts alike all the apertures of the body closed up, and the land was seized with indescribable excitement. In the morning, when the king awoke, in agony and terror, he called all his servants and told his dream in their ears. One of their number said: "O lord and king! Restore this woman unto the man, for he is her husband. It is but his way in a strange land to pretend that she is his sister. Thus did he with the king of Egypt, too, and God sent heavy afflictions upon Pharaoh when he took the woman unto himself. Consider, also, O lord and king, what hath befallen this night in the land; great pain, wailing, and confusion there was, and we know that it came upon us only because of this woman."

There were some among his servants who spake: "Be not afraid of dreams! What dreams make known to man is but falsehood." Then God appeared unto Abimelech again and commanded him to let Sarah go free, otherwise he would be a dead man. Abimelech replied: "Is this Thy way? Then, I ween, the generation of the flood and the generation of the confusion of tongues were innocent, too! The man himself did say unto me, She is my sister, and she, even she herself said, He is my brother, and all the people of their household said the same words." And God said unto him: "Yea, I know that thou hast not yet committed a trespass, for I withheld thee from sinning. Thou didst not know that Sarah was a man's wife. But is it becoming to question a stranger, no sooner does he set foot upon thy territory, about the woman accompanying him, whether she be his wife or his sister? Abraham, who is a prophet, knew beforehand the danger to himself if he revealed the whole truth. But, being a prophet, he also knows that thou didst not touch his wife, and he shall pray for thee, and thou shalt live."

The smoke was still rising from the ruins of Sodom, and Abimelech and his people, seeing it, feared that a like fate might overtake them. The king called Abraham and reproached him for having caused such great misfortune through his false statements concerning Sarah. Abraham excused his conduct by his apprehension that, the fear of God not being in the place, the inhabitants of the land slay him for his wife. Abraham went on and told the history of his whole life, and he said: "When I dwelt in the house of my father, the nations of the world sought to do me harm, but God proved Himself my Redeemer. When the nations of the world tried to lead me astray to idolatry, God revealed Himself to me, and He said, 'Get thee out of thy country, and from thy kindred, and from thy father's house.' And when the nations of the world were about to go astray, God sent two prophets, my kinsmen Shem and Eber, to admonish them."

Abimelech gave rich gifts to Abraham, wherein he acted otherwise than Pharaoh in similar circumstances. The Egyptian king gave gifts to Sarah, but Abimelech was God fearing, and desired that Abraham pray for him. To Sarah he gave a costly robe that covered her whole person, hiding her seductive charms from the view of beholders. At the same time it was a reproach to Abraham, that he had not fitted Sarah out with the splendor due to his wife.

Though Abimelech had done him great injury, Abraham not only granted him the forgiveness he craved, but also he prayed for him to God. Thus he is an exemplar unto all. "Man should be pliant as a reed, not hard like the cedar." He should be easily appeased, and slow to anger, and as soon as he who has sinned against him asks for pardon, he should forgive him with all his heart. Even if deep and serious injury has been done to him, he should not be vengeful, nor bear his brother a grudge in his heart.

Abraham prayed thus for Abimelech: "O Lord of the world! Thou hast created man that he may increase and propagate his kind. Grant that Abimelech and his house may multiply and increase!" God fulfilled Abraham's petition in behalf of Abimelech and his people, and it was the first time it happened in the history of mankind that God fulfilled the prayer of one human being for the benefit of another. Abimelech and his subjects were healed of all their diseases, and so efficacious was the prayer offered by Abraham that the wife of Abimelech, barren hitherto, bore a child.

THE BIRTH OF ISAAC

When the prayer of Abraham for Abimelech was heard, and the king of the Philistines recovered, the angels raised a loud cry, and spoke to God thus: "O Lord of the world! All these years hath Sarah been barren, as the wife of Abimelech was. Now Abraham prayed to Thee, and the wife of Abimelech hath been granted a child. It is just and fair that Sarah should be remembered and granted a child." These words of the angels, spoken on the New Year's Day, when the fortunes of men are determined in heaven for the whole year, bore a result. Barely seven months later, on the first day of the Passover, Isaac was born.

The birth of Isaac was a happy event, and not in the house of Abraham alone. The whole world rejoiced, for God remembered all barren women at the same time with Sarah. They all bore children. And all the blind were made to see, all the lame were made whole, the dumb were made to speak, and the mad were restored to reason. And a still greater miracle happened: on the day of Isaac's birth the sun shone with such splendor as had not been seen since the fall of man, and as he will shine again only in the future world.

To silence those who asked significantly, "Can one a hundred years old beget a son?" God commanded the angel who has charge over the embryos, to give them form and shape, that he fashion Isaac precisely according to the model of Abraham, so that all seeing Isaac might exclaim, "Abraham begot Isaac."

That Abraham and Sarah were blessed with offspring only after they had attained so great an age, had an important reason. It was necessary that Abraham should bear the sign of the covenant upon his body before he begot the son who was appointed to be the father of Israel. And as Isaac was the first child born to Abraham after he was marked with the sign, he did not fail to celebrate his circumcision with much pomp and ceremony on the eighth day. Shem, Eber, Abimelech king of the Philistines, and his whole retinue, Phicol the captain of his host in it--they all were present, and also Terah and his son Nahor, in a word, all the great ones round about. On this occasion Abraham could at last put a stop to the talk of the people, who said, "Look at this old couple! They picked up a foundling on the highway, and they pretend he is their own son, and to make their statement seem credible, they arrange a feast in his honor." Abraham had invited not only men to the celebration, but also the wives of the magnates with their infants, and God permitted a miracle to be done. Sarah had enough milk in her breasts to suckle all the babes there, and they who drew from her breasts had much to thank her for. Those whose mothers had harbored only pious thoughts in their minds when they let them drink the milk that flowed from the breasts of the pious Sarah, they became proselytes when they grew up; and those whose mothers let Sarah nurse them only in order to test her, they grew up to be powerful rulers, losing their dominion only at the revelation on Mount Sinai, because they would not accept the Torah. All proselytes and pious heathen are the descendants of these infants.

Among the guests of Abraham were the thirty-one kings and thirty-one viceroys of Palestine who were vanquished by Joshua at the conquest of the Holy Land. Even Og king of Bashan was present, and he had to suffer the teasing of the other guests, who rallied him upon having called Abraham a sterile mule, who would never have offspring. Og, on his part, pointed at the little boy with contempt, and said, "Were I to lay my finger upon him, he would be crushed." Whereupon God said to him: "Thou makest mock of the gift given to Abraham! As thou livest, thou shalt look upon millions and myriads of his descendants, and in the end thou shalt fall into their hands."

ISHMAEL CAST OFF

When Isaac grew up, quarrels broke out between him and Ishmael, on account of the rights of the first-born. Ishmael insisted he should receive a double portion of the inheritance after the death of Abraham, and Isaac should receive only one portion. Ishmael, who had been accustomed from his youth to use the bow and arrow, was in the habit of aiming his missiles in the direction of Isaac, saying at the same time that he was but jesting. Sarah, however, insisted that Abraham make over to Isaac all he owned, that no disputes might arise after his death, "for," she said, "Ishmael is not worthy of being heir with my son, nor with a man like

Isaac, and certainly not with my son Isaac." Furthermore, Sarah insisted that Abraham divorce himself from Hagar, the mother of Ishmael, and send away the woman and her son, so that there be naught in common between them and her own son, either in this world or in the future world.

Of all the trials Abraham had to undergo, none was so hard to bear as this, for it grieved him sorely to separate himself from his son. God appeared to him in the following night, and said to him: "Abraham, knowest thou not that Sarah was appointed to be thy wife from her mother's womb? She is thy companion and the wife of thy youth, and I named not Hagar as thy wife, nor Sarah as thy bondwoman. What Sarah spoke unto thee was naught but truth, and let it not be grievous in thy sight because of the lad, and because of thy bondwoman." The next morning Abraham rose up early, gave Hagar her bill of divorcement, and sent her away with her son, first binding a rope about her loins that all might see she was a bondwoman.

The evil glance cast upon her stepson by Sarah made him sick and feverish, so that Hagar had to carry him, grown-up as he was. In his fever he drank often of the water in the bottle given her by Abraham as she left his house, and the water was quickly spent. That she might not look upon the death of her child, Hagar cast Ishmael under the willow shrubs growing on the selfsame spot whereon the angels had once spoken with her and made known to her that she would bear a son. In the bitterness of her heart, she spoke to God, and said, "Yesterday Thou didst say to me, I will greatly multiply thy seed, that it shall not be numbered for multitude, and to-day my son dies of thirst." Ishmael himself cried unto God, and his prayer and the merits of Abraham brought them help in their need, though the angels appeared against Ishmael before God. They said, "Wilt Thou cause a well of water to spring up for him whose descendants will let Thy children of Israel perish with thirst?" But God replied, and said, "What is Ishmael at this moment--righteous or wicked?" and when the angels called him righteous, God continued, "I treat man according to his deserts at each moment."

At that moment Ishmael was pious indeed, for he was praying to God in the following words: "O Lord of the world! If it be Thy will that I shall perish, then let me die in some other way, not by thirst, for the tortures of thirst are great beyond all others." Hagar, instead of praying to God, addressed her supplications to the idols of her youth. The prayer of Ishmael was acceptable before God, and He bade Miriam's well spring up, the well created in the twilight of the sixth day of creation. Even after this miracle Hagar's faith was no stronger than before. She filled the bottle with water, because she feared it might again be spent, and no other would be nigh. Thereupon she journeyed to Egypt with her son, for "Throw the stick into the air as thou wilt, it will always land on its point." Hagar had come from Egypt, and to Egypt she returned, to choose a wife for her son.

THE TWO WIVES OF ISHMAEL

The wife of Ishmael bore four sons and a daughter, and afterward Ishmael, his mother, and his wife and children went and returned to the wilderness. They made themselves tents in the wilderness in which they dwelt, and they continued to encamp and journey, month by month and year by year. And God gave Ishmael flocks, and herds, and tents, on account of Abraham his father, and the man increased in cattle. And some time after, Abraham said to Sarah, his wife, "I will go and see my son Ishmael; I yearn to look upon him, for I have not seen him for a long time." And Abraham rode upon one of his camels to the wilderness, to seek his son Ishmael, for he heard that he was dwelling in a tent in the wilderness with all belonging to him. And Abraham went to the wilderness, and he reached the tent of Ishmael about noon, and he asked after him. He found the wife of Ishmael sitting in the tent with her children, and her husband and his mother were not with them. And Abraham asked the wife of Ishmael, saying, "Where has Ishmael gone?" And she said, "He has gone to the field to hunt game." And Abraham was still mounted upon the camel, for he would not alight upon the ground, as he had sworn to his wife Sarah that he would not get off from the camel. And Abraham said to Ishmael's wife, "My daughter, give me a little water, that I may drink, for I am fatigued and tired from the journey." And Ishmael's wife answered, and said to Abraham, "We have neither water nor bread," and she was sitting in the tent, and did not take any notice of Abraham. She did not even ask him who he was. But all the while she was beating her children in the tent, and she was cursing them, and she also cursed her husband Ishmael, and spoke evil of him, and Abraham heard the words of Ishmael's wife to her children, and it was an evil thing in his eyes. And Abraham called to the woman to come out to him from the tent, and the woman came out, and stood face to face with Abraham, while Abraham was still mounted upon the camel.

And Abraham said to Ishmael's wife, "When thy husband Ishmael returns home, say these words to him: A very old man from the land of the Philistines came hither to seek thee, and his appearance was thus and so, and thus was his figure. I did not ask him who he was, and seeing thou wast not here, he spoke unto me, and said, When Ishmael thy husband returns, tell him, Thus did the man say, When thou comest home, put away this tentpin which thou hast placed here, and place another tent-pin in its stead." And Abraham finished his instructions to the woman, and he turned and went off on the camel homeward. And when Ishmael returned to the tent, he heard the words of his wife, and he knew that it was his father, and that his wife had not honored him. And Ishmael understood his father's words that he had spoken to his wife, and he hearkened to the voice of his father, and he divorced his wife, and she went away. And Ishmael afterward went to the land of Canaan, and he took another wife, and he brought her to his tent, to the place where he dwelt.

And at the end of three years, Abraham said, "I will go again and see Ishmael my son, for I have not seen him for a long time." And he rode upon his camel, and went to the wilderness, and he reached the tent of Ishmael about noon. And he asked after Ishmael, and his wife came out of the tent, and she said, "He is not here, my lord, for he has gone to hunt in the fields and feed the camels," and the woman said to Abraham, "Turn in, my lord, into the tent, and eat a morsel of bread, for thy soul must be wearied on account of the journey." And Abraham said to her, "I will not stop, for I am in haste to continue my journey, but give me a little water to drink, for I am thirsty," and the woman hastened and ran into the tent, and she brought out water and bread to Abraham, which she placed before him, urging him to eat and drink, and he ate and drank, and his heart was merry, and he blessed his son Ishmael. And he finished his meal, and he blessed the Lord, and he said to Ishmael's wife: "When Ishmael comes home, say these words to him: A very old man from the land of the Philistines came hither, and asked after thee, and thou wast not here, and I brought him out bread and water, and he ate and drank, and his heart was merry. And he spoke these words to me, When Ishmael thy husband comes home, say unto him, The tent-pin which thou hast is very good, do not put it away from the tent." And Abraham finished commanding the woman, and he rode off to his home, to the land of the Philistines, and when Ishmael came to his tent, his wife went forth to meet him with joy and a cheerful heart, and she told him the words of the old man. Ishmael knew that it was his father, and that his wife had honored him, and he praised the Lord. And Ishmael then took his wife and his children and his cattle and all belonging to him, and he journeyed from there, and he went to his father in the land of the Philistines. And Abraham related to Ishmael all that had happened between him and the first wife that Ishmael had taken, according to what she had done. And Ishmael and his children dwelt with Abraham many days in that land, and Abraham dwelt in the land of the Philistines a long time.

THE COVENANT WITH ABIMELECH

After a sojourn of twenty-six years in the land of the Philistines, Abraham departed thence, and he settled in the neighborhood of Hebron. There he was visited by Abimelech with twenty of his grandees, who requested him to make an alliance with the Philistines.

As long as Abraham was childless, the heathen did not believe in his piety, but when Isaac was born, they said to him, "God is with thee." But again they entertained doubt of his piety when he cast off Ishmael. They said, "Were he a righteous man, he would not drive his first-born forth from his house." But when they observed the impious deeds of Ishmael, they said, "God is with thee in all thou doest." That Abraham was the favorite of God, they saw in this, too, that although Sodom was destroyed and all traffic had come to a standstill in that region, yet Abraham's treasure chambers were filled. For these reasons, the Philistines sought to form an alliance with him, to remain in force for three generations to come, for it is to the third generation that the love of a father extends.

Before Abraham concluded the covenant with Abimelech, king of the Philistines, he reproved him on account of a well, for "Correction leads to love," and "There is no peace without correction." The herdmen of Abraham and those of Abimelech had left their dispute about the well to decision by ordeal: the well was to belong to the party for whose sheep the waters would rise so that they could drink of them. But the shepherds of Abimelech disregarded the agreement, and they wrested the well for their own use. As a witness and a perpetual sign that the well belonged to him, Abraham set aside seven sheep, corresponding to the seven Noachian laws binding upon all men alike. But God said, "Thou didst give him seven sheep. As thou livest, the Philistines shall one day slay seven righteous men, Samson, Hophni, Phinehas, and Saul with his three sons, and they will destroy seven holy places, and they will keep the holy Ark in their country as booty of war for a period of seven months, and furthermore only the seventh generation of thy descendants will be able to rejoice in the possession of the land promised to them." After concluding the alliance with Abimelech, who acknowledged Abraham's right upon the well, Abraham called the place Beer-sheba, because there they swore both of them unto a covenant of friendship.

In Beer-sheba Abraham dwelt many years, and thence he endeavored to spread the law of God. He planted a large grove there, and he made four gates for it, facing the four sides of the earth, east, west, north, and south, and he planted a vineyard therein. If a traveller came that way, he entered by the gate that faced him, and he sat in the grove, and ate, and drank, until he was satisfied, and then he departed. For the house of Abraham was always open for all passers-by, and they came daily to eat and drink there. If one was hungry, and he came to Abraham, he would give him what he needed, so that he might eat and drink and be satisfied; and if one was naked, and he came to Abraham, he would clothe him with the garments of the poor man's choice, and give him silver and gold, and make known to him the Lord, who had created him and set him on earth. After the wayfarers had eaten, they were in the habit of thanking Abraham for his kind entertainment of them, whereto he would reply: "What, ye give thanks unto me! Rather return thanks to your host, He who alone provides food and drink for all creatures." Then the people would ask, "Where is He?" and Abraham would answer them, and say: "He is the Ruler of heaven and earth. He woundeth and He healeth, He formeth the embryo in the womb of the mother and bringeth it forth into the world, He causeth the plants and the trees to grow, He killeth and He maketh alive, He bringeth down to Sheol and bringeth up." When the people heard such words, they would ask, "How shall we return thanks to God and manifest our gratitude unto Him?" And Abraham would instruct them in these words: "Say, Blessed be the Lord who is blessed! Blessed be He that giveth bread and food unto all flesh!" In this manner did Abraham teach those who had enjoyed his hospitality how to praise and thank God. Abraham's house thus became not only a lodging-place for the hungry and thirsty, but also a place of instruction where the knowledge of God and His law were taught.

SATAN ACCUSES ABRAHAM

In spite of the lavish hospitality practiced in the house of Abraham, it happened once that a poor man, or rather an alleged poor man, was turned away empty-handed, and this was the immediate reason for the last of Abraham's temptations, the sacrifice of his favorite son Isaac. It was the day on which Abraham celebrated the birth of Isaac with a great banquet, to which all the magnates of the time were bidden with their wives. Satan, who always appears at a feast in which no poor people participate, and keeps aloof from those to which poor guests are invited, turned up at Abraham's banquet in the guise of a beggar asking alms at the door. He had noticed that Abraham had invited no poor man, and he knew that his house was the right place for him.

Abraham was occupied with the entertainment of his distinguished guests, and Sarah was endeavoring to convince their wives, the matrons, that Isaac was her child in very truth, and not a spurious child. No one concerned himself about the beggar at the door, who thereupon accused Abraham before God.

Now, there was a day when the sons of God came to present themselves before the Lord, and Satan came also among them. And the Lord said unto Satan, "From whence comest thou?" and Satan answered the Lord, and said, "From going to and fro on the earth, and from walking up and down in it." And the Lord said unto Satan, "What hast thou to say concerning all the children of the earth?" and Satan answered the Lord, and said: "I have seen all the children of the earth serving Thee and remembering Thee, when they require aught from Thee. And when Thou givest them what they require from Thee, then they forsake Thee, and they remember Thee no more. Hast Thou seen Abraham, the son of Terah, who at first had no children, and he served Thee and erected altars to Thee wherever he came, and he brought offerings upon them, and he proclaimed Thy name continually to all the children of the earth? And now his son Isaac is born to him, he has forsaken Thee. He made a great feast for all the inhabitants of the land, and the Lord he has forgotten. For amidst all that he has done, he brought Thee no offering, neither burnt offering nor peace offering, neither one lamb nor goat of all that he had killed in the day that his son was weaned. Even from the time of his son's birth till now, being thirty-seven years, he built no altar before Thee, nor brought up any offering to Thee, for he saw that Thou didst give what he requested before Thee, and he therefore forsook Thee." And the Lord said to Satan: "Hast thou considered My servant Abraham? For there is none like him in the earth, a perfect and an upright man before Me for a burnt offering, and that feareth God and escheweth evil. As I live, were I to say unto him, Bring up Isaac thy son before Me, he would not withhold him from Me, much less if I told him to bring up a burnt offering before Me from his flocks or herds." And Satan answered the Lord, and said, "Speak now unto Abraham as Thou hast said, and Thou wilt see whether he will not transgress and cast aside Thy words this day."

God wished to try Isaac also. Ishmael once boasted to Isaac, saying, "I was thirteen years old when the Lord spoke to my father to circumcise us, and I did not transgress His word, which He commanded my father." And Isaac answered Ishmael, saying, "What dost thou boast to me about this, about a little bit of thy flesh which thou didst take from thy body, concerning which the Lord commanded thee? As the Lord liveth, the God of my father Abraham, if the Lord should say unto my father, Take now thy son Isaac and bring him up as an offering before Me, I would not refrain, but I would joyfully accede to it."

THE JOURNEY TO MORIAH

And the Lord thought to try Abraham and Isaac in this matter. And He said to Abraham, "Take now thy son."

Abraham: "I have two sons, and I do not know which of them Thou commandest me to take."

God: "Thine only son."

Abraham: "The one is the only son of his mother, and the other is the only son of his mother."

God: "Whom thou lovest."

Abraham: "I love this one and I love that one."

God: "Even Isaac."

Abraham: "And where shall I go?"

God: "To the land I will show thee, and offer Isaac there for a burnt offering."

Abraham: "Am I fit to perform the sacrifice, am I a priest? Ought not rather the high priest Shem to do it?"

God: "When thou wilt arrive at that place, I will consecrate thee and make thee a priest."

And Abraham said within himself, "How shall I separate my son Isaac from Sarah his mother?" And he came into the tent, and he sate before Sarah his wife, and he spake these words to her: "My son Isaac is grown up, and he has not yet studied the service of God. Now, to-morrow I will go and bring him to Shem and Eber his son, and there he will learn the ways of the Lord, for they will teach him to know the Lord, and to know how to pray unto the Lord that He may answer him, and to know the way of serving the Lord his God." And Sarah said, "Thou hast spoken well. Go, my lord, and do unto him as thou hast said, but remove him not far from me, neither let him remain there too long, for my soul is bound within his soul." And Abraham said unto Sarah, "My daughter, let us pray to the Lord our God that He may do good with us." And Sarah took her son Isaac, and he abode with her all that night, and she kissed and embraced him, and she laid injunctions upon him till morning, and she said to Abraham: "O my lord, I pray thee, take heed of thy son, and place thine eyes over him, for I have no other son nor daughter but him. O neglect him not. If he be hungry, give him bread, and if he be thirsty, give him water to drink; do not let him go on foot, neither let him sit in the sun, neither let him go by himself on the road, neither turn him from whatever he may desire, but do unto him as he may say to thee."

After spending the whole night in weeping on account of Isaac, she got up in the morning and selected a very fine and beautiful garment from those that Abimelech had given to her. And she dressed Isaac therewith, and she put a turban upon his head, and she fastened a precious stone in the top of the turban, and she gave them provisions for the road. And Sarah went out with them, and she accompanied them upon the road to see them off, and they said to her, "Return to the tent." And when Sarah heard the words of her son Isaac, she wept bitterly, and Abraham wept with her, and their son wept with them, a great weeping, also those of their servants who went with them wept greatly. And Sarah caught hold of Isaac, and she held him in her arms, and she embraced him, and continued to weep with him, and Sarah said, "Who knoweth if I shall ever see thee again after this day?"

Abraham departed with Isaac amid great weeping, while Sarah and the servants returned to the tent. He took two of his young men with him, Ishmael and Eliezer, and while they were walking in the road, the young men spoke these words to each other. Said Ishmael to Eliezer: "Now my father Abraham is going with Isaac to bring him up for a burnt offering to the Lord, and when he returneth, he will give unto me all that he possesses, to inherit after him, for I am his first-born." Eliezer answered: "Surely, Abraham did cast thee off with thy mother, and swear that thou shouldst not inherit anything of all he possesses. And to whom will he give all that he has, all his precious things, but unto his servant, who has been faithful in his house, to me, who have served him night and day, and have done all that he desired me?" The holy spirit answered, "Neither this one nor that one will inherit Abraham."

And while Abraham and Isaac were proceeding along the road, Satan came and appeared to Abraham in the figure of a very aged man, humble and of contrite spirit, and said to him: "Art thou silly or foolish, that thou goest to do this thing to thine only son? God gave thee a son in thy latter days, in thine old age, and wilt thou go and slaughter him, who did not commit any violence, and wilt thou cause the soul of thine only son to perish from the earth? Dost thou not know and understand that this thing cannot be from the Lord? For the Lord would not do unto man such evil, to command him, Go and slaughter thy son." Abraham, hearing these words, knew that it was Satan, who endeavored to turn him astray from the way of the Lord, and he rebuked him that he went away. And Satan returned and came to Isaac, and he appeared unto him in the figure of a young man, comely and well-favored, saying unto him: "Dost thou not know that thy silly old father bringeth thee to the slaughter this day for naught? Now, my son, do not listen to him, for he is a silly old man, and let not thy precious soul and beautiful figure be lost from the earth." And Isaac told these words to his father, but Abraham said to him, "Take heed of him, and do not listen to his words, for he is Satan endeavoring to lead us astray from the commands of our God." And Abraham rebuked Satan again, and Satan went from them, and, seeing he could not prevail over them, he transformed himself into a large brook of water in the road, and when Abraham, Isaac, and the two young men reached that place, they saw a brook large and powerful as the mighty waters. And they entered the brook, trying to pass it, but the further they went, the deeper the brook, so that the water reached up to their necks, and they were all terrified on account of the water. But Abraham recognized the place, and he knew that there had been no water there before, and he said to his son: "I know this place, on which there was no brook nor water. Now, surely, it is Satan who doth all this to us, to draw us aside this day from the commands of God." And Abraham rebuked Satan, saying unto him: "The Lord rebuke thee, O Satan. Begone from us, for we go by the command of God." And Satan was terrified at the voice of Abraham, and he went away from them, and the place became dry land again as it was at first. And Abraham went with Isaac toward the place that God had told him.

Satan then appeared unto Sarah in the figure of an old man, and said unto her, "Where did thine husband go?" She said, "To his work." "And where did thy son Isaac go?" he inquired further, and she answered, "He went with his father to a place of study of the Torah." Satan said: "O thou poor old woman, thy teeth will be set on edge on account of thy son, as thou knowest not that Abraham took his son with him on the road to sacrifice him." In this hour Sarah's loins trembled, and all her limbs shook. She was no more of this world. Nevertheless she aroused herself, and said, "All that God hath told Abraham, may he do it unto life and unto peace."

On the third day of his journey, Abraham lifted up his eyes and saw the place at a distance, which God had told him. He noticed upon the mountain a pillar of fire reaching from the earth to heaven, and a heavy cloud in which the glory of God was seen. Abraham said to Isaac, "My son, dost thou see on that mountain which we perceive at a distance that which I see upon it?" And Isaac answered, and said unto his father, "I see, and, lo, a pillar of fire and a cloud, and the glory of the Lord is seen upon the cloud." Abraham knew then that

Isaac was accepted before the Lord for an offering. He asked Ishmael and Eliezer, "Do you also see that which we see upon the mountain?" They answered, "We see nothing more than like the other mountains," and Abraham knew that they were not accepted before the Lord to go with them. Abraham said to them, "Abide ye here with the ass, you are like the ass--as little as it sees, so little do you see. I and Isaac my son go to yonder mount, and worship there before the Lord, and this eve we will return to you." An unconscious prophecy had come to Abraham, for he prophesied that he and Isaac would both return from the mountain. Eliezer and Ishmael remained in that place, as Abraham had commanded, while he and Isaac went further.

THE 'AKEDAH

And while they were walking along, Isaac spake unto his father, "Behold, the fire and the wood, but where then is the lamb for a burnt offering before the Lord?" And Abraham answered Isaac, saying, "The Lord hath chosen thee, my son, for a perfect burnt offering, instead of the lamb." And Isaac said unto his father, "I will do all that the Lord hath spoken to thee with joy and cheerfulness of heart." And Abraham again said unto Isaac his son, "Is there in thy heart any thought or counsel concerning this which is not proper? Tell me, my son, I pray thee! O my son, conceal it not from me." And Isaac answered, "As the Lord liveth, and as thy soul liveth, there is nothing in my heart to cause me to deviate either to the right or the left from the word that He hath spoken unto thee. Neither limb nor muscle hath moved or stirred on account of this, nor is there in my heart any thought or evil counsel concerning this. But I am joyful and cheerful of heart in this matter, and I say, Blessed is the Lord who has this day chosen me to be a burnt offering before Him."

Abraham greatly rejoiced at the words of Isaac, and they went on and came together to that place that the Lord had spoken of. And Abraham approached to build the altar in that place, and Abraham did build, while Isaac handed him stones and mortar, until they finished erecting the altar. And Abraham took the wood and arranged it upon the altar, and he bound Isaac, to place him upon the wood which was upon the altar, to slay him for a burnt offering before the Lord. Isaac spake hereupon: "Father, make haste, bare thine arm, and bind my hands and feet securely, for I am a young man, but thirty-seven years of age, and thou art an old man. When I behold the slaughtering knife in thy hand, I may perchance begin to tremble at the sight and push against thee, for the desire unto life is bold. Also I may do myself an injury and make myself unfit to be sacrificed. I adjure thee, therefore, my father, make haste, execute the will of thy Creator, delay not. Turn up thy garment, gird thy loins, and after that thou hast slaughtered me, burn me unto fine ashes. Then gather the ashes, and bring them to Sarah, my mother, and place them in a casket in her chamber. At all hours, whenever she enters her chamber, she will remember her son Isaac and weep for him."

And again Isaac spoke: "As soon as thou hast slaughtered me, and hast separated thyself from me, and returnest to Sarah my mother, and she asketh thee, Where is my son Isaac? what wilt thou answer her, and what will you two do in your old age?" Abraham answered, and said, "We know we can survive thee by a few days only. He who was our Comfort before thou wast born, will comfort us now and henceforth."

After he had laid the wood in order, and bound Isaac on the altar, upon the wood, Abraham braced his arms, rolled up his garments, and leaned his knees upon Isaac with all his strength. And God, sitting upon His throne, high and exalted, saw how the hearts of the two were the same, and tears were rolling down from the eyes of Abraham upon Isaac, and from Isaac down upon the wood, so that it was submerged in tears. When Abraham stretched forth his hand, and took the knife to slay his son, God spoke to the angels: "Do you see how Abraham my friend proclaims the unity of My Name in the world? Had I hearkened unto you at the time of the creation of the world, when ye spake, What is man, that Thou art mindful of him? And the son of man, that Thou visitest him? who would there have been to make known the unity of My Name in this world?" The angels then broke into loud weeping, and they exclaimed: "The highways lie waste, the wayfaring man ceaseth, he hath broken the covenant. Where is the reward of Abraham, he who took the wayfarers into his house, gave them food and drink, and went with them to bring them on the way? The covenant is broken, whereof Thou didst speak to him, saying, 'For in Isaac shall thy seed be called,' and saying, 'My covenant will I establish with Isaac,' for the slaughtering knife is set upon his throat."

The tears of the angels fell upon the knife, so that it could not cut Isaac's throat, but from terror his soul escaped from him. Then God spoke to the archangel Michael, and said: "Why standest thou here? Let him not be slaughtered." Without delay, Michael, anguish in his voice, cried out: "Abraham! Abraham! Lay not thine hand upon the lad, neither do thou any thing unto him!" Abraham made answer, and he said: "God did command me to slaughter Isaac, and thou dost command me not to slaughter him! The words of the Teacher and the words of the disciple- unto whose words doth one hearken?" Then Abraham heard it said: "By Myself have I sworn, saith the Lord, because thou hast done this thing, and hast not withheld thy son, thine only son, that in blessing I will bless thee, and in multiplying I will multiply thy seed as the stars of the heaven, and as the sand which is upon the sea-shore; and thy seed shall possess the gate of his enemies, and in thy seed shall all the nations of the earth be blessed, because thou hast obeyed My voice."

At once Abraham left off from Isaac, who returned to life, revived by the heavenly voice admonishing Abraham not to slaughter his son. Abraham loosed his bonds, and Isaac stood upon his feet, and spoke the benediction, "Blessed art Thou, O Lord, who quickenest the dead."

Then spake Abraham to God, "Shall I go hence without having offered up a sacrifice?" Whereunto God replied, and said, "Lift up thine eyes, and behold the sacrifice behind thee." And Abraham lifted up his eyes, and, behold, behind him a ram caught in the thicket, which God had created in the twilight of Sabbath eve in the week of creation, and prepared since then as a burnt offering instead of Isaac. And the ram had been running toward Abraham, when Satan caught hold of him and entangled his horns in the thicket, that he might not advance to Abraham. And Abraham, seeing this, fetched him from the thicket, and brought him upon the altar as an offering in the place of his son Isaac. And Abraham sprinkled the blood of the ram upon the altar, and he exclaimed, and said, "This is instead of my son, and may this be considered as the blood of my son before the Lord." And whatsoever Abraham did by the altar, he exclaimed, and said, "This is instead of my son, and may it be considered before the Lord in place of my son." And God accepted the sacrifice of the ram, and it was accounted as though it had been Isaac.

As the creation of this ram had been extraordinary, so also was the use to which all parts of his carcass were put. Not one thing went to waste. The ashes of the parts burnt upon the altar formed the foundation of the inner altar, whereon the expiatory sacrifice was brought once a year, on the Day of Atonement, the day on which the offering of Isaac took place. Of the sinews of the ram, David made ten strings for his harp upon which he played. The skin served Elijah for his girdle, and of his two horns, the one was blown at the end of the revelation on Mount Sinai, and the other will be used to proclaim the end of the Exile, when the "great horn shall be blown, and they shall come which were ready to perish in the land of Assyria, and they that were outcasts in the land of Egypt, and they shall worship the Lord in the holy mountain at Jerusalem."

When God commanded the father to desist from sacrificing Isaac, Abraham said: "One man tempts another, because he knoweth not what is in the heart of his neighbor. But Thou surely didst know that I was ready to sacrifice my son!"

God: "It was manifest to Me, and I foreknew it, that thou wouldst withhold not even thy soul from Me."

Abraham: "And why, then, didst Thou afflict me thus?"

God: "It was My wish that the world should become acquainted with thee, and should know that it is not without good reason that I have chosen thee from all the nations. Now it hath been witnessed unto men that thou fearest God."

Hereupon God opened the heavens, and Abraham heard the words, "By Myself I swear!"

Abraham: "Thou swearest, and also I swear, I will not leave this altar until I have said what I have to say."

God: "Speak whatsoever thou hast to speak!"

Abraham: "Didst Thou not promise me Thou wouldst let one come forth out of mine own bowels, whose seed should fill the whole world?"

God: "Yes."

Abraham: "Whom didst Thou mean?"

God: "Isaac."

Abraham: "Didst Thou not promise me to make my seed as numerous as the sand of the sea-shore?"

God: "Yes."

Abraham: "Through which one of my children?"

God: "Through Isaac."

Abraham: "I might have reproached Thee, and said, O Lord of the world, yesterday Thou didst tell me, In Isaac shall Thy seed be called, and now Thou sayest, Take thy son, thine only son, even Isaac, and offer him for a burnt offering. But I refrained myself, and I said nothing. Thus mayest Thou, when the children of Isaac commit trespasses and because of them fall upon evil times, be mindful of the offering of their father Isaac, and forgive their sins and deliver them from their suffering."

God: "Thou hast said what thou hadst to say, and I will now say what I have to say. Thy children will sin before me in time to come, and I will sit in judgment upon them on the New Year's Day. If they desire that I should grant them pardon, they shall blow the ram's horn on that day, and I, mindful of the ram that was substituted for Isaac as a sacrifice, will forgive them for their sins."

Furthermore, the Lord revealed unto Abraham that the Temple, to be erected on the spot of Isaac's offering, would be destroyed, and as the ram substituted for Isaac extricated himself from one tree but to be caught in another, so his children would pass from kingdom to kingdom--delivered from Babylonia they would be subjugated by Media, rescued from Media they would be enslaved by Greece, escaped from Greece they would serve Rome--yet in the end they would be redeemed in a final redemption, at the sound of the ram's horn, when "the Lord God shall blow the trumpet, and shall go with whirlwinds of the south."

The place on which Abraham had erected the altar was the same whereon Adam had brought the first sacrifice, and Cain and Abel had offered their gifts to God--the same whereon Noah raised an altar to God after he left the ark; and Abraham, who knew that it was the place appointed for the Temple, called it Yireh, for it would be the abiding place of the fear and the service of God. But as Shem had given it the name Shalem, Place of Peace, and God would not give offence to either Abraham or Shem, He united the two names, and called the city by the name Jerusalem.

After the sacrifice on Mount Moriah, Abraham returned to Beer-sheba, the scene of so many of his joys. Isaac was carried to Paradise by angels, and there he sojourned for three years. Thus Abraham returned home alone, and when Sarah beheld him, she exclaimed, "Satan spoke truth when he said that Isaac was sacrificed," and so grieved was her soul that it fled from her body.

THE DEATH AND BURIAL OF SARAH

While Abraham was engaged in the sacrifice, Satan went to Sarah, and appeared to her in the figure of an old man, very humble and meek, and said to her: "Dost thou not know all that Abraham has done unto thine only son this day? He took Isaac, and built an altar, slaughtered him, and brought him up as a sacrifice. Isaac cried and wept before his father, but he looked not at him, neither did he have compassion upon him." After saying these words to Sarah, Satan went away from her, and she thought him to be an old man from amongst the sons of men who had been with her son. Sarah lifted up her voice, and cried bitterly, saying: "O my son, Isaac, my son, O that I had this day died instead of thee I It grieves me for thee! After that I have reared thee and have brought thee up, my joy is turned into mourning over thee. In my longing for a child, I cried and prayed, till I bore thee at ninety. Now hast thou served this day for the knife and the fire. But I console myself, it being the word of God, and thou didst perform the command of thy God, for who can transgress the word of our God, in whose hands is the soul of every living creature? Thou art just, O Lord our God, for all Thy works are good and righteous, for I also rejoice with the word which Thou didst command, and while mine eye weepeth bitterly, my heart rejoiceth." And Sarah laid her head upon the bosom of one of her handmaids, and she became as still as a stone.

She rose up afterward and went about making inquiries concerning her son, till she came to Hebron, and no one could tell her what had happened to her son. Her servants went to seek him in the house of Shem and Eber, and they could not find him, and they sought throughout the land, and he was not there. And, behold, Satan came to Sarah in the shape of an old man, and said unto her, "I spoke falsely unto thee, for Abraham did not kill his son, and he is not dead," and when she heard the word, her joy was so exceedingly violent that her soul went out through joy.

When Abraham with Isaac returned to Beer-sheba, they sought for Sarah and could not find her, and when they made inquiries concerning her, they were told that she had gone as far as Hebron to seek them. Abraham and Isaac went to her to Hebron, and when they found that she was dead, they cried bitterly over her, and Isaac said: "O my mother, my mother, how hast thou left me, and whither hast thou gone? O whither hast thou gone, and how hast thou left me?" And Abraham and all his servants wept and mourned over her a great and heavy mourning," even that Abraham did not pray, but spent his time in mourning and weeping over Sarah. And, indeed, he had great reason to mourn his loss, for even in her old age Sarah had retained the beauty of her youth and the innocence of her childhood.

The death of Sarah was a loss not only for Abraham and his family, but for the whole country. So long as she was alive, all went well in the land. After her death confusion ensued. The weeping, lamenting, and wailing over her going hence was universal, and Abraham, instead of receiving consolation, had to offer consolation to others. He spoke to the mourning people, and said: "My children, take not the going hence of Sarah too much to heart. There is one event unto all, to the pious and the impious alike. I pray you now, give me a burying-place with you, not as a gift, but for money."

In these last few words Abraham's unassuming modesty was expressed. God had promised him the whole land, yet when he came to bury his dead, he had to pay for the grave, and it did not enter his heart to cast aspersions upon the ways of God. In all humility he spoke to the people of Hebron, saying, "I am a stranger and a sojourner with you." Therefore spake God to him, and said, "Thou didst bear thyself modestly. As thou livest, I will appoint thee lord and prince over them."

To the people themselves he appeared an angel, and they answered his words, saying: "Thou art a prince of God among us. In the choice of our sepulchres bury thy dead, among the rich if thou wilt, or among the poor if thou wilt."

Abraham first of all gave thanks to God for the friendly feeling shown to him by the children of Heth, and then he continued his negotiations for the Cave of Machpelah. He had long known the peculiar value of this spot. Adam had chosen it as a burial-place for himself. He had feared his body might be used for idolatrous purposes after his death; he therefore designated the Cave of Machpelah as the place of his burial, and in the depths his corpse was laid, so that none might find it. When he interred Eve there, he wanted to dig deeper, because he scented the sweet fragrance of Paradise, near the entrance to which it lay, but a heavenly voice called to him, Enough! Adam himself was buried there by Seth, and until the time of Abraham the place was guarded by angels, who kept a fire burning near it perpetually, so that none dared approach it and bury his dead therein. Now, it happened on the day when Abraham received the angels in his house, and he wanted to slaughter an ox for their entertainment, that the ox ran away, and in his pursuit of him Abraham entered the Cave of Machpelah. There he saw Adam and Eve stretched out upon couches, candles burning at the head of their resting-places, while a sweet scent pervaded the cave.

Therefore Abraham wished to acquire the Cave of Machpelah from the children of Heth, the inhabitants of the city of Jebus. They said to him. "We know that in time to come God will give these lands unto thy seed, and now do thou swear a covenant with us that Israel shall not wrest the city of Jebus from its inhabitants without their consent." Abraham agreed to the condition, and he acquired the field from Ephron, in whose possession it lay.

This happened the very day on which Ephron had been made the chief of the children of Heth, and he had been raised to the position so that Abraham might not have to have dealings with a man of low rank. It was of advantage to Abraham, too, for Ephron at first refused to sell his field, and only the threat of the children of Heth to depose him from his office, unless he fulfilled the desire of Abraham, could induce him to change his disposition.

Dissembling deceitfully, Ephron then offered to give Abraham the field without compensation, but when Abraham insisted upon paying for it, Ephron said: "My lord, hearken unto me. A piece of land worth four hundred shekels of silver, what is that betwixt me and thee?" showing only too well that the money was of the greatest consequence to him. Abraham understood his words, and when he came to pay for the field, he weighed out the sum agreed upon between them in the best of current coin. A deed, signed by four witnesses, was drawn up, and the field of Ephron, which was in Machpelah, the field, and the cave which was therein, were made sure unto Abraham and his descendants for all times.

The burial of Sarah then took place, amid great magnificence and the sympathy of all. Shem and his son Eber, Abimelech king of the Philistines, Aner, Eshcol, and Mamre, as well as all the great of the land, followed her bier. A seven days' mourning was kept for her, and all the inhabitants of the land came to condole with Abraham and Isaac.

When Abraham entered the cave to place the body of Sarah within, Adam and Eve refused to remain there, "because," they said, "as it is, we are ashamed in the presence of God on account of the sin we committed, and now we shall be even more ashamed on account of your good deeds." Abraham soothed Adam. He promised to pray to God for him, that the need for shame be removed from him. Adam resumed his place, and Abraham entombed Sarah, and at the same time he carried Eve, resisting, back to her place.

One year after the death of Sarah, Abimelech king of the Philistines died, too, at the age of one hundred and ninety-three years. His successor upon the throne was his twelve-year old son Benmelek, who took the name of his father after his accession. Abraham did not fail to pay a visit of condolence at the court of Abimelech.

Lot also died about this time, at the age of one hundred and forty-two. His sons, Moab and Ammon, both married Canaanitish wives. Moab begot a son, and Ammon had six sons, and the descendants of both were numerous exceedingly.

Abraham suffered a severe loss at the same time in the death of his brother Nahor, whose days ended at Haran, when he had reached the age of one hundred and seventy two years.

ELIEZER'S MISSION

The death of Sarah dealt Abraham a blow from which he did not recover. So long as she was alive, he felt himself young and vigorous, but after she had passed away, old age suddenly overtook him. It was he himself who made the plea that age be betrayed by suitable signs and tokens. Before the time of Abraham an old man was not distinguishable externally from a young man, and as Isaac was the image of his father, it happened frequently that father and son were mistaken for each other, and a request meant for the one was preferred to the other. Abraham prayed therefore that old age might have marks to distinguish it from youth, and God granted his petition, and since the time of Abraham the appearance of men changes in old age. This is one of the seven great wonders that have occurred in the course of history.

The blessing of God did not forsake Abraham in old age, either. That it might not be said it had been granted to him only for the sake of Sarah, God prospered him after her death, too. Hagar bore him a daughter, and Ishmael repented of his evil ways and subordinated himself to Isaac. And as Abraham enjoyed undisturbed happiness in his family, so also outside, in the world. The kings of the east and the west eagerly besieged the door of his house in order to derive benefit from his wisdom. From his neck a precious stone was suspended, which possessed the power of healing the sick who looked upon it. On the death of Abraham, God attached it to the wheel of the sun. The greatest blessing enjoyed by him, and by none beside except his son Isaac and Jacob the son of Isaac, was that the evil inclination had no power over him, so that in this life he had a foretaste of the future world.

But all these Divine blessings showered upon Abraham were not undeserved. He was clean of hand, and pure of heart, one that did not lift up his soul unto vanity.

He fulfilled all the commands that were revealed later, even the Rabbinical injunctions, as, for instance, the one relating to the limits of a Sabbath day's journey, wherefor his reward was that God disclosed to him the new teachings which He expounded daily in the heavenly academy.

But one thing lacked to complete the happiness of Abraham, the marriage of Isaac. He therefore called his old servant Eliezer unto himself. Eliezer resembled his master not only externally, in his appearance, but also spiritually. Like Abraham he possessed full power over the evil inclination, and like the master, the servant was an adept in the law. Abraham spake the following words to Eliezer: "I am stricken in age, and I know not the day of my death. Therefore prepare thyself, and go unto my country, and to my kindred, and fetch hither a wife for my son." Thus he spake by reason of the resolution he had taken immediately after the sacrifice of Isaac on Moriah, for he had there said within himself, that if the sacrifice had been executed, Isaac would have gone hence childless. He was even ready to choose a wife for his son from among the daughters of his three friends, Aner, Eshcol, and Mamre, because he knew them to be pious, and he did not attach much importance to aristocratic stock. Then spake God to him, and said: "Concern thyself not about a wife for Isaac. One has already been provided for him," and it was made known to Abraham that Milcah, the wife of his brother Nahor, childless until the birth of Isaac, had then been remembered by God and made fruitful. She bore Bethuel, and he in turn, at the time of Isaac's sacrifice, begot the daughter destined to be the wife of Isaac.

Mindful of the proverb, "Even if the wheat of thine own place be darnel, use it for seed," Abraham determined to take a wife for Isaac from his own family. He argued that as any wife he chose would have to become a proselyte, it would be best to use his own stock, which had the first claim upon him.

Eliezer now said to his master: "Peradventure no woman will be willing to follow me unto this land. May I then marry my own daughter to Isaac?" "No," replied Abraham, "thou art of the accursed race, and my son is of the blessed race, and curse and blessing cannot be united. But beware thou that thou bring not my son again unto the land from whence I came, for if thou broughtest him thither again, it were as though thou tookest him to hell. God who sets the heavens in motion, He will set this matter right, too, and He that took me from my father's house, and that spake unto me, and that swore unto me in Haran, and at the covenant of the pieces, that He would give this land unto my seed, He shall send His excellent angel before thee, and thou shalt take a wife for my son from thence." Eliezer then swore to his master concerning the matter, and Abraham made him take the oath by the sign of the covenant.

THE WOOING OF REBEKAH

Attended by ten men, mounted upon ten camels laden with jewels and trinkets, Eliezer betook himself to Haran under the convoy of two angels, the one appointed to keep guard over Eliezer, the other over Rebekah.

The journey to Haran took but a few hours, at evening of the same day he reached there, because the earth hastened to meet him in a wonderful way. He made a halt at the well of water, and he prayed to God to permit him to distinguish the wife appointed for Isaac among the damsels that came to draw water, by this token, that she alone, and not the others, would give him drink. Strictly speaking, this wish of his was unseemly, for suppose a bondwoman had given him water to drink! But God granted his request. All the damsels said they could not give him of their water, because they had to take it home. Then appeared Rebekah, coming to the well contrary to her wont, for she was the daughter of a king, Bethuel her father being king of Haran. When Eliezer addressed his request for water to drink to this young innocent child, not only was she ready to do his bidding, but she rebuked the other maidens on account of their discourtesy to a stranger. Eliezer noticed, too, how the water rose up to her of its own accord from the bottom of the well, so that she needed not to exert herself to draw it. Having scrutinized her carefully, he felt certain that she was the wife chosen for Isaac. He gave her a nose ring, wherein was set a precious stone, half a shekel in weight, foreshadowing the half-shekel which her descendants would once bring to the sanctuary year by year. He gave her also two bracelets for her hands, of ten shekels weight in gold, in token of the two tables of stone and the Ten Commandments upon them.

When Rebekah, bearing the jewels, came to her mother and to her brother Laban, this one hastened to Eliezer in order to slay him and take possession of his goods. Laban soon learnt that he would not be able to do much harm to a giant like Eliezer. He met him at the moment when Eliezer seized two camels and bore them across the stream. Besides, on account of Eliezer's close resemblance to Abraham, Laban thought he saw Abraham before him, and he said: "Come in, thou blessed of the Lord! It is not becoming that thou shouldst stand without, I have cleansed my house of idols."

But when Eliezer arrived at the house of Bethuel, they tried to kill him with cunning. They set poisoned food before him. Luckily, he refused to eat before he had discharged himself of his errand. While he was telling his story, it was ordained by God that the dish intended for him should come to stand in front of Bethuel, who ate of it and died.

Eliezer showed the document he had in which Abraham deeded all his possessions to Isaac, and he made it known to the kindred of Abraham, how deeply attached to them his master was, in spite of the long years of separation. Yet he let them know at the same time that Abraham was not dependent wholly upon them. He might seek a wife for his son among the daughters of Ishmael or Lot. At first the kindred of Abraham consented to let Rebekah go with Eliezer, but as Bethuel had died in the meantime, they did not want to give Rebekah in marriage without consulting her. Besides, they deemed it proper that she should remain at home at least during the week of mourning for her father. But Eliezer, seeing the angel wait for him, would brook no delay, and he said, "The man who came with me and prospered my way, waits for me without," and as Rebekah professed herself ready to go at once with Eliezer, her mother and brother granted her wish and dismissed her with their blessings. But their blessings did not come from the bottom of their hearts. Indeed, as a rule, the blessing of the impious is a curse, wherefore Rebekah remained barren for years.

Eliezer's return to Canaan was as wonderful as his going to Haran had been. A seventeen days' journey he accomplished in three hours. He left Haran at noon, and he arrived at Hebron at three o'clock in the afternoon, the time for the Minhah Prayer, which had been introduced by Isaac. He was in the posture of praying when Rebekah first laid eyes upon him, wherefore she asked Eliezer what man this was. She saw he was not an ordinary individual. She noticed the unusual beauty of Isaac, and also that an angel accompanied him. Thus her question was not dictated by mere curiosity. At this moment she learnt through the holy spirit, that she was destined to be the mother of the godless Esau. Terror seized her at the knowledge, and, trembling, she fell from the camel and inflicted an injury upon herself.

After Isaac had heard the wonderful adventures of Eliezer, he took Rebekah to the tent of his mother Sarah, and she showed herself worthy to be her successor. The cloud appeared again that had been visible over the tent during the life of Sarah, and had vanished at her death; the light shone again in the tent of Rebekah that Sarah had kindled at the coming in of the Sabbath, and that had burnt miraculously throughout the week; the blessing returned with Rebekah that had hovered over the dough kneaded by Sarah; and the gates of the tent were opened for the needy, wide and spacious, as they had been during the lifetime of Sarah.

For three years Isaac had mourned for his mother, and he could find no consolation in the academy of Shem and Eber, his abiding-place during that period. But Rebekah comforted him after his mother's death, for she was the counterpart of Sarah in person and in spirit.

As a reward for having executed to his full satisfaction the mission with which he had charged him, Abraham set his bondman free. The curse resting upon Eliezer, as upon all the descendants of Canaan, was transformed into a blessing, because he ministered unto Abraham loyally. Greatest reward of all, God found him worthy of entering Paradise alive, a distinction that fell to the lot of very few.

THE LAST YEARS OF ABRAHAM

Rebekah first saw Isaac as he was coming from the way of Beer-lahai-roi, the dwelling-place of Hagar, whither he had gone after the death of his mother, for the purpose of reuniting his father with Hagar, or, as she is also called, Keturah.

Hagar bore him six sons, who, however, did scant honor to their father, for they all were idolaters. Abraham, therefore, during his own lifetime, sent them away from the presence of Isaac, that they might not be singed by Isaac's flame, and gave them the instruction to journey eastward as far as possible. There he built a city for them, surrounded by an iron wall, so high that the sun could not shine into the city. But Abraham provided them with huge gems and pearls, their lustre more brilliant than the light of the sun, which will be used in the Messianic time when "the moon shall be confounded and the sun ashamed." Also Abraham taught them the black art, wherewith they held sway over demons and spirits. It is from this city in the east that Laban, Balaam, and Balaam's father Beor derived their sorceries.

Epher, one of the grandsons of Abraham and Keturah, invaded Lybia with an armed force, and took possession of the country. From this Epher the whole land of Africa has its name. Aram is also a country made habitable by a kinsman of Abraham. In his old age Terah contracted a new marriage with Pelilah, and from this union sprang a son Zoba, who was the father in turn of three sons. The oldest of these, Aram, was exceedingly rich and powerful, and the old home in Haran sufficed not for him and his kinsmen, the sons of Nahor, the brother of Abraham. Aram and his brethren and all that belonged to him therefore departed from Haran, and they settled in a vale, and they built themselves a city there which they called Aram-Zoba, to perpetuate the name of the father and his first-born son. Another Aram, Aram-naharaim, on the Euphrates, was built by Aram son of Kemuel, a nephew of Abraham. Its real name was Petor, after the son of Aram, but it is better known as Aram-naharaim. The descendants of Kesed, another nephew of Abraham, a son of his brother Nahor, established themselves opposite to Shinar, where they founded the city of Kesed, the city whence the Chaldees are called Kasdim.

Though Abraham knew full well that Isaac deserved his paternal blessing beyond all his sons, yet he withheld it from him, that no hostile feelings be aroused among his descendants. He spake, and said: "I am but flesh and blood, here to-day, to-morrow in the grave. What I was able to do for my children I have done. Henceforth let come what God desires to do in His world," and it happened that immediately after the death of Abraham God Himself appeared unto Isaac, and gave him His blessing.

A HERALD OF DEATH

When the day of the death of Abraham drew near, the Lord said to Michael, "Arise and go to Abraham and say to him, Thou shalt depart from life!" so that he might set his house in order before he died. And Michael went and came to Abraham and found him sitting before his oxen for ploughing. Abraham, seeing Michael, but not knowing who he was, saluted him and said to him, "Sit down a little while, and I will order a beast to be brought, and we will go to my house, that thou mayest rest with me, for it is toward evening, and arise in the morning and go whithersoever thou wilt." And Abraham called one of his servants, and said to him: "Go and bring me a beast, that the stranger may sit upon it, for he is wearied with his journey." But Michael said, "I abstain from ever sitting upon any fourfooted beast, let us walk therefore, till we reach the house."

On their way to the house they passed a huge tree, and Abraham heard a voice from its branches, singing, "Holy art thou, because thou hast kept the purpose for which thou wast sent." Abraham hid the mystery in his heart, thinking that the stranger did not hear it. Arrived at his house, he ordered the servants to prepare a meal, and while they were busy with their work, he called his son Isaac, and said to him, "Arise and put water in the vessel, that we may wash the feet of the stranger." And he brought it as he was commanded, and Abraham said, "I perceive that in this basin I shall never again wash the feet of any man coming to us as a guest." Hearing this, Isaac began to weep, and Abraham, seeing his son weep, also wept, and Michael, seeing them weep, wept also, and the tears of Michael fell into the water, and became precious stones.

Before sitting down to the table, Michael arose, went out for a moment, as if to ease nature, and ascended to heaven in the twinkling of an eye, and stood before the Lord, and said to Him: "Lord and Master, let Thy power know that I am unable to remind that righteous man of his death, for I have not seen upon the earth a man like him, compassionate, hospitable, righteous, truthful, devout, refraining from every evil deed." Then the Lord said to Michael, "Go down to My friend Abraham, and whatever he may say to thee, that do thou also, and whatever he may eat, eat thou also with him, and I will cast the thought of the death of Abraham into the heart of Isaac, his son, in a dream, and Isaac will relate the dream, and thou shalt interpret it, and he himself will know his end." And Michael said, "Lord, all the heavenly spirits are incorporeal, and neither eat nor drink, and this man has set before me a table with an abundance of all good things earthly and corruptible. Now, Lord, what shall I do?" The Lord answered him, "Go down to him and take no thought for this, for when thou sittest down with him, I will send upon thee a devouring spirit, and it will consume out of thy hands and through thy mouth all that is on the table."

Then Michael went into the house of Abraham, and they ate and drank and were merry. And when the supper was ended, Abraham prayed after his custom, and Michael prayed with him, and each lay down to sleep upon his couch in one room, while Isaac went to his chamber, lest he be troublesome to the guest. About the seventh hour of the night, Isaac awoke and came to the door of his father's chamber, crying out and saying, "Open, father, that I may touch thee before they take thee away from me." And Abraham wept together with his son, and when Michael saw them weep, he wept likewise. And Sarah, hearing the weeping, called forth from her bedchamber, saying: "My lord Abraham, why this weeping? Has the stranger told thee of thy brother's son Lot, that he is dead? or has aught befallen us?" Michael answered, and said to her, "Nay, my sister Sarah, it is not as thou sayest, but thy son Isaac, methinks, beheld a dream, and came to us weeping, and we, seeing him, were moved in our hearts and wept." Sarah, hearing Michael speak, knew straightway that it was an angel of the Lord, one of the three angels whom they had entertained in their house once before, and therefore she made a sign to Abraham to come out toward the door, to inform him of what she knew. Abraham said: "Thou hast perceived well, for I, too, when I washed his feet, knew in my heart that they were the feet that I had washed at the oak of Mamre, and that went to save Lot." Abraham, returning to his chamber, made Isaac relate his dream, which Michael interpreted to them, saying: "Thy son Isaac has spoken truth, for thou shalt go and be taken up into the heavens, but thy body shall remain on earth, until seven thousand ages are fulfilled, for then all flesh shall arise. Now, therefore, Abraham, set thy house in order, for thou wast heard what is decreed concerning thee." Abraham answered, "Now I know thou art an angel of the Lord, and wast sent to take my soul, but I will not go with thee, but do thou whatever thou art commanded." Michael returned to heaven and told God of Abraham's refusal to obey his summons, and he was again commanded to go down and admonish Abraham not to rebel against God, who had bestowed many blessings upon him, and he reminded him that no one who has come from Adam and Eve can escape death, and that God in His great kindness toward him did not permit the sickle of death to meet him, but sent His chief captain, Michael, to him. "Wherefore, then," he ended, "hast thou said to the chief captain, I will not go with thee?" When Michael delivered these exhortations to Abraham, he saw that it was futile to oppose the will of God, and he consented to die, but wished to have one desire of his fulfilled while still alive. He said to Michael: "I beseech thee, lord, if I must depart from my body, I desire to be taken up in my body, that I may see the creatures that the Lord has created in heaven and on earth." Michael went up into heaven, and spake before the Lord concerning Abraham, and the Lord answered Michael, "Go and take up Abraham in the body and show him all things, and whatever he shall say to thee, do to him as to My friend."

ABRAHAM VIEWS EARTH AND HEAVEN

The archangel Michael went down, and took Abraham upon a chariot of the cherubim, and lifted him up into the air of heaven, and led him upon the cloud, together with sixty angels, and Abraham ascended upon the chariot over all the earth, and saw all things that are below on the earth, both good and bad. Looking down upon the earth, he saw a man committing adultery with a wedded woman, and turning to Michael he said, "Send fire from heaven to consume them." Straightway there came down fire and consumed them, for God had commanded Michael to do whatsoever Abraham should ask him to do. He looked again, and he saw thieves digging through a house, and Abraham said, "Let wild beasts come out of the desert, and tear them in pieces," and immediately wild beasts came out of the desert and devoured them. Again he looked down, and he saw people preparing to commit murder, and he said, "Let the earth open and swallow them," and, as he spoke, the earth swallowed them alive. Then God spoke to Michael: "Turn away Abraham to his own house and let him not go round the whole earth, because he has no compassion on sinners, but I have compassion on sinners, that they may turn and live and repent of their sins, and be saved."

So Michael turned the chariot, and brought Abraham to the place of judgment of all souls. Here he saw two gates, the one broad and the other narrow, the narrow gate that of the just, which leads to life, they that enter through it go into Paradise. The broad gate is that of sinners, which leads to destruction and eternal punishment. Then Abraham wept, saying, "Woe is me, what shall I do? for I am a man big of body, and how shall I be able to enter by the narrow gate?" Michael answered, and said to Abraham, "Fear not, nor grieve, for thou shalt enter by it unhindered, and all they who are like thee." Abraham, perceiving that a soul was adjudged to be set in the midst, asked Michael the reason for it, and Michael answered, "Because the judge found its sins and its righteousness equal, he neither committed it to judgment nor to be saved." Abraham said to Michael, "Let us pray for this soul, and see whether God will hear us," and when they rose up from their prayer, Michael informed Abraham that the soul was saved by the prayer, and was taken by an angel and carried up to Paradise. Abraham said to Michael, "Let us yet call upon the Lord and supplicate His compassion and entreat His mercy for the souls of the sinners whom I formerly, in my anger, cursed and destroyed, whom the earth devoured, and the wild beasts tore in pieces, and the fire consumed, through my words. Now I know that I have sinned before the Lord our God."

After the joint prayer of the archangel and Abraham, there came a voice from heaven, saying, "Abraham, Abraham, I have hearkened to thy voice and thy prayer, and I forgive thee thy sin, and those whom thou thinkest that I destroyed, I have called up and brought them into life by My exceeding kindness, because for a season I have requited them in judgment, and those whom I destroy living upon earth, I will not requite in death."

When Michael brought Abraham back to his house, they found Sarah dead. Not seeing what had become of Abraham, she was consumed with grief and gave up her soul. Though Michael had fulfilled Abraham's wish, and had shown him all the earth and the judgment and recompense, he still refused to surrender his soul to Michael, and the archangel again ascended to heaven, and said unto the Lord: "Thus speaks Abraham, I will not go with thee, and I refrain from laying my hands on him, because from the beginning he was Thy friend, and he has done all things pleasing in Thy sight. There is no man like him on earth, not even Job, the wondrous man." But when the day of the death of Abraham drew nigh, God commanded Michael to adorn Death with great beauty and send him thus to Abraham, that he might see him with his eyes.

While sitting under the oak of Mamre, Abraham perceived a flashing of light and a smell of sweet odor, and turning around he saw Death coming toward him in great glory and beauty. And Death said unto Abraham: "Think not, Abraham, that this beauty is mine, or that I come thus to every man. Nay, but if any one is righteous like thee, I thus take a crown and come to him, but if he is a sinner, I come in great corruption, and out of their sins I make a crown for my head, and I shake them with great fear, so that they are dismayed." Abraham said to him, "And art thou, indeed, he that is called Death?" He answered, and said, "I am the bitter name," but Abraham answered, "I will not go with thee." And Abraham said to Death, "Show us thy corruption." And Death revealed his corruption, showing two heads, the one had the face of a serpent, the other head was like a sword. All the servants of Abraham, looking at the fierce mien of Death, died, but Abraham prayed to the Lord, and he raised them up. As the looks of Death were not able to cause Abraham's soul to depart from him, God removed the soul of Abraham as in a dream, and the archangel Michael took it up into heaven. After great praise and glory had been given to the Lord by the angels who brought Abraham's soul, and after Abraham bowed down to worship, then came the voice of God, saying thus: "Take My friend Abraham into Paradise, where are the tabernacles of My righteous ones and the abodes of My saints Isaac and Jacob in his bosom, where there is no trouble, nor grief, nor sighing, but peace and rejoicing and life unending."

Abraham's activity did not cease with his death, and as he interceded in this world for the sinners, so will he intercede for them in the world to come. On the day of judgment he will sit at the gate of hell, and he will not suffer those who kept the law of circumcision to enter therein.

THE PATRON OF HEBRON

Once upon a time some Jews lived in Hebron, few in number, but pious and good, and particularly hospitable. When strangers came to the Cave of Machpelah to pray there, the inhabitants of the place fairly quarreled with each other for the privilege of entertaining the guests, and the one who carried off the victory rejoiced as though he had found great spoil.

On the eve of the Day of Atonement, it appeared that, in spite of all their efforts, the dwellers at Hebron could not secure the tenth man needed for public Divine service, and they feared they would have none on the holy day. Toward evening, when the sun was about to sink, they descried an old man with silver white beard, bearing a sack upon his shoulder, his raiment tattered, and his feet badly swollen from much walking. They ran to meet him, took him to one of the houses, gave him food and drink, and, after supplying him with new white garments, they all together went to the synagogue for worship. Asked what his name was, the stranger replied, Abraham.

At the end of the fast, the residents of Hebron cast lots for the privilege of entertaining the guest. Fortune favored the beadle, who, the envy of the rest, bore his guest away to his house. On the way, he suddenly disappeared, and the beadle could not find him anywhere. In vain all the Jews of the place went on a quest for him. Their sleepless night, spent in searching, had no result. The stranger could not be found. But no sooner had the beadle lain down, toward morning, weary and anxious, to snatch some sleep, than he saw the lost guest before him, his face luminous as lightning, and his garments magnificent and studded with gems radiant as the sun. Before the beadle, stunned by fright, could open his mouth, the stranger spake, and said: "I am Abraham the Hebrew, your ancestor, who rests here in the Cave of Machpelah. When I saw how grieved you were at not having the number of men prescribed for a public service, I came forth to you. Have no fear! Rejoice and be merry of heart!"

On another occasion Abraham granted his assistance to the people of Hebron. The lord of the city was a heartless man, who oppressed the Jews sorely. One day he commanded them to pay a large sum of money into his coffers, the whole sum in uniform coins, all stamped with the same year. It was but a pretext to kill the Jews. He knew that his demand was impossible of fulfillment.

The Jews proclaimed a fast and day of public prayer, on which to supplicate God that He turn aside the sword suspended above them. The night following, the beadle in a dream saw an awe-inspiring old man, who addressed him in the following words: "Up, quickly! Hasten to the gate of the court, where lies the money you need. I am your father Abraham. I have beheld the affliction wherewith the Gentiles oppress you, but God has heard your groans." In great terror the beadle arose, but he saw no one, yet he went to the spot designated by the vision, and he found the money and took it to the congregation, telling his dream at the same time. Amazed, they counted the gold, precisely the amount required of them by the prince, no more and no less. They surrendered the sum to him, and he who had considered compliance with his demand impossible, recognized now that God is with the Jews, and thenceforth they found favor in his eyes.

Chapter 6

JACOB--THE BIRTH OF ESAU AND JACOB

Isaac was the counterpart of his father in body and soul. He resembled him in every particular--"in beauty, wisdom, strength, wealth, and noble deeds." It was, therefore, as great an honor for Isaac to be called the son of his father as for Abraham to be called the father of his son, and though Abraham was the progenitor of thirty nations, he is always designated as the father of Isaac.

Despite his many excellent qualities, Isaac married late in life. God permitted him to meet the wife suitable to him only after he had successfully disproved the mocking charges of Ishmael, who was in the habit of taunting him with having been circumcised at the early age of eight days, while Ishmael had submitted himself voluntarily to the operation when be was thirteen years old. For this reason God demanded Isaac as a sacrifice when he had attained to full manhood, at the age of thirty-seven, and Isaac was ready to give up his life. Ishmael's jibes were thus robbed of their sting, and Isaac was permitted to marry. But another delay occurred before his marriage could take place. Directly after the sacrifice on Mount Moriah, his mother died, and he mourned her for three years. Finally he married Rebekah, who was then a maiden of fourteen.

Rebekah was "a rose between thorns." Her father was the Aramean Bethuel, and her brother was Laban, but she did not walk in their ways. Her piety was equal to Isaac's. Nevertheless their marriage was not entirely happy, for they lived together no less than twenty years without begetting children. Rebekah besought her husband to entreat God for the gift of children, as his father Abraham had done. At first Isaac would not do her bidding. God had promised Abraham a numerous progeny, and he thought their childlessness was probably Rebekah's fault, and it was her duty to supplicate God, and not his. But Rebekah would not desist, and husband and wife repaired to Mount Moriah together to pray to God there. And Isaac said: "O Lord God of heaven and earth, whose goodness and mercies fill the earth, Thou who didst take my father from his father's house and from his birthplace, and didst bring him unto this land, and didst say unto him, To thee and thy seed will I give the land, and didst promise him and declare unto him, I will multiply thy seed as the stars of heaven and as the sand of the sea, now may Thy words be verified which Thou didst speak unto my father. For Thou art the Lord our God, our eyes are toward Thee, to give us seed of men as Thou didst promise us, for Thou art the Lord our God, and our eyes are upon Thee." Isaac prayed furthermore that all children destined for him might be born unto him from this pious wife of his, and Rebekah made the same petition regarding her husband Isaac and the children destined for her.

Their united prayer was heard. Yet it was chiefly for the sake of Isaac that God gave them children. It is true, Rebekah's piety equalled her husband's, but the prayer of a pious man who is the son of a pious man is far more efficacious than the prayer of one who, though pious himself, is descended from a godless father.

The prayer wrought a great miracle, for Isaac's physique was such that he could not have been expected to beget children, and equally it was not in the course of nature that Rebekah should bear children.

When Rebekah had been pregnant seven months, she began to wish that the curse of childlessness had not been removed from her. She suffered torturous pain, because her twin sons began their lifelong quarrels in her womb. They strove to kill each other. If Rebekah walked in the vicinity of a temple erected to idols, Esau moved in her body, and if she passed a synagogue or a Bet ha-Midrash, Jacob essayed to break forth from her womb. The quarrels of the children turned upon such differences as these. Esau would insist that there was no life except the earthly life of material pleasures, and Jacob would reply: "My brother, there are two worlds before us, this world and the world to come. In this world, men eat and drink, and traffic and marry, and bring up sons and daughters, but all this does not take place in the world to come. If it please thee, do thou take this world, and I will take the other." Esau had Samael as his ally, who desired to slay Jacob in his mother's womb. But the archangel Michael hastened to Jacob's aid. He tried to burn Samael, and the Lord saw it was necessary to constitute a heavenly court for the purpose of arbitrating the case of Michael and Samael. Even the quarrel between the two brothers regarding the birthright had its beginning before they emerged from the womb of their mother. Each desired to be the first to come into the world. It was only when Esau threatened to carry his point at the expense of his mother's life that Jacob gave way.

Rebekah asked other women whether they, too, had suffered such pain during their pregnancy, and when they told her they had not heard of a case like hers, except the pregnancy of Nimrod's mother, she betook herself to Mount Moriah, whereon Shem and Eber had their Bet ha-Midrash. She requested them as well as Abraham to inquire of God what the cause of her dire suffering was. And Shem replied: "My daughter, I confide a secret to thee. See to it that none finds it out. Two nations are in thy womb, and how should thy body contain them, seeing that the whole world will not be large enough for them to exist in it together peaceably? Two nations they are, each owning a world of its own, the one the Torah, the other sin. From the one will spring Solomon, the builder of the Temple, from the other Vespasian, the destroyer thereof. These two are what are needed to raise the number of nations to seventy. They will never be in the same estate. Esau will vaunt lords, while Jacob will bring forth prophets, and if Esau has princes, Jacob will have kings. They, Israel and Rome, are the two nations destined to be hated by all the world. One will exceed the other in strength. First Esau will subjugate the whole world, but in the end Jacob will rule over all. The older of the two will serve the younger, provided this one is pure of heart, otherwise the younger will be enslaved by the older."

The circumstances connected with the birth of her twin sons were as remarkable as those during the period of Rebekah's pregnancy. Esau was the first to see the light, and with him all impurity came from the womb; Jacob was born clean and sweet of body. Esau was brought forth with hair, beard, and teeth, both front and back, and he was blood-red, a sign of his future sanguinary nature. On account of his ruddy appearance he remained uncircumcised. Isaac, his father, feared that it was due to poor circulation of the blood, and he hesitated to perform the circumcision. He decided to wait until Esau should attain his thirteenth year, the age at which Ishmael had received the sign of the covenant. But when Esau grew up, he refused to give heed to his father's wish, and so he was left uncircumcised. The opposite of his brother in this as in all respects, Jacob was born with the sign of the covenant upon his body, a rare distinction. But Esau also bore a mark upon him at birth, the figure of a serpent, the symbol of all that is wicked and hated of God.

The names conferred upon the brothers are pregnant with meaning. The older was called Esau, because he was 'Asui, fully developed when he was born, and the name of the younger was given to him by God, to point to some important events in the future of Israel by the numerical value of each letter. The first letter in Ya'akob, Yod, with the value of ten, stands for the decalogue; the second, 'Ayin, equal to seventy, for the seventy elders, the leaders of Israel; the third, Kof, a hundred, for the Temple, a hundred ells in height; and the last, Bet, for the two tables of stone.

THE FAVORITE OF ABRAHAM

While Esau and Jacob were little, their characters could not be judged properly. They were like the myrtle and the thorn-bush, which look alike in the early stages of their growth. After they have attained full size, the myrtle is known by its fragrance, and the thorn-bush by its thorns.

In their childhood, both brothers went to school, but when they reached their thirteenth year, and were of age, their ways parted. Jacob continued his studies in the Bet ha Midrash of Shem and Eber, and Esau abandoned himself to idolatry and an immoral life. Both were hunters of men, Esau tried to capture them in order to turn them away from God, and Jacob, to turn them toward God. In spite of his impious deeds, Esau possessed the art of winning his father's love. His hypocritical conduct made Isaac believe that his first-born son was extremely pious. "Father," he would ask Isaac, "what is the tithe on straw and salt?" The question made him appear God-fearing in the eyes of his father, because these two products are the very ones that are exempt from tithing. Isaac failed to notice, too, that his older son gave him forbidden food to eat. What he took for the flesh of young goats was dog's meat.

Rebekah was more clear-sighted. She knew her sons as they really were, and therefore her love for Jacob was exceeding great. The oftener she heard his voice, the deeper grew her affection for him. Abraham agreed with her. He also loved his grandson Jacob, for he knew that in him his name and his seed would be called. And he said unto Rebekah, "My daughter, watch over my son Jacob, for he shall be in my stead on the earth and for a blessing in the midst of the children of men, and for the glory of the whole seed of Shem." Having admonished Rebekah thus to keep guard over Jacob, who was destined to be the bearer of the blessing given to Abraham by God, he called for his grandson, and in the presence of Rebekah he blessed him, and said: "Jacob, my beloved son, whom my soul loveth, may God bless thee from above the firmament, and may He give thee all the blessing wherewith He blessed Adam, and Enoch, and Noah, and Shem, and all the things of which He told me, and all the things which He promised to give me may He cause to cleave to thee and to thy seed forever, according to the days of the heavens above the earth. And the spirit of Mastema shall not rule over thee or over thy seed, to turn thee from the Lord, who is thy God from henceforth and forever. And may the Lord God be a father to thee, and mayest thou be His first-born son, and may He be a father to thy people always. Go in peace, my son."

And Abraham had good reason to be particularly fond of Jacob, for it was due to the merits of his grandson that he had been rescued from the fiery furnace.

Isaac and Rebekah, knowing of Abraham's love for their young son, sent their father a meal by Jacob on the last Feast of Pentecost which Abraham was permitted to celebrate on earth, that he might eat and bless the Creator of all things before he died. Abraham knew that his end was approaching, and he thanked the Lord for all the good He had granted him during the days of his life, and blessed Jacob and bade him walk in the ways of the Lord, and especially he was not to marry a daughter of the Canaanites. Then Abraham prepared for death. He placed two of Jacob's fingers upon his eyes, and thus holding them closed he fell into his eternal sleep, while Jacob lay beside him on the bed. The lad did not know of his grandfather's death, until he called him, on awakening next morning, "Father, father," and received no answer.

THE SALE OF THE BIRTHRIGHT

Though Abraham reached a good old age, beyond the limit of years vouchsafed later generations, he yet died five years before his allotted time. The intention was to let him live to be one hundred and eighty years old, the same age as Isaac's at his death, but on account of Esau God brought his life to an abrupt close. For some time Esau had been pursuing his evil inclinations in secret. Finally he dropped his mask, and on the day of Abraham's death he was guilty of five crimes: he ravished a betrothed maiden, committed murder, doubted the resurrection of the dead, scorned the birthright, and denied God. Then the Lord said: "I promised Abraham that he should go to his fathers in peace. Can I now permit him to be a witness of his grandson's rebellion against God, his violation of the laws of chastity, and his shedding of blood? It is better for him to die now in peace."

The men slain by Esau on this day were Nimrod and two of his adjutants. A long-standing feud had existed between Esau and Nimrod, because the mighty hunter before the Lord was jealous of Esau, who also devoted himself assiduously to the chase. Once when he was hunting it happened that Nimrod was separated from his people, only two men were with him. Esau, who lay in ambush, noticed his isolation, and waited until he should pass his covert. Then he threw himself upon Nimrod suddenly, and felled him and his two companions, who hastened to his succor. The outcries of the latter brought the attendants of Nimrod to the spot where he lay dead, but not before Esau had stripped him of his garments, and fled to the city with them.

These garments of Nimrod had an extraordinary effect upon cattle, beasts, and birds. Of their own accord they would come and prostrate themselves before him who was arrayed in them. Thus Nimrod and Esau after him were able to rule over men and beasts.

After slaying Nimrod, Esau hastened cityward in great fear of his victim's followers. Tired and exhausted he arrived at home to find Jacob busy preparing a dish of lentils. Numerous male and female slaves were in Isaac's household. Nevertheless Jacob was so simple and modest in his demeanor that, if he came home late from the Bet ha-Midrash, he would disturb none to prepare his meal, but would do it himself. On this occasion he was cooking lentils for his father, to serve to him as his mourner's meal after the death of Abraham. Adam and Eve had eaten lentils after the murder of Abel, and so had the parents of Haran, when he perished in the fiery furnace. The reason they are used for the mourner's meal is that the round lentil symbolizes death: as the lentil rolls, so death, sorrow, and mourning constantly roll about among men, from one to the other.

Esau accosted Jacob thus, "Why art thou preparing lentils?"

Jacob: "Because our grandfather passed away; they shall be a sign of my grief and mourning, that he may love me in the days to come."

Esau: "Thou fool! Dost thou really think it possible that man should come to life again after he has been dead and has mouldered in the grave?" He continued to taunt Jacob. "Why dost thou give thyself so much trouble?" he said. "Lift up thine eyes, and thou wilt see that all men eat whatever comes to hand--fish, creeping and crawling creatures, swine's flesh, and all sorts of things like these, and thou vexest thyself about a dish of lentils."

Jacob: "If we act like other men, what shall we do on the day of the Lord, the day on which the pious will receive their reward, when a herald will proclaim: Where is He that weigheth the deeds of men, where is He that counteth?"

Esau: "Is there a future world? Or will the dead be called back to life? If it were so, why hath not Adam returned? Hast thou heard that Noah, through whom the world was raised anew, hath reappeared? Yea, Abraham, the friend of God, more beloved of Him than any man, hath he come to life again?"

Jacob: "If thou art of opinion that there is no future world, and that the dead do not rise to new life, then why dost thou want thy birthright? Sell it to me, now, while it is yet possible to do so. Once the Torah is revealed, it cannot be done. Verily, there is a future world, in which the righteous receive their reward. I tell thee this, lest thou say later I deceived thee."

Jacob was little concerned about the double share of the inheritance that went with the birthright. What he thought of was the priestly service, which was the prerogative of the first-born in ancient times, and Jacob was loth to have his impious brother Esau play the priest, he who despised all Divine service.

The scorn manifested by Esau for the resurrection of the dead he felt also for the promise of God to give the Holy Land to the seed of Abraham. He did not believe in it, and therefore he was willing to cede his birthright and the blessing attached thereto in exchange for a mess of pottage. In addition, Jacob paid him in coin, and, besides, he gave him what was more than money, the wonderful sword of Methuselah, which Isaac had inherited from Abraham and bestowed upon Jacob.

Esau made game of Jacob. He invited his associates to feast at his brother's table, saying, "Know ye what I did to this Jacob? I ate his lentils, drank his wine, amused myself at his expense, and sold my birthright to him." All that Jacob replied was, "Eat and may it do thee good!" But the Lord said, "Thou despisest the birthright, therefore I shall make thee despised in all generations." And by way of punishment for denying God and the resurrection of the dead, the descendants of Esau were cut off from the world.

As naught was holy to Esau, Jacob made him swear, concerning the birthright, by the life of their father, for he knew Esau's love for Isaac, that it was strong. Nor did he fail to have a document made out, duly signed by witnesses, setting forth that Esau had sold him the birthright together with his claim upon a place in the Cave of Machpelah.

Though no blame can attach to Jacob for all this, yet he secured the birthright from him by cunning, and therefore the descendants of Jacob had to serve the descendants of Esau.

ISAAC WITH THE PHILISTINES

The life of Isaac was a faithful reflex of the life of his father. Abraham had to leave his birthplace; so also Isaac. Abraham was exposed to the risk of losing his wife; so also Isaac. The Philistines were envious of Abraham; so also of Isaac. Abraham long remained childless; so also Isaac. Abraham begot one pious son and one wicked son; so also Isaac. And, finally, as in the time of Abraham, so also in the time of Isaac, a famine came upon the land.

At first Isaac intended to follow the example of his father and remove to Egypt, but God appeared unto him, and spake: "Thou art a perfect sacrifice, without a blemish, and as a burnt offering is made unfit if it is taken outside of the sanctuary, so thou wouldst be profaned if thou shouldst happen outside of the Holy Land. Remain in the land, and endeavor to cultivate it. In this land dwells the Shekinah, and in days to come I will give unto thy children the realms possessed by mighty rulers, first a part thereof, and the whole in the Messianic time."

Isaac obeyed the command of God, and he settled in Gerar. When he noticed that the inhabitants of the place began to have designs upon his wife, he followed the example of Abraham, and pretended she was his sister. The report of Rebekah's beauty reached the king himself, but he was mindful of the great danger to which he had once exposed himself on a similar occasion, and he left Isaac and his wife unmolested. After they had been in Gerar for three months, Abimelech noticed that the manner of Isaac, who lived in the outer court of the royal palace, was that of a husband toward Rebekah. He called him to account, saying, "It might have happened to the king himself to take the woman thou didst call thy sister." Indeed, Isaac lay under the suspicion of having illicit intercourse with Rebekah, for at first the people of the place would not believe that she was his wife. When Isaac persisted in his statement, Abimelech sent his grandees for them, ordered them to be arrayed in royal vestments, and had it proclaimed before them, as they rode through the city: "These two are man and wife. He that toucheth this man or his wife shall surely be put to death."

Thereafter the king invited Isaac to settle in his domains, and he assigned fields and vineyards to him for cultivation, the best the land afforded. But Isaac was not self-interested. The tithe of all he possessed he gave to the poor of Gerar. Thus he was the first to introduce the law of tithing for the poor, as his father Abraham had been the first to separate the priests' portion from his fortune. Isaac was rewarded by abundant harvests; the land yielded a hundred times more than was expected, though the soil was barren and the year unfruitful. He grew so rich that people wished to have "the dung from Isaac's she-mules rather than Abimelech's gold and silver." But his wealth called forth the envy of the Philistines, for it is characteristic of the wicked that they begrudge their fellow-men the good, and rejoice when they see evil descend upon them, and envy brings hatred in its wake, and so the Philistines first envied Isaac, and then hated him. In their enmity toward him, they stopped the wells which Abraham had had his servants dig. Thus they broke their covenant with Abraham and were faithless, and they have only themselves to blame if they were exterminated later on by the Israelites.

Isaac departed from Gerar, and began to dig again the wells of water which they had digged in the days of Abraham his father, and which the Philistines had stopped. His reverence for his father was so great that he even restored the names by which Abraham had called the wells. To reward him for his filial respect, the Lord left the name of Isaac unchanged, while his father and his son had to submit to new names.

After four attempts to secure water, Isaac was successful; he found the well of water that followed the Patriarchs. Abraham had obtained it after three diggings. Hence the name of the well, Beer-sheba, "the well of seven diggings," the same well that will supply water to Jerusalem and its environs in the Messianic time.

Isaac's success with his wells but served to increase the envy of the Philistines, for he had come upon water in a most unlikely spot and, besides, in a year of drouth. But "the Lord fulfils the desire of them that fear Him." As Isaac executed the will of his Creator, so God accomplished his desire. And Abimelech, the king of Gerar, speedily came to see that God was on the side of Isaac, for, to chastise him for having instigated Isaac's removal from Gerar, his house was ravaged by robbers in the night, and he himself was stricken with leprosy. The wells of the Philistines ran dry as soon as Isaac left Gerar, and also the trees failed to yield their fruit. None could be in doubt but that these things were the castigation for their unkindness.

Now Abimelech entreated his friends, especially the administrator of his kingdom, to accompany him to Isaac and help him win back his friendship. Abimelech and the Philistines spake thus to Isaac: "We have convinced ourselves that the Shekinah is with thee, and therefore we desire thee to renew the covenant which thy father made with us, that thou wilt do us no hurt, as we also did not touch thee." Isaac consented. It illustrates the character of the Philistines strikingly that they took credit unto themselves for having done him no hurt. It shows that they would have been glad to inflict harm upon him, for "the soul of the wicked desireth evil."

The place in which the covenant was made between Isaac and the Philistines was called Shib'ah, for two reasons, because an oath was "sworn" there, and as a memorial of the fact that even the heathen are bound to observe the "seven" Noachian laws.

For all the wonders executed by God for Isaac, and all the good he enjoyed throughout his life, he is indebted to the merits of his father. For his own merits he will be rewarded in future. On the great day of judgment it will be Isaac who will redeem his descendants from Gehenna. On that day the Lord will speak to Abraham, "Thy children have sinned," and Abraham will make reply, "Then let them be wiped out, that Thy Name be sanctified." The Lord will turn to Jacob, thinking that he who had suffered so much in bringing his sons to manhood's estate would display more love for his posterity. But Jacob will give the same answer as Abraham. Then God will say: "The old have no understanding, and the young no counsel. I will now go to Isaac. Isaac," God will address him, "thy children have sinned," and Isaac will reply: "O Lord of the world, sayest Thou my children, and not THINE? When they stood at Mount Sinai and declared themselves ready to execute all Thy bidding before even they heard it, Thou didst call Israel 'My first-born,' and now they are MY children, and not THINE! Let us consider. The years of a man are seventy. From these twenty are to be deducted, for Thou inflictest no punishment upon those under twenty. Of the fifty years that are left, one-half are to be deducted for the nights passed in sleep. There remain only twenty-five years, and these are to be diminished by twelve and a half, the time spent in praying, eating, and attending to other needs in life, during which men commit no sins. That leaves only twelve years and a half. If Thou wilt take these upon Thyself, well and good. If not, do Thou take one-half thereof, and I will take the other half." The descendants of Isaac will then say, "Verily, thou art our true father!" But he will point to God, and admonish them, "Nay, give not your praises to me, but to God alone," and Israel, with eyes directed heavenward, will say, "Thou, O Lord, art our Father; our Redeemer from everlasting is Thy name."

It was Isaac, or, as he is sometimes called, Elihu the son of Barachel, who revealed the wonderful mysteries of nature in his arguments with Job.

At the end of the years of famine, God appeared unto Isaac, and bade him return to Canaan. Isaac did as he was commanded, and he settled in Hebron. At this time he sent his younger son Jacob to the Bet ha-Midrash of Shem and Eber, to study the law of the Lord. Jacob remained there thirty-two years. As for Esau, he refused to learn, and he remained in the house of his father. The chase was his only occupation, and as he pursued beasts, so he pursued men, seeking to capture them with cunning and deceit.

On one of his hunting expeditions, Esau came to Mount Seir, where he became acquainted with Judith, of the family of Ham, and he took her unto himself as his wife, and brought her to his father at Hebron.

Ten years later, when Shem his teacher died, Jacob returned home, at the age of fifty. Another six years passed, and Rebekah received the joyful news that her sister-in-law 'Adinah, the wife of Laban, who, like all the women of his house, had been childless until then, had given birth to twin daughters, Leah and Rachel. Rebekah, weary of her life on account of the woman chosen by her older son, exhorted Jacob not to marry one of the daughters of Canaan, but a maiden of the family of Abraham. He assured his mother that the words of Abraham, bidding him to marry no woman of the Canaanites, were graven upon his memory, and for this reason he was still unmarried, though he had attained the age of sixty-two, and Esau had been urging him for twenty-two years past to follow his example and wed a daughter of the people of the land in which they lived. He had heard that his uncle Laban had daughters, and he was resolved to choose one of them as his wife. Deeply moved by the words of her son, Rebekah thanked him and gave praise unto God with the words: "Blessed be the Lord God, and may His Holy Name be blessed for ever and ever, who hath given me Jacob as a pure son and a holy seed; for he is Thine, and Thine shall his seed be continually and throughout all the generations for evermore. Bless him, O Lord, and place in my mouth the blessing of righteousness, that I may bless him."

And when the spirit of the Lord came over her, she laid her hands upon the head of Jacob and gave him her maternal blessing. It ended with the words, "May the Lord of the world love thee, as the heart of thy affectionate mother rejoices in thee, and may He bless thee."

ISAAC BLESSES JACOB

Esau's marriage with the daughters of the Canaanites was an abomination not only in the eyes of his mother, but also in the eyes of his father. He suffered even more than Rebekah through the idolatrous practices of his daughters in-law. It is the nature of man to oppose less resistance than woman to disagreeable circumstances. A bone is not harmed by a collision that would shiver an earthen pot in pieces. Man, who is created out of the dust of the ground, has not the endurance of woman formed out of bone. Isaac was made prematurely old by the conduct of his daughters-in-law, and he lost the sight of his eyes. Rebekah had been accustomed in the home of her childhood to the incense burnt before idols, and she could therefore bear it under her own roof-tree. Unlike her, Isaac had never had any such experience while he abode with his parents, and he was stung by the smoke arising from the sacrifices offered to their idols by his daughters-in-law in his own house. Isaac's eyes had suffered earlier in life, too. When he lay bound upon the altar, about to be sacrificed by his father, the angels wept, and their tears fell upon his eyes, and there they remained and weakened his sight.

At the same time he had brought the scourge of blindness down upon himself by his love for Esau. He justified the wicked for a bribe, the bribe of Esau's filial love, and loss of vision is the punishment that follows the taking of bribes. "A gift," it is said, "blinds the eyes of the wise."

Nevertheless his blindness proved a benefit for Isaac as well as Jacob. In consequence of his physical ailments, Isaac had to keep at home, and so he was spared the pain of being pointed out by the people as the father of the wicked Esau. And, again, if his power of vision had been unimpaired, he would not have blessed Jacob. As it was, God treated him as a physician treats a sick man who is forbidden to drink wine, for which, however, he has a strong desire. To placate him, the physician orders that warm water be given him in the dark, and he be told that it is wine.

When Isaac reached the age of one hundred and twenty three, and was thus approaching the years attained by his mother, he began to meditate upon his end. It is proper that a man should prepare for death when he comes close to the age at which either of his parents passed out of life. Isaac reflected that he did not know whether the age allotted to him was his mother's or his father's, and he therefore resolved to bestow his blessing upon his older son, Esau, before death should overtake him. He summoned Esau, and he said, "My son," and Esau replied, "Here am I," but the holy spirit interposed: "Though he disguises his voice and makes it sound sweet, put no confidence in him. There are seven abominations in his heart. He will destroy seven holy places--the Tabernacle, the sanctuaries at Gilgal, Shiloh, Nob, and Gibeon, and the first and the second Temple."

Gently though Esau continued to speak to his father, he yet longed for his end to come. But Isaac was stricken with spiritual as well as physical blindness. The holy spirit deserted him, and he could not discern the wickedness of his older son. He bade him sharpen his slaughtering knives and beware of bringing him the flesh of an animal that had died of itself, or had been torn by a beast, and he was to guard also against putting an animal before Isaac that had been stolen from its rightful owner. "Then," continued Isaac, "will I bless him who is worthy of being blessed."

This charge was laid upon Esau on the eve of the Passover, and Isaac said to him: "To-night the whole world will sing the Hallel unto God. It is the night when the storehouses of dew are unlocked. Therefore prepare dainties for me, that my soul may bless thee before I die." But the holy spirit interposed, "Eat not the bread of him that hath an evil eye." Isaac's longing for tidbits was due to his blindness. As the sightless cannot behold the food they eat, they do not enjoy it with full relish, and their appetite must be tempted with particularly palatable morsels.

Esau sallied forth to procure what his father desired, little recking the whence or how, whether by robbery or theft. To hinder the quick execution of his father's order, God sent Satan on the chase with Esau. He was to delay him as long as possible. Esau would catch a deer and leave him lying bound, while he pursued other game. Immediately Satan would come and liberate the deer, and when Esau returned to the spot, his victim was not to be found. This was repeated several times. Again and again the quarry was run down, and bound, and liberated, so that Jacob was able meanwhile to carry out the plan of Rebekah whereby he would be blessed instead of Esau.

Though Rebekah had not heard the words that had passed between Isaac and Esau, they nevertheless were revealed to her through the holy spirit, and she resolved to restrain her husband from taking a false step. She was not actuated by love for Jacob, but by the wish of keeping Isaac from committing a detestable act. Rebekah said to Jacob: "This night the storehouses of dew are unlocked; it is the night during which the celestial beings chant the Hallel unto God, the night set apart for the deliverance of thy children from Egypt, on which they, too, will sing the Hallel. Go now and prepare savory meat for thy father, that he may bless thee before his death. Do as I bid thee, obey me as thou art wont, for thou art my son whose children, every one, will be good and God-fearing--not one shall be graceless."

In spite of his great respect for his mother, Jacob refused at first to heed her command. He feared he might commit a sin, especially as he might thus bring his father's curse down upon him. As it was, Isaac might still have a blessing for him, after giving Esau his. But Rebekah allayed his anxieties, with the words: "When Adam was cursed, the malediction fell upon his mother, the earth, and so shall I, thy mother, bear the imprecation, if thy father curses thee. Moreover, if the worst comes to the worst, I am prepared to step before thy father and tell him, 'Esau is a villain, and Jacob is a righteous man.' "

Thus constrained by his mother, Jacob, in tears and with body bowed, went off to execute the plan made by Rebekah. As he was to provide a Passover meal, she bade him get two kids, one for the Passover sacrifice and one for the festival sacrifice. To soothe Jacob's conscience, she added that her marriage contract entitled her to two kids daily. "And," she continued, "these two kids will bring good unto thee, the blessing of thy father, and they will bring good unto thy children, for two kids will be the atoning sacrifice offered on the Day of Atonement."

Jacob's hesitation was not yet removed. His father, he feared, would touch him and convince himself that he was not hairy, and therefore not his son Esau. Accordingly, Rebekah tore the skins of the two kids into strips and sewed them together, for Jacob was so tall a giant that otherwise they would not have sufficed to cover his hands. To make Jacob's disguise complete, Rebekah felt justified in putting Esau's wonderful garments on him. They were the high priestly raiment in which God had clothed Adam, "the first-born of the world," for in the days before the erection of the Tabernacle all the first-born males officiated as priests. From Adam these garments descended to Noah, who transmitted them to Shem, and Shem bequeathed them to Abraham, and Abraham to his son Isaac, from whom they reached Esau as the older of his two sons. It was the opinion of Rebekah that as Jacob had bought the birthright from his brother, he had thereby come into possession of the garments as well. There was no need for her to go and fetch them from the house of Esau. He knew his wives far too well to entrust so precious a treasure to them; they were in the safe-keeping of his mother. Besides, he used them most frequently in the house of his parents. As a rule, he did not lay much stress upon decent apparel. He was willing to appear on the street clad in rags, but he considered it his duty to wait upon his father arrayed in his best. "My father," Esau was in the habit of saying, "is a king in my sight, and it would ill become me to serve before him in any thing but royal apparel." To the great respect he manifested toward his father, the descendants of Esau owe all their good fortune on earth. Thus doth God reward a good deed.

Rebekah led Jacob equipped and arrayed in this way to the door of Isaac's chamber. There she parted from him with the words, "Henceforward may thy Creator assist thee." Jacob entered, addressing Isaac with "Father," and receiving the response, "Here am I! Who art thou, my son?" he replied equivocally, "It is I, thy first-born son is Esau." He sought to avoid a falsehood, and yet not betray that he was Jacob. Isaac then said: "Thou art greatly in haste to secure thy blessing. Thy father Abraham was seventy-five years old when he was blessed, and thou art but sixty-three." Jacob replied awkwardly, "Because the Lord thy God sent me good speed." Isaac concluded at once that this was not Esau, for he would not have mentioned the name of God, and he made up his mind to feel the son before him and make sure who he was. Terror seized upon Jacob at the words of Isaac, "Come near, I pray thee, that I may feel thee, my son." A cold sweat covered his body, and his heart melted like wax. Then God caused the archangels Michael and Gabriel to descend. The one seized his right hand, the other his left hand, while the Lord God Himself supported him, that his courage might not fail him. Isaac felt him, and, finding his hands hairy, he said, "The voice is Jacob's voice, but the hands are the hands of Esau," words in which he conveyed the prophecy that so long as the voice of Jacob is heard in the houses of prayer and of learning, the hands of Esau will not be able to prevail against him. "Yes," he continued, "it is the voice of Jacob, the voice that imposes silence upon those on earth and in heaven," for even the angels may not raise their voices in praise of God until Israel has finished his prayers.

Isaac's scruples about blessing the son before him were not yet removed, for with his prophetical eye he foresaw that this one would have descendants who would vex the Lord. At the same time, it was revealed to him that even the sinners in Israel would turn penitents, and then he was ready to bless Jacob. He bade him come near and kiss him, to indicate that it would be Jacob who would imprint the last kiss upon Isaac before he was consigned to the grave- he and none other. When Jacob stood close to him, he discerned the fragrance of Paradise clinging to him, and he exclaimed, "See, the smell of my son is as the smell of the field which the Lord hath blessed."

The fragrance emanating from Jacob was not the only thing about him derived from Paradise. The archangel Michael had fetched thence the wine which Jacob gave his father to drink, that an exalted mood might descend upon him, for only when a man is joyously excited the Shekinah rests upon him. The holy spirit filled Isaac, and he gave Jacob his tenfold blessing: "God give thee of the dew of heaven," the celestial dew wherewith God will awaken the pious to new life in days to come; "and of the fatness of the earth," the goods of this world; "and plenty of corn and wine," the Torah and the commandments which bestow the same joy upon man as abundant harvests; "peoples shall serve thee," the Japhethites and the Hamites; "nations shall bow down to thee," the Shemite nations; "thou wilt be lord over thy brethren," the Ishmaelites and the descendants of Keturah; "thy mother's sons will bow down to thee," Esau and his princes; "cursed be every one that curseth thee," like Balaam; "and blessed be every one that blesseth thee," like Moses.

For each blessing invoked upon Jacob by his father Isaac, a similar blessing was bestowed upon him by God Himself in the same words. As Isaac blessed him with dew, so also God: "And the remnant of Jacob shall be in the midst of many peoples as dew from the Lord." Isaac blessed him with the fatness of the earth, so also God: "And he shall give the rain of thy seed, that thou shalt sow the ground withal; and bread of the increase of the ground, and it shall be fat and plenteous." Isaac blessed him with plenty of corn and wine, so also God: "I will send you corn and wine." Isaac said, "Peoples shall serve thee," so also God: "Kings shall be thy nursing fathers, and their queens thy nursing mothers; they shall bow down to thee with their faces to the earth, and lick the dust of thy feet." Isaac said, "Nations shall bow down to thee," so also God: "And He will make thee high above all nations which He hath made, in praise, and in name, and in honor."

To this double blessing his mother Rebekah joined hers: "For He shall give His angels charge over thee, to keep thee in all thy ways. They shall bear thee up in their hands, lest thou dash thy feet against a stone. Thou shalt tread upon the lion and adder; the young lion and the serpent shalt thou trample under feet. Because he hath set his love upon me, therefore will I deliver him; I will set him on high, because he hath known my name."

The holy spirit added in turn: "He shall call upon me, and I will answer him; I will be with him in trouble; I will deliver him, and honor him. With long life will I satisfy him, and show him my salvation."

Jacob left the presence of his father crowned like a bridegroom, adorned like a bride, and bathed in celestial dew, which filled his bones with marrow, and transformed him into a hero and a giant.

Of a miracle done for him at that very moment Jacob himself was not aware. Had he tarried with his father an instant longer, Esau would have met him there, and would surely have slain him. It happened that exactly as Jacob was on the point of leaving the tent of his father, carrying in his hands the plates off which Isaac had eaten, he noticed Esau approaching, and he concealed himself behind the door. Fortunately, it was a revolving door, so that though he could see Esau, he could not be seen by him.

ESAU'S TRUE CHARACTER REVEALED

Esau arrived after a delay of four hours. In spite of all the efforts he had put forth, he had not succeeded in catching any game, and he was compelled to kill a dog and prepare its flesh for his father's meal. All this had made Esau ill-humored, and when he bade his father partake of the meal, the invitation sounded harsh. "Let my father arise," he said, "and eat of his son's venison." Jacob had spoken differently; he had said, "Arise, I pray thee, sit and eat of my venison." The words of Esau terrified Isaac greatly. His fright exceeded that which he had felt when his father was about to offer him as a sacrifice, and he cried out, "Who then is he that hath been the mediator between me and the Lord, to make the blessing reach Jacob?"- words meant to imply that he suspected Rebekah of having instigated Jacob's act.

Isaac's alarm was caused by his seeing hell at the feet of Esau. Scarcely had he entered the house when the walls thereof began to get hot on account of the nearness of hell, which he brought along with him. Isaac could not but exclaim, "Who will be burnt down yonder, I or my son Jacob?" and the Lord answered him, "Neither thou nor Jacob, but the hunter."

Isaac told Esau that the meat set before him by Jacob had had marvellous qualities. Any savor that one desired it possessed, it was even endowed with the taste of the food that God will grant the pious in the world to come. "I know not," he said, "what the meat was. But I had only to wish for bread, and it tasted like bread, or fish, or locusts, or flesh of animals, in short, it had the taste of any dainty one could wish for." When Esau heard the word "flesh," he began to weep, and he said: "To me Jacob gave no more than a dish of lentils, and in payment for it he took my birthright. What must he have taken from thee for flesh of animals?" Hitherto Isaac had been in great anguish on account of the thought that he had committed a wrong in giving his blessing to his younger son instead of the firstborn, to whom it belonged by law and custom. But when he heard that Jacob had acquired the birthright from Esau, he said, "I gave my blessing to the right one!"

In his dismay, Isaac had had the intention of cursing Jacob for having wrested the blessing from him through cunning. God prevented him from carrying out his plan. He reminded him that he would but curse himself, seeing that his blessing contained the words, "Cursed be every one that curseth thee." But Isaac was not willing to acknowledge his blessing valid as applied to Jacob, until he was informed that his second son was the possessor of the birthright. Only then did he say, "Yea, he shall be blessed," whereat Esau cried with an exceeding great and bitter cry. By way of punishment for having been the cause of such distress, a descendant of Jacob, Mordecai, was also made to cry with a loud and bitter cry, and his grief was brought forth by the Amalekite Haman, the descendant of Esau. At the words of Isaac, "Thy brother came with wisdom, and hath taken away thy blessing," Esau spat out in vexation, and said, "He took away my birthright, and I kept silence, and now that he takes away my blessing, should I also keep silence? Is not he rightly named Jacob? for he hath supplanted me these two times."

Isaac continued to speak to Esau: "Behold, I have made him thy lord, he is thy king, and do what thou wilt, thy blessings will still belong to him; all his brethren have I given to him for slaves, and what slaves possess belongs to their owner. There is nothing for it, thou must be content that thou wilt receive thy bread baked from thy master." The Lord took it ill of Isaac that he cheered him with such kind words. "To Mine enemy," He reproached him, "thou sayest, 'What shall I do for thee, my son?' " Isaac replied, "O that he might find grace with Thee!" God: "He is a recreant." Isaac: "Doth he not act righteously when he honors his parents?" God: "In the land of uprightness will he deal wrongfully, he will stretch his hand forth in days to come against the Temple." Isaac: "Then let him enjoy much good in this world, that he may not behold the abiding-place of the Lord in the world to come."

When it became plain to Esau that he could not induce his father to annul the blessing bestowed upon Jacob, he tried to force a blessing for himself by an underhand trick. He said: "Hast thou but one blessing, my father? bless me, even me also, O my father, else it will be said thou hast but one blessing to bestow. Suppose both Jacob and I had been righteous men, had not then thy God had two blessings, one for each?" The Lord Himself made reply: "Silence! Jacob will bless the twelve tribes, and each blessing will be different from every other." But Isaac felt great pity for his older son, and he wanted to bless him, but the Shekinah forsook him, and he could not carry out what he purposed. Thereupon Esau began to weep. He shed three tears--one ran from his right eye, the second from his left eye, and the third remained hanging from his eyelash. God said, "This villain cries for his very life, and should I let him depart empty-handed?" and then He bade Isaac bless his older son.

The blessing of Isaac ran thus: "Behold, of the fat of the earth shall be thy dwelling," by which he meant Greater Greece, in Italy; "and of the dew of heaven from above," referring to Bet-Gubrin; "and by thy sword shalt thou live, and thou shalt serve thy brother," but when he casts off the yoke of the Lord, then shalt thou "shake his yoke from off thy neck," and thou wilt be his master.

The blessing which Isaac gave to his older son was bound to no condition whatsoever. Whether he deserved them or not, Esau was to enjoy the goods of this world. Jacob's blessing, however, depended upon his pious deeds; through them he would have a just claim upon earthly prosperity. Isaac thought: "Jacob is a righteous man, he will not murmur against God, though it should come to pass that suffering be inflicted upon him in spite of his upright life. But that reprobate Esau, if he should do a good deed, or pray to God and not be heard, he would say, 'As I pray to the idols for naught, so it is in vain to pray to God.' " For this reason did Isaac bestow an unconditional blessing upon Esau.

JACOB LEAVES HIS FATHER'S HOUSE

Esau hated his brother Jacob on account of the blessing that his father had given him, and Jacob was very much afraid of his brother Esau, and he fled to the house of Eber, the son of Shem, and he concealed himself there fourteen years on account of his brother Esau, and he continued there to learn the ways of the Lord and His commandments. When Esau saw that Jacob had fled and escaped from him, and Jacob had cunningly obtained the blessing, then Esau grieved exceedingly, and he was also vexed at his father and mother. He also rose up and took his wife, and went away from his father and mother to the land of Seir. There he married his second wife, Basemath, the daughter of Elon the Hittite, and he called her name Adah, saying that the blessing had in that time passed from him. After dwelling in Seir for six months, Esau returned to the land of Canaan, and placed his two wives in his father's house in Hebron. And the wives of Esau vexed and provoked Isaac and Rebekah with their works, for they walked not in the ways of the Lord, but served their fathers' gods of wood and stone, as their fathers had taught them, and they were more wicked than their fathers. They sacrificed and burnt incense to the Baalim, and Isaac and Rebekah became weary of them. And at the end of fourteen years of Jacob's residing in the house of Eber, Jacob desired to see his father and his mother, and he returned home. Esau had forgotten in those days what Jacob had done to him, in having taken the blessing from him, but when Esau saw Jacob returning to his parents, he remembered what Jacob had done to him, and he was greatly incensed against him, and he sought to slay him.

But Esau would not kill Jacob while his father was yet alive, lest Isaac beget another son. He wanted to be sure of being the only heir. However, his hatred against Jacob was so great that he determined to hasten the death of his father and then dispatch Jacob. Such murderous plans Esau cherished in his heart, though he denied that he was harboring them. But God spoke, "Probably thou knowest not that I examine the hearts of men, for I am the Lord that searcheth the heart." And not God alone knew the secret desires of Esau. Rebekah, like all the Mothers, was a prophetess, and she delayed not to warn Jacob of the danger that hung over him. "Thy brother," she said to him, "is as sure of accomplishing his wicked purpose as though thou wert dead. Now therefore, my son, obey my voice, and arise, flee thou to Laban my brother, to Haran, and tarry with him for seven years, until thy brother's fury turn away." In the goodness of her heart, Rebekah could not but believe that the anger of Esau was only a fleeting passion, and would disappear in the course of time. But she was mistaken, his hate persisted until the end of his life.

Courageous as he was, Jacob would not run away from danger. He said to his mother, "I am not afraid; if he wishes to kill me, I will kill him," to which she replied, "Let me not be bereaved of both my sons in one day." By words Rebekah again showed her prophetic gift. As she spoke, so it happened--when their time came, Esau was slain while the burial of Jacob was taking place.

And Jacob said to Rebekah: "Behold, thou knowest that my father has become old and does not see, and if I leave him and go away, he will be angry and will curse me. I will not go; if he sends me, only then will I go."

Accordingly, Rebekah went to Isaac, and amid tears she spoke to him thus: "If Jacob take a wife of the daughters of Heth, what good shall my life do me?" And Isaac called Jacob, and charged him, and said unto him: "Thou shalt not take a wife of the daughters of Canaan, for thus did our father Abraham command us according to the word of the Lord, which He had commanded him, saying, 'Unto thy seed will I give the land; if thy children keep My covenant that I have made with thee, then will I also perform to thy children that which I have spoken unto thee, and I will not forsake them.' Now therefore, my son, hearken to my voice, to all that I shall command thee, and refrain from taking a wife from amongst the daughters of Canaan. Arise, go to Haran, to the house of Bethuel, thy mother's father, and take thee a wife from thence of the daughters of Laban, thy mother's brother. Take heed lest thou shouldst forget the Lord thy God and all His ways in the land to which thou goest, and shouldst join thyself to the people of the land, and pursue vanity, and forsake the Lord thy God. But when thou comest to the land, serve the Lord. Do not turn to the right or to the left from the way which I commanded thee, and which thou didst learn. And may the Almighty God grant thee favor before the people of the land, that thou mayest take a wife there according to thy choice, one who is good and upright in the way of the Lord. And may God give unto thee and thy seed the blessing of thy father Abraham and make thee fruitful and multiply thee, and mayest thou become a multitude of people in the land whither thou goest, and may God cause thee to return to thy land, the land of thy father's dwelling, with children and with great riches, with joy and with pleasure."

As the value of a document is attested by its concluding words, the signature of the witnesses, so Isaac confirmed the blessing he had bestowed upon Jacob. That none might say Jacob had secured it by intrigue and cunning, he blessed him again with three blessings, in these words, "In so far as I am endowed with the power of blessing, I bestow blessing upon thee. May God, with whom there is endless blessing, give thee His, and also the blessing wherewith Abraham desired to bless me, desisting only in order not to provoke the jealousy of Ishmael."

Seeing with his prophetic eye that the seed of Jacob would once be compelled to go into exile, Isaac offered up one more petition, that God would bring the exiles back again. He said, "He shall deliver thee in six troubles, and in the seventh there shall no evil touch thee." And also Rebekah prayed to God in behalf of Jacob: "O Lord of the world, let not the purpose prosper which Esau harbors against Jacob. Put a bridle upon him, that he accomplish not all he wills to do."

When Esau observed that even his father's love had passed from him to Jacob, he went away, to Ishmael, and he addressed him as follows: "Lo, as thy father gave all his possessions to thy brother Isaac, and dismissed thee with empty hands, so my father purposeth to do to me. Make thyself ready then, go forth and slay thy brother, and I will slay mine, and then we two shall divide the whole world between us." And Ishmael replied: "Why dost thou want me to slay thy father? thou canst do it thyself." Esau said: "It hath happened aforetime that a man killed his brother- Cain murdered Abel. But that a son should kill his father is unheard of."

Esau did not really shrink back from parricide, only it chanced not to fit the plan he had hatched. "If Ishmael slays my father," he said to himself, "I am the rightful redeemer, and I shall kill Ishmael to avenge my father, and if, then, I murder Jacob, too, everything will belong to me, as the heir of my father and my uncle." This shows that Esau's marriage with Mahalath, the daughter of Ishmael and grandchild of Abraham, was not concluded out of regard for his parents, who were opposed to his two other wives, daughters of the Canaanites. All he desired was to enter into amicable relations with Ishmael in order to execute his devilish plan.

But Esau reckoned without his host. The night before his wedding with Mahalath Ishmael died, and Nebaioth, the son of Ishmael, stepped into his father's place, and gave away his sister. How little it had been in Esau's mind to make his parents happy by taking a granddaughter of Abraham to wife, appears from the fact that he kept his two other wives, the Canaanitish women. The daughter of Ishmael followed the example of her companions, and thus she but added to the grief caused the parents of Esau by their daughters-in-law. And the opportunity might have been a most favorable one for Esau to turn aside from his godless ways and amend his conduct, for the bridegroom is pardoned on his wedding day for all his sins committed in years gone by.

Scarcely had Jacob left his father's house, when Rebekah began to weep, for she was sorely distressed about him. Isaac comforted her, saying: "Weep not for Jacob! In peace doth he depart, and in peace will he return. The Lord, God Most High, will guard him against all evil and be with him. He will not forsake him all the days of his life. Have no fear for him, for he walketh on the right path, he is a perfect man, and he hath faith in God--he will not perish."

JACOB PURSUED BY ELIPHAZ AND ESAU

When Jacob went away to go to Haran, Esau called his son Eliphaz, and secretly spoke unto him, saying: "Now hasten, take thy sword in thy hand and pursue Jacob, and pass before him in the road, and lurk for him and slay him with thy sword in one of the mountains, and take all belonging unto him, and come back." And Eliphaz was dexterous and expert with the bow, as his father had taught him, and he was a noted hunter in the field and a valiant man. And Eliphaz did as his father had commanded him. And Eliphaz was at that time thirteen years old, and he arose and went and took ten of his mother's brothers with him, and pursued Jacob. And he followed Jacob closely, and when he overtook him, he lay in ambush for him on the borders of the land of Canaan, opposite to the city of Shechem. And Jacob saw Eliphaz and his men pursuing after him, and Jacob stood in the place in which he was going in order to know what it was, for he did not understand their purpose. Eliphaz drew his sword and went on advancing, he and his men, toward Jacob, and Jacob said unto them, "Wherefore have you come hither, and why do you pursue with your swords?" Eliphaz came near to Jacob, and answered as follows, "Thus did my father command me, and now therefore I will not deviate from the orders which my father gave me." And when Jacob saw that Esau had impressed his command urgently upon Eliphaz, he approached and supplicated Eliphaz and his men, saying, "Behold, all that I have, and that which my father and mother gave unto me, that take unto thee and go from me, and do not slay me, and may this thing that thou wilt do with me be accounted unto thee as righteousness." And the Lord caused Jacob to find favor in the sight of Eliphaz and his men, and they hearkened to the voice of Jacob, and they did not put him to death, but took all his belongings, together with the silver and gold that he had brought with him from Beer-sheba. They left him nothing. When Eliphaz and his men returned to Esau, and told him all that had happened to them with Jacob, he was wroth with his son Eliphaz and with his men, because they had not put Jacob to death. And they answered, and said unto Esau, "Because Jacob supplicated us in this matter, not to slay him, our pity was moved toward him, and we took all belonging to him, and we came back." Esau then took all the silver and gold which Eliphaz had taken from Jacob, and he put them by in his house.

Nevertheless Esau did not give up the hope of intercepting Jacob on his flight and slaying him. He pursued him, and with his men occupied the road along which he had to journey to Haran. There a great miracle happened to Jacob. When he observed what Esau's intention was, he turned off toward the Jordan river, and, with eyes directed to God, he cleft the waters with his wanderer's staff, and succeeded in crossing to the other side. But Esau was not to be deterred. He kept up the pursuit, and reached the hot springs at Baarus before his brother, who had to pass by there. Jacob, not knowing that Esau was on the watch for him, decided to bathe in the spring, saying, "I have neither bread nor other things needful, so I will at least warm my body in the waters of the well." While he was in the bath, Esau occupied every exit, and Jacob would surely have perished in the hot water, if the Lord had not caused a miracle to come to pass. A new opening formed of itself, and through it Jacob escaped. Thus were fulfilled the words, "When thou passest through the waters, I will be with thee; when thou walkest through the fire, thou shalt not be burnt," for Jacob was saved from the waters of the Jordan and from the fire of the hot spring.

At the same time with Jacob, a rider, leaving his horse and his clothes on the shore, had stepped into the river to cool off, but he was overwhelmed by the waves, and he met his death. Jacob put on the dead man's clothes, mounted his horse, and went off. It was a lucky chance, for Eliphaz had stripped him of everything, even his clothes, and the miracle of the river had happened only that he might not be forced to appear naked among men.

Though Jacob was robbed of all his possessions, his courage did not fail him. He said: "Should I lose hope in my Creator? I set my eyes upon the merits of my fathers. For the sake of them the Lord will give me His aid." And God said: "Jacob, thou puttest thy trust in the merits of thy fathers, therefore I will not suffer thy foot to be moved; He that keepeth thee will not slumber. Yea, still more! While a keeper watcheth only by day as a rule, and sleepeth by night, I will guard thee day and night, for, behold, He that keepeth Israel shall neither slumber nor sleep. The Lord will keep thee from all evil, from Esau as well as Laban; He will keep thy soul, that the Angel of Death do thee no hurt; He will keep thy going out and thy coming in, He will support thee now thou art leaving Canaan, and when thou returnest to Canaan."

Jacob was reluctant to leave the Holy Land before he received direct permission from God. "My parents," he reflected, "bade me go forth and sojourn outside of the land, but who knows whether it be the will of God that I do as they say, and beget children outside of the Holy Land?" Accordingly, he betook himself to Beer-sheba. There, where the Lord had given permission to Isaac to depart from Canaan and go to Philistia, he would learn the will of the Lord concerning himself.

He did not follow the example of his father and grandfather and take refuge with Abimelech, because he feared the king might force also him into a covenant, and make it impossible for his descendants of many generations to take possession of the Philistine land. Nor could he stay at home, because of his fear that Esau might wrest the birthright and the blessing from him, and to that he would not and could not agree. He was as little disposed to take up the combat with Esau, for he knew the truth of the maxim, "He who courts danger will be overcome by it; he who avoids danger will overcome it." Both Abraham and Isaac had lived according to this rule. His grandfather had fled from Nimrod, and his father had gone away from the Philistines.

THE DAY OF MIRACLES

Jacob's journey to Haran was a succession of miracles. The first of the five that befell for his sake in the course of it was that the sun sank while Jacob was passing Mount Moriah, though it was high noon at the time. He was following the spring that appeared wherever the Patriarchs went or settled. It accompanied Jacob from Beer-sheba to Mount Moriah, a two days' journey. When he arrived at the holy hill, the Lord said to him: "Jacob, thou hast bread in thy wallet, and the spring of waters is near by to quench thy thirst. Thus thou hast food and drink, and here thou canst lodge for the night." But Jacob replied: "The sun has barely passed the fifth of its twelve day stages, why should I lie down to sleep at so unseemly an hour?" But then Jacob perceived that the sun was about to sink, and he prepared to make ready his bed. It was the Divine purpose not to let Jacob pass the site of the future Temple without stopping; he was to tarry there at least one night. Also, God desired to appear unto Jacob, and He shows Himself unto His faithful ones only at night. At the same time Jacob was saved from the pursuit of Esau, who had to desist on account of the premature darkness.

Jacob took twelve stones from the altar on which his father Isaac had lain bound as a sacrifice, and he said: "It was the purpose of God to let twelve tribes arise, but they have not been begotten by Abraham or Isaac. If, now, these twelve stones will unite into a single one, then shall I know for a certainty that I am destined to become the father of the twelve tribes." At this time the second miracle came to pass, the twelve stones joined themselves together and made one, which he put under his head, and at once it became soft and downy like a pillow. It was well that he had a comfortable couch. He was in great need of rest, for it was the first night in fourteen years that he did not keep vigils. During all those years, passed in Eber's house of learning, he had devoted the nights to study. And for twenty years to come he was not to sleep, for while he was with his uncle Laban, he spent all the night and every night reciting the Psalms.

On the whole it was a night of marvels. He dreamed a dream in which the course of the world's history was unfolded to him. On a ladder set up on the earth, with the top of it reaching to heaven, he beheld the two angels who had been sent to Sodom. For one hundred and thirty-eight years they had been banished from the celestial regions, because they had betrayed their secret mission to Lot. They had accompanied Jacob from his father's house thither, and now they were ascending heavenward. When they arrived there, he heard them call the other angels, and say, "Come ye and see the countenance of the pious Jacob, whose likeness appears on the Divine throne, ye who yearned long to see it," and then he beheld the angels descend from heaven to gaze upon him. He also saw the angels of the four kingdoms ascending the ladder. The angel of Babylon mounted seventy rounds, the angel of Media, fifty-two, that of Greece, one hundred and eighty, and that of Edom mounted very high, saying, "I will ascend above the heights of the clouds, I will be like the Most High," and Jacob heard a voice remonstrating, "Yet thou shalt be brought down to hell, to the uttermost parts of the pit." God Himself reproved Edom, saying, "Though thou mount on high as the eagle, and though thy nest be set among the stars, I will bring thee down from thence."

Furthermore, God showed unto Jacob the revelation at Mount Sinai, the translation of Elijah, the Temple in its glory and in its spoliation, Nebuchadnezzar's attempt to burn the three holy children in the fiery furnace, and Daniel's encounter with Bel.

In this, the first prophetic dream dreamed by Jacob, God made him the promise that the land upon which he was lying would be given to him, but the land he lay upon was the whole of Palestine, which God had folded together and put under him. "And," the promise continued, "thy seed will be like unto the dust of the earth.

As the earth survives all things, so thy children will survive all the nations of the earth. But as the earth is trodden upon by all, so thy children, when they commit trespasses, will be trodden upon by the nations of the earth." And, furthermore, God promised that Jacob should spread out to the west and to the east, a greater promise than that given to his fathers Abraham and Isaac, to whom He had allotted a limited land. Jacob's was an unbounded possession.

From this wondrous dream Jacob awoke with a start of fright, on account of the vision he had had of the destruction of the Temple. He cried out, "How dreadful is this place! this is none other but the house of God, wherein is the gate of heaven through which prayer ascends to Him." He took the stone made out of the twelve, and set it up for a pillar, and poured oil upon the top of it, which had flowed down from heaven for him, and God sank this anointed stone unto the abyss, to serve as the centre of the earth, the same stone, the Eben Shetiyah, that forms the centre of the sanctuary, whereon the Ineffable Name is graven, the knowledge of which makes a man master over nature, and over life and death.

Jacob cast himself down before the Eben Shetiyah, and entreated God to fulfil the promise He had given him, and also he prayed that God grant him honorable sustenance. For God had not mentioned bread to eat and raiment to put on, that Jacob might learn to have faith in the Lord. Then he vowed to give the tenth of all he owned unto God, if He would but grant his petition. Thus Jacob was the first to take a vow upon himself, and the first, too, to separate the tithe from his income.

God had promised him almost all that is desirable, but he feared he might forfeit the pledged blessings through his sinfulness, and again he prayed earnestly that God bring him back to his father's house unimpaired in body, possessions, and knowledge, and guard him, in the strange land whither he was going, against idolatry, an immoral life, and bloodshed.

His prayer at an end, Jacob set out on his way to Haran, and the third wonder happened. In the twinkling of an eye he arrived at his destination. The earth jumped from Mount Moriah to Haran. A wonder like this God has executed only four times in the whole course of history.

The first thing to meet his eye in Haran was the well whence the inhabitants drew their supply of water. Although it was a great city, Haran suffered from dearth of water, and therefore the well could not be used by the people free of charge. Jacob's sojourn in the city produced a change. By reason of his meritorious deeds the water springs were blessed, and the city had water enough for its needs.

Jacob saw a number of people by the well, and he questioned them, "My brethren, whence be ye?" He thus made himself a model for all to follow. A man should be companionable, and address others like brothers and friends, and not wait for them to greet him. Each one should strive to be the first to give the salutation of peace, that the angels of peace and compassion may come to meet him. When he was informed that the by-standers hailed from Haran, he made inquiry about the character and vocation of his uncle Laban, and whether they were on terms of friendly intercourse with him. They answered briefly: "There is peace between us, but if thou art desirous of inquiring further, here comes Rachel the daughter of Laban. From her thou canst learn all thou hast a mind to learn." They knew that women like to talk, wherefore they referred him to Rachel.

Jacob found it strange that so many should be standing idle by the well, and he questioned further: "Are you day laborers? then it is too early for you to put by your work. But if you are pasturing your own sheep, why do you not water your flocks and let them feed?" They told him they were waiting until all the shepherds brought their flocks thither, and together rolled the stone from the mouth of the well. While he was yet speaking with them, Rachel came with her father's sheep, for Laban had no sons, and a pest having broken out shortly before among his cattle, so few sheep were left that a maiden like Rachel could easily tend them. Now, when Jacob saw the daughter of his mother's brother approaching, he rolled the great stone from the mouth of the well as easily as a cork is drawn from a bottle--the fourth wonder of this extraordinary day. Jacob's strength was equal to the strength of all the shepherds; with his two arms alone he accomplished what usually requires the united forces of a large assemblage of men. He had been divinely endowed with this supernatural strength on leaving the Holy Land. God had caused the dew of the resurrection to drop down upon him, and his physical strength was so great that even in a combat with the angels he was victorious.

The fifth and last wonder of the day was that the water rose from the depths of the well to the very top, there was no need to draw it up, and there it remained all the twenty years that Jacob abode in Haran.

JACOB WITH LABAN

Rachel's coming to the well at the moment when Jacob reached the territory belonging to Haran was an auspicious omen. To meet young maidens on first entering a city is a sure sign that fortune is favorable to one's undertakings. Experience proves this through Eliezer, Jacob, Moses, and Saul. They all encountered maidens when they approached a place new to them, and they all met with success.

Jacob treated Rachel at once as his cousin, which caused significant whispering among the by-standers. They censured Jacob for his demeanor toward her, for since God had sent the deluge upon the world, on account of the immoral life led by men, great chastity had prevailed, especially among the people of the east. The talk of the men reduced Jacob to tears. Scarcely had he kissed Rachel when he began to weep, for he repented of having done it.

There was reason enough for tears. Jacob could not but remember sadly that Eliezer, his grandfather's slave, had brought ten camels laden with presents with him to Haran, when he came to sue for a bride for Isaac, while he had not even a ring to give to Rachel. Moreover, he foresaw that his favorite wife Rachel would not lie beside him in the grave, and this, too, made him weep.

As soon as Rachel heard that Jacob was her cousin, she ran home to tell her father about his coming. Her mother was no longer among the living, else she would naturally have gone to her. In great haste Laban ran to receive Jacob. He reflected, if Eliezer, the bondman, had come with ten camels, what would not the favorite son of the family bring with him, and when he saw that Jacob was unattended, he concluded that he carried great sums of money in his girdle, and he threw his arms about his waist to find out whether his supposition was true. Disappointed in this, he yet did not give up hope that his nephew Jacob was a man of substance. Perhaps he concealed precious stones in his mouth, and he kissed him in order to find out whether he had guessed aright. But Jacob said to him: "Thou thinkest I have money. Nay, thou art mistaken, I have but words." Then he went on to tell him how it had come about that he stood before him empty-handed. He said that his father Isaac had sent him on his way provided with gold, silver, and money, but he had encountered Eliphaz, who had threatened to slay him. To this assailant Jacob had spoken thus: "Know that the descendants of Abraham have an obligation to meet, they will have to serve four hundred years in a land that is not theirs. If thou slayest me, then you, the seed of Esau, will have to pay the debt. It were better, therefore, to take all I have, and spare my life, so that what is owing may be paid by me. Hence," Jacob continued, "I stand before thee bare of all the substance carried off by Eliphaz."

This tale of his nephew's poverty filled Laban with dismay. "What," he exclaimed, "shall I have to give food and drink for a month or, perhaps, even a year to this fellow, who has come to me empty-handed!" He betook himself to his teraphim, to ask them for counsel upon the matter, and they admonished him, saying: "Beware of sending him away from thy house. His star and his constellation are so lucky that good fortune will attend all his undertakings, and for his sake the blessing of the Lord will rest upon all thou doest, in thy house or in thy field."

Laban was satisfied with the advice of the teraphim, but he was embarrassed as to the way in which he was to attach Jacob to his house. He did not venture to offer him service, lest Jacob's conditions be impossible of fulfilment. Again he resorted to the teraphim, and asked them with what reward to tempt his nephew, and they replied: "A wife is his wage; he will ask nothing else of thee but a wife. It is his nature to be attracted by women, and whenever he threatens to leave thee, do but offer him another wife, and he will not depart.

Laban went back to Jacob, and said, "Tell me, what shall thy wages be?" and he replied, "Thinkest thou I came hither to make money? I came only to get me a wife," for Jacob had no sooner beheld Rachel than he fell in love with her and made her a proposal of marriage. Rachel consented, but added the warning: "My father is cunning, and thou art not his match." Jacob: "I am his brother in cunning." Rachel: "But is deception becoming unto the pious?" Jacob: "Yes, 'with the righteous righteousness is seemly, and with the deceiver deception.' But," continued Jacob, "tell me wherein he may deal cunningly with me." Rachel: "I have an older sister, whom he desires to see married before me, and he will try to palm her off on thee instead of me." To be prepared for Laban's trickery, Jacob and Rachel agreed upon a sign by which he would recognize her in the nuptial night.

Thus warned to be on his guard against Laban, Jacob worded his agreement with him regarding his marriage to Rachel with such precision that no room was left for distortion or guile. Jacob said: "I know that the people of this place are knaves, therefore I desire to put the matter very clearly to thee. I will serve thee seven years for Rachel, hence not Leah; for thy daughter, that thou bringest me not some other woman likewise named Rachel; for the younger daughter, that thou exchangest not their names in the meantime."

Nothing of all this availed: "It profits not if a villain is cast into a sawmill"--neither force nor gentle words can circumvent a rascal. Laban deceived not only Jacob, but also the guests whom he invited to the wedding.

THE MARRIAGE OF JACOB

After Jacob had served Laban seven years, he said to his uncle: "The Lord destined me to be the father of twelve tribes. I am now eighty-four years old, and if I do not take thought of the matter now, when can I?" Thereupon Laban consented to let him have his daughter Rachel to wife, and he was married forty-four years after his brother Esau. The Lord often defers the happiness of the pious, while He permits the wicked to enjoy the fulfilment of their desires soon. Esau, however, had purposely chosen his fortieth year for his marriage; he had wanted to indicate that he was walking in the footsteps of his father Isaac, who had likewise married at forty years of age. Esau was like a swine that stretches out its feet when it lies down, to show that it is cloven-footed like the clean animals, though it is none the less one of the unclean animals. Until his fortieth year Esau made a practice of violating the wives of other men, and then at his marriage he acted as though he were following the example of his pious father. Accordingly, the woman he married was of his own kind, Judith, a daughter of Heth, for God said: "This one, who is designed for stubble, to be burnt by fire, shall take unto wife one of a people also destined for utter destruction." They, Esau and his wife, illustrated the saying, "Not for naught does the raven consort with the crow; they are birds of a feather."

Far different it was with Jacob. He married the two pious and lovely sisters, Leah and Rachel, for Leah, like her younger sister, was beautiful of countenance, form, and stature. She had but one defect, her eyes were weak, and this malady she had brought down upon herself, through her own action. Laban, who had two daughters, and Rebekah, his sister, who had two sons, had agreed by letter, while their children were still young, that the older son of the one was to marry the older daughter of the other, and the younger son the younger daughter. When Leah grew to maidenhood, and inquired about her future husband, all her tidings spoke of his villainous character, and she wept over her fate until her eyelashes dropped from their lids. But Rachel grew more and more beautiful day by day, for all who spoke of Jacob praised and extolled him, and "good tidings make the bones fat."

In view of the agreement between Laban and Rebekah, Jacob refused to marry the older daughter Leah. As it was, Esau was his mortal enemy, on account of what had happened regarding the birthright and the paternal blessing. If, now, Jacob married the maiden appointed for him, Esau would never forgive his younger brother. Therefore Jacob resolved to take to wife Rachel, the younger daughter of his uncle.

Laban was of another mind. He purposed to marry of his older daughter first, for he knew that Jacob would consent to serve him a second period of seven years for love of Rachel. On the day of the wedding he assembled the inhabitants of Haran, and addressed them as follows: "Ye know well that we used to suffer from lack of water, and as soon as this pious man Jacob came to dwell among us, we had water in abundance." "What hast thou in mind to do?" they asked Laban. He replied: "If ye have naught to say against it, I will deceive him and give him Leah to wife. He loves Rachel with an exceeding great love, and for her sake he will tarry with us yet seven other years." "Do as it pleaseth thee," his friends said. "Well, then," said Laban, "let each one of you give me a pledge that ye will not betray my purpose."

With the pledges they left with him, Laban bought wine, oil, and meat for the wedding feast, and he set a meal before them which they had themselves paid for. Because he deceived his fellow-citizens thus, Laban is called Arami, "the deceiver." They feasted all day long, until late at night, and when Jacob expressed his astonishment at the attention shown him, they said to him: "Through thy piety thou didst a great service of lovingkindness unto us, our supply of water was increased unto abundance, and we desire to show our gratitude therefor." And, indeed, they tried to give him a hint of Laban's purpose. In the marriage ode which they sang they used the refrain "Halia," in the hope that he would understand it as Ha Leah, "This is Leah." But Jacob was unsuspicious and noticed nothing.

When the bride was led into the nuptial chamber, the guests extinguished all the candles, much to Jacob's amazement. But their explanation satisfied him. "Thinkest thou," they said, "we have as little sense of decency as thy countrymen?" Jacob therefore did not discover the deception practiced upon him until morning. During the night Leah responded whenever he called Rachel, for which he reproached her bitterly when daylight came. "O thou deceiver, daughter of a deceiver, why didst thou answer me when I called Rachel's name?" "Is there a teacher without a pupil?" asked Leah, in return. "I but profited by thy instruction. When thy father called thee Esau, didst thou not say, Here am I?"

Jacob was greatly enraged against Laban, and he said to him: "Why didst thou deal treacherously with me? Take back thy daughter, and let me depart, seeing thou didst act wickedly toward me." Laban pacified him, however, saying, "It is not so done in our place, to give the younger before the first-born," and Jacob agreed to serve yet seven other years for Rachel, and after the seven days of the feast of Leah's wedding were fulfilled, he married Rachel.

With Leah and Rachel, Jacob received the handmaids Zilpah and Bilhah, two other daughters of Laban, whom his concubines had borne unto him.

THE BIRTH OF JACOB'S CHILDREN

The ways of God are not like unto the ways of men. A man clings close to his friend while he has riches, and forsakes him when he falls into poverty. But when God sees a mortal unsteady and faltering, He reaches a hand out to him, and raises him up. Thus it happened with Leah. She was hated by Jacob, and God visited her in mercy. Jacob's aversion to Leah began the very morning after their wedding, when his wife taunted him with not being wholly free from cunning and craft himself. Then God said, "Help can come to Leah only if she gives birth to a child; then the love of her husband will return to her." God remembered the tears she had shed when she prayed that her doom, chaining her to that recreant Esau, be averted from her, and so wondrous are the uses of prayer that Leah, besides turning aside the impending decree, was permitted to marry Jacob before her sister and be the first to bear him a child. There was another reason why the Lord was compassionately inclined toward Leah. She had gotten herself talked about. The sailors on the sea, the travellers along the highways, the women at their looms, they all gossiped about Leah, saying, "She is not within what her seeming is without. She appears to be pious, but if she were, she would not have deceived her sister." To put an end to all this tattle, God granted her the distinction of bearing a son at the end of seven months after her marriage. He was one of a pair of twins, the other child being a daughter. So it was with eleven of the sons of Jacob, all of them except Joseph were born twins with a girl, and the twin sister and brother married later on. Altogether it was an extraordinary childbirth, for Leah was barren, not formed by nature to bear children.

She called her first-born son Reuben, which means "See the normal man," for he was neither big nor little, neither dark nor fair, but exactly normal. In calling her oldest child Reuben, "See the son," Leah indicated his future character. "Behold the difference," the name implied, "between my first-born son and the first-born son of my father in-law. Esau sold his birthright to Jacob of his own free will, and yet he hated him. As for my first-born son, although his birthright was taken from him without his consent, and given to Joseph, it was nevertheless he who rescued Joseph from the hands of his brethren."

Leah called her second son Shime'on, "Yonder is sin," for one of his descendants was that Zimri who was guilty of vile trespasses with the daughters of Moab.

The name of her third son, Levi, was given him by God Himself, not by his mother. The Lord summoned him through the angel Gabriel, and bestowed the name upon him as one who is "crowned" with the twenty-four gifts that are the tribute due to the priests.

At the birth of her fourth son, Leah returned thanks to God for a special reason. She knew that Jacob would beget twelve sons, and if they were distributed equally among his four wives, each would bear three. But now it appeared that she had one more than her due share, and she called him Jehudah, "thanks unto God." She was thus the first since the creation of the world to give thanks to God, and her example was followed by David and Daniel, the descendants of her son Judah.

When Rachel saw that her sister had borne Jacob four sons, she envied Leah. Not that she begrudged her the good fortune she enjoyed, she only envied her for her piety, saying to herself that it was to her righteous conduct that she owed the blessing of many children. Then she besought Jacob: "Pray unto God for me, that He grant me children, else my life is no life. Verily, there are four that may be regarded as though they were dead, the blind, the leper, the childless, and he who was once rich and has lost his fortune." Jacob's anger was kindled against Rachel, and he said: "It were better thou shouldst address thy petition to God, and not to me, for am I in God's stead, who hath withheld from thee the fruit of the womb?" God was displeased with this answer that Jacob made to his sad wife. He rebuked him with the words: "Is it thus thou wouldst comfort a grief-stricken heart? As thou livest, the day will come when thy children will stand before the son of Rachel, and he will use the same words thou hast but now used, saying, 'Am I in the place of the Lord?' "

Rachel also made reply to Jacob, saying: "Did not thy father, too, entreat God for thy mother with earnest words, beseeching Him to remove her barrenness?" Jacob: "It is true, but Isaac had no children, and I have several." Rachel: "Remember thy grandfather Abraham, thou canst not deny that he had children when he supplicated God in behalf of Sarah!" Jacob: "Wouldst thou do for me what Sarah did for my grandfather?" Rachel: "Pray, what did she?" Jacob: "She herself brought a rival into her house." Rachel: "If that is all that is necessary, I am ready to follow the example of Sarah, and I pray that as she was granted a child for having invited a rival, so may I be blessed, too." Thereupon Rachel gave Jacob Bilhah, her freed handmaid, to wife, and she bore him a son, whom Rachel called Dan, saying, "As the Lord was gracious unto me and gave me a son according to my petition, so He will permit Samson, the descendant of Dan, to judge his people, that it fall not into the hands of the Philistines." Bilhah's second son Rachel named Naphtali, saying, "Mine is the bond that binds Jacob to this place, for it was for my sake that he came to Laban." At the same time she wanted to convey by this name that the Torah, which is as sweet as Nofet, "honeycomb," would be taught in the territory of Naphtali. And the name had still a third meaning: "As God hath heard my fervent prayer for a son, so He will hearken unto the fervent prayer of the Naphtalites when they are beset by their enemies."

Leah, seeing that she had left bearing, while Bilhah, her sister's handmaid, bore Jacob two sons, concluded that it was Jacob's destiny to have four wives, her sister and herself, and their half-sisters Bilhah and Zilpah. Therefore she also gave him her handmaid to wife. Zilpah was the youngest of the four women. It was the custom of that time to give the older daughter the older handmaid, and the younger daughter the younger handmaid, as their dowry, when they got married. Now, in order to make Jacob believe that his wife was the younger daughter he had served for, Laban had given Leah the younger handmaid as her marriage portion. This Zilpah was so young that her body betrayed no outward signs of pregnancy, and nothing was known of her condition until her son was born. Leah called the boy Gad, which means "fortune," or it may mean "the cutter," for from Gad was descended the prophet Elijah, who brings good fortune to Israel, and he also cuts down the heathen world. Leah had other reasons, too, for choosing this name of double meaning. The tribe of Gad had the good fortune of entering into possession of its allotment in the Holy Land before any of the others, and, also, Gad the son of Jacob was born circumcised.

To Zilpah's second son Leah gave the name of Asher, "praise," for, she said, "Unto me all manner of praise is due, for I brought my handmaid into the house of my husband as wife. Sarah did likewise, but only because she had no children, and so it was also with Rachel. But as for me, I had children, and nevertheless I subdued my passion, and without jealousy I gave my handmaid to my husband for wife. Verily, all will praise and extol me." Furthermore she spoke: "As the women will praise me, so the sons of Asher will in time to come praise God for their fruitful possession in the Holy Land."

The next son born unto Jacob was Issachar, "a reward," and once more it was Leah who was permitted to bring forth the child, as a reward from God for her pious desire to have the twelve tribes come into the world. To secure this result, she left no means untried.

It happened once that her oldest son Reuben was tending his father's ass during the harvest, and he bound him to a root of dudaim, and went his way. On returning, he found the dudaim torn out of the ground, and the ass lying dead beside it. The beast had uprooted it in trying to get loose, and the plant has a peculiar quality, whoever tears it up must die. As it was the time of the harvest, when it is permitted for any one to take a plant from a field, and as dudaim is, besides, a plant which the owner of a field esteems lightly, Reuben carried it home. Being a good son, he did not keep it for himself, but gave it to his mother. Rachel desired the dudaim, and she asked the plant of Leah, who parted with it to her sister, but on the condition that Jacob, when he returned from work in the evening, should tarry with her for a while. It was altogether unbecoming conduct in Rachel to dispose thus of her husband. She gained the dudaim, but she lost two tribes. If she had acted otherwise, she would have borne four sons instead of two. And she suffered another punishment, her body was not permitted to rest in the grave beside her husband's.

Jacob came home from the field after night had fallen, for he observed the law obliging a day laborer to work until darkness sets in, and Jacob's zeal in the affairs of Laban was as great in the last seven years, after his marriage, as in the first seven, while he was serving for the hand of Rachel. When Leah heard the braying of Jacob's ass, she ran to meet her husband, and without giving him time to wash his feet, she insisted upon his turning aside into her tent. At first Jacob refused to go, but God compelled him to enter, for unto God it was known that Leah acted from pure, disinterested motives. Her dudaim secured two sons for her, Issachar, the father of the tribe that devotes itself to the study of the Torah, whence his name meaning "reward," and Zebulon, whose descendants carried on commerce, using their profits to enable their brethren of Issachar to keep at their studies. Leah called this last-born son of hers Zebulon, "dwelling-place," for she said, "Now will my husband dwell with me, seeing that I have borne him six sons, and, also, the sons of Zebulon will have a goodly dwelling-place in the Holy Land."

Leah bore once more, and this last time it was a daughter, a man child turned into a woman by her prayer. When she conceived for the seventh time, she spake as follows: "God promised Jacob twelve sons. I bore him six, and each of the two handmaids has borne him two. If, now, I were to bring forth another son, my sister Rachel would not be equal even unto the handmaids." Therefore she prayed to God to change the male embryo in her womb into a female, and God hearkened unto her prayer.

Now all the wives of Jacob, Leah, Rachel, Zilpah, and Bilhah, united their prayers with the prayer of Jacob, and together they besought God to remove the curse of barrenness from Rachel. On New Year's Day, the day whereon God sits in judgment upon the inhabitants of the earth, He remembered Rachel, and granted her a son. And Rachel spake, "God hath taken away my reproach," for all the people had said that she was not a pious woman, else had she borne children, and now that God had hearkened to her, and opened her womb, such idle talk no longer had any reason.

By bearing a son, she had escaped another disgrace. She had said to herself: "Jacob hath a mind to return to the land of his birth, and my father will not be able to hinder his daughters who have borne him children from following their husband thither with their children. But he will not let me, the childless wife, go, too, and he will keep me here and marry me to one of the uncircumcised." She said furthermore, "As my son hath removed my reproach, so Joshua, his descendant, will roll away a reproach from the Israelites, when he circumcises them beyond Jordan."

Rachel called her son Joseph, "increase," saying, "God will give me an additional son." Prophetess as she was, she foresaw she would have a second son. But an increase added on by God is larger than the original capital itself. Benjamin, the second son, whom Rachel regarded merely as a supplement, had ten sons, while Joseph begot only two. These twelve together may be considered the twelve tribes borne by Rachel. Had Rachel not used the form of expression, "The Lord add to me another son," she herself would have begotten twelve tribes with Jacob.

JACOB FLEES BEFORE LABAN

Jacob had only been waiting for Joseph to be born to begin preparations for his journey home. The holy spirit had revealed to him that the house of Joseph would work the destruction of the house of Esau, and, therefore, Jacob exclaimed at the birth of Joseph, "Now I need not fear Esau or his legions.

About this time, Rebekah sent her nurse Deborah, the daughter of Uz, accompanied by two of Isaac's servants, to Jacob, to urge him to return to his father's house, now that his fourteen years of service had come to an end. Then Jacob approached Laban, and spoke, "Give me my wives and my children, that I may go unto mine own place, and to my country, for my mother has sent messengers unto me, bidding me to return to my father's house." Laban answered, saying, "O that I might find favor in thine eyes! By a sign it was made known unto me that God blesseth me for thy sake." What Laban had in mind was the treasure he had found on the day Jacob came to him, and he considered that a token of his beneficent powers. Indeed, God had wrought many a thing in the house of Laban that testified to the blessings spread abroad by the pious. Shortly before Jacob came, a pest had broken out among Laban's cattle, and with his arrival it ceased. And Laban had had no son, but during Jacob's sojourn in Haran sons were born unto him.

All the hire he asked in return for his labor and for the blessings he had brought Laban was the speckled and spotted among the goats of his herd, and the black among the sheep. Laban assented to his conditions, saying, "Behold, I would it might be according to thy word." The arch-villain Laban, whose tongue wagged in all directions, and who made all sorts of promises that were never kept, judged others by himself, and therefore suspected Jacob of wanting to deceive him. And yet, in the end, it was Laban himself who broke his word. No less than a hundred times he changed the agreement between them. Nevertheless his unrighteous conduct was of no avail. Though a three days' journey had been set betwixt Laban's flocks and Jacob's, the angels were wont to bring the sheep belonging to Laban down to Jacob's sheep, and Jacob's droves grew constantly larger and better. Laban had given only the feeble and sick to Jacob, yet the young of the flock, raised under Jacob's tendance, were so excellent in quality that people bought them at a heavy price. And Jacob had no need to resort to the peeled rods. He had but to speak, and the flocks bare according to his desire. What Laban deserved was utter ruin, for having permitted the pious Jacob to work for him without hire, and after his wages had been changed ten times, and ten times Laban had tried to overreach him, God rewarded him in this way. But his good luck with the flocks was only what Jacob deserved. Every faithful laborer is rewarded by God in this world, quite regardless of what awaits him in the world to come. With empty hands Jacob had come to Laban, and he left him with herds numbering six hundred thousand. Their increase had been marvellous, an increase that will be equalled only in the Messianic time.

The wealth and good fortune of Jacob called forth the envy of Laban and his sons, and they could not hide their vexation in their intercourse with him. And the Lord said unto Jacob, "Thy father-in-law's countenance is not toward thee as beforetime, and yet thou tarriest with him? Do thou rather return unto the land of thy fathers, and there I will let My Shekinah rest upon thee, for I cannot permit the Shekinah to reside outside of the Holy Land." Immediately Jacob sent the fleet messenger Naphtali to Rachel and Leah to summon them to a consultation, and he chose as the place of meeting the open field, where none could overhear what was said.

His two wives approved the plan of returning to his home, and Jacob resolved at once to go away with all his substance, without as much as acquainting Laban with his intention. Laban was gone to shear his sheep, and so Jacob could execute his plan without delay.

That her father might not learn about their flight from his teraphim, Rachel stole them, and she took them and concealed them upon the camel upon which she sat, and she went on. And this is the manner they used to make the images: They took a man who was the first-born, slew him and took the hair off his head, then salted the head, and anointed it with oil, then they wrote "the Name" upon a small tablet of copper or gold, and placed it under his tongue. The head with the tablet under the tongue was then put in a house where lights were lighted before it, and at the time when they bowed down to it, it spoke to them on all matters that they asked of it, and that was due to the power of the Name which was written upon it.

THE COVENANT WITH LABAN

Jacob departed and crossed the Euphrates, and set his face toward Gilead, for the holy spirit revealed to him that God would bring help there to his children in the days of Jephthah. Meantime the shepherds of Haran observed that the well, which had been filled to overflowing since the arrival of Jacob in their place, ran dry suddenly. For three days they watched and waited, in the hope that the waters would return in the same abundance as before. Disappointed, they finally told Laban of the misfortune, and he divined at once that Jacob had departed thence, for he knew that the blessing had been conferred upon Haran only for the sake of his son-in-law's merits.

On the morrow Laban rose early, assembled all the people of the city, and pursued Jacob with the intention of killing him when he overtook him. But the archangel Michael appeared unto him, and bade him take heed unto himself, that he do not the least unto Jacob, else would he suffer death himself. This message from heaven came to Laban during the night, for when, in extraordinary cases, God finds it necessary to reveal Himself unto the heathen, He does it only in the dark, clandestinely as it were, while He shows Himself to the prophets of the Jews openly, during daylight.

Laban accomplished the journey in one day for which Jacob had taken seven, and he overtook him at the mountain of Gilead. When he came upon Jacob, he found him in the act of praying and giving praise unto God. Immediately Laban fell to remonstrating with his son-in-law for having stolen away unawares to him. He showed his true character when he said, "It is in the power of my hand to do thee hurt, but the God of thy father spake unto me yesternight, saying, Take heed to thyself that thou speak not to Jacob either good or bad." That is the way of the wicked, they boast of the evil they can do. Laban wanted to let Jacob know that only the dream warning him against doing aught that was harmful to Jacob prevented him from carrying out the wicked design he had formed against him.

Laban continued to take Jacob to task, and he concluded with the words, "And now, though thou wouldst needs be gone, because thou sore longedst after thy father's house, yet wherefore hast thou stolen my gods?" When he pronounced the last words, his grandchildren interrupted him, saying, "We are ashamed of thee, grandfather, that in thy old age thou shouldst use such words as 'my gods.' " Laban searched all the tents for his idols, going first to the tent of Jacob, which was Rachel's at the same time, for Jacob always dwelt with his favorite wife. Finding nothing, he went thence to Leah's tent, and to the tents of the two handmaids, and, noticing that Rachel was feeling about here and there, his suspicions were aroused, and he entered her tent a second time. He would now have found what he was looking for, if a miracle had not come to pass. The teraphim were transformed into drinking vessels, and Laban had to desist from his fruitless search.

Now Jacob, who did not know that Rachel had stolen her father's teraphim in order to turn him aside from his idolatrous ways, was wroth with Laban, and began to chide with him. In the quarrel between them, Jacob's noble character manifested itself. Notwithstanding his excitement, he did not suffer a single unbecoming word to escape him. He only reminded Laban of the loyalty and devotion with which he had served him, doing for him what none other would or could have done. He said: "I dealt wrongfully with the lion, for God had appointed of Laban's sheep for the lion's daily sustenance, and I deprived him thereof. Could another shepherd have done thus? Yes, the people abused me, calling me robber and sneak thief, for they thought that only by stealing by day and stealing by night could I replace the animals torn by wild beasts. And as to my honesty," he continued, "is it likely there is another son-in-law who, having lived with his father-in-law, hath not taken some little thing from the household of his father-in-law, a knife, or other trifle? But thou hast felt about all my stuff, what hast thou found of all thy household stuff? Not so much as a needle or a nail."

In his indignation, and conscious of his innocence, Jacob exclaimed, "With whomsoever thou findest thy gods, he shall not live," words which contained a curse—the thief was cursed with premature death, and therefore Rachel had to die in giving birth to Benjamin. Indeed, the curse would have taken effect at once, had it not been the wish of God that Rachel should bear Jacob his youngest son.

After the quarrel, the two men made a treaty, and with his gigantic strength Jacob set up a huge rock as a memorial, and a heap of stones as a sign of their covenant. In this matter Jacob followed the example of his fathers, who likewise had covenanted with heathen nations, Abraham with the Jebusites, and Isaac with the Philistines. Therefore Jacob did not hesitate to make a treaty with the Arameans. Jacob summoned his sons, calling them brethren, for they were his peers in piety and strength, and he bade them cast up heaps of stones. Thereupon he swore unto his father-in-law that he would take no wives beside his four daughters, either while they were alive or after their death, and Laban, on his part, swore that he would not pass over the heaps or over the pillar unto Jacob with hostile intent, and he took the oath by the God of Abraham, and the God of Nahor, while Jacob made mention of the Fear of Isaac. He refrained from using the term "the God of Isaac," because God never unites His name with that of a living person, for the reason that so long as a man has not ended his years, no trust may be put in him, lest he be seduced by the evil inclination. It is true, when He appeared unto Jacob at Beth-el, God called Himself "the God of Isaac." There was a reason for the unusual phrase. Being blind, Isaac led a retired life, within his tent, and the evil inclination had no power over him any more. But though God had full confidence in Isaac, yet Jacob could not venture to couple the name of God with the name of a living man, wherefore he took his oath by "the Fear of Isaac."

Early in the morning after the day of covenanting, Laban rose up, and kissed his grandchildren and his daughters, and blessed them. But these acts and words of his did not come from the heart; in his innermost thoughts he regretted that Jacob and his family and his substance had escaped him. His true feelings he betrayed in the message which he sent to Esau at once upon his return to Haran, by the hand of his son Beor and ten companions of his son. The message read: "Hast thou heard what Jacob thy brother has done unto me, who first came to me naked and bare, and I went to meet him, and took him to my house with honor, and brought him up, and gave him my two daughters for wives, and also two of my maids? And God blessed him on my account, and he increased abundantly, and had sons and daughters and maidservants, and also an uncommon stock of flocks and herds, camels and asses, also silver and gold in abundance. But when he saw that his wealth increased, he left me while I went to shear my sheep, and he rose up and fled in secrecy. And he put his wives and children upon camels, and he led away all his cattle and substance which he acquired in my land, and he resolved to go to his father Isaac, to the land of Canaan. And he did not suffer me to kiss my sons and daughters, and he carried away my daughters as captives of the sword, and he also stole my gods, and he fled. And now I have left him in the mountain of the brook of Jabbok, he and all belonging to him, not a jot of his substance is lacking. If it be thy wish to go to him, go, and there wilt thou find him, and thou canst do unto him as thy soul desireth."

Jacob had no need to fear either Laban or Esau, for on his journey he was accompanied by two angel hosts, one going with him from Haran to the borders of the Holy Land, where he was received by the other host, the angels of Palestine. Each of these hosts consisted of no less than six hundred thousand angels, and when he beheld them, Jacob said: "Ye belong neither to the host of Esau, who is preparing to go out to war against me, nor the host of Laban, who is about to pursue me again. Ye are the hosts of the holy angels sent by the Lord." And he gave the name Mahanaim, Double-Host, to the spot on which the second army relieved the first.

JACOB AND ESAU PREPARE TO MEET

The message of Laban awakened Esau's old hatred toward Jacob with increased fury, and he assembled his household, consisting of sixty men. With them and three hundred and forty inhabitants of Seir, he went forth to do battle with Jacob and kill him. He divided his warriors into seven cohorts, giving to his son Eliphaz his own division of sixty, and putting the other six divisions under as many of the Horites.

While Esau was hastening onward to meet Jacob, the messengers which Laban had sent to Esau came to Rebekah and told her that Esau and his four hundred men were about to make war upon Jacob, with the purpose of slaying him and taking possession of all he had. Anxious lest Esau should execute his plan while yet Jacob was on the journey, she hastily dispatched seventy-two of the retainers of Isaac's household, to give him help. Jacob, tarrying on the banks of the brook Jabbok, rejoiced at the sight of these men, and he greeted them with the words, "This is God's helping host," wherefore he called the place of their meeting Mahanaim, Host.

After the warriors sent by Rebekah had satisfied his questions regarding the welfare of his parents, they delivered his mother's message unto him, thus: "I have heard, my son, that thy brother Esau hath gone forth against thee on the road, with men of the children of Seir the Horite, and therefore, my son, hearken to my voice, and take counsel with thyself what thou wilt do, and when he cometh up to thee, supplicate him, and do not speak roughly to him, and give him a present from what thou possessest, and from what God has favored thee with. And when he asketh thee concerning thy affairs, conceal nothing from him, perhaps he may turn from his anger against thee, and thou wilt thereby save thy soul, thou and all belonging to thee, for it is thy duty to honor him, since he is thy elder brother."

And when Jacob heard the words of his mother which the messengers had spoken to him, he lifted up his voice and wept bitterly, and did as his mother commanded him.

He sent messengers to Esau to placate him, and they said unto him: "Thus speaketh thy servant Jacob: My lord, think not that the blessing which my father bestowed upon me profited me. Twenty years I served Laban, and he deceived me, and changed my hire ten times, as thou well knowest. Yet did I labor sorely in his house, and God saw my affliction, my labor, and the work of my hands, and afterward He caused me to find grace and favor in the sight of Laban. And through God's great mercy and kindness, I acquired oxen and asses and cattle and men-servants and maid servants. And now I am coming to my country and to my home, to my father and mother, who are in the land of Canaan. And I have sent to let my lord know all this in order to find favor in the eyes of my lord, so that he may not imagine that I have become a man of substance, or that the blessing with which my father blessed me has benefited me."

Furthermore spake the messengers: "Why dost thou envy me in respect to the blessing wherewith my father blessed me? Is it that the sun shineth in my land, and not in thine? Or doth the dew and the rain fall only upon my land, and not upon thine? If my father blessed me with the dew of heaven, he blessed thee with the fatness of the earth, and if he spoke to me, Peoples will serve thee, he hath said unto thee, By thy sword shalt thou live. How long, then, wilt thou continue to envy me? Come, now, let us set up a covenant between us, that we will share equally all the vexations that may occur."

Esau would not agree to this proposal, his friends dissuaded him therefrom, saying, "Accept not these conditions, for God hath said to Abraham, Know of a surety that thy seed shall be a stranger in a land that is not theirs, and shall serve the people thereof, and the aliens shall afflict them four hundred years. Wait, therefore, until Jacob and his family go down into Egypt to pay off this debt."

Jacob also sent word to Esau, saying: "Though I dwelt with that heathen of the heathen, Laban, yet have I not forgotten my God, but I fulfil the six hundred and thirteen commandments of the Torah. If thy mind be set upon peace, thou wilt find me ready for peace. But if thy desire be war, thou wilt find me ready for war. I have with me men of valor and strength, they have but to utter a word, and God fulfils it. I tarried with Laban until Joseph should be born, he who is destined to subdue thee. And though my descendants be held in bondage in this world, yet a day will come when they will rule over their rulers."

In reply to all these gentle words, Esau spoke with arrogance: "Surely I have heard, and truly it has been told unto me what Jacob has been to Laban, who brought him up in his house, and gave him his daughters for wives, and he begot sons and daughters, and abundantly increased in wealth and riches in Laban's house and with his help. And when he saw that his wealth was abundant and his riches were great, he fled with all belonging to him from Laban's house, and he carried away Laban's daughters from their father as captives of the sword, without telling him of it. And not only to Laban hath Jacob done thus, but also unto me hath he done so, and he hath twice supplanted me, and shall I be silent? Now, I have this day come with my camp to meet him, and I will do unto him according to the desire of my heart."

The messengers dispatched by Jacob now returned to him, and reported these words of Esau unto him. They also told him that his brother was advancing against him with an army consisting of four hundred crowned heads, each leading a host of four hundred men. "It is true, thou art his brother, and thou treatest him as a brother should," they said to Jacob, "but he is an Esau, thou must be made aware of his villainy."

Jacob bore in mind the promise of God, that He would bring him back to his father's house in peace, yet the report about his brother's purpose alarmed him greatly. A pious man may never depend upon promises of earthly good. God does not keep the promise if he is guilty of the smallest conceivable trespass, and Jacob feared that he might have forfeited happiness by reason of a sin committed by him. Moreover, he was anxious lest Esau be the one favored by God, inasmuch as he had these twenty years been fulfilling two Divine commands that Jacob had had to disregard. Esau had been living in the Holy Land, Jacob outside of it; the former had been in attendance upon his parents, the latter dwelling at a distance from them. And much as he feared defeat, Jacob also feared the reverse, that he might be victorious over Esau, or might even slay his brother, which would be as bad as to be slain by him. And he was depressed by another apprehension, that his father had died, for he reasoned that Esau would not take such warlike steps against his own brother, were his father still alive.

When his wives saw the anxiety that possessed Jacob, they began to quarrel with him, and reproach him for having taken them away from their father's house, though he knew that such danger threatened from Esau. Then Jacob determined to apply the three means that might save him from the fate impending: he would cry to God for help, appease Esau's wrath with presents, and hold himself in readiness for war if the worst came to the worst.

He prayed to God: "O Thou God of my father Abraham, and God of my father Isaac, God of all who walk in the ways of the pious and do like unto them! I am not worthy of the least of all the mercies, and of all the truth, which Thou hast showed unto Thy servant. O Lord of the world, as Thou didst not suffer Laban to execute his evil designs against me, so also bring to naught the purpose of Esau, who desireth to slay me. O Lord of the world, in Thy Torah which Thou wilt give us on Mount Sinai it is written, And whether it be cow or ewe, ye shall not kill it and her young both in one day. If this wretch should come and murder my children and their mothers at the same time, who would then desire to read Thy Torah which Thou wilt give us on Mount Sinai? And yet Thou didst speak, For the sake of thy merits and for the merits of thy fathers I will do good unto thee, and in the future world thy children shall be as numerous as the sand of the sea."

As Jacob prayed for his own deliverance, so also he prayed for the salvation of his descendants, that they might not be annihilated by the descendants of Esau.

Such was the prayer of Jacob when he saw Esau approaching from afar, and God heard his petition and looked upon his tears, and He gave him the assurance that for his sake his descendants, too, would be redeemed from all distress.

Then the Lord sent three angels, and they went before Esau, and they appeared unto Esau and his people as hundreds and thousands of men riding upon horses. They were furnished with all sorts of weapons, and divided into four columns. And one division went on, and they found Esau coming with four hundred men, and the division ran toward them, and terrified them. Esau fell off his horse in alarm, and all his men separated from him in great fear, while the approaching column shouted after them, "Verily, we are the servants of Jacob, the servant of God, and who can stand against us?" Esau then said unto them, "O, then my lord and brother Jacob is your lord, whom I have not seen these twenty years, and now that I have this day come to see him, do you treat me in this manner?" The angels answered, "As the Lord liveth, were not Jacob thy brother, we had not left one remaining of thee and thy people, but on account of Jacob we will do nothing to thee." This division passed from Esau, and when he had gone from there about a league, the second division came toward him, and they also did unto Esau and his men as the first had done to them, and when they permitted him to go on, the third came and did like the first, and when the third had passed also, and Esau still continued with his men on the road to Jacob, the fourth division came and did to them as the others had done. And Esau was greatly afraid of his brother, because he thought that the four columns of the army which he had encountered were the servants of Jacob.

After Jacob had made an end of praying, he divided all that journeyed with him into two companies, and he set over them Damesek and Alinus, the two sons of Eliezer, the bondman of Abraham, and their sons. Jacob's example teaches us not to conceal the whole of our fortune in one hiding-place, else we run the danger of losing everything at one stroke.

Of his cattle he sent a part to Esau as a present, first dividing it into three droves in order to impress his brother more. When Esau received the first drove, he would think he had the whole gift that had been sent to him, and suddenly he would be astonished by the appearance of the second portion, and again by the third. Jacob knew his brother's avarice only too well.

The men who were the bearers of Jacob's present to Esau were charged with the following message, "This is an offering to my lord Esau from his slave Jacob." But God took these words of Jacob in ill part, saying, "Thou profanest what is holy when thou callest Esau lord." Jacob excused himself; he was but flattering the wicked in order to escape death at his hands.

JACOB WRESTLES WITH THE ANGEL

The servants of Jacob went before him with the present for Esau, and he followed with his wives and his children. As he was about to pass over the ford of Jabbok, he observed a shepherd, who likewise had sheep and camels. The stranger approached Jacob and proposed that they should ford the stream together, and help each other move their cattle over, and Jacob assented, on the condition that his possessions should be put across first. In the twinkling of an eye Jacob's sheep were transferred to the other side of the stream by the shepherd. Then the flocks of the shepherd were to be moved by Jacob, but no matter how many he took over to the opposite bank, always there remained some on the hither shore. There was no end to the cattle, though Jacob labored all the night through. At last he lost patience, and he fell upon the shepherd and caught him by the throat, crying out, "O thou wizard, thou wizard, at night no enchantment succeeds!" The angel thought, "Very well, let him know once for all with whom he has had dealings," and with his finger he touched the earth, whence fire burst forth. But Jacob said, "What! thou thinkest thus to affright me, who am made wholly of fire?"

The shepherd was no less a personage than the archangel Michael, and in his combat with Jacob he was assisted by the whole host of angels under his command. He was on the point of inflicting a dangerous wound upon Jacob, when God appeared, and all the angels, even Michael himself, felt their strength ooze away. Seeing that he could not prevail against Jacob, the archangel touched the hollow of his thigh, and injured him, and God rebuked him, saying, "Dost thou act as is seemly, when thou causest a blemish in My priest Jacob?" Michael said in astonishment, "Why, it is I who am Thy priest!" But God said, "Thou art My priest in heaven, and he is My priest on earth." Thereupon Michael summoned the archangel Raphael, saying, "My comrade, I pray thee, help me out of my distress, for thou art charged with the healing of all disease," and Raphael cured Jacob of the injury Michael had inflicted.

The Lord continued to reproach Michael, saying, "Why didst thou do harm unto My first-born son?" and the archangel answered, "I did it only to glorify Thee," and then God appointed Michael as the guardian angel of Jacob and his seed unto the end of all generations, with these words: "Thou art a fire, and so is Jacob a fire; thou art the head of the angels, and he is the head of the nations; thou art supreme over all the angels, and he is supreme over all the peoples. Therefore he who is supreme over all the angels shall be appointed unto him who is supreme over all the peoples, that he may entreat mercy for him from the Supreme One over all."

Then Michael said unto Jacob, "How is it possible that thou who couldst prevail against me, the most distinguished of the angels, art afraid of Esau?"

When the day broke, Michael said to Jacob, "Let me go, for the day breaketh," but Jacob held him back, saying, "Art thou a thief, or a gambler with dice, that thou fearest the daylight?" At that moment appeared many different hosts of angels, and they called unto Michael: "Ascend, O Michael, the time of song hath come, and if thou art not in heaven to lead the choir, none will sing." And Michael entreated Jacob with supplications to let him go, for he feared the angels of 'Arabot would consume him with fire, if he were not there to start the songs of praise at the proper time. Jacob said, "I will not let thee go, except thou bless me," whereto Michael made reply: "Who is greater, the servant or the son? I am the servant, and thou art the son. Why, then, cravest thou my blessing?" Jacob urged as an argument, "The angels that visited Abraham did not leave without blessing him," but Michael held, "They were sent by God for that very purpose, and I was not." Yet Jacob insisted upon his demand, and Michael pleaded with him, saying, "The angels that betrayed a heavenly secret were banished from their place for one hundred and thirty eight years. Dost thou desire that I should acquaint thee with what would cause my banishment likewise?" In the end the angel nevertheless had to yield; Jacob could not be moved, and Michael took counsel with himself thus: "I will reveal a secret to him, and if God demands to know why I revealed it, I will make answer, Thy children stand upon their wishes with Thee, and Thou dost yield to them. How, then, could I have left Jacob's wish unfulfilled?"

Then Michael spoke to Jacob, saying: "A day will come when God will reveal Himself unto thee, and He will change thy name, and I shall be present when He changeth it. Thy name shall be called no more Jacob, but Israel, for happy thou, of woman born, who didst enter the heavenly palace, and didst escape thence with thy life." And Michael blessed Jacob with the words, "May it be the will of God that thy descendants be as pious as thou art."

At the same time the archangel reminded Jacob that he had promised to give a tithe of his possessions unto God, and at once Jacob separated five hundred and fifty head of cattle from his herds, which counted fifty-five hundred. Then Michael went on, "But thou hast sons, and of them thou hast not set apart the tenth." Jacob proceeded to pass his sons in review: Reuben, Joseph, Dan, and Gad being the first-born, each of his mother, were exempt, and there remained but eight sons, and when he had named them, down to Benjamin, he had to go back and begin over again with Simon, the ninth, and finish with Levi as the tenth.

Michael took Levi with him into heaven, and presented him before God, saying, "O Lord of the world, this one is Thy lot, and the tenth belonging unto Thee," and God stretched forth His hand and blessed Levi with the blessing that his children should be the servants of God on earth as the angels were His servants on high. Michael spoke again, "Doth not a king provide for the sustenance of his servants?" whereupon God appointed for the Levites all that was holy unto the Lord.

Then Jacob spoke to the angel: "My father conferred the blessing upon me that was intended for Esau, and now I desire to know whether thou wilt acknowledge the blessing as mine, or wilt bring charges against me on account of it." And the angel said: "I acknowledge the blessing to be thine by right. Thou didst not gain it by craft and cunning, and I and all the heavenly powers recognize it to be valid, for thou hast shown thyself master over the mighty powers of the heavens as over Esau and his legions."

And even then Jacob would not let the angel depart, he had to reveal his name to him first, and the angel made known to him that it was Israel, the same name that Jacob would once bear.

At last the angel departed, after Jacob had blessed him, and Jacob called the place of wrestling Penuel, the same place to which before he had given the name Mahanaim, for both words have but one meaning, the place of encounter with angels.

THE MEETING BETWEEN ESAU AND JACOB

At the break of day the angel left off from wrestling with Jacob. The dawn on that day was of particularly short duration. The sun rose two hours before his time, by way of compensation for having set early, on the day on which Jacob passed Mount Moriah on his journey to Haran, to induce him to turn aside and lodge for a night on the future Temple place. Indeed, the power of the sun on this same day was altogether remarkable. He shone with the brilliance and ardor with which he was invested during the six days of the creation, and as he will shine at the end of days, to make whole the halt and the blind among the Jews and to consume the heathen. This same healing and devastating property he had on that day, too, for Jacob was cured, while Esau and his princes were all but burnt up by his terrible heat.

Jacob was in dire need of healing lotions for the injury he had sustained in the encounter with the angel. The combat between them had been grim, the dust whirled up by the scuffle rose to the very throne of God. Though Jacob prevailed against his huge opponent, as big as one-third of the whole world, throwing him to the ground and keeping him pinned down, yet the angel had injured him by clutching at the sinew of the hip which is upon the hollow of the thigh, so that it was dislocated, and Jacob halted upon his thigh. The healing power of the sun restored him, nevertheless his children took it upon themselves not to eat the sinew of the hip which is upon the hollow of the thigh, for they reproached themselves with having been the cause of his mishap, they should not have left him alone in that night.

Now, although Jacob had prepared for the worst, for open hostilities even, yet when he saw Esau and his men, he thought it discreet to make separate divisions of the households of Leah, Rachel, and the handmaids, and divide the children unto each of them. And he put the handmaids and their children foremost, and Leah and her children after, and Rachel and Joseph hindermost. It was the stratagem which the fox used with the lion. Once upon a time the king of beasts was wroth with his subjects, and they looked hither and thither for a spokesman who mastered the art of appeasing their ruler. The fox offered himself for the undertaking, saying, "I know three hundred fables which will allay his fury." His offer was accepted with joy. On the way to the lion, the fox suddenly stood still, and in reply to the questions put to him, he said, "I have forgotten one hundred of the three hundred fables." "Never mind," said those accompanying him, "two hundred will serve the purpose." A little way further on the fox again stopped suddenly, and, questioned again, he confessed that he had forgotten half of the two hundred remaining fables. The animals with him still consoled him that the hundred he knew would suffice. But the fox halted a third time, and then he admitted that his memory had failed him entirely, and he had forgotten all the fables he knew, and he advised that every animal approach the king on his own account and endeavor to appease his anger. At first Jacob had had courage enough to enter the lists with Esau in behalf of all with him. Now he came to the conclusion to let each one try to do what he could for himself.

However, Jacob was too fond a father to expose his family to the first brunt of the danger. He himself passed over before all the rest, saying, "It is better that they attack me than my children." After him came the handmaids and their children. His reason for placing them there was that, if Esau should be overcome by passion for the women, and try to violate them, he would thus meet the handmaids first, and in the meantime Jacob would have the chance of preparing for more determined resistance in the defense of the honor of his wives. Joseph and Rachel came last, and Joseph walked in front of his mother, though Jacob had ordered the reverse. But the son knew both the beauty of his mother and the lustfulness of his uncle, and therefore he tried to hide Rachel from the sight of Esau.

In the vehemence of his rage against Jacob, Esau vowed that he would not slay him with bow and arrow, but would bite him dead with his mouth, and suck his blood. But he was doomed to bitter disappointment, for Jacob's neck turned as hard as ivory, and in his helpless fury Esau could but gnash his teeth. The two brothers were like the ram and the wolf. A wolf wanted to tear a ram in pieces, and the ram defended himself with his horns, striking them deep into the flesh of the wolf. Both began to howl, the wolf because he could not secure his prey, and the ram from fear that the wolf renew his attacks. Esau bawled because his teeth were hurt by the ivory-like flesh of Jacob's neck, and Jacob feared that his brother would make a second attempt to bite him.

Esau addressed a question to his brother. "Tell me," he said, "what was the army I met?" for on his march against Jacob he had had a most peculiar experience with a great host of forty thousand warriors. It consisted of various kinds of troops, armor-clad soldiers walking on foot, mounted on horses, and seated in chariots, and they all threw themselves upon Esau when they met. He demanded to know whence they came, and the strange soldiers hardly interrupted their savage onslaught to reply that they belonged to Jacob. Only when Esau told them that Jacob was his brother did they leave off, saying, "Woe to us if our master hears that we did thee harm." This was the army and the encounter Esau inquired about as soon as he met his brother. But the army was a host of angels, who had the appearance of warriors to Esau and his men. Also the messengers sent by Jacob to Esau had been angels, for no mere human being could be induced to go forth and face the recreant.

Jacob now gave Esau the presents intended for him, a tenth of all his cattle, and also pearls and precious stones, and, besides, a falcon for the chase. But even the animals refused to give up their gentle master Jacob and become the property of the villain Esau. They all ran away when Jacob wanted to hand them over to his brother, and the result was that the only ones that reached Esau were the feeble and the lame, all that could not make good their escape.

At first Esau declined the presents offered to him. Naturally, that was a mere pretense. While refusing the gifts with words, he held his hand outstretched ready to receive them. Jacob took the hint, and insisted that he accept them, saying: "Nay, I pray thee, if now I have found grace in thy sight, then receive my present at my hand, forasmuch as I have seen thy face, as I have seen the face of angels, and thou art pleased with me." The closing words were chosen with well-calculated purpose. Jacob wanted Esau to derive the meaning that he had intercourse with angels, and to be inspired with awe. Jacob was like the man invited to a banquet by his mortal enemy who has been seeking an opportunity to slay him. When the guest divines the purpose for which he has been brought thither, he says to the host: "What a magnificent and delicious meal this is! But once before in my life did I partake of one like it, and that was when I was bidden by the king to his table"-- enough to drive terror to the heart of the would-be slayer. He takes good care not to harm a man on such intimate terms with the king as to be invited to his table!

Jacob had valid reason for recalling his encounter with the angel, for it was the angel of Esau who had measured his strength with Jacob's, and had been overcome.

As Esau accepted the presents of Jacob willingly on this first occasion, so he continued to accept them for a whole year; daily Jacob gave him presents as on the day of their meeting, for, he said, " 'A gift doth blind the eyes of the wise,' and how much more doth it blind the wicked! Therefore will I give him presents upon presents, perhaps he will let me alone." Besides, he did not attach much value to the possessions he had acquired outside of the Holy Land. Such possessions are not a blessing, and he did not hesitate to part with them.

Beside the presents which Jacob gave Esau, he also paid out a large sum of money to him for the Cave of Machpelah. Immediately upon his arrival in the Holy Land he sold all he had brought with him from Haran, and a pile of gold was the proceeds of the sale. He spoke to Esau, saying: "Like me thou hast a share in the Cave of Machpelah, wilt thou take this pile of gold for thy portion therein?" "What care I for the Cave?" returned Esau. "Gold is what I want," and for his share in Machpelah he took the gold realized from the sale of the possessions Jacob had accumulated outside of the Holy Land. But God "filled the vacuum without delay," and Jacob was as rich as before.

Wealth was not an object of desire to Jacob. He would have been well content, in his own behalf and in behalf of his family, to resign all earthly treasures in favor of Esau and his family. He said to Esau: "I foresee that in future days suffering will be inflicted by thy children upon mine. But I do not demur, thou mayest exercise thy dominion and wear thy crown until the time when the Messiah springs from my loins, and receives the rule from thee." These words spoken by Jacob will be realized in days to come, when all the nations will rise up against the kingdom of Edom, and take away one city after another from him, one realm after another, until they reach Bet-Gubrin, and then the Messiah will appear and assume his kingship. The angel of Edom will flee for refuge to Bozrah, but God will appear there, and slay him, for though Bozrah is one of the cities of refuge, yet will the Lord exercise the right of the avenger therein. He will seize the angel by his hair, and Elijah will slaughter him, letting the blood spatter the garments of God. All this Jacob had in mind when he said to Esau, "Let my lord, I pray thee, pass over before his servant, until I come unto my lord unto Seir." Jacob himself never went to Seir. What he meant was the Messianic time when Israel shall go to Seir, and take possession thereof.

Jacob tarried in Succoth a whole year, and he opened a house of learning there. Then he journeyed on to Shechem, while Esau betook himself to Seir, saying to himself, "How long shall I be a burden to my brother?" for it was during Jacob's sojourn at Succoth that Esau received daily presents from Jacob.

And Jacob, after abiding these many years in a strange land, came to Shechem in peace, unimpaired in mind and body. He had forgotten none of the knowledge he had acquired before; the gifts he gave to Esau did not encroach upon his wealth; the injury inflicted by the angel that wrestled with him had been healed, and likewise his children were sound and healthy.

Jacob entered Shechem on a Friday, late in the afternoon, and his first concern was to lay out the boundaries of the city, that the laws of the Sabbath might not be transgressed. As soon as he was settled in the place, he sent presents to the notables. A man must be grateful to a city from which he derives benefits. No less did the common people enjoy his bounty. For them he opened a market where he sold all wares at low prices.

Also he lost no time in buying a parcel of ground, for it is the duty of every man of substance who comes to the Holy Land from outside to make himself the possessor of land there. He gave a hundred lambs for his estate, a hundred yearling sheep, and a hundred pieces of money, and received in return a bill of sale, to which he attached his signature, using the letters Yod-He for it. And then he erected an altar to God upon his land, and he said, "Thou art the Lord of all celestial things, and I am the lord of all earthly things." But God said, "Not even the overseer of the synagogue arrogates privileges in the synagogue, and thou assumest lordship with a high hand? Forsooth, on the morrow thy daughter will go abroad, and she shall be humbled."

THE OUTRAGE AT SHECHEM

While Jacob and his sons were sitting in the house of learning, occupied with the study of the Torah, Dinah went abroad to see the dancing and singing women, whom Shechem had hired to dance and play in the streets in order to entice her forth. Had she remained at home, nothing would have happened to her. But she was a woman, and all women like to show themselves in the street. When Shechem caught sight of her, he seized her by main force, young though she was, and violated her in beastly fashion.

This misfortune befell Jacob as a punishment for his excessive self-confidence. In his negotiations with Laban, he had used the expression, "My righteousness shall answer for me hereafter." Besides, on his return to Palestine, when he was preparing to meet his brother, he concealed his daughter Dinah in a chest, lest Esau desire to have her for wife, and he be obliged to give her to him. God spoke to him, saying: "Herein hast thou acted unkindly toward thy brother, and therefore Dinah will have to marry Job, one that is neither circumcised nor a proselyte. Thou didst refuse to give her to one that is circumcised, and one that is uncircumcised will take her. Thou didst refuse to give her to Esau in lawful wedlock, and now she will fall a victim to the ravisher's illicit passion."

When Jacob heard that Shechem had defiled his daughter, he sent twelve servants to fetch Dinah from Shechem's house, but Shechem went out to them with his men, and drove them from his house, and he would not suffer them to come unto Dinah, and he kissed and embraced her before their eyes. Jacob then sent two maidens of his servants' daughters to remain with Dinah in the house of Shechem. Shechem bade three of his friends go to his father Hamor, the son of Haddakum, the son of Pered, and say, "Get me this damsel to wife." Hamor tried at first to persuade his son not to take a Hebrew woman to wife, but when Shechem persisted in his request, he did according to the word of his son, and went forth to communicate with Jacob concerning the matter. In the meanwhile the sons of Jacob returned from the field, and, kindled with wrath, they spoke unto their father, saying, "Surely death is due to this man and his household, because the Lord God of the whole earth commanded Noah and his children that man shall never rob nor commit adultery. Now, behold, Shechem has ravaged and committed fornication with our sister, and not one of all the people of the city spake a word to him." And whilst they were speaking, Hamor came to speak to Jacob the words of his son concerning Dinah, and after he ceased to speak, Shechem himself came to Jacob and repeated the request made by his father. Simon and Levi answered Hamor and Shechem deceitfully, saying: "All you have spoken unto us we will do. And, behold, our sister is in your house, but keep away from her until we send to our father Isaac concerning this matter, for we can do nothing without his counsel. He knows the ways of our father Abraham, and whatever he saith unto us we will tell you, we will conceal nothing from you."

Shechem and his father went home thereafter, satisfied with the result achieved, and when they had gone, the sons of Jacob asked him to seek counsel and pretext in order to kill all the inhabitants of the city, who had deserved this punishment on account of their wickedness. Then Simon said to them: "I have good counsel to give you. Bid them be circumcised. If they consent not, we shall take our daughter from them, and go away. And if they consent to do this, then, when they are in pain, we shall attack them and slay them." The next morning Shechem and his father came again to Jacob, to speak concerning Dinah, and the sons of Jacob spoke deceitfully to them, saying: "We told our father Isaac all your words, and your words pleased him, but he said, that thus did Abraham his father command him from God, that any man that is not of his descendants, who desireth to take one of his daughters to wife, shall cause every male belonging to him to be circumcised."

Shechem and his father hastened to do the wishes of the sons of Jacob, and they persuaded also the men of the city to do likewise, for they were greatly esteemed by them, being the princes of the land.

On the next day, Shechem and his father rose up early in the morning, and they assembled all the men of the city, and they called for the sons of Jacob, and they circumcised Shechem, his father, his five brothers, and all the males in the city, six hundred and forty-five men and two hundred and seventy-six lads. Haddakum, the grandfather of Shechem, and his six brothers would not be circumcised, and they were greatly incensed against the people of the city for submitting to the wishes of the sons of Jacob.

In the evening of the second day, Shechem and his father sent to have eight little children whom their mothers had concealed brought to them to be circumcised. Haddakum and his six brothers sprang at the messengers, and sought to slay them, and sought to slay also Shechem, Hamor, and Dinah. They chided Shechem and his father for doing a thing that their fathers had never done, which would raise the ire of the inhabitants of the land of Canaan against them, as well as the ire of all the children of Ham, and that on account of a Hebrew woman. Haddakum and his brothers finished by saying: "Behold, to-morrow we will go and assemble our Canaanitish brethren, and we will come and smite you and all in whom you trust, that there shall not be a remnant left of you or them."

When Hamor and his son Shechem and all the people of the city heard this, they were sore afraid, and they repented what they had done, and Shechem and his father answered Haddakum and his brothers: "Because we saw that the Hebrews would not accede to our wishes concerning their daughter, we did this thing, but when we shall have obtained our request from them, we will then do unto them that which is in your hearts and in ours, as soon as we shall become strong."

Dinah, who heard their words, hastened and dispatched one of her maidens whom her father had sent to take care of her in Shechem's house, and informed Jacob and his sons of the conspiracy plotted against them. When the sons of Jacob heard this, they were filled with wrath, and Simon and Levi swore, and said, "As the Lord liveth, by to-morrow there shall not be a remnant left In the whole city."

They began the extermination by killing eighteen of the twenty young men who had concealed themselves and were not circumcised, and two of them fled and escaped to some lime pits that were in the city. Then Simon and Levi slew all the city, not leaving a male over, and while they were looking for spoils outside of the city, three hundred women rose against them and threw stones and dust upon them, but Simon single-handed slew them all, and returned to the city, where he joined Levi. Then they took away from the people outside of the city their sheep, their oxen, their cattle, and also the women and the little children, and they led all these away, and took them to the city to their father Jacob. The number of women whom they did not slay, but only took captive, was eighty-five virgins, among them a young damsel of great beauty by the name of Bunah, whom Simon took to wife. The number of the males which they took captive and did not slay was forty-seven, and all these men and women were servants to the sons of Jacob, and to their children after them, until the day they left Egypt.

A WAR FRUSTRATED

When Simon and Levi had gone from the city, the two young men who had concealed themselves in the lime pits, and were not slain amongst the people of the city, rose up, and they found the city desolate, without a man, only weeping women, and they cried out, saying, "Behold, this is the evil which the sons of Jacob did who destroyed one of the Canaanite cities, and were not afraid of all the land of Canaan."

They left the city and went to Tappuah, and told the inhabitants all that the sons of Jacob had done to the city of Shechem. Jashub, the king of Tappuah, sent to Shechem to see whether these young men told the truth, for he did not believe them, saying, "How could two men destroy a large city like Shechem?" The messengers of Jashub returned, and they reported, "The city is destroyed, not a man is left there, only weeping women, neither are there flocks and cattle there, for all that was in the city was taken away by the sons of Jacob."

Jashub wondered thereat, for the like had not been heard from the days of Nimrod, and not even from the remotest times, that two men should be able to destroy so large a city, and he decided to go to war against the Hebrews, and avenge the cause of the people of Shechem. His counsellors said to him: "If two of them laid waste a whole city, surely if thou goest against them, they all will rise up against us, and destroy us. Therefore, send to the kings round about, that we all together fight against the sons of Jacob, and prevail against them."

The seven kings of the Amorites, when they heard the evil that the sons of Jacob had done to the city of Shechem, assembled together, with all their armies, ten thousand men, with drawn swords, and they came to fight against the sons of Jacob. And Jacob was greatly afraid, and he said to Simon and Levi, "Why have you brought such evil upon me? I was at rest, and you provoked the inhabitants of the land against me by your acts."

Then Judah spoke to his father: "Was it for naught that Simon and Levi killed the inhabitants of Shechem? Verily, it was because Shechem dishonored our sister, and transgressed the command of our God to Noah and his children, and not one of the inhabitants of the city interfered in the matter. Now, why art thou afraid, and why art thou displeased at my brethren? Surely, our God, who delivered the city of Shechem and its people into their hand, He will also deliver into our hands all the Canaanitish kings who are coming against us. Now cast away thy fears, and pray to God to assist us and deliver us."

Judah then addressed his brethren, saying: "The Lord our God is with us! Fear naught, then! Stand ye forth, each man girt with his weapons of war, his bow and his sword, and we will go and fight against the uncircumcised. The Lord is our God, He will save us."

Jacob, his eleven sons, and one hundred servants belonging to Isaac, who had come to their assistance, marched forward to meet the Amorites, a people exceedingly numerous, like unto the sand upon the sea-shore. The sons of Jacob sent unto their grandfather Isaac, at Hebron, requesting him to pray unto the Lord to protect them from the hand of the Canaanites, and he prayed as follows: "O Lord God, Thou didst promise my father, saying, I will multiply thy seed as the stars of heaven, and also me Thou didst promise that Thou wouldst establish Thy word to my father. Now, O Lord, God of the whole world, pervert, I pray Thee, the counsel of these kings, that they may not fight against my sons, and impress the hearts of their kings and their people with the terror of my sons, and bring down their pride that they turn away from my sons. Deliver my sons and their servants from them with Thy strong hand and outstretched arm, for power and might are in Thy hands to do all this."

Jacob also prayed unto God, and said: "O Lord God, powerful and exalted God, who hast reigned from days of old, from then until now and forever! Thou art He who stirreth up wars and causeth them to cease. In Thy hand are power and might to exalt and to bring low. O may my prayer be acceptable unto Thee, that Thou mayest turn to me with Thy mercies, to impress the hearts of these kings and their people with the terror of my sons, and terrify them and their camps, and with Thy great kindness deliver all those that trust in Thee, for Thou art He who subdues the peoples under us, and the nations under our feet."

God heard the prayers of Isaac and Jacob, and He filled the hearts of all the advisers of the Canaanite kings with great fear and terror, and when the kings, who were undecided whether to undertake a campaign against the sons of Jacob, consulted them, they said: "Are you silly, or is there no understanding in you, that you propose to fight with the Hebrews? Why do you take delight in your own destruction this day? Behold, two of them came to the city of Shechem without fear or terror, and they put all the inhabitants of the city to the sword, no man stood up against them, and how will you be able to fight with them all?"

The royal counsellors then proceeded to enumerate all the mighty things God had done for Abraham, Jacob, and the sons of Jacob, such as had not been done from days of old and by any of the gods of the nations. When the kings heard all the words of their advisers, they were afraid of the sons of Jacob, and they would not fight against them. They turned back with their armies on that day, each to his own city. But the sons of

Jacob kept their station that day till evening, and seeing that the kings did not advance to do battle with them in order to avenge the inhabitants of Shechem whom they had killed, they returned home.

The wrath of the Lord descended upon the inhabitants of Shechem to the uttermost on account of their wickedness. For they had sought to do unto Sarah and Rebekah as they did unto Dinah, but the Lord had prevented them. Also they had persecuted Abraham when he was a stranger, and they had vexed his flocks when they were big with young, and Eblaen, one born in his house, they had handled most shamefully. And thus they did to all strangers, taking away their wives by force.

THE WAR WITH THE NINEVITES

The destruction of Shechem by Simon and Levi terrified the heathen all around. If two sons of Jacob had succeeded in ruining a great city like Shechem, they argued, what would Jacob and all his sons accomplish acting together? Jacob meanwhile left Shechem, hindered by none, and with all his possessions he set out, to betake himself to his father Isaac. But after an eight days' march he encountered a powerful army, which had been dispatched from Nineveh to levy tribute upon the whole world and subjugate it. On coming in the vicinity of Shechem, this army heard to what the city had been exposed at the hands of the sons of Jacob, and fury seized the men, and they resolved to make war upon Jacob.

But Jacob said to his sons: "Fear not, God will be your helper, and He will fight for you against your enemies. Only you must put away from you the strange gods in your possession, and you must purify yourselves, and wash your garments clean."

Girt with his sword, Jacob advanced against the enemy, and in the first onslaught he slew twelve thousand of the weak in the army. Then Judah spake to him, and said, "Father, thou art tired and exhausted, let me fight the enemy alone." And Jacob replied, saying, "Judah, my son, I know thy strength and thy bravery, that they are exceeding great, so that none in the world is like unto thee therein." His countenance like a lion's and inflamed with wrath, Judah attacked the army, and slew twelve myriads of tried and famous warriors. The battle raged hot in front and in the rear, and Levi his brother hastened to his aid, and together they won a victory over the Ninevites. Judah alone slew five thousand more soldiers, and Levi dealt blows right and left with such vigor that the men of the enemy's army fell like grain under the scythe of the reaper.

Alarmed about their fate, the people of Nineveh said: "How long shall we fight with these devils? Let us return to our land, lest they exterminate us root and branch, without leaving a remnant." But their king desired to restrain them, and he said: "O ye heroes, ye men of might and valor, have you lost your senses that you ask to return to your land? Is this your bravery? After you have subdued many kingdoms and countries, ye are not able to hold out against twelve men? If the nations and the kings whom we have made tributary to ourselves hear of this, they will rise up against us as a man, and make a laughing-stock of us, and do with us according to their desire. Take courage, ye men of the great city of Nineveh, that your honor and your name be exalted, and you become not a mockery in the mouth of your enemies."

These words of their king inspired the warriors to continue the campaign. They sent messengers to all the lands to ask for help, and, reinforced by their allies, the Ninevites assaulted Jacob a second time. He spoke to his sons, saying, "Take courage and be men, fight against your enemies." His twelve sons then took up their stand in twelve different places, leaving considerable intervals between one and another, and Jacob, a sword in his right hand and a bow in his left, advanced to the combat. It was a desperate encounter for him. He had to ward off the enemy to the right and the left. Nevertheless he inflicted a severe blow, and when a band of two thousand men beset him, he leapt up in the air and over them and vanished from their sight. Twenty-two myriads he slew on this day, and when evening came he planned to flee under cover of darkness. But suddenly ninety thousand men appeared, and he was compelled to continue the fight. He rushed at them with his sword, but it broke, and he had to defend himself by grinding huge rocks into lime powder, and this he threw at the enemy and blinded them so that they could see nothing. Luckily, darkness was about to fall, and he could permit himself to take rest for the night.

In the morning, Judah said to Jacob, "Father, thou didst fight the whole of yesterday, and thou art weary and exhausted. Let me fight this day." When the warriors caught sight of Judah's lion face and his lion teeth, and heard his lion voice, they were greatly afraid. Judah hopped and jumped over the army like a flea, from one warrior to the next, raining blows down upon them incessantly, and by evening he had slain eighty thousand and ninety-six men, armed with swords and bows. But fatigue overcame him, and Zebulon took up his station at his brother's left hand, and mowed down eighty thousand of the enemy. Meantime Judah regained some of his strength, and, rising up in wrath and fury, and gnashing his teeth with a noise like unto thunder claps in midsummer, he put the army to flight. It ran a distance of eighteen miles, and Judah could enjoy a respite that night.

But the army reappeared on the morrow, ready for battle again, to take revenge on Jacob and his children. They blew their trumpets, whereupon Jacob spake to his sons, "Go forth and fight with your enemies." Issachar and Gad said that this day they would take the combat upon themselves, and their father bade them do it while their brothers kept guard and held themselves in readiness to aid and relieve the two combatants when they showed signs of weariness and exhaustion.

The leaders of the day slew forty-eight thousand warriors, and put to flight twelve myriads more, who concealed themselves in a cave. Issachar and Gad fetched trees from the woods, piled the trunks up in front of the opening of the cave, and set fire to them. When the fire blazed with a fierce flame, the warriors spoke, saying: "Why should we stay in this cave and perish with the smoke and the heat? Rather will we go forth and fight with our enemies, then we may have a chance of saving ourselves." They left the cave, going through openings at the side, and they attacked Issachar and Gad in front and behind. Dan and Naphtali saw the plight of their brothers and ran to their assistance. They laid about with their swords, hewing a way for themselves to Issachar and Gad, and, united with them, they, too, opposed the foe.

It was the third day of the conflict, and the Ninevites were reinforced by an army as numerous as the sand on the sea-shore. All the sons of Jacob united to oppose it, and they routed the host. But when they pursued after the enemy, the fugitives faced about and resumed the battle, saying: "Why should we run away? Let us rather fight them, perhaps we may be victorious, now they are weary." A stubborn combat ensued, and when Jacob saw the vehement attack upon his children, he himself sprang into the thick of the battle and dealt blows right and left. Nevertheless the heathen were victorious, and succeeded in separating Judah from his brethren. As soon as Jacob was aware of the peril of his son, he whistled, and Judah responded, and his brethren hastened to his aid. Judah was fatigued and parched with thirst, and there was no water for him to drink, but he dug his finger into the ground with such force that water gushed out in the sight of the whole army. Then said one warrior to another, "I will flee before these devils, for God fights on their side," and he and all the army fled precipitately, pursued by the sons of Jacob. Soldiers without number they slew, and then they went back to their tents. On their return they noticed that Joseph was missing, and they feared he had been killed or taken captive. Naphtali ran after the retreating enemy, to make search for Joseph, and he found him still fighting against the Ninevite army. He joined Joseph, and killed countless soldiers, and of the fugitives many drowned, and the men that were besetting Joseph ran off and left him in safety.

At the end of the war Jacob continued his journey, unhindered, to his father Isaac.

THE WAR WITH THE AMORITES

At first the people that lived round about Shechem made no attempt to molest Jacob, who had returned thither after a while, together with his household, to take up his abode there and establish himself. But at the end of seven years the heathen began to harass him. The kings of the Amorites assembled together against the sons of Jacob to slay them in the Valley of Shechem. "Is it not enough," they said, "that they have slain all the men of Shechem? Should they be permitted now to take possession of their land, too?" and they advanced to render battle.

Judah leapt into the midst of the ranks of the foot soldiers of the allied kings, and slew first of all Jashub, the king of Tappuah, who was clad in iron and brass from top to toe. The king was mounted, and from his horse he cast his spears downward with both hands, in front of him and in back, without ever missing his aim, for he was a mighty warrior, and he could throw javelins with one hand or the other. Nevertheless Judah feared neither him nor his prowess. He ran toward him, snatching a stone of sixty sela'im from the ground and hurling it at him. Jashub was at a distance of one hundred and seventy-seven ells and one-third of an ell, and, protected with iron armor and throwing spears, he moved forward upon Judah. But Judah struck him on his shield with the stone, and unhorsed him. When the king attempted to rise, Judah hastened to his side to slay him before he could get on his feet. But Jashub was nimble, he stood ready to attack Judah, shield to shield, and he drew his sword to cut off Judah's head. Quickly Judah raised his shield to catch the blow upon it, but it broke in pieces. What did Judah now? He wrested the shield of his opponent away from him, and swung his sword against Jashub's feet, cutting them off above the ankles. The king fell prostrate, his sword slipped from his grasp, and Judah hastened to him and severed his head from his body.

While Judah was removing the armor of his slain adversary, nine of Jashub's followers appeared. Judah slung a stone against the head of the first of them that approached him, with such force that he dropped his shield, which Judah snatched from the ground and used to defend himself against his eight assailants. His brother Levi came and stood next to him, and shot off an arrow that killed Elon, king of Gaash, and then Judah killed the eight men. And his father Jacob came and killed Zerori king of Shiloh. None of the heathen could prevail against these sons of Jacob, they had not the courage to stand up before them, but took to flight, and the sons of Jacob pursued after them, and each slew a thousand men of the Amorites on that day, before the going down of the sun. And the other sons of Jacob set forth from the Hill of Shechem, where they had taken up their stand, and they also pursued after them as far as Hazor. Before this city they had another severe encounter with the enemy, more severe than that in the Valley of Shechem. Jacob let his arrows fly, and slew Pirathon king of Hazor, and then Pasusi king of Sartan, Laban king of Aram, and Shebir king of Mahanaim.

Judah was the first to mount the walls of Hazor. As he approached the top, four warriors attacked him, but he slew them without stopping in his ascent, and before his brother Naphtali could bring him succor. Naphtali followed him, and the two stood upon the wall, Judah to the right and Naphtali to the left, and thence they dealt out death to the warriors. The other sons of Jacob followed their two brothers in turn, and made an end of exterminating the heathen host on that day. They subjugated Hazor, slew the warriors thereof, let no man escape with his life, and despoiled the city of all therein.

On the day following they went to Sartan, and again a bloody battle took place. Sartan was situated upon high land, and the hill before the city was likewise very high, so that none could come near unto it, and also none could come near unto the citadel, because the wall thereof was high. Nevertheless they made themselves masters of the city. They scaled the walls of the citadel, Judah on the east side being the first to ascend, then Gad on the west side, Simon and Levi on the north, and Reuben and Dan on the south, and Naphtali and Issachar set fire to the hinges upon which the gates of the city were hung.

In the same way the sons of Jacob subdued five other cities, Tappuah, Arbel, Shiloh, Mahanaim, and Gaash, making an end of all of them in five days. On the sixth day all the Amorites assembled, and they came to Jacob and his sons unarmed, bowed down before them, and sued for peace. And the sons of Jacob made peace with the heathen, who ceded Timna to them, and all the land of Harariah. In that day also Jacob concluded peace with them, and they made restitution to the sons of Jacob for all the cattle they had taken, two head for one, and they restored all the spoil they had carried off. And Jacob turned to go to Timna, and Judah went to Arbel, and thenceforth the Amorites troubled them no more.

ISAAC BLESSES LEVI AND JUDAH

If a man voweth a vow, and he does not fulfil it in good time, he will stumble through three grave sins, idolatry, unchastity, and bloodshed. Jacob had been guilty of not accomplishing promptly the vow he had taken upon himself at Beth-el, and therefore punishment overtook him--his daughter was dishonored, his sons slew men, and they kept the idols found among the spoils of Shechem. Therefore, when Jacob prostrated himself before God after the bloody outrage at Shechem, He bade him arise, and go to Beth-el and accomplish the vow he had vowed there. Before Jacob set out for the holy place to do the bidding of God, he took the idols which were in the possession of his sons, and the teraphim which Rachel had stolen from her father, and he shivered them in pieces, and buried the bits under an oak upon Mount Gerizim, uprooting the tree with one hand, concealing the remains of the idols in the hollow left in the earth, and planting the oak again with one hand.

Among the destroyed idols was one in the form of a dove, and this the Samaritans dug up later and worshipped.

On reaching Beth-el he erected an altar to the Lord, and on a pillar he set up the stone whereon he had rested his head during the night which he had passed there on his journey to Haran. Then he bade his parents come to Beth-el and take part in his sacrifice. But Isaac sent him a message, saying, "O my son Jacob, that I might see thee before I die," whereupon Jacob hastened to his parents, taking Levi and Judah with him. When his grandchildren stepped before Isaac, the darkness that shrouded his eyes dropped away, and he said, "My son, are these thy children, for they resemble thee?" And the spirit of prophecy entered his mouth, and he grasped Levi with his right hand and Judah with his left in order to bless them, and he spoke these words to Levi: "May the Lord bring thee and thy seed nigh unto Him before all flesh, that ye serve in His sanctuary like the Angel of the Face and the Holy Angels. Princes, judges, and rulers shall they be unto all the seed of the children of Jacob. The word of God they will proclaim in righteousness, and all His judgments they will execute in justice, and they will make manifest His ways unto the children of Jacob, and unto Israel His paths." And unto Judah he spake, saying: "Be ye princes, thou and one of thy sons, over the sons of Jacob. In thee shall be the help of Jacob, and the salvation of Israel shall be found in thee. And when thou sittest upon the throne of the glory of thy justice, perfect peace shall reign over all the seed of the children of my beloved Abraham."

On the morrow, Isaac told his son that he would not accompany him to Beth-el on account of his great age, but he bade him not delay longer to fulfil his vow, and gave him permission to take his mother Rebekah with him to the holy place. And Rebekah and her nurse Deborah went to Beth-el with Jacob.

JOY AND SORROW IN THE HOUSE OF JACOB

Deborah, the nurse of Rebekah, and some of the servants of Isaac had been sent to Jacob by his mother, while he still abode with Laban, to summon him home at the end of his fourteen years' term of service. As Jacob did not at once obey his mother's behest, the two servants of Isaac returned to their master, but Deborah remained with Jacob then and always. Therefore, when Deborah died in Beth-el, Jacob mourned for her, and he buried her below Beth-el under the palm-tree, the same under which the prophetess Deborah sat later, when the children of Israel came to her for judgment.

But a short time elapsed after the death of the nurse Deborah, and Rebekah died, too. Her passing away was not made the occasion for public mourning. The reason was that, as Abraham was dead, Isaac blind, and Jacob away from home, there remained Esau as the only mourner to appear in public and represent her family, and beholding that villain, it was feared, might tempt a looker-on to cry out, "Accursed be the breasts that gave thee suck." To avoid this, the burial of Rebekah took place at night.

God appeared unto Jacob to comfort him in his grief, and with Him appeared the heavenly family. It was a sign of grace, for all the while the sons of Jacob had been carrying idols with them the Lord had not revealed Himself to Jacob. At this time God announced to Jacob the birth of Benjamin soon to occur, and the birth of Manasseh and Ephraim, who also were to be founders of tribes, and furthermore He told him that these three would count kings among their descendants, Saul and Ish-bosheth, of the seed of Benjamin, Jeroboam the Ephraimite, and Jehu of the tribe of Manasseh. In this vision, God confirmed the change of his name from Jacob to Israel, promised him by the angel with whom he had wrestled on entering the Holy Land, and finally God revealed to him that he would be the last of the three with whose names the Name of God would appear united, for God is called only the God of Abraham, the God of Isaac, and the God of Jacob, and never the God of any one else.

In token of this revelation from God, Jacob set up a pillar of stone, and he poured out a drink offering thereon, as in a later day the priests were to offer libations in the Temple on the Feast of Tabernacles, and the libation brought by Jacob at Beth-el was as much as all the waters in the Sea of Tiberias.

At the time when Deborah and Rebekah died, occurred also the death of Rachel, at the age of thirty-six, but not before her prayer was heard, that she bear Jacob a second son, for she died in giving birth to Benjamin. Twelve years she had borne no child, then she fasted twelve days, and her petition was granted her. She brought forth the youngest son of Jacob, whom he called Benjamin, the son of days, because he was born in his father's old age, and with him a twin sister was born.

Rachel was buried in the way to Ephrath, because Jacob, gifted with prophetic spirit, foresaw that the exiles would pass this place on their march to Babylon, and as they passed, Rachel would entreat God's mercy for the poor outcasts.

Jacob journeyed on to Jerusalem.

During Rachel's lifetime, her couch had always stood in the tent of Jacob. After her death, he ordered the couch of her handmaid Bilhah to be carried thither. Reuben was sorely vexed thereat, and he said, "Not enough that Rachel alive curtailed the rights of my mother, she must needs give her annoyance also after death!" He went and took the couch of his mother Leah and placed it in Jacob's tent instead of Bilhah's couch. Reuben's brothers learned of his disrespectful act from Asher. He had found it out in one way or another, and had told it to his brethren, who ruptured their relations with him, for they would have nothing to do with an informer, and they did not become reconciled with Asher until Reuben himself confessed his transgression. For it was not long before Reuben recognized that he had acted reprehensibly toward his father, and he fasted and put on sackcloth, and repented of his misdeed. He was the first among men to do penance, and therefore God said to him: "Since the beginning of the world it hath not happened that a man hath sinned and then repented thereof. Thou art the first to do penance, and as thou livest, a prophet of thy seed, Hosea, shall be the first to proclaim, 'O Israel, return.'"

ESAU'S CAMPAIGN AGAINST JACOB

When Isaac felt his end approaching, he called his two sons to him, and charged them with his last wish and will, and gave them his blessing. He said: "I adjure you by the exalted Name, the praised, honored, glorious, immutable, and mighty One, who hath made heaven and earth and all things together, that ye fear Him, and serve Him, and each shall love his brother in mercy and justice, and none wish evil unto the other, now and henceforth unto all eternity, all the days of your life, that ye may enjoy good fortune in all your undertakings, and that ye perish not."

Furthermore he commanded them to bury him in the Cave of Machpelah, by the side of his father Abraham, in the grave which he had dug for himself with his own hands. Then he divided his possessions between his two sons, giving Esau the larger portion, and Jacob the smaller. But Esau said, "I sold my birthright to Jacob, and I ceded it to him, and it belongs unto him." Isaac rejoiced greatly that Esau acknowledged the rights of Jacob of his own accord, and he closed his eyes in peace.

The funeral of Isaac was not disturbed by any unseemly act, for Esau was sure of his heritage in accordance with the last wishes expressed by his father. But when the time came to divide Isaac's possessions between the two brothers, Esau said to Jacob, "Divide the property of our father into two portions, but I as the elder claim the right of choosing the portion I desire." What did Jacob do? He knew well that "the eye of the wicked never beholds treasures enough to satisfy it," so he divided their common heritage in the following way: all the material possessions of his father formed one portion, and the other consisted of Isaac's claim upon the Holy Land, together with the Cave of Machpelah, the tomb of Abraham and Isaac. Esau chose the money and the other things belonging to Isaac for his inheritance, and to Jacob were left the Cave and the title to the Holy Land. An agreement to this effect was drawn up in writing in due form, and on the strength of the document Jacob insisted upon Esau's leaving Palestine. Esau acquiesced, and he and his wives and his sons and daughters journeyed to Mount Seir, where they took up their abode.

Though Esau gave way before Jacob for the nonce, he returned to the land to make war upon his brother. Leah had just died, and Jacob and the sons borne by Leah were mourning for her, and the rest of his sons, borne unto him by his other wives, were trying to comfort them, when Esau came upon them with a powerful host of four thousand men, well equipped for war, clad in armor of iron and brass, all furnished with bucklers, bows, and swords. They surrounded the citadel wherein Jacob and his sons dwelt at that time with their servants and children and households, for they had all assembled to console Jacob for the death of Leah, and they sat there unconcerned, none entertained a suspicion that an assault upon them was meditated by any man. And the great army had already encircled their castle, and still none within suspected any harm, neither Jacob and his children nor the two hundred servants. Now when Jacob saw that Esau presumed to make war upon them, and sought to slay them in the citadel, and was shooting darts at them, he ascended the wall of the citadel and spake words of peace and friendship and brotherly love to Esau. He said: "Is this the consolation which thou hast come to bring me, to comfort me for my wife, who hath been taken by death? Is this in accordance with the oath thou didst swear twice unto thy father and thy mother before they died? Thou hast violated thy oath, and in the hour when thou didst swear unto thy father, thou wast judged." But Esau made reply: "Neither the children of men nor the beasts of the field swear an oath to keep it unto all eternity, but on every day they devise evil against one another, when it is directed against an enemy, or when they seek to slay an adversary. If the boar will change his skin and make his bristles as soft as wool, or if he can cause horns to sprout forth on his head like the horns of a stag or a ram, then shall I observe the tie of brotherhood with thee."

Then spoke Judah to his father Jacob, saying: "How long wilt thou stand yet wasting words of peace and friendship upon him? And he attacks us unawares, like an enemy, with his mail-clad warriors, seeking to slay us." Hearing these words, Jacob grasped his bow and killed Adoram the Edomite, and a second time he bent his bow, and the arrow struck Esau upon the right thigh. The wound was mortal, and his sons lifted Esau up and put him upon his ass, and he came to Adora, and there he died.

Judah made a sally to the south of the citadel, and with him were Naphtali and Gad, aided by fifty of Jacob's servants; to the east Levi and Dan went forth with fifty servants; Reuben, Issachar, and Zebulon with fifty servants, to the north; and Simon, Benjamin, and Enoch, the last the son of Reuben, with fifty servants, to the west. Judah was exceedingly brave in battle. Together with Naphtali and Gad he pressed forward into the ranks of the enemy, and captured one of their iron towers. On their bucklers they caught the sharp missiles hurled against them in such numbers that the light of the sun was darkened by reason of the rocks and darts and stones. Judah was the first to break the ranks of the enemy, of whom he killed six valiant men, and he was accompanied on the right by Naphtali and by Gad on the left. They also hewed down two soldiers each, while their troop of servants killed one man each. Nevertheless they did not succeed in forcing the army away from the south of the citadel, not even when all together, Judah and his brethren, made an united attack upon the enemy, each of them picking out a victim and slaying him. And they were still unsuccessful in a third combined attack, though this time each killed two men.

When Judah saw now that the enemy remained in possession of the field, and it was impossible to dislodge them, he girded himself with strength, and an heroic spirit animated him. Judah, Naphtali, and Gad united, and together they pierced the ranks of the enemy, Judah slaying ten of them, and his brothers each eight. Seeing this, the servants took courage, and they joined their leaders and fought at their side. Judah laid about him to right and to left, always aided by Naphtali and Gad, and so they succeeded in forcing the enemy one ris further to the south, away from the citadel. But the hostile army recovered itself, and maintained a brave stand against all the sons of Jacob, who were faint from the hardships of the combat, and could not continue to fight. Thereupon Judah turned to God in prayer, and God hearkened unto his petition, and He helped them. He set loose a storm from one of His treasure chambers, and it blew into the faces of the enemy, and filled their eyes with darkness, and they could not see how to fight. But Judah and his brothers could see clearly, for the wind blew upon their backs. Now Judah and his two brothers wrought havoc among them, they hewed the enemy down as the reaper mows down the stalks of grain and heaps them up for sheaves.

After they had routed the division of the army assigned to them on the south, they hastened to the aid of their brothers, who were defending the east, north, and west of the citadel with three companies. On each side the wind blew into the faces of the enemy, and so the sons of Jacob succeeded in annihilating their army. Four hundred were slain in battle, and six hundred fled, among the latter Esau's four sons, Reuel, Jeush, Lotan, and Korah. The oldest of his sons, Eliphaz, took no part in the war, because he was a disciple of Jacob, and therefore would not bear arms against him.

The sons of Jacob pursued after the fleeing remnant of the army as far as Adora. There the sons of Esau abandoned the body of their father, and continued their flight to Mount Seir. But the sons of Jacob remained in Adora over night, and out of respect for their father they buried the remains of his brother Esau. In the morning they went on in pursuit of the enemy, and besieged them on Mount Seir. Now the sons of Esau and all the other fugitives came and fell down before them, bowed down, and entreated them without cease, until they concluded peace with them. But the sons of Jacob exacted tribute from them.

THE DESCENDANTS OF ESAU

The worthiest among the sons of Esau was his first-born Eliphaz. He had been raised under the eyes of his grandfather Isaac, from whom he had learnt the pious way of life. The Lord had even found him worthy of being endowed with the spirit of prophecy, for Eliphaz the son of Esau is none other than the prophet Eliphaz, the friend of Job. It was from the life of the Patriarchs that he drew the admonitions which he gave unto Job in his disputes with him. Eliphaz spake: "Thou didst ween thyself the equal of Abraham, and thou didst marvel, therefore, that God should deal with thee as with the generation of the confusion of tongues. But Abraham stood the test of ten temptations, and thou faintest when but one toucheth thee. When any that was not whole came to thee, thou wouldst console him. To the blind thou wouldst say, If thou didst build thyself a house, thou wouldst surely put windows in it, and if God hath denied thee light, it is but that He may be glorified through thee in the day when 'the eyes of the blind shall be opened.' To the deaf thou wouldst say, If thou didst fashion a water pitcher, thou wouldst surely not forget to make ears for it, and if God created thee without hearing, it is but that He may be glorified through thee in the day when 'the ears of the deaf shall be unstopped.' In such wise thou didst endeavor to console the feeble and the maimed. But now it is come unto thee, and thou art troubled. Thou sayest, I am an upright man, why doth He chastise me? But who, I pray thee, ever perished, being innocent? Noah was saved from the flood, Abraham from the fiery furnace, Isaac from the slaughtering knife, Jacob from angels, Moses from the sword of Pharaoh, and Israel from the Egyptians that were drowned in the Sea. Thus shall all the wicked fare."

Job answered Eliphaz, and said, "Look at thy father Esau!"

But Eliphaz returned: "I have nothing to do with him, the son should not bear the iniquity of the father. Esau will be destroyed, because he executed no good deeds, and likewise his dukes will perish. But as for me, I am a prophet, and my message is not unto Esau, but unto thee, to make thee render account of thyself." But God rebuked Eliphaz, and said: "Thou didst speak harsh words unto My servant Job. Therefore shall Obadiah, one of thy descendants, utter a prophecy of denunciation against thy father's house, the Edomites."

The concubine of Eliphaz was Timna, a princess of royal blood, who had asked to be received into the faith of Abraham and his family, but they all, Abraham, Isaac, and Jacob, had rejected her, and she said, "Rather will I be a maid servant unto the dregs of this nation, than mistress of another nation," and so she was willing to be concubine to Eliphaz. To punish the Patriarchs for the affront they had offered her, she was made the mother of Amalek, who inflicted great injury upon Israel.

Another one of Esau's descendants, Anah, had a most unusual experience. Once when he was pasturing his father's asses in the wilderness, he led them to one of the deserts on the shores of the Red Sea, opposite the wilderness of the nations, and while he was feeding the beasts, a very heavy storm came from the other side of the sea, and the asses could not move. Then about one hundred and twenty great and terrible animals came out from the wilderness at the other side of the sea, and they all came to the place where the asses were, and they placed themselves there. From the middle down, these animals were in the shape of a man, and from the middle up some had the likeness of bears, some of apes, and they all had tails behind them like the tail of the dukipat, from between their shoulders reaching down to the earth. The animals mounted the asses, and they rode away with them, and unto this day no eye hath seen them. One of them approached Anah, and smote him with its tail, and then ran off.

When Anah saw all this, he was exceedingly afraid on account of his life, and he fled to the city, where he related all that had happened to him. Many sallied forth to seek the asses, but none could find them. Anah and his brothers went no more to the same place from that day forth, for they were greatly afraid on account of their lives.

This Anah was the offspring of an incestuous marriage; his mother was at the same time the mother of his father Zibeon. And as he was born of an unnatural union, so he tried to bring about unnatural unions among animals. He was the first to mix the breed of the horse and the ass and produce the mule. As a punishment, God crossed the snake and the lizard, and they brought forth the habarbar, whose bite is certain death, like the bite of the white she-mule.

The descendants of Esau had eight kings before there reigned any king over the descendants of Jacob. But a time came when the Jews had eight kings during whose reign the Edomites had none and were subject to the Jewish kings. This was the time that intervened between Saul, the first Israelitish king, who ruled over Edom, and Jehoshaphat, for Edom did not make itself independent of Jewish rule until the time of Joram, the son of Jehoshaphat. There was a difference between the kings of Esau's seed and the kings of Jacob's seed. The Jewish people always produced their kings from their own midst, while the Edomites had to go to alien peoples to secure theirs. The first Edomite king was the Aramean Balaam, called Bela in his capacity as ruler of Edom. His successor Job, called Jobab also, came from Bozrah, and for furnishing Edom with a king this city will be chastised in time to come. When God sits in judgment on Edom, Bozrah will be the first to suffer punishment.

The rule of Edom was of short duration, while the rule of Israel will be unto all times, for the standard of the Messiah shall wave forever and ever.

Volume 2

Chapter 1

JOSEPH--THE FAVORITE SON

Jacob was not exempt from the lot that falls to the share of all the pious. Whenever they expect to enjoy life in tranquillity, Satan hinders them. He appears before God, and says: "Is it not enough that the future world is set apart for the pious? What right have they to enjoy this world, besides?" After the many hardships and conflicts that had beset the path of Jacob, he thought he would be at rest at last, and then came the loss of Joseph and inflicted the keenest suffering. Verily, few and evil had been the days of the years of Jacob's pilgrimage, for the time spent outside of the Holy Land had seemed joyless to him. Only the portion of his life passed in the land of his fathers, during which he was occupied with making proselytes, in accordance with the example set him by Abraham and Isaac, did he consider worth while having lived, and this happy time was of short duration. When Joseph was snatched away, but eight years had elapsed since his return to his father's house.

And yet it was only for the sake of Joseph that Jacob had been willing to undergo all the troubles and the adversity connected with his sojourn in the house of Laban. Indeed, Jacob's blessing in having his quiver full of children was due to the merits of Joseph, and likewise the dividing of the Red Sea and of the Jordan for the Israelites was the reward for his son's piety. For among the sons of Jacob Joseph was the one that resembled his father most closely in appearance, and, also, he was the one to whom Jacob transmitted the instruction and knowledge he had received from his teachers Shem and Eber. The whole course of the son's life is but a repetition of the father's. As the mother of Jacob remained childless for a long time after her marriage, so also the mother of Joseph. As Rebekah had undergone severe suffering in giving birth to Jacob, so Rachel in giving birth to Joseph. As Jacob's mother bore two sons, so also Joseph's mother. Like Jacob, Joseph was born circumcised. As the father was a shepherd, so the son. As the father served for the sake of a woman, so the son served under a woman. Like the father, the son appropriated his older brother's birthright. The father was hated by his brother, and the son was hated by his brethren. The father was the favorite son as compared with his brother, so was the son as compared with his brethren. Both the father and the son lived in the land of the stranger. The father became a servant to a master, also the son. The master whom the father served was blessed by God, so was the master whom the son served. The father and the son were both accompanied by angels, and both married their wives outside of the Holy Land. The father and the son were both blessed with wealth. Great things were announced to the father in a dream, so also to the son. As the father went to Egypt and put an end to famine, so the son. As the father exacted the promise from his sons to bury him in the Holy Land, so also the son. The father died in Egypt, there died also the son. The body of the father was embalmed, also the body of the son. As the father's remains were carried to the Holy Land for interment, so also the remains of the son. Jacob the father provided for the sustenance of his son Joseph during a period of seventeen years, so Joseph the son provided for his father Jacob during a period of seventeen years.

Until he was seventeen years old, Joseph frequented the Bet ha-Midrash, and he became so learned that he could impart to his brethren the Halakot he had heard from his father, and in this way he may be regarded as their teacher. He did not stop at formal instruction, he also tried to give them good counsel, and he became the favorite of the sons of the handmaids, who would kiss and embrace him.

In spite of his scholarship there was something boyish about Joseph. He painted his eyes, dressed his hair carefully, and walked with a mincing step. These foibles of youth were not so deplorable as his habit of bringing evil reports of his brethren to his father. He accused them of treating the beasts under their care with cruelty--he said that they ate flesh torn from a living animal--and he charged them with casting their eyes upon the daughters of the Canaanites, and giving contemptuous treatment to the sons of the handmaids Bilhah and Zilpah, whom they called slaves.

For these groundless accusations Joseph had to pay dearly. He was himself sold as a slave, because he had charged his brethren with having called the sons of the handmaids slaves, and Potiphar's wife cast her eyes upon Joseph, because he threw the suspicion upon his brethren that they had cast their eyes upon the Canaanitish women. And how little it was true that they were guilty of cruelty to animals, appears from the fact that at the very time when they were contemplating their crime against Joseph, they yet observed all the rules and prescriptions of the ritual in slaughtering the kid of the goats with the blood of which they besmeared his coat of many colors.

JOSEPH HATED BY HIS BRETHREN

Joseph's talebearing against his brethren made them hate him. Among all of them Gad was particularly wrathful, and for good reason. Gad was a very brave man, and when a beast of prey attacked the herd, over which he kept guard at night, he would seize it by one of its legs, and whirl it around until it was stunned, and then he would fling it away to a distance of two stadia, and kill it thus. Once Jacob sent Joseph to tend the flock, but he remained away only thirty days, for he was a delicate lad and fell sick with the heat, and he hastened back to his father. On his return he told Jacob that the sons of the handmaids were in the habit of slaughtering the choice cattle of the herd and eating it, without obtaining permission from Judah and Reuben. But his report was not accurate. What he had seen was Gad slaughtering one lamb, which he had snatched from the very jaws of a bear, and he killed it because it could not be kept alive after its fright. Joseph's account sounded as though the sons of the handmaids were habitually inconsiderate and careless in wasting their father's substance.

To the resentment of the brethren was added their envy of Joseph, because their father loved him more than all of them. Joseph's beauty of person was equal to that of his mother Rachel, and Jacob had but to look at him to be consoled for the death of his beloved wife. Reason enough for distinguishing him among his children. As a token of his great love for him, Jacob gave Joseph a coat of many colors, so light and delicate that it could be crushed and concealed in the closed palm of one hand. The Hebrew name of the garment, Passim, conveys the story of the sale of Joseph. The first letter, Pe, stands for Potiphar, his Egyptian master; Samek stands for Soharim, the merchantmen that bought Joseph from the company of Ishmaelites to whom his brethren had sold him; Yod stands for these same Ishmaelites; and Mem, for the Midianites that obtained him from the merchantmen, and then disposed of him to Potiphar. But Passim. has yet another meaning, "clefts." His brethren knew that the Red Sea would be cleft in twain in days to come for Joseph's sake, and they were jealous of the glory to be conferred upon him. Although they were filled with hatred of him, it must be said in their favor that they were not of a sullen, spiteful nature. They did not hide their feelings, they proclaimed their enmity openly.

Once Joseph dreamed a dream, and he could not refrain from telling it to his brethren. He spoke, and said: "Hear, I pray you, this dream which I have dreamed. Behold, you gathered fruit, and so did I. Your fruit rotted, but mine remained sound. Your seed will set up dumb images of idols, but they will vanish at the appearance of my descendant, the Messiah of Joseph. You will keep the truth as to my fate from the knowledge of my father, but I will stand fast as a reward for the self-denial of my mother, and you will prostrate yourselves five times before me."

The brethren refused at first to listen to the dream, but when Joseph urged them again and again, they gave heed to him, and they said, "Shalt thou indeed reign over us? or shalt thou indeed have dominion over us?" God put an interpretation into their mouths that was to be verified in the posterity of Joseph. Jeroboam and Jehu, two kings, and Joshua and Gideon, two judges, have been among his descendants, corresponding to the double and emphatic expressions used by his brethren in interpreting the dream.

Then Joseph dreamed another dream, how the sun, the moon, and eleven stars bowed down before him, and Jacob, to whom he told it first, was rejoiced over it, for he understood its meaning properly. He knew that he himself was designated by the sun, the name by which God had called him when he lodged overnight on the holy site of the Temple. He had heard God say to the angels at that time, "The sun has come." The moon stood for Joseph's mother, and the stars for his brethren, for the righteous are as the stars. Jacob was so convinced of the truth of the dream that he was encouraged to believe that he would live to see the resurrection of the dead, for Rachel was dead, and her return to earth was clearly indicated by the dream. He went astray there, for not Joseph's own mother was referred to, but his foster-mother Bilhah, who had raised him.

Jacob wrote the dream in a book, recording all the circumstances, the day, the hour, and the place, for the holy spirit cautioned him, "Take heed, these things will surely come to pass." But when Joseph repeated his dream to his brethren, in the presence of his father, Jacob rebuked him, saying, "I and thy brethren, that has some sense, but I and thy mother, that is inconceivable, for thy mother is dead." These words of Jacob called forth a reproof from God. He said, "Thus thy descendants will in time to come seek to hinder Jeremiah in delivering his prophecies." Jacob may be excused, he had spoken in this way only in order to avert the envy and hate of his brethren from Joseph, but they envied and hated him because they knew that the interpretation put upon the dream by Jacob would be realized.

JOSEPH CAST INTO THE PIT

Once the brethren of Joseph led their father's flocks to the pastures of Shechem, and they intended to take their ease and pleasure there. They stayed away a long time, and no tidings of them were heard. Jacob began to be anxious about the fate of his sons. He feared that a war had broken out between them and the people of Shechem, and he resolved to send Joseph to them and have him bring word again, whether it was well with his brethren. Jacob desired to know also about the flocks, for it is a duty to concern oneself about the welfare of anything from which one derives profit. Though he knew that the hatred of his brethren might bring on unpleasant adventures, yet Joseph, in filial reverence, declared himself ready to go on his father's errand. Later, whenever Jacob remembered his dear son's willing spirit, the recollection stabbed him to the heart. He would say to himself, "Thou didst know the hatred of thy brethren, and yet thou didst say, Here am I."

Jacob dismissed Joseph, with the injunction that he journey only by daylight, saying furthermore, "Go now, see whether it be well with thy brethren, and well with the flock; and send me word"--an unconscious prophecy. He did not say that he expected to see Joseph again, but only to have word from him. Since the covenant of the pieces, God had resolved, on account of Abraham's doubting question, that Jacob and his family should go down into Egypt to dwell there. The preference shown to Joseph by his father, and the envy it aroused, leading finally to the sale of Joseph and his establishment in Egypt, were but disguised means created by God, instead of executing His counsel directly by carrying Jacob down into Egypt as a captive.

Joseph reached Shechem, where he expected to find his brethren. Shechem was always a place of ill omen for Jacob and his seed--there Dinah was dishonored, there the Ten Tribes of Israel rebelled against the house of David while Rehoboam ruled in Jerusalem, and there Jeroboam was installed as king. Not finding his brethren and the herd in Shechem, Joseph continued his journey in the direction of the next pasturing place, not far from Shechem, but he lost his way in the wilderness. Gabriel in human shape appeared before him, and asked him, saying, "What seekest thou?" And he answered, "I seek my brethren." Whereto the angel replied, "Thy brethren have given up the Divine qualities of love and mercy. Through a prophetic revelation they learned that the Hivites were preparing to make war upon them, and therefore they departed hence to go to Dothan. And they had to leave this place for other reasons, too. I heard, while I was still standing behind the curtain that veils the Divine throne, that this day the Egyptian bondage would begin, and thou wouldst be the first to be subjected to it." Then Gabriel led Joseph to Dothan.

When his brethren saw him afar off, they conspired against him, to slay him. Their first plan was to set dogs on him. Simon then spoke to Levi, "Behold, the master of dreams cometh with a new dream, he whose descendant Jeroboam will introduce the worship of Baal. Come now, therefore, and let us slay him, that we may see what will become of his dreams." But God spoke: "Ye say, We shall see what will become of his dreams, and I say likewise, We shall see, and the future shall show whose word will stand, yours or Mine."

Simon and Gad set about slaying Joseph, and he fell upon his face, and entreated them: "Have mercy with me, my brethren, have pity on the heart of my father Jacob. Lay not your hands upon me, to spill innocent blood, for I have done no evil unto you. But if I have done evil unto you, then chastise me with a chastisement, but your hands lay not upon me, for the sake of our father Jacob." These words touched Zebulon, and he began to lament and weep, and the wailing of Joseph rose up together with his brother's, and when Simon and Gad raised their hands against him to execute their evil design, Joseph took refuge behind Zebulon, and supplicated his other brethren to have mercy upon him. Then Reuben arose, and he said, "Brethren, let us not slay him, but let us cast him into one of the dry pits, which our fathers dug without finding water." That was due to the providence of God; He had hindered the water from rising in them in order that Joseph's rescue might be accomplished, and the pits remained dry until Joseph was safe in the hands of the Ishmaelites.

Reuben had several reasons for interceding in behalf of Joseph. He knew that he as the oldest of the brethren would be held responsible by their father, if any evil befell him. Besides, Reuben was grateful to Joseph for having reckoned him among the eleven sons of Jacob in narrating his dream of the sun, moon, and stars. Since his disrespectful bearing toward Jacob, he had not thought himself worthy of being considered one of his sons. First Reuben tried to restrain his brethren from their purpose, and he addressed them in words full of love and compassion. But when he saw that neither words nor entreaties would change their intention, he begged them, saying: "My brethren, at least hearken unto me in respect of this, that ye be not so wicked and cruel as to slay him. Lay no hand upon your brother, shed no blood, cast him into this pit that is in the wilderness, and let him perish thus.

Then Reuben went away from his brethren, and he hid in the mountains, so that he might be able to hasten back in a favorable moment and draw Joseph forth from the pit and restore him to his father. He hoped his reward would be pardon for the transgression he had committed against Jacob. His good intention was frustrated, yet Reuben was rewarded by God, for God gives a recompense not only for good deeds, but for good intentions as well. As he was the first of the brethren of Joseph to make an attempt to save him, so the city of Bezer in the tribe of Reuben was the first of the cities of refuge appointed to safeguard the life of the innocent that seek help. Furthermore God spake to Reuben, saying: "As thou wast the first to endeavor to restore a child unto his father, so Hosea, one of thy descendants, shall be the first to endeavor to lead Israel back to his heavenly Father."

The brethren accepted Reuben's proposition, and Simon seized Joseph, and cast him into a pit swarming with snakes and scorpions, beside which was another unused pit, filled with offal. As though this were not enough torture, Simon bade his brethren fling great stones at Joseph. In his later dealings with this brother Simon, Joseph showed all the forgiving charitableness of his nature. When Simon was held in durance in Egypt as a hostage, Joseph, so far from bearing him a grudge, ordered crammed poultry to be set before him at all his meals.

Not satisfied with exposing Joseph to the snakes and scorpions, his brethren had stripped him bare before they flung him into the pit. They took off his coat of many colors, his upper garment, his breeches, and his shirt. However, the reptiles could do him no harm. God heard his cry of distress, and kept them in hiding in the clefts and the holes, and they could not come near him. From the depths of the pit Joseph appealed to his brethren, saying: "O my brethren, what have I done unto you, and what is my transgression? Why are you not afraid before God on account of your treatment of me? Am I not flesh of your flesh, and bone of your bone? Jacob your father, is he not also my father? Why do you act thus toward me? And how will you be able to lift up your countenance before Jacob? O Judah, Reuben, Simon, Levi, my brethren, deliver me, I pray you, from the dark place into which you have cast me. Though I committed a trespass against you, yet are ye children of Abraham, Isaac, and Jacob, who were compassionate with the orphan, gave food to the hungry, and clothed the naked. How, then, can ye withhold your pity from your own brother, your own flesh and bone? And though I sinned against you, yet you will hearken unto my petition for the sake of my father. O that my father knew what my brethren are doing unto me, and what they spake unto me!"

To avoid hearing Joseph's weeping and cries of distress, his brethren passed on from the pit, and stood at a bow-shot's distance. The only one among them that manifested pity was Zebulon. For two days and two nights no food passed his lips on account of his grief over the fate of Joseph, who had to spend three days and three nights in the pit before he was sold. During this period Zebulon was charged by his brethren to keep watch at the pit. He was chosen to stand guard because he took no part in the meals. Part of the time Judah also refrained from eating with the rest, and took turns at watching, because he feared Simon and Gad might jump down into the pit and put an end to Joseph's life.

While Joseph was languishing thus, his brethren determined to kill him. They would finish their meal first, they said, and then they would fetch him forth and slay him. When they had done eating, they attempted to say grace, but Judah remonstrated with them: "We are about to take the life of a human being, and yet would bless God? That is not a blessing, that is contemning the Lord. What profit is it if we slay our brother? Rather will the punishment of God descend upon us. I have good counsel to give you. Yonder passeth by a travelling company of Ishmaelites on their way to Egypt. Come and let us sell him to the Ishmaelites, and let not our hand be upon him. The Ishmaelites will take him with them upon their journeyings, and he will be lost among the peoples of the earth. Let us follow the custom of former days, for Canaan, too, the son of Ham, was made a slave for his evil deeds, and so will we do with our brother Joseph."

THE SALE

While the brethren of Joseph were deliberating upon his fate, seven Midianitish merchantmen passed near the pit in which he lay. They noticed that many birds were circling above it, whence they assumed that there must be water therein, and, being thirsty, they made a halt in order to refresh themselves. When they came close, they heard Joseph screaming and wailing, and they looked down into the pit and saw a youth of beautiful figure and comely appearance. They called to him, saying: "Who art thou? Who brought thee hither, and who cast thee into this pit in the wilderness?" They all joined together and dragged him up, and took him along with them when they continued on their journey. They had to pass his brethren, who called out to the Midianites: "Why have you done such a thing, to steal our slave and carry him away with you? We threw the lad into the pit, because he was disobedient. Now, then, return our slave to us." The Midianites replied: "What, this lad, you say, is your slave, your servant? More likely is it that you all are slaves unto him, for in beauty of form, in pleasant looks, and fair appearance, he excelleth you all. Why, then, will you speak lies unto us? We will not give ear unto your words, nor believe you, for we found the lad in the wilderness, in a pit, and we took him out, and we will carry him away with us on our journey." But the sons of Jacob insisted, "Restore our slave to us, lest you meet death at the edge of the sword."

Unaffrighted, the Midianites drew their weapons, and, amid war whoops, they prepared to enter into a combat with the sons of Jacob. Then Simon rose up, and with bared sword he sprang upon the Midianites, at the same time uttering a cry that made the earth reverberate. The Midianites fell down in great consternation, and he said: "I am Simon, the son of the Hebrew Jacob, who destroyed the city of Shechem alone and unaided, and together with my brethren I destroyed the cities of the Amorites. God do so and more also, if it be not true that all the Midianites, your brethren, united with all the Canaanite kings to fight with me, cannot hold out against me. Now restore the boy you took from us, else will I give your flesh unto the fowls of the air and to the beasts of the field."

The Midianites were greatly afraid of Simon, and, terrified and abashed, they spake to the sons of Jacob with little courage: "Said ye not that ye cast this lad into the pit because he was of a rebellious spirit? What, now, will ye do with an insubordinate slave? Rather sell him to us, we are ready to pay any price you desire." This speech was part of the purpose of God. He had put it into the heart of the Midianites to insist upon possessing Joseph, that he might not remain with his brethren, and be slain by them. The brethren assented, and Joseph was sold as a slave while they sat over their meal. God spake, saying: "Over a meal did ye sell your brother, and thus shall Ahasuerus sell your descendants to Haman over a meal, and because ye have sold Joseph to be a slave, therefore shall ye say year after year, Slaves were we unto Pharaoh in Egypt."

The price paid for Joseph by the Midianites was twenty pieces of silver, enough for a pair of shoes for each of his brethren. Thus "they sold the righteous for silver, and the needy for a pair of shoes." For so handsome a youth as Joseph the sum paid was too low by far, but his appearance had been greatly changed by the horrible anguish he had endured in the pit with the snakes and the scorpions. He had lost his ruddy complexion, and he looked sallow and sickly, and the Midianites were justified in paying a small sum for him.

The merchantmen had come upon Joseph naked in the pit, for his brethren had stripped him of all his clothes. That he might not appear before men in an unseemly condition, God sent Gabriel down to him, and the angel enlarged the amulet banging from Joseph's neck until it was a garment that covered him entirely. Joseph's brethren were looking after him as he departed with the Midianites, and when they saw him with clothes upon him, they cried after them, "Give us his raiment! We sold him naked, without clothes." His owners refused to yield to their demand, but they agreed to reimburse the brethren with four pairs of shoes, and Joseph kept his garment, the same in which he was arrayed when he arrived in Egypt and was sold to Potiphar, the same in which he was locked up in prison and appeared before Pharaoh, and the same he wore when he was ruler over Egypt.

As an atonement for the twenty pieces of silver taken by his brethren in exchange for Joseph, God commanded that every first-born son shall be redeemed by the priest with an equal amount, and, also, every Israelite must pay annually to the sanctuary as much as fell to each of the brethren as his share of the price.

The brethren of Joseph bought shoes for the money, for they said: "We will not eat it, because it is the price for the blood of our brother, but we will tread upon him, for that he spake, he would have dominion over us, and we will see what will become of his dreams." And for this reason the ordinance has been commanded, that he who refuseth to raise up a name in Israel unto his brother that hath died without having a son, shall have his shoe loosed from off his foot, and his face shall be spat upon. Joseph's brethren refused to do aught to preserve his life, and therefore the Lord loosed their shoes from off their feet, for, when they went down to Egypt, the slaves of Joseph took their shoes off their feet as they entered the gates, and they prostrated themselves before Joseph as before a Pharaoh, and, as they lay prostrate, they were spat upon, and put to shame before the Egyptians.

The Midianites pursued their journey to Gilead, but they soon regretted the purchase they had made. They feared that Joseph had been stolen in the land of the Hebrews, though sold to them as a slave, and if his kinsmen should find him with them, death would be inflicted upon them for the abduction of a free man. The high-handed manner of the sons of Jacob confirmed their suspicion, that they might be capable of man theft. Their wicked deed would explain, too, why they had accepted so small a sum in exchange for Joseph. While discussing these points, they saw, coming their way, the travelling company of Ishmaelites that had been observed earlier by the sons of Jacob, and they determined to dispose of Joseph to them, that they might at least not lose the price they had paid, and might escape the danger at the same time of being made captives for the crime of kidnapping a man. And the Ishmaelites bought Joseph from the Midianites, and they paid the same price as his former owners had given for him.

JOSEPH'S THREE MASTERS

As a rule the only merchandise with which the Ishmaelites loaded their camels was pitch and the skins of beasts. By a providential dispensation they carried bags of perfumery this time, instead of their usual ill-smelling freight, that sweet fragrance might be wafted to Joseph on his journey to Egypt. These aromatic substances were well suited to Joseph, whose body emitted a pleasant smell, so agreeable and pervasive that the road along which he travelled was redolent thereof, and on his arrival in Egypt the perfume from his body spread over the whole land, and the royal princesses, following the sweet scent to trace its source, reached the place in which Joseph was. Even after his death the same fragrance was spread abroad by his bones, enabling Moses to distinguish Joseph's remains from all others, and keep the oath of the children of Israel, to inter them in the Holy Land.

When Joseph learned that the Ishmaelites were carrying him to Egypt, he began to weep bitterly at the thought of being removed so far from Canaan and from his father. One of the Ishmaelites noticed Joseph's weeping and crying, and thinking that he found riding uncomfortable, he lifted him from the back of the camel, and permitted him to walk on foot. But Joseph continued to weep and sob, crying incessantly, "O father, father!" Another one of the caravan, tired of his lamentations, beat him, causing only the more tears and wails, until the youth, exhausted by his grief, was unable to move on. Now all the Ishmaelites in the company dealt out blows to him. They treated him with relentless cruelty, and tried to silence him by threats. God saw Joseph's distress, and He sent darkness and terror upon the Ishmaelites, and their hands grew rigid when they raised them to inflict a blow. Astonished, they asked themselves why God did thus unto them upon the road. They did not know that it was for the sake of Joseph.

The journey was continued until they came to Ephrath, the place of Rachel's sepulchre. Joseph hastened to his mother's grave, and throwing himself across it, he groaned and cried, saying: "O mother, mother, that didst bear me, arise, come forth and see how thy son hath been sold into slavery, with none to take pity upon him. Arise, see thy son, and weep with me over my misfortune, and observe the heartlessness of my brethren. Awake, O mother, rouse thyself from thy sleep, rise up and prepare for the conflict with my brethren, who stripped me even of my shirt, and sold me as a slave to merchantmen, who in turn sold me to others, and without mercy they tore me away from my father. Arise, accuse my brethren before God, and see whom He will justify in the judgment, and whom He will find guilty. Arise, O mother, awake from thy sleep, see how my father is with me in his soul and in his spirit, and comfort him and ease his heavy heart."

Joseph wept and cried upon the grave of his mother, until, weary from grief, he lay immovable as a stone. Then he heard a voice heavy with tears speak to him from the depths, saying: "My son Joseph, my son, I heard thy complaints and thy groans, I saw thy tears, and I knew thy misery, my son. I am grieved for thy sake, and thy affliction is added to the burden of my affliction. But, my son Joseph, put thy trust in God, and wait upon Him. Fear not, for the Lord is with thee, and He will deliver thee from all evil. Go down into Egypt with thy masters, my son; fear naught, for the Lord is with thee, O my son." This and much more like unto it did the voice utter, and then it was silent. Joseph listened in great amazement at first, and then he broke out in renewed tears. Angered thereby, one of the Ishmaelites drove him from his mother's grave with kicks and curses. Then Joseph entreated his masters to take him back to his father, who would give them great riches as a reward. But they said, "Why, thou art a slave! How canst thou know where thy father is? If thou hadst had a free man as father, thou wouldst not have been sold twice for a petty sum." And then their fury against him increased, they beat him and maltreated him, and he wept bitter tears.

Now God looked upon the distress of Joseph, and He sent darkness to enshroud the land once more. A storm raged, the lightning flashed, and from the thunderbolts the whole earth trembled, and the Ishmaelites lost their way in their terror. The beasts and the camels stood still, and, beat them as their drivers would, they refused to budge from the spot, but crouched down upon the ground. Then the Ishmaelites spake to one another, and said: "Why hath God brought this upon us? What are our sins, what our trespasses, that such things befall us?" One of them said to the others: "Peradventure this hath come upon us by reason of the sin which we have committed against this slave. Let us beg him earnestly to grant us forgiveness, and if then God will take pity, and let these storms pass away from us, we shall know that we suffered harm on account of the injury we inflicted upon this slave."

The Ishmaelites did according to these words, and they said unto Joseph: "We have sinned against God and against thee. Pray to thy God, and entreat Him to take this death plague from us, for we acknowledge that we have sinned against Him." Joseph fulfilled their wish, and God hearkened to his petition, and the storm was assuaged. All around became calm, the beasts arose from their recumbent position, and the caravan could proceed upon its way. Now the Ishmaelites saw plainly that all their trouble had come upon them for the sake of Joseph, and they spoke one to another, saying: "We know now that all this evil hath happened to us on account of this poor fellow, and wherefore should we bring death upon ourselves by our own doings? Let us take counsel together, what is to be done with the slave." One of them advised that Joseph's wish be fulfilled, and he be taken back to his father. Then they would be sure of receiving the money they had paid out for him. This plan was rejected, because they had accomplished a great part of their journey, and they were not inclined to retrace their steps. They therefore resolved upon carrying Joseph to Egypt and selling him there. They would rid themselves of him in this way, and also receive a great price for him.

They continued their journey as far as the borders of Egypt, and there they met four men, descendants of Medan, the son of Abraham, and to these they sold Joseph for five shekels. The two companies, the Ishmaelites and the Medanites, arrived in Egypt upon the same day. The latter, hearing that Potiphar, an officer of Pharaoh, the captain of the guard, was seeking a good slave, repaired to him at once, to try to dispose of Joseph to him. Potiphar was willing to pay as much as four hundred pieces of silver, for, high as the price was, it did not seem too great for a slave that pleased him as much as Joseph. However, he made a condition. He said to the Medanites: "I will pay you the price demanded, but you must bring me the person that sold the slave to you, that I may be in a position to find out all about him, for the youth seems to me to be neither a slave nor the son of a slave. He appears to be of noble blood. I must convince myself that he was not stolen." The Medanites brought the Ishmaelites to Potiphar, and they testified that Joseph was a slave, that they had owned him, and had sold him to the Medanites. Potiphar rested satisfied with this report, paid the price asked for Joseph, and the Medanites and the Ishmaelites went their way.

JOSEPH'S COAT BROUGHT TO HIS FATHER

No sooner was the sale of Joseph an accomplished fact than the sons of Jacob repented of their deed. They even hastened after the Midianites to ransom Joseph, but their efforts to overtake them were vain, and they had to accept the inevitable. Meantime Reuben had rejoined his brethren. He had been so deeply absorbed in penances, in praying and studying the Torah, in expiation of his sin against his father, that he had not been able to remain with his brethren and tend the flocks, and thus it happened that he was not on the spot when Joseph was sold. His first errand was to go to the pit, in the hope of finding Joseph there. In that case he would have carried him off and restored him to his father clandestinely, without the knowledge of his brethren. He stood at the opening and called again and again, "Joseph, Joseph!" As he received no answer, he concluded that Joseph had perished, either by reason of terror or as the result of a snake bite, and he descended into the pit, only to find that he was not there, either living or dead. He mounted to the top again, and rent his clothes, and cried out, "The lad is not there, and what answer shall I give to my father, if he be dead?" Then Reuben returned unto his brethren, and told them that Joseph had vanished from the pit, whereat he was deeply grieved, because he, being the oldest of the sons, was responsible to their father Jacob. The brethren made a clean breast of what they had done with Joseph, and they related to him how they had tried to make good their evil deed, and how their efforts had been vain.

Now there remained nothing to do but invent a plausible explanation for their brother's disappearance to give to Jacob. First of all, however, they took an oath not to betray to his father or any human being what they had actually done with Joseph. He who violated the oath would be put to the sword by the rest. Then they took counsel together about what to say to Jacob. It was Issachar's advice to tear Joseph's coat of many colors, and dip it in the blood of a little kid of the goats, to make Jacob believe that his son had been torn by a wild beast. The reason he suggested a kid was because its blood looks like human blood. In expiation of this act of deception, it was ordained that a kid be used as an atonement sacrifice when the Tabernacle was dedicated.

Simon opposed this suggestion. He did not want to relinquish Joseph's coat, and he threatened to hew down any one that should attempt to wrest it from him by force. The reason for his vehemence was that he was very much enraged against his brethren for not having slain Joseph. But they threatened him in turn, saying, "If thou wilt not give up the coat, we shall say that thou didst execute the evil deed thyself." At that Simon surrendered it, and Naphtali brought it to Jacob, handing it to him with the words: "When we were driving our herds homeward, we found this garment covered with blood and dust on the highway, a little beyond Shechem. Know now whether it be thy son's coat or not." Jacob recognized Joseph's coat, and, overwhelmed by grief, he fell prostrate, and long lay on the ground motionless, like a stone. Then he arose, and set up a loud cry, and wept, saying, "It is my son's coat."

In great haste Jacob dispatched a slave to his sons, to bid them come to him, that he might learn more about what had happened. In the evening they all came, their garments rent, and dust strewn upon their heads. When they confirmed all that Naphtali had told him, Jacob broke out in mourning and lamentation: "It is my son's coat; an evil beast hath devoured him; Joseph is without doubt torn in pieces. I sent him to you to see whether it was well with you, and well with the flock. He went to do my errand, and while I thought him to be with you, the misfortune befell." Thereto the sons of Jacob made reply: "He came to us not at all. Since we left thee, we have not set eyes on him."

After these words, Jacob could doubt no longer that Joseph had been torn by wild beasts, and he mourned for his son, saying: "O my son Joseph, my son, I sent thee to inquire after the welfare of thy brethren, and now thou art torn by wild beasts. It is my fault that this evil chance hath come upon thee. I am distressed for thee, my son, I am sorely distressed. How sweet was thy life to me, and how bitter is thy death! Would God I had died for thee, O Joseph, my son, for now I am distressed on thy account. O my son Joseph, where art thou, and where is thy soul? Arise, arise from thy place, and look upon my grief for thee. Come and count the tears that roll down my cheeks, and bring the tale of them before God, that His wrath be turned away from me. O Joseph, my son, how painful and appalling was thy death! None hath died a death like thine since the world doth stand. I know well that it came to pass by reason of my sins. O that thou wouldst return and see the bitter sorrow thy misfortune hath brought upon me! But it is true, it was not I that created thee, and formed thee. I gave thee neither spirit nor soul, but God created thee. He formed thy bones, covered them with flesh, breathed the breath of life into thy nostrils, and then gave thee unto me. And God who gave thee unto me, He hath taken thee from me, and from Him hath this dispensation come upon me. What the Lord doeth is well done!" In these words and many others like them Jacob mourned and bewailed his son, until he fell to the ground prostrate and immovable.

When the sons of Jacob saw the vehemence of their father's grief, they repented of their deed, and wept bitterly. Especially Judah was grief-stricken. He laid his father's head upon his knees, and wiped his tears away as they flowed from his eyes, while he himself broke out in violent weeping. The sons of Jacob and their wives all sought to comfort their father. They arranged a great memorial service, and they wept and mourned over Joseph's death and over their father's sorrow. But Jacob refused to be comforted.

The tidings of his son's death caused the loss of two members of Jacob's family. Bilhah and Dinah could not survive their grief. Bilhah passed away the very day whereon the report reached Jacob, and Dinah died soon after, and so he had three losses to mourn in one month.

He received the tidings of Joseph's death in the seventh month, Tishri, and on the tenth day of the month, and therefore the children of Israel are bidden to weep and afflict their souls on this day. Furthermore, on this day the sin offering of atonement shall be a kid of the goats, because the sons of Jacob transgressed with a kid, in the blood of which they dipped Joseph's coat, and thus they brought sorrow upon Jacob.

When he had recovered somewhat from the stunning blow which the tidings of his favorite son's death had dealt him, Jacob rose up from the ground and addressed his sons, tears streaming down his cheeks all the while. "Up," he said, "take your swords and your bows, go out in the field, and make search, perhaps you will find the body of my son, and you will bring it to me, so that I may bury it. Keep a lookout, too, for beasts of prey, and catch the first you meet. Seize it and bring it to me. It may be that God will have pity upon my sorrow, and put the beast between your hands that hath torn my child in pieces, and I will take my revenge upon it."

The sons of Jacob set out on the morrow to do the bidding of their father, while he remained at home and wept and lamented for Joseph. In the wilderness they found a wolf, which they caught and brought to Jacob alive, saying: "Here is the first wild beast we encountered, and we have brought it to thee. But of thy son's corpse we saw not a trace." Jacob seized the wolf, and, amid loud weeping, he addressed these words to him: "Why didst thou devour my son Joseph, without any fear of the God of the earth, and without taking any thought of the grief thou wouldst bring down upon me? Thou didst devour my son without reason, he was guilty of no manner of transgression, and thou didst roll the responsibility for his death upon me. But God avengeth him that is persecuted."

To grant consolation to Jacob, God opened the mouth of the beast, and he spake: "As the Lord liveth, who hath created me, and as thy soul liveth, my lord, I have not seen thy son, and I did not rend him in pieces. From a land afar off I came to seek mine own son, who suffered a like fate with thine. He hath disappeared, and I know not whether he be dead or alive, and therefore I came hither ten days ago to find him. This day, while I was searching for him, thy sons met me, and they seized me, and, adding more grief to my grief over my lost son, they brought me hither to thee. This is my story, and now, O son of man, I am in thy hands, thou canst dispose of me this day as seemeth well in thy sight, but I swear unto thee by the God that bath created me, I have not seen thy son, nor have I torn him in pieces, never hath the flesh of man come into my mouth." Astonished at the speech of the wolf, Jacob let him go, unhindered, whithersoever he would, but he mourned his son Joseph as before.

It is a law of nature that however much one may grieve over the death of a dear one, at the end of a year consolation finds its way to the heart of the mourner. But the disappearance of a living man can never be wiped out of one's memory. Therefore the fact that he was inconsolable made Jacob suspect that Joseph was alive, and he did not give entire credence to the report of his sons. His vague suspicion was strengthened by something that happened to him. He went up into the mountains, hewed twelve stones out of the quarry, and wrote the names of his sons thereon, their constellations, and the months corresponding to the constellations, a stone for a son, thus, "Reuben, Ram, Nisan," and so for each of his twelve sons. Then he addressed the stones and bade them bow down before the one marked with Reuben's name, constellation, and month, and they did not move. He gave the same order regarding the stone marked for Simon, and again the stones stood still. And so he did respecting all his sons, until he reached the stone for Joseph. When he spoke concerning this one, "I command you to fall down before Joseph," they all prostrated themselves. He tried the same test with other things, with trees and sheaves, and always the result was the same, and Jacob could not but feel that his suspicion was true, Joseph was alive.

There was a reason why God did not reveal the real fate of Joseph to Jacob. When his brethren sold Joseph, their fear that the report of their iniquity might reach the ears of Jacob led them to pronounce the ban upon any that should betray the truth without the consent of all the others. Judah advanced the objection that a ban is invalid unless it is decreed in the presence of ten persons, and there were but nine of them, for Reuben and Benjamin were not there when the sale of Joseph was concluded. To evade the difficulty, the brothers counted God as the tenth person, and therefore God felt bound to refrain from revealing the true state of things to Jacob. He had regard, as it were, for the ban pronounced by the brethren of Joseph. And as God kept the truth a secret from Jacob, Isaac did not feel justified in acquainting him with his grandson's fate, which was well known to him, for he was a prophet. Whenever he was in the company of Jacob, he mourned with him, but as soon as he quitted him, he left off from manifesting grief, because he knew that Joseph lived.

Jacob was thus the only one among Joseph's closest kinsmen that remained in ignorance of his son's real fortunes, and he was the one of them all that had the greatest reason for regretting his death. He spoke: "The covenant that God made with me regarding the twelve tribes is null and void now. I did strive in vain to establish the twelve tribes, seeing that now the death of Joseph hath destroyed the covenant. All the works of God were made to correspond to the number of the tribes--twelve are the signs of the zodiac, twelve the months, twelve hours hath the day, twelve the night, and twelve stones are set in Aaron's breastplate--and now that Joseph hath departed, the covenant of the tribes is set at naught."

He could not replace the lost son by entering into a new marriage, for he had made the promise to his father-in-law to take none beside his daughters to wife, and this promise, as he interpreted it, held good after the death of Laban's daughters as well as while they were alive.

Beside grief over his loss and regret at the breaking of the covenant of the tribes, Jacob had still another reason for mourning the death of Joseph. God had said to Jacob, "If none of thy sons dies during thy lifetime, thou mayest look upon it as a token that thou wilt not be put in Gehenna after thy death." Thinking Joseph to be dead, Jacob had his own fate to bewail, too, for he now believed that he was doomed to Gehenna. His mourning lasted all of twenty-two years, corresponding to the number of the years he had dwelt apart from his parents, and had not fulfilled the duty of a son toward them.

In his mourning Jacob put sackcloth upon his loins, and therein be became a model for the kings and princes in Israel, for David, Ahab, Joram, and Mordecai did likewise when a great misfortune befell the nation.

JUDAH AND HIS SONS

When the sons of Jacob saw how inconsolable their father was, they went to Judah, and said to him, "This great misfortune is thy fault." Judah replied: "It was I that asked you, What profit is it if we slay our brother and conceal his blood? and now you say the sin lies at my door." The brethren continued to argue: "But it was thou that didst say, Come and let us sell him to the Ishmaelites, and we followed thy advice. Hadst thou said, Let us restore him to his father, we had heeded these words of thine as well."

The brethren hereupon deprived Judah of his dignity, for hitherto he had been their king, and they also excluded him from their fellowship, and he had to seek his fortune alone. Through the mediation of his chief shepherd Hirah, he became acquainted with the Canaanitish king of Adullam, Barsan by name. Though he was well aware of the corruption of the generations of Canaan, he permitted passion to get the better of him, and took a Canaanite to wife. The Adullamite king gave a banquet in his honor, at which his daughter Bath-shua poured the wine, and intoxicated by wine and passion Judah took her and married her. Judah's action may be compared to that of the lion who passes a carrion and eats of it, though a cur preceding him on the way had refused to touch it. Even Esau came in time to acknowledge that the daughters of Canaan were wicked, and the lion Judah must needs take one of them to wife. The holy spirit cried out against Judah when he married the Canaanite woman of Adullam, saying, "The glory of Israel went down in Adullam."

The first-born son of Judah from this marriage was named Er, "the childless," a suitable name for him that died without begetting any issue. At Judah's desire, Er married Tamar, a daughter of Aram, the son of Shem, but because she was not a Canaanitish woman, his mother used artifices against her, and he did not know her, and an angel of the Lord killed him on the third day after his wedding. Then Judah gave Tamar to his second son Onan, the marriage taking place before the week of the wedding festivities for Er had elapsed. A whole year Onan lived with Tamar without knowing her, and when, finally, Judah uttered threats against him on that account, he did, indeed, have intercourse with her, but, giving heed to the injunctions of his mother, he took care not to beget any children with her. He, too, died on account of his iniquity, and his name Onan "mourning," was well chosen, for very soon was his father called upon to mourn for him. Now Judah conceived the plan of marrying Tamar to his youngest son Shelah, but his wife would not permit it. She hated Tamar because she was not of the daughters of Canaan like herself, and while Judah was away from home, Bath-shua chose a wife for her son Shelah from the daughters of Canaan. Judah was very angry at Bath-shua for what she had done, and also God poured out His wrath upon her, for on account of her wickedness she had to die, and her death happened a year after that of her two sons.

Now that Bath-shua was dead, Judah might have carried out his wish and married Tamar to his youngest son. But he waited for Shelah to grow up, because he feared for his life, seeing that Tamar had brought death to two husbands before him. So she remained a widow in her father's house for two years. Endowed with the gift of prophecy, Tamar knew that she was appointed to be the ancestress of David and of the Messiah, and she determined to venture upon an extreme measure in order to make sure of fulfilling her destiny. Accordingly, when the holy spirit revealed to her that Judah was going up to Timnah, she put off from her the garments of her widowhood, and sat in the gate of Abraham's tent, and there she encountered Judah. All the time she lived in the house of her father-in-law, he had never seen her face, for in her virtue and chastity she had always kept it covered, and now when Judah met her, he did not recognize her. It was as a reward for her modesty that God made her to become the mother of the royal line of David, and the ancestress of Isaiah, and his father Amoz as well, both of whom were prophets and of royal blood.

Judah passed Tamar by without paying any attention to her, and she raised her eyes heavenward, and said, "O Lord of the world, shall I go forth empty from the house of this pious man?" Then God sent the angel that is appointed over the passion of love, and he compelled Judah to turn back. With prophetic caution, Tamar demanded that, as a pledge for the reward he promised her, he leave with her his signet, his mantle, and his staff, the symbols of royalty, judgeship, and Messiahship, the three distinctions of the descendants of Tamar from her union with Judah. When Judah sent her the promised reward, a kid of the goats, by the hand of his friend, in order to receive the pledges from her hand, Tamar could not be found, and he feared to make further search for her, lest he be put to shame. But Tamar, who soon discerned that she was with child, felt very happy and proud, for she knew that she would be the mother of kings and redeemers.

When her state became known, she was forcibly dragged before the court, in which Isaac, Jacob, and Judah sat as judges. Judah, being the youngest of the judges and the least considerable in dignity, was the first to give a decision, for thus it is prescribed in criminal cases, that the prominent judges overawe not the lesser and influence their decisions unduly. It was the opinion of Judah that the woman was liable to the penalty of death by burning, for she was the daughter of the high priest Shem, and death by fire is the punishment ordained by the law for a high priest's daughter that leads an unchaste life.

The preparations for her execution were begun. In vain Tamar searched for the three pledges she had received from Judah, she could not find them, and almost she lost hope that she would be able to wring a confession from her father-in-law. She raised her eyes to God, and prayed: "I supplicate Thy grace, O God, Thou who givest ear to the cry of the distressed in the hour of his need, answer me, that I may be spared to bring forth the three holy children, who will be ready to suffer death by fire, for the sake of the glory of Thy Name." And God granted her petition, and sent the angel Michael down to succor her. He put the pledges in a place in which Tamar could not fail to see them, and she took them, and threw them before the feet of the judges, with the words: "By the man whose these are am I with child, but though I perish in the flames, I will not betray him. I hope in the Lord of the world, that He will turn the heart of the man, so that he will make confession thereof." Then Judah rose up, and said: "With your permission, my brethren, and ye men of my father's house, I make it known that with what measure a man metes, it shall be measured unto him, be it for good or for evil, but happy the man that acknowledgeth his sins. Because I took the coat of Joseph, and colored it with the blood of a kid, and then laid it at the feet of my father, saying, Know now whether it be thy son's coat or not, therefore must I now confess, before the court, unto whom belongeth this signet, this mantle, and this staff. But it is better that I be put to shame in this world than I should be put to shame in the other world, before the face of my pious father. It is better that I should perish in a fire that can be extinguished than I should be cast into hell fire, which devoureth other fires. Now, then, I acknowledge that Tamar is innocent. By me is she with child, not because she indulged in illicit passion, but because I held back her marriage with my son Shelah." Then a heavenly voice was heard to say: "Ye are both innocent! It was the will of God that it should happen!"

The open confession of Judah induced his oldest brother Reuben to make public acknowledgment of the sin he had committed against his father, for he had kept it a secret until then.

Tamar gave birth to twin sons, Perez and Zerah, both resembling their father in bravery and piety. She called the first Perez, "mighty," because she said, "Thou didst show thyself of great power, and it is meet and proper that thou shouldst be strong, for thou art destined to possess the kingdom." The second son was called Zerah, because he appeared from out of the womb before his brother, but he was forced back again to make way for Perez. These two, Perez and Zerah. were sent out as spies by Joshua, and the line that Rahab bound in the window of her house as a token to the army of the Israelites, she received from Zerah. It was the scarlet thread that the midwife had bound upon his hand, to mark him as the child that appeared first and withdrew.

THE WIVES OF THE SONS OF JACOB

Judah was the first of the sons of Jacob to enter wedlock. After the sale of Joseph to the Midianites, his brethren had said to Judah, "If conditions were as before, our father would provide wives for us now. As it is, he is entirely absorbed by his grief for Joseph, and we must look about for wives ourselves. Thou art our chief, and thou shouldst marry first."

Judah's marriage with Alit the daughter of the noble merchant Shua, which was consummated at Adullam, the residence of his friend Hirah, or, as he was called later, Hiram, king of Tyre, was not happy. His two oldest sons died, and shortly thereafter his wife also. It was Judah's punishment for having begun a good deed and left it unfinished, for "he who begins a good deed, and does not execute it to the end, brings down misfortune upon his own head." Judah had rescued Joseph from death, but it was his suggestion to sell him into slavery. Had he urged them to restore the lad to his father, his brethren would have obeyed his words. He was lacking in constancy to persist until he had completed the work of Joseph's deliverance, which he had begun.

In the same year, the year of Joseph's misfortune, all his other brethren married, too. Reuben's wife was named Elyoram, the daughter of the Canaanite Uzzi of Timnah. Simon married his sister Dinah first, and then a second wife. When Simon and Levi massacred the men of Shechem, Dinah refused to leave the city and follow her brethren, saying, "Whither shall I carry my shame?" But Simon swore he would marry her, as he did later, and when she died in Egypt, he took her body to the Holy Land and buried it there. Dinah bore her brother a son, and from her union with Shechem, the son of Hamor, sprang a daughter, Asenath by name, afterward the wife of Joseph. When this daughter was born to Dinah, her brethren, the sons of Jacob, wanted to kill her, that the finger of men might not point at the fruit of sin in their father's house. But Jacob took a piece of tin, inscribed the Holy Name upon it, and bound it about the neck of the girl, and he put her under a thornbush, and abandoned her there. An angel carried the babe down to Egypt, where Potiphar adopted her as his child, for his wife was barren. Years thereafter, when Joseph travelled through the land as viceroy, the maidens threw gifts at him, to make him turn his eyes in their direction and give them the opportunity of gazing upon his beauty. Asenath possessed nothing that would do as a present, therefore she took off the amulet suspended from her neck, and gave it to him. Thus Joseph became acquainted with her lineage, and he married her, seeing that she was not an Egyptian, but one connected with the house of Jacob through her mother.

Beside the son of Dinah, Simon had another son, whose name was Saul, by Bunah, the damsel he had taken captive in the campaign against Shechem.

Levi and Issachar married two daughters of Jobab, the grandson of Eber; the wife of the former was named Adinah, the wife of the latter, Aridah. Dan's wife was Elflalet, a daughter of the Moabite Hamudan. For a long time their marriage remained childless, finally they had a son, whom they called Hushim. Gad and Naphtali married women from Haran, two sisters, daughters of Amoram, a grandson of Nahor. Naphtali's wife, Merimit, was the older of the two, and the younger, the wife of Gad, was named Uzit.

Asher's first wife was Adon, the daughter of Ephlal, a grandson of Ishmael. She died childless, and he married a second wife, Hadorah, a daughter of Abimael, the grandson of Shem. She had been married before, her first husband having been Malchiel, also a grandson of Shem, and the issue of this first marriage was a daughter, Serah by name. When Asher brought his wife to Canaan, the three year old orphan Serah came with them. She was raised in the house of Jacob, and she walked in the way of pious children, and God gave her beauty, wisdom, and sagacity.

Zebulon's wife was Maroshah, the daughter of Molad, a grandson of Midian, the son of Abraham by Keturah.

For Benjamin, when he was but ten years old, Jacob took Mahlia to wife, the daughter of Aram, the grandson of Terah, and she bore him five sons. At the age of eighteen he married a second wife, Arbat, the daughter of Zimran, a son of Abraham by Keturah, and by her also he had five sons.

JOSEPH THE SLAVE OF POTIPHAR

When Joseph was sold as a slave to the Ishmaelites, he kept silent out of respect for his brethren, and did not tell his masters that he was a son of Jacob, a great and powerful man. Even when he came to the Midianites with the Ishmaelites, and the former asked after his parentage, he still said he was a slave, only in order not to put his brethren to shame. But the most distinguished of the Midianites rebuked Joseph, saying, "Thou art no slave, thy appearance betrayeth thee," and he threatened him with death unless he acknowledged the truth. Joseph, however, was steadfast, he would not act treacherously toward his brethren.

Arrived in Egypt, the owners of Joseph could come to no agreement regarding him. Each desired to have sole and exclusive possession of him. They therefore decided to leave him with a shopkeeper until they should come back to Egypt again with their merchandise. And God let Joseph find grace in the sight of the shopkeeper. All that he had, his whole house, he put into Joseph's hand, and therefore the Lord blessed him with much silver and gold, and Joseph remained with him for three months and five days.

At that time there came from Memphis the wife of Potiphar, and she cast her eyes upon Joseph, of whose comeliness of person she had heard from the eunuchs. She told her husband how that a certain shopkeeper had grown rich through a young Hebrew, and she added: "But it is said that the youth was stolen away out of the land of Canaan. Go, therefore, and sit in judgment upon his owner, and take the youth unto thy house, that the God of the Hebrews may bless thee, for the grace of heaven rests upon the youth."

Potiphar summoned the shopkeeper, and when he appeared before him, he spoke harshly to him, saying: "What is this I hear? that thou stealest souls from the land of Canaan, and dost carry on traffic with them?" The shop-keeper protested his innocence, and he could not be made to recede from his assertion, that a company of Ishmaelites had left Joseph in his charge temporarily, until they should return. Potiphar had him stripped naked and beaten, but he continued to reiterate the same statement.

Then Potiphar summoned Joseph. The youth prostrated himself before this chief of the eunuchs, for he was third in rank of the officers of Pharaoh. And he addressed Joseph, and said, "Art thou a slave or a free-born man?" and Joseph replied, "A slave." Potiphar continued to question him, "Whose slave art thou?" Joseph: "I belong to the Ishmaelites." Potiphar: "How wast thou made a slave?" Joseph: "They bought me in the land of Canaan."

But Potiphar refused to give credence to what he said, and he had also him stripped and beaten. The wife of Potiphar, standing by the door, saw how Joseph was abused, and she sent word to her husband, "Thy verdict is unjust, for thou punishest the free-born youth that was stolen away from his place as though he were the one that had committed a crime." As Joseph held firmly to what he had said, Potiphar ordered him to prison, until his masters should return. In her sinful longing for him, his wife wanted to have Joseph in her own house, and she remonstrated with her husband in these words: "Wherefore dost thou keep the captive, nobly-born slave a prisoner? Thou shouldst rather set him at liberty and have him serve thee." He answered, "The law of the Egyptians does not permit us to take what belongs to another before all titles are made clear," and Joseph stayed in prison for twenty-four days, until the return of the Ishmaelites to Egypt.

Meanwhile they had heard somewhere that Joseph was the son of Jacob, and they therefore said to him: "Why didst thou pretend that thou wast a slave? See, we have information that thou art the son of a powerful man in Canaan, and thy father mourns for thee in sackcloth." Joseph was on the point of divulging his secret, but he kept a check upon himself for the sake of his brethren, and he repeated that he was a slave.

Nevertheless the Ishmaelites decided to sell him, that he be not found in their hands, for they feared the revenge of Jacob, who, they knew, was in high favor with the Lord and with men. The shopkeeper begged the Ishmaelites to rescue him from the legal prosecution of Potiphar, and clear him of the suspicion of man theft. The Ishmaelites in turn had a conference with Joseph, and bade him testify before Potiphar that they had bought him for money. He did so, and then the chief of the eunuchs liberated him from prison, and dismissed all parties concerned.

With the permission of her husband, Potiphar's wife sent a eunuch to the Ishmaelites, bidding him to buy Joseph, but he returned and reported that they demanded an exorbitant price for the slave. She dispatched a second eunuch, charging him to conclude the bargain, and though they asked one mina of gold, or even two, he was not to be sparing of money, he was to be sure to buy the slave and bring him to her. The eunuch gave the Ishmaelites eighty pieces of gold for Joseph, telling his mistress, however, that he had paid out a hundred pieces. Joseph noticed the deception, but he kept silent, that the eunuch might not be put to shame.

Thus Joseph became the slave of the idolatrous priest Potiphar, or Poti-phera, as he was sometimes called. He had secured possession of the handsome youth for a lewd purpose, but the angel Gabriel mutilated him in such manner that he could not accomplish it. His master soon had occasion to notice that Joseph was as pious as he was beautiful, for whenever he was occupied with his ministrations, he would whisper a prayer: "O Lord of the world, Thou art my trust, Thou art my protection. Let me find grace and favor in Thy sight and in the sight of all that see me, and in the sight of my master Potiphar." When Potiphar noticed the movement of his lips, he said to Joseph, "Dost thou purpose to cast a spell upon me?" "Nay," replied the youth, "I am beseeching God to let me find favor in thine eyes."

His prayer was heard. Potiphar convinced himself that God was with Joseph. Sometimes he would make a test of Joseph's miraculous powers. If he brought him a glass of hippocras, he would say, "I would rather have wine mixed with absinthe," and straightway the spiced wine was changed into bitter wine. Whatever he desired, he could be sure to get from Joseph, and he saw clearly that God fulfilled the wishes of his slave. Therefore he put all the keys of his house into his hand, and he knew not aught that was with him, keeping back nothing from Joseph but his wife. Seeing that the Shekinah rested upon him, Potiphar treated Joseph not as a slave, but as a member of his family, for he said, "This youth is not cut out for a slave's work, he is worthy of a prince's place." Accordingly, he provided instruction for him in the arts, and ordered him to have better fare than the other slaves.

Joseph thanked God for his new and happy state. He prayed, "Blessed art Thou, O Lord, that Thou hast caused me to forget my father's house." What made his present fortunes so agreeable was that he was removed from the envy and jealousy of his brethren. He said: "When I was in my father's house, and he gave me something pretty, my brethren begrudged me the present, and now, O Lord, I thank Thee that I live amid plenty." Free from anxieties, he turned his attention to his external appearance. He painted his eyes, dressed his hair, and aimed to be elegant in his walk. But God spake to him, saying, "Thy father is mourning in sackcloth and ashes, while thou dost eat, drink, and dress thy hair. Therefore I will stir up thy mistress against thee, and thou shalt be embarrassed." Thus Joseph's secret wish was fulfilled, that he might be permitted to prove his piety under temptation, as the piety of his fathers had been tested.

JOSEPH AND ZULEIKA

"Throw the stick up in the air, it will always return to its original place." Like Rachel his mother, Joseph was of ravishing beauty, and the wife of his master was filled with invincible passion for him." Her feeling was heightened by the astrologic forecast that she was destined to have descendants through Joseph. This was true, but not in the sense in which she understood the prophecy. Joseph married her daughter Asenath later on, and she bore him children, thus fulfilling what had been read in the stars."

In the beginning she did not confess her love to Joseph. She tried first to seduce him by artifice. On the pretext of visiting him, she would go to him at night, and, as she had no sons, she would pretend a desire to adopt him. Joseph then prayed to God in her behalf, and she bore a son. However, she continued to embrace him as though he were her own child, yet he did not notice her evil designs. Finally, when he recognized her wanton trickery, he mourned many days, and endeavored to turn her away from her sinful passion by the word of God. She, on her side, often threatened him with death, and surrendered him to castigations in order to make him amenable to her will, and when these means had no effect upon Joseph, she sought to seduce him with enticements. She would say, "I promise thee, thou shalt rule over me and all I have, if thou wilt but give thyself up to me. and thou shalt be to me the same as my lawful husband." But Joseph was mindful of the words of his fathers, and he went into his chamber, and fasted, and prayed to God, that He would deliver him from the toils of the Egyptian woman.

In spite of the mortifications he practiced, and though he gave the poor and the sick the food apportioned to him, his master thought he lived a luxurious life, for those that fast for the glory of God are made beautiful of countenance.

The wife of Potiphar would frequently speak to her husband in praise of Joseph's chastity in order that he might conceive no suspicion of the state of her feelings. And, again, she would encourage Joseph secretly, telling him not to fear her husband, that he was convinced of his purity of life, and though one should carry tales to him about Joseph and herself, Potiphar would lend them no credence. And when she saw that all this was ineffectual, she approached him with the request that he teach her the word of God, saying, "If it be thy wish that I forsake idol worship, then fulfil my desire, and I will persuade that Egyptian husband of mine to abjure the idols, and we shall walk in the law of thy God." Joseph replied, "The Lord desireth not that those who fear Him shall walk in impurity, nor hath He pleasure in the adulterer."

Another time she came to him, and said, "If thou wilt not do my desire, I will murder the Egyptian and wed with thee according to the law." Whereat Joseph rent his garment, and he said, "O woman, fear the Lord, and do not execute this evil deed, that thou mayest not bring destruction down upon thyself, for I will proclaim thy impious purposes to all in public."

Again, she sent him a dish prepared with magic spells, by means of which she hoped to get him into her power. But when the eunuch set it before him, he saw the image of a man handing him a sword together with the dish, and, warned by the vision, he took good care not to taste of the food. A few days later his mistress came to him, and asked him why he had not eaten of what she had sent him. He reproached her, saying, "How couldst thou tell me, I do not come nigh unto the idols, but only unto the Lord? The God of my fathers hath revealed thy iniquity to me through an angel, but that thou mayest know that the malice of the wicked has no power over those who fear God in purity, I shall eat thy food before thine eyes, and the God of my fathers and the angel of Abraham will be with me." The wife of Potiphar fell upon her face at the feet of Joseph, and amid tears she promised not to commit this sin again.

But her unholy passion for Joseph did not depart from her, and her distress over her unfulfilled wish made her look so ill that her husband said to her, "Why is thy countenance fallen?" And she replied, "I have a pain at my heart, and the groanings of my spirit oppress me."

Once when she was alone with Joseph, she rushed toward him, crying, "I will throttle myself, or I will jump into a well or a pit, if thou wilt not yield thyself to me." Noticing her extreme agitation, Joseph endeavored to calm her with these words, "Remember, if thou makest away with thyself, thy husband's concubine, Asteho, thy rival, will maltreat thy children, and extirpate thy memory from the earth." These words, gently spoken, had the opposite effect from that intended. They only inflamed her passion the more by feeding her hopes. She said: "There, seest thou, thou dost love me now! It sufficeth for me that thou takest thought for me and for the safety of my children. I expect now that my desire will be fulfilled." She did not know that Joseph spoke as he did for the sake of God, and not for her sake.

His mistress, or, as she was called, Zuleika, pursued him day after day with her amorous talk and her flattery, saying: "How fair is thy appearance, how comely thy form! Never have I seen so well-favored a slave as thou art." Joseph would reply: "God, who formed me in my mother's womb, hath created all men."

Zuleika: "How beautiful are thine eyes, with which thou hast charmed all Egyptians, both men and women!"

Joseph: "Beautiful as they may be while I am alive, so ghastly they will be to look upon in the grave."

Zuleika: "How lovely and pleasant are thy words! I pray thee, take thy harp, play and also sing, that I may hear thy words."

Joseph: "Lovely and pleasant are my words when I proclaim the praise of my God."

Zuleika: "How beautiful is thy hair! Take my golden comb, and comb it."

Joseph: "How long wilt thou continue to speak thus to me? Leave off! It were better for thee to care for thy household."

Zuleika: "There is nothing in my house that I care for, save thee alone."

But Joseph's virtue was unshaken. While she spoke thus, he did not so much as raise his eyes to look at his mistress. He remained equally steadfast when she lavished gifts upon him, for she provided him with garments of one kind for the morning, another for noon, and a third kind for the evening. Nor could threats move him. She would say, "I will bring false accusations against thee before thy master," and Joseph would reply, "The Lord executeth judgment for the oppressed." Or, "I will deprive thee of food;" whereupon Joseph, "The Lord giveth food to the hungry." Or, "I will have thee thrown into prison;" whereupon Joseph, "The Lord looseth the prisoners." Or, "I will put heavy labor upon thee that will bend thee double;" whereupon Joseph, "The Lord raiseth up them that are bowed down." Or, "I will blind thine eyes;" whereupon Joseph, "The Lord openeth the eyes of the blind."

When she began to exercise her blandishments upon him, he rejected them with the words, "I fear my master." But Zuleika would say, "I will kill him." Joseph replied with indignation, "Not enough that thou wouldst make an adulterer of me, thou wouldst have me be a murderer, besides?" And he spoke furthermore, saying, "I fear the Lord my God!"

Zuleika: "Nonsense! He is not here to see thee!

Joseph: "Great is the Lord and highly to be praised, and His greatness is unsearchable."

Thereupon she took Joseph into her chamber, where an idol hung above the bed. This she covered, that it might not be a witness of what she was about to do. Joseph said: "Though thou coverest up the eyes of the idol, remember, the eyes of the Lord run to and fro through the whole earth. Yes," continued Joseph, "I have many reasons not to do this thing for the sake of God. Adam was banished from Paradise on account of violating a light command; how much more should I have to fear the punishment of God, were I to commit so grave a sin as adultery! The Lord is in the habit of choosing a favorite member of our family as a sacrifice unto Himself. Perhaps He desireth to make choice of me, but if I do thy will, I make myself unfit to be a sacrifice unto God. Also the Lord is in the habit of appearing suddenly, in visions of the night, unto those that love Him. Thus did He appear unto Abraham, Isaac, and Jacob, and I fear that He may appear unto me at the very moment while I am defiling myself with thee. And as I fear God, so I fear my father, who withdrew the birthright from his first-born son Reuben, on account of an immoral act, and gave it to me. Were I to fulfil thy desire, I would share the fate of my brother Reuben."

With such words, Joseph endeavored to cure the wife of his master of the wanton passion she had conceived for him, while he took heed to keep far from a heinous sin, not from fear of the punishment that would follow, nor out of consideration for the opinion of men, but because he desired to sanctify the Name of God, blessed be He, before the whole world. It was this feeling of his that Zuleika could not comprehend, and when, finally, carried away by passion, she told him in unmistakable language what she desired, and he recoiled from her, she said to Joseph: "Why dost thou refuse to fulfil my wish? Am I not a married woman? None will find out what thou hast done." Joseph replied: "If the unmarried women of the heathen are prohibited unto us, how much more their married women? As the Lord liveth, I will not commit the crime thou biddest me do." In this Joseph followed the example of many pious men, who utter an oath at the moment when they are in danger of succumbing to temptation, and seek thus to gather moral courage to control their evil instincts."

When Zuleika could not prevail upon him, to persuade him, her desire threw her into a grievous sickness, and all the women of Egypt came to visit her, and they said unto her, "Why art thou so languid and wasted, thou that lackest nothing? Is not thy husband a prince great and esteemed in the sight of the king? Is it possible that thou canst want aught of what thy heart desireth?" Zuleika answered them, saying, "This day shall it be made known unto you whence cometh the state wherein you see me."

She commanded her maid-servants to prepare food for all the women, and she spread a banquet before them in her house. She placed knives upon the table to peel the oranges, and then ordered Joseph to appear, arrayed in costly garments, and wait upon her guests. When Joseph came in, the women could not take their eyes off him, and they all cut their hands with the knives, and the oranges in their hands were covered with blood, but they, not knowing what they were doing, continued to look upon the beauty of Joseph without turning their eyes away from him.

Then Zuleika said unto them: "What have ye done? Behold, I set oranges before you to eat, and you have cut your hands." All the women looked at their hands, and, lo, they were full of blood, and it flowed down and stained their garments. They said to Zuleika, "This slave in thy house did enchant us, and we could not turn our eyes away from him on account of his beauty." She then said: "This happened to you that looked upon him but a moment, and you could not refrain yourselves! How, then, can I control myself in whose house he abideth continually, who see him go in and out day after day? How, then, should I not waste away, or keep from languishing on account of him!" And the women spake, saying: "It is true, who can look upon this beauty in the house, and refrain her feelings? But he is thy slave! Why dost thou not disclose to him that which is in thy heart, rather than suffer thy life to perish through this thing?" Zuleika answered them: "Daily do I endeavor to persuade him, but he will not consent to my wishes. I promised him everything that is fair, yet have I met with no return from him, and therefore I am sick, as you may see."

Her sickness increased upon her. Her husband and her household suspected not the cause of her decline, but all the women that were her friends knew that it was on account of the love she bore Joseph, and they advised her all the time to try to entice the youth. On a certain day, while Joseph was doing his master's work in the house, Zuleika came and fell suddenly upon him, but Joseph was stronger than she, and he pressed her down to the ground. Zuleika wept, and in a voice of supplication, and in bitterness of soul, she said to Joseph: "Hast thou ever known, seen, or heard of a woman my peer in beauty, let alone a woman with beauty exceeding mine? Yet I try daily to persuade thee, I fall into decline through love of thee, I confer all this honor upon thee, and thou wilt not hearken unto my voice! Is it by reason of fear of thy master, that he punish thee? As the king liveth, no harm shall come upon thee from thy master on account of this thing. Now, therefore, I pray thee, listen to me, and consent unto my desire for the sake of the honor that I have conferred upon thee, and take this death away from me. For why should I die on account of thee?" Joseph remained as steadfast under these importunities as before. Zuleika, however, was not discouraged; she continued her solicitations unremittingly, day after day, month after month, for a whole year, but always without the least success, for Joseph in his chastity did not permit himself even to look upon her, wherefore she resorted to constraint. She had an iron shackle placed upon his chin, and he was compelled to keep his head up and look her in the face."

JOSEPH RESISTS TEMPTATION

Seeing that she could not attain her object by entreaties or tears, Zuleika finally used force, when she judged that the favorable chance had come. She did not have long to wait. When the Nile overflowed its banks, and, according to the annual custom of the Egyptians, all repaired to the river, men and women, people and princes, accompanied by music, Zuleika remained at home under pretense of being sick. This was her long-looked-for opportunity, she thought. She rose up and ascended to the hall of state, and arrayed herself in princely garments. She placed precious stones upon her head, onyx stones set in silver and gold, she beautified her face and her body with all sorts of things for the purifying of women, she perfumed the hall and the whole house with cassia and frankincense, spread myrrh and aloes all over, and afterward sat herself down at the entrance to the hall, in the vestibule leading to the house, through which Joseph had to pass to his work.

And, behold, Joseph came from the field, and he was on the point of entering the house to do his master's work, but when he reached the place where Zuleika sat, and saw all she had done, he turned back. His mistress, perceiving it, called out to him, "What aileth thee, Joseph? Go to thy work, I will make room for thee, that thou mayest pass by to thy seat." Joseph did as she bade him, he entered the house, took his seat, and set about his master's work as usual. Then Zuleika stood before him suddenly in all her beauty of person and magnificence of raiment, and repeated the desire of her heart. It was the first and the last time that

Joseph's steadfastness deserted him, but only for an instant. When he was on the point of complying with the wish of his mistress, the image of his mother Rachel appeared before him, and that of his aunt Leah, and the image of his father Jacob. The last addressed him thus: "In time to come the names of thy brethren will be graven upon the breastplate of the high priest. Dost thou desire to have thy name appear with theirs? Or wilt thou forfeit this honor through sinful conduct? For know, he that keepeth company with harlots wasteth his substance." This vision of the dead, and especially the image of his father, brought Joseph to his senses, and his illicit passion departed from him.

Astonished at the swift change in his countenance, Zuleika said, "My friend and true-love, why art thou so affrighted that thou art near to swooning?

Joseph: "I see my father!"

Zuleika: "Where is he? Why, there is none in the house."

Joseph: "Thou belongest to a people that is like unto the ass, it perceiveth nothing. But I belong to those who can see things."

Joseph fled forth, away from the house of his mistress, the same house in which aforetime wonders had been done for Sarah kept a captive there by Pharaoh. But hardly was he outside when the sinful passion again overwhelmed him, and he returned to Zuleika's chamber. Then the Lord appeared unto him, holding the Eben Shetiyah in His hand, and said to him: "If thou touchest her, I will cast away this stone upon which the earth is founded, and the world will fall to ruin." Sobered again, Joseph started to escape from his mistress, but Zuleika caught him by his garment, and she said: "As the king liveth, if thou wilt not fulfil my wish, thou must die," and while she spoke thus, she drew a sword with her free hand from under her dress, and, pressing it against Joseph's throat, she said, "Do as I bid thee, or thou diest." Joseph ran out, leaving a piece of his garment in the hands of Zuleika as he wrenched himself loose from the grasp of the woman with a quick, energetic motion.

Zuleika's passion for Joseph was so violent that, in lieu of its owner, whom she could not succeed in subduing to her will, she kissed and caressed the fragment of cloth left in her hand. At the same time she was not slow to perceive the danger into which she had put herself, for, she feared, Joseph might possibly betray her conduct, and she considered ways and means of obviating the consequences of her folly.

Meanwhile her friends returned from the Nile festival, and they came to visit her and inquire after her health. They found her looking wretchedly ill, on account of the excitement she had passed through and the anxiety she was in. She confessed to the women what had happened with Joseph, and they advised her to accuse him of immorality before her husband, and then he would be thrown into prison. Zuleika accepted their advice, and she begged her visitors to support her charges by also lodging complaints against Joseph, that he had been annoying them with improper proposals.

But Zuleika did not depend entirely upon the assistance of her friends. She planned a ruse, besides, to be sure of convincing her husband of Joseph's guilt. She laid aside her rich robes of state, put on her ordinary clothes, and took to her sick-bed, in which she had been lying when the people left to go to the festival. Also she took Joseph's torn garment, and laid it out next to her. Then she sent a little boy to summon some of the men of her house, and to them she told the tale of Joseph's alleged outrage, saying: "See the Hebrew slave, whom your master hath brought in unto my house, and who attempted to do violence to me to-day! You had scarcely gone away to the festival when be entered the house, and making sure that no one was here he tried to force me to yield to his lustful desire. But I grasped his clothes, tore them, and cried with a loud voice. When he heard that I lifted up my voice and cried, he was seized with fear, and be fled, and got him out, but he left his garment by me." The men of her house spake not a word, but, in a rage against Joseph, they went to their master, and reported to him what had come to pass. In the meantime the husbands of Zuleika's friends had also spoken to Potiphar, at the instigation of their wives, and complained of his slave, that he molested them.

Potiphar hastened home, and he found his wife in low spirits, and though the cause of her dejection was chagrin at not having succeeded in winning Joseph's love, she pretended that it was anger at the immoral conduct of the slave. She accused him in the following words: "O husband, mayest thou not live a day longer, if thou dost not punish the wicked slave that hath desired to defile thy bed, that hath not kept in mind who he was when he came to our house, to demean himself with modesty, nor hath he been mindful of the favors he hath received from thy bounty. He did lay a privy design to abuse thy wife, and this at the time of observing a festival, when thou wouldst be absent." These words she spoke at the moment of conjugal intimacy with Potiphar, when she was certain of exerting an influence upon her husband.

Potiphar gave credence to her words, and he had Joseph flogged unmercifully. While the cruel blows fell upon him, he cried to God, "O Lord, Thou knowest that I am innocent of these things, and why should I die to-day on account of a false accusation by the hands of these uncircumcised, impious men?" God opened the mouth of Zuleika's child, a babe of but eleven months, and he spoke to the men that were beating Joseph, saying: "What is your quarrel with this man? Why do you inflict such evil upon him? Lies my mother doth speak, and deceit is what her mouth uttereth. This is the true tale of that which did happen," and the child proceeded to tell all that had passed--how Zuleika had tried first to persuade Joseph to act wickedly, and then had tried to force him to do her will. The people listened in great amazement. But the report finished, the child spake no word, as before.

Abashed by the speech of his own infant son, Potiphar commanded his bailiffs to leave off from chastising Joseph, and the matter was brought into court, where priests sat as judges. Joseph protested his innocence, and related all that had happened according to the truth, but Potiphar repeated the account his wife had given him. The judges ordered the garment of Joseph to be brought which Zuleika had in her possession, and they examined the tear therein. It turned out to be on the front part of the mantle, and they came to the conclusion that Zuleika had tried to hold him fast, and had been foiled in her attempt by Joseph, against whom she was now lodging a trumped up charge. They decided that Joseph had not incurred the death penalty, but they condemned him to incarceration, because he was the cause of a stain upon Zuleika's fair name."

Potiphar himself was convinced of Joseph's innocence, and when he cast him into prison, he said to him, "I know that thou art not guilty of so vile a crime, but I must put thee in durance, lest a taint cling to my children."

JOSEPH IN PRISON

By way of punishment for having traduced his ten brethren before his father, Joseph had to languish for ten years in the prison to which the wiles of traducers had in turn condemned him. But, on the other hand, as he had sanctified the Name of God before the world by his chastity and his steadfastness, he was rewarded. The letter He, which occurs twice in the Name of God, was added to his name. He had been called Joseph, but now he was called also Jehoseph.

Though he was bound in prison, Joseph was not yet safe from the machinations of his mistress, whose passion for him was in no wise lessened. In truth it was she that had induced her husband to change his intention regarding Joseph; she urged him to imprison the slave rather than kill him, for she hoped that as a prisoner he could be made amenable to her wishes more easily. She spake to her husband, saying: "Do not destroy thy property. Cast the slave in prison and keep him there until thou canst sell him, and receive back the money thou didst pay out for him." Thus she had the opportunity of visiting Joseph in his cell and trying to persuade him to do her will. She would say, "This and that outrage have I executed against thee, but, as thou livest, I will put yet other outrages upon thee if thou dost not obey me." But Joseph replied, "The Lord executeth judgment for the oppressed."

Zuleika: "I will push matters so far that all men will hate thee."

Joseph: "The Lord loveth the righteous."

Zuleika: "I will sell thee into a strange land."

Joseph: "The Lord preserveth the strangers."

Then she would resort to enticements in order to obtain her desire. She would promise to release him from prison, if he would but grant her wish. But he would say, "Better it is to remain here than be with thee and commit a trespass against God." These visits to Joseph in prison Zuleika continued for a long time, but when, finally, she saw that all her hopes were vain, she let him alone.

As the mistress persisted in her love for Joseph, so his master, her husband, could not separate himself from his favorite slave. Though a prisoner, Joseph continued to minister to the needs of Potiphar, and he received permission from the keeper of the prison to spend some of his time in his master's house. In many other ways the jailer showed himself kindly disposed toward Joseph. Seeing the youth's zeal and conscientiousness in executing the tasks laid upon him, and under the spell of his enchanting beauty, he made prison life as easy as possible for his charge. He even ordered better dishes for him than the common prison fare, and he found it superfluous caution to keep watch over Joseph, for he could see no wrong in him, and he observed that God was with him, in good days and in bad. He even appointed him to be the overseer of the prison, and as Joseph commanded, so the other prisoners were obliged to do.

For a long time the people talked of nothing but the accusation raised against Joseph by his mistress. In order to divert the attention of the public from him, God ordained that two high officers, the chief butler and the chief baker, should offend their lord, the king of Egypt, and they were put in ward in the house of the captain of the guard. Now the people ceased their talk about Joseph, and spoke only of the scandal at court. The charges laid at the door of the noble prisoners were that they had attempted to do violence to the daughter of Pharaoh, and they had conspired to poison the king himself. Besides, they had shown themselves derelict in their service. In the wine the chief butler had handed to the king to drink, a fly had been discovered, and the bread set upon the royal board by the chief baker contained a little pebble." On account of all these transgressions they were condemned to death by Pharaoh, but for the sake of Joseph it was ordained by Divine providence that the king should first detain them in prison before he ordered their execution. The Lord had enkindled the wrath of the king against his servants only that the wish of Joseph for liberty might be fulfilled, for they were the instruments of his deliverance from prison, and though they were doomed to death, yet in consideration of the exalted office they had held at court, the keeper of the prison accorded them privileges, as, for instance, a man was detailed to wait upon them, and the one appointed thereto was Joseph. 1]

The chief butler and the chief baker had been confined in prison ten years, when they dreamed a dream, both of them, but as for the interpretation, each dreamed only that of the other one's dream. In the morning when Joseph brought them the water for washing, he found them sad, depressed in spirits, and, in the manner of the sages, he asked them why they looked different on that day from other days. They said unto him, "We have dreamed a dream this night, and our two dreams resemble each other in certain particulars, and there is none that can interpret them." And Joseph said unto them: "God granteth understanding to man to interpret dreams. Tell them me, I pray you." It was as a reward for ascribing greatness and credit to Him unto whom it belongeth that Joseph later attained to his lofty position.

The chief butler proceeded to tell his dream: "In my dream, behold, a vine was before me; and in the vine were three branches; and it was as though it budded, and its blossoms shot forth, and the clusters thereof brought forth ripe grapes; and Pharaoh's cup was in my hand; and I took the grapes, and pressed them into Pharaoh's cup, and I gave the cup into Pharaoh's hand." The chief butler was not aware that his dream contained a prophecy regarding the future of Israel, but Joseph discerned the recondite meaning, and he interpreted the dream thus: The three branches are the three Fathers, Abraham, Isaac, and Jacob, whose descendants in Egypt will be redeemed by three leaders, Moses, Aaron, and Miriam; and the cup given into the hand of Pharaoh is the cup of wrath that he will have to drain in the end. This interpretation of the dream Joseph kept for himself, and he told the chief butler nothing thereof, but out of gratitude for the glad tidings of the deliverance of Israel from the bondage of Egypt, he gave him a favorable interpretation of his dream, and begged him to have him in his remembrance, when it should be well with him, and liberate him from the dungeon in which he was confined.

When the chief baker heard the interpretation of the butler's dream, he knew that Joseph had divined its meaning correctly, for in his own he had seen the interpretation of his friend's dream, and he proceeded to tell Joseph what he had dreamed in the night: "I also was in my dream, and, behold, three baskets of white bread were on my head; and in the uppermost basket there was of all manner of bake-meats for Pharaoh; and the birds did eat them out of the basket upon my head." Also this dream conveyed a prophecy regarding the future of Israel: The three baskets are the three kingdoms to which Israel will be made subject, Babylon, Media, and Greece; and the uppermost basket indicates the wicked rule of Rome, which will extend over all the nations of the world, until the bird shall come, who is the Messiah, and annihilate Rome. Again Joseph kept the prophecy a secret. To the chief baker he gave only the interpretation that had reference to his person, but it was unfavorable to him, because through his dream Joseph had been made acquainted with the suffering Israel would have to undergo.

And all came to pass, as Joseph had said, on the third day. The day whereon he explained the meaning of their dreams to the two distinguished prisoners, a son was born unto Pharaoh and to celebrate the joyous event, the king arranged a feast for his princes and servants that was to last eight days. He invited them and all the people to his table, and he entertained them with royal splendor. The feast had its beginning on the third day after the birth of the child, and on that occasion the chief butler was restored in honor to his butlership, and the chief baker was hanged, for Pharaoh's counsellors had discovered that it was not the butler's fault that the fly had dropped into the king's wine, but the baker had been guilty of carelessness in allowing the pebble to get into the bread. Likewise it appeared that the butler had had no part in the conspiracy to poison the king, while the baker was revealed as one of the plotters, and he had to expiate his crime with his life.

PHARAOH'S DREAMS

Properly speaking, Joseph should have gone out free from his dungeon on the same day as the butler. He had been there ten years by that time, and had made amends for the slander he had uttered against his ten brethren. However, he remained in prison two years longer. "Blessed is the man that trusteth in the Lord, and whose hope is the Lord," but Joseph had put his confidence in flesh and blood. He had prayed the chief butler to have him in remembrance when it should be well with him, and make mention of him unto Pharaoh, and the butler forgot his promise, and therefore Joseph had to stay in prison two years more than the years originally allotted to him there. The butler had not forgotten him intentionally, but it was ordained of God that his memory should fail him. When he would say to himself, If thus and so happens, I will remember the case of Joseph, the conditions he had imagined were sure to be reversed, or if he made a knot as a reminder, an angel came and undid the knot, and Joseph did not enter his mind.

But "the Lord setteth an end to darkness," and Joseph's liberation was not delayed by a single moment beyond the time decreed for it. God said, "Thou, O butler, thou didst forget Joseph, but I did not," and He caused Pharaoh to dream a dream that was the occasion for Joseph's release.

In his dream Pharaoh saw seven kine, well-favored and fat-fleshed, come up out of the Nile, and they all together grazed peaceably on the brink of the river, In years when the harvest is abundant, friendship reigns among men, and love and brotherly harmony, and these seven fat kine stood for seven such prosperous years. After the fat kine, seven more came up out of the river, ill-favored and lean-fleshed, and each had her back turned to the others, for when distress prevails, one man turns away from the other. For a brief space Pharaoh awoke, and when he went to sleep again, he dreamed a second dream, about seven rank and good ears of corn, and seven ears that were thin and blasted with the east wind, the withered cars swallowing the full ears. He awoke at once, and it was morning, and dreams dreamed in the morning are the ones that come true.

This was not the first time Pharaoh had had these dreams. They had visited him every night during a period of two years, and he had forgotten them invariably in the morning. This was the first time he remembered them, for the day had arrived for Joseph to come forth from his prison house. Pharaoh's heart beat violently when he called his dreams to mind on awaking. Especially the second one, about the ears of corn, disquieted him. He reflected that whatever has a mouth can eat, and therefore the dream of the seven lean kine that ate up the seven fat kine did not appear strange to him. But the ears of corn that swallowed up other ears of corn troubled his spirit. He therefore called for all the wise men of his land, and they endeavored in vain to find a satisfactory interpretation. They explained that the seven fat kine meant seven daughters to be born unto Pharaoh, and the seven lean kine, that he would bury seven daughters; the rank ears of corn meant that Pharaoh would conquer seven countries, and the blasted ears, that seven provinces would rebel against him. About the ears of corn they did not all agree. Some thought the good ears stood for seven cities to be built by Pharaoh, and the seven withered ears indicated that these same cities would be destroyed at the end of his reign.

Sagacious as he was, Pharaoh knew that none of these explanations hit the nail on the head. He issued a decree summoning all interpreters of dreams to appear before him on pain of death, and he held out great rewards and distinctions to the one who should succeed in finding the true meaning of his dreams. In obedience to his summons, all the wise men appeared, the magicians and the sacred scribes that were in Mizraim, the city of Egypt, as well as those from Goshen, Raamses, Zoan, and the whole country of Egypt, and with them came the princes, officers, and servants of the king from all the cities of the land.

To all these the king narrated his dreams, but none could interpret them to his satisfaction. Some said that the seven fat kine were the seven legitimate kings that would rule over Egypt, and the seven lean kine betokened seven princes that would rise up against these seven kings and exterminate them. The seven good ears of corn were the seven superior princes of Egypt that would engage in a war for their overlord, and would be defeated by as many insignificant princes, who were betokened by the seven blasted ears.

Another interpretation was that the seven fat kine were the seven fortified cities of Egypt, at some future time to fall into the hands of seven Canaanitish nations, who were foreshadowed in the seven lean kine. According to this interpretation, the second dream supplemented the first. It meant that the descendants of Pharaoh would regain sovereign authority over Egypt at a subsequent period, and would subdue the seven Canaanitish nations as well.

There was a third interpretation, given by some: The seven fat kine are seven women whom Pharaoh would take to wife, but they would die during his lifetime, their loss being indicated by the seven lean kine. Furthermore, Pharaoh would have fourteen sons, and the seven strong ones would be conquered by the seven weaklings, as the blasted ears of corn in his dream had swallowed up the rank ears of corn.

And a fourth: "Thou wilt have seven sons, O Pharaoh, these are the seven fat kine. These sons of thine will be killed by the seven powerful rebellious princes. But then seven minor princes will come, and they will kill the seven rebels, avenge thy descendants, and restore the dominion to thy family."

The king was as little pleased with these interpretations as with the others, which he had heard before, and in his wrath he ordered the wise men, the magicians and the scribes of Egypt, to be killed, and the hangmen made ready to execute the royal decree.

However, Mirod, Pharaoh's chief butler, took fright, seeing that the king was so vexed at his failure to secure an interpretation of his dreams that he was on the point of giving up the ghost. He was alarmed about the king's death, for it was doubtful whether the successor to the throne would retain him in office. He resolved to do all in his power to keep Pharaoh alive. Therefore he stepped before him, and spake, saying, "I do remember two faults of mine this day, I showed myself ungrateful to Joseph, in that I did not bring his request before thee, and also I saw thee in distress by reason of thy dream, without letting thee know that Joseph can interpret dreams. When it pleased the Lord God to make Pharaoh wroth with his servants, the king put me in ward in the house of the captain of the guard, me and the chief baker. And with us there was a simple young man, one of the despised race of the Hebrews, slave to the captain of the guard, and he interpreted our dreams to us, and it came to pass, as he interpreted to us, so it was. Therefore, O king, stay the hand of the hangmen, let them not execute the Egyptians. The slave I speak of is still in the dungeon, and if the king will consent to summon him hither, he will surely interpret thy dreams."

JOSEPH BEFORE PHARAOH

"Accursed are the wicked that never do a wholly good deed." The chief butler described Joseph contemptuously as a "slave" in order that it might be impossible for him to occupy a distinguished place at court, for it was a law upon the statute books of Egypt that a slave could never sit upon the throne as king, nor even put his foot in the stirrup of a horse.

Pharaoh revoked the edict of death that he had issued against the wise men of Egypt, and he sent and called Joseph. He impressed care upon his messengers, they were not to excite and confuse Joseph, and render him unfit to interpret the king's dream correctly. They brought him hastily out of the dungeon, but first Joseph, out of respect for the king, shaved himself, and put on fresh raiment, which an angel brought him from Paradise, and then he came in unto Pharaoh.

The king was sitting upon the royal throne, arrayed in princely garments, clad with a golden ephod upon his breast, and the fine gold of the ephod sparkled, and the carbuncle, the ruby, and the emerald flamed like a torch, and all the precious stones set upon the king's head flashed like a blazing fire, and Joseph was greatly amazed at the appearance of the king. The throne upon which he sat was covered with gold and silver and with onyx stones, and it had seventy steps. If a prince or other distinguished person came to have an audience with the king, it was the custom for him to advance and mount to the thirty-first step of the throne, and the king would descend thirty-six steps and speak to him. But if one of the people came to have speech with the king, he ascended only to the third step, and the king would come down four steps from his seat, and address him thence. It was also the custom that one who knew all the seventy languages ascended the seventy steps of the throne to the top, but if a man knew only some of the seventy languages, he was permitted to ascend as many steps as he knew languages, whether they were many or, few. And another custom of the Egyptians was that none could reign over them unless he was master of all the seventy languages.

When Joseph came before the king, he bowed down to the ground, and he ascended to the third step, while the king sat upon the fourth from the top, and spake with Joseph, saying: "O young man, my servant beareth witness concerning thee, that thou art the best and most discerning person I can consult with. I pray thee, vouchsafe unto me the same favors which thou didst bestow on this servant of mine, and tell me what events they are which the visions of my dreams foreshow. I desire thee to suppress naught out of fear, nor shalt thou flatter me with lying words, or with words that please me. Tell me the truth, though it be sad and alarming."

Joseph asked the king first whence he knew that the interpretation given by the wise men of his country was not true, and Pharaoh replied, "I saw the dream and its interpretation together, and therefore they cannot make a fool of me." In his modesty Joseph denied that he was an adept at interpreting dreams. He said, "It is not in me; it is in the hand of God, and if it be the wish of God, He will permit me to announce tidings of peace to Pharaoh." And for such modesty he was rewarded by sovereignty over Egypt, for the Lord doth honor them that honor Him. Thus was also Daniel rewarded for his speech to Nebuchadnezzar:

"There is a God in heaven that revealeth secrets, but as for me, this secret is not revealed to me for any wisdom that I have more than any living, but to the intent that the interpretation may be made known to the king, and that thou mayest know the thoughts of thy heart."

Then Pharaoh began to tell his dream, only he omitted some points and narrated others inaccurately in order that he might test the vaunted powers of Joseph. But the youth corrected him, and pieced the dreams together exactly as they had visited Pharaoh in the night, and the king was greatly amazed. Joseph was able to accomplish this feat, because he had dreamed the same dream as Pharaoh, at the same time as he. Thereupon Pharaoh retold his dreams, with all details and circumstances, and precisely as he had seen them in his sleep, except that he left out the word Nile in the description of the seven lean kine, because this river was worshipped by the Egyptians, and he hesitated to say that aught that is evil had come from his god.

Now Joseph proceeded to give the king the true interpretation of the two dreams. They were both a revelation concerning the seven good years impending and the seven years of famine to follow them. In reality, it had been the purpose of God to bring a famine of forty-two years' duration upon Egypt, but only two years of this distressful period were inflicted upon the land, for the sake of the blessing of Jacob when he came to Egypt in the second year of the famine. The other forty years fell upon the land at the time of the prophet Ezekiel.

Joseph did more than merely interpret the dreams. When the king gave voice to doubts concerning the interpretation, he told him signs and tokens. He said: "Let this be a sign to thee that my words are true, and my advice is excellent: Thy wife, who is sitting upon the birthstool at this moment, will bring forth a son, and thou wilt rejoice over him, but in the midst of thy joy the sad tidings will be told thee of the death of thine older son, who was born unto thee but two years ago, and thou must needs find consolation for the loss of the one in the birth of the other."

Scarcely had Joseph withdrawn from the presence of the king, when the report of the birth of a son was brought to Pharaoh, and soon after also the report of the death of his first-born, who had suddenly dropped to the floor and passed away. Thereupon he sent for all the grandees of his realm, and all his servants, and he spake to them, saying: "Ye have heard the words of the Hebrew, and ye have seen that the signs which he foretold were accomplished, and I also know that he hath interpreted the dream truly. Advise me now how the land may be saved from the ravages of the famine. Look hither and thither whether you can find a man of wisdom and understanding, whom I may set over the land, for I am convinced that the land can be saved only if we heed the counsel of the Hebrew." The grandees and the princes admitted that safety could be secured only by adhering to the advice given by Joseph, and they proposed that the king, in his sagacity, choose a man whom he considered equal to the great task. Thereupon Pharaoh said: "If we traversed and searched the earth from end to end, we could find none such as Joseph, a man in whom is the spirit of God. If ye think well thereof, I will set him over the land which he hath saved by his wisdom."

The astrologers, who were his counsellors, demurred, saying, "A slave, one whom his present owner hath acquired for twenty pieces of silver, thou proposest to set over us as master?" But Pharaoh maintained that Joseph was not only a free-born man beyond the peradventure of a doubt, but also the scion of a noble family. However, the princes of Pharaoh were not silenced, they continued to give utterance to their opposition to Joseph, saying: "Dost thou not remember the immutable law of the Egyptians, that none may serve as king or as viceroy unless he speaks all the languages of men? And this Hebrew knows none but his own tongue, and how were it possible that a man should rule over us who cannot even speak the language of our land? Send and have him fetched hither, and examine him in respect to all the things a ruler should know and have, and then decide as seemeth wise in thy sight."

Pharaoh yielded, he promised to do as they wished, and he appointed the following day as the time for examining Joseph, who had returned to his prison in the meantime, for, on account of his wife, his master feared to have him stay in his house. During the night Gabriel appeared unto Joseph, and taught him all the seventy languages, and he acquired them quickly after the angel had changed his name from Joseph to Jehoseph. The next morning, when he came into the presence of Pharaoh and the nobles of the kingdom, inasmuch as he knew every one of the seventy languages, he mounted all the steps of the royal throne, until he reached the seventieth, the highest, upon which sat the king, and Pharaoh and his princes rejoiced that Joseph fulfilled all the requirements needed by one that was to rule over Egypt.

The king said to Joseph: "Thou didst give me the counsel to look out a man discreet and wise, and set him over the land of Egypt, that he may in his wisdom save the land from the famine. As God hath showed thee all this, and as thou art master of all the languages of the world, there is none so discreet and wise as thou. Thou shalt therefore be the second in the land after Pharaoh, and according unto thy word shall all my people go in and go out; my princes and my servants shall receive their monthly appanage from thee; before thee the people shall prostrate themselves, only in the throne will I be greater than thou."

THE RULER OF EGYPT

Now Joseph reaped the harvest of his virtues, and according to the measure of his merits God granted him reward. The mouth that refused the kiss of unlawful passion and sin received the kiss of homage from the people; the neck that did not bow itself unto sin was adorned with the gold chain that Pharaoh put upon it;

the hands that did not touch sin wore the signet ring that Pharaoh took from his own hand and put upon Joseph's; the body that did not come in contact with sin was arrayed in vestures of byssus; the feet that made no steps in the direction of sin reposed in the royal chariot, and the thoughts that kept themselves undefiled by sin were proclaimed as wisdom.

Joseph was installed in his high position, and invested with the insignia of his office, with solemn ceremony. The king took off his signet ring from his hand, and put it upon Joseph's hand, and arrayed him in princely apparel, and set a gold crown upon his head, and laid a gold chain about his neck. Then he commanded his servants to make Joseph to ride in his second chariot, which went by the side of the chariot wherein sat the king, and he also made him to ride upon a great and strong horse of the king's horses, and his servants conducted him through the streets of the city of Egypt. Musicians, no less than a thousand striking cymbals and a thousand blowing flutes, and five thousand men with drawn swords gleaming in the air formed the vanguard. Twenty thousand of the king's grandees girt with gold-embroidered leather belts marched at the right of Joseph, and as many at the left of him. The women and the maidens of the nobility looked out of the windows to gaze upon Joseph's beauty, and they poured down chains upon him, and rings and jewels, that he might but direct his eyes toward them. Yet he did not look up, and as a reward God made him proof against the evil eye, nor has it ever had the power of inflicting harm upon any of his descendants. Servants of the king, preceding him and following him, burnt incense upon his path, and cassia, and all manner of sweet spices, and strewed myrrh and aloes wherever he went. Twenty heralds walked before him, and they proclaimed: "This is the man whom the king bath chosen to be the second after him. All the affairs of state will be administered by him, and whoever resisteth his commands, or refuseth to bow down to the ground before him, he will die the death of the rebel against the king and the king's deputy."

Without delay the people prostrated themselves, and they cried, "Long live the king, and long live the deputy of the king!" And Joseph, looking down from his horse upon the people and their exultation, exclaimed, his eyes directed heavenward: "The Lord raiseth up the poor out of the dust, and lifteth up the needy from the dunghill. O Lord of hosts, blessed is the man that trusteth in Thee."

After Joseph, accompanied by Pharaoh's officers and princes, had journeyed through the whole city of Egypt, and viewed all there was therein, he returned to the king on the selfsame day, and the king gave him fields and vineyards as a present, and also three thousand talents of silver, and a thousand talents of gold, and onyx stones and bdellium, and many other costly things. The king commanded, moreover, that every Egyptian give Joseph a gift, else he would be put to death. A platform was erected in the open street, and there all deposited their presents, and among the things were many gold and silver, as well as precious stones, carried thither by the people and also the grandees, for they saw that Joseph enjoyed the favor of the king. Furthermore, Joseph received one hundred slaves from Pharaoh, and they were to do all his bidding, and he himself acquired many more, for he resided in a spacious palace. Three years it took to build it. Special magnificence was lavished upon the hall of state, which was his audience chamber, and upon the throne fashioned of gold and silver and inlaid with precious stones, whereon there was a representation of the whole land of Egypt and of the river Nile. And as Joseph multiplied in riches, so he increased also in wisdom, for God added to his wisdom that all might love and honor him. Pharaoh called him Zaphenath-paneah, he who can reveal secret things with ease, and rejoiceth the heart of man therewith. Each letter of the name Zaphenath-paneah has a meaning, too. The first, Zadde, stands for Zofeh, seer; Pe for Podeh, redeemer; Nun for Nabi, prophet; Taw for Tomek, supporter; Pe for Poter, interpreter of dreams; Ain for Arum, clever; Nun for Nabon, discreet; and Het for Hakam, wise.

The name of Joseph's wife pointed to her history in the same way. Asenath was the daughter of Dinah and Hamor, but she was abandoned at the borders of Egypt, only, that people might know who she was, Jacob engraved the story of her parentage and her birth upon a gold plate fastened around her neck. The day on which Asenath was exposed, Potiphar went walking with his servants near the city wall, and they heard the voice of a child. At the captain's bidding they brought the baby to him, and when he read her history from the gold plate, he determined to adopt her. He took her home with him, and raised her as his daughter. The Alef in Asenath stands for On, where Potiphar was priest; the Samek for Setirah, Hidden, for she was kept concealed on account of her extraordinary beauty; the Nun for Nohemet, for she wept and entreated that she might be delivered from the house of the heathen Potiphar; and the Taw for Tammah, the perfect one, on account of her pious, perfect deeds.

Asenath had saved Joseph's life while she was still an infant in arms. When Joseph was accused of immoral conduct by Potiphar's wife and the other women, and his master was on the point of having him hanged, Asenath approached her foster-father, and she assured him under oath that the charge against Joseph was false. Then spake God, "As thou livest, because thou didst try to defend Joseph, thou shalt be the woman to bear the tribes that he is appointed to beget.

Asenath bore him two sons, Manasseh and Ephraim, during the seven years of plenty, for in the time of famine Joseph refrained from all indulgence in the pleasures of life. They were bred in chastity and fear of God by their father, and they were wise, and well-instructed in all knowledge and in the affairs of state, so that they became the favorites of the court, and were educated with the royal princes.

Before the famine broke over the land, Joseph found an opportunity of rendering the king a great service. He equipped an army of four thousand six hundred men, providing all the soldiers with shields and spears and bucklers and helmets and slings. With this army, and aided by the servants and officers of the king, and by the people of Egypt, he carried on a war with Tarshish in the first year after his appointment as viceroy. The people of Tarshish had invaded the territory of the Ishmaelites, and the latter, few in number at that time, were sore pressed, and applied to the king of Egypt for help against their enemies. At the head of his host of heroes, Joseph marched to the land of Havilah, where he was joined by the Ishmaelites, and with united forces they fought against the people of Tarshish, routed them utterly, settled their land with the Ishmaelites, while the defeated men took refuge with their brethren in Javan. Joseph and his army returned to Egypt, and not a man had they lost.

In a little while Joseph's prophecy was confirmed: that year and the six following years were years of plenty, as he had foretold. The harvest was so ample that a single ear produced two heaps of grain, and Joseph made circumspect arrangements to provide abundantly for the years of famine. He gathered up all the grain, and in the city situated in the middle of each district he laid up the produce from round about, and had ashes and earth strewn on the garnered food from the very soil on which it had been grown; also he preserved the grain in the ear; all these being precautions taken to guard against rot and mildew. The inhabitants of Egypt also tried, on their own account, to put aside a portion of the superabundant harvest of the seven fruitful years against the need of the future, but when the grievous time of dearth came, and they went to their storehouses to bring forth the treasured grain, behold, it had rotted, and become unfit for food. The famine broke in upon the people with such suddenness that the bread gave out unexpectedly as they sat at their tables, they had not even a bite of bran bread.

Thus they were driven to apply to Joseph and beseech his help, and he admonished them, saying, "Give up your allegiance to your deceitful idols, and say, Blessed is He who giveth bread unto all flesh." But they refused to deny their lying gods, and they betook themselves to Pharaoh, only to be told by him, "Go unto Joseph; what he saith to you, do!" For this Pharaoh was rewarded. God granted him long life and a long reign, until he became arrogant, and well-merited punishment overtook him.

When the Egyptians approached Joseph with the petition for bread, he spoke, saying, "I give no food to the uncircumcised. Go hence, and circumcise yourselves, and then return hither." They entered the presence of Pharaoh, and complained to him regarding Joseph, but he said as before, "Go unto Joseph!" And they replied, "We come from Joseph, and he hath spoken roughly unto us, saying, Go hence and circumcise yourselves! We warned thee in the beginning that he is a Hebrew, and would treat us in such wise." Pharaoh said to them: "O ye fools, did he not prophesy through the holy spirit and proclaim to the whole world, that there would come seven years of plenty to be followed by seven years of dearth? Why did you not save the yield of one or two years against the day of your need?"

Weeping, they made reply: "The grain that we put aside during the good years hath rotted."

Pharaoh: "Have ye nothing over of the flour of yesterday?"

The Egyptians: "The very bread in the basket rotted!"

Pharaoh: "Why?"

The Egyptians: "Because Joseph willed thus!"

Pharaoh: "O ye fools, if his word hath power over the grain, making it to rot when he desireth it to rot, then also must we die, if so be his wish concerning us. Go, therefore, unto him, and do as he bids you."

JOSEPH'S BRETHREN IN EGYPT

The famine, which inflicted hardships first upon the wealthy among the Egyptians, gradually extended its ravages as far as Phoenicia, Arabia, and Palestine. Though the sons of Jacob, being young men, frequented the streets and the highways, yet they were ignorant of what their old home-keeping father Jacob knew, that corn could be procured in Egypt. Jacob even suspected that Joseph was in Egypt. His prophetic spirit, which forsook him during the time of his grief for his son, yet manifested itself now and again in dim visions, and he was resolved to send his sons down into Egypt. There was another reason. Though he was not yet in want, he nevertheless had them go thither for food, because he was averse from arousing the envy of the sons of Esau and Ishmael by his comfortable state. For the same reason, to avoid friction with the surrounding peoples, he bade his sons not appear in public with bread in their hands, or in the accoutrements of war. And as he knew that they were likely to attract attention, on account of their heroic stature and handsome appearance, he cautioned them against going to the city all together through the same gate, or, indeed, showing themselves all together anywhere in public, that the evil eye be not cast upon them.

The famine in Canaan inspired Joseph with the hope of seeing his brethren. To make sure of their coming, he issued a decree concerning the purchase of corn in Egypt, as follows: "By order of the king and his deputy, and the princes of the realm, be it enacted that he who desireth to buy grain in Egypt may not send his slave hither to do his bidding, but he must charge his own sons therewith. An Egyptian or a Canaanite that hath bought grain and then selleth it again shall be put to death, for none may buy more than he requireth for the needs of his household. Also, who cometh with two or three beasts of burden, and loads them up with grain, shall be put to death."

At the gates of the city of Egypt, Joseph stationed guards, whose office was to inquire and take down the name of all that should come to buy corn, and also the name of their father and their grandfather, and every evening the list of names thus made was handed to Joseph. These precautions were bound to bring Joseph's brethren down to Egypt, and also acquaint him with their coming as soon as they entered the land.

On their journey his brethren thought more of Joseph than of their errand. They said to one another: "We know that Joseph was carried down into Egypt, and we will make search for him there, and if we should find him, we will ransom him from his master, and if his master should refuse to sell him, we will use force, though we perish ourselves."

At the gates of the city of Egypt, the brethren of Joseph were asked what their names were, and the names of their father and grandfather. The guard on duty happened to be Manasseh, the son of Joseph. The brethren submitted to being questioned, saying "Let us go into the town, and we shall see whether this taking down of our names be a matter of taxes. If it be so, we shall not demur; but if it be something else, we shall see to-morrow what can be done in the case."

On the evening of the day they entered Egypt, Joseph discovered their names in the list, which he was in the habit of examining daily, and he commanded that all stations for the sale of corn be closed, except one only. Furthermore, even at this station no sales were to be negotiated unless the name of the would-be purchaser was first obtained. His brethren, with whose names Joseph furnished the overseer of the place, were to be seized and brought to him as soon as they put in appearance.

But the first thought of the brethren was for Joseph, and their first concern, to seek him. For three days they made search for him everywhere, even in the most disreputable quarters of the city. Meantime Joseph was in communication with the overseer of the station kept open for the sale of corn, and, hearing that his brethren had not appeared there, he dispatched some of his servants to look for them, but they found them neither in Mizraim, the city of Egypt, nor in Goshen, nor in Raamses. Thereupon he sent sixteen servants forth to make a house to house search for them in the city, and they discovered the brethren of Joseph in a place of ill-fame and haled them before their master.

JOSEPH MEETS HIS BRETHREN

A large crown of gold on his head, apparelled in byssus and purple, and surrounded by his valiant men, Joseph was seated upon his throne in his palace. His brethren fell down before him in great admiration of his beauty, his stately appearance, and his majesty. They did not know him, for when Joseph was sold into slavery, he was a beardless youth. But he knew his brethren, their appearance had not changed in aught, for they were bearded men when he was separated from them.

He was inclined to make himself known to them as their brother, but an angel appeared unto him, the same that had brought him from Shechem to his brethren at Dothan, and spoke, saying, "These came hither with intent to kill thee." Later, when the brethren returned home, and gave an account of their adventures to Jacob, they told him that a man had accused them falsely before the ruler of Egypt, not knowing that he who incited Joseph against them was an angel. It was in reference to this matter, and meaning their accuser, that Jacob, when he dispatched his sons on their second expedition to Egypt, prayed to God, "God Almighty give you mercy before the man."

Joseph made himself strange unto his brethren, and he took his cup in his hand, knocked against it, and said, "By this magic cup I know that ye are spies." They replied, "Thy servants came from Canaan into Egypt for to buy corn."

Joseph: "If it be true that ye came hither to buy corn, why is it that each one of you entered the city by a separate gate?"

The brethren: "We are ALL the sons of one man in the land of Canaan, and he bade us not enter a city together by the same gate, that we attract not the attention of the people of the place." Unconsciously they had spoken as seers, for the word ALL included Joseph as one of their number.

Joseph: "Verily, ye are spies! All the people that come to buy corn return home without delay, but ye have lingered here three days, without making any purchases, and all the time you have been gadding about in the disreputable parts of the city, and only spies are wont to do thus."

The brethren: "We thy servants are twelve brethren, the sons of Jacob, the son of Isaac, the son of the Hebrew Abraham. The youngest is this day with our father in Canaan, and one hath disappeared. Him did we look for in this land, and we looked for him even in the disreputable houses."

Joseph: "Have ye made search in every other place on earth, and was Egypt the only land left? And if it be true that he is in Egypt, what should a brother of yours be doing in a house of ill-fame, if, indeed, ye are the descendants of Abraham, Isaac, and Jacob?"

The brethren: "We did hear that some Ishmaelites stole our brother, and sold him into slavery in Egypt, and as our brother was exceeding fair in form and face, we thought he might have been sold for illicit uses, and therefore we searched even the disreputable houses to find him."

Joseph: "You speak deceitful words, when you call yourselves sons of Abraham. By the life of Pharaoh, ye are spies, and you did go from one disreputable house to another that none might discover you."

The expression "by the life of Pharaoh" might have betrayed Joseph's real feeling to his brethren, had they but known his habit of taking this oath only when he meant to avoid keeping his word later.

Joseph continued to speak to his brethren: "Let us suppose you should discover your brother serving as a slave, and his master should demand a high sum for his ransom, would you pay it?"

The brethren: "Yes!"

Joseph: "But suppose his master should refuse to surrender him for any price in the world, what would you do?"

The brethren: "If he yields not our brother to us, we will kill the master, and carry off our brother."

Joseph: "Now see how true my words were, that ye are spies. By your own admission ye have come to slay the inhabitants of the land. Report hath told us that two of you did massacre the people of Shechem on account of the wrong done to your sister, and now have ye come down into Egypt to kill the Egyptians for the sake of your brother. I shall be convinced of your innocence only if you consent to send one of your number home and fetch your youngest brother hither."

His brethren refused compliance, and Joseph caused them to be put into prison by seventy of his valiant men, and there they remained for three days. God never allows the pious to languish in distress longer than three days, and so it was a Divine dispensation that the brethren of Joseph were released on the third day, and were permitted by Joseph to return home, on condition, however, that one of them remain behind as hostage.

The difference between Joseph and his brethren can be seen here. Though he retained one of them to be bound in the prison house, he still said, "I fear God," and dismissed the others, but when he was in their power, they gave no thought to God. At this time, to be sure, their conduct was such as is becoming to the pious, who accept their fate with calm resignation, and acknowledge the righteousness of God, for He metes out reward and punishment measure for measure. They recognized that their present punishment was in return for the heartless treatment they had dealt out to Joseph, paying no heed to his distress, though he fell at the feet of each of them, weeping, and entreating them not to sell him into slavery. Reuben reminded the others that they had two wrongs to expiate, the wrong against their brother and the wrong against their father, who was so grieved that he exclaimed, "I will go down to the grave to my son mourning."

The brethren of Joseph knew not that the viceroy of Egypt understood Hebrew, and could follow their words, for Manasseh stood and was an interpreter between them and him.

Joseph decided to keep Simon as hostage in Egypt, for he had been one of the two--Levi was the other--to advise that Joseph be put to death, and only the intercession of Reuben and Judah had saved him. He did not detain Levi, too, for he feared, if both remained behind together, Egypt might suffer the same fate at their hands as the city of Shechem. Also, he preferred Simon to Levi, because Simon was not a favorite among the sons of Jacob, and they would not resist his detention in Egypt too violently, while they might annihilate Egypt, as aforetime Shechem, if they were deprived of Levi, their wise man and high priest. Besides, it was Simon that had lowered Joseph into the pit, wherefore he had a particular grudge against him.

When the brethren yielded to Joseph's demand, and consented to leave their brother behind as hostage, Simon said to them, "Ye desire to do with me as ye did with Joseph!" But they replied, in despair: "What can we do? Our households will perish of hunger." Simon made answer, "Do as ye will, but as for me, let me see the man that will venture to cast me into prison." Joseph sent word to Pharaoh to let him have seventy of his valiant men, to aid him in arresting robbers. But when the seventy appeared upon the scene, and were about to lay hands on Simon, he uttered a loud cry, and his assailants fell to the floor and knocked out their teeth. Pharaoh's valiant men, as well as all the people that stood about Joseph, fled affrighted, only Joseph and his son Manasseh remained calm and unmoved. Manasseh rose up, dealt Simon a blow on the back of his neck, put manacles upon his hands and fetters upon his feet, and cast him into prison. Joseph's brethren were greatly amazed at the heroic strength of the youth, and Simon said, "This blow was not dealt by an Egyptian, but by one belonging to our house."

He was bound and taken to prison before the eyes of the other brethren of Joseph, but as soon as they were out of sight, Joseph ordered good fare to be set before him, and he treated him with great kindness.

Joseph permitted his nine other brethren to depart, carrying corn with them in abundance, but he impressed upon them that they must surely return and bring their youngest brother with them. On the way, Levi, who felt lonely without his constant companion Simon, opened his sack, and he espied the money he had paid for the corn. They all trembled, and their hearts failed them, and they said, "Where, then, is the lovingkindness of God toward our fathers Abraham, Isaac, and Jacob, seeing that He hath delivered us into the hands of the Egyptian king, that he may raise false accusations against us?" And Judah said, "Verily, we are guilty concerning our brother, we have sinned against God, in that we sold our brother, our own flesh, and why do ye ask, Where, then, is the lovingkindness of God toward our fathers?"

Reuben spoke in the same way: "Spake I not unto you, saying, Do not sin against the child, and ye would not hear? And now the Lord doth demand him of us. How can you say, Where, then, is the lovingkindness of God toward our fathers, though you have sinned against Him?"

They proceeded on their journey home, and their father met them on the way. Jacob was astonished not to see Simon with them, and in reply to his questions, they told him all that had befallen them in Egypt. Then Jacob cried out: "What have ye done? I sent Joseph to you to see whether it be well with you, and ye said, An evil beast hath devoured him. Simon went forth with you for to buy corn, and you say, The king of Egypt hath cast him into prison. And now ye will take Benjamin away and kill him, too. Ye will bring down my gray hairs with sorrow to the grave."

The words of Jacob, which he uttered, "Me have ye bereaved of my children," were meant to intimate to his sons that he suspected them of the death of Joseph and of Simon's disappearance as well, and their reports concerning both he regarded as inventions. What made him inconsolable was that now, having lost two of his sons, he could not hope to see the Divine promise fulfilled, that he should be the ancestor of twelve tribes. He was quite resolved in his mind, therefore, not to let Benjamin go away with his brethren under any condition whatsoever, and he vouchsafed Reuben no reply when he said, "Slay my two sons, if I bring him not to thee." He considered it beneath his dignity to give an answer to such balderdash. "My first-born son," he said to himself, "is a fool. What will it profit me, if I slay his two sons? Does he not know that his sons are equally mine?" Judah advised his brethren to desist from urging their father then; he would consent, he thought, to whatever expedients were found necessary, as soon as their bread gave out, and a second journey to Egypt became imperative.

THE SECOND JOURNEY TO EGYPT

When the supplies bought in Egypt were eaten up, and the family of Jacob began to suffer with hunger, the little children came to him, and they said, "Give us bread, that we die not of hunger before thee." The words of the little ones brought scorching tears to the eyes of Jacob, and he summoned his sons and bade them go again down into Egypt and buy food. But Judah spake unto him, "The man did solemnly protest unto us, saying that we should not see his face, except our brother Benjamin be with us, and we cannot appear before him with idle pretexts." And Jacob said, "Wherefore dealt ye so ill with me as to tell the man whether ye had yet a brother?" It was the first and only time Jacob indulged in empty talk, and God said, "I made it My business to raise his son to the position of ruler of Egypt, and he complains, and says, Wherefore dealt ye so ill with-me?" And Judah protested against the reproach, that he had initiated the Egyptian viceroy in their family relations, with the words: "Why, he knew the very wood of which our baby coaches are made! Father," he continued, "if Benjamin goes with us, he may, indeed, be taken from us, but also he may not. This is a doubtful matter, but it is certain that if he does not go with us, we shall all die of hunger. It is better not to concern thyself about what is doubtful, and guide thy actions by what is certain. The king of Egypt is a strong and mighty king, and if we go to him without our brother, we shall all be put to death. Dost thou not know, and hast thou not heard, that this king is very powerful and wise, and there is none like unto him in all the earth? We have seen all the kings of the earth, but none like unto the king of Egypt. One would surely say that among all the kings of the earth there is none greater than Abimelech king of the Philistines, yet the king of Egypt is greater and mightier than he, and Abimelech can hardly be compared with one of his officers. Father, thou hast not seen his palace and his throne, and all his servants standing before him. Thou hast not seen that king upon his throne, in all his magnificence and with his royal insignia, arrayed in his royal robes, with a large golden crown upon his head. Thou hast not seen the honor and the glory that God hath given unto him, for there is none like unto him in all the earth. Father, thou hast not seen the wisdom, the understanding, and the knowledge that God has given in his heart. We heard his sweet voice when he spake unto us. We know not, father, who acquainted him with our names, and all that befell us. He asked also concerning thee, saying, Is your father still alive, and is it well with him? Thou hast not seen the affairs of the government of Egypt regulated by him, for none asketh his lord Pharaoh about them. Thou hast not seen the awe and the fear that he imposes upon all the Egyptians. Even we went out from his presence threatening to do unto Egypt as unto the cities of the Amorites, and exceedingly wroth by reason of all his words that he spake concerning us as spies, yet when we came again before him, his terror fell upon us all, and none of us was able to speak a word to him, great or small. Now, therefore, father, send the lad with us, and we will arise and go down into Egypt, and buy food to eat, that we die not of hunger."

Judah offered his portion in the world to come as surety for Benjamin, and thus solemnly he promised to bring him back safe and sound, and Jacob granted his request, and permitted Benjamin to go down into Egypt with his other sons. They also carried with them choice presents from their father for the ruler of Egypt, things that arouse wonder outside of Palestine, such as the murex, which is the snail that produces the Tyrian purple, and various kinds of balm, and almond oil, and pistachio oil, and honey as hard as stone. Furthermore, Jacob put double money in their hand to provide against a rise in prices in the meantime. And after all these matters were attended to, he spake to his sons, saying: "Here is money, and here is a present, and also your brother. Is there aught else that you need?" And they replied, Yes, we need this, besides, that thou shouldst intercede for us with God." Then their father prayed: "O Lord, Thou who at the time of creation didst call Enough! to heaven and earth when they stretched themselves out further and further toward infinity, set a limit to my sufferings, too, say unto them, Enough! God Almighty give you mercy before the ruler of Egypt, that he may release unto you Joseph, Simon, and Benjamin."

This prayer was an intercession, not only for the sons of Jacob, but also for their descendants--that God would deliver the Ten Tribes in time to come, as He delivered the two, Judah and Benjamin, and after He permitted the destruction of two Temples, He would grant endless continuance to the third.

Jacob also put a letter addressed to the viceroy of Egypt into the hands of his son. The letter ran thus: "From thy servant Jacob, the son of Isaac, the grandson of Abraham, prince of God, to the mighty and wise king Zaphenathpaneah, the ruler of Egypt, peace! I make known unto my lord the king that the famine is sore with us in the land of Canaan, and I have therefore sent my sons unto thee, to buy us a little food, that we may live, and not die. My children surrounded me, and begged for something to eat, but, alas, I am very old, and I cannot see with mine eyes, for they are heavy with the weight of years, and also on account of my never-ceasing tears for my son Joseph, who hath been taken from me. I charged my sons not to pass through the gate all together at the same time, when they arrived in the city of Egypt, in consideration of the inhabitants of the land, that they might not take undue notice of them. Also I bade them go up and down in the land of Egypt and seek my son Joseph, mayhap they would find him there.

"This did they do, but thou didst therefore account them as spies. We have heard the report of thy wisdom and sagacity. How, then, canst thou look upon their countenances, and yet declare them to be spies? Especially as we have heard thou didst interpret Pharaoh's dream, and didst foretell the coming of the famine, are we amazed that thou, in thy discernment, couldst not distinguish whether they be spies or not.

"And, now, O my lord king, I send unto thee my son Benjamin, as thou didst demand of my other sons. I pray thee, take good care of him until thou sendest him back to me in peace with his brethren. Hast thou not heard, and dost thou not know, what our God did unto Pharaoh when he took our mother Sarah unto himself? Or what happened unto Abimelech on account of her? And what our father Abraham did unto the nine kings of Elam, how he killed them and exterminated their armies, though he had but few men with him? Or hast thou not heard what my two sons Simon and Levi did to the eight cities of the Amorites, which they destroyed on account of their sister Dinah? Benjamin consoled them for the loss of Joseph. What, then, will they do unto him that stretcheth forth the hand of power to snatch him away from them?

"Knowest thou not, O king of Egypt, that the might of our God is with us, and that He always hearkens unto our prayers, and never forsakes us? Had I called upon God to rise up against thee when my sons told me how thou didst act toward them, thou and thy people, ye all would have been annihilated ere Benjamin could come down to thee. But I reflected that Simon my son was abiding in thy house, and perhaps thou wast doing kindnesses unto him, and therefore I invoked not the punishment of God upon thee. Now my son

Benjamin goeth down unto thee with my other sons. Take heed unto thyself, keep thy eyes directed upon him, and God will direct His eye upon all thy kingdom.

"I have said all now that is in my heart. My sons take their youngest brother down into Egypt with them, and do thou send them all back to me in peace."

This letter Jacob put into the keeping of Judah, charging him to deliver it to the ruler of Egypt. His last words to his sons were an admonition to take good care of Benjamin and not leave him out of their sight, either on the journey or after their arrival in Egypt. He bade farewell to them, and then turned in prayer to God, saying: "O Lord of heaven and earth! Remember Thy covenant with our father Abraham. Remember also my father Isaac, and grant grace unto my sons, and deliver them not into the hands of the king of Egypt. O my God, do it for the sake of Thy mercy, redeem my sons and save them from the hands of the Egyptians, and restore their two brethren unto them."

Also the women and the children in the house of Jacob prayed to God amid tears, and entreated Him to redeem their husbands and their fathers out of the hands of the king of Egypt.

JOSEPH AND BENJAMIN

Great was the joy of Joseph when his brethren stood before him and Benjamin was with them. In his youngest brother he saw the true counterpart of his father. He ordered his son Manasseh, the steward of his house, to bring the men into the palace, and make ready a meal for them. But he was to take care to prepare the meat dishes in the presence of the guests, so that they might see with their own eyes that the cattle had been slaughtered according to the ritual prescriptions, and the sinew of the hip which is upon the hollow of the thigh had been removed.

The dinner to which Joseph invited his brethren was a Sabbath meal, for he observed the seventh day even before the revelation of the law. The sons of Jacob refused the invitation of the steward, and a scuffle ensued. While he tried to force them into the banqueting hall, they tried to force him out, for they feared it was but a ruse to get possession of them and their asses, on account of the money they had found in their sacks on their return from their first journey to Egypt. In their modesty they put the loss of their beasts upon the same level as the loss of their personal liberty. To the average man property is as precious as life itself.

Standing at the door of Joseph's house, they spake to the steward, and said: "We are in badly reduced circumstances. In our country we supported others, and now we depend upon thee to support us." After these introductory words, they offered him the money they had found in their sacks. The steward reassured them concerning the money, saying, "However it may be, whether for the sake of your own merits, or for the sake of the merits of your fathers, God hath caused you to find a treasure, for the money ye paid for the corn came into my hand." Then he brought Simon out to them. Their brother looked like a leather bottle, so fat and rotund had he grown during his sojourn in Egypt. He told his brethren what kind treatment had been accorded unto him. The very moment they left the city he had been released from prison, and thereafter he had been entertained with splendor in the house of the ruler of Egypt.

When Joseph made his appearance, Judah took Benjamin by the hand, and presented him to the viceroy, and they all bowed down themselves to him to the earth. Joseph asked them concerning the welfare of their father and their grandfather, and they made reply, "Thy servant our father is well; he is yet alive," and Joseph knew from their words that his grandfather Isaac was no more. He had died at the time when Joseph was released from prison, and the joy of God in the liberation of Joseph was overcast by His sorrow for Isaac. Then Judah handed his father's letter to Joseph, who was so moved at seeing the well-known handwriting that he had to retire to his chamber and weep. When he came back, he summoned Benjamin to approach close to him, and he laid his hand upon his youngest brother's head, and blessed him with the words, "God be gracious unto thee, my son." His father had once mentioned "the children which God hath graciously given Thy servant," and as Benjamin was not among the children thus spoken of, for he was born later, Joseph compensated him now by blessing him with the grace of God.

The table was set in three divisions, for Joseph, for his brethren, and for the Egyptians. The sons of Jacob did not venture to eat of the dishes set before them, they were afraid they might not have been prepared according to the ritual prescriptions--a punishment upon Joseph for having slandered his brethren, whom he once charged with not being punctilious in the observance of the dietary laws. The Egyptians, again, could not sit at the same table with the sons of Jacob, because the latter ate the flesh of the animals to which the former paid divine worship.

When all was ready, and the guests were to be seated, Joseph raised his cup, and, pretending to inhale his knowledge from it, he said, "Judah is king, therefore let him sit at the head of the table, and let Reuben the first-born take the second seat," and thus he assigned places to all his brethren corresponding to their dignity and their age. Moreover, he seated the brothers together who were the sons of the same mother, and when he reached Benjamin, he said, "I know that the youngest among you has no brother borne by his own mother, next to whom he might be seated, and also I have none, therefore he may take his place next to me."

The brethren marvelled one with another at all this. During the meal, Joseph took his portion, and gave it to Benjamin, and his wife Asenath followed his example, and also Ephraim and Manasseh, so that Benjamin had four portions in addition to that which he had received like the other sons of Jacob.

Wine was served at the meal, and it was the first time in twenty-two years that Joseph and his brethren tasted of it, for they had led the life of Nazarites, his brethren because they regretted the evil they had done to Joseph, and Joseph because he grieved over the fate of his father.

Joseph entered into conversation with his brother Benjamin. He asked him whether he had a brother borne by his own mother, and Benjamin answered, "I had one, but I do not know what hath become of him." Joseph continued his questions: "Hast thou a wife?"

Benjamin: "Yes, I have a wife and ten sons."

Joseph: "And what are their names? "

Benjamin: "Bela, and Becher, and Ashbel, Gera, and Naaman, Ehi, and Rosh, Muppim, and Huppim, and Ard."

Joseph: "Why didst thou give them such peculiar names?"

Benjamin: "In memory of my brother and his sufferings: Bela, because my brother disappeared among the peoples; Becher, he was the first-born son of my mother; Ashbel, he was taken away from my father; Gera, he dwells a stranger in a strange land; Naaman, he was exceedingly lovely; Ehi, he was my only brother by my father and my mother together; Rosh, he was at the head of his brethren; Muppim, he was beautiful in every respect; Huppim, he was slandered; and Ard, because he was as beautiful as a rose."

Joseph ordered his magic astrolabe to be brought to him, whereby he knew all things that happen, and he said unto Benjamin, "I have heard that the Hebrews are acquainted with all wisdom, but dost thou know aught of this?" Benjamin answered, "Thy servant also is skilled in all wisdom, which my father hath taught me." He then looked upon the astrolabe, and to his great astonishment he discovered by the aid of it that he who was sitting upon the throne before him was his brother Joseph. Noticing Benjamin's amazement, Joseph asked him, "What hast thou seen, and why art thou astonished?" Benjamin said, "I can see by this that Joseph my brother sitteth here before me upon the throne." And Joseph said: "I am Joseph thy brother! Reveal not the thing unto our brethren. I will send thee with them when they go away, and I will command them to be brought back again into the city, and I will take thee away from them. If they risk their lives and fight for thee, then shall I know that they have repented of what they did unto me, and I will make myself known unto them. But if they forsake thee, I will keep thee, that thou shouldst remain with me. They shall go away, and I will not make myself known unto them."

Then Joseph inquired of Benjamin what his brethren had told their father after they had sold him into slavery, and he heard the story of the coat dipped in the blood of a kid of the goats. "Yes, brother," spoke Joseph, "when they had stripped me of my coat, they handed me over to the Ishmaelites, who tied an apron around my waist, scourged me, and bade me run off. But a lion attacked the one that beat me, and killed him, and his companions were alarmed, and they sold me to other people."

Dismissed by Joseph with kind, words, his brethren started on their homeward journey as soon as the morning was light, for it is a good rule to "leave a city after sunrise, and enter a city before sundown." Besides, Joseph had a specific reason for not letting his brethren depart from the city during the night. He feared an encounter between them and his servants, and that his men might get the worst of it, for the sons of Jacob were like the wild beasts, which have the upper hand at night.

THE THIEF CAUGHT

They were not yet far beyond the city gates, when Joseph dispatched Manasseh, the steward of his house, to follow after them, and look for the silver cup that he had concealed in Benjamin's sack. He knew his brethren well, he did not venture to let them get too far from the city before he should attempt to force their return. He hoped that the nearness of the city would intimidate them and make them heed his commands. Manasseh therefore received the order to bring them to a halt, by mild speech if he could, or by rough speech if he must, and carry them back to the city. He acted according to his instructions. When the brethren heard the accusation of theft, they said: "With whomsoever of thy servants the cup be found, let him die, and we also will be my lord's bondmen." And Manasseh said, "As you say, so were it proper to do, for if ten persons are charged with theft, and the stolen object is found with one of them, all are held responsible. But I will not be so hard. He with whom the cup is found shall be the bondman, and the rest shall be blameless."

He searched all the sacks, and in order not to excite the suspicion that he knew where the cup was, he began at Reuben, the eldest, and left off at Benjamin, the youngest, and the cup was found in Benjamin's sack. In a rage, his brethren shouted at Benjamin, "O thou thief and son of a thief! Thy mother brought shame upon our father by her thievery, and now thou bringest shame upon us." But he replied, "Is this matter as evil as the matter of the kid of the goats--as the deed of the brethren that sold their own brother into slavery?"

In their fury and vexation, the brethren rent their clothes. God paid them in their own coin. They had caused Jacob to tear his clothes in his grief over Joseph, and now they were made to do the same on account of their own troubles. And as they rent their clothes for the sake of their brother Benjamin, so Mordecai, the descendant of Benjamin, was destined to rend his on account of his brethren, the people of Israel. But because mortification was inflicted upon the brethren through Manasseh, the steward of Joseph, the allotment of territory given to the tribe of Manasseh was "torn" in two, one-half of the tribe had to live on one side of the Jordan, the other half on the other side. And Joseph, who had not shrunk from vexing his brethren so bitterly that they rent their clothes in their abasement, was punished, in that his descendant Joshua was driven to such despair after the defeat of Ai that he, too, rent his clothes.

Convicted of theft beyond the peradventure of a doubt, the brethren of Joseph had no choice but to comply with the steward's command and return to the city. They accompanied him without delay. Each of them loaded his ass himself, raising the burden with one hand from the ground to the back of the beast, and then they retraced their steps cityward, and as they walked, they rapped Benjamin roughly on the shoulder, saying, "O thou thief and son of a thief, thou hast brought the same shame upon us that thy mother brought upon our father." Benjamin bore the blows and the abusive words in patient silence, and he was rewarded for his humility. For submitting to the blows upon his shoulder, God appointed that His Shekinah should "dwell between his shoulders," and He also called him "the beloved of the Lord."

Joseph's brethren returned to the city without fear. Though it was a great metropolis, in their eyes it appeared but as a hamlet of ten persons, which they could wipe out with a turn of the hand. They were led into the presence of Joseph, who, contrary to his usual habit, was not holding a session of the court in the forum on that day. He remained at home, that his brethren might not be exposed to shame in public. They fell to the earth before him, and thus came true his dream of the eleven stars that made obeisance to him. But even while paying homage to Joseph, Judah was boiling inwardly with suppressed rage, and he said to his brethren, "Verily, this man hath forced me to come back hither only that I should destroy the city on this day."

Guarded by his valiant men on the right and on the left, Joseph addressed his brethren, snarling, "What deed is this that ye have done, to steal away my cup? I know well, ye took it in order to discover with its help the whereabouts of your brother that hath disappeared." Judah was spokesman, and he replied: "What shall we say unto my lord concerning the first money that he found in the mouth of our sacks? What shall we speak concerning the second money that also was in our sacks? And how shall we clear ourselves concerning the cup? We cannot acknowledge ourselves guilty, for we know ourselves to be innocent in all these matters. Yet we cannot avow ourselves innocent, because God hath found out the iniquity of thy servants, like a creditor that goes about and tries to collect a debt owing to him. Two brothers take care not to enter a house of mirth and festivity together, that they be not exposed to the evil eye, but we all were caught together in one place, by reason of the sin which we committed in company."

Joseph: "But if your punishment is for selling Joseph, why should this brother of yours suffer, the youngest, he that had no part in your crime.

Judah: "A thief and his companions are taken together."

Joseph: "If you could prevail upon yourselves to report to your father concerning a brother that had not stolen, and had brought no manner of shame upon you, that a wild beast had torn him, you will easily persuade yourselves to say it concerning a brother that hath stolen, and hath brought shame upon you. Go hence, and tell your father, 'The rope follows after the water bucket.' But," continued Joseph, shaking his purple mantle, "God forbid that I should accuse you all of theft. Only the youth that stole the cup in order to divine his brother's whereabouts shall remain with me as my bondman; but as for you, get you up in peace unto your father."

The holy spirit called out, "Great peace have they which love thy law!"

The brethren all consented to yield Benjamin to the ruler of Egypt, only Judah demurred, and he cried out, "Now it is all over with peace!" and he prepared to use force, if need be, to rescue Benjamin from slavery.

JUDAH PLEADS AND THREATENS.

Joseph dismissed his brethren, and carried Benjamin off by main force, and locked him up in a chamber. But Judah broke the door open and stood before Joseph with his brethren. He determined to use in turn the three means of liberating Benjamin at his disposal. He was prepared to convince Joseph by argument, or move him by entreaties, or resort to force, in order to accomplish his end.

He spake: "Thou doest a wrong unto us. Thou who didst say, 'I fear God,' thou showest thyself to be like unto Pharaoh, who hath no fear of God. The judgments which thou dost pronounce are not in accordance with our laws, nor are they in accordance with the laws of the nations. According to our law, a thief must pay double the value of what he hath stolen. Only, if he hath no money, he is sold into slavery, but if he hath the money, he maketh double restitution. And according to the law of the nations, the thief is deprived of all he owns. Do so, but let him go free. If a man buys a slave, and then discovers him to be a thief, the transaction is void. Yet thou desirest to make one a slave whom thou chargest with being a thief. I suspect thee of wanting to keep him in thy power for illicit purposes, and in this lustfulness thou resemblest Pharaoh. Also thou art like Pharaoh in that thou makest a promise and keepest it not. Thou saidst unto thy servants, Bring thy youngest brother down unto me, that I may set mine eyes upon him. Dost thou call this setting thine eyes upon him? If thou didst desire nothing beside a slave, then wouldst thou surely accept our offer to serve thee as bondmen instead of Benjamin. Reuben is older than he, and I exceed him in strength. It cannot but be as I say, thou hast a lustful purpose in mind with our brother.

"Therefore let these words of mine which I am about to speak find entrance into thy heart: For the sake of the grandmother of this lad were Pharaoh and his house stricken with sore plagues, because he detained her in his palace a single night against her will. His mother died a premature death, by reason of a curse which his father uttered in inconsiderate haste. Take heed, then, that this man's curse strike thee not and slay thee. Two of us destroyed the whole of a city on account of one woman, how much more would we do it for the sake of a man, and that man the beloved of the Lord, in whose allotment it is appointed that God shall dwell!

"If I but utter a sound, death-dealing pestilence will stalk through the land as far as No. In this land Pharaoh is the first, and thou art the second after him, but in our land my father is the first, and I am the second. If thou wilt not comply with our demand, I will draw my sword, and hew thee down first, and then Pharaoh."

When Judah gave utterance to this threat, Joseph made a sign, and Manasseh stamped his foot on the ground so that the whole palace shook. Judah said, "Only one belonging to our family can stamp thus!" and intimidated by this display of great strength, he moderated his tone and manner. "From the very beginning," he continued to speak, "thou didst resort to all sorts of pretexts in order to embarrass us. The inhabitants of many countries came down into Egypt to buy corn, but none of them didst thou ask questions about their family relations. In sooth, we did not come hither to seek thy daughter in marriage, or peradventure thou desirest an alliance with our sister? Nevertheless we gave thee an answer unto all thy questions."

Joseph replied: "Verily, thou canst talk glibly! Is there another babbler like thee among thy brethren? Why dost thou speak so much, while thy brethren that are older than thou, Reuben, Simon, and Levi, stand by silent?"

Judah: "None of my brethren has so much at stake as I have, if Benjamin returns not to his father. I was a surety to my father for him, saying, If I bring him not unto thee, and set him before thee, then let me bear the blame forever, in this world and in the world to come.

The other brethren withheld themselves intentionally from taking part in the dispute between Judah and Joseph, saying, "Kings are carrying on a dispute, and it is not seemly for us to interfere between them." Even the angels descended from heaven to earth to be spectators of the combat between Joseph the bull and Judah the lion, and they said, "It lies in the natural course of things that the bull should fear the lion, but here the two are engaged in equal, furious combat."

In reply to Judah, when he explained that his great interest in Benjamin's safety was due to the pledge he had given to his father, Joseph spoke: "Why wast thou not a surety for thy other brother, when ye sold him for twenty pieces of silver? Then thou didst not regard the sorrow thou wast inflicting upon thy father, but thou didst say, A wild beast hath devoured Joseph. And yet Joseph had done no evil, while this Benjamin has committed theft. Therefore, go up and say unto thy father, The rope hath followed after the water bucket."

These words had such an effect upon Judah that he broke out in sobs, and cried aloud, "How shall I go up to my father, and the lad be not with me?" His outcry reached to a distance of four hundred parasangs, and when Hushim the son of Dan heard it in Canaan, he jumped into Egypt with a single leap and joined his voice with Judah's, and the whole land was on the point of collapsing from the great noise they produced. Joseph's valiant men lost their teeth, and the cities of Pithom and Raamses were destroyed, and they remained in ruins until the Israelites built them up again under taskmasters. Also Judah's brethren, who had kept quiet up to that moment, fell into a rage, and stamped on the ground with their feet until it looked as though deep furrows had been torn in it by a ploughshare. And Judah addressed his brethren, "Be brave, demean yourselves as men, and let each one of you show his heroism, for the circumstances demand that we do our best."

Then they resolved to destroy Mizraim, the city of Egypt, and Judah said, "I will raise my voice, and with it destroy Egypt."

Reuben: "I will raise my arm, and crush it out of existence."

Simon: "I will raise my hand, and lay waste its palaces."

Levi: "I will draw my sword, and slay the inhabitants of Egypt."

Issachar: "I will make the land like unto Sodom."

Zebulon: "Like unto Gomorrah will I render it."

Dan: "I will reduce it to a desert."

Then Judah's towering rage began to show signs of breaking out: his right eye shed tears of blood; the hair above his heart grew so stiff that it pierced and rent the five garments in which he was clothed; and he took brass rods, bit them with his teeth, and spat them out as fine powder. When Joseph observed these signs, fear befell him, and in order to show that he, too, was a man of extraordinary strength, he pushed with his foot against the marble pedestal upon which he sat, and it broke into splinters. Judah exclaimed, "This one is a hero equal to myself!" Then he tried to draw his sword from its scabbard in order to slay Joseph, but the weapon could not be made to budge, and Judah was convinced thereby that his adversary was a God-fearing man, and he addressed himself to the task of begging him to let Benjamin go free, but he remained inexorable.

Judah then said: "What shall we say unto our father, when he seeth that our brother is not with us, and he will grieve over him?"

Joseph: "Say that the rope hath followed after the water bucket."

Judah: "Thou art a king, why dost thou speak in this wise, counselling a falsehood? Woe unto the king that is like thee!"

Joseph: "Is there a greater falsehood than that ye spake concerning your brother Joseph, whom you sold to the Midianites for twenty pieces of silver, telling your father, An evil beast bath devoured him?"

Judah: "The fire of Shechem burneth in my heart, now will I burn all thy land with fire."

Joseph: "Surely, the fire kindled to burn Tamar, thy daughter-in-law, who did kill thy sons, will extinguish the fire of Shechem."

Judah: "If I pluck out a single hair from my body, I will fill the whole of Egypt with its blood."

Joseph: "Such is it your custom to do; thus ye did unto your brother whom you sold, and then you dipped his coat in blood, brought it to your father, and said, An evil beast hath devoured him, and here is his blood."

When Judah heard this, he was exceedingly wroth, and he took a stone weighing four hundred shekels that was before him, cast it toward heaven with one hand, caught it with his left hand, then sat upon it, and the stone turned into dust. At the command of Joseph, Manasseh did likewise with another stone, and Joseph said to Judah: "Strength hath not been given to you alone, we also are powerful men. Why, then, will ye all boast before us?" Then Judah sent Naphtali forth, saying, "Go and count all the streets of the city of Egypt and come and tell me the number," but Simon interposed, saying, "Let not this thing trouble you, I will go to the mount, and take up one huge stone from the mount, throw it over the whole of Mizraim, the city of Egypt, and kill all therein."

Hearing all these words, which they spake aloud, because they did not know that he understood Hebrew, Joseph bade his son Manasseh make haste and gather together all the inhabitants of Egypt, and all the valiant men, and let them come to him on horseback and afoot. Meantime Naphtali had gone quickly to execute Judah's bidding, for he was as swift as the nimble hart, he could run across a field of corn without breaking an ear. And he returned and reported that the city of Egypt was divided into twelve quarters. Judah bade his brethren destroy the city; he himself undertook to raze three quarters, and he assigned the nine remaining quarters to the others, one quarter to each.

In the meantime Manasseh had assembled a great army, five hundred mounted men and ten thousand on foot, among them four hundred valiant heroes, who could fight without spear or sword, using only their strong, unarmed hands. To inspire his brethren with more terror, Joseph ordered them to make a loud noise with all sorts of instruments, and their appearance and the hubbub they produced did, indeed, cause fear to fall upon some of the brethren of Joseph. Judah, however, called to them, "Why are you terrified, seeing that God grants us His mercy?" He drew his sword, and uttered a wild cry, which threw all the people into consternation, and in their disordered flight many fell over each other and perished, and Judah and his brethren followed after the fleeing people as far as the house of Pharaoh. Returning to Joseph, Judah again broke out in loud roars, and the reverberations caused by his cries were so mighty that all the city walls in

Egypt and in Goshen fell in ruins, the pregnant women brought forth untimely births, and Pharaoh was flung from his throne. Judah's cries were heard at a great distance, as far off as Succoth.

When Pharaoh learnt the reason of the mighty uproar, he sent word to Joseph that he would have to concede the demands of the Hebrews, else the land would suffer destruction. "Thou canst take thy choice," were the words of Pharaoh, "between me and the Hebrews, between Egypt and the land of the Hebrews. If thou wilt not heed my command, then leave me and go with them into their land."

JOSEPH MAKES HIMSELF KNOWN

Seeing that his brethren were, indeed, on the point of destroying Egypt, Joseph resolved to make himself known to them, and he cast around for a proper opening, which would lead naturally to his announcement. At his behest, Manasseh laid his hand upon Judah's shoulder, and his touch allayed Judah's fury, for he noticed that he was in contact with a kinsman of his, because such strength existed in no other family. Then Joseph addressed Judah gently, saying: "I should like to know who advised him to steal the cup. Could it have been one of you?" Benjamin replied: "Neither did they counsel theft, nor did I touch the cup." "Take an oath upon it," demanded Joseph, and Benjamin complied with his brother's request: "I swear that I did not touch the cup! As true as my brother Joseph is separated from me; as true as I had nothing to do with the darts that my brethren threw at him; as true as I was not one of those to take off his coat; as true as I had no part in the transaction by which he was given over to the Ishmaelites; as true as I did not help the others dip his coat in blood; so true is my oath, that they did not counsel theft, and that I did not commit theft."

Joseph: "How can I know that this oath of thine taken upon thy brother's fate is true?"

Benjamin: "From the names of my ten sons, which I gave them in memory of my brother's life and trials, thou canst see how dearly I loved him. I pray thee, therefore, do not bring down my father with sorrow to the grave."

Hearing these words of abiding love, Joseph could refrain himself no longer. He could not but make himself known unto his brethren. He spake these words to them: "Ye said the brother of this lad was dead. Did you yourselves see him dead before you?" They answered, "Yes!"

Joseph: "Did you stand beside his grave?"

The brethren: "Yes!"

Joseph: "Did you throw clods of earth upon his corpse?"

The brethren: "No."

Then Joseph reflected, saying to himself: "My brethren are as pious as aforetime, and they speak no lies. They said I was dead, because when they abandoned me, I was poor, and 'a poor man is like unto a dead man;' they stood beside my grave, that is the pit into which they cast me; but they did not say that they had shovelled earth upon me, for that would have been a falsehood."

Turning to his brethren, he said: "Ye lie when ye say that your brother is dead. He is not dead. You sold him, and I did buy him. I shall call him, and set him before your eyes," and he began to call, "Joseph, son of Jacob, come hither! Joseph, son of Jacob, come hither! Speak to thy brethren who did sell thee." The others turned their eyes hither and thither, to the four corners of the house, until Joseph called to them: "Why look ye here and there? Behold, I am Joseph your brother! "Their souls fled away from them, and they could make no answer, but God permitted a miracle to happen, and their souls came back to them.

Joseph continued, "Ye see it with your own eyes, and also my brother Benjamin seeth it with his eyes, that I speak with you in Hebrew, and I am truly your brother." But they would not believe him. Not only had he been transformed from a smooth-faced youth into a bearded man since they had abandoned him, but also the forsaken youth now stood before them the ruler of Egypt. Therefore Joseph bared his body and showed them that he belonged to the descendants of Abraham.

Abashed they stood there, and in their rage they desired to slay Joseph as the author of their shame and their suffering. But an angel appeared and flung them to the four corners of the house. Judah raised so loud an outcry that the walls of the city of Egypt tumbled down, the women brought forth untimely births, Joseph and Pharaoh both rolled down off their thrones, and Joseph's three hundred heroes lost their teeth, and their heads remained forever immobile, facing backward, as they had turned them to discover the cause of the tumult. Yet the brethren did not venture to approach close to Joseph, they were too greatly ashamed of their behavior toward their brother. He sought to calm them, saying, "Now be not grieved, nor angry with yourselves, that ye sold me hither, for God did send me before you to preserve life."

Even such kind words of exhortation did not banish their fear, and Joseph continued to speak, "As little as I harbor vengeful thoughts in my heart against Benjamin, so little do I harbor them against you."And still his brethren were ill at case, and Joseph went on, "Think you that it is possible for me to inflict harm upon you? If the smoke of ten candles could not extinguish one, how can one extinguish ten?"

At last the brethren were soothed, and they went up to Joseph, who knew each by name, and, weeping, he embraced and kissed them all in turn. The reason why he wept was that his prophetic spirit showed him the descendants of his brethren enslaved by the nations. Especially did he weep upon Benjamin's neck, because he foresaw the destruction decreed for the two Temples to be situated in the allotment of Benjamin. And Benjamin also wept upon Joseph's neck, for the sanctuary at Shiloh, in the territory of Joseph which was likewise doomed to destruction.

Pharaoh was well pleased with the report of the reconciliation between Joseph and the Hebrews, for he had feared that their dissensions might cause the ruin of Egypt, and he sent his servants to Joseph, that they take part in his joy. Also he sent word to Joseph that it would please him well if his brethren took up their abode in Egypt, and he promised to assign the best parts of the land to them for their dwelling-place.

Not all the servants of Pharaoh were in agreement with their master concerning this invitation to the Hebrews. Many among them were disquieted, saying, "If one of the sons of Jacob came hither, and he was advanced to a high position over our heads, what evil will happen to us when ten more come hither?"

Joseph gave all his brethren two changes of raiment, one for use on the ordinary days of the week and one for use on the Sabbath, for, when the cup was found with Benjamin, they had rent their clothes, and Joseph would not have his brethren go about in torn garments. But to Benjamin he gave five changes of raiment, though not in order to distinguish him above his brethren. Joseph remembered only too well what mischief his father had caused by giving him the coat of many colors, thereby arousing the envy of his brethren. He desired only to intimate that Mordecai, a descendant of Benjamin, would once be arrayed in five royal garments.

Joseph presented his brethren, apparelled in their gold and silver embroidered clothes, before Pharaoh, who was well pleased to become acquainted with them when he saw that they were men of heroic stature and handsome appearance. He gave them wagons, to bring their families down into Egypt, but as they were ornamented with images of idols, Judah burnt them, and Joseph replaced them with eleven other wagons, among them the one he had ridden in at his accession to office, to view the land of Egypt. This was to be used by his father on his journey to Egypt. For each of his brothers' children, he sent raiments, and also one hundred pieces of silver for each, but for each of the children of Benjamin he sent ten changes of raiment. And for the wives of his brethren he gave them rich garments of state, such as were worn by the wives of the Pharaohs, and also ointments and aromatic spices. To his sister Dinah he sent silver and gold embroidered clothes, and myrrh, aloes, and other perfumes, and such presents he gave also to the wife and the daughters-in-law of Benjamin. For themselves and for their wives the brethren received all sorts of precious stones and jewelled ornaments, like those that are worn by the Egyptian nobility.

Joseph accompanied his eleven brethren to the frontier, and there he took leave of them with the wish that they and all their families come down to Egypt, and he enjoined upon them, besides, three maxims to be observed by travellers: Do not take too large steps; do not discuss Halakic subjects, that you lose not your way; and enter the city at the latest with the going down of the sun.

JACOB RECEIVES THE GLAD TIDINGS

In blithe spirits the sons of Jacob journeyed up to the land of Canaan, but when they reached the boundary line, they said to one another, "How shall we do? If we appear before our father and tell him that Joseph is alive, he will be greatly frightened, and he will not be inclined to believe us." Besides, Joseph's last injunction to them had been to take heed and not startle their father with the tidings of joy.

On coming close to their habitation, they caught sight of Serah, the daughter of Asher, a very beautiful maiden, and very wise, who was skilled in playing upon the harp. They summoned her unto them and gave her a harp, and bade her play before Jacob and sing that which they should tell her. She sat down before Jacob, and, with an agreeable melody, she sang the following words, accompanying herself upon the harp: "Joseph, my uncle, liveth, he ruleth over the whole of Egypt, he is not dead!" She repeated these words several times, and Jacob grew more and more pleasurably excited. His joy awakened the holy spirit in him, and he knew that she spoke the truth. The spirit of prophecy never visits a seer when he is in a state of lassitude or in a state of grief; it comes only together with joy. All the years of Joseph's separation from him Jacob had had no prophetic visions, because he was always sad, and only when Serah's words reawakened the feeling of happiness in his heart, the prophetic spirit again took possession of him. Jacob rewarded her therefor with the words, "My daughter, may death never have power over thee, for thou didst revive my spirit." And so it was. Serah did not die, she entered Paradise alive. At his bidding, she repeated the words she had sung again and again, and they gave Jacob great joy and delight, so that the holy spirit waxed stronger and stronger within him.

While he was sitting thus in converse with Serah, his sons appeared arrayed in all their magnificence, and with all the presents that Joseph had given them, and they spake to Jacob, saying: "Glad tidings! Joseph our brother liveth! He is ruler over the whole land of Egypt, and he sends thee a message of joy." At first Jacob would not believe them, but when they opened their packs, and showed him the presents Joseph had sent to all, he could not doubt the truth of their words any longer.

Joseph had had a premonition that his father would refuse to give his brethren credence, because they had tried to deceive him before, and "it is the punishment of the liar that his words are not believed even when he speaks the truth." He had therefore said to them, "If my father will not believe your words, tell him that when I took leave of him, to see whether it was well with you, he had been teaching me the law of the heifer whose neck is broken in the valley." When they repeated this, every last vestige of Jacob's doubt disappeared, and he said: "Great is the steadfastness of my son Joseph. In spite of all his sufferings he has remained constant in his piety. Yea, great are the benefits that the Lord hath conferred upon me. He saved me from the hands of Esau, and from the hands of Laban, and from the Canaanites who pursued after me. I have tasted many joys, and I hope to see more, but never did I hope to set eyes upon Joseph again, and now I shall go down to him and behold him before my death."

Then Jacob and the members of his family put on the clothes Joseph had sent, among them a turban for Jacob, and they made all preparations to journey down into Egypt and dwell there with Joseph and his family. Hearing of his good fortune, the kings and the grandees of Canaan came to wait upon Jacob and express sympathy with him in his joy, and he prepared a three days' banquet for them.

Jacob, however, would not go down into Egypt without first inquiring whether it was the will of God that he should leave the Holy Land. He said, "How can I leave the land of my fathers, the land of my birth, the land in which the Shekinah dwells, and go into an unclean land, inhabited by slaves of the sons of Ham, a land wherein there is no fear of God?" Then he brought sacrifices in honor of God, in the expectation that a Divine vision would descend upon him and instruct him whether to go down into Egypt or have Joseph come up to Canaan. He feared the sojourn in Egypt, for he remembered the vision he had had at Beth-el on leaving his father's house, and he said to God: "I resemble my father. As he was greedy in filling his maw, so am I, and therefore I would go down into Egypt in consequence of the famine. As my father preferred one son to the other, so had I a favorite son, and therefore I would go down into Egypt to see Joseph. But in this I do not resemble my father, he had only himself to provide for, and my house consists of seventy souls, and therefore am I compelled to go down into Egypt. The blessing which my father gave me was not fulfilled in me, but in my son Joseph, whom peoples serve, and before whom nations bow down."

Then the Shekinah addressed Jacob, calling his name twice in token of love, and bidding him not to fear the Egyptian slavery foretold for the descendants of Abraham, for God would have pity upon the suffering of his children and deliver them from bondage. God furthermore said, "I will go down into Egypt with thee," and the Shekinah accompanied Jacob thither, bringing the number of the company with which he entered Egypt up to seventy. But as Jacob entertained fears that his descendants would stay there forever, God gave him the assurance that He would lead him forth together with all the pious that were like unto him. And God also told Jacob that Joseph had remained steadfast in his piety even in Egypt, and he might dismiss all doubts from his mind on this score, for it was his anxiety on this account that had induced Jacob to consider going down into Egypt; he wanted only to make sure of Joseph's faithfulness, and then return home, but God commanded him to go thither and remain there.

Before Jacob left Canaan, he went to Beer-sheba, to hew down the cedars that Abraham had planted there, and take them with him to Egypt. For centuries these cedar trees remained in the possession of his descendants; they carried them with them when they left Egypt, and they used them in building the Tabernacle.

Although Joseph had put wagons at the disposal of his brethren for the removal of his family from Canaan to Egypt, they yet carried Jacob upon their arms, for which purpose they divided themselves into three divisions, one division after the other assuming the burden. As a reward for their filial devotion, God redeemed their descendants from Egypt.

Judah was sent on ahead by his father, to erect a dwelling in Goshen, and also a Bet ha-Midrash, that Jacob might set about instructing his sons at once after his arrival. He charged Judah with this honorable task in order to compensate him for a wrong he had done him. All the years of Joseph's absence he had suspected Judah of having made away with Rachel's son. How little the suspicion was justified he realized now when Judah in particular had been assiduous in securing the safety of Benjamin, the other son of Rachel. Jacob therefore said to Judah: "Thou hast done a pious, God-bidden deed, and hast shown thyself to be a man capable of carrying on negotiations with Joseph. Complete the work thou hast begun! Go to Goshen, and together with Joseph prepare all things for our coming. Indeed," continued Jacob, "thou wast the cause of our going down into Egypt, for it was at thy suggestion that Joseph was sold as a slave, and, also, through thy descendants Israel will be led forth out of Egypt."

When Joseph was informed of the approach of his father, he rejoiced exceedingly, chiefly because his coming would stop the talk of the Egyptians, who were constantly referring to him as the slave that had dominion over them. "Now," thought Joseph, "they will see my father and my brethren, and they will be convinced that I am a free-born man, of noble stock."

In his joy in anticipation of seeing his father, Joseph made ready his chariot with his own hands, without waiting for his servants to minister to him, and this loving action redounded later to the benefit of the Israelites, for it rendered of none effect Pharaoh's zeal in making ready his chariot himself, with his own hands, to pursue after the Israelites.

JACOB ARRIVES IN EGYPT

When the Egyptian nobles observed their viceroy completing his preparations to meet his father, they did the same. Indeed, Joseph had issued a proclamation throughout the land, threatening with death all that did not go forth to meet Jacob. The procession that accompanied him was composed of countless men, arrayed in byssus and purple, and marching to the sound of all sorts of musical instruments. Even the women of Egypt had a part in the reception ceremonies. They ascended to the roofs of the houses and the walls of the cities, ready to greet Jacob with the music of cymbals and timbrels.

Joseph wore the royal crown upon his head, Pharaoh had yielded it to him for the occasion. He descended from his chariot when he was at a distance of about fifty ells from his father, and walked the rest of the way on foot, and his example was followed by the princes and nobles of Egypt. When Jacob caught sight of the approaching procession, he was rejoiced, and even before he recognized Joseph, he bowed down before him, but for permitting his father to show him this mark of honor, punishment was visited upon Joseph. He died an untimely death, before the years of life assigned to him had elapsed.

That no harm befall Jacob from a too sudden meeting with him, Joseph sent his oldest son ahead with five horses, the second son following close after him in the same way. As each son approached, Jacob thought he beheld Joseph, and so he was prepared gradually to see him face to face.

Meantime Jacob had espied, from where he was seated, a man in royal robes among the Egyptians, a crown upon his head, and a purple mantle over his shoulders, and he asked Judah who it might be. When he was told that it was Joseph, his joy was great over the high dignity attained by his son.

By this time Joseph had come close to his father, and he bowed himself before him down to the earth, and all the people with him likewise prostrated themselves. Then Joseph fell upon his father's neck, and he wept bitterly. He was particularly grieved that he had permitted his father to bow down before him but a little while before without hindering it. At the very moment when Joseph embraced his father, Jacob was reciting the Shema', and he did not allow himself to be interrupted in his prayer, but then he said, "When they brought me the report of the death of Joseph, I thought I was doomed to double death--that I should lose this world and the world to come as well. The Lord had promised to make me the ancestor of twelve tribes, and as the death of my son rendered it impossible that this promise should be realized, I feared I had incurred the doom by my own sins, and as a sinner I could not but expect to forfeit the future world, too. But now that I have beheld thee alive, I know that my death will be only for the world here below."

Such was the manner of Jacob's arrival in Egypt. He came with his whole family, sixty-nine persons they were in all, but the number was raised to seventy by the birth of Jochebed, afterward the mother of Moses, which took place when the cavalcade had advanced to the space between the one and the other city wall. All the males in his family were married men; even Pallu and Hezron, the latter of whom was but one year old at the time of their migration, and the former but two years, had the wives with them that had been chosen for them by their parents. In general, all the sons and grandsons of Jacob had married young, some of them had been fathers at the age of seven.

Joseph took some from among his brethren, and presented them to Pharaoh. He chose the weakest of them, that the king might not be tempted to retain them in his service as warriors. And as he did not desire his family to live at close quarters with the Egyptians and perhaps amalgamate with them, he introduced them as shepherds. The Egyptians worshipped the constellation of the rain, and paid divine honors to animals, and they kept aloof from shepherds. Pharaoh therefore was inclined to grant Joseph's wish, to give them the pasture land of Goshen for their sojourning place, the land that was theirs by right, for the Pharaoh that took Sarah away from Abraham by force had given it to her as her irrevocable possession.

In their conversation with Pharaoh the brethren of Joseph made it plain to the Egyptian king that it was not their intention to remain in Egypt forever, it was to be only a temporary dwelling-place.

Then Joseph set Jacob his father before Pharaoh, and when the king saw him, he said to Og, who happened to be with him at that moment, "Seest thou! Thou wast wont to call Abraham a sterile mule, and here is his grandson with a family of seventy persons!" Og would not believe his own eyes, he thought Abraham was standing before him, so close was the resemblance between Jacob and his progenitor. Then Pharaoh asked about Jacob's age, to find out whether he actually was Jacob, and not Abraham. And Jacob said unto Pharaoh, "The days of the years of my pilgrimage are an hundred and thirty years," using the word pilgrimage in reference to life on earth, which the pious regard as a temporary sojourn in alien lands. "Few and evil," he continued, "have been the days of the years of my life. In my youth I had to flee to a strange land on account of my brother Esau, and now, in my old age, I must again go to a strange land, and my days have not attained unto the days of the years of the life of my fathers in the days of their pilgrimage." These words sufficed to convince Pharaoh and Og that the man standing before them was not Abraham, but his grandson.

When Jacob uttered the words, "The days of the years of my pilgrimage have been few and evil," God said to him: "Jacob, I saved thee out of the hands of Esau and Laban, I restored Joseph unto thee, and made him to be a king and a ruler, and yet thou speakest of few and evil days. Because of thy ingratitude, thou wilt not attain unto the days of the years of the life of thy fathers," and Jacob died at an age thirty-three years less than his father Isaac's.

On going out from the presence of Pharaoh, Jacob blessed the king with the words, "May the years still in store for me be given unto thee, and may the Nile overflow its banks henceforth again and water the land." His words were fulfilled. In order to show that the pious are a blessing for the world, God caused the Nile to rise above its bed and fructify the land of Egypt.

JOSEPH'S KINDNESS AND GENEROSITY

Jacob and his family now settled in the land of Goshen, and Joseph provided them with all things needful, not only with food and drink, but also with clothing, and in his love and kindness he entertained his father and his brethren daily at his own table. He banished the wrong done to him by his brethren from his mind, and he besought his father to pray to God for them, that He should forgive their great transgression. Touched by this noble sign of love, Jacob cried out, "O Joseph, my child, thou hast conquered the heart of thy father Jacob."

Joseph had other virtues, besides. The title "the God-fearing one," borne only by him, Abraham, Job, and Obadiah, he gained by reason of his kindness of heart and his generosity. Whatever he gave his brethren, he gave with a "good eye," a liberal spirit. If it was bread for food, it was sure to be abundant enough, not only to satisfy the hunger of all, but also for the children to crumble, as is their habit.

But Joseph was more than a helper to his family. As a shepherd pastures his flock, so he provided for the whole world during the years of famine. The people cursed Pharaoh, who kept the stores of corn in his treasure chambers for his own use, and they blessed Joseph, who took thought for the famishing, and sold grain to all that came. The wealth which he acquired by these sales was lawful gain, for the prices were raised, not by him, but by the Egyptians themselves. One part of his possessions, consisting of gold and silver and precious stones, Joseph buried in four different places, in the desert near the Red Sea, on the banks of the Euphrates, and in two spots in the desert in the vicinity of Persia and Media. Korah discovered one of the hiding-places, and the Roman emperor Antoninus, the son of Severus, another. The other two will never be found, because God has reserved the riches they hold for the pious, to be enjoyed by them in the latter days, the days of the Messiah. The remainder of Joseph's possessions he gave away, partly to his brethren and their families, and partly to Pharaoh, who put them into his treasury.

The wealth of the whole world flowed into Egypt at that time, and it remained there until the exodus of the Israelites. They took it along, leaving Egypt like a net without fish. The Israelites kept the treasure until the time of Rehoboam, who was deprived of it by the Egyptian king Shishak, and he in turn had to yield it to Zerah, the king of Ethiopia. Once more it came into possession of the Jews when King Asa conquered Zerah, but this time they held it for only a short while, for Asa surrendered it to the Aramean king Ben-hadad, to induce him to break his league with Baasha, the king of the Ten Tribes. The Ammonites, in turn, captured it from Ben-hadad, only to lose it in their war with the Jews under Jehoshaphat. Again it remained with the Jews, until the time of King Ahaz, who sent it to Sennacherib as tribute money. Hezekiah won it back, but Zedekiah, the last king of the Jews, lost it to the Chaldeans, from whom it came to Persia, thence to the Greeks, and finally to the Romans, and with the last it remained for all time.

The people were soon left without means to purchase the corn they needed. In a short time they had to part with their cattle, and when the money thus secured was spent, they sold their land to Joseph, and even their persons. Many of them would cover themselves with clay and appear before Joseph, and say to him, "O lord king, see me and see my possessions!" And so Joseph bought all the land of Egypt, and the inhabitants became his tenants, and they gave a fifth of their ingatherings unto joseph.

The only class of the people permitted to remain in possession of their land were the priests. Joseph owed them gratitude, for they had made it possible for him to become the ruler over Egypt. The Egyptians had hesitated to make him their viceroy, because they shrank from choosing a man accused of adultery for so high an office. It was the priests that made the suggestion to examine Joseph's torn garment, which his mistress had submitted as evidence of his guilt, and see whether the rent was in front or in back. If it was in back, it would show his innocence--he had turned to flee, and his temptress had clutched him so that the garment tore. But if the tear was in front, then it would be a proof of his guilt--he had used violence with the woman, and she had torn the mantle in her efforts to defend her honor. The angel Gabriel came and transferred the rent from the fore part to the back, and the Egyptians were convinced of Joseph's innocence, and their scruples about raising him to the kingship were removed.

As soon as the Egyptians learnt of the advantageous position of the priests, they all tried to prove themselves members of the caste. But Joseph investigated the lists in the archives, and determined the estate of every citizen.

The priests were favored in another way. Beside remaining in possession of their land, they received daily portions from Pharaoh, wherefore God said, "The priests that serve idols receive all they need every day, how much more do the sons of Abraham, Isaac, and Jacob, who are My priests, deserve that I should give them what they need every day."

The rest of the inhabitants of Egypt, who had to part with their land, were not permitted to remain in their native provinces. Joseph removed them from their own cities, and settled them in others. His purpose herein was to prevent the Egyptians from speaking of his brethren derogatorily as "exiles the sons of exiles"; he made them all equally aliens. For the same reason, God later, at the time of the going forth of the Israelites from Egypt, caused all nations to change their dwelling-places about, so that the Israelites could not be reproached with having had to leave their home. And, finally, when Sermacherib carried the Jews away from their land into exile, it also happened that this king first mixed up the inhabitants of all the countries of the world.

JACOB'S LAST WISH

In return for the seventeen years that Jacob had devoted to the bringing up of Joseph, he was granted seventeen years of sojourn with his favorite son in peace and happiness. The wicked experience sorrow after joy; the pious must suffer first, and then they are happy, for all's well that ends well, and God permits the pious to spend the last years of their lives in felicity.

When Jacob felt his end approach, he summoned Joseph to his bedside, and he told him all there was in his heart. He called for Joseph rather than one of his other sons, because he was the only one in a position to execute his wishes.

Jacob said to Joseph: "If I have found grace in thy sight, bury me not, I pray thee, in Egypt. Only for thy sake did I come down into Egypt, and for thy sake I spoke, Now I can die. Do this for me as a true service of love, and not because thou art afraid, or because decency demands it. And when I sleep with my fathers, thou shalt bury me in their burying-place. Carry me out of the land of idolatry, and bury me in the land where God hath caused His Name to dwell, and put me to rest in the place in which four husbands and wives are to be buried, I the last of them."

Jacob desired not to be buried in Egypt for several reasons. He knew that the soil of Egypt would once swarm with vermin, and it revolted him to think of his corpse exposed to such uncleanness. He feared, moreover, that his descendants might say, "Were Egypt not a holy land, our father Jacob had never permitted himself to be buried there," and they might encourage themselves with this argument to make choice of Egypt as a permanent dwelling-place. Also, if his grave were there, the Egyptians might resort to it when the ten plagues came upon them, and if he were induced to pray for them to God, he would be advocating the cause of the Lord's enemies. If, on the other hand, he did not intercede for them, the Name of God would be profaned among the heathen, who would say, "Jacob is a useless saint!" Besides, it was possible that God might consider him, the "scattered sheep" of Israel, as a sacrifice for the Egyptians, and remit their punishment. From his knowledge of the people, another fear was justified, that his grave would become an object of idolatrous veneration, and the same punishment is appointed by God for the idols worshipped as for the idolaters that worship them.

If Jacob had good reasons for not wanting his body to rest in the soil of Egypt, he had equally good reasons for wanting it to rest in the Holy Land. In the Messianic time, when the dead will rise, those buried in Palestine will awaken to new life without delay, while those buried elsewhere will first have to roll from land to land through the earth, hollowed out for the purpose, until they reach the Holy Land, and only then will their resurrection take place. But over and beyond this, Jacob had an especial reason for desiring to have his body interred in Palestine. God had said to him at Beth-el, "The land whereon thou liest, to thee will I give it, and to thy seed," and hence he made every endeavor to "lie" in the Holy Land, to make sure it would belong to him and his descendants. Nevertheless he bade Joseph strew some Egyptian earth over his dead body.

Jacob expressed these his last wishes three times. Such is the requirement of good breeding in preferring a request.

In the last period of Jacob's life, one can see how true it is that "even a king depends upon favors in a strange land." Jacob, the man for the sake of whose merits the whole world was created, for the sake of whom Abraham was delivered from the fiery furnace, had to ask services of others while he was among strangers, and when Joseph promised to do his bidding, he bowed himself before his own son, for it is a true saying, "Bow before the fox in his day," the day of his power.

He was not satisfied with a simple promise from Joseph, that he would do his wish; he insisted upon his taking an oath by the sign of the covenant of Abraham, putting a hand under his thigh in accordance with the ceremony customary among the Patriarchs! But Joseph said: "Thou treatest me like a slave. With me thou hast no need to require an oath. Thy command sufficeth." Jacob, however, urged him, saying: "I fear Pharaoh may command thee to bury me in the sepulchre with the kings of Egypt. I insist that thou takest an oath, and then I will be at peace." Joseph gave in, though he would not submit to the ceremony that Eliezer had used to confirm the oath he took at the request of his master Abraham. The slave acted in accordance with the rules of slavery, the free man acted in accordance with the dictates of freedom. And in a son that thing would have been unseemly which was becoming in a slave.

When Joseph swore to bury his father in Palestine, he added the words, "As thou commandest me to do, so also will I beg my brethren, on my death-bed, to fulfil my last wish and carry my body from Egypt to Palestine."

Jacob, noticing the Shekinah over the bed's head, where she always rests in a sick room, bowed himself upon the bed's head, saying, "I thank thee, O Lord my God, that none who is unfit came forth from my bed, but my bed was perfect." He was particularly grateful for the revelation God had vouchsafed him concerning his first-born son Reuben, that he had repented of his trespass against his father, and atoned for it by penance. He was thus assured that all his sons were men worthy of being the progenitors of the twelve tribes, and he was blessed with happiness such as neither Abraham nor Isaac had known, for both of them had had unworthy as well as worthy sons.

Until the time of Jacob death had always come upon men suddenly, and snatched them away before they were warned of the imminent end by sickness. Once Jacob spoke to God, saying, "O Lord of the world, a man dies suddenly, and he is not laid low first by sickness, and he cannot acquaint his children with his wishes regarding all he leaves behind. But if a man first fell sick, and felt that his end were drawing nigh, he would have time to set his house in order." And God said, "Verily, thy request is sensible, and thou shalt be the first to profit by the new dispensation," and so it happened that Jacob fell sick a little while before his death.

His sickness troubled him grievously, for he had undergone much during his life. He had worked day and night while he was with Laban, and his conflicts with the angel and with Esau, though he came off victor from both, had weakened him, and he was not in a condition to endure the hardships of disease.

THE BLESSING OF EPHRAIM AND MANASSEH

All the years of Jacob's sojourn in Egypt, Asenath, the wife of Joseph, was his constant nurse. When she saw his end drawing nigh, she spoke to Joseph: "I have heard that one who is blessed by a righteous man is as though he had been blessed by the Shekinah. Therefore, bring thy sons hither, that Jacob give them his blessing."

Though Joseph was a devoted and loving son to his father, he was not in constant attendance upon him, because he wanted to avoid giving him the opportunity of inquiring into the circumstances of his coming to Egypt. He was apprehensive that Jacob might curse his sons and bring death upon them, if he discovered the facts connected with their treacherous dealings with Joseph. He took good care therefore never to be alone with his father. But as he desired to be kept informed of his welfare, he arranged a courier service between himself and Jacob.

Now when Joseph received the news of his father's having fallen sick, through his messenger, as well as through Ephraim, whom Jacob was instructing in the Torah, he hastened to the land of Goshen, taking his two sons with him. He desired to have certainty upon five points: Would his father bless his two sons, who were born in Egypt, and, if so, would he appoint them to be heads of tribes? Would he assign the rights of the first-born unto himself, and, if so, would he divest Reuben of such rights altogether? And why had his father buried his mother Rachel by the wayside, and not carried her body to the family tomb at Machpelah?

Jacob had also entertained doubts on five points, when he was about to emigrate from Canaan to Egypt: He did not know whether his descendants would lose themselves among the people of Egypt; whether he would die there and be buried there; and whether he would be permitted to see Joseph and see the sons of Joseph. God gave him the assurance, saying, "I will go down with thee into Egypt, and I will surely bring thee up again after thy death, and thy descendants also, and Joseph shall put his hand upon thine eyes." When the time approached for the fulfilment of the Divine promise, God appeared unto Jacob, and He said, "I promised to fulfil thy wish, and the time of fulfilment hath come."

The holy spirit made known to Jacob that Joseph was coming to him, and he strengthened himself, and sat upon the bed in order to pay due respect to the representative of the government. Though Joseph was his son, he was also viceroy, and entitled to special marks of honor. Besides, Jacob desired to make the impression of being a man in good health. He wanted to avoid the possibility of having his blessing of Joseph and Joseph's sons questioned as the act of an irresponsible person.

He strengthened himself spiritually as well as physically, by prayer to God, in which he besought Him to let the holy spirit descend upon him at the time of his giving the blessing to the sons of Joseph.

When Joseph appeared in the company of his two sons, his father said to him: "In all the seventeen years thou hast been visiting me, thou didst never bring thy sons with thee, but now they have come, and I know the reason. If I bless them, I shall act in opposition to the word of God, who promised to make me the progenitor of twelve tribes, for if I adopt them as my sons, there will be fourteen tribes. But if I do not bless them, it will plunge thee in sorrow. So be it, I will bless them. But think not I do it because thou didst support me all these years. There is quite another reason. When I left my father's house to go to Haran, I offered up a prayer at Beth-el, and I promised to give unto God the tenth of all I owned. So far as my material possessions are concerned, I kept my vow, but I could not give the tithe of my sons, because according to the law I had to withdraw from the reckoning the four sons, Reuben, Joseph, Dan, and Gad, that are the first-born children of their mothers. When I returned, God again appeared unto me in Beth-el, and He said, Be fruitful and multiply. But after this blessing no son was born unto me except Benjamin alone, and it cannot be but that God meant Manasseh and Ephraim when He spoke of 'a nation and a company of nations.' If now I have found favor in thy sight, thy two sons Ephraim and Manasseh, even as Reuben and Simon, shall be mine, and then I shall be able to give a tenth part of my ten sons unto the Lord, and I shall leave this world free from the sin of not keeping my vow to the Lord concerning the tithe-giving."

Joseph consented to do his father's will, and Jacob tithed his sons, consecrating Levi to the Holy One, and appointing him to be the chief of his brethren. He enjoined his sons to have a care that there should never fail them a son of Levi in the priestly succession. And it happened that. of all the tribes Levi was the only one that never proved faithless to the covenant of the fathers.

Thus Jacob adopted Manasseh and Ephraim to be his own sons, even as Reuben and Simon were his sons. They were entitled like the others to a portion in the Holy Land, and like the others they were to bear standards on their journey through the desert.

Satisfied as to Jacob's intentions concerning his sons, Joseph asked his father about his mother's burial-place, and Jacob spoke, saying: "As thou livest, thy wish to see thy mother lying by my side in the grave doth not exceed mine own. I had joy in life only as long as she was alive, and her death was the heaviest blow that ever fell upon me." Joseph questioned him: "Perhaps thou didst have to bury her in the way, because she died during the rainy season, and thou couldst not carry her body through the rain to our family sepulchre?" "No," replied Jacob, "she died in the spring time, when the highways are clean and firm." Joseph: "Grant me permission to take up her body now and place it in our family burial-place." Jacob: "No, my son, that thou mayest not do. I was unwilling to bury her in the way, but the Lord commanded it." The reason of the command was that God knew that the Temple would be destroyed, and Israel would be carried away into banishment, and the exiles would ask the Patriarchs to intercede for them with God, but God would not hearken unto them. On their way to the land of the stranger they would pass the grave of Rachel, and they would throw themselves upon it, and beseech their mother to make intercession for them with God. And Rachel would pray to God in their behalf: "O Lord of the world, look upon my tears, and have compassion upon my children. But if Thou wilt not take pity on them, then indemnify me for the wrong done to me." Unto her prayer God will hearken, and He will have mercy upon Israel. Therefore was Rachel buried in the way.

Now Jacob desired to bless the sons of Joseph, but the holy spirit made him to see Jeroboam, the descendant of Ephraim, and Jehu, the descendant of Manasseh, how they would seduce Israel to idolatry, and the Shekinah forsook him as he was about to lay his hands upon the heads of his grandsons. He said to Joseph, "Is it possible that thou didst not marry the mother of thy children according to the law?" Joseph thereupon brought his wife Asenath to his father, and pointing to her marriage contract, he said, "This one is my wife, whom I married as is proper, with a marriage contract and due ceremony. I pray thee, my father, bless my sons if only for the sake of this pious woman."

Jacob bade his grandsons approach close to him, and he kissed and embraced them, in the hope that his joy in them would lure back the holy spirit, but his hope was vain. Joseph concluded that the time was not favorable for blessing, and he decided to go away until a more propitious opportunity presented itself, first, however, proving to his father that his sons had been initiated in the covenant of Abraham.

Outside of his father's chamber, alone with his sons, he threw himself down before God and besought Him to show him mercy, and he bade his sons do likewise, saying, "Be not content with your high station, for worldly honors are but for a time. Entreat God to be merciful and let the Shekinah descend upon my father, that he bless you both." Then spake God to the holy spirit: "How long yet shall Joseph suffer? Reveal thyself quickly, and enter into Jacob, that he may be able to bestow blessings."

In the words of Jacob, "Ephraim and Manasseh, even as Reuben and Simon, shall be mine," Joseph had noticed his father's preference for his younger son Ephraim. It made him very anxious about his older son's birthright, and he was careful to put the two lads before his father in such wise that Manasseh should stand opposite Jacob's right hand, and Ephraim opposite his left hand. But Ephraim, on account of his modesty, was destined for greater things than his older brother Manasseh, and God bade the holy spirit prompt Jacob to give the birthright to Ephraim. Now when Joseph observed his father put his right hand upon Ephraim's head, he made an attempt to remove it unto Manasseh's head. But Jacob warded him off, saying: "What, thou wouldst displace my hand against my will, the hand that overcame the prince of the angel hosts, who is as large as one-third of the world! I know things not known to thee--I know what Reuben did to Bilhah, and what Judah did to Tamar. How much more do I know things known to thee! Thinkest thou I know not what thy brethren did to thee, because thou wouldst betray nothing whenever I asked thee? I know it, Manasseh also shall become great, the judge Gideon shall descend from him, but his younger brother will be the ancestor of Joshua, who will bring the sun and the moon to a standstill, though they have dominion over the whole earth from end to end." Thus did Jacob set Ephraim the younger above Manasseh the older, and thus did it remain unto all times. In the list of the generations, Manasseh comes after Ephraim, and so it was in the allotment of the portions in the Holy Land, and so it was in the placing of the camps and the standards of the tribes, and in the dedication of the Tabernacle--everywhere Ephraim preceded Manasseh.

The blessing bestowed upon his grandchildren by Jacob was as follows: "O that it be the will of God that ye walk in the ways of the Lord like unto my fathers Abraham and Isaac, and may the angel that hath redeemed me from all evil give his aid unto Joshua and Gideon, and reveal himself unto them. May your names be named on Israel, and like unto fishes may you grow into a multitude in the midst of the earth, and as fishes are protected by the water, so may you be protected by the merits of Joseph."

The words "like unto fishes" were used by Jacob for the purpose of intimating the manner of death awaiting the Ephraimites, the descendants of Joseph. As fish are caught by their mouth, so the Ephraimites were in later days to invite their doom by their peculiar lisp. At the same time, Jacob's words contained the prophecy that Joshua the son of the man Nun, the "fish," would lead Israel into the Holy Land. And in his words lay still another prophecy, with reference to the sixty thousand men children begot in the same night as Moses, all cast into the river with him, and saved for the sake of his merits. The number of boys thrown to the fishes in the river that night was equal to the number of men in Israel upon the earth.

Ephraim received a special and separate blessing from his grandfather. Jacob said to him, "Ephraim, my son, thou art the head of the Academy, and in the days to come my most excellent and celebrated descendants will be called Ephrati after thee."

Joseph received two gifts from his father. The first was Shechem, the city that Jacob had defended, with sword and bow, against the depredations of the Amorite kings when they tried to take revenge upon his sons for the outrage committed there. And the second gift was the garments made by God for Adam and passed from hand to hand, until they came into the possession of Jacob. Shechem was his reward, because, with his chastity, he stemmed the tide of immorality that burst loose in Shechem first of all. Besides, he had a prior claim upon the city. Shechem, son of Hamor, the master of the city, had given it to Dinah as a present, and the wife of Joseph, Asenath, being the daughter of Dinah, the city belonged to him by right.

Adam's clothes Jacob had received from Esau. He had not taken them from his brother by force, but God had caused them to be given to him as a reward for his good deeds. They had belonged to Nimrod. Once when the mighty hunter caught Esau in his preserves, and forbade him to go on the chase, they agreed to determine by combat what their privileges were. Esau had taken counsel with Jacob, and he had advised him never to fight with Nimrod while he was clothed in Adam's garments. The two now wrestled with each other, and at the time Nimrod was not dressed in Adam's clothes. The end was that he was slain by Esau. Thus the garments worn by Adam fell into the hands of Esau, from him they passed into Jacob's, and he bequeathed them to Joseph.

Jacob also taught Joseph three signs whereby to distinguish the true redeemer, who should deliver Israel from the bondage of Egypt. He would proclaim the Ineffable Name, appoint elders, and use the word Pakod in addressing the people.

THE BLESSING OF THE TWELVE TRIBES

When Joseph and his two sons left Jacob, his brethren, envious of the bountiful blessings bestowed upon the three, said, "The whole world loveth a favorite of fortune, and our father hath blessed Joseph thus because he is a ruler of men." Then spoke Jacob: "They that seek the Lord shall not want any good thing. I have blessings enough for all."

Jacob summoned his sons from the land of Egypt, and bade them come to him at Raamses, first, however, commanding them to make themselves clean, that the blessing he was about to bestow might attach itself to them. Another one of his commands was that they were to establish an Academy, by the members of which they were to be governed.

When his sons were brought into his presence by the angels, Jacob spoke, saying, "Take heed that no dissensions spring up among you, for union is the first condition of Israel's redemption," and he was on the point of revealing the great secret to them concerning the end of time, but while they were standing around the golden bed whereon their father lay, the Shekinah visited him for a moment and departed as quickly, and with her departed also all trace of the knowledge of the great mystery from the mind of Jacob. He had the same experience as his own father Isaac, who also had loss of memory inflicted upon him by God, to prevent him from revealing the secret at the end of time to Esau, when he summoned him to receive his blessing.

The accident made Jacob apprehensive that his sons were not pious enough to be considered worthy of the revelation concerning the Messianic era, and he said to them, "Ishmael and the sons of Keturah were the blemished among the issue of my grandfather Abraham; my father Isaac begot a blemished issue in Esau, and I fear now that among you, too, there is one that harbors the intention to serve idols." The twelve men spake, and said: "Hear, O Israel, our father, the Eternal our God is the One Only God. As thy heart is one and united in avouching the Holy One, blessed be He, to be thy God, so also are our hearts one and united in avouching Him." Whereto Jacob responded, "Praised be the Name of the glory of His majesty forever and ever!" And although the whole mystery of the Messianic time was not communicated to the sons of Jacob, yet the blessing of each contained some reference to the events of the future.

These were the words addressed by Jacob to his oldest son: "Reuben, thou art my first-born, my might, and the beginning of my strength! Thy portion should have been three crowns. Thou shouldst have had the double heritage of thy primogeniture, and the priestly dignity, and the royal power. But by reason of thy sin, the birthright is conferred upon Joseph, kingship upon Judah, and the priesthood upon Levi. My son, I know no healing remedy for thee, but the man Moses, who will ascend to God, he will make thee whole, and God will forgive thy sin. I bless thee--may thy descendants be heroes in the Torah and heroes in war. Though thou must lose thy birthright, yet wilt thou be the first to enter into possession of thy allotment in the Holy Land, and in thy territory shall be the first of the cities of refuge, and always shall thy name stand first in the list of the families of the tribes. Yea, thou shalt also be the first whose heritage will be seized by the enemy, and the first to be carried away into the lands of exile."

After Reuben had had his "ears pulled" thus, he retired, and Jacob called his sons Simon and Levi to his side, and he addressed them in these words: "Brethren ye were of Dinah, but not of Joseph, whom you sold into slavery. The weapons of violence wherewith ye smote Shechem were stolen weapons, for it was not seemly for you to draw the sword. That was Esau's portion. To him was it said, By thy sword shalt thou live. Into the council of the tribe of Simon my soul will not come when they foregather at Shittim to do vicious deeds, and my glory will not be united unto the assembly of Korah, the descendants of Levi. In their anger Simon and Levi slew the prince of Shechem, and in their self-will they sold Joseph the bull into slavery. Accursed was the city of Shechem when they entered to destroy it. If they remain united, no ruler will be able to stand up before them, no war will prosper against them. Therefore will I divide and scatter their possession among the possessions of the other tribes. The descendants of Simon will many of them be poor men, who will wander from tribe to tribe and beg for bread, and also Levi's tribe will gather its tithes and gifts from all the others."

The words of Jacob, "I will divide them in Jacob," spoken of Simon and Levi, were fulfilled on Simon in particular. When twenty-four thousand of Simon fell at Shittim, the widows they left behind married husbands of all the other tribes. Nevertheless Jacob did not dismiss Simon and Levi without blessing them; the tribe of Simon was to bring forth the teachers and the beadles needed by all Israel, and Levi, the scholars that would expound the Torah and render decisions according to its teachings.

When the remaining sons of Jacob heard the rebukes dealt out by their father to these three, they feared to hear like reproaches, and they tried to slip away from his presence. Especially Judah was alarmed, that his father might taunt him with his trespass touching Tamar. But Jacob spoke thus to him: "Judah, thou dost deserve thy name. Thy mother called thee Jehudah, because she gave praise to God at thy birth, and so shall thy brethren praise thee, and they all will call themselves by thy name. And as thou didst confess thy sin openly, so also thy descendants, Achan, David, and Manasseh, will make public avowal of their sins, and the Lord will hear their prayer. Thy hands will send darts after the fleeing foe, and thy father's sons shall pay thee respect. Thou hast the impudence of a dog and the bravery of a lion. Thou didst save Joseph from death, and Tamar and her two sons from the flames. No people and no kingdom will be able to stand up against thee. Rulers shall not cease from the house of Judah, nor teachers of the law from his posterity, until his descendant Messiah come, and the obedience of all peoples be unto him. How glorious is Messiah of the House of Judah! His loins girded, he will go out to do battle with his enemies. No king and no ruler will prevail against him. The mountains will be dyed red with their blood, and the garments of Messiah will be like the garments of him that presseth wine. The eyes of Messiah will be clearer than pure wine, for they will never behold unchastity and bloodshed; and his teeth will be whiter than milk, for never will they bite aught that is taken by violence."

Though Issachar was the older, Zebulon came next to be blessed, as a reward for the sacrifice he had made for his brother's sake, for when Issachar chose the study of the Torah as his vocation, Zebulon decided to devote himself to business and support his brother with the profits of his trade, that he might give himself up to the law undisturbed. His blessing was that he would conquer the seacoast as far as Zidon.

"Issachar," said Jacob, "will take upon himself the burden of the study of the Torah, and all the other tribes will come to him and ask him to decide their doubts on legal questions, and his descendants will be the members of the Sanhedrin and the scholars that will occupy themselves with fixing the calendar." Jacob blessed Issachar also with the blessing, that the fruits of his land should be exceedingly large, and this brought a heavenly as well as an earthly profit in its train, for when the heathen to whom the fruits were sold marvelled thereat, the Jewish merchants explained that their extraordinary size was due to the merits of the tribe of Issachar, whom God rewarded for their devotion to the Torah, and thus many of the heathen were induced to convert to Judaism.

In blessing Dan, Jacob's thoughts were occupied chiefly with his descendant Samson, who, like unto God, without any manner of assistance, conferred victory upon his people. Jacob even believed the strong, heroic man to be the Messiah, but when Samson's death was revealed to him, he exclaimed, "I wait for Thy salvation, O Lord, for Thy help is unto all eternity, while Samson's help is only for a time. The redemption" continued Jacob, "will not be accomplished by Samson the Danite, but by Elijah the Gadite, who will appear at the end of time."

Asher's blessing was the beauty of his women, who would be sought in marriage by kings and high priests.

In Naphtali's land all fruits would ripen quickly, and they would be brought as presents to kings, and gain royal favor for the givers. This blessing was fulfilled in the plain of Gennesaret. At the same time Naphtali's blessing was a prophecy concerning his descendant Deborah, who was like a hind let loose against Sisera to conquer him, and she gave goodly words in her song of Israel's victory. Naphtali himself deserved the description applied to Deborah, for he was swift as a hart to do the will of God, and he was a fleet messenger unto his father and the tribes. They sent him whithersoever they would, and he executed their errands with dispatch. He served the brethren of Joseph as herald, to announce unto Jacob the glad tidings, "Joseph is yet alive," and when the stricken father saw him approach, he said, "Lo, here cometh Naphtali the lovable, who proclaimeth peace."

Joseph's blessing exceeded the blessing of all his brethren. Jacob spoke: "O son whom I bred up, Joseph, whom I raised, and who wast strong to resist the enticements of sin, thou didst conquer all the magicians and the wise men of Egypt by thy wisdom and thy pious deeds. The daughters of princes cast their jewels before thee, to draw thine eyes upon them when thou didst pass through the land of Egypt, but thou didst not look their way, and therefore wast thou made the father of two tribes. The magicians and the wise men of Egypt sought to defame thee before Pharaoh and slander thee, but thou didst set thy hope in the Almighty. Therefore may He who appeared unto me as El Shaddai bless thee and grant thee fertile soil and much cattle. May the blessing thy father giveth thee now, and the blessing that his fathers Abraham and Isaac gave him, and that called forth the envy of the great of the world, Ishmael, Esau, and the sons of Keturah--may all these blessings be a crown upon the head of Joseph, and a chain upon the neck of him that was the ruler of Egypt, and yet diminished not the honor due to his brethren."

The slander of which Jacob spoke referred to what Potiphar had said of Joseph before Pharaoh. He had complained, saying, "Why didst thou appoint my slave, whom I did buy for twenty pieces of silver, to be ruler over the Egyptians?" Joseph had then taken up his own defense, saying: "When thou didst buy me as a slave, thou didst commit a capital crime. Only a descendant of Canaan may be sold as a slave, and I am a descendant of Shem, and a prince besides. If thou wilt convince thyself of the truth of my words, do but compare me with the likeness of my mother Sarah that Pharaoh had made of her!" They brought Sarah's likeness, and, verily, it appeared that Joseph resembled his ancestress, and all were convinced of his noble lineage.

The blessing that Jacob bestowed upon Benjamin contains the prophecy that his tribe would provide Israel with his first ruler and his last ruler, and so it was, for Saul and Esther both belonged to the tribe of Benjamin. Likewise Benjamin's heritage in the Holy Land harbors two extremes: Jericho ripens its fruits earlier than any other region in Palestine, while Beth-el ripens them latest. In Benjamin's blessing, Jacob referred also to the service in the Temple, because the Holy Place was situated in the territory of Benjamin. And when Jacob called his youngest son a wolf that ravineth, he was thinking of the judge Ehud, the great scholar, a Benjamite, who conquered Eglon king of Moab, and also he had in mind the Benjamites that captured their wives by cunning and force.

Again, if he called Benjamin a wolf, Judah a lion, and Joseph a bull, he wanted to point to the three kingdoms known as wolf, lion, and bull, the doom of which was and will be sealed by the descendants of his three sons: Babylon, the kingdom of the lion, fell through the hands of Daniel of the tribe of Judah; Media, the wolf, found its master in the Benjamite Mordecai; and the bull Joseph will subdue the horned beast, the kingdom of wickedness, before the Messianic time.

THE DEATH OF JACOB

After Jacob had blessed each of his sons separately, he addressed himself to all of them together, saying: "According to my power did I bless you, but in future days a prophet will arise, and this man Moses will bless you, too, and he will continue my blessings where I left off." He added, besides, that the blessing of each tribe should redound to the good of all the other tribes: the tribe of Judah should have a share in the fine wheat of the tribe of Benjamin, and Benjamin should enjoy the goodly barley of Judah. The tribes should be mutually helpful, one to another.

Moreover, he charged them not to be guilty of idolatry in any form or shape and not to let blasphemous speech pass their lips, and he taught them the order of transporting his bier, thus: "Joseph, being king, shall not help to bear it, nor shall Levi, who is destined to carry the Ark of the Shekinah. Judah, Issachar, and Zebulon shall grasp its front end, Reuben, Simon, and Gad its right side, Ephraim, Manasseh, and Benjamin the hindmost end, and Dan, Asher, and Naphtali its left side." And this was the order in which the tribes, bearing each its standard, were to march through the desert, the Shekinah dwelling in the midst of them.

Jacob then spake to Joseph, saying: "And thou, my son Joseph, forgive thy brethren for their trespass against thee, forsake them not, and grieve them not, for the Lord hath put them into thine hands, that thou shouldst protect them all thy days against the Egyptians."

Also he admonished his sons, saying that the Lord would be with them if they walked in His ways, and He would redeem them from the hands of the Egyptians. "I know," he continued, "great suffering will befall your sons and your grandsons in this land, but if you will obey God, and teach your sons to know Him, then He will send you a redeemer, who will bring you forth out of Egypt and lead you into the land of your fathers."

In resignation to the will of God, Jacob awaited his end, and death enveloped him gently. Not the Angel of Death ended his life, but the Shekinah took his soul with a kiss. Beside the three Patriarchs, Abraham, Isaac, and Jacob, only Moses, Aaron, and Miriam breathed their last in this manner, through the kiss of the Shekinah. And these six, together with Benjamin, are the only ones whose corpses are not exposed to the ravages of the worms, and they neither corrupt nor decay.

Thus Jacob departed this world, and entered the world to come, a foretaste of which he had enjoyed here below, like the other two Patriarchs, and none beside among men. In another respect their life in this world resembled their life in the world to come, the evil inclination had no power over them, either here or there, wherein David resembled them.

Joseph ordered his father's body to be placed upon a couch of ivory, covered with gold, studded with gems, and hung with drapery of byssus and purple. Fragrant wine was poured out at its side, and aromatic spices burnt next to it. Heroes of the house of Esau, princes of the family of Ishmael, and the lion Judah, the bravest of his sons, surrounded the sumptuous bier of Jacob. "Come," said Judah to his brethren, "let us plant a high cedar tree at the head of our father's grave, its top shall reach up to the skies, its branches shall shade all the inhabitants of the earth, and its roots shall grow down deep into the earth, unto the abyss. For from him are sprung twelve tribes, and from him will arise kings and rulers, chapters of priests prepared to perform the service of the sacrifices, and companies of Levites ready to sing psalms and play upon sweet instruments."

The sons of Jacob tore their garments and girded their loins with sackcloth, threw themselves upon the ground, and strewed earth upon their heads until the dust rose in a high cloud. And when Asenath, the wife of Joseph, heard the tidings of Jacob's death, she came, and with her came the women of Egypt, to weep and mourn over him. And the men of Egypt that had known Jacob repaired thither, and they mourned day after day, and also many journeyed down into Egypt from Canaan, to take part in the seventy days' mourning made for him.

The Egyptians spake to one another, saying, "Let us lament for the pious man Jacob, because the affliction of the famine was averted from our land on account of his merits," for instead of ravaging the land for forty-two years according to the decree of God, the famine had lasted but two years, and that was due to the virtues of Jacob.

Joseph ordered the physicians to embalm the corpse. This he should have refrained from doing, for it was displeasing to God, who spoke, saying: "Have I not the power to preserve the corpse of this pious man from corruption? Was it not I that spoke the reassuring words, Fear not the worm, O Jacob, thou dead Israel?" Joseph's punishment for this useless precaution was that he was the first of the sons of Jacob to suffer death. The Egyptians, on the other hand, who devoted forty days to embalming the corpse and preparing it for burial, were rewarded for the veneration they showed. Before He destroyed their city, God gave the Ninevites a forty days' respite on account of their king, who was the Pharaoh of Egypt. And for the three score and ten days of mourning that the heathen made for Jacob, they were recompensed at the time of Ahasuerus. During seventy days, from the thirteenth of Nisan, the date of Haman's edict ordering the extermination of the Jews, until the twenty-third of Siwan, when Mordecai recalled it, they were permitted to enjoy absolute power over the Jews.

When all preparations for the burial of Jacob had been completed, Joseph asked permission of Pharaoh to carry the body up into Canaan. But he did not himself go to put his petition before Pharaoh, for he could not well appear before the king in the garb of a mourner, nor was he willing to interrupt his lamentation over his father for even a brief space and stand before Pharaoh and prefer his petition. He requested the family of Pharaoh to intercede for him with the king for the additional reason that he was desirous of enlisting the favor of the king's relations, lest they advise Pharaoh not to fulfil his wish. He acted according to the maxim, "Seek to win over the accuser, that he cause thee no annoyance."

Joseph applied first to the queen's hairdresser, and she influenced the queen to favor him, and then the queen put in a good word for him with the king. At first Pharaoh refused the permission craved by Joseph, who, however, urged him to consider the solemn oath he had given his dying father, to bury him in Canaan. Pharaoh desired him to seek absolution from the oath. But Joseph rejoined, "Then will I apply also for absolution from the oath I gave thee," referring to an incident in his earlier history. The grandees of Egypt had advised Pharaoh against appointing Joseph as viceroy, and they did not recede from this counsel until Joseph, in his conversation with the Egyptian king, proved himself to be master of the seventy languages of the world, the necessary condition to be fulfilled before one could become ruler over Egypt. But the conversation proved something else, that Pharaoh himself was not entitled to Egyptian kingship, because he lacked knowledge of Hebrew. He feared, if the truth became known, Joseph would be raised to his own place, for he knew Hebrew beside all the other tongues. In his anxiety and distress, Pharaoh made Joseph swear an oath never to betray the king's ignorance of Hebrew. Now when Joseph threatened to have himself absolved from this oath as well as the one to his dying father, great terror overwhelmed him, and he speedily granted Joseph permission to go up to Canaan and bury his father there.

Moreover, Pharaoh issued a decree in all parts of the land menacing those with death who would not accompany Joseph and his brethren upon their journey to Canaan with their father's remains, and accordingly the procession that followed the bier of Jacob was made up of the princes and nobles of Egypt as well as the common people. The bier was borne by the sons of Jacob. In obedience to his wish not even their children were allowed to touch it. It was fashioned of pure gold, the border thereof inlaid with onyx stones and bdellium, and the cover was gold woven work joined to the bier with threads that were held together with hooks of onyx stones and bdellium. Joseph placed a large golden crown upon the head of his father, and a golden sceptre he put in his hand, arraying him like a living king.

The funeral cortege was arranged in this order: First came the valiant men of Pharaoh and the valiant men of Joseph, and then the rest of the inhabitants of Egypt. All were girt with swords and clothed in coats of mail, and the trappings of war were upon them. The weepers and mourners walked, crying and lamenting, at some distance from the bier, and the rest of the people went behind it, while Joseph and his household followed together after it, with bare feet and in tears, and Joseph's servants were close to him, each man with his accoutrements and weapons of war. Fifty of Jacob's servants preceded the bier, strewing myrrh upon the road in passing, and all manner of perfumes, so that the sons of Jacob trod upon the aromatic spices as they carried the body forward.

Thus the procession moved on until it reached Canaan. It halted at the threshing-floor of Atad, and there they lamented with a very great and sore lamentation. But the greatest honor conferred upon Jacob was the presence of the Shekinah, who accompanied the cortege.

The Canaanites had no intention at first to take part in the mourning made for Jacob, but when they saw the honors shown him, they joined the procession of the Egyptians, loosing the girdles of their garments as a sign of grief. Also the sons of Esau, Ishmael, and Keturah appeared, though their design in coming was to seize the opportunity and make war upon the sons of Jacob, but when they saw Joseph's crown suspended from the bier, the Edomite and Ishmaelite kings and princes followed his example, and attached theirs to it, too, and it was ornamented with thirty-six crowns.

Nevertheless the conflict was not averted; it broke out in the end between the sons of Jacob and Esau and his followers. When the former were about to lower the body of their father into the Cave of Machpelah, Esau attempted to prevent it, saying that Jacob had used his allotted portion of the tomb for Leah, and the only space left for a grave belonged to himself. For, continued Esau, "though I sold my birthright unto Jacob, I yet have a portion in the tomb as a son of Isaac." The sons of Jacob, however, were well aware of the fact that their father had acquired Esau's share in the Cave, and they even knew that a bill of sale existed, but Esau, assuming properly that the document was left behind in Egypt, denied that any such had ever been made out, and the sons of Jacob sent Naphtali, the fleet runner, back to Egypt to fetch the bill. Meantime, while this altercation was going on between Esau and the others, Hushim the son of Dan arose and inquired in astonishment why they did not proceed with the burial of Jacob, for he was deaf and had not understood the words that had passed between the disputants. When he heard what it was all about, and that the ceremonies were interrupted until Naphtali should return from Egypt with the bill of sale, he exclaimed, with indignation, "My grandfather shall lie here unburied until Naphtali comes back!" and he seized a club and dealt Esau a vigorous blow, so that he died, and his eyes fell out of their sockets and dropped upon Jacob's knees, and Jacob opened his own eyes and smiled. Esau being dead, his brother's burial could proceed without hindrance, and Joseph interred him in the Cave of Machpelah in accordance with his wish.

His other children had left all arrangements connected with the burial of their father's body to their brother Joseph, for they reflected that it was a greater honor for Jacob if a king concerned himself about his remains rather than simple private individuals.

The head of Esau, as he lay slain by the side of Jacob's grave, rolled down into the Cave, and fell into the lap of Isaac, who prayed to God to have mercy upon his son, but his supplications were in vain. God spoke, saying, "As I live, he shall not behold the majesty of the Lord."

THE SONS OF JACOB AT WAR WITH THE SONS OF ESAU

Jacob having been interred with royal pomp, and the seven days' period of mourning over, the conflict between the sons of Jacob and the sons of Esau broke out anew. In the skirmish that had ensued when Esau advanced a claim upon a place in the Cave of Machpelah, while his brother's remains still lay unburied, he lost forty of his men, and after his death fortune favored his sons as little. Eighty of their followers were slain, while of the sons of Jacob not one was lost. Joseph succeeded in capturing Zepho the son of Eliphaz and fifty of his men, and he clapped them in chains and carried them off to Egypt. Thereupon the rest of the attacking army led by Eliphaz fled to Mount Seir, taking with them the headless corpse of Esau, to bury it in his own territory. The sons of Jacob pursued after them, but they slew none, out of respect for the remains of Esau.

On the third day a great army gathered together, consisting of the inhabitants of Seir and the children of the East, and they marched down into Egypt with the purpose of making war upon Joseph and his brethren. In the battle that came off, this army was almost totally destroyed, not less than six hundred thousand men were mowed down by Joseph and his warriors, and the small remnant fled precipitately. Returned to their own country after this fatal campaign, the sons of Esau and the sons of Seir fell to quarrelling among themselves, and the sons of Seir demanded that their former allies leave the place, because it was they that had brought misfortune upon the country.

The sons of Esau thereupon dispatched a messenger in secret to their friend Agnias, king of Africa, begging his aid against the sons of Seir. He granted their request, and sent them troops consisting of foot-soldiers and mounted men. The sons of Seir, on their part, also sought allies, and they secured the help of the children of the East, and of the Midianites, who put warriors at their disposal. In the encounters that ensued between the hostile forces, the sons of Esau were defeated again and again, partly on account of treachery in their own ranks, for their men sometimes deserted to the enemy while the combat was on. At last, however, in the battle that took place in the desert of Paran, the sons of Esau gained a decisive victory. They massacred all the warriors of the sons of Seir, and the Midianites and the children of the East were put to flight.

Thereafter the sons of Esau returned to Seir, and they slew all the inhabitants of the place, men, women, and children, sparing only fifty lads and maidens. The former they used as slaves, and the latter they took to wife. They also enriched themselves with the spoils, seizing all the possessions of the sons of Seir, and the whole land was divided among the five sons of Esau. Now these descendants of Esau determined to put a king over themselves, but in consequence of the treachery committed during the war there prevailed such hatred and bitterness among them that they decided never to appoint a ruler from their own people. Their choice fell upon Bela, the son of Beor, one of the warriors sent to them by King Agnias. His peer could not be found among the allied troops for bravery, wisdom, and handsome appearance. They set the royal crown upon his head, built a palace for him, and gave him gifts of silver, gold, and gems, until he lived in great opulence. He reigned happily for thirty years, and met his death then in a war against Joseph and his brethren.

This war came about because the sons of Esau could not banish from their memory the disgrace of the defeat inflicted upon them by Joseph and his people. Having enlisted the aid of Agnias, and of the Ishmaelites and other nations of the East, they set forth on a second campaign against Egypt, in the hope of delivering Zepho and his followers from the hands of Joseph. In spite of their enormous host--they had no less than eight hundred thousand men of infantry and cavalry--they were defeated at Raamses by Joseph and his brethren and their little company of six hundred men. Beside their king Bela, they left one-fourth of their army upon the field. The loss of their king discouraged them grievously, and they took to flight, hard pressed by Joseph, who cut down many of the fugitives.

When he returned from the battle, Joseph ordered manacles and fetters to be put upon Zepho and his followers, and their captivity was made more bitter unto them than it had been before.

The sons of Esau appointed Jobab of Bozrah to succeed their dead king Bela. His reign lasted ten years, but they desisted from all further attempts at waging war with the sons of Jacob. Their last experience with them had been too painful, but the enmity they cherished against them was all the fiercer, and their hatred never abated.

Their third king was Husham, and he ruled over them for twenty years. During his reign Zepho succeeded in making good his escape from Egypt. He was received kindly by Agnias, king of Africa, and appointed commander-in-chief of his troops. He used every means of persuasion to induce his sovereign lord to enter into a war with Egypt, but in vain, for Agnias was only too well acquainted with the strength and heroism of the sons of Jacob. For many years he resisted Zepho's arguments and blandishments. Indeed, as it was, Agnias had his hands full with other warlike enterprises. It had happened about this time that a man of the land of Kittim, 'Uzi by name, whom his countrymen venerated as a god, died in the city of Pozimana, and he left behind a fair and clever daughter. Agnias heard of Yaniah's beauty and wisdom, and he sued for her hand, and his request was granted him by the people of Kittim.

The messengers of Agnias were hastening away from Kittim, bearing to their master the promise of the inhabitants that Yaniah should become his wife, when Turnus, king of Benevento, arrived on the same errand. His suit was rejected, for the people of Kittim were afraid-to break the promise given to Agnias. In his anger, Turnus went to Sardinia to make war upon King Lucus, a brother of Agnias, intending to deal with the latter as soon as the other was rendered harmless. Hearing of the design hatched by Turnus, Agnias hastened to Sardinia to the assistance of his brother, and a battle took place in the Valley of Campania. Against Turnus were arrayed Agnias, his brother Lucus, and the son of the latter, Niblos, whom his father had appointed commander-in-chief of the Sardinian troops. In the first encounter, Turnus was the victor, and the Sardinians lost their general Niblos. But in the second engagement the army of Turnus was routed completely, and he himself was left dead on the field. His army fled, pursued closely by Agnias as far as the cross-road between Rome and Albano. Niblos' body was put inside of a golden statue, and his father erected a high tower over his grave, and another over the grave of Turnus, and these two buildings, connected by a marble pavement, stand opposite to each other, on the cross-road at which Agnias left off from following after the fugitive army.

The king of Africa went on to the city of Benevento, but he took no harsh measures against it and its inhabitants, because it belonged to the land of Kittim at that time. Thenceforth, however, bands of soldiers from Africa made incursions, now and again, into the land of Kittim, under the lead of Zepho, the captain of the African army. Agnias meantime went to Pozimana, to solemnize his marriage with Yaniah, and he returned with her to his capital in Africa.

ZEPHO KING OF KITTIM

All this time Zepho did not leave off urging Agnias to invade Egypt, and he succeeded finally in persuading the king to consider his wish, and a great army was equipped against Egypt and the sons of Jacob. Among the shield-bearers was Balaam, the fifteen year old son of Beor, a wise youth and an adept in magic, and the king bade him acquaint him with the issue of the war upon which they were entering. Balaam took wax and moulded the figures of men, to represent the army of Agnias and the army of the Egyptians, and he plunged them into magic water and let them swim, and it appeared that the African army was subdued by the Egyptians. Agnias accordingly gave up the campaign, and Zepho, seeing that his sovereign could not be persuaded into war with the sons of Jacob, fled the country and betook himself to Kittim.

The people of Kittim received him with great honors, and they offered him much money to stay with them and conduct their wars. It happened once while Zepho was in the mountains of Koptiziah, where the inhabitants of Kittim had taken refuge before the troops of the African king, that he had to go on a search for an ox that had strayed away, and he discovered a cave the opening of which was barred by a great stone. He shivered the stone in pieces, and entering the cave he saw an animal formed like a man above and a he-goat below, and he killed the strange beast, which was in the very act of devouring his lost ox. There was great rejoicing among the people of Kittim, for the monster had long been doing havoc among their cattle, and in gratitude they set aside one day of the year, which they called by Zepho's name, in honor of their liberator, and all the people brought him presents and offered sacrifices to him.

At this time it came to pass that Yaniah, the wife of King Agnias, fell into a grievous sickness, and the physicians ascribed her illness to the climate, and to the water of Africa, to which she, a native of the land of Kittim, could not get accustomed, because she had been in the habit of using the water of the river Forma, which her forefathers had drawn to her house through a conduit. Agnias sent to the land of Kittim and had some of the water of the Forma brought to Africa. Finding it much lighter than the water of his own country, he built a huge canal from the land of Kittim. to Africa, and the queen henceforth had all the Forma water she needed. Besides, he took earth and stone from Kittim, and built a palace for Yaniah, and she recovered from her illness.

Meantime Zepho had won a decisive victory over the African troops that had made an incursion into the land of Kittim, and the people chose him as king. His first undertaking was a campaign against the sons of Tubal and the Islands of the Sea, and again he was successful, he subdued them completely. On his return, the people built a great palace for Zepho, and they renewed his kingship, and he continued until his death to reign as king of Kittim and of Italy.

During the first thirteen years of his reign, the Africans made no attempt to disturb the peace of Kittim, but then they invaded the land, only to be severely repulsed by Zepho, who pursued the troops up to the very borders of Africa, and Agnias the king was in such consternation that he did not venture to make reprisals for some time. When he finally made a second attempt, his troops were annihilated by Zepho down to the very last man. Now Agnias, in despair, assembled all the inhabitants of Africa, as numerous as the sand on the sea-shore, and he united his great host with the army of his brother Lucus, and thus he made his third attempt upon Zepho and the people of the land of Kittim.

Alarmed, Zepho wrote to his brethren in Seir, and entreated their king Hadad to send him aid. But the people of Seir had concluded an alliance with Agnias as far back as under their first king Bela, and they refused Zepho's request, and the king of Kittim had to face the host of eight hundred thousand men mustered by Agnias with his little band of three thousand. Then the people of Kittim spake to their king Zepho, saying: "Pray for us unto the God of thy ancestors. Peradventure He may deliver us from the hand of Agnias and his army, for we have heard that He is a great God, and He delivers all that trust in Him." Zepho prayed unto the Lord, saying: "O Lord, God of Abraham and Isaac, my fathers, this day may it be made known that Thou art a true God, and all the gods of the nations are vain and useless. Remember now this day unto me Thy covenant with Abraham our father, which our ancestors related unto us, and do graciously with me this day for the sake of Abraham and Isaac, our fathers, and save me and the sons of Kittim from the hand of the king of Africa, who hath come against us for battle."

God gave ear unto Zepho's prayer, and in the first day's battle one-half of the African army fell. Agnias forthwith dispatched a decree to his country, ordering, on penalty of death and confiscation of property, that all the males of the land, including boys that had passed their tenth year, were to join the army and fight against the people of Kittim. In spite of these new accessions, three hundred thousand strong, Agnias was beaten again by Zepho in the second battle. The African general Sosipater having fallen slain, the troops broke into flight, at their head Agnias with Lucus the brother and Asdrubal the son of Agnias. After this dire defeat the Africans made no further attempt to disturb the peace of Kittim, and their incursions ceased forever.

In spite of the great victory that Zepho had won with the help of God, the king of Kittim walked in the idolatrous ways of the people whom he ruled, and in the ways of the sons of Esau, for, as saith the proverb of the ancients, "Out of the wicked cometh forth wickedness," and Zepho was not other than the rest of the sons of Esau.

The severe defeat inflicted upon Agnias drove Balaam from Africa to Kittim, and he was received with great honors by Zepho, who welcomed him on account of his deep wisdom.

Now Zepho thought the time had arrived for him to carry out his plan of vengeance against the posterity of Jacob, all the more as in the meantime Joseph had died, and also his brethren and the valiant men of Pharaoh had passed away. He was joined in the enterprise by Hadad, the king of Edom, and by the nations of the East and the Ishmaelites. The allied army was so vast that the space it covered as it stood in rank and file was equal to a three days' journey. It formed in battle array in the Valley of Pathros, and it was met by three hundred thousand Egyptians and one hundred and fifty Israelites from Goshen. But the Egyptians did not trust the Israelites, they feared their defection to the sons of Esau and Ishmael. They therefore made an agreement with them that the Israelites were not to come to the help of the Egyptians until it appeared that the enemy were getting the upper hand.

Zepho, who had a high opinion of Balaam's ability, desired him to use his magic arts and find out what would be the outcome of the war, but Balaam's knowledge failed him, he could not satisfy the king's wish. The Egyptians got the worst of the first encounter between the two hostile armies, but the aspect of things changed as soon as they summoned the Israelites to aid them. The Israelites prayed to God to support them with His help, and the Lord heard their prayer. Then they threw themselves upon Zepho and his allies, and after they had cut down several thousand men, such dismay and confusion took hold of the enemy that they fled hastily, pursued by the Israelites as far as the boundary of the country. The Egyptians, instead of coming to the assistance of the Israelites, had taken to flight, leaving the small band of their allies to dispose of the huge host of their adversaries. Embittered by such treatment, the Israelites slew as many as two hundred Egyptians, under the pretext that they thought they belonged to the enemy.

THE NATIONS AT WAR

Hadad, the king of Edom, who had failed to gain fame and honor in the Egyptian campaign, was favored by fortune in another war, a war against Moab. The Moabites shrank from meeting Hadad alone, and they made an alliance with the Midianites. In the thick of the fight the Moabites fled from the field of battle, leaving the Midianites to their fate, and these deserted allies of theirs were cut down to a man by Hadad and his Edomites. The Moabites saved their skins, and suffered only the inconvenience of having to pay tribute. To avenge the faithlessness practiced against them, the Midianites, supported by their kinsmen, the sons of Keturah, gathered a mighty army, and attacked the Moabites the following year. But Hadad came to their assistance, and again he inflicted a severe defeat upon the Midianites, who had to give up their plan of revenge against Moab. This is the beginning of the inveterate enmity between the Moabites and the Midianites. If a single Moabite is caught in the land of Midian, he is killed without mercy, and a Midianite in Moab fares no better.

After the death of Hadad, the Edomites installed Samlah of Masrekah as their king, and he reigned eighteen years. It was his desire to take up the cause of Agnias, the old ally of the Edomites, and chastise Zepho for having gone to war with him, but his people, the Edomites, would not permit him to undertake aught that was inimical to their kinsman, and Samlah had to abandon the plan. In the fourteenth year of Samlah's reign, Zepho died, having been king of Kittim for fifty years. His successor was Janus, one of the people of Kittim, who enjoyed an equally long reign.

Balaam had made his escape to Egypt after the death of Zepho, and he was received there with great demonstrations of honor by the king and all the nobles, and Pharaoh appointed him to be royal counsellor, for he had heard much about his exceeding great wisdom.

In the Edomite kingdom, Samlah was succeeded by Saul of Pethor, a youth of surpassing beauty, whose reign lasted forty years. His successor upon the throne was Baal Hamon, king for thirty-eight years, during which period the Moabites rose up against the Edomites, to whom they had been paying tribute since the time of Hadad, and they succeeded in throwing off the yoke of the stranger.

The times were troubled everywhere. Agnias, the king of Africa, died, and also the death of Janus occurred, the king of Kittim. The successors to these two rulers, Asdrubal, the son of Agnias, and Latinus, the king of Kittim, then entered upon a long drawn out war of many years. At first the fortune of war favored Latinus. He sailed to Africa in ships, and inflicted one defeat after another upon Asdrubal, and finally this king of Africa lost his life upon the battlefield. After destroying the canal from Kittim to Africa built many years before by Agnias, Latinus returned to his own country, taking with him as his wife Ushpiziwnah, the daughter of Asdrubal, who was so wondrously beautiful that her countrymen wore her likeness upon their garments.

Latinus did not enjoy the fruits of his victory long. Anibal, the younger brother of Asdrubal and his successor in the royal power, went to Kittim in ships and carried on a series of wars lasting eighteen years, in the course of which he killed off eighty thousand of the people of Kittim, not sparing the princes and the nobles. At the end of this protracted period he went back to Africa, and reigned over his people in quiet and peace.

The Edomites, during the forty-eight years of the reign of Hadad, the successor of Baal Hamon, fared no better than the people of Kittim. Hadad's first undertaking was to reduce the Moabites again under the sovereignty of Edom, but he had to desist, because he could not offer successful resistance to a newly chosen king of theirs, one of their own people, who enlisted the aid of their kinsmen the Ammonites. The allies commanded a great host, and Hadad was overwhelmed. These wars were followed by others between Hadad of Edom. and Abimenos of Kittim. The latter was the attacking party, and he invaded Seir with a mighty army. The sons of Seir were defeated abjectly, their king Hadad was taken captive, and then executed by Abimenos, and Seir was made a province subject to Kittim and ruled by a governor.

Thus ended the independence of the sons of Esau. Henceforth they had to pay tribute to Kittim, over which Abimenos ruled until his death, in the thirty-eighth year of his reign.

JOSEPH'S MAGNANIMITY

As Joseph was returning from the burial of his father in the Cave of Machpelah, he passed the pit into which his brethren had once cast him, and he looked into it, and said, "Blessed be God who permitted a miracle to come to pass for me here!" The brethren inferred from these words of gratitude, which Joseph but uttered in compliance with the injunctions of the law, that he cherished the recollection of the evil they had done him, and they feared, that now their father was dead, their brother would requite them in accordance with their deeds. They observed, moreover, that since their father was no more, Joseph had given up the habit of entertaining them at his table, and they interpreted this as a sign of his hatred of them. In reality, it was due to Joseph's respect and esteem for his brethren. "So long as my father was alive," Joseph said to himself, "he bade me sit at the head of the table, though Judah is king, and Reuben is the first-born. It was my father's wish, and I complied with it. But now it is not seemly that I should have the first seat in their presence, and yet, being ruler of Egypt, I cannot yield my place to any other." He thought it best therefore not to have the company of his brethren at his meals.

But they, not fathoming his motives, sent Bilhah to him with the dying message of their father, that he was to forgive the transgression and the sin of his brethren. For the sake of the ways of peace they had invented the message; Jacob had said nothing like it. Joseph, on his part, realized that his brethren spoke thus only because they feared he might do harm unto them, and he wept that they should put so little trust in his affection. When they appeared, and fell down before his face, and said, "Thou didst desire to make one of us a slave unto thyself. Behold, we all are ready to be thy servants," he spoke to them gently, and tried to convince them that he harbored no evil design against them. He said: "Be not afraid, I will do you no harm, for I fear God, and if ye think I failed to have you sit at my table because of enmity toward you, God knows the intentions of my heart, He knows that I acted thus out of consideration for the respect I owe to you."

Furthermore he said: "Ye are like unto the dust of the earth, the sand on the sea-shore, and the stars in the heavens. Can I do aught to put these out of the world? Ten stars could effect nothing against one star, how much less can one star effect anything against ten? Do you believe that I have the power of acting contrary to the laws of nature? Twelve hours hath the day, twelve hours the night, twelve months the year, twelve constellations are in the heavens, and also there are twelve tribes! You are the trunk and I am the head--of what use the head without the trunk? It is to my own good that I should treat you with fraternal affection. Before your advent, I was looked upon as a slave in this country--you proved me a man of noble birth. Now, if I should kill you, my claims upon an aristocratic lineage would be shown to be a lie. The Egyptians would say, He was not their brother, they were strangers to him, he but called them his brethren to serve his purpose, and now he hath found a pretext to put them out of the way. Or they would hold me to be a man of no probity. Who plays false with his own kith and kin, how can he keep faith with others? And, in sooth, how can I venture to lay hand upon those whom God and my father both have blessed?"

As Joseph's dealings were kind and gentle with his brethren, so he was the helper and counsellor of the Egyptians, and when Pharaoh departed this life, Joseph being then a man of seventy-one years of age, the king's last wish was that he might be a father unto his son and successor Magron, and administer the affairs of state for him. Some of the Egyptians desired to make Joseph king after the death of Pharaoh, but this plan met with opposition on the part of others. They objected to an alien on the throne, and so the royal title was left to Magron, called Pharaoh, according to the established custom the name given to all the Egyptian kings. But Joseph was made the actual ruler of the land, and though he was only viceroy in Egypt, he reigned as king over the lands outside of Egypt as far as the Euphrates, parts of which Joseph had acquired by conquest. The inhabitants of these countries brought their yearly tribute to him and other presents besides, and thus did Joseph rule for forty years, beloved of all, and respected by the Egyptians and the other nations, and during all that time his brethren dwelt in Goshen, happy and blithe in the service of God. And in his own family circle Joseph was happy also; he lived to act as godfather at the circumcision of the sons of his grandson Machir.

His end was premature as compared with that of his brethren; at his death he was younger than any of them at their death. It is true, "Dominion buries him that exercises it." He died ten years before his allotted time, because, without taking umbrage, he had permitted his brethren to call his father his "servant" in his presence.

ASENATH

God gives every man the wife he deserves, and so Asenath was worthy of being the helpmeet of Joseph the pious. Her father was Potiphar, one of Pharaoh's magnates, ranking among the most distinguished of them by reason of wisdom, wealth, and station. His daughter was slender like unto Sarah, beautiful like Rebekah, and radiant in appearance like Rachel. Noblemen and princes sued for her hand when she was eighteen years of age. Even Pharaoh's appointed successor, his first-born son, demanded her in marriage, but his father refused to comply with his wish, because he did not consider her a proper wife for one destined to sit upon the throne. The daughter of the Moabite king, he insisted, was a more suitable match for him. But Asenath rejected every proposal of marriage, and avoided all intercourse with men. With seven maidens born the same day as herself, she lived in retirement in a magnificent palace adjoining that of her parents.

It happened in the first of the seven years of plenty that Joseph planned to visit the place in which Potiphar resided, and he sent word to him that he would put up with him, at his house. Potiphar was enchanted with the honor in prospect for him, and also with the opportunity it would afford him of bringing about a marriage between Asenath and Joseph. But when he disclosed his plan to his daughter, she rejected it with indignation. "Why shouldst thou desire to see me united with a vagabond, a slave," she cried out, "one that does not even belong to our nation, but is the son of a Canaanitish herdsman, a fellow that attempted to violate the honor of his mistress, and in punishment for this misdemeanor was thrown into prison, to be liberated thence by Pharaoh for interpreting his dream? Nay, father, never will I become his wife. I am willing to marry the son of Pharaoh, the future ruler and king of Egypt."

Potiphar promised his daughter not to speak of the plan again. At that moment Joseph's arrival was announced, and Asenath left the presence of her parents and withdrew to her own apartments. Standing by the window, she saw Joseph pass, and she was so transported with his divine beauty and his indescribably noble carriage that she burst into tears, and said: "Poor, foolish me, what shall I do? I permitted myself to be misled by friends, who told me that Joseph was the son of a Canaanitish shepherd. Now I behold the splendor that emanates from him like unto the splendor of the sun, illuminating our house with his rays. In my audacity and folly I had looked down upon him, and had spoken absurd nonsense against him. I knew not that he was a son of God, as he must be, for among men such beauty as his does not exist. I pray Thee, O God of Joseph, grant me pardon! It was my ignorance that made me speak like a fool. If my father will give me in marriage to Joseph, I will be his forever."

Meantime Joseph had taken his seat at Potiphar's table, and he observed a maiden looking at him from one of the palace windows. He commanded that she be ordered away, for he never permitted women to gaze at him or come near to him. His supernatural beauty always fascinated the noble Egyptian ladies, and they were untiring in the efforts they made to approach him. But their attempts were vain. He cherished the words of his father Jacob, who had admonished his son to keep aloof from the women of the Gentiles.

Potiphar explained to Joseph that the maiden at the window was his virgin daughter, who never permitted men to abide near her; he was the first man she had ever looked upon. The father continued and made the request of Joseph, to allow his daughter to pay him her respects. Joseph granted the favor he desired, and Asenath appeared and greeted him with the words, "Peace be with thee, thou blessed of God Most High," whereunto Joseph returned the salutation, "Be thou blessed of the Lord, from whom flow all blessings."

Asenath desired also to kiss Joseph, but he warded off the intimate greeting with the words: "It is not meet that a God-fearing man, who blesses the living God, and eats the blessed bread of life, who drinks of the blessed cup of immortality and incorruptibility, and anoints himself with the fragrant oil of holiness, should kiss a woman of a strange people, who blesses dead and unprofitable idols, and eats the putrid bread of idolatry, which chokes the soul of man, who drinks the libations of deceit, and anoints herself with the oil of destruction."

These words uttered by Joseph touched Asenath unto tears. Out of compassion with her, he bestowed his blessing upon her, calling upon God to pour out His spirit over her and make her to become a member of His people and His inheritance, and grant her a portion in the life eternal.

THE MARRIAGE OF JOSEPH

The appearance and the speech of Joseph made so deep an impression upon Asenath that no sooner had she reached her apartment than she divested herself of her robes of state and took off her jewels, and put on sackcloth instead, strewed ashes upon her head, and supplicated God amid tears to grant her pardon for her sins. In this manner she spent seven days and seven nights in her chamber. Not even her seven attendants were permitted to enter her presence during the time of her penance. The morning of the eighth day an angel appeared unto her, and bade her put away her sackcloth and ashes and array herself in state, for this day she had been born anew, he said, to eat the blessed bread of life, to drink of the cup of life immortal, and anoint herself with the oil of life eternal. Asenath was about to set food and drink before her guest, when she perceived a honeycomb of wondrous form and fragrance. The angel explained to her that it had been produced by the bees of Paradise, to serve as food for the angels and the elect of God. He took a small portion of it for himself, and the rest he put into Asenath's mouth, saying: "From this day forth thy body shall bloom like the eternal flowers in Paradise, thy bones shall wax fat like the cedars thereof, strength inexhaustible shall be thine, thy youth shall never fade, and thy beauty never perish, and thou shalt be like unto a metropolis surrounded by a wall." At the request of Asenath, the angel blessed also her seven attendants, with the words, "May the Lord bless you and make you to be seven pillars in the City of Refuge."

Thereupon the angel left her, and she saw him ascend heavenward in a chariot of fire drawn by four steeds of fire. Now she knew that she had not been entertaining a human being, but an angel.

The celestial messenger had scarcely departed, when a visit from Joseph was announced, and she hastened to array and adorn herself for his reception. When she washed her face, she caught sight of it in the water, and saw it to be of such beauty as never before, so great had been the transformation wrought by the angel. When Joseph came, he did not recognize her. He asked her who she was, whereto she replied, "I am thy maid-servant Asenath! I have cast away my idols, and this day a visitant came to me from heaven. He gave me to eat of the bread of life and to drink of the blessed cup, and he spake these words unto me, 'I give thee unto Joseph as his affianced wife, that he may be thy affianced husband forever.' And furthermore he said, 'Thy name shall not any more be called Asenath, but thy name shall be City of Refuge, whither the nations shall flee for safety.' And he added, 'I go to Joseph, to tell him all these things that have reference to thee.' Now, my lord, thou knowest whether the man was with thee and spoke to thee in my behalf."

Joseph confirmed all she had said, and they embraced and kissed each other in token of their betrothal, which they celebrated by a banquet with Potiphar and his wife. The wedding took place later in the presence of Pharaoh, who set a golden crown upon the head of the bridegroom and the bride, gave them his blessing, and made a seven days' feast in their honor, to which he invited the magnates and princes of Egypt and of other countries. And during the seven days of the wedding festivities the people were prohibited, under penalty of death, from doing any manner of work; they all were to join in the celebration of Joseph's marriage.

KIND AND UNKIND BRETHREN

On the twenty-first day of the second month in the second of the seven years of famine, Jacob came down to Egypt, and his daughter-in-law Asenath visited him. She marvelled not a little at his beauty and strength. His shoulders and his arms were like an angel's, and his loins like a giant's. Jacob gave her his blessing, and with her husband she returned home, accompanied by the sons of Leah, while the sons of the handmaids, remembering the evil they had once done unto Joseph, kept aloof. Levi in particular had conceived a fondness for Asenath. He was especially close to the Living God, for he was a prophet and a sage, his eyes were open, and he knew how to read the celestial books written by the finger of God. He revealed to Asenath that he had seen her future resting-place in heaven, and it was built upon a rock and encompassed by a diamond wall.

On their journey they met the son of Pharaoh, his successor to the throne, and he was so transported with Asenath's beauty, that he made the plan of murdering Joseph in order to secure possession of his wife. He summoned Simon and Levi, and by blandishments and promises sought to induce them to put Joseph out of the way. Simon was so enraged that he would have felled him at once, had not his brother Levi, who was endowed with the gift of prophecy, divined his purpose, and frustrated it by stepping upon his foot, while whispering: "Why art thou so angry, and so wroth with the man? We that fear God may not repay evil with evil." Turning to the son of Pharaoh, he told him that nothing would induce them to execute the wickedness he had proposed; rather he advised him not to undertake aught against Joseph, else he would kill him with the sword that had served him in his slaughter of the inhabitants of Shechem. The culprit was seized with frantic alarm, and fell down before Simon and Levi to entreat their mercy. Levi raised him tip, saying, "Fear not, but abandon thy wicked plan, and harbor no evil design against Joseph."

Nevertheless the son of Pharaoh did not give up his criminal purpose. He approached the sons of Bilhah and Zilpah, and sought to accomplish through them what had failed with Simon and Levi. He called them into his presence, and told them of a conversation between Joseph and Pharaoh that he had overheard. The former had said that he waited but to learn of the death of his father Jacob in order to do away with the sons of the handmaids, because they had been the ones to sell him into slavery. Their wrath excited against Joseph by these words, the sons of Bilhah and Zilpah assented to the proposition of the son of Pharaoh. It was arranged that the latter should kill Pharaoh, the friend of Joseph, while they would fall upon their brother, and put him out of the way. They were furnished with six hundred able warriors and fifty spearmen for the purpose. The first part of the plan, the murder of Pharaoh, failed. The palace guard would not allow even the successor to the throne to enter his father's bedchamber, and he had to depart without having effected his object.

Now Dan and Gad gave him the advice to take up his station with fifty archers in a secret place that Asenath had to pass on her homeward journey. Thence he could make a successful attack upon her suite, and gain possession of her. Naphtali and Asher did not care to have anything to do with this hostile enterprise against Joseph, but Dan and Gad forced them into it, insisting that all the sons of the handmaids must stand together as men and repel the danger that threatened them.

TREACHERY PUNISHED

From their ambush the forces of the son of Pharaoh fell upon Asenath and her six hundred attendants. They succeeded in hewing down the vanguard, and Asenath had to take to flight. To her alarm she encountered the son of Pharaoh with fifty mounted men. Benjamin, seated in the same chariot with her, came to her rescue, for in spite of his youth he was exceedingly courageous. He descended from the chariot, gathered pebbles, and, throwing them at the son of Pharaoh, struck him on his forehead and inflicted a severe wound. The charioteer aided him by keeping him supplied with pebbles, which he cast at the fifty riders with such expert skill that he slew forty-eight of them with as many missiles. Meantime the sons of Leah arrived on the spot and came to Asenath's aid, for Levi, with his prophetic spirit, had seen what was happening, and summoning his five brothers he had hastened thither. These six attacked the troops in ambush and cut them down. But the danger to Asenath was by no means removed. At this moment the sons of the handmaids threw themselves upon her and Benjamin with drawn swords. It was their intention to kill them both, and flee to cover in the depths of the woods. But as soon as Asenath supplicated God for aid, the swords dropped from the hands of her assailants, and they saw that the Lord was on the side of Asenath. They fell at her feet and entreated her grace. She allayed their anxiety with the words: "Be courageous and have no fear of your brethren, the sons of Leah. They are God-fearing men. Do but keep yourselves in hiding until their wrath is appeased."

When the sons of Leah appeared, Asenath fell down before them, and amid tears she adjured them to spare the sons of the handmaids and not repay with evil the evil they had meditated. Simon would not hear of making concessions. He insisted that the measure of their sins was full, and they must pay for them with their lives, for they had been the ones that had sold Joseph into slavery, and brought down untold misfortune upon Jacob and his sons. But Asenath did not leave off, and her urgent petitions won the day. She succeeded in calming the anger of Simon, and in Levi she had a secret ally, for this prophet knew the hiding-place of the sons of the handmaids, and he did not betray it to Simon, lest his wrath be increased at the sight of them. It was also Levi that restrained Benjamin from giving the death blow to the heavily wounded son of Pharaoh. So far from permitting harm to be done to him, he washed his wounds, put him into a chariot, and took him to Pharaoh, who thanked Levi from his heart for his services of loving-kindness. Levi's efforts were vain, three days later the son of Pharaoh died of the wounds inflicted by Benjamin, and from grief over the loss of his first-born Pharaoh followed him soon after, departing this life at the age of one hundred and seventy-seven years. His crown he left to Joseph, who ruled over Egypt for forty-eight years thereafter. He in turn handed the crown on to the grandchild of Pharaoh, an infant in arms at the time of his grandfather's death, toward whom Joseph had acted in a father's stead all his life.

THE DEATH AND BURIAL OF JOSEPH

On his death-bed Joseph took an oath of his brethren, and he bade them on their death-bed likewise take an oath of their sons, to carry his bones to Palestine, when God should visit them and bring them up out of the land of Egypt. He said: "I that am a ruler could take my father's body up to the Holy Land while it was still intact. Of you I do but make the request that ye carry my bones from hence, and you may inter them in any spot in Palestine, for I know that the burial-place of the fathers was appointed to be the tomb only of the three Patriarchs and their three wives."

Joseph took the oath, to carry his remains along with them when they left Egypt, from his brethren, and not from his sons, to bury him at once in Palestine, for he feared the Egyptians would not give the latter permission to transport his bones even if they recalled what Joseph had been allowed to do with his father's body. They would object that Joseph had been the viceroy, and a wish preferred by one of so high an estate could not be denied. Furthermore, he adjured his brethren not to leave Egypt until a redeemer should appear and announce his message with the words, "Pakod--I have surely visited you"--a tradition which Joseph had received from his father, who had it from Isaac, and Isaac in turn had beard it from Abraham. And he told them that God would redeem Israel through Moses as through the Messiah, in this world as in the world to come, and the Egyptian redemption would begin in Tishri, when Israel would be freed from slave labor, and would be completed in the following Nisan, when they would leave Egypt.

Joseph also admonished his brethren to walk in the ways of the Lord, so that they might become worthy of His grace and help. Especially he impressed upon his brethren and his sons the virtue of chastity and a steadfast moral life. He told them all that had happened to him, the hatred of his brethren, the persecutions of the wife of Potiphar, the slander, envy, and malice of the Egyptians, to show how that those who fear the Lord are not forsaken by Him in darkness, or bondage, or tribulation, or distress. "I was sold into slavery," he said, "but the Lord delivered me; I was thrown into prison, but His strong hand helped me. I was tortured by hunger, but the Lord Himself gave me sustenance. I was alone, and God comforted me. And as for you, if ye will walk in the ways of chastity and purity in patience and humility of heart, the Lord will dwell among you, for He loveth a chaste life, and if you, my children, will observe the commandments of the Lord, He will raise you up here, in this world, and bless you there, in the world to come. If men seek to do evil unto you, pray for them, and you will be delivered from all evil by the Lord. On account of my forbearing patience I received the daughter of my master to wife, and her dowry was a hundred talents of gold, and God gave me also beauty like the beauty of a flower, more than all the children of Jacob, and He preserved me unto mine old age in vigor and beauty, for in all things did I resemble Jacob."

Joseph continued and told them the visions he had had, in which the future of Israel was revealed to him, and then he closed with the words: "I know that the Egyptians will oppress you after my death, but God will execute vengeance for your sakes, and He will lead you to the land of promise of your fathers. But ye shall surely carry my bones with you from hence, for if my remains are taken to Canaan, the Lord will be with you in the light, and Behar will be with the Egyptians in the darkness. Also take with you the bones of your mother Zilpah, and bury them near the sepulchre of Bilhah and Rachel."

These words ended, he stretched out his feet, and slept his last eternal sleep, and the whole of Israel mourned him, and the whole of Egypt was in great grief, for he had been a compassionate friend to the Egyptians, too, and he had done good unto them, and given them wise counsel and assistance in all their undertakings.

Joseph's wish, that his bones should rest in the Holy Land, was fulfilled when the Israelites went forth from Egypt, and no less a personage than Moses applied himself to its execution. Such was Joseph's reward for the devotion he had displayed in the interment of his father's body, for he had done all things needful himself, leaving naught to others. Therefore so great a man as Moses busied himself with the realization of Joseph's wish.

For three days and three nights preceding the exodus Moses hunted up and down through the land of Egypt for Joseph's coffin, because he knew that Israel could not leave Egypt without heeding the oath given to Joseph. But his trouble was in vain; the coffin was nowhere to be found. Serah, the daughter of Asher, met Moses, tired and exhausted, and in answer to her question about the cause of his weariness, he told her of his fruitless search. Serah took him to the Nile river, and told him that the leaden coffin made for Joseph by the Egyptians had been sunk there after having been scaled up on all sides. The Egyptians had done this at the instigation and with the help of the magicians, who, knowing that Israel could not leave the country without the coffin, had used their arts to put it in a place whence it could not be removed.

Moses now took Joseph's cup, and he cut four flat pieces from it, and engraved a lion on one of them, an eagle on the second, a bull on the third, and a human figure on the fourth. He threw the first, with the lion, into the river, saying at the same time, "Joseph, Joseph, the hour for the redemption of Israel hath arrived, the Shekinah lingers here only for thy sake, the clouds of glory await thy coming. If thou wilt show thyself, well and good; if not, then we are clear from our oath." But the coffin did not appear.

Then Moses threw the second plate into the water, that with the figure of the eagle, repeating the same words, but again the coffin did not rise from the bed of the Nile, and there it remained, too, when he threw in the third plate bearing the figure of the bull, and called upon Joseph a third time to come forth. But the fourth plate with the human figure and the fourth invocation to Joseph brought the coffin to the surface of the water. Moses seized it, and in joy he bore it off. While Israel had been busy gathering gold and silver from the Egyptians, Moses had been thinking of nothing but Joseph's coffin, and his happiness was great that he had been permitted to fulfil the wish of Joseph.

During the forty years of wandering through the desert, the coffin was in the midst of Israel, as a reward for Joseph's promise to his brethren, "I will nourish you and take care of you." God had said, "As thou livest, for forty years they will take care of thy bones."

All this time in the desert Israel carried two shrines with them, the one the coffin containing the bones of the dead man Joseph, the other the Ark containing the covenant of the Living God. The wayfarers who saw the two receptacles wondered, and they would ask, "How doth the ark of the dead come next to the ark of the Ever-living?" The answer was, "The dead man enshrined in the one fulfilled the commandments enshrined in the other. In the latter it is written, I am the Lord thy God, and he said, Am I in the place of God? Here it is written, Thou shalt have no other gods before My face, and he said, I fear God. Here it is written, Thou shalt not take the name of the Lord thy God in vain, and therefore he did not swear by God, but said, By the life of

Pharaoh. Here it is written, Remember the Sabbath day, and he said to the overseer of his palace on Friday, Slay and make ready, meaning for the Sabbath. Here it is written, Honor thy father and thy mother, and he said, when his father desired to send him to his brethren, Here am I, although he knew it was perilous for him to go. Here it is written, Thou shalt not kill, and he refrained from murdering Potiphar when Potiphar's wife urged him to do it. Here it is written, Thou shalt not commit adultery, and he scorned the adulterous proposals of Potiphar's wife. Here it is written, Thou shalt not steal, and he stole nothing from Pharaoh, but gathered up all the money and brought it unto Pharaoh's house. Here it is written, Thou shalt not bear false witness against thy neighbor, and he told his father nothing of what his brethren had done to him, though what he might have told was the truth. Here it is written, Thou shalt not covet, and he did not covet Potiphar's wife."

On their arrival in the Holy Land, the Israelites buried the bones of Joseph in Shechem, for God spake to the tribes, saying, "From Shechem did ye steal him, and unto Shechem, shall ye return him."

God, who is so solicitous about the dead bodies of the pious, is even more solicitous about their souls, which stand before Him like angels, and do their service ministering unto Him.

Chapter 2

THE SONS OF JACOB--SIGNIFICANT NAMES

Jacob raised all his sons in the fear of God, and taught them the ways of a pious life, using severity when there was need to make his lessons impressive. He reaped the fruits of his labor, for all his sons were godly men of stainless character. The ancestors of the twelve tribes resembled their fathers in piety, and their acts were no less significant than those of Abraham, Isaac, and Jacob. Like these three, they deserve to be called the Fathers of Israel. God made a covenant with them as He had made with the three Patriarchs, and to this covenant their descendants owe their preservation.

The very names of the tribes point to the redemption of Israel. Reuben is so called, because God "sees" the affliction of His people; Simon, because He "hears" its groaning; Levi, He "joins" Himself unto His people when Israel suffers; Judah, Israel will "thank" God for its deliverance; Issachar, it will be "rewarded" for its suffering with a recompense; Zebulon, God will have a "dwelling-place" in Israel; Benjamin, He swore by His "right hand" to succor His people; Dan, He will "judge" the nation that subjugates Israel; Naphtali, He bestowed the Torah upon Israel, and she drops sweetness like the "honeycomb"; Gad, the Lord gave manna unto Israel, and it was like "coriander" seed; Asher, all nations will call Israel "happy"; and Joseph, because God will "add" a second redemption of Israel to the first--redemption from the wicked kingdom at the end as from Egypt in former times.

Not only the names of Jacob's sons are significant, but the names of their sons as well. Thus the names of the sons of Issachar express the activities of the tribe known for its learning above all the others. The oldest was called Tola, "worm"; as the silk worm is distinguished for its mouth, with which it spins, so also the men of the tribe of Issachar for the wise words of their mouth. The second is Puah, "madder plant"; as this plant colors all things, so the tribe of Issachar colors the whole world with its teachings. The third is Jashub, "the returning one," for through the teachings of Issachar Israel will be turned back to its Heavenly Father; and Shimron, the fourth, is "the observing one," to indicate that the tribe of Issachar observes the Torah.

The names of the sons of Gad likewise interpret the history of the tribe. During Israel's sojourn in Egypt, it had strayed from the right path, but when Aaron appeared as prophet and monitor, and called unto the Israelites to cast away the abominations of their eyes and forsake the idols of Egypt, they hearkened unto his words. Hence the double name Ozni and Ezbon borne by one of the sons of Gad, for this tribe "hearkened" to the word of God, and fulfilled His "will."

The grandsons of Asher bear the names Heber and Malchiel, because they were the "associates" of kings, and their inheritance yielded "royal dainties."

Partly the history of the tribe of Benjamin can be read in the names of its chiefs. It consisted originally of ten divisions, descended from Benjamin's ten sons, but five of them perished in Egypt on account of their ungodly ways, from which no admonition availed to turn them aside. Of the five families remaining, two, the descendants of Bela and those of Ashbel, had always been God-fearing; the others, the Ahiramites, the Shephuphamites, and the Huphamites, repented of their sins, and in accordance with the change in their conduct had been the change in their names. Ehi had become Ahiram, because the breach with the "Exalted" One was healed; Muppira was called Shephupham, because they "afflicted" themselves in their penance; and Huppim was turned into Hupham, to indicate that they had "cleansed" themselves from sin. As a reward for their piety, the family springing from Bela was permitted to have two subdivisions, the Ardites and the Naamites. Their names point them out as men that know well how the fear of God is to be manifested, whose deeds are exceedingly lovely.

Naphtali was another tribe of steadfast piety, and the names of his sons testify thereto: Jahzeel, because the tribesmen raised a "partition wall" between God and the idols, inasmuch as they trusted in God and contemned the idols; Guni, because God was their "protection"; and Jezer and Shillem designate the Naphtalites as men devoted to God with all their hearts.

REUBEN'S TESTAMENT

Two years after the death of Joseph, Reuben fell sick. Feeling that his end was nigh, he called together his sons, his grandsons, and his brethren, to give them his last admonitions from out of the fulness of his experience. He spake: "Hear, my brethren, and do ye, my children, give ear unto Reuben your father in the commands that I enjoin upon you. And, behold, I adjure you this day by the God of heaven that ye walk not in the follies of youth and the fornications to which I was addicted, and wherewith I defiled the bed of my father Jacob. For I tell you now that for seven months the Lord afflicted my loins with a terrible plague, and if my father Jacob had not interceded for me, the Lord had swept me away. I was twenty years of age when I did what was evil before the Lord, and for seven months I was sick unto death. Then I did penance for seven years in the innermost depths of my soul. Wine and strong drink I drank not, the flesh of animals passed not my lips, dainties I tasted not, because I mourned over my sins, for they were great."

He admonished those gathered around him to beware of the seven tempter spirits, which are the spirit of fornication, gluttony, strife, love of admiration, arrogance, falsehood, and injustice. He cautioned them especially against unchastity, saying: "Pay no heed to the glances of a woman, and remain not alone with a married woman, and do not occupy yourselves with the affairs of women. Had I not seen Bilhah bathe in a secluded spot, I had not fallen into the great sin I committed, for after my thoughts had once grasped the nakedness of woman, I could not sleep until I had accomplished the abominable deed. For when our father Jacob went to his father Isaac, while we sojourned in Eder, not far from Ephrath, which is Beth-lehem, Bilhah was drunken with wine, and she lay asleep, uncovered, in her bedchamber, and I entered in and saw her nakedness and committed the sin, and I went out again, leaving her asleep. But an angel of God revealed my impious act to my father Jacob at once. He came back and mourned over me, and never again did he approach Bilhah. Unto the very last day of his life, I had not the assurance to look my father in the face or to speak to my brethren regarding my disgrace, and even now my conscience tortures me on account of my sin. Nevertheless my father spake words of comfort to me, and prayed to God in my behalf, that the wrath of the Lord might depart from me, as He showed me."

Reuben admonished his children impressively to join themselves to Levi, "because he will know the law of the Lord," he said, "and he will give ordinances for judgment, and bring sacrifices for all Israel, until the consummation of the times, as the anointed high priest of whom the Lord spake."

After announcing his last will to his sons, Reuben departed this life at the age of one hundred and twenty-five years. His body was laid in a coffin until his sons bore it away from Egypt, and carried it up to Hebron, where they buried it in the Double Cave.

SIMON'S ADMONITION AGAINST ENVY

As Reuben confessed his sin upon his death-bed, and warned his children and his family to be on their guard against unchastity, the vice that had brought about his fall, so Simon, when he was about to die, assembled his sons around him, and confessed the sin he had committed. He had been guilty of boundless envy of Joseph, and he spoke: "I was the second son begotten by my father Jacob, and my mother Leah called me Simon, because the Lord had heard her prayer. I waxed strong, and shrank from no manner of deed, and I was afraid of naught, for my heart was hard, and my liver unyielding, and my bowels without mercy. And in the days of my youth I was jealous of Joseph, for our father loved him more than all the rest of us, and I resolved to kill him. For the prince of temptation sent the spirit of jealousy to take possession of me, and it blinded me so that I did not consider Joseph to be my brother, and I spared not even my father Jacob. But his God and the God of his fathers sent His angel and saved him out of my hands.

When I went to Shechem to fetch ointment for the herds, and Reuben was in Dothan, where all our supplies and stores were kept, our brother Judah sold Joseph to the Ishmaelites. On his return, when he heard what had happened, Reuben was very sad, for he had been desirous of saving Joseph and bringing him back to our father. But as for me, my wrath was enkindled against Judah, that he had let him escape alive. My anger abode with me all of five months. But the Lord restrained me from using the power of my hands, for my right hand withered for the length of seven days. Then I knew that what had happened was for the sake of Joseph. I repented and prayed to God to restore my hand and withhold me henceforth from all sorts of defilement, envy, and folly. For two years I gave myself up to fasting and the fear of God, for I perceived that redemption from jealousy could come only through the fear of God.

My father, seeing me downcast, asked to know the cause of my sadness, and I replied that I was suffering with my liver, but in truth I was mourning more than all my brethren, seeing that I had been the cause of Joseph's sale. And when we went down into Egypt, and Joseph bound me as a spy, I was not grieved, for I knew in my heart that my suffering was just retribution. But Joseph was good, the spirit of God dwelt within him. Compassionate and merciful as he was, he bore me no resentment for my evil deeds toward him, but he loved me with the same love he showed the others. He paid due honor to us all, and gave us gold, and cattle, and produce. And now, my dear children, do ye love one another, each one his brother, with a clean heart, and remove the spirit of jealousy from the midst of you."

Like Reuben, so also Simon adjured his sons to beware of unchastity, for this vice is the mother of all evil. It separates man from God, and abandons him to Behar. These were the closing words of his exhortation: "In the writings of Enoch I saw that your sons would be corrupted through unchastity, and they would maltreat the sons of Levi with the sword. But they will not be able to do aught against Levi, for the war he will wage is the war of the Lord, and he will vanquish all your armies. As a small remnant you will be scattered among Levi and Judah, and none among you will rise to be a judge or a king of our people, as, my father Jacob prophesied in his blessing."

Having completed his admonitions to his sons, Simon passed away and was gathered to his fathers, at the age of one hundred and twenty years. His sons placed him in a coffin made of imperishable wood, so that they might carry his bones to Hebron, as they did, in secret, during the war between the Egyptians and the Canaanites. Thus did all the tribes during the war; they took the remains each of its founder from Egypt to Hebron. Only the bones of Joseph remained in Egypt until the Israelites went out of the land, for the Egyptians guarded them in their royal treasure chambers. Their magicians had warned them that whenever Joseph's bones should be removed from Egypt, a great darkness would envelop the whole land, and it would be a dire misfortune for the Egyptians, for none would be able to recognize his neighbor even with the light of a lamp.

THE ASCENSION OF LEVI

When it was disclosed to Levi that he was about to die, he gathered all his children around him, to tell them the story of his life, and he also prophesied unto them what they would do, and what would happen to them until the judgment day. He spoke: "When we were pasturing the flocks in Abel-Meholah, the spirit of understanding of the Lord came upon me, and I saw all mankind, how they corrupt their ways, and that injustice builds up walls for herself, and impiety sits enthroned upon the towers. And I fell to grieving over the generations of men, and I prayed to the Lord to save me. Sleep enshrouded me, and I beheld a tall mountain, and lo! the heavens opened, and an angel of God addressed me, and said: 'Levi, enter!'

"I entered the first heaven, and I saw a great sea hanging there, and farther on I saw a second heaven, brighter and more resplendent than the first. I said to the angel, 'Why is this so?' And the angel said to me, 'Marvel not at this, for thou shalt see another heaven, brilliant beyond compare, and when thou hast ascended thither, thou shalt stand near the Lord, and thou shalt be His minister, and declare His mysteries to men; and of the Lord's portion shall be thy life, and He shall be thy field and vineyard and fruits and gold and silver.'

"Then the angel explained the uses of the different heavens to me, and all that happens in each, and he proclaimed the judgment day. He opened the gates of the third heaven, where I beheld the holy Temple, and God seated upon the Throne of Glory. The Lord spake to me: 'Levi, upon thee have I bestowed the blessing of the priesthood, until I come and dwell in the midst of Israel.' Then the angel carried me back to earth, and gave me a shield and a sword, saying, 'Execute vengeance upon Shechem for Dinah, and I will be with thee, for the Lord hath sent me.' I asked the angel what his name was, and he replied: 'I am the angel that intercedes for the people of Israel, that it may not be destroyed utterly, for every evil spirit attacks it.'

"When I awoke, I betook myself to my father, and on the way, near Gebal, I found a brass shield, such as I had seen in my dream. Then I advised my father and my brother Reuben to bid the sons of Hamor circumcise themselves, for I was quivering with rage on account of the abominable deed they had done. I slew Shechem first of all, and then Simon slew Hamor, and all my other brothers came out and destroyed the whole city. Our father took this in ill part, and in his blessing he remembered our conduct. Although we did a wrong thing in acting thus against his wishes, yet I recognized it to be the judgment of God upon the people of Shechem on account of their sins, and I said to my father: 'Be not wroth, my lord, for God will exterminate the Canaanites through this, and he will give the land to thee and to thy seed after thee. Henceforth Shechem will be called the city of imbeciles, for as a fool is mocked at, so have we made a mockery of them.'

"When we journeyed to Beth-lehem, and had been abiding there for seventy days, another vision was vouchsafed me, like unto the former. I saw seven men clad in white, and they spake to me, saying: 'Rise up, and array thyself in the priestly garments, set the crown of righteousness upon thy head, and put on the ephod of understanding, and the robe of truth, and the mitre-plate of faith, and the mitre of dignity, and the shoulderpieces of prophecy.' And each of the men brought a garment unto me and invested me therewith, and spake: 'Henceforth be the priest of the Lord, thou and thy seed unto eternity. And ye shall eat all that is lovely to look upon, and the table of the Lord thy descendants will appropriate for themselves, and from them will come high priests, judges, and scholars, for all that is holy will be guarded by their mouth.'

"Two days after I was visited by this dream, Judah and I repaired to our grandfather Isaac, who blessed me in accordance with the words I had heard. Jacob also had a vision, and he saw, too, that I was appointed to be the priest of God, and through me he set apart a tenth of his possessions unto the Lord. And when we established ourselves in Hebron, the residence of Isaac, our grandfather taught me the law of the priesthood, and admonished me to hold myself aloof from unchastity.

At the age of twenty-eight years I took Milcah to wife, and she bore me a son, and I named him Gershom, because we were strangers in the land. But I perceived he would not be in the first ranks of men. My second son was born unto me in my thirty-fifth year, and he saw the light of the world at sunrise, and I beheld him in a vision standing among the proud of the assembly, and therefore I gave him the name Kohath. The third son my wife bore me in the fortieth year of my life, and I called his name Merari, because bitter had been her travail in bearing him. My daughter Jochebed was born in Egypt, when I was sixty-three years old, and I called her thus because I was known honorably among my brethren in those days. And in my ninety-fourth year, Amram took Jochebed to wife, he that was born on the same day with her."

Thereupon Levi admonished his children to walk in the ways of the Lord, and fear Him with all their heart, and he told them what he had learnt from the writings of Enoch, that his descendants would sin against the Lord in times to come, and they would suffer the Divine punishment for their transgression, and then God would raise up a new priest, unto whom all the words of the Lord would be revealed. His last words were: "And now, my children, ye have heard all I have to say. Choose, now, light or darkness, the law of the Lord or the works of Beliar." And his sons made answer, "Before the Lord we will walk according to His law." Then Levi spake, "The Lord is witness and the angels are witnesses, I am witness and ye are witnesses, concerning the word of your mouth." And his sons replied, "We are witnesses."

Thus Levi ceased to admonish his sons. He stretched out his feet, and was gathered unto his fathers, at the age of one hundred and thirty-seven years, a greater age than any of his brethren attained.

JUDAH WARNS AGAINST GREED AND UNCHASTITY

The last words addressed by Judah to his sons were the following: "I was the fourth son begotten by my father, and my mother called me Judah, saying, 'I thank the Lord that He hath given me a fourth son.' I was zealous in my youth and obedient to my father in all things. When I grew up to manhood, he blessed me, saying, 'Thou wilt be king, and wilt prosper in all thy ways.' The Lord granted me His grace in whatever I undertook, in the field and in the house. I could speed as swiftly as the hind, and overtake it, and prepare a dish of it for my father. A deer I could catch on the run, and all the animals of the valley. A wild mare I could outstrip, hold it, and bridle it. A lion I slew, and snatched a kid from its jaws. A bear I caught by the paw, and flung it adown the cliff, and it lay beneath crushed. I could keep pace with the wild boar, and overtake it, and as I ran I seized it, and tore it to pieces. A leopard sprang at my dog in Hebron, and I grasped its tail, and hurled it away from me, and its body burst on the coast at Gaza. A wild steer I found grazing in the field. I took it by its horns, swung it round and round until it was stunned, and then I cast it to the ground and killed it."

Judah continued and told his children of his heroism in the wars that the sons of Jacob had waged with the kings of Canaan and with Esau and his family. In all these conflicts he bore a distinguished part, beyond the achievements of the others. His father Jacob was free from all anxiety when Judah was with his brethren in their combats, because he had had a vision showing him an angel of strength standing at the side of Judah on all his ways.

Judah did not conceal his shortcomings, either. He confessed how drunkenness and passion had betrayed him first into marriage with a Canaanitish woman, and then into improper relations with his daughter-in-law Tamar. He said to his children:

"Do not walk after the desire of your hearts, and vaunt not the valiant deeds of your youth. This, too, is evil in the eyes of the Lord. For while I boasted that the face of a beautiful woman had never allured me in the wars, and reviled my brother Reuben for his transgression with Bilhah, the spirit of passion and unchastity gained possession of me, and I took Bath-shua to wife, and trespassed with Tamar, though she was the affianced of my son. First I said to Bath-shua's father, 'I will take counsel with my father Jacob, to know whether I should marry thy daughter,' but he was a king, and he showed me an untold heap of gold accredited to his daughter, and he adorned her with the magnificence of women, in gold and pearls, and he bade her pour the wine at the meal. The wine turned my eyes awry, and passion darkened my heart. In mad love for her, I violated the command of the Lord and the will of my father, and I took her to wife. The Lord gave me a recompense according to the counsel of my heart, for I had no joy in the sons she bore me.

"And now, my children, I pray you, do not intoxicate yourselves with wine, for wine twists the understanding away from the truth, and confuses the sight of the eyes. Wine led me astray, so that I felt no shame before the throngs of people in the city, and I turned aside and went in to Tamar in the presence of them, and committed a great sin. And though a man be a king, if he leads an unchaste life, he loses his kingship. I gave Tamar my staff, which is the stay of my tribe, and my girdle-cord, which is power, and my signet-diadem, which is the glory of my kingdom. I did penance for all this, and unto old age I drank no wine, and ate no flesh, and knew no sort of pleasure. Wine causes the secret things of God and man to be revealed unto the stranger. Thus did I disclose the commands of the Lord and the mysteries of my father Jacob to the Canaanite woman Bath-shua, though God had forbidden me to betray them. I also enjoin you not to love gold, and not to look upon the beauty of women, for through money and through beauty I was led astray to Bath-shua the Canaanite. I know that my stock will fall into misery through these two things, for even the wise men among my sons will be changed by them, and the consequence will be that the kingdom of Judah will be diminished, the domain that the Lord gave me as a reward for my obedient conduct toward my father, for never did I speak in contradiction of him, but I did all things according to his words. And Isaac, my father's father, blessed me with the blessing that I should be ruler in Israel, and I know that the kingdom will arise from me. In the books of Enoch the just I read all the evil that ye will do in the latter days. Only beware, my children, of unchastity and greed, for love of gold leads to idolatry, causing men to call them gods that are none, and dethroning the reason of man. On account of gold I lost my children, and had I not mortified my flesh, and humbled my soul, and had not my father Jacob offered up prayers for me, I had died childless. But the God of my fathers, the merciful and gracious One, saw that I had acted unwittingly, for the ruler of deception had blinded me, and I was ignorant, being flesh and blood, and corrupt through sins, and in the moment when I considered myself invincible, I recognized my weakness."

Then Judah revealed to his sons, in clear, brief words, the whole history of Israel until the advent of the Messiah, and his final speech was: "My children, observe the whole law of the Lord; in it is hope for all that keep His ways. I die this day at the age of one hundred and nineteen years before your eyes. None shall bury me in a costly garment, nor shall ye cut my body to embalm it, but ye shall carry me to Hebron."

Having spoken these words, Judah sank into death.

ISSACHAR'S SINGLENESS OF HEART

When Issachar felt his end approach, he summoned his sons, and he said to them: "Hearken, my children, unto your father Issachar, and listen to the words of him that is beloved of the Lord. I was born unto Jacob as his fifth son, as a reward for the dudaim. Reuben brought the dudaim from the field. They were fragrant apples, which grew in the land of Haran upon an eminence below a gully. Rachel met Reuben, and she took the dudaim away from him. The lad wept, and his cries brought his mother Leah to his side, and she addressed Rachel thus: 'Is it a small matter that thou hast taken away my husband? and wouldst thou take away my son's dudaim also?' And Rachel said, 'See, Jacob shall be thine to-night for thy son's dudaim.' But Leah insisted, 'Jacob is mine, and I am the wife of his youth,' whereupon Rachel, 'Be not boastful and overweening. To me he was betrothed first, and for my sake he served our father fourteen years. Thou art not his wife, thou wast taken to him by cunning instead of me, for our father deceived me, and put me out of the way the night of thy nuptials, so that Jacob could not see me. Nevertheless, give me the dudaim, and thou mayest have Jacob for a night.'

"Then Leah bore me, and I was called Issachar, on account of the reward Rachel had given to my mother. At that time an angel of the Lord appeared to Jacob, and he spoke: 'Rachel will bear only two sons, for she rejected the espousal of her husband, and chose continence! But Leah bore six sons, for the Lord knew that she desired to be with her husband, not because she was prompted by the evil inclination, but for the sake of children. Rachel's prayer also was fulfilled, on account of the dudaim, for although she desired to eat of the apples, she did not touch them, but put them in the house of the Lord, and gave them to the priest of the Most High that was in those days.

"When I grew up, my children, I walked in the integrity of my heart, and I became a husbandman, cultivating the land for my father and my brethren, and I gathered the fruit from the fields in their due time. My father blessed me, because he saw that I walked in singleness of heart. I was not married to a wife until I was thirty years old, for the hard work I did consumed my strength, and I had no desire unto woman, but, overwhelmed by fatigue, I would sink into sleep. My father was well pleased at all times with my rectitude. If my work was crowned with good results, I brought the firstfruits of my labor to the priest of the Lord, the next harvest went to my father, and then I thought of myself. The Lord doubled the possessions in my hand, and Jacob knew that God aided me for the sake of my singleness of heart, for in my sincerity I gave of the produce of the land to the poor and the needy.

"And now hearken unto me, my children, and walk in singleness of heart, for upon it resteth the favor of the Lord at all times. The simple man longeth not for gold, he doth not defraud his neighbor, he hath no desire for meats and dainties of many kinds, he careth not for sumptuous dress, he hopeth not for long life, he waiteth only upon the will of God. The spirits of deception have no power over him, for he looketh not upon the beauty of woman, lest he defile his understanding with corruption. Jealousy cometh not into his thoughts, envy doth not sear his soul, and insatiable greed doth not make him look abroad for rich gain. Now, then, my children, observe the law of the Lord, attain to simplicity, and walk in singleness of heart, without meddling with the affairs of others. Love the Lord and love your neighbors, have pity upon the poor and the feeble, bow your backs to till the ground, occupy yourselves with work upon the land, and bring gifts unto the Lord in gratitude. For the Lord hath blessed you with the best of the fruits of the field, as he hath blessed all the saints from Abel down to our day.

"Know, my children, that in the latter time your sons will abandon the paths of probity, and will be ruled by greed. They will forsake rectitude and practice craft, they will depart from the commands of the Lord and follow after Beliar, they will give up husbandry and pursue their evil plans, they will be scattered among the heathen and serve their enemies. Tell this unto your children, so that, if they sin, they may repent speedily, and return to the Lord, for He is merciful, and He will take them out to bring them back unto their land.

"I am one hundred and twenty-two years old, and I can discern no sin in myself. Save my wife, I have known no woman. I was guilty of no unchastity through the lifting up of eyes. I drank no wine, that I might not be led astray, I did not covet what belonged to my neighbor, guile had no place in my heart, lies did not pass my lips. I sighed along with all that were heavy-laden, and to the poor I gave my bread. I loved the Lord with all my might, and mankind I also loved. Do ye likewise, my children, and all the spirits of Beliar will flee from you, no deed done by the wicked will have power over you, and ye will vanquish all the wild beasts, for ye have with you the Lord of heaven."

And Issachar bade his children carry him up to Hebron, and bury him there by his fathers in the Cave, and he stretched out his feet, and fell into the sleep of eternity, full of years, healthy of limb, and in the possession of all his faculties.

ZEBULON EXHORTS UNTO COMPASSION

When Zebulon attained the age of one hundred and fourteen years, which was two years after the death of Joseph, he called his sons together, and admonished them, in these words, to lead a life of piety: "I am Zebulon, a precious gift for my parents, for when I was born, my father became very rich, by means of the streaked rods, in herds of sheep and herds of cattle. I am conscious of no sin in me, and I remember no wrong done by me, unless it be the unwitting sin committed against Joseph, in that I did not, out of consideration for my brethren, disclose to my father what had happened to his favorite son, though in secret I mourned exceedingly. I feared my brethren, because they had agreed that he who betrayed the secret should be slain with the sword. When they planned to kill Joseph, I besought them amid tears not to sin thus.

"And now, my children, hearken unto me. I exhort you to observe the commands of the Lord, and have mercy upon your neighbors, and act compassionately, not only toward men, but also toward dumb brutes. For on account of my mercifulness the Lord blessed me; all my brethren fell sick at one time or another, but I escaped without any illness. Also the sons of my brethren had to endure disease, and they were nigh unto death for the sake of Joseph, because they had no pity in their hearts. But my sons were preserved in perfect health, as ye well know. And when I was in Canaan, catching fish at the shores of the sea for my father Jacob, many were drowned in the waters of the sea, but I came away unharmed. For ye must know that I was the first to build a boat for rowing upon the sea, and I plied along the coasts in it, and caught fish for my father's household, until we went down into Egypt. Out of pity I would share my haul with the poor stranger, and if he was sick or well on in years, I would prepare a savory dish for him, and I gave unto each according to his needs, sympathizing with him in his distress and having pity upon him. Therefore the Lord brought numerous fish to my nets, for he that gives aught to his neighbor, receives it back from the Lord with great increase. For five years I fished in the summer, and in the winter I pastured the flocks with my brethren.

"Now, my children, have pity and compassion on all men, that the Lord may have pity and compassion on you, for in the measure in which man has mercy with his fellow-men, God has mercy with him. When we came down into Egypt, Joseph did not visit upon us the wrong he had suffered. Take him as your model, and remember not a wrong done unto you, else unity is rent asunder, and the bonds of kinship are torn, and the soul is disquieted. Observe the water! If it runs on undivided, it carries down stone, wood, and sand along with it. But if it is divided and flows through many channels, the earth sucks it up, and it loses its force. If you separate, one from the other, you will be like divided waters. Be not cleft into two heads, for all that the Lord hath made has but one head. He has given two shoulders unto his creatures, two hands, and two feet, but all these organs obey one head."

Zebulon ended his exhortation unto unity with an account of the divisions in Israel, whereof he had read in the writings of the fathers, that they would come about in future days, and bring sore suffering upon Israel. However, he spoke encouraging words to his children, saying: "Be not grieved over my death, and do not lose heart at my departure from you, for I shall arise again in the midst of you, and I shall live joyously among the people of my tribe, those who observe the law of the Lord. As for the godless, the Lord will bring everlasting fire down upon them, and exterminate them unto all generations. Now I hasten hence unto my eternal rest with my fathers. But ye, fear ye the Lord your God with all your might all the days of your life."

Having made an end of saying these words, he sank into the sleep of death, and his sons put him into a coffin, wherein they carried him up to Hebron later, to bury him there next to his fathers.

DAN'S CONFESSION

When Dan assembled his family at the last of his life, he spake: "I confess before you this day, my children, that I had resolved to kill Joseph, that good and upright man, and I rejoiced over his sale, for his father loved him more than he loved the rest of us. The spirit of envy and boastfulness goaded me on, saying, 'Thou, too, art the son of Jacob,' and one of the spirits of Behar stirred me up, saying, 'Take this sword, and slay Joseph, for once he is dead thy father will love thee.' It was the spirit of anger that was seeking to persuade me to crush Joseph, as a leopard crunches a kid between its teeth. But the God of our father Jacob did not deliver him into my hand, to let me find him alone, and He did not permit me to execute this impious deed, that two tribes in Israel might not be destroyed.

"And now, my children, I am about to die, and I tell it unto you in truth, if you take not heed against the spirit of lies and anger, and if ye love not truth and generosity, you will perish. The spirit of anger casts the net of error around its victim, and it blinds his eyes, and the spirit of lies warps his mind, and clouds his vision. Evil is anger, it is the grave of the soul. Desist from anger and hate lies, that the Lord may dwell among you, and Behar flee from your presence. Speak the truth each unto his neighbor, and you will not fall into anger and trouble, but you will be at peace, and the Lord of peace you will have with you, and no war will vanquish you.

"I speak thus, for I know that in the latter days you will fall off from God, and you will kindle the wrath of Levi, and rise in rebellion against Judah, but you will not accomplish aught against them, for the angel of the Lord is their guide, and Israel will perish through them. And if you turn recreant to the Lord, you will execute every kind of evil thing, and do the abominations of the heathen, committing unchastity with the wives of the godless, while the tempter spirits are at work among you. Therefore you will be carried away into captivity, and in the lands of exile you will suffer all the plagues of Egypt and all the tribulations of the heathen. But when you return to the Lord, you will find mercy. He will take you into His sanctuary, and grant you peace.

"And now, my children, fear the Lord, and be on your guard against Satan and his spirits. Keep aloof from every evil deed, cast anger away from you and every sort of lie, love truth and forbearance, and what ye have heard from your father, tell unto your children. Avoid all manner of unrighteousness, cling to the integrity of the law of the Lord, and bury me near my fathers."

Having spoken these words, he kissed his children, and fell asleep.

NAPHTALI'S DREAMS OF THE DIVISION OF THE TRIBES

In the hundred and thirty-second year of his life, Naphtali invited all his children to a banquet. The next morning when he awoke, he told them that he was dying, but they would not believe him. He, however, praised the Lord, and assured them again that his death was due after the banquet of the day before. Then he addressed his last words to his children:

"I was born of Bilhah, and because Rachel had acted with cunning, and had given Jacob Bilhah instead of herself, I was called Naphtali. Rachel loved me, for I was born upon her knees, and while I was still very young, she was in the habit of kissing me and saying, 'O that I had a brother unto thee from mine own body, one in thine image.' Therefore Joseph resembled me in all respects, in accordance with Rachel's prayer. My mother Bilhah was a daughter of Rotheus, a brother of Deborah, Rebekah's nurse, and she was born the same day as Rachel. As for Rotheus, he was of the family of Abraham, a Chaldean, God-fearing, and a free man of noble birth, and when he was taken captive, he was bought by Laban and married to his slave Aina. She bore Rotheus a daughter, and he called her Zilpah, after the name of the village in which he was taken captive. His second daughter he called Bilhah, saying, 'My daughter is impetuous,' for hardly was she born when she hastened to suckle.

"I was fleet of foot like a deer, and my father Jacob appointed me to be his messenger, and in his blessing he called me a hind let loose. As the potter knows the vessel he fashions, how much it is to hold, and uses clay accordingly, so the Lord makes the body in conformity with the soul, and to agree with the capacity of the body He plans the soul. The one corresponds to the other down to the third of a hair-breadth, for the whole of creation was made by weight, and measure, and rule. And as the potter knows the use of every vessel he fashions, so the Lord knows the body of His creature, unto what point it will be steadfast in the good, and at what point it will fall into evil ways. Now, then, my children, let your conduct be well-ordered unto good in the fear of God, do naught that is ill-regulated or untimely, for though ye tell your eye to hear, it yet cannot, and as little can ye do deeds of light while you abide in darkness."

Furthermore Naphtali said unto his children: "I give you no command concerning my silver, or my gold, or any other possession that I bequeath to you. And what I command you is not a hard matter, which you cannot do, but I speak unto you concerning an easy thing, which you can execute." Then his sons answered, and said, "Speak, father, for we are listening to thy words." Naphtali continued: "I give you no commandment except regarding the fear of God, that you should serve Him and follow after Him." Then the sons of Naphtali asked: "Wherefore does He require our service?" and he replied, saying: "He needs no creature, but all creatures need Him. Nevertheless He hath not created the world for naught, but that men should fear Him, and none should do unto his neighbor what he would not have others do unto him." His sons asked again, "Father, hast thou observed that we strayed from the ways of the Lord to the right or to the left?" Naphtali replied: "God is witness, and so am I witness for you, that it is as you say. But I fear regarding future times, that you may depart from the ways of the Lord, and follow after the idols of the stranger, and walk in the statutes of the heathen peoples, and join yourselves unto the sons of Joseph instead of the sons of Levi and Judah." The sons of Naphtali spoke, "What reason hast thou for commanding this thing unto us?" Naphtali: "Because I know that the sons of Joseph will one day turn recreant to the Lord, the God of their fathers, and it is they that will lead the sons of Israel into sin, and cause them to be driven away from their inheritance, their beautiful land, to a land that is not ours, even as it was Joseph that brought the Egyptian bondage down upon us.

"I will tell ye, my children, the vision I had while I was yet a shepherd of flocks. I saw my brethren pasturing the herds with me, and our father approached, and said: 'Up, my sons, each one take what he can in my presence!' We answered, and said to him, 'What shall we take? We see nothing but the sun, the moon, and the stars.' Then our father said: 'These shall ye take!' Levi, hearing this, snatched up an ox-goad, sprang up to the sun, sat upon him, and rode. Judah did likewise. He jumped up to the moon, and rode upon her. And the other nine tribes did the same, each rode upon his star or his planet in the heavens. Joseph remained behind alone on the earth, and our father Jacob said to him, 'My son, why hast thou not done like thy brethren?' Joseph answered, 'What right have men born of woman to be in the heavens, seeing that in the end they must stay on earth?' While Joseph was speaking thus, a tall steer appeared before him. He had great pinions like the wings of the stork, and his horns were as long as those of the reem. Jacob urged his son, 'Up, Joseph, mount the steer!' Joseph did as his father bade him, and Jacob went his way. For the space of two hours Joseph displayed himself upon the steer, sometimes galloping, sometimes flying, until he reached Judah. Then Joseph unfolded the standard in his hand, and began to rain blows down upon Judah with it, and when his brother demanded the reason for this treatment, he said, 'Because thou hast twelve rods in thine hand, and I have but one. Give thine to me, and peace shall prevail between us!' But Judah refused to do his bidding, and Joseph beat him until he dropped ten rods, and only two remained in his clutch. Joseph now invited his brethren to abandon Judah and follow after him. They all did thus, except Benjamin, who stayed true to Judah. Levi was grieved over the desertion of Judah, and he descended from the sun. Toward the end of the day a storm broke out, and it scattered the brethren, so that no two were together. When I gave an account of my vision to my father Jacob, he said, 'It is but a dream, it can neither help nor harm.'

"A short while thereafter another vision was revealed to me. I saw all of us together with our father at the shores of the sea, and a ship appeared in the midst of the sea, and it had neither sailors nor other crew. Our father spake, 'Do you see what I see?' And when we answered that we did, he commanded us to follow him. He took off his clothes, and sprang into the sea, and we sprang after him. Levi and Judah were the first to scale the side of the ship. Our father cried after them, 'See what is written upon the mast,' for there is no ship that does not bear the name of the owner upon the mast. Levi and Judah scrutinized the writing, and what they read was this, 'This ship and all the treasures therein belong unto the son of Barachel.' Jacob thanked God for having blessed him, not only on land, but also upon the sea, and he said to us, 'Stretch forth your hands, and whatsoever each one seizes shall be his!' Levi caught hold of the big mast, Judah of the second mast, next to Levi's, and the other brethren, with the exception of Joseph, took the oars, and Jacob himself seized the two rudders, wherewith to guide the ship. He bade Joseph take an oar, too, but he refused to do his father's bidding, and Jacob gave him one of the rudders. After our father had instructed us each one in what we had to do, he disappeared, whereupon Joseph took possession of the second rudder, too. All went smoothly for a time, as long as Judah and Joseph acted together in harmony with each other, and Judah kept Joseph informed in what direction to steer. But a quarrel broke out between them, and Joseph did not guide the vessel in the way his father had commanded him, and Judah attempted to direct him, and the vessel was wrecked upon a rock. Levi and Judah descended from the masts, and likewise the other brethren left the ship and escaped to the shore. At this moment Jacob appeared, and he found us scattered in all directions, and we reported to him how Joseph had caused the vessel to run aground, because he had refused, out of jealousy of Judah and Levi, to steer it according to their instructions. Then Jacob asked us to show him the spot where we had lost the ship, of which only the masts were visible above the water. He emitted a whistle summoning us all, and he swam out into the water, and raised the vessel as before. Turning to Joseph, he spake thus, 'My son, never do that again, never permit jealousy of thy brethren to master thee. Nearly it happened that all thy brethren perished because of thee.'

"When I told my father what I had seen in this vision, he clasped his hands, and tears flowed from his eyes, and be said: 'My son, for that the vision was doubled unto thee twice, I am dismayed, and I shudder for my son Joseph. I loved him more than all of you, but by reason of his perverseness ye will be carried away into captivity, and scattered among the nations. Thy first and thy second vision had the same meaning, the vision is one.'

"Therefore, my sons, I command you not to join yourselves unto the sons of Joseph, but ye shall join yourselves unto the sons of Levi and Judah. I tell you, too, that my inheritance shall be of the best of Palestine, the middle of the earth. You will eat, and the delectable gifts of my portion will satisfy you. But I warn you not to kick in your prosperity and not to become perverse, resisting the commands of God, who satisfies you with the best of His land, and not to forget your God, whom your father Abraham chose when the families of the earth were divided in the days of Peleg. The Lord descended with seventy angels, at their head Michael, and he commanded them to teach the seventy languages unto the seventy families of Noah. The angels did according to the behest of God, and the holy Hebrew language remained only in the house of Shem and Eber, and in the house of their descendant Abraham. On this day of teaching languages, Michael came to each nation separately, and told it the message with which God had charged him, saying: 'I know the rebellion and the confusion ye have enacted against God. Now, make choice of him whom you will serve, and whom will you have as your mediator in heaven?' Then spake Nimrod the wicked, 'In my eyes there is none greater than he that taught me the language of Cush.' The other nations also answered in words like these, each one designated its angel. But Abraham said: 'I choose none other than Him that spake and the world was. In Him I will have faith, and my seed forever and ever.' Thenceforth God put every nation in the care of its angel, but Abraham and his seed He kept for Himself.

"Therefore I adjure you not to go astray and serve other gods beside Him whom our fathers made choice of. You can perceive somewhat of His power in the creation of man. From head to foot is man wonderfully made. With his ears he hears, with his eyes he sees, with his brain he comprehends, with his nose he smells, with the tubes of his throat he utters sounds, with his gullet he swallows food, with his tongue he articulates, with his mouth he forms words, with his hands he does his work, with his heart he meditates, with his spleen he laughs, with his liver he waxes angry, with his stomach he crushes his food, with his feet he walks, with his lungs he breathes, and with his kidneys he makes resolves, and none of his organs undergoes a change in function, each performs its own. Therefore it behooves man to take to heart who it is that hath created him, and who hath developed him from a foul-smelling drop in the womb of woman, who hath brought him to the light of the world, who hath given sight to his eyes, and who hath bestowed the power of motion upon his feet, who maketh him to stand upright, who hath infused the breath of life into him, and who hath imparted of His own pure spirit unto him. Happy the man, therefore, that polluteth not the holy spirit of God within him by doing evil deeds, and well for him if he returns it to his Creator as he received it."

After Naphtali had charged his children thus, and with many other lessons like these, he enjoined them to carry his remains to Hebron, to be buried there near his fathers. Then he ate and drank with rejoicing, covered his face, and died, and his sons did according to all that their father Naphtali had commanded them.

GAD'S HATRED

In the hundred and twenty-fifth year of his life Gad assembled his sons, and he spake to them: "I am the ninth son of Jacob, and I was a valiant shepherd of the flocks. I guarded the herds, and when a lion or any other wild beast approached, I pursued it, gripped it by the foot, flung it a stone's throw from me, and killed it thus. Once, for a space of thirty days, Joseph tended the flocks with us, and when he returned to our father, he told him that the sons of Zilpah and Bilhah slaughtered the best of the herds, and used the flesh without the knowledge of Reuben and Judah. He had seen me snatch a lamb out of the jaws of a bear, kill the bear, and slaughter the lamb, for it was too badly injured to live. I was wroth with Joseph for his talebearing, until he was sold into Egypt. I would neither look upon him nor hear aught about him, for to our very faces he, blamed us, because we had eaten the lamb without seeking the permission of Judah first. And whatever Joseph told our father, he believed.

"Now I confess my sin, that ofttimes I longed to kill him, for I hated him from the bottom of my heart, and on account of his dreams I hated him still more, and I desired to destroy him from off the land of the living. But Judah sold him by stealth to the Ishmaelites. Thus the God of our fathers saved him out of our hands, and He did not permit us to commit an abominable outrage in Israel.

"Hear now, my children, the words of truth, that ye may practice justice and the whole law of the Most High, and permit yourselves not to be tempted by the spirit of hatred. Evil is hatred, for it is the constant companion of deception, it always contradicts the truth. A little thing it magnifies into a great thing, light it takes for darkness, the sweet it calls bitter, and it teaches slander, enkindles anger, brings on war and violence, and fills the heart with devilish poison. I tell you my own experience, my children, that ye may drive hatred out of your hearts, and cleave to the love of the Lord. Righteousness banishes hatred, and humility kills it, for he that fears to give umbrage to the Lord, desires not to do wrong even in his thoughts. This is what I recognized at the last, after I had done penance on account of Joseph, for true atonement, pleasing to God, enlightens the eyes, illumines the soul with knowledge, and creates a counsel of salvation. My penance came in consequence of a sickness of the liver that God inflicted upon me. Without the prayers of my father Jacob, my spirit would have departed from me, for through the organ wherewith man transgresses, he is punished. As my liver had felt no mercy for Joseph, unmerciful suffering was caused unto me by my liver. My judgment lasted eleven months, as long as my enmity toward Joseph.

"And now, my children, each of you shall love his brother, and ye shall uproot hatred from your hearts by loving one another in word and deed and the thoughts of the soul. For I spake peaceably with Joseph in the presence of our father, but when I went out from before him, the spirit of hatred darkened my understanding, and stirred up my soul to murder him. If you see one that hath more good fortune than you, do not grieve, but pray for him, that his happiness may be perfect, and if one of the wicked even should grow rich in substance, like Esau, my father's brother, do not envy him. Wait for the end of the Lord.

"This also tell unto your children, that they shall honor Judah and Levi, for from them the Lord will cause a savior to arise unto Israel. For I know that in the end your children will fall off from God, and they will take part in all wickedness, malice, and corruptness, before the Lord."

After Gad had rested a little while, he spake again, "My children, hearken unto your father, and bury me with my fathers." Then he drew up his feet, and slept in peace. After five years, his sons carried his remains to Hebron unto his fathers.

ASHER'S LAST WORDS

In the hundred and twenty-fifth year of his life, while be was still robust in health, Asher summoned his children unto him, and admonished them to walk in the ways of virtue and the fear of God. He spake: "Hearken, ye sons of Asher, unto your father, and I will show you all that is right before God. Two ways hath God put before the children of men, and two inclinations hath He bestowed upon them, two kinds of actions and two aims. Therefore all things are in twos, the one opposite to the other. But ye, my children, ye shall not be double, pursuing both goodness and wickedness. Ye shall cling only to the ways of goodness, for the Lord taketh delight in them, and men yearn after them. And flee from wickedness, for thus you will destroy the evil inclination. Heed well the commands of the Lord, by following truth with a single mind. Observe the law of the Lord, and have not the same care for wicked things as for good things. Rather keep your eyes upon what is truly good, and guard it through all the commands of the Lord. The end of man, when he meets the messengers of God and of Satan, shows whether he was righteous or unrighteous in his life. If his soul goes out with agitation, she will be plagued by the evil spirit, whom she served with her lusts and her evil deeds; but if she departs tranquilly, the angel of peace will lead her to life eternal.

"Be not like Sodom, my children, which recognized not the angels of the Lord, that ye be not delivered into the hands of your enemies, and your land be cursed, and your sanctuary destroyed, and you be scattered to the four corners of the earth, and scorned in the confusion like stale water, until the Most High shall visit the earth, and break the heads of the dragons in the waters. Tell this, my sons, unto your children, that they be not disobedient toward God, for I read in the tablets of the heavens that you will be contumacious and act impiously toward Him, in that you will have no care for the law of God, but you will heed human laws, and they are corrupted by reason of man's godlessness. Therefore ye will be dispersed abroad like unto Gad and Dan, my brethren, and you will not know either your land, or your tribe, or your tongue. Nevertheless the Lord will gather you in His faithfulness, for the sake of His gracious mercy, and for the sake of Abraham, Isaac, and Jacob."

And when he had made an end of saying these words, he commanded them to bury him in Hebron. And he sank into sweet sleep, and died. His sons did as he had commanded, and they carried him up and buried him with his fathers.

BENJAMIN EXTOLS JOSEPH

Benjamin was one hundred and twenty-five years old, and he called his children to come to him. When they appeared, he kissed them, and spake: "As Isaac was born unto Abraham in his old age, so was I born unto Jacob when he was stricken in years. Therefore I was called Benjamin, 'the son of days.' My mother Rachel died at my birth, and Bilhah her slave suckled me. Rachel had no children for twelve years after bearing Joseph. Therefore she prayed to God, and fasted twelve days, and she conceived and bare me. Our father loved Rachel fondly, and he had longed greatly to have two sons by her.

"When I came down to Egypt, and my brother Joseph recognized me, he asked me, 'What said my brethren to my father regarding me?' And I told him that they had sent Jacob his coat stained with blood, and had said, 'Know now whether this be thy son's coat or not.' And Joseph said: 'This is what happened to me. Canaanitish merchantmen stole me away with violence, and on the way they wanted to hide my coat, to make it seem as though a wild beast had met me and slain me. But he who was about to conceal it, was torn by a lion, whereupon his companions, in great fear, sold me to the Ishmaelites. My brethren, thou seest, did not deceive my father with a lie.' In this wise Joseph tried to keep the deed of our brethren a secret from me. He also summoned my brethren, and enjoined them not to make known to our father what they had done to him, and bade them repeat the tale he had told me.

"Now, my children, love ye the Lord, the God of heaven and earth, and observe His commandments, taking that good and pious man Joseph as your model. Until the day of his death he would not have divulged what his brethren had done to him, and although God revealed their action to Jacob, he continued to deny it. Only after many efforts, when Jacob adjured him to confess the truth, he was induced to speak out. Even then he besought our father Jacob to pray for our brethren, that God account not the evil they had done to him as a sin. And Jacob exclaimed, 'O my good child Joseph, thou hast shown thyself more merciful than I was!'

"My children, have you observed the mercy of the good man? Imitate it with pure intention, that ye, too, may wear crowns of glory. A good man has not an envious eye, he has mercy with all, even with sinners, though their evil designs be directed against him, and by his good deeds he conquers the evil, since it was ordained of God. If you do good, the unclean spirits will depart from you, and even the wild beasts will stand in fear of you. The inclination of a good man lies not in the power of the tempter spirit Behar, for the angel of peace guides his soul. Flee before the malice of Beliar, whose sword is drawn to slay all that pay him obedience, and his sword is the mother of seven evils, bloodshed, corruptness, error, captivity, hunger, panic, and devastation. Therefore God surrendered Cain to seven punishments. Once in a hundred years the Lord brought a castigation upon him. His afflictions began when he was two hundred years old, and in his nine hundredth year he was destroyed by the deluge, for having slain his righteous brother Abel. And those who are like unto Cain will be chastised forever with the same punishments as his.

"Know now, my children, that I am about to die. Practice truth and righteousness, and observe the law of the Lord and also His commandments. This I bequeath unto you as your sole heritage, and you shall leave it to your children as an eternal possession. Thus Abraham, Isaac, and Jacob did, they transmitted it unto us, saying, 'Observe the commands of God, until the Lord shall reveal His salvation in the sight of all the heathen.' Then you will see Enoch, Noah, Shem, Abraham, Isaac, and Jacob rise up with rejoicing to new life at the right hand of God, and we brethren, the sons of Jacob, will arise also, each of us at the head of his tribe, and we will pay homage to the King of the heavens."

After Benjamin had made an end of speaking thus, he said: "I command you, my children, to carry my bones up out of Egypt and bury me near my fathers."

And when he had made an end of saying these things, he fell asleep at a good old age, and they put his body into a coffin, and in the ninety-first year of their sojourning in Egypt, his sons and the sons of his brethren brought up the bones of their father, in secret, and buried them in Hebron, at the feet of their fathers. Then they returned from the land of Canaan, and they dwelt in Egypt until the day of the exodus from the land.

Chapter 3

JOB--JOB AND THE PATRIARCHS

Job, the most pious Gentile that ever lived, one of the few to bear the title of honor "the servant of God," was of double kin to Jacob. He was a grandson of Jacob's brother Esau, and at the same time the son-in-law of Jacob himself, for he had married Dinah as his second wife. He was entirely worthy of being a member of the Patriarch's family, for he was perfectly upright, one that feared God, and eschewed evil. Had he not wavered in his resignation to the Divine will during the great trial to which he was subjected, and murmured against God, the distinction would have been conferred upon him of having his name joined to the Name of God in prayer, and men would have called upon the God of Job as they now call upon the God of Abraham, Isaac, and Jacob. But he was not found steadfast like the three Fathers, and he forfeited the honor God had intended for him.

The Lord remonstrated with him for his lack of patience, saying: "Why didst thou murmur when suffering came upon thee? Dost thou think thyself of greater worth than Adam, the creation of Mine own hands, upon whom together with his descendants I decreed death on account of a single transgression? And yet Adam murmured not. Thou art surely not more worthy than Abraham, whom I tempted with many trials, and when he asked, 'Whereby shall I know that I shall inherit the land?' and I replied, 'Know of a surety that thy seed will be a stranger in a land that is not theirs, and shall serve them; and they shall afflict them four hundred years,' he yet murmured not. Thou dost not esteem thyself more worthy than Moses, dost thou? Him I would not grant the favor of entering the promised land, because he spake the words, 'Hear now, ye rebels; shall we bring you forth water out of this rock?' And yet he murmured not. Art thou more worthy than Aaron, unto whom I showed greater honor than unto any created being, for I sent the angels themselves out of the Holy of Holies when he entered the place? Yet when his two sons died, he murmured not."

The contrast between Job and the Patriarchs appears from words spoken by him and words spoken by Abraham. Addressing God, Abraham said, "That be far from Thee to do after this manner, to slay the righteous with the wicked, that so the righteous should be as the wicked," and Job exclaimed against God, "It is all one; therefore I say, He destroyeth the perfect and the wicked." They both received their due recompense, Abraham was rewarded and Job was punished.

Convinced that his suffering was undeserved and unjust, Job had the audacity to say to God: "O Lord of the world, Thou didst create the ox with cloven feet and the ass with unparted hoof, Thou hast created Paradise and hell, Thou createst the righteous and also the wicked. There is none to hinder, Thou canst do as seemeth good in Thy sight." The friends of Job replied: "It is true, God hath created the evil inclination, but He hath also given man the Torah as a remedy against it. Therefore the wicked cannot roll their guilt from off their shoulders and put it upon God."

The reason Job did not shrink from such extravagant utterances was because he denied the resurrection of the dead. He judged of the prosperity of the wicked and the woes of the pious only by their earthly fortunes. Proceeding from this false premise, he held it to be possible that the punishment falling to his share was not at all intended for him. God had slipped into an error, He imposed the suffering upon him that had been appointed unto a sinner. But God spake to him, saying: "Many hairs have I created upon the head of man, yet each hair hath its own sac, for were two hairs to draw their nourishment from the same sac, man would lose the sight of his eyes. It hath never happened that a sac hath been misplaced. Should I, then, have mistaken Job for another? I let many drops of rain descend from the heavens, and for each drop there is a mould in the clouds, for were two drops to issue from the same mould, the ground would be made so miry that it could not bring forth any growth. It hath never happened that a mould hath been misplaced. Should I, then, have mistaken Job for another? Many thunderbolts I hurl from the skies, but each one comes from its own path, for were two to proceed from the same path, they would destroy the whole world. It hath never happened that a path hath been misplaced. Should I, then, have mistaken Job for another? The gazelle gives birth to her young on the topmost point of a rock, and it would fall into the abyss and be crushed to death, if I did not send an eagle thither to catch it up and carry it to its mother. Were the eagle to appear a minute earlier or later than the appointed time, the little gazelle would perish. It hath never happened that the proper minute of time was missed. Should I, then, have mistaken Job for another? The hind has a contracted womb, and would not be able to bring forth her young, if I did not send a dragon to her at the right second, to nibble at her womb and soften it, for then she can bear. Were the dragon to come a second before or after the right time, the hind would perish. It hath never happened that I missed the right second. Should I, then, have mistaken Job for another?"

Notwithstanding Job's unpardonable words, God was displeased with his friends for passing harsh judgment upon him. "A man may not be held responsible for what he does in his anguish," and Job's agony was great, indeed.

JOB'S WEALTH AND BENEFACTIONS

Job was asked once what he considered the severest affliction that could strike him, and he replied, "My enemies' joy in my misfortune, and when God demanded to know of him, after the accusations made by Satan, what he preferred, poverty or physical suffering, he chose pain, saying, "O Lord of the whole world, chastise my body with suffering of all kinds, only preserve me from poverty." Poverty seemed the greater scourge, because before his trials he had occupied a brilliant position on account of his vast wealth. God graciously granted him this foretaste of the Messianic time. The harvest followed close upon the ploughing of his field; no sooner were the seeds strewn in the furrows, than they sprouted and grew and ripened produce. He was equally successful with his cattle. His sheep killed wolves, but were themselves never harmed by wild beasts. Of sheep he had no less than one hundred and thirty thousand, and he required eight hundred dogs to keep guard over them, not to mention the two hundred dogs needed to secure the safety of his house. Besides, his herds consisted of three hundred and forty thousand asses and thirty-five hundred pairs of oxen. All these possessions were not used for self-indulgent pleasures, but for the good of the poor and the needy, whom he clothed, and fed, and provided with all things necessary. To do all this, he even had to employ ships that carried supplies to all the cities and the dwelling-places of the destitute. His house was furnished with doors on all its four sides, that the poor and the wayfarer might enter, no matter from what direction they approached. At all times there were thirty tables laden with viands ready in his house, and twelve besides for widows only, so that all who came found what they desired. Job's consideration for the poor was so delicate that he kept servants to wait upon them constantly. His guests, enraptured by his charitableness, frequently offered themselves as attendants to minister to the poor in his house, but Job always insisted upon paying them for their services. If he was asked for a loan of money, to be used for business purposes, and the borrower promised to give a part of his profits to the poor, he would demand no security beyond a mere signature. And if it happened that by some mischance or other the debtor was not able to discharge his obligation, Job would return the note to him, or tear it into bits in his presence.

He did not rest satisfied at supplying the material needs of those who applied to him. He strove also to convey the knowledge of God to them. After a meal he was in the habit of having music played upon instruments, and then he would invite those present to join him in songs of praise to God. On such occasions he did not consider himself above playing the cithern while the musicians rested.

Most particularly Job concerned himself about the weal and woe of widows and orphans. He was wont to pay visits to the sick, both rich and poor, and when it was necessary, he would bring a physician along with him. If the case turned out to be hopeless, he would sustain the stricken family with advice and consolation. When the wife of the incurably sick man began to grieve and weep, he would encourage her with such words as these: "Trust always in the grace and lovingkindness of God. He hath not abandoned thee until now, and He will not forsake thee henceforth. Thy husband will be restored to health, and will be able to provide for his family as heretofore. But if--which may God forefend--thy husband should die, I call Heaven to witness that I shall provide sustenance for thee and thy children." Having spoken thus, he would send for a notary, and have him draw up a document, which he signed in the presence of witnesses, binding himself to care for the family, should it be bereaved of its head. Thus he earned for himself the blessing of the sick man and the gratitude of the sorrowing wife.

Sometimes, in case of necessity, Job could be severe, too, especially when it was a question of helping a poor man obtain his due. If one of the parties to a suit cited before his tribunal was known to be a man of violence, he would surround himself with his army and inspire him with fear, so that the culprit could not but show himself amenable to his decision.

He endeavored to inculcate his benevolent ways upon his children, by accustoming them to wait upon the poor. On the morrow after a feast he would sacrifice bountifully to God, and together with the pieces upon the altar his offerings would be divided among the needy. He would say: "Take and help yourselves, and pray for my children. It may be that they have sinned, and renounced God, saying in the presumption of their hearts: 'We are the children of this rich man. All these things are our possessions. Why should we be servants to the poor?'"

SATAN AND JOB

The happy, God-pleasing life led by Job for many years excited the hatred of Satan, who had an old grudge against him. Near Job's house there was an idol worshipped by the people. Suddenly doubts assailed the heart of Job, and he asked himself: "Is this idol really the creator of heaven and earth? How can I find out the truth about it?" In the following night he perceived a voice calling: "Jobab! Jobab! Arise, and I will tell thee who he is whom thou desirest to know. This one to whom the people offer sacrifices is not God, he is the handiwork of the tempter, wherewith he deceives men." When he heard the voice, Job threw himself on the ground, and said: "O Lord, if this idol is the handiwork of the tempter, then grant that I may destroy it. None can hinder me, for I am the king of this land."

Job, or, as he is sometimes called, Jobab, was, indeed, king of Edom, the land wherein wicked plans are concocted against God, wherefore it is called also Uz, "counsel."

The voice continued to speak. It made itself known as that of an archangel of God, and revealed to Job that he would bring down the enmity of Satan upon himself by the destruction of the idol, and much suffering with it. However, if he remained steadfast under them, God would change his troubles into joys, his name would become celebrated throughout the generations of mankind, and he would have a share in the resurrection to eternal life. Job replied to the voice: "Out of love of God I am ready to endure all things unto the day of my death. I will shrink back from naught." Now Job arose, and accompanied by fifty men he repaired to the idol, and destroyed it.

Knowing that Satan would try to approach him, he ordered his guard not to give access to any one, and then he withdrew to his chamber. He had guessed aright. Satan appeared at once, in the guise of a beggar, and demanded speech with Job. The guard executed his orders, and forbade his entering. Then the mendicant asked him to intercede for him with Job for a piece of bread. Job knew it was Satan, and he sent word to him as follows, "Do not expect to eat of my bread, for it is prohibited unto thee," at the same time putting a piece of burnt bread into the hand of the guard for Satan. The servant was ashamed to give a beggar burnt bread, and he substituted a good piece for it. Satan, however, knowing that the servant had not executed his master's errand, told him so to his face, and he fetched the burnt bread and handed it to him, repeating the words of Job. Thereupon Satan returned this answer, "As the bread is burnt, so I will disfigure thy body." Job replied: "Do as thou desirest, and execute thy plan. As for me, I am ready to suffer whatever thou bringest down upon me."

Now Satan betook himself to God, and prayed Him to put Job into his power, saying: "I went to and fro in the earth, and walked up and down in it, and I saw no man as pious as Abraham. Thou didst promise him the whole land of Palestine, and yet he did not take it in ill part that he had not so much as a burial-place for Sarah. As for Job, it is true, I found none that loveth Thee as he does, but if Thou wilt put him into my hand, I shall succeed in turning his heart away from Thee." But God spake, "Satan, Satan, what hast thou a mind to do with my servant Job, like whom there is none in the earth?" Satan persisted in his request touching Job, and God granted it, He gave him full power over Job's possessions.

This day of Job's accusation was the New Year's Day, whereon the good and the evil deeds of man are brought before God.

JOB'S SUFFERING

Equipped with unlimited power, Satan endeavored to deprive Job of all he owned. He burnt part of his cattle, and the other part was carried off by enemies. What pained Job more than this was that recipients of his bounty turned against him, and took of his belongings.

Among the adversaries that assailed him was Lilith, the queen of Sheba. She lived at a great distance from his residence, it took her and her army three years to travel from her home to his. She fell upon his oxen and his asses, and took possession of them, after slaying the men to whose care Job had entrusted them. One man escaped alone. Wounded and bruised, he had only enough life in him to tell Job the tale of his losses, and then he fell down dead. The sheep, which had been left unmolested by the queen of Sheba, were taken away by the Chaldeans. Job's first intention was to go to war against these marauders, but when he was told that some of his property had been consumed by fire from heaven, he desisted, and said, "If the heavens turn against me, I can do nothing."

Dissatisfied with the result, Satan disguised himself as the king of Persia, besieged the city of Job's residence, took it, and spoke to the inhabitants, saying: "This man Job hath appropriated all the goods in the world, leaving naught for others, and he hath also torn down the temple of our god, and now I will pay him back for his wicked deeds. Come with me and let us pillage his house." At first the people refused to hearken to the words of Satan. They feared that the sons and daughters of Job might rise up against them later, and avenge their father's wrongs. But after Satan had pulled down the house wherein the children of Job were assembled, and they lay dead in the ruins, the people did as he bade them, and sacked the house of Job.

Seeing that neither the loss of all he had nor the death of his children could change his pious heart, Satan appeared before God a second time, and requested that Job himself, his very person, be put into his hand. God granted Satan's plea, but he limited his power to Job's body, his soul he could not touch. In a sense Satan was worse off than Job. He was in the position of the slave that has been ordered by his master to break the pitcher and not spill the wine.

Satan now caused a terrific storm to burst over the house of Job. He was cast from his throne by the reverberations, and he lay upon the floor for three hours. Then Satan smote his body with leprosy from the sole of his foot unto his crown. This plague forced Job to leave the city, and sit down outside upon an ash-heap, for his lower limbs were covered with oozing boils, and the issue flowed out upon the ashes. The upper part of his body was encrusted with dry boils, and to ease the itching they caused him, he used his nails, until they dropped off together with his fingertips, and he took him a potsherd to scrape himself withal. His body swarmed with vermin, but if one of the little creatures attempted to crawl away from him, he forced it back, saying, "Remain on the place whither thou wast sent, until God assigns another unto thee." His wife, fearful that he would not bear his horrible suffering with steadfastness, advised him to pray to God for death, that he might be sure of going hence an upright man. But he rejected her counsel, saying, "If in the days of good fortune, which usually tempts men to deny God, I stood firm, and did not rebel against Him, surely I shall be able to remain steadfast under misfortune, which compels men to be obedient to God." And Job stuck to his resolve in spite of all suffering, while his wife was not strong enough to bear her fate with resignation to the will of God.

Her lot was bitter, indeed, for she had had to take service as a water-carrier with a common churl, and when her master learnt that she shared her bread with Job, he dismissed her. To keep her husband from starving, she cut off her hair, and purchased bread with it. It was all she had to pay the price charged by the bread merchant, none other than Satan himself, who wanted to put her to the test. He said to her, "Hadst thou not deserved this great misery of thine, it had not come upon thee." This speech was more than the poor woman could bear. Then it was that she came to her husband, and amid tears and groans urged him to renounce God and die. Job, however, was not perturbed by her words, because he divined at once that Satan stood behind his wife, and seduced her to speak thus. Turning to the tempter, he said: "Why dost thou not meet me frankly? Give up thy underhand ways, thou wretch." Thereupon Satan appeared before Job, admitted that he had been vanquished, and went away abashed.

THE FOUR FRIENDS

The friends of Job lived in different places, at intervals of three hundred miles one from the other. Nevertheless they all were informed of their friend's misfortune at the same time, in this way: Each one had the pictures of the others set in his crown, and as soon as any one of them met with reverses, it showed itself in his picture. Thus the friends of Job learnt simultaneously of his misfortune, and they hastened to his assistance.

The four friends were related to one another, and each one was related to Job. Eliphaz, king of Teman, was a son of Esau; Bildad, Zophar, and Elihu were cousins, their fathers, Shuah, Naamat, and Barachel, were the sons of Buz, who was a brother of Job and a nephew of Abraham.

When the four friends arrived in the city in which Job lived, the inhabitants took them outside the gates, and pointing to a figure reclining upon an ash-heap at some distance off, they said, "Yonder is Job." At first the friends would not give them credence, and they decided to look more closely at the man, to make sure of his identity. But the foul smell emanating from Job was so strong that they could not come near to him. They ordered their armies to scatter perfumes and aromatic substances all around. Only after this had been done for hours, they could approach the outcast close enough to recognize him.

Eliphaz was the first to address Job, "Art thou indeed Job, a king equal in rank with ourselves?" And when Job said Aye, they broke out into lamentations and bitter tears, and all together they sang an elegy, the armies of the three kings, Eliphaz, Bildad, and Zophar, joining in the choir. Again Eliphaz began to speak, and he bemoaned Job's sad fortune, and depicted his friend's former glory, adding the refrain to each sentence, "Whither hath departed the splendor of thy throne?"

After listening long to the wailing and lamenting of Eliphaz and his companions, Job spake, saying: "Silence, and I will show you my throne and the splendor of its glory. Kings will perish, rulers disappear, their pride and lustre will pass like a shadow across a mirror, but my kingdom will persist forever and ever, for glory and magnificence are in the chariot of my Father."

These words aroused the wrath of Eliphaz, and he called upon his associates to abandon Job to his fate and go their way. But Bildad appeased his anger, reminding him that some allowance ought to be made for one so sorely tried as Job. Bildad put a number of questions to the sufferer in order to establish his sanity. He wanted to elicit from Job how it came about that God, upon whom he continued to set his hopes, could inflict such dire suffering. Not even a king of flesh and blood would allow a guardsman of his that had served him loyally to come to grief. Bildad desired to have information from Job also concerning the movements of the heavenly bodies.

Job had but one answer to make to these questions: man cannot comprehend Divine wisdom, whether it reveal itself in inanimate and brute nature or in relation to human beings. "But," continued Job, "to prove to you that I am in my right mind, listen to the question I shall put to you. Solid food and liquids combine inside of man, and they separate again when they leave his body. Who effects the separation?" And when Bildad conceded that he could not answer the question, Job said, "If thou canst not comprehend the changes in thy body, how canst thou hope to comprehend the movements of the planets?"

Zophar, after Job had spoken thus to Bildad, was convinced that his suffering had had no effect upon his mind, and he asked him whether he would permit himself to be treated by the physicians of the three kings, his friends. But Job rejected the offer, saying, "My healing and my restoration come from God, the Creator of all physicians."

While the three kings were conversing thus with Job, his wife Zitidos made her appearance clad in rags, and she threw herself at the feet of her husband's friends, and amid tears she spoke, saying: "O Eliphaz, and ye other friends of Job, remember what I was in other days, and how I am now changed, coming before you in rags and tatters." The sight of the unhappy woman touched them so deeply that they could only weep, and not a word could they force out of their mouths. Eliphaz, however, took his royal mantle of purple, and laid it about the shoulders of the poor woman. Zitidos asked only one favor, that the three kings should order their soldiers to clear away the ruins of the building under which her children lay entombed, that she might give their remains decent burial. The command was issued to the soldiers accordingly, but Job said, "Do not put yourselves to trouble for naught. My children will not be found, for they are safely bestowed with their Lord and Creator." Again his friends were sure that Job was bereft of his senses. He arose, however, prayed to God, and at the end of his devotions, he bade his friends look eastward, and when they did his bidding, they beheld his children next to the Ruler of heaven, with crowns of glory upon their heads. Zitidos prostrated herself, and said, "Now I know that my memorial resides with the Lord." And she returned to the house of her master, whence she had absented herself for some time against his will. He had forbidden her to leave it, because he had feared that the three kings would take her with them.

In the evening she lay down to sleep next to the manger for the cattle, but she never rose again, she died there of exhaustion. The people of the city made a great mourning for her, and the elegy composed in her honor was set down in writing and recorded.

JOB RESTORED

More and more the friends of Job came to the conclusion that he had incurred Divine punishment on account of his sins, and as he asseverated his innocence again and again, they prepared angrily to leave him to his fate. Especially Elihu was animated by Satan to speak scurrilous words against Job, upbraiding him for his unshakable confidence in God. Then the Lord appeared to them, first unto Job, and revealed to him that Elihu was in the wrong, and his words were inspired by Satan. Next he appeared unto Eliphaz, and to him He spake thus: "Thou and thy friends Bildad and Zophar have committed a sin, for ye did not speak the truth concerning my servant Job. Rise up and let him bring a sin offering for you. Only for his sake do I refrain from destroying you."

The sacrifice offered by Job in behalf of his friends was accepted graciously by God, and Eliphaz broke out into a hymn of thanksgiving to the Lord for having pardoned the transgression of himself and his two friends. At the same time he announced the damnation of Elihu, the instrument of Satan.

God appeared to Job once more, and gave him a girdle composed of three ribands, and he bade him tie it around his waist. Hardly had he put it on when all his pain disappeared, his very recollection of it vanished, and, more than this, God made him to see all that ever was and all that shall ever be.

After suffering sevenfold pain for seven years Job was restored to strength. With his three friends he returned to the city, and the inhabitants made a festival in his honor and unto the glory of God. All his former friends joined him again, and he resumed his old occupation, the care of the poor, for which he obtained the means from the people around. He said to them, "Give me, each one of you, a sheep for the clothing of the poor, and four silver or gold drachmas for their other needs." The Lord blessed Job, and in a few days his wealth had increased to double the substance he had owned before misfortune overtook him. Zitidos having died during the years of his trials, he married a second wife, Dinah, the daughter of Jacob, and she bore him seven sons and three daughters. He had never had more than one wife at a time, for he was wont to say, "If it had been intended that Adam should have ten wives, God would have given them to him. Only one wife was bestowed upon him, whereby God indicated that he was to have but one, and therefore one wife suffices for me, too."

When Job, after a long and happy life, felt his end approaching, he gathered his ten children around him, and told them the tale of his days. Having finished the narrative, he admonished them in these words: "See, I am about to die, and you will stand in my place. Forsake not the Lord, be generous toward the poor, treat the feeble with consideration, and do not marry with the women of the Gentiles."

Thereupon he divided his possessions among his sons, and to his daughters he gave what is more precious than all earthly goods, to each of them one riband of the celestial girdle he had received from God. The magic virtue of these ribands was such that no sooner did their possessors tie them around their waists than they were transformed into higher beings, and with seraphic voices they broke out into hymns after the manner of the angels.

For three days Job lay upon his bed, sick though not suffering, for the celestial girdle made him proof against pain. On the fourth day he saw the angels descend to fetch his soul. He arose from his bed, handed a cithern to his oldest daughter Jemimah, "Day," a censer to the second one, Keziah, "Perfume," and a cymbal to the third, Amalthceas, "Horn," and bade them welcome the angels with the sound of music. They played and sang and praised the Lord in the holy tongue. Then he appeared that sits in the great chariot, kissed Job, and rode away bearing his soul with him eastward. None saw them depart except the three daughters of Job.

The grief of the people, especially the poor, the widows, and the orphans, was exceeding great. For three days they left the corpse unburied, because they could not entertain the thought of separating themselves from it.

As the name of Job will remain imperishable unto all time, by reason of the man's piety, so his three friends were recompensed by God for their sympathy with him in his distress. Their names were preserved, the punishment of hell was remitted unto them, and, best of all, God poured out the holy spirit over them. But Satan, the cause of Job's anguish, the Lord cast down from heaven, for he had been vanquished by Job, who amid his agony had thanked and praised God for all He had done unto him.

Chapter 4

MOSES IN EGYPT--THE BEGINNING OF THE EGYPTIAN BONDAGE

As soon as Jacob was dead, the eyes of the Israelites were closed, as well as their hearts. They began to feel the dominion of the stranger, although real bondage did not enslave them until some time later. While a single one of the sons of Jacob was alive, the Egyptians did not venture to approach the Israelites with evil intent. It was only when Levi, the last of them, had departed this life that their suffering commenced. A change in the relation of the Egyptians toward the Israelites had, indeed, been noticeable immediately after the death of Joseph, but they did not throw off their mask completely until Levi was no more. Then the slavery of the Israelites supervened in good earnest.

The first hostile act on the part of the Egyptians was to deprive the Israelites of their fields, their vineyards, and the gifts that Joseph had sent to his brethren. Not content with these animosities, they sought to do them harm in other ways. The reason for the hatred of the Egyptians was envy and fear. The Israelites had increased to a miraculous degree. At the death of Jacob the seventy persons he had brought down with him had grown to the number of six hundred thousand, and their physical strength and heroism were extraordinary and therefore alarming to the Egyptians. There were many occasions at that time for the display of prowess. Not long after the death of Levi occurred that of the Egyptian king Magron, who had been bred up by Joseph, and therefore was not wholly without grateful recollection of what he and his family had accomplished for the welfare of Egypt. But his son and successor Malol, together with his whole court, knew not the sons of Jacob and their achievements, and they did not scruple to oppress the Hebrews.

The final breach between them and the Egyptians took place during the wars waged by Malol against Zepho, the grandson of Esau. In the course of it, the Israelites had saved the Egyptians from a crushing defeat, but instead of being grateful they sought only the undoing of their benefactors, from fear that the giant strength of the Hebrews might be turned against them.

PHARAOH'S CUNNING

The counsellors and elders of Egypt came to Pharaoh, and spake unto him, saying: "Behold, the people of the children of Israel are greater and mightier than we. Thou hast seen their strong power, which they have inherited from their fathers, for a few of them stood up against a people as many as the sand of the sea, and not one hath fallen. Now, therefore, give us counsel what to do with them, until we shall gradually destroy them from among us, lest they become too numerous in the land, for if they multiply, and there falleth out any war, they will also join themselves with their great strength unto our enemies, and fight against us, destroy us from the land, and get them up out of the land."

The king answered the elders, saying: "This is the plan advised by me against Israel, from which we will not depart. Behold, Pithom and Raamses are cities not fortified against battle. It behooves us to fortify them. Now, go ye and act cunningly against the children of Israel, and proclaim in Egypt and in Goshen, saying: 'All ye men of Egypt, Goshen, and Pathros! The king has commanded us to build Pithom and Raamses and fortify them against battle. Those amongst you in all Egypt, of the children of Israel and of all the inhabitants of the cities, who are willing to build with us, shall have their wages given to them daily at the king's order.'

"Then go ye first, and begin to build Pithom and Raamses, and cause the king's proclamation to be made daily, and when some of the children of Israel come to build, do ye give them their wages daily, and after they shall have built with you for their daily wages, draw yourselves away from them day by day, and one by one, in secret. Then you shall rise up and become their taskmasters and their officers, and you shall have them afterward to build without wages. And should they refuse, then force them with all your might to build. If you do this, it will go well with us, for we shall cause our land to be fortified after this manner, and with the children of Israel it will go ill, for they will decrease in number on account of the work, because you will prevent them from being with their wives."

The elders, the counsellors, and the whole of Egypt did according to the word of the king. For a month the servants of Pharaoh built with Israel, then they withdrew themselves gradually, while the children of Israel continued to work, receiving their daily wages, for some men of Egypt were still carrying on the work with them. After a time all the Egyptians had withdrawn, and they had turned to become the officers and taskmasters of the Israelites. Then they refrained from giving them any pay, and when some of the Hebrews refused to work without wages, their taskmasters smote them, and made them return by force to labor with their brethren. And the children of Israel were greatly afraid of the Egyptians, and they came again and worked without pay, all except the tribe of Levi, who were not employed in the work with their brethren. The children of Levi knew that the proclamation of the king was made to deceive Israel, therefore they refrained from listening to it, and the Egyptians did not molest them later, since they had not been with their brethren at the beginning, and though the Egyptians embittered the lives of the other Israelites with servile labor, they did not disturb the children of Levi. The Israelites called Malol, the king of Egypt, Maror, "Bitterness," because in his days the Egyptians embittered their lives with all manner of rigorous service.

But Pharaoh did not rest satisfied with his proclamation and the affliction it imposed upon the Israelites. He suspended a brick-press from his own neck, and himself took part in the work at Pithom and Raamses. After this, whenever a Hebrew refused to come and help with the building, alleging that he was not fit for such hard service, the Egyptians would retort, saying, "Dost thou mean to make us believe thou art more delicate than Pharaoh?"

The king himself urged the Israelites on with gentle words, saying, "My children, I beg you to do this work and erect these little buildings for me. I will give you great reward therefor." By means of such artifices and wily words the Egyptians succeeded in overmastering the Israelites, and once they had them in their power, they treated them with undisguised brutality. Women were forced to perform men's work, and men women's work.

The building of Pithom and Raamses turned out of no advantage to the Egyptians, for scarcely were the structures completed, when they collapsed, or they were swallowed by the earth, and the Hebrew workmen, besides having to suffer hardships during their erection, lost their lives by being precipitated from enormous heights, when the buildings fell in a heap.

But the Egyptians were little concerned whether or not they derived profit from the forced labor of the children of Israel. Their main object was to hinder their increase, and Pharaoh therefore issued an order, that they were not to be permitted to sleep at their own homes, that so they might be deprived of the opportunity of having intercourse with their wives. The officers executed the will of the king, telling the Hebrews that the reason was the loss of too much time in going to and fro, which would prevent them from completing the required tale of bricks. Thus the Hebrew husbands were kept apart from their wives, and they were compelled to sleep on the ground, away from their habitations.

But God spake, saying: "Unto their father Abraham I gave the promise, that I would make his children to be as numerous as the stars in the heavens, and you contrive plans to prevent them from multiplying. We shall see whose word will stand, Mine or yours." And it came to pass that the more the Egyptians afflicted them, the more they multiplied, and the more they spread abroad. And they continued to increase in spite of Pharaoh's command, that those who did not complete the required tale of bricks were to be immured in the buildings between the layers of bricks, and great was the number of the Israelites that lost their lives in this way. Many of their children were, besides, slaughtered as sacrifices to the idols of the Egyptians. For this reason God visited retribution upon the idols at the time of the going forth of the Israelites from Egypt. They had caused the death of the Hebrew children, and in turn they were shattered, and they crumbled into dust."

THE PIOUS MIDWIVES

When now, in spite of all their tribulations, the children of Israel continued to multiply and spread abroad, so that the land was full of them as with thick underbrush--for the women brought forth many children at a birth--the Egyptians appeared before Pharaoh again, and urged him to devise some other way of ridding the land of the Hebrews, seeing that they were increasing mightily, though they were made to toil and labor hard. Pharaoh could invent no new design; he asked his counsellors to give him their opinion of the thing. Then spake one of them, Job of the land of Uz, which is in Aram-naharaim, as follows: "The plan which the king invented, of putting a great burden of work upon the Israelites, was good in its time, and it should be executed henceforth, too, but to secure us against the fear that, if a war should come to pass, they may overwhelm us by reason of their numbers, and chase us forth out of the land, let the king issue a decree, that every male child of the Israelites shall be killed at his birth. Then we need not be afraid of them if we should be overtaken by war. Now let the king summon the Hebrew midwives, that they come hither, and let him command them in accordance with this plan."

Job's advice found favor in the eyes of Pharaoh and the Egyptians." They preferred to have the midwives murder the innocents, for they feared the punishment of God if they laid hands upon them themselves. Pharaoh cited the two midwives of the Hebrews before him, and commanded them to slay all men children, but to save the daughters of the Hebrew women alive," for the Egyptians were as much interested in preserving the female children as in bringing about the death of the male children. They were very sensual, and were desirous of having as many women as possible at their service."

However, the plan, even if it had been carried into execution, was not wise, for though a man may marry many wives, each woman can marry but one husband. Thus a diminished number of men and a corresponding increase in the number of women did not constitute so serious a menace to the continuance of the nation of the Israelites as the reverse case would have been.

The two Hebrew midwives were Jochebed, the mother of Moses, and Miriam, his sister. When they appeared before Pharaoh, Miriam exclaimed: "Woe be to this man when God visits retribution upon him for his evil deeds." The king would have killed her for these audacious words, had not Jochebed allayed his wrath by saying: "Why dost thou pay heed to her words? She is but a child, and knows not what she speaks." Yet, although Miriam was but five years old at the time, she nevertheless accompanied her mother, and helped her with her offices to the Hebrew women, giving food to the new-born babes while Jochebed washed and bathed them.

Pharaoh's order ran as follows: "At the birth of the child, if it be a man child, kill it; but if it be a female child, then you need not kill it, but you may save it alive." The midwives returned: "How are we to know whether the child is male or female?" for the king had bidden them kill it while it was being born. Pharaoh replied: "If the child issues forth from the womb with its face foremost, it is a man child, for it looks to the earth, whence man was taken; but if its feet appear first, it is a female, for it looks up toward the rib of the mother, and from a rib woman was made."

The king used all sorts of devices to render the midwives amenable to his wishes. He approached them with amorous proposals, which they both repelled, and then he threatened them with death by fire. But they said within themselves: "Our father Abraham opened an inn, that he might feed the wayfarers, though they were heathen, and we should neglect the children, nay, kill them? No, we shall have a care to keep them alive." Thus they failed to execute what Pharaoh had commanded. Instead of murdering the babes, they supplied all their needs. If a mother that had given birth to a child lacked food and drink, the midwives went to well-to-do women, and took up a collection, that the infant might not suffer want. They did still more for the little ones. They made supplication to God, praying: "Thou knowest that we are not fulfilling the words of Pharaoh, but it is our aim to fulfil Thy words. O that it be Thy will, our Lord, to let the child come into the world safe and sound, lest we fall under the suspicion that we tried to slay it, and maimed it in the attempt." The Lord hearkened to their prayer, and no child born under the ministrations of Shiphrah and Puah, or Jochebed and Miriam, as the midwives are also called, came into the world lame or blind or afflicted with any other blemish.

Seeing that his command was ineffectual, he summoned the midwives a second time, and called them to account for their disobedience. They replied: "This nation is compared unto one animal and another, and, in sooth, the Hebrews are like the animals. As little as the animals do they need the offices of midwives." These two God-fearing women were rewarded in many ways for their good deeds. Not only that Pharaoh did them no harm, but they were made the ancestors of priests and Levites, and kings and princes. Jochebed became the mother of the priest Aaron and of the Levite Moses, and from Miriam's union with Caleb sprang the royal house of David. The hand of God was visible in her married life. She contracted a grievous sickness, and though it was thought by all that saw her that death would certainly overtake her, she recovered, and God restored her youth, and bestowed unusual beauty upon her, so that renewed happiness awaited her husband, who had been deprived of the pleasures of conjugal life during her long illness. His unexpected joys were the reward of his piety and trust in God. And another recompense was accorded to Miriam: she was privileged to bring forth Bezalel, the builder of the Tabernacle, who was endowed with celestial wisdom.

THE THREE COUNSELLORS

In the one hundred and thirtieth year after Israel's going down to Egypt Pharaoh dreamed that he was sitting upon his throne, and he lifted up his eyes, and he beheld an old man before him with a balance in his hand, and he saw him taking all the elders, nobles, and great men of Egypt, tying them together, and laying them in one scale of the balance, while he put a tender kid into the other. The kid bore down the pan in which it lay until it hung lower than the other with the bound Egyptians. Pharaoh arose early in the morning, and called together all his servants and his wise men to interpret his dream, and the men were greatly afraid on account of his vision. Balaam the son of Beor then spake, and said: "This means nothing but that a great evil will spring up against Egypt, for a son will be born unto Israel, who will destroy the whole of our land and all its inhabitants, and he will bring forth the Israelites from Egypt with a mighty hand. Now, therefore, O king, take counsel as to this matter, that the hope of Israel be frustrated before this evil arise against Egypt."

The king said unto Balaam: "What shall we do unto Israel? We have tried several devices against this people, but we could not prevail over it. Now let me hear thy opinion."

At Balaam's instance, the king sent for his two counsellors, Reuel the Midianite and Job the Uzite, to hear their advice. Reuel spoke: "If it seemeth good to the king, let him desist from the Hebrews, and let him not stretch forth his hand against them, for the Lord chose them in days of old, and took them as the lot of His inheritance from amongst all the nations of the earth, and who is there that hath dared stretch forth his hand against them with impunity, but that their God avenged the evil done unto them?" Reuel then proceeded to enumerate some of the mighty things God had performed for Abraham, Isaac, and Jacob, and he closed his admonition with the words: "Verily, thy grandfather, the Pharaoh of former days, raised Joseph the son of Jacob above all the princes of Egypt, because he discerned his wisdom, for through his wisdom he rescued all the inhabitants of the land from the famine, after which he invited Jacob and his sons to come down to Egypt, that the land of Egypt and the land of Goshen be delivered from the famine through their virtues. Now, therefore, if it seem good in thine eyes, leave off from destroying the children of Israel, and if it be not thy will that they dwell in Egypt, send them forth from here, that they may go to the land of Canaan, the land wherein their ancestors sojourned."

When Pharaoh heard the words of Jethro-Reuel, he was exceedingly wroth with him, and he was dismissed in disgrace from before the king, and he went to Midian.

The king then spoke to Job, and said: "What sayest thou, Job, and what is thy advice respecting the Hebrews?" Job replied: "Behold, all the inhabitants of the land are in thy power. Let the king do as seemeth good in his eyes."

Balaam was the last to speak at the behest of the king, and he said: "From all that the king may devise against the Hebrews, they will be delivered. If thou thinkest to diminish them by the flaming fire, thou wilt not prevail over them, for their God delivered Abraham their father from the furnace in which the Chaldeans cast him. Perhaps thou thinkest to destroy them with a sword, but their father Isaac was delivered from being slaughtered by the sword. And if thou thinkest to reduce them through hard and rigorous labor, thou wilt also not prevail, for their father Jacob served Laban in all manner of hard work, and yet he prospered. If it please the king, let him order all the male children that shall be born in Israel from this day forward to be thrown into the water. Thereby canst thou wipe out their name, for neither any of them nor any of their fathers was tried in this way.

THE SLAUGHTER OF THE INNOCENTS

Balaam's advice was accepted by Pharaoh and the Egyptians. They knew that God pays measure for measure, therefore they believed that the drowning of the men children would be the safest means of exterminating the Hebrews, without incurring harm themselves, for the Lord had sworn unto Noah never again to destroy the world by water. Thus, they assumed, they would be exempt from punishment, wherein they were wrong, however. In the first place, though the Lord had sworn not to bring a flood upon men, there was nothing in the way of bringing men into a flood. Furthermore, the oath of God applied to the whole of mankind, not to a single nation. The end of the Egyptians was that they met their death in the billows of the Red Sea. "Measure for measure"--as they had drowned the men children of the Israelites, so they were drowned.

Pharaoh now took steps looking to the faithful execution of his decree. He sent his bailiffs into the houses of the Israelites, to discover all new-born children, wherever they might be. To make sure that the Hebrews should not succeed in keeping the children hidden, the Egyptians hatched a devilish plan. Their women were to take their little ones to the houses of the Israelitish women that were suspected of having infants. When the Egyptian children began to cry or coo, the Hebrew children that were kept in hiding would join in, after the manner of babies, and betray their presence, whereupon the Egyptians would seize them and bear them off.

Furthermore, Pharaoh commanded that the Israelitish women employ none but Egyptian midwives, who were to secure precise information as to the time of their delivery, and were to exercise great care, and let no male child escape their vigilance alive. If there should be parents that evaded the command, and preserved a new-born boy in secret, they and all belonging to them were to be killed.

Is it to be wondered at, then, that many of the Hebrews kept themselves away from their wives? Nevertheless those who put trust in God were not forsaken by Him. The women that remained united with their husbands would go out into the field when their time of delivery arrived, and give birth to their children and leave them there, while they themselves returned home. The Lord, who had sworn unto their ancestors to multiply them, sent one of His angels to wash the babes, anoint them, stretch their limbs, and swathe them. Then he would give them two smooth pebbles, from one of which they sucked milk, and from the other honey. And God caused the hair of the infants to grow down to their knees and serve them as a protecting garment, and then He ordered the earth to receive the babes, that they be sheltered therein until the time of their growing up, when it would open its mouth and vomit forth the children, and they would sprout up like the herb of the field and the grass of the forest. Thereafter each would return to his family and the house of his father.

When the Egyptians saw this, they went forth, every man to his field, with his yoke of oxen, and they ploughed up the earth as one ploughs it at seed time. Yet they were unable to do harm to the infants of the children of Israel that had been swallowed up and lay in the bosom of the earth. Thus the people of Israel increased and waxed exceedingly. And Pharaoh ordered his officers to go to Goshen, to look for the male babes of the children of Israel, and when they discovered one, they tore him from his mother's breast by force, and thrust him into the river." But no one is so valiant as to be able to foil God's purposes, though he contrive ten thousand subtle devices unto that end. The child foretold by Pharaoh's dreams and by his astrologers was brought up and kept concealed from the king's spies. It came to pass after the following manner.

THE PARENTS OF MOSES

When Pharaoh's proclamation was issued, decreeing that the men children of the Hebrews were to be cast into the river, Amram, who was the president of the Sanhedrin, decided that in the circumstances it was best for husbands to live altogether separate from their wives. He set the example. He divorced his wife, and all the men of Israel did likewise, for he occupied a place of great consideration among his people, one reason being that he belonged to the tribe of Levi, the tribe that was faithful to its God even in the land of Egypt, though the other tribes wavered in their allegiance, and attempted to ally themselves with the Egyptians, going so far as to give up Abraham's sign of the covenant. To chastise the Hebrews for their impiety, God turned the love of the Egyptians for them into hatred, so that they resolved upon their destruction. Mindful of all that he and his people owed to Joseph's wise rule, Pharaoh refused at first to entertain the malicious plans proposed by the Egyptians against the Hebrews. He spoke to his people, "You fools, we are indebted to these Hebrews for whatever we enjoy, and you desire now to rise up against them?" But the Egyptians could not be turned aside from their purpose of ruining Israel. They deposed their king, and incarcerated him for three months, until he declared himself ready to execute with determination what they had resolved upon, and he sought to bring about the ruin of the children of Israel by every conceivable means. Such was the retribution they had drawn down upon themselves by their own acts.

As for Amram, not only did he belong to the tribe of Levi, distinguished for its piety, but by reason of his extraordinary piety he was prominent even among the pious of the tribe. He was one of the four who were immaculate, untainted by sin, over whom death would have had no power, had mortality not been decreed against every single human being on account of the fall of the first man and woman. The other three that led the same sinless life were Benjamin, Jesse the father of David, and Chileab the son of David. If the Shekinah was drawn close again to the dwelling-place of mortals, it was due to Amram's piety. Originally the real residence of the Shekinah was among men, but when Adam committed his sin, she withdrew to heaven, at first to the lowest of the seven heavens. Thence she was banished by Cain's crime, and she retired to the second heaven. The sins of the generation of Enoch removed her still farther off from men, she took up her abode in the third heaven; then, successively, in the fourth, on account of the malefactors in the generation of the deluge; in the fifth, during the building of the tower of Babel and the confusion of tongues; in the sixth, by reason of the wicked Egyptians at the time of Abraham; and, finally, in the seventh, in consequence of the abominations of the inhabitants of Sodom. Six righteous men, Abraham, Isaac, Jacob, Levi, Kohath, and Amram, drew the Shekinah back, one by one, from the seventh to the first heaven, and through the seventh righteous man, Moses, she was made to descend to the earth and abide among men as aforetime.

Amram's sagacity kept pace with his piety and his learning. The Egyptians succeeded in enslaving the Hebrews by seductive promises. At first they gave them a shekel for every brick they made, tempting them to superhuman efforts by the prospect of earning much money. Later, when the Egyptians forced them to work without wages, they insisted upon having as many bricks as the Hebrews had made when their labor was paid for, but they could demand only a single brick daily from Amram, for he had been the only one whom they had not led astray by their artifice. He had been satisfied with a single shekel daily, and had therefore made only a single brick daily, which they had to accept afterward as the measure of his day's work.

As his life partner, Amram chose his aunt Jochebed, who was born the same day with him. She was the daughter of Levi, and she owed her name, "Divine Splendor," to the celestial light that radiated from her countenance. She was worthy of being her husband's helpmeet, for she was one of the midwives that had imperilled their own lives to rescue the little Hebrew babes. Indeed, if God had not allowed a miracle to happen, she and her daughter Miriam would have been killed by Pharaoh for having resisted his orders and saved the Hebrew children alive. When the king sent his hangmen for the two women, God caused them to become invisible, and the bailiffs had to return without accomplishing their errand.

The first child of the union between Amram and Jochebed, his wife, who was one hundred and twenty-six years old at the time of her marriage, was a girl, and the mother called her Miriam, "Bitterness," for it was at the time of her birth that the Egyptians began to envenom the life of the Hebrews. The second child was a boy, called Aaron, which means, "Woe unto this pregnancy!" because Pharaoh's instructions to the midwives, to kill the male children of the Hebrews, was proclaimed during the months before Aaron's birth.

THE BIRTH OF MOSES

When Amram separated from his wife on account of the edict published against the male children of the Hebrews, and his example was followed by all the Israelites, his daughter Miriam said to him: "Father, thy decree is worse than Pharaoh's decree. The Egyptians aim to destroy only the male children, but thou includest the girls as well. Pharaoh deprives his victims of life in this world, but thou preventest children from being born, and thus thou deprivest them of the future life, too. He resolves destruction, but who knows whether the intention of the wicked can persist? Thou art a righteous man, and the enactments of the righteous are executed by God, hence thy decree will be upheld."

Amram recognized the justice of her plea, and he repaired to the Sanhedrin, and put the matter before this body. The members of the court spoke, and said: "It was thou that didst separate husbands and wives, and from thee should go forth the permission for re-marriage." Amram then made the proposition that each of the members of the Sanhedrin return to his wife, and wed her clandestinely, but his colleagues repudiated the plan, saying, "And who will make it known unto the whole of Israel? "

Accordingly, Amram stood publicly under the wedding canopy with his divorced wife Jochebed, while Aaron and Miriam danced about it, and the angels proclaimed, "Let the mother of children be joyful!" His re-marriage was solemnized with great ceremony, to the end that the men that had followed his example in divorcing their wives might imitate him now in taking them again unto themselves. And so it happened.

Old as Jochebed was, she regained her youth. Her skin became soft, the wrinkles in her face disappeared, the warm tints of maiden beauty returned, and in a short time she became pregnant.

Amram was very uneasy about his wife's being with child; he knew not what to do. He turned to God in prayer, and entreated Him to have compassion upon those who had in no wise transgressed the laws of His worship, and afford them deliverance from the misery they endured, while He rendered abortive the hope of their enemies, who yearned for the destruction of their nation. God had mercy on him, and He stood by him in his sleep, and exhorted him not to despair of His future favors. He said further, that He did not forget their piety, and He would always reward them for it, as He had granted His favor in other days unto their forefathers. "Know, therefore," the Lord continued to speak, "that I shall provide for you all together what is for your good, and for thee in particular that which shall make thee celebrated; for the child out of dread of whose nativity the Egyptians have doomed the Israelite children to destruction, shall be this child of thine, and be shall remain concealed from those who watch to destroy him, and when he has been bred up, in a miraculous way, he shall deliver the Hebrew nation from the distress they are under by reason of the Egyptians. His memory shall be celebrated while the world lasts, and not only among the Hebrews, but among strangers also. And all this shall be the effect of My favor toward thee and thy posterity. Also his brother shall be such that he shall obtain My priesthood for himself, and for his posterity after him, unto the end of the world."

After he had been informed of these things by the vision, Amram awoke, and told all unto his wife Jochebed.

His daughter Miriam likewise had a prophetic dream, and she related it unto her parents, saying: "In this night I saw a man clothed in fine linen. 'Tell thy father and thy mother,' he said, 'that he who shall be born unto them, shall be cast into the waters, and through him the waters shall become dry, and wonders and miracles shall be performed through him, and he shall save My people Israel, and be their leader forever.'"

During her pregnancy, Jochebed observed that the child in her womb was destined for great things. All the time she suffered no pain, and also she suffered none in giving birth to her son, for pious women are not included in the curse pronounced upon Eve, decreeing sorrow in conception and in childbearing.

At the moment of the child's appearance, the whole house was filled with radiance equal to the splendor of the sun and the moon. A still greater miracle followed. The infant was not yet a day old when he began to walk and speak with his parents, and as though he were an adult, he refused to drink milk from his mother's breast.

Jochebed gave birth to the child six months after conception. The Egyptian bailiffs, who kept strict watch over all pregnant women in order to be on the spot in time to carry off their new-born boys, had not expected her delivery for three months more. These three months the parents succeeded in keeping the babe concealed, though every Israelitish house was guarded by two Egyptian women, one stationed within and one without. At the end of this time they determined to expose the child, for Amram was afraid that both he and his son would be devoted to death if the secret leaked out, and he thought it better to entrust the child's fate to Divine Providence. He was convinced that God would protect the boy, and fulfil His word in truth.

MOSES RESCUED FROM THE WATER

Jochebed accordingly took an ark fashioned of bulrushes, daubed it with pitch on the outside, and lined it with clay within. The reason she used bulrushes was because they float on the surface of the water, and she put pitch only on the outside, to protect the child as much as possible against the annoyance of a disagreeable odor. Over the child as it lay in the ark she spread a tiny canopy, to shade the babe, with the words, "Perhaps I shall not live to see him under the marriage canopy." And then she abandoned the ark on the shores of the Red Sea. Yet it was not left unguarded. Her daughter Miriam stayed near by, to discover whether a prophecy she had uttered would be fulfilled. Before the child's birth, his sister had foretold that her mother would bring forth a son that should redeem Israel. When he was born, and the house was filled with brilliant light, Amram kissed her on her head, but when he was forced into the expedient of exposing the child, he beat her on her head, saying, "My daughter, what hath become of thy prophecy?" Therefore Miriam stayed, and strolled along the shore, to observe what would be the fate of the babe, and what would come of her prophecy concerning him.

The day the child was exposed was the twenty-first of the month of Nisan, the same on which the children of Israel later, under the leadership of Moses, sang the song of praise and gratitude to God for the redemption from the waters of the sea. The angels appeared before God, and spoke: "O Lord of the world, shall he that is appointed to sing a song of praise unto Thee on this day of Nisan, to thank Thee for rescuing him and his people from the sea, shall he find his death in the sea to-day?" The Lord replied: "Ye know well that I see all things. The contriving of man can do naught to change what bath been resolved in My counsel. Those do not attain their end who use cunning and malice to secure their own safety, and endeavor to bring ruin upon their fellow-men. But he who trusts Me in his peril will be conveyed from profoundest distress to unlooked-for happiness. Thus My omnipotence will reveal itself in the fortunes of this babe.

At the time of the child's abandonment, God sent scorching heat to plague the Egyptians, and they all suffered with leprosy and smarting boils. Thermutis, the daughter of Pharaoh, sought relief from the burning pain in a bath in the waters of the Nile. But physical discomfort was not her only reason for leaving her father's palace. She was determined to cleanse herself as well of the impurity of the idol worship that prevailed there.

When she saw the little ark floating among the flags on the surface of the water, she supposed it to contain one of the little children exposed at her father's order, and she commanded her handmaids to fetch it. But they protested, saying, "O our mistress, it happens sometimes that a decree issued by a king is unheeded, yet it is observed at least by his children and the members of his household, and dost thou desire to transgress thy father's edict?" Forthwith the angel Gabriel appeared, seized all the maids except one, whom he permitted the princess to retain for her service, and buried them in the bowels of the earth.

Pharaoh's daughter now proceeded to do her own will. She stretched forth her arm, and although the ark was swimming at a distance of sixty ells, she succeeded in grasping it, because her arm was lengthened miraculously. No sooner had she touched it than the leprosy afflicting her departed from her. Her sudden restoration led her to examine the contents of the ark, and when she opened it, her amazement was great.

She beheld an exquisitely beautiful boy, for God had fashioned the Hebrew babe's body with peculiar care, and beside it she perceived the Shekinah. Noticing that the boy bore the sign of the Abrahamic covenant, she knew that he was one of the Hebrew children, and mindful of her father's decree concerning the male children of the Israelites, she was about to abandon the babe to his fate. At that moment the angel Gabriel came and gave the child a vigorous blow, and he began to cry aloud, with a voice like a young man's. His vehement weeping and the weeping of Aaron, who was lying beside him, touched the princess, and in her pity she resolved to save him. She ordered an Egyptian woman to be brought, to nurse the child, but the little one refused to take milk from her breast, as he refused to take it from one after the other of the Egyptian women fetched thither. Thus it had been ordained by God, that none of them might boast later on, and say, "I suckled him that holds converse now with the Shekinah." Nor was the mouth destined to speak with God to draw nourishment from the unclean body of an Egyptian woman.

Now Miriam stepped into the presence of Thermutis, as though she had been standing there by chance to look at the child, and she spoke to the princess, saying, "It is vain for thee, O queen, to call for nurses that are in no wise of kin to the child, but if thou wilt order a woman of the Hebrews to be brought, he may accept her breast, seeing that she is of his own nation." Thermutis therefore bade Miriam fetch a Hebrew woman, and with winged steps, speeding like a vigorous youth, she hastened and brought back her own mother, the child's mother, for she knew that none present was acquainted with her. The babe, unresisting, took his mother's breast, and clutched it tightly. The princess committed the child to Jochebed's care, saying these words, which contained an unconscious divination: "Here is what is thine." Nurse the boy henceforth, and I will give thee two silver pieces as thy wages.

The return of her son, safe and sound, after she had exposed him, was Jochebed's reward from God for her services as one of the midwives that had bidden defiance to Pharaoh's command and saved the Hebrew children alive.

By exposing their son to danger, Amram and Jochebed had effected the withdrawal of Pharaoh's command enjoining the extermination of the Hebrew men children. The day Moses was set adrift in the little ark, the astrologers had come to Pharaoh and told him the glad tidings, that the danger threatening the Egyptians on account of one boy, whose doom lay in the water, had now been averted. Thereupon Pharaoh cried a halt to the drowning of the boys of his empire. The astrologers had seen something, but they knew not what, and they announced a message, the import of which they did not comprehend. Water was, indeed, the doom of Moses, but that did not mean that he would perish in the waters of the Nile. It had reference to the waters of Meribah, the waters of strife, and how they would cause his death in the desert, before he had completed his task of leading the people into the promised land. Pharaoh, misled by the obscure vision of his astrologers, thought that the future redeemer of Israel was to lose his life by drowning, and to make sure that the boy whose appearance was foretold by the astrologers might not escape his fate, he had ordered all boys, even the children of the Egyptians, born during a period of nine months to be cast into the water.

On account of the merits of Moses, the six hundred thousand men children of the Hebrews begotten in the same night with him, and thrown into the water on the same day, were rescued miraculously together with him, and it was therefore not an idle boast, if he said later, "The people that went forth out of the water on account of my merits are six hundred thousand men."

THE INFANCY OF MOSES

For two years the child rescued by Pharaoh's daughter stayed with his parents and kindred. They gave him various names. His father called him Heber, because it was for this child's sake that he had been "reunited" with his wife. His mother's name for him was Jekuthiel, "because," she said, "I set my hope upon God, and He gave him back to me." To his sister Miriam he was Jered, because she had "descended" to the stream to ascertain his fate. His brother Aaron called him Abi Zanoah, because his father, who had "cast off" his mother, had taken her back for the sake of the child to be born. His grandfather Kohath knew him as Abi Gedor, because the Heavenly Father had "built up" the breach in Israel, when He rescued him, and thus restrained the Egyptians from throwing the Hebrew men children into the water. His nurse called him Abi Soco, because he had been kept concealed in a "tent" for three months, escaping the pursuit of the

Egyptians. And Israel called him Shemaiah ben Nethanel, because in his day God would "hear" the sighs of the people, and deliver them from their oppressors, and through him would He "give" them His own law.

His kindred and all Israel knew that the child was destined for great things, for he was barely four months old when he began to prophesy, saying, "In days to come I shall receive the Torah from the flaming torch."

When Jochebed took the child to the palace at the end of two years, Pharaoh's daughter called him Moses, because she had "drawn" him out of the water, and because he would "draw" the children of Israel out of the land of Egypt in a day to come. And this was the only name whereby God called the son of Amram, the name conferred upon him by Pharaoh's daughter. He said to the princess: "Moses was not thy child, yet thou didst treat him as such. For this I will call thee My daughter, though thou art not My daughter," and therefore the princess, the daughter of Pharaoh, bears the name Bithiah, "the daughter of God." She married Caleb later on, and he was a suitable husband for her. As she stood up against her father's wicked counsels, so Caleb stood up against the counsel of his fellow-messengers sent to spy out the land of Canaan. For rescuing Moses and for her other pious deeds, she was permitted to enter Paradise alive.

That Moses might receive the treatment at court usually accorded to a prince, Bithiah pretended that she was with child for some time before she had him fetched away from his parents' house." His royal foster-mother caressed and kissed him constantly, and on account of his extraordinary beauty she would not permit him ever to quit the palace. Whoever set eyes on him, could not leave off from looking at him, wherefore Bithiah feared to allow him out of her sight.

Moses' understanding was far beyond his years; his instructors observed that he disclosed keener comprehension than is usual at his age. All his actions in his infancy promised greater ones after he should come to man's estate, and when he was but three years old, God granted him remarkable size. As for his beauty, it was so attractive that frequently those meeting him as he was carried along on the road were obliged to turn and stare at him. They would leave what they were about, and stand still a great while, looking after him, for the loveliness of the child was so wondrous that it held the gaze of the spectator. The daughter of Pharaoh, perceiving Moses to be an extraordinary lad, adopted him as her son, for she had no child of her own. She informed her father of her intention concerning him, in these words: "I have brought up a child, who is divine in form and of an excellent mind, and as I received him through the bounty of the river in a wonderful way, I have thought it proper to adopt him as my son and as the heir of thy kingdom." And when she had spoken thus, she put the infant between her father's hands, and he took him and hugged him close to his breast.

MOSES RESCUED BY GABRIEL

When Moses was in his third year, Pharaoh was dining one day, with the queen Alfar'anit at his right hand, his daughter Bithiah with the infant Moses upon her lap at his left, and Balaam the son of Beor together with his two sons and all the princes of the realm sitting at table in the king's presence. It happened that the infant took the crown from off the king's head, and placed it on his own. When the king and the princes saw this, they were terrified, and each one in turn expressed his astonishment. The king said unto the princes, "What speak you, and what say you, O ye princes, on this matter, and what is to be done to this Hebrew boy on account of this act?"

Balaam spoke, saying: "Remember now, O my lord and king, the dream which thou didst dream many days ago, and how thy servant interpreted it unto thee. Now this is a child of the Hebrews in whom is the spirit of God. Let not my lord the king imagine in his heart that being a child he did the thing without knowledge. For he is a Hebrew boy, and wisdom and understanding are with him, although he is yet a child, and with wisdom has he done this, and chosen unto himself the kingdom of Egypt. For this is the manner of all the Hebrews, to deceive kings and their magnates, to do all things cunningly in order to make the kings of the earth and their men to stumble.

"Surely thou knowest that Abraham their father acted thus, who made the armies of Nimrod king of Babel and of Abimelech king of Gerar to stumble, and he possessed himself of the land of the children of Heth and the whole realm of Canaan. Their father Abraham went down into Egypt, and said of Sarah his wife, She is my sister, in order to make Egypt and its king to stumble.

"His son Isaac did likewise when he went to Gerar, and he dwelt there, and his strength prevailed over the army of Abimelech, and he intended to make the kingdom of the Philistines to stumble, by saying that Rebekah his wife was his sister.

"Jacob also dealt treacherously with his brother, and took his birthright and his blessing from him. Then he went to Paddan-aram, to Laban, his mother's brother, and he obtained his daughters from him cunningly, and also his cattle and all his belongings, and he fled away and returned to the land of Canaan, to his father.

"His sons sold their brother Joseph, and he went down into Egypt and became a slave, and he was put into prison for twelve years, until the former Pharaoh delivered him from the prison, and magnified him above all the princes of Egypt on account of his interpreting the king's dreams. When God caused a famine to descend upon the whole world, Joseph sent for his father, and he brought him down into Egypt his father, his brethren, and all his father's household, and he supplied them with food without pay or reward, while he acquired Egypt, and made slaves of all its inhabitants.

"Now, therefore, my lord king, behold, this child has risen up in their stead in Egypt, to do according to their deeds and make sport of every man, be he king, prince, or judge. If it please the king, let us now spill his blood upon the ground, lest he grow up and snatch the government from thine hand, and the hope of Egypt be cut off after he reigns. Let us, moreover, call for all the judges and the wise men of Egypt, that we may know whether the judgment of death be due to this child, as I have said, and then we will slay him."

Pharaoh sent and called for all the wise men of Egypt, and they came, and the angel Gabriel was disguised as one of them. When they were asked their opinion in the matter, Gabriel spoke up, and said: "If it please the king, let him place an onyx stone before the child, and a coal of fire, and if he stretches out his hand and grasps the onyx stone, then shall we know that the child hath done with wisdom all that he bath done, and we will slay him. But if he stretches out his hand and grasps the coal of fire, then shall we know that it was not with consciousness that he did the thing, and he shall live."

The counsel seemed good in the eyes of the king, and when they had placed the stone and the coal before the child, Moses stretched forth his hand toward the onyx stone and attempted to seize it, but the angel Gabriel guided his hand away from it and placed it upon the live coal, and the coal burnt the child's hand, and he lifted it up and touched it to his mouth, and burnt part of his lips and part of his tongue, and for all his life he became slow of speech and of a slow tongue.

Seeing this, the king and the princes knew that Moses had not acted with knowledge in taking the crown from off the king's head, and they refrained from slaying him. God Himself, who protected Moses, turned the king's mind to grace, and his foster-mother snatched him away, and she had him educated with great care, so that the Hebrews depended upon him, and cherished the hope that great things would be done by him. But the Egyptians were suspicious of what would follow from such an education as his.

At great cost teachers were invited to come to Egypt from neighboring lands, to educate the child Moses. Some came of their own accord, to instruct him in the sciences and the liberal arts. By reason of his admirable endowments of mind, he soon excelled his teachers in knowledge. His learning seemed a process of mere recollecting, and when there was a difference of opinion among scholars, he selected the correct one instinctively, for his mind refused to store up anything that was false.

But he deserves more praise for his unusual strength of will than for his natural capacity, for he succeeded in transforming an originally evil disposition into a noble, exalted character, a change that was farther aided by his resolution, as he himself acknowledged later. After the wonderful exodus of the Israelites from Egypt, a king of Arabia sent an artist to Moses, to paint his portrait, that he might always have the likeness of the divine man before him. The painter returned with his handiwork, and the king assembled his wise men, those in particular who were conversant with the science of physiognomy. He displayed the portrait before them, and invited their judgment upon it. The unanimous opinion was that it represented a man covetous, haughty, sensual, in short, disfigured by all possible ugly traits. The king was indignant that they should pretend to be masters in physiognomy, seeing that they declared the picture of Moses, the holy, divine man, to be the picture of a villain. They defended themselves by accusing the painter in turn of not having produced a true portrait of Moses, else they would not have fallen into the erroneous judgment they had expressed. But the artist insisted that his work resembled the original closely.

Unable to decide who was right, the Arabian king went to see Moses, and he could not but admit that the portrait painted for him was a masterpiece. Moses as he beheld him in the flesh was the Moses upon the canvas. There could be no doubt but that the highly extolled knowledge of his physiognomy experts was empty twaddle. He told Moses what had happened, and what he thought of it. He replied: "Thy artist and thy experts alike are masters, each in his line. If my fine qualities were a product of nature, I were no better than a log of wood, which remains forever as nature produced it at the first. Unashamed I make the confession to thee that by nature I possessed all the reprehensible traits thy wise men read in my picture and ascribed to me, perhaps to a greater degree even than they think. But I mastered my evil impulses with my strong will, and the character I acquired through severe discipline has become the opposite of the disposition with which I was born. Through this change, wrought in me by my own efforts, I have earned honor and commendation upon earth as well as in heaven."

THE YOUTH OF MOSES

One day--it was after he was grown up, and had passed beyond the years of childhood--Moses went to the land of Goshen, in which lived the children of Israel. There he saw the burdens under which his people were groaning, and he inquired why the heavy service had been put upon them. The Israelites told him all that had befallen, told him of the cruel edict Pharaoh had issued shortly before his birth, and told him of the wicked counsels given by Balaam against themselves as well as against his person when he was but a little boy and had set Pharaoh's crown upon his head. The wrath of Moses was kindled against the spiteful adviser, and he tried to think out means of rendering him harmless. But Balaam, getting wind of his ill-feeling, fled from Egypt with his two sons, and betook himself to the court of Kikanos king of Ethiopia.

The sight of his enslaved people touched Moses unto tears, and he spoke, saying: "Woe unto me for your anguish! Rather would I die than see you suffer so grievously." He did not disdain to help his unfortunate brethren at their heavy tasks as much as lay in his power. He dismissed all thought of his high station at court, shouldered a share of the burdens put upon the Israelites, and toiled in their place. The result was that he not only gave relief to the heavily-laden workmen, but he also gained the favor of Pharaoh, who believed that Moses was taking part in the labor in order to promote the execution of the royal order. And God said unto Moses: "Thou didst relinquish all thy other occupations, and didst join thyself unto the children of Israel, whom thou dost treat as brethren; therefore will I, too, put aside now all heavenly and earthly affairs, and hold converse with thee."

Moses continued to do all he could to alleviate the suffering of his brethren to the best of his ability. He addressed encouraging words to them, saying: "My dear brethren, bear your lot with fortitude! Do not lose courage, and let not your spirit grow weary with the weariness of your body. Better times will come, when tribulation shall be changed into joy. Clouds are followed by sunshine, storms by calm, all things in the world tend toward their opposites, and nothing is more inconstant than the fortunes of man."

The royal favor, which the king accorded him in ever-increasing measure, he made use of to lighten the burden laid upon the children of Israel. One day he came into the presence of Pharaoh, and said: "O my lord, I have a request to make of thee, and my hope is that thou wilt not deny it." "Speak," replied the king. "It is an admitted fact," said Moses, "that if a slave is not afforded rest at least one day in the week, he will die of overexertion. Thy Hebrew slaves will surely perish, unless thou accordest them a day of cessation from work." Pharaoh fulfilled the petition preferred by Moses, and the king's edict was published in the whole of Egypt and in Goshen, as follows: "To the sons of Israel! Thus saith the king: Do your work and perform your service for six days, but on the seventh day you shall rest; on it ye shall do no labor. Thus shall ye do unto all times, according to the command of the king and the command of Moses the son of Bithiah." And the day appointed by Moses as the day of rest was Saturday, later given by God to the Israelites as the Sabbath day.

While Moses abode in Goshen, an incident of great importance occurred. To superintend the service of the children of Israel, an officer from among them was set over every ten, and ten such officers were under the surveillance of an Egyptian taskmaster. One of these Hebrew officers, Dathan by name, had a wife, Shelomith, the daughter of Dibri, of the tribe of Dan, who was of extraordinary beauty, but inclined to be very loquacious. Whenever the Egyptian taskmaster set over her husband came to their house on business connected with his office, she would approach him pleasantly and enter into conversation with him. The beautiful Israelitish woman enkindled a mad passion in his breast, and he sought and found a cunning way of satisfying his lustful desire. One day he appeared at break of dawn at the house of Dathan, roused him from his sleep, and ordered him to hurry his detachment of men to their work. The husband scarcely out of sight, he executed the villainy he had planned, and dishonored the woman, and the fruit of this illicit relation was the blasphemer of the Name whom Moses ordered to execution on the march through the desert.

At the moment when the Egyptian slipped out of Shelomith's chamber, Dathan returned home. Vexed that his crime had come to the knowledge of the injured husband, the taskmaster goaded him on to work with excessive vigor, and dealt him blow after blow with the intention to kill him. Young Moses happened to visit the place at which the much-abused and tortured Hebrew was at work. Dathan hastened toward him, and complained of all the wrong and suffering the Egyptian had inflicted upon him. Full of wrath, Moses, whom the holy spirit had acquainted with the injury done the Hebrew officer by the Egyptian taskmaster, cried out to the latter, saying: "Not enough that thou hast dishonored this man's wife, thou aimest to kill him, too?" And turning to God, he spoke further: "What will become of Thy promise to Abraham, that his posterity shall be as numerous as the stars, if his children are given over to death? And what will become of the revelation on Sinai, if the children of Israel are exterminated?"

Moses wanted to see if someone would step forward, and, impelled by zeal for the cause of God and for God's law, would declare himself ready to avenge the outrage. He waited in vain. Then he determined to act himself. Naturally enough he hesitated to take the life of a human being. He did not know whether the evil-doer might not be brought to repentance, and then lead a life of pious endeavor. He also considered, that there would perhaps be some among the descendants to spring from the Egyptian for whose sake their wicked ancestor might rightfully lay claim to clemency. The holy spirit allayed all his doubts. He was made to see that not the slightest hope existed that good would come either from the malefactor himself or from any of his offspring. Then Moses was willing to requite him for his evil deeds. Nevertheless he first consulted the angels, to hear what they had to say, and they agreed that the Egyptian deserved death, and Moses acted according to their opinion.

Neither physical strength nor a weapon was needed to carry out his purpose. He merely pronounced the Name of God, and the Egyptian was a corpse. To the bystanders, the Israelites, Moses said: "The Lord compared you unto the sand of the sea-shore, and as the sand moves noiselessly from place to place, so I pray you to keep the knowledge of what hath happened a secret within yourselves. Let nothing be heard concerning it."

The wish expressed by Moses was not honored. The slaying of the Egyptian remained no secret, and those who betrayed it were Israelites, Dathan and Abiram, the sons of Pallu, of the tribe of Reuben, notorious for their effrontery and contentiousness. The day after the thing with the Egyptians happened, the two brothers began of malice aforethought to scuffle with each other, only in order to draw Moses into the quarrel and create an occasion for his betrayal. The plan succeeded admirably. Seeing Dathan raise his hand against Abiram, to deal him a blow, Moses exclaimed, "O thou art a villain, to lift up thy hand against an Israelite, even if he is no better than thou." Dathan replied: "Young man, who hath made thee to be a judge over us, thou that hast not yet attained to years of maturity? We know very well that thou art the son of Jochebed, though people call thee the son of the princess Bithiah, and if thou shouldst attempt to play the part of our master and judge, we will publish abroad the thing thou didst unto the Egyptian. Or, peradventure, thou harborest the intention to slay us as thou didst slay him, by pronouncing the Name of God?"

Not satisfied with these taunts, the noble pair of brothers betook themselves to Pharaoh, and spoke before him, "Moses dishonoreth thy royal mantle and thy crown," to which Pharaoh returned, saying, "Much good may it do him!" But they pursued the subject. "He helps thine enemies, Pharaoh," they continued, whereupon he replied, as before, "Much good may it do him!" Still they went on, "He is not the son of thy daughter." These last words did not fail of making an impression upon Pharaoh. A royal command was issued for the arrest of Moses, and he was condemned to death by the sword.

The angels came to God, and said, "Moses, the familiar of Thine house, is held under restraint," and God replied, "I will espouse his cause." "But," the angels urged, "his verdict of death has been pronounced--yes, they are leading him to execution," and again God made reply, as before, "I will espouse his cause."

Moses mounted the scaffold, and a sword, sharp beyond compare, was set upon his neck ten times, but it always slipped away, because his neck was as hard as ivory. And a still greater miracle came to pass. God sent down the angel Michael, in the guise of a hangman, and the human hangman charged by Pharaoh with the execution was changed into the form of Moses. This spurious Moses the angel killed with the very sword with which the executioner had purposed to slay the intended victim. Meantime Moses took to flight. Pharaoh ordered his pursuit, but it was in vain. The king's troops were partly stricken with blindness partly with dumbness. The dumb could give no information about the abiding-place of Moses, and the blind, though they knew where it was, could not get to it.

THE FLIGHT

An angel of God took Moses to a spot removed forty days' journey from Egypt, so far off that all fear was banished from his mind. Indeed, his anxiety had never been for his own person, but only on account of the future of Israel. The subjugation of his people had always been an unsolved enigma to him. Why should Israel, he would ask himself, suffer more than all the other nations? But when his personal straits initiated him in the talebearing and back-biting that prevailed among the Israelites, then he asked himself, Does this people deserve to be redeemed? The religious conditions among the children of Israel were of such kind at that time as not to permit them to hope for Divine assistance. They refused to give ear to Aaron and the five sons of Zerah, who worked among them as prophets, and admonished them unto the fear of God. It was on account of their impiety that the heavy hand of Pharaoh rested upon them more and more oppressively, until God had mercy upon them, and sent Moses to deliver them from the slavery of Egypt.

When he succeeded in effecting his escape from the hands of the hangman, Moses had no idea that a royal throne awaited him. It was nevertheless so. A war broke out at this time between Ethiopia and the nations of the East that had been subject to it until then. Kikanos, the king, advanced against the enemy with a great army. He left Balaam and Balaam's two sons, Jannes and Jambres, behind, to keep guard over his capital and take charge of the people remaining at home. The absence of the king gave Balaam the opportunity of winning his subjects over to his side, and he was put upon the throne, and his two sons were set over the army as generals. To cut Kikanos off from his capital, Balaam and his sons invested the city, so that none could enter it against their will. On two sides they made the walls higher, on the third they dug a network of canals, into which they conducted the waters of the river girding the whole land of Ethiopia, and on the fourth side their magic arts collected a large swarm of snakes and scorpions. Thus none could depart, and none could enter.

Meantime Kikanos succeeded in subjugating the rebellious nations. When he returned at the head of his victorious army, and espied the high city wall from afar, he and his men said: "The inhabitants of the city, seeing that the war detained us abroad for a long time, have raised the walls and fortified them, that the kings of Canaan may not be able to enter." On approaching the city gates, which were barred, they cried out to the guards to open them, but by Balaam's instructions they were not permitted to pass through. A skirmish ensued, in which Kikanos lost one hundred and thirty men. On the morrow the combat was continued, the king with his troops being stationed on the thither bank of the river. This day he lost his thirty riders, who, mounted on their steeds, had attempted to swim the stream. Then the king ordered rafts to be constructed for the transporting of his men. When the vessels reached the canals, they were submerged, and the waters, swirling round and round as though driven by mill wheels, swept away two hundred men, twenty from each raft. On the third day they set about assaulting the city from the side on which the snakes and scorpions swarmed, but they failed to reach it, and the reptiles killed one hundred and seventy men. The king desisted from attacking the city, but for the space of nine years he surrounded it, so that none could come out or go in.

While the siege was in progress, Moses appeared in the king's camp on his flight before Pharaoh, and at once found favor with Kikanos and his whole army. He exercised an attraction upon all that saw him, for he was slender like a palm-tree, his countenance shone as the morning sun, and his strength was equal to a lion's. So deep was the king's affection for him that he appointed him to be commander-in-chief of his forces.

At the end of the nine years Kikanos fell a prey to a mortal disease, and he died on the seventh day of his illness. His servants embalmed him, buried him opposite to the city gate toward the land of Egypt, and over his grave they erected a magnificent structure, strong and high, upon the walls whereof they engraved all the mighty deeds and battles of the dead king.

Now, after the death of Kikanos, his men were greatly grieved on account of the war. One said unto the other, "Counsel us, what shall we do at this time? We have been abiding in the wilderness, away from our homes, for nine years. If we fight against the city, many of us will fall dead; and if we remain here besieging it, we shall also die. For now all the princes of Aram and of the children of the East will hear that our king is dead, and they will attack us suddenly, and they will fight with us until not a remnant will be left. Now, therefore, let us go and set a king over us, and we will remain here besieging the city until it surrenders unto us."

THE KING OF ETHIOPIA

They could find none except Moses fit to be their king. They hastened and stripped off each man his upper garment, and cast them all in a heap upon the ground, making a high place, on top of which they set Moses. Then they blew with trumpets, and called out before him: "Long live the king! Long live the king!" And all the people and the nobles swore unto him to give him Adoniah for wife, the Ethiopian queen, the widow of Kikanos. And they made Moses king over them on that day.

They also issued a proclamation, commanding every man to give Moses of what he possessed, and upon the high place they spread a sheet, wherein each one cast something, this one a gold nose ring, that one a coin, and onyx stones, bdellium, pearls, gold, and silver in great abundance.

Moses was twenty-seven years old when he became king over Ethiopia, and he reigned for forty years. On the seventh day of his reign, all the people assembled and came before him, to ask his counsel as to what was to be done to the city they were besieging. The king answered them, and said: "If you will hearken to my words, the city will be delivered into our hands. Proclaim with a loud voice throughout the whole camp, unto all the people, saying: 'Thus saith the king! Go to the forest and fetch hither of the young of the stork, each man one fledgling in his hand. And if there be any man that transgresseth the word of the king, not to bring a bird, he shall die, and the king shall take all belonging to him.' And when you have brought them, they shall be in your keeping. You shall rear them until they grow up, and you shall teach them to fly as the hawk flieth."

All the people did according to the word of Moses, and after the young storks had grown to full size, he ordered them to be starved for three days. On the third day the king said unto them, "Let every man put on his armor and gird his sword upon him. Each one shall mount his horse, and each shall set his stork upon his hand, and we will rise up and fight against the city opposite to the place of the serpents."

When they came to the appointed spot, the king said to them, "Let each man send forth his young stork, to descend upon the serpents." Thus they did, and the birds swooped down and devoured all the reptiles and destroyed them. After the serpents were removed in this way, the men fought against the city, subdued it, and killed all its inhabitants, but of the people besieging it there died not one.

When Balaam saw that the city had fallen into the hands of the besiegers, he exercised his magic arts, which enabled him to fly through the air, and he carried with him his two sons, Jannes and Jambres, and his eight brothers, and they all took refuge in Egypt.

Seeing that they had been saved by the king, and the city had been taken by his good counsel, the people became more than ever attached to him. They set the royal crown upon his head, and gave him Adoniah, the widow of Kikanos to wife. But Moses feared the stern God of his fathers, and he went not in unto Adoniah, nor did he turn his eyes toward her, for he remembered how Abraham had made his servant Eliezer swear, saying unto him, "Thou shalt not take a wife for my son of the daughters of the Canaanites, among whom I dwell." He also remembered what Isaac did when Jacob fled before his brother Esau, how he commanded his son, saying, "Thou shalt not take a wife from the daughters of Canaan, nor ally thyself by marriage with any of the children of Ham, for the Lord our God gave Ham the son of Noah and all his seed as slaves to the children of Shem and Japheth forever."

At that time Aram and the children of the East heard that Kikanos the king of Ethiopia had died, and they rose up against the Ethiopians, but Moses went forth with a mighty army to fight against the rebellious nations, and he subdued them, first the children of the East and then Aram.

Moses continued to prosper in his kingdom. He conducted the government in justice, righteousness, and integrity, and his people loved and feared him.

In the fortieth year of his reign, while he was sitting upon his throne one day, surrounded by all the nobles, Adoniah the queen, who was seated before him, rose up, and spake: "What is this thing which you, the people of Ethiopia, have done these many days? Surely you know that during the forty years this man hath reigned over you, he hath not approached me, nor hath he worshipped the gods of Ethiopia. Now, therefore, let this man reign over you no more, for he is not of our flesh. Behold, Monarchos my son is grown up, let him reign over you. It is better for you to serve the son of your lord than a stranger, a slave of the king of Egypt."

A whole day the people and the nobles contended with one another, whether to pay heed to the words of the queen. The officers of the army remained faithful to Moses, but the people of the cities were in favor of crowning the son of their former lord as king. The following morning they rose up and made Monarchos, the son of Kikanos, king over them, but they were afraid to stretch forth their hand against Moses, for the Lord was with him. They also remembered the oath they had sworn unto Moses, and therefore they did him no harm. Moreover, they gave many presents to him, and dismissed him with great honor.

When Moses left Ethiopia, in the sixty-seventh year of his age, it was the time appointed by God in the days of old to bring Israel forth from the affliction of the children of Ham. But fearing to return to Egypt on account of Pharaoh, Moses journeyed to Midian.

JETHRO

In the city of Midian, named thus for a son of Abraham by Keturah, the man Jethro had lived for many years, doing a priest's service before the idols. As time went on, he grew more and more convinced of the vanity of idol worship. His priesthood became repugnant to him, and he resolved to give up his, charge. He stood before his townsmen, and said, "Until now I performed your service before the idols, but I have grown too old for the duties of the office. Choose, therefore, whomever you would choose in my place." Speaking thus, he delivered to the people all the paraphernalia appertaining to the idol worship, and bade them transfer them to the one to whom in their discretion they should entrust his position. Suspecting Jethro's hidden motives, the people put him under the ban, and none might venture to do him the slightest service. Not even would the shepherds pasture his flocks, and there was nothing for him to do but impose this work upon his seven daughters.

Jethro's transformation from an idolatrous priest into a God-fearing man is conveyed by his seven names. He was called Jether, because the Torah contains an "additional" section about him; Jethro, he "overflowed" with good deeds. Hobab, "the beloved son of God"; Reuel, "the friend of God"; Heber, "the associate of God"; Putiel, "he that hath renounced idolatry"; and Keni, he that was "zealous" for God, and "acquired" the Torah.

In consequence of the hostile relation between Jethro and the inhabitants of the city, his daughters were in the habit of making their appearance at the watering troughs before the other shepherds came thither. But the ruse was not successful. The shepherds would drive them away, and water their own flocks at the troughs that the maidens had filled. When Moses arrived in Midian, it was at the well that he made halt, and his experience was the same as Isaac's and Jacob's. Like them he found his helpmeet there. Rebekah had been selected by Eliezer as the wife of Isaac, while she was busy drawing water for him; Jacob had seen Rachel first, while she was watering her sheep, and at this well in Midian Moses met his future wife Zipporah.

The rudeness of the shepherds reached its climax the very day of Moses' arrival. First they deprived the maidens of the water they had drawn for themselves, and attempted to do violence to them, and then they threw them into the water with intent to kill them. At this moment Moses appeared, dragged the maidens out of the water, and gave the flocks to drink, first Jethro's and then the flocks of the shep-herds, though the latter did not deserve his good offices. True, he did them the service with but little trouble to himself, for he had only to draw a bucketful, and the water flowed so copiously that it sufficed for all the herds, and it did not cease to flow until Moses withdrew from the well, --the same well at which Jacob had met Rachel, his future wife, and the same well that God created at the beginning of the world, the opening of which He made in the twilight of the first Sabbath eve.

Jethro's daughters thanked Moses for the assistance he had afforded them. But Moses warded off their gratitude, saying, "Your thanks are due to the Egyptian I killed, on account of whom I had to flee from Egypt. Had it not been for him, I should not be here now."

MOSES MARRIES ZIPPORAH

One of the seven maidens whom Moses saw at the well attracted his notice in particular on account of her modest demeanor, and he made her a proposal of marriage. But Zipporah repulsed him, saying, "My father has a tree in his garden with which he tests every man that expresses a desire to marry one of his daughters, and as soon as the suitor touches the tree, he is devoured by it."

Moses: "Whence has he the tree?"

Zipporah: "It is the rod that the Holy One, blessed be He, created in the twilight of the first Sabbath eve, and gave to Adam. He transmitted it to Enoch, from him it descended to Noah, then to Shem, and Abraham, and Isaac, and finally to Jacob, who brought it with him to Egypt, and gave it to his son Joseph. When Joseph died, the Egyptians pillaged his house, and the rod, which was in their booty, they brought to Pharaoh's palace. At that time my father was one of the most prominent of the king's sacred scribes, and as such he had the opportunity of seeing the rod. He felt a great desire to possess it, and he stole it and took it to his house. On this rod the Ineffable Name is graven, and also the ten plagues that God will cause to visit the Egyptians in a future day. For many years it lay in my father's house. One day he was walking in his garden carrying it, and he stuck it in the ground. When he attempted to draw it out again, he found that it had sprouted, and was putting forth blossoms. That is the rod with which he tries any that desire to marry his daughters. He insists that our suitors shall attempt to pull it out of the ground, but as soon as they touch it, it devours them."

Having given him this account of her father's rod, Zipporah went home, accompanied by her sisters, and Moses followed them.

Jethro was not a little amazed to see his daughters return so soon from the watering troughs. As a rule, the chicanery they had to suffer from the shepherds detained them until late. No sooner had he heard their report about the wonder-working Egyptian than he exclaimed, "Mayhap he is one of the descendants of Abraham, from whom issueth blessing for the whole world." He rebuked his daughters for not having invited the stranger that had done them so valuable a service to come into their house, and he ordered them to fetch him, in the hope that he would take one of his daughters to wife.

Moses had been standing without all this time, and had allowed Jethro's daughters to describe him as an Egyptian, without protesting and asserting his Hebrew birth. For this God punished him by causing him to die outside of the promised land. Joseph, who had proclaimed in public that he was a Hebrew, found his last resting-place in the land of the Hebrews, and Moses, who apparently had no objection to being considered an Egyptian, had to live and die outside of that land.

Zipporah hastened forth to execute her father's wish, and no sooner had she ushered him in than Moses requested her hand in marriage. Jethro replied, "If thou canst bring me the rod in my garden, I will give her to thee." Moses went out, found the sapphire rod that God had bestowed upon Adam when he was driven forth from Paradise, the rod that had reached Jethro after manifold vicissitudes, and which he had planted in the garden. Moses uprooted it and carried it to Jethro, who conceived the idea at once that he was the prophet in Israel concerning whom all the wise men of Egypt had foretold that he would destroy their land and its inhabitants. As soon as this thought struck him, he seized Moses, and threw him into a pit, in the expectation that he would meet with death there.

And, indeed, he would have perished, if Zipporah had not devised a stratagem to save his life. She said to her father: "Would it were thy will to hearken unto my counsel. Thou hast no wife, but only seven daughters. Dost thou desire my six sisters to preside over thy household? Then shall I go abroad with the sheep. If not, let my sisters tend the flocks, and I shall take care of the house." Her father said: "Thou hast spoken well. Thy six sisters shall go forth with the sheep, and thou shalt abide in the house and take care of it, and all that belongeth to me therein."

Now Zipporah could provide Moses with all sorts of dainties as he lay in the pit, and she did it for the space of seven years. At the expiration of this period, she said to her father: "I recollect that once upon a time thou didst cast into yonder pit a man that had fetched thy rod from the garden for thee, and thou didst commit a great trespass thereby. If it seemeth well to thee, uncover the pit and look into it. If the man is dead, throw his corpse away, lest it fill the house with stench. But should he be alive, then thou oughtest to be convinced that he is one of those who are wholly pious, else he had died of hunger."

The reply of Jethro was: "Thou hast spoken wisely. Dost thou remember his name?" And Zipporah rejoined, "I remember he called himself Moses the son of Amram." Jethro lost no time, he opened the pit, and called out, "Moses! Moses!" Moses replied, and said: "Here am I!" Jethro drew him up out of the pit, kissed him, and said: "Blessed be God, who guarded thee for seven years in the pit. I acknowledge that He slayeth and reviveth, that thou art one of the wholly pious, that through thee God will destroy Egypt in time to come, lead His people out of the land, and drown Pharaoh and his whole army in the sea."

Thereupon Jethro gave much money to Moses, and he bestowed his daughter Zipporah upon him as wife, giving her to him under the condition that the children born of the marriage in Jethro's house should be divided into two equal classes, the one to be Israelitish, the other Egyptian. When Zipporah bore him a son, Moses circumcised him, and called him Gershom, as a memorial of the wonder God had done for him, for although he lived in a "strange" land, the Lord had not refused him aid even "there."

Zipporah nursed her first child for two years, and in the third year she bore a second son. Remembering his compact with Jethro, Moses realized that his father-in-law would not permit him to circumcise this one, too, and he determined to return to Egypt, that he might have the opportunity of bringing up his second son as an Israelite. On the journey thither, Satan appeared to him in the guise of a serpent, and swallowed Moses down to his extremities. Zipporah knew by this token that the thing had happened because her second son had not been circumcised, and she hastened to make good the omission. As soon as she sprinkled the blood of the circumcision on her husband's feet, a heavenly voice was heard to cry to the serpent, commanding him, "Spew him out!" and Moses came forth and stood upon his feet. Thus Zipporah saved Moses' life twice, first from the pit and then from the serpent.

When Moses arrived in Egypt, he was approached by Dathan and Abiram, the leaders of the Israelites, and they spake: "Comest thou hither to slay us, or dost thou purpose to do the same with us as thou didst with the Egyptian?" This drove Moses straightway back to Midian, and there he remained two years more, until God revealed Himself at Horeb, and said to him, "Go and bring forth My children out of the land of Egypt.

A BLOODY REMEDY

The latter years of Israel's bondage in Egypt were the worst. To punish Pharaoh for his cruelty toward the children of Israel, God afflicted him with a plague of leprosy, which covered his whole body, from the crown of his bead to the soles of his feet. Instead of being chastened by his disease, Pharaoh remained stiffnecked, and he tried to restore his health by murdering Israelitish children. He took counsel with his three advisers, Balaam, Jethro, and Job, how he might be healed of the awful malady that had seized upon him. Balaam spoke, saying, "Thou canst regain thy health only if thou wilt slaughter Israelitish children and bathe in their blood." Jethro, averse from having a share in such an atrocity, left the king and fled to Midian. Job, on the other hand, though he also disapproved of Balaam's counsel, kept silence, and in no wise protested against it, wherefor God punished him with a year's suffering. But afterward He loaded him down with all the felicities of this life, and granted him many years, so that this pious Gentile might be rewarded in this world for his good deeds and not have the right to urge a claim upon the beatitude of the future life.

In pursuance of the sanguinary advice given by Balaam, Pharaoh had his bailiffs snatch Israelitish babes from their mothers' breasts, and slaughter them, and in the blood of these innocents he bathed. His disease afflicted him for ten years, and every day an Israelitish child was killed for him. It was all in vain; indeed, at the end of the time his leprosy changed into boils, and he suffered more than before.

While he was in this agony, the report was brought to him that the children of Israel in Goshen were careless and idle in their forced labor. The news aggravated his suffering, and he said: "Now that I am ill, they turn and scoff at me. Harness my chariot, and I will betake myself to Goshen, and see the derision wherewith the children of Israel deride me." And they took and put him upon a horse, for he was not able to mount it himself. When he and his men had come to the border between Egypt and Goshen, the king's steed passed into a narrow place. The other horses, running rapidly through the pass, pressed upon each other until the king's horse fell while he sate upon it, and when it fell, the chariot turned over on his face, and also the horse lay upon him. The king's flesh was torn from him, for this thing was from the Lord, He had heard the cries of His people and their affliction. The king's servants carried him upon their shoulders, brought him back to Egypt, and placed him on his bed.

He knew that his end was come to die, and the queen Alfar'anit and his nobles gathered about his bed, and they wept a great weeping with him.

The princes and his counsellors advised the king to make choice of a successor, to reign in his stead, whomsoever he would choose from among his sons. He had three sons and two daughters by the queen Alfar'anit, beside children from concubines. The name of his first-born was Atro, the name of the second Adikam, and of the third Moryon. The name of the older daughter was Bithiah, and of the other, Akuzit. The first-born of the sons of the king was an idiot, precipitate and heedless in all his actions. Adikam, the second son, was a cunning and clever man, and versed in all the wisdom of Egypt, but ungainly in appearance, fleshy and short of stature; his height was a cubit and a space, and his beard flowed down to his ankles.

The king resolved that Adikam should reign in his stead after his death. When this second son of his was but ten years old, he had given him Gedidah, the daughter of Abilat, to wife, and she bore him four sons. Afterward Adikam went and took three other wives, and begot eight sons and three daughters.

The king's malady increased upon him greatly, and his flesh emitted a stench like a carcass cast into the field in summer time in the heat of the sun. When he saw that his disorder had seized upon him with a strong grip, he commanded his son Adikam to be brought to him, and they made him king over the land in his place.

At the end of three years the old king died in shame and disgrace, a loathing to all that saw him, and they buried him in the sepulchre of the kings of Egypt in Zoan, but they did not embalm him, as was usual with kings, for his flesh was putrid, and they could not approach his body on account of the stench, and they buried him in haste. Thus the Lord requited him with evil for the evil he had done in his days to Israel, and he died in terror and shame after having reigned ninety-four years.

Adikam was twenty years old when he succeeded his father, and he reigned four years. The people of Egypt called him Pharaoh, as was their custom with all their kings, but his wise men called him Akuz, for Akuz is the word for "short" in the Egyptian language, and Adikam was exceedingly awkward and undersized. The new

Pharaoh surpassed his father Malol and all the former kings in wickedness, and he made heavier the yoke upon the children of Israel. He went to Goshen with his servants, and increased their labor, and he said unto them, "Complete your work, each day's task, and let not your hands slacken from the work from this day forward, as you did in the day of my father." He placed officers over them from amongst the children of Israel, and over these officers he placed taskmasters from amongst his servants. And he put before them a measure for bricks, according to the number they were to make day by day, and whenever any deficiency was discovered in the measure of their daily bricks, the taskmasters of Pharaoh would go to the women of the children of Israel, and take their infants from them, as many as the number of bricks lacking in the measure, and these babes they put into the building instead of the missing bricks. The taskmasters forced each man of the Israelites to put his own child in the building. The father would place his son in the wall, and cover him over with mortar, all the while weeping, his tears running down upon his child.

The children of Israel sighed every day on account of their dire suffering, for they had thought that after Pharaoh's death his son would lighten their toil, but the new king was worse than his father. And God saw the burden of the children of Israel, and their heavy work, and He determined to deliver them.

However, it was not for their own sake that God resolved upon the deliverance of the children of Israel, for they were empty of good deeds, and the Lord foreknew that, once they were redeemed, they would rise up against Him, and even worship the golden calf. Yet He took mercy upon them, for He remembered His covenant with the Fathers, and He looked upon their repentance for their sins, and accepted their promise, to fulfil the word of God after their going forth from Egypt even before they should hear it.

After all, the children of Israel were not wholly without merits. In a high degree they possessed qualities of extraordinary excellence. There were no incestuous relations among them, they were not evil-tongued, they did not change their names, they clung to the Hebrew language, never giving it up, and great fraternal affection prevailed among them. If one happened to finish the tale of his bricks before his neighbors, he was in the habit of helping the others. Therefore God spake, "They deserve that I should have mercy upon them, for if a man shows mercy unto another, I have mercy upon him."

THE FAITHFUL SHEPHERD

When Jethro bestowed his daughter Zipporah upon Moses as his wife, he said to his future son-in-law: "I know that thy father Jacob took his wives, the daughters of Laban, and went away with them against their father's will. Now take an oath that thou wilt not do the same unto me," and Moses swore not to leave him without his consent, and he remained with Jethro, who made him the shepherd of his flocks. By the way he tended the sheep, God saw his fitness to be the shepherd of His people, for God never gives an exalted office to a man until He has tested him in little things. Thus Moses and David were tried as shepherds of flocks, and only after they had proved their ability as such, He gave them dominion over men.

Moses watched over the flocks with loving care. He led the young animals to pasture first, that they might have the tender, juicy grass for their food; the somewhat older animals he led forth next, and allowed them to graze off the herbs suitable for them; and finally came the vigorous ones that had attained their full growth, and to them he gave the hard grass that was left, which the others could not eat, but which afforded good food for them. Then spake God, "He that understandeth how to pasture sheep, providing for each what is good for it, he shall pasture My people."

Once a kid escaped from the flock, and when Moses followed it, he saw how it stopped at all the water courses, and he said to it: "Poor kid, I knew not that thou wast thirsty, and wast running after water! Thou art weary, I ween," and he carried it back to the herd on his shoulder. Then said God: "Thou hast compassion with a flock belonging to a man of flesh and blood! As thou livest, thou shalt pasture Israel, My flock."

Not only did Moses take heed that no harm should come to the herds under his charge, but he was also careful that they cause no injury to men. He always chose an open meadow as his pasturing place, to prevent his sheep from grazing in private estates.

Jethro had no reason to be dissatisfied with the services rendered to him by his son-in-law. During the forty years Moses acted as his shepherd not one sheep was attacked by wild beasts, and the herds multiplied to an incredible degree. Once he drove the sheep about in the desert for forty days, without finding a pasturing place for them. Nevertheless he did not lose a single sheep.

Moses' longing for the desert was irresistible. His prophetic spirit caused him to foresee that his own greatness and the greatness of Israel would manifest themselves there. In the desert God's wonders would appear, though it would be at the same time the grave of the human herd to be entrusted to him in the future, and also his own last resting-place. Thus he had a presentiment at the very beginning of his career that the desert would be the scene of his activity, which not only came true in the present order of things, but also will be true in the latter days, when he will appear in the desert again, to lead into the promised land the generation, arisen from their graves, that he brought forth from Egyptian bondage.

Wandering through the desert, he reached Mount Horeb, which is called by six names, each conveying one of its distinctions. It is "the mountain of God," wherein the Lord revealed His law; "Basban," for God "came there"; "a mountain of humps," for the Lord declared all the other mountains unfit for the revelation, as "crookbackt" animals are declared unfit for sacrifices; "mountain of abode," because it is the mountain that God desired for His "abode"; Sinai, because the "hatred" of God against the heathen began at the time when Israel received the law thereon; and Horeb, "sword," because there the sword of the law was drawn upon the sinners.

THE BURNING THORN-BUSH

When Moses drew near to Mount Horeb, he was aware at once that it was a holy place, for he noticed that passing birds did not alight upon it. At his approach the mountain began to move, as though to go forward and meet him, and it settled back into quietude only when his foot rested upon it. The first thing Moses noticed was the wonderful burning bush, the upper part of which was a blazing flame, neither consuming the bush, nor preventing it from bearing blossoms as it burnt, for the celestial fire has three peculiar qualities: it produces blossoms, it does not consume the object around which it plays, and it is black of color. The fire that Moses saw in the bush was the appearance of the angel Michael, who had descended as the forerunner of the Shekinah herself to come down presently. It was the wish of God to hold converse with Moses, who, however, was not inclined to permit any interruption of the work under his charge. Therefore God startled him with the wonderful phenomenon of the burning thorn-bush. That brought Moses to a stop, and then God spoke with him.

There were good reasons for selecting the thorn-bush as the vessel for a Divine vision. It was "clean," for the heathen could not use it to make idols. God's choosing to dwell in the stunted thorn-bush conveyed the knowledge to Moses that He suffers along with Israel. Furthermore, Moses was taught that there is nothing in nature, not even the insignificant thorn-bush, that can exist without the presence of the Shekinah. Besides, the thorn-bush may be taken as the symbol for Israel in several respects. As the thorn-bush is the lowliest of all species of trees, so the condition of Israel in the exile is the lowliest as compared with that of all the other nations, but as the thorn-bush releases no bird that alights upon it without lacerating its wings, so the nations that subjugate Israel will be punished. Also, as a garden hedge is made of the thorn-bush, so Israel forms the hedge for the world, the garden of God, for without Israel the world could not endure. Furthermore, as the thorn-bush bears thorns and roses alike, so Israel has pious and impious members, and as the thorn-bush requires ample water for its growth, so Israel can prosper only through the Torah, the celestial water. And the thorn-bush, the leaf of which consists of five leaflets, was to indicate to Moses that God had resolved to redeem Israel only for the sake of the merits of five pious men, Abraham, Isaac, Jacob, Aaron, and Moses. The numbers represented by the letters composing the Hebrew word for thorn-bush, Seneh, add up to one hundred and twenty, to convey that Moses would reach the age of one hundred and twenty years, and that the Shekinah would rest on Mount Horeb for one hundred and twenty days. Finally, in order to give Moses an illustration of His modesty, God descended from the exalted heavens and spake to him from a lowly thorn-bush instead of the summit of a lofty mountain or the top of a stately cedar tree.

THE ASCENSION OF MOSES

The vision of the burning bush appeared to Moses alone; the other shepherds with him saw nothing of it. He took five steps in the direction of the bush, to view it at close range, and when God beheld the countenance of Moses distorted by grief and anxiety over Israel's suffering, He spake, "This one is worthy of the office of pasturing My people."

Moses was still a novice in prophecy, therefore God said to Himself, "If I reveal Myself to him in loud tones, I shall alarm him, but if I reveal Myself with a subdued voice, he will hold prophecy in low esteem," whereupon he addressed him in his father Amram's voice. Moses was overjoyed to hear his father speak, for it gave him the assurance that. he was still alive. The voice called his name twice, and he answered, "Here am I! What is my father's wish?" God replied, saying, "I am not thy father. I but desired to refrain from terrifying thee, therefore I spoke with thy father's voice. I am the God of thy father, the God of Abraham, the God of Isaac, and the God of Jacob." These words rejoiced Moses greatly, for not only was his father Amram's name pronounced in the same breath with the names of the three Patriarchs, but it came before theirs, as though he ranked higher than they.

Moses said not a word. In silent reverence before the Divine vision he covered his face, and when God disclosed the mission with which He charged him, of bringing the Israelites forth from the land of Egypt, he answered with humility, "Who am I, that I should go unto Pharaoh, and bring forth the children of Israel out of Egypt?" Thereupon spake God, "Moses, thou art meek, and I will reward thee for thy modesty. I will deliver the whole land of Egypt into thine hand, and, besides, I will let thee ascend unto the throne of My glory, and look upon all the angels of the heavens."

Hereupon God commanded Metatron, the Angel of the Face, to conduct Moses to the celestial regions amid the sound of music and song, and He commanded him furthermore to summon thirty thousand angels, to serve as his body-guard, fifteen thousand to right of him and fifteen thousand to left of him. In abject terror Moses asked Metatron, "Who art thou?" and the angel replied, "I am Enoch, the son of Jared, thy ancestor, and God has charged me to accompany thee to His throne." But Moses demurred, saying, "I am but flesh and blood, and I cannot look upon the countenance of an angel," whereupon Metatron changed Moses' flesh into torches of fire, his eyes into Merkabah wheels, his strength into an angel's, and his tongue into a flame, and he took him to heaven with a retinue of thirty thousand angels, one half moving to right of them and one half to left of them.

In the first heaven Moses saw streams upon streams of water, and he observed that the whole heaven consisted of windows, at each of which angels were stationed. Metatron named and pointed out all the windows of heaven to him: the window of prayer and the window of supplication; of weeping and of joy; plenitude and starvation; wealth and poverty; war and peace; conception and birth; showers and soft rains; sin and repentance; life and death; pestilence and healing; sickness and health; and many windows more.

In the second heaven Moses saw the angel Nuriel, standing three hundred parasangs high, with his retinue of fifty myriads of angels, all fashioned out of water and fire, and all keeping their faces turned toward the Shekinah while they sang a song of praise to God. Metatron explained to Moses, that these were the angels set over the clouds, the winds, and the rains, who return speedily, as soon as they have executed the will of their Creator, to their station in the second of the heavens, there to proclaim the praise of God.

In the third heaven Moses saw an angel, so tall it would take a human being five hundred years to climb to his height. He had seventy thousand heads, each head having as many mouths, each mouth as many tongues, and each tongue as many sayings, and he together with his suite of seventy thousand myriads of angels made of white fire praised and extolled the Lord. "These," said Metatron to Moses, "are called Erelim, and they are appointed over the grass, the trees, the fruits, and the grain, but as soon as they have done the will of their Creator, they return to the place assigned to them, and praise God."

In the fourth heaven Moses saw a Temple, the pillars thereof made of red fire, the staves of green fire, the thresholds of white fire, the boards and clasps of flaming fire, the gates of carbuncles, and the pinnacles of rubies. Angels were entering the Temple and giving praise to God there. In response to a question from Moses Metatron told him that they presided over the earth, the sun, the moon, the stars, and the other celestial bodies. and all of them intone songs before God. In this heaven Moses noticed also the two great planets, Venus and Mars, each as large as the whole earth, and concerning these he asked unto what purpose they had been created. Metatron explained thereupon, that Venus lies upon the sun to cool him off in summer, else he would scorch the earth, and Mars lies upon the moon, to impart warmth to her, lest she freeze the earth.

Arrived in the fifth heaven, Moses saw hosts of angels, whose nether parts were of snow and their upper parts of fire, and yet the snow did not melt nor was the fire extinguished, for God had established perfect harmony between the two elements. These angels, called Ishim, have had nothing to do since the day of their creation but praise and extol the Lord.

In the sixth of the heavens were millions and myriads of angels praising God, they were called 'Irin and kadishim, "Watchers" and "Holy Ones," and their chief was made of hail, and he was so tall, it would take five hundred years to walk a distance equal to his height.

In the last heaven Moses saw two angels, each five hundred parasangs in height, forged out of chains of black fire and red fire, the angels Af, "Anger," and Hemah, "Wrath," whom God created at the beginning of the world, to execute His will. Moses was disquieted when he looked upon them, but Metatron embraced him, and said, "Moses, Moses, thou favorite of God, fear not, and be not terrified," and Moses became calm. There was another angel in the seventh heaven, different in appearance from all the others, and of frightful mien. His height was so great, it would have taken five hundred years to cover a distance equal to it, and from the crown of his head to the soles of his feet he was studded with glaring eyes, at the sight of which the beholder fell prostrate in awe. "This one," said Metatron, addressing Moses, "is Samael, who takes the soul away from man." "Whither goes he now?" asked Moses, and Metatron replied, "To fetch the soul of Job the pious." Thereupon Moses prayed to God in these words, "O may it be Thy will, my God and the God of my fathers, not to let me fall into the hands of this angel."

Here, in the highest heaven, he saw also the seraphim with their six wings. With two they cover their face, that they gaze not upon the Shekinah; and with two their feet, which, being like a calf's feet, they hide, to keep secret Israel's transgression of the golden calf. With the third pair of wings they fly and do the service of the Lord, all the while exclaiming, "Holy, holy, holy is the Lord of hosts; the whole earth is full of His glory." The wings of these angels are of prodigious size, it would take a man five hundred years to traverse their length and their breadth, as from one end of the earth to the other.

And Moses saw in the seventh heaven the holy Hayyot, which support the throne of God; and he beheld also the angel Zagzagel, the prince of the Torah and of wisdom, who teaches the Torah in seventy languages to the souls of men, and thereafter they cherish the precepts contained therein as laws revealed by God to Moses on Sinai. From this angel with the horns of glory Moses himself learnt all the ten mysteries."

Having seen what there is in the seven heavens, he spoke to God, saying, "I will not leave the heavens unless Thou grantest me a gift," and God replied, "I will give thee the Torah, and men shall call it the Law of Moses."

MOSES VISITS PARADISE AND HELL

When Moses was on the point of departing from heaven, a celestial voice announced: "Moses, thou camest hither, and thou didst see the throne of My glory. Now thou shalt see also Paradise and hell," and God dispatched Gabriel on the errand of showing hell to him. Terrified by its fires, when he caught sight of them as he entered the portals of hell, Moses refused to go farther. But the angel encouraged him, saying, "There is a fire that not only burns but also consumes, and that fire will protect thee against hell fire, so that thou canst step upon it, and yet thou wilt not be seared."

As Moses entered hell, the fire withdrew a distance of five hundred parasangs, and the Angel of Hell, Nasargiel, asked him, "Who art thou?" and he answered, "I am Moses, the son of Amram."

Nasargiel: "This is not thy place, thou belongest in Paradise."

Moses: "I came hither to see the manifestation of the power of God."

Then said God to the Angel of Hell, "Go and show hell unto Moses, and how the wicked are treated there." Immediately he went with Moses, walking before him like a pupil before his master, and thus they entered hell together, and Moses saw men undergoing torture by the Angels of Destruction: some of the sinners were suspended by their eyelids, some by their ears, some by their hands, and some by their tongues, and they cried bitterly. And women were suspended by their hair and by their breasts, and in other ways, all on chains of fire. Nasargiel explained: "These hang by their eyes, because they looked lustfully upon the wives of their neighbors, and with a covetous eye upon the possessions of their fellow-men. These hang by their ears because they listened to empty and vain speech, and turned their ear away from hearing the Torah. These hang by their tongues, because they talked slander, and accustomed their tongue to foolish babbling. These hang by their feet, because they walked with them in order to spy upon their fellow-men, but they walked not to the synagogue, to offer prayer unto their Creator. These hang by their hands, because with them they robbed their neighbors of their possessions, and committed murder. These women hang by their hair and their breasts, because they uncovered them in the presence of young men, so that they conceived desire unto them, and fell into sin."

Moses heard hell cry with a loud and a bitter cry, saying to Nasargiel: "Give me something to eat, I am hungry."--Nasargiel: "What shall I give thee?"--Hell: "Give me the souls of the pious."--Nasargiel: "The Holy One, blessed be He, will not deliver the souls of the pious unto thee."

Moses saw the place called Alukah, where sinners were suspended by their feet, their heads downward, and their bodies covered with black worms, each five hundred parasangs long. They lamented, and cried: "Woe unto us for the punishment of hell. Give us death, that we may die!" Nasargiel explained: "These are the sinners that swore falsely, profaned the Sabbath and the holy days, despised the sages, called their neighbors by unseemly nicknames, wronged the orphan and the widow, and bore false witness. Therefore bath God delivered them to these worms."

Moses went thence to another place, and there he saw sinners prone on their faces, with two thousand scorpions lashing, stinging, and tormenting them, while the tortured victims cried bitterly. Each of the scorpions had seventy thousand heads, each head seventy thousand mouths, each mouth seventy thousand stings, and each sting seventy thousand pouches of poison and venom, which the sinners are forced to drink down, although the anguish is so racking that their eyes melt in their sockets. Nasargiel explained: "These are the sinners who caused the Israelites to lose their money, who exalted themselves above the community, who put their neighbors to shame in public, who delivered their fellow-Israelites into the hands of the Gentiles, who denied the Torah of Moses, and who maintained that God is not the Creator of the world."

Then Moses saw the place called Tit ba-Yawen, in which the sinners stand in mud up to their navels, while the Angels of Destruction lash them with fiery chains, and break their teeth with fiery stones, from morning until evening, and during the night they make their teeth grow again, to the length of a parasang, only to break them anew the next morning. Nasargiel explained: "These are the sinners who ate carrion and forbidden flesh, who lent their money at usury, who wrote the Name of God on amulets for Gentiles, who used false weights, who stole money from their fellow-Israelites, who ate on the Day of Atonement, who ate forbidden fat, and animals and reptiles that are an abomination, and who drank blood."

Then Nasargiel said to Moses: "Come and see how the sinners are burnt in hell," and Moses answered, "I cannot go there," but Nasargiel replied, "Let the light of the Shekinah precede thee, and the fire of hell will have no power over thee." Moses yielded, and he saw how the sinners were burnt, one half of their bodies being immersed in fire and the other half in snow, while worms bred in their own flesh crawled over them, and the Angels of Destruction beat them incessantly. Nasargiel explained: "These are the sinners who committed incest, murder, and idolatry, who cursed their parents and their teachers, and who, like Nimrod and others, called themselves gods." In this place, which is called Abaddon, he saw the sinners taking snow by stealth and putting it in their armpits, to relieve the pain inflicted by the scorching fire, and he was convinced that the saying was true, "The wicked mend not their ways even at the gate of hell."

As Moses departed from hell, he prayed to God, "May it be Thy will, O Lord my God and God of my fathers, to save me and the people of Israel from the places I have seen in hell." But God answered him, and said,

"Moses, before Me there is no respecting of persons and no taking of gifts. Whoever doeth good deeds entereth Paradise, and he that doeth evil must go to hell."

At the command of God, Gabriel now led Moses to Paradise. As he entered, two angels came toward him, and they said to him, "Thy time is not yet arrived to leave the world," and Moses made answer, "What ye say is true, but I have come to see the reward of the pious in Paradise." Then the angels extolled Moses, saying: "Hail, Moses, servant of God! Hail, Moses, born of woman, that hast been found worthy to ascend to the seven heavens! Hail to the nation to which thou belongest!"

Under the tree of life Moses saw the angel Shamshiel, the prince of Paradise, who led him through it, and showed him all there is therein. He saw seventy thrones made of precious stones, standing on feet of fine gold, each throne surrounded by seventy angels. But one of them was larger than all the others, and it was encircled by one hundred and twenty angels. This was the throne of Abraham, and when Abraham beheld Moses, and heard who he was, and what his purpose was in visiting Paradise, he exclaimed, "Praise ye the Lord, for He is good, for His mercy endureth forever."

Moses asked Shamshiel about the size of Paradise, but not even he who is the prince thereof could answer the question, for there is none that can gauge it. It can neither be measured nor fathomed nor numbered. But Shamshiel explained to Moses about the thrones, that they were different one from the other, some being of silver, some of gold, some of precious stones and pearls and rubies and carbuncles. The thrones made of pearls are for the scholars that study the Torah day and night for her own sake; those of precious stones are for the pious, those of rubies for the just, those of gold for the repentant sinners, and those of silver for the righteous proselytes. "The greatest of them all," continued Shamshiel, "is the throne of Abraham, the next in size the thrones of Isaac and Jacob, then come the thrones of the prophets, the saints, and the righteous, each in accordance with a man's worth, and his rank, and the good deeds he has performed in his lifetime." Moses asked then for whom the throne of copper was intended, and the angel answered, "For the sinner that has a pious son. Through the merits of his son he receives it as his share."

Again Moses looked, and he beheld a spring of living water welling up from under the tree of life and dividing into four streams, which passed under the throne of glory, and thence encompassed Paradise from end to end. He also saw four rivers flowing under each of the thrones of the pious, one of honey, the second of milk, the third of wine, and the fourth of pure balsam.

Beholding all these desirable and pleasant things, Moses felt great joy, and he said, "Oh, how great is Thy goodness, which Thou hast laid up for them that fear Thee, which Thou hast wrought for them that put their trust in Thee, before the sons of men!" And Moses left Paradise, and returned to the earth.

At the moment of his departure, a heavenly voice cried aloud: "Moses, servant of the Lord, thou that art faithful in His house, even as thou hast seen the reward that is laid up for the pious in the world to come, so also thou wilt be worthy of seeing the life of the world that shall be in the future time. Thou and all Israel, ye shall see the rebuilding of the Temple and the advent of the Messiah, behold the beauty of the Lord, and meditate in His Temple."

In the world to come Moses, beside sharing the joys of Israel, will continue his activity as the teacher of Israel, for the people will go before Abraham and request him to instruct them in the Torah. He will send them to Isaac, saying, "Go to Isaac, he hath studied more of the Torah than ever I studied," but Isaac, in turn, will send them to Jacob, saying, "Go to Jacob, he hath had more converse with the sages than ever I had." And Jacob will send them to Moses, saying, "Go to Moses, he was instructed in the Torah by God Himself."

In the Messianic time, Moses will be one of the seven shepherds that shall be the leaders of Israel with the Messiah.

MOSES DECLINES THE MISSION

When Moses turned aside to see the great sight, that the bush was not consumed, he heard a voice calling to him, "Draw not nigh hither." These words were to convey that the dignity to be conferred upon him God intended for Moses personally, not for his descendants, and further he was warned not to arrogate honors appointed for others, as the priesthood, which was to belong to Aaron and Aaron's descendants, or royalty, which was to appertain to David and the house of David.

Again the voice spake: "Put off thy shoes from off thy feet, for the place whereon thou standest is holy ground." These words conveyed the desire of God that he cut asunder every bond uniting him with earthly concerns, he was even to give up his conjugal life. Hereupon the angel Michael spoke to God: "O Lord of the world, can it be Thy purpose to destroy mankind? Blessing can prevail only if male and female are united, and yet Thou biddest Moses separate from his wife." God answered, saying, "Moses has begot children, he has done his duty toward the world. I desire him to unite himself now with the Shekinah, that she may descend upon earth for his sake."

God spake furthermore, addressing Moses, "Thou seest only what is to happen in the near future, that Israel is to receive the Torah on Mount Sinai, but I behold what cometh after, bow the people will worship the steer, the figure of which they will see upon My chariot, even while My revelation will be made on Sinai. Thus they will excite My wrath. Nevertheless, though I know all the perverseness of their hearts, wherein they will rebel against Me in the desert, I will redeem them now, for I accord unto man the treatment he merits for his present actions, not what he will deserve in the future. I promised their father Jacob, 'I will go down with thee into Egypt, and I will also surely bring thee up again,' and now I will betake myself thither, to bring Israel up in accordance with My words unto Jacob, and bear them to the land I swore unto their fathers, that their seed should inherit it. So long as the time of affliction that I had appointed unto his seed in My revelation to Abraham was not past, I hearkened not to the supplication and the groaning of his children, but now the end hath come. Therefore, go before Pharaoh, that he dismiss My people. If thou dost not bring about the redemption, none other will, for there is none other that can do it. In thee doth Israel hope, and upon thee doth Israel wait. The matter lieth in thine hands alone."

Moses, however, refused to take the mission upon himself. He said to God, "Thy promise unto Jacob was, 'I will surely bring thee up again out of Egypt.' Thou didst undertake to do it Thyself, and now it is Thy purpose to send me thither. And how, indeed, were it possible for me to accomplish this great matter, to bring the children of Israel up out of Egypt? How could I provide them with food and drink? Many are the women in childbirth among them, many are the pregnant women and the little children. Whence shall I procure dainties for those who have borne babes, whence sweetmeats for the pregnant, and whence tidbits for the little ones? And how may I venture to go among the Egyptian brigands and murderers? for Thou art bidding me to go to mine enemies, to those who lie in wait to take my life. Why should I risk the safety of my person, seeing that I know not whether Israel possesses merits making them worthy of redemption?' I have reckoned up the years with care, and I have found that but two hundred and ten have elapsed since the covenant of the pieces made with Abraham, and at that time Thou didst ordain four hundred years of oppression for his seed."

But God overturned all his objections. He spake to Moses, saying: "I will be with thee. Whatever thou desirest I will do, so that the redemption will in very truth be realized through Me, in accordance with My promise to Jacob. The little ones that Israel will carry up out of Egypt I will provide with food for thirty days. This shall prove to thee in what manner I will supply the needs of all. And as I will be at thy side, thou hast no need to fear any man. Respecting thy doubt, whether Israel deserves to be redeemed, this is My answer: they will be permitted to go forth from Egypt on account of the merits they will acquire at this mountain, whereon they will receive the Torah through thee. And thy reckoning of the end is not correct, for the four hundred years of bondage began with the birth of Isaac, not with the going down of Jacob into Egypt. Therefore the appointed end hath come."

Persuaded now of God's unalterable resolve to use him as His instrument in the redemption of Israel from Egypt, Moses entreated God to impart to him the knowledge of His Great Name, that he be not confounded if the children of Israel ask for it. God answered, saying: "Thou desirest to know My Name? My Name is according to My acts. When I judge My creatures, I am called Elohim, "judge"; when I rise up to do battle against the sinners, I am Lord Zebaot, "the Lord of hosts"; when I wait with longsuffering patience for the improvement of the sinner, My name is El Shaddai; when I have mercy upon the world, I am Adonai. But unto the children of Israel shalt thou say that I am He that was, that is, and that ever will be, and I am He that is with them in their bondage now, and He that shall be with them in the bondage of the time to come."

In reply to the latter words of God, Moses said, "Sufficient unto the day is the evil thereof," and God assented thereto. He admitted that it was not proper to force the knowledge of future suffering upon Israel in a present that was itself full of evil and sorrow. And the Lord said to Moses: "My words about the future were meant for thee alone, not also for them. Tell the children of Israel, besides, that at My behest an angel can stretch his hand from heaven and touch the earth with it, and three angels can find room under one tree, and My majesty can fill the whole world, for when it was My will, it appeared to Job in his hair, and, again, when I willed otherwise, it appeared in a thorn-bush."

But the most important communication from God to Moses concerning the Divine Names were the words to follow: "In mercy I created the world; in mercy I guide it; and with mercies I will return to Jerusalem. But unto the children of Israel thou shalt say that My mercy upon them is for the sake of the merits of Abraham, Isaac, and Jacob."

When Moses heard these words, he spoke to God, saying, "Are there men that transgress after death?" and when God assured him that it was not possible for the dead to sin, Moses asked again, "Why, then, is it that Thou didst reveal Thyself to me at the first as the God of my father, and now Thou passest him over?" Whereupon God said, "In the beginning it was My purpose to address thee with flattering words, but now thou hearest the whole and exact truth, I am only the God of Abraham, the God of Isaac, and the God of Jacob."

Moses prayed to God, entreating Him to reveal His Great and Holy Name unto him, so that he might call upon Him with it and secure the fulfilment of all his wishes. The Lord granted the prayer of Moses, and when the celestials knew that He had revealed the secret of the Ineffable Name, they cried out, "Blessed art Thou, O Lord, gracious Giver of knowledge!"

God is always regardful of the honor of the elders of a people, and He bade Moses assemble those of Israel and announce the approaching redemption to them. And as God knew beforehand how Pharaoh's obduracy would display itself, He made it known to Moses at once, lest he reproach God later with the Egyptian king's frowardness.

MOSES PUNISHED FOR HIS STUBBORNNESS

In spite of all these safeguards, Moses was not yet ready to accept the mission God wished to impose upon him. He persisted in urging his fears, saying: "But, behold, they will not believe me, nor hearken unto my voice, for they will say, 'The Lord hath not appeared unto thee. And the Lord said unto him, "What is that in thine hand?" And he said, "A rod." And the Lord said: "Thou deservest to be castigated with it. If thou didst not intend to take My mission upon thyself, thou shouldst have said so in the beginning. Instead, thou didst hold back with thy refusal, until I revealed to thee the great secret of the Ineffable Name, that thou mightest know it if the children of Israel should ask thee concerning it. And now thou sayest, I will not go. Now, therefore, if thou wilt not execute My charge to thee, it will be executed by this rod. It was My wish to distinguish thee and make thee My instrument for doing many miracles. But thou deservest a punishment for having suspected My children of lack of faith. The children of Israel are believers and sons of believers, but thou wilt show thyself of little faith in thy career, and as thou followest the example of the slanderous serpent, so shalt thou be punished with leprosy, wherewith the serpent was punished."

The Lord now bade Moses put his hand into his bosom and take it out again, and when he took it out, behold, his hand was leprous, as white as snow. And God bade him put his hand into his bosom again, and it turned again as his other flesh. Beside being a chastisement for his hasty words, the plague on his hand was to teach him that as the leper defiles, so the Egyptians defiled Israel, and as Moses was healed of his uncleanness, so God would cleanse the children of Israel of the pollution the Egyptians had brought upon them.

The second wonder connected with the rod of Moses likewise conveyed a double meaning, in that it pointed to the coming redemption of Israel, and taught Moses a specific lesson. At the bidding of God, Moses cast his rod on the ground, and it became a serpent, to show him that when he traduced Israel, he was following the example of the abusive serpent, and also to show him that the great dragon that lieth in the midst of the rivers of Egypt, though he was now hacking into Israel with his teeth, would be rendered harmless like the rod of wood, which has no power to bite.

And, again, through the third miracle he was bidden to perform, God conveyed to Moses what would happen in the latter years of his own life. The sign He gave him was to make known to him that, before the water came, blood would flow from the rock at Meribah, when Moses should strike it after uttering the hasty, impatient words that were destined to bring death down upon him.

For seven days God urged Moses to undertake the mission He desired him to execute. He resorted to persuasion, that the heathen might not say, that He abused His power as the Ruler of the world, forcing men to do His service against their will. But Moses remained obdurate, he could not be won over. He said: "Thou doest a wrong unto me in sending me to Pharaoh. In the palace of the Egyptian king there are persons that know how to speak the seventy languages of the world. No matter what language a man may use, there is someone that understands him. If I should come as Thy representative, and they should discover that I am not able to converse in the seventy languages, they will mock at me, and say, 'Behold this man, he pretends to be the ambassador of the Creator of the world, and he cannot speak the seventy languages.'" To this God made reply, as follows: "Adam, who was taught by none, could give names to the beasts in the seventy languages. Was it not I that made him to speak?"

Moses was not yet satisfied, he continued to urge objections, and he said: "O Lord of the world, Thou wouldst charge me with the task of chastising Egypt and redeeming Israel, and I am ready to be Thy messenger. But is it seemly that a man should execute two errands at once? Nay, my Lord, for this two men are needed." God made answer, and said, "Moses, I know well whom thou hast in mind with thy request, to be thy companion in the mission I assign to thee. Know, therefore, that the holy spirit hath already come upon thy brother Aaron, and even now he is awaiting thee on the way of Egypt, and when his eyes rest upon thee he will rejoice."

Furthermore God spake to Moses, saying, "When I appeared unto thee the first time, thou wast meek, and didst hide thy face, not to see the vision. Whence cometh now this effrontery of thine, that thou addressest Me as a servant his master? Thou speakest too many words by far. Perchance thou thinkest I have no messengers, hosts, seraphim, ofanim, ministering angels, and Merkabah wheels, to send to Egypt, to bring My children thence, that thou sayest, 'Send by the hand of him whom Thou wilt send.' In sooth, thou deservest severe chastisement. But what can I do, seeing that I am the Master of mercy? If thou escapest unpunished, thou owest it to thy father Amram, who rendered great services in behalf of the preservation of the Israelitish people in Egypt."

But Moses replied: "O Lord of the world, I a prophet and the son of a prophet obeyed Thy words only after much hesitation, and I cannot expect Pharaoh, a wicked man and the son of a wicked man, and the Egyptians, a disobedient people and the sons of a disobedient people, to give ear to my words. O Lord of the world, Thou dost send me to Egypt to redeem sixty myriads of Thy people from the oppression of the Egyptians. If it were a question of delivering a couple of hundred men, it were a sufficiently difficult enterprise. How much severer is the task of freeing sixty myriads from the dominion of Pharaoh! If Thou hadst called upon the Egyptians to give up their evil ways soon after they began to enslave Israel, they might have heeded Thy admonitions. But if I should go and speak to them now, after they have been ruling over Israel these two hundred and ten years, Pharaoh would say, 'If a slave has served his master for ten years, and no protest has made itself heard from any quarter, how can a man conceive the idea suddenly of having him set at liberty?' Verily, O Lord of the world, the task Thou puttest upon me is too heavy for my strength."

Moses said furthermore: "I am not an eloquent man, nor can I see of what avail words can be in this matter. Thou art sending me to one that is himself a slave, to Pharaoh of the tribe of Ham, and a slave will not be corrected by words. I consent to go on Thy errand only if Thou wilt invest me with the power of chastising Pharaoh with brute force." To these words spoken by Moses, God made reply: "Let it not fret thee that thou art not an eloquent speaker. It is I that made the mouth of all that speak, and I that made men dumb. One I make to see, another I make blind; one I make to hear, another I make deaf. Had I willed it so, thou hadst been a man of ready speech. But I desired to show a wonder through thee. Whenever I will it, the words I cast into thy mouth shall come forth without hesitation. But what thou sayest about a slave, that he cannot be corrected by words, is true, and therefore I give thee My rod for Pharaoh's castigation."

But Moses still stood his ground. He raised other objections. "His grandchild," he said, "is closer to a man than his nephew. Nevertheless when Lot was taken captive, Thou didst send angels to the aid of Abraham's nephew. But now, when the life of sixty myriads of Abraham's lineal descendants is at stake, Thou sendest me, and not the angels. When the Egyptian bondwoman Hagar was in distress, Thou didst dispatch five angels to stand by her, and to redeem sixty myriads of the children of Sarah Thou dost dispatch me. O Lord, send, I pray Thee, by the hand of him whom Thou wilt send in days to come." To this God answered, saying, "I said not that I would send thee to Israel, but to Pharaoh, and that one whom thou madest mention of, I will send to Israel at the end of days--Elijah will appear to them before the great and terrible day."

If Moses refused to do the errand of the Lord, there was a reason. God had revealed to him the treasures of the Torah, of wisdom, and of knowledge, and the whole world's future. Now he beheld in the inner chamber of God rows of scholars and judges interpreting the Torah in forty-nine different ways as they sat in the court of hewn stones; and he saw, besides, Rabbi Akiba explaining the meaning of the crowns upon the letters. Then said Moses: "I do not care to be God's messenger. Let Him rather send one of these great scholars." Then God ordered the Angel of Wisdom to carry Moses to a place of myriads of scholars, all interpreting the Torah, and all making use of the formula: This is a Halakah revealed to Moses on Mount Sinai. Now Moses recognized that even the greatest scholars of future generations would be dependent upon him, and then, at last, he was ready to execute the mission God desired to lay upon him.

But Moses had to pay dear for having hesitated in the execution of the Divine bidding. God said to him: "It was appointed that thou shouldst be priest, and Aaron should be the Levite. Because thou hast refused to execute My will, thou shalt be the Levite, and Aaron shall be priest,"--a punishment that did not fall upon Moses personally, but only upon his descendants, all of whom are Levites. As for himself, he performed a priest's service in the Tabernacle.

Moses had said to God, "Thou hast been speaking to me now these many days, nevertheless I am still slow of speech and of a slow tongue." For this he received another punishment. God said to him: "I might change thee into a new man, and heal thee of thy imperfect speech, but because thou hast uttered such words, I refrain from curing thee."

THE RETURN TO EGYPT

When Moses finally gave in, and declared himself ready to go to Egypt as God's messenger, his acceptance was still conditional upon the promise of God to fulfil all his wishes, and God granted whatsoever he desired, except immortality and entering the Holy Land. God also allayed his fears regarding the danger that threatened him from his whilom enemies Dathan and Abiram, on account of whom he had had to flee from Egypt. He told him that they had sunk to the estate of poor and insignificant men, bereft of the power of doing him harm.

Moses was loyal to the oath he had given his father-in-law Jethro, never to return to Egypt without securing his consent. His first concern therefore was to go back to Midian and obtain his permission, which Jethro gave freely. Then Moses could set out on his journey. He tarried only to take his wife and his children with him, which made his father-in-law say, "Those who are in Egypt are to leave it, and thou desirest to take more thither?" Moses replied: "Very soon the slaves held in bondage in Egypt will be redeemed, and they will go forth from the land, and gather at Mount Sinai, and hear the words, 'I am the Lord thy God,' and should my sons not be present there?" Jethro acknowledged the justice of Moses' words, and he said to him, "Go in peace, enter Egypt in peace, and leave the land in peace."

At last Moses sallied forth upon his journey to Egypt, accompanied by his wife and his children. He was mounted upon the very ass that had borne Abraham to the Akedah on Mount Moriah, the ass upon which the Messiah will appear riding at the end of days. Even now, his journey begun, Moses was but half-hearted about his mission. He travelled leisurely, thinking: "When I arrive in Egypt and announce to the children of Israel that the end of the term of Egyptian slavery has come, they will say, 'We know very well that our bondage must last four hundred years, and the end is not yet,' but if I were to put this objection before God, He would break out in wrath against me. It is best for me to consume as much time as possible on the way thither."

God was ill pleased with Moses for this artifice, and He spake to him, saying, "Joseph prophesied long ago that the oppression of Egypt would endure only two hundred and ten years." For his lack of faith Moses was punished while he was on the road to Egypt. The angels Af and Hemah appeared and swallowed his whole body down to his feet, and they gave him up only after Zipporah, nimble as a "bird," circumcised her son Gershom, and touched the feet of her husband with the blood of the circumcision. The reason why their son had remained uncircumcised until then was that Jethro had made the condition, when he consented to the marriage of his daughter with Moses, that the first son of their union should be brought up as a Gentile.

When Moses was released by the angels, he attacked them, and he slew Hemah, whose host of angels, however, held their own before the assailant.

The Divine voice heard by Moses in Midian telling him to return to his brethren in Egypt fell at the same time upon the ear of Aaron, dwelling in Egypt, and it bade him "go into the wilderness to meet Moses." God speaketh marvellously with His voice, and therefore the same revelation could be understood one way in Midian and another way in Egypt.

The greeting of the two brothers was very cordial. Envy and jealousy had no place between them. Aaron was rejoiced that God had chosen his younger brother to be the redeemer of Israel, and Moses was rejoiced that his older brother had been divinely appointed the high priest in Israel. God knew their hearts, for at the time when He charged him with the Egyptian mission, Moses had said, "All these years Aaron has been active as a prophet in Israel, and should I now encroach upon his province and cause him vexation?" But God reassured him, saying, "Moses, thy brother Aaron will surely not be vexed, he will rather rejoice at thy mission, yea, he will come forth and meet thee."

Aaron showed his joy freely at seeing his brother once more, after their separation of many years. As for his joy in the distinction accorded to Moses, it was too great to be expressed in all its depth and extent. For his kind, generous spirit, he received a reward from God, in that he was permitted to bear the Urim and Thummim upon his heart, "for," God said, "the heart that rejoiced at the exalting of a brother shall wear the Urim and Thummim."

Aaron ran to meet his brother, and embraced him, and asked where he had spent all the years of their separation. When he was told in Midian, he continued to question him, saying, "Who are these that are travelling with thee?"

Moses: "My wife and my sons."

Aaron: "Whither goest thou with them?"

Moses: "To Egypt."

Aaron: "What! Great enough is our sorrow through those who have been in Egypt from the beginning, and thou takest more to the land?"

Moses recognized that Aaron was right, and he sent his wife and his sons back to his father-in-law Jethro.

He was no less magnanimous than Aaron. If the elder brother felt no envy on account of the younger brother's dignity, the younger brother did not withhold from the other the teachings and revelations he had received. Immediately after meeting with Aaron, Moses told him all that God had taught him, even the awful secret of the Ineffable Name communicated to him on Mount Horeb.

In obedience to the command of God, the elders of the people were assembled, and before them Moses performed the wonders that were to be his credentials as the redeemer sent to deliver the people.

Nevertheless, the deeds he did were not so potent in convincing them of the reality of the mission as the words wherein God had announced the approaching redemption to him, which he repeated in their ears. The elders knew that Jacob had imparted to Joseph the secret mark designating the redeemer, and Joseph had in turn confided it to his brethren before his death. The last surviving one of the brethren, Asher, had revealed it to his daughter Serah, in the following words: "He that will come and proclaim the redemption with the words of God, 'I have surely visited you, and seen that which is done to you in Egypt,' he is the true redeemer." Serah was still alive at Moses' return, and the elders betook themselves to her, and told her the words of Moses announcing the redemption. When she heard that his words had been the same as those Asher had quoted, she knew that he was the promised redeemer, and all the people believed in him.

Thereupon Moses invited the elders to go to Pharaoh with him, but they lacked the courage to appear before the king. Though they started out with Moses, they dropped off stealthily on the way, one by one, and when Moses and Aaron stood in the presence of the king, they found themselves alone, deserted by all the others. The elders did not go out free. Their punishment was that God did not permit them to ascend the holy mountain with Moses. They durst accompany him on the way to God only as far as they had accompanied him on the way to Pharaoh, and then they had to tarry until he came again.

MOSES AND AARON BEFORE PHARAOH

The day Moses and Aaron made their appearance before Pharaoh happened to be the anniversary of his birth, and he was surrounded by many kings, for he was the ruler of the whole world, and this was the occasion on which the kings of the earth came to do him homage. When the attendants announced Moses and Aaron, Pharaoh inquired whether the two old men had brought him crowns, and, receiving a negative reply, he ordered that they were not to be admitted to his presence, until he had seen and dismissed all the others desirous of paying him their respects.

Pharaoh's palace was surrounded by a vast army. It was built with four hundred entrances, one hundred on each side, and each of them guarded by sixty thousand soldiers. Moses and Aaron were overawed by this display of power, and they were afraid. But the angel Gabriel appeared, and he led them into the palace, observed by none of the guards, and Pharaoh decreed severe punishment upon the inattentive sentinels for having admitted the old men without his permission. They were dismissed, and others put in their places. But the same thing happened the next day. Moses and Aaron were within the palace, and the new guard had not been able to hinder their passing. Pharaoh questioned his servants, how it had been possible for the two old men to enter, and they said: "We know it not! Through the doors they did not come. Surely, they must be magicians."

Not enough that the palace was guarded by a host, at each entrance two lions were stationed, and in terror of being torn to pieces none dared approach the doors, and none could go within until the lion tamer came and led the beasts away. Now Balaam and all the other sacred scribes of Egypt advised that the keepers loose the lions at the approach of Moses and Aaron. But their advice availed naught. Moses had but to raise his rod, and the lions bounded toward him joyously, and followed at his feet, gambolling like dogs before their master on his return home.

Within the palace, Moses and Aaron found seventy secretaries busy with Pharaoh's correspondence, which was carried on in seventy languages. At the sight of the messengers of Israel, they started up in great awe, for the two men resembled angels. In stature they were as the cedars of Lebanon, their countenances radiated splendor like the sun, the pupils of their eyes were like the sphere of the morning star, their beards like palm branches, and their mouths emitted flames when they opened them for speech. In their terror, the secretaries flung down pen and paper, and prostrated themselves before Moses and Aaron.

Now the two representatives of the children of Israel stepped before Pharaoh, and they spake, "The God of the Hebrews hath met with us; let us go, we pray thee, three days' journey into the wilderness, and sacrifice unto the Lord our God, lest He fall upon us with pestilence or with the sword." But Pharaoh answered, saying: "What is the name of your God? Wherein doth His strength consist, and His power? How many countries, how many provinces, how many cities hath He under His dominion? In how many campaigns was

He victorious? How many lands did He make subject to Himself? How many cities did He capture? When He goeth to war, how many warriors, riders, chariots, and charioteers doth He lead forth?" Whereto Moses and Aaron replied: "His strength and His power fill the whole world. His voice heweth out flames of fire; His words break mountains in pieces. The heaven is His throne, and the earth His footstool. His bow is fire, His arrows are flames, His spears torches, His shield clouds, and His sword lightning flashes. He created the mountains and the valleys, He brought forth spirits and souls, He stretched out the earth by a word, He made the mountains with His wisdom, He forms the embryo in the womb of the mother, He covers the heavens with clouds, at His word the dew and the rain descend earthward, He causes plants to grow from the ground, He nourishes and sustains the whole world, from the horns upon the rem down to the eggs of vermin. Every day He causes men to die, and every day He calls men into life."

Pharaoh answered, and said: "I have no need of Him. I have created myself, and if ye say that He causes dew and rain to descend, I have the Nile, the river that hath its source under the tree of life, and the ground impregnated by its waters bears fruit so huge that it takes two asses to carry it. and it is palatable beyond description, for it has three hundred different tastes."

Then Pharaoh sent to fetch the books of the chronicles of his kingdom from his archives, wherein are recorded the names of the gods of all the nations, to see whether the name of the God of the Hebrews was among them. He read off: "The gods of Moab, the gods of Ammon, the gods of Zidon--I do not find your God inscribed in the archives!" Moses and Aaron exclaimed: "O thou fool! Thou seekest the Living in the graves of the dead. These which thou didst read are the names of dumb idols, but our God is the God of life and the King of eternal life."

When Pharaoh said the words, "I know not the Lord," God Himself made answer, saying: "O thou rascal! Thou sayest to My ambassadors, 'I know not the strength and the power of your God'? Lo, I will make thee to stand, for to show thee My power, and that My Name may be declared throughout all the earth."

Having searched his list of the gods of the nations in vain for a mention of the God of the Hebrews, Pharaoh cited before him the wise men of Egypt, and he said to them: "Have ye ever heard the name of the God of these people?" They replied, "We have been told that He is a son of the wise, the son of ancient kings." Then spake God, saying, "O ye fools! Ye call yourselves wise men, but Me ye call only the son of the wise. Verily, I will set at naught all your wisdom and your understanding."

Pharaoh persisted in his obduracy, even after Moses and Aaron had performed the miracle of the rod. At the time when the two Hebrews succeeded in entering the palace, guarded as it was by lions, Pharaoh had sent for his magicians, at their head Balaam and his two sons Jannes and Jambres, and when they appeared before him, he told them of the extraordinary incident, how the lions had followed the two old men like dogs, and fawned upon them. It was Balaam's opinion that they were simply magicians like himself and his companions, and he prayed the king to have them come before him together with themselves, to test who were the master magicians, the Egyptians or the Hebrews.

Pharaoh called for Moses and Aaron, and he said to them: "Who will believe you when you say that you are the ambassadors of God, as you pretend to be, if you do not convince men by performing wonders?" Thereupon Aaron cast his rod to the ground, and it became a serpent. Pharaoh laughed aloud. "What," he exclaimed, "is this all your God can do? It is the way of merchants to carry merchandise to a place if there is none of it there, but would anyone take brine to Spain or fish to Accho? It seems you do not know that I am an adept in all sorts of magic!" He ordered little school children to be brought, and they repeated the wonder done by Moses and Aaron; indeed, Pharaoh's own wife performed it. Jannes and Jambres, the sons of Balaam, derided Moses, saying, "Ye carry straw to Ephrain!" whereto Moses answered, "To the place of many vegetables, thither carry vegetables."

To show the Egyptians that Aaron could do something with his rod that their magicians could not imitate, God caused the serpent into which His rod had been changed to swallow up all the rods of the magicians. But Balaam and his associates said: "There is nothing marvellous or astonishing in this feat. Your serpent has but devoured our serpents, which is in accordance with a law of nature, one living being devours another. If thou wishest us to acknowledge that the spirit of God worketh in thee, then cast thy rod to the earth, and if, being wood, it swallows up our rods of wood, then we shall acknowledge that the spirit of God is in thee." Aaron stood the test. After his rod had resumed its original form, it swallowed up the rods of the Egyptians, and yet its bulk showed no increase. This caused Pharaoh to reflect, whether this wonderful rod of Aaron might not swallow up also him and his throne. Nevertheless he refused to obey the behest of God, to let Israel go, saying, "Had I Jacob-Israel himself here before me, I should put trowel and bucket on his shoulder." And to Moses and Aaron, he said, "Because ye, like all the rest of the tribe of Levi, are not compelled to labor, therefore do ye speak, 'Let us go and sacrifice to the Lord.' If you had asked for a thousand people, or two thousand, I should have fulfilled your request, but never will I consent to let six hundred thousand men go away."

THE SUFFERING INCREASES

Beside refusing to dismiss the children of Israel, he ordered, on the very day of Moses and Aaron's audience with him, that the people be required to deliver the prescribed tale of bricks, though the taskmasters were not as heretofore to give them straw to make brick. Another decree was, that the children of Israel were not to be permitted to rest on the Sabbath, for Pharaoh knew that they used the leisure for reading the rolls that described their redemption. All this was a part of God's plan, the oppression of Israel was to be increased the closer the end approached. As they wandered up and down the land of Egypt gathering the straw they needed for the due tale of bricks, they were maltreated by the Egyptians if they caught them on their fields. Such unkind acts perpetrated by the whole people made it impossible for them to cast the entire blame for the bondage of Israel upon Pharaoh. All the Egyptians showed cruelty to the Israelites on their straw foraging expeditions, and therefore the Divine punishment descended upon all alike.

This frightful time of Israel's extreme suffering lasted six months. Meantime Moses went to Midian, leaving Aaron alone in Egypt. When Moses returned at the end of the reign of terror, two of the Israelitish officers accosted him and Aaron, and heaped abuse upon them for having increased the woes of their people rather than diminished them. They spake, saying, "If ye are truly the ambassadors of God, then may He judge between us and Pharaoh. But if you are seeking to bring about the redemption of Israel on your own account, then may God judge between you and Israel. You are responsible for the widespread stench now issuing from the Israelitish corpses used as bricks for building when our tale was not complete. The Egyptians had but a faint suspicion that we were waiting for our redemption. It is your fault if they are fully conscious of it now. We are in the quandary of the poor sheep that has been dragged away by a wolf. The shepherd pursues the robber, catches up with him, and tries to snatch the sheep from his jaws, and the wretched victim, pulled this way by the wolf and that way by the shepherd, is torn to pieces. Thus Israel fares between you and Pharaoh."

The two officers that spake these stinging words were Dathan and Abiram, and it was neither the first nor the last time they inflicted an injury upon Moses. The other Israelitish officers were gentle and kind; they permitted themselves to be beaten by the taskmasters rather than prod the laborers of their own people put under their surveillance.

The cruel suffering to which his people was exposed caused Moses to speak to God thus: "I have read the book of Genesis through, and I found the doom in it pronounced upon the generation of the deluge. It was a just judgment. I found also the punishments decreed against the generation of the confusion of tongues, and against the inhabitants of Sodom. These, too, were just. But what hath this nation of Israel done unto Thee, that it is oppressed more than any other nation in history? Is it because Abraham said, 'Whereby shall I know that I shall inherit the land?' and Thou didst rebuke him for his small faith, saying, 'Know of a surety that thy seed shall be a stranger in a land that is not theirs'? Why, then, are not the descendants of Esau and Ishmael held in bondage, too? Are they not likewise of the seed of Abraham? But if Thou wilt say, 'What concern is it of mine?' then I ask Thee, Why didst Thou send me hither as Thy messenger? Thy great, exalted, and terrible Name is feared in all the earth, yet Pharaoh heard me pronounce it, and he refuses obedience. I know Thou wilt redeem Israel in Thine own good time, and it is of little moment to Thee that now they are immuring living Israelites in these buildings."

Were He a God of justice only, the Lord would have slain Moses for the audacity of his last words, but in view of his having spoken as he had only out of compassion with Israel, the Lord dealt graciously with him. He answered Moses, saying, "Thou shalt see what I will do to Pharaoh," words conveying to Moses, that although he would be witness to the chastisement of Pharaoh, he would not be present at that of the thirty-one kings of Canaan. Thus he was rebuked for the unbecoming language he had used in addressing God. At the same time God's words were a rejoinder to another speech by Moses. He had said: "O Lord of the world, I know well that Thou wilt bring Thy children forth from Egypt. O that Thou wouldst make use of another instrument, for I am not worthy of being the redeemer of Thy children." God made answer thereto: "Yes, Moses, thou art worthy thereof. Through thee My children will be brought forth out of Egypt. Thou shalt see what I will do to Pharaoh."

At the same time God called him to account for having so little faith. He said: "O for the departed, their like cannot be found any more! I appeared unto Abraham, Isaac, and Jacob, as El Shaddai, God Almighty, but I was not known to them by My name Adonai, God All-Merciful, as I appeared unto thee. Nevertheless they did not cast aspersions upon My acts. I spake to Abraham, 'Unto thee will I give the land,' but when he was about to bury Sarah, he had to pay out silver and buy a resting-place for her body; and yet he did not find fault with Me. I spake to Isaac, 'Unto thee, and unto thy seed, I will give all these lands,' but when he desired water to drink, he had to strive with the herdsmen of Gerar; and yet he did not find fault with Me. I spake to Jacob, 'The land whereon thou liest, to thee will I give it, and to thy seed,' but when he wanted to spread his tent, he had to acquire a parcel of ground for an hundred pieces of money; and yet he did not find fault with Me. None of them asked to know My Name. But thou didst demand to know it at the very first, when I desired to send thee down into Egypt, and after I revealed it to thee, thou didst speak, saying, 'Thou didst tell me that Thou art called Compassionate and Gracious, Longsuffering and Merciful, but as soon as I pronounced this Name before Pharaoh, misfortune descended upon the people of Israel.' Now I desire to fulfil My covenant with the three Patriarchs, and give their posterity the promised land, as a reward for the unquestioning faith of the Fathers, and also as a reward to the people, who, in spite of their suffering, did not find fault with My deeds. For this will I give them the land, which they do not deserve to possess for other reasons. I swear that I will do thus!" God pronounced this oath, to banish all fear from the mind of Moses, that He might act only in accordance with His attribute of justice, and thus delay the redemption of Israel for a time, on account of the sins of the people.

Now the redemption of Israel was a settled fact. But before Moses and Aaron could start on the work of delivering their people, God called various points to their attention, which He bade them consider in their undertaking. He spake to them, saying: "My children are perverse, passionate, and troublesome. You must be prepared to stand their abuse, to the length of being pelted with stones by them. I send you to Pharaoh, and although I will punish him according to his deserts, yet you must not fail in the respect due to him as a ruler. Furthermore, be careful to take the elders of the people into your counsel, and let your first step toward redemption be to make the people give up the worship of idols."

The last was a most difficult task, and the words of God concerning it wrung the exclamation from Moses: "See, the children of Israel will not hearken unto me. How, then, should Pharaoh hearken unto me?" It was the third time Moses declined to go on the errand of God. Now the Divine patience was exhausted, and Moses was subjected to punishment. At first God had revealed Himself only to Moses, and the original intention had been that he alone was to perform all the miracles, but henceforth the word of God was addressed to Aaron as well, and he was given a share in doing the wonders.

MEASURE FOR MEASURE

God divided the ten punishments decreed for Egypt into four parts, three of the plagues He committed to Aaron, three to Moses, one to the two brothers together, and three He reserved for Himself. Aaron was charged with those, that proceeded from the earth and the water, the elements that are composed of more or less solid parts, from which are fashioned all the corporeal, distinctive entities, while the three entrusted to Moses were those that proceeded from the air and the fire, the elements that are most prolific of life.

The Lord is a man of war, and as a king of flesh and blood devises various stratagems against his enemy, so God attacked the Egyptians in various ways. He brought ten plagues down upon them. When a province rises up in rebellion, its sovereign lord first sends his army against it, to surround it and cut off the water supply. If the people are contrite, well and good; if not, he brings noise makers into the field against them. If the people are contrite, well and good; if not, he orders darts to be discharged against them. If the people are contrite, well and good; if not, he orders his legions to assault them. If the people are contrite, well and good; if not, he causes bloodshed and carnage among them. If the people are contrite, well and good; if not, he directs a stream of hot naphtha upon them. If the people are contrite, well and good; if not, he hurls projectiles at them from his ballistae. If the people are contrite, well and good; if not, he has scaling-ladders set up against their walls. If the people are contrite, well and good; if not, he casts them into dungeons. If the people are contrite, well and good; if not, he slays their magnates.

Thus did God proceed against the Egyptians. First He cut off their water supply by turning their rivers into blood. They refused to let the Israelites go, and He sent the noisy, croaking frogs into their entrails. They refused to let the Israelites go, and He brought lice against them, which pierced their flesh like darts. They refused to let the Israelites go, and He sent barbarian legions against them, mixed hordes of wild beasts. They refused to let the Israelites go, and He brought slaughter upon them, a very grievous pestilence. They refused to let the Israelites go, and He poured out naphtha over them, burning blains. They refused to let the Israelites go, and He caused His projectiles, the hail, to descend upon them. They refused to let the Israelites go, and He placed scaling-ladders against the wall for the locusts, which climbed them like men of war. They refused to let the Israelites go, and He cast them into dungeon darkness. They refused to let the Israelites go, and He slew their magnates, their first-born sons.

The plagues that God sent upon the Egyptians corresponded to the deeds they had perpetrated against the children of Israel. Because they forced the Israelites to draw water for them, and also hindered them from the use of the ritual baths, He changed their water into blood.

Because they had said to the Israelites, "Go and catch fish for us," He brought frogs up against them, making them to swarm in their kneading-troughs and their bed-chambers and hop around croaking in their entrails. It was the severest of all the ten plagues.

Because they had said to the Israelites, "Go and sweep and clean our houses, our courtyards, and our streets," He changed the dust of the air into lice, so that the vermin lay piled up in heaps an ell high, and when the Egyptians put on fresh garments, they were at once infested with the insects.

The fourth plague was an invasion of the land by hordes of all sorts of wild animals, lions, wolves, panthers, bears, and others. They overran the houses of the Egyptians, and when they closed their doors to keep them out, God caused a little animal to come forth from the ground, and it got in through the windows, and split open the doors, and made a way for the bears, panthers, lions, and wolves, which swarmed in and devoured the people down to the infants in their cradles. If an Egyptian entrusted his ten children to an Israelite, to take a walk with them, a lion would come and snatch away one of the children, a bear would carry off the second, a serpent the third, and so on, and in the end the Israelite returned home alone. This plague was brought upon them because they were in the habit of bidding the Israelites go and catch wolves and lions for their circuses, and they sent them on such errands, to make them take up their abode in distant deserts, where they would be separated from their wives, and could not propagate their race.

Then God brought a grievous murrain upon their cattle, because they had pressed the Israelites into their service as shepherds, and assigned remote pasturing places to them, to keep them away from their wives. Therefore the murrain came and carried off all the cattle in the flocks the Israelites were tending.

The sixth plague was a boil breaking forth with blains upon man and upon beast. This was the punishment of the Egyptians, because they would say to the children of Israel, "Go and prepare a bath for us unto the delight of our flesh and our bones." Therefore they were doomed to suffer with boils that inflamed their flesh, and on account of the itch they could not leave off scratching. While the Egyptians suffered thus, the children of Israel used their baths.

Because they had sent the Israelites forth into the fields, to plough and sow, hail was sent down upon them, and their trees and crops were destroyed.

They had been in the habit of saying to the Israelites, "Go forth, plant ye trees for us, and guard the fruit thereon." Therefore God brought the locusts into the Egyptian border, to eat the residue of that which was escaped, which remained unto them from the hail, for the teeth of the locust are the teeth of a lion, and he hath the jaw teeth of a great lion.

Because they would throw the Israelites into dungeons, God brought darkness upon them, the darkness of hell, so that they had to grope their way. He that sat could not rise up on his feet, and he that stood could not sit down. The infliction of darkness served another purpose. Among the Israelites there were many wicked men, who refused to leave Egypt, and God determined to put them out of the way. But that the Egyptians might not say they had succumbed to the plague like themselves, God slew them under cover of the darkness, and in the darkness they were buried by their fellow-Israelites, and the Egyptians knew nothing of what had happened. But the number of these wicked men had been very great, and the children of Israel spared to leave Egypt were but a small fraction of the original Israelitish population.

The tenth plague was the slaying of the first-born, and it came upon the Egyptians because of their intention to murder the men children of the Israelites at their birth, and, finally, Pharaoh and his host were drowned in the Red Sea, because the Egyptians had caused the men children of the Israelites to be exposed in the water.

Each of the plagues inflicted upon Egypt had another parallel in the cruel treatment accorded to the Israelites. The first was a punishment for the arrogant words spoken by Pharaoh, "My Nile river is mine own, and I have made it for myself."

The plague of the frogs God brought down upon the Egyptians, "because," He said, "the frogs, which sometimes inhabit the water, shall take vengeance upon the Egyptians for having desired to destroy the nation destined to be the bearers of the Torah, and the Torah is likened unto water."

God sent vermin upon them, saying, "Let the lice made of the dust of the earth take vengeance upon the Egyptians for having desired to destroy the nation whose seed is like unto the dust of the earth."

Hordes of beasts, lions and wolves and swarms of serpents, came down upon them, "because," God said, "these animals shall take vengeance upon the Egyptians for having desired to destroy the nation that is likened unto lions, wolves, and serpents."

A fatal pestilence was brought upon them, "because," God said, "death shall take vengeance upon the Egyptians for having desired to destroy the nation that faces death for the glorification of the Name of God."

They were made to suffer with burning blains, "because," God said, "the boils coming from the ashes of the furnace shall take vengeance upon the Egyptians for having desired to destroy the nation whose ancestor Abraham walked into the fiery furnace for the glorification of the Name of God."

He made hail to descend upon them, "because," He said, "the white hail shall take vengeance upon the Egyptians for having desired to destroy a nation whose sins shall be white."

The locusts came upon them, "because," God said, "the locusts, which are My great army, shall take vengeance upon the Egyptians for having desired to destroy the nation that is called My hosts."

"Darkness," said God, "which is divided from the light, shall come and take vengeance upon the Egyptians for desiring to destroy the nation upon which shineth the light of the Lord, while gross darkness covers the other peoples."

The tenth plague, the slaying of the first-born, God inflicted, saying, "I will take vengeance upon the Egyptians for having desired to destroy the nation that is My first-born. As the night divided itself for Abraham, that his enemies might be vanquished, so I will pass through Egypt in the middle of the night, and as Abraham was proved by ten temptations, so I will send ten plagues upon Egypt, the enemy of his children."

THE PLAGUES BROUGHT THROUGH AARON

From the infliction of the first of the plagues until the passing of the last, after which the Egyptians yielded all that Moses and Aaron demanded, there elapsed a whole year, for twelve months is the term set by God for the expiation of sins. The deluge lasted one year; Job suffered one year; sinners must endure hell tortures for one year, and the judgment upon Gog at the end of time will be executed for the length of one year.

Moses announced the first plague to Pharaoh one morning when the king was walking by the river's brink. This morning walk enabled him to practice a deception. He called himself a god, and pretended that he felt no human needs. To keep up the illusion, he would repair to the edge of the river every morning, and ease nature there while alone and unobserved. At such a time it was that Moses appeared before him, and called out to him, "Is there a god that hath human needs?" "Verily, I am no god," replied Pharaoh, "I only pretend to be one before the Egyptians, who are such idiots, one should consider them asses rather than human beings."

Then Moses made known to him that God would turn the water into blood, if he refused to let Israel go. In the warning we can discern the difference between God and man. When a mortal harbors the intention to do an injury to an enemy, he lies in wait for the moment when he can strike an unexpected blow. But God is outspoken. He warned Pharaoh and the Egyptians in public whenever a plague was about to descend, and each warning was repeated by Moses for a period of three weeks, although the plague itself endured but a single week.

As Pharaoh would not lay the warning to heart, the plague announced by Moses was let loose upon him and his people--the waters were turned into blood. It is a well-known proverb, "Beat the idols, and the priests are in terror." God smote the river Nile, which the Egyptians worshipped as their god, in order to terrify Pharaoh and his people and force them to do the Divine will.

To produce the plague, Aaron took his rod, and stretched out his hand over the waters of Egypt. Moses had no part in performing the miracle, for God had said to him, "The water that watched over thy safety when thou wast exposed in the Nile, shall not suffer harm through thee."

Aaron had scarcely executed the Divine bidding, when all the water of Egypt became blood, even such as was kept in vessels of wood and in vessels of stone. The very spittle of an Egyptian turned into blood no sooner had he ejected it from his mouth, and blood dripped also from the idols of the Egyptians.

The transformation of the waters into blood was intended mainly as a punishment for the oppressors, but it was at the same time a source of profit for the oppressed. It gave the Israelites the opportunity of amassing great wealth. The Egyptians paid them large sums for their water, for if an Egyptian and an Israelite drew water from the same trough, the portion carried off by the Egyptian was bound to be useless, it turned into blood. To be sure, nothing helped the Egyptians in their distress, for though they drank water from the same cup as an Israelite, it became blood in their mouth.

However, this plague did not impress Pharaoh as a punishment inflicted in the name of God, because with the help of the Angels of Destruction the magicians of Egypt produced the same phenomenon of changing water into blood. Therefore he hearkened not unto the words of Moses.

The next was the plague of the frogs, and again it was Aaron that performed the wonder. He stretched forth his hand with his rod over the rivers, and caused frogs to come up upon the land of Egypt. Moses, whose life had been preserved by the water, was kept from poisoning his savior with the reptiles. At first only a single frog appeared, but he began to croak, summoning so many companions that the whole land of Egypt swarmed with them. Wherever an Egyptian took up his stand, frogs appeared, and in some mysterious way they were able to pierce the hardest of metals, and even the marble palaces of the Egyptian nobles afforded no protection against them. If a frog came close to them, the walls split asunder immediately. "Make way," the frogs would call out to the stone, "that I may do the will of my Creator," and at once the marble showed a rift, through which the frogs entered, and then they attacked the Egyptians bodily, and mutilated and overwhelmed them. In their ardor to fulfil the behest of God, the frogs cast themselves into the red-hot flames of the bake-ovens and devoured the bread. Centuries later, the three holy children, Hananiah, Mishael, and Azariah, were ordered by Nebuchadnezzar to pay worship to his idols on penalty of death in the burning furnace, and they said, "If the frogs, which were under no obligation to glorify the Name of God, nevertheless threw themselves into the fire in order to execute the Divine will concerning the punishment of the Egyptians, how much more should we be ready to expose our lives to the fire for the greater glory of His Name!" And the zealous frogs were not permitted to go unrewarded. While the others were destroyed from Pharaoh and the Egyptian houses at the moment appointed as the last of the plague, God saved those in the bake-ovens alive, the fire had no power to do them the least harm.

Now, although the Egyptian magicians also brought up frogs upon the land of Egypt through the help of demons, Pharaoh nevertheless declared himself ready to let the people go, to sacrifice unto the Lord. The difference between this plague and the first was, that water turned into blood had not caused him any personal inconvenience, while the swarms of frogs inflicted physical suffering, and he gave the promise to Moses to let Israel go, in the hope of ridding himself of the pain he experienced. And Moses in turn promised to entreat God for him on the following day. It could not be done at once, because the seven days' term had not yet elapsed. The prayer offered by Moses in behalf of Pharaoh was granted, all the frogs perished, and their destruction was too swift for them to retire to the water. Consequently the whole land was filled with the stench from the decaying frogs, for they had been so numerous that every man of the Egyptians gathered together four heaps of them. Although the frogs had filled all the market-places and stables and dwellings, they retreated before the Hebrews as if they had been able to distinguish between the two nations, and had known which of them it was proper to abuse, and which to treat with consideration. Beside sparing the Hebrews in the land of Egypt, the frogs kept within the limits of the land, in no wise trenching upon the territory of the neighboring nations. Indeed, they were the means of settling peaceably an old boundary dispute between Egypt and Ethiopia. Wherever they appeared, so far extended the Egyptian domain; all beyond their line belonged to Ethiopia.

Pharaoh was like the wicked that cry to God in their distress, and when their fortunes prosper slide back into their old, impious ways. No sooner had the frogs departed from him, his houses, his servants, and his people, than he hardened his heart again, and refused to let Israel go. Thereupon God sent the plague of the lice, the last of those brought upon Egypt through the mediation of Aaron. Moses could have no part in it, "for," said God, "the earth that afforded thee protection when she permitted thee to hide the slain Egyptian, shall not suffer through thine hand."

The Egyptian magicians having boasted that they were able to produce the first two plagues,--an empty boast it was, for they did not bring them about with their enchantments, but only because Moses willed them to do it,--God put them to shame with the third plague. They tried in vain to imitate it. The demons could not aid them, for their power is limited to the production of things larger than a barley grain, and lice are smaller. The magicians had to admit, "This is the finger of God." Their failure put an end once for all to their attempts to do as Moses did.

But Pharaoh's heart was hardened, and God spake to Moses, saying, "This wicked fellow remains hard of heart, in spite of the three plagues. The fourth shall be much worse than those which have preceded it. Go to him, therefore, and warn him, it would be well for him to let My people go, that the plague come not upon him."

THE PLAGUES BROUGHT THROUGH MOSES

The fourth plague was also announced to the king early in the morning by the river's brink. Pharaoh went thither regularly, for he was one of the magi, who need water for their enchantments. Moses' daily morning visits were beginning to annoy him, and he left the house early, in the hope of circumventing his monitor. But God, who knows the thoughts of man, sent Moses to Pharaoh at the very moment of his going forth.

The warning of the plague that was imminent not having had any effect upon Pharaoh, God sent the fourth plague upon Egypt, a mixed horde of wild animals, lions, bears, wolves, and panthers, and so many birds of prey of different kinds that the light of the sun and the moon was darkened as they circled through the air.

These beasts came upon the Egyptians as a punishment for desiring to force the seed of Abraham to amalgamate with the other nations. God retaliated by bringing a mixture upon them that cost them their life.

As Pharaoh had been the first of the Egyptians to lay evil plans against the children of Israel, so he was the first upon whom descended punishment. Into his house the mixed horde of beasts came first of all, and then into the houses of the rest of the Egyptians. Goshen, the land inhabited by the Israelites, was spared entirely, for God put a division between the two peoples. It is true, the Israelites had committed sins enough to deserve punishment, but the Holy One, blessed be He, permitted the Egyptians to act as a ransom for Israel.

Again Pharaoh expressed his willingness to let the children of Israel sacrifice unto their God, but they were to stay in the land and do it, not go outside, into the wilderness. Moses pointed out to Pharaoh how unbecoming it would be for the Israelites to sacrifice, before the very eyes of his people, the animals that the Egyptians worshipped as gods. Then Pharaoh consented to let them go beyond the borders of his land, only they were not to go very far away, and Moses, to mislead him, asked for a three days' journey into the wilderness. But, again, when Moses had entreated God on Pharaoh's behalf, and the horde of wild beasts had vanished, the king hardened his heart, and did not let the people go.

The cessation of the fourth plague was as miraculous as the plague itself. The very animals that had been slain by the Egyptians in self-defense returned to life and departed from the land with the rest. This was ordained to prevent the wicked oppressors from profiting by the punishment even so much as the value of the hides and the flesh of the dead animals. It had not been so with the useless frogs, they had died on the spot, and their carcasses had remained where they fell.

The fifth plague inflicted by God upon the Egyptians was a grievous pestilence, which mowed down the cattle and beasts chiefly, yet it did not spare men altogether. This pestilence was a distinct plague, but it also accompanied all the other plagues, and the death of many Egyptians was due to it. The Israelites again came off unscathed. Indeed, if an Israelite had a just claim upon a beast held by an Egyptian, it, too, was spared, and the same good fortune waited upon such cattle as was the common property of Israelites and Egyptians.

The sixth plague, the plague of boils, was produced by Moses and Aaron together in a miraculous way. Each took a handful of ashes of the furnace, then Moses held the contents of the two heaps in the hollow of one of his hands, and sprinkled the ashes tip toward the heaven, and it flew so high that it reached the Divine throne. Returning earthward, it scattered over the whole land of Egypt, a space equal to four hundred square parasangs. The small dust of the ashes produced leprosy upon the skin of the Egyptians, and blains of a peculiar kind, soft within and dry on top.

The first five plagues the magicians had tried to imitate, and partly they had succeeded. But in this sixth plague they could not stand before Moses, and thenceforth they gave up the attempt to do as he did. Their craft had all along been harmful to themselves. Although they could produce the plagues, they could not imitate Moses in causing them to disappear. They would put their hands into their bosom, and draw them out white with leprosy, exactly like Moses, but their flesh remained leprous until the day of their death. And the same happened with all the other plagues that they imitated: until their dying day they were afflicted with the ills they produced.

As Pharaoh had wittingly hardened his heart with each of the first five plagues, and refused to turn from his sinful purpose, God punished him thereafter in such wise that he could not mend his ways if he would. God said, "Even though he should desire to do penance now, I will harden his heart until he pays off the whole of his debt."

Pharaoh had observed that whenever he walked on the brink of the Nile, Moses would intercept him. He therefore gave up his morning walk. But God bade Moses seek the king in his palace in the early hours of the day and urge him to repent of his evil ways. Therefore Moses spake to him as follows, in the name of God: "O thou villain! Thou thinkest that I cannot destroy thee from the world. Consider, if I had desired it, instead of smiting the cattle, I might have smitten thee and thy people with the pestilence, and thou wouldst have been cut off from the earth. I inflicted the plague only in such degree as was necessary to show thee My power, and that My Name may be declared throughout all the earth. But thou dost not leave off treading My people underfoot. Behold, to-morrow when the sun passes this point,"--whereat Moses made a stroke upon the wall--"I will cause a very grievous hail to pour down, such as will be only once more, when I annihilate Gog with hail, fire, and brimstone."

But God's lovingkindness is so great that even in His wrath He has mercy upon the wicked, and as His chief object was not to injure men and beasts, but to damage the vegetation in the fields of the Egyptians, He bade Moses admonish Pharaoh to send and hasten in his cattle and all that he had in the field. But the warning fell on heedless ears. Job was the only one to take it to heart, while Pharaoh and his people regarded not the word of the Lord. Therefore the Lord let the hail smite both man and beast, instead of confining it to the herbs and the trees of the field, as He had intended from the first.

As a rule, fire and water are elements at war with each other, but in the hailstones that smote the land of Egypt they were reconciled. A fire rested in the hailstones as the burning wick swims in the oil of a lamp; the surrounding fluid cannot extinguish the flame. The Egyptians were smitten either by the hail or by the fire. In the one case as the other their flesh was seared, and the bodies of the many that were slain by the hail were consumed by the fire. The hailstones heaped themselves up like a wall, so that the carcasses of the slain beasts could not be removed, and if the people succeeded in dividing the dead animals and carrying their flesh off, the birds of prey would attack them on their way home, and snatch their prize away. But the vegetation in the field suffered even more than man and beast, for the hail came down like an axe upon the trees and broke them. That the wheat and the spelt were not crushed was a miracle.

Now, at last, Pharaoh acknowledged, and said, "The Lord is righteous, and I and my people are wicked. He was righteous when He bade us hasten in our cattle from before the hail, and I and my people were wicked, for we heeded not His warning, and men and beasts were found in the field by the hail, and slain." Again he begged Moses to supplicate God in his behalf, that He turn the plague away, and he promised to let the children of Israel go. Moses consented to do his will, saying, however: "Think not that I do not know what will happen after the plague is stayed. I know that thou and thy servants, ye will fear the Lord God, once His punishment is removed, as little as ye feared Him before. But to show His greatness, I will pray to Him to make the hail to cease."

Moses went a short distance out of the city from Pharaoh, and spread abroad his hands unto the Lord, for he did not desire to pray to God within, where there were many idols and images. At once the hail remained suspended in the air. Part of it dropped down while Joshua was engaged in battle with the Amorites, and the rest God will send down in His fury against Gog. Also the thunders ceased at Moses' intercession, and were stored up for a later time, for they were the noise which the Lord made the host of the Syrians to hear at the siege of Samaria, wherefore they arose and fled in the twilight.

As Moses had foreseen, so it happened. No sooner had the hail stopped than Pharaoh abandoned his resolve, and refused to let Israel go. Moses lost no time in announcing the eighth plague to him, the plague of the locusts. Observing that his words had made an impression upon the king's counsellors, he turned and went out from Pharaoh, to give them the opportunity of discussing the matter among themselves. And, indeed, his servants urged Pharaoh to let the Israelites go and serve the Lord their God. But, again, when Moses insisted that the whole people must go, the young and the old, the sons and the daughters, Pharaoh demurred, saying, "I know it to be customary for young men and old men to take part in sacrifices, but surely not little children, and when you demand their presence, too, you betray your evil purpose. It is but a pretense, your saying that you will go a three days' journey into the wilderness, and then return. You mean to escape and never come back. I will have nothing more to do with the matter. My god Baal-zephon will oppose you in the way, and hinder you on your journey." Pharaoh's last words were a dim presentiment. As a magician he foresaw that on their going forth from Egypt the children of Israel would find themselves in desperate straits before the sanctuary of Baal-zephon.

Pharaoh was not content with merely denying the request preferred by Moses and Aaron. He ordered them to be forcibly expelled from the palace. Then God sent the plague of the locusts announced by Moses before. They ate every herb of the land, and all the fruit of the trees that the hail had left, and there remained not any green thing. And again Pharaoh sent for Moses and Aaron, to ask their forgiveness, both for his sin against the Lord God, in not having hearkened unto His word, and for his sin against them, in having chased them forth and intended to curse them. Moses, as before, prayed to God in Pharaoh's behalf, and his petition was granted, the plague was taken away, and in a rather surprising manner. When the swarms of locusts began to darken the land, the Egyptians caught them and preserved them in brine as a dainty to be eaten. Now the Lord turned an exceeding strong west wind, which took up the locusts, and drove them into the Red Sea. Even those they were keeping in their pots flew up and away, and they had none of the expected profit.

The last plague but one, like those which had preceded it, endured seven days. All the time the land was enveloped in darkness, only it was not always of the same degree of density. During the first three days, it was not so thick but that the Egyptians could change their posture when they desired to do so. If they were sitting down, they could rise up, and if they were standing, they could sit down. On the fourth, fifth, and sixth days, the darkness was so dense that they could not stir from their place. They either sat the whole time, or stood; as they were at the beginning, so they remained until the end. The last day of darkness overtook the Egyptians, not in their own land, but at the Red Sea, on their pursuit of Israel. The darkness was not of the ordinary, earthly kind; it came from hell, and it could be felt. It was as thick as a dinar, and all the time it prevailed a celestial light brightened the dwellings of the children of Israel, whereby they could see what the Egyptians were doing under cover of the darkness. This was of great advantage to them, for when they were about to go forth from the land, and they asked their neighbors to lend them raiment, and jewels of gold and jewels of silver, for the journey, the Egyptians tried to deny having any in their possession. But the children of Israel, having spied out all their treasures during the days of darkness, could describe the objects they needed with accuracy, and designate their hiding-places. The Egyptians reasoned that the words of the Israelites could be taken implicitly as they spoke them, for if they had had any idea of deceiving them, asking for a loan when they intended to keep what they laid hands on, they might have taken unobserved during the days of darkness whatever: they desired. Hence the Egyptians felt no hesitation in lending the children of Israel all the treasures they asked for.

The darkness was of such a nature that it could not be dispelled by artificial means. The light of the fire kindled for household uses was either extinguished by the violence of the storm, or else it was made invisible and swallowed up in the density of the darkness. Sight, that most indispensable of all the external senses, though unimpaired, was deprived of its office, for nothing could be discerned, and all the other senses were overthrown like subjects whose leader has fallen. None was able to speak or to hear, nor could anyone venture to take food, but they lay themselves down in quiet and hunger, their outward senses in a trance. Thus they remained, overwhelmed by the affliction, until Moses had compassion on them again, and besought God in their behalf, who granted him the power of restoring fine weather, light instead of darkness and day instead of night.

Intimidated by this affliction, Pharaoh permitted the people to go, the little ones as well as the men and the women, only he asked that they let their flocks and their herds be stayed. But Moses said: "As thou livest, our cattle also shall go with us. Yea, if but the hoof of an animal belongs to an Israelite, the beast shall not be left behind in Egypt." This speech exasperated Pharaoh to such a degree that he threatened Moses with death in the day he should see his face again.

At this very moment the Lord appeared unto Moses, and bade him inform Pharaoh of the infliction of the last plague, the slaying of the first-born. It was the first and the last time that God revealed Himself in the royal palace. He chose the residence of Pharaoh on this occasion that Moses might not be branded as a liar, for he had replied to Pharaoh's threat of killing him if he saw his face again, with the words, "Thou hast spoken well; I will see thy face again no more."

With a loud voice Moses proclaimed the last plague, closing his announcement with the words: "And all these thy servants shall come down unto me and bow down themselves unto me, saying, Get thee out: and all the people that follow thee; and after that I will go out." Moses knew well enough that Pharaoh himself would come and urge him to lead Israel forth with as great haste as possible, but he mentioned only the servants of the king, and not the king himself, because he never forgot the respect due to a ruler.

THE FIRST PASSOVER

When the time approached in which, according to the promise made to Abraham, his children would be redeemed, it was seen that they had no pious deeds to their credit for the sake of which they deserved release from bondage. God therefore gave them two commandments, one bidding them to sacrifice the paschal lamb and one to circumcise their sons. Along with the first they received the calendar in use among the Jews, for the Passover feast is to be celebrated on the fifteenth day of the month of Nisan, and with this month the year is to begin. But the computations for the calendar are so involved that Moses could not understand them until God showed him the movements of the moon plainly. There were three other things equally difficult, which Moses could comprehend only after God made him to see them plainly. They were the compounding of the holy anointing oil, the construction of the candlestick in the Tabernacle, and the animals the flesh of which is permitted or prohibited. Also the determination of the new moon was the subject of special Divine teaching. That Moses might know the exact procedure, God appeared to him in a garment with fringes upon its corners, bade Moses stand at His right hand and Aaron at His left, and then, citing Michael and Gabriel as witnesses, He addressed searching questions to the angels as to how the new moon had seemed to them. Then the Lord addressed Moses and Aaron, saying, "Thus shall My children proclaim the new moon, on the testimony of two witnesses and through the president of the court.

When Moses appeared before the children of Israel and delivered the Divine message to them, telling them that their redemption would come about in this month of Nisan, they said: "How is it possible that we should be redeemed? Is not the whole of Egypt full of our idols? And we have no pious deeds to show making us worthy of redemption." Moses made reply, and said: "As God desires your redemption, He pays no heed to your idols; He passes them by. Nor does He look upon your evil deeds, but only upon the good deeds of the pious among you."

God would not, indeed, have delivered Israel if they had not abandoned their idol worship. Unto this purpose He commanded them to sacrifice the paschal lamb. Thus they were to show that they had given up the idolatry of the Egyptians, consisting in the worship of the ram. The early law was different from the practice of later times, for they were bidden to select their sacrificial animal four days before the day appointed for the offering, and to designate it publicly as such, to show that they did not stand in awe of the Egyptians.

With a heavy heart the Egyptians watched the preparations of the Israelites for sacrificing the animals they worshipped. Yet they did not dare interpose an objection, and when the time came for the offering to be made, the children of Israel could perform the ceremonies without a tremor, seeing that they knew, through many days' experience, that the Egyptians feared to approach them with hostile intent. There was another practice connected with the slaughter of the paschal lamb that was to show the Egyptians how little the Israelites feared them. They took of the blood of the animal, and openly put it on the two side posts and on the lintel of the doors of their houses.

Moses communicated the laws regulating the Passover sacrifice to the elders, and they in turn made them known to the people at large. The elders were commended for having supported the leader at his first appearance, for their faith in Moses caused the whole people to adhere to him at once. Therefore God spake, saying: "I will reward the elders for inspiring the people with confidence in Moses. They shall have the honor of delivering Israel. They shall lead the people to the Passover sacrifice, and through this the redemption will be brought about."

The ceremonies connected with the Passover sacrifice had the purpose of conveying instruction to Israel about the past and the future alike. The blood put on the two side posts and on the lintel of their doors was to remind them of Abraham, Isaac, and Jacob; and the bunch of hyssop for sprinkling the blood on the doors was to imply that, although Israel's position among the peoples of the earth is as lowly as that of the hyssop among the plants, yet this little nation is bound together like the bunch of hyssop, for it is God's peculiar treasure.

The paschal sacrifice afforded Moses the opportunity for inducing the children of Israel to submit themselves to circumcision, which many had refused to do until then in spite of his urgent appeals. But God has means of persuasion. He caused a wind to blow that wafted the sweet scents of Paradise toward Moses' paschal lamb, and the fragrance penetrated to all parts of Egypt, to the distance of a forty days' journey. The people were attracted in crowds to Moses' lamb, and desired to partake of it. But he said, "This is the command of God, 'No uncircumcised person shall eat thereof,'" and they all decided to undergo circumcision. When the Lord passed through the land of Egypt, He blessed every Israelite for his fulfilment of the two commands, the command of the paschal sacrifice and the command regarding circumcision."

The Lord performed a great miracle for the Israelites. As no sacrifice may be eaten beyond the borders of the Holy Land, all the children of Israel were transported thither on clouds, and after they had eaten of the sacrifice, they were carried back to Egypt in the same way.

THE SMITING OF THE FIRST-BORN

When Moses announced the slaying of the first-born, the designated victims all repaired to their fathers, and said: "Whatever Moses hath foretold has been fulfilled. Let the Hebrews go, else we shall all die." But the fathers replied, "It is better for one of every ten of us to die, than the Hebrews should execute their purpose." Then the first-born repaired to Pharaoh, to induce him to dismiss the children of Israel. So far from granting their wish, he ordered his servants to fall upon the first-born and beat them, to punish them for their presumptuous demand. Seeing that they could not accomplish their end by gentle means, they attempted to bring it about by force.

Pharaoh and all that opposed the wishes of the first-born were of the opinion that the loss of so inconsiderable a percentage of the population was a matter of small moment. They were mistaken in their calculation, for the Divine decree included not only the first-born sons, but also the first-born daughters, and not only the first-born of the marriages then existing, but also the first-born issuing from previous alliances of the fathers and the mothers, and as the Egyptians led dissolute lives, it happened not rarely that each of the ten children of one woman was the first-born of its father. Finally, God decreed that death should smite the oldest member of every household, whether or not he was the first-born of his parents. What God resolves is executed. At the exact instant marking the middle of the night, so precise that only God Himself could determine and discern it, He appeared in Egypt, attended by nine thousand myriads of the Angels of Destruction who are fashioned some of hail and some of flames, and whose glances drive terror and trembling to the heart of the beholder. These angels were about to precipitate themselves into the work of annihilation, but God restrained them, saying, "My wrath will not be appeased until I Myself execute vengeance upon the enemies of Israel."

Those among the Egyptians who gave credence to Moses' words, and tried to shield their first-born children from death, sent them to their Hebrew neighbors, to spend the fateful night with them, in the hope that God would exempt the houses of the children of Israel from the plague. But in the morning, when the Israelites arose from their sleep, they found the corpses of the Egyptian fugitives next to them. That was the night in which the Israelites prayed before lying down to sleep: "Cause us, O Lord our God, to lie down in peace, remove Satan from before us and from behind us, and guard our going out and our coming in unto life and unto peace," for it was Satan that had caused frightful bloodshed among the Egyptians.

Among the slain there were, beside the Egyptian first-born, also the first-born of other nationalities residing in Egypt, as well as the Egyptian first-born dwelling outside of their own land. Even the long dead of the first-born were not spared. The dogs dragged their corpses out of their graves in the houses, for it was the Egyptian custom to inter the dead at home. At the appalling sight the Egyptians mourned as though the bereavement had befallen them but recently. The very monuments and statues erected to the memory of the first-born dead were changed into dust, which was scattered and flew out of sight. Moreover, their slaves had to share the fate of the Egyptians, and no less the first-born of the captive that was in the dungeon, for none was so low but he hated the Hebrews, and rejoiced when the Egyptians decreed their persecution. The female slaves that ground corn between mill-stones were in the habit of saying, "We do not regret our servitude, if only the Israelites are gagged, too.

In dealing out punishment to these aliens in the land of Egypt, God showed that He was at once the Master of the land and the Lord over all the gods of the nations, for if the slaves and the captives of war had not been smitten, they would have said, "Mighty is our god, who helped us in this plague." For the same reason all the idols of the Egyptians were swept out of existence in that night. The stone idols were ground into dust, the wooden idols rotted, and those made of metal melted away, and so the Egyptians were kept from ascribing their chastisement to the wrath of their own gods. Likewise the Lord God slew the first-born of the cattle, for the Egyptians paid worship to animals, and they would have attributed their misfortunes to them. In all these ways the Lord showed them that their gods were but vanity.

THE REDEMPTION OF ISRAEL FROM EGYPTIAN BONDAGE

Pharaoh rose up in the night of the smiting of the first-born. He waited not for the third hour of the morning, when kings usually arise, nor did he wait to be awakened, but he himself roused his slaves from their slumber, and all the other Egyptians, and together they went forth to seek Moses and Aaron. He knew that Moses had never spoken an untruth, and as he had said, "I will see thy face again no more," he could not count upon Moses' coming to him. There remained nothing for him to do but go in search of the Israelitish leader. He did not know where Moses lived, and he had great difficulty and lost much time in looking for his house, for the Hebrew lads of whom he made inquiries when he met them in the street played practical jokes on him, misdirected him, and led him astray. Thus he wandered about a long time. all the while weeping and crying out, "O my friend Moses, pray for me to God!"

Meanwhile Moses and Aaron and all Israel beside were at the paschal meal, drinking wine as they sat and leaned to one side, and singing songs in praise of God, the Hallel, which they were the first to recite. When Pharaoh finally reached the door of the house wherein Moses abode, he called to him, and from Moses the question came back, "Who art thou, and what is thy name?"--"I am Pharaoh, who stands here humiliated."-- Moses asked again: "Why dost thou come to me thyself? Is it the custom of kings to linger at the doors of common folk?"--"I pray thee, my lord," returned Pharaoh, "come forth and intercede for us, else there will not remain a single being in Egypt."--"I may not come forth, for God bath commanded us, 'None of you shall go out of the door of his house until the morning.'" --But Pharaoh continued to plead: "Do but step to the window, and speak with me," and when Moses yielded to his importunities, and appeared at the window, the king addressed these words to him: "Thou didst say yesterday, 'All the first-born in the land of Egypt will die,' but now as many as nine-tenths of the inhabitants have perished."

Pharaoh was accompanied by his daughter Bithiah, Moses' foster-mother. She reproached him with ingratitude, in having brought down evil upon her and her countrymen. And Moses answered, and said: "Ten plagues the Lord brought upon Egypt. Hath evil accrued to thee from any of them? Did one of them affect thee?" And when Bithiah acknowledged that no harm had touched her, Moses continued to speak, "Although thou art thy mother's first-born, thou shalt not die, and no evil shall reach thee in the midst of Egypt." But Bithiah said, "Of what advantage is my security to me, when I see the king, my brother, and all his household, and his servants in this evil plight, and look upon their first-born perishing with all the first-born of Egypt?" And Moses returned, "Verily, thy brother and his household and the other Egyptians would not hearken to the words of the Lord, therefore did this evil come upon them.

Turning to Pharaoh, Moses said: "In spite of all that hath happened, I will teach thee something, if thou desirest to learn, and thou wilt be spared, and thou wilt not die. Raise thy voice, and say: 'Ye children of Israel, ye are your own masters. Prepare for your journey, and depart from among my people. Hitherto ye were the slaves of Pharaoh, but henceforward ye are under the authority of God. Serve the Lord your God!'" Moses made him say these words three times, and God caused Pharaoh's voice to be heard throughout the land of Egypt, so that all the inhabitants, the home-born and the aliens, knew that Pharaoh had released the children of Israel from the bondage in which they had languished. And all Israel sang, "Hallelujah, praise, O ye servants of the Lord, praise the Name of the Lord," for they belonged to the Lord, and no more were the servants of Pharaoh.

Now the king of Egypt insisted upon their leaving the land without delay. But Moses objected, and said: "Are we thieves, that we should slink away under cover of the night? Wait until morning." Pharaoh, however, urged and begged Moses to depart, confessing that he was anxious about his own person, for he was a first-born son, and he was terrified that death would strike him down, too. Moses dissipated his alarm, though he substituted a new horror, with the words, "Fear not, there is worse in store for thee!" Dread seized upon the whole people; every one of the Egyptians was afraid of losing his life, and they all united their prayers with Pharaoh's, and begged Moses to take the Israelites hence. And God spake, Ye shall all find your end, not here, but in the Red Sea!"

THE EXODUS

Pharaoh and the Egyptians let their dead lie unburied, while they hastened to help the Israelites load their possessions on wagons, to get them out of the land with as little delay as possible. When they left, they took with them, beside their own cattle, the sheep and the oxen that Pharaoh had ordered his nobles to give them as presents. The king also forced his magnates to beg pardon of the Israelites for all they had suffered, knowing as he did that God forgives an injury done by man to his fellow only after the wrong-doer has recovered the good-will of his victim by confessing and regretting his fault. "Now, depart!" said Pharaoh to the Israelites, "I want nothing from you but that you should pray to God for me, that I may be saved from death."

The hatred of the Egyptians toward the Israelites changed now into its opposite. They conceived affection and friendship for them, and fairly forced raiment upon them, and jewels of silver and jewels of gold, to take along with them on their journey, although the children of Israel had not yet returned the articles they had borrowed from their neighbors at an earlier time. This action is in part to be explained by the vanity of Pharaoh and his people. They desired to pretend before the world that they were vastly rich, as everybody would conclude when this wealth of their mere slaves was displayed to observers. Indeed, the Israelites bore so much away from Egypt that one of them alone might have defrayed the expense of building and furnishing the Tabernacle.

On their leaving the land only the private wealth of the Egyptians was in their hands, but when they arrived at the Red Sea they came into possession of the public treasure, too, for Pharaoh, like all kings, carried the moneys of the state with him on his campaigns, in order to be prepared to hire a relay of mercenaries in case of defeat. Great as the other treasure was, the booty captured at the sea far exceeded it.

But if the Israelites loaded themselves down with goods and jewels and money, it was not to gratify love of riches, or, as any usurer might say, because they coveted their neighbors' possessions. In the first place they could look upon their plunder as wages due to them from those they had long served, and, secondly, they were entitled to retaliate on those at whose hands they had suffered wrong. Even then they were requiting them with an affliction far slighter than any one of all they had endured themselves.

The plagues did not stay the cruelty of the Egyptian oppressors toward the Hebrews. It continued unabated until the very end of their sojourn in the land. On the day of the exodus, Rachel the daughter of Shuthelah gave birth to a child, while she and her husband together were treading the clay for bricks. The babe dropped from her womb into the clay and sank out of sight. Gabriel appeared, moulded a brick out of the clay containing the child, and carried it to the highest of the heavens, where he made it a footstool before the Divine throne. In that night it was that God looked upon the suffering of Israel, and smote the first-born of the Egyptians, and it is one of the four nights that God has inscribed in the Book of Memorial. The first of the four is that in which God appeared to create the world; all was waste and void, and darkness brooded over the abyss, until the Lord came and spread light round about by His word. The second night is that in which God appeared unto Abraham at the covenant of the pieces. In the third night He appeared in Egypt, slaying the first-born of the Egyptians with His right hand, and protecting the first-born of the Israelites with His left. The fourth night recorded will be that in which the end of the redemption will be accomplished, when the iron yoke of the wicked kingdom will be broken, and the evil-doers will be destroyed. Then will Moses come from the desert, and the Messiah from Rome, each at the head of his flock, and the word of God will mediate between them, causing both to walk with one accord in the same direction.

Israel's redemption in future days will happen on the fifteenth of Nisan, the night of Israel's redemption from Egypt, for thus did Moses say, "In this night God protected Israel against the Angels of Destruction, and in this night He will also redeem the generations of the future."

Though the actual deliverance from Egypt took place in that night, the Hebrews did not leave the land until the following day.

During the same night God requited the Egyptians for their evil deeds in the sight of all the people, the night being as bright as day at the time of the summer solstice. Not one could escape the general chastisement, for by Divine dispensation none was absent from home at the time, so that none could fail to see the chastisement.

The angels in heaven learnt what was happening on earth. When they were about to begin their song of praise to God, He silenced them with the words, "My children on earth are singing now," and the celestial hosts had to stop and listen to the song of Israel.

Great as the joy of the Hebrews was at their deliverance from the Egyptian bondage, it was exceeded by that of Pharaoh's people at seeing their slaves depart, for with them went the dread of death that had obsessed them. They were like the portly gentleman riding an ass. The rider feels uncomfortable and longs for the moment of alighting, but his longing cannot compare in intensity with that of the ass groaning under the corpulent burden, and when their journey's end is reached, the ass rejoices more than his master. So the Egyptians were happier to be rid of the Hebrews than these were to be free.

In general, the Israelites were not in a joyous mood. The strength of men is readily exhausted, mentally and physically, by the strain of a sudden change from slavery to freedom. They did not recover vigor and force until they heard the angel hosts sing songs of praise and joy over the redemption of Israel and the redemption of the Shekinah, for so long as the chosen people is in exile, the Shekinah, who dwells among Israel, is also, as it were, in exile. At the same time, God caused the earth to exhale and send aloft a healing fragrance, which cured them of all their diseases.

The exodus of the Israelites began at Raamses, and although the distance from there to the city of Mizraim, where Moses abode, was a forty days' journey, yet they heard the voice of their leader urging them to leave the land. They covered the distance from Raamses to Succoth, a three days' march, in an instant. In Succoth God enveloped them in seven clouds of glory, four hovering in front, behind, and at the two sides of them, one suspended above them, to keep off rain, hail, and the rays of the sun, and one under them to protect them against thorns and snakes. The seventh cloud preceded them, and prepared the way for them, exalting the valleys and making low every mountain and hill. Thus they wandered through the wilderness for forty years. In all that time no artificial lighting was needed; a beam from the celestial cloud followed them into the darkest of chambers, and if one of the people had to go outside of the camp, even thither he was accompanied by a fold of the cloud, covering and protecting him. Only, that a difference might be made between day and night, a pillar of fire took the place of the cloud in the evening. Never for an instant were the people without the one or the other to guide them: the pillar of fire glowed in front of them before the pillar of cloud retired, and in the morning the cloud was there before the fire vanished. The clouds of glory and the pillar of fire were sent for the protection of Israel alone, for none beside, not for the heathen and not for the mixed multitude that went up with them; these had to walk outside of the cloud enclosure.

The cavalcade consisted of six hundred thousand heads of families afoot, each accompanied by five children on horseback, and to these must be added the mixed multitude, exceeding the Hebrews vastly in number.

So profound was Israel's trust in the Lord, that they followed Moses unmurmuringly into the wilderness, without supplying themselves with provisions. The only edibles they took were the remains of the unleavened bread and the bitter herbs, and these not to satisfy their hunger, but because they were unwilling to separate themselves from what they had prepared lovingly at the command of God. These possessions were so dear to them that they would not entrust them to the beasts of burden, they carried them on their own shoulders.

Volume 3

Chapter 1

Moses In the Wilderness

THE LONG ROUTE

The exodus would have been impossible if Joseph's bones had remained behind. Therefore Moses made it his concern to seek their resting-place, while the people had but the one thought of gathering in the treasures of the Egyptians. But it was not an easy matter to find Joseph's body. Moses knew that he had been interred in the mausoleum of the Egyptian kings, but there were so many other bodies there that it was impossible to identify it. Moses' mother Jochebed came to his aid. She led him to the very spot where Joseph's bones lay. As soon as he came near them, he knew them to be what he was seeking, by the fragrance they exhaled and spread around. But his difficulties were not at an end. The question arose, how he was to secure possession of the remains. Joseph's coffin had been sunk far down into the ground, and he knew not how to raise it from the depths. Standing at the edge of the grave, he spoke these words. "Joseph, the time hath come whereof thou didst say, 'God will surely visit you, and ye shall carry up my bones from hence.'" No sooner had this reminder dropped from his lips than the coffin stirred and rose to the surface.

And even yet the difficulties in Moses' way were not removed wholly. The Egyptian magicians had stationed two golden dogs at Joseph's coffin, to keep watch, and they barked vehemently if anyone ventured close to it. The noise they made was so loud it could be heard throughout the land, from end to end, a distance equal to a forty day's journey. When Moses came near the coffin, the dogs emitted their warning sound, but he silenced them at once with words, "Come, ye people, and behold the miracle! The real, live dogs did not bark, and these counterfeit dogs produced by magic attempt it!" What he said about real, live dogs and their refraining from barking had reference to the fact that the dogs of the Egyptians did not move their tongues against any of the children of Israel, through they had barked all the time the people were engaged in burying the bodies of their smitten first-born. As a reward God gave the Israelites the law, to cast to the dogs the flesh they themselves are forbidden to eat, for the Lord withholds due recompense from none of His creatures. Indeed, the dogs received a double reward, for their excrements are used in tanning the hides from which the Torah scrolls are made, as well as the Mezuzot and the phylacteries.

Joseph's coffin in the possession of Moses, the march of the Israelites could begin. The Egyptians put no manner of obstacle in their way. Pharaoh himself accompanied them, to make sure that they were actually leaving the land, and now he was so angry at his counselors for having advised against letting the Israelites depart that he slew them.

For several reasons God did not permit the Israelites to travel along the straight route to the promised land. He desired them to go to Sinai first and take the law upon themselves there, and, besides, the time divinely appointed for the occupation of the land by the Gentiles had not yet elapsed. Over and above all this, the long sojourn in the wilderness was fraught with profit for the Israelites, spiritually and materially. If they had reached Palestine directly after leaving Egypt, they would have devoted themselves entirely each to the cultivation of his allotted parcel of ground, and no time would have been left for the study of the Torah. In the wilderness they were relieved of the necessity of providing for their daily wants, and they would give all their efforts to acquiring the law. On the whole, it would not have been advantageous to process at once to the Holy Land and take possession thereof, for when the Canaanites heard that the Israelites were making for Palestine, they burnt the crops, felled the trees, destroyed the buildings, and choked the water springs, all in order to render the land uninhabitable. Hereupon God spake, and said: "I did not promise their fathers to give a devastated land unto their see, but a land full of all good things. I will lead them about in the wilderness for forty years, and meanwhile the Canaanites will have time to repair the damage they have done." Moreover, the many miracles preformed for the Israelites during the journey through the wilderness had made their terror to fall upon the other nations, and their hearts melted, and there remained no more spirit in any man. They did not venture to attack the Israelites, and the conquest of the land was all the easier.

Nor does this exhaust the list of reasons for preferring the longer route through the desert. Abraham had sworn a solemn oath to live at peace with the Philistines during a certain period, and the end of the term had not yet arrived. Besides, there was the fear that the sight of the land of the Philistines would awaken sad recollections in the Israelites, and drive them back into Egypt speedily, for once upon a time it had been the scene of a bitter disappointment to them. they had spent one hundred and eighty years in Egypt, in peace and prosperity, not in the least molested by the people. Suddenly Ganon came, a descendant of Joseph, of the tribe of Ephraim, and he spake, "The Lord hat appeared unto me, and He bade me lead you forth out of Egypt." The Ephraimites were the only ones to heed his words. Proud of their royal lineage as direct descendants of Joseph, and confident to their valor in war, for they were great heroes, they left the land and betook themselves to Palestine. They Carried only weapons and gold and silver. They had taken no provisions, because they expected to buy food and drink on the way or capture them by force if the owners would not part with them for money.

After a day's march they found themselves in the neighborhood of Gath, at the place where the shepherds employed by the residents of the city gathered with the flocks. the Ephraimites asked them to sell them some sheep, which they expected to slaughter in order to satisfy their hunger with them, but the shepherds refused to have business dealings with them, saying, "Are the sheep ours, or does the cattle belong to us, that we could part with them for money?" Seeing that they could not gain their point by kindness, the Ephraimites used force. The outcries of the shepherds brought the people of Gath to their aid. A violent encounter, lasting a whole day, took place between the Israelites and the Philistines. The people of Gath realized that alone they would not be able to offer successful resistance to the Ephraimites, and they summoned the people of the other Philistine cities to join them. The following day an army of forty thousand stood ready to oppose the Ephraimites. Reduced in strength, as they were, by their three days' fast, they were exterminated root and branch. Only ten of them escaped with their bare life, and returned to Egypt, to bring Ephraim word of the disaster that had overtaken his posterity, and he mourned many days.

This abortive attempt of the Ephraimites to leave Egypt was the first occasion for oppressing Israel. Thereafter the Egyptians exercised force and vigilance to keep them in their land. As for the disaster of the Ephraimites, it was well-merited punishment, because they had paid no heed to the wish of the father Joseph, who had adjured his descendants solemnly on his deathbed not to think of quitting the land until the redeemer should appear. Their death was followed by disgrace, for their bodies lay unburied for many years on the battlefield near Gath, and the purpose of God in directing the Israelites to choose the longer route from Egypt to Canaan, was to spare them the sight of those dishonored corpses. Their courage might have deserted them, and out of apprehension of sharing the fate of their brethren they might have hastened back to the land of slavery.

PHARAOH PURSUES THE HEBREWS

When Pharaoh permitted Israel to depart, he was under the impression that they were going only a three days' journey into the wilderness for the purpose of offering sacrifices. He sent officers with them, whose duty was to bring them back at the appointed time. The exodus took place on a Thursday. On the following Sunday the king's watchers noticed that the Israelites, so far from preparing for a return, were making arrangements looking to a long sojourn in the desert. They remonstrated and urged them to go back. The Israelites maintained that Pharaoh had dismissed them for good, but the officers would not be put off with their mere assertions. They said, "Willy-nilly, you will have to do as the powers that be command." To such arrogance the Israelites would not submit, and they fell upon the officers, slaying some and wounding others. The maimed survivors went back to Egypt, and report the contumacy of the Israelites to Pharaoh. Meantime Moses, who did not desire the departure of his people to have the appearance of flight before the Egyptians, gave the signal to turn back to Pi-hahiroth. Those of little faith among the Israelites tore their hair and their garments in desperation, though Moses assured them that by the word of God they were free men, and no longer slaves to Pharaoh. Accordingly, they retraced their steps to Pi-hahiroth, where two rectangular rocks form an opening, within which the great sanctuary of Baal-zephon was situated. The rocks are shaped like human figures, the one a man and the other a woman, and they were not chiseled by human hands, but by the Creator Himself. The place had been called Pithom in earlier times, but later, on account of the idols set up there, it received the name Hahiroth. Of set purpose God had left Baal-zephon uninjured, alone of all the Egyptian idols. He wanted the Egyptian people to think that this idol was possessed of exceeding might, which it exercised to prevent the Israelites from journeying on. To confirm them in their illusory belief, God caused wild beasts to obstruct the road to the wilderness, and they took it for granted that their idol Baal-zephon had ordained their appearance.

Pi-hahiroth was famous, besides, on account of the treasures heaped up there. The wealth of the world which Joseph had acquired through the sale of corn he had stored up during the seven years of plenty, he had divided into three parts. The first part he surrendered to Pharaoh. The second part he concealed in the wilderness, where it was found by Korah, though it disappeared again, not to come to view until the Messianic time, and then it will be for the benefit of the pious. The third part Joseph hid in the sanctuary of Baal-zephon, whence the Hebrews carried it off as booty.

When Amalek and the magicians brought the information to Pharaoh, that the Israelites had resolved not to return to Egypt, his heart and the heart of his whole people turned against them. The very counselors that had persuaded him to dismiss the children of Israel spake now as follows: " If we had only been smitten with the plaques, we could have resigned ourselves to our fate. Or if, besides being smitten with the plagues, we had been compelled to let the Hebrews depart from the land, that, too, we could have been borne with patience. But to be smitten with the plagues, to be compelled to let our slaves depart from us, and to sit by and see them go off with our riches, that is more than we can endure."

Now that the children of Israel had gone from them the Egyptians recognized how valuable an element they had been in their country. In general, the time of the exodus of Israel was disastrous for their former masters. In addition to losing their dominion over the Israelites, the Egyptians had to deal with mutinies that broke out among many other nations tributary to them, for hitherto Pharaoh had been the ruler of the whole world. The king resorted to blandishments and promises, to induce the people to make war against the Israelites, saying, "As a rule the army marches forth first, and the king follows in security, but I will precede you; and as a rule the king has the first choice of the booty, and as much of it as he desires, but I will take no more than any one of you, and on my return from the war I will divide my treasures of silver, gold, and precious stones among you."

In his zeal Pharaoh did not wait to have his chariot made ready for him he did it with his own hands, and his nobles followed his example. Samael granted Pharaoh assistance, putting six hundred chariots manned with his own hosts at his disposal. These formed the vanguard, and they were joined by all the Egyptians, with their vast assemblages of chariots and warriors, no less than three hundred of their men to one of the children of Israel, each equipped with their different sorts of weapons. The general custom was for two charioteers to take turns at driving a car, but to overtake the Israelites more surely and speedily, Pharaoh ordered three to be assigned to each. The result was that they covered in one day the ground which it had taken the Israelites three to traverse.

The mind of the Egyptians was in no wise directed toward spoil and plunder in this expedition. Their sole and determined purpose was to exterminate Israel, kith and kin. As the heathen lay great stress upon omens when they are about to start out on a campaign, God caused all their preparations to proceed smoothly, without the slightest untoward circumstance. Everything pointed to a happy issue. Pharaoh, himself an adept in magic, had a presentiment that dire misfortune would befall the children of Israel in the wilderness, that they would lose Moses there, and there the whole generation that had departed from Egypt would find its grave. Therefore he spoke to Dathan and Abiram, who remained behind in Egypt, saying: "Moses is leading them, but he himself knows not whither. Verily, the congregation of Israel will lift up their voice in the wilderness, and cry, and there they will be destroyed." He thought naturally that these visions had reference to an imminent future, to the time of his meeting with his dismissed slaves. But his error was profound-he was hurrying forward to his own destruction.

When he reached the sanctuary of Baal-zephon, Pharaoh, in his joy at finding him spared while all the other idols in Egypt had been annihilated, lost no time, but hastened to offer sacrifices to him, and he was comforted, "for," he said, "Baal-zephon approves my purpose of drowning the children of Israel in the sea."

When the Israelites beheld the huge detachments of the Egyptian army moving upon them, and when they considered that in Migdol there were other troops stationed, besides, more, indeed, than their own numbers, men, women, and children all told, great terror overwhelmed them. What affrighted them most, was the sight of the Angel of Egypt darting through the air as he flew to the assistance of the people under his tutelage. They turned to Moses, saying: "What has thou done to us? Now they will requite us for all that hath happened-that their first-born were smitten, and that we ran off with their money, which was thy fault, for thou didst bid up borrow gold and silver from our Egyptian neighbors and depart with their property."

The situation of the Israelites was desperate. Before them was the sea, behind them the Egyptians, on both sides the wild beasts of the desert. The wicked among them spoke to Moses, saying, "While we were in Egypt, we said to thee and to Aaron, 'The Lord look upon you, and judge, because ye have made our savor to be abhorred in the eyes of Pharaoh and in the eyes of his servants, to put a sword in their hand to slay us.' Then there died many of our brethren during the days of darkness, which was worse than the bondage in which the Egyptians kept us. Nevertheless our fate in the desert will be sadder than theirs. They at least were mourned, and their bodies ere buried, but our corpses will lie exposed, consumed in the day by drought and by frost in the night."

Moses in his wisdom knew how to pacify the thousands and myriads under his leadership. He impressed them with the words, "Fear ye not, stand still, and see the salvation of the Lord." "When will His salvation come?" questioned the people, and he told them it would appear the following day, but they protested, "We cannot wait until to-morrow." Then Moses prayed to God, and the Lord showed him the angel hosts standing ready to hasten to the assistance of the people.

They were not agreed as to what they were to do. There were four contending parties. The opinion of the first party was that they seek death by drowning in the sea; of the second, that they return to Egypt; the third was in favor of a pitched battle with the enemy, and the fourth thought it would be a good plan to intimidate the Egyptians by noise and a great hubbub. To the first Moses said, "Stand still, and see the salvation of the Lord;" to the second, "The Egyptians whom ye have seen to-day, ye shall see them again no more forever;" to the third, "The Lord shall fight for you;" and to the fourth, "Ye shall hold your peace." "What, then, shall we do?" these asked their leader, and Moses answered them, saying, "Ye shall bless, praise, extol, adore and glorify Him that is the Lord of war!" Instead of the sword and the five sorts of arms which they bore, they mad use of their mouth, and it was of greater avail than all possible weapons of war. The Lord hearkened unto their prayer, for which He had but been waiting.

Moses also addressed himself to God, saying: "O Lord of the world! I am like the shepherd who, having undertaken to pasture a flock, has been heedless enough to drive his sheep to the edge of a precipice, and then is in a despair how to get them down again. Pharaoh is behind my flock Israel, in the south is Baal-zephon, in the north Midgol, and before us the sea lies spread out. Thou knowest, O Lord, that it is beyond human strength and human contrivance to surmount the difficulties standing in our way. Thine alone is the work of procuring deliverance for this army, which left Egypt at Thy appointment. We despair of all other assistance or device, and we have recourse only to our hope in Thee. If there be any escape possible, we look up to Thy providence to accomplish it for us." With such words Moses continued to make fervent supplication to God to succor Israel in their need. But God cut short his prayer, saying: "Moses, My children are in distress-the sea blocks the way before them, the enemy is in hot pursuit after them, and thou standest here and prayest. Sometimes long prayer is good, but sometimes it is better to be brief. If I gathered the waters together unto one place, and let the dry land appear for Adam, a single human being, should I not do the same for this holy congregation? I will save them if only for the sake of the merits of Abraham, who stood ready to sacrifice his son Isaac unto Me, and for the sake of My promise to Jacob. The sun and the moon are witnesses that I will cleave the sea for the seed of the children of Israel, who deserve My help for going after Me in the wilderness unquestioningly. Do thou but see to it that they abandon their evil thought of returning to Egypt, and then it will not be necessary to turn to Me and entreat My help."

Moses, however, was still very much troubled in mind, on account of Samael, who had not left off lodging accusations before God against Israel since the exodus from Egypt. The Lord adopted the same procedure in dealing with the accuser as the experienced shepherd, who, at the moment of transferring his sheep across a stream, was faced by a ravening wolf. The shepherd threw a strong ram to the wolf, and while the two engaged in combat, the rest of the flock was carried across the water, and then the shepherd returned and snatch the wolf's supposed prey away from him. Samael said to the Lord: "Up to this time the children of Israel were idol worshippers, and now Thou proposest so great a thing as dividing the sea for them?" What did the Lord do? He surrendered Job to Samael, saying, "While he busies himself with Job, Israel will pass through the sea unscathed, and as soon as they are in safety, I will rescue Job from the hands of Samael."

Israel had other angel adversaries, besides. Uzza, the tutelary Angel of the Egyptians, appeared before God, and said, "O Lord of the world! I have a suit with this nation which Thou hast brought forth out to Egypt. If it seemeth well to Thee, let their angel Michael appear, and contend with me before Thee." The Lord summoned Michael, and Uzza stated his charges against Israel: "O Lord of the world! Thou didst decree concerning this people of Israel that is hall be held in bondage by my people, the Egyptians, for a period of four hundred years. But they had dominion over them only eighty-six years, therefore the time of their going forth hath not yet arrived. If it be Thy will, give me permission to take them back to Egypt, that they may continue in slavery for the three hundred and fourteen years that are left, and Thy word be fulfilled. As Thou are immutable, so let Thy decree be immutable!"

Michael was silent, for he knew not how to controvert these words, and it seemed as if Uzza had won his suit. But the Lord Himself espoused the cause of Israel, and He said to Uzza: "The duty of serving thy nation was laid upon My children only on account of an unseemly word uttered by Abraham. When I spoke to him, saying, 'I am the Lord that brought thee out of Ur of the Chaldees, to give thee this land to inherit it,' he made answer, 'Whereby shall I know that I shall inherit it?' Therefore did I say to him, 'Thy seed shall be a stranger.' But it is well-known and manifest before Me that they were 'strangers' from the day of Isaac's birth, and. reckoning thence, the period of four hundred years has elapsed, and thou hast no right to keep My children in bondage any longer."

THE SEA DIVIDED

God spake to Moses, saying, "Why dost thou stand here praying? My children's prayer has anticipated thine. For thee there is naught to do but lift up thy rod and stretch out thine hand over the sea, and divide it." Moses replied: "Thou commandest me to divide the sea, and lay bare the dry ground in the midst of it, and yet Thou didst Thyself make it a perpetual decree, that the sand shall be placed for the bound of the sea." And again God spake to Moses: "Thou has not read the beginning of the Torah. I, yea, I, did speak, 'Let the waters under the heaven be gathered together unto one place, and let the dry land appear,' and at that time I made the condition that the waters shall divide before Israel. Take the rod that I gave unto thee, and go to the sea upon Mine errand, and speak thus: 'I am the messenger sent by the Creator of the world! Uncover thy paths, O sea, for My children, that they may go through the midst of thee on dry ground.'"

Moses spoke to the sea as God had bidden him, but it replied, "I will not do according to thy words, for thou are only a man born of woman, and, besides, I am three days older than thou, O man, for I was brought forth on the third day of creation, and thou on the sixth." Moses lost no time, but carried back to God the words the sea has spoken, and the Lord said" "Moses, what does a master do with an intractable servant?" "He beats him with a rod," said Moses. "Do thus!" ordered God. "Lift up thy rod, and stretch out thine hand over the sea and divide it."

Thereupon Moses raised up his rod-the rod that had been created at the very beginning of the world, on which were graven in plain letters the great and exalted Name, the names of the ten plagues inflicted upon the Egyptians, and the names of the three Fathers, the six Mothers, and the twelve tribes of Jacob. This rod he lifted up, and stretched it out over the sea.

The sea, however, continued in its perverseness, and Moses entreated God to give His command direct to it. But God refused, saying: "Were I to command the sea to divide, it would never again return to its former estate. Therefore, do thou convey My order to it, that it be not drained dry forever. But I will let a semblance of My strength accompany thee, and that will compel its obedience." When the sea saw the Strength of God at the right hand of Moses, it spoke to the earth saying, "Make hollow places for me, that I may hide myself therein before the Lord of all created things, blessed be He." Noticing the terror of the sea, Moses said to it: "For a whole day I spoke to thee at the bidding of the Holy One, who desired thee to divide, but thou didst refuse to pay heed to my words; even when I showed thee my rod, thou didst remain obdurate. What hath happened now that thou skippest hence?" The sea replied, "I am fleeing, not before thee, but before the Lord of all created things, that His Name be magnified in all the earth." And the waters of the Red Sea divided, and not they alone, but all the waters in heaven and on earth, in whatever vessel it was, in cisterns, in wells, in caves, in casks, in pitchers, in drinking cups, and in glasses, and none of these waters returned to their former estate until Israel has passed through the sea on dry land.

The angel Gabriel was eager to drown the Egyptians during the same night, but God bade him wait until early the next day, until the hour of the morning watch, when Abraham had made himself ready to set out for the sacrifice of his son. Gabriel succeeded, however, in holding back the turbulent water about to sweep over Israel. To the wall of water on the right, he called, "Beware of Israel, who will receive the law in time to come from the right hand of the Lord," and turning to the wall of water on the left, he said, "Beware of Israel, who will wind the phylacteries about their left hand in time to come." The water behind he admonished, "Beware of Israel, who will let the Zizit drop down upon their back in time to come," and to the water towering in front of them, he called, "Beware of Israel, who bear the sign of the covenant upon their bodies."

God caused the sea to go back by a strong east wind, the wind He always makes use of when He chastises the nations. The same east wind had brought the deluge; it had laid the tower of Babel in ruins; it was to cause the destruction of Samaria, Jerusalem, and Tyre; and it will, in future, be the instrument for castigating Rome drunken with pleasure; and likewise the sinners in Gehenna are punished by means of the east wind. All night long God made it to blow over the sea. To prevent the enemy from inflicting harm upon the Israelites, He enveloped the Egyptians in profound darkness, so impenetrable it could be felt, and none could move or change his posture. He that sat when it fell could not arise from his place, and he that stood could not sit down. Nevertheless, the Egyptians could see that the Israelites were surrounded by bright light, and were enjoying a banquet where they stood, and when they tried to speed darts and arrows against them, the missiles were caught up by the cloud and by the angels hovering between the two camps, and no harm came to Israel.

THE PASSAGE THROUGH THE RED SEA

On the morning after the eventful night, though the sea was not yet made dry land, the Israelites, full of trust in God, were ready to cast themselves into its waters. The tribes contended with one another for the honor of being the first to jump. Without awaiting the outcome of the wordy strife, the tribe of Benjamin sprang in, and the princes of Judah were so incensed at having been deprived of pre-eminence in danger that they pelted the Benjamites with stones. God knew that the Judaeans and the Benjamites were animated by a praiseworthy purpose. The ones like the others desired but to magnify the Name of God, and He rewarded both tribes: in Benjamin's allotment the Shekinah took up her residence, and the royalty of Israel was conferred upon Judah.

When God saw the two tribes in the waves of the sea, He called upon Moses, and said: "My beloved are in danger of drowning, and thou standest by and prayest. Bid Israel go forward, and thou lift up thy rod over the sea, and divide it." Thus it happened, and Israel passed through the sea with its water cleft in twain.

The dividing of the sea was but the first of ten miracles connected with the passage of the Israelites through it. The others were that the waters united in a vault above their heads; twelve paths opened up, one for each of the tribes; the water became transparent as glass, and each tribe could see the others; the soil underfoot was dry, but it changed into clay when the Egyptians stepped upon it; the walls of water transformed into rocks, against which the Egyptians were thrown and dashed to death, while before the Israelites could slake their thirst; and, finally, the tenth wonder was, that this drinking water was congealed in the heart of the sea as soon as they had satisfied their need.

And there were other miracles, besides. The sea yielded the Israelites whatever their hearts desired. If a child cried as it lay in the arms of its mother, she needed but to stretch out her hand and pluck and apple or some fruit and quiet it. The waters were piled up to the height of sixteen hundred miles, and they could be seen by all the nations of the earth.

The great wonder of Israel's passage through the sea took place in the presence of the three Fathers and the six Mothers, for God had fetched them out of their graves to the shores of the Red Sea, to be witnesses of the marvelous deeds wrought in behalf of their children.

Wonderful as were the miracles connected with the rescue of the Israelites from the waters of the sea, those performed when the Egyptians were drowned were no less remarkable. First of all God felt called upon to defend Israel's cause before Uzza, the Angel of the Egyptians, who would not allow his people to perish in the waters of the sea. He appeared on the spot at the very moment when God wanted to drown the Egyptians, and he spake: "O Lord of the world! Thou are called just and upright, and before Thee there is no wrong, no forgetting, no respecting of persons. Why, then, dost Thou desire to make my children perish in the sea? Canst Thou say that my children drowned or slew a single one of Thine? If it be on account of the rigorous slavery that my children imposed upon Israel, then consider that Thy children have received their wages, in that they took their silver and golden vessels from them."

Then God convoked all the members of His celestial family, and He spake to the angel hosts: "Judge ye in truth between Me and yonder Uzza, the Angel of the Egyptians. At the first I brought a famine upon his people, and I appointed My friend Joseph over them, who saved them through his sagacity, and they all became his slaves. Then My children went down into their land as strangers, in consequence of the famine, and they made the children of Israel to serve with rigor in all manner of hard work there is in the world. They groaned on account of their bitter service, and their cry rose up to Me, and I sent Moses and Aaron, My faithful messengers, to Pharaoh. When they came before the king of Egypt, they spake to him, 'Thus said the Lord, the God of Israel, Let My people go, that they may hold a feast unto Me in the wilderness.' In the presence of the kings of the East and of the West, the sinner began to boast, saying: 'Who is the Lord, that I should hearken unto His voice, to let Israel go? Why comes He not before me, like all the kings of the world, and why doth He not bring me a present like the others? This God of whom you speak, I know Him not at all. Wait and let me search my lists, and see whether I can find His Name.' But his servants said, 'We have heard that He is the son of the wise, the son of ancient kings.' Then Pharaoh asked My messengers, 'What are the works of this God?' and they replied, 'He is the God of gods, the Lord of lords, who created the heaven and the earth.' But Pharaoh doubted their words, and said, 'There is no God in all the world that can accomplish such works besides me, for I made myself, and I made the Nile river.' Because he denied Me thus, I sent ten plagues upon him, and he was compelled to let My children go. Yet, in spite of all, he did not leave off from his wicked ways, and he tried to bring them back under his bondage. Now, seeing all that hath happened to him, and that he will not acknowledge Me as God and Lord, does he not deserve to be drowned in the sea with his host?"

The Celestial family called out when the Lord had ended His defense, "Thou hast every right to drown him in the sea!"

Uzza heard their verdict, and he said: "O Lord of all the worlds! I know that my people deserve the punishment Thou has decreed, but may it please Thee to deal with them according to Thy attribute of mercy, and take pity upon the work of Thy hands, for Thy tender mercies are over all Thy works!"

Almost the Lord had yielded to Uzza's entreaties, when Michael gave a sign to Gabriel that mad him fly to Egypt swiftly and fetch thence a brick for which a Hebrew child had been used as a mortar. Holding this incriminating object in his had, Gabriel stepped into the presence of God, and said: "O Lord of the world! Wilt Thou have compassion with the accursed nation that has slaughtered Thy children so cruelly?" Then the Lord turned Himself away from His attribute of mercy, and seating Himself upon His throne of justice He resolved to drown the Egyptians in the sea.

The first upon whom judgement was executed was the Angel of Egypt-Uzza was thrown into the sea. A similar fate overtook Rahab, the Angel of the Sea, with his hosts. Rahab had made intercession before God in behalf of the Egyptians. He had said: "Why shouldst Thou drown the Egyptians? Let is suffice the Israelites that Thou hast saved them out of the hand of their masters." At that God dealt Rahab and his army a blow, under which they staggered and fell dead, and then He cast their corpses in the sea, whence its unpleasant odor.

THE DESTRUCTION OF THE EGYPTIANS

At the moment when the last of the Israelites stepped out of the bed of the sea, the first of the Egyptians set foot into it, but in the same instant the waters surged back into their wonted place, and all the Egyptians perished.

But drowning was not the only punishment decreed upon them by God. He undertook a thoroughgoing campaign against them. When Pharaoh was preparing to persecute the Israelites, he asked his army which of the saddle beasts was the swiftest runner, that one he would use, and they said: "There is none swifter than thy piebald mare, whose like is to be found nowhere in the world." Accordingly, Pharaoh mounted the mare, and pursued after the Israelites seaward. And while Pharaoh was inquiring of his army as to the swiftest animal to mount, God was questioning the angels as to the swiftest creature to use to the detriment of Pharaoh. And the angels answered: "O Lord of the world! All thing are Thine, and all are Thine handiwork. Thou knowest well, and it is manifest before Thee, that among all Thy creatures there is none so quick as the wind that comes from under the throne of Thy glory," and the Lord flew swiftly upon the wings of the wind.

The angels now advanced to support the Lord in His war against the Egyptians. Some brought swords, some arrows, and some spears. But God warded them off, saying, "Away! I need no help!" The arrows sped by Pharaoh against the children of Israel were answered by the Lord with fiery darts directed against the Egyptians. Pharaoh's army advanced with gleaming swords, and the Lord sent out lightnings that discomfited the Egyptians. Pharaoh hurled missiles, and the Lord discharged hailstones and coals of fire against him. With trumpets, sackbuts, and horns the Egyptians made their assault, and the Lord thundered in the heavens, and the Most High uttered His voice. In vain the Egyptians marched forward in orderly battle array; the Lord deprived them of their standards, and they were thrown into wild confusion. To lure them into the water, the Lord caused fiery steeds to swim out upon the sea, and the horses of the Egyptians followed them, each with a rider upon his back.

Now the Egyptians tried to flee to their land in their chariots drawn by she-mules. As they had treated the children of Israel in a way contrary to nature, so the Lord treated them now. Not the she-mules pulled the chariots but the chariots, though fire from heaven had consumed their wheels, dragged the men and the beasts into the water. The chariots were laden with silver, gold, and all sorts of costly things, which the river Pishon, as it flows forth from Paradise, carries down into the Gihon. Thence the treasures float into the Red Sea, and by its waters they were tossed into the chariots of the Egyptians. It was the wish of Israel, and for this reason He caused the chariots to roll down into the sea, and the sea in turn to cast them out upon the opposite shore, at the feet of the Israelites.

And the Lord fought against the Egyptians also with the pillar of cloud and the pillar of fire. The former made the soil miry, and the mire was heated to the boiling point by the latter, so that the hoofs of the horses dropped from their feet, and they could not budge from the spot.

The anguish and the torture that God brought upon the Egyptians at the Red Sea caused them by far more excruciating pain than the plagues they had endured in Egypt, for at the sea He delivered them into the hands of the Angels of Destruction, who tormented them pitilessly. Had God not endowed the Egyptians with a double portion of strength, they could not have stood the pain a single moment.

The last judgement executed upon the Egyptians corresponded to the wicked designs harbored against Israel by the three different parties among them when they set out in pursuit of their liberated slaves. The first party had said, "We will bring Israel back to Egypt;" the second had said, "We will strip them bare," and the third had said, "We will slay them all." The Lord blew upon the first with His breath, and the sea covered them; the second party He shook into the sea, and the third He pitched into the depths of the abyss. He tossed them about as lentils are shaken up and down in a saucepan; the upper ones are made to fall to the bottom, the lower ones fly to the top. This was the experience of the Egyptians. And worse still, first the rider and his beast were whisked high up in the air, and then the two together, the rider sitting upon the back of the beast, were hurled to the bottom of the sea.

The Egyptians endeavored to save themselves from the sea by conjuring charms, for they were great magicians. Of the ten measures of magic allotted to the world, they had taken nine for themselves. And, indeed, they succeeded for the moment; they escaped out of the sea. But immediately the sea said to itself, "How can I allow the pledge entrusted to me by God to be taken from me?" And the water rushed after the Egyptians, and dragged back every man of them.

Among the Egyptians were the two arch-magicians Jannes and Jambres. They made wings for themselves, with which they flew up to heaven. They also said to Pharaoh: "If God Himself hath done this thing, we can effect naught. But if this work has been put into the hands of His angel, then we will shake his lieutenants into the sea." They proceeded at once to use their magic contrivances, whereby they dragged the angels down. These cried up to God: "Save us, O God, for the waters are come in unto our soul! Speak Thy word that will cause the magicians to drown in the mighty waters." And Gabriel cried to God, "By the greatness of Thy glory dash Thy adversaries to pieces." Hereupon God bade Michael go and execute judgement upon the two magicians. The archangel seized hold of Jannes and Jambres by the locks of their hair, and he shattered them against the surface of the water.

Thus all the Egyptians were drowned. Only one was spared-Pharaoh himself. When the children of Israel raised their voices to sing a song of praise to God at the shores of the Red Sea, Pharaoh heard it as he was jostled hither and thither by the billows, and he pointed his finger heavenward, and called out: "I believe in Thee, O God! Thou art righteous, and I and My people are wicked, and I acknowledge now that there is no god in the world beside Thee." Without a moments delay, Gabriel descended and laid and iron chain about Pharaoh's neck, and holding him securely, he addressed him thus: "Villain! Yesterday thou didst say, 'Who is the Lord that I should hearken to His voice?' and now thou sayest, 'The Lord is righteous.'" With that he let him drop into the depths of the sea, and there he tortured him for fifty days, to make the power of God known to him. At the end of the time he installed him as king of the great city of Nineveh, and after the lapse of many centuries, when Jonah came to Nineveh, and prophesied the overthrow of the city on account of the evil done by the people, it was Pharaoh who, seized by fear and terror, covered himself with sackcloth, and sat in ashes, and with his own mouth made proclamation and published this decree through Nineveh: "Let neither man nor beast, herd nor flock, taste anything; let them not feed nor drink water; for I know there is no god beside Him in all the world, all His words are truth, and all His judgements are true and faithful."

Pharaoh never died, and never will die. He always stands at the portal of hell, and when the kings of the nations enter, he makes the power of God known to them at once, in these words: "O ye fools! Why have ye not learnt knowledge from me? I am denied the Lord God, and He brought ten plagues upon me, sent me to the bottom of the sea, kept me there for fifty days, released me then, and brought me up. Thus I could not but believe in Him."

God caused the Egyptians to be washed ashore in their death struggle. There were four reasons for this. The Israelites were not to say that as they themselves had escaped, so also the Egyptians had passed through the sea dryshod, only the latter had gone in another direction, and therefore had vanished from sight. The Egyptians, on the other hand, were not to think that the children of Israel had been drowned in the sea like themselves. In the third place, the Israelites were to have, as their booty, the silver, gold, and other precious things with which the Egyptians were decked; and, finally, the Israelites were to enjoy the satisfaction of seeing their enemies suffer. With their finger thy could point them out one by one, saying, "This one way my taskmaster, who beat me with those fists of his at which the dogs are now gnawing, and yonder Egyptian, the dogs are chewing the feet with which he kicked me."

As they lay on the shore in their last agony, they had to witness their own destruction and the victory of the Israelites, and they also beheld the suffering of their brethren that had remained behind in Egypt, for God poured out His punishment over the whole people, whether in Egypt or at the Red Sea. As for the corpses by the shores of the sea, they did not remain unburied, the earth swallowed them, by way of reward for Pharaoh's having acknowledged the justice of the chastisement that had been inflicted upon king and people. Before their corpses had been disposed of in this way, there had been a quarrel between the earth and the sea. The sea said to the earth, "Take thy children unto thyself," and the earth retorted, "Keep those whom thou hast slain." The sea hesitated to do as the earth bade, for fear that God would demand them back on the day of judgement; and the earth hesitated, because it remembered with terror the curse that had been pronounced upon it for having sucked up Abel's blood. Only after God swore and oath, not to punish it for receiving the corpses of the Egyptians, would the earth swallow them.

THE SONG AT THE SEA

Mighty is faith, for the spirit of God came upon the Israelites as a reward for their trust in God, and in His servant Moses; and it was in this exaltation that they sang to the Lord a song that moved Him to grant forgiveness for all their sins. This song was the second of the nine songs that in the course of history of Israel sang to their God. They assembled to sing the first in Egypt, on the night when they were freed from captivity; their second was the song of triumph by the Red Sea; their third, when the well sprang up in the wilderness; Moses sang the fourth before his death; the fifth was Joshua's song after his victory over the five Amorite Kings; Deborah and Barak sang the sixth when they conquered Sisera; the seventh was David's psalm of thanksgiving to God for his deliverance out of the hand of all his enemies; the eighth was Solomon's song at the dedication of the Temple; the ninth Jehoshaphat sang as, trusting in God, he went to battle against the Moabites and the Ammonites. The tenth and last song, however, will be that grand and mighty song, when Israel will raise their voice in triumph at their future deliverance, for that will be the final release of Israel for all time.

When Israel prepared to sound their praises to God for delivering them from destruction in the Red Sea, God, to show His recognition of Israel's fulfillment of the token of the Abrahamic covenant, bade the angels who came to intone their song, wait: "Let My children sing first," He said. This incident with the angels is like the story of the king who, upon returning from a victorious campaign, was told that his son and his servant were waiting with wreaths in their hands, and were asking who should first crown him. The king said, "O ye fools, to question if my servant should walk before my son! No, let my son come first!"

This was the second time the angels were obliged to retire before Israel. When Israel stood by the Red Sea, before them the rolling waters, and behind them the hosts of Egypt, then, too, the angels appeared, to sing their daily song of praise to the Lord, but God called to them, "Forbear! My children are in distress, and you would sing!"

But even after the men had completed their song, it was not yet given to the angels to raise their voices, for after the men followed the women of Israel, and only then came the turn of the angels. Then they began to murmur, and said, "Is it not enough that the men have preceded us? Shall the women come before us also?" But God replied, "As surely as ye live, so it is."

At first Israel requested their leader Moses to begin the song, but he declined, saying, "No, ye shall begin it, for it is a greater mark of honor to be praised by the multitude than by a single one." At once the people sang: "We will glorify the Eternal, for He has shown us signs and tokens. When the Egyptians passed the decree against us, and said, 'Every son that is born ye shall cast into the river,' our mothers went into the field, and Thou didst bid a sleep to fall upon them, and they bore us without any pain; and the angels descended from Heaven, washed and anointed us, and robed us in many-colored silken garments, and placed in our hands two lumps, one of butter and one of honey. When our mothers awoke and saw us washed, anointed, and clothed in silk, then they praised Thee, and said, 'Praise be God who has not turned His grace and His lasting love from the seed of our father Abraham; and now behold! they are in Thy hand, do with them as Thou wilt.' And they departed. When the Egyptians saw us, they approached to kill us, but Thou in Thy great mercy didst bid the earth swallow us and set us in another place, where we were not seen by the Egyptians, and lo! in this way didst Thou save us from their hand. When we grew up, we wandered in troops to Egypt, where each recognized his parents and his family. All this hast Thou done for us, therefore will we sing of Thee."

Thereupon Moses said: "Ye have given thanks to the Holy One, blessed be He, and not I will praise His name, for to me also has He shown signs and tokens. The Lord is my strength and my song, and He is become my salvation; He is my God, and I will prepare Him and habitation; my father's God, and I will exalt Him."

The song by the Red Sea was as much the song of Moses as of all Israel, for the great leader counted as not less than all the other Israelites together, and, besides, he had composed a large portion of the song. In virtue of the spirit of God that possessed them while they sang, Moses and the people mutually supplemented each other, so that, as soon as Moses spoke half the verse, the people repeated it, and linked the second complementary part to it. So Moses began with the half verse, "I will sing unto the Lord, for He hath triumphed gloriously," whereupon the people answered, "The horse and his rider hath He thrown into the sea." And in this wise developed the whole song.

But not alone the adults took part in this song, even the sucklings dropped their mothers' breasts to join in singing; yea, even the embryos in the womb joined the melody, and the angels' voices swelled the song. God so distinguished Israel during the passage through the Red Sea, that even the children beheld His glory, yea, even the woman slave saw more of the presence of God by the Red Sea than the Prophet Ezekiel was ever permitted to behold.

They closed the song with the words: "Let us set the crown of glory upon the head of our Deliverer, who suffers all things to perish, but does not Himself decay, who changes all things, but is Himself unchanged. His is the diadem of sovereignty, for He is the King of kings in this world, and His is the sovereignty of the world to come; it is His and will be His in all eternity." Thereupon Moses spake to Israel, "Ye have seen all the signs, all miracles and works of glory that the Holy One, blessed be He, hath wrought for you, but even more will He do for you in the world to come; for not like unto this world is the world of the hereafter; for in this world war and suffering, evil inclination, Satan, and the Angel of Death hold sway; but in the future would, there will be neither suffering nor enmity, neither Satan nor the Angel of Death, neither groans nor oppression, nor evil inclination."

As Moses and the race that wandered from Egypt with him sang a song to the Lord by the Red Sea, so shall they sing again in the world to come. In the world to come, all generations will pass before the Lord and will ask Him who should first intone the song of praise, whereupon He will reply: "In the past it was the generation of Moses that offered up to me a song of praise. Let them do it now once more, and as Moses conducted the song by the Red Sea, so shall he do in the world of the hereafter."

In other respects, too, it shall be in the world to come as it was at the time of the song by the sea. For when Israel intoned the song of praise, God put on a festive robe, on which were embroidered all the promises for a happy future to Israel. Among them were written: "Then shall thy light break forth as the morning"; "Then said they among the heathen. 'The Lord hath done great things for them,'" and many similar promises. But when Israel sinned, God rent the festive robe, and He will not restore it, or put it on until the coming of the future world.

After the men had completed the song, the women under the guidance of Miriam sang the same song to the accompaniment of music and dancing. The Israelites had had perfect faith, that God would perform for them miracles and deeds of glory, hence they had provided themselves with timbrels and with flutes, that they might have them at hand to glorify the anticipated miracles. Then Miriam said to the women, "Let us sing unto the Lord, for strength and sublimity are His; He lords it over the lordly, and He resents presumption. He hurled Pharaoh's horses and chariots into the sea, and drowned them, because wicked Pharaoh in his presumption pursued God's people, Israel."

THE AWFUL DESERT

Just as Israel had displayed sullenness and lack of faith upon approaching the sea, so did they upon leaving it. Hardly had they seen that the Egyptians met death in the waters of the sea, when they spoke to Moses, and said: "God had led us from Egypt only to grant us five tokens: To give us the wealth of Egypt, to let us walk in clouds of glory, to cleave the sea for us, to take vengeance on the Egyptians, and to let us sing Him a song of praise. Now that all this has taken place, let us return to Egypt." Moses answered: "The Eternal said, 'The Egyptians whom ye have seen to-day, yes shall see them again no more forever.'" But the people were not yet content, and said, "Now the Egyptians are all dead, and therefore we can return to Egypt." Then Moses said, "You must now redeem your pledge, for God said, 'When thou hast brought forth the people out of Egypt, ye shall serve God upon this mountain.'" Still the people remained headstrong, and without giving heed to Moses, they set out on the road to Egypt, under the guidance of an idol that they had brought with them out of Egypt, and had even retained during their passage through the sea. Only through sheer force was Moses able to restrain them from their sinful transgression. This was the second of the ten temptations with which Israel tempted God during their wanderings through the desert.

There was one other difficulty with the people that Moses had to overcome: The sea cast up many jewels, pearls and other treasures that had belonged to the Egyptians, drowned in its waves, and Israel found it hard to tear themselves away from the spot that brought them such riches. Moses, however, said, "Do you really believe that the sea will continue to yield you pearls and jewels?"

From the sea they passed to the desert Shur, a horrible and dreadful wilderness, full of snakes, lizards, and scorpions, extending over hundreds of miles. So deadly is the nature of the snakes that dwell in the desert, that if one of them merely glides over the shadow of a flying bird, the bird falls into pieces. It was in this desert that the following happened to King Shapor: A cohort that he sent through this desert was swallowed by a snake, and the same fate overtook a second and a third cohort. Upon the advice of his sages, he then filled the hides of animals with hot coals wrapped in straw, and had these cast before the snake until it expired.

It was then a proof of Israel's great faith in their God, that they obeyed Moses, and without murmur or delay followed him into this frightful wilderness. Therefore did God reward them for their trust in Him, for not only were they not harmed by the snakes and scorpions during their many years stay in the desert, but they were even relieved of the fear of the reptiles, for as soon as the snakes saw the Israelites, they meekly lay down upon the sand. For three days they marched through the desert, uncomplaining, but when their supply of water gave out, the people murmured against Moses, saying, "What shall we drink?" While crossing through the Red Sea they had provided themselves with water, for, miraculously, the sea flowed sweet for them; and now when the supply was becoming exhausted, they began to give expression to their dissatisfaction. On this occasion they again betrayed their faintheartedness, for instead of seeking advice from their leader Moses, they began to murmur against him and against God, even though at present they had not yet suffered from lack of water. So poorly did they stand the test to which God has put them, for in fact the very ground upon which they trod had running water beneath it, but they were not aware of this. God had desired to see how they would act under these conditions.

The people were all the more exasperated because their joy, when they sighted the springs and hastened to draw from the, turned to keenest disappointment when they tasted of the water and found it bitter. These deluded hopes cast them down spiritually as well as physically, and grieved them, not so much for their own sakes as for those of their young children, to whose pleas for water they could not listen without tears. Some of the thoughtless and fickle of faith among them uttered the accusation that even the former kindness had been granted them so much as a benefit, but rather with a view to the present and much greater privation. These said that death by the hand of the enemy is to be thrice preferred to perishing by thirst; for by the wise man, speedy and painless departure from life is in no way to be distinguished from immortality; the only real death, however, is slow and painful dying, for the dread lies not in being dead, but in dying.

While they indulged in these lamentations, Moses prayed to God to forgive the faint of heart their unseemly words, and, furthermore, to supply the general want. Mindful of the distress of the people, Moses did not pray long, but uttered his request in a few words; and quickly, as he had prayed, was his prayer answered. God bade him take a piece of a laurel tree, write upon it the great and glorious name of God, and throw it into the water, whereupon the water would become drinkable and sweet.

The ways of the Holy One, blessed be He, differ from the ways of man: Man turns bitter to sweet by the agency of some sweet stuff, but God transformed the bitter water through the bitter laurel tree. When Israel beheld this miracle, they asked forgiveness of their heavenly Father, and said: "O Lord of the world! We sinned against Thee when we murmured about the water." Not through this miracle alone, however, has Marah become a significant spot for Israel, but, especially, because there God gave to Israel important percepts, like the Sabbath rest, marriage and civil laws, and said to the people: "If you will observe these statutes, you will receive many more, the Ten Commandments, the Halakot, and the Haggadot; the Torah, however, will bring you happiness and life. If you will diligently endeavor to walk through life uprightly, so that you will be virtuous in your dealing with men, I will value it as if you had fulfilled all commandments, and will put upon you none of those diseases that I brought Egypt. If, however, you will not be mindful of My laws, and will be visited by diseases, then will I be you physician and will make you well, for as soon as you will observe the laws, shall the diseases vanish."

The cause for the want of water at Marah had been that for three days the people had neglected the study of the Torah, and it was for this reason that the prophets and elders of Israel instituted the custom of reading from the Torah on Saturday, Monday and Thursday, at the public service, so that three days might never again pass without a reading from the Torah.

From Marah they moved on to Elim. From a distance palm trees made the place look inviting enough, but when the people came close, they were again disappointed; there were not more than three score and ten palm tress, and there were of stunted growth owing to a lack of water, for in spite of the presence of twelve wells of water, the soil was so barren and sandy that the wells were not sufficient to water it. Here again the marvelous intercession of God in favor of the fate of Israel is shown, for the scant supply of water at Elim, which had hardly sufficed for seventy palm trees, satisfied sixty myriads of the wandering people that stayed there for several days.

The men of understanding could at this place see a clear allusion to the fortune of the people; for there are twelve tribes of the people, each of which, if it prove God-fearing, will be a well of water, inasmuch as its piety will constantly and continually bring forth beautiful deeds; the leaders of the people, however, are seventy, and they recall the noble palm tree, for in outward appearance as well as in its fruits, it is the most beautiful of trees, whose seat of life does not lie buried deep in the roots, as with other plants, but soars high, set like the heart in the midst of its branches, by which it is surrounded as a queen under the protection of her bodyguard. The soul of him who has tasted piety possesses a similar spirit; it has learned to look up and ascend, and itself ever busy with spiritual things and the investigation of Divine beauty, disdains earthly things, and considers them only a childish play, whereas that aspiration alone seems serious.

It was at Elim, where, at the creation of the world, God had made the twelve wells of water, and the seventy palm trees, to correspond to the twelve tribes and the seventy elders of Israel, that Israel first took up the study of the law, for there they studied the laws given them at Marah.

THE HEAVENLY FOOD

The bread which Israel had taken along out of Egypt sufficed for thirty-one days, and when they had consumed it, the whole congregation of the children of Israel murmured against their leader Moses. It was not only immediate want that oppressed them, but despair of a food supply for the future; for when they saw the vast, extensive, utterly barren wilderness before them, their courage gave way, and they said: "We migrated, expecting freedom, and now we are not even free from the cares of subsistence; we are not, as out leader promised, the happiest, but in truth the most unfortunate of men. After our leader's words had keyed us to the highest pitch of expectation, and had filled out ears with vain hopes, he tortures us with famine and does not provide even the necessary food. With the name of a new settlement he has deceived this great multitude; after he had succeeded in leading us from a well-known to an uninhabited land, he now plans to send us to the underworld, the last road of life. 'Would to God we had died by the hand of the Lord during the three days of darkness in the land of Egypt when we sat by the flesh-pots, and when we did eat bread to the full.'" In their exasperation they spoke untruths, for in reality they had suffered from want of food in Egypt, too, as the Egyptians had not given them enough to eat.

In spite of the railings against him, Moses was not so much indignant about their words as about the fickleness of the people. After those many quite extraordinary experiences they had no right to expect merely the natural and the probable, but should cheerfully have trusted him; for, truly, in the sight of all, they had been shown the most tangible proofs of his reliability. When, on the other hand, Moses considered their distress, he forgave them; for he told himself that a multitude is by nature fickle, and allows itself to be easily influenced by impressions of the moment, which cast the past into oblivion, and engender despair of the future.

God also forgave the unworthy conduct of Israel, and instead of being angry with them because they murmured against Him, when it should have been their duty to pray to Him, He was ready to grant them aid, saying to Moses, "They act according to their lights, and I will act according to Mine; not later than to-morrow morning manna will descend from heaven."

As a reward for Abraham's readiness, in answer to the summons to sacrifice Isaac, when he said, "Here am I," God promised manna to the descendants of Abraham with the same words, "Here I am." In the same way, during their wanderings through the wilderness, God repaid the descendants of Abraham for what their ancestor had done by the angels who visited him. He himself had fetched bread for them, and likewise God Himself caused bread to rain from heaven; he himself ran before them on their way, and likewise God moved before Israel; he had water fetched for them, and likewise God, through Moses, caused water to flow from the rock; he bade them seek shade under the tree, and likewise God had a cloud spread over Israel. Then God spoke to Moses: "I will immediately reveal Myself without Jacob, 'I will rain bread from My treasure in heaven for you; and the people shall go out and gather a certain rate every day.'"

There were good reasons for not exceeding a day's ration in the daily downpour of manna. First, that they might be spared the need of carrying it on their wanderings; secondly, that they might daily receive it hot; and, lastly, that they might day by day depend upon God's aid, and in this way exercise themselves in faith.

While the people were still abed, God fulfilled their desire, and rained down manna for them. For this food had been created on the second day of creation, and ground by the angels, it later descended for the wanderers in the wilderness. The mills are stationed in the third heaven, where manna is constantly being ground for the future use of the pious; for in the future world manna will be set before them. Manna deserves its name, "bread of the angels," not only because it is prepared by them, but because those who partake of it become equal to the angels in strength, and, furthermore, like them, have no need of easing themselves, as manna is entirely dissolved in the body. Not until they sinned, did they have to ease themselves like ordinary mortals.

Manna also showed its heavenly origin in the miraculous flavor it possessed. There was no need of cooking or baking it, nor did it require any other preparation, and still it contained the flavor of every conceivable dish. One had only to desire a certain dish, and no sooner had he thought of it, than manna had the flavor of the dish desire. The same food had a different taste to every one who partook of it, according to his age; to the little children it tasted like milk, to the strong youths like bread, to the old men like honey, to the sick like barley steeped in oil and honey.

As miraculous as the taste of manna was it descent from heaven. First came a north wind to sweep the floor of the desert; then a rain to wash it quite clean; then dew descended upon it, which was congealed into a solid substance by the wind, that it might serve as a table for the heaven-descending gold. But, that no insects or vermin might settle on the manna, the frozen dew formed not only a tablecloth, but also a cover for the manna, so that it lay enclosed there as in a casket, protected from soiling or pollution above and below.

THE GATHERING OF THE MANNA

With an easy mind every individual might perform his morning prayer in his house and recite the Shema', then betake himself to the entrance of his tent, and gather manna for himself and all his family. The gathering of manna caused little trouble, and those among the people who were too lazy to perform even the slightest work, went out while manna fell, so that it fell straight into their hands. The manna lasted until the fourth hour of the day, when it melted; but even the melted manna was not wasted, for out of it formed the rivers, from which the pious will drink in the hereafter. The heathen even then attempted to drink out of these streams, but the manna that tasted so deliciously to the Jews, had a quite bitter taste in the mouth of the heathen. Only indirectly could they partake of the enjoyment of manna: They used to catch the animals that drank the melted manna, and even it this form it was so delicious that the heathen cried, "Happy is the people that is in such a case." For the descent of manna was not a secret to the heathen, as it settled at such enormous heights that the kings of the East and of the West could see how Israel received its miraculous food.

The mass of the manna was in proportion to its height, for as much descended day by day, as might have satisfied the wants of sixty myriads of people, through two thousand years. Such profusion of manna fell over the body of Joshua alone, as might have sufficed for the maintenance of the whole congregation. Manna, indeed, had the peculiarity of falling to every individual in the same measure; and when, after gathering, they measured it, they found that there was an omer for every man.

Many lawsuits were amicably decided through the fall of manna. If a married couple came before Moses, each accusing the other of inconstancy, Moses would say to them, "To-morrow morning judgement will be given." If, then, manna descended for the wife before the house of her husband, it was known that he was in the right; but if her share descended before the house of her own parents, she was in the right.

The only days on which manna did not descend were the Sabbaths and the holy days, but then a double portion fell on the preceding day. These days had the further distinction that, while they lasted, the color of the manna sparkled more than usual, and it tasted better than usual. The people, however, were fainthearted, and on the very first Sabbath, they wanted to go out as usual to gather manna in the morning, although announcement had been made that God would send them no food on that day. Moses, however, restrained them. They attempted to do it again toward evening, and again Moses restrained them with the words, "To-day ye shall not find it in the field." At these words they were greatly alarmed, for they feared that they might not receive it any more at all, but their leader quieted them with the words, "To-day ye shall not find any of it, but assuredly to-morrow; in this world ye shall not receive manna on the Sabbath, but assuredly in the future world."

The unbelieving among them did not hearken to the words of God, and went out on the Sabbath to find manna. Here-upon God said to Moses: "Announce these words to Israel: I have led you out of Egypt, have cleft the sea for you, have sent you manna, have caused the well of water to spring up for you, have sent the quails to come up to you, have battled for you against Amalek, and wrought other miracles for you, and still you do not obey My statutes and commandments. You have not even the excuse that I imposed full many commandments upon you, for all that I bade you do at Marah, was to observe the Sabbath, but you have violated it." "If," continues Moses, "you will observe the Sabbath, God will give you three festivals in the months of Nisan, Siwan, and Tishri; and as a reward for the observance of the Sabbath, you will receive six gifts from God: the land of Israel, the future world, the new world, the sovereignty of the dynasty of David, the institution of the priests and the Levites; and, furthermore, as a reward for the observance of the Sabbath, you shall be freed from the three great afflictions: from the sufferings of the times of Gog and Magog, from the travails of the Messianic time, and from the day of the great Judgement."

When Israel heard these exhortations and promises, they determined to observe the Sabbath, and did so. They did not know, to be sure, what they had lost through their violation of the first Sabbath. Had Israel then observed the Sabbath, no nation would ever have been able to exercise any authority over them.

This, moreover, was not the only sin that Israel committed during this time, for some among them also broke the other commandment in regard to manna, that it, not to store it away from day to day. These sinners were none other than the infamous pair, Dathan and Abiram, who did not hearken to the word of God, but saved the manna for the following day. But if they fancied they could conceal their sinful deed, they were mistaken, for great swarms of worms bred from the manna, and these moved in a long train from their tents to the other tents, so that everyone perceived what these two had done.

To serve future generations as a tangible proof of the infinite power of God, the Lord bade Moses lay an earthen vessel full of manna before the Holy Ark, and this command was carried out by Aaron in the second year of the wanderings through the desert. When, many centuries later, the prophet Jeremiah exhorted his contemporaries to study the Torah, and they answered his exhortations, saying, "How shall we then maintain ourselves?" the prophet brought forth the vessel with manna, and spoke to them, saying: "O generation, see ye the word of the Lord; see what it was that served your fathers as food when they applied themselves to the study of the Torah. You, too, will God support in the same way, if you will but devote yourselves to the study of the Torah.

When the imminent destruction of the Temple was announced to King Josiah, he concealed the Holy Ark, and with it also the vessel with manna, as well as the jug filled with sacred oil, which was used by Moses for anointing the sacred implements, and other sacred objects. In the Messianic time the prophet Elijah will restore all these concealed objects.

Israel received three gifts during their wanderings through the desert: the well, the clouds of glory, and the manna; the first for the merits of Miriam, the second for those of Aaron, and the third for those of Moses. When Miriam died, the well disappeared for a time, but it reappeared as a reward for the merits of Aaron and Moses; when Aaron dies, the clouds of glory disappeared for a time, but reappeared owing to the merits of Moses. But when the last-named died, the well, the clouds of glory, and the manna disappeared forever. Throughout forty years, however, manna served them not only as food, but also as provender for their cattle, for the dew that preceded the fall of manna during the night brought grain for their cattle. Manna also replaced perfume for them, for it shed and excellent fragrance upon those who ate of it.

In spite of all the excellent qualities of manna, they were not satisfied with it, and demanded that Moses and Aaron give them flesh to eat. These replied: "We might put up with you if you murmured only against us, but you murmur against the Eternal. Come forward, that you may hear the judgment of God." At once God appeared to Moses, and said to him: "It is revealed to Me what the congregation of Israel have said, and what they will say, but tell them this: You have demanded two things; you have desired bread, and I gave it to you, because man cannot exist without it; but now, filled to satiety, you demand flesh; this also will I give you, so that you might not say if your wish were denied. 'God cannot grant it,' but at some future time you shall make atonement for it; I am a judge and shall assign punishment for this."

In the meantime, however, God granted their wish, and toward evening thick swarms of quails came up from the sea, and covered the whole camp, taking their flight quite low, not two ells above the ground, so that they might be easily caught. Contrary to the manna, which fell in the morning, the quails did not come before evenfall; with a radiant countenance God gave them the former, as their desire for bread was justified, but with a darkened mien, under cover of night, He sent quails. Now, because the one food came in the morning and the second in the evening, Moses instituted the custom among his people of taking two meals a day, one in the morning and one in the evening; and he set the meal with the use of meat for the evening. At the same time he taught them the prayer in which they were to offer thanks after eating manna, which read: "Blessed be Thou, O God our Lord, King of the world, who in Thy bounty, dost provide for all the world; who, in Thy grace, goodwill, and mercy, dost grant food to every creature, for Thy grace is everlasting. Thanks to Thy bounty we have never lacked food, nor ever shall lack it, for Thy great name's sake. For Thou suppliest and providest for all; Thou are bountiful, and nourishest all Thy creatures which Thou has made. Blessed be Thou, O God, that dost provide for all."

MIRIAM'S WELL

Relieved as they were of all the cares of subsistence through the gift of manna, it was plainly the duty of the Israelites to devote themselves exclusively to the study of the Torah. When, therefore, they slackened in the performance of this duty, punishment in the form of lack of water immediately overtook them. This was the first time that they actually experienced this want, for at Marah nothing more than alarm that this need might come upon them, had caused them to murmur and complain. In their distress they once more unreasonably cast reproaches upon their leader, and disputed with him, saying: "Wherefore is this, children, that thou hast brought us up out of Egypt, to kill us, and our children, and our cattle with thirst?" Moses replied: "As often as you quarrel with me, you tempt God, but God performeth wonders and excellent deeds for you, as often as you dispute with me, that His name may sound in glory throughout the world."

In spite of the injury they had done him, Moses prayed to God that He might aid them in their distress and also stand by him. "O Lord of the world!" said he, "I am surely doomed to die. Thou biddest me not to be offended with them, but if I obey Thy words, I shall certainly be killed by them." God, however, replied: "Try thou to act like Me; as I return good for evil, so do thou return to them good for evil, and forgive their trespass; go on before the people, and We shall see who dares touch thee." Hardly had Moses shown himself to the people, when all of them rose reverently from their seats, whereupon God said to Moses: "How often have I told thee not to be angry with them, but to lead them, as a shepherd leads his flock; it is for their sake that I have set thee on this height, and only for their sake wilt thou find grace, goodwill, and mercy in My sight."

Then God bade him go with some elders to the rock on Horeb, and fetch water out of it. The elders were to accompany him there, that they might be convinced that he was not bringing water from a well, but smiting it from a rock. To accomplish this miracle, God bade him smite the rock with his rod, as the people labored under the impression that this rod could only bring destruction, for through its agency Moses had brought the ten plagues upon the Egyptians in Egypt, and at the Red Sea; now they were to see that it could work good also. Upon God's bidding, Moses told the people to choose from which rock they wished water to flow, and hardly had Moses touched with his sapphire rod the rock which they had chosen, when plenteous water flowed from it. The spot where this occurred, God called Massah, and Meribah, because Israel had there tried their God, saying, "If God is Lord over all, as over us; if He satisfies our needs, and will further show us that He knows our thoughts, then will we serve Him, but not otherwise."

The water that flowed for them on this spot served not only as a relief for their present need, but on this occasion there was revealed to them a well of water, which did not abandon them in all their forty years' wandering, but accompanied them on all their marches. God wrought this great miracle for the merits of the prophetess Miriam, wherefore also it was called "Miriam's Well." But his well dates back to the beginning of the world, for God created it on the second day of the creation, and at one time it was in the possession of Abraham. It was this same well that Abraham demanded back from Abimelech, king of the Philistines, after the king's servants had violently taken it away. But when Abimelech pretended not to know anything about it, saying, "I wot not who hath done this thing," Abraham said: "Thou and I will send sheep to the well, and he shall be declared the rightful owner of the well, for whose sheep the water will spout forth to water them. And," continued Abraham, "from that same well shall the seventh generation after me, the wanderers in the desert, draw their supply."

This well was in the shape of a sieve-like rock, out of which water gushes forth as from a spout. It followed them on all their wanderings, up hill and down dale, and wherever they halted, it halted, too, and it settled opposite the Tabernacle. Thereupon the leaders of the twelve tribes would appear, each with his staff and chant these words to the well, "Spring up, O well, sing ye unto it; nobles of the people digged it by the direction of the lawgiver with their staves." Then the water would gush forth from the depths of the well, and shoot up high as pillars, then discharge itself into great streams that were navigable, and on these rivers the Jews sailed to the ocean, and hauled all the treasures of the world therefrom.

The different parts of the camp were separated by these rivers, so that women, visiting each other, were obliged to make use of ships. Then the water discharged itself beyond the encampment, where it surrounded a great plain, in which grew every conceivable kind of plant and tree; and these trees, owing to the miraculous water, daily bore fresh fruits. This well brought fragrant herbs with it, so that the women had no need of perfumes on the march, for the herbs they gathered served this purpose. This well furthermore threw down soft, fragrant kinds of grass that served as pleasant couches for the poor, who had no pillows or bedclothes. Upon the entrance to the Holy Land this well disappeared and was hidden in a certain spot of the Sea of Tiberias. Standing upon Carmel, and looking over the sea, one can notice there a sieve-like rock, and that is the well of Miriam. Once upon a time it happened that a leper bathed at this place of the Sea of Tiberias, and hardly had he come in contact with the waters of Miriam's well when he was instantly healed.

AMALEK'S WAR AGAINST ISRAEL

As a punishment because they had not had sufficient faith in God, and had doubted whether He could fulfill all their wishes, and had grown negligent in the study of the Torah and in the observance of the laws, God turned Amalek against them during their sojourn in Rephidim, where they had committed these sins. God dealt with them as did that man with his son, whom he bore through the river on his shoulders. Whenever the child saw something desirable, he said, "Father, buy it for me," and he fulfilled the child's wish. After the son had in this way received many beautiful things from his father, he called to a passing stranger with these words, "Hast thou perhaps seen my father?" Then, indignantly, the father said to his son: "O thou fool, that sittest on my shoulder! All that thou didst desire, did I procure for thee, and now dost thou ask of that man, 'Hast thou seen my father?'" Thereupon the father threw the child off his shoulder, and a dog came and bit him. So did Israel fare. When they moved out of Egypt, God enveloped them in seven clouds of glory; they wished for bread, and He gave them manna; they wished for flesh, and He gave them quails. After all their wishes had been granted, they began to doubt, saying, "Is the Lord among us, or not?" Then God answered, "You doubt My power; so surely as you live shall you discover it; the dog will soon bite you." Then came Amalek.

This enemy of Israel bore the name Amalek to denote the rapidity with which he moved against Israel, for like a swarm of locusts he flew upon them; and the name furthermore designates the purpose of this enemy, who came to suck the blood of Israel. This Amalek was a son of Eliphaz, the first-born son of Esau, and although the descendants of Jacob had been weaker and more insignificant in earlier times, Amalek had left them in peace, for he had excellent reasons to delay his attack. God had revealed to Abraham that his seed would have to serve in the land of the Egyptians, and had put the payment of this debt upon Isaac, and after his death, upon Jacob and his descendants. The wicked Amalek now said to himself, "If I destroy Jacob and his descendants, God will impose the Egyptians bondage upon, me, grandson of Esau, descendant of Abraham." Therefore he kept himself in restraint as long as Israel dwelt in Egypt, but only after the bondage predicted to the seed of Abraham had been served in full, did he set out to accomplish the war of annihilation against Israel, which his grandfather Esau had enjoined upon him.

No sooner had he heard of Israel's departure from Egypt, then he set out against them and met them by the Red Sea. There, indeed, he could work them no ill, for Moses uttered against him the Ineffable Name; and so great was his confusion, that he was forced to retreat without having effected his object. Then, for some time, he tried lying hidden in ambush, and in this wise molesting Israel, but as length he gave up this game of hide-and-seek, and with a bold front revealed himself as the open enemy of Israel. Not alone, however, did he himself declare war upon Israel, but he also seduced all the heathen nations to assist him in his enterprise against Israel. Although these declined to war upon Israel, fearing that they might have to fare like the Egyptians, they agreed to the following plan of Amalek. He said: "Follow my expedition. Should Israel conquer me, there will still be plenty of time for you to flee, but should success crown my attempt, join your fate to mine, in my undertaking against Israel." So Amalek now marched from his settlement in Seir, which was no less than four hundred parasangs away from the encampment of the Jews; and although five nations, the Hittites, the Hivites, the Jebusites, the Amorites, and the Canaanites, had their dwellings between his home and the camp of the Jews, he insisted upon being the first to declare war upon Israel.

God punished Israel, who had shown themselves an ungrateful people, by sending against them an enemy that was ungrateful, too, never recalling that he owed his life to the sons of Jacob, who had had him in their power after their brilliant victory over Esau and his followers.

In his expedition against Israel he made use of his kinsman. Before going over to open attack, he lured many unsuspecting Jews to death by his kindly words. He had fetched from Egypt the table of descent of the Jews; for every Jew had there to mark his name on the bricks produced by him, and these lists lay in the Egyptian archives. Familiar with the names of the different Jewish families, Amalek appeared before the Jewish camp, and calling the people by name, he invited them to leave the camp, and come out to him. "Reuben! Simeon! Levi! etc.," he would call, "come out to me, your brother, and transact business with me."

Those who answered the enticing call, found certain death at his hands; and not only did Amalek kill them, but he also mutilated their corpses, following the example of his grandsire Esau, by cutting off a certain part of the body, and throwing it toward heaven with the mocking words, "Here shalt Thou have what Thou desirest." In this way did he jeer at the token of the Abrahamic covenant.

So long as the Jews remained within the encampment, he could, of course, do them no harm, for the cloud enveloped them, and under its shelter they were as well fortified as a city that is surrounded by a solid wall. The cloud, however, covered those only who were pure, but the unclean had to stay beyond it, until they were cleansed by a ritual bath, and these Amalek caught and killed. The sinners, too, particularly the tribe of Dan, who were all worshippers of idols, were not protected by the cloud, and therefore exposed to the attacks of Amalek.

Moses did not himself set out to battle against this dangerous foe of Israel, but he sent his servant Joshua, and for good reasons. Moses knew that only a descendant of Rachel, like the Ephraimite Joshua, could conquer the descendant of Esau. All the sons of Jacob had taken part in the unbrotherly act of selling Joseph as a slave, hence none of their descendants might stand up in battle against the descendant of Esau; for they who had themselves acted unnaturally to a brother, could hardly hope for God's assistance in a struggle with the unbrotherly Edomites. Only the descendants of Joseph, the man who had been generous and good to his brothers, might hope that God would grant them aid against the unbrotherly descendants of Esau. In many other respects, too, Joseph was the opposite of Esau, and his services stood his descendants in good stead in their battles against the descendants of Esau. Esau was the firstborn of his father, but through his evil deeds he lost his birthright; Joseph, on the other hand, was the youngest of his father's sons, and through his good deeds was he found worthy of enjoying the rights of a firstborn son. Joseph had faith in the resurrection, while Esau denied it; hence God said, "Joseph, the devout, shall be the one to visit merited punishment on Esau, the unbelieving." Joseph associated with two wicked men, Potiphar and Pharaoh, yet he did not follow their example; Esau associated with two pious men, his father and his brother, yet he did not follow their example. "Hence," said God, "Joseph, who did not follow example of wicked men, shall visit punishment upon him who did not follow the example of pious men." Esau soiled his life with lewdness and murder; Joseph was chaste and shunned bloodshed, hence God delivered Esau's descendants into the hands of Joseph's descendants. And, as in the course of history only the descendants of Joseph were victorious over the descendants of Esau, so will it be in the future, at the final reckoning between the angel of Esau and the angels of the Jews. The angel of Reuben will be rebuffed by the angel of Esau with these words, "you represent on who had illegal relations with his father's wife"; the angels of Simeon and Levi will have the listen to this reproof, "You represent people who slew the inhabitants of Shechem"; the angel of Judah will be repulsed with the words, "Judah had illicit relations with his daughter-in-law." And the angels of the other tribes will be repulsed by Esau's angel, when he points out to them that they all took part in selling Joseph. The only one whom he will not be able to repulse will be Joseph's angel, to whom he will be delivered and by whom he will be destroyed; Joseph will b the flame and Esau the straw burned in the flame.

AMALEK DEFEATED

Moses now instructed Joshua in regard to his campaign against Amalek, saying, "Choose us out men and go out, fight with Amalek." The words "choose us" characterize the modesty of Moses, who treated his disciple Joshua as an equal; in these words he has taught us that the honor of our disciples should stand as high as our own. Joshua did not at first want to expose himself to danger and leave the protection of the cloud, but Moses said to him, "Abandon the cloud and set forth against Amalek, if ever thou dost hope to set the crown upon thy head." He commanded him to choose his warriors from among the pious and God-fearing, and promised him that he would set a fast day for the following day, and implore God, in behalf of the good deeds of the Patriarchs and the wives of the Patriarchs, to stand by Israel in this war.

Joshua acted in accordance with these commands and set out against Amalek, to conquer whom required not only skillful strategy, but also adeptness in the art of magic. For Amalek was a great magician and knew that propitious and the unpropitious hour of each individual, and in this way regulated his attacks against Israel; he attacked that one at night, whose death had been predicted for a night, and him whose death had been preordained for a day did he attack by day.

But in this art, too, Joshua was his match, for he, too, knew how to time properly the attack upon individuals, and he destroyed Amalek, his sons, the armies he himself commanded, and those under the leadership of his sons. But in the very heat of battle, Joshua treated his enemies humanely, he did not repay like with like. Far was it from him to follow Amalek's example in mutilating the corpses of the enemy. Instead with a sharp sword he cut off the enemies' heads, an execution that does not dishonor.

But only through the aid of Moses, did Joshua with his victory. Moses did not go out into battle, but through his prayer and through his influence upon the people in inspiring them with faith, the battle was won. While the battle raged between Israel and Amalek, Moses was stationed on a height, where, supported by the Levite Aaron and the Judean Hur, the representatives of the two noble tribes Levi and Judah, he fervently implored God's aid. He said: "O Lord of the world! Through me has Thou brought Israel out of Egypt, through me hast Thou cleft the sea, and through me has Thou wrought miracles; so do Thou now work miracles for me, and lend me victory to Israel, for I well know that while all other nations fight only to the sixth hour of the day, this sinful nation stand in battle ranks till sunset." Moses did not consider it sufficient to pray alone to God, but he raised his hands toward heaven as a signal for the whole nation to follow his example and trust in God. As often as he then raised his hands to heaven and the people prayed with him, trusting that God would lend them victory, they were indeed victorious; as often, however, as Moses let down his hands and the people ceased prayer, weakening in their faith in God, Amalek conquered. But it was hard for Moses constantly to raise his hands. This was God's way of punishing him for being somewhat negligent in the preparations for the war against Amalek. Hence Aaron and Hur were obliged to hold up his arms and assist him in his prayer. As, furthermore, he was unable to stand all that time, he seated himself on a stone, disdaining a soft and comfortable seat, saying, "So long as Israel is in distress, I shall share it with them."

At evenfall, the battle was not yet decided, therefore Moses prayed to God that He might stay the setting of the sun and thus enable Israel to draw the battle to a close. God granted this prayer, for the sun did not set until Israel had completely destroyed their enemy. Thereupon Moses blessed Joshua with the words, "Some day the sun shall stand still for thy sake, as it did to-day for mine," and this blessing was later fulfilled at Gibeon, when the sun stood still to help Joshua in his battle against the Amorites.

Although Amalek had not received the merited punishment from the hands of Joshua, still his enterprise against Israel had not been entirely unavailing. The miraculous exodus of Israel out of Egypt, and especially the cleaving of the sea, had created such alarm among the heathens, that none among them had dared to approach Israel. But this fear vanished as soon as Amalek attempted to compete in battle with Israel. Although he was terrible beaten, still the fear of the inaccessibility of Israel was gone. It was with Amalek as with that foolhardy wight who plunged into a scalding-hot tub. He scalded himself terribly, yet the tub became cold through his plunge into it. Hence God was not content with the punishment Amalek received in the time of Moses, but swore by His throne and by His right hand that He would never forget Amalek's misdeeds, that in this world as well as in the time of the Messiah He would visit punishment upon him, and would completely exterminate him in the future world. So long as the seed of Amalek exist, the face of God is, as it were, covered, and will only then come to view, when the seed of Amalek shall have been entirely exterminated.

God had at first left the war against Amalek in the hands of His people, therefore He bade Joshua, the future leader of the people, never to forget the war against Amalek; and if Moses had listened intently, he would have perceived from this command of God that Joshua was destined to lead the people into the promised land. But later, when Amalek took part in the destruction of Jerusalem, God Himself took up the war against Amalek, saying, "By My throne I vow not to leave a single descendant of Amalek under the heavens, yea, no one shall even be able to say that this sheep or that wether belonged to an Amalekite."

God bade Moses impress upon the Jews to repulse no heathen should he desire conversion, but never to accept an Amalekite as a proselyte. It was in consideration of this word of God that David slew the Amalekite, who announced to him the death of Saul and Jonathan; for he saw in him only a heathen, although he appeared in the guise of a Jew.

Part of the blame for the destruction of Amalek falls upon his father, Eliphaz. He used to say to Amalek: "My son, dost thou indeed know who will posses this world and the future world?" Amalek paid no attention to his allusion to the future fortune of Israel, and his father urged it no more strongly upon him, although it would have been his duty to instruct his son clearly and fully. He should have said to him: "My son, Israel will posses this world as well as the future world; dig wells then for their use and build road for them, so that thou mayest be judged worthy to share in the future world." But as Amalek had not been sufficiently instructed by his father, in his wantonness he undertook to destroy the whole world. God, who tries the reins and the heart, said to him: "O thou fool, I created thee after all the seventy nations, but for thy sins thou shalt be the first to descend into hell."

To glorify the victory over Amalek, Moses built an altar, which God called "My Miracle," for the miracle God wrought against Amalek in the war of Israel was, as it were, a miracle for God. For so long as the Israelites dwell in sorrow, God feels with them, and a joy for Israel is a joy for God, hence, too, the miraculous victory over Israel's foe was a victory for God.

JETHRO

"Smite a scorner, and the simple will beware." The destruction of Amalek brought Jethro to his senses. Jethro was originally in the same plot with Amalek, both having incited Pharaoh against Israel, but when he saw that Amalek lost this world and the other, he repented of his sinful ways, saying: "There is nothing left to me but to go over to the God of Israel"; and although he dwelt in the greatest wealth and honor, he determined to set out for the desert, to Moses and his God. Arrived at the camp of Israel, he could not enter it, for it was enveloped by a cloud that none could pierce, hence he wrote a letter to Moses and shot it off with an arrow, so that it fell into the camp. The letter read: "I adjure thee, by thy two sons and by thy God, to come to meet me and receive me kindly. If thou wilt not do if for my sake, do it for thy wife's sake; and if thou wilt not do it for her sake, do it for thy sons' sake." For Jethro brought with him his daughter Zipporah, from whom Moses had been divorced, as well as her two sons, her only children, for after her separation from Moses, she had wed no other man.

At first Moses was inclined to give no ear to this letter, but God said to him: "I, through whose word the world came into being, I bring men to Me and do not thrust them back. I permitted Jethro to approach Me, and did not push him from Me. So do thou, too, receive this man, who desires to betake himself under the wings of the Shekinah, let him approach, and do not repulse him." God herewith taught Moses that one should repulse with the left hand, and beckon with the right.

Moses, Aaron, Nadab, and Abihu, together with the seventy elders of Israel, carrying with them the sacred Ark, hastened to welcome Jethro kindly; and Moses so honored his father-in-law as to make an obeisance before him and kiss him. Before Moses told his father-in-law of the great miracles God had wrought for Egypt, such as the exodus from Egypt, the cleaving of the sea, the rain of manna, and the rest, he offered him the greeting of peace; for great is peace, that precedes event he praise of God. After the peace-greeting, Moses, to draw his father-in-law nearer to true faith in God and His revelation, began to relate to him the miracles that God had wrought for them at the exodus from Egypt, during the passing through the Red Sea, and during the war with Amalek. He said, moreover, "In the manna that God gives us we perceive the taste of bread, of meat, of fish, in short, of all the dishes there are. Out of the well that God gives us we draw a drink that possesses the taste of old wine as well as new, of milk and of honey, in short, of all the beverages that exist." "We shall," Moses continued, "receive six other gifts from God, the land of Israel, the future world, the new world, the sovereignty of David, the institution of priests, and of Levites."

When Jethro heard all this, he determined to become a Jew and to believe in the only God, and although he felt a pang at heart upon hearing that the Egyptians had perished-for no one should scoff at a heathen before a proselyte who is not a Jew of ten generation's standing-still he burst into a song of praise to God for the deeds He had one for His people. In truth, it reflects shame upon Moses and the sixty myriads of Jews that they had not given thanks to God for the release from Egypt, until Jethro came and did so. He said: "Praised be God who delivered Moses and Aaron, as well as the whole nation of Israel, from the bondage of Pharaoh, that great dragon, and of the Egyptians. Truly, great is the Lord before all gods, for whereas formerly not a single slave succeeded in escaping from Egypt, He led sixty myriads out of Egypt. There is no god whom I had not, at some time in my life, worshipped, but not I must admit that none is like the God of Israel. This God had not been unbeknown to me heretofore, but now I know Him better, for His fame will sound throughout the world, because He visited upon the Egyptians exactly what they had planned to undertake against Israel. They wanted to destroy Israel by water, and by water were they destroyed."

With sacrifices and a feast was the arrival of Jethro celebrated, for after he had made the burnt offering not far from the bush of thorns that had been unscathed by fire, Jethro prepared a feast of rejoicing for the whole people, at which Moses did not consider it below the dignity to wait on the guests in person. In this he followed the example of Abraham, who in person waited on the three angels, though they appeared in the guise of idolatrous Arabs.

Abraham like Moses sought to follow in the ways of the Lord, to provide each according to his wants, and to grant to everybody what he lacks, whether he be a righteous man, or an idolater, who through his sins conjures up God's wrath.

To this feast the people sat down according to their tribes. They ate, drank and were merry, while Aaron and Jethro with their relatives sang songs of thanksgiving to God, and praised Him as the Creator and Donor of their lives and their liberty. At the same time they gave due appreciation to Moses, through whose courage everything had happily come to pass. In his words of gratitude to Moses, Jethro also gave expression to many glorious eulogies on the people of Israel, but he especially extolled Moses, who through difficulties and dangers had shown so much courage in the salvation of his friends.

Chapter 2

THE INSTALLATION OF ELDERS

Jethro, who had come to Moses shortly before the revelation on Mount Sinai, stayed with his son-in-law for more than a year. In the first months, however, he had no opportunity of observing Moses in the capacity of judge, for Moses spent the time from the day of the revelation to the tenth day of Tishri almost entirely in heaven. Hence Jethro could not be present at a court proceeding of his before the eleventh day of Tishri, the first day after Moses' return from heaven. Jethro now perceived how Moses sat like a king upon his throne, while the people, who brought their lawsuits before him, stood around him. This so displeased him that he said to his son-in-law: "Why sittest thou thyself alone, and all the people stand by thee from morning until even?" Moses answered: "Because the people come unto me to enquire of God. It is not in my honor that they stand, but in honor of God, whose judgement they would know. When they are in doubt over a case of clean or unclean, or when there is a dispute between two parties, which they desire to have settled exactly according to the law, or in conformity with a compromise, they come to me; and when the parties at dispute leave me, they part as friends and no longer enemies. I expound to the people, besides, the words of God and His decisions."

On the day that Moses again took up his activity as a judge, and Jethro had for the first time the chance of observing him, came the mixed multitude with the pleas that they, like the other Israelites, wanted their share in the Egyptians booty. Moses' method, first seen by him in practice, struck Jethro as most absurd, and he therefore said: "The thing that thou doest is not good," through delicacy softening his real opinion, "It is bad" to "It is not good." "The people," he continued, "will surely unbraid thee and Aaron, his two sons Nadab and Abihu, and the seventy elders, if thou continuest in this fashion. But if thou hearkenest now to my voice, thou wilt fare well, provided God approves of my plan. This is, that thou shalt be 'the vessel of the revelations of God,' and shalt lay the revelations of God before the people, as often as thou receivest them; so that they may understand the exposition of the Torah, as well as its decisions. And thou shalt instruct them how to pray in the synagogues, how to tend the sick, how to bury their dead, how to render the services of friendship to one another, how to practice justice, and how, in some cases, not to insist on strict justice. But as for trying the people as a judge, thou shouldst, in accordance with thy prophetic insight, choose men that are possessed of wisdom, fear of God, modesty, hate of covetousness, love of truth, love of humanity, and a good name, and these shall devote all their time to trials, and to the study of the study of the Torah. If God approve my plan, then wilt thou and Aaron, his sons and the seventy elders, and all the people dwell in peace."

This counsel of Jethro's found great favor in Moses' eyes, for he had been only too well aware of the difficulties and annoyances with which he had had to contend. The people were very disputatious, being willing to spend seventy silverlings in litigation costs for the sake of gaining one silverling, and did their utmost to lengthen their disputes at law. When on say that Moses was about to cast a decision against him, he demanded that his lawsuit be adjourned, declaring that had witnesses and other proofs, which he would bring forward on the next occasion. But they were not merely litigious and disputatious, they were also spiteful, and vented their temper on Moses. If Moses went out early, they would say: "Behold the son of Amram, who betakes himself early to the gathering of manna, that he may get the largest grains." If he went out late, they would say: "Behold the son of Amram, he goes through the multitude, to gather in marks of hone." But if he chose a path aside from the crowd, they said: "Behold the son of Amram, who makes it impossible for us to follow the simple commandment, to hone a sage." Then Moses said: "If I did this you were not content, and if I did that you were not content! I can no longer bear you alone. 'The Eternal, your God, hath multiplied you, and behold, ye are this day as the stars of heaven for multitude. The Lord, God of you fathers, make you a thousand times so many as ye are, and bless you, as he hath promised you!"

The Israelites were not content with this blessing of Moses, and said to him: "O our teacher Moses, we do not desire thee to bless us, we have had much greater blessings given to us. God spoke to our father Abraham: 'I will bless thee and in multiplying I will multiply thy seed as the stars of the heaven, and as the sand which is upon the sea shore,' and thou dost limit our blessings." Moses cried: "I am only a creature of flesh and blood, limited in my powers, hence is my blessing limited. I give you my blessing, but the blessing of God remains preserved for ye, and He will bless you unlimitedly, and multiply you as the fish of the sea and the sands on the seashore, as the star in the sky and the plants on the earth."

After he had bestowed his blessing upon them, he asked them to propose capable pious men, that he might appoint them as judges and leaders over them. He said: "If a man were to present himself to me as a candidate for this position of honor, I alone should not be able to decide to what tribe he belonged, and whence he came; but you know them, and hence it is advisable for you to propose them. Do not think, however, that I feel I must abide by your choice, for it depends solely upon me, whether or not I shall appoint them."

The people were very eager to carry this plan of Moses into execution, and requested him to settle the matter as quickly as possible. But their motive was self-interested, for every one among them said: "Moses will now appoint about eighty thousand officials. If I myself should not be among them, surely my son will be, and if not he, my grandson, and with a gift of some kind it will be an easy matter to induce such a judge to look after my interests at court." Moses, of course, was not deceived about their true sentiments; still, he paid no further attention to them, and picked out the best men among the people, though they were not possessed of nearly all the good qualities Jethro had thought essential for judges and leaders of people. With kindly words he invited them to assume their offices, and said: "Blessed are ye that are judged worthy of being leader of the children of Abraham, Isaac, and Jacob, of a people whom God called His friends, His brothers, His flock, and other titles of love." He impressed upon them that they must possess much patience, and must not become impatient if a lawsuit is brought before them more than once. "Heretofore," he said, "you belonged to yourselves, but from now you belong to the people; for you judge between every man, and his brother and his neighbor. If ye are to appoint judges, do so without respect of persons. Do not say 'I will appoint that man because he is a handsome man or a strong man, because he is my kinsman, or because he is a linguist.' Such judges will declare the innocent guilty and the guilty innocent, not through wickedness, but through ignorance; and God will reckon the appointment of such judges against you, as a perversion of justice, on account of your respect of persons. If a wealthy man and a poor man come before you to court, do not say: 'Why should I insult the rich man for so small a matter? I will rather give judgement in his favor, and then, outside the court, tell him to give the poor man what he demands, as he is in the right.' But do not, on the other hand, if the poor man is in the wrong, say: 'The rich man is obliged to assist the poor anyhow, I will now decide in favor of the poor, that in a decent way he may, without begging, obtain money from his rich fellow-man.' Do not, moreover, say: 'I fear to pronounce judgement, lest that man kill my son, burn my barn, or destroy my plants,' for the judgement is God's."

After these admonitions, Moses instructed the new judges in legal procedure, in both civil and criminal cases, and at the same time urged the people no to deny the judges the veneration due him. For great is the importance of justice. For him who hates it, there is no remedy; but the judge who decides conscientiously is the true peacemaker, for the weal of Israel, of the commonwealth, and indeed of all living creatures.

JETHRO REWARDED

Although the installation of elders on Moses' part came to pass in accordance with the command of God, still it was Jethro upon whose advice Moses besought God to lighten his burden, and to permit him partly to transfer the leadership of the people to others. Hence he did not conceal the name of the adviser, but announced it to all the people, and immortalized him as such in the Holy Scriptures; for he deemed it praiseworthy to appreciate duly the merits of others. It had, however, been part of God's scheme to reward Jethro for the love he bore the Torah; and for this reason did He allow it to come to pass that Moses had to have his attention called to the plan of installing the elders through his father-in-law, that the Holy Scriptures might devote a whole chapter to the plan of Jethro.

This, however, is not the only reward for Jethro's piety, who, in his love for the Torah, excelled all proselytes. A miracle occurred on the very first day of his arrival in camp for manna in his honor descended at the noon hour, the hour of his arrival; and, moreover, in as great quantities as was wont to rain down for sixty myriads of Israelites. He did not have to exert himself to gather the food, for it came over his body, so all he had to do was to carry his hand to his mouth to partake of it. Jethro, nevertheless, did not remain with Moses, but returned to his native land. Moses, of course, tried to persuade his father-in-law to stay. He said to him: "Do not think that we shall continue to move thus slowly through the desert, nay, we shall now move directly to the promised land." Only to urge Jethro to stay longer with them did Moses use the words "we move," so that his father-in-law might believe that Moses too would enter the promised land, for otherwise he would hardly have allowed himself to be persuaded to join the march to Palestine. Moses continued: "I do not want to mislead thee, hence I will tell thee that the land will be divided only among the twelve tribes, and that thou has no claim to possession of lands; but God bade us be kind to the proselytes, and to thee we shall be kinder than to all other proselytes." Jethro, however, was not to be persuaded by his son-in-law, considering himself in duty bound to return to his native land. For the inhabitants of his city had for many years made a habit of having him store their valuable, as none possessed their confidence in such a measure as he. If he had stayed still longer with Moses, people would have declared that he had absconded with all these things and fled to Moses to share it with him, and that would have been a blot on his fair name and that of Moses. Jethro had furthermore made many debts during the year in which he came to Moses, for, owing to the hail God had sent upon Egypt before the exodus of Israel, a great famine had arisen in Jethro's home too, and he had found himself obliged to lend money for the support of the poor. If he were not now to return to his home, people would say that he had run away in order to evade his creditors, and such talk concerning a man of piety would have been desecration of the Divine Name. So he said to Moses: "There are people who have a fatherland, but no property there; there are also property-holders who have no family; but I have a fatherland, and have property there as well as a family; hence I desire to return to my fatherland, my property, and my family." But Moses would not yield so soon, and said to his father-in-law: "If thou dost not accompany us as a favor, I will command thee to do so, that the Israelites might not say thou hadst been converted to our religion only in the expectation of receiving a share in the promised land, but hadst returned to thy home when thou didst discover that proselytes have no claim on property in the Holy Land. Through thy refusal to move with us, thou wilt give the heathens an opportunity to say that the Jews do not accept proselytes, since they did not accept even their own king's father-in-law, but allowed him to return to his own land. Thy refusal will injure the glory of God, for the heathens will keep away from the true faith. But if thou wilt wander with us, I assure thee that they seed shall share with us the Temple, the Torah, and the future reward of the pious. How canst thou, moreover, who hast seen all the miracles of God wrought for us during the march through the desert; who wert a witness of the way in which even the Egyptians became fond of us-how canst thou now depart from us? It is a sufficient motive for thee to remain with us, in order to officiate as a member of the Sanhedrin, and teach the Torah. We, on our part, want to retain thee, only that thou mightest in difficult cases enlighten our eyes; for thou wert the man who gave us good and fair counsel, to which God Himself could not refuse His assent." Jethro replied: "A candle may glow in the dark, but not when the sun and the moon; of what avail would my candle-light be? I had, therefore, better return to my home city that I may make proselytes of its inhabitants, instruct them in the Torah, and lead them under the wings of the Shekinah." Amid great marks of honor, and provided with rich gifts, Jethro returned to his home, where he converted his kinsmen and his compatriots to the belief in the true God, as he had intended.

The descendants of Jethro later settled in Palestine, where the fruitful land of Jericho was allotted to them as a dwelling place. After the capture of Palestine, the tribes, by mutual consent, agreed that the fertile strip of land at Jericho should fall to the share of the tribe on whose land the Temple was to be erected. But when its erection was postponed for a long time, they agreed to allot this piece of land to Jethro's sons, because they, being proselytes, had no other possession in the Holy Land. Four hundred and eighty years did the descendants of Jethro dwell in Jericho, when, upon the erection of the Temple at Jerusalem, they relinquished it to the tribe of Judah, who claimed it as an indemnity for the site of the Temple.

Jethro's descendants inherited his devotion to the Torah, like him dedicating their lives entirely to its study. So long as Joshua lived, they sat at this master's feet, but when he died, they said: "We left our fatherland and came here only for the sake of studying the Torah; if we were now to spend our time in cultivating the soil, when should we study the Torah?" They therefore gave up their dwelling-place in Jericho, and moved to the cold barren wilderness, to Jabez, who there had his house of instruction. But when they there beheld the priests, the Levites, and the noblest of the Jews, they said, "How can we, proselytes, presume to sit beside these?" Instead of sitting within the house of instruction, they remained at the entrance of it, where they listened to the lectures, and in this manner made further progress in the study of the Torah. They were rewarded for their piety, their prayer was heard by God, and their good deeds served as a protection to Israel; and on account of their pious actions they were called "the families of the scribes," the Tirathites, the Shimeathites, and the Suchathites, names designating their piety and devotion to the Torah.

One of the descendants of Jethro was Jonadab, son of Rechab, who, when he heard from a prophet that God would destroy the Temple, bade all his children, as a toke of mourning, to drink no wine, use no oil for anointing themselves, nor cut their hair, nor dwell in houses. The Rechabites obeyed this command of their sire, and as a reward for this, God made a covenant with them that their descendants should always be members of the Sanhedrin, and teachers of Israel. The covenant with the Rechabites was even stronger than that with David, for to the house of the latter God promised to keep the covenant only if his descendants were pious, but He made an unconditional covenant with the Rechabites. God rewarded them for their devotion to Him in this way, although they did not belong to the Jewish nation. From this one can gather how great would have been their reward if they had been Israelites.

THE TIME IS AT HAND

Moses sent his father-in-law Jethro back to his home, shortly before the revelation on Mount Sinai. He thought: "When God gave us a single commandment of the Torah in Egypt, the Passover, He said, 'There shall no stranger eat thereof.' Surely Jethro may not look on when God bestows on us the whole Torah." Moses was right: God did not want Jethro to be present at the revelation. He said: "Israel was in Egypt, bound to work with clay and bricks, at the same time as Jethro was sitting at home in peace and quiet. He who suffers with the community shall share their future joys, but he who does not share the sufferings of the community shall not take part in their rejoicing."

God had not only good cause to delay the giving of the Torah until after the departure of Jethro, but the time He chose to bestowing it was also chosen for a good reason. Just as a female proselyte, or a woman freed from captivity, or an emancipated slave, may not enter wedlock before she has for three months lived as a free Jewess, so God also waited three months after the deliverance of Israel from the bondage and the slavery of Egypt, before His union with Israel on Mount Sinai. God furthermore treated His bride as did that king who went to the marriage ceremony only after he had overwhelmed his chosen bride with many gifts. So did Israel first receive manna, the well, and the quails, and not till then was the Torah granted them. Moses, who had received this promise when God had first appeared to him, viz., "When thou has brought forth the people out of Egypt, ye shall serve God upon this mountain"-waited most longingly for the promised time, saying, "When will this time come to pass?" When the time drew near, God said to Moses, "The time is at hand when I shall bring about something entirely new."

This new miracle of which God spoke was the healing of all the sick among the Jews. God had wanted to give the Torah to the Jews immediately after the exodus from Egypt, but among them were found many that were lame, halt, or deaf; wherefore God said: "The Torah is without a blemish, hence would I not bestow it on a nation that has in it such as are burdened with defects. Nor do I want to wait until their children shall have grown to manhood, for I do not desire any longer to delay the delight of the Torah." For these reasons nothing was left Him to do, but to heal those afflicted with disease. In the time between the exodus from Egypt and the revelation on Mount Sinai, all the blind among the Israelites regained their sight, all the halt became whole, so that the Torah might be given to a sound and healthy people. God wrought for that generation the same miracle which He will hereafter bring about in the future world, when "the eyes of the blind shall be opened, the ears of the deaf shall be unstopped, the lame man leap as an hart, and the tongues of the dumb sing." Not only physically was this generation free from blemishes, but spiritually, too, it stood on a high plane, and it was the combined merits of such a people that made them worthy of their high calling. Never before or after lived a generation as worthy as this of receiving the Torah. Had there been but one missing, God would not have given them the Torah: "for He layeth up wisdom for the righteous; He is a buckler to them that walk uprightly."

For one other reason did God delay the revelation of the Torah. He had intended giving them the Torah immediately after their exodus from Egypt, but at the beginning of the march through the desert, great discord reigned among them. Nor was harmony established until the new moon of the third month, when they arrived at Mount Sinai; whereupon God said: "The ways of the Torah are ways of loveliness, and all its paths are paths of peace; I will yield the Torah to a nation that dwells in peace and amity." This decision of God, now to give them the Torah, also shows how mighty is the influence of penance. For they had been sinful upon their arrival at Mount Sinai, continuing to tempt God and doubting His omnipotence. After a short time, however, they changed in spirit; and hardly had they reformed, when God found them worthy of revealing to them the Torah.

The third month was chosen for the revelation, because everything that is closely connected with the Torah and with Israel is triple in number. The Torah consists of three parts, the Pentateuch, the Prophets, and the Hagiographa; similarly the oral law consists of Midrash, Halakah, and Haggadah. The communications between God and Israel were carried on by three, Moses, Aaron, and Miriam. Israel also is divided into three divisions, priests, Levites, and laymen; and they are, furthermore, the descendants of the three Patriarchs, Abraham, Isaac, and Jacob. For God has a preference for "the third": It was the third of Adam's sons, Seth, who became the ancestor of humanity, and so too it was the third among Noah's sons, Shem, who attained high station. Among the Jewish kings, too, it was the third, Solomon, whom God distinguished before all others. The number three plays a particularly important part in the life of Moses. He belonged to the tribe of Levi, which is not only the third of the tribes, but has a name consisting of three letters. He himself was the third of the children of the family; his own name consists of three letters; in his infancy he had been concealed by his mother throughout three months; and in the third month of the year, after a preparation of three days, did he receive the Torah on a mountain, the name of which consists of three letters.

THE GENTILES REFUSE THE TORAH

The mountain on which God made his revelation bears six names: It is called the Desert Sin, because God there announced His commandments; it is called the Desert Kadesh, because Israel was sanctified there; the Desert Kadmut because the pre-existing Torah was there revealed; the Desert Paran because Israel there was greatly multiplied; the Desert Sinai because the hatred of God against the heathens began there, for the reason that they would not accept the Torah; and for this same reason is it called Horeh, because the annihilation of the heathens was there decreed by God. For the wrath of God against the heathens dates from their refusal to accept the Torah offered them.

Before God gave Israel the Torah, He approached every tribe and nation, and offered them the Torah, that hereafter they might have no excuse to say, "Had the Holy one, blessed be He, desired to give us the Torah, we should have accepted it." He went to the children of Esau and said, "Will ye accept the Torah?" They answered Him, saying, "What is written therein?" He answered them, "Thou shalt not kill." Then they all said: "Wilt Thou perchance take from us the blessing with which our father Esau was blessed? For he was blessed with the words, 'By thy sword shalt thou live." We do not want to accept the Torah." Thereupon He went to the children of Lot and said to them, "Will ye accept the Torah?" They said, "What is written therein?" He answered, "Thou shalt not commit unchastity." They said: "From unchastity do we spring; we do no want to accept the Torah." Then He went to the children of Ishmael and said to them, "Do ye want to accept the Torah?" They said to Him, "What is written therein?" He answered, "Thou shalt not steal." They said: "Wilt Thou take from us the blessing with which our father was blessed? God promised him: 'His hand will be against every man.' We do not want to accept the Thy Torah." Thence He went to all the other nations, who likewise rejected the Torah, saying: "We cannot give up the law of our fathers, we do not want Thy Torah, give it to Thy people Israel." Upon this He came to Israel and spoke to them, "Will ye accept the Torah?" They said to Him, "What is written therein?" He answered, "Six hundred and thirteen commandments." They said: "All that the Lord has spoken will we do and be obedient." "O Lord of the world!" they continued, "We acted in accordance with Thy commandments before they were revealed to us. Jacob fulfilled the first of the Ten Commandments by bidding his sons put away strange gods that were among them. Abraham obeyed the commandment not to take the name of the Lord in vain, for he said: 'I have lifted up mine hand unto the Lord, the most high God.' Joseph fulfilled the commandment to remember the Sabbath and keep it holy; and when his brothers came to him, he had everything for their welcome prepared on Friday. Isaac observed the law to honor his father and his mother, when he allowed Abraham to bind him on the altar as a sacrifice. Judah observed the commandment not to kill when he said to his brothers, 'What profit is it if we slay our brother and conceal his blood?' Joseph observed the law: 'Thou shalt not commit adultery,' when he repulsed the desire of the wife of Potiphar. The other sons of Jacob observed the commandment: 'Thou shalt not steal,' saying: 'How then should we steal out of thy lord's house silver and gold?' Abraham observed the commandment: 'Thou shalt not bear false witness,' for he was a true witness, and bore witness before all the world that Thou art the Lord of all creation. It was Abraham, also, who observed the last of the Ten Commandments 'Thou shalt not covet,' saying: 'I will not take from a thread even to a shoe-latchet.'"

THE CONTEST OF THE MOUNTAINS

While the nations and peoples were refusing to accept the Torah, the mountains among themselves were fighting for the honor of being chosen as the spot for the revelation. One said: "Upon me shall the Shekinah of God rest, and mine shall be this glory," whereupon the other mountain replied: "Upon me shall the Shekinah rest, and mine shall be this glory." The mountain of Tabor said to the mountain of Hermon: "Upon me shall the Shekinah rest, mine shall be this glory, for in times of old, when in the days of Noah the flood came over the earth, all the mountains that are under the heavens were covered with water, whereas it did not reach my head, nay, not even my shoulder. All the earth was sunk under water, but I, the highest of the mountains, towered high above the waters, hence I am called upon to bear the Shekinah." Mount Hermon replied to Mount Tabor: "Upon me shall the Shekinah rest, I am the destined one, for when Israel wished to pass through the Red Sea, it was I who enabled them to do so, for I settled down between the two shores of the sea, and they moved from one side to the other, through my aid, so that not even their clothes became wet." Mount Carmel was quite silent, but settled down on the shore of the sea, thinking: "If the Shekinah is to repose on the sea, it will rest upon me, and if it is to repose on the mainland, it will rest upon me." Then a voice out of the high heavens rang out and said: "The Shekinah shall not rest upon these high mountains that are so proud, for it is not God's will that the Shekinah should rest upon high mountains that quarrel among themselves and look upon one another with disdain. He prefers the low mountains, and Sinai among these, because it is the smallest and most insignificant of all. Upon it will He let the Shekinah rest." The other mountains hereupon said to God, "Is it possible that Thou are partial, and wilt give us no reward for our good intention?" God replied: "Because ye have striven in My honor will I reward ye. Upon Tabor will I grant aid to Israel at the time of Deborah, and upon Carmel will I give aid to Elijah."

Mount Sinai was given the preference not for its humility alone, but also because upon it there had been no worshipping of idols; whereas the other mountains, owing to their height, had been employed as sanctuaries by the idolaters. Mount Sinai has a further significance, too, for it had been originally a part of Mount Moriah, on which Isaac was to have been sacrificed; but Sinai separated itself from it, and came to the desert. Then God said: "Because their father Isaac lay upon this mountain, bound as a sacrifice, it is fitting that upon it his children receive the Torah." Hence God now chose this mountain for a brief stay during the revelation, for after the Torah had been bestowed, He withdrew again to heaven. In the future world, Sinai will return to its original place, Mount Moriah, when "the mountain of the Lord's house shall be established in the top of the mountains, and shall be exalted above the hills."

Just as Sinai was chosen as the spot for the revelation owing to its humility, so likewise was Moses. When God said to Moses, "Go, deliver Israel," he in his great humility, said: "Who am I that I should go to Pharaoh and lead the children of Israel out of Egypt? There are nobler and wealthier than I." But God replied: "Thou are a great man, thee have I chosen out of all Israel. Of thee shall the prophet of the future say, 'I have laid help upon one that is mighty; I have exalted on chosen out of the people.'" Moses in his humility, however, still stood apart and would not accept the office offered him, until God said to him "Why dost thou stand apart? If they are not to be delivered by thee, by none other will they be delivered." When, likewise, at God's command Moses had erected the Tabernacle, he did not enter it, out of great humility, until God said to him, "Why dost thou stand outside? Thou are worthy to serve Me."

THE TORAH OFFERED TO ISRAEL

On the second day of the third month, Moses received word form God to betake himself to Mount Sinai, for without this direct summons he would not have gone there. This time, as at all times, when God desired to speak with Moses, He twice called him by name, and after he had answered, "Here I am," God's revelation to him followed. When Moses had been carried to God in a cloud, which was always ready to bear him to God and the restore him to men, God said to him: "Go and acquaint the women of Israel with the principles of Judaism, and try with kindly words to persuade them to accept the Torah; but expound the full contents of the Torah to the men, and with them speak solemn words concerning it."

There were several reasons for his going to the women first. God said: "When I created the world, I gave My commandment concerning the forbidden fruit to Adam only, and not to his wife Eve, and this omission had the effect that she tempted Adam to sin. Hence it appears advisable that the women first hear My commandments, and the men will then follow their counsel." God, furthermore, knew that women are more scrupulous in their observance of religious percepts, and hence He first addressed Himself to them. Then, too, God expected the women to instruct their children in the ways of the Torah, wherefore He sent His messenger first to them.

The words that Moses was to address to the women as well as to the men, to the Sanhedrin as well as to the people, were as follows: "You yourselves have seen-for it is not from writings, or through tradition, or from the mouths of others that ye learn it-what I did for you in Egypt; for although they were idolaters, slayers of men, and men of lewd living, still I punished them not for these sins, but only for the wrong done to you. But ye will I carry on the wings of eagles, on the day of the revelation at Sinai, and ye will I bring to Me when the Temple shall be erected. Since I have wrought for you so many miracles, even before you had received the Torah and observed the laws, how many more miracles will I work for you, when you will have received the Torah and observed the laws! The beginning of all things is hard, but as soon as you will have grown accustomed to obedience, all else will be easy to you. If you will now observe the Abrahamic covenant, the Sabbath, and the commandment against idolatry, then will you be My possession; for although everything belongs to Me, Israel will be My especial possession, because I led them out of Egypt, and freed them from bondage. With respect to Israel, God is like one who receive many fields as an heritage, but one he purchased himself, and the one he earned was dearest to his heart. I will reign alone over you, as My possession, I and none other, so long as you keep yourselves aloof from other peoples. If not, other peoples shall reign over you. But if you obey Me, you shall be a nation, not only free from care, but also a nation of priests, and a holy nation."

If Israel had not sinned through worshipping the Golden Calf, there would be among them no caste of priests, the nation would have been a nation of priests, and it was only after their sin that the greater part of the people lost the right to priesthood.

God now instructed Moses to transmit to the people His words without adding to them or diminishing from them, in the precise order and in the same tongue, the Hebrew. Moses hereupon betook himself to the people to deliver his message, without first seeing his family. He first addressed the word of God to the elders, for he never forgot the honor due the elders. Then, in simple and well arranged form, he repeated it to all the people, including the women. Joyfully and of his own impulse, every Israelite declared himself willing to accept the Torah, whereupon Moses returned to God to inform Him of the decision of the people. For although God, being omniscient, had no need of hearing from Moses the answer of the people, still propriety demands that one who is sent on a message return to make a report of his success to him who sent him. God hereupon said to Moses: "I will come to thee in a thick cloud and repeat to thee the commandments that I gave thee on Marah, so that what thou tellest them may seem to the people as important as what they hear from Me. But not only in thee shall they have faith, but also in the prophets and sages that will come after thee."

Moses then returned to the people once more, and explained to them the serious effects that disregard of the law would have upon them. The first time he spoke to them about the Torah, he expounded its excellencies to them, so as to induce them to accept it; but now he spoke to them of the terrible punishments they would bring upon themselves, if they did not observe the laws. The people did not, however, alter their resolution, but were full of joy in the expectation of receiving the Torah. They only wished Moses to voice to God their desire to hear Him impart His words directly to them, so they said to Moses, "We want to hear the words of our King from Himself." They were not even content with this, but wanted to see the Divine presence, for "hearing is not like seeing." God granted both their wishes, and commanded Moses to tell them to prepare themselves during the next two days for receiving the Torah.

ISRAEL PREPARES FOR THE REVELATION

Just as one who is to be admitted to Judaism must first submit to the three ceremonies of circumcision, baptism, and sacrifice, so Israel did not receive the Torah until they had performed these three ceremonies. They had already undergone circumcision in Egypt. Baptism was imposed upon them two days before the revelation on Mount Sinai. On the day preceding the revelation Moses recorded in a book the covenant between Israel and their God, and on the morning of the day of the revelation, sacrifices were offered as a strengthening of the covenant.

As there were no priests at that time, the service was performed by the elders of Israel, who in spite of their age performed their duty with youthful vigor. Moses erected an altar on Mount Sinai, as well as twelve memorial pillars, one for each tribe, and then bade them bring bulls, as a burnt offering and a peace offering. The blood of these animals was then separated exactly into two halves. This was attended to by the angel Michael, who guided Moses' hand, and so conducted the separation of the blood that there might be not a drop more in one half than in the other. God upon this said to Moses: "Sprinkle the one half of the blood upon the people, as a token that they will not barter My glory for the idols of other peoples; and sprinkle the other half on the altar, as a token that I will not exchange them for any other nation." Moses did as he was bidden, and lo! the miracle came to pass that the blood of a few animals sufficed to sprinkle every single Israelite.

Before this covenant between God and Israel had been made, Moses read aloud to the people all of the Torah, that they might know exactly what they were taking upon themselves. This covenant was made a second time in the desert of Moab by Moses, and a third time by Joshua after the entrance into the promised land, on the mountains of Gerizim and Ebal.

Although the people had now clearly expressed their desire to accept the Torah, still God hesitated to give it to them, saying: "Shall I without further ado give you the Torah? Nay, bring Me bondsmen, that you will observe it, and I will give you the Torah." Israel: "O Lord of the world! Our fathers are bondsmen for us." God: "Your fathers are My debtors, and therefore not good bondsmen. Abraham said, 'Whereby shall I know it?' and thus proved himself lacking in faith. Isaac loved Esau, whom I hated, and Jacob did not immediately upon his return from Padan-Aram keep his vow that he had made upon his way there. Bring Me good bondsmen and I will give you the Torah." Israel: "Our prophets shall be our bondsmen." God: "I have claims against them, for 'like foxes in the deserts became your prophets.' Bring Me good bondsmen and I will give you the Torah." Israel: "We will give Thee our children as bondsmen." God: "Well, then, these are good bondmen, on whose bond I will give you the Torah." Hereupon the Israelites brought their wives with their babes at their breasts, and their pregnant wives, and God made the bodies of the pregnant women transparent as glass, and He addressed the children in the womb with these words: "Behold, I will give your fathers the Torah. Will you be surety for them that they will observe it?" They answered: "Yea." He furthermore said: "I am your God." They answered: "Yea." "Ye shall have no other gods." They said: "Nay." In this wise the children in the womb answered every commandment with "Yea," and every prohibition with "Nay." As it was the little children upon whose bond God gave His people the Torah, it comes to pass that many little children die when Israel does not observe the Torah.

THE REVELATION ON MOUNT SINAI

From the first day of the third month, the day on which Israel arrived at Mount Sinai, a heavy cloud rested upon them, and every one except Moses was forbidden to ascend the mountain, yea, they durst not even stay near it, lest God smite those who pushed forward, with hail or fiery arrows. The day of the revelation announced itself as an ominous day even in the morning, for diverse rumblings sounded from Mount Sinai. Flashes of lightning, accompanied by an ever swelling peal of horns, moved the people with mighty fear and trembling. God bent the heavens, moved the earth, and shook the bounds of the world, so that the depths trembled, and the heavens grew frightened. His splendor passed through the four portals of fire, earthquake, storm and hail. The kings of the earth trembled in their palaces, and they all came to the villain Balaam, and asked him if God intended the same fate for them as for the generation of the flood. But Balaam said to them: "O ye fools! The Holy One, blessed be He, has long since promised Noah never again to punish the world with a flood." The kings of the heathen, however, were not quieted, and furthermore said: "God has indeed promised never again to bring a flood upon the world, but perhaps He now means to destroy it by means of fire." Balaam said: "Nay, God will not destroy the world either through fire or through water. The commotion throughout nature was caused through this only, that He is not about to bestow the Torah upon His people. 'The Eternal will give strength unto His people.'" At this all the kings shouted, "May the Eternal bless His people with peace," and each one, quieted in spirit, went to his house.

Just as the inhabitants of the earth were alarmed at the revelation, and believed the end of all time had arrived, so too did the earth. She thought the resurrection of the dead was about to take place, and she would have to account for the blood of the slain that she had absorbed, and for the bodies of the murdered whom she covered. The earth was not calmed until she heard the first words of the Decalogue.

Although phenomena were perceptible on Mount Sinai in the morning, still God did not reveal Himself to the people until noon. For owing to the brevity of the summer nights, and the pleasantness of the morning sleep in summer, the people were still asleep when God had descended upon Mount Sinai. Moses betook himself to the encampment and awakened them with these words: "Arise from your sleep, the bridegroom is at hand, and is waiting to lead his bride under the marriage-canopy." Moses, at the head of the procession, hereupon brought the nation to its bridegroom, God, to Sinai, himself going up the mountain. He said to God: "Announce Thy words, Thy children are ready to obey them." These words of Moses rang out near and far, for on the occasion, his voice, when he repeated the words of God to the people, had as much power as the Divine voice that he heard.

It was not indeed quite of their own free will that Israel declared themselves ready to accept the Torah, for when the whole nation, in two divisions, men and women, approached Sinai, God lifted up this mountain and held it over the heads of the people like a basket, saying to them: "If you accept the Torah, it is well, otherwise you will find you grave under this mountain." They all burst into tears and poured out their heart in contrition before God, and then said: "All that the Lord hath said, will we do, and be obedient." Hardly had they uttered these words of submission to God, when a hundred and twenty myriads of angels descended, an provided every Israelite with a crown and a girdle of glory-Divine gifts, which they did not lose until they worshipped the Golden Calf, when the angels came and took the gifts away from them. At the same time with these crowns and girdles of glory, a heavenly radiance was shed over their faces, but this also they later lost through their sins. Only Moses retained it, whose face shone so brightly, that if even to-day a crack were made in his tomb, the light emanating from his corpse would be so powerful that it could not but destroy all the world.

After God had bestowed upon Israel these wonderful gifts, He wanted to proceed to the announcement of the Torah, but did not desire to do so while Moses was with Him, that the people might not say it was Moses who had spoken out of the cloud. Hence He sought an excuse to be rid of him. He therefore said to Moses: "Go down, warn the people, that they shall not press forward to see, for if even one of them were to be destroyed, the loss to Me would be as great as if all creation had been destroyed. Bid Nadab and Abihu also, as well as the first born that are to perform priestly duties, beware that they do not press forward." Moses, however, desirous of remaining with God, replied: "I have already warned the people and set the bounds beyond which they may not venture." God hereupon said to Moses: "Go, descend and call upon Aaron to come up with thee, but let him keep behind thee, while the people do not move beyond the positions thou hadst assigned them." Hardly had Moses left the mountain, when God revealed the Torah to the people.

This was the sixth revelation of God upon earth since the creation of the world. The tenth and last is to take place on the Day of Judgement.

The heavens opened and Mount Sinai, freed from the earth, rose into the air, so that its summit towered into the heavens, while a thick cloud covered the sides of it, and touched the feet of the Divine Throne. Accompanying God on one side, appeared twenty-two thousand angels with crowns for the Levites, the only tribe that remained true to God while the rest worshipped the Golden Calf. On the second side were sixty myriads, three thousand five hundred and fifty angels, each bearing a crown of fire for each individual Israelite. Double this number of angels was on the third side, whereas on the fourth side they were simply innumerable. For God did not appear from one direction, but from all four simultaneously, which, however, did not prevent His glory from filling the heaven as well as all the earth. In spite of these innumerable hosts of angels there was no crowding on Mount Sinai, no mob, there was room for all the angels that had appeared in honor of Israel and the Torah. They had, however, at the same time received the order to destroy Israel in case they intended to reject the Torah.

THE FIRST COMMANDMENT

The first word of God on Sinai was Anoki, "It is I." It was not a Hebrew word, but and Egyptian word that Israel first heard from God. He treated them as did that king his home-coming son, whom, returning from a long stay over sea, he addressed in the language the son had acquired in a foreign land. So God addressed Israel in Egyptian, because it was the language they spoke. At the same time Israel recognized in this word "Anoki," that is was God who addressed them. For when Jacob had assembled his children around his death-bed, he warned them to be mindful of the glory of God, and confided to them the secrets that God would hereafter reveal to them with the word "Anoki." He said: "With the word 'Anoki' He addressed my grandfather Abraham; with the word 'Anoki' He addressed my father Isaac, and with the word 'Anoki' He addressed me. Know, then, that when He will come to you, and will so address, you, it will be He, but not otherwise."

When the first commandment had come out of the mouth of God thunder and lightning proceeded from His mouth, a torch was at His right, and a torch at His left, and His voice flew through the air, saying: "My people, My people, House of Israel! I am the Eternal, you God, who brought you out of the land of Egypt." When Israel heard the awful voice, they flew back in their horror twelve miles, until their souls fled from them. Upon this the Torah turned to God, saying: "Lord of the world! Hast Thou given me to the living, or to the dead?" God said: "To the living." The Torah: "But they are all dead." God: "For thy sake will I restore them to life." Hereupon He let fall upon them the dew that will hereafter revive the dead, and they returned to life.

The trembling of heaven and earth that set in upon the perception of the Divine voice, alarmed Israel so greatly that they could hardly stand on their feet. God hereupon sent to every one of them two angels; on lay his hand upon the heart of each, that his soul might not depart, and on to lift the head of each, that he might behold his Maker's splendor. They beheld the glory of God as well as the otherwise invisible word when it emanated from the Divine vision, and rolled forward to their ears, whereupon they perceived these words: "Wilt thou accept the Torah, which contains two hundred and forty-eight commandments, corresponding to the number of the members of they body?" They answered: "Yea, yea." Then the word passed from the ear to the mouth; it kissed the mouth, then rolled again to the ear again to the ear, and called to it: "Wilt thou accept the Torah, which contains three hundred and sixty-five prohibitions, corresponding to the days of the year?" And when they replied, "Yea, yea," again the word turned from the ear to the mouth and kissed it. After the Israelites had in this wise taken upon themselves the commandments and the prohibitions, God opened the seven heavens and the seven earths, and said: "Behold, these are My witnesses that there is none like Me in the heights or on earth! See that I am the Only One, and that I have revealed Myself in My splendor and My radiance! If anyone should say to you, 'Go, serve other gods,' then say: 'Can one who has seen his Maker, face to face, in His splendor, in His glory and His strength, leave Him and become an idolater?' See, it is I that have delivered you out of the house of bondage; it is I that cleaved the seas before you and led you on dry land, while I submerged you enemies in the depths. I am the God of the dry land as well as the sea, of the past as well as of the future, the God of this world as well as of the future worlds. I am the God of all nations, but only with Israel is My name allied. If they fulfil My wishes, I, the Eternal, am merciful, gracious and long suffering, and abundant in goodness and truth; but if you are disobedient, then will I be a stern judge. If you had not accepted the Torah, no punishment could have fallen upon you were you not to fulfil it, but now that you have accepted it, you must obey it."

In order to convince Israel of the unity and uniqueness of God, He bade all nature stand still, that all might see that there is nothing beside Him. When God bestowed the Torah, no bird sang, no ox lowed, the Ofannim did not fly, the Seraphim uttered not their "Holy, holy, holy," the sea did not roar, no creature uttered a sound-all listened in breathless silence to the words announced by an echoless voice, "I am the Lord you God."

These words as well as the others, made know by God on Mount Sinai, were not heard by Israel alone, but by the inhabitants of all the earth. The Divine voice divided itself into the seventy tongues of men, so that all might understand it; but whereas Israel could listen to the voice without suffering harm, the souls of the heathens almost fled from them when they heard it. When the Divine voice sounded, all the dead in Sheol were revived, and betook themselves to Sinai; for the revelation took place in the presence of the living as well as of the dead, yea, even the souls of those who were not yet born were present. Every prophet, every sage, received at Sinai his share of the revelation, which in the course of history was announced by them to mankind. All heard indeed the same words, but the same voice, corresponding to the individuality of each, was God's way of speaking with them. And as the same voice sounded differently to each one, so did the Divine vision appear differently to each, wherefore God warned them not to ascribe the various forms to various beings, saying: "Do not believe that because you have seen Me in various forms, there are various gods, I am the same that appeared to you at the Red Sea as a God of war, and at Sinai as a teacher."

THE OTHER COMMANDMENTS REVEALED ON SINAI

After Israel had accepted the first commandment with a "Yea," God said: "As you have now acknowledged Me as you sovereign, I can now give you commands: Thou shalt not acknowledge the gods of other nations as such, for they bring no advantage to those who adore them; this thou shalt not do while I exist. I have given you my Torah in order to lend sovereignty to you, hence you must not kindle My wrath by breaking My covenant through idolatry. You shall not worship dead idols, but Him who kills and restores to life, and in whose hand are all living things. Do not learn the works of other nations, for their works are vanity. I, the Eternal, you God, rule over zeal and am not ruled by it; I wait until the fourth generation to visit punishment. But those who love Me, or fear Me, will I reward even unto the thousandth generation."

When Moses heard these words, according to which God would visit upon the descendants the sins of their fathers only if the consecutive generations were one after another sinful, he cast himself upon the ground and thanked God for it; for he knew it never occurred among Israel that three consecutive generations were sinful.

The third commandment read: "O My people of Israel, none among you shall call the name of the Lord in vain, for he who swears falsely by the name of the Lord shall not go unpunished on the great Judgement Day." Swearing falsely has terrible consequences not only for the one who does it, but it endangers all the world. For when God created the world, He laid over the abyss a shard, on which is engraved the Ineffable Name, that the abyss may not burst forth and destroy the world. But as often as on swears falsely in God's name, the letters of the Ineffable Name fly away, and as there is then nothing to restrain the abyss, the waters burst forth from it to destroy the world. This would surely come to pass, if God did not sent the angel Ya'asriel, who has charge of the seventy pencils, to engrave anew the Ineffable Name on the shard.

God said then to Israel, "If you accept My Torah and observe My laws, I will give you for all eternity a thing most precious that I have in My possession." "And what," replied Israel, "is that precious thing which Thou wilt give us if we obey Thy Torah?" God: "The future world." Israel: "But even in this world should we have a foretaste of that other." God: "The Sabbath will give you this foretaste. Be mindful of the Sabbath on the seventh day of the creation of the world." For when the world was created, the seventh day came before God, and said to Him: "All that Thou has created is in couples, why not I?" Whereupon God replied, "The community of Israel shall be thy spouse." Of this promise that God had made to the seventy day, He reminded the people on Mount Sinai, when he gave them the fourth commandment, to keep the Sabbath holy.

When the nations of the earth heard the first commandment, they said: "There is no king that does not like to see himself acknowledged as sovereign, and just so does God desire His people to pledge unto Him their allegiance." At the second commandment they said: "No king suffers a king beside himself, nor does the God of Israel." At the third commandment they said: "Is there a king that would like to have people swear false oaths by his name?" At the fourth commandment they said: "No King dislikes to see his birthday celebrated." But when the people heard the fifth commandment, "Honor thy father and thy mother," they said: "According to our laws, if a man enrolls himself as a servant of the king, he thereby disowns his parents. God, however, makes it a duty to honor father and mother; truly, for this is honor due to Him."

It was with these words that the fifth commandment was emphasized: "Honor thy parents to whom thou owest existence, as thou honorest Me. Honor the body that bore thee, and the breasts that gave thee suck, maintain thy parents, for thy parents took part in thy creation." For man owes his existence to God, to his father, and to his mother, in that he receives from each of his parents five of the parts of his body, and ten from God. The bones, the veins, the nails, the brain, and the white of the eye come from the father. The mother gives him skin, flesh, blood, hair, and the pupil of the eye. God gives him the following: breath, soul, light of countenance, sight, hearing, speech, touch, sense, insight, and understanding. When a human being honors his parents, God says: "I consider it as if I had dwelled among men and they had honored Me," but if people do not honor their parents, God say: "It is good that I do not dwell among men, or they would have treated Me superciliously, too."

God not only commanded to love and fear parents as Himself, but in some respects He places the honor due to parents even higher than that due Him. A man is only then obliged to support the poor or to perform certain religious ceremonies, if he has the wherewithal, but it is the duty of each one even to go begging at men' doors, if he cannot otherwise maintain his parents.

The sixth commandment said: "O My people Israel, be no slayers of men, do not associate with murderers, and shun their companionship, that your children may not learn the craft of murder." As a penalty for deeds of murder, God will send a devastating war over mankind. There are two divisions in Sheol, an inner and an outer. In the latter are all those who were slain before their time. There they stay until the course of the time predestined them is run; and every time a murder has been committed, God says: "Who has slain this person and has forced Me to keep him in the outer Sheol, so that I must appear unmerciful to have removed him from earth before his time?" On the Judgement Day the slain will appear before God, and will implore Him: "O Lord of the world! Thou hast formed me, Thou hast developed me, Thou hast been gracious unto me while I was in the womb, so that I left it unharmed. Thou in Thy great mercy hast provided for me. O Lord of all worlds! Grant me satisfaction from this villain that knew no pity for me." Then God's wrath will be kindled against the murderer, into Gehenna will he throw him and damn him for all eternity, while the slain will see satisfaction given him, and be glad.

The seventh commandment says: "O My people of Israel, be not adulterers, nor the accomplices or companions of adulterers, that your children after you may not be adulterers. Commit no unchaste deeds, with your hands, feet, eyes, or ears, for as a punishment therefore the plague will come over the world."

This is the eighth commandment: "Be not thief, nor the accomplice or companion of thieves, that your children may not become thieves." As a penalty for robbery and theft famine will come upon the world. God may forgive idolatry, but never theft, and He is always ready to listen to complaints against forgers and robbers.

The ninth commandment reads: "O My people of Israel, bear not false witness against your companions, for in punishment for this the clouds will scatter, so that there may be no rain, and famine will ensue owing to drought." God is particularly severe with a false witness because falsehood is the one quality that God did not create, but is something that men themselves produces.

The content of the tenth commandment is: "O My people Israel, covet not the possessions of your neighbors, for owing to this sin will the government take their possessions from the people, so that even the wealthiest will become poor and will have to go into exile." The tenth commandment is directed against a sin that sometimes leads to a trespassing of all the Ten Commandments. If a man covets his neighbor's wife and commits adultery, he neglects the first commandment: "I am the Eternal, thy God," for he commits his crime in the dark and thinks that none sees him, not even the Lord, whose eyes float over all the world, and see good as well as evil. He oversteps the second commandment: "Thou shalt not have strange gods besides Me..., I am a jealous God," who is wroth against faithlessness, whether toward Me, or toward men. He breaks the third commandment: "Thou shalt not take the name of the Lord in vain," for he swears he has not committed adultery, but he did so. He is the cause of profanation of the Sabbath, the consecration of which God commands in the fourth commandment, because in his illegal relation he generates descendants who will perform priestly duties in the Temple on the Sabbath, which, being bastards, they have no right to do. The fifth commandment will be broken by the children of the adulterer, who will honor as a father a strange man, and will not even know their true father. He breaks the sixth commandment: "Thou shalt not kill," if he is surprised by the rightful husband, for every time a man goes to a strange woman, he does so with the consciousness that this may lead to his death or the death of his neighbor. The trespassing of the seventh commandment: "Thou shalt not commit adultery," is the direct outcome of a forbidden coveting. The eighth commandment: "Thou shalt not steal," is broken by the adulterer, for he steals another man's fountain of happiness. The ninth commandment" "Thou shalt not bear false witness," is broken by the adulterous woman, who pretends that the fruit of her criminal relations is the child of her husband. In this way, the breaking of the tenth commandment has not only led to all the other sins, but has also the evil effect that the deceived husband leaves his whole property to one who is not his son, so that the adulterer robs him of his possessions as well as of his wife.

THE UNITY OF THE TEN COMMANDMENTS

The Ten Commandments are so closely interwoven, that the breaking of one leads to the breaking of another. But there is a particularly strong bond of union between the first five commandments, which are written on one table, and the last five, which were on the other table. The first commandment: "I am the Lord, thy God," corresponds to the sixth: "Thou shalt not kill," for the murderer slays the image of God. The second: "Thou shalt have no strange gods before me," corresponds to the seventh: "Thou shalt not commit adultery," for conjugal faithlessness is as grave a sin as idolatry, which is faithlessness to God. The third commandment: "Thou shalt not take the name of the Lord in vain," corresponds to the eighth: "Thou shalt not steal," for theft leads to false oath. The fourth commandment: "Remember the Sabbath day, to keep it holy," corresponds to the ninth: "Thou shalt not bear false witness against thy neighbor," for he who bears false witness against his neighbor commits as grave a sin as if he had borne false witness against God, saying that He had not created the world in six days and rested on the seventh, the Sabbath. The fifth commandment: "Honor thy father and thy mother," corresponds to the tenth: "Covet not thy neighbor's wife," for one who indulges this lust produces children who will not honor their true father, but will consider a stranger their father.

The Ten Commandments, which God first revealed on Mount Sinai, correspond in their character to the ten words of which He had made use at the creation of the world. The first commandment: "I am the Lord, thy God," corresponds to the first word at the creation: "Let there be light," for God is the eternal light. The second commandment: "Thou shalt have no strange gods before me," corresponds to the second word: "Let there be a firmament in the midst of the waters, and let it divide the waters from the waters." For God said: "Choose between Me and the idols; between Me, the fountain of living waters, and the idols, the stagnant waters." The third commandment: "Thou shalt not take the name of thy God in vain" corresponds to the word: "Let the waters be gathered together," for as little as water can be gathered in a cracked vessel, so can a man maintain his possession which he has obtained through false oaths. The fourth commandment: "Remember to keep the Sabbath holy," corresponds to the word: "Let the earth bring forth grass," for he who truly observes the Sabbath will receive good things from God without having to labor for them, just as the earth produces grass that need not be sown. For at the creation of man it was God's intention that he be free from sin, immortal, and capable of supporting himself by the products of the soil without toil. The fifth commandment: "Honor thy father and thy mother," corresponds to the word: "Let there be lights in the firmament of the heaven," for God said to man: "I gave thee two lights, thy father and thy mother, treat them with care." The sixth commandment: "Thou shalt not kill," corresponds to the word: "Let the waters bring forth abundantly the moving creature," for God said: "Be not like the fish, among whom the great swallow the small." The seventh commandment: "Thou shalt not commit adultery," corresponds to the word: "Let the earth bring forth the living creature after his kind," for God said: "I chose for thee a spouse, abide with her." The eighth commandment: "Thou shalt not steal," corresponds to the word: "Behold, I have given you every herb-bearing seed," for none, said God, should touch his neighbor's goods, but only that which grows free as the grass, which is the common property of all. The ninth commandment: "Thou shalt not bear false witness against thy neighbor," corresponds to the word: "Let us make man in our image." Thou, like thy neighbor, art made in My image, hence bear not false witness against thy neighbor. The tenth commandment: "Thou shalt not covet the wife of thy neighbor," corresponds to the tenth word of the creation: "It is not good for man to be alone," for God said: "I created thee a spouse, and let not one among ye covet his neighbor's wife."

MOSES CHOSEN AS INTERMEDIATOR

After Israel had heard the Ten Commandments, they supposed that God would on this occasion reveal to them all the rest of the Torah. But the awful vision on Mount Sinai, where they heard the visible and saw the audible-the privilege was granted them that even the slave women among them saw more than the greatest prophet of later times-this vision has so exhausted them that they would surely have perished, had they heard another word from God. They therefore went to Moses and implored him to be the intermediator between them and God. God found their wish right, so that He not only employed Moses as His intermediator, but determined in all future times to send prophets to Israel as messengers of His words. Turning to Moses, God said: "All that they have spoken is good. If it were possible, I would even now dismiss the Angel of Death, but death against humanity has already been decreed by Me, hence it must remain. Go, say unto them: 'Return to your tents,' but stay thou with Me." In these words God indicated to Israel that they might again enter upon conjugal relations, from which they has abstained throughout three days, while Moses should forever have to deny himself all earthly indulgences.

Moses in his great wisdom now knew how, in a few words, to calm the great excitement of the myriads of men, saying to them: "God gave you the Torah and wrought marvels for you, in order, through this and through the observances of the laws which He imposed upon you, to distinguish you before all other nations on earth. Consider, however, that whereas up to this time you have been ignorant, and your ignorance served as your excuse, you now know exactly what to do and what not to do. Until now you did not know that the righteous are to be rewarded and the godless to be punished in the future world, but now you know it. But as long as you will have a feeling of shame, you will not lightly commit sins." Hereupon the people withdrew twelve miles from Mount Sinai, while Moses stepped quite close before the Lord.

In the immediate proximity of God are the souls of the pious, a little farther Mercy and Justice, and close to these was the position Moses was allowed to occupy. The vision of Moses, owing to his nearness to God, was clear and distinct, unlike that of the other prophets, who saw but dimly. He is furthermore distinguished from all the other prophets, that he was conscious of his prophetic revelations, while they were unconscious in the moments of prophecy. A third distinction of Moses, which he indeed shared with Aaron and Samuel, was that God revealed Himself to him in a pillar of cloud.

In spite of these great marks of favor to Moses, the people still perceived the difference between the first two commandments, which they heard directly from God, and those that they learned through Moses' intercession. For when they heard the words, "I am the Eternal, thy Lord," the understanding of the Torah became deep-rooted in their hearts, so that they never forgot what they thus learned. But they forgot some of the things Moses taught, for as man is a being of flesh and blood, and hence ephemeral, so are his teachings ephemeral. They hereupon came to Moses, saying: "O, if He would only reveal Himself once more! O that once more He would kiss us with the kisses of His mouth! O that understanding of the Torah might remain firm in our hearts as before!" Moses answered: "It is no longer possible now, but it will come to pass in the future world, when He will put His law in their inward parts, and write it in their hearts."

Israel had another reason for regretting the choice of an intermediator between themselves and God. When they heard the second commandment: "Thou shalt have no strange gods beside Me," the evil impulse was torn out from their hearts. But as soon as they requested Moses to intercede for them, the evil impulse set in once more in its old place. In vain, however, did they plead with Moses to restore the former direct communication between them and God, so that the evil impulse might be taken from them. For he said: "It is no longer possible now, but in the future world He will 'take out of your flesh the stony heart.'"

Although Israel had now heard only the first two commandments directly from God, still the Divine apparition had and enormous influence upon this generation. Never in the course of their lives was any physical impurity heard of among them, nor did any vermin succeed in infesting their bodies, and when they died, their corpses remained free from worms and insects.

MOSES AND THE ANGELS STRIVE FOR THE TORAH

The day on which God revealed Himself on Mount Sinai was twice as long as ordinary days. For on that day the sun did not set, a miracle that was four times more repeated for Moses' sake. When this long day had drawn to its close, Moses ascended the holy mountain, where he spent a week to rid himself of all mortal impurity, so that he might betake himself to God into heaven. At the end of his preparations, God called him to come to Him. Then a cloud appeared and lay down before him, but he knew not whether to ride upon it or merely to hold fast to it. Then suddenly the mouth of the cloud flew open, and he entered into it, and walked about in the firmament as a man walks about on earth. Then he met Kemuel, the porter, the angel who is in charge of twelve thousand angels of destruction, who are posted at the portals of the firmament. He spoke harshly to Moses, saying: "What dost thou here, son of Amram, on this spot, belonging to the angels of fire?" Moses answered: "Not of my own impulse do I come here, but with the permission of the Holy One, to receive the Torah and bear it down to Israel." As Kemuel did not want to let him pass, Moses struck him and destroyed him out of the world, whereupon he went on his way until the angel Hadarniel came along.

This angel is sixty myriads of parasangs taller than his fellows, and at every word that passes out of his mouth, issue twelve thousand fiery lightning flashes. When he beheld Moses he roared at him: "What dost thou here, son of Amram, here on the spot of the Holy and High?" When Moses heard his voice, he grew exceedingly frightened, his eyes shed tears, and soon he would have fallen from the cloud. But instantly the pity of God for Moses was awakened, and He said to Hadarniel: "You angels have been quarrelsome since the day I created you. In the beginning, when I wanted to create Adam, you raised complaint before Me and said,

'What is man that Thou are mindful of him!' and My wrath was kindled against you and I burned scores of you with My little finger. Now again ye commence strife with the faithful one of My house, whom I have bidden to come up here to receive the Torah and carry it down to My chosen children Israel, although you know that if Israel did not receive the Torah, you would no longer be permitted to dwell in heaven." When Hadarniel heard this, he said quickly to the Lord: "O Lord of the world! It is manifest and clear to Thee, that I was not aware he came hither with Thy permission, but since I now know it, I will be his messenger and go before him as a disciple before his master." Hadarniel hereupon, in a humble attitude, ran before Moses as a disciple before his master, until he reached the fire of Sandalfon, when he spoke to Moses, saying: "Go, turn about, for I may not stay in this spot, or the fire of Sandalfon will scorch me."

This angel towers above his fellows by so great height, that it would take five hundred years to cross over it. He stands behind the Divine Throne and binds garlands for his Lord. Sandalfon does not know the abiding spot of the Lord either, so that he might set the crown on His head, but he charms the crown, so that it rises of its own accord until it reposes on the head of the Lord. As soon as Sandalfon bids the crown rise, the hosts on high tremble and shake, the holy animals burst into paeans, the holy Seraphim roar like lions and say: "Holy, holy, holy is the Lord of hosts, the whole earth is full of His glory." When the crown has reached the Throne of Glory, the wheels of the Throne are instantly set in motion, the foundations of its footstool tremble, and all the heavens are seized with trembling and horror. As soon as the crown now passes the Throne of Glory, to settle upon its place, all the heavenly hosts open their mouths, saying: "Praised be the glory of the Eternal from His place." And when the crown has reached its destination, all the holy animals, the Seraphim, the wheels of the Throne, and the hosts on high, the Cherubim and the Hashmalim speak with one accord: "The Eternal is King, the Eternal was King, the Eternal will be King in all eternity."

Now when Moses beheld Sandalfon, he was frightened, and in his alarm came near to falling out of the cloud. In tears he imploringly begged God for mercy, and was answered. In His bountiful love of Israel, He Himself descended from the Throne of His glory and stood before Moses, until he had passed the flames of Sandalfon.

After Moses had passed Sandalfon, he ran across Rigyon, the stream of fire, the coals of which burn the angels, who dip into them every morning, are burned, and then arise anew. This stream with the coals of fire is generated beneath the Throne of Glory out of the perspiration of the holy Hayyot, who perspire fire out of fear of God. God, however, quickly drew Moses past Rigyon without his suffering any injury.

As he passed on he met the angel Gallizur, also called Raziel. He it is who reveals the teachings to his Maker, and makes known in the world what is decreed by God. For he stands behind the curtains that are drawn before the Throne of God, and sees and hears everything. Elijah on Horeb hears that which Raziel calls down into the world, and passes his knowledge on. This angel performs other functions in heaven. He stands before the Throne with outspread wings, and in this way arrests the breath of the Hayyot, the heat of which would otherwise scorch all the angels. He furthermore puts the coals of Rigyon into a glowing brazier, which he holds up to kings, lords, and princes, and from which their faces receive a radiance that makes men fear them. When Moses beheld him, he trembled, but God led him past unhurt.

He then came to a host of Angels of Terror that surround the Throne of Glory, and are the strongest and mightiest among the angels. These now wished to scorch Moses with their fiery breath, but God spread His radiance of splendor over Moses, and said to him: "Hold on tight to the Throne of My Glory, and answer them." For as soon as the angels became aware of Moses in heaven, they said to God: "What does he who is born of woman here?" And God's answer was as follows: "He has come to receive the Torah." They furthermore said: "O Lord, content Thyself with the celestial beings, let them have the Torah, what wouldst Thou with the dwellers of the dust?" Moses hereupon answered the angels: "It is written in the Torah: 'I am the Eternal, thy Lord, that have led thee out of the land of Egypt and out of the house of bondage.' Were ye perchance enslaved in Egypt and then delivered, that ye are in need of the Torah? It is further written in the Torah: 'Thou shalt have no other gods.' Are there perchance idolaters among ye, that ye are in need of the Torah? It is written: 'Thou shalt not utter the name of the Eternal, thy God, in vain,' Are there perchance business negotiations among ye, that ye are in need of the Torah to teach you the proper form of invocation? It is written: 'Remember to keep the Sabbath holy.' Is there perchance any work among you, that ye are in need of the Torah? It is written: 'Honor thy father and thy mother.' Have ye perchance parents, that ye are in need of the Torah? It is written: 'Thou shalt not kill.' Are there perchance murderers among ye, that ye are in need of the Torah? It is written: 'Thou shalt not commit adultery.' Are there perchance women among ye, that ye are in need of the Torah? It is written: 'Thou shalt not steal.' Is there perchance money in heaven, that ye are need of the Torah? It is written: 'Thou shalt not bear false witness against thy neighbor.' Is there perchance any false witness among ye, that ye are in need of the Torah? It is written: 'Covet not the house of thy neighbor.' Are there perchance houses, fields, or vineyards among ye, that ye are in need of the Torah?" The angels hereupon relinquished their opposition to the delivering of the Torah into the hands of Israel, and acknowledged that God was right to reveal it to mankind, saying: "Eternal, our Lord, how excellent is Thy name in all the earth! Who hast set Thy glory upon the heavens."

Moses now stayed forty days in heaven to learn the Torah from God. But when he started to descend and beheld the hosts of the angels of terror, angels of trembling, angels of quaking, and angels of horror, then through his fear he forgot all he had learned. For this reason God called the angel Yefefiyah, the prince of the Torah, who handed over to Moses the Torah, "ordered in all things and sure." All the other angels, too, became his friends, and each bestowed upon him a remedy as well as the secret of the Holy Names, as they are contained in the Torah, and as they are applied. Even the Angel of Death gave him a remedy against death. The applications of the Holy Names, which the angels through Yefefiyah, the prince of the Torah, and Metatron, the prince of the Face, taught him, Moses passed on to the high-priest Eleazar, who passed them to his son Phinehas, also known as Elijah.

MOSES RECEIVES THE TORAH

When Moses reached heaven, he found God occupied ornamenting the letters in which the Torah was written, with little crown-like decorations, and he looked on without saying a word. God then said to him: "In thy home, do not people know the greeting of peace?" Moses: "Does it behoove a servant to address his Master?" God: "Thou mightest at least have wished Me success in My labors." Moses hereupon said: "Let the power of my Lord be great according as Thou hast spoken." Then Moses inquired as the significance of the crowns upon the letter, and was answered: "Hereafter there shall live a man called Akiba, son of Joseph, who will base in interpretation a gigantic mountain of Halakot upon every dot of these letters." Moses said to God: "Show me this man." God: "Go back eighteen ranks." Moses went where he was bidden, and could hear the discussions of the teacher sitting with his disciples in the eighteenth rank, but was not able to follow these discussions, which greatly grieved him. But just then he heard the disciples questioning their master in regard to a certain subject: "Whence dost thou know this?" And he answered, "This is a Halakah given to Moses on Mount Sinai," and not Moses was content. Moses returned to God and said to Him: "Thou has a man like Akiba, and yet dost Thou give the Torah to Israel through me!" But God answered: "Be silent, so has it been decreed by Me." Moses then said: "O Lord of the world! Thou has permitted me to behold this man's learning, let see also the reward which will be meted out to him." God said: "Go, return and see." Moses saw them sell the flesh of the martyr Akiba at the meat market. He said to God: "Is this the reward for such erudition?" But God replied: "Be silent, thus have I decreed."

Moses then saw how God wrote the word "long-suffering" in the Torah, and asked: "Does this mean that Thou hast patience with the pious?" But God answered: "Nay, with sinners also am I long-suffering." "What!" exclaimed Moses, "Let the sinners perish!" God said no more, but when Moses implored God's mercy, begging Him to forgive the sin of the people of Israel, God answered him: "Thou thyself didst advice Me to have no patience with sinners and to destroy them." "Yea," said Moses, "but Thou didst declare that Thou art long-suffering with sinners also, let now the patience of the Lord be great according as Thou has spoken."

The forty days that Moses spent in heaven were entirely devoted to the study of the Torah, he learned the written as well as the oral teaching, yea, even the doctrines that an able scholar would some day propound were revealed to him. He took an especial delight in hearing the teachings of the Tanna Rabbi Eliezer, and received the joyful message that this great scholar would be one of his descendants.

The study of Moses was so planned for the forty days, that by day God studied with him the written teachings, and by night the oral. In this way was he enabled to distinguish between night and day, for in heaven "the night shineth as the day." There were other signs also by which he could distinguish night from day; for if he heard the angels praise God with "Holy, holy, holy, is the Lord of hosts," he knew that it was day; but if they praised Him with "Blessed be the Lord to whom blessing is due," he knew it was night. Then, too, if he saw the sun appear before God and cast itself down before Him, he knew that it was night; if, however, the moon and the stars cast themselves at His feet, he knew that it was day. He could also tell time by the occupation of the angels, for by day they prepared manna for Israel, and by night they sent it down to earth. The prayers he heard in heaven served him as another token whereby he might know the time, for if he heard the recitation of the Shema' precede prayer, he knew that it was day, but if the prayer preceded the recitation of the Shema', then it was night.

During his stay with Him, God showed Moses all the seven heavens, and the celestial temple, and the four colors that he was to employ to fit up the tabernacle. Moses found it difficult to retain the color, whereupon God said to him: "Turn to the right," and as he turned, he saw a host of angels in garments that had the color of the sea. "This," said God, "is violet." Then He bade Moses turn to the left, and there he saw angels dressed in red, and God said: "This is royal purple." Moses hereupon turned around to the rear, and saw angels robed in a color that was neither purple nor violet, and God said to him: "This color is crimson." Moses then turned about and saw angels robed in white, and God said to him: "This is the color of twisted linen."

Although Moses now devoted both night and day to the study of the Torah, he still learned nothing, for hardly had he learned something from God when he forgot it again. Moses thereupon said to God: "O Lord of the world! Forty days have I devoted to studying the Torah, without having profited anything by it." God therefore bestowed the Torah upon Moses, and now he could descend to Israel, for now he remembered all that he had learned.

Hardly had Moses descended from heaven with the Torah, when Satan appeared before the Lord and said: "Where, forsooth, is the place where the Torah is kept?" For Satan knew nothing of the revelation of God on Sinai, as God had employed him elsewhere on purposes, that he might not appear before him as an accuser, saying: "Wilt Thou give the Torah to a people that forty days later will worship the Golden Calf?" In answer to Satan's question regarding the whereabouts of the Torah, God said: "I gave the Torah to Earth." To earth, then, Satan betook himself with his query: "Where is the Torah?" Earth said: "God knows of its course, He knoweth its abiding-place, for 'He looketh to the ends of the earth, and seeth under the whole heaven.'" Satan now passed on to the sea to seek for the Torah, but the sea also said: "It is not with me," and the abyss said: "It is not in me." Destruction and death said: "We have heard the fame thereof with our ears." Satan now returned to God and said: "O Lord of the world! Everywhere have I sought the Torah, but I found it not." God replied: "Go, seek the son of Amram." Satan now hastened to Moses and asked him: "Where is the Torah that God hath given thee?" Whereupon Moses answered: "Who am I, that the Holy One, blessed be He, should have given me the Torah?" God hereupon spoke to Moses: "O Moses, thou utterest a falsehood." But Moses answered: "O Lord of the world! Thou hast in Thy possession a hidden treasure that daily delights Thee. Dare I presume to declare it my possession?" Then God said: "As a reward for thy humility, the Torah shall be named for thee, and it shall henceforth be known as the Torah of Moses."

Moses departed from the heavens with the two tables on which the Ten Commandments were engraved, and just the words of it are by nature Divine, so too are the tables on which they are engraved. These were created by God's own hand in the dusk of the first Sabbath at the close of the creation, and were made of a sapphire-like stone. On each of the two tables are the Ten Commandments, four times repeated, and in such wise were they engraved that the letters were legible on both sides, for, like the tables, the writing and the pencils for inscription, too, were of heavenly origin. Between the separate commandments were noted down all the precepts of the Torah in all their particulars, although the tables were not more than six hands in length and as much in width. It is another of the attributes of the tables, that although they are fashioned out of the hardest stone, they can still be rolled up like a scroll. When God handed the tables to Moses, He seized them by the top third, whereas Moses took hold of the bottom third, but on third remained open, and it was in this way that the Divine radiance was shed upon Moses' face.

THE GOLDEN CALF

When God revealed Himself upon Mount Sinai, all Israel sang a song of jubilation to the Lord, for their faith in God was on this occasion without bounds and unexampled, except possibly at the time of the Messiah, when they likewise will cherish this firm faith. The angels, too, rejoiced with Israel, only God was down-cast on this day and sent His voice "out of thickest darkness," in token of His sorrow. The angels hereupon said to God: "Is not the joy that Thou hast created Thine?" But God replied: "You do not know what the future will bring." He knew that forty days later Israel would give the lie to the words of God: "Thou shalt have no other gods before Me," and would adore the Golden Calf. And truly, God had sufficient cause to grow sad at this thought, for the worship of the Golden Calf had more disastrous consequences for Israel than any other of their sins. God had resolved to give life everlasting to the nation that would accept the Torah, hence Israel upon accepting the Torah gained supremacy over the Angel of Death. But they lost this power when they worshipped the Golden Calf. As a punishment for this, their sin, they were doomed to study the Torah in suffering and bondage, in exile and unrest, amid cares of life and burdens, until, in the Messianic time and in the future world, God will compensate them for all their sufferings. But until that time there is no sorrow that falls to Israel's lot that is not in part a punishment for their worship of the Golden Calf.

Strange as it may seem that Israel should set out to worship this idol at the very time when God was busied with the preparation of the two tables of the law, still the following circumstances are to be considered. When Moses departed from the people to hasten to God to receive the Torah, he said to them: "Forty days from to-day I will bring you the Torah." But at noon on the fortieth day Satan came, and with a wizard's trick conjured up for the people a vision of Moses lying stretched out dead on a bier that floated midway between earth and heaven. Pointing to it with their fingers, they cried: "This is the man Moses that bought us up out of the land of Egypt." Under the leadership of the magicians Jannes and Jambres, they appeared before Aaron, saying: "The Egyptians were wont to carry their gods about with them, to dance and play before them, that each might be able to behold his gods; and now we desire that thou shouldst make us a god such as the Egyptians had." When Hur, the son of Miriam, whom Moses during his absence had appointed joint leader of the people with Aaron, owing to his birth which placed him among the notables of highest rank, beheld this, he said to them: "O ye frivolous ones, you are no longer mindful of the many miracles God wrought for you." In their wrath, the people slew this pious and noble man; and, pointing out his dead body to Aaron, they said to him threateningly: "If thou wilt make us a god, it is well, if not we will dispose of thee as of him." Aaron had no fear for his life, but he thought: "If Israel were to commit so terrible a sin as to slay their priest and prophet, God would never forgive them." He was willing rather to take a sin upon himself than to cast the burden of so wicked a deed upon the people. He therefore granted them their wish to make them a god, but he did it in such a way that he still cherished the hope that this thing might not come to pass. Hence he demanded from them not their own ornaments for the fashioning of the idol, but the ornaments of their wives, their sons, and their daughters, thinking: "If I were to tell them to bring me gold and silver, they would immediately do so, hence I will demand the earrings of their wives, their sons, and their daughters, that through their refusal to give up their ornaments, the matter might come to nought." But Aaron's assumption was only in part true; the women indeed did firmly refuse to give up their jewels for the making of a monster that is of no assistance to his worshippers. As a reward for this, God gave the new moons as holidays to women, and in the future world too they will be rewarded for their firm faith in God, in that, like the new moons, they too, may monthly be rejuvenated. But when the men saw that no gold or silver for the idol was forthcoming from the women, they drew off their own earrings that they wore in Arab fashion, and brought these to Aaron.

No living calf would have shaped itself out of the gold of these earrings, if a disaster had not occurred through an oversight of Aaron. For when Moses at the exodus of Israel from Egypt set himself to lifting the coffin of Joseph out of the depths of the Nile, he employed the following means: He took four leaves of silver, and engraved on each the image of one of the beings represented at the Celestial Throne,-the lion, the man, the eagle, and the bull. He then cast on the river the leaf with the image of the lion, and the waters of the river became tumultuous, and roared like a lion. He then threw down the leaf with the image of man, and the scattered bones of Joseph united themselves into an entire body; and when he cast in the third leaf with the image of the eagle, the coffin floated up to the top. As he had no use for the fourth leaf of silver with the image of the bull, he asked a woman to store it away for him, while he was occupied with the transportation of the coffin, and later forgot to reclaim the leaf of silver. This was now among the ornaments that the people brought to Aaron, and it was exclusively owing to this bull's image of magical virtues, that a golden bull arose out of the fire into which Aaron put the gold and silver.

When the mixed multitude that had joined Israel in their exodus from Egypt saw this idol conducting itself like a living being, they said to Israel: "This is thy God, O Israel." The people then betook themselves to the seventy members of the Sanhedrin and demanded that they worship the bull that had led Israel out of Egypt. "God," said they, "had not delivered us out of Egypt, but only Himself, who had in Egypt been in captivity." The members of the Sanhedrin remained loyal to their God, and were hence cut down by the rabble. The twelve heads of the tribes did not answer the summons of the people any more than the members of the Sanhedrin, and were therefore rewarded by being found worthy of beholding the Divine vision.

But the people worshipped not only the Golden Calf, they made thirteen such idols, one each for the twelve tribes, and one for all Israel. More than this, they employed manna, which God in His kindness did not deny them even on this day, as an offering to their idols. The devotion of Israel to this worship of the bull is in part explained by the circumstance that while passing through the Red Sea, they beheld the Celestial Throne, and most distinctly of the four creatures about the Throne, they saw the ox. It was for this reason that they hit upon the notion that the ox had helped God in the exodus from Egypt, and for this reason did they wish to worship the ox beside God.

The people then wanted to erect an altar for their idol, but Aaron tried to prevent this by saying to the people: "It will be more reverential to your god if I build the altar in person," for he hoped that Moses might appear in the meantime. His expectation, however, was disappointed, for on the morning of the following day, when Aaron had at length completed the altar, Moses was not yet at hand, and the people began to offer sacrifices to their idol, and to indulge in lewdness.

MOSES BLAMED FOR ISRAEL'S SIN

When the people turned from their God, He said to Moses, who was still in heaven: "'Go, get thee down; for thy people, which thou broughtest out of the land of Egypt, have corrupted themselves.'" Moses, who until then had been superior to the angels, now, owing to the sins of Israel, feared them greatly. The angels, hearing that God meant to send him from His presence, wanted to kill him, and only by clinging to the Throne of God, who covered him with His mantle, did he escape from the hands of the angels, that they might do him no harm. He had particularly hard struggle with the five Angels of Destruction: Kezef, Af, Hemah, Mashhit, and Haron, whom God had sent to annihilate Israel. Moses then hastened to the three Patriarchs, Abraham, Isaac, and Jacob, and said to them: "If ye are men who are participators of the future life, stand by me in this hour, for your children are as a sheep that is led to the slaughter." The three Patriarchs united their prayers with those of Moses, who said to God; "Hast Thou not made a vow to these three to multiply their seed as the stars, and are they now to be destroyed?" In recognition of the merits of these three pious men, God called away three of the Angels of Destruction, leaving only two: whereupon Moses further importuned God: "For the vow Thou madest to Israel, take from them the angel Mashhit;" and God granted his prayer. Moses continued: "For the vow Thou madest me, take from them also the angel Haron." God now stood by Moses, so that he was able to conquer this angel, and he thrust him down deep into the earth in a spot that is possession of the tribe of Gad, and there held him captive.

So long as Moses lived this angel was held in check by him, and if he tried, even when Israel sinned, to rise out of the depths, open wide his mouth, and destroy Israel with his panting, all Moses had to do was to utter the name of God, and Haron, or as he is sometimes called, Peor, was drawn once more into the depths of the earth. At Moses' death, God buried him opposite the spot where Peor is bound. For should Peor, if Israel sinned, reach the upper world and open his mouth to destroy Israel with his panting, he would, upon seeing Moses' grave, be so terror-stricken, that he would fall back into the depths once more.

Moses did indeed manage the Angels of Destruction, but it was a more difficult matter to appease God in His wrath. He addressed Moses harshly, crying: "The grievous sins of men had once caused Me to go down from heaven to see their doings. Do thou likewise go down from heaven now. It is fitting that the servant be treated as his master. Do thou now go down. Only for Israel's sake have I caused this honor to fall to thy lot, but now that Israel has become disloyal to Me, I have not further reason thus to distinguish thee." Moses hereupon answered: "O Lord of the world! Not long since didst Thou say to me: 'Come now, therefore, and I will send thee that thou mayest bring forth My people out of Egypt;' and now Thou callest them my people. Nay, whether pious or sinful, they are Thy people still." Moses continued: "What wilt Thou now do with them?" God answered: "I will consume them, and I will make of thee a great nation." "O Lord of the world!" replied Moses, "If the three-legged bench has no stability, how then shall the one-legged stand? Fulfil not, I implore Thee, the prophecies of the Egyptian magicians, who predicted to their king that the star 'Ra'ah' would move as a harbinger of blood and death before the Israelites." Then he began to implore mercy for Israel: "Consider their readiness to accept the Torah, whereas the sons of Esau rejected it." God: "But they transgressed the precepts of the Torah; one day were they loyal to Me, then instantly set to work to make themselves the Golden Calf." Moses: "Consider that when in Thy name I came to Egypt and announced to them Thy name, they at once believed in me, and bowed down their heads and worshipped Thee." God: "But they now bow down their heads before their idol." Moses: "Consider that they sent Thee their young men to offer Thee burnt offerings." God: "They now offered sacrifices to the Golden Calf." Moses: "Consider that on Sinai they acknowledged that Thou are their God." God: "They now acknowledge that the idol is their god."

All these arguments with God did not help Moses; he even had to put up with having the blame for the Golden Calf laid on his shoulders. "Moses," said God, "when Israel was still in Egypt, I gave thee the commission to lead them out of the land, but not take with thee the mixed multitude that wanted to join them. But thou in thy clemency and humility didst persuade Me to accept the penitent that do penance, and didst take with thee the mixed multitude. I did as thou didst beg me, although I knew what the consequences would be, and it is now these people, 'thy people,' that have seduced Israel to idolatry." Moses now thought it would be useless to try to secure God's forgiveness for Israel, and was ready to give up his intercession, when God, who in reality meant to preserve Israel, but only like to hear Moses pray, now spoke kindly to Moses to let him see that He was not quite inaccessible to his exhortations, saying: "Even in Egypt did I foresee what this people would do after their deliverance. Thou foresawest only the receiving of the Torah on Sinai, but I foresaw the worship of the Calf as well." With these words, God let Moses perceive that the defection of Israel was no surprise to Him, as He had considered it even before the exodus from Egypt; hence Moses now gathered new courage to intercede for Israel. He said: "O Lord of the world! Israel has indeed created a rival for Thee in their idol, that Thou are angry with them. The Calf, I supposed, shall bid stars and moon to appear, while Thou makest the sun to rise; Thou shalt send the dew and he will cause the wind to blow; Thou shalt send down the rain, and he shall bid the plants to grow." God: "Moses, thou are mistaken, like them, and knowest not that the idol is absolutely nothing." "If so," said Moses, "why art Thou angry with Thy people for that which is nothing?" "Besides," he continued, "Thou didst say Thyself that it was chiefly my people, the mixed multitude, that was to blame for this sin, why then are Thou angry with Thy people? If Thou are angry with them only because they have not observed the Torah, then let me vouch for the observance of it on the part of my companions, such as Aaron and his sons, Joshua and Caleb, Jair and Machir, as well as many pious men among them, and myself." But God said: "I have vowed that 'He that sacrificeth unto any god, save unto the Lord only, he shall be utterly destroyed,' and a vow that has once passe My lips, I can not retract." Moses replied: "O Lord of the world! Has not Thou given us the law of absolution from a vow, whereby power is given to a learned man to absolve any one from his vows? But every judge who desires to have his decisions accounted valid, must subject himself to the law, and Thou who has prescribed the law of absolution from vows through a learned man, must subject Thyself to this law, and through me be absolved from Thy vow." Moses thereupon wrapped his robe about him, seated himself, and bade God let him absolve Him from his vow, bidding Him say: "I repent of the evil that I had determined to bring upon My people." Moses then cried out to Him: "Thou are absolved from Thine oath and vow."

THE PUNISHMENT OF THE SINNERS

When Moses descended from Sinai, he there found his true servant Joshua, who had awaited him on the slope of the mountain throughout all the forty days during which Moses stayed in heaven, and together they repaired to the encampment. On approaching it, they heard cries of the people, and Joshua remarked to Moses: "There is a noise of war in the camp," but Moses replied: "Is it possible that thou, Joshua, who art one day destined to be the leader of sixty myriads of people, canst not distinguish among the different kinds of dins? This is no cry of Israel conquering, nor of their defeated foe, but their adoration of an idol." When Moses had now come close enough to the camp to see what was going on there, he thought to himself: "How now shall I give to them the tables and enjoin upon them the prohibition of idolatry, for the very trespassing of which, Heaven will inflict capital punishment upon them?" Hence, instead of delivering to them the tables, he tried to turn back, but the seventy elders pursued him and tried to wrest the tables from Moses. But his strength excelled that of the seventy others, and he kept the tables in his hands, although these were seventy Seah in weight. All at once, however, he saw the writing vanish from the tables, and at the same time became aware of their enormous weight; for while the celestial writing was upon them, they carried their own weight and did not burden Moses, but with the disappearance of the writing all this changes. Now all the more did Moses feel loath to give the tables without their contents to Israel, and besides he thought: "If God prohibited one idolatrous Israelite from partaking of the Passover feast, how much more would He be angry if I were now to give all the Torah to an idolatrous people?" Hence, without consulting God, he broke the tables. God, however, thanked Moses for breaking the tables.

Hardly had Moses broken the tables, when the ocean wanted to leave its bed to flood the world. Moses now "took the Calf which they had made, and burnt it in the fire, and ground it to powder, and strewed it upon the water," saying to the waters: "What would ye upon the dry land?" And the waters said: "The world stands only through the observance of the Torah, but Israel has not been faithful to it." Moses hereupon said to the water" "All that have committed idolatry shall be yours. Are you now satisfied with these thousands?" But the waters were not to be appeased by the sinners that Moses cast into them, and the ocean would not retreat to its bed until Moses made the children of Israel drink of it.

The drinking of these waters was one of the forms of capital punishment that he inflicted upon the sinners. When, in answer to Moses' call: "Who is on the Lord's side? Let him come unto me," all the sons of Levi gathered themselves together unto him-they who had not taken part in the adoration of the Golden Calf,-Moses appointed these Levites as judges, whose immediate duty it was to inflict the lawful punishment of decapitation upon all those who had been seen by witnesses to be seduced to idolatry after they had been warned not to do so. Moses gave the command as though he had been commissioned to do so by God. This was not actually so, but he did it in order to enable the judges appointed by him to punish all the guilty in the course of one day, which otherwise, owing to the procedure of Jewish jurisprudence, could not well have been possible. Those who, according to the testimony of witnesses, had been seduced to idolatry, but who could not be proven to have been warned beforehand, were not punished by temporal justice, they died of the water that Moses forced them to drink; for this water had upon them the same effect as the curse-bringing water upon the adulterous woman. But those sinners, too, against whom no witnesses appeared, did not escape their fate, for upon them God sent the plague to carry them off.

MOSES INTERCEDES FOR THE PEOPLE

Those who were executed by these judgements numbered three thousand, so that Moses said to God: "O Lord of the world! Just and merciful art Thou, and all Thy deeds are deeds of integrity. Shall six hundred thousand people-not to mention all who are below twenty years of age, and all the many proselytes and slaves-perish for the sake of three thousand sinners?" God could no longer withhold His mercy, and determined to forgive Israel their sins. It was only after long and fervent prayers that Moses succeeded in quite propitiating God, and hardly had he returned from heaven, when he again repaired thither to advance before God his intercession for Israel. He was ready to sacrifice himself for the sake of Israel, and as soon as punishment had been visited on the sinners, he turned to God with the words: "O Lord of the world! I have now destroyed both the Golden Calf and its idolaters, what cause for ill feeling against Israel can now remain? The sins these committed came to pass because Thou hadst heaped gold and silver upon them, so that the blames is not wholly theirs. 'Yet now, if Thou wilt, forgive their sin; and if not, blot me, I pray Thee, out of Thy book which Thou has written.'"

These bold words of Moses were not without consequences for him, for although God thereupon replied: "Whosoever hath sinned against Me, him will I blot out of My blood," still it was on account of this that his name was omitted from one section of the Pentateuch. But for Israel his words created an instant revulsion of feeling in God, who now addressed him kindly, and promised that he would send His angel, who would lead the people into the promised land. These words indicated to Moses that God was not yet entirely appeased, and he could further see this in the punishment that fell upon Israel on that day. Their weapons, which every man among them had received at the revelation on Sinai, and which had miraculous virtues, having the name of God engraved upon them, were taken from them by the angels, and their robes of purple likewise. When Moses saw from this that God's wrath was still upon Israel, and that He desired to have nothing further to do with them, he removed his tent a mile away from the camp, saying to himself: "The disciple may not have intercourse with people whom the master has excommunicated."

Not only the people went out o this tent whenever they sought the Lord, but the angels also, the Seraphim, and the heavenly hosts repaired thither, the sun, the moon, and the other heavenly bodies, all of whom knew that God was to be found there, and that the tent of Moses was the spot where they were to appear before their Creator. God, however, was not at all pleased to see Moses keep himself aloof from the people, and said to him: "According to our agreement, I was to propitiate thee every time thou wert angry with the people, and thou wert to propitiate Me when My wrath was kindled against them. What is now to become of these poor people, if we be both angry with them? Return, therefore, into the camp to the people. But if thou wilt not obey, remember that Joshua is in the camp at the sanctuary, and he can well fill thy place." Moses replied: "It is for Thy sake that I am angry with them, and now I see that still Thou canst not forsake them." "I have," said God, "already told thee, that I shall send and angel before them." But Moses, by no means content with this assurance, continued to importune God not to entrust Israel to an angel, but to conduct and guide them in person.

Forty days and forty nights, from the eighteenth day of Tammus to the twenty-eight day of Ab, did Moses stay in heaven, beseeching and imploring God to restore Israel once more entirely into His favor. But all his prayers and exhortations were in vain, until at the end of forty days he implored God to set the pious deeds of the three Patriarchs and of the twelve sons of Jacob to the account of their descendants; and only then was his prayer answered. H said: "If Thou art angry with Israel because they transgressed the Ten Commandments, be mindful for their sake of the ten tests to which Thou didst subject Abraham, and through which he nobly passed. If Israel deserves at Thy hands punishment by fire for their sin, remember the fire of the limekiln into which Abraham let himself be cast for the glory of Thy name. If Israel deserves death by sword, remember the readiness with which Isaac laid down his neck upon the altar to be sacrificed to Thee. If they deserve punishment by exile, remember for their sake how their father Jacob wandered into exile from his paternal home to Haran." Moses furthermore said to God: "Will the dead ever be restored to life?" God in surprise retorted: "Hast thou become a heretic, Moses, that thou dost doubt the resurrection?" "If," said Moses, "the dead never awaken to life, then truly Thou art right to wreak vengeance upon Israel; but if the dead are to be restored to life hereafter, what wilt Thou then say to the fathers of this nation, if they ask Thee what has become of the promise Thou hadst made to them? I demand nothing more for Israel," Moses continued, "than what Thou were willing to grant Abraham when he pleaded for Sodom. Thou wert willing to let Sodom survive if there were only ten just men therein, and I am now about to enumerate to Thee ten just men among the Israelites: myself, Aaron, Eleazar, Ithamar, Phinehas, Joshua, and Caleb." "But that is only seven," objected God. Moses, not at all abashed, replied: "But Thou hast said that the dead will hereafter be restored to life, so count with these the three Patriarchs to make the number ten complete." Moses' mention of the names of the three Patriarchs was of more avail than all else, and God granted his prayer, forgave Israel their transgression, and promised to lead the people in person.

THE INSCRUTABLE WAYS OF THE LORD

Moses still cherished three other wishes: that the Shekinah might dwell with Israel; that the Shekinah might not dwell with other nations; and lastly, that he might learn to know the ways of the Lord whereby He ordained good and evil in the world, sometimes causing suffering to the just and letting the unjust enjoy happiness, whereas at other times both were happy, or both were destined to suffer. Moses laid these wishes before God in the moment of His wrath, hence God bade Moses wait until His wrath should have blown over, and then He granted him his first two wishes in full, but his third in part only. God showed him the great treasure troves in which are stored up the various rewards for the pious and the just, explaining each separated one to him in detail: in this one were the rewards of those who give alms; in that one, of those who bring up orphans. In this way He showed him the destination of each one of the treasures, until at length they came to one of gigantic size. "For whom is this treasure?" asked Moses, and God answered: "Out of the treasures that I have shown thee I give rewards to those who have deserved them by their deeds; but out of this treasure do I give to those who are not deserving, for I am gracious to those also who may lay no claim to My graciousness, and I am bountiful to those who are not deserving of My bounty."

Moses now had to content himself with the certainty that the pious were sure of their deserts; without, however, learning from God, how it sometimes comes to pass that evil doers, too, are happy. For God merely stated that He also shows Himself kind to those who do not deserve it, but without further assigning the why and the wherefore. But the reward to the pious, too, was only in part revealed to him, for he beheld the joys of Paradise of which they were to partake, but not the real reward that is to follow the feast in Paradise; for truly "eye hath not seen, beside the Lord, what He hath prepared for him that waiteth for Him."

By means of the following incident God showed Moses how little man is able to fathom the inscrutable ways of the Lord. When Moses was on Sinai, he saw from that station a man who betook himself to a river, stooped down to drink, lost his purse, and without noticing it went his way. Shortly after, another man cam, found the money, pocketed it, and took to his heels. When the owner of the purse became aware of his loss, he returned to the river, where he did not find his money, but saw a man, who came there by chance to fetch water. To him he said: "Restore to me the money that a little while ago I left here, for none can have taken it if not thou." When the man declared that he had found none of the money nor seen any of it, the owner slew him. Looking with horror and amazement on this injustice on earth, Moses said to God: "I beseech Thee, show my Thy ways. Why has this man, who was quite innocent, been slain, and why hath the true thief gone unpunished?" God replied: "The man who found the money and kept it merely recovered his own possession, for he who had lost the purse by the river, had formerly stolen it from him; but the one who seemed to be innocently slain is only making atonement for having at one time murdered the father of his slayer." In this way, God granted the request of Moses, "to show him His ways," in part only. He let him look into the future, and let him see every generation and it sages, every generation and its prophets, every generation and its expounders of the Scriptures, every generation and its leaders, ever generation and its pious men. But when Moses said: "O Lord of the world! Let me see by what law Thou dost govern the world; for I see that many a just man is lucky, but many a one is not; many a wicked man is lucky, but many a one is not; many a rich man is happy, but many a one is not; many a poor man is happy, but many a one is not;" then God answered: "Thou canst not grasp all the principles which I apply to the government of the world, but some of them shall I impart to thee. When I see human beings who have no claim to expectations from Me either for their own deeds or for those of their fathers, but who pray to Me and implore Me, then do I grant their prayers and give them what they require from subsistence."

Although God had now granted all of his wishes, still Moses received the following answer to his prayer, "I beseech Thee, show me Thy glory": "Thou mayest not behold My glory, or else thou wouldst perish, but in consideration of My vow to grant thee all thy wishes, and in view of the fact that thou are in possession of the secret of My name, I will meet thee so far as to satisfy thy desire in part. Lift the opening of the cave, and I will bid all the angels that serve Me pass in review before thee; but as soon as thou hearest the Name, which I have revealed to thee, know then that I am there, and bear thyself bravely and without fear.'

God has a reason for not showing His glory to Moses. He said to him: "When I revealed Myself to thee in the burning bush, thou didst not want to look upon Me; now thou are willing, but I am not."

THE THIRTEEN ATTRIBUTES OF GOD

The cave in which Moses concealed himself while God passed in review before him with His celestial retinue, was the same in which Elijah lodged when God revealed Himself to him on Horeb. If there had been in it an opening even as tiny as a needle's point, both Moses and Elijah would have been consumed by the passing Divine light, which was of an intensity so great that Moses, although quite shut off in the cave, nevertheless caught the reflection of it, so that from its radiance his face began to shine. Not without great danger, however, did Moses earn this distinction; for as soon as the angels heard Moses request God to show him His glory, they were greatly incensed against him, and said to God: "We, who serve Thee night and day, may not see Thy glory, and he, who is born of woman, asks to see it!" In their anger they made ready to kill Moses, who would certainly have perished, had not God's hand protected him from the angels. Then God appeared in the cloud.

It was the seventh time that He appeared on earth, and taking the guise of a precentor of a congregation, He said to Moses: "Whenever Israel hath sinned, and calleth Me by the following thirteen attributes, I will forgive them their sins. I am the Almighty God who provides for all creatures. I am the Merciful One who restrains evil from human kind. I am the Gracious One who helps in time of need. I am the Long-Suffering to the upright as well as to the wicked. I am Bountiful to those whose own deed do not entitle them to lay claim to rewards. I am Faithful to those who have a right to expect good from Me; and preserve graciousness unto the two-thousandth generation. I forgive misdeeds and even atrocious actions, in forgiving those who repent." When Moses heard this, and particularly that God is long-suffering with sinners, he prayed: "O forgive, then, Israel's sin which they committed in worshipping the Golden Calf." Had Moses now prayed, "Forgive the sins of Israel unto the end of all time," God would have granted that too, as it was a time of mercy; but as Moses asked forgiveness for this one sin only, this one only was pardoned, and God said: "I have pardoned according to thy word."

The day on which God showed Himself merciful to Moses and to His people, was the tenth day of Tishri, the day on which Moses was to receive the tables of the law from God for the second time, and all Israel spent it amid prayer and fasting, that the evil spirit might not again lead them astray. Their ardent tears and exhortations, joined with those of Moses, reached heaven, so that God took pity upon them and said to them: "My children, I swear by my lofty Name that these your tears shall be tears of rejoicing for you; that this day shall be a day of pardon, of forgiveness, and of the canceling of sins for you, for your children, and your children's children to the end of all generations."

This day was not set for the annual Day of Atonement, without which the world could not exist, and which will continue even in the future world when all other holy days will cease to be. The Day of Atonement, however, is not only a reminiscence of the day on which God was reconciled to Israel and forgave them their sins, but it is also the day on which Israel finally received the Torah. For after Moses has spent forty days in prayer, until God finally forgave Israel their sins, he began to reproach himself for having broken the tables of the law, saying" "Israel asked me to intercede for them before God, but who will, on account of my sin, intercede before God for my sake?" Then God said to him: "Grieve not for the loss of the first two tables, which contained only the Ten Commandments. The second tables that I am now ready to give thee, shall contain Halakot, Midrash, and Haggadot."

At the new moon of the month Elul, Moses had the trumpet sounded throughout the camp, announcing to the people that he would once more betake himself to God for forty days to receive the second tables from Him, so that they might be alarmed by his absence; and he stayed in heaven until the tenth day of Tishri, on which day he returned with the Torah and delivered it to Israel.

THE SECOND TABLES

Whereas the first tables had been given on Mount Sinai amid great ceremonies, the presentation of the second tables took place quietly, for God said: "There is nothing lovelier than quiet humility. The great ceremonies on the occasion of presenting the first tables had the evil effect of directing an evil eye toward them, so that they were finally broken." In this also were the second tables differentiated from the first, that the former were the work of God, and the latter, the work of man. God dealt with Israel like the king who took to himself to wife and drew up the marriage contract with his own hand. One day the king noticed his wife engaged in very intimate conversation with a slave; and enraged at her unworthy conduct, he turned here out of his house. Then he who had given the bride away at the wedding came before the king and said to him: "O sire, dost thou not know whence thou didst take thy bride? She had been brought up among the slaves, and hence is intimate with them." The king allowed himself to be appeased, saying to the other: "Take paper and let a scribe draw up a new marriage contract, and here take my authorization, signed in my own hand." Just so did Israel fare with their God when Moses offered the following excuse for their worship of the

Golden Calf: "O Lord, dost Thou not know whence Thou hast brought Israel, out of a land of idolaters?" God replied: "Thou desirest Me to forgive them. Well, then, I shall do so, now fetch Me hither tables on which I may write the words that were written on the first. But to reward thee for offering up thy life for their sake, I shall in the future send thee along with Elijah, that both of you together may prepare Israel for the final deliverance."

Moses fetched the tables out of a diamond quarry which God pointed out to him, and the chips that fell, during the hewing, from the precious stone made a rich man of Moses, so that he now possessed all the qualifications of a prophet-wealth, strength, humility, and wisdom. In regard to the last-named be it said, that God given in Moses' charge all the fifty gates of wisdom except one.

As the chips falling from the precious stone were designed for Moses alone, so too had originally the Torah, written on these tables, been intended only Moses and his descendants; but he was benevolent of spirit, and imparted the Torah to Israel. The wealth that Moses procured for himself in fashioning the Torah, was a reward for having taken charge of the corpse of Joseph while all the people were appropriating to themselves the treasures of Egyptians. God now said: "Moses deserves the chips from the tables. Israel, who did not occupy themselves with labors of piety, carried off the best of Egypt at the time of their exodus. Shall Moses, who saw to the corpse of Joseph, remain poor? Therefore will I make him rich through these chips."

During the forty days he spent in heaven, Moses received beside the two tables all the Torah-the Bible, Mishnah, Talmud, and Haggadah, yea, even all that ever clever scholars would ask their teacher was revealed to him. When he now received the command from God to teach all this to Israel, he requested God to write down all the Torah and to give it to Israel in that way. But God said: "Gladly would I give them the whole in writing, but it is revealed before Me that the nations of the world will hereafter read the Torah translated into Greek, and will say: 'We are the true Israel, we are the children of God.' Then I shall say to the nations: 'Ye claim to be MY children, do ye not know that those only are My children to whom I have confided My secret, the oral teaching?'" This was the reason why the Pentateuch only was given to Moses in writing, and the other parts of the Torah by word of mouth. Hence the covenant God made with Israel reads: "I gave ye a written and an oral Torah. My covenant with you says that ye shall study the written Torah as a written thing, and the oral as an oral; but in case you confound the one with the other you will not be rewarded. For the Torah's sake alone have I made a covenant with you; had ye not accepted the Torah, I should not have acknowledged you before all other nations. Before you accepted the Torah, you were just like all other nations, and for the Torah's sake alone have I lifted you above the others. Even your king, Moses, owes the distinction he enjoys in this world and in the world hereafter to the Torah alone. Had you not accepted the Torah, then should I have dissolved the upper and the under worlds into chaos."

Forty days and forty nights Moses now devoted to the study of the Torah, and in all the time he ate no bread and drank no water, acting in accordance with the proverb, "If thou enterest a city, observe its laws." The angels followed this maxim when they visited Abraham, for they there ate like men; and so did Moses, who being among angels, like the angels partook of no food. He received nourishment from radiance of the Shekinah, which also sustains the holy Hayyot that bear the Throne. Moses spent the day in learning the Torah from God, and the night in repeating what he had learned. In this way he set an example for Israel, that they might occupy themselves with the Torah by night and by day.

During this time Moses also wrote down the Torah, although the angels found it strange that God should have given him the commission to write down the Torah, and gave expression to their astonishment in the following words, that they addressed to God: "How is it that Thou givest Moses permission to write, so that he may write whatever he will, and say to Israel, 'I gave you the Torah, I myself wrote it, and then gave it to you?'" But God answered: "Far be it from Moses to do such a thing, he is a faithful servant!"

When Moses had complete the writing of the Torah, he wiped his pen on the hair of his forehead, and from this heavenly ink that cleaved to his forehead originated the beams of light that radiated from it. In this way God fulfilled to Moses the promise: "Before all thy people I will do marvels, such as have not been done in all the earth, nor in any nation." On Moses' return from heaven, the people were greatly amazed to see his face shining, and there was fear, too, in their amazement. This fear was a consequence of their sin, for formerly they had been able to bear without fear the sight of "the glory of the Lord that was like devouring fire," although it consisted of seven sheaths of fire, laid one over another; but after their transgression they could not even bear to look upon the countenance of the man who had been the intermediator between themselves and God. But Moses quieted them, and instantly set about imparting to the people the Torah he had received from God.

His method of instruction was as follows: first came Aaron, to whom he imparted the word of God, and as soon as he had finished with Aaron, came the sons of Aaron, Eleazar and Ithamar, and he instructed them, while Aaron sat at his right hand, listening. When he had finished with the sons of Aaron, the elders appeared to receive instruction, while Eleazar sat at the right hand of his father, and Ithamar at the left hand of Moses, and listened; and when he had finished with the elders, the people came and received instruction, whereupon Moses withdrew. Then Aaron went over what had been taught, and his sons likewise, and the elders, until every one, from Aaron down to every man out of the people, had four times repeated what he had learned, for in this way had God bidden Moses impress the Torah four times upon Israel.

THE CENSUS OF THE PEOPLE

At sight of the rays that emanated from Moses' face, the people said to him: "We were humbled by God owing to that sin we had committed. God, thou sayest, had forgiven us, and is reconciled to us. Thou, Moses, were include in our humiliation, and we see that He has once more exalted thee, whereas, in spite of the reconciliation with God, we remain humbled." Hereupon Moses betook himself to God and said; "When Thou didst humble them, Thou didst humble me also, hence shouldst Thou now raise them too, if Thou has raised me." God replied: "Truly, as I have exalted thee, so will I exalt them also; record their number, and through this show the world how near to My heart is the nation that before all others acknowledged Me as their king, singing by the Red Sea: 'This is my God, and I will exalt Him.'" Moses then said to God: "O Lord of the world! Thou hast so many nation in Thy world, but Thou carest nothing about recording their numbers, and only Israel dost Thou bid me count." God replied: "All these multitudes do not belong to Me, they are doomed to the destruction of Gehenna, but Israel is My possession, and as a man most prizes the possession he paid for most dearly, so is Israel most dear to Me, because I have with great exertions made it My own." Moses further said to God: "O Lord of the world! To our father Abraham Thou made the following promises: 'And I will make thy seed as the stars in the heavens,' but now Thou biddest me number Israel. If their forefather Abraham could not count them, how, then, should I?" But God quieted Moses, saying: "Thou needest not actually count them, but if thou wouldst determine their number, add together the numerical value of the names of the tribes, and the result will be their number." And truly in this way did Moses procure the sum total of the Jews, which amounted to sixty myriads less three thousand, the three thousand having been swept away by the plague in punishment for their worship of the Golden Calf. Hence the difference between the number at the exodus from Egypt, when Moses had counted them for the first time, and the number at the second census, after the losses incurred by the plague. God treated Israel as did that king his herd, who ordered the shepherds tell the tale of the sheep when he heard that wolves had been among them and had killed some, having this reckoning made in order to determine the amount of his loss.

The occasions on which, in the course of history, Israel were numbered, are as follows: Jacob counted his household upon entering Egypt; Moses counted Israel upon the exodus from Egypt; after the worship of the Golden Calf; at the arrangement into camp divisions; and at the distribution of the promised land. Saul twice instituted a census of the people, the first time when he set out against Nahash, the Ammonite, and the second time when he set out in war upon Amalek. It is significant of the enormous turn in the prosperity of the Jews during Saul's reign, that at the first census every man put down a pebble, so that the pebbles might be counted, but at the second census the people were so prosperous that instead of putting down a pebble, every man brought a lamb. There was a census in the reign of David, which, however, not having been ordered by God, had unfortunate consequences both for the king and for the people. Ezra instituted the last census when the people returned from Babylon to the Holy Land. Apart from these nine censuses, God will Himself count His people in the future time when their number will be so great that no mortal will be able to count them.

There was an offering to the sanctuary connected with the second census in Moses' time, when every one above twenty years of age had to offer up half a shekel. For God said to Moses: "They indeed deserve death for having made the Golden Calf, but let each one offer up to the Eternal atonement money for his soul, and in this way redeem himself from capital punishment." When the people heard this, they grieved greatly, for they thought: "In vain did we exert ourselves in taking booty from the Egyptians, if we are not to yield up our hard-earned possessions as atonement money. The law prescribes that a man pay fifty shekels of silver for dishonoring a woman, and we who have dishonored the word of God, should have to pay at least an equal amount. The law furthermore decrees that if an ox kill a servant, his owner shall pay thirty shekels of silver, hence every Israelite should have to discharge such a sum, for 'we changed our glory into the similitude of an ox that eateth grass.' But these two fines would not suffice, for we slandered God, He who brought us out of Egypt, by calling out to the Calf, 'This is thy God, that brought thee up out of Egypt,' and slander is punishable by law with one hundred shekels of silver." God who knew their thoughts, said to Moses: "Ask them why they are afraid. I do not ask of them to pay as high a fine as he who dishonors or seduces a woman, nor the penalty of a slanderer, nor that of the owner of a goring ox, all that I ask of them is this," and hereupon he showed Moses at the fire a small coin that represented the value of half a shekel. This coin each one of those who had passed through the Red Sea was to give as an offering.

There were several reasons why God asked particularly for the value of half a shekel as a penalty. As they committed their sin, the worship of the Golden Calf, in the middle, that is the half of the day, so they were to pay half of a shekel; and, furthermore, as they committed their sin in the sixth hour of the day, so were they to pay half a shekel, which is six grains of silver. This half shekel, furthermore, contains ten gerahs, and is hence the corresponding fine for those who trespassed the Ten Commandments. The half shekel was also to be an atonement for the sin committed by the ten sons of Jacob, who sold their brother Joseph as a slave, for whom each had received half a shekel as his share.

THE ERECTION OF THE TABERNACLE COMMANDED

When, on that memorable Day of Atonement, God indicated His forgiveness to Israel with the words, "I have forgiven them according as I have spoken," Moses said: "I now feel convinced that Thou hast forgiven Israel, but I wish Thou wouldst show the nations also that Thou are reconciled with Israel." For these were saying: "How can a nation that heard God's word on Sinai, 'Thou shalt have no other gods before Me,' and that forty days later called out to the Calf, 'This is thy god, O Israel,' expect that God would ever be reconciled to them?" God therefore said to Moses: "As truly as thou livest, I will let My Shekinah dwell among them, so that all my know that I have forgiven Israel. My sanctuary in their midst will be a testimony of My forgiveness of their sins, and hence it may well be called a 'Tabernacle of Testimony.'"

The erection of a sanctuary among Israel was begun in answer to a direct appeal from the people, who said to God: "O Lord of the world! The kings of the nations have palaces in which are set a table, candlesticks, and other royal insignia, that their king may be recognized as such. Shalt not Thou, too, our King, Redeemer, and Helper, employ royal insignia, that all the dwellers of the earth may recognize that Thou are their King?" God replied: "My children, the kings of the flesh and blood need all these things, but I do not, for I need neither food nor drink; nor is light necessary to Me, as can well be seen by this, that My servants, the sun and the moon, illuminate all the world with the light they receive from Me; hence ye need do none of these things for Me, for without these signs of honor will I let all good things fall to your lot in recognition of the merits of your fathers." But Israel answered: "O Lord of the world! We do not want to depend on our fathers. 'Doubtless Thou are our Father, though Abraham be ignorant of us, and Israel acknowledge us not." God hereupon said: "If you now insist upon carrying out your wish, do so, but do it in the way I command you. It is customary in the world that whosoever had a little son, cares for him, anoints him, washes him, feeds him, and carries him, but as soon as the son is come of age, he provides for his father a beautiful dwelling, a table, and a candlestick. So long as you were young, did I provide for you, washed you, fed you with bread and meat, gave you water to drink, and bore you on eagles' wings; but now that you are come of age, I wish you to build a house for Me, set therein a table and a candlestick, and make an altar of incense within it." God then gave them detailed instruction for furnishing the Tabernacle, saying to Moses; "Tell Israel that I order them to build Me a tabernacle not because I lack a dwelling, for, even before the world had been created, I had erected My temple in the heavens; but only as a token of My affection for you will I leave My heavenly temple and dwell among you, 'they shall make Me a sanctuary, that I may dwell among them.'"

At these last words Moses seized by a great fear, such as had taken possession of him only on two other occasions. Once, when God said to him, "Let each give a ransom for his soul," when, much alarmed, he said: "If a man were to give all that he hath for his soul, it would not suffice." God quieted him with the words, "I do not ask what is due Me, but only what they can fulfil, half a shekel will suffice." Then again, fear stirred Moses when God said to him: "Speak to Israel concerning My offering, and My bread for My sacrifices made by fire," and he said trembling, "Who can bring sufficient offerings to Thee? 'Lebanon is not sufficient to burn, nor the beast thereof sufficient for a burnt offering.'" Then again God quieted him with the words, "I demand not according to what is due Me, but only that which they can fulfil, one sheep as a morning sacrifice, and one sheep as an evening sacrifice." The third time, God was in the midst of giving Moses instructions concerning the building of the sanctuary, when Moses exclaimed in fear: "Behold, the heaven and heaven of heavens cannot contain Thee, how much less this sanctuary that we are to build Thee?" And this time also God quieted him with the words, "I do not ask what is due Me, but only that which they can fulfil; twenty boards to the north, as many to the south, eight in the west, and I shall then so draw My Shekinah together that it may find room under them." God was indeed anxious to have a sanctuary erected to Him, it was the condition on which He led them out of Egypt, yea, in a certain sense the existence of all the world depended on the construction of the sanctuary, for when the sanctuary had been erected, the world stood firmly founded, whereas until then it had always been swaying hither and thither. Hence the Tabernacle in its separate parts also corresponded to the heaven and the earth, that had been created on the first day. As the firmament had been created on the second day to divide the waters which were under the firmament from the waters which were above, so there was a curtain in the Tabernacle to divide between the holy and the most holy. As God created the great sea on the third say, so did He appoint the laver in the sanctuary to symbolize it, and as He had on that day destined the plant kingdom as nourishment for man, so did He now require a table with bread in the Tabernacle. The candlestick in the Tabernacle corresponded to the two luminous bodies, the sun and the moon, created on the fourth day; and the seven branches of the candlestick corresponded to the seven planets, the Sun, Venus, Mercury, the Moon, Saturn, Jupiter, and Mars. Corresponding to the birds created on the fifth day, the Tabernacle contained the Cherubim, that had wings like birds. On the sixth, the last day of creation, man had been created in the image of God to glorify his Creator, and likewise was the high priest anointed to minister in the Tabernacle before the Lord and Creator.

Chapter 3

THE MATERIALS FOR THE CONSTRUCTION OF THE TABERNACLE

When, on the Day of Atonement, God said to Moses, "Let them make Me a sanctuary, that I may dwell among them," that the nations of the world might see that He has forgiven Israel their sin, the worship of the Golden Calf, it was gold He bade them bring for the adornment of the sanctuary. God said: "The gold of the Tabernacle shall serve as an expiation for the gold they employed in the construction of the Golden Calf. Besides gold, let them bring Me twelve other materials for the construction of the Tabernacle: 'silver, brass, and blue, and purple, and scarlet, fine linen, and goats' hair, and rams' skins dyed red, and badgers' skins, and shittim wood, oil for the light, spices for anointing-oil, and for sweet incense, onyx stones and stones to be set in the ephod and in the breastplate.'" To these instructions, God added these words: "But do not suppose that you are giving Me these thirteen objects as gifts, for thirteen deed did I perform for you in Egypt, which these thirteen objects now repay. For 'I clothed you with broidered work, and shod you with badgers' skins, and girded you about with fine linen, and I covered you with silk. I decked you also with ornaments, and I put bracelets upon your arms, and chains about your necks. And I put jewels on your foreheads, and earrings in your ears, and a beautiful crown upon your heads.' But in the future world, in return for these thirteen offerings to the Tabernacle, you shall receive thirteen gifts from Me, when 'I shall create upon every dwelling place of Mount Zion, and upon her assemblies, a cloud and smoke by day, and the shining of a flaming fire by night, for upon all the glory shall be a defence. And there shall be a tabernacle for a shadow in the daytime from the heat, and for a place of refuge, and for a covert, from storms and from rain.'" God continued: "Give your contributions to the sanctuary with a willing heart. Do not think that you need give anything out of your pockets, for all you have belongs to Me, through whom you received it in you passage through the Red Sea, when you took their wealth from the Egyptians. I demand nothing from the other nations, but from you I do so, because it was I that led you out of Egypt. But you shall erect a sanctuary to Me not in this world only, but in the future world also. At first the Torah dwelt with Me, but now that it is in your possession, you must let Me dwell among you with the Torah."

Through the various objects God bade them dedicate to the sanctuary, the course of their history was indicated. The gold signified their yoke under Babylon, "the head of golds;" the silver pointed toward the sovereignty of Persia and Media, who through silver tried to bring about the destruction of Israel; brass stood for the Greek Empire, that like this metal is of inferior quality, its rule also was less significant than that of its predecessors in the sovereignty over the world; the ram's skins dyed red indicate the sovereignty of "red Rome." God now said to Israel: "Although you now behold the four nations that will hold sway over you, still shall I send you help out of your bondage, 'oil for the light,' the Messiah, who will enlighten the eyes of Israel, and who will make use of 'spices for anointing-oil,' for he will anoint the high priest, that once again 'I may accept you with your sweet savour.'"

When Moses was in heaven, God showed him the Tabernacle, as well as models for all the holy vessels therein, hence Moses naturally supposed that he was destined to be the builder of the Tabernacle. But he was mistaken, for when he was about to leave heaven, God said to Moses: "Thee have I appointed king, and it does not behoove a king to execute works in person, but to give people directions. Therefore thou are not to execute the building of the Tabernacle in person, but thou art to give them thy directions to be executed." Moses now asked God whom he should select as the man to carry out his orders, whereupon God fetched out the book of Adam and laid it before Moses. In this book he found recorded all the generations, from the creation of the world to the resurrection of the dead, and the kings, leaders, and prophets set down beside every generation. Then God said to Moses: "In that hour did I decree every man's calling, and Bezalel was then appointed to his task."

BEZALEL

Bezalel was, first of all, of a noble line. His father Hur was a son of Caleb from his union with Miriam, Moses' sister, that Hur who gave his life to restrain Israel from the worship of the Golden Calf. As a reward for his martyrdom, his son Bezalel was to build the Tabernacle, and one of his later descendants, King Solomon, was to build the Temple at Jerusalem. Bezalel was not only of a distinguished family, he was himself a man of distinction, possessed of wisdom, insight, and understanding. By means of these three God created the world; Bezalel erected the Tabernacle. Through their aid was the Temple complete, and even in the future world will it be wisdom, insight, and understanding, these three that God will employ to set up the new Temple. Bezalel, furthermore, had wisdom in the Torah, insight into the Halakah, and understanding in the Talmud, but more than this, he was well versed in secret lore, knowing as he did the combination of letters by means of which God created heaven and earth. The name Bezalel, "in the shadow of God," was most appropriate for this man whose wisdom made clear to him what none could know save one who dwelt "in the shadow of God."

Moses had an instant opportunity of testing the wisdom of this builder appointed by God. God had bidden Moses first to erect the Tabernacle, then the Holy Ark, and lastly to prepare the furnishings of the Tabernacle; but Moses, to put Bezalel's wisdom to the test, ordered him to construct first the Holy Ark, then the furnishings of the Tabernacle, and only then the sanctuary. Hereupon wise Bezalel said to Moses: "O our teacher Moses, it is the way of man first to build his house, and only then to provide its furnishings. Thou biddest me first provide furnishings and then build a sanctuary. What shall I do with the furnishings when there is no sanctuary ready to receive them?" Moses, delighted with Bezalel's wisdom, replied: "Now truly, the command was given just as thou sayest. Wert thou, perchance, 'in the shadow of God,' that thou knewest it?"

Although God knew that Bezalel was the right man for the erection of the Tabernacle, still He asked Moses, "Dost thou consider Bezalel suited to this task?" Moses replied: "O Lord of the world! If Thou considerest him suitable, then surely do I!" But God said: "Go, nevertheless, and ask Israel if they approve My choice of Bezalel." Moses did as he was bidden, and the people assented in these words: "If Bezalel is judged good enough by God and by thee, assuredly he is approved by us." As the builder of the Tabernacle, God gave Bezalel five other names to bear. He called him Reaiah, "to behold," for Bezalel was beheld by God, by Moses, and by Israel, as the one who had been decreed for his activity since the beginning of the world. He called him "the son of Shobal," because he had erected the Tabernacle that towered high, like a dove-cote. He called him Jahath, "the Trembler," because he made the sanctuary, the seat of the fear of God. He called him Ahamai, because, through his work, the sanctuary, Israel, and God were united; and finally Lahad, as the one who brought splendor and loftiness it Israel, for the sanctuary is the pride and splendor of Israel.

At the side of Bezalel, the noble Judean, worked Oholiab, of the insignificant tribe of Dan, to show that "before God, the great and the lowly are equal." And as the Tabernacle rose, thanks to the combined efforts of a Judean and a Danite, so too did the Temple of Jerusalem, which was built at the command of the Judean Solomon by the Danite Hiram. As the head-workers of the Tabernacle were filled with the holy spirit of God in order to accomplish their task aright, so too were all who aided in its construction, yes, even the beasts that were employed on this occasion possessed wisdom, insight, and understanding.

THE ARK WITH THE CHERUBIM

The very first thing that Bezalel constructed was the Ark of the Covenant, contrary to Moses' order, first to erect the Tabernacle and then to supply its separate furnishings. He succeeded in convincing Moses that it was the proper thing to begin with the Ark, saying: "What is the purpose of this Tabernacle?" Moses: "That God may let His Shekinah rest therein, and so teach the Torah to His people Israel." Bezalel: "And where dost thou keep the Torah?" Moses: "As soon as the Tabernacle shall have been complete, we shall make the Ark for keeping the Torah." Bezalel: "O our teacher Moses, it does not become the dignity of the Torah that in the meanwhile it should lie around like this, let us rather first make the Ark, put the Torah into it, and then continue with the erection of the Tabernacle, for the Tabernacle exists only for the sake of the Torah." Moses saw the justice of this argument, and Bezalel began his work with the construction of the Ark. In this he followed the example of God, who created light before all the rest of the creation. So Bezalel first constructed the Ark that contains the Torah, the light that illuminates this world and the other world; and only then followed the rest. The Ark consisted of three caskets, a gold one, the length of then spans and a fractional part; within this a wooden one, nine spans long, and within this wooden one, one of gold, eight spans long, so that within and without the wooden was overlaid with the golden caskets. The Ark contained the two tables of the Ten Commandments as well as the Ineffable Name, and all His other epithets. The Ark was an image of the celestial Throne, and was therefore the most essential part of the Tabernacle, so that even during the march it was spread over with a cloth wholly of blue, because this color is similar to the color of the celestial Throne. It was through the Ark, also, that all the miracles on the way through the desert had been wrought. Two sparks issued from the Cherubim that shaded the Ark, and these killed all the serpents and scorpions that crossed the path of the Israelites, and furthermore burned all thorns that threatened to injure the wanderers on their march through the desert. The smoke rising from these scorched thorns, moreover, rose straight as a column, and shed a fragrance that perfumed all the world, so that the nations exclaimed: "Who is this that cometh out of the wilderness like pillars of smoke, perfumed with myrrh and frankincense, with all powders of the merchant?"

Apart from this Ark, which was kept in the Tabernacle, they had another ark, in which were contained the tables broken by Moses, which they carried with them whenever they went to war. The Ark that Bezalel constructed was also used again in Solomon's Temple, for he retained the Ark used by Moses in the Tabernacle, even though all the other furnishings of the Temple were fashioned anew. It remained there up to the time of the destruction of the Temple by Nebuchadnezzar, when it was concealed under the pavement of the wood-house, that it might not fall into the hands of the enemy. This place remained a secret for all time. Once a priest, noticing about the wood-house that something lay hidden under it, called out to his colleagues, but was suddenly stricken dead before divulging the secret.

On the Ark were the Cherubim with their faces of boys and their wings. Their number was two, corresponding to the two tables, and to the two sacred names of God, Adonai and Elohim, which characterized Him as benevolent and as powerful. The face of each Cherub measured one span, and the wings extended each ten spans, making twenty-two spans in all, corresponding to the twenty-two letters of the Hebrew alphabet. It was "from between the two Cherubim" that God communed with Moses, for the Shekinah never wholly descended to earth any more than any mortal ever quite mounted into the heaven, even Moses and Elijah stood a slight distance from heaven; for, "The heaven, even the heavens, are the Lord's: but the earth hath He given to the children of men." Therefore God chose the Cherubim that were ten spans above the earth as the place where the Shekinah betook itself to commune with Moses. The heads of the Cherubim were slightly turned back, like that of a scholar bidding his master farewell; but as a token of God's delight in His people Israel, the faces of the Cherubim, by a miracle, "looked one to another" whenever Israel were devoted to their Lord, yea, even clasped one another like a loving couple. During the festivals of the pilgrimage the priest used to raise the curtain from the Holy of Holies to show the pilgrims how much their God loved them as they could see in the embrace of the two Cherubim.

A tow-fold miracle came to pass when the Cherubim were brought into the Temple by Solomon: the two staves that were attached to the Ark extended until they touched the curtain, so that two protuberances like a woman's breasts became visible at the back of it, and the wings of the Cherubim furthermore extended until they reached the ceiling of the Holy of Holies.

THE TABLE AND THE CANDLESTICK

While the number of Cherubim was the same in the Temple as in the Tabernacle, Solomon had, on the other hand, ten tables set up in the Temple in place of the one fashioned by Moses. This was because the one table sufficed to bring sustenance to Israel so long as they were maintained by manna in the desert; but as the demand for food was greater after they settled in the promised land, Solomon had ten tables set up. But in the Temple also did the table of Moses retain its ancient significance, for only upon it was the shewbread placed, and it stood in the center, whereas the tables fashioned by Solomon stood five to the south and five to the north. For from the south come "the dews of blessing and the rains of plenty," while all evil comes from the north; hence Solomon said: "The tables on the south side shall cause the rains of plenty and the dews of blessing to come upon the earth, while the tables on the north side shall keep off all evil from Israel."

Moses had great difficulty with the construction of the candlestick, for although God had given him instructions about it, he completely forgot these when he descended from heaven. He hereupon betook himself to God once more to be shown, but in vain, for hardly had he reached earth, when he again forgot. When he betook himself to God the third time, God took a candlestick of fire and plainly showed him every single detail of it, that he might now be able to reconstruct the candlestick for the Tabernacle. When he found it still hard to form a clear conception of the nature of the candlestick, God quieted him with these words" "Go to Bezalel, he will do it aright." And indeed, Bezalel had no difficulty in doing so, and instantly executed Moses' commission. Moses cried in amazement: "God showed me repeatedly how to make the candlestick, yet I could not properly seize the idea; but thou, without having had it shown thee by God, couldst fashion it out of thy own fund of knowledge. Truly dost thou deserve thy name Bezalel, 'in the shadow of God,' for thou dost act as if thou hadst been 'in the shadow of God' while He was showing me the candlestick."

The candlestick was later set up in the Temple of Solomon, and although he set up ten other candlesticks, still this one was the first to be lighted. Solomon chose the number ten because it corresponds to the number of Words revealed on Sinai; and each of these candlesticks had seven lamps, seventy in all, to correspond to the seventy nations. For while these lamps burned the power of these nations was held in check, but on the day on which these lamps are extinguished the power of the nations is increased. The candlestick stood toward the south, and the table to the north of the sanctuary, the table to indicate the delights of which the pious would partake in Paradise, which lies to the north; the light of the candlestick to symbolize the light of the Shekinah, for in the future world there will be but one delight, to gaze at the light of the Shekinah. On account of its sacredness the candlestick was one of the five sacred objects that God concealed at the destruction of the Temple by Nebuchadnezzar, and that He will restore when in His loving-kindness He will erect His house and Temple. These sacred objects are: the Ark, the candlestick, the fire of the altar, the Holy Spirit of prophecy, and the Cherubim.

THE ALTAR

One of the most miraculous parts of the Tabernacle was the altar. For when God bade Moses make an altar of shittim wood and overlay it with brass, Moses said to God: "O Lord of the world! Thou badest me make the altar of wood and overlay it with brass, but Thou didst also bid me have 'a fire kept burning upon the altar continually.' Will not the fire destroy the overlay of brass, and then consume the wood of the altar?" God replied: "Moses, thou judgest by the laws that apply to men, but will these also apply to Me? Behold, the angels that are of burning flame. Beside them are My store-houses of snow and My store-houses of hail. Doth the water quench their fire, or doth their fire consume the water? Behold, also, the Hayyot that are of fire. Above their heads extends a terrible sea of ice that no mortal can traverse in less than five hundred years. Yet doth the water quench their fire, or doth their fire consume the water? For, 'I am the Lord who maketh peace between these elements in My high places.' But thou, because I have bidden thee to have 'a fire kept burning upon the altar continually,' art afraid that the wood might be consumed by the fire. Dead things come before Me, and leave Me imbued with life, and thou are afraid the wood of the altar might be consumed! Thine own experience should by now have taught thee better; thou didst pierce the fiery chambers of heaven, thou didst enter among the fiery hosts on high, yea, thou didst even approach Me, that 'am a consuming fire.' Surely thou shouldst then have been consumed by fire, but thou wert unscathed because thou didst go into the fire at My command; no more shall the brass overlay of the altar be injured by fire, even though it be no thicker than a denarium."

In the words, "Dead things come before Me and leave Me imbued with life," God alluded to the three following incidents. The rod of Aaron, after it had lain for a night in the sanctuary, "brought forth buds, and bloomed blossoms, and even yielded almonds." The cedars that Hiram, king of Tyre, sent to Solomon for the building of the Temple, as soon as the incense of the sanctuary reached them, thrilled green anew, and throughout centuries bore fruits, by means of which the young priests sustained themselves. Not until Manasseh brought the idol into the Holy of Holies, did these cedars wither and cease to bear fruit. The third incident to which God alludes was the stretching of the staves of the Ark when Solomon set them in the Holy of Holies, and the staves, after having been apart of the Ark for four hundred and eighty years, suddenly extended until they touched the curtain.

Solomon erected a new altar for offerings, but knowing how dear to God was the altar erected by Moses, the brazen altar, he at least retained the same name for his altar. But in the following words it is evident how much God prized the altar erected by Moses, for He said: "To reward Israel for having had 'a fire kept burning upon the altar continually,' I shall punish 'the kingdom laden with crime' by fire 'that shall not be quenched night or day; the smoke thereof shall go up forever.'"

Beside the brazen altar there was also one of gold, which corresponded to the human soul, while the former corresponded to the body; and as gold is more valuable than brass, so also is the soul greater than the body. But both altars were used daily, as man must also serve his Maker with both body and soul. On the brazen altar sacrifices were offered, as the body of man, likewise, is nourished by food; but on the golden altar, spices and sweet incense, for the soul takes delight in perfumes only.

The materials employed for the constructions of the Tabernacle, the skins and the wood, were not of the common order. God created the animal Tahash exclusively for the needs of the Tabernacle, for it was so enormous that out of one skin could be made a curtain, thirty cubits long. This species of animal disappeared as soon as the demands of the Tabernacle for skins were satisfied. The cedars for the Tabernacle, also, were obtained in no common way, for whence should they have gotten cedars in the desert? They owed these to their ancestor Jacob. When he reached Egypt, he planted a cedar-grove and admonished his sons to do the same, saying: "You will in the future be released from bondage in Egypt, and God will then demand that you erect Him a sanctuary to thank Him for having delivered you. Plant cedar trees, then, that when God will bid you build Him a sanctuary, you may have in your possession the cedars required for its construction." His sons acted in accordance with the bidding of their father, and upon leaving Egypt took along the cedars for the anticipated erection of the sanctuary. Among these cedars was also that wonderful cedar out of which was wrought "the middle bar in the midst of the boards, that reached from end to end," and which Jacob took with him from Palestine when he emigrated to Egypt, and then left to remain among his descendants. When the cedars were selected for the construction of the Tabernacle, they intoned a song of praise to God for this distinction.

But not all the twenty-four species of cedar might be used for the Tabernacle, nay, not even the seven most excellent among them were found worthy, but only the species shittim might be used. For God, who foresees all, knew that Israel would in the future commit a great sin at Shittim, and therefore ordained that shittim wood be used for the Tabernacle to serve as atonement for the sin committed at Shittim. Shittim furthermore signifies "follies," hence Israel were to construct the place of penance for their folly in adoring the Golden Calf, out of shittim wood, to atone for this "folly." And finally, the letters of which the wood "Shittim" is composed, stand for Shalom, "peace," Tobah, "good," Yesh'uah. "salvation," and Mehillah, "forgiveness." The boards that were made for the Tabernacle out of shittim wood never decayed, but endure in all eternity.

THE SYMBOLICAL SIGNIFICANCE OF THE TABERNACLE

The separate parts of the Tabernacle had each a symbolical significance, for to all that is above there is something corresponding below. There are stars above, but likewise below, where "a star shall come out of Jacob;" God has His hosts above, and likewise below, His people Israel, "the hosts of the Lord;" above there are Ofannim, and on earth likewise there is an Ofan; above, God has Cherubim, and likewise below in the sanctuary of Israel; God hath His dwelling above, but likewise below; and, lastly, God hath stretched out the heavens above like a curtain, and below, in the sanctuary, were curtains of goats' hair.

The number of curtains, also, corresponds to those in heaven, for just as there are eleven upper heavens, so also were there eleven curtains of goats' hair. The size of the Tabernacle was seventy cubits, corresponding to the seventy holy days celebrated annually by the Jews, to wit: fifty-two Sabbaths, seven days of Passover, eight of Tabernacles, and a day each for Pentecost, the Day of Atonement, and New Year's Day. The number of vessels amounted to seventy also; as likewise God, Israel, and Jerusalem bear seventy names; and as, correspondingly, in the time between the building of the first and of the second Temple, there were seventy consecutive Sanhedrin.

Like the Tabernacle, so the altar, too had its symbolical significance. Its length and its breadth were five cubits each, corresponding respectively to the five Commandments on the two tables of the law. Its height was three cubits, corresponding to the three deliverers God sent to deliver Israel from Egypt,-Moses, Aaron, and Miriam. It had four horns in the corners thereof, to atone for the sins of the people that on Sinai receive four horns, "the horn of the Torah," "the horn of the Shekinah," "the horn of Priesthood," and "the horn of the Kingdom."

In the Tabernacle, as later in the Temple, gold, silver, and brass were employed, but not iron. God meant to indicate by the exclusion of iron that "in the future time," "the golden Babylon, the silver Media, and the brazen Greece," would be permitted to bestow the gifts on the new Temple, but not "the iron Rome." It is true that Babylon also destroyed the sanctuary of God, like Rome, but not with such fury and such thorough-going wrath as Rome, whose sons cried: "Raze it, raze it, even to the foundations thereof," and for this reason Rome may not contribute to the Messianic Temple. And as God will reject the gifts of Rome, so also will the Messiah, to whom all the nations of the earth will have to offer gifts. Egypt will come with her gifts, and although the Messiah will at first refuse to accept anything from the former taskmaster of Israel, God will say to him: "The Egyptians granted My children an abode in their land, do not repulse them." Then the Messiah will accept their gift. After Egypt will follow her neighbor, Ethiopia, with her gifts, thinking that if the Messiah accepted gifts from the former taskmaster of Israel, he will also accept gifts from her. Then the Messiah will also accept Ethiopia's gifts. After these two kingdoms will follow all others with their gifts, and all will be accepted save those from Rome. This kingdom will be sorely disappointed, for, depending upon their kinship with Israel, they will expect kind treatment from the Messiah, who had graciously received the other nations not connected with Israel. But God will call out to the Messiah: "Roar at this monster that devours the fat of nations, that justifies its claims for recognition through being a descendant of Abraham by his grandson Esau, the nation that forgives all for the sake of money, that kept Israel back from the study of the Torah, and tempted them to deeps that are in accord with the wishes of Satan."

THE PRIESTLY ROBES

Simultaneously with the construction of the Tabernacle and its vessels, were fashioned the priestly robes for Aaron and his sons. It was at this time that God made known Aaron's appointment to the office of high priest, saying: "Go and appoint a high priest." Moses: "Out of which tribe?" God: "Of the tribe of Levi." Moses was most happy upon hearing that the high priest was to be chosen out of his tribe, and his joy was increased when God added: "Appoint thy brother Aaron as high priest." This choice of Aaron was, of course, also a disappointment to Moses, who had hoped God would appoint him as His high priest, but God had designed this dignity for Aaron to reward him for his pious deeds when Israel worshipped the Golden Calf. For when Moses returned from Sinai and saw the Calf fashioned by Aaron, he thought his brother was no better than the rest of the people, and had, like them, devoted himself to idolatry. But God knew that Aaron's participation in the construction of the Calf was merely due to the pious motive of delaying the people until Moses should return, hence He even then said to Aaron: "I am fully aware of they motive, and, as truly as thou livest, I shall appoint thee as warden over the sacrifices that My children offer Me." In consideration of Moses' feelings, God gave into his hands the appointment of Aaron, saying to him: "I might have installed thy brother as high priest without having informed thee of it, but I relinquish his appointment to thee, that thou mayest have an opportunity of showing the people thy humility, in that thou dost not seek this high office for thyself." At God's bidding, Aaron and his two sons were now chosen as priest, and, moreover, not for a limited period, but Aaron and his house were invested with the priesthood for all eternity. As soon as these were installed as priests, Moses set to work to instruct them thoroughly in the priestly laws.

God ordered the following eight garments as Aaron's garb: coat, breeches, mitre, girdle, breastplate, ephod, robe, and golden plate; but his sons needed only the first four garments. All these garments had expiatory virtues, and each expiated a definite sin. The coat atoned for murder, the breeches for unchastity, the mitre for pride, the girdle for theft, the breastplate for partial verdicts, the ephod for idolatry, the bells on the robe for slander, and the golden plate for effrontery.

The breastplate and the ephod were set with precious stones, which were the gifts of the noble to the sanctuary, though, to be exact, they were in reality a gift from God. For precious stones and pearls had rained down with the manna, which the noble among Israel had gathered up and laid away until the Tabernacle was erected, when they offered them as gifts.

The ephod had only two precious stones, one on each shoulder, and on each of these stones were engraved the names of the six tribes in the following order: Reuben, Levi, Issachar, Naphtali, Gad, Jehoseph, on the right shoulder-piece; Simeon, Judah, Zebulun, Dan, Asher, Benjamin, on the left shoulder. The name Joseph was spelled Jehoseph, a device by which the two stones had exactly the same number of letters engraved upon them. On the breast plate were twelve precious stones, on which the names of the three Patriarchs preceded those of the twelve tribes, and at the end were engraved the words, "All these are the twelve tribes of Israel."

THE STONES IN THE BREASTPLATE

The twelve stones differed not only in color, but also in certain qualities peculiar to each, and both quality and color had especial reference to the tribe whose name it bore. Reuben's stone was the ruby, that has the property, when grated by a woman and tasted by her, of promoting pregnancy, for it was Reuben who found the mandrakes which induce pregnancy.

Simeon's stone was the smaragd, that has the property of breaking as soon as an unchaste woman looks at it, a fitting stone for the tribe whose sire, Simeon, was kindles to wrath by the unchaste action of Shechem. It was at the same time a warning to the tribe of Simeon, that committed whoredom at Shittim with the daughters of Moab, to be mindful of chastity, and like its stone, to suffer no prostitution.

Levi's stone was the carbuncle, that beams like lightning, as, likewise, the faces of that tribe beamed with piety and erudition. This stone has the virtue of making him who wears it wise; but true wisdom is the fear of God, and it was this tribe alone that did not join in the worship of the Golden Calf.

Judah's stone was the green emerald, that has the power of making its owner victorious in battle, a fitting stone for this tribe from which springs the Jewish dynasty of kings, that routed its enemies. The color green alludes to the shame that turned Judah's countenance green when he publicly confessed his crime with Tamar.

Issachar's stone was the sapphire, for this tribe devoted themselves completely to the study of the Torah, and it is this very stone, the sapphire, out of which the two tables of the law were hewn. This stone increases strength of vision and heals many diseases, as the Torah, likewise, to which this tribe was so devoted, enlightens the eye and makes the body well.

The white pearl is the stone of Zebulun, for with his merchant ships he sailed the sea and drew his sustenance from the ocean from which the pearl, too, is drawn. The pearl has also the quality of bringing its owner sleep, and it is all the more to the credit of this tribe that they nevertheless spent their nights on commercial ventures to maintain their brother-tribe Issachar, that lived only for the study of the Torah. The pearl is, furthermore, round, like the fortune of the rich, that turns like a wheel, and in this way the wealthy tribe of Zebulun were kept in mind of the fickleness of fortune.

Dan's stone was a species of topaz, in which was visible the inverted face of a man, for the Danites were sinful, turning good to evil, hence the inverted face in their stone.

The turquoise was Naphtali's stone, for it gives its owner speed in riding, and Naphtali was "a hind let loose."

Gad's stone was the crystal, that endows its owner with courage in battle, and hence served this warlike tribe that battled for the Lord as an admonition to fear none and build on God.

The chrysolite was Asher's stone, and as this stone aids digestion and makes its owner sturdy and fat, so were the agricultural products of Asher's tribe of such excellent quality that they made fat those who ate of them.

Joseph's stone was the onyx, that has the virtue of endowing him who wears it with grace, and truly, by his grace, did Joseph find favor in the eyes of all.

Jasper was Benjamin's stone, and as this stone turns color, being now red, now green, now even black, so did Benjamin's feelings vary to his brothers. Sometimes he was angry with them for having sold into slavery Joseph, the only other brother by his mother Rachel, and in this mood he came near betraying their deed to his father; but, that he might not disgrace his brothers, he did not divulge their secret. To this discretion on his part alludes the Hebrew name of his stone, Yashpeh, which signifies, "There is a mouth," for Benjamin, though he had a mouth, did not utter the words that would have covered his brothers with disgrace.

The twelve stones in the breastplate, with their bright colors, were of great importance in the oracular sentences of the high priest, who by means of these stones made the Urim and Tummim exercise their functions. For whenever the king or the head of the Sanhedrin wished to get directions from the Urim and Tummim he betook himself to the high priest. The latter, robed in his breastplate and ephod, bade him look into his face and submit his inquiry. The high priest, looking down on his breastplate, then looked to see which of the letters engraved on the stones shone out most brightly, and then constructed the answer out of these letters. Thus, for example, when David inquired of the Urim and Tummim if Saul would pursue him, the high priest Abiathar beheld gleaming forth the letter Yod in Judah's name, Resh in Reuben's name, and Dalet in Dan's name, hence the answer read as follows: Yered, "He will pursue."

The information of this oracle was always trustworthy, for the meaning of the name Urim and Tummim is in the fact that "these answers spread light and truth," but not every high priest succeeded in obtaining them. Only a high priest who was permeated with the Holy Spirit, and over whom rested the Shekinah, might obtain an answer, for in other cases the stones withheld their power. But if the high priest was worthy, he received an answer to every inquiry, for on these stones were engraved all the letters of the alphabet, so that all conceivable words could be constructed from them.

THE COMPLETION OF THE TABERNACLE

On the eleventh day of Tishri Moses assembled the people, and informed them that it was God's wish to have a sanctuary among them, and each man was bidden to bring to the sanctuary any offering he pleased. At the same time he impressed upon them that, however pious a deed participation in the construction of the Tabernacle might be, still they might under no circumstances break the Sabbath to hasten to building of the sanctuary. Moses thereupon expounded to them the kind of work that was permissible on the Sabbath, and the king that was prohibited, for there were not less then thirty-nine occupations the pursuit of which on the Sabbath was punishable by death. Owing to the importance of keeping the Sabbath, Moses imparted the precepts concerning it directly to the great masses of the people that he had gathered together, and not to the elders alone. In this he acted according to God's command, who said to him: "Go, Moses, call together great assemblages and announce the Sabbath laws to them, that the future generations may follow thy example, and on Sabbath days assemble the people in the synagogues and instruct them in the Torah, that they may know what is prohibited and what is permitted, that My name may be glorified among My children." In the spirit of this command did Moses institute that on every holy day there might be preaching in the synagogues, and instruction concerning the significance of the special holy day. He summoned the people to these teachings with the words: "If you will follow my example, God will count it for you as if you had acknowledged God as your king throughout the world."

The stress laid on the observance of the Sabbath laws was quite necessary, for the people were so eager to deliver up their contributions, that on the Sabbath Moses had to have an announcement proclaimed that they were to take nothing out of their houses, as the carrying of things on the Sabbath is prohibited. For Israel is a peculiar people, that answered the summons to fetch gold for the Golden Calf, and with no less zeal answered the summons of Moses to give contributions for the Tabernacle. They were not content to bring things out of their houses and treasuries, but forcibly snatched ornaments from their wives, their daughters, and their sons, and brought them to Moses for the construction of the Tabernacle. In this way they thought they could cancel their sin in having fashioned the Golden Calf; then had they used their ornaments in the construction of the idol, and now they employed them for the sanctuary of God.

The women, however, were no less eager to contribute their mite, and were especially active in producing the woolen hangings. They did this in no miraculous a way, that they spun the wool while it was still upon the goats. Moses did not at first want to accept contributions from the women, but these brought their cloaks and their mirrors, saying: "Why dost thou reject our gifts? If thou doest so because thou wantest in the sanctuary nothing that women use to enhance their charms, behold, here are our cloaks that we use to conceal ourselves from the eyes of the men. But if thou are afraid to accept from us anything that might be not our property, but our husbands', behold, here are our mirrors that belong to us alone, and not to our husbands." When Moses beheld the mirrors, he waxed very angry, and bade the women to be driven from him, exclaiming: "What right in the sanctuary have these mirrors that exist only to arouse sensual desires?" But God said to Moses: "Truly dearer to Me than all other gifts are these mirrors, for it was these mirrors that yielded Me My hosts. When in Egypt the men were exhausted from their heavy labors, the women were wont to come to them with food and drink, take out their mirrors, and caressingly say to their husbands: 'Look into the mirror, I am much more beautiful than thou,' and in this way passion seized the men so that they forgot their cares and united themselves with their wives, who thereupon brought many children into the world. Take now these mirrors and fashion out of them the laver that contains the water for the sanctifying of the priests." Furthermore out of this laver was fetched the water that a woman suspected of adultery had to drink to prove her innocence. As formerly the mirrors had been used to kindle conjugal affection, so out of them was made the vessel for the water that was to restore broken peace between husband and wife.

When Moses upon God's command made known to the people that whosoever was of a willing heart, man or woman, might bring an offering, the zeal of the women was so great, that they thrust away the men and crowded forward with their gifts, so that in two days all that was needful for the construction of the

Tabernacle was in Moses' hands. The princes of the tribes came almost too late with their contributions, and at the last moment they brought the precious stones for the garments of Aaron, that they might not be entirely unrepresented in the sanctuary. But God took their delay amiss, and for this reason they later sought to be the first to offer up sacrifices in the sanctuary.

After everything had been provided for the construction of the Tabernacle, Bezalel set to work with the devotion of his whole soul, and as a reward for this, the Holy Scriptures speak of him only as the constructor of the sanctuary, although many others stood by him in this labor. He began his work by fashioning the boards, then attended to the overlaying of them, and when he had completed these things, he set to work to prepare the curtains, then completed the Ark with the penance-cover belonging to it, and finally the table for the shewbread, and the candlestick.

THE SETTING UP OF THE TABERNACLE

The work on the Tabernacle progressed rapidly, for everything was ready in the month of Kislew, but it was not set up until three months later. The people were indeed eager to set up the sanctuary at once and to dedicate it, but God bade Moses wait until the first day of the month of Nisan, because that was Isaac's birthday, and God wished the joy of dedication to take place on this day of joy. The mockers among Israel, of course, to whom this was not known, made fun of Moses, saying: "Of course, is it possible that the Shekinah should rest over the work of Amram's sons?"

In regard to the Tabernacle, Moses had to suffer much besides from the fault-finders and wicked tongues. If he showed himself upon the street, they called out to one another: "See what a well-fed neck, what sturdy legs the son of Amram has, who eats and drinks from our money!" The other would answer: "Dost thou believe that one who has construction of the Tabernacle in his hands will remain a poor man?" Moses said nothing, but resolved, as soon as the Tabernacle should have been completed, to lay an exact account before the people, which he did. But when it came to giving his account, he forgot one item of seven hundred seventy-five shekels which he had expended for hooks upon which to hang the curtains of the Tabernacle. Then, as he suddenly raised his eyes, he saw the Shekinah resting on the hooks and was reminded of his omission of this expenditure. Thereafter all Israel became convinced that Moses was a faithful and reliable administrator.

As the people had brought much more material than was necessary for the Tabernacle, Moses erected a second Tabernacle outside the encampment on the spot where God had been accustomed to reveal Himself to him, and this "Tabernacle of revelation" was in all details like the original sanctuary in the camp.

When everything was ready, the people were very much disappointed that the Shekinah did not rest upon their work, and the betook themselves to the wise men who had worked on the erection of the Tabernacle, and said to them: "Why do ye sit thus idle, set up the Tabernacle, that the Shekinah may dwell among us." These now attempted to put up the Tabernacle, but did not succeed, for hardly did they believe it was up, when it fell down again. Now all went to Bezalel and his assistant Oholiab, saying to them: "Do you now set up the Tabernacle, you who constructed it, and perhaps it will then stand." But when even these two master-builders did not succeed in setting up the Tabernacle, the people began to find fault, and say: "See now what the son of Amram has brought upon us. We spent our money and went through a great deal of trouble, all because he assured us that the Holy One, blessed be He, would descend from His place with the angels and dwell among us under 'the hangings of goats' hair,' but it has all been in vain." The people now went to Moses, saying: "O our teacher Moses, we have done all thou has bidden us do, we gave all thou didst ask of us. Look now upon this completed work, and tell us if we have omitted aught, or have done aught we should have refrained from doing, examine it with care and answer us." Moses had to admit that all had been done according to his instructions. "But if it be so," continued the people, "why then cannot the Tabernacle stand? Bezalel and Oholiab failed to set it up, and all the wise men as well!" This communication sorely grieved Moses, who could not understand why the Tabernacle could not be set up. But God said to him: "Thou wert sorry to have had no share in the erection of the Tabernacle, which the people supplied with material, and on which Bezalel, Oholiab, and the other wise men labored with the work of their hands. For this reason did it come to pass that none could set up the Tabernacle, for I want all Israel to see that it cannot stand if thou dost not set it up." Moses replied: "O Lord of the world! I do not know how to put it up." But God answered: "Go, get busy with its setting-up, and while thou art busy at it, it will rise of its own accord." And so it came to pass. Hardly had Moses put his hand upon the Tabernacle, when it stood erect, and the rumors among the people that Moses had arbitrarily put up the Tabernacle without the command of God ceased forevermore.

THE CONSECRATION OF THE PRIESTS

Before the sanctuary and its vessels were dedicated for service, they were anointed with holy oil. On this occasion the miracle came to pass that twelve lugs of oil sufficed not only to anoint the sanctuary and its vessels, and Aaron and his two sons throughout the seven days of their consecration, but with this same oil were anointed all the successors of Aaron in the office of high priest, and several kings until the days of Josiah.

An especial miracle occurred when Aaron was anointed and on his pointed beard two drops of holy oil hung pendant like two pearls. These drops did not even disappear when he trimmed his beard, but rose to the roots of the hair. Moses at first feared that the useless waste of these drops of holy oil on Aaron's beard might be considered sacrilege, but a Divine voice quieted him. A Divine voice quieted Aaron, also, who likewise feared the accident that had turned the holy oil to his personal use.

The anointing of Aaron and his two sons was not the only ceremony that consecrated them as priests, for during a whole week did they have to live near the Tabernacle, secluded from the outer world. During this time Moses performed all priestly duties, even bringing sacrifices for Aaron and his sons, and sprinkling them with the blood of these sacrifices. It was on the twenty-third day of Adar that God bade Moses consecrate Aaron and his sons as priests, saying to him: "Go, persuade Aaron to accept his priestly office, for he is a man whom shuns distinctions. But effect his appointment before all Israel, that he may be honored in this way, and at the same time warn the people that after the choice of Aaron none may assume priestly rights. Gather thou all the congregation together unto the door of the Tabernacle." At these last words Moses exclaimed: "O Lord of the world! How shall I be able to assemble before the door of the Tabernacle, a space that measures only two seah, sixty myriads of adult men and as many youths?" But God answered: "Dost thou marvel at this? Greater miracles than this have I accomplished. The heaven was originally as thin and as small as the retina of the eye, still I caused it to stretch over all the world from one end to the other. In the future world, too, when all men from Adam to the time of the Resurrection will be assembled in Zion, and the multitude will be so great that one shall call to the other, 'The place is too strait for me, give place to me that I may dwell,' on that day will I so extend the holy city that all will conveniently find room there."

Moses did as he was bidden, and in presence of all the people took place the election of Aaron and his sons as priests, whereupon these retired for a week to the door of the Tabernacle. During this week, in preparing the burnt offering and the sin offering, Moses showed his brother Aaron and Aaron's sons how to perform the different priestly functions in the sanctuary. Moses made a sin offering because he feared that among the gifts out of which the sanctuary had been constructed, there might have been ill-gotten gains, and God loves justice and hates loot as an offering, Moses through a sin offering sought to obtain forgiveness for a possible wrong. During this week, however, the sanctuary was only temporarily used. Moses would set it up mornings and evenings, then fold it together again, and it was not until this week had passed that the sanctuary was committed to the general use. After that it was not folded together except when they moved from on encampment to another.

These seven days of retirement were assigned to Aaron and his sons not only as a preparation for their regular service, they had another significance also. God, before bringing the flood upon the earth, observed the seven days preceding as a week of mourning, and in the same way He bade Aaron and his sons live in absolute retirement for a week, as is the duty of mourners, for a heavy loss awaited them-the death of Nadab and Abihu, which took place on the joyous day of their dedication.

THE DAY OF THE TEN CROWNS

The first day of Nisan was an eventful day, "a day that was distinguished by ten crowns." It was the day on which the princes of the tribes began to bring their offerings; it was the first day on which Shekinah came to dwell among Israel; the first day on which sacrifice on any but the appointed place was forbidden; the first day on which priests bestowed their blessing upon Israel; the first day for regular sacrificial service; the first day on which the priests partook of certain portions of the offering; the first day on which the heavenly fire was seen on the altar; it was besides the first day of the week, a Sunday, the first day of the first month of the year.

It was on this day after "the week of training" for Aaron and his sons that God said to Moses: "Thinkest thou that thou are to be high priest because thou hast been attending to priestly duties during this week? Not so, call Aaron and announce to him that he has been appointed high priest, and at the same time call the elders and in their presence announce his elevation to this dignity, that none may say Aaron himself assumed this dignity." Following the example of God, who on Sinai distinguished Aaron before all others, saying, "And thou shalt come up, thou and Aaron with thee, but let not the priests and the people break through," Moses went first to Aaron, then to Aaron's sons, and only then to the elders, to discuss with them the preparations for the installation of Aaron into office.

When Moses approached Aaron with the news of God's commission to appoint him as high priest, Aaron said: "What! Thou hadst all the labor of erecting the Tabernacle, and I am now to be its high priest!" But Moses replied: "As truly as thou livest, although thou art to be high priest, I am as happy as if I had been chosen myself. As thou didst rejoice in my elevation, so do I now rejoice in thine." Moses continued: "My brother Aaron, although God had become reconciled to Israel and has forgiven them their sin, still, through thy offering must thou close the mouth of Satan, that he may not hate thee when thou enterest the sanctuary. Take then a young calf as a sin-offering, for as thou didst nearly lose thy claim to the dignity of high priest through a calf, so shalt thou now through the sacrifice of a calf be established in thy dignity." Then Moses turned to the people, saying: "You have two sins to atone for: the selling of Joseph, whose coat you fathers smeared with the blood of a kid to convince their father that its owner had been torn to pieces by a wild beast, and the sin you committed through the worship of the Golden Calf. Take, then, a kid to atone for the guilt you brought upon yourselves with a kid, and take a calf to atone for the sin you committed through a calf. But to make sure that God had become reconciled to you, offer up a bull also, and thereby acknowledge that you are slaughtering before God your idol, the bull that you had erstwhile worshipped." The people, however, said to Moses: "What avails it this nation to do homage to its king, who is invisible?" Moses replied: "For this very reason did God command you to offer these sacrifices, so that He may show Himself to you." At these words they rejoiced greatly, for through them they knew that God was now completely reconciled to them, and they hastened to bring the offerings to the sanctuary. Moses admonished them with the words: "See to it now that you drive evil impulse from your hearts, that you now have but one thought and one resolution, to serve God; and that your undivided services are devoted singly and solely to the one God, for He is the God of gods and the Lord of lords. If you will act according to my words, 'the glory of the Lord shall appear unto you.'"

But Aaron in his humility still did not dare to enter on his priestly activities. The aspect of the horned altar filled him with fear, for it reminded him of the worship of the bull by Israel, an incident in which he felt he had not been altogether without blame. Moses had to encourage him to step up to the altar and offer the sacrifices. After Aaron had offered up the prescribed sacrifices, he bestowed his blessing upon the people with lifted hands, saying: "The Eternal bless thee and keep thee: The Eternal make His face shine upon thee and be gracious unto thee: The Eternal lift up His countenance upon thee and give thee peace."

In spite of the offerings and the blessings, there was still no sign of the Shekinah, so that Aaron, with a heavy heart, thought, "God is angry with me, and it is my fault that the Shekinah had not descended among Israel, I merely owe it to my brother Moses that to my confusion I entered the sanctuary, for my service did not suffice to bring down the Shekinah." Upon this Moses went with his brother into the sanctuary a second time, and their united prayers had the desired effect, there came "a fire out from before the Lord, and consumed upon the altar well-nigh one hundred and sixteen years, and neither was the wood of the altar consumed, nor its brazen overlay molten.

When the people saw the heavenly fire, the evident token of God's grace and His reconciliation with them, they shouted, and fell on their faces, and praised God, intoning in His honor a song of praise. Joy reigned not only on earth, but in heaven also, for on this day God's joy over the erection of the sanctuary was as great as had been His joy on the first day of creation over His works, heaven and earth. For, in a certain sense, the erection of the Tabernacle was the finishing touch to the creation of the world. For the world exists for the sake of three things, the Torah, Divine service, and works of love. From the creation of the world to the revelation on Sinai the world owed its existence to the love and grace of God; from the revelation to the erection of the sanctuary, the world owed its existence to the Torah and to love, but only with the erection of the Tabernacle did the world secure its firm basis, for now it had three feet whereupon to rest, the Torah, Divine service, and love. From another point of view, too, is the day of consecration of the sanctuary to be reckoned with the days of creation, for at the creation of the world God dwelt with mortals and withdrew the Shekinah to heaven only on account of the sin of the first two human beings. But on the day of consecration of the Tabernacle the Shekinah returned to its former abode, the earth. The angels therefore lamented on this day, saying: "Now God will leave the celestial hosts and will dwell among mortals." God indeed quieted them with the words, "As truly as ye live, My true dwelling will remain on high," but He was not quite in earnest when He said so, for truly earth is His chief abode. Only after the Tabernacle on earth had been erected did God command the angels to build one like it in heaven, and it is this Tabernacle in which Metatron offers the souls of the pious before God as an expiation for Israel, at the time of the exile when His earthly sanctuary is destroyed.

This day marks an important change in the intercourse between God and Moses. Before this, the voice of God would strike Moses' ear as if conducted through a tube, and on such an occasion the outer would recognized only through Moses' reddened face that he was receiving a revelation; now, at the consecration of the sanctuary, this was changed. For when, on this day, he entered the sanctuary, a sweet, pleasant and lovely voice rang out toward him, whereupon he said: "I will hear what God the Lord will speak." Then he heard the words: "Formerly there reigned enmity between Me and My children, formerly there reigned anger between Me and My children, formerly there reigned hatred between Me and My children; but now love reigns between Me and My children, friendship reigns between Me and My children, peace reigns between Me and My children."

It was evident that peace reigned, for on this day the undisturbed freedom of movement over the world, which had until then been accorded the demons, was taken from them. Until then these were so frequently met with, that Moses regularly recited a special prayer whenever going to Mount Sinai, entreating God to protect him from the demons. But as soon as the Tabernacle had been erected, they vanished. Not entirely, it is true, for even now these pernicious creatures may kill a person, especially within the period from the seventeenth day of Tammuz to the ninth day of Ab, when the demons exercise their power. The most dangerous one among them is Keteb, the sight of whom kill men as well as animals. He rolls like a ball and had the head of a calf with a single horn on his forehead.

Just as God destroyed the power of these demons through the Tabernacle, so too, through the priestly blessing that He bestowed upon His people before the consecration of the sanctuary, did He break the spell of the evil eye, which might otherwise have harmed them now as it had done at the revelation on Sinai. The great ceremonies on that occasion had turned the eyes of all the world upon Israel, and the evil eye of the nations brought about the circumstance of the breaking of the two tables. As God blessed His people on this occasion, so too did Moses, who upon the completion of the Tabernacle blessed Israel with the words: "The Eternal God of you fathers make you a thousand times so many more as ye are, and bless you, as He hath promised you!" The people made answer to this blessing, saying: "Let the beauty of the Lord our God be upon us: and establish Thou the work of our hands upon us; yea the work of our hands establish Thou it."

THE INTERRUPTED JOY

The happiest of women on this day was Elisheba, daughter of Amminadab, for beside the general rejoicing at the dedication of the sanctuary, five particular joys fell to her lot: her husband, Aaron, was high priest; her brother-in-law, Moses, king; her son, Eleazar, head of the priests; her grandson, Phinehas, priest of war; and her brother, Nahshon, prince of his tribe. But how soon was her joy turned to grief! Her two sons, Nadab and Abihu, carried away by the universal rejoicing at the heavenly fire, approached the sanctuary with the censers in their hands, to increase God's love for Israel through this act of sacrifice, but paid with their lives for this offering. From the Holy of Holies issued two flames of fire, as thin as threads, then parted into four, and two each pierced the nostrils of Nadab and Abihu, whose souls were burnt, although no external injury was visible.

The death of these priests was not, however, unmerited, for in spite of their piety they had committed many a sin. Even at Sinai they had not conducted themselves properly, for instead of following the example of Moses, who had turned his face away from the Divine vision in the burning bush, they basked in the Divine vision of Mount Sinai. Their fate had even been decreed, but God did not want to darken the joy of the Torah by their death, hence He waited for the dedication of the Tabernacle. On this occasion God acted like the king who, discovering on the day of his daughter's wedding that the best-man was guilty of a deadly sin, said: "If I cause the best-man to be executed on the spot, I shall cast a shadow on my daughter's joy. I will rather have him executed on my day of gladness than on hers." God inflicted the penalty upon Nadab and Abihu "in the day of gladness of His heart," and not on the day on which the Torah espoused Israel.

Among the sins for which they had to atone was their great pride, which was expressed in several ways. They did not marry, because they considered no woman good enough for them, saying: "Our father's brother is king, our father is high priest, our mother's brother is prince of his tribe, and we are heads of the priests. What woman is worthy of us?" And many a woman remained unwed, waiting for these youths to woo her. In their pride they even went so far in sinful thoughts as to wish for the time when Moses and Aaron should die and they would have the guidance of the people in their hands. But God said: "'Boast not thyself of to-morrow;' many a colt has died and his hide had been used as cover for his mother's back." Even in the performance of the act that brought death upon them, did they show their pride, for they asked permission of neither Moses nor Aaron whether they might take part in the sacrificial service. What is more, Nadab and Abihu did not even consult with each other before starting out on this fatal deed, they performed it independently of each other. Had they previously taken counsel together, or had they asked their father and their uncle, very likely they would never have offered the disastrous sacrifice. For they were neither in a proper condition for making an offering, nor was their offering appropriate. They partook of wine before entering the sanctuary, which if forbidden to priests; they did not wear the prescribed priestly robes, and, furthermore, they had not sanctified themselves with water out of the laver for washing. They made their offering, moreover, in the Holy of Holies, to which admittance had been prohibited, and used "strange fire," and the offering was all in all out of place because they had had no command from God to offer up incense at that time. Apart from this lists of sins, however, they were very pious men, and their death grieved God more than their father Aaron, not alone because it grieves God to see a pious father lose his sons, but because they actually were worthy and pious youths.

When Aaron heard of the death of his sons, he said: "All Israel saw Thee at the Red Sea as well as at Sinai without suffering injury thereafter; but my sons, whom Thou didst order to dwell in the Tabernacle, a place that a layman may not enter without being punished by death-my sons entered the Tabernacle to behold Thy strength and Thy might, and they died!" God hereupon said to Moses: "Tell Aaron the following: 'I have shown thee great favor and have granted thee great honor through this, that thy sons have been burnt. I assigned to thee and thy sons a place nearer to the sanctuary, before all others, even before thy brother Moses. But I have also decreed that whosoever enters the Tabernacle without having been commanded, he shall be stricken with leprosy. Wouldst thou have wished thy sons, to whom the innermost places had been assigned, to sit as lepers outside the encampment as a penalty for having entered the Holy of Holies?" When Moses imparted these words to his brother, Aaron said: "I thank Thee, O God, for that which Thou hast shown me in causing my sons to die rather then having them waste their lives as lepers. It behooves me to thank Thee and praise Thee, 'because Thy lovingkindness is better than life, my lips shall praise Thee.'"

Moses endeavored to comfort his brother in still another way, saying: "Thy sons died to glorify the name of the Lord, blessed be His name, for on Sinai God said to me: 'And there will I meet with the children of Israel, the Tabernacle shall be sanctified by those that glorify Me.' I knew that this sanctuary of God was to be sanctified by the death of those that stood near it, but I thought either thou or I was destined for this, but now I perceive that thy sons were nearer to God than we." These last words sufficed to induce Aaron to control his grief over the loss of his sons, and like the true wise man he silently bore the heavy blow of fate without murmur or lament. God rewarded him for his silence by addressing him directly, and imparting an important priestly law to him.

Aaron could not take part in the burial of Nadab and Abihu, for a high priest is not permitted to take part in a funeral procession, even if the deceased be a near kinsman. Eleazar and Ithamar, also, the surviving sons of Aaron, were not permitted to mourn or attend the funeral on the day of their dedication as priests, so that Aaron's cousins, the Levites Mishael and Elzaphan, the next of kin after these had to attend to the funeral. These two Levites were the sons of a very worthy father, who was not only by descent a near kinsman of Aaron, but who was also closely akin to Aaron in character. As Aaron pursued peace, so too did his uncle Uzziel, father to Mishael and Elzaphan. Being Levites they might not enter the place where the heavenly fire had met their cousins, hence an angel had thrust Nadab and Abihu out of the priestly room, and they did not die until they were outside it, so that Mishael and Elzaphan might approach them.

Whereas the whole house of Israel was bidden to bewail the death of Nadab and Abihu, for "the death of a pious man is greater misfortune to Israel than the Temple's burning to ashes,"-Aaron and his sons, on the other hand, were permitted to take no share in the mourning, and Moses bade them eat of the parts of the offering due them, as if nothing had happened. Now when Moses saw that Aaron had burnt to ashes one of the three sin offerings that were offered on that day, without himself or his sons having partaken of it, his wrath was kindled against his brother, but in consideration of Aaron's age and his office Moses addressed his violent words not to Aaron himself, but to his sons. He reproached them with having offended against God's commandment in burning one sin offering and eating of the other two. He asked them, besides, if they were not wise enough to profit by the example of their deceased brothers, who paid for their arbitrary actions with their lives, particularly since they also had been doomed to death, and owed their lived only to his prayer, which had power to preserve for their father half the number of sons. Moses' reproof, however, was unjustified, for Aaron and his sons had done what the statutes required, but Moses had on this occasion, as on two others, owing to his wrath, forgotten the laws which he himself had taught Israel. Hence Aaron opposed him decidedly and pointed out his error to him. Moses, far from taking Aaron's reprimand amiss, caused a herald to make an announcement throughout the camp: "I have falsely interpreted the law, and Aaron, my brother, has corrected me. Eleazar and Ithaman also knew the law, but were silent out of consideration for me." As a reward for their considerateness, God thereupon revealed important laws to Moses with a special injunction to tell them to Aaron as well as to Eleazar and Ithamar.

THE GIFTS OF THE PRINCES

When Moses called on the people to make their offerings for the erection of the sanctuary, it sorely vexed the princes of the tribes that he had not summoned them particularly. Hence they withheld their contributions, waiting for the people to give according to their powers, so that they might step in and make up the deficiency, and all should observe that without them the Tabernacle could not have been completed. But they were mistaken, for in their ready devotion the people provided all needful things for the sanctuary, and when the princes of the tribes perceived their mistake and brought their contributions, it was too late. All that they could do was to provide the jewels for the robes of the high priest, but they could no longer take a hand in the erection of the Tabernacle. On the day of the dedication they tried to make partial amends for letting slip their opportunity, by following the advice of the tribe of Issachar, renowned for wisdom and erudition, to bring wagons for the transportation of the Tabernacle. These princes of the tribes were no upstarts or men newly risen to honor, they were men who even in Egypt had been in office and exposed to the anger of the Egyptians; they had also stood at Moses' side when he undertook the census of the people. They now brought as an offering to Moses six covered wagons, fully equipped, and even painted blue, the color of the sky, and also twelve oxen to draw the wagons. The number of wagons as well as of oxen had been set with purpose. The six wagons corresponded to the six days of creation; to the six Mothers, Sarah, Rebekah, Rachel, Leah, Billhah, and Zilpah; to the six laws that the Torah prescribes exclusively for the king; to the six orders of the Mishnah, and to the six heavens. The number of the oxen corresponded to the twelve constellations, and to the twelve tribes. Moses did not at first want to accept the teams, but God not only bade him accept them, He also ordered him to address the princes kindly, and to thank them for their gifts. Moses now even thought the Shekinah had deserted him and would rest on the princes of the tribes, assuming that they had received direct communication from God to make this offering to the sanctuary. But God said to Moses: "If it had been a direct command from Me, then I should have ordered thee to tell them, but they did this on their own initiative, which indeed meets with My wish." Moses now accepted the gifts, not without misgivings, fearing lest a wagon should break, or an ox die, leaving the tribe or that unrepresented by a gift. But God assured him that no accident should occur to either wagon or ox,--yes, a great miracle came to pass in regard to these wagons and oxen, for the animals live forever without ailing or growing old, and the wagons likewise endure to all eternity.

Moses then distributed the wagons among the Levites so that the division of the sons of Gershon received two wagons, with the transportation of the heavy portions of the Tabernacle, boards, bars, and similar things, whereas the former, having the lighter portions, had enough with two wagons. The third division of Levites, the sons of Kohath, received no wagons, for they were entrusted with the transportation of the Holy Ark, which might not be lifted upon a wagon, but was to be borne upon their shoulders. David, who forgot to observe this law and had the Ark lifted upon a wagon, paid heavily for his negligence, for the priests who tried to carry the Ark to the wagon were flung down upon the ground. Ahithophel then called David's attention to the need of following the example of Kohath's sons, who bore the Ark on their shoulders through the desert, and David ordered them to do the same.

But the princes of the tribes were not content with having provided the means for transporting the sanctuary, they wanted to be the first, on the day of dedication, to present offerings. As with the wagons, Moses was doubtful whether or not to permit them to bring their offerings, for theses were of an unusual kind that were not ordinarily permissible. But God bade him accept the dedication offerings of the princes, though Moses was still in doubt whether to let all the twelve princes make their offerings on the same day, or to set a special day for each, and if so, in what order they should make their offerings. God thereupon revealed to him that each one of the princes of the tribes were to sacrifice on a special day, and that Nahshon, the prince of Judah, was to make the start. He was rewarded in this way for the devotion he had shown God during the passage through the Red Sea. When Israel, beset by the Egyptians, reached the sea, the tribes among themselves started quarreling who should first go into the sea. Then suddenly Nahshon, the prince of Judah, plunged into the sea, firmly trusting that God would stand by Israel in their need.

Nahshon's offering was one silver changer that had been fashioned for the sanctuary, the weight whereof was an hundred and thirty shekels; on bowl of equal size, but of lighter weight, of seventy shekels; both of them full of fine flour mingles with oil for a meat offering. Furthermore, one spoon of ten shekels of gold, full of incense; on young bullock, the picked of his herd; one excellent ram, and one lamb a year old, these three for a burnt offering; and a kid of the goats for a sin offering, to atone for a possible uncleanness in the sanctuary. These sacrifices and gifts Nahshon offered out of his own possessions, not out of those of his tribe. God's acceptance of the offerings of the princes of the tribes shows how dear they were to God; for at no other time was and individual allowed to offer up incense, as Nahshon and his fellows did. They also brought sin offerings, which is ordinarily not permitted unless on is conscious of having committed a sin. Finally the prince of the tribe of Ephraim brought his offering on the seventh day of the dedication, which was on a Sabbath, though ordinarily none but the daily sacrificed may be offered on the Sabbath.

The offerings of all the princes of the tribes were identical, but they had a different significance for each tribe. From the time of Jacob, who foretold it to them, every tribe knew his future history to the time of the Messiah, hence at the dedication every prince brought such offerings as symbolized the history of his tribe.

Nahshon, the prince of Judah, brought a silver charger and a silver bowl, the one to stand for the sea, the other for the mainland, indicating that out of his tribe would spring such men as Solomon and the Messiah, who would rule over all the world, both land and sea. The golden spoon of ten shekels signified the ten generations from Perez, son of Judah, to David, first of Judean kings, all whose actions were sweet as the incense contained in the spoon. The three burnt offerings, the bullock, the ram, and the lamb, corresponded to the three Patriarchs, Abraham, Isaac, and Jacob, whereas the kid of the goats was to atone for the sin of Judah, who sought to deceive his father with the blood of a kid. The two oxen of the peace offering pointed to David and Solomon, and the three small cattle of the peace offering, the rams, the goats, and the lambs, corresponded to the descendants and successors of these two Judean kings, who may also be classified in three groups, the very pious, the very wicked, and those who were neither pious nor wicked.

On the second day of the dedication appeared the prince of the tribe of Reuben and wanted to present his offering, saying: "Tis enough that Judah was permitted to offer sacrifice before me, surely it is not time for our tribe to present our offerings." But Moses informed him that God had ordained that the tribes should present offerings in the order in which they moved through the desert, so that the tribe of Issachar followed Judah. This tribe had altogether good claims to be among the first to offer sacrifices, for, in the first place, this tribe devoted itself completely to the study of the Torah, so that the great scholars in Israel were among them; and then, too, it was this tribe that had proposed to the others that bringing of the dedication offerings. As this was the tribe of erudition, its gifts symbolized things appertaining to the Torah. The silver charger and the silver bowl corresponded to the written and to the oral Torah; and both vessels alike are filled with fine flour, for the two laws are not antagonistic, but form a unity and contain the loftiest teachings. The fine flour was mingled with oil, just as knowledge of the Torah should be added to good deeds; for he who occupies himself with the Torah, who works good deeds, and keeps himself aloof from sin, fills his Creator with delight. The golden spoon of ten shekels symbolizes the two tables on which God with His palm wrote the Ten Commandments, and which contained between the commandments all the particulars of the Torah, just as the spoon was filled with incense. The three burnt offerings, the bullock, the ram, and the lamb corresponded to the three groups of priests, Levites and Israelites, whereas the kid of the goats alluded to the proselytes, for the Torah was revealed not only for Israel but for all the world; and "a proselyte who studies the Torah is no less than a high priest." The two oxen of the peace offering corresponded to the oral and the written Torah, the study of which brings peace on earth and peace in heaven.

After Nahshon, the temporal king, and Nethanel the spiritual king, came the turn of Eliab, the prince of the tribe of Zebulun. This tribe owed its distinction to the circumstance that it followed commerce and through the profits thereof was enabled to maintain the tribe of Issachar, which, entirely devoted to study, could not support itself. The charger and bowl that he presented to the sanctuary symbolize the food and drink with which Zebulun provide the scholar-tribe Issachar. The spoon indicated the border of the sea, which Jacob in his blessing had bestowed on Zebulun as his possession, and the ten shekels of its weight corresponded to the ten words of which this blessing consisted. The tow oxen point to the two blessings which Moses bestowed upon Zebulun, as the three small cattle, the ram, the goat, and the lamb, corresponded to the three things which gave Zebulun's possessions distinction before all others, the tunny, the purple snail, and white glass.

After the tribes that belonged to Judah's camp division had brought their offerings, followed Reuben and the tribes belonging to his division. The gifts of the tribe of Reuben symbolized the events in the life of their forefather Reuben. The silver charger recalled Reuben's words when he saved Joseph's life, whom the other brothers wanted to kill, for "the tongue of the just is as choice silver." The silver bowl, from which was sprinkled the sacrificial blood, recalled the same incident, for it was Reuben who advised his brothers to throw Joseph into the pit rather than to kill him. The spoon of ten shekels of gold symbolized the deed of Reuben, who restrained Jacob's sons from bloodshed, hence the gold out of which the spoon was fashioned had a blood-red color. The spoon was filled with incense, and so too did Reuben fill his days with fasting and prayer until God forgave his sin with Billhah, and "his prayer was set forth before God as incense." As penance for this crime, Reuben offered the kid of goats as a sin offering, whereas the two oxen of the peace offering corresponded to the two great deeds of Reuben, the deliverance of Joseph, and the long penance for his sin.

Just as Reuben interceded to save his brother Joseph's life so did Simeon rise up for his sister Dinah when he took vengeance upon the inhabitants of Shechem for the wrong they had done her. Hence the prince of the tribe of Simeon followed the prince of the tribe of Reuben. As the sanctuary was destined to punish unchastity among Israel, so were the gifts of the tribe whose sire figured as the avenger of unchastity symbolical of the different parts of the Tabernacle. The charger corresponded to the court that surrounded the Tabernacle, and therefore weighed one hundred and thirty shekels, to correspond to the size of the court that measured one hundred cubits, of which the Tabernacle occupied thirty. The bowl of seventy shekels corresponded to the empty space of the Tabernacle. These two, the charger and the bowl, were filled with fine flour mingled with oil, because in the court of the Tabernacle were offered up meat offerings, mingled with oil, whereas in the Tabernacle was the shewbread of fine flour, and the candlestick filled with oil. The spoon of ten shekels of gold corresponded to the scroll of the Torah and the tables with the Ten Commandments that rested in the Ark. The sacrificial animals, the bullock, the ram, the lamb, and the kid corresponded to the four different kinds of curtains and hangings that were used in the sanctuary, and that were fashioned our of the hides of these animals. The two oxen of the peace offering pointed to the two curtains, the one in front of the Tabernacle, the other in front of the court, whereas the three kinds of small cattle that were used as offerings corresponded to the three curtains of the court, one to the north, one to the south, one to the west of it; and as each of these was five cubits long, so were five of each kind presented as offerings.

As Simeon, sword in hand, battled for his sister, so, by force of arms, did the tribe of Gad set out to gain the land beyond the Jordan for their brethren. Therefore did their prince follow Shelumiel, prince of Simeon, with his offerings. This tribe, so active in gaining the promised land, symbolized in its gifts the exodus from Egypt, which alone made possible the march of Palestine. The charger of the weight of a hundred and thirty shekels alluded to Jochebed, who at the age of one hundred and thirty years bore Moses, who had symbolical connection with the bowl, for he was thrown into the Nile. This bowl weighed seventy shekels, as Moses extended his prophetic spirit over the seventy elders; and as the bowl was filled with fine flour, so did Moses' prophetic spirit in no way diminish because the seventy elders shared in prophecy. The three burnt offerings recalled the three virtues Israel possessed in Egypt, which were instrumental in their deliverance-they did not alter their Hebrew names, they did not alter their Hebrew language, and they lived a live of chastity. The sin offerings were to atone for the idolatry to which they were addicted in Egypt, so that God did not permit their deliverance until they had renounced idolatry. The two oxen of the peace offering corresponded to Jacob and Joseph, for whose sake God had delivered Israel out of Egypt. They brought, besides, fifteen heads of small cattle as sacrifice, because God was mindful of His vow to the three Patriarchs and the twelve fathers of the tribes, and released Israel out of bondage.

A special distinction was granted to the tribe of Ephraim, for God allowed their prince to make his offering on the Sabbath, a day on which otherwise none but the daily offerings were allowed to be offered. This distinction the tribe of Ephraim owed to its ancestor Joseph in recognition of his strict observance of the Sabbath as governor of Egypt. The gifts of this tribe represent the history of Jacob and of Joseph, for the descendants of the latter owed much to Jacob's love for his son Joseph. The charger alluded to Jacob, the bowl to Joseph, and as both these vessels were filled with fine flour mingled with oil, so too were both Jacob and Joseph very pious men, and the course of their lives ran evenly. The spoon symbolized Jacob's right hand, which he laid on the head of Ephraim to bless him; the spoon was filled with incense; Jacob laid his right hand upon Ephraim and not upon his elder brother Manasseh because he knew that the former was worthy of the distinction. The three burnt offerings corresponded to the three Patriarchs, whereas the kid of goats stood for Joseph, whose coat had been smeared with a kid's blood. The two oxen of the peace offering indicated the two blessings that the sons of Joseph had received from their grandfather, Jacob, and the three kinds of small cattle that were offered as peace offerings corresponded to the three generations of Ephraim that Joseph was permitted to see before his death.

Joseph not only observed the Sabbath, he was also chaste, not to be tempted by Potiphar's wife, and he was faithful in the service of his master. God therefore said to Joseph: "Thou hast kept the seventh commandment, 'Thou shalt not commit adultery,' and has not committed adultery with Potiphar's wife; and thou hast also kept the following commandment, the eighth, 'Thou shalt not steal,' for thou didst still neither Potiphar's money nor his conjugal happiness, hence there will come a time when I shall give thee the reward due thee. When, hereafter, the princes of the tribes will offer their offerings at the dedication of the altar, the two princes among thy descendants shall one after the other offer their offerings, the one on the seventh, the other on the eighth day of the dedication, as a reward because thou didst observe the seventh and the eighth commandments." The prince of the tribe of Manasseh now followed that of Ephraim, trying like the preceding, symbolically to represent Jacob's and Joseph's lives. The charger, one hundred and thirty shekels in weight, indicated that Jacob at the age of one hundred and thirty years migrated to Egypt for the sake of Joseph. The bowl of seventy shekels corresponded to Joseph who caused seventy souls of the Hebrews to migrated to Egypt. The spoon of ten shekels of gold indicated the ten portions of land that fell to Manasseh. The three burnt offerings corresponded to the three generations of Manasseh that Joseph was permitted to see before his death, whereas the kid of the goats recalled Jair, son of Manasseh, who died childless. The two oxen of the peace offering indicated that the possessions of the tribe of Manasseh were to be divided into two parts, one on this side the Jordan, and one beyond it. The three kinds of small cattle for peace offerings corresponded to the triple attempt of Joseph to influence his father in favor of Manasseh, whereas the five head of each indicated the five daughters of Zelophehad, the only women who, like men, received their shares in the distribution of the promised land.

As the sanctuary stood first in Shiloh, Joseph's possession, then in Jerusalem, Benjamin's possession, so did this tribe with its sacrifices follow Joseph's tribes. The charger signified Rachel, the mother of Benjamin, who bore him to Jacob when he was a hundred years old, and in memory of this, as well as of Benjamin's attainment of thirty years when he came to Egypt, the weight of the charger amounted to one hundred and thirty shekels. The bowl indicated the cup Joseph employed to discover his brothers' sentiments toward Benjamin, and both vessels, charger and cup, were filled with fine flour, for both Joseph's and Benjamin's lands were found worthy being sited for God's sanctuary. The spoon of then shekels of gold full of incense corresponded to the ten sons of Benjamin, all of whom were pious men. The three burnt offering corresponded to the three temples erected in Jerusalem, Benjamin's property, the Temple of Solomon, the Temple of the exiles returned from Babylon, and the Temple to be erected by the Messiah. The sin offering, the kid of the goats, points to the building of the Temple by the wicked king Herod, who atoned for his execution of the learned men by the erection of the santuary. The two oxen of the peace offering corresponded to the two deliverers of the Jews that sprang from the tribe of Benjamin, Mordecai, and Esther. The five heads each of the three kinds of small cattle for a peace offering symbolized the triple distinction of Benjamin and his tribe by five gifts. The gift of honor that Joseph gave his brother Benjamin five times exceeded that of all his other brothers; when Joseph made himself known to his brothers, he gave Benjamin five changes of raiment, and so too did the Benjamite Mordecai receive from Ahasuerus five garments of state.

In his blessing Jacob likened Dan to Judah, hence the tribe of Dan stood at the head of the fourth camp of Israel, and their prince offered his gifts before those of Asher and Naphtali. Jacob in his blessing to Dan thought principally of the great hero, Samson, hence the gifts of this tribe allude chiefly to the history of this Danite judge. Samson was a Nazirite, and to this alluded the silver charger for storing bread, for it is the duty of a Nazirite, at the expiration of the period of his vow, to present bread as an offering. To Samson, too, alluded the bowl, in Hebrew called Mizrak, "creeping," for he was lame of both feet, and hence could only creep and crawl. The spoon of ten shekels of gold recalled the ten laws that are imposed upon Nazirites, and that Samson had to obey. The three burnt offerings had a similar significance, for Samson's mother received three injunctions from the angel, who said to her husband, Manoah: "She may not eat of anything that cometh of the vine, neither let her drink wine or strong drink, nor eat any unclean thing." The sin offering, which consisted of a kid, called in Hebrew, Sa'ir, corresponded to the admonition given to Samson's mother, not to shave his hair, in Hebrew Se'ar. The two oxen corresponded to the two pillars of which Samson took hold to demolish the house of the Philistines; whereas the three kinds of small cattle that were presented as offerings symbolized the three battles that Samson undertook against the Philistines.

The judge must pronounce judgement before it be executed, hence, too, the tribe of Asher, "the executors of justice," followed Dan, the judges. The name Asher also signifies "good fortune," referring to the good fortune of Israel that was chosen to the God's people, and in accordance with this name also do the gifts of the prince of the tribe of Asher allude to the distinction of Israel. The charger, one hundred and thirty shekels of silver in weight, corresponds to the nations of the world, whom, however, God repudiated, choosing Israel in their stead. The bowl of seventy shekels corresponds to the seventy pious souls of whom Israel consisted when they moved to Egypt. Both vessels were filled with fine flour. God sent His prophets to the other nations as well as to Israel, but Israel alone declared itself willing to accept the Torah. This nation accepted "the spoon of then shekels of gold filled with incense," every man among them being willing to accept the Ten Commandments and the Torah. The three burnt offerings corresponded to the three crowns that Israel received from their God, the crown of the Torah, the crown of the Priesthood, and the crown of the Kingdom, for which reason also golden crowns were fashioned on the Ark in which the Torah was kept, on the altar on which the priests offered sacrifices, and on the table that symbolized the kingdom. But the highest of all is the crown of a good name, which a man earns through good deeds, for the crucial test is not the study of the Torah, but the life conforming to it. For this reason also there was a sin offering among the offerings, corresponding to the crown of good deeds, for these alone can serve as an expiation. The two oxen indicate the two Torot that God gave His people, the written and the oral, whereas the fifteen peace offerings of small cattle correspond to the three Patriarchs and the twelve fathers of the tribes, for these fifteen God had chosen.

As Jacob blessed after Asher and the Naphtali, so too did these two tribes succeed each other in the offerings at the dedication of the Tabernacle. Naphtali, Jacob's son, was a very affectionate son, who was ever ready to execute his father's every command. The prince of the tribe of Naphtali followed his ancestor's example, and by his gifts to the sanctuary sought to recall the three Patriarchs and their wives. "One silver charger, the weight whereof was an hundred and thirty shekels," symbolized Sarah, who was unique among her sex in her piety, and who almost attained the age of hundred and thirty years. A silver bowl for sprinkling blood recalled Abraham, who was thrown far away form his home. The weight of the bowl was seventy shekels, as Abraham also was seventy years old when God made with him the covenant between the pieces. The charger and the bowl were both filled with fine flour mingled with oil, as also Abraham and Sarah were imbued with a love for good and pious deeds. The spoon of ten shekels of gold alludes to Abraham as well, for Abraham conquered the evil inclination and resisted the ten temptations, whereas the three burnt offerings and the sin offering corresponded to the offerings made by Abraham at the covenant between the pieces. The two oxen for the peace offering indicate Isaac and Rebekah, whereas the three kinds of small cattle allude to Jacob, Leah, and Rachel, but the sum total of the offerings of these three species was fifteen, corresponding to these three and the twelve fathers of the tribes.

Apart from the significance that the offerings of the tribal princes had for each individual tribe respectively, they also symbolized the history of the world from the time of Adam to the erection of the Tabernacle. The silver charger indicated Adam, who lived nine hundred and thirty years, and the numerical equivalent of the letters of Kaarat Kesef, "silver charger," amounts to the same. Corresponding to the weight of "an hundred and thirty shekels," Adam begat his son Seth, the actual father of the future generations, at the age of a hundred and thirty years. The silver bowl alludes to Noah, for, as it weighed seventy shekels, so too did seventy nations spring from Noah. Both these vessels were filled with fine flour, as Adam and Noah were both full of good deeds. The spoon "of ten shekels of gold" corresponded to the ten words of God by which the world was created, to the ten Sefirot, to the ten lists of generations in the Scriptures, to the ten essential constituent parts of the human body, to the ten miracles God wrought for Israel in Egypt, to the ten miracles Israel experienced by the Red Sea. The three burnt offerings were meant to recall the three Patriarchs. The kid of goats indicated Joseph; the two oxen corresponded to Moses and Aaron; the five rams to the five distinguished sons of Zerah: Zimri, Ethan, Heman, Calcol, and Dara; whereas the five goats and the five lambs symbolized the five senses of mankind by means of which the existence of things is determined.

The sum total of the gifts of the twelve princes of the tribes had also a symbolical significance. The twelve chargers correspond to the twelve constellations; the twelve bowls of the twelve months; the twelve spoons to the twelve guides of men, which are: the heart, that bestows understanding and insight; the kidneys, that give counsels, good as well as evil; the mouth, that cuts all kinds of food; the tongue, that renders speech impossible; the palate, that tastes the flavors of food; the windpipe, that renders possible breathing and the utterance of sounds; the esophagus, that swallows food and drink; the lungs, that absorbs fluids; the liver, that promotes laughter; the crop, that grinds all food; and the stomach, that affords pleasant sleep. "All the silver of the vessels that weighed two thousand and four hundred shekels" corresponded to the years that had passed from the creation of the world to the advent of Moses in the fortieth year of his life. All the gold of the spoons, the weight of which was an hundred and twenty shekels, corresponds to the years of Moses' life, for he died at the age of a hundred and twenty.

The different species of animals offered as sacrifices corresponded to the different ranks of the leaders of Israel. The twelve bullocks to the kings, the twelve rams to the princes of the tribes, the twelve kids of the goats to the governors, and the twelve sheep to the government officials. The twenty-four oxen for a peace offering corresponded to the books of the Scriptures, and the divisions of the priests, and were also meant to serve as atonement for the twenty-four thousand men, who, owing to their worship of Peor, died of the plague. The sixty rams of the peace offering corresponded to the sixty myriads of Israel's fighting hosts; the sixty he-goats to the sixty empires; and the sixty he-lambs to the building of the second Temple that measured sixty cubits in height and sixty in width.

The gifts of the twelve princes of the tribes were not only equal in number, but also in the size and width of the objects bestowed, every tribe making exactly the same offering to the sanctuary. None among them wished to outrival the others, but such harmony reigned among them and such unity of spirit that God valued the service of each as if he had brought not only his own gifts but also those of his companions. As a reward for this mutual regard and friendship, God granted them the distinction of permitting them to present their offerings even on the Sabbath day.

THE REVELATIONS IN THE TABERNACLE

"Honor pursues him who tries to escape it." Moses in his humility felt that his mission as leader of the people ended with the erection of the Tabernacle, as Israel could now satisfy all their spiritual needs without his aid. But God said: "As truly as thou livest, I have for thee a far greater task than any thou hast yet accomplished, for thou shalt instruct My children about 'clean and unclean,' and shalt teach them how to offer up offerings to Me." God hereupon called Moses to the Tabernacle, to reveal to him there the laws and teachings. Moses in his humility did not dare to enter the Tabernacle, so that God had to summon him to enter. Moses, however, could not enter the sanctuary while a cloud was upon it, this being a sign "that the demons held sway," but waited until the cloud had moved on. The voice that called Moses came from heaven in the form of a tube of fire and rested over the two Cherubim, whence Moses perceived its sound. This voice was a powerful as at the revelation at Sinai when the souls of all Israel escaped in terror, still it was audible to none but Moses. Not even the angels heard it, for the words of God were destined exclusively for Moses. Aaron, too, with the exception of three cases in which God revealed Himself to him, never received His commands except through the communications of Moses. God would call Moses twice caressingly words by name, and when he had answered, "Here am I," God's words were revealed to him, and every commandment as a special revelation. God always allowed a pause to take place between the different laws to be imparted, that Moses might have time rightly to grasp what was told him.

On the first day of the dedication of the Tabernacle, not lest than eight important sections of laws were communicated to Moses by God. As a reward for his piety, Aaron and his descendants to all eternity received the laws of sanctity, which are a special distinction of the priests, and these laws were revealed on this day. It was on this day, also, that Aaron and his sons received the gifts of the priests, for although even at the revelation on Sinai Israel had set them aside, still they were not given to Aaron and his sons until this day when the sanctuary was anointed.

The second law revealed on this day was the separation of the Levites from among the children of Israel, that they might be dedicated to the sanctuary. "For God elevated no man to an office unless He has tried him and found him worthy of his calling." He did not say, "and the Levites shall be Mine," before He had tried this tribe, and found them worthy. In Egypt none but the tribe of Levi observed the Torah and clung to the token of the Abrahamic covenant, while the others tribes, abandoning both Torah and token of covenant, like the Egyptians, practiced idolatry. In the desert, also, it was this tribe alone that did not take part in the worship of the Golden Calf. Justly, therefore, did God's choice fall upon this godly tribe, who on this day were consecrated as the servants of God and His sanctuary.

The ceremonies connected with the consecration of the Levites had much in common with the regulations for cleansing of lepers. Originally, the firstborn had been the servants of the sanctuary, but, owing to the worship of the Golden Calf, they lost this prerogative, and the Levites replaced them. It was for this reason that the Levites were obliged to observe regulations similar to those for the cleansing of lepers, because they took the place of men who by their sins had defiled themselves. The offerings that the Levites brought on this occasion consisted of two bullocks, on for a burnt offering whenever the congregation, seduced by others, commits idolatry; and Israel would not have worshipped the Golden Calf had not the mixed multitude misled them. "But whosoever worships an idol, by this act renounces the whole Torah," hence did the Levites have to offer up another bullock for a sin offering, in accordance with the law that "if the whole congregation of Israel have done somewhat against any of the commandments of the Lord concerning things which should not be done, and are guilty, then they shall offer up a young bullock for the sin." As the Levites had been chosen "to do the service of the children of Israel in the Tabernacle of the congregation, and to make an atonement for the children of Israel," God ordered all the congregation of Israel to be present at the consecration of the Levites, for whosoever had a sin offering up for himself must in person bring it to the Tabernacle. Therefore, too, did the elders of Israel have to put their hands upon the Levites, according to the prescription that the elders must put their hands upon the sin of the congregation. Aaron, like the elders, participated in the ceremony of the consecration, lifting up every single Levite as a token that he was now dedicated to the sanctuary. Aaron's extraordinary strength is proven by the fact that he was able to lift up twenty-tow thousand men in one day.

THE CLEANSING OF THE CAMP

The third law revealed on this day was the command that the children of Israel put out of the camp every leper and every unclean person. When Israel moved out of Egypt, the majority of the people were afflicted with physical defects and diseases, contracted during their work on the structures they had been compelled to erect in Egypt. One had his hand crushed by a falling stone, another's eye blinded by splashing of loam. It was a battered and crippled host that reached Sinai, eager to receive the Torah, but God said: "Does it become the glory of the Torah that I should bestow it on a race of cripples? Nor do I want to await the coming of another, sound generation, for I desire no further delay of the revelation of the Torah." Hereupon God sent angels to heal all among Israel that were diseased or afflicted with defects, so that all the children of Israel were sound and whole when they received the Torah. They remained in this condition until they worshipped the Golden Calf, when all their diseases returned as a punishment for their defection from God. Only the women, during their stay in the desert, were exempt from the customary ailments to which women are subject, as a reward for being the first who declared themselves ready to accept the Torah. When the Tabernacle had been consecrated, God now said to Moses: "So long as you had not yet erected the Tabernacle, I did not object to having the unclean and the lepers mingle with the rest of the people, but now that the sanctuary is erected, and that My Shekinah dwells among you, I insist upon your separating all these from among you, that they may not defile the camp in the midst of which I dwell."

The law in regard to lepers was particularly severe, for they were denied the right of staying within the camp, whereas the unclean were prohibited merely from staying near the sanctuary. The lepers were the very ones who had worshipped the Golden Calf, and had as a consequence been smitten with this disease, and it was for this reason that God separated them from the community. Thirteen sins are punished with leprosy by God: blasphemy, unchastity, murder, false suspicion, pride, illegal appropriation of the rights of others, slander, theft, perjury, profanation of the Divine Name, idolatry, envy, and contempt of the Torah. Goliath was stricken with leprosy because he reviled God; the daughters of Zion became leprous in punishment of their unchastity; leprosy was Cain's punishment for the murder of Abel. When Moses said to God, "But behold, they will not believe me," God replied: "O Moses, art thou sure that they will not believe thee? They are believers and the sons of believers. Thou who didst suspect them wrongly, put not they hand into thy bosom,.....and he put his hand into his bosom: and when he took it out, behold, his hand was leprous as snow. " Uzziah presumed upon the rights of the priesthood, and went into the Temple to burn incense upon the altar of incense. He was just about to commit the offence, when "the leprosy brake forth in his forehead." Leprosy fell upon Naaman, who had grown arrogant because of his heroic deeds. For slandering Moses Miriam became leprous as snow; and Gehazi was punished by leprosy because he frustrated the purpose of Elisha, who desired to accept nothing from Naaman in order that the cure might redound to the glory of God.

Another important law revealed on this day referred to the celebration of "the second Passover feast." Mishael and Elzaphan, who had attended to the burial of Nadab and Abihu, were godly men, anxious to fulfil the commandments of God, hence they went to the house where Moses and Aaron instructed the people, and said to them: "We are defiled by the dead body of a man; wherefore are we kept back that we may not offer an offering of the Lord in His appointed season among the children of Israel?" Moses at first answered that they might not keep the Passover owing to their condition of uncleanness, but they argued with him, asking that even if, owing to their condition, they might not partake of the sacrificial meat, they might, at least, be permitted to participate in the offering of the paschal lamb by having the blood of the offering sprinkled for them. Moses admitted that he could not pass judgement on this case before receiving instruction concerning it from God. For Moses had the rare privilege of being certain of receiving revelations from God whenever he applied to Him. He therefore bade Mishael and Elzaphan await God's judgement concerning their case, and sentence was indeed revealed immediately.

It was on this day also that God said to Moses: "A heavy blow of fate had fallen upon Aaron to-day, but instead of murmuring he thanked Me for the death that robbed him of his two sons, which proves his trust in My justice toward them, who had deserved punishment more severe. Go then, and comfort him; and at the same time tell him 'that he come not at all times into the holy place within the vail before the mercy seat, which is upon the Ark.'" These last words greatly aggrieved Moses, who not thought: "Woe is me! For it seems as if Aaron had lost his rank, since he may not at all times enter the sanctuary. The statement of the periods for his admission into the sanctuary is also so indeterminate that I am not at all sure whether they are to recur hourly, or daily, or annually, every twelve years, perhaps even seventy, or not at all." But God replied: "Thou art mistaken, I was not thinking of fixing a certain time. Whether hour, or day or year, for Aaron may enter the sanctuary at any time, but when he does so, he must observe certain ceremonies." The ceremonies that Aaron, as well as every other high priest, had to perform on the Day of Atonement before his entrance into the Holy of Holies were symbolical of the three Patriarchs, of the four wives of the Patriarchs, and of the twelve tribes. Only by depending upon the merits of these pious men and women might the high priest venture to enter the Holy of Holies without having to fear the angels that filled this space. These were obliged to retreat upon the entrance of the high priest, and even Satan had to flee whenever he beheld the high priest, and did not dare to accuse Israel before God.

Aaron's grief about the death of his sons was turned to joy when God, on the day of their death, granted him the distinction of receiving a direct revelation from the Lord, which prohibited both him and his sons from drinking wine or strong drink when they went into the Tabernacle.

On this day, also, Moses received the revelation concerning the red heifer, whose significance was never vouchsafed to any other human being beside himself. On the following day, under the supervision of Eleazar, Aaron's son, it was slaughtered and burned. Although, beside this one, a number of other red heifers were provided in future generations, this one was distinguished by having its ashes kept forever, which, mingled with the ashes of other red heifers, were always used for the purification of Israel. But it is in this world alone that the priest can purify the unclean by sprinkling with this water of purification, whereas in the future world God will sprinkle clean water upon Israel, "that thy may be cleansed from all their filthiness, and from all their idols."

THE LIGHTING OF THE CANDLESTICK

The eighth law revealed on this day was the lighting of the candlestick. After all the princes of the tribes had brought their gifts to the sanctuary, and God had bidden Moses to let them offer each his offering, one a day, throughout twelve days, Aaron, profoundly agitated, thought: "Woe is me! It seems as if, owing to my sin, my tribe has been excluded by God from participating in the dedication of the sanctuary." Hereupon God said to Moses: "Go to Aaron and say to him, 'Do not fear that thou art slighted, and art deemed inferior to the other princes of the tribes. Thou, on the contrary, shalt enjoy a greater glory than all of these, for thou art to light the lamps of the candlestick in the sanctuary.'" When Israel heard God's command that the lights of the sanctuary be lighted, they said: "O Lord of the world! Thou biddest us make a light for Thee that are the light of the world, and with whom light dwelleth." But God replied: "Not because I need your light do I bid you burn lamps before Me, but only the I might thereby distinguish you in the eyes of the nations that will say,

'Behold the people of Israel, that hold up a light before Him who bestoweth light upon the world.' By your own eye-sight can you see how little need I have of your light. You have the white of the eye and the black of the eye, and it is by means of this dark part of the eye that you are enabled to see, and not through the light part of the white of the eye. How should I, that am all light, have need of your light!" God furthermore said: "A mortal of flesh and blood lights one light by means of another that is burning, I have brought forth light out of darkness: 'In the beginning darkness was upon the face of the deep,' whereupon I spake, 'Let there be light: and there was light.' Shall I now be in need of your illumination? Nay, I commanded you to light the candles in the sanctuary that I might distinguish you and give you another opportunity of doing a pious deed, the execution of which I will reward in the future world by letting a great light shine before you; and, furthermore, if you will let the candles shine before Me in My sanctuary, I shall protect from all evil your spirit, 'the candle of the Lord.'"

Simultaneously with the command to light the sanctuary, Moses received the instruction to celebrate the Sabbath by the lighting of candles, for God said to him: "Speak unto the children of Israel; if you will observe My command to light the Sabbath candles, I shall permit you to live to see Zion illuminated, when you will no longer require the light of the sun, but My glory will shine before you so that the nations will follow your light."

Aaron was distinguished not only by being selected to dedicate the sanctuary through the lighting of the candles, God ordered Moses to communicate to his brother the following revelation: "The sanctuary will on another occasion also be dedicated by the lighting of the candles, and then it will be done by the descendants, the Hasmoneans, for whom I will perform miracles and to whom I will grant grace. Hence there is greater glory destined for thee than for all the other princes of the tribes, for their offerings to the sanctuary shall be employed only so long as it endures, but the lights of the Hanukkah festival will shine forever; and, moreover, thy descendants shall bestow the priestly blessing upon Israel even after the destruction of the Temple."

The candlestick that Aaron lighted in the sanctuary, was not the common work of mortal hands, but was wrought by a miracle. When God bade Moses fashion a candlestick, he found it difficult to execute the command, not knowing how to set to work to construct it in all its complicated details. God therefore said to Moses: "I shall show thee a model." He then took white fire, red fire, and green fire, and black fire, and out these four kinds of fires He fashioned a candlestick with its bowls, its knops, and its flowers. Even then Moses was not able to copy the candlestick, whereupon God drew its design upon his palm, saying to him: "look at this, and imitate the design I have drawn on thy palm." But even that did not suffice to teach Moses how to execute the commission, whereupon God bade him cast a talent of gold into the fire. Moses did as he was bidden, and the candlestick shaped itself out of the fire. As on this occasion, so upon other occasions also did God have to present the things tangibly before Moses in order to make certain laws intelligible to him. In this way, for example, at the revelation concerning clean and unclean animals, God showed one specimen of each to Moses, saying: "This ye shall eat, and this ye shall not eat."

Chapter 4

THE TWELVE PRINCES OF THE TRIBES

God in His love for Israel had frequent censuses taken of them, so that He might accurately estimate His possession. In scarcely half a year they were twice counted, once shortly before the erection of the Tabernacle, and the second time a month after its dedication. On the first day of the month of Iyyar, Moses received instructions to take a census of all men over twenty who were physically fit to go to war. He was ordered to take Aaron as his assistant, so that in case he should overlook some of the men Aaron might remind him of them, for "two are better than one." They were also to take as their subordinate assistants Eleazar and Ithamar, Aaron's sons, and a man each from the several tribes. These twelve men were appointed not only to conduct the census, but also to look after the spiritual welfare of their respective tribes, the sins of which would be upon their heads unless, with all their powers, they strove to prevent them. Moses and Aaron nevertheless adjured the princes of the tribes, in spite of their high rank, not to tyrannize over the people, whereas, on the other hand, they admonished the people to pay all due respect to their superiors.

The names of these twelve princes of the tribes indicated the history of the tribes they represented. The prince of the tribe Reuben was called Elizur, "my God is a rock," referring to the ancestor of this tribe, Reuben, Jacob's son, who sinned, but, owing to his penance, was forgiven by God, who bore his sin as a rock bears the house built upon it. The name of Elizur's father was Shedeur, "cast into the fire," because Reuben was converted to repentance and atonement through Judah, who confessed his sin when his daughter-in-law Tamar was about to be cast into the fire.

The prince of the tribe of Simeon was named Shelumiel, "my God is peace," to indicate that in spite of the sin of Zimri, head of this tribe, through whom four and twenty thousand men among Israel died, God nevertheless made peace with this tribe.

The prince of the tribe of Judah bore the name Nahshon, "wave of the sea," the son of Amminadab, "prince of My people," because the prince received this dignity as a reward for having plunged into the waves of the Red Sea to glorify God's name.

The tribe of Issachar had for its prince Nethanel, "God gave," for this tribe devoted its life to the Torah given by God to Moses. Accordingly Nethanel was called the son of Zuar, "burden," for Issachar assumed the burden of passing judgement on the lawsuits of the other tribes.

Corresponding to the occupation of the tribe of Zebulun, its prince was called Eliab, "the ship," son of Helon, "the sand," for this tribe spent its life on ships, seeking "treasures hidden in the sand."

Elishama, son of Ammihud, the name of the prince of the tribe of Ephraim, points to the history of Joseph, their forefather. God said: "Elishama, 'he obeyed Me,' who bade him be chaste and not covet his master's wife that wanted to tempt him to sin, and Ammihud, 'Me he honored,' and none other."

The other tribe of Joseph, Manasseh, also named their prince in reference to their forefather, calling him Gamaliel, son of Pedahzur, which signifies, "God rewarded Joseph for his piety by releasing him from bondage and making him ruler over Egypt."

The prince of the tribe of Benjamin was named Abidan, "my father decreed," son of Gideoni, "mighty hosts," referring to the following incident. When Rachel perceived that she would die at the birth of her son, she called him "son of faintness," supposing that a similar fate would overtake him, and that he was doomed through weakness to die young. But Jacob, the child's father, decreed otherwise, and called him Benjamin, "son of might and of many years."

The prince of the tribe of Dan bore the name Ahiezer, "brother of help," son of Ammishaddai, "My people's judge," because he was allied with the helpful tribe of Judah at the erection of the Tabernacle, and like this ruling tribe brought forth a mighty judge in the person of Samson.

The tribe of Asher was distinguished by the beauty of its women, which was so excellent that even the old among them were fairer and stronger than the young girls of the other tribes. For this reason kings chose the daughters of this tribe to be their wives, and these, through their intercession before the kings, saved the lives of many who had been doomed to death. Hence the name of the prince of the tribe of Asher, Pagiel, "the interceder," son of Ochran, "the afflicted," for the women of the tribe of Asher, through their intercession, obtained grace for the afflicted.

The prince of the tribe of Gad bore the name Eliasaph, "God multiplied;" son of Deuel, "God is a witness." To reward them for passing over the Jordan and not returning to their property on this side of the river until the promised land was won, their wealth was multiplied by God; for when, upon returning, they found the enemy at home, God aided them and they gained all their enemies possessions. God was furthermore witness that this tribe had no wicked motive when they erected an altar on their land.

The prince of the tribe of Naphtali was called Ahira, "desirable meadow," son of Enan, "clouds;" for the land of this tribe was distinguished by its extraordinary excellence. Its products were exactly what their owners "desired," and all this owing to the plenty of water, for the "clouds" poured plentiful rain over their land.

At the census of the people the tribes were set down in the order in which they put up their camp and moved in their marches. The tribes of Judah, Issachar, and Zebulun formed the first group, the royal tribe of Judah being associated with the tribe of learned men, Issachar, and with Zebulun, which through its generosity enabled Issachar to devote itself to the study of the Torah. The second group consisted of Reuben, Simeon, and Gad. The sinful tribe of Simeon was supported on the right by the penance of Reuben and on the left by the strength of Gad. The tribes of Ephraim, Manasseh, and Benjamin formed a group by themselves, for these before all the other tribes were destined to appear gloriously against Amalek. The Ephraimite Joshua was the first who was victorious against Amalek, the Benjamite Saul followed his example in his war against Agag, king of Amalek, and, under the leadership of men out of the tribe of Manasseh, the tribe of Simeon at the time of king Jehoshaphat succeeded in destroying the rest of the Amalekites, and to take possession formed the last group, and for the following reason were united in this way. The tribe of Dan had already at the time of the exodus from Egypt been possessed of the sinful thought to fashion an idol. To counteract this "dark thought" Asher was made its comrade, from whose soil came "the oil for lighting;" and that Dan might participate in the blessing, Naphtali, "full with the blessing of the Lord," became its second companion.

At this third census the number of men who were able to go to war proved to be exactly the same as the second census, taken in the same year. Not one among Israel had died during this period, from the beginning of the erection of the Tabernacle to its dedication, when the third census took place. But no conclusive evidence concerning the sum total of the separate tribes can be drawn from this number of men able to go to war, because the ration of the two sexes varied among the different tribes, as, for example, the female sex in the tribe of Naphtali greatly outnumbered the male.

THE CENSUS OF THE LEVITES

Moses at the census did not take into consideration the tribe of Levi, because God had not commanded him to select a prince for this tribe as for all others, hence he drew the conclusion that they were not to be counted. Naturally he was not sure of his decision in this matter, and wavered whether or not to include the Levites in the number, when God said to him: "Do not muster the tribe of Levi, nor number them among the children of Israel." At these words Moses was frightened, for he feared that his tribe was considered unworthy of being counted with the rest, and was therefore excluded by God. But God quieted him, saying: "Do not number the Levites among the children of Israel, number them separately." There was several reasons for numbering the Levites separately. God foresaw that, owing to the sin of the spies who were sent to search the land, all men who were able to go to war would perish in the wilderness, "all that were numbered of them, according to their whole number, from twenty years old and upward." Now had the Levites been included in the sum total of Israel, the Angel of Death would have held sway over them also, wherefore God excluded them from the census of all the tribes, that they might in the future be exempt from the punishment visited upon the others, and might enter the promised land. The Levites were, furthermore, the body-guard of God, to whose care the sanctuary was entrusted-another reason for counting them separately. God in this instance conducted Himself like the king who ordered one of his officers to number his legions, but added: "Number all the legions excepting only the legion that is about me."

The extent of God's love for Levi is evident through the command given to Moses, to number in the tribe of Levi "all males from a month old and upward," whereas in the other tribes none were numbered save men able to go to war, from twenty years and upward. Upon other occasions God had even the embryos among the Levites numbered. This occurred upon Jacob's entrance into Egypt, when the number seventy for his family was attained only by including Jochebed who was still in the womb; and similarly at a future time upon the return of the exiles from Babylon. For at that time only twenty-three of the priestly sections returned, hence to complete their number they had to include Bigvai, who belonged to the missing section, even though he was still in the womb.

When Moses was ordered to number among the Levites all children from a month old and upward, he said to God: "Thou biddest me count them from a month old and upward. Shall I now wander about their courts and houses and count each child, seeing that Thou givest me such a command?" But God replied: "Do thou what thou canst do, and I will do what I can do." It now came to pass that whenever Moses betook himself to a Levite tent he found the Shekinah awaiting him, tell him exactly the number of children without his having to count them.

In the choice of this tribe God showed His preference for the seventh, for Levi was the seventh pious man, starting from Adam, to wit: Adam, Noah, Enoch, Abraham, Isaac, Jacob, and Levi. As in this instance, so in many others did God indicate His love for the seventh. He sits enthroned in the seventh heaven; of the seven worlds the seventh alone is inhabited by human beings; of the early generations the seventh was the most excellent, for it produces Enoch. Moses, seventh among the Patriarch, was judged worthy of receiving the Torah. David, seventh son of Jesse, was chosen as king. In periods of time, also, the seventh was the favorite. The seventh day is the Sabbath; the seventh month, Tishri, is the month of the holy days; the seventh year is the Sabbatical year of rest, and every seventh Sabbatical year of rest is the year of jubilee.

Another reason for numbering even the youngest boys among the Levites was that the tribe of Levi as a whole had the responsibility of atoning for the sin of the first-born among the children of Israel. For it was these who until the time of the worship of the Golden Calf performed the services of the priesthood, and their privilege was taken from them owing to this, their sin. This prerogative was then conferred upon the tribe of Levi, who, moreover, dedicating themselves, man for man, to the service of the Lord, served as an atonement for the first-born of Israel, that they might not be destroyed as they deserved.

The exchange of Levites in place of the first-born did, however, present a difficulty. For God had communicated the number of Levites to Moses in the following way: "Their number amounts to as many as the number of My legion." For, when God came down upon Sinai, twenty-two thousand angels surrounded Him, and just as many men did the Levites number. Outside of these there were three hundred first-born among the Levites that could not well be offered in exchange for the first-born among the other tribes, because their standing was the same as theirs. As the number of first-born among the other tribes exceeded the number of Levites by two hundred seventy-three, this surplus remained without actual atonement. Hence God ordered Moses to take from them five shekels apiece by the poll as redemption money, and give it to the priests. The sum was fixed upon by God, who said: "Ye sold the first-born of Rachel for five shekels, and for this reason shall ye give as redemption money for every first-born among ye five shekels."

To avoid quarrels among the first-born, as otherwise each one would try to lay the payment of redemption money upon his neighbor, Moses wrote upon twenty-two thousand slips of paper the word "Levi," and upon two hundred seventy-three the words "five shekels," all of which were then thrown into an urn and mixed. Then every first-born had to draw one of the slips. If he drew a slip with "Levi" he was not obliged to remit any payment, but if he drew "five shekels," he had to pay that sum to the priests.

THE FOUR DIVISIONS OF THE LEVITES

Apart from the census of all male Levites, Moses now took another census of the men from the ages of thirty to fifty, for only at this age were the Levites permitted to perform service in the Tabernacle throughout their march through the desert, a law that indeed ceased to hold good when Israel settled in the Holy Land. These officiating Levites, as well as the priests, were divided by Moses into eight sections, a number that was not doubled until the prophet Samuel increased it to sixteen, to which David again added eight, so that there were later twenty-four divisions among the Levites and priests.

The most distinguished among the Levites were the sons of Kohath, whose charge during the march through the desert was the Holy of Holies, and among the vessels particularly the Holy Ark. This latter was a dangerous trust, for out of the staves attached to it would issue sparks that consumed Israel's enemies, but now and then this fire wrought havoc among the bearers of the Ark. It therefore became a customary thing, when the camp was about to be moved, for Kohath's sons to hasten into the sanctuary and seek to pack up the different portions of it, each one planning cautiously to shift the carrying of the Ark upon another. But this even more kindled God's anger against them, and He slew many of the Kohathites because they ministered to the Ark with an unwilling heart. To avert the danger that threatened them, God ordered Aaron and his sons to enter first into the sanctuary, and "to appoint to the Kohathites, every one, his service and his burden, that they might not go in to see when the holy things are covered, lest they die." This was done because previous to this command the sons of Kohath had been accustomed to feast their eyes on the sight of the Ark, which brought them instantaneous death. But, according to this order, Aaron and his sons first took apart the different portions of the sanctuary, covered the Ark, and not till then called the sons of Kohath to bear the burden.

During the march the Levites might wear no shoes, but had to walk barefoot because they carried and ministered to holy objects. The Kohathites had, moreover, to walk backwards, for they might not turn their backs to the Holy Ark. They were, furthermore, owing to their offices as bearers of the Ark, distinguished by being the first of the Levites to be numbered in the census, although in other respects the sons of Gershon led, for Gershon was the first-born of Levi.

When giving the commission to count the sons of Kohath, God explicitly mentioned that Moses should undertake the census with Aaron, but He did not do so when He ordered the numbering of the sons of Gershon. Moses now thought that God had done this intentionally because the former were directly under Aaron's supervision while the Gershonites were not. Nevertheless, out of respect to his brother, he bade his brother, as well as, out of courtesy, the princes of the tribes to be present at the numbering of the Levites, but he did not tell Aaron that he did so in the name of God. In this Moses erred, for God wished Aaron to be present at the numbering of the Levites. For this reason, when He ordered the census of the third division, Merari's sons, to be taken, He expressly mentioned Aaron's name. At the apportionment of the service among the individual Levites, however, Aaron paid attention only to the sons of Kohath, each of whom had his special task allotted to him, whereas Moses appointed their tasks to the sons of Gershon and Merari. The highest chief of the Levites, however, was Eleazar, who was "to have the oversight of them that keep the charge of the santuary." But despite his high position, Eleazar was modest enough to participate in the service in person. During their marches from place to place, he himself would carry all needful things for the daily offering. In his right hand he carried the oil for the candlestick, in his left hand the incense, on his are the things that were made in the pans, and, attached to his girdle, the phial with the oil for ointment. Ithamar, Eleazar's brother, also had a duty in the sanctuary, for it was he to whom the guidance of the service of Gershon's and Merari's sons was assigned. For these must perform none but the service God had specially assigned to them, as no Gershonite might perform the duty of a Merarite, and vice versa, and each individual, too, had his special duty, that no quarrel might arise among them.

THE FOUR STANDARDS

When God appeared upon Sinai, He was surrounded by twenty-two thousand angels, all in full array and divided into groups, each of which had its own standard. Looking upon these angel hosts, Israel wished like them to be divided into groups with standards, and God fulfilled their wish. After Moses had completed the census of the people, God said to Him: "Fulfill their wish and provide them with standards as they desire. 'Every man of the children of Israel shall pitch by his own standard, with the ensign of their father's house; far off about the Tabernacle of the congregation shall they pitch.'" This commission greatly agitated Moses, who thought: "Now will there be much strife among the tribes. If I bid the tribe of Judah pitch in the East, it will surely state its preference for the South, and every tribe will likewise choose any direction but the one assigned to it." But God said to Moses: "Do not concern thyself with the position of the standards of the tribes, for they have no need of thy direction. Their father Jacob before his death ordered them to group themselves about the Tabernacle just as his sons were to be grouped about his bier at the funeral procession." When Moses now told the people to divide themselves in groups round about the Tabernacle, they did it in the manner Jacob had bidden them.

"The Lord by wisdom hath founded the earth; by understanding hath He established the heavens." The division of the tribes of Israel according to four standards, as well as their subdivision at each standard, is not arbitrary and accidental, it corresponds to the same plan and direction as that of which God made use in heaven. The celestial Throne is surrounded by four angels: to the right Michael, in front Gabriel, to the left

Uriel, and to the rear Raphael. To these four angels corresponded the four tribes of Reuben, Judah, Dan, and Ephraim, the standard bearers. Michael earned his name, "Who is like unto God," by exclaiming during the passage of Israel through the Red Sea, "Who is like unto Thee, O Lord, among the gods?" and he made a similar statement when Moses completed the Torah, saying: "There is none like unto the God of Jeshurun." In the same way Reuben bore upon his standard the words, "Hear, O Israel: the Lord our God is one Lord," hence Reuben's position with his standard to the right of the sanctuary corresponded exactly to Michael's post at the right of the celestial Throne. Gabriel, "God is mighty," stands in front of the Throne, as Judah, "mightiest among his brethren," was the standard bearer in front of the camp. Dan, the tribe "from which emanated dark sin," stood at the left side of the camp with his standard, corresponding to the angel Uriel, "God is my light," for God illuminated the darkness of sin by the revelation of the Torah, in the study of which this angel instructed Moses, and devotion to which is penance for sin. The tribe of Ephraim was the standard bearer to the rear of the camp, occupying the same position as Raphael, "God heals," holds the celestial Throne; for this tribe, from which sprang Jeroboam, was in need of God's healing for the wound that this wicked king dealt Israel.

God had other reasons for the divisions of the tribes that He decreed, for He said to Moses: "In the East whence comes the light shall the tribe of Judah, whence arises the light of sovereignty, pitch its camp, and with them the tribe of Issachar, with whom dwells the light of the Torah, and Zebulum, shining through the wealth. From the South come the dews of blessing and the rains of plenty, hence shall Reuben pitch on this side, for this tribe owes its existence to the penitent deeds of its forefather, penance being that which causes God to send His blessing upon the world. Beside Reuben shall stand the warlike tribe of Gad, and between these two Simeon, in order that this tribe, made weak by its sins, might be protected on either side by the piety of Reuben and the heroism of Gad. In the West are storehouses of snow, the storehouses of hail, of cold, and of heat, and as powerless as are mortals against these forces of nature, so ineffectual shall be the enemies of the tribes of Ephraim, Manasseh, and Benjamin, for which reason their post was to the West of the camp. From the North comes the darkness of sin, for this tribe alone will declare itself willing to accept the idols of Jeroboam, hence its place is to the North of the camp. To illuminate its darkness, put beside it shining Asher, and Naphtali, filled with God's plenty."

The four standards were distinguished from one another by their different colors, and by the inscriptions and figures worked upon each. The color of Judah's standard corresponded to the color of the three stones in the breastplate of the high priest, on which were engraved the names of Judah, Issachar, and Zebulun, and was composed of red, green, and fiery red. Judah's name, as well as Issachar's and Zebulun's, was inscribed on the banner, and beside the names was this inscription: "Rise up, Lord, and let Thine enemies be scattered; and let them that hate Thee flee before Thee." The standard of Reuben, about which gathered also the tribes of Simeon and Gad, was the color of the emerald, the sapphire, and the sabhalom, for on these three stones were the names of these tribes engraved on the breastplate of the high priest. Besides the names of Reuben, Simeon, and Gad the following device was wrought on the second standard, "Hear, O Israel: the Lord our God is one Lord." The third standard, around which rallied the tribes of Ephraim, Manasseh, and Benjamin, bore the color of the diamond, the turquoise, and the amethyst, for on these three stones in the high priest's breastplate were engrave the names of these three tribes. On this standard beside the names of these three tribes was the motto, "And the cloud of the Lord was upon them by day, when they went out of camp." As on the breastplate of the high priest the stones chrysolite, beryl and panther-stone bore the names of Dan, Asher, and Naphtali, so too did the fourth standard, round which these three tribes gathered, bear a color resembling these three stones. This standard contained the names of Dan, Asher, and Naphtali, and the device: "Return, O Lord, unto the many thousands of Israel."

The standards had also other distinguishing characteristics. Judah's standard bore in its upper part the figure of a lion, for its forefather had been characterized by Jacob as "a lion's whelp," and also sword-like hooks of gold. On these hooks God permitted a strip of the seventh cloud of glory to rest, in which were visible the initials of the names of the three Patriarchs, Abraham, Isaac, and Jacob, the letters being radiations from the Shekinah. Reuben's standard had in its upper part the figure of a man, corresponding to the mandrakes that Reuben, forefather of this tribe, found, for this plant had the form of a manikin. The hooks on this standard were like those on the standard of Judah, but the second letters of the names of the three Patriarchs, Bet,

Zade, and 'Ayyin were seen above them in the cloud. In the standard of Ephraim was fashioned the form of a fish, for Jacob had blessed the forefather of this tribe by telling him to multiply like a fish; in all other respects it was like the other two standards, save the above the sword-like hooks of gold were seen the third letters in the names of the Patriarchs, Resh, Het, and Kof. Dan's standard contained the form of a serpent, for "Dan shall be a serpent by the way," was Jacob's blessing for this tribe; and the gleaming letters over the hooks were: Mem for Abraham, Kof for Isaac, and Bet for Jacob. The letter He of Abraham's name was not indeed visible over the standards, but was reserved by God for a still greater honor. For, over the Holy Ark, God let a pillar of cloud rest, and in this were visible the letter Yod and He, spelling the name Yah, by means of which God had created the world. This pillar of cloud shed sunlight by day and moonlight by night, so that Israel, who were surrounded by clouds, might distinguish between night and day. These two sacred letters, Yod, He, would on week-days fly about in the air over the four standards, hovering now upon this, now upon that. But as soon as Friday was over and the Sabbath began, these letters stood immovable on the spot where they chanced to be at that moment, and remained in this rigid position from the first moment of the Sabbath to the last.

Whenever God wanted Israel to break up camp and move on, He would send on from its place over the Ark the cloud in which beamed the two sacred letters Yod and He in the direction in which Israel was to march, and the four strips of cloud over the standards would follow. As soon as the priests saw the clouds in motion, they blew the trumpets as a signal for starting, and the winds thereupon from all sides breathed myrrh and frankincense.

Although it was the clouds that gave the signal for taking down and pitching tents, still they always awaited the word of Moses. Before starting the pillar of cloud would contract and stand still before Moses, waiting for him to say: "Rise up, Lord, and let Thine enemies be scattered; and let them that hate Thee flee before Thee," whereupon the pillar of cloud would be set in motion. It was the same when they pitched camp. The pillar of cloud would contract and stand still before Moses, waiting for him to say: "Return, O Lord, unto the many thousands of Israel," whereupon it would expand first over the tribes that belonged to the standard of Judah, and then over the sanctuary, within and without.

THE CAMP

The camp was in the form of a square, twelve thousand cubits on each side, and in the middle was the space, four thousand cubits in size, for the sanctuary, and the dwelling place of priests and Levites. In the East of the sanctuary lived Moses, Aaron, and Aaron's sons; the Levites of the family of Kohath lived in the South, the sons of Gershon in the West, and the sons of Merari in the North. Each of theses divisions had for its dwelling place a space of a hundred cubits, while each group of three tribes that joined under one standard had a space of four thousand cubits. This was only for the dwelling place of the people, the cattle were outside the encampment, and the cloud of glory separated the dwelling places of the human beings from those of the animals. Rivers surrounded the camp from without, and so also were the different groups separated one from the other by rivers. But in order that on the Sabbath, when riding was prohibited, intercourse among the different parts of the camp might not be rendered impossible, there were bridges of boards over the rivers. The purple color of the cloud of glory was reflected in the waters of the rivers, so that it spread afar a radiance like that of the sun and the stars. The heathens, whenever they beheld these wondrous radiant waters, were frightened and feared Israel, but at the same time praised God for the miracles He wrought for Israel.

These were miracles that were visible to the outer world as well, but there were others that were known to Israel alone. During their forty years' march they had no need of change of raiment. The robe of purple which the angels clothed each one among them at their exodus from Egypt remained ever new; and as a snail's shell grows with it, so did their garments grow with them. Fire could not injure these garments, and though they wore the same things throughout forty years, still they were not annoyed by vermin, yes, even the corpses of this generation were spared by worms.

During their marches, as well as in their stay at a certain place, they had not only the four standards that divided them into four groups of three tribes each, each individual tribe had furthermore its own special spot and its special ensign. Reuben's flag was red, and on it were pictured mandrakes. Simeon's flag was green, with a picture of the city of Shechem upon it, for the forefather of the tribe had conquered this city. Judah's flag was azure, and bore the form of a lion. Issachar's flag was black, and had two figures, the sun and the moon, for from this tribe sprung the learned men who busied themselves with astronomy and the science of the calendar. Zebulun's flag was white, with the form of a ship, for this tribe devoted to navigation. Dan's flag had a color like a sapphire, with the figure of a serpent. Naphtali's flag was a dull red, the color of wine, and on it was the figure of a hind, in memory of its forefather, who was like "a hind let loose." Ashere's flag was red like fire, and had the token of an olive tree, because this tribe had much olive oil of excellent quality. The two tribes descended from Joseph,-Ephraim, and Manasseh-both flags of the same deep black color with a representation of Egypt, but they had other forms besides. Ephraim's had the picture of a bull, to symbolize Joshua, sprung of this tribe, whose glory was like "the firstling of his bullock, that pusheth the people together to the ends of the earth;" whereas Manasseh's was that of a unicorn, symbolizing the judge Gideon that sprang from this tribe, "who with his horns of unicorns pushed the people." Benjamin's flag had a color composed of all the other eleven colors, and a wolf for his token, Jacob having described this tribe a "a wolf that ravineth." The different colors of the flags corresponded to the colors of the stones set in the breastplate of the high priest, on which were engraved the names of the twelve tribes. Reuben's stone had a red color like his flag, Simeon's flag was green like the color of his stone, and in this way with all the tribes the color of stones and of flags harmonized.

THE BLASPHEMER AND THE SABBATH-BREAKER

When Israel received the Torah from God, all the other nations envied them and said: "Why were these choosen by God out of all the nations?" But God stopped their mouths, replying: "Bring Me your family records, and My children shall bring their family records." The nations could not prove the purity of their families, but Israel stood without a blemish, every man among them ready to prove his pure descent, so that the nations burst into praise at Israel's family purity, which was rewarded by God with the Torah for this its excellence.

How truly chastity and purity reigned among Israel was shown by the division of the people into groups and tribes. Among all these thousands was found only a single man who was not of pure descent, and who therefore at the pitching of the standards could attach himself to none of the groups. This man was the son of Shelomith, a Danite woman, and the Egyptian, whom Moses, when a youth of eighteen, had slain for having offered violence to Shelomith, the incident that had necessitated Moses' flight from Egypt. It had happened as follows: When Moses came to Goshen to visit his parents, he witnessed how an Egyptian struck an Israelite, and the latter, knowing that Moses was in high favor at Pharaoh's court, sought his assistance, appealing to him with these words: "O, my lord, this Egyptian by night forced his way into my house, bound me with chains, and in my presence offered violence to my wife. Now he wants to kill me besides." Indignant at this infamous action of the Egyptian, Moses slew him, so that the tormented Israelite might go home. The latter, on reaching his house, informed his wife that he intended getting a divorce from her, as it was not proper for a member of the house of Jacob to live together with a woman that had been defiled. When the wife told her brothers of her husband's intentions, they wanted to kill their brother-in-law, who eluded them only by timely flight.

The Egyptian's violence was not without issue, for Shelomith gave birth to a son whom she reared as a Jew, even though his father had been and Egyptian. When the division of the people according to the four standard took place, this son of Shelomith appeared among the Danites into whose division he meant to be admitted, pointing out to them that his mother was a woman of the tribe of Dan. The Danites, however, rejected him, saying: "The commandment of God says, 'each man by his own standard, with the ensign of his father's house.' Paternal, not maternal descent decides a man's admission to a tribe." As this man was not content with this answer, his case was brought to Moses' court, who also passed judgement against him. This so embittered him the he blasphemed the Ineffable Name which he had heard on Mount Sinai, and cursed Moses. He at the same time ridiculed the recently announced law concerning the shewbread that was to be set on the table in the sanctuary every Sabbath, saying: "It behooves a king to eat fresh bread daily, and no stale bread."

At the same time as the crime blasphemy was committed by the son of Shelomith, Zelophehad committed another capital crime. On a Sabbath day he tore trees out of the ground although he had been warned by witnesses not to break the Sabbath. The overseers whom Moses had appointed to enforce the observance of the Sabbath rest seized him and brought him to the school, where Moses, Aaron, and other leaders of the people studied the Torah.

In both these cases Moses was uncertain how to pass judgement, for, although he knew that capital punishment must follow the breaking of the Sabbath, still the manner of capital punishment in this case had not yet been revealed to him. Zelophehad was in the meantime kept in prison until Moses should learn the details of the case, for the laws says that a man accused of a capital charge may not be given liberty of person. The sentence that Moses received from God was to execute Zelophehad in the presence of all the community by stoning him. This was accordingly done, and after the execution his corps was for a short time suspended from the gallows.

The sin of the Sabbath-breaker was the occasion that gave rise to God's commandment of Zizit to Israel. For He said to Moses, "dost thou know how it came to pass that this man broke the Sabbath?" Moses: "I do not know." God: "On week days he wore phylacteries on his head and phylacteries on his arm to remind him of his duties, but on the Sabbath day, on which no phylacteries may be worn, he had nothing to call his duties to his mind, and he broke the Sabbath. Go now, Moses, and find for Israel a commandment the observance of which is not limited to week days only, but which will influence them on Sabbath days and on holy days as well." Moses selected the commandment of Zizit, the sight of which will recall to the Israelites all the other commandments of God.

Whereas in the case of the Sabbath breaker Moses had been certain that the sin was punishable by death, and had been certain that the sin was punishable by death, and had been in doubt only concerning the manner of execution, in the case of the blasphemer matters were different. Here Moses was in doubt concerning the nature of the crime, for he was not even sure if it was at all a capital offence. Hence he did not have these two men imprisoned together, because one of them was clearly a criminal, whereas the status of the other was undetermined. But God instructed Moses that the blasphemer was also to be stoned to death, and that this was to be the punishment for blasphemers in the future.

There were two other cases beside these two in Moses' career on which he could not pass judgement without appealing to God. These were the claims of Zelophehad's daughters to the inheritance of their father, and the case of the unclean that might not participate in the offering of the paschal lamb. Moses hastened in his appeal to God concerning the two last mentioned cases, but took his time with the two former, for on these depended human lives. In this Moses set the precedent to the judges among Israel to dispatch civil cases with all celerity, but to proceed slowly in criminal cases. In all these cases, however, he openly confessed that he did not at the time know the proper decision, thereby teaching the judges of Israel to consider it no disgrace, when necessary, to consult others in cases when they were not sure of true judgement.

THE UNGRATEFUL MULTITUDE

When God commanded Israel to set out from Sinai and continue their march, the Israelites were glad, for during their stay in that place they had throughout eleven days received new laws daily, and they hoped that after having departed from the holy mountain they would receive no further laws. Hence, instead of making a day's march from Sinai, as God had commanded them, they marched incessantly for three days, in order to be as far as possible from the holy spot. They behaved like a boy who runs quickly away after dismissal from school, that his teacher might not call him back. Although this antipathy to His laws vexed God, He did not therefore forsake them, but let the Ark move before them as long as they desired to continue the march. For it was by this token that the Israelites knew that the Shekinah was among them, as God had promised them. As often as they broke camp or pitched camp Moses would say to them: "Do what the Shekinah within the Ark bids you do." But they would not believe Moses that the Shekinah dwelt among them unless he spoke the words: "Rise up, Lord, and let Thine enemies be scattered; and let them that hate Thee flee before Thee," whereupon the Ark would begin to move, and they were convinced of the presence of the Shekinah. The Ark furthermore gave the signal for breaking camp by soaring up high, and then swiftly moving before the camp at a distance of three days' march, until it found a suitable spot upon which Israel might encamp.

Hardly had they departed from Sinai when they once more began to lead the wicked course of life that they had for a time abandoned. They began to seek a pretext to renounce God and again to be addicted to idolatry. They complained about the forced marches which at God's command they had been obliged to make after their departure from Sinai, and in this way showed their ingratitude to God who wanted them as quickly as possible to reach the Holy Land, and for this reason allowed them to cover an eleven days' distance in three days. Their murmurs and complaints, however, were not silent, but quite loud, for they were anxious that God should hear their wicked words. In punishment for their defamation of the Divine glory, God sent upon them a fire emanating from the very glory.

Upon twelve occasions did God send a Divine fire upon earth, six times as a token of honor and distinction, but as many times as a punishment. To the first class belong the fire at the consecration of the Tabernacle, at the offering of Gideon as at that of Manoah and of David; at the dedication of Solomon's Temple, and at the offering of Elijah upon Mount Carmel. The six fatal fires are the following: the fire that consumed Nadab and Abihu; that which wrought havoc among the murmuring and complaining multitude; the fire that consumed the company of Korah; the fire that destroyed Job's sheep, and the two fires that burned the first and second troops which Ahaziah sent against Elijah.

This celestial fire wrought the greatest havoc among the idolatrous tribe of Dan, and among the mixed multitude that had joined the Israelites upon their exodus from Egypt. The elders of the people turned to Moses, saying: "Rather deliver us as a sheep to the slaughter, but not to a celestial fire that consumes earthly fire." They should by right have prayed to God themselves, but in this instance they were like the king's son who had kindled his father's anger against him, and who not hastened to his father's friend, begging him to intercede for him. So did Israel say to Moses: "Go thou to God and pray for us." Moses instantly granted their wish, and God without delay heard Moses' prayer and halted the destroying fire. But God did not simply take the fire away from Israel and put it elsewhere, for it was of such a nature that it would gradually have spread on all sides and finally have destroyed everything. It had in this way caused the destruction in Israel, for, beginning at one end of the camp, it spread so rapidly that one could at no time tell how far it had gone. That the presence of this Divine fire might continue to restrain Israel from sin, God did not allow it to rise back to heaven, but it found its place on the altar of the Tabernacle, where it consumed all the offerings that were brought during Israel's stay in Egypt. This is the same fire that destroyed Aaron's sons as well as Korah's company, and it is the Divine fire that every mortal beholds in the moment of his death.

On this occasion also it was evident that pious men are greater than the angels, for Moses took bundles of wool and laid them upon the Divine fire, which thereupon went out. He then said to the people: "If you repent of your sin, then the fire will go out, but otherwise it will burst forth and consume you."

THE FLESH-POTS OF EGYPT

Not mindful of the punishment by fire, Israel still did not mend their ways, but soon again began to murmur against God. As so often before, it was again the mixed multitude that rebelled against God and Moses, saying: "Who shall give up flesh to eat? We remember the fish that we did eat in Egypt freely; the cucumbers, and the melons, and the leeks, and the onions, and the garlic. But now our soul is dried away: there is nothing at all, beside this manna before our eyes." But all this murmuring and these complaints were only a pretext to sever themselves from God, for first of all, they actually possessed many herds and much cattle, enough plentifully to satisfy their lusting after flesh if they had really felt it; and manna, furthermore, had the flavor of every conceivable kind of food, so all they had to do while eating it was to wish for a certain dish and they instantly perceived in manna the taste of the desired food. It is true that manna never gave them the flavor of the five vegetables they mentioned, but they should have been grateful to God for sparing them the taste of these vegetables injurious to health. Here they showed their perversity in being dissatisfied with measures for which they should have been grateful to God. Manna displeased them because it did not contain the flavor injurious to health, and they also objected to it because it remained in their bodies, wherefore they said: "The manna will swell in our stomachs, for can there be a human being that takes food without excreting it!" God had, as a special mark of distinction, given them this food of the angels, which is completely dissolved in the body, and of which they could always partake without injury to their health. It is a clear proof of the excellent taste of manna that a later time, when the last manna fell on the day of Moses' death, they ate of it for forty days, and would not make use of other food until the manna had been exhausted to the last grain, clearly showing that the taking of any different food was disagreeable. But while manna was at hand in abundance, they complained about seeing before them, morning and evening, no other food than manna.

The true state of affairs was that they had a lurking dissatisfaction with the yoke of the law. It is certain that they had not had in Egypt better food for which they now longed, for their taskmasters, far from giving them dainties, gave them not even straw for making bricks. But in Egypt they had lived undisturbed by laws, and it was this unrestrained life that they desired back. Especially hard for them were the new laws on marriage, for in Egypt they had been accustomed to marry those closely related by blood, from whom they were now obliged to separate. They now trooped together in families, and awaiting the moment when Moses, about to leave the house of study, would have to pass them, they began to murmur publicly, accusing him of being to blame for all the sufferings they had been obliged to bear. Upon his advice, they said, had they abandoned a most fruitful land, and instead of enjoying the great fortune promised to them, they were now wandering about in misery, suffering thirst from lack of water, and were apprehensive of dying of starvation in case the supply of manna should cease. When these and similar abuses were uttered against Moses, one out of the people stepped forth and exhorted them not so soon to forget the many benefactions they had known from Moses, and not to despair of God's aid and support. But the multitude upon this became even more excited, and raged and shouted more violently than ever against Moses. This conduct of Israel called forth God's wrath, but Moses, instead of interceding for the people, began to complain of their treatment of him, and announced to God that he could not now execute the commission he had undertaken in Egypt, namely, to lead Israel in spite of all reverses, until he had reached the promised land. He now begged God to relieve him of the leadership of the people in some way, and at the same time to stand by him in his present predicament, that he might satisfy the people's desire for flesh.

THE APPOINTMENT OF THE SEVENTY ELDERS

The sad predicament of Moses on this occasion is partly traceable to the fact that he had to face alone the murmurs and complaints of the people without the accustomed assistance of the seventy elders. Since the exodus from Egypt the seventy elders of the people had always been at his side, but these had recently been killed by the fire from heaven at Taberah, so that he now stood all alone. This death overtook the elders because like Nadab and Abihu they had not shown sufficient reverence in ascending Mount Sinai on the day of the revelation, when, in view of the Divine vision, they conducted themselves in an unseemly manner. Like Nadab and Abihu the elder would have received instantaneous punishment for their offense, had not God been unwilling to spoil the joyful day of the revelation by their death. But they had to pay the penalty nevertheless: Nadab and Abihu, by being burned at the consecration of the Tabernacle, and the elders similarly, at Taberah.

As Moses now utterly refused to bear the burden of the people alone, God said to him: "I gave thee sufficient understanding and wisdom to guide My children alone, that thou mightest be distinguished by this honor. Thou, however, wishest to share this guidance with others. Go, then, and expect no help from Me, 'but I will take of the spirit that is upon thee and will put it upon them; and they shall bear the burden of the people with thee, that thou bear it not thyself alone'"

God bade Moses choose as his helpers in the guidance of the people such men as had already been active leaders and officers in Egypt. In the days of Egyptian bondage it frequently happened that the officers of the children of Israel were beaten if the people had not fulfilled their task in making bricks, but "he that is willing to sacrifice himself for the benefit of Israel shall be rewarded with honor, dignity, and the gift of the Holy Spirit." The officers suffered in Egypt for Israel, and were now found worthy of having the Holy Spirit come upon them. God moreover said to Moses: "With kindly words welcome the elders to their new dignity, saying, 'Hail to you that are deemed worthy by God of being fit for this office.' At the same time, however, speak seriously with them also, saying, 'Know ye that the Israelites are a troublesome and stiff-necked people, and that you must ever be prepared to have them curse you or cast stones at you'"

God commanded the selection of the elders to take place at the Tabernacle, that Israel might reverence them, saying, "Surely these are worthy men," but they were not permitted with Moses to enter the Tabernacle and hear God's word. The people were however mistaken in assuming that God's word reached the ears of the elders, for He spoke with Moses alone, even though the prophetic spirit came upon them also.

Now when Moses wished to proceed to the selection of the seventy elders, he was in a sore predicament because he could not evenly divide the number seventy among the twelve tribes, and was anxious to show no partiality to one tribe over another, which would lead to dissatisfaction among Israel. Bezalel, son of Uri, however, gave Moses good advice. He took seventy slips of paper on which was written "elder," and with them two blank slips, and mixed all these in an urn. Seventy-two elders, six to each tribe, now advance and each drew a slip. Those whose slips were marked "elder" were elected, while those who had drawn blank slips were rejected, but in such a wise that they could not well accuse Moses of partiality.

By this method of appointment, it came to pass that there were six elders for each tribe except the tribe of Levi. The names of those chosen were: from the tribe of Reuben,-Hanoch, Carmi, Pallu, Zaccur, Eliab, Nemuel; from the tribe of Simeon,-Jamin, Jachin, Zohar, Ohad, Shaul, Zimri; from the tribe of Levi,-Amram, Hananiah, Nethanel, Sithri; from the tribe of Judah,-Zerah, Dan, Jonadab, Bezalel, Shephatiah, Nahshon; from the tribe of Issachar,-Zuar, Uzza, Igal, Palti, Othniel, Haggi; from the tribe of Zebulun,-Sered, Elon, Sodi, Oholiab, Elijah, Nimshi; from the tribe of Benjamin,-Senaah, Kislon, Elidad, Ahitub, Jediael, Mattaniah; from the tribe of Joseph,-Jair, Joezer, Malchiel, Adoniram, Abiram, Sethur; from the tribe of Dan,-Gedaliah, Jogli, Ahinoam, Ahiezer, Daniel, Seraiah; from the tribe of Naphtali,-Elhanan, Eliakim, Elishama, Semachiah, Zabdi, Johanan; from the tribe of Gad,-Haggai, Zarhi, Keni, Mattathiah, Zechariah, Shuni; from the tribe of Asher,-Pashhur, Shelomi, Samuel, Shalom, Shecaniah, Abihu.

Moses gathered these seventy elders of novel extraction and of lofty and pious character round about the tent in which God used to reveal Himself, bidding thirty of them take their stand on the south side, thirty on the northern, and ten on the eastern, whereas he himself stood on the western side. For this tent was thirty cubits long and ten cubits wide, so that a cubit each was apportioned to the elders. God was so pleased with the appointment of the elders that, just as on the day of the revelation, He descended from heaven and permitted the spirit of prophecy to come upon the elders, so that they received the prophetic gift to the end of their days, as God had put upon them of the spirit of Moses. But Moses' spirit was not diminished by this, he was like a burning candle from which many others are lighted, but which is not therefore diminished; and so likewise was the wisdom of Moses unimpaired. Even after the appointment of the elders did Moses remain the leader of the people, for he was the head of this Sanhedrin of seventy members which he guided and directed.

The position of the elders was not of the same rank as that of Moses, for he was the king of Israel, and it was for this reason that God had bidden him to secure trumpets, to use them for the calling of the assembly, that this instrument might be blown before him as before a king. Hence shortly before Moses' death these trumpets were recalled from use, for his successor Joshua did not inherit from him either his kingly dignity or these royal insignia. Not until David's time were the trumpets used again which Moses had fashioned in the desert.

ELDAD AND MEDAD

When Moses had completed the appointment of the elders and had asked them to accompany him to the Tabernacle, there to receive the Holy Spirit, Eldad and Medad, two of these elders, in their humility, did not obey his summons, but hid themselves, deeming themselves unworthy of this distinction. God rewarded them for their humility by distinguishing them five-fold above the other elders. These prophesied what would take place on the following day, announcing the appearance of the quails, but Eldad and Medad prophesied what was still veiled in the distant future. The elders prophesied only on this one day, but Eldad and Medad retained the gift for life. The elders died in the desert, whereas Eldad and Medad were the leaders of the people after the death of Joshua. The elders are not mentioned by name in the Scriptures, whereas theses two are called by name. The elders, furthermore, had received the prophetic gift from Moses, whereas Eldad and Medad received it directly from God.

Eldad now began to make prophecies, saying: "Moses will die, and Joshua the son of Nun will be his successor as leader of the people, whom he will lead into the land of Canaan, and to whom he will give it as a possession." Medad's prophecy was as follows: "Quails will come from the sea and will cover the camp of Israel, but they will bring evil to the people." Besides these prophecies, both together announced the following revelation: "At the end of days there will come up out of the land of Magog a king to whom all nations will do homage. Crowned kings, princes, and warriors with shields will gather to make war upon those returned from exile in the land of Israel. But God, the Lord, will stand by Israel in their need and will slay all their enemies by hurling a flame from under His glorious Throne. This will consume the souls in the hosts of the king of Magog, so that their bodies will drop lifeless upon the mountains of the land of Israel, and will become a prey to the beasts of the field and the fowls of the air. Then will all the dead among Israel arise and rejoice in the good that at the beginning of the world was laid up for them, and will receive the reward for their good deeds."

When Gershon, Moses' son, heard these prophecies of Eldad and Medad, he hurried to his father and told him of them. Joshua was now greatly agitated about the prophecy that Moses was to die in the desert and that he as to be his successor, and said to Moses: "O lord, destroy these people that prophesy such evil news!" But Moses replied: "O Joshua, canst thou believe that I begrudge thee thy splendid future? It is my wish that thou mayest be honored as much as I have been and that all Israel be honored like thee."

Eldad and Medad were distinguished not only by their prophetic gift, but also by their noble birth, being half-brothers of Moses and Aaron. When the marriage laws were revealed, all those who had been married to relatives by blood had to be divorced from them, so that Amram, too, had to be separated from his wife Jochebed, who was his aunt, and he married another woman. From this union sprang Eldad, "not of an aunt," and Medad, "in place of an aunt," so called by Amram to explain by these names why he had divorced his first wife, his aunt.

THE QUAILS

The prophecy of these men concerning the quails turned out as they had predicted, the quails being, as God had foretold to Moses, no blessing for the people. For God said to Moses: "Tell the people to be prepared for impending punishment, they shall eat flesh to satiety, but then they shall loathe it more than they now lust for it. I know, however, how they came to have such desires. Because My Shekinah is among them they believe that they may presume anything. Had I removed My Shekinah from their midst they would never have cherished so foolish a desire." Moses, knowing that the granting of the people's wish would be disastrous to them, said to God: "O Lord, why, pray, dost Thou first give them flesh, and then, in punishment for their sin, slay them? Who ever heard any one say to an ass, 'Here is a measure of wheat; eat it, for we want to cut off they head?' Or to a man, 'Here is a loaf of bread for thee; take it, and go to hell with it?'" God replied: "Well, then, what wouldst thou do?" Moses: "I will go to them and reason with them that they may desist from their lusting after flesh." God: "I can tell thee beforehand that thy endeavors in this matter will be fruitless." Moses betook himself to the people, saying to them: "Is the Lord's hand waxed short? Behold, He smote the rock, that the waters gushed out, and the streams overflowed; He can give bread also; can He not provide flesh for His people?" The people, however, said: "Thou are only trying to soothe us; God cannot grant our wish." But they erred vastly, for hardly had the pious among them retired to their tents, when upon the godless, who had remained in the open, came down quails in masses as thick as snowflakes, so that many more were kill by the descent of the quails than later by the tasting of them. The quails came in such masses that they completely filled the space between heaven and earth, so that they even covered the sun's disk, and settled down on the north side and the south side of the camp, as it were a day's journey, lying, however, not directly upon the ground but two cubits above it, that people might not have to stoop to gather them up. Considering this abundance, it is not surprising that even the halt that could not go far, and the lazy the would not, gathered each a hundred kor. These vast quantities of flesh did not, however, benefit them, for hardly had they tasted of it, when they gave up the ghost. This was the punishment for the grave sinners, while the better ones among them enjoyed the taste of the flesh for a month before they died, whereas the pious without suffering harm caught the quails, slaughtered them, and ate of them. This was the heaviest blow that had fallen upon Israel since their exodus from Egypt, and in memory of the many men who had died because of their forbidden lusting after flesh, they changed the name of the place where this misfortune occurred to Kibroth-hattaavah, "Graves of those who lusted." The winds that went forth to bring the quails was so powerful a storm that it could have destroyed the world, so great was God's anger against the ungrateful people, and it was only due to the merits of Moses and Aaron that this wind finally left the world upon its hinges.

AARON AND MIRIAM SLANDER MOSES

When the seventy elders were appointed, and the spirit of the Lord came upon them, all the women lighted the candles of joy, to celebrate by this illumination the elevation of these men to the dignity of prophets. Zipporah, Moses' wife, saw the illumination, and asked Miriam to explain it. She told her the reason, and added, "Blessed are the women who behold with their eyes how their husbands are raised to dignity." Zipporah answered, "It would be more proper to say, 'Woe to the wives of these men who must now abstain from all conjugal happiness!'" Miriam: "How does thou know this?" Zipporah: "I judge so from the conduct of thy brother, for ever since he was chosen to receive Divine revelations, he no longer knows his wife." Miriam hereupon went to Aaron, and said to him: "I also received Divine revelations, but without being obliged to separated myself from my husband," whereupon Aaron agreed, saying " I, too, received Divine revelations, without, however, being obliged to separated myself from my wife." Then both said: "Our fathers also received revelations, but without discontinuing their conjugal life. Moses abstains from conjugal joys only out of pride, to show how holy a man he is." Not only did they speak evil of Moses to each other, but hastened to him and told him to his face their opinion of his conduct. But he, who could be self-assured and stern when it touched a matter concerning God's glory, was silent to the undeserved reproached they heaped upon him, knowing that upon God's bidding he had foresworn earthly pleasures. God therefore said: "Moses is very meek and pays no attention to the injustice meted out to him, as he did when My glory was detracted from, and boldly stepped forth and exclaimed, 'Who is on the Lord's side? Let him come unto me.' I will therefore now stand by him."

It is quite true that this was not the only occasion on which Moses proved himself humble and gentle, for it was part of his character. Never among mortals, counting even the three Patriarchs, was there more meek a man than he. The angels alone excelled him in humility, but no human being; for the angels are so humble and meek, that when the assemble to praise God, each angel calls to the other and asks him to precede him, saying among themselves: "Be thou the first, thou are worthier than I."

God carried out His intention to uphold Moses' honor, for just as Aaron was with his wife and Miriam with her husband, a Divine call suddenly reached Amram's three children, one voice that simultaneously called, "Aaron!" "Moses!" and "Miriam!"-a miracle that God's voice alone can perform. The call went to Moses also, that the people might not think that Aaron and Miriam had been chosen to take Moses' place. He was ready to hearken to God's words, but not so his brother and his sister, who had been surprised in the state of uncleanness, and who therefore, upon hearing God's call, cried, "Water, water," that they might purify themselves before appearing before God. They then left their tents and followed the voice until God appeared in a pillar of cloud, a distinction that was conferred also upon Samuel. The pillar of cloud did not, however, appear in the Tabernacle, where it always rested whenever God revealed Himself to Moses, and this was due to the following reasons. First of all, God did not want to create the impression of having removed Moses from his dignity, and of giving it to his brother and sister, hence He did not appear to them in the holy place. At the same time, moreover, Aaron was spared the disgrace of being reproached by God in his brother's presence, for Moses did not follow his brother and sister, but awaited God's word in the sanctuary. But there was still another reason why God did not want Moses to be present during His conference with Aaron and Miriam-"Never praise a man to his face." As God wanted to praise Moses before Aaron and Miriam, He preferred to do so in his absence.

Hardly had God addressed Aaron and Miriam, when they began to interrupt Him, whereupon He said to them: "Pray, contain yourselves until I have spoken." In these words He taught people the rule of politeness, never to interrupt. He then said: "Since the creation of the world hath the word of God ever appeared to any prophet otherwise than in a dream? Not so with Moses, to whom I have shown what is above and what is below; what it before and what it behind; what was and what will be. To him have I revealed all that is in the water and all that is upon the dry land; to him did I confide the sanctuary and set him above the angels. I Myself ordered him to abstain from conjugal life, and the word he received was revealed to him clearly and not in dark speeches, he saw the Divine presence from behind when It passed by him. Wherefore then were ye not afraid to speak against a man like Moses, who is, moreover, My servant? Your censure is directed to Me, rather than to him, for 'the receiver is no better than the thief,' and if Moses is not worthy of his calling, I, his Master, deserve censure."

MIRIAM'S PUNISHMENT

God now gently rebuked Aaron and Miriam for their transgression, and did not give vent to His wrath until He had shown them their sin. This was an example to man never to show anger to his neighbor before giving his reason for his anger. The effects of God's wrath were shown as soon as He had departed from them, for while He was with them, His mercy exceeded His anger, and nothing happened to them, but when He was not long with them, punishment set in. Both Aaron and Miriam became leprous, for this is the punishment ordained for those who speak ill of their neighbors. Aaron's leprosy, however, lasted for a moment only, for his sin had not been as great as that of his sister, who started the talk against Moses. His disease vanished as soon as he looked upon his leprosy. Not so with Miriam. Aaron in vain tried to direct his eyes upon her leprosy and in this way to heal her, for in her case the effect was the reverse; as soon as he looked upon her the leprosy increased, and nothing remained but to call for Moses' assistance, who was ready to give it before being called upon. Aaron thereupon turned to his brother with the following words: "Think not that the leprosy is on Miriam's body only, it is as if it were on the body of our father Amram, of whose flesh and blood she is." Aaron did not, however, try to extenuate their sin, saying to Moses: "Have we, Miriam and I, ever done harm to a human being?" Moses: "No." Aaron: "If we have done evil to no strange people, how then canst thou believe that we wished to harm thee? For a moment only did we forget ourselves and acted in an unnatural way toward our brother. Shall we therefore lose our sister? If Miriam's leprosy doth not now vanish, she must pass all her life as a leper, for only a priest who is not a relative by blood of the leper may under certain conditions declare her clean, but all the priests, my sons and I, are her relatives by blood. The life of a leper is as of one dead, for as a corpse makes unclean all that comes in contact with it, so too the leper. Alas!" so Aaron closed his intercession, "Shall our sister, who was with us in Egypt, who with us intoned the song at the Red Sea, who took upon herself the instruction of the women while we instructed the men, shall she now, while we are about to leave the desert and enter the promised land, sit shut out from the camp?"

These words of Aaron, however, were quite superfluous, for Moses had determined, as soon as his sister became diseased, to intercede for her with God, saying to himself: "It is not right that my sister should suffer and I dwell in contentment." He now drew a circle about himself, stood up, and said a short prayer to God, which he closed with the words: "I will not go from this spot until Thou shalt have healed my sister. But if Thou do not heal her, I myself shall do so, for Thou hast already revealed to me, how leprosy arises and how it disappears." This prayer was fervent, spoken with his whole heart and soul, though very brief. Had he spoken long, some would have said: "His sister is suffering terribly and he, without heeding her, spends his time in prayer." Others again would have said: "He prayeth long for his sister, but for us he prayeth briefly." God said to Moses: "Why dost thou shout so?" Moses: "I know what suffering my sister is enduring. I remember the chain which my hand was chained, for I myself once suffered from this disease." God: "If a king, or if her father had but spit in her face, should she not be ashamed seven days? I, the King of kings, have spit in her face, and she should be ashamed at least twice seven days. For thy sake shall seven days be pardoned her, but the other seven days let her be shut out from the camp." For want of priest who, according to the tenets of the law, must declare a leper clean after the healing, God Himself assumed this part, declaring Miriam unclean for a week, and clean after the passing of that period.

Although leprosy came to Miriam as a punishment for her sin, still this occasion served to show how eminent a personage she was. For the people were breaking camp and starting on the march when, after having saddled their beasts of burden for the march, upon turning to see the pillar of cloud moving before them, they missed the sight of it. They looked again to see if Moses and Aaron were in the line of procession, but they were missing, nor was there anywhere to be seen a trace of the well that accompanied them on their marches. Hence they were obliged to return again to camp, where they remained until Miriam was healed. The clouds and the well, the sanctuary and the sixty myriads of the people, all had to wait a week in this spot until Miriam recovered. Then the pillar of cloud moved on once more and the people knew that they had not been permitted to proceed on their march only because of this pious prophetess. This was a reward for the kind deed Miriam had done when the child Moses was thrown into the water. Then Miriam for some time walked up and down along the shore to wait the child's fate, and for this reason did the people wait for her, nor could they move on until she had recovered.

THE SENDING OF THE SPIES

The punishment that God brought upon Miriam was meant as a lesson of the severity with which God punishes slander. For Miriam spoke no evil of Moses in the presence of any one except her brother Aaron. She had moreover no evil motive, but a kindly intention, wishing only to induce Moses to resume his conjugal life. She did not even dare to rebuke Moses to his face, and still, even in spite of her great piety, Miriam was not spared this heavy punishment. Her experience, nevertheless, did not awe the wicked man who, shortly after this incident, made an evil report of the promised land, and by their wicked tongues stirred up the whole people in rebellion against God, so that they desired rather to return to Egypt than to enter Palestine. The punishment that God inflicted upon the spies as well as upon the people they had seduced was well deserved, for had they not been warned of slander by Miriam's example, there might still have been some excuse. In that case they might have been ignorant of the gravity of the sin of slander, but now they had no excuse to offer.

When Israel approached the boundaries of Palestine, they appeared before Moses, saying: "We will send men before us, and they shall search out the land, and bring us word again by what way we must go up, and into what cities we shall come." This desire caused God to exclaim: "What! When you went through a land of deserts and of pits, you had no desire for scouts, but now that you are about to enter a land full of good things, now you wish to send out scouts. Not only was the desire in itself unseemly, but also the way in which they presented their request to Moses; for instead of approaching as they had been accustomed, letting the older men be the spokesmen of the younger they appeared on this occasion without guidance or order, the young crowding out the old, and these pushing away their leaders. Their bad conscience after making this request-for they knew that their true motive was lack of faith in God-caused them to invent all sorts of pretexts for their plans. They said to Moses: "So long as we are in the wilderness, the clouds act as scouts for us, for they move before us and show us the way, but as these will not proceed with us into the promised land, we want men to search out the land for us." Another plea that they urged for their desire was this. They said: "The Canaanites fear an attack from us and therefore hid their treasures. This is the reason why we want to sent spies there in time, to discover for us where they are hiding their treasures." They sought in other ways to give Moses the impression that their one wish was exactly to carry out the law. They said: "Hast not thou taught us that an idol to which homage is no longer paid may be used, but otherwise it must be destroyed? If we now enter Palestine and find idols, we shall not know which of them were adored by the Canaanites and must be destroyed, and which of them were no longer adored, so that we might use them." Finally they said the following to Moses: "Thou, our teacher, hast taught us that God 'would little by little drive the Canaanites before us.' If this be so, we must send out spies to find out which cities we must attack first." Moses allowed himself to be influenced by their talk, and he also liked the idea of sending out spies, but not wishing to act arbitrarily he submitted to God the desire of the people. God answered: "It is not the first time that they disbelieve My promises. Even in Egypt they ridiculed Me, it is now become a habit with them, and I know what their motive in sending spies is. If thou wishest to send spies do so, but do not pretend that I have ordered thee."

Moses hereupon chose one man from every tribe with the exception of Levi, and sent these men to spy out the land. These twelve men were the most distinguished and most pious of their respective tribes, so that even God gave His assent to the choice of every man among them. But hardly had these men been appointed to their office when they made the wicked resolve to bring up an evil report of the land, and dissuade the people from moving to Palestine. Their motive was a purely personal one, for they thought to themselves that they would retain their offices at the head of the tribes so long as they remained in the wilderness, but would be deprived of them when they entered Palestine.

SIGNIFICANT NAMES

Significant of the wickedness of these men are their names, all of which point to their godless action. The representative of the tribe of Reuben was called Shammua, the son of Zaccur, because he did not obey God, which was counted against him just as if he had pursued sorcery. Shaphat, the son of Hori, was Simeon's representative. His name signifies, "He did not conquer his evil inclination, and hence went out empty-handed, without having received a possession in the land of Israel." The tribe of Issachar was represented by Igal, the son of Joseph. He bore this name because he soiled the reputation of the Holy Land, and therefore died before his time. Benjamin's representative was Palti, the son of Raphu, so called because "he spat out the good qualities that had previously been his, and therefore wasted away." The name of Gaddiel, the son of Sodi, Zebulun's representative, signifies, "He spoke infamous things against God in executing the secret plan of the spies." Manasseh's representative, Gaddi, the son of Susi, was so called because he blasphemed God and aroused His wrath; for it was he who said of the land, "it eateth up its inhabitants." But the worst one among them was Ammiel, the son of Gemalli, the representative of Dan, for it was he who said, "The land is so strong that not even God could go up against it," hence his name, which means, "He cast a shadow upon God's strength," and he was punished according to his wicked words, for he did not enter the promised land. Asher's representative was Sethur, the son of Michael, who had resolved to act against God and instead of saying, "Who is like unto God?" he said, "Who is God?" Naphtali's representative was named Nahbi, the son of Vophsi, for he suppressed the truth, and faith found no room in his mouth, for he brought forth lies against God. The last of these spies, Gad's representative, bore the name Geuel, the son of Machi, for he was humbled because he urged untruths against God.

As the ten sinners were name in accordance with their actions, so too did the names of the two pious spies among them correspond to their pious actions. Judah's representative was name Caleb, the son of Jephunneh, because "he spoke what he felt in his heart and turned aside from the advice of the rest of the spies." The pious representative of Ephraim was Hoshea, the son of Nun, a fitting name for him, for he was full of understanding and was not caught like a fish by the spies. Moses who perceived, even when he sent out the spies, the evil intentions they harbored, changed Hoshea's name to Joshua, saying: "May God stand by thee, that thou mayest not follow the counsel of the spies."

This change of name that was brought about by the prefixing of the letter Yod at last silenced the lamentations of this letter. For ever since God had changed Sarai's name to Sarah, the letter Yod used to fit about the celestial Throne and lament: "Is it perchance because I am the smallest among the letters that Thou has taken me away from the name of the pious Sarah?" God quieted this letter, saying: "Formerly thou wert in a woman's name, and, moreover, at the end. I will not affix thee to a man's name, and, moreover, at the beginning." This promise was redeemed when Hoshea's name was changed to Joshua.

When the spies set out on their way, they received instructions from Moses how to conduct themselves, and what in particular, they were to note. He ordered them not to walk on the highways, but to go along private pathways, for although the Shekinah would follow them, they were still to incur no needless danger. If they entered a city, however, they were not to slink like thieves in alleyways, but to show themselves in public and answer those who asked what they wanted by saying: "We came only to buy some pomegranates and grapes." They were emphatically to deny that they had any intention of destroying the idols or of felling the sacred trees. Moses furthermore said: "Look about carefully what manner of land it is, for some lands produce strong people and some weak, some lands produce many people and some few. If you find the inhabitants dwelling in open places, then know that they are mighty warriors, and depending upon their strength have no fear of hostile attack. If, however, they live in a fortified place, they are weaklings, and in their fear of strangers seek shelter within their walls. Examine also the nature of the soil. If it be hard, know then that it it fat; but if it be soft, it is lean." Finally he bade them inquire whether Job was still alive, for if he was dead, then they assuredly needed not to fear the Canaanites, as there was not a single pious man among them whose merits might be able to shield them. And truly when the spies reached Palestine, Job died, and they found the inhabitants of the land at his grave, partaking of the funeral feast.

THE SPIES IN PALESTINE

On the twenty-seventh day of Siwan Moses sent out the spies from Kadesh-Barnea in the wilderness of Paran, and following his directions they went first to the south of Palestine, the poorest part of the Holy Land. Moses did like the merchants, who first show the poorer wares, and then the better kind; so Moses wished the spies to see better parts of the land the farther they advanced into it. When they reached Hebron, they could judge what a blessed land this was that had been promised them, for although Hebron was the poorest tract in all Palestine, it was still much better than Zoan, the most excellent part of Egypt. When, therefore, the sons of Ham built cities in several lands, it was Hebron that they erected first, owing to its excellence, and not Zoan, which they built in Egypt fully seven years later.

Their progress through the land was on the whole easy, for God had wished it so, that as soon as the spies entered a city, the plague struck it, and the inhabitants, busied with the burial of their dead, had neither time nor inclination to concern themselves with the strangers. Although they met with no evil on the part of the inhabitants, still the sight of the three giants, Ahiman, Sheshai, and Talmai inspired them with terror. These were so immensely tall that the sun reached only to their ankles, and they received their names in accordance with their size and strength. The strongest among them was Ahiman, beholding whom one fancied oneself standing at the foot of a mountain that was about to fall, and exclaimed involuntarily, "What is this that is coming upon me?" Hence the name Ahiman. Strong as marble was the second brother, wherefore he was called Sheshai, "marble." The mighty strides of the third brother threw up plots from the ground when he walked, hence he was called Talmi, "plots." Not only the sons of Anak were of such strength and size, but his daughters also, whom the spies chanced to see. For when these reached the city inhabited by Anak, that was called Kiriath-Arba, "City of Four," because the giant Anak and his three sons dwelt there, they were struck with such terror by them that they sought a hiding place. But what they had believed to be a cave was only the rind of a huge pomegranate that the giant's daughter had thrown away, as they later, to their horror, discovered. For this girl, after having eaten the fruit, remembered that she must not anger her father by letting the rind lie there, so she picked it up with the twelve men in it as one picks up an egg shell, and threw it into the garden, never noticing that she had thrown with it twelve men, each measuring sixty cubits in height. When they left their hiding place, they said to one another: "Behold the strength of these women and judge by their standard the men!"

They soon had an opportunity of testing the strength of the men, for as soon as the three giants heard of the presence of the Israelite men, they pursued them, but the Israelites found out with what manner of men they were dealing even before the giants had caught up with them. One of the giants shouted, and the spies fell down as men dead, so that it took a long time for the Canaanites to restore them to life by the aid of friction and fresh air. The Canaanites hereupon said to them: "Why do you come here? Is not the whole world your God's, and did not He parcel it out according to His wish? Came ye here with the purpose of felling the sacred trees?" The spied declared their innocence, whereupon the Canaanites permitted them to go their ways unmolested. As a reward for this kind deed, the nation to which these giants belonged has been preserved even to this day.

They would certainly not have escaped from the hands of the giants, had not Moses given them two weapons against them, his staff and the secret of the Divine Name. These two brought them salvation whenever they felt they were in danger from the giants. For these were none other than the seed of the angels fallen in the antediluvian era. Sprung from their union with the daughters of men, and being half angels, half men, these giants were only half mortal. They lived very long, and then half their body withered away. Threatened by an eternal continuance of this condition, half life, and half death, they preferred either to plunge into the sea, or by magic herb which they knew to put an end to their existence. They were furthermore of such enormous size that the spies, listening one day while the giants discussed them, heard them say, pointing to the Israelites: "There are grasshoppers by the trees that have the semblance of men," for "so they were in their sight."

The spies, with the exception of Joshua and Caleb, had resolved from the start to warn the people against Palestine, and so great was their influence that Caleb feared he would yield to it. He therefore hastened to Hebron where the three Patriarchs lie, and, standing at their graves, said: "Joshua is proof against the pernicious influence of the spies, for Moses had prayed to God for him. Send up prayers now, my fathers, for me, that God in His mercy may keep me far from the counsel of the spies."

There had always been a clash between Caleb and his comrades during their crossing through Palestine. For whereas he insisted upon taking along the fruits of the land to show their excellence to the people, they strongly opposed this suggestion, wishing as they did to keep the people from gaining an impression of the excellence of the land. Hence they yielded only when Caleb drew his sword, saying: "If you will not take of the fruits, either I shall slay you, or you will slay me." They hereupon cut down a vine, which was so heavy that eight of them had to carry it, putting upon each the burden of one hundred and twenty seah. The ninth spy carried a pomegranate, and the tenth a fig, which they brought from a place that had once belonged to Eshcol, one of Abraham's friends, but Joshua and Caleb carried nothing at all, because it was not consistent with their dignity to carry a burden. This vine was of such gigantic size that the wine pressed from its grapes sufficed for all the sacrificial libations of Israel during the forty years' march.

After the lapse of forty days they returned to Moses and the people, after having crossed through Palestine from end to end. By natural means it would not, of course, have been possible to traverse all the land in so short a time, by God made it possible by "bidding the soil to leap for them," and they covered a great distance in a short time. God knew that Israel would have to wander in the wilderness forty years, a year for every day the spies had spent in Palestine, hence He hastened their progress through the land, that Israel might not have to stay too long in the wilderness.

THE SLANDEROUS REPORT

When Moses heard that the spies had returned from their enterprise, he went to his great house of study, where all Israel too assembled, for it was a square of twelve miles, affording room to all. There too the spies betook themselves and were requested to give their report. Pursuing the tactics of slanderers, they began by extolling the land, so that they might not by too unfavorable a report arouse the suspicion of the community. They said: "We came unto the land whither thou sentest us, and surely it floweth with milk and honey." This was not an exaggeration, for honey flowed from the trees under which the goats grazed, out of whose udders poured mile, so that both mile and honey moistened the ground. But they used these words only as an introduction, and the passed on to their actual report, which they had elaborated during those forty days, and by means of which they hoped to be able to induce the people to desist from their plan of entering Palestine. "Nevertheless," they continued, "the people be strong that dwell in the land, and the cities are walled, and very great: and moreover we saw children of Anak there." Concerning the latter they spoke an untruth with the intention of inspiring Israel with fear, for the sons of Anak dwelt in Hebron, whither Caleb alone had gone to pray at the graves of the Patriarchs, at the same time as the Shekinah went there to announce to the Patriarch that their children were now on the way to take possession of the land which had been promised to them of yore. To intensify to the uttermost their fear of the inhabitants of Palestine, they furthermore said: "The Amalekites dwell in the land of the South." They threatened Israel with Amalek as one threatens a child with a strap that had once been employed to chastise him, for they had had bitter experiences with Amalek. The statement concerning Amalek was founded on fact, for although southern Palestine had not originally been their home, still they had recently settled there in obedience to the last wish of their forefather Esau, who had bidden them cut off Israel from their entrance into the promised land. "If, however," continued the spies in their report, "you are planning to enter the land from the mountain region in order to evade Amalek, let us inform you that the Hittites, and the Jebussites, and the Amorites dwell in the mountains; and if you plan to go there by sea, let us inform you that the Canaanites dwell by the sea, and along the Jordan."

As soon as the spies had completed their report, Joshua arose to contradict them, but they gave him no chance to speak, calling out to him: "By what right dost thou, foolish man, presume to speak? Thou hast neither sons nor daughters, so what dost thou care if we perish in our attempt to conquer the land? We, on the other hand, have to look out for our children and wives." Joshua, therefore, very much against his will, had to be silent. Caleb now considered in what way he could manage to get a hearing without being shouted down as Joshua had been.

Caleb had given his comrades an entirely false impression concerning his sentiments, for when these formed the plan to try to make Israel desist from entering Palestine, they drew him into their council, and he pretended to agree with them, whereas he even then resolved to intercede for Palestine. Hence, when Caleb arose, the spies were silent, supposing he would corroborate their statements, a supposition which his introductory words tended to strengthen. He began: "Be silent, I will reveal the truth. This is not all for which we have to thank the son of Amram." But to the amazement of the spies, his next words praised, not blamed, Moses. He said: "Moses-it is he who drew us up out of Egypt, who clove the sea for us, who gave us manna as food." In this way he continued his eulogy on Moses, closing with the words: "We should have to obey him even if he bade us ascend to heaven upon ladders!" These words of Caleb were heard by all the people, for his words were so mighty that they could be heard twelve miles off. It was this same powerful voice that had saved the life of the spies. For when the Canaanites first took note of them and suspected them of being spies, the three giants, Ahiman, Sheshai, and Talmai pursued them and caught up with them in the plain of Judea. When Caleb, hidden behind a fence, saw that the giants were at their heels, he uttered such a shout that the giants fell down in a swoon because of the frightful din. When they had recovered, the giants declared that they had pursued the Israelites not because of the fruits, but because they had suspected them of the wish to burn their cities.

Caleb's mighty voice did not, however, in the least impress the people or the spies, for the latter, far from retracting their previous statements, went so far as to say: "We be not able to go up against the people; for they are stronger than we, they are so strong that even God can not get at them. The land through which we had gone to search it is a land that eateth up the inhabitants thereof through disease; and all the people that we saw in it are men of wicked traits. And here we saw men upon sight of whom we almost swooned in fright, the giants, the sons of Anak, which come of giants: and we were in our own sight as grasshoppers, and so we were in their sight." At these last words, God said: "I have not objection to your saying, 'We were in our own sight as grasshoppers,' but I take it amiss if you say, 'And so we were in their sight,' for how can you tell how I made you appear in their sight? How do you know if you did not appear to them to be angels?"

THE NIGHT OF TEARS

The words of the spies were heard by willing ears. The people believed them implicitly, and when called to task by Moses, replied: "O our teacher Moses, if there had been only two spies or three, we should have had to give credence to their words, for the law tells us to consider the testimony of even two as sufficient, whereas in this case there are fully ten! Our brethren have made us faint of heart. Because the Lord hated us, He hath brought us forth out of the land of Egypt, to deliver us into the hand of the Amorites, to destroy us." By these words the Israelites revealed that they hated God, and for this reason did they believe that they were hated by Him, for "whatever a man wisheth his neighbor, doth he believe that his neighbor wisheth him." They even tried to convince Moses that God hated them. They said: "If an earthly king has two sons and two fields, on watered by a river, and the other dependent upon rains, will he not five the one that is watered by the river to his favorite son, and give the other, less excellent field to his other son? God led us out of Egypt, a land that is not dependent upon rain, only to give us the land of Canaan, which produces abundantly only if the rains fall."

Not only did the spies in the presence of Moses and Aaron voice their opinion that is was not advisable to attempt conquering Palestine, but they employed every means of inciting the people into rebellion against Moses and God. On the following evening every one of them betook himself to his house, donned his mourning cloths, and began to weep bitterly and to lament. Their housemates quickly ran toward them and in astonishment asked their reason for these tears and lamentations. Without interrupting their wailings, they answered" "Woe is me for ye, my sons, and woe is me for ye, my daughters and daughters-in-law, that are doomed to be dishonored by the uncircumcised and to be given as a prey to their lusts. These men that we have beheld are not like unto mortals. Strong and mighty as angels are they; one of them might well slay a thousand of us. How dare we look into the iron faces of men so powerful that a nail of theirs is sufficient to stop up a spring of water!" At these words all the household, sons, daughters, and daughters-in-law, burst into tears and loud lamentations. Their neighbors came running to them and joined in the wails and sobs until they spread throughout all the camp, and all the sixty myriads of people were weeping. When the sound of their weeping reached heaven, God said: "Ye weep to-day without a cause, I shall see to it that in the future ye shall have a cause to weep on this day." It was then that God decreed to destroy the Temple on the ninth day of Ab, the day on which Israel in the wilderness wept without cause, so that this day became forever a day of tears.

The people were not, however, content with tears, they resolved to set up as leaders in place of Moses and Aaron, Dathan and Abiram, and under their guidance to return to Egypt. But worse than this, not only did they renounce their leader, but also their God, for they denied Him and wished to set up and idol for their God. Not only the wicked ones among them such as the mixed multitude demurred against Moses and Aaron, but those also who had heretofore been pious, saying: "Would to God that we had died in the land of Egypt! Or would to God we had died in this wilderness!" When Joshua and Caleb heard these speeches of the people teeming with blasphemy, they rent their garments and tried to restrain the people from their sinful enterprise, exhorting them particularly to have fear of the Canaanites, because the time was at hand when God had promised Abraham to give the land of Canaan to his descendants, and because there were no pious men among the inhabitants of the land for whose sake God would have been willing to leave it longer in their possession. They also assured the people that God had hurled from heaven the guardian angel of the inhabitants of Palestine, so that they were now impotent. The people, however, replied: "We do not believe you; the other spies have our weal and woe more at heart than you." Nor were the admonitions of Moses of more avail, even though he brought them a direct message from God to have no fear of the Canaanites. In vain did he say to them, "He who wrought all those miracles for you in Egypt and during your stay in the wilderness will work miracles for you as well when you will enter the promised land. Truly the past ought to inspire you with trust in the future." The only answer the people had to this was, "Had we heard this report of the land from strangers, we should not have given it credit, but we have heard it from men whose sons are our sons, and whose daughters are our daughters." In their bitterness against their leaders they wanted to lay hands upon Moses and Aaron, whereupon God sent His cloud of glory as a protection to them, under which they sought refuge. But far from being brought to a realization of their wicked enterprise by this Divine apparition, they cast stones at the cloud, hoping in this way to kill Moses and Aaron. This outrage on their part completely wore out God's patience, and He determined upon the destruction of the spies, and a severe punishment of the people misled by them.

INGRATITUDE PUNISHED

God now appeared to Moses, bidding him convey the following words to the people: "You kindle My anger on account of the very benefits I conferred upon you. When I clove the sea for you that you might pass through, while the Egyptians stuck in the loam at its bottom, you said to one another, 'In Egypt we trod loam, and He led us out of Egypt, only that we might again tread it.' I gave you manna as food, which made you strong and fat, but you, perceiving of it, said: 'How comes it to pass that twenty days a human being dies if after four or five days he does not excrete food he had taken. Surely we are doomed to die.' When the spies came to Palestine, I arranged it so that as soon as they entered the city its king or governor dies, in order that the inhabitants, occupied with the burial of their ruler, might not take account of the spies' presence and kill them. Instead of being thankful for this, the spies returned and reported, 'The land through which we have gone to search it, is a land that eateth up the inhabitants thereof.' To you I gave the Torah; for your sake I said to the Angel of Death, 'Continue to hold sway over the rest of the world, but not over this nation that I have chosen as My people.' Truly I had hopes that after all this you would sin no more, and like Myself and the angels would live eternally, without ever tasting death. You, however, in spite of the great opportunity that I offered you, conducted yourselves like Adam. Upon him also did I lay a commandment, promising him life eternal on condition he observed it, but he brought ruin upon himself by trespassing My commandment and eating of the tree. To him I said, 'Dust thou art, and unto dust shalt thou return.' Similar was My experience with you. I said, 'You are angels,' but you conducted yourselves like Adam in your sins, and hence like Adam you must die. I had thought and hoped you would follow example of the Patriarchs, but you act like the inhabitants of Sodom, who in punishment for their sins were consumed by fire." "If," continued God, turning to Moses, "they suppose that I have need of swords or spears to destroy them, they are mistaken. As through the word I created the world, so can I destroy the world by it, which would be a proper punishment for them. As through their words and their talk they angered Me, so shall the word kill them, and thou shalt be their heir, for 'I will make of thee a greater nation and mightier than they.'" Moses said: "If the chair with three legs could not withstand the moment of Thy wrath, how then shall a chair that have but one leg endure? Thou are about to destroy the seed of the three Patriarchs; how then may I hope that my seed is to fare better? This is not the only reason for which Thou shouldst preserve Israel, as there are other considerations why Thou shouldst do so. Were Thou to destroy Israel, the Edomites, Moabites, and all the inhabitants of Canaan would say that Thou hadst done this only because Thou wert not able to maintain Thy people, and therefore Thou didst destroy them. These will furthermore declare that the gods of Canaan are mightier than those of Egypt, that Thou hadst indeed triumphed over the river gods of Egypt, but that Thou wert not the peer of the rain gods of Canaan. Worse even than this, the nations of the world will accuse Thee of continuous cruelty, saying, 'He destroyed the generation of the flood through water; He rased to the ground the builders of the tower, as well as the inhabitants of Sodom; and no better then theirs was the fate of the Egyptians, whom He drowned in the sea. Now He hath also ruined Israel whom He had called, 'My firstborn son,' like Lilith who, when she can find no strange children, slays her own. So did He slay His own son." Moses furthermore said: "Every pious man makes a point of cultivating a special virtue. Do Thou also in this instance bring Thy special virtue to bear." God: "And what is My special virtue?" Moses: "Long-suffering, love, and mercy, for Thou art wont to be long-suffering with them that kindle Thy wrath, and to have mercy for them. In Thy very mercy is Thy strength best shown. Mete out to Thy children, then, justice in small measure only, but mercy in great measure."

Moses well knew that mercy was God's chief virtue. He remembered that he had asked God, when he interceded for Israel after their sin of the Golden Calf, "Pray tell me by what attribute of Thine Thou rulest the world." God answered: "I rule the world with loving-kindness, mercy, and long-suffering." "Can it be," said Moses, "that Thy long-suffering lets sinners off with impunity?" To this question Moses had received no answer, hence he felt he might now say to God: "Act now as Thou didst then assent. Justice, that demands the destruction of Israel, is on one side of the scales, but it is exactly balance by my prayer on the other side. Let us now see how the scales will balance." God replied: "As truly as thou livest, Moses, thy prayer shall dip the scales to the side of mercy. For thy sake must I cancel My decision to annihilate the children of Israel, so that the Egyptians will exclaim, 'Happy the servant to whose wish his master defers.' I shall, however, collect My debt, for although I shall not annihilate Israel all at once, they shall make partial annual payments during the following forty years. Say to them, 'Your carcasses shall fall in this wilderness; and all that were numbered of you, according to your whole number, from twenty years old and upward, which have murmured against Me. And your children shall be wanderers in the wilderness forty years, and shall bear you whoredoms, until your carcasses be consumed in the wilderness.'"

This punishment was not, however, as severe as it might appear, for none among them died below the ages of sixty, whereas those who had at the time of the exodus from Egypt been either below twenty or above sixty were entirely exempt from this punishment. Besides only such were smitten as had followed the counsel of the spies, whereas the others, and the Levites and the women were exempt. Death, moreover, visited the transgressors in such fashion that they were aware it was meant as punishment for their sins. Throughout all the year not one among them died. On the eighth day of the month of Ab, Moses would have a herald proclaim throughout the camp, "Let each prepare his grave." They dug their graves, and spent there the following night, the same night on which, following the counsel of the spies, they had revolted against God and Moses. In the morning a herald would once more appear and cry: "Let the living separate themselves from the dead." Those that were still alive arose, but about fifteen thousand of them remained dead in their graves. After forty years, however, when the herald repeated his customary call the ninth day of Ab, all arose, and there was not a single dead man among them. At first they thought they had made a miscalculation in their observation of the moon, that is was not the ninth day of Ab at all, and that this was the reason why their lives had been spared. Hence they repeated their preparations for death until the fifteenth day of Ab. Then the sight of the full moon convinced them that the ninth day of Ab had gone by, and that their punishment had been done away with. In commemoration of the relief from this punishment, they appointed the fifteenth day of Ab to be a holy day.

THE YEARS OF DISFAVOR

Although God had now cancelled His resolution to annihilate Israel, He was not yet quite reconciled with them, and they were out of favor during the following years of their march through the desert, as was made evident by several circumstances. During these years of disfavor the north wind did not blow, with the result that the boys who were born in the desert could not be circumcised, as the absence of the wind produced and excessively high temperature, a condition that made it very dangerous for the young boys to have this operation performed upon them. As the law, however, prohibits the offering of the paschal lamb unless the boys have been circumcised, Israel could not properly observe the feast of Passover after the incident of the spies. Moses also felt the effects of the disfavor, for during this time he received from God none but the absolutely essential directions, and no other revelations. This was because Moses, like all other prophets, received this distinction only for the sake of Israel, and when Israel was in disgrace, God did not communicate with him affectionately. Indeed Moses' fate, to die in the desert without entering the promised land, had been decreed simultaneously with the fate of the generation led by him out of Egypt.

But the most terrible punishment of all fell upon the spies who, with their wicked tongues, had brought about the whole disaster. God repaid them measure for measure. Their tongues stretched to so great a length that they touched the navel; and worms crawled out of their tongues, and pierced the navel; in this horrible fashion these men died. Joshua and Caleb, however, who had remained true to God and had not followed the wicked counsel of their colleagues, were not only exempted from death, but were furthermore rewarded by God, by receiving in the Holy Land the property that had been allotted to the other spies. Caleb was forty years of age at the time when he was sent out as a spy. He had married early, and at the age of ten had begot a son, still at the age of eighty-five he was sturdy enough to enjoy his possession in the Holy Land.

God's mercy is also extended to sinners, hence He bade Moses say to the people: "The Amalekites and the Canaanites are now dwelling in the valley, to-morrow turn you, and get you into the wilderness by the way of the Red Sea." God did this because He had firmly resolved, in the event of a war between Israel and the inhabitants of Palestine, not to aid the former. Knowing that in this cast their annihilation was sure, He commanded them to make no attempt to enter the land by force. "It had been My intention," said God, "to exalt you, but now if you were to attempt to make war upon the inhabitants of Palestine, you would suffer humiliation." The people did not, however, hearken to the words of God that Moses communicated to them, and all at once formed in battle array in order to advance against the Amorites. They thought that after they had confessed their sin of having been misled by the spies, God would stand by them in their battles, so they said to Moses: "Surely these few drops have not filled the bucket." Their transgression against God seemed to them only a peccadillo that had long since been forgiven. They were, however, mistaken. Like bees the enemies swarmed down upon them, and whereas these had in former times fallen dead of fright upon hearing the names of the Israelites, now a blow from them sufficed to kill the Israelites. Their attempt to wage war without the Holy Ark in their midst proved a miserable failure. Many of them, and Zelophehad among these, met their death, and as many others returned to camp covered with wounds. The wailing and weeping of the people was of no avail, God persisted in His resolve, and they brought upon themselves grave punishment for this new proof of disobedience, for God said to Moses: "If I were to deal with them now in accordance with strict justice, they should never enter the land. After a while, however, I shall let them 'possess the land, which I sware unto their fathers to give unto them.'"

In order to comfort and encourage Israel in their dejection, Moses received directions to announce the law of sacrifices, and other precepts laid down for the life in the Holy Land, that the people might see that God did not mean to be angry with them forever. When Moses announced the laws to them, a dispute arose between the Israelites and the proselytes, because the former declared that they alone and not the others were to make offerings to God in His sanctuary. God hereupon called Moses, and said to him: "Why do these always quarrel one with another?" Moses replied: "Thou knowest why." God: "Have I not said to thee, 'One law and one ordinance shall be for you and for the stranger that sojourneth with you?'"

Although the forty years' march through the desert was a punishment for the sin of Israel, still it had one advantage. At the time when Israel departed from Egypt, Palestine was in poor condition; the trees planted in the time of Noah were old and withered. Hence God said: "What! Shall I permit Israel to enter an uninhabitable land? I shall bid them wander in the desert for forty years, that the Canaanites may in the meantime fell the old trees and plant new ones, so that Israel, upon entering the land, may find it abounding in plenty." So did it come to pass, for when Israel conquered Palestine, they found the land not only newly cultivated, but also filled to overflowing with treasures. The inhabitants of this land were such misers that they would not indulge in a drop of oil for their gruel; if an egg broke, they did not use it, but sold it for cash. The hoardings of these miserly Canaanites God later gave to Israel to enjoy and to use.

Chapter 5

THE REBELLION OF KORAH

The Canaanites were not the only ones who did not enjoy their wealth and money, for a similar fate was decreed for Korah. He had been the treasurer of Pharaoh, and possessed treasures so vast that he employed three hundred white mules to carry the keys of his treasures: but "let not the rich man boast of his riches," for Korah through his sin lost both life and property. Korah had obtained possession of his riches in the following way: When Joseph, during the lean years, through the sale of grain amassed great treasures, he erected three great buildings, one hundred cubits wide, one hundred cubits long, and one hundred cubits wide, one hundred high, filled them with money and delivered them to Pharaoh, being too honest to leave even five silver shekels of this money to his children. Korah discovered one of these three treasuries. On account of his wealth he became proud, and his pride brought about his fall. He believed Moses had slighted him by appointing his cousin Elizaphan as chief of the Levite division of Kohathites. He said: "My grandfather had four sons, Amram, Ishar, Hebron, and Uzziel. Amram, as the firstborn, had privileges of which his sons availed themselves, for Aaron is high priest and Moses is king; but have not I, the son of Izhar, the second son of Kohath, the rightful claim to be prince of the Kohathites? Moses, however, passed me by and appointed Elizaphan, whose father was Uzziel, the youngest son of my grandfather. Therefore will I now stir up rebellion against Moses, and overthrow all institutions founded by him." Korah was far too wise a man to believe that God would permit success to a rebellion against Moses, and stand by indifferently, but the very insight that enabled him to look into the future became his doom. He saw with his prophetic eye that Samuel, a man as great as both Aaron and Moses together, would be one of his descendants; and furthermore that twenty-four descendants of his, inspired by the Holy Spirit, would compose psalms and sing them in the Temple. This brilliant future of his descendants inspired him with great confidence in his undertaking, for he thought to himself that God would not permit the father of such pious men to perish. His eye did not, however, look sharply enough into the future, or else he would also have known that his sons would repent of the rebellion against Moses, and would for this reason be deemed worthy of becoming the fathers of prophets and Temple singers, whereas he was to perish in this rebellion.

The names of this unfortunate rebel corresponded to his deed and to his end. He was called Korah, "baldness," for through the death of his horde he caused a baldness in Israel. He was the son of Izhar, "the heat of the noon," because he caused the earth to be made to boil "like the heat of noon;" and furthermore he was designated as the son of Kohath, for Kohath signifies "bluntness," and through his sin he made "his children's teeth be set on edge." His description as the son of Levi, "conduct," points to his end, for he was conducted to hell.

Korah, however, was not the only one who strove to overthrow Moses. With him were, first of all, the Reubenites, Dathan and Abiram, who well deserve their names, for the one signifies, "transgressor of the Divine law," and the other, "the obdurate." There were, furthermore, two hundred fifty men, who by their rank and influence belonged to the most prominent people in Israel; among them even the princes of the tribes. In the union of the Reubenites with Korah was verified the proverb, "Woe to the wicked, woe to his neighbor." For Korah, one of the sons of Kohath, had his station to the south of the Tabernacle, and as the Reubenites were also encamped there, a friendship was struck up between them, so that they followed him in his undertaking against Moses.

The hatred Korah felt against Moses was still more kindled by his wife. When, after the consecration of the Levites, Korah returned home, his wife noticed that the hairs of his head and of his body had been shaved, and asked him who had done all this to him. He answered, "Moses," whereupon his wife remarked: "Moses hates thee and did this to disgrace thee." Korah, however, replied: "Moses shaved all the hair of his own sons also." But she said: "What did the disgrace of his own sons matter to him if he only felt he could disgrace thee? He was quite ready to make that sacrifice." As at home, so also did Korah fare with others, for, hairless as he was, no one at first recognized him, and when people at last discovered who was before them, they asked him in astonishment who had so disfigured him. In answer to their inquiries he said, "Moses did this, who besides took hold of my hands and feet to lift me, and after he had lifted me, said, 'Thou art clean.' But his brother Aaron he adorned like a bride, and bade him take his place in the Tabernacle." Embittered by what they considered as insult offered him by Moses, Korah and his people exclaimed: "Moses is king, his brother did he appoint as high priest, his nephews as heads of the priests, he allots to the priest the heave offering and many other tributes." Then he tried to make Moses appear ridiculous in the eyes of the people. Shortly before this Moses had read to the people the law of the fringes in the borders of their garments. Korah now had garments of purple made for the two hundred fifty men that followed him, all of whom were chief justices. Arrayed thus, Korah and his company appeared before Moses and asked him if they were required to attach fringes to the corners of these garments. Moses answered, "Yea." Korah then began this argument. "If," said he, "one fringe of purple suffices to fulfil this commandment, should not a whole garment of purple answered the requirements of the law, even if there be no special fringe of purple in the corners?" He continued to lay before Moses similar artful questions: "Must a Mezuzah be attached to the doorpost of the house filled with the sacred Books?" Moses answered, "Yea," Then Korah said: "The two hundred and seventy sections of the Torah are not sufficient, whereas the two sections attached to the door-post suffice!" Korah put still another question: "If upon a man's skin there show a bright spot, the size of half a bean, is he clean or is he unclean?" Moses: "Unclean." "And," continued Korah, "if the spot spread and cover all the skin of him, is he then clean or unclean?" Moses: "Clean." "Laws so irrational," said Korah, "cannot possibly trace their origin from God. The Torah that thou didst teach to Israel is not therefore God's work, but thy work, hence art thou no prophet and Aaron is no high priest!"

KORAH ABUSES MOSES AND THE TORAH

Then Korah betook himself to the people to incite them to rebellion against Moses, and particularly against the tributes to the priests imposes upon the people by him. That the people might now be in a position to form a proper conception of the oppressive burden to these tasks, Korah told them the following tale that he had invented: "There lived in my vicinity a widow with two daughters, who owned for their support a field whose yield was just sufficient for them to keep body and soul together. When this woman set out to plow her field, Moses appeared and said: 'Thou shalt not plow with an ox and an ass together.' When she began to sow, Moses appeared and said: 'Thou shalt not sow with divers seeds.' When the first fruits showed in the poor widow's field, Moses appeared and bade her bring it to the priests, for to them are due 'the first of all the fruit of the earth'; and when at length the time came for he to cut it down, Moses appeared and ordered her 'not wholly to reap the corners of the field, not to gather the gleanings of the harvest, but to leave them for the poor.' When she had done all that Moses had bidden her, and was about to thrash the grain, Moses appeared once more, and said: 'Give me the heave offerings, the first and the second tithes to the priest.' When at last the poor woman became aware of the fact that she could not now possibly maintain herself from the yield of the field after the deduction of all the tributes that Moses had imposed upon her, she sold the field and with the proceeds purchased ewes, in the hope that she might now undisturbed have the benefit of the wool as well as the younglings of the sheep. She was, however, mistaken. When the firstling of the sheep was born, Aaron appeared and demanded it, for the firstborn belongs to the priest. She had a similar experience with the wool. At shearing time Aaron reappeared and demanded 'the first of the fleece of the sheep,' which, according to Moses' law, was his. But not content with this, he reappeared later and demanded one sheep out of every ten as a tithe, to which again, according to the law, he had a claim. This, however, was too much for the long-suffering woman, and she slaughtered the sheep, supposing that she might now feel herself secure, in full possession of the meat. But wide of the mark! Aaron appeared, and, basing his claim on the Torah, demanded the shoulder, the two cheeks, and the maw. 'Alas!' exclaimed the woman, 'The slaughtering of the sheep did not deliver me out of thy hands! Let the meat then be consecrated to the sanctuary.' Aaron said, 'Everything devoted in Israel is mine. It shall then be all mine.' He departed, taking with him the meat of the sheep, and leaving behind him the widow and her daughters weeping bitterly. Such men," said Korah, concluding his tale, "are Moses and Aaron, who pass their cruel measures as Divine laws."

Pricked on by speeches such as these, Korah's horde appeared before Moses and Aaron, saying: "Heavier is the burden that ye lay upon us than was that of the Egyptians; and moreover as, since the incident of the spies, we are forced annually to offer as a tribute to death fifteen thousand men, it would have been better for us had we stayed in Egypt." They also reproached Moses and Aaron with an unjustified love of power, saying: "Upon Sinai all Israel heard the words of God, 'I am thy Lord.' Wherefore then lift ye up yourselves above the congregation of the Lord?" They knew no bounds in their attacks upon Moses, they accused him of leading an immoral life and even warned their wives to keep far from him. They did not, moreover, stop short at words, but tried to stone Moses, when at last he sought protection from God and called to Him for assistance. He said: "I do not care if they insult me or Aaron, but I insist that the insult of the Torah be avenged. 'If these men die the common death of all men,' I shall myself become a disbeliever and declare the Torah was not given by God."

MOSES PLEADS IN VAIN WITH KORAH

Moses took Korah's transgression much to heart, for he thought to himself that perhaps, after the many sins of Israel, he might not succeed in obtaining God's pardon for them. He did not therefore have this matter decided immediately, but admonished the people to wait until the following day, having a lingering hope that Korah's horde, given time for calm reflection, might themselves perceive their sin to which an excess of drink might have carried them away. Hence he said to them: "I may not now appear before the Lord, for although He partakes of neither food nor drink, still He will not judge such actions of ours as we have committed after feasting and revelling. But 'to-morrow the Lord will show who are His.' Know ye now that just as God has set definite bounds in nature between day and night, between light and darkness, so also has He separated Israel from the other nations, and so also has he separated Aaron from the rest of Israel. If you can obliterate the boundary between light and darkness, then only you remove the boundary of separation between Israel and the rest, but not otherwise. Other nations have many religions, many priests, and worship in many temples, but we have one God, one Torah, one law, one altar, and one high priest, whereas ye are two hundred fifty men, each of whom is imbued with the desire of becoming the high priest, as I too should like to be high priest, if such a thing were possible. But to prove Aaron's claim to his dignity, 'this do; take you censers, Korah, and all his company; and put fire therein, and put incense upon them before the Lord to-morrow.' The offering of incense is the most pleasant offering before the Lord, but for him who hath not been called this offering holds a deadly poison, for it consumed Nadab and Abihu. But I exhort ye not to burden your souls with a deadly sin, for none but the man God will choose as high priest out of the number of you will remain alive, all others will pay with their lives at the offering of incense." These last words of Moses, however, far from restraining them, only strengthened Korah in his resolve to accomplish his undertaking, for he felt sure that God would choose him, and none other. He had a prophetic presentiment that he was destined to be the forefather of prophets and Temple singers, and for this reason thought he was specially favored by God.

When Moses perceived that Korah was irreclaimable, he directed the rest of his warning to those other Levites, the men of Korah's tribe, who, he feared, would join Korah in his rebellion. He admonished them to be satisfied with the honors God had granted them, and not to strive for priestly dignity. He concluded his speech with a last appeal to Korah to cause no schism in Israel, saying; "Had Aaron arbitrarily assumed the priestly dignity, you would do right to withstand his presumption, but it was God, whose attributes are sublimity, strength, and sovereignty, who clothed Aaron with this dignity, so that those who are against

Aaron are in reality against God." Korah made no answer to all these words, thinking that the best course for him to follow would be to avoid picking an argument with so great a sage as Moses, feeling sure that in such a dispute he should be worsted and, contrary to his own conviction, be forced to yield to Moses.

Moses, seeing that is was useless to reason with Korah, sent a messenger to Dathan and Abiram, summoning them to appear before his court. He did this because the law required that the accused be summoned to appear before the judge, before the judgement may be passed upon him, and Moses did not wish these men to be punished without a hearing. These, however, made answer to the messenger sent by Moses, "We will not come up!" This shameless answer held an unconscious prophecy. They went not up, but, as their end showed, down, to hell. Not only, moreover, did they refuse to comply with Moses' demand, they sent the following message in answer to Moses: "Why dost thou set thyself up as master over us? What benefit didst thou bring to us? Thou didst lead us out of Egypt, a land 'like the garden of the Lord,' but hast not brought us to Canaan, leaving us in the wilderness where we are daily visited by the plague. Even in Egypt didst thou try to assume the leadership, just as thou doest not. Thou didst beguile the people in their exodus from Egypt, when thou didst promise to lead them to a land of milk and honey; in their delusion they followed thee and were disappointed. Now dost thou attempt to persuade us as thou didst persuade them, but thou shalt not succeed, for we will not come and obey thy summons."

The shamelessness of these two men, who declined even to talk about their transgression with Moses, aroused his wrath to the uttermost, for a man does get a certain amount of satisfaction out of discussing the dispute with this opponents, whereas he feels badly if he cannot discuss the matter. In his anger he said to God: "O Lord of the world! I well know that these sinners participated in the offerings of the congregation that were offered for all Israel, but as they have withdrawn themselves from the community, accept not Thou their share of the offering and let it not be consumed by the heavenly fire. It was I whom they treated so, I who took no money from the people for my labors, even when payment was my due. It is customary for anyone who works for the sanctuary to receive pay for his work, but I traveled to Egypt on my own ass, and took none of theirs, although I undertook the journey in their interests. It is customary for those that have a dispute to go before a judge, but I did not wait for this, and went straight to them to settle their disputes, never declaring the innocent guilty, or the guilty innocent."

When he now perceived that his words had no effect upon Korah and his horde, he concluded his words with a treat to the ring leaders: "Be thou and all thy company before the Lord, thou and they, and Aaron, to-morrow."

Korah spent the night before the judgement in trying to win over the people to his side, and succeeded in so doing. He went to all the other tribes, saying to them: "Do not think I am seeking a position of honor for myself. No, I wish only that this honor may fall to the lot of each in turn, whereas Moses is now king, and his brother high priest." On the following morning, all the people, and not Korah's original company alone, appeared before the Tabernacle and began to pick quarrels with Moses and Aaron. Moses now feared that God would destroy all the people because they had joined Korah, hence he said to God: "O Lord of the world! If a nation rebels against a king of flesh and blood because ten or twenty men have cursed the king or his ambassadors, then he sends his hosts to massacre the inhabitants of the land, innocent as well as guilty, for he is not able with certainty to tell which among them honored the king and which among them cursed him. But Thou knowest the thought of man, and what his heart and kidneys counsel him to do, the workings of Thy creatures' minds lie open before Thee, so that Thou knowest who had the spirit of each one.' Shall one man sin, and wilt thou be wroth with all the congregation?'" God hereupon said to Moses "I have heard the prayer for the congregation. Say then, to them, 'Get you up from about the Tabernacle of Korah, Dathan, and Abiram.'"

Moses did not immediately carry out these instructions, for he tried once again to warn Dathan and Abiram of the punishment impending upon them, but they refused to give heed to Moses, and remained within their tents. "Now," said Moses, "I have done all I could, and can do nothing more." Hence, turning to the congregation, he said: "Depart, I pray you, from the tents of these wicked men, that even in their youth deserved death as a punishment for their actions. In Egypt they betrayed the secret of my slaying an Egyptian: at the Red Sea it was they that angered God by their desire to return to Egypt; in Alush they broke the Sabbath, and now they trooped together to rebel against God. They now well deserve excommunication, and the destruction of all their property. 'Touch, therefore, nothing of theirs, lest ye be consumed in all their sins.'"

The community obeyed the words of Moses and drew back from the dwellings of Dathan and Abiram. These, not at all cowed, were not restrained from their wicked intention, but stood at the doors of their tents, abusing and calumniating Moses. Moses hereupon said to God: "If these men die upon their beds like all men, after physicians have attended to them and acquaintances have visited them, then shall I publicly avow 'that the Lord hath not sent me' to do all these works, but that I have done them of mine own mind." God replied: "What wilt thou have Me do?" Moses: "If the Lord hath already provided the earth with a mouth to swallow them, it is well, if not, I pray Thee, do so now." God said: "Thou shalt decree a thing, and it shall be established unto thee."

Moses was not the only one to insist upon exemplary punishment of the horde of Korah. Sun and Moon appeared before God, saying: "If Thou givest satisfaction to the son of Amram, we shall set out on our course around the world, but not otherwise." God, however, hurled lightnings after them, that they might go about their duties, saying to them: "You have never championed My cause, but not you stand up for a creature of flesh and blood." Since that time Sun and Moon have always to be driven to duty, never doing it voluntarily because they do not wish to look upon the sins of man upon earth.

KORAH AND HIS HORDE PUNISHED

God did not gainsay satisfaction of His faithful servant. The mouth of hell approached the spot upon which Dathan, Abiram, and their families stood, and the ground under their feet grew so precipitous that they were not able to stand upright, but rolled to the opening and went quickly into the pit. Not these wicked people alone were swallowed by the earth, but their possessions also. Even their linen that was the launderer's or a pin belonging to them rolled toward the mouth of the earth and vanished therein. Nowhere upon earth remained a trace of them or of their possessions, and even their names disappeared from the documents upon which they were written. They did not, however, meet an immediate death, but sank gradually into the earth, the opening of which adjusted itself to the girth of each individual. The lower extremities disappeared first, then the opening widened, and the abdomen followed, until in this way the entire body was swallowed. While they were sinking thus slowly and painfully, they continued to cry: "Moses is truth and his Torah is truth. We acknowledge that Moses is rightful king and true prophet, that Aaron is legitimate high priest, and that the Torah has been given by God. Now deliver us, O our teacher Moses!" These words were audible throughout the entire camp, so that all might be convinced of the wickedness of Korah's undertaking.

Without regard to these followers of Korah, who were swallowed up by the earth, the two hundred and fifty men who had offered incense with Aaron found their death in the heavenly fire that came down upon their offering and consumed them. But he who met with the most terrible form of death was Korah. Consumed at the incense offering, he then rolled in the shape of a ball of fire to the opening in the earth, and vanished. There was a reason for this double punishment of Korah. Had he received punishment by burning alone, then those who had been swallowed by the earth, and who had failed to see Korah smitten by the same punishment, would have complained about God's injustice, saying: "It was Korah who plunged us into destruction, yet he himself escaped it." Had he, on the other hand, been swallowed by the earth without meeting death by fire, then those whom the fire had consumed would have complained about God injustice that permitted the author of their destruction to go unpunished. Now, however, both those who perished by fire and those who were swallowed up by the earth witnessed their leader share their punishment.

This terrible death did not, however, suffice to atone for the sins of Korah and his company, for their punishment continues in hell. They are tortured in hell, and at the end of thirty days, hell again casts them up near to the surface of the earth, on the spot where they had been swallowed. Whosoever on that day puts his ear to the ground upon that spot hears the cry. "Moses is truth, and his Torah is truth, but we are liars." Not until after the Resurrection will their punishment cease, for even in spite of their grave sin they were not given over to eternal damnation.

For a time Korah and his company believed that they should never know relief from these tortures of hell, but Hannah's words encouraged them not to despair. In reference to them she announced the prophecy, "The Lord bringeth low, to Sheol, and lifteth up." At first they had no real faith in this prophecy, but when God destroyed the Temple, and sank its portals deep into the earth until they reached hell, Korah and his company clung to the portals, saying: "If these portals return again upward, then through them shall we also return upward." God hereupon appointed them as keepers of these portals over which they will have to stand guard until they return to the upper world.

ON AND THE THREE SONS OF KORAH SAVED

God punished discord severely, for although the decree of Heaven does not otherwise punish any one below twenty years of age, at Korah's rebellion the earth swallowed alive even children that were only a day old-men, women, and children, all together. Out of all the company of Korah and their families only four persons escaped ruin, to wit: On, the son of Peleth, and Korah's three sons. As it was Korah's wife who through her inciting words plunged her husband into destruction, so to his wife does On owe his salvation. Truly to these two women applies the proverb: "Every wise woman buildeth her house: but the foolish plucketh it down with her own hands." On, whose abilities had won him distinction far beyond that of his father, had originally joined Korah's rebellion. When he arrived home and spoke of it to his wife, she said to him: "What benefit shalt thou reap from it? Either Moses remains master and thou art his disciple, or Korah becomes master and thou art his disciple." On saw the truth of this argument, but declared that he felt it incumbent upon himself to adhere to Korah because he had given him his oath, which he could not now take back. His wife quieted him, however, entreating him to stay at home. To be quite sure of him, however, she gave him wine to drink, whereupon he fell into a deep sleep of intoxication. His wife now carried out her work of salvation, saying to herself: "All the congregation are holy, and being such, they will approach no woman whose hair is uncovered." She now showed herself at the door of the tent with streaming hair, and whenever one out of the company of Korah, about to go to On, saw the woman in this condition, he started back, and owing to this schemer husband had no part in the rebellion. When the earth opened to swallow Korah's company, the bed on which On still slept began to rock, and to roll to the opening in the earth. On's wife, however, seized it, saying: "O Lord of the world! My husband made a solemn vow never again to take part in dissensions. Thou that livest and endurest to all eternity canst punish him hereafter if ever he prove false to his vow." God heard her plea, and On was saved. She now requested On to go to Moses, but he refused, for he was ashamed to look into Moses' face after he had rebelled against him. His wife then went to Moses in his stead. Moses at first evaded her, for he wished to have nothing to do with women, but as she wept and lamented bitterly, she was admitted and told Moses all that had occurred. He now accompanied her to her house, at the entrance of which he cried: "On, the son of Peleth, step forth, God will forgive thee thy sins." It is with reference to this miraculous deliverance and to his life spent in doing penance that this former follower of Korah was called On, "the penitent," son of Peleth, "miracle." His true name was Nemuel, the son of Eliab, a brother of Dathan and Abiram.

More marvelous still than that of On was the salvation of Korah's three sons. For when the earth yawned to swallow Korah and his company, these cried: "Help us, Moses!" The Shekinah hereupon said: "If these men were to repent, they should be saved; repentance do I desire, and naught else." Korah's three sons now simultaneously determined to repent their sin, but they could not open their mouths, for round about them burned the fire, and below them gaped hell. God was, however, satisfied with their good thought, and in the sight of all Israel, for their salvation, a pillar arose in hell, upon which they seated themselves. There did they sit and sing praises and song to the Lord sweeter than ever mortal ear had heard, so that Moses and all Israel hearkened to them eagerly. They were furthermore distinguished by God in receiving from Him the prophetic gift, and they then announced in their songs events that were to occur in the future world. They said: "Fear not the day on which the Lord will 'take hold of the ends of the earth, and the wicked be shaken out of it,' for the pious will cling to the Throne of Glory and will find protection under the wings of the Shekinah. Fear not, ye pious men, the Day of Judgement, for the judgement of sinners will have as little power over you as it had over us when all the others perished and we were saved."

ISRAEL CONVINCED OF AARON'S PRIESTHOOD

After the death of the two hundred and fifty followers of Korah, who perished at the offering of incense, Eleazar, the son of Aaron, was ordered "to take up the censers out of the burning," in which the souls, not the bodies of the sinners were burned, that out of these brasen plates he made a covering for the altar. Eleazar, and not his father, the high priest, received this commission, for God said: "The censer brought death upon two of Aaron's sons, therefore let the third now fetch forth the censer and effect expiation for the sinners." The covering of the altar fashioned out of the brass of these censers was "to be a memorial unto the children of Israel, to the end that no stranger, which is not of the seed of Aaron, come near to burn incense before the Lord." Such a one was not, however, to be punished like Korah and his company, but in the same way as Moses had once been punished by God, with leprosy. This punishment was visited upon king Uzziah, who tried to burn incense in the Temple, asserting that it was the king's task to perform the service before the King of all. The heavens hastened to the scene to consume him, just as the celestial fire had once consumed the two hundred and fifty men, who had wrongfully assumed the rights of priesthood; the earth strove to swallow him as it had once swallowed Korah and his company. But a celestial voice announced: "Upon none save Korah and his company came punishments like these, upon no others. This man's punishment shall be leprosy." Hence Uzziah became a leper.

Peace was not, however, established with the destruction of Korah and his company, for on the very day that followed the terrible catastrophe, there arose a rebellion against Moses, that was even more violent than the preceding one. For although the people were now convinced that nothing came to pass without the will of God, still they thought God was doing all this for Moses' sake. Hence they laid at his door God's violent anger against them, blaming not the wickedness of those who had been punished, but Moses, who, they said, had excited God's revengefulness against them. They accused Moses of having brought about the death of so many of the noblest among them as a punishment for the people, only that they might not again venture to call him to account, and that he might thereby ensure his brother's possession of the priestly office, since no one would hereafter covet it, seeing that on its account the noblest among them had met so terrible a fate. The kinsmen of those who had perished stirred the flame of resentment and spurred on the people to set a limit to Moses' love of power, insisting that the public welfare and the safety of Israel demanded such measures. These unseemly speeches and their unceasing, incorrigible perverseness brought upon them God's wrath to such a degree that He wanted to destroy them all, and bade Moses and Aaron go away from the congregation that He might instantly set about their ruin.

When Moses saw that "there was wrath gone out from the Lord, and the plague was begun," he called Aaron to him, saying: "Take thy censer and put fire therein from off the altar, and lay incense thereon, and carry it quickly unto the congregation, and make atonement for them." This remedy against death Moses had learned from the Angel of Death himself at the time he was staying in heaven to receive the Torah. At that time he had received a gift from each one of the angels, and that of the Angel of Death had been the revelation of the secret that incense can hold him at bay. Moses, in applying this remedy, had in mind also the purpose of showing the people the injustice of their superstition concerning the offering of incense. They called it death-bearing because it had brought death upon Nadab and Abihu, as well as upon the two hundred and fifty followers of Korah. He now wished to convince them that it was this very incense that prevented the plague, and to teach them that it is sin that brings death. Aaron, however, did not know why he employed incense, and therefore said to Moses: "O my lord Moses, hast thou perchance my death in view? My sons were burned because they put strange fires into the censers. Shall I now fetch holy fire from the altar and carry it outside? Surely I shall meet death through this fire!" Moses replied: "Go quickly and do as I have bidden thee, for while thou dost stand and talk, they die." Aaron hastened to carry out the command given to him, saying: "Even if it be my death, I obey gladly if I can only serve Israel thereby."

The Angel of Death had meanwhile wrought terrible havoc among the people, like a reaper mowing down line after line of them, allowing not one of the line he touched to escape, whereas, on the other hand, not a single man died before he reached the row in which the man stood. Aaron, censer in hand, now appeared, and stood up between the ranks of the living and those of the dead, holding the Angel of Death at bay. The latter now addressed Aaron, saying: "Leave me to my work, for I have been sent to do it by God, whereas thou dost bid me stop in the name of a creature that is only of flesh and blood." Aaron did not, however, yield, but said: "Moses acts only as God commands him, and if thou wilt not trust him, behold, God and

Moses are both in the Tabernacle, let us both betake ourselves thither." The Angel of Death refused to obey his call, whereupon Aaron seized him by force and, thrusting the censer under his face, dragged him to the Tabernacle where he locked him in, so that death ceased.

In this way Aaron paid off a debt to Moses. After the worship of the Golden Calf, that came to pass not without some guilt on Aaron's part, God had decreed that all four of Aaron's sons were to die, but Moses stood up between the living and the dead, and through his prayer succeeded in saving two out of the four. In the same way Aaron now stood up between the living and the dead to ward off from Israel the Angel of Death.

God in His kindness now desired the people once and for all to be convinced of the truth that Aaron was the elect, and his house the house of priesthood, hence he bade Moses convince them in the following fashion. Upon God's command, he took a beam of wood, divided it into twelve rods, bade every prince of a tribe in his own hand write his name on one of the rods respectively, and laid up the rods over night before the sanctuary. Then the miracle came to pass that the rod of Aaron, the prince of the tribe of Levi, bore the Ineffable Name which caused the rod to bloom blossoms over night and to yield ripe almonds. When the people, who all night had been pondering which tribe should on the morrow be proven by the rod of its prince to be the chosen one, betook themselves early in the morning to the sanctuary, and saw the blossoms and almonds upon the rod of Aaron, they were at last convinced that God had destined the priesthood for his house. The almonds, which ripen more quickly than any other fruit, at the same time informed them that God would quickly bring punishment upon those who should venture to usurp the powers of priesthood. Aaron's rod was then laid up before the Holy Ark by Moses. It was this rod, kings used until the time of the destruction of the Temple, when, in miraculous fashion, it disappeared. Elijah will in the future fetch it forth and hand it over to the Messiah.

THE WATERS OF MERIBAH

Korah's rebellion took place during Israel's sojourn in Kadesh-Barnea, whence, a short time before, the spies had been sent out. They remained in this place during nineteen years, and then for as long a time wandered ceaselessly from place to place through the desert. When at last the time decreed by God for their stay in the wilderness was over, and the generation that God had said must die in the desert had paid its penalty for its sin, they returned again to Kadesh-Barnea. They took delight in this place endeared to them by long years of habitation, and settled down in the expectation of a cheerful and agreeable time. But the prophetess Miriam now dies, and the loss of the woman, who occupied a place as high as that of her brothers, Moses and Aaron, at once became evident in a way that was perceived by the pious as well as by the godless. She was the only woman who died during the march through the desert, and this occurred for the following reasons. She was a leader of the people together with her brothers, and as these two were not permitted to lead the people into the promised land, she had to share their fate. The well, furthermore, that had provided Israel with water during the march through the desert, had been a gift of God to the people as a reward for the good deeds of this prophetess, and as this gift had been limited to the time of the march through the desert, she had to die shortly before the entrance into the promised land.

Hardly had Miriam died, when the well also disappeared and a dearth of water set in, that all Israel might know that only owing to the merits of the pious prophetess had they been spared a lack of water during the forty years of the march. While Moses and Aaron were now plunged in deep grief for their sister's death, a mob of the people collected to wrangle with them on account of the dearth of water. Moses, seeing the multitudes of people approaching from the distance, said to his brother Aaron: "What may all these multitudes desire?" The other replied: "Are not the children of Abraham, Isaac, and Jacob kind-hearted people and the descendants of kind-hearted people? They come to express their sympathy." Moses, however, said: "Thou are not able to distinguish between a well-ordered procession and this motley multitude; were these people assembled in an orderly procession, they would move under the leadership of the rules of thousands and the rulers of hundreds, but behold, they move in disorderly troops. How then can their intentions be to console with us!"

The two brothers were not long to remain in doubt concerning the purpose of the multitude, for they stepped up to them and began to pick a quarrel with Moses, saying: "It was a heavy blow for us when fourteen thousand and seven hundred of our men died of the plague; harder still to bear was the death of those who were swallowed up by the earth, and lost their lives in an unnatural way; the heaviest blow of all, however, was the death of those who were consumed at the offering of incense, whose terrible end is constantly recalled to us by the covering of the altar, fashioned out of the brasen plates that came of the censers used by those unfortunate ones. But we bore all these blows, and even wish we had all perished simultaneously with them instead of becoming victims to the tortures of death by thirst."

At first they directed their reproaches against Moses alone, since Aaron, on account of his extraordinary love of peace and his kind-heartedness, was the favorite of the people, but once carried away by suffering and rage, they started to hurl their accusations against both of the brothers, saying: "Formerly your answer to us had always been that sorrows came upon us and that God did not stand by us because there were sinful and godless men among us. Now that we are 'a congregation of the Lord,' why have ye nevertheless led us to this poor place where there is not water, without which neither man nor beast can live? Why do not ye exhort God to have pity upon us since the well of Miriam had vanished with her death?"

"A righteous man regardeth the life of his beast," and the fact that these people, so near to death, still considered the sufferings of their beasts shows that they were, notwithstanding their attitude toward Moses and Aaron, really pious men. And, in truth, God did not take amiss their words against Moses and Aaron, "for God holds no man accountable for that which he utters in distress." For the same reason neither Moses nor Aaron made reply to the accusations hurled against them, but hastened to the sanctuary to implore God's mercy for His people. They also considered that the holy place would shelter them in case the people meant to lay hands upon them. God actually did appear at once, and said to them: "Hasten from this place; My children die of thirst, and ye have nothing better to do than to mourn the death of an old woman!" He then bade Moses "to speak unto the rock that it may give forth water," but impressed upon them the command to bring forth neither honey nor oil out of the rock, but water only. This was to prove God's power, who can pour out of the rock not only such liquids as are contained in it, but water too, that never otherwise issues from a rock. He also ordered Moses to speak to the rock, but not to smite it with his rod. "For," said God, "the merits of them that sleep in the Cave of Machpelah suffice to cause their children to receive water out of the rock."

Moses then fetched out of the Tabernacle the holy rod on which was the Ineffable Name of God, and, accompanied by Aaron, betook himself to the rock to bring water out of it. On the way to the rock all Israel followed him, halting at any rock by the way, fancying that they might fetch water out of it. The grumblers now went about inciting the people against Moses, saying: "Don't you know that the son of Amram had once been Jethro's shepherd, and all shepherds have knowledge of the places in the wilderness that are rich in water? Moses will now try to lead us to such a place where there is water, and then he will cheat us and declare he had causes the water to flow out of a rock. If he actually is able to bring forth water out of rocks, then let him fetch it out of any one of the rocks upon which we fix." Moses could easily have done this, for God said to him: "Let them see the water flow out of the rock they have chosen," but when, on the way to the rock, he turned around and perceived that instead of following him they stood about in groups around different rocks, each group around some rock favored by it, he commanded them to follow him to the rock upon which he had fixed. They, however, said: "We demand that thou bring us water out of the rock we have chosen, and if thou wilt not, we do not care to fetch water out of another rock."

MOSES' ANGER CAUSES HIS DOOM

Throughout forty years Moses had striven to refrain from harshly addressing the people, knowing that if but a single time he lost patience, God would cause him to die in the desert. On this occasion, however, he was mastered by his rage, and shouted at Israel the words: "O ye madmen, ye stiffnecked ones, that desire to teach their teacher, ye that shoot upon your leaders with your arrows, do ye think that out of this rock that ye have chosen, we shall be able to bring forth water? I vow that I shall let water flow out of that rock only that I have chosen." He addressed these harsh words not to a few among Israel, but to all the people, for God had brought the miracle to pass that the small space in front of the rock held all Israel. Carried away by anger, Moses still further forgot himself, and instead of speaking to the rock as God had commanded him, he struck a rock chosen by himself. As Moses had not acted according to God's command, the rock did not at once obey, and sent forth only a few drops of water, so that the mockers cried: "Son of Amram, is this for the sucklings and for them that are weaned from the milk?" Moses now waxed angrier still, and for a second time smote the rock, from which gushed streams so mighty that many of his enemies me their death in the currents, and at the same time water poured out of all the stones and rocks of the desert. God here upon said to Moses: "Thou and Aaron believed Me not, I forbade you to smite the rock, but thou didst smite it; ye sanctified Me not in the eyes of the children of Israel because ye did not fetch water out of any one of the rocks, as the people wished; ye trespassed against Me when ye said, 'Shall we bring forth water out of this rock?' and ye acted contrary to My command because ye did not speak to the rock as I had bidden ye. I vow, therefore, that 'ye shall not bring this assembly into the land which I have given them,' and not until the Messianic time shall ye two lead Israel to the Holy Land." God furthermore said to Moses: "Thou shouldst have learned from the life of Ishmael to have greater faith in Me; I bade the well to spring up for him, even though he was only a single human being, on account of the merits of his father Abraham. How much more than hadst thou a right to expect, thou who couldst refer to the merits of the three Patriarchs as well as to the people's own, for they accepted the Torah and obeyed many commandments. Yea, even from thine own experience shouldst thou have drawn greater faith in My will to aid Israel. When in Rephidim thou didst say to Me, 'They be almost ready to stone me,' did not I not reply to thee, 'Why dost thou accuse My children? God with thy rod before the people, and thou shalt smite the rock, and there shall come water out of it.' If I wrought for them miracles such as these when they had not yet accepted the Torah, and did not yet have faith in Me, shouldst thou not have known how much more I would do for them now?"

God "taketh the wise in their own craftiness." He had long before this decreed that Moses die in the desert, and Moses' offense in Kadesh was only a pretext God employed that He might not seem to be unjust. But He gave to Moses himself the true reason why He did not permit him to enter the promised land, saying: "Would it perchance redound to thy glory if thou wert to lead into the land a new generation after thou hadst led out of Egypt the sixty myriads and buried them in the desert? People would declare that the generation of the desert has no share in future world, therefore stay with them, that at their head thou mayest after the Resurrection enter the promised land." Moses now said to God: "Thou hast decreed that I die in the desert like the generation of the desert that angered Thee. I implore Thee, write in Thy Torah wherefore I have been thus punished, that future generations may not say I had been like the generations of the desert." God granted this wish, and in several passages of the Scriptures set forth what had really been the offense on account of which Moses had been prohibited from entering the promised land. It was due only to the transgression at the rock in Kadesh, where Moses failed to sanctify God in the eyes of the children of Israel; and God was sanctified by allowing justice to take its course without respect of persons, and punishing Moses. Hence this place was called Kadesh, "sanctity," and En Mishpat, "fountain of justice," because on this spot judgement was passed upon Moses, and by this sentence God's name was sanctified.

As water had been the occasion for the punishment of Moses, God did not say that that which He had created on the second day of the creation "was good," for on that day He had created water, and that which brought about Moses' death was not good.

If the death doomed for Moses upon this occasion was a very severe punishment, entirely out of proportion to his offense, then still more so was the death destined for Aaron at the same time. For he had been guilty of no other offense than that of joining Moses at his transgression, and "who so joins a transgressor, is as bad as the transgressor himself." On this occasion, as usual, Aaron showed his absolute devotion and his faith in God's justice. He might have said, "I have not sinned; why am I to be punished?" but he conquered himself and put up no defense, wherefore Moses greatly praised him.

EDOM'S UNBROTHERLY ATTITUDE TOWARD ISRAEL

From Kadesh Moses sent ambassadors to the king of Edom, requesting him to permit Israel to travel through his territory. "For," thought Moses, "When our father Jacob with only a small troop of men planned to return to his father's house, which was not situated in Esau's possessions, he previously sent a messenger to him to ask his permission. How much more then does it behoove us, a people of great numbers, to refrain from entering Edom's territory before receiving his sanction to do so!"

Moses' ambassadors had been commissioned to bear the following message to the king of Edom: "From the time of our grandfather Abraham, there was a promissory note to be redeemed, for God had imposed it upon him that in Egypt his seed should be enslaved and tortured. It had been thy duty, as well as ours, to redeem this note, and thou knowest that we have done our duty whereas thou wert not willing. God had, as thou knowest, promised Abraham that those who had been in bondage in Egypt should receive Canaan for their possession as a reward. That land, therefore, is ours, who were in Egypt, and thou who didst shirk the redemption of the debt, hast now claim to our land. Let us then pass through thy land until we reach ours. Know also that the Patriarchs in their grave sympathized with our sufferings in Egypt, and whenever we called out to God He heard us, and sent us one of His ministering angels to lead us out of Egypt. Consider, then, that all thy weapons will avail thee naught if we implore God's aid, who will then at once overthrow thee and thy hosts, for this is our inheritance, and 'the voice of Jacob' never proves ineffectual. That thou mayest not, however, plead that our passage through thy land will bring thee only annoyances and no gain, I promise thee that although we draw drink out of a well that accompanies us on our travels, and are provided with food through the manna, we shall, nevertheless, by water and food from thy people, that ye may profit by our passage."

This was no idle promise, for Moses had actually asked the people to be liberal with their money, that the Edomites might not take them to be poor slaves, but might be convinced that in spite of their stay in Egypt, Israel was a wealthy nation. Moses also pledged himself to provide the cattle with muzzles during their passage through Edom, that they might do no damage to the land of the dwellers there. With these words he ended his message to the king of Edom: "To the right and to the left of thy land may we pillage and slaughter, but in accord with God's words, we may not touch thy possession." But all these prayers and pleadings of Moses were without avail, for Edom's answer was in the form of a threat: "Ye depend upon your inheritance, upon 'the voice of Jacob' which God answers, and I too shall depend upon my inheritance, 'the hand and sword of Esau.'" Israel now had to give up their attempt to reach their land through Edom's territory, not, however, through fear, but because God had prohibited them from bringing war upon the Edomites, even before they had heard from the embassy that Edom had refused them the right of passage.

The neighborhood of the godless brings disaster, as Israel was to experience, for they lost the pious Aaron on the boundary of Edom, and buried him on Mount Hor. The cloud that used to precede Israel, had indeed been accustomed to level all the mountains, that they might move on upon level ways, but God retained three mountains in the desert: Sinai, as the place of the revelation; Nebo, as the burial-place of Moses; and Hor, consisting of a twin mountain, as a burial-place for Aaron. Apart from these three mountains, there were none in the desert, but the cloud would leave little elevations on the place where Israel pitched camp, that the sanctuary might thereupon be set up.

THE THREE SHEPHERDS

Aaron died four months after the death of his sister Miriam, whereas Moses died nearly a year after his sister. Her death took place on the first day of Nisan, and that of Moses on the seventh day of Adar in the same year. Although the death of these three did not take place in the same month, God spoke of them saying, "And I cut off the three shepherds in one month," for He had determined upon their death in one month. It is God's way to classify people into related groups, and the death of these three pious ones was not determined upon together with hat of the sinful generation of wanderers in the desert, but only after this generations had died, was sealed the doom of the three. Miriam died first, and the same fate was decreed for her brothers as a consequence of her death.

Miriam's death plunged all into deep mourning, Moses and Aaron wept in their apartments and the people wept in the streets. For six hours Moses was ignorant of the disappearance of Miriam's well with Miriam's death, until the Israelites went to him, saying, "How long wilt thou sit here and weep?" He answered, "Shall I not weep for my sister, who had died?" They replied, "While thou are weeping for one soul, weep at the same time for us all." "Why?" asked he. They said, "We have no water to drink." Then he rose up from the ground, went out and saw the well without a drop of water. He now began to quarrel with them, saying, "Have I not told ye, 'I am not able to bear you myself alone'? Ye have rulers of thousands, rulers of hundreds, rulers of fifties, and rulers of tens, princes, chiefs, elders, and magnates, let these attend to your needs." Israel, however, said: "All rests with thee, for it is thou who didst lead us out of Egypt and brought 'us in unto this evil place; it is no place of seed or of figs, or of vines, or of pomegranates; neither is there any water to drink.' If thou wilt give us water, it is well, if not, we shall stone thee." When Moses heard this, he fled from them and betook himself to the Tabernacle. There God said to him: "What ails thee?" and Moses replied: "O Lord of the world! Thy children want to stone me, and had I not escaped, they would have stoned me by now." God said: "Moses, how much longer wilt thou continue to calumniate My children? Is it not enough that at Horeb thou didst say, 'They be ready to stone me,' whereupon I answered thee, 'Go up before them and I will see whether they stone thee or not!' 'Take the rod and assemble the congregation, thou and Aaron thy brother, and speak ye unto the rock before their eyes, that it give forth its water.'"

Moses now went to seek for the rock, followed by all Israel, for he did not know which was the rock out of which God had said water was to flow. For the rock out of which Miriam's well flowed vanished among the rest of the rocks in such a way that Moses was not able to distinguish it among the number. On the way they saw a rock that dripped, and they took up their places in front of it. When Moses saw that the people stood still, he turned around and they said to him: "How long wilt thou lead us on?" Moses: "Until I fetch ye forth water out of the rock." The people: "Give us water at once, that we may drink." Moses: "How long do ye quarrel? Is there a creature in all the world that so rebels against its Maker as ye do, when it is certain that God will give ye water out of a rock, even though I do not know which one that may be!" The people: "Thou wert a prophet and our shepherd during our march through the desert, and now thou sayest, 'I know not out of which rock God will give ye water.'"

Moses hereupon assembled them about a rock, saying to himself: "If I now speak to the rock, bidding it bring forth water, and it bring forth none, I shall subject myself to humiliation in the presence of the community, for they will say, 'Where is thy wisdom?'" Hence he said to the people: "Ye know that God can perform miracles for ye, but He hath hidden from me out of which rock He will let the water flow forth. For whenever the time comes that God wished a man not to know, then his wisdom and understanding are of no avail to him." Moses then lifted his rod and let it quietly slide down upon the rock which he laid it, uttering, as if addressing Israel, the words, "Shall we bring you forth water out of this rock?" The rock of its own accord now began to give forth water, whereupon Moses struck upon it with his rod, but then water no longer flowed forth, but blood. Moses hereupon said to God: "This rock brings forth no water," and God instantly turned to the rock with the question: "Why dost thou bring forth not water, but blood?" The rock answered: "O Lord of the world! Why did Moses smite me?" When God asked Moses why he had smitten the rock, he replied: "That it might bring forth water." God, however, said to Moses: "Had I bidden thee to smite the rock? I had only said, 'Speak to it.'" Moses tried to defend himself by saying, "I did speak to it, but it brought forth nothing." "Thou," God replied, "hast given Israel the instruction, 'In righteousness shalt thou judge thy neighbor'; why then, didst not thou judge the rock 'in righteousness,' the rock that in Egypt supported thee when out of it thou didst such honey? Is this the manner in which thou repayest it? Not only wert thou unjust to the rock, but thou didst also call My children fools. If then thou are a wise man, it does not become thee as a wise man to have anything further to do with fools, and therefore thou shalt not with them learn to know the land of Israel." At the same time God added, "Neither thou, nor thy brother, nor thy sister, shall set foot upon the land of Israel." For even in Egypt God had warned Moses and Aaron to refrain from calling the Israelites fools, and as Moses, without evoking a protest from Aaron, at the water of Kadesh, called them fools, the punishment of death was decreed for him and his brother. When God had informed Moses of the impending punishment due to him and his brother, He turned to the rock, saying: "Turn thy blood into water," and so it came to pass.

PREPARING AARON FOR IMPENDING DEATH

As a sign of especial favor God communicates to the pious the day of their death, that they may transmit their crowns to their sons. But God considered it particularly fitting to prepare Moses and Aaron for impending death, saying: "These two pious men throughout their lifetime did nothing without consulting Me, and I shall not therefore take them out of this world without previously informing them."

When, therefore, Aaron's time approached, God said to Moses: "My servant Moses, who hast been 'faithful in all Mine house,' I have an important matter to communicate to thee, but it weighs heavily upon Me." Moses: "What is it?" God: "Aaron shall be gathered unto his people; for he shall not enter into the land which I have given unto the children of Israel, because ye rebelled against My word at the waters of Meribah." Moses replied: "Lord of the world! It is manifest and known before the Throne of Thy glory, that Thou art Lord of all the world and of Thy creatures that in this world Thou hast created, so that we are in Thy hand, and in Thy hand it lies to do with us as Thou wilt. I am not, however, fit to go to my brother, and repeat to him Thy commission, for he is older than I, and how then shall I presume to go up to my older brother and say, 'Go up unto Mount Hor and die there!'" God answered Moses: "Not with the lip shalt thou touch this matter, but 'take Aaron and Eleazar his son, and bring them up unto Mount Hor.' Ascend thou also with them, and there speak with thy brother sweet and gentle words, the burden of which will, however, prepare him for what awaits him. Later when ye shall all three be upon the mountain, 'strip Aaron of his garments, and put them upon Eleazar his son, and Aaron shall be gathered unto his people, and shall die there.' As a favor to Me prepare Aaron for his death, for I am ashamed to tell him of it Myself."

When Moses heard this, there was a tumult in his heart, and he knew not what to do. He wept so passionately that his grief for the impending loss of his brother brought him to the brink of death himself. As a faithful servant of God, however, nothing remained for him to do, but to execute his Master's command, hence he betook himself to Aaron to the Tabernacle, to inform him of his death.

Now it had been customary during the forty years' march through the desert for the people daily to gather, first before the seventy elders, then under their guidance before the princes of the tribes, then for all of them to appear before Eleazar and Aaron, and with these to go to Moses to present to him their morning greeting. On this day, however, Moses made a change in this custom, and after having wept through the night, at the cock's crow summoned Eleazar before him and said to him: "Go and call to me the elders and the princes, for I have to convey to them a commission from the Lord." Accompanied by these men, Moses not betook himself to Aaron who, seeing Moses when he arose, asked: "Why hast thou made a change in the usual custom?" Moses: "God hath bidden me to make a communication to thee." Aaron: "Tell it to me." Moses: "Wait until we are out of doors." Aaron thereupon donned his eight priestly garments and both went out.

Now it had always been the custom for Moses whenever he went from his house to the Tabernacle to walk in the center, with Aaron at his right, Eleazar at his left, then the elders at both sides, and the people following in the rear. Upon arriving within the Tabernacle, Aaron would seat himself as the very nearest at Moses' right hand, Eleazar at his left, and the elders and princes in front. On this day, however, Moses changed this order; Aaron walked in the center, Moses at his right hand, Eleazar at his left, the elders and princes at both sides, and the rest of the people following.

When the Israelites saw this, they rejoiced greatly, saying: "Aaron now has a higher degree of the Holy Spirit than Moses, and therefore does Moses yield to him the place of honor in the center." The people loved Aaron better than Moses. For ever since Aaron had become aware that through the construction of the Golden Calf he had brought about the transgression of Israel, it was his endeavor through the following course of life to atone for his sin. He would go from house to house, and whenever he found one who did not know how to recite his Shema', he taught him the Shema'; if one did not know how to pray he taught him how to pray; and if he found one who was not capable of penetrating into the study of the Torah, he initiated him into it. He did not, however, consider his task restricted 'to establishing peace between God and man,' but strove to establish peace between the learned and the ignorant Israelites, among the scholars themselves, among the ignorant, and between man and wife. Hence the people loved him very dearly, and rejoiced when they believed he had now attained a higher rank than Moses.

Having arrived at the Tabernacle, Aaron now wanted to enter, but Moses held him back, saying: "We shall now go beyond the camp." When they were outside the camp, Aaron said to Moses: "Tell me the commission God hath given thee." Moses answered: "Wait until we reach the mountain." At the foot of the mountain

Moses said to the people: "Stay here until we return to you; I, Aaron, and Eleazar will go to the top of the mount, and shall return when we shall have heard the Divine revelation." All three now ascended.

AARON'S DEATH

Moses wanted to inform his brother of his impending death, but knew not how to go about it. At length he said to him: "Aaron, my brother, hath God given anything into thy keeping?" "Yes," replied Aaron. "What, pray?" asked Moses. Aaron: "The altar and the table upon which is the shewbread hath He given into my charge." Moses: "It may be that He will now demand back from thee all that He hath given into thy keeping." Aaron: "What, pray?" Moses: "Hath He not entrusted a light to thee?" Aaron: "Not one light only but all seven of the candlestick that now burn in the sanctuary." Moses had, of course, intended to call Aaron's attention to the soul, "the light of the Lord," which God had given into his keeping and which He now demanded back. As Aaron, in his simplicity, did not notice the allusion, Moses did not go into further particulars, but remarked to Aaron: "God hath with justice called thee an innocent, simple-hearted man."

While they were thus conversing, a cave opened up before them, whereupon Moses requested his brother to enter it, and Aaron instantly acquiesced. Moses was now in a sad predicament, for, to follow God's command, he had to strip Aaron of his garments and to put them upon Eleazar, but he knew not how to broach the subject to his brother. He finally said to Aaron: "My brother Aaron, it is not proper to enter the cave into which we now want to descend, invested in the priestly garments, for they might there become unclean; the cave is very beautiful, and it is therefore possible that there are old graves in it." Aaron replied, "Thou art right." Moses then stripped his brother of his priestly garments, and put them upon Aaron's son, Eleazar.

As it would have been improper if Aaron had been buried quite naked, God brought about the miracle that, as soon as Moses took off one of Aaron's garments, a corresponding celestial garment was spread over Aaron, and when Moses had stripped him of all his priestly garments, he found himself arrayed in eight celestial garments. A second miracle came to pass in the stripping of Aaron's garments, for Moses was enabled to take off the undermost garments before the upper. This was done in order to satisfy the law that priests may never use their upper garments as undergarments, a thing Eleazar would have had to do, had Moses stripped off Aaron's outer garments first and with these invested his son.

After Eleazar had put on the high priest's garments, Moses and Aaron said to him: "Wait for us here until we return out of the cave," and both entered it. At their entrance they beheld a couch spread, a table prepared, and a candle lighted, while ministering angels surrounded the couch. Aaron then said to Moses: "How long, O my brother, wilt thou still conceal the commission God hath entrusted to thee? Thou knowest that He Himself, when for the first time He addressed thee, with His own lips declared of me, 'When he seeth thee, he will be glad in his heart.' Why, then, dost thou conceal the commission God hath entrusted to thee? Even if it were to refer to my death, I should take it upon myself with a cheerful countenance." Moses replied: "As thou thyself dost speak of death, I will acknowledge that God's words to me do concern thy death, but I was afraid to make it known to thee. But look now, thy death is not as that of the other creatures of flesh and blood; and not only is thy death a remarkable one, but see! The ministering angels have come to stand by thee in thy parting hour."

When he spoke of the remarkable death that awaited Aaron, Moses meant to allude to the fact that Aaron, like his sister Miriam and later Moses, was to die not through the Angel of Death, but by a kiss from God. Aaron, however, said: "O my brother Moses, why didst not thou make this communication to me in the presence of my mother, my wife, and my children?" Moses did not instantly reply to this question, but tried to speak words of comfort and encouragement to Aaron, saying: "Dost thou not know, my brother, that thou didst forty years ago deserve to meet thy death when thou didst fashion the Golden Calf, but then I stood before the Lord in prayer and exhortation, and saved thee from death. And now I pray that my death were as thine! For when thou diest, I bury thee, but when I shall die, I shall have no brother to bury me. When thou diest, thy sons will inherit thy position, but when I die, strangers will inherit my place." With these and similar words Moses encouraged his brother, until he finally looked forward to his end with equanimity.

Aaron lay down upon the adorned couch, and God received his soul. Moses then left the cave, which immediately vanished, so that none might know or understand how it had happened. When Eleazar saw Moses return alone, he said to him: "O my teacher, where is my father?" Moses replied: "He has entered Paradise." Then both descended from the mountain into the camp. When the people saw Moses and Eleazar return without Aaron, they were not at all in the mood to lend faith to the communication of Aaron's death. They could not at all credit that a man who had overcome the Angel of Death was now overcome by him. Three opinions were then formed among the people concerning Aaron's absence. Some declared that Moses had killed Aaron because he was jealous of his popularity; some thought Eleazar had killed his father to become his successor as high priest; and there was also some who declared that he had been removed from earth to be translated to heaven. Satan had so incited the people against Moses and Eleazar that they wanted to stone them. Moses hereupon prayed to God, saying: "Deliver me and Eleazar from this unmerited suspicion, and also show to the people Aaron's bier, that they may not believe him to be still alive, for in their boundless admiration for Aaron they may even make a God of him." God then said to the angels: "Lift up on high the bier upon which lies My friend Aaron, so that Israel may know he is dead and my not lay hand upon Moses and Eleazar." The angels did as they were bidden, and Israel then saw Aaron's bier floating in the air, while God before it and the angels behind intoned a funeral song for Aaron. God lamented in the words, "He entereth into peace; they rest in their beds, each one that walketh in his uprightness," whereas the angels said: "The law of truth was in his mouth, and unrighteousness was not found in his lips: he walked with Me in peace and uprightness, and did turn many away from iniquity."

THE GENERAL MOURNING FOR AARON

When Israel beheld the funeral rites prepared in honor of Aaron by God and by the angels, they also prepared a funeral ceremony of thirty days in which all the people, men and women, adults and children, took part. This universal mourning had its foundation not only in Israel's emulation of the Divine mourning and of the ceremonies arranged by Moses and Eleazar, or in their wish to show their reverence for the deceased high priest, but first and foremost in the truth that the people deeply loved Aaron and deeply felt his death. They mourned for him even more than they did later for Moses; for the latter only a part of the people shed tears, but for Aaron, everyone. Moses, as a judge, was obliged to mete out justice to the guilty, so that he had enemies among the people, men who could not forget that he had pronounced them guilty in court. Moses, furthermore, was sometimes severe with Israel when he held up to them their sins, but never Aaron. The latter "loved peace and pursued peace, loved men and brought them near to the Torah. In his humility, he did not consider his dignity hurt by offering greetings first even to the lowliest, yes, he did not even fail in offering his greeting when he was certain that the man before him was wicked and godless. The lament of the angels for Aaron as one "who did turn many away from iniquity" was therefore well justified. This kindliness of his led many a sinner to reform, who at the moment when he was about to commit a sin thought to himself: "How shall I be able to lift up my eyes to Aaron's face? I, to whom Aaron was so kind, blush to do evil." Aaron recognized his especial task as that of the peace-maker. If he discovered that two men had fallen out, he hastened first to the one, then to the other, saying to each: "My son, dost thou not know what he is doing with whom thou hast quarreled? He beats at his heart, rends his garments in grief, and says, 'Woe is me! How can I ever again lift up my eyes and look upon my companion against whom I have acted so?'" Aaron would then speak to each separately until both the former enemies would mutually forgive each other, and as soon as they were again face to face salute each other as friends. If Aaron heard that husband and wife lived in discord, he would hasten to the husband, saying: "I come to thee because I hear that thou and thy wife live in discord, wherefore thou must divorce her. Keep in mind, however, that if thou shouldst in place of thy present wife marry another, it is very questionable if thy second wife will be as good as this one; for at your first quarrel she will throw up to thee that thou art a quarrelsome man, as was shown by thy divorce from thy first wife." Many thousands of unions were saved from impending rupture by the efforts and urgings of Aaron, and the sons born to the couples brought together anew usually received Aaron's name, owing, as they did, their existence to his intercession. Not less than eighty thousand youths bearing his name took part in the mourning for Aaron.

When Moses beheld the deep-felt sorrow of the heavenly beings and of men for Aaron, he burst into passionate weeping, and said: "Woe is me, that am now left all alone! When Miriam died, none came to show her the last marks of honor, and only I, Aaron, and his sons stood about her bier, wept for her, mourned her, and buried her. At Aaron's death, I and his sons were present at his bier to show him the last marks of honor. But alas! How shall I fare? Who will be present at my death? I have neither father nor mother, neither brother nor sister,-who then will weep for me?" God, however, said to him: "Be not afraid, Moses, I Myself shall bury thee amid great splendor, and just as the cave in which Aaron lied has vanished, that none may know the spot where Aaron is buried, so too shall no mortal know thy burial place. As the Angel of Death had no power over Aaron, who died 'by the kiss,' so shall the Angel of Death have no power over thee, and thou shalt die 'by the kiss.'" Moses grew calm at these words, knowing at last that he had his place among the blessed pious. Blessed are thy, for not only does God in person gather them to Him, but as soon as they are dead, the angels go joyously to meet them and with beaming faces go to greet them, saying, "Enter into peace."

THE FALSE FRIENDS

When Moses and Eleazar returned from the mountain without Aaron, Israel said to Moses: "We shall not release thee from this spot until thou showest us Aaron, dead or alive." Moses prayed to God, and He opened the cave and all Israel saw within it Aaron, lying dead upon a bier. They instantly felt what they had lost in Aaron, for when they turned to look at the camp, they saw that the clouds of glory that had covered the site of the camp during their forty years' march had vanished. They perceived, therefore, that God had sent these clouds for Aaron's sake only, and hence, with Aaron's death, had caused them to vanish. These among Israel who had been born in the desert, having now, owing to the departure of the clouds of glory, for the first time beheld the sun and moon, wanted to fall down before them and adore them, for the clouds had always hidden the sun and the moon from them, and the sight of them made a most awful impression upon them. But God said to them: "Have I not commanded you in My Torah: 'Take ye therefore good heed unto yourselves...lest thou lift up thine eyes unto heaven, and when thou seest the sun and the moon and the stars, even all the host of heaven, thou be drawn away and worship them, and serve them?' For it is God that led thee out of the furnace of Egypt, that thou mightest be the people of His inheritance."

The disappearance of the clouds of glory inspired Israel with terror, for now they were unaided against the attacks of enemies, whereas none had been able to enter into the camp of Israel while the clouds covered them. This fear was not, indeed, ungrounded, for hardly did Amalek learn that Aaron was dead and that the clouds of glory had vanished, when he at once set about harassing Israel. Amalek acted in accordance with the counsel his grandsire Esau had given him, for his words to his grandson had been: "In spite of all my pains, I did not succeed in killing Jacob, therefore be thou mindful of avenging me upon his descendants." "But how, alas!" said Amalek, "Shall I be able to compete with Israel?" Esau made answer: "Look well, and as soon as thou seest Israel stumble, leap upon them." Amalek looked upon this legacy as the guiding star of his actions. When Israel trespassed, saying with little faith, "Is the Lord among us, or not?" Amalek instantly appeared. Hardly had Israel been tempted by its spies wickedly to exclaim, "Let us make a captain, and let us return into Egypt," when Amalek was upon the scene to battle with Israel. In later times also Amalek followed this policy, and when Nebuchadnezzar moved to Jerusalem in order to destroy it, Amalek took up his position one mile away from the holy city, saying: "If Israel should conquer, I should declare that I had come to assist them, but should Nebuchadnezzar be victorious, then shall I cut off the flight of the fleeing Israelites." His hopes were realized, for Nebuchadnezzar was victorious, and standing at the crossway, he cut down the fleeing Israelites, and added insult to injury by hurling invectives against God and the people, and ridiculing them.

When, after Aaron's death, Amalek no longer considered Israel dangerous, since the clouds had disappeared, he instantly set about making war upon them. Amalek did not, however, go in open warfare against Israel, but tried through craft to attain what he dared not hope for in open warfare. Concealing their weapons in their garments, the Amalekites appeared in Israel's camp as if they meant to condole with them for Aaron's death, and the unexpectedly attacked them. Not content with this, the Amalekites disguised themselves in Canaanite costume and spoke the speech of the latter, so that the Israelites might not be able to tell if they had before them Amalekites, as their personal appearance seemed to show, or Canaanites, as their dress and speech indicated. The reason for this disguise was that Amalek knew that Israel had inherited the legacy from their ancestor Isaac that God always answered their prayer, hence Amalek said: "If we now appear as Canaanites, they will implore God to send them aid against the Canaanites, and we shall slay them." But all these wiles of Amalek were of no avail. Israel couched their prayer to God in these words: "O Lord of the world! We know not with what nation we are now waging war, whether with Amalek or with Canaan, but whichsoever nation it be, pray visit punishment upon it." God heard their prayer and, promising to stand by them, ordered them totally to annihilate their enemy, saying: "Although ye are now dealing with Amalek, do not treat him like Esau's other sons, against whom ye may not war, but try totally to destroy them, as if they were Canaanites." Israel acted according to this command, slaying the Amalekites in battle, and dedicating their cities to God. Amalek's only gain in this enterprise was that, at the beginning of the war, they seized a slave woman who had once belonged to them, but who later passed over into the possession of the Israelites.

For Israel this attack of Amalek had indeed serious consequences, for as soon as they perceived the approach of the enemy, they were afraid to continue the march to Palestine, being now no longer under the protection of the clouds, that vanished with Aaron's death; hence they determined to return to Egypt. They actually carried out part of this project by retreating eight stations, but the Levites pursued them, and in Moserah there arose a bitter quarrel between those who wanted to return to Egypt and the Levites who insisted upon the continuance of the march to Palestine. Of the former, eight tribal divisions were destroyed in this quarrel, five Benjamite, and one each of the Simeonite, Gadite, and Asherite divisions, while of the Levites one division was completely extirpated, and three others decimated in such a way that they did not recover until the days of David. The Levites were finally victorious, for even their opponents recognized that it had been folly on their part to desire to return to Egypt, and that their loss had been only a punishment because they had not arranged a mourning ceremony adequate to honor a man of Aaron's piety. They thereupon celebrated a grand mourning ceremony for Aaron in Moserah, and it is for this reason that people later spoke of this place as the place where Aaron died, because the great mourning rites took place there.

THE BRAZEN SERPENT

Owing to the king of Edom's refusal to permit Israel to pass through his land, they were obliged, at the very point when they believed themselves at the end of their march, to continue it, so as to go around the land of Edom. The people, weary of the many years' marches, now became peevish, saying: "We had already been close to the promised land, and now must turn about once more! It was the same with our fathers who, close to their goal, had to turn back and roam about for thirty-eight years. Thus will it be with us!" In their dejection they set about murmuring against God and Moses, "master and servant being to them as one." They complained that they were entirely thrown upon manna as a means of sustenance. This last mentioned complaint came from those in regard to whom God had vowed that they should never see the land which He had sworn unto the Patriarchs. These people could not bear the sight of the products of Palestine's soil, dying as soon as they beheld them. Now that they had arrived at the outskirts of the promised land, the merchants brought into the camp of the Israelites the native products, but these, unable to partake of them, still had to continue to gather sustenance exclusively from manna.

Then a voice sounding from the heavens became audible upon earth, making this announcement: "Come hither and behold, O ye men! Come hither and hearken, ye the serpent with the words, 'Dust shalt thou eat,' yet it complained not of its food. But ye, My people that I have led out of Egypt, for whom I caused manna to rain down from heaven, and quails to fly from the sea, and a spring to gush forth from the abyss, ye do murmur against Me on account of manna, saying, 'Our soul loatheth this light bread.' Let now the serpents come, that complained not, even though whatever food they ate tasted only of the dust, and let them bite those who murmur though they have a food that possesses every conceivable flavor. The serpent, which was the first creature to slander its Maker and was therefore punished, shall now punish this people, which, not profiting by the example of the serpent's punishment, blasphemes its Creator by declaring that the heavenly food that He sends them would finally bring them death." The very serpents that during the forty years' march had been burned by the cloud of glory and lay heaped up high round about the camp, these same serpents now bit the people so terribly that their poison burned the souls of those whom they attacked.

When Moses betook himself to those who had been bitten, hearing that they were too ill to come to him, they, conscious of their guilt, said to him: "We have sinned, because we have spoken against the Lord and against thee; pray unto the Lord, that He take away the serpents from us." Such was the meekness of Moses, that he instantly forgave the people's transgression in regard to himself, and at once implored God's aid. God also, however, forgave their sin as soon as they had shown penitence, and thus set an example to man likewise to grant forgiveness when it is requested.

As a healing for those who had been bitten, God now bade Moses to make a serpent of brass, and put it upon a pole, that it might come to pass that every one who was bitten might look upon it and live. Moses did as he was bidden, and made a serpent of brass. As soon as he hurled it on high, it remained floating in the air, so that all might be able to look upon it. He mad the serpent brass, because in Hebrew Nahash signifies "snake" and Nehoshet, "brass"; hence Moses made the serpent of a substance that had a sound similar to that of the object fashioned out of it. It was not, however, the sight of the serpent of brass that brought with it healing and life; but whenever those who had been bitten by the serpents raised their eyes upward and subordinated their hearts to the will of the heavenly Father, they were healed; if they gave no thought to God, they perished.

Looking upon the serpent of brass brought about healing not only to those who had been bitten by serpents, but also to those who had been bitten by dogs or other animals. The cure of the latter was effected even more quickly than that of the former, for a casual glance sufficed for them, whereas the former were healed only after a long and insistent gaze.

AT ARNON

The murmurs of the people, on account of which God sent upon them the serpents, took place in Zalmonah, a place where grew only thorns and thistles. Thence they wandered on to Punon, where God's punishment overtook them. In the following two stations also, in Oboth and Iye-abarim, they continued their hostile actions against God, who for this reason was full of wrath against them, and did not look upon them again with favor until they reached Arnon. God's favor was instantly shown during Israel's passage through the valley of Arnon, where He wrought for Israel miracles as great as those of yore at the passage through the Red Sea. This valley was formed by two lofty mountains that lay so close together that people upon the two summits of them could converse with one another. But in passing from one mountain to the other, one had to cover a distance of seven miles, having first to descend into the valley, and then again to ascend the other mountain. The Amorits, knowing that Israel should now have to pass through the valley, assembled in innumerable multitudes, and a part of them hid in the caves, of which there were many on the slopes of the mountain, while another part of them awaited Israel in the valley below, hoping to attack and destroy them unexpectedly from above and from below in their passage through the valley. God, however, frustrated this plan, bringing it to pass that Israel did not descend into the valley at all, but stayed above, through the following miracle. For whereas the mountain on the one side of the valley was full of caves, the other consisted entirely of pointed rocks; and God moved this rocky mountain so close up to the other, that the jutting rocks of the one entered into the caves of the other, and all the Amorites that were concealed within them were crushed.

It was the rocky mountain that was moved, and not the other, for this same rocky mountain was the beginning of the promised land, and at the approach of Israel from the other mountain, which was Moabite, the land leaped to meet them, for it awaited them most longingly.

An old proverb says: "If you give a piece of bread to a child, tell its mother about it." God, likewise, wanted Israel to know the great miracles He had accomplished for their sake, for they had no inkling of the attack the heathens had planned to make upon them. God therefore bade the well that had reappeared since their stay in Beeroth to flow past the caves and wash out parts of the corpses in great numbers. When Israel not turned to look upon the well, they perceived it in the valley of the Arnon, shining like the moon, and drawing corpses with it. Not until then did they discover the miracles that had been wrought for them. Not only did the mountains at first move together to let them pass, and then again move apart, but God saved them from great peril. They now intoned a song of praise to the well that revealed to them the great miracle.

When, at the passage through the Red Sea, Israel wanted to intone a song of praise, Moses did not let them do it alone, but first sang to them the song they were to sing to the Lord. For then Israel was young, and could only repeat what its teacher Moses sang before them, but when the nation reached Arnon, it was fully grown, after its forty years' march through the desert. Now the Israelites sang their own song, saying: "O Lord of the world! It behooves Thee to work miracles for us, whereas it is our duty to intone to Thee songs of praise." Moses had no part in the song of praise to the well, for the well had given occasion to his death in the desert, and no man can be expected to sing about his executioner. As Moses wanted have nothing to do with this song, God demanded that His own name also be not mentioned in it, acting in this instances like the king who was invited to a prince's table, but refused the invitation when he learned that his friend was not to be present at the feast. The song to the well was as follows: "This is the well that the Patriarchs of the world, Abraham, Isaac, and Jacob, have digged, the princes olden times have searched, the heads of the people, the lawgivers of Israel, Moses and Aaron, have made its water to run with their staves. In the desert Israel received it as a gift, and after they had received it, it followed Israel upon all their wanderings, to lofty mountains and deep valleys. Not until they came to the boundary of Moab did it disappear, because Israel did not observe the words of the Torah."

Israel sang a song to the well alone, and not to manna, because they had on several occasions railed against the heavenly food, and therefore God said: "I do not wish ye to find fault with manna, nor yet to have ye praise it now," and He would not permit them to sing a song of praise to manna.

SIHON, THE KING OF THE AMORITES

The crushing of those concealed in the caves of the mountain at Arnon was only the beginning of the miracles God wrought for Israel during their conquest of the land. It was at Arnon, too, that Sihon, the king of the Amorites, and his people who, hardly a month after Aaron's death, rushed upon Israel, were completely destroyed by them. This Amorite king, and likewise Og, the king of Basham, were sons of Ahiah, whose father Shemhazai was one of the fallen angels. In accordance with his celestial origin Sihon was a giant who none could withstand, for he was of enormous stature, taller than any tower in all the world, his thigh-bone alone measuring eighteen cubits, according to the big cubit of that time. In spite of his huge size he was also fleet of foot, wherefore he was called Sihon, "foal," to indicate the celerity with which he moved, for his true name was Arad.

Moses was sorely afraid of waging war against this giant, but God put Sihon's and Og's guardian angels in chains, and then said to Moses: "Behold, I have begun to deliver up Sihon and his land before thee: begin to possess, that thou mayest inherit his land." For indeed after the angels of Sihon and his people had fallen, Moses had nothing more to fear, for his enemies were thus delivered into his hands. God assured Moses that "He would begin to put the dread of him and the fear of him upon the peoples that are under the whole heaven," by bidding the sun to stand still during his war against Sihon, that all the world might see that God battled for Moses.

Moses now asked if he might before waging war send ambassadors to Sihon to request him to permit Israel to pass through the land. God replied: "How now! I commanded thee, 'Rise up, contend with him in battle, begin to possess his land!' and thou wantest to send him messengers of peace?" Moses, however, replied: "I desire only to follow Thy example when Thou didst wish to lead Israel out of Egypt, and yet didst send me to Pharaoh with the message to let Israel, Thy people, pass out, even though Thou couldst have consumed all of Egypt with one flash of lightning. When Thou didst reveal the Torah, too, Thou didst offer it to the heathen nations for acceptance before giving it to Israel." God saw the justice of Moses' words, and commanded him never in the future to declare war upon a city before previously urging the people to surrender in peace.

Moses hereupon sent a missive to Sihon in which he requested him to permit Israel to pass through the land, promising him that he would see to it that the people should go along by the king's highway, so that he need have no cause to fear any deeds of violence upon married women, or seductions of girls. "We shall even," continued Moses, "pay for the water that is otherwise given freely, and likewise buy food-stuffs from thee at good prices." This letter to Sihon contained at its close, notwithstanding, the communication that the Israelites would bring war upon Sihon in case he did not permit them to pass through. Moses' assumption, however, that Sihon should permit Israel to pass through sounded in Sihon's ears like a summons to the keeper of a vineyard to permit one to harvest it. Sihon's answer therefore was as follows: "I and my brother Og receive tribute from all the other Canaanite kings to keep off their enemies from access to the land, and now you ask me to give you free access to Canaan!"

War between Sihon and Moses ensued, and ended in a brilliant victory for Israel. Sihon and his son, who equaled him in heroic strength, found their death in this fray. God had so brought it to pass that Israel had no need of laboriously waging war upon one city after another in Sihon's land, He had brought all the hosts of this Amorite king together into Heshbon. When this city therefore and the hosts within it were destroyed, all the rest of Sihon's land lay open before them. Israel's victory was all the more marvelous, because Heshbon was an exceptionally well fortified city, so that, had gnats been its inhabitants, it could not have been captured by mortal means, much less so when manned by the hero Sihon and his heroic warriors. This victory was made possible only by the fact that God visited them with convulsions so terrible that they rolled up and writhed in pain, unable to stand in the battle lines, so that Israel could cut them down while they were half dead from convulsive pains. God also drew masks over their faces, so that they could not see plainly, and taking one another for Israelites, slew their own people.

With the fall of Heshbon Israel came into possession of all the land of Sihon, with the exception of Jazer, and Moses therefore sent spies to that city. The men whom he sent there, Caleb and Phinehas, were not only capable warriors, but also pious men. They said: "Moses once sent spies who brought great misfortune upon all their generations, we will attack this city, trusting in God, and we are sure we shall not perish, because Moses has prayed for our welfare." They thereupon attacked Jazer, conquered it, and when upon the day after Moses had sent them out they returned to him, they informed him that they had conquered Jazer and slain its inhabitants.

THE GIANT OG

The war with Sihon took place in the month of Elul. In the following month of Tishri they rested on account of the holy days, but immediately after these they set out to battle against Og. This king did not hasten to his brother's aid, although he was only one day's distance from him, for he felt sure Sihon could conquer Israel without his assistance. He erred in this, however, as in some other matters. In the war of the four kings against the five, it was Og who had brought to Abraham news of his nephew Lot's bondage, assuming that Abraham would surely hasten to his kinsman's aid, be killed in battle, and thus enable Og to get possession of the beautiful Sarah. God, however, leaves no man unrewarded or unpunished. To reward him for hastening with quick steps to advise Abraham of Lot's captivity, God granted him life for five hundred years, but he was eventually killed because it was only a wicked motive that had induced him to perform this service for Abraham. He did not, as he had hoped, gain Sarah, but was slain by her descendant Moses.

The battle against Og took place in Edrei, the outskirts of which Israel reached toward nightfall. On the following morning, however, barely at gray dawn, Moses arose and prepared to attack the city, but looking toward the city wall, he cried in amazement, "Behold, in the night they have built up a new wall about the city!" Moses did not see clearly in the misty morning, for there was no wall, but only the giant Og who sat upon the wall with his feet touching the ground below. Considering Og's enormous stature, Moses' mistake was pardonable, for as a grave-digger of later times related, Og's thigh-bone alone measured more than three parasangs. "Once," so records Abba Saul, "I hunted a stag which fled into the thigh bone of a dead man. I pursued it and ran along three parasangs of the thigh-bone, yet had not reached its end." This thigh-bone, as was later established, was Og's.

This giant never in all his days made use of a wooden chair or bed, as these would have broken down beneath his weight, but sat upon iron chairs and lay upon iron beds. He was not only of gigantic build and strength, but of a breadth also that was completely out of proportion even with his height, for his breadth was one half his height, whereas the normal proportion of breadth to height is as one to three. In his youth Og had been a slave to Abraham, who had received him as a gift from Nimrod, for Og is none other than Eliezer, Abraham's steward. One day, when Abraham rebuked him and shouted at him, Eliezer was so frightened that one of his teeth fell out, and Abraham fashioned out of it a bed in which he always slept. Og daily devoured a thousand oxen or an equal number of other animals, and drank correspondingly, requiring daily not less than a thousand measures of liquids. He remained in Abraham's service until Isaac's marriage, when Abraham gave him his freedom as a reward for having undertaken the labor of wooing Rebekah for his son, and of fetching her to his house. God also rewarded him in this world, that this wicked wight might not lay claim to a reward in the world to come. He therefore made a king of him. During his reign he founded sixty cities, that he surrounded with high walls, the lowest of which was not less than sixty miles in height.

Moses now feared to wage war against Og, not only on account of his giant strength and huge size, which Moses had now witnessed with his own eyes, but he also thought: "I am only one hundred and twenty years old, whereas he is more than five hundred. Surely he could never have attained so great an age, had he not performed meritorious deeds." Moses also remembered that Og was the only giant that had escaped the hand of Amraphel, and he perceived in this a token of God's special favor toward Og. Moses feared, moreover, that Israel in the recent war against Sihon might have committed sins, so that God would not now stand by them. "The pious are always afraid of the consequences of sin, and therefore do not rely upon the assurances God had made to them;" hence Moses now feared to advance upon Og even though God had promised him aid against his enemies. God, however, said to him: "What is thy hand, his destruction has been decreed since the moment when he looked with evil eyes upon Jacob and his family when they arrived in Egypt." For even then God had said to him: "O thou wicked knave, why dost thou look upon them with all evil eye? Verily, thine eye shall burst, for thou shalt fall into their hands."

Og met his death in the following fashion. When he discovered that Israel's camp was three parasangs in circumference, he said: "I shall now tear up a mountain of three parasangs, and cast it upon Israel's camp, and crush them." He did as he had planned, pulled up a mountain of three parasangs, laid it upon his head, and came marching in the direction of the Israelite camp, to hurl it upon them. But what did God do? He caused ants to perforate the mountain, so that is slipped from Og's head down upon his neck, and when he attempted to shake it off, he teeth pushed out and extended to left and right, and did not let the mountain pass, so that he now stood there with the mountain, unable to throw it from him. When Moses saw this, he took an axe twelve cubits long, leaped ten cubits into the air, and dealt a blow to Og's ankle, which caused the giant's death.

This was the end of the last of the giants, who was not only last in time, but also in significance, for despite his height and strength, he was the most insignificant of the giants who perished in the flood.

With Og's death all his lands fell to the lot of the Israelites without another sword's stroke, for God has so ordained it that al of Og's warriors were with him at his encounter with Israel, and after Israel had conquered these, only women and children remained in all the land. Had Israel been obliged to advance upon every city individually, they would never have finished, on account of the number of the cities and the strength of the hosts of the Amorites.

Not alone Sihon and Og, the kings of the Amorites, were such giants and heroes, but all the Amorites. When Hadrian conquered Jerusalem, he boasted of his victory, whereupon Rabba Johanan, the son of Zakkai, said to hi: "Boast not of thy victory over Jerusalem, for, had not God conquered it for thee, thou shouldst never have gained it." He thereupon led Hadrian to a cave where he showed him the corpses of the Amorites, each of which was eighteen cubits, and said: "When we were worthy of victory, these fell into our hands, but now, on account of our sins, dost thou rule over us."

The victory over Sihon and his hosts was as great as that over Pharaoh and his hosts, and so was the victory over Og and his hosts. Each of these victories was as important as that over the thirty-one kings that Joshua later captured, and it would well have behooved Israel to sing songs of praise to their Lord as after Pharaoh's destruction. David later made good this omission, for he intoned a song of praise in gratitude for the victory God had lent to Israel over Sihon and Og.

Without direct assistance from God these victories would not have been possible, but He sent hornets upon them, and their destruction was irrevocable. Two hornets pursued ever Amorite; one bit one eye, the second the other eye, and the poison of these little creatures consumed those bitten by them. These hornets remained on the east side of the Jordan, and did not pursue Israel's march to the regions west of the Jordan, nevertheless they wrought great havoc among the Canaanites of the region west of the Jordan. The hornets stood on the eastern bank of the Jordan, and spat their venom across to the opposite bank, so that the Canaanites that were hit became blind and were disarmed.

When God promised Moses to send an angel to Israel, he declined the offer with the words: "If Thy presence go not with me, carry us not up hence," whereupon God replied: "Thou complainest because I desire to send only an angel to assist thee to conquer the land. As truly as thou livest, I shall now send thee not even an angel, but a hornet to destroy the enemies of Israel. It is, however, for thy sake alone that I deliver the enemy into Israel's hands, and not as if Israel deserved it through their own good deeds."

Og's bed, fashioned out of ivory, that measured nine arms' length, taking the giant's arm as a standard, Og had preserved in the Ammonite city Rabbah, for he knew that Israel would penetrate neither to the land of the Ammonites nor of the Moabites, because God had prohibited them from coming too close to Lot's descendants. He likewise forbade them to wage war with the Edomites; in this way Esau, a son kind to his father Isaac, was rewarded by not having his descendants, the Edomites, molested by Israel. God said to Israel: "In this world ye shall have no sway over the mountain Seir, Edom's realm, but in the future world, when ye shall be released, then shall ye obtain possession of it. Until then, however, beware of the sons of Esau, even when they fear ye, much more so when ye shall dwell scattered among them."

MOSES' SPEECH OF ADMONITION

As Abraham before his death spoke to his son Isaac, he to his son Jacob, and Jacob in turn to his sons, words admonishing them to walk in the ways of the Lord, so Moses also did not depart from this world without previously calling Israel to account for their sins, and admonishing them to observe the commandments of the Lord. Moses' speech of admonition had a greater effect than the revelation of the Decalogue upon Mount Sinai, for whereas Israel, shortly after they had said on Sinai, "We shall do according as we have heard," transgressed by worshipping the Golden Calf, Moses' words of admonition had left a powerful impression upon them, and he restored them to God and the Torah. God therefore said, "As a reward to thee because thy words of exhortation have brought Israel to follow Me, I shall designate these words as thine, even though thou didst speak them only in execution of My command."

Moses did not, however, make his speech of exhortation to the people until after the victory of Sihon and Og, for Moses thought: "Were I to have called them to account before these victories, they would have answered, 'He is trying to recall to us our sins because he is unable to lead us into the promised land against Sihon and Og, and he is seeking our sins as an excuse.'" But after Moses had proven what he could do, he could safely venture to recall to the people their sins. He now assembled all classes of Israel, the nobles as well as the common people, saying to them: "I will now give you a severe rebuke for your sins, and if any one have something to offer as an excuse, let him now advance it." In this way he shut off the possibility of their saying later on, "Had we heard the words of the son of Amram, we should have answered each word fourfold and fivefold."

Moses now recounted the ten temptations with which they tempted God: how at the Red Sea they had repented having followed Him, and had even turned back three stations on the way to Egypt; how even after the miracle that clove the Red sea for them, they had so little faith in God as to say, "Just as at this spot we passed unharmed through the Red Sea, so also did the Egyptians in another part of it." At Marah and at Rephidim they tried God on account of the dearth of water, and as they twice rebelled against God on account of water, so also did they on account of manna. They infringed upon the two laws God had given them in regard to manna, storing it from one day to the next, and going to gather it on the Sabbath, although God had strictly forbidden both. On account of their lust for flesh also they twice transgressed, murmuring for flesh at the same time as they received manna, although manna completely satisfied their needs; and after God had granted their wish and had sent them quails, they remains content for a short time only, and then again demanded quails, until God granted them that wish also. "But the worst of all," Moses told them, "was the worship of the Golden Calf. And not only that, but again in Paran, misled by the spies, ye transgressed in desiring to make an idol, and under its guidance to return to Egypt."

Moses then pointed out to them that it was owing to their sin that they had strayed about in the desert for forty years, for otherwise God would have brought them to Palestine on the same day as He had led them out of Egypt. He not only reproached Israel with the sins they had committed against God, but also with the evil they had worked Moses himself, mentioning how they had thrown their infants into his lap, saying, "What food hast thou for these?" On this occasion it was evident how good and pious a nation was that before Moses, for all the sins he enumerated to them had been committed not by them, but by their fathers, all of whom had in the meantime died, yet they were silent, and made no answer to this severe reprimand their leader gave them. Moses did not, however, merely admonish the people to walk in the ways of the Lord, but he said to Israel: "I am near to death, Whosoever hath learned from me a verse, a chapter, or a law, let him come to me and learn it anew," whereupon he repeated all the Torah, and that, too, in the seventy languages of the world, that not Israel alone but all the heathen peoples, too, might hear the teachings of God.

BALAK, KING OF MOAB

"God allows nothing to stay unrewarded, not even a respectable word remains without its reward." The older of Lot's two daughters had called her son that was conceived in guilt, Moab, "by the father," whereas the younger, for the sake of decency, called her son Ammon, "son of my people," and she was rewarded for her sense of propriety. For when Moses wanted to overrun the descendants of Lot with war, God said to him: "My plans differ from thine. Two doves shall spring from this nation, the Moabite Ruth and the Ammonite Naomi, and for this reason must these two nations be spared."

The treatment God bade Israel accord to these two nations was not, however, uniform. In regard to Moab, God said, "Vex not Moab, neither contend with them in battle," which portended that Israel was not to wage war against the Moabites, but that they might rob them or reduce them to servitude. In regard to the sons of Ammon, on the other hand, God forbade Israel to show these descendants of Lot's younger daughter even the slightest sign of hostility, or in any way to alarm them, so that Israel did not even show themselves in battle array to the Ammonites.

Israel's hostile, though not warlike, attitude toward Moab inspired these people and their kings with great fear, so much so that they seemed to be strangers in their own land, fearing as they did that they should have to fare like the Egyptians; for the Israelites had come to Egypt as strangers, but had in time possessed themselves of the land so that the Egyptians had to rent their dwelling-places from them. Their fear was still further increased by their belief that Israel would pay no attention to God's command to them not to wage war against Lot's descendants. This assumption of theirs was based on the fact the Israel had taken possession of the kingdoms of Sihon and Og, even though these had originally been part of Ammon's and Moab's possessions. Heshbon, Sihon's capital city, had formerly belonged to Moab; but the Amorites, thanks to Balaam and his father Beor's support, had taken from Moab these and some other regions. The Amorites had hired these two sorcerers to curse Moab, with the result that the Moabites were miserably defeated in the war against Sihon. "Woe to thee, Moab! Thou art undone, O people of Chemosh!" These and similar utterances were the ominous words that Balaam and his father employed against Moab. Chemosh was a black stone in the form of a woman, that the Moabites worshipped as their god.

As part of Moab passed into Sihon's possession so did a part of Ammon fall into Og's hands, and because Israel had appropriated these land, the Moabites feared they would filch from them all their land. In great alarm they therefore gathered together in their fastnesses, in which they knew themselves to be safe from Israel's attacks. Their fear was in reality quite without foundation, for Israel never dreamed of transgressing God's command by waging war upon Lot's descendants. They might without compunction keep the former provinces of Moab and Ammon because they took them not from these, but from Sihon and Og, who had captured them.

At this time the king of Moab was Balak, who was formerly a vassal of Sihon, and in that capacity was known as Zur. After Sihon's death he was chosen king, though he was not worthy of a rank so high. Favored by fortune, he received royal dignity, a position that his father had never filled. Balak was a fitting name for this king, for he set about destroying the people of Israel, wherefore he was also called the son of Zippor, because he flew as swiftly as a bird to curse Israel. Balak was a great magician, who employed for his sorcery the following instrument. He constructed a bird with its feet, trunk, and head of gold, its mouth of silver, and its wings of bronze, and for a tongue he supplied it with the tongue of the bird Yadu'a. This bird was now placed by a window where the sun shone by day and the moon by night, and there it remained for seven days, throughout which burnt offerings were offered before it, and ceremonies performed. At the end of this week, the bird's tongue would begin to move, and if pricked by a golden needle, would divulge great secrets. It was this bird that had imparted to Balak all his occult lore. One day, however, a flame that suddenly leaped up burned the wings of this bird, which greatly alarmed Balak, for he thought that Israel's proximity had destroyed his instrument of sorcery.

The Moabites now perceiving that Israel conquered their enemies by supernatural means said, "Their leader had been bred in Midian, let us therefore inquire of the Midianites about his characteristics." When the elders of Midian were consulted, they replied, "His strength abides in his mouth." "Then," said the Moabites, "we shall oppose to him a man whose strength lies in his mouth as well," and the determined to call upon Balaam's support. The union of Moab and Midian establishes the truth of the proverb: "Weasel and Cat had a feast of rejoicing over the flesh of the unfortunate Dog." For there had always been irreconcilable enmity between Moab and Midian, but they united to bring ruin upon Israel, just as Weasel and Cat had united to put an end to their common enemy Dog.

Chapter 6

BALAAM, THE HEATHEN PROPHET

The man whom the Moabites and Midianites believed to be Moses' peer was none other than Laban, Israel's arch-enemy, who in olden days had wanted to root out entirely Jacob and all his family, and who had later on incited Pharaoh and Amalek against the people of Israel to bring about their destruction. Hence, too, the name Balaam, "Devourer of Nations," for he was determined to devour the nation of Israel. Just at this time Balaam was at the zenith of his power, for his curse had brought upon the Moabites their defeat at the hands of Sihon, and his prophecy that his compatriot Balak should wear the royal crown had just been fulfilled, so that all the kings sent ambassadors to seek advice from him. He had gradually developed from an interpreter of dreams to a sorcerer, and had not attained the still greater dignity of prophet, thus even surpassing his father, who had indeed been prophet too, but not so notable a one as his son.

God would permit the heathens to have no ground for exculpation, for saying in the future world, "Thou hadst kept us far from Thee." To them, as well as to Israel, he gave kings, sages, and prophets; but whereas the former showed themselves worthy of their high trust, the latter proved themselves unworthy of it. Both Solomon and Nebuchadnezzar were rulers over all the world: the former built the Temple and composed many hymns and prayers, the latter destroyed the Temple and cursed and blasphemed the Lord, saying, "I will ascend above the heights of the clouds; I will be like the Most High." Both David and Haman received great treasures from God, but the former employed them to secure a site for God's sanctuary, whereas the latter with his tried to destroy the whole nation. Moses was Israel's prophet, and Balaam was prophet of the heathens: but how great a contrast between these two! Moses exhorted his people to keep from sin, whereas Balaam counseled the nations to give up their moral course of life and to become addicted to lewdness. Balaam was also different from the Israelite prophet in his cruelty. They had such pity for the nations that misfortune among the heathens caused them suffering and sorrow, whereas Balaam was so cruel that he wanted to destroy an entire nation without any cause.

Balaam's course of life and his actions show convincingly why God withdrew from the heathen the gift of prophecy. For Balaam was the last of the heathen prophets. Shem had been the first whom God had commissioned to communicate His words to the heathens. This was after the flood, when God said to Shem: 'Shem, had My Torah existed among the previous ten generations, I suppose I should not have destroyed the world by the flood. Go now, announce to the nations of the earth My revelations, ask them if they will not accept My Torah." Throughout four hundred years did Shem go about as a prophet, but the nations of the earth did not heed him. The prophets that labored after him among the heathens were Job and his four friends, Eliphaz, Zophar, Bildad, and Elihu, as well as Balaam, all of whom were descendants of Nahor, Abraham's brother, from his union with Milcah. In order that the heathens might not say, "Had we had a prophet like Moses, we should have received the Torah," God gave them Balaam as a prophet, who in no way was inferior to Moses either in wisdom or in the gift of prophecy. Moses was indeed the greatest prophet among the Israelites, but Balaam was his peer among the heathens. But although Moses excelled the heathen prophet in that God called him without any previous preparation, whereas the other could obtain Divine revelations only through sacrifices, still Balaam had one advantage over the Israelite prophet. Moses had to pray to God "to shew him His ways," whereas Balaam was the man who could declare of himself that he "knew the knowledge of the Most High." But because, in spite of his high prophetic dignity, Balaam had never done anything good or kind, but through his evil tongue had almost destroyed all the world, God vowed a vow to His people that He would never exchange them for any other people or nation, and that He would never permit them to dwell in any land other than Palestine.

BALAK'S MESSENGERS TO BALAAM

Balak now sent messengers to Balaam with the following message: "Think not that I ask thy help against Israel exclusively in my own interests, and that thou canst expect from me alone honor and rewards for thy service, but rest assured that all nations will then honor thee, that Canaanites as well as Egyptians will cast themselves at thy feet when thou shalt have destroyed Israel. This people that hath gone out of Egypt hath covered with earth Sihon and Og, the eyes that guarded the whole land, and now they are about to destroy us as well. They are not, indeed, greater heroes than we, nor are their host more numerous than ours, but they conquer as soon as they open their lips in prayer, and that we cannot do. Try now to see if I may not gradually become their master, so that I may at least lead a certain per cent of them to destruction, be it only a twenty-fourth part of them."

Balak himself was even a greater magician and soothsayer than Balaam, but he lacked the gift of properly grasping prophetic observations. He knew through his sorcery that he was to be the cause of the death of twenty-four thousand Israelites, but he did not know in what way Israel was to suffer so great a loss, hence he requested Balaam to curse Israel, hoping by this curse to be able to restrain Israel from entering the Holy Land.

Balak's messengers to Balaam consisted of the elders of Moab and Midian. The latter were themselves great magicians, and by their art established the truth, that should Balaam obey Balak's summons, their mission against Israel would be successful, but should he hesitate even for a moment to follow them, nothing was to be expected from him. When they now reached Balaam and he bade them stay over night to await his answer, the elders of Midian instantly returned, for they knew that they had now nothing to expect from him. They said: "Is there such a father as hates his son? God is the father of Israel, He loves them. Shall He now, owing to a curse from Balaam turn His love into hatred?" Indeed, had the matter depended on Balaam's wishes, he would doubtless instantly have acquiesced and followed Balak's summons, for he hated Israel more than Balak, and was much pleased with the commission of the Moabite king. The elders that Balak had sent had besides in their possession all needful instruments of magic, so that Balaam might have no excuse for not instantly following them, but Balaam had, of course, to bide his time and first find out if God would permit him to go to Balak, hence he bade the Moabite messengers stay over night, because God never appears to heathen prophets save at night. As Balaam expected, God appeared by night and asked Balaam, "Who are these people with thee?"

Balaam was one of the three men whom God put to the test and who miserably failed to pass it. When God appeared to Cain and asked, "Where is Abel thy brother?" he tried to deceive God. He should have replied, "Lord of the world! What is hidden and what is open, both alike are known to Thee. Why then dost Thou inquire after my brother?" But instead of this he replied, "I know not. Am I my brother's keeper?" God therefore said to him: "Thou hast spoken thin own sentence. The voice of thy brother's blood crieth unto Me from the ground, and now cursed art thou." Hezekiah acted like Cain when the messengers from the king of Babylon came to him, and Isaiah the prophet asked him, "What said these men? And from whence came they unto thee?" Hezekiah should have answered, "Thou art a prophet of God, why dost thou ask me?" But instead of giving this answer, he replied haughtily and boastfully, "They are come from a far country unto me, even from Babylon." On account of this haughty answer Isaiah announced to the king this prophecy: "Behold, the days come, that all that is in thine house shall be carried to Babylon; and of thy sons that shall issue from thee, they shall be eunuchs in the palace of the king of Babylon."

The scoundrel Balaam, too, should have made answer to God's question, "What men are these with thee?" by saying, "Lord of the world! Everything lies open before Thee, and nothing is hidden from Thee, why then dost Thou ask me?" But he, on the other hand, made quite a different answer and started to boast, saying to God: "Although Thou dost not distinguish me, and dost not spread my fame over the world, still the kings seek me: Balak, the king of Moab, hath sent to ask me to curse Israel." Then God said, "Because thou speakest thus, thou shalt not curse the people," and added, "O thou wicked rascal! I said of Israel, He that toucheth them, toucheth the apple of My eye,' and yet thou wishest to touch them and curse them! Therefore shall thine eye be blinded." Thus Balaam became blind of one eye, as he had already been lame of one foot. Balaam now perceiving that God did not wish him to curse Israel said, "If it be so, then I shall bless them." God: "They have not need of thy blessing, for they are blessed." God said to Balaam as one says to a bee: "Neither thy honey nor thy sting."

BALAAM ACCEPTS BALAK'S INVITATION

On the following morning Balaam gave the elders of Moab his answer, saying that he would not follow Balak's call, but not betraying to them the truth, that God hat forbidden him to curse Israel. He said instead, "God said to me, 'Go not with these men, for that would be beneath thy dignity, but await nobler ambassadors.'" Balaam's plan was to insult Balak, so that he should send no further messengers to him, and no one might discover that he could accomplish nothing beyond the word of God. His expectations, however, were disappointed. The ambassadors in their turn, not quite painstaking in their representation of the truth, told their king that Balaam considered it beneath his dignity to appear in their escort, making no mention of God, but speaking as if the refusal came simply and exclusively from Balaam.

Balak thereupon sent more honorable ambassadors to Balaam, until he was at last obliged to admit that he could undertake nothing against God's command. Even then, it is true, he did not admit that his acceptance or refusal of Balak's invitation depended entirely upon God, but declared that he could, if he wished, do as he chose, but did not choose to transgress God's prohibition. In his second embassy Balak promised Balaam more for his service than he had offered him the first time. Balaam's answer was as follows: "If Balak would give me his house full of silver and gold, I cannot go beyond the word of the Lord my God." These words characterize the man, who had three bad qualities: a jealous eye, a haughty spirit, and a greedy soul. His jealousy was the reason why he wanted to curse Israel, whom he envied for their good fortune; in his haughtiness, he told the first messengers the falsehood that God would not let him go with them because it would be beneath his dignity; and his avarice was expressed in his answer to the second embassy in which he not only surreptitiously mentioned Balak's gold and silver, but spoke his mind by explaining to them that their master could not adequately compensate him for his service, saying, "If Balak were to hire hosts against Israel, his success would still be doubtful, whereas he should be certain of success if he hired me!"

He did not, however, give even the second embassy a decisive answer, but said to them also, "I cannot go beyond the word of the Lord my God, to do less or more. Now therefore I pray you, tarry ye also here this night, that I may know what the Lord will speak unto me more." These words of his held unconscious prophecies: "I cannot go beyond the word of the Lord," was as much as to say that he could not put the blessings of God to Israel to naught. "Tarry ye also here this night," contained the prophecy that this second embassy would be as much disappointed as the first, for although Balaam accompanied the second messengers, still he had no power to curse Israel, but only to bless them. Finally, the words, "What the Lord will speak unto me more," held a prediction that God would bestow even more benedictions upon the Israelites through him.

"God permits man to go upon the way he chooses to go." When God appeared to Balaam the first time he said to him, "Thou shalt not go with them;" but when Balaam still did not relinquish his desire to go to Balak,

God would not interfere. Hence, at His second appearance, God said to Balaam, "If the men be come to call thee, rise up, go with them; but only the word which I speak unto thee, that shalt thou do."

"Audacity prevails even before God." Balaam's steadfast insistence upon his wish wrested from God his consent to Balaam's journey to Moab. He warned him of its consequences, saying to him: "I take no pleasure in the destruction of sinners, but if thou are bound to go to thy destruction, do so! Whosoever leads righteous men astray upon an evil way, will fall into the ditch of his own digging!" Balaam was misled by God's behavior toward him, and thus plunged into destruction. When God first appeared to him and asked him, "What men are these with thee?" this blasphemer thought: "God know them not. It seems clear that there are times when He is not aware of what goes on, and I shall now be able to do with His children as I wish." Balaam was misled by God because he had with his words seduced to unchastity people who had up to his time lived in purity. God's apparent change of decision, that first prohibited him from going to Balak, and then permitted him to do so, completely bewildered him, so that he thought, "God at first said to me, 'Go thou not with them,' but the second time He said, 'Go with them.' So too will He change His words, 'Curse them not,' into 'Curse them.'" Just as Balaam was confused by God, so too were the magicians that Balak had sent to him. At the first visit these had through their magic lore established that he would accept Balak's invitation, but God made him decline it; at the second time, on the other hand, they established that he would not accept the invitation, and God made him obey their summons.

BALAAM'S ASS

Balaam could hardly await the morning, rejoicing no less than Balak's messengers at God's consent to his journey to Balak, and still hoping that he might succeed in bringing disaster upon Israel. In his haste to set out, he himself saddled his ass although he did not lack servants, whereupon God said: "O thou villain, their ancestor Abraham forestalled thee, for he too rose up early in the morning and in person saddled his ass to lead Isaac to sacrifice in fulfillment of the command that had reached him."

The ass that Balaam took with him had been created on the sixth day of the creation. He had received it as a gift from Jacob, that he might not give evil counsel to Pharaoh concerning Jacob's children. It was upon his advice, nevertheless, that Pharaoh forced the Israelites to make bricks. He took his two sons, Jannes and Jambres, for it behooves a noble man always to have at least two companions upon any journey that he undertakes.

Although God had now granted him permission to go on the journey, still His wrath was kindled when he set out. God said, "Behold, this man! He knows that I read each man's heart, and knows also that he departeth only to curse Israel." This wickedness on his part had the result that even the Angel of Mercy turned against him as an enemy, standing in his way. At first the ass alone perceived the angel, and not Balaam, for God has so arranged it that human beings may not perceive the angels that surround them or else they would through terror lose their reason. The ass, on the other hand, instantly perceived the angel. He at first stood in her way as she was in the middle of the road, so that she could turn aside on both sides; then she perceived him when the road narrowed, and she could turn to one side only; and finally she reached a spot where there was no road at all to which she could turn either on this side or on that. This was to teach Balaam the following lesson: if he wished to curse Abraham's children, he should have leeway on both sides, Ishmael's children and Keturah's children; if he wanted to curse Isaac's children, one side would still be open to him, Esau's children; but if he wanted to curse Jacob's children, he should never bring it to pass, for they are protected on both sides, on the one hand by Abraham and Isaac, on the other by Jacob and Levi, while God watches over them from above. "The wall on this side, and on that side," through which place he had to pass, were furthermore to indicate to him that he could not become master over Israel, who have in their possession the tables of the law, "that were written on both their sides." When the ass reached the wall that Jacob and Laban had erected as a token that they "would never pass over it for harm," she thrust her feet against it, to punish him for having broken his agreement with Jacob.

Balaam, who had with blows attempted to make the ass walk straight ahead, flew into a rage when she lay down altogether and would not budge from the spot, so that he smote her all the more. Then the Lord opened the mouth of the ass, and permitted her to use speech, a gift that she had possessed ever since her creation, but had not until then used. She said, "What have I done unto thee, that thou has smitten me these three times?" The first words of the ass were so chosen as to call Balaam's attention to the wickedness and uselessness of his undertaking against Israel; "Three times" was to remind him that he wished to curse a nation that "three times" in every year arranged pilgrimages to the Lord. The ass's speech was altogether to serve as a warning to Balaam to beware of his mouth, and not to curse Israel. The ass, through her speaking, was to instruct him that the mouth and the tongue are in God's hand.

Balaam answered the ass in the language in which she had addressed him, in Hebrew, which he did not, however, speak fluently. He said, "Because thou hast mocked me: I would there were a sword in mine hand, for now I had killed thee." The ass thereupon replied, "Thou canst not kill me save with a sword in thy hand; how then wilt thou destroy an entire nation with thy mouth!" Balaam was silent, knowing no reply. The ass did not only make him ridiculous in the eyes of the elders of Moab that accompanied him, but she also exposed him as a liar. For when the ambassadors asked him why he had not chosen a horse rather than an ass for his journey, he answered that his saddle horse was in the pasture. Then the ass interrupted him, saying, "Am not I thine ass upon which thou hast ridden all thy life long?" Balaam: "I use thee as a beast of burden, but not for the saddle." The ass: "Nay, upon me has thou ridden since thine earliest day, and thou hast always treated me with as much affection as a man treats his wife." Balaam had now to admit that the ass had spoken the truth.

Balak's princes were much amazed at this extraordinary miracle, but the ass died the moment she had spoken what she had to say. God did this for two reasons, firstly because He feared that the heathens might worship this ass were she to stay alive; and secondly because God wanted to spare Balaam the disgrace of having people point to his ass and say, "This is she that worsted Balaam." By this action it can be seen how highly God prizes the honor or pious men, if He even sought to spare the honor of this villain. It is out of consideration to mankind, also, that God has closed the mouth of animals, for were they to speak, man could not well use them for his service, since the ass, the most stupid of all animals, when she spoke, confounded Balaam, the wisest of the wise.

BALAAM RUNS INTO HIS OWN DESTRUCTION

While all this was going on, Balaam still did not perceive that God's angel stood before him. God meant to show him that in His hand is not only the tongue of man, but his eye as well, so that as long as He chooses, man will fail to see what is directly before his nose. But God suddenly permitted Balaam to see the angel with a sword drawn in his hand, and Balaam fell flat on his face. For, being uncircumcised, Balaam might not listen to the words of God or of an angel, standing erect; hence, upon perceiving the angel, who instantly began to address him, Balaam cast himself upon the ground. The sword in the angel's hand did not signify that he meant to strike Balaam, for a breath from his mouth would have sufficed to kill myriads, but it was to point out the following truth to Balaam: "The mouth was given to Jacob, but to Esau and to the other nations, the sword. Thou are about to change thy profession, and to go out against Israel with his own weapon, and therefore shalt thou find death through the sword that is thy own weapon."

The angel now said to Balaam: "If I have been commissioned to demand restitution from thee for the injustice thou hast offered to the ass, that can show neither meritorious deeds of her own nor of her fathers, how much the more must I stand up as the avenger of an entire nation, that have their own merits and can refer to the merits of their fathers. But to return to the ass, why didst thou smite her, that turned from the road only because she saw me and was frightened?" Balaam was a shrewd sinner, for he knew that Divine punishment could be averted only by penitence, and that the angels have no power to touch a man who, after sinning, says, "I have sinned." Hence he said to the angel, "I have sinned," but added, "I did not set out until God said to me, 'Rise up, go with them;' and now thou sayest to me, 'Return.' But this is the Lord's way. Did He not also at first tell Abraham to sacrifice his son, and then He caused an angel to call out to him, 'Lay not thine hand upon the lad?' It is His custom first to give a command, and the through an angel to recall it. So also did He indeed say to me, 'Go with them;' but if it displeaseth thee, I shall turn back." The angel replied: "All that I have done was to thy advantage, but if thou are bound to plunge into destruction, do so, go with these people, but destruction is decreed for all of you. Think not, however, that thou shalt do as thou wilt, for thou shalt have to say what I desire thee to speak, and to restrain what I wish to remain unuttered."

In spite of the warnings he had received from God and the angel, he was not to be restrained from taking this fatal step, but in his hatred toward Israel still cherished the hope that he should succeed in obtaining God's consent to curse Israel, and he continued his journey in this happy expectation.

BALAAM WITH BALAK

Whensoever God wished to humble an evil-doer, He at first exalts him, to fill him with pride. So too He humbled Balaam after exalting him, for at first Balak had sent princes of little distinction to him, whereupon God said to him, "Thou shalt not go with them." When, however, he sent many renowned princes to him, God said to Balaam, "Go with them," but this journey brought him nothing but humiliation and ruin, for he fared in accordance with the proverb, "Pride goeth before destruction, and an haughty spirit before a fall." God does this so that men might not say, "Whom hath God destroyed? Surely not that insignificant person," hence God exalts sinners before their fall.

When Balaam approached the Moabite boundaries, he sent messengers to Balak to announce his arrival, and Balak went forth to his country's border to meet him. Pointing to the boundary lines, Balak said to Balaam: "These have been fixed since Noah's days, that no nation might push into the realm of another, but Israel set out to destroy the boundaries, as their attitude toward Sihon and Og shows, into whose kingdoms they entered." He then greeted him with the words: "Did I not twice sent unto thee to call thee? Wherefore camest not thou unto me? Am I not able indeed to promote thee to honor?" Balak unconsciously uttered a prophecy, for in truth Balaam went hence in disgrace and dishonor, and not covered with glory, as he could not fulfil the other's wish to curse Israel. It should now have been Balaam's duty, had he really desired to be of service to the king of Moab, to say to him, "Why dost thou attempt to do what will bring thee misfortune, and finally utter ruin?" But he spoke quite differently instead, boastfully bragging with his gift of prophecy, pointing out that he was the last prophet among the heathens. "And," continued he, "I, the last prophet among the heathens, shall thus counsel thee. The ancestor of that nation erected to God an altar upon which, thrice annually, he offered up seven oxen and seven rams; do thou, then, erect seven altars, and offer up on each seven oxens and seven rams." God laughed when he heard this counsel, saying: "Every beast of the forest is Mine, and the cattle upon a thousand hills. I know all the fowls of the mountains: and the wild beasts of the field are Mine. If I were hungry, I would not tell thee: for the world is Mine, and the fullness thereof. Will I eat the flesh of bulls, or drink the blood of goats?"

Balak led his guest from the border-line to the interior of the land, taking pains to show him great multitudes of the people, having bazaars erected for that purpose. Pointing to these multitudes, among which there were also may children, Balak said, "Look thou, how Israel plan to destroy these multitudes of people that have done them no injury."

Balak slew for Balaam's welcome one ox and one sheep, proving the proverb, "The pious promise little and do much, the wicked promise much and do little." Balak had sent word to Balaam, saying, "I will promote thee unto very great honor;" yet when he arrived, he offered him for food only one ox and one sheep. Suppressing his rage, Balaam thought, "Is that all that he offers me! He will have to pay for this to-morrow," for he instantly determined to have him offer up many sacrifices on the following day to punish him for having treated him in so niggardly a fashion.

BALAAM'S SACRIFICES REFUSED

On the following morning Balak took Balaam and brought him upon into the high places of Baal. For Balak was even a greater magician and soothsayer than Balaam, who allowed himself like a blind man to be led by him. He led him to this spot because through his magic lore he knew that Israel was to suffer a great misfortune upon the heights of Baalpeor, and he thought it was to be Balaam's curse that would effect this disaster upon them. The relation of these two men to each other was like that between two men, one of whom has a knife in his hand, but does not know what part of the body to strike for slaughter, and the other knows the part of the body, but has no knife. Balak knew the place where disaster awaited Israel, but did not know how it was to be brought about, whereas Balaam knew how evil is conjured up, but did not know the places set for disaster, to which Balak had to lead him. Balaam's superiority over Balak and the other magicians lay in this, that he could accurately determine the moment in which God is wrathful, and it was for this reason that his curse was always effective because he knew how to curse at the very instant of God's anger. It is true that God is angry for one instant every day, to wit, during the third hour of the day, when the kings with crowns upon their head worship the sun, but this moment is of infinitesimally short duration. Fully eighty-five thousand and eighty-eight such moments make an hour, so that no mortal save Balaam had ever been able to fix that moment, although this point of time has its outward manifestations in nature, for while it lasts, the cock's comb becomes absolutely white, without even the smallest stripe of red. God's love for Israel, however, is so great that during the time that Balaam prepared to curse Israel, He did not wax angry at all, so that Balaam waited in vain for the moment of wrath.

Balaam now tried to obtain God's consent for Israel's curse through sacrifices, and hence bade Balak erect seven altars upon the high place of Baal, corresponding to the seven altars that since Adam had been erected by seven pious men, to wit: Adam, Abel, Noah, Abraham, Isaac, Jacob, and Moses. When the altars had been erected, he said to God: "Why didst Thou favor these people, if not for the sacrificed that they offered Thee? Were it not better for Thee to be adored by seventy nations than by one?" But the Holy Spirit answered, "'Better is a dry morsel and quietness therewith, than an house full of sacrifices and strife.' Dearer to Me is a dry offering of meal than all these many flesh offerings by which thou strivest to stir up strife between Me and Israel."

Now was Balaam's fate decided, for by his conduct he put himself into direct opposition to God, and hence his destruction was decreed, and from that moment the holy spirit of prophecy left him and he was nothing more than a magician. For Israel's sake, however, God granted him the honor of His revelation, but He did so grudgingly, as one loathes to touch an unclean thing. Hence He would not permit Balaam to come to Him, but rather appeared to Balaam. God's different treatment of Balaam and of Moses at the revelation is evident, for whereas the latter betook himself to the sanctuary to hear God's words, the former received God's revelation at any place whatsoever. It characterizes God's attitude toward them. Two men once knocked at a magnate's door, the one being a friend, who had a request to make, and the other a leprous beggar. The magnate said, "Let my friend enter, but I shall send the beggar's alms to the door, that he may not enter and pollute my palace." God called Moses to Him, whereas He did not desire Balaam to come to Him, but betook Himself there.

He found Balaam at the seven altars that he had erected, and said to him, "What doest thou here?" whereupon Balaam answered, "I have erected for Thee as many altars as the three fathers of Israel, and I have offered upon them bullocks and rams." God, however, said to him: "'Better is a dinner of herbs where love is, than a stalled ox and hatred therewith.' Pleasanter to Me is the meal of unleavened bread and herbs that the Israelites took in Egypt, than the bullocks that thou offerest out of enmity. O thou knave, if I wished for offerings, I should order Michael and Gabriel to bring them to Me, thou are mistaken if thou believest that I should accept offerings from the nations of the world, for I have vowed a vow to accept such from Israel alone." God thereupon handed him over to an angel who entered and settled in his throat, and would not permit Balaam to speak when he wanted to curse Israel.

BALAAM EXTOLS ISRAEL

Balaam now turned back to Balak, who awaited him with his princes. He now wanted to begin to curse Israel, but his mouth, far from being able to utter the words, was on the contrary compelled to praise and bless Israel. He said: "I found myself upon the high places, in company with the Patriarchs, and thou, Balak, hast cast me down from the heights; through thee did I lose the gift of prophecy. Both of us are ungrateful men if we wish to undertake evil against Israel, for, had it not been for their father Abraham, for whose sake God saved Lot out of the ruin of the cities, there should not be no Balak, for thou are one of Lot's descendants. And had it not been for Jacob, I, Laban's descendant, should not now be on earth, for no sons were born unto Laban until after Jacob had come into his house. Thou didst bring me out of Aram to curse Israel, but it was this land that their father Abraham left, laden with blessings, and it was this land also that their father Jacob entered, laden with blessings. Shall now a curse come upon them from this land? How can I curse them if he that curseth them bringeth a curse upon himself? Thou, moreover, wishest me even to curse Jacob. Hadst thou urged me to curse a nation that were only the descendants of Abraham or of Isaac, I might have been able to do so; but to curse Jacob's descendants is as bad as if a man were to come to a king and say to him, 'The crown that thou wearest upon thy head is worthless.' Would such a man be permitted to live? 'The Lord's portion is His people; Jacob is the lot of His inheritance.' 'In Israel,' said the Lord, 'will I be glorified.' How now should I curse them? How shall I curse whom God hath not cursed? Even when they have been worthy of a curse, they have not been cursed. When Jacob went in to receive the blessings, he went in through craft and said to his father, 'I am Esau, thy firstborn.' Doth not he deserve a curse out of whose mouth issueth a lie? Yet, far from being cursed, he was even blessed. Ordinarily a legion that stirs up sedition against their king is declared guilty by death, but Israel had denied God, saying, 'These be thy gods, O Israel.' Should they not then have been destroyed? God, however, did not even at that moment withdraw from them His love, but left to them the clouds of glory, manna, and the well, even after they had adored the Calf. Howsoever often they sinned and God threatened them with a curse, still He did not say that He would bring it upon them, whereas in His promises of blessings He always tells them that He Himself would send them upon Israel. How shall I curse when God doth not curse!

"Israel is a nation of whom God thought even before the creation of the world. It is the rock upon which the world is founded. For, when God was considering the scheme of the creation, He thought, 'How can I create the world if the idolatrous generation of Enosh and the generation of the flood will arouse My anger?' He was about to desist from the creation of the world, when He saw before Him Abraham's form, and He said, 'Now I have a rock upon which I can build, one upon which I can found the world.' How, too, should I curse this nation that are protected and surrounded by the merits of the Patriarchs and the wives of the Patriarchs as if by lofty mountains and steep hills, so that if Israel sin, God forgives them as soon as Moses prays to Him to be mindful of the Patriarchs!

"I was in error when I believed Israel could be easily attacked, but now I know that they have taken deep root in the earth, and cannot be uprooted. God forgives them many sins out of consideration for their having preserved the token of the Abrahamic covenant; and as powerless as I am to curse them alone, just as powerless am I to curse them together with another nation, for 'it is a people that shall dwell alone, and shall not be reckoned among the nations.' Israel is distinguished from all other nations by their custom, by their food, by the token of the covenant upon their bodies, and by the token upon their doorposts, wherefore God doth not judge them at the same time with other nations, for He judges the latter in the darkness of the night, but the former in bright daylight. Israel is a separate people, alone they enjoy the blessings God gives them, no other nation rejoices with Israel. So too in the Messianic time Israel will quite alone rejoice in delights and pleasures, whereas in the present world it may also partake of the universal welfare of the nations.

"I am not able to accomplish anything against a nation that zealously fulfils God's commandments, and that owes its existence to the devotion with which the wives of the Patriarchs obeyed the commandments of God. 'Let me die the death of the righteous, and let my last end be like his!'" Balaam in these words spoke an unconscious prophecy, to wit, that he should be entitled to participate in the fate of the righteous, to his share in the future world, if he died the death of the righteous, a natural death, but not otherwise. He died, however, a violent death, and thus lost his share in the future world.

BALAAM'S HOPES DISAPPOINTED

When Balak saw that Balaam, instead of cursing, praised and exalted Israel, he led him to the top of Pisgah, hoping that he might there succeed in cursing Israel. By means of his sorcery, Balak had discovered that Pisgah was to be a place of misfortune for Israel, hence he thought the Balaam would there utter his curse against Israel. He was, however, mistaken; the disaster that there awaited Israel was the death of their leader Moses, who died there, and God refused to grant Balaam's wish on this spot also.

God indeed appeared to Balaam, but what He said to him was: "Go again unto Balak, and bless Israel." Balaam now did not wish to return to Balak at all, to disappoint him a second time, but God compelled him to return to Balak and communicate to him the blessings of Israel. Balaam now turned back to Balak, whom he found standing by his burnt offering. But whereas on the first occasion the king had awaited Balaam, surrounded by all his princes, Balaam now saw only a few notables surrounding Balak. Most of the princes had deserted their king without awaiting Balaam, for they expected nothing further from him after the first disappointment he had caused them. Balak as well did not now receive him as kindly, but mockingly asked, "What hath the Lord spoken?" hinting in this way that Balaam was unable to say what he wished, but only what God willed.

Balaam replied to these scornful words of Balak: "Rise up, Balak. Thou mayest not be seated when God's words are spoken. God is not like a man of flesh and blood, that makes friends and disowns them, as soon as he finds such as are better than they. God is not so, for He doth not cancel the vow He had made to the Patriarchs, for He promised to bestow Canaan upon their descendants, and He fulfilleth His promise. He always fulfils what He hath promised to Israel, but allows the evil with which He threatens them to be unfulfilled as soon as they repent them of their sins. God sees not their sins, but He seeth their good deeds. Thou, Balak, sayest to me, 'Come, curse Jacob for me,' but a thief can enter a vineyard that hath a keeper only if the keeper sleeps, but 'He that keepeth Israel neither sleepeth nor slumbereth,' and how then can I enter their vineyard? If, however, thou dost think that I cannot harm Israel on account of Moses, who is their keeper, know then that his successor will be as invincible as he, for through the sound of trumpets he will overthrow the walls of Jericho.

"Thou, Balak, furthermore sayest, 'A people hath gone forth out of Egypt,' but they have not only gone forth, 'God brought them forth out of Egypt,' who combines in Himself the powers of the angels and of the invisible demons. Swift as the flight of a bird doth fortune as well as misfortune come upon Israel; if they sin, God suddenly plunges them down, but if they act well in the sight of the Lord, God exalts them as quickly as a cloud. Thou, Balak, hast repeatedly tried to discover in what spot thou shouldst be able to work them woe, but they will have nothing to do with sorceries, they baffle and put to naught the sorceries and prophecies of other nations by their pious deeds. When they set forth into battle, they practice no magic, but the high priest, clad in the Urim and Tummin, consults God about the outcome of the battle. There will even be a time when Israel will sit before the Lord like a pupil before his master, and will receive the revelation of the secrets of the Torah from him, so that even the angels will consult Israel concerning the secrets revealed to them by God, for the angels are not permitted to approach God as closely as the Israelites in the Messianic time.

"There is not indeed upon the earth a nation like Israel. The last thing they do before going to sleep is to devote themselves to the study of the Torah and the fulfillment of its laws, and this also is their first occupation upon awakening. As soon as they arise, they recite the Shema' and adore God, and not until after they have done this, do they go about their business. If evil spirits come to attack them, or if disaster threatens them, they worship their God, and as soon as they utter the words, 'The Lord our God is one Lord,' the harmful spirits become powerless against them and whisper after them the words, 'Praised be the Name of the Glory of His Kingdom, for ever and ever.' When at night they retire, they against recite the Shema', whereupon the angels of the day pass on the trust of guarding them to the angels of night, and when, upon awakening they again worship their Lord, the angels of the night again pass them on to be guarded by the angels of day."

When Balak for the second time saw that Balaam, instead of cursing, blessed Israel, he brought him to the top of Peor, thinking that peradventure it would please God to have him curse them from thence. For by his sorcery Balak had discovered that a great disaster was to fall upon Israel on the top of Peor, and thought that this disaster might be their curse from Balaam. He was, however, mistaken in this supposition, for the disaster in that spot was none other than Israel's sin with the daughters of Moab, and God's punishment for this.

CURSES TURNED TO BLESSINGS

Balaam, on the other hand, made no further attempts to induce God to curse Israel, but thought he might be able to bring misfortune upon Israel by enumerating the sins they had committed in the desert, and in this way to conjure up God's wrath against them. But the desert had also been the place where Israel had accepted the Torah, hence the mention of the desert called up God's love instead of His wrath. Balaam himself, when he let his eyes wander over the camp of Israel, and perceived how their tents were so pitched that no one might see what was going on in the homes of the others, found himself compelled to burst into praises of Israel; and, under the inspiration of the prophetic spirit, the curses he had intended to speak were changed in his mouth into blessings, and he spoke of the extent and importance of the kingdom of Israel. But whereas Moses blessed his people in a low, quiet voice, Balaam spoke his words of blessing in a very loud voice, so that all the other nations might hear and out of envy make war upon Israel. Balaam's blessings were therefore accounted to him not as blessings, but as curses. God said: "I have promised Abraham, 'And I will bless them that bless thee, and him that curseth thee will I curse,' hence will I account Balaam's blessings as curses." And indeed all of Balaam's blessing later turned to curses, except his blessing that houses of teaching and of prayer should never be missing among Israel.

The words that Balaam announced were heard by all the inhabitants of the earth, such power did God lend to his voice, for He knew that at some future time there would be a man born of woman who would pass himself for a god and would mislead all the world. Hence God permitted all the world to hear Balaam's words, that said: "God is not a man, and the man that passeth himself for God lieth. But he that will mislead the world by declaring that he will disappear for a time and then reappear will promise what he can never fulfil. Woe then to that nation that will lend ear to the man who will pass himself for God." Balaam furthermore announced the events that would come to pass at the time of David's sovereignty; and also what will happen at the end of days, in the time of Messiah, when Rome and all other nations will be destroyed by Israel, excepting only the descendants of Jethro, who will participate in Israel's joy and sorrows. Yea, the Kenites are to be the ones to announce to Israel the arrival of the Messiah, and the sons of the Kenite Jonadab are to be the first at the time of the Messiah to bring offerings at the Temple and to announce to Jerusalem its deliverance. This was Balaam's last prophecy. After this, the prophetic spirit left Balaam, and God in this way granted Moses' wish to reserve the gift of prophecy as a special distinction to Israel. Balaam was the last prophet of the nations.

BALAAM'S WICKED COUNSEL

Although Balaam had not been able to fulfil Balak's wish and curse Israel, still he did not leave him before giving him advice as to how he might bring ruin to Israel, saying: "The God of this people loathes unchastity; but they are very eager to possess linen garments. Pitch tents, then, and at their entrances have old women offer these articles for sale. Induce them in this way to enter the interior of the tents where they will be surprised by young harlots, who will seduce them to unchastity, so that God may punish them for their sin."

"Throw the stick up in the air it will always return to its original place." The Moabite nation that owes its existence to the illegal relations of Lot with his daughter could not deny its origin, and followed Balaam's counsel to tempt Israel to unchastity. They pitched tents, filled them with pretty women, whom they provided with valuable things, and had old women take up their posts at the doors of the tents, whose task it was to lure the passing Israelites into the interior. If an Israelite passed to buy something of the Moabites, the old women at the entrance to the tent would thus address him, "Dost thou not wish to buy linen garments that were made in Bet-Shan?" Then they would show him a sample of the goods, and name the price, and finally add, "Go within, and thou wilt see wares still more beautiful." If he went within, he was received by a young woman who was richly adorned and perfumed, who would at first set for him a price much lower than the value of the goods, and then invite him to do as if he were at home, and to choose the article he liked best. While he sat there, he was treated with wine, and the young woman invited him to drink with the words: "Why do we love ye while you hate us? Are we not all descendants of one man? Was not Terah our ancestor as much as yours? If thou wilt not eat of our sacrifices or what we have cooked, here are calves and fowl that thou mayest slaughter in accordance with thy law." But as soon as the Israelite had allowed himself to be persuaded to drink, he was absolutely in the hands of the shameless woman. Intoxicated with wine, his passion for the woman was soon kindled, but she agreed to satisfy his desires only after he had first worshipped Peor, the god of the Moabites. Now the worship of this idol consisted in nothing else than the complete baring of the body, hence the Israelites, seeing no evil in it, declared themselves willing to follow the summons of the Moabite women; and in this way they were seduced both to unchastity and to idolatry by the Moabite women. At first the men were ashamed and committed this whoredom with the Moabite women in secret, but they soon lost this feeling of shame and betook themselves two by two to their lewd actions.

Israel's moral degeneration is to be partly explained by this, that the place where they found themselves was apt to tempt them to lewdness. For there are springs whose waters have various effects upon those who partake of them. One kind of water strengthens, another weakens; one makes beautiful, another makes ugly; one makes chaste, another brings about lewdness. Now there was in Shittim, where the Israelites then dwelt, the "Well of Lewdness," out of which the inhabitants of Sodom had erstwhile fetched water, but from which, since the destruction of the sinful cities, no one had drunk, and for this reason the people had until then been chaste. But Israel, as soon as they tasted of this water, gave up their chaste manner of life. This disastrous spring will lose its force only in the Messianic time when God will cause it to dry up.

PHINEHAS, ZEALOUS FOR GOD

When the people's shamelessness became more and more widespread, God commanded Moses to appoint judges to punish the sinners, and as it was difficult to discover these through the agency of witnesses, God marked them by causing the cloud of glory that lay spread over the camp of Israel to disappear from the sinners. Those that were not covered by the cloud of glory were thus clearly marked as sinners. God appointed as judges and executioners the seven myriads eight thousand six hundred officers of the people, giving them the order that each of them execute two sinners. These carried out Moses' command and stoned the sinners, whose corpses then hung upon the gallows for a few minutes. This was the legal punishment, for these sinners had not only committed whoredom with the women of Moab, but had worshipped the Moabit idol Peor; and idolatry is punishable with death by stoning.

While the judges administered their stern offices, the tribe of Simeon approached their prince, Zimri, and said to him, "People are being executed, and thou sittest still as if nothing were going on." He thereupon took with him twenty-four thousand men, and betook himself to Cozbi, Balak's daughter, and without considering God or men, he requested her in the presence of many people to yield herself to him, to satisfy his evil desires. Now Balak had ordered his daughter Cozbi to employ her beauty only for the sake of enticing Moses, thinking, "Whatever evil may be decreed by God against Israel, Moses will be brought to naught, but if my daughter should succeed in seducing him to sin, then all Israel will be in my hand." Hence Cozbi said to Zimri: "My father ordered me to be obedient to the wishes of Moses alone, and to none other; for he is a king, and so is my father, and a king's daughter is fit for none but a king." Zimri, however, replied: "I am a greater man the Moses, for he is chief only of the third tribe of Israel, whereas I am prince of the tribe of Simeon, the second of the Israelite tribes, and if thou wilt, I will convince thee that I am a greater man than Moses, for I will take thee to myself in his presence, without paying attention to his prohibition."

Zimri then seized Cozbi by the locks of her hair, and brought her before Moses, whom he then addressed as follows: "Tell me, son of Amram, is this woman permitted me, or is she forbidden me?" Moses said, "She is forbidden to thee." Zimri answered: "Art thou really the faithful expounder of the Torah, whose reliability God praised with the words, 'He is faithful in all Mine house?' How then canst thou assert that she is forbidden me, for then thy wife would be forbidden to thee, for she is a Midianite like this woman, and this one is a noble woman of a noble family, whereas thy wife is the daughter of an idolatrous priest." At those words, Moses, Eleazar, and the elders began to weep, for they knew not how to make answer to Zimri's insolent words, nor what they could do to restrain this sinner from the accomplishment of his sin. God said to Moses: "Where is thy wisdom? Thou didst need to utter only one word, and Korah and all his company were swallowed by the earth. Canst thou now do nothing better than to weep?" The Holy Spirit exclaimed at Moses' perplexity and silence, "The stouthearted are spoiled, they have slept their sleep."

God, who calls the pious to strict account, punished Moses for the lack of decision that he displayed on this occasion, by leaving his burial-place unknown to mankind. While Moses and other pious men were irresolute and deliberated whether or not Zimri deserved death, Phinehas said to Moses: "O my great-uncle, didst thou not teach me, when thou didst return from Mount Sinai, that is was the zealot's task for the sake of God's law to slay those who commit unchastity with non-Jewish women?" Phinehas took the liberty of pointing out the law to his teacher Moses who had forgotten it, because, "when God's name is profaned, no man should consider the respect due to a teacher," wherefore Phinehas thought now only of establishing God's law, and in doing this it was necessary to recall it to Moses' mind. Moses indeed did not take it all amiss, but said to

Phinehas, "Let the reader of the letter be its bearer also," words by which he called upon Phinehas himself to visit punishment upon the sinners.

Phinehas was now for a time in doubt whether he should dare to punish the sinners, for it was to be expected that he would eventually meet his death in this way, being one against two, Zimri and his mistress Cozbi. When, however, the plague that God had sent upon Israel on account of their sins spread more and more rapidly, Phinehas determined to risk his life in trying to kill the sinners. "For," said he to himself, "the horse goes willingly into battle, and is ready to be slain only to be of service to its master. How much more does it behoove me to expose myself to death in order to sanctify God's name!" He found himself all the more impelled to act thus because he could not well leave the punishment of the sinners to others. He said: "The tribe of Reuben can effect nothing in this instance, because their grandsire Reuben was himself suspected of an unchaste action; nothing is to be expected from the tribe of Simeon, for it follows the sinful example of its prince Zimri; the tribe of Judah cannot well be of use in this matter, because their grandsire Judah committed unchastity with his daughter-in-law Tamar; Moses himself is doomed to impotence because his wife Zipporah is a Midianite woman. Hence there remains nothing but for me to interpose."

TWELVE MIRACLES

Phinehas now, prepared at the risk of his own life to punish Zimri for his sin, left the house of teaching where he had until now debated the case of Zimri with Moses and all other pious men, and had himself provided with a lance, having none with him because no armed man may enter a house of teaching. That his weapon might not betray him, he detached the upper iron part of the lance and hid it in his bosom, and leaned upon the wooden shaft as if it were a staff. When he reached the house where Zimri and Cozbi were giving extravagant play to their passions, the people said to him, "Whence, Phinehas, and whither?" He replied, "Do ye not know that the tribe of Levi is always to be found where the tribe of Simeon is?" Then they permitted him to enter the house, but said, "It seems that even the Pharisees now permit intercourse with the heathen women." When Phinehas had entered, he drew his lance, "and thrust both of them through, the man of Israel, and the woman through her belly."

Phinehas's fear that these two might attack him was not realized, for God performed no less than twelve miracles for Phinehas, which not only made it impossible for the sinners to attack him, but also showed the people that his action found favor in the sight of the Lord. The first miracle was that an angel would not allow the sinful couple to separate when Phinehas surprised them; the second miracle was that the angel stopped their mouths so that they could not cry out for help; the third miracle was that Phinehas's lance struck the man's and the woman's pudenda; the fourth miracle was that the upper, iron part of the lance extended, so that Phinehas could at one thrust pierce the man as well as the woman; the fifth miracle was that Phinehas's arm was sufficiently strong to lift both upon the point of his lance; the sixth miracle was that the wooden shaft of the lance sustained the weight of two persons; the seventh miracle was that the two bodies remained poised upon the lance and did not fall off; the eighth miracle was that the angel turned the shameless pair around, so that all might see that Phinehas had surprised them in flagranti; the ninth miracle was that no blood flowed from them although they had been thrust through, or else Phinehas would have been polluted; the tenth miracle was that the shameless couple did not give up the ghost so long as Phinehas bore them upon the point of his lance, as he would otherwise have been polluted by their corpses; the eleventh miracle was that the angel raised the doorposts of the room so that Phinehas might pass through with the sinners upon the point of his lance, and the twelfth miracle was that when the tribe of Simeon prepared to avenge Prince Zimri's death upon Phinehas, the angel sent a plague upon them, so that they were impotent against him.

Phinehas was not, however, content with having punished the sinners, but tried also to reconcile God with Israel. He threw the two dead bodies upon the ground, saying to God, "Why, alas! Hast Thou on account of the sins of these two slain twenty-four thousand Israelites!" For this was the number that had been snatched away by the plague that God had sent upon Israel for their sins. The angels now wanted to plunge Phinehas into death for his bold words, but God bade them desist, saying, "Leave him in peace, he is a zealot, the son of a zealot, and an appeaser of wrath, the son of an appeaser of wrath."

PHINEHAS REWARDED

While God expressed His entire satisfaction with Phinehas's act, if found many adversaries among Israel, who would scornfully call after him, "Behold, this man, the grandson of one who fattened calves to offer them up to an idol, daring to slay a prince among Israel!" This spiteful remark referred to the fact that Phinehas was descended on his mother's side not only from Joseph, but from Jethro also who, before his conversion to Judaism, had been a priest of idols. God therefore said to Moses, "Phinehas the son of Eleazar, the son of Aaron the priest, hast turned My wrath away from the children of Israel, hence I offer him My greeting of peace, for it was he who, zealous for My sake, preserved the seed of Abraham." The reason God designated Phinehas as the son of Eleazar and the grandson of Aaron was that He wanted to stop the mouths of Phinehas's detractors, who pretended that he was nothing but a grandson of the heathen priest Jethro, ignoring the fact that he was at the same time the grandson of Aaron, the high priest before the Lord. God was not content with the greeting of peace, but bade Moses tell Phinehas: "With thy mouth hast thou defended Israel, therefore as thy priest's portion shalt thou receive the jawbone of animals; with thy lance didst thou aim at the bellies of the shameless couple, hence shalt thou receive the bellies of the animals; and as with thy arm thou didst labor to slay the sinners, so for thy portion shalt thou receive the shoulder of the animals. As, moreover, thou didst strive to make peace among mankind, so shalt thou bestow the priestly blessing upon My children, and bless them with peace." As a reward for his pious deed Phinehas was appointed by God as a priest with all the rights of priesthood, that enabled him to lay claim to the twenty-four tributes to priests.

But the highest reward to Phinehas was that God granted him everlasting priesthood. For Phinehas is none other than the prophet of Elijah. His task it is to make atonement for Israel, and without tasting of death, he constantly discharges the duties of his everlasting priesthood until the resurrection of the dead, offering up daily two sacrifices for the children of Israel, and upon the skins of these animals recording the events of each day. God furthermore said to Phinehas: "Thou hast in this world established peace between Me and Israel; in the future world also shalt thou establish peace between Me and them." He was therefore destined to be the forerunner of the Messiah to establish before his coming peace on earth.

When Israel addicted themselves to an immoral life at shittim, the nations of the world rejoiced greatly, for they knew that God had distinguished Israel before all other nations, and had given them the Torah, only because their life had been moral. "Now," said they, "the crown has been taken from Israel's head, their pride is departed, for now they are no better then we." God, however, raised up Israel from their fall by sending the plague upon the sinners at Shittim, and thus purified Israel from them, so that they could again, as of yore, be proud of their family purity, through which they had been distinguished from all other nations.

God therefore ordered them to take a census, to show in this way that Israel remained true to the traditions of their ancestor Abraham by keeping their family life pure. This census showed that several tribes had lost entire divisions since the time that passed between the entrance of Israel into Egypt, and their entrance into the promised land. Among the tribes that had perished were such as had already lost their lives in Egypt, those, namely, who had died during the days of darkness because they were such sinners that they did not want to leave Egypt. But heaviest of all were the losses in the tribes of Benjamin and of Simeon, for in the battle between the Levites and the other tribes after Aaron's death, when the latter, for fear of the Canaanites, wanted to return to Egypt, the Benjamites lost no less than seven divisions. All of the twenty-four thousand men that died from the plague at Shittim belonged, however, to the tribe of Simeon which, at the end of the march through the desert, had dwindles down to less than half its number. The tribe of Dan, on the other hand, had turned out to be very fruitful, for whereas at the entrance of Egypt it had consisted of only one division, it later exceeded in number all the other tribes, except the tribe of Judah.

THE DAUGHTERS OF ZELOPHEHAD

But there was another purpose beside that of establishing Israel's family purity in taking the census at Arbot-Moab. For when God at the exodus from Egypt put his people into Moses' hands, He entrusted them to him after having counted them, and not when Moses was about to depart from this world, he wanted to return the flock that God had entrusted to him, truly numbered, into God's hand.

After the number of the nation had been determined, God ordered Moses to divide the promised land among them according to their numbers. Jacob had indeed upon his death-bed determined what parts of the land were to fall to the lot of each tribe, but in order that the tribes might not quarrel among themselves, God decreed that the assignments be made by lot. After the conquest of the land Joshua and Eleazar saw to the drawing of lots. On this occasion the miracle came to pass that whenever Eleazar drew a lot from the urn, the lot itself announced the words, "I am the lot of Thus-and-So." In this way was avoided the possibility of having the malcontents declare that Eleazar had, at the drawing of lots, been partial to his friends and had assigned to them the lots they wished for.

When Zelophehad's daughters, that had lived piously and wisely like their father and their ancestors, heard that the land was being divided among the male members of the tribe, but not among the female, they took counsel together, discussing what they could do, so that they might not find themselves come out empty-handed. They said: "God's love is not like the love of a mortal father; the latter prefers his sons to his daughters, but He that created the world extends His love to women as well as to men, 'His tender mercies are over all His works.'" They now hoped that God would take pity on them and give them their share of the promised land, which they loved with as great devotion as their grandsire Joseph, who had upon his death-bed exhorted his children to transfer his body to the Holy Land.

Being wise and learned, they waited for a propitious time to lay their case before Moses, and opportunity which they found when Moses in house of teaching recited the law concerning the levirate marriage. They now advanced and said: "If we are as good as our brothers, then do we lay claim to our father's inheritance, and to his share of the land; but if we are not to be considered as sons, then should our mother have to marry her brother-in-law, as our father has left no issue, since we do not count." They furthermore pointed out that their father had been neither one of the spies nor one of Korah's followers, who had, owing to their sins, lost claim to their share of the land, but that he had found his death when a number of men, in spite of Moses' warnings, had presumed to storm the mountain occupied by the Amalekites and the Canaanites. "Had our father," continued they, "left behind him a son, and the latter were now also dead, then should we lay no claim to inheritance if this son had left a living child, were it even a daughter; but as we are our father's only descendants, give us, we pray, 'a possession among the brethren of our father.'"

The fervent longing of these women to have a share in the Holy Land shows how much better and more pious were the women of this generation than the men. The latter said, "Let us make a captain, and let us return to Egypt," whereas the women said, "Give us a possession among the brethren of our father." But not only during the rebellion that was kindled by the spies did the women remain true to Moses and to their God, but on other occasions also it was they who tried to build up what the men had torn down. at the worship of the Golden Calf, too, they tried to restrain the men from sin, hence it was the men only that had to die in the desert because they had been tempted to rebellion by the spies, whereas the women entered into the promised land. Among them also there was even to be found a woman as old as Jochebed-the daughter of Levi by his union with Otah-who survived her sons Moses and Aaron, as well as her daughter Miriam, and who was permitted to enter the promised land at the age of two hundred and fifty years.

The daughters of Zelophehad did not bring their request directly to Moses, but at first urged their plea before the lowest officers, the captains of tens. These, however, said: "This is an important matter since it touches upon laws of inheritance, hence it does not become us to decide this matter; greater men than we must settle it." Hence they sent them to the captains of fifties. When these saw that out of consideration for them the captains of tens would not pass judgement, they sent the daughters of Zelophehad on to the captains of hundreds, that were their superiors. But these too, out of consideration for the higher judges, would not settle this matter, and so the daughters of Zelophehad came to the captains of thousands, who sent them to the princes of the tribes, until they came at last to the highest authority, to Moses. Now Moses might well have decided this case without further ado, but in his meekness he thought, "There is still a higher authority than I, to wit, God," and he bade them await God's judgement. The answer that he received from God was as follows: "The daughters of Zelophehad have the law on their side, for what they desire is in accordance with the law that was written in heaven by Me; give them therefore their father's inheritance, and also two parts of their grandfather Hepher's possessions, for their father Zelophehad was his firstborn and was therefore entitled to a double share."

The daughters of Zelophehad, who in spite of their years-the youngest of them had attained forty-had not yet been married, now entered into wedlock, and according to God's bidding that Moses communicated to them, they married their uncle's sons, although they were free to marry whomsoever they chose.

"God works good through the good, and evil through the evil." The chapter of the laws of God that was published by Moses as an addition to the incident of Zelophehad's daughters would have been given without them also, but God rewarded these women for their piety by making them the direct occasion of this chapter of the law. At the same time this case of these women was to teach several lessons to Moses. He who, since he had been made God's messenger to the people, had lived apart from his wife was not to grow too conceited on account of the sacrifice he had made to his sacred calling; hence in the last year of his life there appeared before him the daughters of Zelophehad, who of their own accord had not married because they had not found mates that they considered suitable. Then, too, Moses could not answer the legal question that the daughters of Zelophehad had presented to him, and had to ask God's counsel, which was a second lesson to Moses. At the appointment of the elders, Moses earnestly told them, "The cause that is too hard for ye, bring to me, and I will hear it," and in punishment of these boastful words God so brought it to pass that he could give no answer to this request of the women, whereupon God said to him, "Didst not thou say, 'the cause that is too hard for ye, bring it to me?' and now thou canst not properly settle this legal question of the women."

A similar punishment for a similar offense was visited upon David who, well aware of his erudition, said, "The laws of the Torah do I grasp as easily and as quickly as songs." God then said, "As truly as thou livest, thou shalt hereafter forget a Biblical law that even the school children know." So, too, it came to pass that when he had the Holy Ark fetched from Gibeah to Zion, he forgot the Biblical instruction that the Ark may be carried only upon the shoulder, and had it lifted upon a wagon. Then occurred the miracle that the Ark leaped of itself into the air, whereas the oxen that pulled the wagon fell down, whereupon Uzzah, to whom the transportation of the Ark had been entrusted, stretched out his hand to prevent the Ark from falling and himself fell dead upon the ground, for "a sin that is committed is ignorance of the law is accounted as if it had been intentional." Uzzah should have been mindful of the law that the Ark was not to be lifted upon a cart, hence his punishment. God thereupon said to David, "Didst thou not say, 'Thy statutes have been my songs?' and thou hast not even mastered the words of the Bible, 'Unto the sons of Kohath he gave none: because the service of the sanctuary belonged unto them; they bare it upon their shoulders.'"

THE APPOINTMENT OF JOSHUA

When Moses heard God's decision in the case of the daughters of Zelophehad, which turned out in their favor so that they inherited their father's property, he thought, "This s a propitious time to urge a plea before the Lord, for if daughters are to inherit their father, then must my sons inherit my office." He then began to pray to God that his successors, who, he hoped, were also to be his descendants, might be worthy leaders of their people. He said: "O my Lord, before whom come the spirits of all human beings, so that Thou knowest the spirit of each-whose spirit is proud, and whose spirit is meek; whose spirit is patient and whose spirit is restive; mayest Thou set over Thy community a man who is gifted with strength, with wisdom, with beauty, and with decorum, so that his conduct may not give offense to the people. O Lord of the world! Thou knowest each man's views, and knowest that each man has a view of his own, hence, as I am about to depart from this world, I pray Thee, appoint a leader over them that will know how to deal with each man according to his views."

Moses, being a truly pious man, thought when he saw his end approach, not of himself, but of the welfare of the community, for whom he implored a good and worthy leader. Hence he furthermore said to God: "Let not my successor share my fate, for although I accepted the guidance of the people only after long hesitation, owing to Thy urgings and requests, still I shall not be permitted to lead them into the promised land. Mayest Thou then deal differently with my successor than Thou hast dealt with me, and permit him not only to lead the people in the desert, but to take them into the promised land. He, however, shall be a man 'which may go out before them,' who, unlike the kings of the heathens, that sent their legions to war but themselves remain at home, shall himself lead Israel to war. But he shall also be a man 'which may come in before them;' may it be granted him to see the number of those returning from war no less than that of those going into war. O Lord of the world!" continued Moses, "Thou hast led Israel out of Egypt, not to punish them for their sins, but to forgive them, and Thou hast not led them out of Egypt that they may be without leaders, but that they may indeed have leaders. I insist, therefore, that Thou shouldst tell me whether or not Thou wilt grant them a leader."

This is one of the five occasions upon which Moses implored God to give him an answer to his question. When he saw that his appearance before Pharaoh only occasioned him to bring greater and greater cruelties upon Israel, he said to God, "Tell me if Thou wilt now deliver them, or not." He also demanded God's answer to the question, "Shall I now fall into their hands or not?" when at Rephindim, on account of the dearth of water, he was threatened by the people. The third occasion was when he prayed to God for Miriam's recovery, and said, "Tell me, wilt Thou heal her or not?" And lastly when, after long and fervent prayer, he asked God whether he should be permitted to enter into the Holy Land, he said, "Let me know if I am to enter the Holy Land or not."

God fulfilled this wish of Moses, saying: "Thou hast now requested to be informed concerning thy immediate successor. I shall do more than this, and show thee all the judges and prophets that I will allow to arise for My children from not on to the resurrection of the dead." Then He showed Moses his successor Joshua, his successor's successor, Othniel, and all the other judges and prophets. Then God added these words: "Of all these that I have shown thee, each will have his individual spirit and his individual knowledge, but such a man as thou now wishest for thy successor, whose spirit is to embrace in itself the spirits of sixty myriads of Israel, so that he may speak to each one of them according to his understanding, such a man as this will not arise until the end of time. The Messiah will be inspired with a spirit that in itself will embrace the spirits of all mankind.

But now, concerning thy immediate successor, know then that he that watcheth the fig tree shall eat of its fruits, and he that waiteth upon his master will be promoted to honor, and thy sons shall not inherit the leadership because they concerned themselves little with the Torah. Joshua shall be thy successor, who served thee with devotion and showed thee great veneration, for at morn and eve he put up the benches in thy house of teaching and spread the carpets over them; he served thee as far as he was able, and Israel shall now know that he will therefore receive his reward. Take then Joshua, a man such as thou didst wish as a successor, whom thou hast proven, and who knows how to deal with people of every tendency, 'and lay thy hand upon him.' Give him an opportunity, while thou art still alive, to speak in public and to pronounce the law, so that Israel may not after thy death contemptuously say of thy successor, 'As long as his teacher was alive, he dared not pronounce judgement, and now he wishes to do so!' Although Joshua, who is not of thy kin, is to be thy successor, I shall nevertheless be mindful of the law that 'no inheritance shall remove from one tribe to another tribe,' for the dignity of leadership is to be reserved for thy family; Joshua 'shall stand even before Eleazar the priest, thy brother's son, who shall ask counsel for him according to the judgement of the Urim.'"

After Moses in kindly words had induced Joshua to accept the leadership after his death, pointing out to him the great rewards that in the future world await the leaders of Israel, 'he took Joshua, and set him before Eleazar the priest, and before all the congregation,' that all might thereafter acknowledge him as his successor. He then bade Joshua, who had been sitting on the floor like all the rest, rise and set himself upon a bench beside him. Joshua seated himself with the words, "Blessed be the Lord that hath through Moses bestowed the Torah upon Israel." Moses honored Joshua furthermore by interrupting his discourse as soon as Joshua enter the house of teaching, and resuming it only when he had taken his seat. Moses also bade a herald proclaim throughout the camp, "This man Joshua is worthy of being appointed by God as His shepherd."

Moses distinguished Joshua not because God had ordered him to do so, but because he was sincerely glad to pass his dignity on to him, just as a father is glad to leave his possessions to his son. So, too, whereas God had bidden Moses to lay only one hand upon Joshua's head and in this way put his honor upon him, Moses fulfilled God's command by laying both his hands upon Joshua, and by this action bestowed upon him not only insight and understanding, but also a radiant countenance like that of Moses, from whose face issued rays like those of the sun. In giving all these qualities to Joshua, Moses lost nothing. Moses' wisdom was like a torch, whereas Joshua's may be compared to a candle only, and just as a torch loses none of its intensity if a candle is lighted therefrom, so little was Moses' wisdom diminished by the wisdom he gave to Joshua. The rays, too, that emanated from Joshua's countenance were weaker than those from Moses', and not until the crossing of the Jordan did they attain their full intensity, so that upon beholding them, "the people feared him as they feared Moses."

Joshua's appointment by God as Moses' successor had been Moses' most cherished wish, but he had not ventured to give expression to it, for he was mindful of the punishment God had sent over him when he had entreated Him to sent Aaron instead of himself to deliver Israel out of Egypt, and from that time he feared to make any proposals whatsoever to God. He was like the child who had once been burned by a coal, and the seeing a brightly sparkling jewel, took it to be a burning coal, and dared not touch it.

MOSES' LEGACY TO JOSHUA

After Moses had announced Joshua as his successor before all the congregation, he disclosed to him that the course of his own life was run, and that he would now depart to his fathers. At his inheritance he gave to Joshua a book of prophecy, which Joshua was to anoint with cedar-oil, and in an earthen vessel to lay upon the spot that from the creation of the world God had created for it, so that His name might there be invoked. This book contained in brief outline the history of Israel from the entrance into the promised land to the establishment of God's kingdom upon earth, when, in wrath and indignation on account of His children, the Lord will rise from His Throne of power and proceed from His holy dwelling.

When Joshua heard the words of Moses as they are written in his Holy Scriptures, he rent his garments and fell at Moses' feet, who, himself in tears, yet comforted him. Joshua, however, said: "How canst thou comfort me concerning the bitter word that thou hast spoken, which abound in sobs and tears, that thou are to depart from thy people? What place will receive thee? What monument will point to thy grave? Or who will dare to remove thy corpse from one place to another as if it were an ordinary mortal's? All dying men receive a grave upon earth according to their rank, but thy grave extends from sunrise to sunset, from South to North; all the world is thy tomb. Thou goest. Who not, O master, shall care for this people? Who shall take pity upon them and be a guide upon their way? Who shall pray for them incessantly, that I may lead them into the land of their fathers? How shall I provide food for them according to their wish, or drink according to their desire? From the beginning they numbered sixty myriads, and now, thanks to thy prayers, they have greatly multiplied. Whence shall I draw insight and understanding to give them judgement and counsel? Even the kings of the Amorites, hearing that we desire to attack them, will say, 'Let us not set out against them, for there is now no longer among them the many-sided, incomprehensible and sacred spirit, worthy of the Lord, the ever-faithful master of the word, the Divine prophet of all the world, the most consummate master of this age. If now our enemies once more transgress before the Lord, they will have no defender to offer up prayers for them before God, as Moses had done, the great messenger who at all hours of the day kneeled down and prayed, lifting up his eyes to Him who rules all the world, and constantly reminding Him of His covenant with the Patriarchs, and appeasing Him with invocation.' For thus will the Amorites speak saying, 'He is no longer among them; arise then and let us wipe them from the face of the earth.' But what then, O my lord Moses, will become of this people?"

When Joshua has spoken these words, he cast himself once more at Moses' feet. Moses seized his hand, raised him to a seat before them, and answered him, saying: "Do not underestimate thyself, O Joshua, but be light of heart, and pay heed to my words. All the nations that dwell in the universe hath God created, and us also. Them and us did He foresee from the beginning of the creation of the universe even unto the end of the world, and He overlooked nothing, even down to the smallest, but He at the same time foresaw and foredoomed everything. All that was to happen in this universe did God foresee and foredoom, and lo! it cometh to pass. He appointed me for them and for their sins, that for them I might make prayer and exhortation. Not for my fitness or my strength was I chosen, but only through the grace of His mercy and His long-suffering. For I assure thee, Joshua, not on account of the excellence of this people wilt thou destroy the heathens; all the fastnesses of heaven and the foundations of the universe were created and approved by God, and are beneath the ring of His right hand. Those, therefore, that maintain and fulfil God's commandments thrive and prosper, but those who sin and neglect the commandments will now receive the promised possessions, and will be punished by the heathens with many plagues. But that He should wholly destroy or abandon them is impossible, for God will step forth, who foresaw everything even to eternity, and whose covenant is firmly founded, in accordance with the oath which He swore to the Patriarchs. Then the hands of the angel will be filled and he will be appointed chief, and he will forthwith avenge them of their enemies."

MOSES' LAST CAMPAIGN

Balaam's prophecy, "He shall not lie down until he eat of the prey, and drink the blood of the slain," was very quickly fulfilled. Shortly before his death, before he lay down to everlasting sleep, it was granted Moses to rejoice in the death of Balaam and the five Midianite kings allied to him. Israel's sinful profanation at Shittim, occasioned by Balaam's wicked advice, sorely smote Moses' heart. God had appointed Moses as lord of the angels, who through fire and cloud had to step aside to make room for him and let him pass, yea, at his appearance they rose from their seats to do him honor. As he had power over the angels, so too did he rule the sea, which he clove at will and then commanded to resume its former guise, and the treasures of hail, which he employed to sent hail over the Egyptians. Now this man, who was sovereign over the angels and over the forces of nature, could only weep when Israel committed whoredom with the daughters of Moab and Midian. To comfort Moses, God now said: "As truly as thou livest, thou shalt not depart out of this world until thou shalt have avenged those who tempted Israel to sin. 'Avenge the children of Israel of the Midianites: afterward shalt thou be gathered unto thy people.'" God at the same time reproached Moses for his despair and lack of energy at Shittim, saying: "When all the tribes of Israel, save the tribe of Levi, were against thee, thou didst not then lack courage to stand up against all the people on account of the worship of the Golden Calf; how much more then at Shittim, when all Israel save only one tribe, the tribe of Simeon, were on thy side, shouldst thou have proven thyself sufficiently strong to keep back the sinners from their sin!" When Moses received the command to wage war upon the people that had tempted Israel to sin, he said to God: "Yesterday didst Thou say to me, 'Vex not Moab,' and now Thou sayest, 'Avenge the children of Israel.'" God, however, replied: "When I said, 'Vex not Moab,' I named these people after their grandsire, the son of Lot, but not that through their own fault they have lost the claim to kind treatment from Israel, I shall no longer think of their grandsire Abraham's kinsman, but shall call them Midianim, 'they that lost their claim.'"

Lot's descendants now not only had no further claims to exemption, but a command was given to Moses to treat them with still greater hostility than the other nations. Until then it had been Israel's duty not to fight against a city of the heathens unless they had first proclaimed peace to it and the heathens had refused to accept it, but now they were instantly to proceed to hostility; and whereas they had formerly been prohibited from destroying the trees that surrounded a city, they were now ruthlessly to destroy all that lay in their path. This wrath of God against those who had tempted Israel to sin was justified, for "the tempter to sin is him of this world alone, but he that tempts another deprives him of this world and the world beyond." Two nations, the Egyptians and the Edomites, attacked Israel with the sword, but God nevertheless said, "Thou shalt not abhor an Edomite; thou shalt not abhor an Egyptian." The Moabites and Ammonites, on the other hand, tempted Israel to sin, hence God's word concerning them was as follows: "An Ammonite or Moabite shall not enter into the assembly of the Lord, even to the tenth generation."

Israel received the command to make war upon the Midianites at the same time as that to fight the Moabites, but whereas Moses at once waged war against Midian, it was not until David's time that a relentless war was waged against Moab. There was several reasons why the Midianites were to receive their punishment before the Moabites. Firstly, Moab's hatred against Israel was not quite without foundation, for although the Israelites had not attacked them in war, still they had inspired them with great fear by pillaging the Moabite region, hence the Moabites tried by every means to be rid of Israel. Midian, on the other hand, had no cause for undertaking hostilities against Israel, and yet they not only joined the Moabites, but outdid them in their hatred against Israel. Furthermore Moab wanted to kill Israel, but Midian wanted to tempt them to sin, which is worse than death. The delay in punishing Moab also corresponded in other ways to God's plan, for the Moabite Ruth was destined to become the mother of the dynasty of David, hence God said to Israel: "Wait yet a while in this matter of the war against the Moabites: I have lost something valuable among them. As soon as I have found it, ye shall avenge yourselves of them."

God indicated that the war against Midian would be Moses' last in these words, "Avenge the children of Israel of the Midianites: afterward shalt thou be gathered unto thy people." The connection between the war and Moses' death is as follows. When God announced to Moses that he was to die on this side of the Jordan, Moses implored God with the words: "O Lord of the world! Is it right that death should so soon overtake me, that have seen Thy ways, Thy actions, and Thy path?" God replied, saying: "Moses, if a long life were better for men, surely I should not then have permitted thy ancestors to taste of death; but it is better for thee if thou are taken from this world than if thou wert to remain in it." Moses was not, however, satisfied with this answer from God, whereupon God said: "Well then, thou mayest live many years longer, yea, thou shalt live even to a thousand years, but know thou that Israel will not then conquer their foes, and that Midian will not be brought under their yoke." In this way was Moses made to yield by God, for he thought, "Whether I die to-day or to-morrow matters little, for death will come to me at last. I would rather see Israel conquer their foes and bring Midian under their yoke than that I should live longer." God therefore bade Moses avenge Israel of the Midianites, if he was thereupon ready to die.

Moses then thought: "I know that if I were now to go into battle against the Midianites, the people would declare that I wished for my own death, since God made it dependent upon the punishing of the Midianites, and my life is assured me as long as ever I wish to put it off." This consideration did not, however, determine him, for, fully aware that his enterprise of war would hasten his death, he nevertheless set about the execution of this war as soon as God commanded him. Wherever the execution of a Divine command, or the possibility of furthering Israel's cause was concerned, Moses gave no thought to himself, even though it touched his life. Not so Joshua. When he came to Canaan, he thought: "If I wage an incessant war upon the Canaanites, I shall certainly die as soon as I shall have conquered them, for Moses also died immediately after his conquest of Midian." He therefore proceeded very slowly in his conquest of the Holy Land, so that he might be sure of a long life. But, "however many thought there may be in man's heart, God's words prevails," and whereas Joshua hoped to become very aged, he died ten years before the time God had originally allotted to him, for, although he would otherwise have attained his master's age, he now died at the age of a hundred and ten.

THE COMPLETE ANNIHILATION OF MIDIAN

Whereas Moses, disregarding the expected consequences of the war upon himself, gladly went into battle, Israel did not want to obey his summons to war. The people of whom Moses had on one occasion said, "They be almost ready to stone me," when they now learned that their leader Moses was to die at the end of this war, tried to evade it, saying that they preferred to forego impending victory rather than to lose their leader, and each one hid himself, so as not to be picked out for this war. God therefore bade Moses cast lots to decide their going into battle, and those whose lots were drawn had to follow the call to arms even against their will. Moses' summons to battle was as follows: "Arm ye men from among you for the war, to execute the Lord's vengeance on Midain." Moses spoke of the Lord's revenge, whereas God designated this war against Midian as Israel's revenge. For Moses said to God: "Lord of the world! If we had worshipped the stars and planets, the Midianites should not have hated us, they hate us only on account of the Torah and the commandments that Thou hast given us, hence must Thou avenge Thyself of them."

Moses did not in person lead the war against Midian, for he was mindful of the proverb, "Cast no stone into the well from which thou hast drawn water," and he who as a fugitive from Egypt had sought refuge in Midian, did not wish to make war upon that land. He relinquished the leadership of the people to Phinehas, for "he that beginneth a good deed shall also complete it," and it was Phinehas who had begun God's war against the Midianites by slaying the princess Cozbi, Zimri's mistress, hence the task of completing this war fell to his lot. Phinehas, as a descendant of Joseph, had, moreover, a special reason for wishing to take revenge upon the Midianites, as those had been Midianites who had sold Joseph as a slave in Egypt.

The forces under Phinehas's command consisted of thirty-six thousand men, one third to take active part in battle, one third to guard the baggage, and one third to pray, whose duty it was in the course of battle to implore God to lend victory to the warriors of Israel. Moses passed on to Phinehas not only the Holy Ark, which Israel always takes into battle, but also the Urim and Tummim, that he might, if necessary, consult God. Outside of this Phinehas also received the gold plate of the mitre from the high priest's forehead, for Moses said to him: "The knave Balaam will by means of his sorceries fly into the air, and will even enable the five Midianite kings to fly with him, therefore shall ye hold up to them the plate of pure gold upon which is engraved God's name, and they will fall to earth." They did as Moses commanded, and truly Balaam and the five kings fell to earth. They then executed Balaam according to the four forms prescribed by the Jewish laws. They hanged him, kindled a fire beneath the gallows, struck off his head with a sword, and then dropped him from the gallows into the fire below. Although Israel undertook the war against Midian upon God's bidding, to take vengeance for the wrong that had been done them, still their method of warfare was most humane. They attacked the cities of the Midianites from three sides only, so as not entirely to cut off flight. Victory was on the side of Israel, into whose possession fell the cities with all their temples, idols, and palaces. The same fate overtook all the five kings of Midian. All were slain alike just as all had made a common cause of the wish to destroy Israel. Balaam who had come to Midian from his home in Mesopotamia in order to receive his reward for his counsel not to fight Israel, but to tempt them to sin, instead of a reward, met with death at the hands of the Jews.

THE GRUESOME END OF BALAAM

This arch-magician at first tried to escape Israel's power by sorcery. For when he saw Phinehas and the leaders of the hosts of Israel, he flew into the air, a feat which he accomplished by magic arts, but particularly through the assistance of his wizard sons, Jannes and Jambres. At the sight of Balaam flying high in the air, Phinehas shouted to his army, "Is there any one among us who is able to fly after this villain?" The Danite Zaliah, a past master in the art of sorcery, followed this summons, and flew high into the air. Balaam, however, surpassed him, and took a path in the air on which Zaliah could not follow, and after the former had soared through five different layers of air, he had quite vanished from Zaliah's ken, who knew not what to do. Phinehas, however, came to his aid. By means of a magical invocation he dispelled the clouds that covered Balaam, and then Zaliah forced Balaam to descend to earth and appear before Phinehas. He began to implore Phinehas to spare his life, promising never again to try to curse Israel, but Phinehas replied: "Art not thou the Aramean Laban who tried to destroy our father Jacob? Then thou didst pass on to Egypt to destroy Jacob's seed, and when they removed from Egypt thou didst incite the wicked Amalek to harass us, and not thou didst attempt to curse Israel. But when thou sawest that thy endeavor to curse them was without avail, since God would not hear thee, thou gavest Balak the despicable advice to deliver up the daughters of his land to prostitution, and thereby to tempt Israel to sin, and wert in part successful, for twenty-four thousand Israelites died in consequence of their sin with the daughters of Moab. In vain therefore dost thou plead that thy life by spared." He then ordered Zaliah to kill Balaam, admonishing him, however, to be sure not to kill him through the holy name of God, as it does not befit so great a sinner to meet his death in such a way. Zaliah now tried in vain to kill Balaam, for through his magic wiles he was proof against every weapon, until Phinehas at last gave Zaliah a sword on both sides of which was engraved a serpent, with the words, "Kill him with that to which he belongs-through this he will die," and with this sword Balaam was killed.

His corpse was not buried, but his bones rotted, and from then arose several species of harmful snakes, that bring disaster to human beings; and even the worms that devoured his flesh were turned into snakes. The magicians made use of these snakes for three different types of enchantment, for the heads, the bodies, and the tails, had each a different effect. One of the questions that the Queen of Sheba put to Solomon was how to withstand these three different kinds of enchantment, and the wise king knew even this secret, which he then imparted to her.

THE VICTORIOUS RETURN FROM THE WAR

After the close of the campaign against Midian, the warriors returned with rich spoils to the camp of Israel, but they were such pious and honorable men that they did not lay claim to the booty, but rendered it all up, so that it might be impartially divided among all. As there were honest and conscientious in their relations between man and man, so likewise were they very strict in their observance of religious statutes. Throughout the time of war not a single one of them neglected even the slightest religious ceremony, were it only to put on the phylactery of the forehead before that of the arm. But they were especially careful never again to be tempted by the Midianite women. If they entered a house to take its treasures from it, they did so in pairs, one blackening the faces of the women, and the other seizing their ornaments. In vain would the Midianite women cry, "Are we not creatures of God, that ye treat us thus?" whereupon the Israelites would say, "Were not ye the cause that so many of us found their death?" Justly therefore could these pious men say to Moses: "Thy servants have taken the sum of the men of war which are under our charge, and not one among us had committed a sin or an unchaste action. We have therefore brought the Lord's oblation to make atonement for our souls." Moses thereupon said in surprise, "Ye contradict yourselves, what need of atonement is there if no man among you is guilty of sin?" They replied: "It is true, our teacher Moses, two by two did we approach the women, one blackening their faces, and the other taking off their ear-rings, but even though we committed no sin with the Midianite women, still the heat of passion was kindled in us when we took hold of the women, and therefore by an offering do we seek to make atonement." Moses thereupon set out to praise them, saying: "Even the common men among you are filled with good and pious deeds, for a man that was under conditions that enabled him to sin, but controlled himself, had done a pious deed, not to speak of the pious and chaste men among you whose pious deeds are legion."

As among those who had been slain in Midian there was a Jewish apostate, the warriors were polluted, and hence might not enter the camp, but had to stay without. Moses in his meekness did not, however, wait for them to come to him, but hastened to them. When, however, he heard that they had killed only the men but not the women, his wrath was kindled against the leaders of the army, for, "Upon the leaders falls the blame for the faults of the people." He reproached them, pointing out to them that it had been the women who really had brought disaster upon Israel at Shittim. But Phinehas replied: "Our teacher Moses, we acted according to thy instructions, thou didst bid us only 'avenge ourselves of the Midianites,' but madest not mention of the women of Midian." Moses then ordered them to execute all the women of the Midianites that were ripe for marriage, but to spare the young girls. In order to determine the difference in age, all were led past the gold plate of the mitre on the high priest's forehead, and this had the effect of making those who had been doomed to death grow pale.

In punishment for Moses' outburst of anger God caused him to forget to communicate to the soldiers outside the camp the laws of purification. These were then announced by Eleazar, Aaron's son. It was not, however, proper for him to pronounce a law in the presence of his teacher Moses, and he was accordingly punished for his lack of reverence to his teacher Moses. God had previously said that whenever Joshua wanted to inquire of God, he was "to stand before Eleazar the priest, and inquire of him by judgement of the Urim and Tummin." But this did not come about. In all his long career, Joshua had no need of asking Eleazar's counsel, so that the latter lost the honor that had been intended from him.

The occasion that led to the war against Midian had been Israel's seduction by the Midianite women, but these had succeeded only by having first intoxicated the sinners with wine. Phinehas, to make sure that this might not be repeated in the future, put the earthly as well as the heavenly ban upon all those who should drink the wine of the heathens, for the latter used it only as libations to their idols and for immoral purposes. In pronouncing this ban, he called upon the Ineffable Name and upon the holy writing of the two tables against its transgressors.

WEALTH THAT BRINGETH DESTRUCTION

God gave three gifts to the world, wisdom, strength and wealth. If they come from God, they are a blessing, otherwise they bring ruin. The world had two great sages, Balaam among the Gentiles, and Ahithophel among the Jews, but both of these, on account of their wisdom, lost this world as well as the world beyond. There were two great heroes in the world, Samson in Israel, and Goliath among the Gentiles, but both met death on account of their strength. There were two wealthy men in the world, Korah among the Jews, and Haman among the Gentiles, and both perished on account of their wealth. A similar fate overtook the two and a half tribes that stayed on the hither side of the Jordan. These had grown very rich in cattle through the spoils of the Midianites, and therefore preferred the pasture land on the hither side of the Jordan as their inheritance. But later on their wealth brought them destruction, because, choosing on their brethren, they were afterwards the first that were driven from their dwelling place into exile.

How intent these people were upon their possessions is shown in the words with which they presented their wish to Moses, saying, "We will build sheepfolds here for our cattle, and cities for our little ones," showing that they rated the cattle higher than their children, for they thought of the animals before they considered their children. Moses did not indeed call them to account for this, but showed them in unmistakable words that it was their duty first to consider men and then animals, by saying in his reply to these tribes, "Build you cities for your little ones, and folds for your sheep."

The land which these tribes had selected was indeed of great excellence, as even the names of the cities indicate. One was called Ataroth, "garlanded with fruits;" a second, Dibon, "flowing with honey;" a third, Jazer, "help," for its possession was a great help to those who owned it. These other cities in this region that were names on account of the excellence of the soil were: Nimrah, "gaily colored," for the ground of this city was gaily colored with fruits; Sebam, "perfume," whose fruits scattered a fragrance like perfume; and Nebo, "produce," because it was distinguished for its excellent product. This last mentioned city, like Baalmeon, did not retain its name when it passed into Israel's possession, for they wanted to have not cities that bore the names of idols, and therefore gave them new names. Many another town as well received a new name from the Israelites, just as Nobah gave his own name to the city of Kenath that he had gained by arms, hoping in this way to immortalize his name, for he had no children. His name was, however, not preserved in this way, for after the death of the conqueror, the old name of Kenath returned again.

It was among the possessions of these two and a half tribes also that Moses shortly before his death founded the cities of refuge. Moses in this instance illustrates the proverb, "Whosoever loves pious deeds, never has enough of them." Although God had told Moses that he would never cross to the other side of the Jordan, he still insisted upon at least determining the site for the asylum in the region of the East Jordan. God gave Moses the law concerning the cities of refuge in accordance with Israel's wish. For the people said to God: "Lord of the world! Thou didst promise us a long course of life as a reward for fulfilling the commandments, but supposing now that a man hath slain another unintentionally, and the avenger of the blood slays him, he will die before his time." God then said to Moses: "As truly as thou livest, they speak wisely. Appoint therefore several cities for cities of refuge, 'that the manslayer might flee thither, which slayeth his neighbor unawares.'" Moses rejoiced greatly at this statute, and instantly set about its execution, for "he that hath tasted of a food knoweth its flavor," and Moses who had erstwhile been obliged to flee on account of having slain an Egyptian, knew the feelings of the man who is pursued on account of a manslaughter that he had committed unawares.

MOSES' DEATH IRREVOCABLY DOOMED

When God in wrath against Moses and Aaron vowed, "Therefore ye shall not bring this assembly into the land which I have given them," Moses forbore to implore God to do away with this sentence, acting in accordance with the percept, "Do not attempt to dissolve thy neighbor's vow in the moment he hath made it." Moses waited forty years before he approached God with the request to permit him to enter the promised land with Israel. This occurred when he had received God's command to appoint Joshua as his successor, for he now perceived that God had actually resolved to execute His sentence. For although God had ten times decreed that Moses was to die in the desert, still Moses had not troubled much about it, even when the resolution had been sealed in the heavenly court. He thought: "How often did Israel sin, and yet, when I prayed for them, He annulled the punishment He had decreed; surely God should accept my prayer, if I-a man who never sinned-should pray to Him." Moses had also a special reason for assuming that God had changed His determination concerning him, and would not permit him to enter the promised land, for he had been permitted to enter the part of Palestine lying on this side of the Jordan, the land of Sihon and of Og, and from this he reasoned that God had not irrevocably decreed punishment for him, and that it might therefore now be recalled He was strengthened in this assumption by the fact that after the conquest of the east-Jordanic region God revealed to him the instructions as to how the land was to be divided, and it seemed to him as if he were in person to carry out these instructions. He was, however, mistaken, for shortly after these laws had been revealed to him, God informed him that he was to look upon the promised land from Mount Abarin, as he should never enter it.

When God saw that Moses was not much concerned about the impending punishment, He sealed the command He had issued against him, and swore by His Ineffable Name that Moses should not march into the land. Moses thereupon put on sackcloth, threw himself upon the ashes, and prayed not less than fifteen hundred prayers for the annulment of the Divine resolve against him. He drew a circle about himself, stood in the center of it, and said, "I will not move from this spot until judgement shall have been suspended." Heaven and earth, as well as all the forms of creation, trembled and said, "Perhaps it is God's wish to destroy this world, to create a new universe." But a voice sounded from heaven and said: "God's wish to destroy the world has not yet come, the commotion in nature is due to this that 'in God's hand is the soul of all living things and the spirit of all flesh,' even the spirit of the man Moses, whose end is not at hand."

God then bade them proclaim in heaven, and in all the celestial courts of justice, that they should not accept Moses' prayers, and that no angel was to carry Moses' prayer to Him, because Moses' doom of death had been sealed by Him. God quickly called before Him the Angel Akraziel, who is the celestial herald, and bade him proclaim the following in heaven: "Descend at once and lock every single gate in heaven, that Moses' prayer may not ascend into it." Then, at Moses' prayer, trembled heaven and earth, all the foundations thereof and the creatures therein, for his prayer was like a sword that slashed and rends, and can in no wise be parried, for in it was the power of the Ineffable Name that Moses had learned from his teacher Zagzagel, the teacher and scribe of the celestial beings. But when the Galgalim and Seraphim saw that God did not accept Moses' prayer, and without taking consideration of him did not grant his prayer for longer life, they all opened their mouths, saying: "Praised be the glory of the Lord from its place, for there is no injustice before Him, no forgetfulness, no respect of persons toward the small or the great."

MOSES' PRAYER FOR SUSPENSION OF JUDGMENT

Moses began his long but fruitless prayer by saying: "Lord of the world! Consider how much I had to bear for the sake of Israel until they became the people of Thy claim and of Thy possession. I suffered with them, shall I not then take part in their rejoicing? Look Thou, by forbidding me to enter the promised land, Thou givest the lie to Thy Torah, for it says, 'In his day thou shalt give the laborer his hire.' Where, then, is my hire for the forty years during which I labored for the sake of Thy children, and for their sake suffered much sorrow in Egypt, in the desert, and at the giving of the Torah and the commandments? With them I suffered pain, shall not I behold their good fortune as well? But Thou tellest me that I may not cross the Jordan! All the time that we were in the desert I could not sit quietly in the academy, teaching and pronouncing judgement, but not that I should be able to do so, Thou tellest me that I may not."

He continued: "May the mercy in Thee precede Thy justice, so that my prayer may be answered, for I well know that 'there is no mercy in justice,' Thou Thyself didst tell me when I asked Thee how Thou didst conduct the world, 'I owe nothing to any creature, and what I do for them is a free gift on My part,' therefore as a free gift, grant now my prayer to me. Thou Thyself didst point out to me that it is Thy desire that people should pray to Thee to cancel punishment that was laid upon them. When Israel committed that terrible sin, the worship of the Golden Calf, Thou didst say to me, 'Let Me alone, that I may destroy them, and blot out their name from under heaven.' I then thought, 'Who can restrain God, that He should say, "Let Me?" It is plain that He desires me to pray for His children;' and I prayed, and was answered. The prayer of the individual for the community was answered, but not so the prayer of the community for the one individual! Is it because I called Israel, 'rebels?' But in this I only followed Thy example, for Thou too didst call them, 'the sons of rebellion.'

"Thou didst call me, as well as Leviathan, thy servant; I sent up prayers to Thee, and Leviathan likewise, and him didst Thou answer, for Thou madest a covenant with him that Thou keepest, but the covenant that Thou madest with me Thou breakest, for Thou didst say, 'Die in the mount whither thou goest up.' In the Torah Thy words are: 'If the servant shall plainly say, I love my master, my wife, and my children; I will not go out free: then his master shall bring him unto the judges; and he shall serve him for ever.' I implore Thee now, 'hear my cry, O God; attend unto my prayer.' Thou are not in the position of a judge of flesh and blood who, when granting a prayer, has to consider that he may be compelled by his superior to repeal his answer, Thou canst do what Thou wilt, for where on earth or in heaven is there one so mighty that he can do such deed as Thine in Egypt, or who can perform such mighty deeds as Thou didst at the Red Sea? I pray Thee, therefore, let me behold the land that, in spite of the slander of the spies, I praised, and Jerusalem and the Temple also.

"When, in answer to the proposition Thou madest me to go into Egypt and deliver Israel, I said, 'I can not do it, for I made a vow to Jethro never to leave him,' Thou didst release me from that vow. O Lord of the world! As then Thou didst absolve me of my vow, saying, 'Go, return into Egypt,' so do Thou now absolve Thyself from Thy vow, and permit me to enter the land of Israel." Then God answered: "Thou hast a master to absolve thee from thy vow, but I have no master." Moses then said: "Thy judgement against me reads that I shall not as king enter the promised land, for to me and to Aaron Thou didst say, "Ye shall not bring this assembly into the land which I have given them.' Permit me then, at least, to enter it as a common citizen." "That," said the Lord, "is impossible. The king shall not enter it degraded to the rank of a common citizen." "Well, then," said Moses, "if I may not even go into the land as a common citizen, let me at least enter into the promised land by the Paneas Grotto, that runs from the east bank to the west bank of the Jordan." But this request, too, God denied him, saying, "Thou shalt not go from this bank of the Jordan to the other." "If this request also is to be denied me," begged Moses, "grant me at least that after my death my bones may be carried to the other side of the Jordan." But God said, "Nay, not even thy bones shall cross the Jordan." "O Lord of the world!" exclaimed Moses, "If Joseph's bones were permitted to be carried into the promised land, why not mine?" God replied, "Whosoever acknowledges his country shall be buried therein, but whosoever does not acknowledge his country shall not be buried therein. Joseph pledged allegiance to his country when he said, 'For indeed I was stolen away out of the land of the Hebrews,' and therefore also does he deserve to have his bones brought to the land of Israel, but thou didst in silence hear the daughters of Jethro say to their father, 'An Egyptian delivered us out of the hands of the shepherds,' without correcting them by saying, 'I am a Hebrew;' and therefore shall not even thy bones be brought into the land of Israel."

Moses furthermore said to God: "O Lord of the world! With the word, 'Behold' did I begin Thy praise, saying, 'Behold, the heaven and the heaven of heavens is the Lord's' and with that very world, 'Behold,' dost thou seal my death, saying, 'Behold, thy days approach that thou must die.'" God replied to this: "A wicked man in his envy sees only the profits, but not the expenditures of his neighbor. Dost thou not recall that when I wanted to send thee to Egypt, thou didst also decline My request with the word, 'Behold,' saying, 'Behold, they will not believe me.' Therefore did I say, 'Behold, thy days approach that thou must die.'" "As furthermore," continued God, "thou didst say to the sons of Levi when they asked thy forgiveness, 'Enough, ye take too much upon ye, ye sons of Levi,' so too shall I answer thy prayer for forgiveness, 'Let it suffice thee; speak no more unto Me of this matter.'"

"O Lord of the world!" again pleaded Moses, "Wilt not Thou recall the time when thou didst say to me, 'Come now, therefore, and I will send thee unto Pharaoh, that thou mayest bring forth My people the children of Israel out of Egypt.' Let them be led by me into their land as I led them out of the land of bondage." But to this also God found a reply: "Moses, wilt not thou recall the time when thou didst say to Me, 'O my Lord, send, I pray Thee by the hand of him whom Thou wild send?' 'With the measure that a man uses, shall measure be given him.' I announce death to thee with the word, 'Behold,' saying 'Behold, thy days approach that thou must die,' because I wanted to point out to thee that thou diest only because thou are a descendant of Adam, upon whose sons I had pronounced death with the word, 'Behold,' saying to the angels: 'Behold, the man is become as one of us, to know good and evil; and now, lest he put forth his hand, and take also of the tree of life, and eat, and live forever.'"

Moses then said, "O Lord of the world! To the first man didst Thou give a command that could easily be obeyed, and yet he disobeyed it, and thereby merited death; but I have not transgressed any of Thy commandments." God: "Behold, Abraham also, who sanctified My name in the world, died." Moses: "Yea, but from Abraham issued Ishmael, whose descendants arouse thy anger." God: "Isaac, also, who laid his neck upon the altar to be offered as a sacrifice to Me, died." Moses: "But from Isaac issued Esau who will destroy the Temple and burn Thy house." God: "From Jacob issued twelve tribes that did not anger Me, and ye he died." Moses: "But he did not ascend into heaven, his feet did not tread the clouds, Thou didst not speak with him face to face, and he did not receive the Torah out of Thy hand." God: "'Let it suffice thee; speak no more unto Me of this matter,' speak not many words, for only 'a fool multiplieth words.'" Moses: "O Lord of the world! Future generations will perchance say, 'Had not God found evil in Moses, He would not have taking him out of the world.'" God: "I have already written in My Torah, 'And there hath not arisen since a prophet in Israel like unto Moses.'" Moses: "Future generations will perhaps say that I had probably acted in accordance with Thy will in my youth, while I was active as a prophet, but that in my old age, when my prophetic activities ceased, I no longer did Thy will."

Moses: "Lord of the world! Let me, I pray, enter into the Land, live there two or three years, and then die." God: "I have resolved that thou shalt not go there." Moses: "If I may not enter it in my lifetime, let me reach it after my death." God: "Nay, neither dead nor alive shalt thou go into the land." Moses: "Why this wrath against me?" God: "Because ye sanctified Me not in the midst of the children of Israel." Moses: "With all Thy creatures dost Thou deal according to Thy quality of mercy, forgiving them their sins, once, twice, and thrice, but me Thou wilt not forgive even one single sin!" God: "Outside of this sin of which thou are aware, thou hast committed six other sins with which I have not until now reproached thee. At the very first, when I appeared to thee, thou didst say, 'O my Lord, send I pray Thee, by the hand of him whom Thou wilt send,' and didst refuse to obey My command to go to Egypt. Secondly thou didst say, 'For since I came to Pharaoh to speak in Thy name, he hath evil entreated this people; neither hast Thou delivered Thy people at all,' accusing Me thereby of having only harmed Israel, instead of aiding them. Thirdly didst thou say, 'If these men die the common death of all men, then the Lord hath not sent me,' so that thou didst arouse doubts among Israel if thou wert really My ambassador. Fourthly didst thou say, 'But if the Lord make a new thing,' doubting if God could do so. Fifthly didst thou say to Israel, 'Hear now, ye rebels,' and in this way didst insult My children. Sixthly didst thou say, 'And behold, ye are risen up in your fathers' stead, an increase of sinful men.' Were Abraham, Isaac, and Jacob, Israel's fathers, perchance sinful men, that thou didst thus address their children?" Moses: "I only followed Thy example, for Thou, too, didst say, 'The censers of these sinners.'" God: "But I did not characterize their fathers as sinners."

Moses: "O Lord of the world! How often did Israel sin before Thee, and when I begged and implored mercy for them, Thou forgavest them, but me Thou wilt not forgive! For my sake Thou forgavest the sins of sixty myriads, and not thou wilt not forgive my sin?" God: "The punishment that is laid upon the community is different from the punishment that is laid upon the individual, for I am not so severe in my treatment of the community as I am in dealing with an individual. But know, furthermore, that until now fate had been in thy power, but now fate is no longer in thy power." Moses: "O Lord of the world! Rise up from the Throne of Justice, and seat Thyself upon the Throne of Mercy, so that in Thy mercy, Thou mayest grant me life, during which I may atone for my sins by suffering that Thou shalt bring upon me. Hand me not over to the sword of the Angel of Death. If Thou wild grant my prayer, then shall I sound Thy praises to all the inhabitants of the earth; I do not wish to die, 'but live and declare the works of the Lord.'" God replied: "'This is the gate of the Lord; the righteous shall enter into it,' this is the gate into which the righteous must enter as well as other creatures, for death had been decreed for man since the beginning of the world."

Moses, however, continued to importune God, saying: "With justice and with mercy hast Thou created the world and mankind, may mercy now conquer justice. In my youth Thou didst begin by showing me Thy power in the bush of thorns, and now, in my old age, I beseech Thee, treat me not as an earthly king treats his servant. When a king of flesh and blood had a servant, he loves him as long as he is young and strong, but casts him off when he is grown old. But Thou, 'cast me not off in the time of old age.' Thou didst show Thy power at the revelation of the Ten Commandments, and thy strong hand in the ten plagues that Thou didst bring upon Egypt. Thou didst create everything, and in Thy hand doth it lie to kill and to give life, there is none who can do these works, nor is there strength like Thine in the future world. Let me then proclaim Thy majesty to the coming generations, and tell them that through me Thou didst cleave the Red Sea, and give the Torah to Israel, that throughout forty years Thou didst cause manna to rain from heaven for Israel, and water to rise from the well." For Moses thought that if his life were spared, he should be able everlastingly to restrain Israel from sin and to hold them forever in faith to the one God. But God said: "' Let it suffice thee.' If thy life were to be spared, men should mistake thee, and make a god of thee, and worship thee." "Lord of the world!" replied Moses, "Thou didst already test me at the time when the Golden Calf was made and I destroyed it. Why then should I die?" God: "Whose son art thou?" Moses: "Amram's son." God: "And whose son was Amram?" Moses: "Izhar's son." God: "And whose son was he?" Moses: "Kohath's son." God: "And whose son was he?" Moses: "Levi's son." God: "And from whom did all of these descend?" Moses: "From Adam." God: "Was the life of any one of these spared?" Moses: "They all died." God: "And thou wishest to live on?" Moses: "Lord of the world! Adam stole the forbidden fruit and ate of it, and it was on this account that Thou didst punish him with death, but did I ever steal aught from Thee? Thou Thyself didst write of me, 'My servant Moses, who is faithful in all Mine house.'" God: "Art thou worthier than Noah?" Moses: "Yes; when Thou sentest the flood over his generation he did not beg Thy mercy for them, but I did say to Thee, 'Yet now, if Thou wilt forgive their sin; and if not, blot me, I pray Thee, out of Thy book which Thou hast written.'"

God: "Was it I perchance, that counseled thee to slay the Egyptian?" Moses: "Thou didst slay all the firstborn of Egypt, and shall I die on account of one single Egyptian that I slew?" God: "Art thou perchance My equal? I slay and restore to life, but canst thou perchance revive the dead?"

GOD TRIES TO COMFORT MOSES CONCERNING HIS

DEATH

That Moses might not take his approaching end too much to heart, God tried to comfort him by pointing out to him that in his lifetime he had received such distinctions from his Creator as no man before him, and that still greater distinctions awaited him in the future world. God said: "Dost not thou remember the great honor I showed thee? Thou didst say to Me, 'Arise,' and I arose; thou saidst, 'Turn about,' and I turned about; for thy sake too did I invert the order of heaven and earth, for the order of heaven it is to send down dew and rain, and earth's order is it to produce bread, but thou didst say to Me, 'I do not wish it so, but bid heaven to send down bread, and earth to bring forth water,' and I acted in accordance with thy wish; I caused bread to rain from heaven, and the well 'sprung up.' Thou didst say, 'If the Lord make a new thing, and the ground open her mouth, and swallow them up, then ye shall understand that the Lord hath sent me,' and I fulfilled thy wish, and it swallowed them. I had also spoken, 'He that sacrificeth unto any god, save unto the Lord only, shall be utterly destroyed,' but when Israel sinned with the Golden Calf and I meant to deal with them according to My words, thou wouldst not let Me, saying: 'Pardon, I pray Thee, the iniquity of this people,' and I forgave them as thou didst ask Me. More than this, the Torah is named after Me, it is the Torah of the Lord, but I named it after Thy name, saying, 'It is the Torah of My servant Moses.' The children of Israel also are named after Me, 'for unto Me the children of Israel are servants; they are My servants,' but I called them after thy name. I distinguished thee still more, for just as there is neither food nor drink for Me, so also didst thou stay in heaven forty days and forty nights, and in all that time, 'didst neither eat bread, nor drink water.' I am God, and see, 'I made thee a god to Pharaoh;' I have prophets, and thou hast a prophet, for I said to thee, 'and Aaron, thy brother, shall be thy prophet.' Again, no being may see Me, and thee too did I make so that 'the people were afraid to come nigh thee,' and as I said to thee, 'thou shalt see My back: but My face shall not be seen,' so too did the people see the back of thee. I glorified the Torah with twenty-two letters, and with all these letters did I glorify thee. I sent thee to Pharaoh, and thou didst lead Israel out of Egypt; through thee did I bestow the Sabbath upon Israel, and the law of circumcision; I gave thee the Ten Commandments, I covered thee with the cloud, I gave thee the two tables of stone, which thou didst break; I made thee unique in the world; I gave thee the Torah as an inheritance, and honored thee more than all the seventy elders."

Moses had to acknowledge that extraordinary marks of honor had been his. He said: "Lord of the world! Thou didst set me on high, and didst bestow upon me so many benefits that I cannot enumerate one of a thousand, and all the world knows how Thou didst exalt me and honor me, and all the world knows as well that Thou art the One God, the only One in Thy world, that there is none beside Thee, and that there is nothing like Thee. Thou didst create those above and those below, Thou art the beginning and the end. Who can enumerate Thy deeds of glory? Do one of these, I beseech Thee, that I may pass over the Jordan." God said: "'Let it suffice, speak no more unto Me of this matter.' It is better for thee to die here, than that thou shouldst cross the Jordan and die in the land of Israel. There in a tomb fashioned by men, on a bier made by men, and by the hands of men wouldst thou be buried; but now shalt thou be buried in a tomb fashioned by

God, on a bier made by God, and shalt be buried by the hands of God. O My son Moses, much honor had been stored up for thee in the future world, for thou wilt take part in all the delights of Paradise, where are prepared three hundred and ten worlds, which I have created for every pious man that through love of Me devoted himself to the Torah. And as in this world I appointed thee over the sixty myriads of Israel, so in the future world shall I appoint thee over the fifty-five myriads of pious men. Thy days, O Moses, will pass, when thou art dead, but thy light will not fade, for thou wilt never have need of the light of sun or moon or stars, nor wilt thou require raiment or shelter, or oil for thy head, or shoes for thy feet, for My majesty will shine before thee, My radiance will make thy face beam, My sweetness will delight thy palate, the carriages of My equipage shall serve as vehicles for thee, and one of My many scepters upon which is engraved the Ineffable Name, one that I had employed in the creation of the world, shall I give to thee, the image of which I had already given thee in this world."

THE INTERCESSIONS FOR MOSES

When Moses saw that God lent no ear to his prayers, he sought to invoke God's mercy through the pleadings of others. "To everything there is a season, and a time to every purpose under the heaven." So long as the course of Moses' days had not yet been run, everything was in his power, but when his time was over, he sought for some one to appeal to God's mercy for him. He now betook himself to Earth and said: "O Earth, I pray thee, implore God's mercy for me. Perhaps for thy sake will He take pity upon me and let me enter into the land of Israel." Earth, however, replied: "I am 'without form and void,' and then too I shall son 'wax old like a garment.' How then should I venture to appear before the King of kings? Nay, thy fate is like mine, for 'dust thou art, and unto dust shalt thou return.'"

Moses hastened to Sun and Moon, and implored them to intercede for him with God, but they replied: "Before we pray to God for thee, we must pray for ourselves, for 'the moon shall be confounded, and the sun ashamed.'"

Moses then took his request to the Stars and the Planets, but these, too, replied: "Before we venture to plead for thee, we must plead for ourselves, for 'all the host of heaven shall be dissolved.'"

Moses then went to the Hills and the Mountains, beseeching them, "Pray appeal to God's mercy for me," and they, too, replied: "We too have to implore God's mercy for ourselves, for He said, 'The mountains shall depart, and the hills be removed.'"

He then laid his plea before Mount Sinai, but the latter said: "Didst thou not see with thine eyes and record in the Torah that, 'Mount Sinai was altogether in smoke, because the Lord descended upon it in a fire?' How then shall I approach the Lord?"

He then went to the Rivers, and sought their intercession before the Lord, but they replied: "'The Lord made a way in the sea, and a path in the mighty waters.' We cannot save ourselves out of His hand, and how then should we aid thee?"

Then he went to the Deserts, and to all the Elements of Nature, but in vain sought to secure their aid. Their answer was : "All go unto one place; all are of the dust, and turn to dust again."

The Great Sea was the last to which he brought his request, but it replied: "Son of Amram, what ails thee today? Art not thou the son of Amram that erstwhile came to me with a staff, beat me, and clove me into twelve parts, while I was powerless against thee, because the Shekinah accompanied thee at thy right hand? What has happened, then, that thou comest before me now pleading?" Upon being reminded of the miracles that he had accomplished in his youth, Moses burst into tears and said, "Oh, that I were as in months past, as in the days when God preserved me!" And turning to the sea, he made answer: "In those days, when I stood beside thee, I was king of the world, and I commanded, but not I am a suppliant, whose prayers are unanswered."

When Moses perceived the Heaven and Earth, Sun and Moon, Stars and Planets, Mountains and Rivers turned a deaf ear to his prayers, he tried to implore mankind to intercede for him before God. He went first to his disciple Joshua, saying: "O my son, be mindful of the love with which I treated thee by day and by night, teaching thee mishnah and halakah, and all arts and sciences, and implore now for my sake God's mercy, for perhaps through thee He may take pity upon me, and permit me to enter the land of Israel." Joshua began to weep bitterly, and beat his palms in sorrow, but when he wanted to begin to pray, Samael appeared and stopped his mouth, saying, "Why dost thou seek to oppose the command of God, who is 'the Rock, whose work is perfect, and all whose ways are judgement?'" Joshua then went to Moses and said, "Master, Samael will not let me pray." At these words Moses burst into loud sobs, and Joshua, too, wept bitterly.

Moses then went to his brother's son, Eleazar, to whom he said: "O my son, be mindful of the days when God was angry with thy father on account of the making of the Golden Calf, and I save him through my prayer. Pray now thou to God for me, and perhaps God will take pity upon me, and let me enter into the land of Israel." But when Eleazar, in accordance with Moses' wish, began to pray, Samael appeared and stopped his mouth, saying to him, "How canst thou think of disregarding God's command?" Then Eleazar reported to Moses that he could not pray for him.

He now tried to invoke Caleb's aid, but him, too, Samael prevented from praying to God. Moses then went to the seventy elders and the other leaders of the people, he even implored every single man among Israel to pray for him, saying: "Remember the wrath which the Lord nursed against your fathers, but I brought it to pass that God relinquished His plan to destroy Israel, and forgave Israel their sins. Now, I pray ye, betake yourselves to the sanctuary of God and exhort His pity for me, that He may permit me to enter into the land of Israel, for 'God never rejects the prayer of the multitude.'"

When the people and their leaders heard these words of Moses, they broke out into mournful weeping, and in the Tabernacle with bitter tears they entreated God to answer Moses' prayer, so that their cries rose even to the Throne of Glory. But then one hundred and eighty four myriads of angels under the leadership of the great angels Zakun and Lahash descended and snatched away the words of the suppliants, that they might not reach God. The angel Lahash indeed tried to restore to their place the words which the other angels had snatched away, so that they might reach God, but when Samael learned of this, he fettered Lahash with chains of fire and brought him before God, where he received sixty blows of fire and was expelled from the inner chamber of God because, contrary to God's wish, he had attempted to aid Moses in the fulfillment of his desire. When Israel now saw how the angels dealt with their prayers, they went to Moses and said, "The angels will not let us pray for thee."

When Moses saw that neither the world nor mankind could aid him, he betook himself to the Angel of the Face, to whom he said, "Pray for me, that God may take pity upon me, and that I may not die." But the angel replied: "Why, Moses, dost thou exert thyself in vain? Standing behind the curtain that is drawn before the Lord, I heard that thy prayer in this instance is not to be answered." Moses now laid his hand upon his head and wept bitterly, saying, "To whom shall I now go, that he might implore God's mercy for me?"

God was now very angry with Moses because he would not resign himself to the doom that had been sealed, but His wrath vanished as soon as Moses spoke the words: "The Lord, the Lord, a God full of compassion and gracious, slow to anger, and plenteous in mercy and truth; keeping mercy for thousands, forgiving iniquity and transgression and sin." God now said kindly to Moses: "I have registered two vows, one that thou are to die, and the second that Israel is to perish. I cannot cancel both vows, if therefore thou choosest to live, Israel must be ruined." "Lord of the world!" replied Moses, "Thou approachest me artfully; Thou seizest the rope at both ends, so that I myself must now say, 'Rather shall Moses and a thousand of his kind perish, than a single soul out of Israel!' But will not all men exclaim, 'Alas! The feet that trod the heavens, the face that beheld the Face of the Shekinah, and the hands that received the Torah, shall not be covered with dust!'" God replied: "Nay, the people will say: ' If a man like Moses, who ascended into heaven, who was peer of the angels, with whom God spoke face to face, and to whom He gave the Torah-if such a man cannot justify himself before God, how much less can an ordinary mortal of flesh and blood, who appears before God without having done good deeds or studied the Torah, justify himself?' I want to know," He added, "why thou are so much aggrieved at thy impending death." Moses: "I am afraid of the sword of the Angel of Death." God: "If this is the reason then speak no more in this matter, for I will not deliver thee into his hand." Moses, however, would not yield, but furthermore said, "Shall my mother Jochebed, to whom my life brought so much grief, suffer sorrow after my death also?" God: "So was it in My mind even before I created the world, and so is the course of the world; every generation has its learned men, every generation has its leaders, every generation has its guides. Up to now it was thy duty to guide the people, but not the time it ripe for thy disciple Joshua to relieve thee of the office destined for him."

MOSES SERVES JOSHUA

Moses now said to himself: "If God has determined that I may not enter the land of Israel, and I am thus to lose the reward for the many precepts that may be observed only in the Holy Land, for no other reason than because the time has come for my disciple Joshua to go to the front of Israel and lead them into the land, then were it better for me to remain alive, to enter the land, and relinquish to Joshua the leadership of the people." What now did Moses do? From the first day of Shebat to the sixth of Adar, the day before his death, he went and served Joshua from morning until evening, as a disciple his mater. These thirty-six days during which Moses served his former disciple corresponded to the equal number of years during which he had been served by Joshua.

The way in which Moses ministered to Joshua was as follows. During the period he arose at midnight, went to Joshua's door, opened it with a key, and taking a shirt from which he shook out the dust, laid it near to Joshua's pillow. He then cleaned Joshua's shoes and placed them beside the bed. Then he took his undergarment, his cloak, his turban, his golden helmet, and his crown of pearls, examined them to see if they were in good condition, cleaned and polished them, arranged them aright, and laid them on a golden chair. He then fetched a pitcher of water and a golden basin and placed them before the golden chair, so to wash himself. He then caused Joshua's rooms, which he furnished like his own, to be swept and put into order, the ordered the golden throne to be brought in, which he covered with a linen and a woolen cloth, and with other beautiful and costly garments, as in the custom with kings. After all these preparations had been made, he bade the herald proclaim: "Moses stands at Joshua's gate and announces that whosoever wishes to hear God's word should betake himself to Joshua, for he, according to God's word, is the leader of Israel."

When the people heard the herald, they trembled and shook, and pretended to have a headache, so that they might not have to go to Joshua. Every one of them said, in tears, "Woe to thee, O land, when thy king is a child!" But a voice from heaven resounded, crying, "When Israel was a child, then I loved him," and Earth, too, opened her mouth, and said, "I have been young, and now am old, yet have I not seen the righteous forsaken." While the people refused to lend ear to the herald's summons, the elders of Israel, the leaders of the troops, the princes of the tribes, and the captains of thousands, of hundreds, and of tens appeared at Joshua's tent, and Moses assigned to each his place according to his rank.

In the meantime approached the hour when Joshua was wont to arise, whereupon Moses entered his room and extended his hand to him. When Joshua saw that Moses served him, he was ashamed to have his master minister to him, and taking the shirt out of Moses' hand, and dressing himself, trembling, he cast himself to Moses' feet and said: "O my master, be not the cause wherefore I should die before half my time is done, owing to the sovereignty God has imposed upon me." But Moses replied: "Fear not, my son, thou sinnest not if thou are served by me. With the measure wherewith thou didst mete out to me, do I mete out to thee; as with a pleasant face thou didst serve me, so shall I serve thee. It was I that taught thee, 'Love thy neighbor as thyself,' and also, 'Let thy pupil's honor be as dear to thee as thine own.'" Moses did not rest until Joshua seated himself upon the golden chair, and then Moses served Joshua, who still resisted, in every needful way. After he was through with all this, he laid upon Joshua, who still resisted, his rays of majesty, which he had received from his celestial teacher Zagzagel, scribe of the angels, at the close of his instruction in all the secrets of the Torah.

When Joshua was completely dressed and ready to go out, they reported to him and to Moses that all Israel awaited them. Moses thereupon laid his hand upon Joshua to lead him out of the tent, and quite against Joshua's wish insisted upon giving precedence to him as they stepped forth. When Israel saw Joshua precede Moses, they all trembled, arose, and made room for these two to proceed to the place of the great, where stood the golden throne, upon which Moses seated Joshua against his will. All Israel burst into tears when they saw Joshua upon the golden throne, and he said amid tears, "why all this greatness and honor to me?"

In this way did Moses spend the time from the first day of Shebat to the sixth of Adar, during which time he expounded the Torah to the sixty myriads of Israel in seventy languages.

Chapter 7

THE LAST DAY OF MOSES' LIFE

On the seventh day of Adar, Moses knew that on this day he should have to die, for a heavenly voice resounded, saying, "Take heed to thyself, O Moses, for thou hast only one more day to live." What did Moses now do? On this day he wrote thirteen scrolls of the Torah, twelve for the twelve tribes, and one he put into the Holy Ark, so that, if they wished to falsify the Torah, the one in the Ark might remain untouched. Moses thought, "If I occupy myself with the Torah, which is the tree of life, this day will draw to a close, and the impending doom will be as naught." God, however, beckoned to the sun, which firmly opposed itself to Moses, saying, "I will not set, so long as Moses lives." When Moses had completed writing the scrolls of the Torah, not even half the day was over. He then bade the tribes come to him, and from his hand receive the scrolls of the Torah, admonishing the men and women separately to obey the Torah and its commands. The most excellent among the thirteen scrolls was fetched by Gabriel, who brought it to the highest heavenly court to show the piety of Moses, who had fulfilled all that is written in the Torah. Gabriel passed with it through all the heavens, so that all might witness Moses' piety. It is this scroll of the Torah out of which the souls of the pious read on Monday and Thursday, as well as on the Sabbath and holy days.

Moses on this day showed great honor and distinction to his disciple Joshua in the sight of all Israel. A herald passed before Joshua through all the camp, proclaiming, "Come and hear the words of the new prophet that hath arisen for us to-day!" All Israel approached to honor Joshua. Moses then gave the command to fetch hither a golden throne, a crown of pearls, a royal helmet, and a robe of purple. He himself set up the rows of benches for the Sanhedrin, for the heads of the army, and for the priests. Then Moses betook himself to Joshua, dressed him, put the crown on his head, and bade him be seated upon the golden throne to deliver from it a speech to the people. Joshua then spoke the following words which he first whispered to Caleb, who then announced it in a loud voice to the people. He said: "Awaken, rejoice, heavens of heavens, ye above; sound joyously, foundations of earth, ye below. Awaken and proclaim aloud, ye orders of creation; awaken and sing, ye mountains everlasting. Exult and shout in joy, ye hills of earth, awaken and burst into songs of triumph, ye hosts of heaven. Sing and relate, ye tents of Jacob, sing, ye dwelling place of Israel. Sing and hearken to all the words that come from your King, incline you heart to all His words, and gladly take upon yourselves and your souls the commandments of your God. Open your mouth, let your tongue speak, and give honor to the Lord that is your Helper, give thanks to your Lord and put your trust in Him. For He is One, and hath no second, there is none like Him among the gods, not one among the angels is like Him, and beside Him is there none that is your Lord. To His praise there are no bounds; to His fame no limit, no end; to His miracles no fathoming; to His works no number. He kept the oath that He swore to the Patriarchs, through our teacher Moses. He fulfilled the covenant with them, and the love and the vow He had made them, for He delivered us through many miracles, led us from bondage to freedom, clove for us the sea, and bestowed upon us six hundred and thirteen commandments."

When Joshua had completed his discourse, a voice resounded from heaven, and said to Moses, "Thou hast only five hours more of life." Moses called out to Joshua, "Stay seated like a king before the people!" Then both began to speak before all Israel; Moses read out the text and Joshua expounded. There was no difference of opinion between them, and the words of the two matched like the pearls in a royal crown. But Moses' countenance shone like the sun, and Joshua's like the moon.

While Joshua and all Israel still sat before Moses, a voice from heaven became audible and said, "Moses, thou hast now only four hours of life." Now Moses began to implore God anew: "O Lord of the world! If I must die only for my disciple's sake, consider that I am willing to conduct myself as if I were his pupil; let it be as if he were high priest, and I a common priest; he is king, and I his servant." God replied: "I have sworn by My great name, which ' the heaven and heaven of heavens cannot contain,' that thou shalt not cross the Jordan." Moses: "Lord of the world! Let me at least, by the power of the Ineffable Name, fly like a bird in the air; or make me like a fish transform my two arms to fins and my hair to scales, that like a fish I may leap over the Jordan and see the land of Israel." God: "If I comply with thy wish, I shall break My vow." Moses: "Lord of the world! Lead me upon the pinions of the clouds about three parasangs high beyond the Jordan, so that the clouds be below me, and I from above may see the land." God replied: "This, too, seems to Me like a breaking of My vow." Moses: "Lord of the world! Cut me up, limb by limb, throw me over the Jordan, and then revive me, so that I may see the land." God: "That, too, would be as if I had broken My vow." Moses: "Let me skim the land with my glance." God: "In this point will I comply with thy wish. 'Thou shalt see the land before thee; but thou shalt not go thither.'" God thereupon showed him all the land of Israel, and although it was a square of four hundred parasangs, still God imparted such strength to Moses' eyes that he could oversee all the land. What lay in the deep appeared to him above, the hidden was plainly in view, the distant was close at hand, and he saw everything.

MOSES BEHOLDS THE FUTURE

Pointing to the land, God said: "'This is the land which I sware unto Abraham, unto Isaac, and unto Jacob, saying, I will give it unto thy seed;' to them did I promise it, but to thee do I show it." But he saw not only the land. God pointed with His finger to every part of the Holy Land, and accurately described it to Moses, saying, "This is Judah's share, this Ephraim's," and in this way instructed him about the division of the land. Moses learned from God the history of the whole land, and the history of every part of it. God showed it to him as it would appear in its glory, and how it would appear under the rule of strangers. God revealed to him not only the complete history of Israel that was to take place in the Holy Land, but also revealed to him all its creation to the Day of Judgement, when the resurrection of the dead will take place. Joshua's war with the Canaanites, Israel's deliverance from the Philistines through Samson, the glory of Israel in David's reign, the building of the Temple under Solomon, and its destruction, the line of kings from the house of David, and the line of prophets from the house of Rahab, the destruction of Gog and Magog on the plain of Jericho, all this and much more, was it given Moses to see. And as God showed him the events in the world, so too did he show him Paradise with its dwellers of piety, and hell with the wicked men that fill it.

The place whence Moses looked upon the Holy Land was a mountain that bore four names: Nebo, Abarim, Hor, and Pisgah. The different appellations are due to the fact that the kingdoms accounted it as a special honor to themselves if they had possessions in the Holy Land. This mountain was divided among four kingdoms, and each kingdom had a special name for its parts. The most appropriate name seems to be Nebo, for upon it died three sinless nebi'im, "prophets," Moses, Aaron and Miriam.

To this mountain, upon God's command, Moses betook himself at noon of the day on which he died. On this occasion, as upon two others, God had His commands executed at noon to show mankind that they could not hinder the execution of God's orders, even if they chose to do so. Had Moses gone to die on Mount Nebo at night, Israel would have said: "He could well do so in the night when we knew of nothing. Had we known that he should go to Nebo to his death, we should not have let him go. Verily, we should not have permitted him to die, who led us out of Egypt, who clove the sea for us, who caused manna to rain down and the well to spring up, who bade the quails to fly to us, and performed many other great miracles." God therefore bade Moses go to his grave on mount Nebo in bright daylight, at noon hour, saying, "Let him who wishes to prevent it try to do so."

For a similar reason did Israel's exodus from Egypt take place in the noon hour, for, had they departed at night, the Egyptians would have said: "They were able to do this in the darkness of the night because we knew nothing of it. Had we known, we should not have permitted them to depart, but should have compelled them by force of arms to stay in Egypt." God therefore said: "I shall lead out Israel to the noon hour. Let him who wishes to prevent it try to do so."

Noah, too, entered the ark at the noon hour for a similar reason. God said: "If Noah enters the ark at night, his generation will declare: 'He could do so because we were not aware of it, or we should not have permitted him to enter the ark alone, but should have taken our hammers and axes, and crushed the ark.' Therefore," said God, "do I wish him to enter the ark at the noon hour. Let him who wishes to prevent it try to do so."

God's command to Moses to betake himself to Mount Nebo, and there to die, was couched in the following words: means not destruction, but elevation. 'Die in the mount whither thou goest up;' go up all alone, and let no one accompany thee. Aaron's son Eleazar accompanied him to his tomb, but no man shall witness the distinction and reward that await thee at thy death. There shalt thou be gather to thy people, to the fathers of Israel, Abraham, Isaac, and Jacob, and to thy fathers, Kohath and Amram, as well as to thy brother Aaron and thy sister Miriam, just as Aaron thy brother died in mount Hor, and was gathered unto his people." For when Aaron was to die, Moses drew off one by one his garments, with which he invested Aaron's son Eleazar, and after he had taken off all his garments, he clothed him in his death robe. Then he said to Aaron: "Aaron, my brother, enter the cave," and he entered. "Get upon the couch," said Moses, and Aaron did so. "Close thine eyes," and he closed them. "Stretch out thy feet," and Aaron did so, and expired. At sight of this painless and peaceful death, Moses said: "Blessed is the man that dies such a death!" When therefore Moses' end drew nigh, God said: "Thou shalt die the death that thou didst wish, as peacefully and with as little pain as thy brother Aaron."

MOSES MEETS THE MESSIAH IN HEAVEN

Moses received still another special distinction on the day of his death, for on that day God permitted him to ascend to the lofty place of heaven, and showed him the reward that awaited him in heaven, and the future. The Divine attribute of Mercy appeared there before him and said to him: "I bring glad tidings to thee, at which thou wilt rejoice. Turn to the Throne of Mercy and behold!" Moses turned to the Throne of Mercy and saw God build the Temple of jewels and pearls, while between the separate gems and pearls shimmered the radiance of the Shekinah, brighter than all jewels. And in this Temple he beheld the Messiah, David's son, and his own brother Aaron, standing erect, and dressed in the robe of the high priest. Aaron then said to Moses: "Do not draw near, for this is the place where the Shekinah dwells, and know that no one may enter here before he have tasted of death and his soul have been delivered to the Angel of Death."

Moses now fell upon his face before God, saying, "Permit me to speak to Thy Messiah before I die." God then said to Moses: "Come, I shall teach thee My great name, that the flames of the Shekinah consume thee not." When the Messiah, David's son, and Aaron beheld Moses approach them, they knew that God had taught him the great name, so they went to meet him and saluted him with the greeting: "Blessed be he that cometh in the name of the Lord." Moses thereupon said to Messiah: "God told me that Israel was to erect a Temple to Him upon earth, and I now see Him build His own Temple, and that, too, in heaven!" The Messiah replied: "Thy father Jacob saw the Temple that will be erected on earth, and also the Temple that God rears with His own hand in heaven, and he clearly understood that it was the Temple God constructed with His own hand in heaven as house of jewels, of pearls, and of the light of the Shekinah, that was to be preserved for Israel to all eternity, to the end of all generations. This was in the night when Jacob slept upon a stone, and in his dream beheld one Jerusalem upon earth, and another in heaven. God then said to Jacob, 'My son Jacob, to-day I stand above thee as in the future thy children will stand before Me.' At the sight of these two Jerusalems, the earthly and the heavenly, Jacob said: 'The Jerusalem on earth is nothing, this is not the house that will be preserved for my children in all generations, but in truth that other house of God, that He builds with His own hands.' But if thou sayest," continued the Messiah, "that God with His own hands builds Himself a Temple in heaven, know then that with His hands also He will build the Temple upon earth."

When Moses heard these words from the mouth of the Messiah, he rejoiced greatly, and lifting up his face to God, he said, "O Lord of the world! When will this Temple built here in heaven come down to earth below?" God replied: "I have made known the time of the event to no creature, either to the earlier ones or to the later, how then should I tell thee?" Moses said: "Give me a sign, so that out of the happenings in the world I may gather when that time will approach," God: "I shall first scatter Israel as with a shovel over all the earth, so that they may be scattered among all nations in the four corners of the earth, and then shall I "set My hand again the second time,' and gather them in that migrated with Jonah, the son of Amittai, to the land of Pathros, and those that dwell in the land of Shinar, Hamath, Elam, and the islands of the sea."

When Moses had heard this, he departed from heaven with a joyous spirit. The Angel of Death followed him to earth, but could not possess himself of Moses' soul, for he refused to give it up to him, delivering it to none but God Himself.

THE LAST HOURS OF MOSES

When Moses had finished looking upon the land and the future, he was one hour nearer to death. A voice sounded from heaven and said, "Make no fruitless endeavors to live." Moses, however, did not desist from prayer, saying to God: "Lord of the world! Let me stay on this side of the Jordan with the sons of Reuben and the sons of God, that I may be as one of them, while Joshua as king at the head of Israel shall enter into the land beyond the Jordan." God replied: "Dost thou wish Me to make as naught the words in the Torah that read, 'Three times in the year all thy males shall appear before the Lord God?' If Israel sees that thou dost not make a pilgrimage to the sanctuary, they will say, 'If Moses, through whom the Torah and the laws were given to us, does not make the pilgrimage to the sanctuary, how much less do we need to do so!' Thou wouldst then cause nonobservance of My commandments. I have, furthermore, written in the Torah through thee, 'At the end of every seven years, in the set time of the year of release, when all Israel is come to appear before the Lord thy God, in the place which He shall choose, thou shalt read this law before all Israel in their hearing.' If thou wert to live thou shouldst put Joshua's authority in the eyes of all Israel to naught, for they would say, 'Instead of learning the Torah and hearing it from the mouth of the disciple, let us rather go to the teacher and learn from him.' Israel will then abandon Joshua and go to thee, so that thou wouldst cause rebellion against My Torah, in which is written that the king shall read before all Israel the Torah in the set time of the year of release."

In the meanwhile still another hour had passed, and a voice sounded from heaven and said: "How long wilt thou endeavor in vain to avert the sentence? Thou has not only two hours more of life." The wicked Samael, head of evil spirits, had eagerly awaited the moment of Moses' death, for he hoped to take his soul like that of all other mortals, and he said continually, "When will the moment be at hand when Michael shall weep and I shall triumph?" When now only two hours remained before Moses' death, Michael, Israel's guardian angel, began to weep, and Samael was jubilant, for now the moment he had awaited so long was very close. But Michael said to Samael: "'Rejoice not against me, mine enemy: when I fall, I shall arise; when I sit in darkness, the Lord shall be a light unto me.' Even if I fell on account of Moses's death, I shall arise again through Joshua when he will conquer the one and thirty kings of Palestine. Even if I sit in darkness owing to the destruction of the first and second Temples, the Lord shall be my light on the day of the Messiah."

In the meanwhile still another hour had passed, and a voice resounded from heaven and said, "Moses, thou hast only one hour more of life!" Moses thereupon said: "O Lord of the world! Even if Thou wilt not let me enter into the land of Israel, leave me at least in this world, that I may live, and not die." God replied, "If I should not let thee die in this world, how then can I revive thee hereafter for the future world? Thou wouldst, moreover, then give the lie to the Torah, for through thee I wrote therein, 'neither is there any that can deliver out of My hand.'" Moses continued to pray: "O Lord of the world! If thou dost not permit me to enter into the land of Israel, let me live like the beasts of the field, and feed on herbs, and drink water, let me live and see the world: let me be as one of these." But God said, "Let it suffice thee!" Still Moses continued: "If Thou wilt not grant me this, let me at least live in this world like a bird that flies in the four directions of the world, and each day gathers its food from the ground, drinks water out of the streams, and at eve returns to its nest." But even this last prayer of his was denied, for God said, "Thou hast already made too many words."

Moses now raised up his voice in weeping, and said, "To whom shall I go that will now implore mercy to me?" He went to every work of creation and said, "Implore mercy for me." But all replied: "We cannot even implore mercy for ourselves, for God 'hath made everything beautiful in its time,' but afterward, 'all go unto one place, all are of the dust, and all turn to dust again,' 'for the heaven shall vanish away like smoke, and the earth shall wax old like a garment.'"

When Moses saw that none of the works of creation could aid him, he said: "He is 'the Rock, His work is perfect, for all His ways are judgement: A God of faithfulness and without iniquity, just and right is He.'"

When Moses saw that he could not escape death, he called Joshua, and in the presence of all Israel addressed him as follows: "Behold, my son, the people that I deliver into thy hands, is the people of the Lord. It is still in its youth, and hence is inexperienced in the observance of its commandments; beware, therefore, lest thou speak harshly to them, for they are the children of the Holy One, who called them, 'My firstborn son, Israel'; and He loved them before all other nations." But God, on the other hand, at once said to Joshua: "Joshua, thy teacher Moses has transferred his office to thee. Follow now in his footsteps, take a rod and hit upon the head, 'Israel is a child, hence I love him,' and 'withhold not correction from the child.'"

Joshua now said to Moses: "O my teacher Moses, what will become of me? If I give to the one a share upon a mountain, he will be sure to want one in the valley, and he to whom I give his share in the valley will wish it to be upon a mountain." Moses, however, quieted him, saying, "Be not afraid, for God hath assured me that there will be peace at the distribution of the land." Then Moses said: "Question me regarding all the laws that are not quite clear to thee, for I shall be taken from thee, and thou shalt see me no more." Joshua replied, "When, O my master, by night or by day, have I ever left thee, that I should be in doubt concerning anything that thou hast taught me?" Moses said, "Even if thou hast no questions to ask to me, come hither, that I may kiss thee." Joshua went to Moses, who kissed him and wept upon his neck, and a second time blessed him, saying, "Mayest thou be at peace, and Israel be at peace with thee."

THE BLESSING OF MOSES

The people now came to Moses and said, "The hour of thy death is at hand," and he replied: "Wait until I have blessed Israel. All my life long they had no pleasant experiences with me, for I constantly rebuked them and admonished them to fear God and fulfil the commandments, therefore do I not now wish to depart out of this world before I have blessed them." Moses had indeed always cherished the desire of blessing Israel, but the Angel of Death had never permitted him to satisfy his wish, so shortly before dying, he enchained the Angel of Death, cast him beneath his feet, and blessed Israel in spite of their enemy, saying, "Save Thy people, and bless Thine inheritance: feed them also, and bear them up for ever."

Moses was not the first to bestow blessings, as former generations had also done so, but no blessing was as effective as his. Noah blessed his sons, but it was a divided blessing, being intended for Shem, whereas Ham, instead of being blessed, was cursed. Isaac blessed his sons, but his blessings led to a dispute, for Esau envied Jacob his blessings. Jacob blessed his sons, but even his blessing was not without a blemish, for in blessing he rebuked Reuben and called him to account for the sins he had committed. Even the number of Moses' blessings excelled that of his predecessors. For when God created the world, He blessed Adam and Eve, and this blessing remained upon the world until the flood, when it ceased. When Noah left the ark, God appeared before him and bestowed upon him anew the blessing that had vanished during the flood, and this blessing rested upon the world until Abraham came into the world and received a second blessing from God, who said, "And I will make of thee a great nation, and I will bless them that bless thee, and curse him that curseth thee." God then said to Abraham: "Henceforth it no longer behooves Me to bless My creatures in person, but I shall leave the blessings to thee: he whom thou blessest, shall be blessed by Me." Abraham did not, however, bless his own son Isaac, in order that the villain Esau might not have a share in that blessing. Jacob, however, received not only two blessings from his father, but one other besides from the angel with whom he wrestled, and one from God; and the blessing also that had been Abraham's to bestow upon his house went to Jacob. When Jacob blessed his sons, he passed on to them the five blessings he had received, and added one other. Balaam should really have blessed Israel with seven benedictions, corresponding to the seven altars he had erected, but he envied Israel greatly, and blessed them with only three blessings. God thereupon said: "Thou villain that begrudgest Israel their blessings! I shall not permit thee to bestow upon Israel all the blessing that are their due. Moses, who had 'a benevolent eye,' shall bless Israel." And so, too, it came to pass. Moses added a seventh blessing to the six benedictions with which Jacob had blessed his twelve sons. This was not, however, the first time that Moses blessed the people. He blessed them at the erection of the Tabernacle, then at its consecration, a third time at the installation of the judges, and a fourth time on the day of his death.

Before bestowing his blessing upon Israel, however, Moses intoned a song in God's praise, for it is fitting to glorify God's name before asking a favor of Him, and as Moses was about to ask God to bless Israel, he first proclaimed His grandeur and His majesty.

He said: "When God first revealed Himself to Israel to bestow the Torah upon them, He appeared to them not from one direction, but from all four at once. He 'came from Sinai,' which is in the South, 'and rose from Seir unto them,' that is in the East; 'He shined forth from mount Paran,' that is in the North, 'and he came from the ten thousands of holy' angels that dwell in the West. He proclaimed the Torah not only in the language of Sinai, that is Hebrew, but also in the tongue of Seir, that is Roman, as well as in Paran's speech, that is Arabic, and in the speech of Kadesh, that is Aramaic, for He offered the Torah not to Israel alone, but to all the nations of the earth. These, however, did not want to accept it, hence His wrath against them, and His especial love for Israel who, despite their awed fear and trembling upon God's appearance on Sinai, still accepted the Torah. Lord of the World!" continued Moses, "When Israel shall have been driven out of their land, be mindful still of the merits of their Patriarchs and stand by them, deliver them in Thy mercy from 'the yoke of the nations,' and from death, and guide them in the future world as Thou didst lead them in the desert."

At these words Israel exclaimed, "The Torah that Moses brought to us at the risk of his life is our bride, and no other nation may lay claim to it. Moses was our king when the seventy elders assembled, and in the future the Messiah will be our king, surrounded by seven shepherds, and he will gather together once more the scattered tribes of Israel." Then Moses said: "God first appeared in Egypt to deliver His people, then at Sinai to give them the Torah, and He will appear a third time to take vengeance at Edom, and will finally appear to destroy Gog."

After Moses had praised and glorified God, he began to implore His blessing for the tribes. His first prayer to God concerned Reuben, for whom he implored forgiveness for his sin with Bilhah. He said: "May Reuben come to life again in the future world for his good deed in saving Joseph, and may he not remain forever dead on account of his sin with Bilhah. May Reuben's descendants also be heroes in war, and heroes in their knowledge of the Torah." God granted this prayer and forgave Reuben's sin in accordance with the wish of the other tribes, who begged God to grant forgiveness to their eldest brother. Moses at once perceived that God had granted his prayer, for all the twelve stones in the high priest's breastplate began to gleam forth, whereas formerly Reuben's stone had given forth no light. When Moses saw that God had forgiven Reuben's sin, he at once set about trying to obtain God's pardon for Judah, saying, "Was it not Judah that through his penitent confession of his sin with his daughter-in-law Tamar induced Reuben, too, to seek atonement and repentance!" The sin for which Moses asked God to forgive Judah was that he had never redeemed his promise to bring Benjamin back to his father. Owing to this sin, his corpse fell to pieces, so that its bones rolled about in their coffin during the forty years' march in the desert. But as soon as Moses prayed to God, saying, "Hear, Lord, the voice of Judah," the bones joined together once more, but his sin was not quite forgiven, for he was not yet admitted to the heavenly academy. Therefore Moses continued to pray: "Bring him in unto his people," and he was admitted. It did not, indeed, benefit him, for in punishment of his sin, God brought it to pass that he could not follow the discussion of the scholars in heaven, much less take part in them, whereupon Moses prayed: "Let his hands be sufficient for him," and them he no longer sat as one dumb in the heavenly academy. But still his sin was not quite forgiven, for Judah could not succeed in being victorious in the disputes of the learned, hence Moses prayed, "And Thou shalt be an help against his adversaries." It was only then that Judah's sin was quite forgiven, and that he succeeded in disputes with his antagonists in the heavenly academy.

As Moses prayed for Judah, so too did he pray for his seed, and especially for David and the royal dynasty of David. He said: "When David, king of Israel, shall be in need, and shall pray to Thee, then, 'Hear, Lord, his voice, and Thou shalt be an help against his adversaries,' 'bring him' then back 'to his people' in peace; and when alone he shall set out into battle against Goliath, 'let his hands be sufficient for him, and Thou shalt be an help against his adversaries.'" Moses at the same time prayed God to stand by the tribe of Judah, whose chief weapon in war was the bow, that their 'hands might be sufficient,' that they might vigorously and with good aim speed the arrow.

As Moses had never forgiven Simeon their sin with the daughters of Moab, he bestowed upon them no blessing, but this tribe also was not quite forgotten, for he included this tribe in his blessing for Judah, praying to God, that He might hear Judah's voice whenever he should pray for the tribe of Simeon when they should be in distress, and that furthermore He should give them their possession in the Holy Land beside Judah's.

Simeon and Levi "drank out of the same cup," for both together in their wrath slew the inhabitants of Shechem, but whereas Levi made amends for his sin, Simeon added another new one. It was the Levites who, in their zeal for God, slew those that worshipped the Golden Calf; it was a Levite, Phinehas, moreover, who in his zeal for God slew the wicked prince of the tribe of Simeon, and his mistress. Hence Moses praised and blessed the tribe of Levi, whereas he did not even consider Simeon with a word.

His words first referred to Aaron, prince of the tribe of Levi. He said: "Well may Thy Urim and Tummim belong to Aaron, who ministered services of love to Thy children, who stood every test that Thou didst put upon him, and who at the 'waters of rebellion' became the victim of a wrong accusation." God had then decreed against Aaron that he was to die in the desert, although not he, but Moses had trespassed against Him, saying to Israel, "Hear now, ye rebels." As Aaron, prince of the tribe of Levi, when Israel was still in Egypt, declaimed passionately against the people because they worshipped idols, so too all the tribe of Levi stood up by God's standard when Israel worshipped the Golden Calf in the desert, and slew the idolaters, even if they were their half-brothers or their daughters sons. The Levites also were the only ones who, in Egypt as in the desert, remained true to God and His teachings, did not abandon the token of the covenant, and were not tempted to rebellion by the spies. "Hence," continued Moses, "shall the Levites be the only ones from whose mouth shall issue judgement and instruction for Israel. 'Thy shall put incense' in the Holy of Holies, 'and whole burnt offerings upon His altar.' Their sacrifices shall reconcile Israel with God, and they themselves shall be blessed with earthly goods. Thou, Lord, 'smitest through the loins of them that rise up against them' that dispute the priestly rights of this tribe, Thou didst destroy Korah, and they 'that hated them' like king Uzziah, 'shall not rise again.' 'Bless, Lord, the substance of the Levites who give from the tithes that they receive one-tenth to the priests. Mayest Thou accept sacrifice from the hands of the priest Elijah upon mount Carmel, 'smite the loins' of his enemy Ahab, break the neck of the latter's false prophets, and may the enemies of the high priest Johanan rise not again."

"Benjamin," said Moses, "is the beloved of the Lord, whom he will always shield, and in whose possession the sanctuary shall stand, in this world as well as in the time of the Messiah, and in the future world."

Moses blessed Joseph's tribe with the blessing that their possession might be the most fruitful and blessed land on earth; dew shall ever be there, and many wells spring up. It shall constantly be exposed to the gentle influences of sun and moon, that the fruits may ripen early. "I wish him," said Moses, "that the blessings given him by the Patriarchs and the wives of the Patriarchs may be fulfilled." And so, too, it came to pass, for the land of the tribe of Joseph possessed everything, and nothing within it was lacking. This was the reward to Joseph for having fulfilled the will of God that was revealed to Moses in the bush of thorns; and also because as king of Egypt he treated his brothers with high honors although they had thrust him from their midst. Moses furthermore blessed Joseph by promising him that, as he had been the first of Jacob's sons to come to Egypt, he was also to be the first in the future world to appear in the Holy Land. Moses proclaimed the heroism of Joseph's seed in the words: "As it is a vain thing to try to force the firstling bullock to labor, so little shall Joseph's sons be yoked into service by the empires; as the unicorn with his horns pushes away all other animals, so, too, shall Joseph's sons rule the nations, even to the ends of the earth. The Ephraimite Joshua shall destroy myriads of heathens, and the Manassite Gideon thousands of them."

Zebulun was the tribe that before all the other tribes devoted itself to commerce, and in this way acted as the agent between Israel and the other nations, selling the products of Palestine to the latter, and foreign wares to the former. Hence the blessing that Moses bestowed upon them. "'Rejoice, Zebulun, in thy going out' on commercial enterprises; at thy instance shall many nations pray upon the sacred mountain of the Temple and offer their sacrifices." For the people that came into Zebulun's realms on matters of business used to go from thence to Jerusalem to look upon the sanctuary of the Jews, and many of them were converted through the grand impression that the life in the holy city made upon them. Moses furthermore blessed this tribe by giving them an estate by the sea, which might yield them costly fish and the purple shell, and the sand of whose shores might furnish them the material for glass. The other tribes were therefore dependent upon Zebulun for these articles, which they could not obtain from any one else, for whosoever attempted to rob Zebulun of them, was doomed to bad luck in business. It is the "Sea of Chaifa" also, within Zebulun's territory, where all the treasures of the ocean were brought to shore; for whenever a ship is wrecked at sea, the ocean sends it and its treasures to the sea of Chaifa, where it is hoarded for the pious until the Judgement Day. One other blessing of Zebulun was that it would always be victorious in battle, whereas the tribe of Issachar, closely bound up with it, was blessed by its distinction in the "tents of learning." For Issachar was "the tribe of scholars and of judges," wherefore Moses blessed them, saying that in "the future time," Israel's great house of instruction as well as the great Sanhedrin would be located in this tribe.

The tribe of Gad, dwelling on the boundary of the land of Israel, received the benediction that in "the future time" it would be as strong in battle as it had been at the first conquest of Palestine, and would hereafter stand at the head of Israel on their return to the Holy Land, as it had done on their first entrance into the land. Moses praised this tribe for choosing its site on this side the Jordan because that place had been chosen to hold Moses' tomb. Moses indeed died on mount Nebo, which is Reuben's possession, but his body was taken from Nebo by the pinions of the Shekinah, and brought to Gad's territory, a distance of four miles, amid the lamentations of the angels, who said, "He shall enter into peace and rest in his bed."

Dan, who like Gad had his territory on the boundary of the land, was also blessed with strength and might, that he might ward off the attacks of Israel's enemies. He was also blessed in receiving his territory in the Holy Land in two different sections of it.

Naphtali's blessing read: "O Naphtali, satisfied with favor, and full with the blessing of the Lord: possess thou the west and the south." This blessing was verified, for the tribe of Naphtali had in its possession an abundance of fish and mushrooms, so that they could maintain themselves without much labor; and the valley of Gennesaret furthermore was their possession, whose fruits were renowned for their extraordinary sweetness. But Naphtali was blessed not with material blessings only, but also with spiritual; for it was the great house of instruction at Tiberias to which Moses alluded when he said of Naphtali, "he is 'full with the blessings of the Lord.'"

Moses called Asher the favorite of his brethren, for it was this tribe that in the years of release provided nourishment for all Israel, as its soil was so productive that what grew of its own accord sufficed to sustain all. But Moses blessed Asher in particular with a land rich in olives, so that oil flowed in streams through Asher's land. Hence Moses blessed him the words: "The treasures of all lands shall flow to thee, for the nations shall give thee gold and silver for thine oil." He blessed Asher moreover with many sons, and with daughters that preserved the charms of youth in their old age.

As Moses uttered eleven benedictions, so likewise did he compose eleven psalms, corresponding to the eleven tribes blessed by him. These psalms of Moses were later received into David's Psalter, where the psalms of Adam, Melchizedek, Abraham, Solomon, Asaph, and the three sons of Korah also found their place. Moses' first psalms says, "'Thou turnest man to destruction; and sayest, Return, ye children of men,' and forgivest the forefather of the tribe of Reuben who sinned, but returned again to God." Another one of Moses' psalms reads, "He that dwelleth in the secret place of the most High shall abide under the shadow of the Almighty," which corresponds to the tribe of Levi that dwelled in the sanctuary, the shadow of the Almighty. To the tribe of Judah, whose name signifies, "Praise the Lord," belongs the psalm, "It is a good thing to give thanks unto the Lord." The psalm: "The Lord is apparelled with majesty," is Benjamin's, for the sanctuary stood in his possession, hence this psalm closes with the words, "Holiness becometh Thine house, O Lord, forevermore." The psalm: "O Lord, Thou God to whom vengeance belongeth; Thou God to whom vengeance belongeth, shine forth," was composed by Moses for the tribe of Gad; for Elijah, a member of this tribe, was to destroy the foundations of the heathens, and to wreak upon them the vengeance of the Lord. To the tribe of learned men, Issachar, goes the psalm: "O come, let us sing unto the Lord: let us make a joyful noise to the rock of our salvation," for it is this tribe that occupy themselves with the Torah, the book of praise.

MOSES PRAYS FOR DEATH

Moses still had many other blessings for every single tribe, but when he perceived that his time had drawn to a close, he included them all in one blessing, saying, "Happy art thou, O Israel: Who is like unto thee, a people saved by the Lord, the shield of thy help, and that is the sword of thy excellency!" With these words he at the same time answered a question that Israel had put to him, saying, "O tell us, our teacher Moses, what is the blessing that God will bestow upon us in the future world?" He replied: "I cannot describe it to you, but all I can say is, happy ye that such is decreed for ye!" Moses at the same time begged God that in the future world He might restore to Israel the heavenly weapon that He had taken from them after the worship of the Golden Calf. God said, "I swear that I shall restore it to them."

When Moses had finished his blessing, he asked Israel to forgive his sternness toward them, saying: "Ye have had much to bear from me in regard to the fulfillment of the Torah and its commandments, but forgive me now." They replied: "Our teacher, our lord, it is forgiven." It was not their turn to ask his forgiveness, which they did in these words: "We have often kindled thine anger and have laid many burdens upon thee, but forgive us now." He said, "It is forgiven."

In the meanwhile people came to him and said, "The hour has come in which thou departest from the world." Moses said, "Blessed be His name that liveth and endureth in all eternity!" Turning to Israel, he then said, "I pray ye, when ye shall have entered into the land of Israel, remember me still, and my bones, and say, 'Woe to the son of Amram that ran before us like a horse, but whose bones remained in the desert.'" Israel said to Moses: "O our teacher, what will become of us when thou art gone?" He replied: "While I was with ye, God was with ye; yet think not that all the signs and miracles that He wrought through me were performed for my sake, for much rather were they done for your sake, and for His love and mercy, and if ye have faith in Him, He will work your desires. 'Put not your trust in princes, nor in the son of man, in whom there is no help,' for how could ye expect help from a man, a creature of flesh and blood, that cannot shield himself from death? Put, therefore, your trust in Him through whose word arose the world, for He liveth and endureth in all eternity. Whether ye be laden with sin, or not, 'pour your heart before Him,' and turn to Him." Israel said: "'The Lord, He is God; the Lord, He is God.' God is our strength and our refuge."

Then a voice sounded from heaven and said, "Why, Moses, dost thou strive in vain? Thou had but one-half hour more of life in the world." Moses, to whom God had now shown the reward of the pious in the future world, and the gates of salvation and of consolation that He would hereafter open to Israel, now said: "Happy art thou, O Israel: who is like unto thee, a people saved by the Lord!" He then bade farewell to the people, weeping aloud. He said: "Dwell in peace, I shall see ye again at the Resurrection," and so he went forth from them, weeping aloud. Israel, too, broke into loud lamentations, so that their weeping ascended to the highest heavens.

Moses took off his outer garment, rent his shirt, strewed dust upon his head, covered it like a mourner, and in this condition betook himself to his tent amid tears and lamentations, saying: "Woe to my feet that may not enter the land of Israel, woe to my hands that may not pluck of its fruits! Woe to my palate that may not taste the fruits of the land that flows with milk and honey!"

Moses then took a scroll, wrote upon it the Ineffable Name, and the book of the song, and betook himself to Joshua's tent to deliver it to him. When he arrived at Joshua's tent, Joshua was seated, and Moses remained standing before him in a bowed attitude without being noticed by Joshua. For God brought this to pass in order that Moses, on account of this disrespectful treatment, might himself wish for death. For when Moses had prayed to God to let him live, were it only as a private citizen, God granted his prayer, saying to him, "If thou hast no objection to subordinating thyself to Joshua, then mayest thou live," and in accordance with this agreement, Moses had betaken himself to hear Joshua's discourse.

The people who had gathered as usual before Moses' tent to hear from him the word of God, failed to find him there, and hearing that he had gone to Joshua, went there likewise, where they found Moses standing and Joshua seated. "What art thou thinking of," they called out to Joshua, "that thou art seated, while thy teacher Moses stands before thee in a bowed attitude and with folded hands?" In their anger and indignation against Joshua, they would instantly have slain him, had not a cloud descended and interposed itself between the people and Joshua. When Joshua noticed that Moses stood before him, he instantly arose, and cried in tears: "O my father and teacher Moses, that like a father didst rear me from my youth, and that didst instruct me in wisdom, why dost thou do such a thing as will bring upon me Divine punishment?" The people now besought Moses as usual to instruct them in the Torah, but he replied, "I have no permission to do so." They did not, however, cease importuning him, until a voice sounded from heaven and said, "Learn from Joshua." The people now consented to acknowledge Joshua as their teacher, and seated themselves before him to hear his discourse. Joshua now began his discourse with Moses sitting at his right, and Aaron's sons, Eleazar and Ithamar, at this left. But hardly had Joshua begun his lecture with the words, "Praised be God that taketh delight in the pious and their teachings," when the treasures of wisdom vanished from Moses and passed over into Joshua's possession, so that Moses was not even able to follow his disciple Joshua's discourse. When Joshua had finished his lecture, Israel requested Moses to review with them what Joshua had taught, but he said, "I know not how to reply to your request!" He began to expound Joshua's lecture to them, but could not, for he had not understood it. He now said to God: "Lord of the world! Until not I wished for life, but now I long to die. Rather a hundred deaths, than one jealousy."

SAMAEL CHASTISED BY MOSES

When God perceived that Moses was prepared to die, He said to the angel Gabriel, "Go, fetch Me Moses' soul." But he replied, "How should I presume to approach and take the soul of him that outweighs sixty myriads of mortals!" God then commissioned the angel Michael to fetch Moses' soul, but he amid tears refused on the same grounds as Gabriel. God then said to the angel Zagzagel, "Fetch Me Moses' soul!" He replied, "Lord of the world! I was his teacher and he my disciple, how then should I take his soul!" Then Samael appeared before God and said: "Lord of the world! Is Moses, Israel's teacher, indeed greater than Adam whom thou didst create in Thine image and Thy likeness? Is Moses greater, perchance, than Thy friend Abraham, who to glorify Thy name cast himself into the fiery furnace? Is Moses greater, perchance, than Isaac, who permitted himself to be bound upon the altar as a sacrifice to Thee? Or is he greater than Thy firstborn Jacob, or than his twelve sons, Thy saplings? Not one of them escaped me, give me therefore permission to fetch Moses' soul." God replied: "Not one of all these equals him. How, too, wouldst thou take his soul? From his face? How couldst thou approach his face that had looked upon My Face! From his hands? Those hands received the Torah, how then shouldst thou be able to approach them! From his feet? His feet touched My clouds, how then shouldst thou be able to approach them! Nay, thou canst not approach him at all." But Samael said, "However it be, I pray Thee, permit me to fetch his soul! " God said, "Thou had My consent."

Samael now went forth from God in great glee, took his sword, girded himself with cruelty, wrapped himself in wrath, and in a great rage betook himself to Moses. When Samael perceived Moses, he was occupied in writing the Ineffable Name. Dart of fire shot from his mouth, the radiance of his face and of his eyes shone like the sun, so that he seemed like an angel of the hosts of the Lord, and Samael in fear and trembling thought, "It was true when the other angels declared that they could not seize Moses' soul!"

Moses who had known that Samael would come, even before his arrival, now lifted his eyes and looked upon Samael, whereupon Samael's eyes grew dim before the radiance of Moses' countenance. He fell upon his face, and was seized with the woes of a woman giving birth, so that in his terror he could not open his mouth. Moses therefore addressed him, saying: "Samael, Samael! 'There is no peace, saith my God, to the wicked!' Why dost thou stand before me? Get thee hence at once, or I shall cut off thy head." In fear and trembling Samael replied: "Why art thou angry with me, my master, give me thy soul, for thy time to depart from the world is at hand." Moses: "Who sent thee to me?" Samael: "He that created the world and the souls." Moses: "I will not give thee my soul." Samael: "All souls since the creation of the world were delivered into my hands." Moses: "I am greater than all others that came into the world, I have had a greater communion with the spirit of God than thee and thou together." Samael: "Wherein lies thy preeminence?" Moses: "Dost thou not know that I am the son of Amram, that came circumcised out of my mother's womb, that at the age of three days not only walked, but even talked with my parents, that took no milk from my mother until she received her pay from Pharaoh's daughter? When I was three months old, my wisdom was so great that I made prophecies and said, 'I shall hereafter from God's right hand receive the Torah.' At the age of six months I entered Pharaoh's palace and took off the crown from his head. When I was eighty years old, I brought the ten plagues upon Pharaoh and the Egyptians, slew their guardian angel, and led the sixty myriads of Israel out of Egypt. I then clove the sea into twelve parts, led Israel through the midst of them, and drowned the Egyptians in the same, and it was not thou that took their souls, but I. It was I, too, that turned the bitter water into sweet, that mounted into heaven, and there spoke face to face with God! I hewed out two tables of stone, upon which God at my request wrote the Torah. One hundred and twenty days and as many nights did I dwell in heaven, where I dwelled under the Throne of Glory; like an angel during all this time I ate no bread and drank no water. I conquered the inhabitants of heaven, made known there secrets to mankind, received the Torah from God's right hand, and at His command wrote six hundred and thirteen commandments, which I then taught to Israel. I furthermore waged war against the heroes of Sihon and Og, that had been created before the flood and were so tall that the waters of the flood did not even reach their ankles. In battle with them I bade sun and moon to stand still, and with my staff slew the two heroes. Where, perchance, is there in the world a mortal who could do all this? How darest thou, wicked one, presume to wish to seize my pure soul that was given me in holiness and purity by the Lord of holiness and purity? Thou hast no power to sit where I sit, or to stand where I stand. Get thee hence, I will not give thee my soul."

Samael now in terror returned to God and reported Moses' words to Him. God's wrath against Samael was now kindled, and He said to him: "Go, fetch Me Moses soul, for if thou dost not do so, I shall discharge thee from thine office of taking men's souls, and shall invest another with it." Samael implored God, saying: "O Lord of the world, whose deed are terrible, bid me go to Gehenna and there turn uppermost to undermost, and undermost to uppermost, and I shall at once do so without a moment's hesitation, but I cannot appear before Moses." God: "Why not, pray?" Samael: "I cannot do it because he is like the princes in thy great chariot. Lightning-flashes and fiery darts issue from his mouth when he speaks with me, just as it is with the Seraphim when they laud, praise and glorify Thee. I pray Thee, therefore, send me not to him, for I cannot appear before him." But God in wrath said to Samael: "Go, fetch Me Moses' soul," and while he set about to execute God's command, the Lord furthermore said: "Wicked one! Out of the fire of Hell was thou created, and to the fire of Hell shalt thou eventually return. First in great joy didst thou set out to kill Moses, but when thou didst perceive his grandeur and his greatness, thou didst say, 'I cannot undertake anything against him.' It is clear and manifest before Me that thou wilt now return from him a second time in shame and humiliation."

Samael now drew his sword out of its sheath and in a towering fury betook himself to Moses, saying, "Either I shall kill him or he shall kill me." When Moses perceived him he arose in anger, and with his staff in his hand, upon which was engraved the Ineffable Name, set about to drive Samael away. Samael fled in fear, but Moses pursued him, and when he reached him, he struck him with his staff, blinded him with the radiance of his face, and then let him run on, covered with shame and confusion. He was not far from killing him, but a voice resounded from heaven and said, "Let him live, Moses, for the world is in need of him," so Moses had to content himself with Samael's chastisement.

GOD KISSES MOSES' SOUL

In the meanwhile Moses' time was at an end. A voice from heaven resounded, saying: "Why, Moses, dost thou strive in vain? Thy last second is at hand." Moses instantly stood up for prayer, and said: "Lord of the world! Be mindful of the day on which Thou didst reveal Thyself to me in the bush of thorns, and be mindful also of the day when I ascended into heaven and during forty days partook of neither food nor drink. Thou, Gracious and Merciful, deliver me not into the hand of Samael." God replied: "I have heard thy prayer. I Myself shall attend to thee and bury thee." Moses now sanctified himself as do the Seraphim that surround the Divine Majesty, whereupon God from the highest heavens revealed Himself to receive Moses' soul. When Moses beheld the Holy One, blessed he His Name, he fell upon his face and said: "Lord of the world! In love didst Thou create the world, and in love Thou guidest it. Treat me also with love, and deliver me not into the hands of the Angel of Death." A heavenly voice sounded and said: "Moses, be not afraid. 'Thy righteousness shall go before thee; the glory of the Lord shall be thy reward.'"

With God descended from heaven three angels, Michael, Gabriel, and Zagzagel. Gabriel arranged Moses' couch, Michael spread upon it a purple garment, and Zagzagel laid down a woolen pillow. God stationed Himself over Moses' head, Michael to his right, Gabriel to his left, and Zagzagel at his feet, whereupon God addressed Moses: "Cross thy feet," and Moses did so. He then said, "Fold thy hands and lay them upon thy breast," and Moses did so. Then God said, "Close thine eyes," and Moses did so. Then God spake to Moses' soul: "My daughter, one hundred and twenty years had I decreed that thou shouldst dwell in this righteous man's body, but hesitate not now to leave it, for thy time is run." The soul replied: "I know that Thou art the God of spirits and of souls, and that in Thy hand are the souls of the living and of the dead. Thou didst create me and put me into the body of this righteous man. Is there anywhere in the world a body so pure and holy as this it? Never a fly rested upon it, never did leprosy show itself upon it. Therefore do I love it, and do not wish to leave it." God replied: "Hesitate not, my daughter! Thine end hath come. I Myself shall take thee to the highest heavens and let thee dwell under the Throne of My Glory, like the Seraphim, Ofannim, Cherubim, and other angels." But the soul replied: "Lord of the world! I desire to remain with this righteous man; for whereas the two angels Azza and Azazel when they descended from heaven to earth, corrupted their way of life and loved the daughters of the earth, so that in punishment Thou didst suspend them between heaven and earth, the son of Amram, a creature of flesh and blood, from the day upon which Thou didst reveal Thyself from the bush of thorns, has lived apart from his wife. Let me therefore remain where I am." When Moses saw that his soul refused to leave him, he said to her: "Is this because the Angel of Death wished to show his power over thee?" The soul replied: "Nay, God doth not wish to deliver me into the hands of death." Moses: "Wilt thou, perchance, weep when the others will weep at my departure?" The soul: "The Lord 'hath delivered mine eyes from tears.'" Moses: "Wilt thou, perchance, go into Hell when I am dead?" The soul: "I will walk before the Lord in the land of the living." When Moses heard these words, he permitted his soul to leave him, saying to her: "Return unto thy rest, O my soul; for the Lord hath dealt bountifully with thee." God thereupon took Moses' soul by kissing him upon the mouth.

Moses activity did not, however, cease with his death, for in heaven he is one of the servants of the Lord. God buried Moses' body in a spot that remained unknown even to Moses himself. Only this is know concerning it, that a subterranean passage connects it with the graves of the Patriarchs. Although Moses' body lies dead in its grave, it is still as fresh as when he was alive.

THE MOURNING FOR MOSES

When Moses died, a voice resounded from heaven throughout all the camp of Israel, which measured twelve miles in length by twelve in width, and said, "Woe! Moses is dead. Woe! Moses is dead." All Israel who, throughout thirty days before Moses' decease, had wept his impending death now arranged a three months' time of mourning for him. But Israel were not the only mourners for Moses, God himself wept for Moses, saying, "Who will rise up for Me against the evil-doers? Who will stand up for Me against the workers of iniquity?" Metatron appeared before God and said: "Moses was thine when he lived, and he is Thine in his death." God replied: "I weep not for Moses' sake, but for the loss Israel suffered through his death. How often had they angered Me, but he prayed for them and appeased My wrath." The angels wept with God, saying, "But where shall wisdom be found?" The heavens lamented: "The godly man is perished out of the earth." The earth wept: "And there is none upright among men." Stars, planets, sun, and moon wailed: "The righteous perisheth, and no man layeth it to heart," and God praised Moses' excellence in the words: "Thou hast said of Me, 'The Lord He is God: there is none else,' and therefore shall I say of thee, 'And there arose not a prophet in Israel like unto Moses.'"

Among mortals, it was particularly Jochebed, Moses' mother, and Joshua, his disciple, that deeply mourned Moses' death. They were not indeed certain if Moses were dead, hence they sought him everywhere. Jochebed went first to Egypt and said to that land, "Mizraim, Mizraim, hast thou perchance seen Moses?" But Mizraim replied, "As truly as thou livest, Jochebed, I have not seen him since the day when he slew all the firstborn here." Jochebed then betook herself to the Nile, saying, "Nile, Nile, hast thou perchance seen Moses?" But Nile replied, "As truly as thou livest, Jochebed, I have not seen Moses since the day when he turned my water to blood." Then Jochebed went to the sea and said, "Sea, sea, hast thou perchance seen Moses?" The sea replied, "As truly as thou livest, Jochebed, I have not seen him since the day when he led the twelve tribes through me." Jochebed thereupon went to the desert and said, "Desert, desert, hast thou perchance seen Moses?" The desert replied, "As truly as thou livest, Jochebed, I have not seen him since the day whereupon he caused manna to rain down upon me." Then Jochebed went to Sinai, and said, "Sinai, Sinai, hast thou perchance seen Moses?" Sinai said, "As truly as thou livest, Jochebed, I have not seen him since the day whereon he descended from me with the two tables of the law." Jochebed finally went to the rock and said, "Rock, rock, hast thou perchance seen Moses?" The rock replied, "As truly as thou livest, I have not seen him since the day when with his staff he twice smote me."

Joshua, too, sought his teacher Moses in vain, and in his grief for Moses' disappearance he rent his garments, and crying aloud, called ceaselessly, "'My father, my father, the chariot of Israel and the horsemen thereof.' 'But where shall wisdom be found?'" But God said to Joshua: "How long wilt thou continue to seek Moses in vain? He is dead, but indeed it is I that have lost him, and not thou."

SAMAEL'S VAIN SEARCH

Samael, the Angel of Death, had not heard that God had taken Moses' soul from his body and received it under the Throne of Glory. Believing that Moses was still among the living, he betook himself to Moses' house in order to seize his soul, for he feared to return before God without having executed His command to take Moses' soul. He did not, however, find Moses in his accustomed place, so he hastened into the land of Israel, thinking, "Long did Moses pray to be permitted to enter this land, and perhaps he is there." He said to the land of Israel, "Is Moses perchance with thee?" But the land replied, "Nay, he is not found in the land of the living."

Samael then thought: "I know that God once said to Moses, 'Lift up thy rod and divide the sea,' so perhaps he is by the sea." He hastened to the sea and said, "Is Moses here?" The sea replied: "He is not here, and I have not seen him since the day when he clove me into twelve parts, and with the twelve tribes passed through me."

Samael then betook himself to Gehenna asking, "Hast thou seen Moses, the son of Amram?" Gehenna replied, "With mine ears have I heard the cry, but I have not seen him."

He betook himself to Sheol, Abaddon, and Tit-ha-Yawen, to whom he said, "Have ye seen the son of Amram?" They replied: "Through Pharaoh, king of Egypt, have we heard his call, but we have not seen him."

He betook himself to the Abyss and asked, "Hast thou seen the son of Amram?" The answer arose, "I have not seen him, but heard indeed his call."

He asked Korah's sons, that dwell with the Abyss, "Have ye seen the son of Amram?" They replied. "We have not seen him since the day upon which at Moses' bidding the earth opened its mouth and swallowed us."

He betook himself to the clouds of glory and asked, "Is Moses perchance with you?" They answered, "He is his from the eyes of all living."

He went to the heavens and asked, "Have ye seen the son of Amram?" The answer was, "We have not seen him since at God command he mounted to us to receive the Torah."

He hastened to Paradise, but when the angels that guard its gates beheld Samael, they drove him away and said, "Wicked one! Wicked one! 'This is the gate of the Lord; the righteous shall enter into it.'" Samael thereupon flew over the gates of Paradise and asked Paradise, "Hast thou perchance seen Moses?" Paradise answered, "Since in Gabriel's company he visited me to look upon the reward of the pious, I have not seen him."

He went to the tree of life, but even at the distance of three hundred parasangs, it cried out to him: "Approach me not." He therefore asked from afar, "Hast thou seen the son of Amram?" The tree replied, "Since the day on which he came to me to cut him a staff, I have not seen him."

He betook himself to the tree of the knowledge of good and evil, and said, "Hast thou seen the son of Amram?" The tree replied, "Since the day on which he came to me to get a writing reed, wherewith to write the Torah, I have not seen him."

He betook himself to the mountains with his query. These replied, "Since he hewed the two tables out of us, we have not seen him."

He went to the deserts and asked, "Have ye seen the son of Amram?" These replied, "Since he has ceased to lead Israel to pasture upon us, we have not seen him."

He betook himself to mount Sinai, for he thought God had formerly commanded Moses to ascend it, and that he might now be there. He asked Sinai, "Hast thou seen the son of Amram?" Sinai said, "Since the day on which out of God's right hand he received the Torah upon me, I have not seen him."

He betook himself to the birds and said, "Have ye seen Moses?" They replied, "Since the say whereupon he separated the birds into clean and unclean we have not seen him." He went to the quadrupeds and asked: "Have ye seen Moses?" They answered: "Since the day on which he determined which beasts might be eaten, and which might not, we have not seen him." The answer of the birds and beasts referred to the day on which God assembled all the species of animals, led them before Moses, and instructed him which of these were clean and which were not, which might, and which might not be eaten.

Samael then betook himself to the "Court of the Dead," where the angel Dumah guards the souls of the deceased, and asked the angel, "Hast thou seen the son of Amram?" He replied: "I heard the words of lamentation for him in heaven, but I have not seen him."

He betook himself to the angels and asked, "Have ye seen the son of Amram?" These made the same reply as Dumah, and advised him to go to the mortals, who might possibly give him information concerning Moses' whereabouts.

He betook himself to the mortals and asked, "Where is Moses?" These replied: "Our teacher Moses is not like human beings. He is the peer of the angels of ministry, for he ascended into heaven and dwelt in heaven like the angels, 'he hath gathered the wind in his fists' like an angel, and God took his soul to Himself in the place of His sanctity. What connection then hast thou with the son of Amram?"

MOSES EXCELS ALL PIOUS MEN

The special distinction that God granted to Moses at his death was well merited, for Moses outweighed all other pious men. When Moses died, Adam appeared and said, "I am greater than thou, for I was created in God's image." But Moses replied: "I am nevertheless superior to thee, for the glory that thou didst receive from God was taken from thee, whereas I retained the radiance of my face forever."

Noah then said to Moses: "I am greater than thou, for I was preserved out of the generation of the flood." Moses replied: "I am superior to thee, for thou didst save thyself alone, and hadst not the power to save thy generations, but I saved myself and also saved my generation at the time when they transgressed with the Golden Calf."

Abraham said to Moses, "I am greater than thou, for I fed the wanderers." Moses: "I am superior to thee, for thou didst feed the uncircumcised whereas I fed the circumcised; and thou, moreover, didst feed them in a land of habitations, whereas I fed Israel in the desert."

Isaac said to Moses: "I am greater than thou, for I bared my neck upon the altar and beheld the Face of the Shekinah." Moses replied: "Still am I superior to thee, for thou didst indeed behold the Face of the Shekihah, but thine eyes grew dim, whereas I talked with the Shekinah face to face, and yet neither did mine eyes grow dim nor my strength wane."

Jacob said, "I am greater than thou, for I wrestled with the angel and conquered him." Moses replied: "Thou didst wrestle with the angel upon thy territory, but I mounted to the angels into their own territory, and still they feared me."

Joseph said to Moses, "I am greater than thou, for my master's wife could not tempt me to sin." Moses replied: "Still am I superior to thee, for thou didst restrain thyself from a strange woman, whereas I abstained from intercourse with my own wife."

The degreed of Moses' superiority over the other pious men can be seen by following. Adam died because he has been seduced by the serpent, whereas Moses fashioned a serpent out of brass at sight of which everyone that had been bitten by a snake recovered. Noah offered a sacrifice to God that was accepted, but he himself was not admitted to God's presence. When Moses, on the other hand, offered a sacrifice in Israel's name, God said to him, "Know that twice daily I shall dwell with ye." Abraham had been the cause for Israel's bondage in Egypt, for that was the punishment for his words, "'Whereby shall I know that I shall inherit 'the land?" Moses, on the other hand, it was that delivered Israel out of Egyptian bondage. Jacob indeed conquered in his struggle with the angel, but the blow that the angel dealt him put Jacob's thigh out of joint forever, whereas Moses inspired the angels with such fear that as soon as they beheld him in heaven, they fled.

But Moses not only surpassed all other human beings, he surpassed also the entire creation that God had brought forth in six days. On the first day God created light, but Moses mounted into heaven and seized the spiritual light, the Torah. On the second day God created the firmament, whereby He decreed that the earth was not to enter the realm of the firmament, nor the firmament the realm of the earth, but Moses scaled the firmament even though he belonged to earth. On the third day God created the sea, but as soon as the sea caught sight of Moses, it retreated before him affrighted. On the fourth day God created the sun and the moon to illuminate the earth, but Moses said to God: "I do not wish sun and moon to give light to Israel, Thou Thyself shalt do so," and God granted his prayer. On the fifth day God created the animals, but Moses slaughtered whatever animals he wanted for Israel's needs. When, therefore, God laid all the objects of creation on one side of the scales, and Moses upon the other, Moses outweighed them. Moses was justly called, "the man of God," for he was half man and half God.

But not in this world alone was Moses the great leader and teacher of his people, he shall be the same in the future world, in accordance with the promise God made him shortly before his death. God said: "Thou that didst lead My children in this world, shalt also lead them in the future world.

Volume 4

Chapter 1

I. JOSHUA

THE SERVANT OF MOSES

The early history of the first Jewish conqueror in some respects is like the early history of the first Jewish legislator. Moses was rescued from a watery grave, and raised at the court of Egypt. Joshua, in infancy, was swallowed by a whale, and, wonderful to relate, did not perish. At a distant point of the sea-coast the monster spewed him forth unharmed. He was found by compassionate passers-by, and grew up ignorant of his descent. The government appointed him to the office of hangman. As luck would have it, he had to execute his own father. By the law of the land the wife of the dead man fell to the share of his executioner, and Joshua was on the point of adding to parricide another crime equally heinous. He was saved by a miraculous sign. When he approached his mother, milk flowed from her breasts. His suspicions were aroused, and through the inquiries he set a foot regarding his origin, the truth was made manifest.

Later Joshua, who was so ignorant that he was called a fool, became the minister of Moses, and God rewarded his faithful service by making him the successor to Moses. He was designated as such to Moses when, at the bidding of his master, he was carrying on war with the Amalekites. In this campaign God's care of Joshua was plainly seen. Joshua had condemned a portion of the Amalekites to death by lot, and the heavenly sword picked them out for extermination. Yet there was as great a difference between Moses and Joshua as between the sun and the moon. God did not withdraw His help from Joshua, but He was by no means so close to him as to Moses. This appeared immediately after Moses had passed away. At the moment when the Israelitish leader was setting out on his journey to the great beyond, he summoned his successor and bade him put questions upon all points about which he felt uncertain. Conscious of his own industry and devotion, Joshua replied that he had no questions to ask, seeing that he had carefully studied the teachings of Moses. Straightway he forgot three hundred Halakot, and doubts assailed him concerning seven hundred others. The people threatened Joshua's life, because he was not able to resolve their difficulties in the law. It was vain to turn to God, for the Torah once revealed was subject to human, not to heavenly, authority. Directly after Moses' death, God commanded Joshua to go to war, so that the people might forget its grievance against him. But it is false to think that the great conqueror was nothing more than a military hero. When God appeared to him, to give him instructions concerning the war, He found him with the Book of Deuteronomy in his hand, whereupon God called to him: "Be strong and of good courage; the book of the law shall not depart out of thy mouth."

ENTERING THE PROMISED LAND

The first step in preparation for war was the selection of spies. To guard against a repetition of what had happened to Moses, Joshua chose as his messengers Caleb and Phinehas, on whom he could place dependence in all circumstances. They were accompanied on their mission by two demons, the husbands of the she-devils Lilith and Mahlah. When Joshua was planning his campaign, these devils offered their services to him; they proposed that they be sent out to reconnoitre the land. Joshua refused the offer, but formed their appearance so frightfully that the residents of Jericho were struck with fear of them. In Jericho the spies put up with Rahab. She had been leading an immoral life for forty years, but at the approach of Israel, she paid homage to the true God, lived the life of a pious convert, and, as the wife of Joshua, became the ancestress of eight prophets and of the prophetess Huldah. She had opportunity in her own house of beholding the wonders of God. When the king's bailiffs came to make their investigations, and Rahab wanted to conceal the Israelitish spies, Phinehas calmed her with the words: "I am a priest, and priests are like angels, visible when they wish to be seen, invisible when they do not wish to be seen."

After the return of the spies, Joshua decided to pass over the Jordan. The crossing of the river was the occasion for wonders, the purpose of which was to clothe him with authority in the eyes of the people. Scarcely had the priests, who at this solemn moment took the place of the Levites as bearers of the Ark, set foot in the Jordan, when the waters of the river were piled up to a height of three hundred miles. All the peoples of the earth were witnesses of the wonder. In the bed of the Jordan Joshua assembled the people around the Ark. A Divine miracle caused the narrow space between its staves to contain the whole concourse. Joshua then proclaimed the conditions under which God would give Palestine to the Israelites, and he added, if these conditions were not accepted, the waters of the Jordan would descend straight upon them. Then they marched through the river. When the people arrived on the further shore, the holy Ark, which had all the while been standing in the bed of the river, set forward of itself, and, dragging the priests after it, overtook the people.

The day continued eventful. Unassailed, the Israelites marched seventy miles to Mount Gerizim and Mount Ebal, and there performed the ceremony bidden by Moses in Deuteronomy: six of the tribes ascended Mount Gerizim, and six Mount Ebal. The priests and the Levites grouped themselves about the holy Ark in the vale between the two peaks. With their faces turned toward Gerizim, the Levites uttered the words: "Happy the man that maketh no idol, an abomination unto the Lord," and all the people answered Amen. After reciting twelve blessings similar to this in form, the Levites turned to Mount Ebal, and recited twelve curses, counterparts of the blessings, to each of which the people responded again with Amen. Thereupon an altar was erected on Mount Ebal with the stones, each weighing forty seim, which the Israelites had taken from the bed of the river while passing through the Jordan. The altar was plastered with lime, and the Torah written upon it in seventy languages, so that the heathen nations might have the opportunity of learning the law. At the end it was said explicitly that the heathen outside of Palestine, if they would but abandon the worship of idols, would be received kindly by the Jews.

All this happened on one day, on the same day on which the Jordan was crossed, and the assembly was held on Gerizim and Ebal, the day on which the people arrived at Gilgal, where they left the stones of which the altar had been built. At Gilgal Joshua performed the rite of circumcision on those born in the desert, who had remained uncircumcised on account of the rough climate and for other reasons. And here it was that the manna gave out. It had ceased to fall at the death of Moses, but the supply that had been stored up had lasted some time longer. As soon as the people were under the necessity of providing for their daily wants, they grew negligent in the study of the Torah. Therefore the angel admonished Joshua to loose his shoes from off his feet, for he was to mourn over the decline of the study of the Torah, and bare feet are a sign of mourning. The angel reproached Joshua in particular with having allowed the preparations for war to interfere with the study of the Torah and with the ritual service. Neglect of the latter might be a venial sin, but neglect of the former is worthy of condign punishment. At the same time the angel assured Joshua that he had come to aid him, and he entreated Joshua not to draw back from him, like Moses, who had refused the good offices of the angel. He who spoke to Joshua was none other than the archangel Michael.

CONQUEST OF THE LAND

Joshua's first victory was the wonderful capture of Jericho. The whole of the city was declared anathema, because it had been conquered on the Sabbath day. Joshua reasoned that as the Sabbath is holy, so also that which conquered on the Sabbath should be holy. The brilliant victory was followed by the luckless defeat at Ai. In this engagement perished Jair, the son of Manasseh, whose loss was as great as if the majority of the Sanhedrin had been destroyed. Presently Joshua discovered that the cause of the defeat was the sinfulness of Israel, brought upon it by Achan, who had laid hands on some of the spoils of Jericho. Achan was a hardened transgressor and criminal from of old. During the life of Moses he had several times appropriated to his own use things that had been declared anathema, and he had committed other crimes worthy of the death penalty. Before the Israelites crossed the Jordan, God had not visited Achan's sins upon the people as a whole, because at that time it did not form a national unit yet. But when Achan abstracted an idol and all its appurtenances from Jericho, the misfortune of Ai followed at once.

Joshua inquired of God, why trouble had befallen Israel, but God refused to reply. He was no tale-bearer; the evil-doer who had caused the disaster would have to be singled out by lot. Joshua first of all summoned the high priest from the assembly of the people. It appeared that, while the other jewels in his breastplate gleamed bright, the stone representing the tribe of Judah was dim. By lot Achan was set apart from the members of his tribe. Achan, however, refused to submit to the decision by lot. He said to Joshua: "Among all living men thou and Phinehas are the most pious. Yet, if lots were cast concerning you two, one or other of you would be declared guilty. Thy teacher Moses has been dead scarcely one month, and thou has already begun to go astray, for thou hast forgotten that a man's guilt can be proved only through two witnesses."

Endued with the holy spirit, Joshua divined that the land was to be assigned to the tribes and families of Israel by lot, and he realized that nothing ought to be done to bring this method of deciding into disrepute. He, therefore, tried to persuade Achan to make a clean breast of his transgression. Meantime, the Judeans, the tribesmen of Achan, rallied about him, and throwing themselves upon the other tribes, they wrought fearful havoc and bloodshed. This determined Achan to confess his sins. The confession cost him his life, but it saved him from losing his share in the world to come.

In spite of the reverses at Ai, the terror inspired by the Israelites grew among the Canaanitish peoples. The Gibeonites planned to circumvent the invaders, and form an alliance with them. Now, before Joshua set out on his campaign, he had issued three proclamations: the nation that would leave Canaan might depart unhindered; the nation that would conclude peace with the Israelites, should do it at once; and the nation that would choose war, should make its preparations. If the Gibeonites had sued for the friendship of the Jews when the proclamation came to their ears, there would have been no need for subterfuges later. But the Canaanites had to see with their own eyes what manner of enemy awaited them, and all the nations prepared for war. The result was that the thirty-one kings of Palestine perished, as well as the satraps of many foreign kings, who were proud to own possessions in the Holy Land. Only the Girgashites departed out of Palestine, and as a reward for their docility God gave them Africa as an inheritance.

The Gibeonites deserved no better fate than all the rest, for the covenant made with them rested upon a misapprehension, yet Joshua kept his promise to them, in order to sanctify the name of God, by showing the world how sacred an oath is to the Israelites. In the course of events it became obvious that the Gibeonites were by no means worthy of being received into the Jewish communion, and David, following Joshua's example, excluded them forever, a sentence that will remain in force even in the Messianic time.

THE SUN OBEYS JOSHUA

The task of protecting the Gibeonites involved in the offensive and defensive alliance made with them, Joshua fulfilled scrupulously. He had hesitated for a moment whether to aid the Gibeonites in their distress, but the words of God sufficed to recall him to his duty. God said to him: "If thou dost not bring near them that are far off, thou wilt remove them that are near by." God granted Joshua peculiar favor in his conflict with the assailants of the Gibeonites. The hot hailstones which, at Moses' intercession, had remained suspended in the air when they were about to fall upon the Egyptians, were now cast down upon the Canaanites. Then happened the great wonder of the sun's standing still, the sixth of the great wonders since the creation of the world.

The battle took place on a Friday. Joshua knew it would pain the people deeply to be compelled to desecrate the holy Sabbath day. Besides, he noticed that the heathen were using sorcery to make the heavenly hosts intercede for them in the fight against the Israelites. He, therefore, pronounced the Name of the Lord, and the sun, moon and stars stood still. The sun at first refused to obey Joshua's behest, seeing that he was older than man by two days. Joshua replied that there was no reason why a free-born youth should refrain from enjoining silence upon an old slave whom he owns, and had not God given heaven and earth to our father Abraham? Nay, more than this, had not the sun himself bowed down like a slave before Joseph? "But," said the sun, "who will praise God if I am silent?" Whereupon Joshua: "Be thou silent, and I will intone a song of praise." And he sang thus:

1. Thou hast done mighty things, O Lord, Thou has performed great deeds. Who is like unto Thee? My lips shall sing unto Thy name.

2. My goodness and my fortress, my refuge, I will sing a new song unto Thee, with thanksgiving I will sing unto Thee, Thou art the strength of my salvation.

3. All the kings of the earth shall praise Thee, the princes of the world shall sing unto Thee, the children of Israel shall rejoice in Thy salvation, they shall sing and praise Thy power.

4. In Thee, O God, did we trust; we said, Thou art our God, for Thou wast our shelter and our strong tower against our enemies.

5. To Thee we cried, and we were not ashamed; in Thee we trusted, and we were delivered; when we cried unto Thee, Thou didst hear our voice, Thou didst deliver our souls from the sword.

6. Thou hast shown unto us Thy mercy, Thou didst give unto us Thy salvation, Thou didst rejoice our hearts with Thy strength.

7. Thou wentest forth for our salvation; with the strength of Thy arm Thou didst redeem Thy people; Thou did console us from the heavens of Thy holiness, Thou didst save us from tens of thousands.

8. Sun and moon stood still in heaven, and Thou didst stand in Thy wrath against our oppressors, and Thou didst execute Thy judgements upon them.

9. All the princes of the earth stood up, the kings of the nations had gathered themselves together, they were not moved at Thy presence, they desired Thy battles.

10. Thou didst rise against them in Thine anger, and Thou didst bring down Thy wrath upon them, Thou didst destroy them in Thy fury, and Thou didst ruin them in Thy rage.

11. Nations raged from fear of Thee, kingdoms tottered because of Thy wrath, Thou didst wound kings in the day of Thine anger.

12. Thou didst pour out Thy fury upon them, Thy wrathful anger took hold of them, Thou didst turn their iniquity upon them, and Thou didst cut them off in their wickedness.

13. They spread a trap, they fell therein, in the net they hid their foot was caught.

14. Thine hand found all Thine enemies, who said, through their sword they possessed the land, through their arm thy dwelt in the city.

15. Thou didst fill their faces with shame, Thou didst bring their horns down to the ground.

16. Thou didst terrify them in Thy wrath, and thou didst destroy them from before Thee.

17. The earth quaked and trembled from the noise of Thy thunder against them; Thou didst not withhold their souls from earth, and Thou didst bring down their lives to the grave.

18. Thou didst pursue them in Thy storm, Thou didst consume them in the whirlwind, Thou didst turn their rain into hail, they fell in floods, so that they could not rise.

19. Their carcasses were like rubbish cast out in the middle of the streets.

20. They were consumed, and they perished before Thee, Thou hast delivered Thy people in Thy might.

21. Therefore our hearts rejoice in Thee, our souls exult in Thy salvation.

22. Our tongues shall relate Thy might, we will sing and praise Thy wondrous works.

23. For Thou didst save us from our enemies, Thou didst deliver us from those who rose up against us, Thou didst destroy them from before us, and depress them beneath our feet.

24. Thus shall all Thine enemies perish, O Lord, and the wicked shall be like chaff driven by the wind, and Thy beloved shall be like trees planted by the waters.

WAR WITH THE ARMENIANS

Joshua's victorious course did not end with the conquest of the land. His war with the Armenians, after Palestine was subdued, marked the climax of his heroic deeds. Among the thirty-one kings whom Joshua had slain, there was one whose son, Shobach by name, was king of Armenia. With the purpose of waging war with Joshua, he united the forty-five kings of Persia and Media, and they were joined by the renowned hero Japheth. The allied kings in a letter informed Joshua of their design against him as follow: "The noble, distinguished council of the kings of Persia and Media to Joshua, peace! Thou wolf of the desert, we well know what thou didst to our kinsmen. Thou didst destroy our palaces; without pity thou didst slay young and old; our fathers thou didst mow down with the sword; and their cities thou didst turn into desert. Know, then, that in the space of thirty days, we shall come to thee, we, the forty-five kings, each having sixty thousand warriors under him, all them armed with bows and arrows, girt about with swords, all of us skilled in the ways of war, and with us the hero Japheth. Prepare now for the combat, and say not afterward that we took thee at unawares."

The messenger bearing the letter arrived on the day before the Feast of Weeks. Although Joshua was greatly wrought up by the contents of the letter, he kept his counsel until after the feast, in order not to disturb the rejoicing of the people. Then, at the conclusion of the feast, he told the people of the message that had reached him, so terrifying that even he, the veteran warrior, trembled at the heralded approach of the enemy. Nevertheless Joshua determined to accept the challenge. From the first words his reply was framed to show the heathen how little their fear possessed him whose trust was set in God. The introduction to his epistle reads as follows: "In the Name of the Lord, the God of Israel, who saps the strength of the iniquitous warrior, and slays the rebellious sinner. He breaks up the assemblies of marauding transgressors, and He gathers together in council the pious and the just scattered abroad, He the God of all gods, the Lord of all lords, the God of Abraham, Isaac, and Jacob. God is the Lord of war! From me, Joshua, the servant of God, and from the holy and chosen congregation to the impious nations, who pay worship to images, and prostrate themselves before idols: No peace unto you, saith my God! Know that ye acted foolishly to awaken the slumbering lion, to rouse up the lion's whelp, to excite his wrath. I am ready to pay you your recompense. Be ye prepared to meet me, for within a week I shall be with you to slay your warriors to a man."

Joshua goes on to recite all the wonders God had done for Israel, who need fear no power on earth; and he ends his missive with the words: "If the hero Japheth is with you, we have in the midst of us the Hero of heroes, the Highest above all the high."

The heathen were not a little alarmed at the tone of Joshua's letter. Their terror grew when the messenger told of the exemplary discipline maintained in the Isrealitish army, of the gigantic stature of Joshua, who stood five ells high, of his royal apparel, of his crown graven with the Name of God. At the end of seven days Joshua appeared with twelve thousand troops. When the mother of King Shobach, who was a powerful witch, espied the host, she exercised her magic art, and enclosed the Isrealitish army in seven walls. Joshua thereupon sent forth a carrier pigeon to communicate his plight to Nabiah, the king of the trans-Jordanic tribes. He urged him to hasten to his help and bring the priest Phinehas and the sacred trumpets with him. Nabiah did not tarry. Before the relief detachment arrived, his mother reported to Shobach that she beheld a star arise out of the East against which her machinations were vain. Shobach threw his mother from the wall, and he himself was soon afterward killed by Nabiah. Meantime Phinehas arrived, and, at the sound of his trumpets, the wall toppled down. A pitched battle ensued, and the heathen were annihilated.

ALLOTMENT OF THE LAND

At the end of seven years of warfare, Joshua could at last venture to parcel out the conquered land among the tribes. This was the way he did it. The high priest Eleazar, attended by Joshua and all the people, and arrayed in the Urim and Thummim, stood before two urns. One of the urns contained the names of the tribes, the other the names of the districts into which the land was divided. The holy spirit caused him to exclaims "Zebulon." When he put his hand into the first urn, lo, he drew forth the word Zebulon, and from the other came the word Accho, meaning the district of Accho. Thus it happened with each tribe in succession. In order that the boundaries might remain fixed, Joshua had had the Hazubah planted between the districts. The rootstock of this plant once established in a spot, it can be extirpated only with the greatest difficulty. The plough may draw deep furrows over it, yet it puts forth new shoots, and grows up again amid the grain, still marking the old division lines.

In connection with the allotment of the land Joshua issued ten ordinances intended, in a measure, to restrict the rights in private property: Pasturage in the woods was to be free to the public at large. Any one was permitted to gather up bits of wood in the field. The same permission to gather up all grasses, wherever they might grow, unless they were in a field that had been sown with fenugreek, which needs grass for protection. For grafting purposes twigs could be cut from any plant except the olive-trees. Water springs belonged to the whole town. It was lawful for any one to catch fish in the Sea of Tiberias, provided navigation was not impeded. The area adjacent to the outer side of a fence about a field might be used by any passer-by to ease nature. From the close of the harvest until the seventeenth day of Marheshwan fields could be crossed. A traveler who lost his way among vineyards could not be held responsible for the damage done in the effort to recover the right path. A dead body found in a field was to be buried on the spot where it was found.

The allotment of the land to the tribes and subdividing each district among the tribesmen took as much time as the conquest of the land.

When the two tribes and a half from the land beyond Jordan returned home after an absence of fourteen years, they were not a little astonished to hear that the boys who had been too young to go to the wars with them had in the meantime shown themselves worthy of the fathers. They had been successful in repulsing the Ishmaelitish tribes who had taken advantage of the absence of the men capable of bearing arms to assault their wives and children.

After a leadership of twenty-eight years, marked with success in war and in peace, Joshua departed this life. His followers laid the knives he had used in circumcising the Israelites into his grave, and over it they erected a pillar as a memorial of the great wonder of the sun's standing still over Ajalon. However, the mourning for Joshua was not so great as might justly have been expected. The cultivation of the recently conquered land so occupied the attention of the tribes that they came nigh forgetting the man to whom chiefly they owed their possession of it. As a punishment for their ingratitude, God, soon after Joshua's death, brought also the life of the high priest Eleazar and of the other elders to a close, and the mount on which Joshua's body was interred began to tremble, and threatened to engulf the Jews.

Chapter 2

II. THE JUDGES

THE FIRST JUDGE

After the death of Joshua the Israelites inquired to God whether they were to go up against the Canaanites in war. They were given the answer: "If ye are pure of heart, go forth unto the combat; but if your hearts are sullied with sin, then refrain." They inquired furthermore how to test the heart of the people. God ordered them to cast lots and set apart those designated by lot, for they would be the sinful among them. Again, when the people besought God to give it a guide and leader, an angel answered: "Cast lots in the tribe of Caleb." The lot designated Kenaz, and he was made prince over Israel.

His first act was to determine by lot who were the sinners in Israel, and what their inward thought. He declared before the people: "If I and my house be set apart by lot, deal with us as we deserve, burn us with fire." The people assenting, lots were cast, and 345 of the tribe of Judah were singled out, 560 of Reuben, 775 of Simon, 150 of Levi, 665 of Issachar, 545 of Zebulon, 380 of Gad, and 665 of Asher, 480 of Manasseh, 448 of Ephraim, and 267 of Benhamin. So 6110 persons were confined in prison, until God should let it be know what was to be done with them. The united prayers of Kenaz, Eleazar the high priest, and the elders of the congregation, were answered thus: "Ask these men now to confess their iniquity, and they shall be burnt with fire." Kenaz thereupon exhorted them: "Ye know that Achan, the son of Zabdi, committed the trespass of taking the anathema, but the lot fell upon him, and he confessed his sin. Do ye likewise confess your sins, that ye may come to life with those whom God will revive on the day of the resurrection."

One of the sinful, a man by the name of Elah, said in reply thereto: "If thou desirest to bring forth the truth, address thyself to each of the tribes separately." Kenaz began with his own, the tribe of Judah. The wicked of Judah confessed to the sin of worshipping the golden calf, like unto their forefathers in the desert. The Reubenites had burnt sacrifices to idols. The Levites said: "We desired to prove whether the Tabernacle is holy." Those of the tribe of Issachar replied: "We consulted idols to know what will become of us." The sinners of Zebulon: "We desired to eat the flesh of our sons and daughters, to know whether the Lord loves them." The Danites admitted, they had taught their children out of the books of the Amorites, which they had hidden then under Mount Abarim, where Kenaz actually found them. The Naphtalites confessed to the same transgression, only they had concealed the books in the tent of Elah, and there they were found by Kenaz. The Gadites acknowledged having led an immoral life, and the sinners of Asher, that they had found, and had hidden under Mount Shechem, the seven golden idols called by the Amorites the holy nymphs the same seven idols which had been made in a miraculous way after the deluge by the seven sinners, Canaan, Put, Shelah, Nimrod, Elath, Diul, and Shuah. They were of precious stones from Havilah, which radiated light, making night bright as day. Besides, they possessed a rare virtue: if a blind Amorite kissed one of the idols, and at the same time touched its eyes, his sight was restored. After the sinners of Asher, those of Manasseh made their confession they had desecrated the Sabbath. The Ephraimites owned to having sacrificed their children to Moloch. Finally, the Benjamites said: "We desired to prove whether the law emanated from God or from Moses."

At the command of God these sinners and all their possessions were burnt with fire at the brook of Pishon. Only the Amorite books and the idols of precious stones remained unscathed. Neither fire nor water could do them harm. Kenaz decided to consecrate the idols to God, but a revelation came to him, saying: "If God were to accept what has been declared anathema, why should not man?" He was assured that God would destroy the things over which human hands had no power. Kenaz, acting under Divine instruction, bore them to the summit of a mountain, where an altar was erected. The books and the idols were placed upon it, and the people offered many sacrifices and celebrated the whole day as a festival. During the night following, Kenaz saw dew rise from the ice in Paradise and descend upon the books. The letters of their writing were obliterated by it, and then an angel came and annihilated what was left. During the same night an angel carried off the seven gems, and threw them to the bottom of the sea. Meanwhile a second angel brought twelve other gems, engraving the names of the twelve sons of Jacob upon them, one name upon each. No two of these gems were alike: the first, to bear the name of Reuben, was like sardius; the second, for Simon, like topaz; the third, Levi, like emerald; the fourth, Judah, like carbuncle; the fifth, Issachar, like sapphire; the sixth, Zebulon, like jasper; the seventh, Dan, like ligure; the eighth, Naphtali, like amethyst; the ninth, Gad, like agate; the tenth, Asher, like chrysolite; the eleventh, Joseph, like beryl; and the twelfth, Benjamin, like onyx.

Now God commanded Kenaz to deposit twelve stones in the holy Ark, and there they were to remain until such time as Solomon should build the Temple, and attach them to the Cherubim. Furthermore, this Divine communication was made to Kenaz: "And it shall come to pass, when the sin of the children of men shall have been completed by defiling My Temple, the Temple they themselves shall build, that I will take these stones, together with the tables of the law, and put them in the place whence they were removed of old, and there they shall remain until the end of all time, when I will visit the inhabitants of the earth. Then I will take them up, and they shall be an everlasting light to those who love me and keep my commandments."

When Kenaz bore the stones to the sanctuary, they illumined the earth like unto the sun at midday.

CAMPAIGNS OF KENAZ

After these preparations Kenaz took the field against the enemy, with three hundred thousand men. The first day he slew eight thousand of the foe, and the second day five thousand. But not all the people were devoted to Kenaz. Some murmured against him, and calumniating him, said: "Kenaz stays at home, while we expose ourselves on the field." The servants of Kenaz reported these words to him. He ordered the thirty-seven men who had railed against him to be incarcerated, and he swore to kill them, if God would but grant him assistance for the sake of His people.

Thereupon he assembled three hundred men of his attendants, supplied them with horses, and bade them be prepared to make a sudden attack during the night, but to tell none of the plans he harbored in his mind. The scouts sent ahead to reconnoitre reported that the Amorites were too powerful for him to risk an engagement. Kenaz, however, refused to be turned away from his intention. At midnight he and his three hundred trusty attendants advanced upon the Amorite camp. Close upon it, he commanded his men to halt, but to resume their march and follow him when they should hear the notes of the trumpet. If the trumpet was not sounded, they were to return home.

Alone Kenaz ventured into the very camp of the enemy. Praying to God fervently, he asked that a sign be given him: "Let this be the sign of the salvation Thou wilt accomplish for me this day: I shall draw my sword from its sheath, and brandish it so that it glitters in the camp of the Amorites. If the enemy recognize it as the sword of Kenaz, then I shall know Thou wilt deliver them into my hand; if not, I shall understand Thou hast not granted my prayer, but dost purpose to deliver me into the hand of the enemy for my sins."

He heard the Amorites say: "Let us proceed to give battle to the Israelites, for our sacred gods, the nymphs, are in their hands, and will cause their defeat." When he heard these words, the spirit of God came over Kenaz. He arose and swung his sword above his head. Scarce had the Amorites seen it gleam in the air when they exclaimed: "Verily, this is the sword of Kenaz, who has come to inflict wounds and pain. But we know that our gods, who are held by the Israelites, will deliver them into our hands. Up, then, to battle!" Knowing that God had heard his petition, Kenaz threw himself upon the Amorites, and mowed down forty-five thousand of them, and as many perished at the hands of their own brethren, for God had sent the angel Gabriel to his aid, and he had struck the Amorites blind, so that they fell upon one another. On account of the vigorous blows dealt by Kenaz on all sides, his sword stuck to his hand. A fleeing Amorite, whom he stopped, to ask him how to loose it, advised him to slay a Hebrew, and let his warm blood flow over his hand. Kenaz accepted his advice, but only in part: instead of a Hebrew, he slew the Amorite himself, and his blood freed his hand from the sword.

When Kenaz came back to his men, he found them sunk in profound sleep, which had overtaken them that they might not see the wonders done for their leader. They were not a little astonished, on awakening, to behold the whole plain strewn with the dead bodies of the Amorites. Then Kenaz said to them: "Are the ways of God like unto the ways of man? Through me the Lord hath sent deliverance to this people. Arise now and go back to your tents." The people recognized that a great miracle had happened, and they said: "Now we know that God hath wrought salvation for His people; He hath no need of numbers, but only of holiness."

On his return from the campaign, Kenaz was received with great rejoicing. The whole people now gave thanks to God for having put him over them as their leader. They desired to know how he had won the great victory. Kenaz only answered: "Ask those who were with me about my deeds." His men were thus forced to confess that they knew nothing, only, on awakening, they had seen the plain full of dead bodies, without being able to account for their being there. Then Kenaz turned to the thirty-seven men imprisoned, before he left for the war, for having cast aspersions upon him. "Well," he said, "what charge have you to make against me?" Seeing that death was inevitable, they confessed they were of the sort of sinners whom Kenaz and the people had executed, and God had now surrendered them to him on account of their misdeeds. They, too, were burnt with fire.

Kenaz reigned for a period of fifty-seven years. When he felt his end draw nigh, he summoned the two prophets, Phinehas and Jabez, together with the priest Phinehas, the son of Eleazar. To these he spake: "I know the heart of this people, it will turn from following after the Lord. Therefore do I testify against it." Phinehas, the son of Eleazar, replied: "As Moses and Joshua testified, so do I testify against it; for Moses and Joshua prophesied concerning the vineyard, the beautiful planting of the Lord, which knew not who had planted it, and did not recognize Him who cultivated it, so that the vineyard was destroyed, and brought forth no fruit. These are the words my father commanded me to say unto this people."

Kenaz broke out into loud wailing, and with him the elders and the people, and they wept until eventide, saying: "Is it for the iniquity of the sheep that the shepherd must perish? May the Lord have compassion upon His inheritance that it may not work in vain."

The spirit of God descended upon Kenaz, and he beheld a vision. He prophesied that this world would continue to exist only seven thousand years, to be followed then by the Kingdom of Heaven. These words spoken, the prophetical spirit departed from him, and he straightway forgot what he had uttered during his vision. Before he passed away, he spoke once more, saying: "If such be the rest which the righteous obtain after their death, it were better for them to die than live in this corrupt world and see its iniquities."

As Kenaz left no male heirs, Zebul was appointed his successor. Mindful of the great service Kenaz had performed for the nation, Zebul acted a father's part toward the three unmarried daughters of his predecessor. At his instance, the people assigned a rich marriage portion to each of them; they were given great domains as their property. The oldest of the three, Ethema by name, he married to Elizaphan; the second, Pheila, to Odihel; and the youngest, Zilpah, to Doel.

Zebul, the judge, instituted a treasury at Shiloh. He bade the people bring contributions, whether of gold or of silver. They were only to take heed not to carry anything thither that had originally belonged to an idol. His efforts were crowned with success. The free-will offerings to the temple treasure amounted to twenty talents of gold and two hundred and fifty talents of silver.

Zebul's reign lasted twenty-five years. Before his death he admonished the people solemnly to be God-fearing and observant of the law.

OTHNIEL

Othniel was a judge of a very different type. His contemporaries said, that before the sun of Joshua went down, the sun of Othniel, his successor in the leadership of the people, appeared on the horizon. The new leader's real name was Judah; Othniel was one of his epithets, as Jabez was another.

Among the judges, Othniel represents the class of scholars. His acumen was so great that he was able, by dint of dialect reasoning, to restore the seventeen hundred traditions which Moses had taught the people, and which had been forgotten in the time of mourning for Moses. Nor was his zeal for the promotion of the study of the Torah inferior to his learning. The descendants of Jethro left Jericho, the district assigned to them, and journeyed to Arad, only that thy might sit at the feed to Othniel. His wife, the daughter of his half-brother Caleb, was not so well pleased with him. She complained to her father that her husband's house was bare of all earthly goods, and his only possession was knowledge of the Torah.

The first event to be noted in Othniel's forty years' reign is his victory over Adoni-bezek. This chief did not occupy a prominent position among the Canaanitish rulers. He was not even accounted a king, nevertheless he had conquered seventy foreign kings. The next event was the capture of Luz by the Israelites. The only way to gain entrance into Luz was by a cave, and the road to the cave lay through a hollow almond tree. If the secret approach to the city had not been betrayed by one of its residents, it would have been impossible for the Israelites to reach it. God rewarded the informer who put the Israelites in the way of capturing Luz. The city he founded was left unmolested both by Sennacherib and Nebuchadnezzar, and not event the Angel of Death has power over its inhabitants. They never die, unless, weary of life, they leave the city.

The same good fortune did not mark Othniel's reign throughout. For eight years Israel suffered oppression at the hands of Cushan, the evil-doer who in former days had threatened to destroy the patriarch Jacob, as he was now endeavoring to destroy the descendants of Jacob, for Cushan is only another name for Laban.

Othniel, however, was held so little answerable for the causes that had brought on the punishment of the people, that God granted him eternal life; he is one of the few who reached Paradise alive.

BOAZ AND RUTH

The story of Ruth came to pass a hundred years after Othniel's reign. Conditions in Palestine were of such a nature that if a judge said to a man, "Remove the mote from thine eye," his reply was, "Do thou remove the beam from thine own." To chastise the Israelites God sent down them one of the ten seasons of famine which He had ordained, as disciplinary measures for mankind, from the creation of the world until the advent of Messiah. Elimelech and his sons, who belonged to the aristocracy of the land, attempted neither to improve the sinful generation whose transgressions had called forth the famine, nor alleviated the distress that prevailed about them. They left Palestine, and thus withdrew themselves from the needy who had counted upon their help. They turned their faced to Moab. There, on account of their wealth and high descent, they were made officers in the army. Mahlon and Chilion, the sons of Elimelech, rose to still higher distinction, they married the daughters of the Moabite king Eglon But this did not happen until after the death of Elimelech, who was opposed to intermarriage with the heathen. Neither the wealth nor the family connections of the two men helped them before God. First they sank into poverty, and, as they continued in their sinful ways, God took their life.

Naomi, their mother, resolved to return to her home. Her two daughters-in-law were very dear to her on account of the love they had borne her sons, a love strong even in death, for they refused to marry again. Yet she would not take them with her to Palestine, because she foresaw contemptuous treatment in store for them as Moabitish women. Orpah was easily persuaded to remain behind. She accompanied her mother-in-law a distance of four miles, and then she took leave of her, shedding only four tears as she bade her farewell. Subsequent events showed that she had not been worthy of entering into the Jewish communion, for scarcely had she separated from Naomi when she abandoned herself to an immoral life. But with God nothing goes unrewarded. For the four miles which Orpah travelled with Naomi, she was recompensed by bringing forth four giants, Goliath and his three brothers.

Ruth's bearing and history were far different. She was determined to become a Jewess, and her decision could not be shaken by what Naomi, in compliance with the Jewish injunction, told her of the difficulties of the Jewish law. Naomi warned her that the Israelites had been enjoined to keep Sabbaths and feast days, and that the daughters of Israel were not in the habit of frequenting the threatres and circuses of the heathen. Ruth only affirmed her readiness to follow Jewish customs. And when Naomi said: "We have one Torah, one law, one command; the Eternal our God is one, there is none beside Him," Ruth answered: "Thy people shall be my people, thy God my God." So the two women journeyed together to Bethlehem. They arrived there on the very day on which the wife of Boaz was buried, and the concourse assembled for the funeral saw Naomi as she returned to her home.

Ruth supported herself and her mother-in-law sparsely with the ears of grain which she gathered in the fields. Association with so pious a woman as Naomi had already exercised great influence upon her life and ways. Boaz was astonished to notice that if the reapers let more than two ears fall, in spite of her need she did not pick them up, for the gleaning assigned to the poor by law does not refer to quantities of more than two ears inadvertently dropped at one time. Boaz also admired her grace, her decorous conduct, her modest demeanor. When he learned who she was, he commended her for her attachment to Judaism. To his praise she returned: "Thy ancestors found no delight even in Timna, the daughter of a royal house. As for me, I am a member of a low people, abominated by thy God, and excluded from the assembly of Israel." For the moment Boaz failed to recollect the Halakah bearing on the Moabites and Ammonites. A voice from heaven reminded him that only their males were affected by the command of exclusion. This he told to Ruth, and he also told her of a vision he had had concerning her descendants. For the sake of the good she had done to her mother-in-law, kings and prophets would spring from her womb.

Boaz showed kindness not only to Ruth and Naomi, but also to their dead. He took upon himself the decent burial of the remains of Elimelech and his two sons. All this begot in Naomi the thought that Boaz harbored the intention of marrying Ruth. She sought to coax the secret, if such there was, from Ruth. When she found that nothing could be elicited from her daughter-in-law, she made Ruth her partner in a plan to force Boaz into a decisive step. Ruth adhered to Naomi's directions in every particular, except that she did not wash and anoint herself and put on fine raiment, until after she had reached her destination. She feared to attract the attention of the lustful, if she walked along the road decked out in unusual finery.

The moral conditions in those days were very reprehensible. Though Boaz was high-born and a man of substance, yet he slept on the threshing-floor, so that his presence might act as a check upon profligacy. In the midst of his sleep, Boaz was startled to find some one next to him. At first he thought it was a demon. Ruth calmed his disquietude with these words: "Thou art the head of the court, thy ancestors were princes, thou art thyself an honorable man, and a kinsman of my dead husband. As for me, who am in the flower of my years, since I left the home of my parents where homage is rendered unto idols, I have been constantly menaced by the dissolute young men around. So I have come hither that thou, who art the redeemer, mayest spread out thy skirt over me." Boaz gave her the assurance that if his older brother Tob failed her, he would assume the duties of a redeemer. The next day he came before the tribunal of the Sanhedrin to have the matter adjusted. Tob soon made his appearance, for an angel led him to the place where he was wanted, that Boaz and Ruth might not have long to wait. Tob, who was not learned in the Torah, did not know that the prohibition against the Moabites had reference only to males. Therefore, he declined to marry Ruth. So she was taken to wife by the octogenarian Boaz. Ruth herself was forty years old at the time of her second marriage, and it was against all expectations that her union with Boaz should be blessed with offspring, a son Obed the pious. Ruth lived to see the glory of Solomon, but Boaz died on the day after the wedding.

DEBORAH

Not long after Ruth, another ideal woman arose in Israel, the prophetess Deborah.

When Ehud died, there was none to take his place as judge, and the people fell off from God and His law. God, therefore, sent an angel to them with the following message: "Out of all the nations on earth, I chose a people for Myself, and I thought, so long as the world stands, My glory will rest upon them. I sent Moses unto them, My servant, to teach them goodness and righteousness. But they strayed from My ways. And now I will arouse their enemies against them, to rule over them, and they will cry out: 'Because we forsook the ways of our fathers, hath this come over us.' Then I will send a woman unto them, and she will shine for them as a light for forty years."

The enemy whom God raised up against Israel was Jabin, the king of Hazor, who oppressed him sorely. But worse than the king himself was his general Sisera, one of the greatest heroes know to history. When he was thirty years old, he had conquered the whole world. At the sound of his voice the strongest of walls fell in a heap, and the wild animals in the woods were chained to the spot by fear. The proportions of his body were vast beyond description. If he took a bath in the river, and dived beneath the surface, enough fish were caught in his beard to feed a multitude, and it required no less than nine hundred horses to draw the chariot in which he rode.

To rid Israel of this tyrant, God appointed Deborah and her husband Barak. Barak was an ignoramus, like most of his contemporaries. It was a time singularly deficient to scholars. In order to do something meritorious in connection with the Divine service, he carried candles, at his wife's instance, to the sanctuary, wherefrom he was called Lipidoth, "Flames." Deborah was in the habit of making the wicks on the candles very thick, so that they might burn a long time. Therefore God distinguished her. He said: "Thou takest pains to shed light in My house, and I will let thy light, thy flame, shine abroad in the whole land." Thus it happened that Deborah became a prophetess and a judge. She dispensed judgement in the open air, for it was not becoming that men should visit a woman in her house.

Prophetess though she was, she was yet subject to the frailties of her sex. Her self-consciousness was inordinate. She sent for Barak to come to her instead of going to him, and in her song she spoke more of herself than was seemly. The result was that the prophetical spirit departed from her for a time while she was composing her song.

The salvation of Israel was effected only after the people, assembled on the Mount of Judah, had confessed their sins publicly before God and besought His help. A seven days' fast was proclaimed for men and women, for young and old. Then God resolved to help the Israelites, not for their sakes, but for the sake of keeping the oath he had sworn to their forefathers, never to abandon their seed. Therefore He sent Deborah unto them.

The task allotted to Deborah and Barak, to lead the attack upon Sisera, was by no means slight. It is comparable with nothing less than Joshua's undertaking to conquer Canaan. Joshua had triumphed over only thirty-one of the sixty-two kings of Palestine, leaving at large as many as he had subdued. Under the leadership of Sisera these thirty-one unconquered kings opposed Israel. No less than forty thousand armies, each counting a hundred thousand warriors, were arrayed against Deborah and Barak. God aided Israel with water and fire. The river Kishon and all the fiery hosts of heaven except the star Meros fought against Sisera. The Kishon had long before been pledged to play its part in Sisera's overthrow. When the Egyptians were drowned in the Red Sea, God commanded the Angel of the Sea to cast their corpses on the land, that the Israelites might convince themselves of the destruction of their foes, and those of little faith might not say afterward that the Egyptians like the Israelites had reached dry land. The Angel of the Sea complained of the impropriety of withdrawing a gift. God mollified him with the promise of future compensation. The Kishon was offered as security that he would received half as many bodies again as he was now giving up. When Sisera's troops sought relief from the scorching fire of the heavenly bodies in the coolness of the waters of the Kishon, God commanded the river to redeem its pledge. And so the heathen were swept down into the Sea by the waves of the river Kishon, whereat the fishes in the Sea exclaimed: "And the truth of the Lord endureth forever."

Sisera's lot was no better than the lot of the men. He fled from the battle on horseback after witnessing the annihilation of his vast army. When Jael saw him approach, she went to meet him arrayed in rich garments and jewels. She was unusually beautiful, and her voice was the most seductive ever a woman possessed. These are the words she addressed to him: "Enter and refresh thyself with food, and sleep until evening, and then I will send my attendants with thee to accompany thee, for I know thou wilt not forget me, and thy recompense will not fail." When Sisera, on stepping into her tent, saw the bed strewn with roses which Jael had prepared for him, he resolved to take her home to his mother as his wife, as soon as his safety should be assured.

He asked her for milk to drink, saying: "My soul burns with the flame which I saw in the stars contending for Israel." Jael went forth to milk her goat, meantime supplicating God to grant her His help: "I pray to Thee, O Lord, to strengthen Thy maid-servant against the enemy. By this token shall I know that Thou wilt aid me if, when I enter the house, Sisera will awaken and ask for water to drink." Scarcely had Jael crossed the threshold when Sisera awakened and begged for water to quench his burning thirst. Jael gave him wine mixed with water, which caused him to drop into a sound sleep again. The woman then took a wooden spike in her left hand, approached the sleeping warrior, and said: "This shall be the sign that Thou wilt deliver him into my hand if I draw him from the bed down on the ground without awaking him." She tugged at Sisera, and in very truth he did not awaken even when he dropped from the bed to the floor. Then Jael prayed: "O God, strengthen the arm of Thy maid-servant this day, for Thy sake, for the sake of Thy people, and for the sake of those that hope in Thee." With a hammer she drove the spike into the temple of Sisera, who cried out as he was expiring: "O that I should lose my life by the hand of a woman!" Jael's mocking retort was: "Descend to hell and join thy fathers, and tell them that thou didst fall by the hand of a woman."

Barak took charge of the body of the dead warrior, and he sent it to Sisera's mother, Themac, with the message: "Here is thy son, whom thou didst expect to see returning laden with booty." He had in mind the vision of Themac and her women-in-waiting. When Sisera went forth to battle, their conjuring tricks had shown him to them as he lay on the bed of a Jewish woman. This they had interpreted to mean that he would return with Jewish captives. "One damsel, two damsels for ever man." they had said. Great, therefore, was the disappointment of Sisera's mother. No less than a hundred cries did she utter over him.

Deborah and Barak thereupon intoned a song of praise, thanking God for the deliverance of Israel out of the power of Sisera, and reviewing the history of the people since the time of Abraham.

After laboring for the weal of her nation for forty years, Deborah departed this life. Her last words to the weeping people were an exhortation not to depend upon the dead. They can do nothing for the living. So long as a man is alive, his prayers are efficacious for himself and for others. They avail naught once he is dead.

The whole nation kept a seventy days' period of mourning in honor of Deborah, and the land was at peace for seven years.

GIDEON

Elated by the victory over Sisera, Israel sang a hymn of praise, the song of Deborah, and God, to reward them for their pious sentiments, pardoned the transgression of the people. But they soon slipped back into the old ways, and the old troubles harassed them. Their backsliding was due to the witchcraft of a Midianite priest named Aud. He made the sun shine at midnight, and so convinced the Israelites that the idols of Midian were mightier than God, and God chastised them by delivering them into the hands of the Midianties. They worshipped their own images reflected in the water, and they were stricken with dire poverty. They could not bring so much as a meal offering, the offering of the poor. On the eve of one Passover, Gideon uttered the complaint: "Where are all the wondrous works which God did for our fathers in this night, when he slew the first-born of the Egyptians, and Israel went forth from slavery with joyous hearts?" God appeared unto him, and said: "Thou who art courageous enough to champion Israel, thou art worthy that Israel should be saved for thy sake."

An angel appeared, and Gideon begged him for a sign, that he would achieve the deliverance of Israel. He excused his petition with the precedent of Moses, the first prophet, who likewise has asked for a sign. The angel bade him pour water on the rock, and then gave him the choice of how he would have the water transformed. Gideon desired to see one-half changed into blood, and one-half into fire. Thus it happened. The blood and the fire mingled with each other, yet the blood did not quench the fire, nor did the fire dry out the blood. Encouraged by this and other signs, Gideon undertook to carry on the war against the Midianites with a band of three hundred God-fearing men, and he was successful. Of the enemy one hundred and twenty thousand corpses covered the field, and all the rest fled precipitately.

Gideon enjoyed the privilege of bringing salvation to Israel because he was a good son. His old father feared to thresh his grain on account of the Midianites, and Gideon once went out to him in the field and said: "Father, thou art too old to do this work; go thou home, and I shall finish thy task for thee. If the Midianites should surprise me out here, I can run away, which thou canst not do, on account of thy age."

The day on which Gideon gained his great victory was during the Passover, and the cake of barley bread that turned the camp of the enemy upside down, of which the Midianite dreamed, was a sign that God would espouse the cause of His people to reward them for bringing a cake of barley bread as an 'Omer offering.

After God had favored Israel with great help through him, Gideon had an ephod made. In the high priest's breastplate, Joseph was represented among the twelve tribes by Ephraim alone, not by Manasseh, too. To wipe out this slight upon his own tribe, Gideon made an ephod bearing the name of Manasseh. He consecrated it to God, but after his death homage was paid to it as an idol. In those days the Israelites were so addicted to the worship of Beelzebub that they constantly carried small images of this god with them in their pockets, and every now and then they were in the habit of bringing the image forth and kissing it fervently. Of such idolaters were the vain and light fellows who helped Abimelech, the son of Gideon by his concubine from Shechem, to assassinate the other sons of his father. But God is just. As Abimelech murdered his brothers upon a stone, so Abimelech himself met his death through a millstone. It was proper, then, that Jotham, in his parable, should compare Abimelech to a thorn-bush, while he characterized his predecessors, Othniel, Deborah, and Gideon, as an olive-tree, or a fig-tree, or a vine. This Jotham, the youngest of the sons of Gideon, was more than a teller of parables. He knew then that long afterward the Samaritans would claim sanctity for Mount Gerizim, on account of the blessing pronounced from it upon the tribe. For this reason he chose Gerizim from which to hurl his curse upon Shechem and it inhabitants.

The successor to Abimelech equalled, if he did not surpass, him in wickedness. Jair erected an altar unto Baal, and on penalty of death he forced the people to prostrate themselves before it. Only seven men remained firm in the true faith, and refused to the last to commit idolatry. Their names were Deuel, Abit Yisreel, Jekuthiel, Shalom, Ashur, Jehonadab, and Shemiel. They said to Jair: "We are mindful of the lessons given us by our teachers and our mother Deborah. 'Take ye heed,' they said, 'that your heart lead you not astray to the right or to the left. Day and night ye shall devote yourselves to the study of the Torah.' Why, then, dost thou seek to corrupt the people of the Lord, saying, 'Baal is God, let us worship him'? If he really is what thou sayest, then let him speak like a god, and we will pay him worship." For the blasphemy they had uttered against Baal, Jair commanded that the seven men be burnt. When his servants were about to carry out his order, God sent the angel Nathaniel, the lord over the fire, and he extinguished the fire though not before the servants of Jair were consumed by it. Not only did the seven men escape the danger of suffering death by fire, but the angel enabled them to flee unnoticed, by striking all the people present with blindness. Then the angel approached Jair, and said to him: "Hear the words of the Lord ere thou diest. I appointed thee as prince over my people, and thou didst break My covenant, seduce My people, and seek to burn My servants with fire, but they were animated and freed by the living, the heavenly fire. As for thee, thou wilt die, and die by fire, a fire in which thou wilt abide forever."

Thereupon the angel burnt him with a thousand men, whom he had taken in the act of paying homage to Baal.

JEPHTHAH

The first judge of any importance after Gideon was Jephthah. He, too, fell short of being the ideal Jewish ruler. His father had married a woman of another tribe, an unusual occurrence in a time when a woman who left her tribe was held in contempt. Jephthah, the offspring of this union, had to bear the consequences of his mother's irregular conduct. So many annoyances were put upon him that he was forced to leave his home and settle in a heathen district.

At first Jephthah refused to accept the rulership which the people offered him in an assembly at Mizpah, for he had not forgotten the wrongs to which he had been subjected. In the end, however, he yielded, and placed himself at the head of the people in the war against Getal, the king of the Ammonites. At his departure, he vowed before God to sacrifice to Him whatsoever came forth out of the doors of his house to meet him when he returned a victor from the war.

God was angry and said: "So Jephthah has vowed to offer unto me the first thing that shall meet him! If a dog were the first to meet him, would a dog be sacrificed to me? Now shall the vow of Jephthah be visited on his first-born, on his own offspring, yea, his prayer shall be visited on his only daughter. But I assuredly shall deliver my people, not for Jephthah's sake, but for the sake of the prayers of Israel."

The first to meet him after his successful campaign was his daughter Sheilah. Overwhelmed by anguish, the father cried out: "Rightly was the name Sheilah, the one who is demanded, given to thee, that thou shouldst be offered up as a sacrifice. Who shall set my heart in the balance and my soul as the weight, that I may stand and see whether that which happened to me is joy or sorrow? But because I opened my mouth to the Lord, and uttered a vow, I cannot take it back." Then Sheilah spoke, saying: "Why dost thou grieve for my death, since the people was delivered? Dost thou not remember what happened in the day of our forefathers, when the father offered his son as a burnt offering, and the son did not refuse, but consented gladly, and the offerer and the offered were both full of joy? Therefore, do as thou hast spoken. But before I die I will ask a favor of thee. Grant me that I may go with my companions upon the mountains, sojourn among the hills, and tread upon the rocks to shed my tears and deposit there the grief for my lost youth. The trees of the field shall weep for me, and the beasts of the field mourn for me. I do not grieve for my death, nor because I have to yield up my life, but because when my father vowed his heedless vow, he did not have me in mind. I fear, therefore, that I may not be an acceptable sacrifice, and that my death shall be for nothing." Sheilah and her companions went forth and told her case to the sages of the people, but none of them could give her any help. Then she went up to Mount Telag, where the Lord appeared to her at night, saying unto her: "I have closed the mouth of the sages of my people in this generation, that they cannot answer the daughter of Jephthah a word; that my vow be fulfilled and nothing of what I have thought remain undone. I know her to be wiser than her father, and all the wise men, and now her soul shall be accepted at her request, and her death shall be very precious before My face all the time." Sheilah began to bewail her fate in these words: "Hearken, ye mountains, to my lamentations, and ye hills, to the tears of my eyes, and ye rocks, testify to the weeping of my soul. My words will go up to heaven, and my tears will be written in the firmament. I have not been granted the joy of wedding, nor was the wreath of my betrothal completed. I have not been decked with ornaments, nor have I been scented with myrrh and with aromatic perfumes. I have not been anointed with the oil that was prepared for me. Alas, O mother, it was in vain thou didst give birth to me, the grave was destined to be my bridal chamber. The oil thou didst prepare for me will be spilled, and the white garments my mother sewed for me, the moth will eat them; the bridal wreath my nurse wound for me will wither, and my garments in blue and purple, the worms will destroy them, and my companions will all their days lament over me. And now, ye trees, incline your branches and weep over my youth; ye beasts of the forest, come and trample upon my virginity, for my years are cut off, and the days of my life grow old in darkness."

Her lamentations were of as little avail as her arguments with her father. In vain she sought to prove to him from the Torah that the law speaks only of animal sacrifices, never of human sacrifices. In vain she cited the example of Jacob, who had vowed to give God a tenth of all the possessions he owned, and yet did not attempt later to sacrifice one of his sons. Jephthah was inexorable. All he would yield was a respite during which his daughter might visit various scholars, who were to decide whether he was bound by his vow. According to the Torah his vow was entirely invalid. He was not even obliged to pay his daughter's value in money. But the scholars of his time had forgotten this Halakah, and they decided that he must keep his vow. The forgetfulness of the scholars was of God, ordained as a punishment upon Jephthah for having slaughtered thousands of Ephraim.

One man there was living at the time who, if he had been questioned about the case, would have been able to give a decision. This was the high priest Phinehas. But he said proudly: "What! I, a high priest, the son of a high priest, should humiliate myself and go to an ignoramus!" Jephthah on the other hand said: "What! I, the chief of the tribes of Israel, the first prince of the land, should humiliate myself and go to one of the rank and file!" So only the rivalry between Jephthah and Phinehas caused the loss of a young life. Their punishment did not miss them. Jephthah dies a horrible death. Limb by limb his body was dismembered. As for the high priest, the holy spirit departed from him, and he had to give up his priestly dignity.

As it had been Jephthah's task to ward off the Ammonites, so his successor Abdon was occupied with protecting Israel against the Moabites. The king of Moab sent messengers to Abdon, and they spoke thus: "Thou well knowest that Israel took possession of cities that belonged to me. Return them." Abdon's reply was: "Know ye not how the Ammonites fared? The measure of Moab's sins, it seems, out against the enemy, slew forty-five thousand of their number, and routed the rest.

SAMSON

The last judge but one, Samson, was not the most important of the judges, but he was the greatest hero of the period and, except Goliath, the greatest hero of all times. He was the son of Manoah of the tribe of Dan, and his wife Zelalponit of the tribe of Judah, and he was born to them at a time when they had given up all hope of having children. Samson's birth is a striking illustration of the shortsightedness of human beings. The judge Ibzan had not invited Manoah and Zelalponit to any of the one hundred and twenty feasts in honor of the marriage of his sixty children, which were celebrated at his house and at the house of their parents-in-law, because he thought that "the sterile she-mule" would never be in a position to repay his courtesy. It turned out that Samson's parents were blessed with an extraordinary son, while Ibzan saw his sixty children die during his lifetime.

Samson's strength was superhuman, and the dimensions of his body were gigantic he measured sixty ells between the shoulders. Yet he had one imperfection, he was maimed in both feet. The first evidence of his gigantic strength he gave when he uprooted two great mountains, and rubbed them against each other. Such feats he was able to perform as often as the spirit of God was poured out over him. Whenever this happened, it was indicated by his hair. In began to move and emit a bell-like sound, which could be heard far off. Besides, while the spirit rested upon him, he was able with one stride to cover a distance equal to that between Zorah and Eshtaol. It was Samson's supernatural strength that made Jacob think that he would be the Messiah. When God showed him Samson's latter end, then he realized that the new era would not be ushered in by the hero-judge.

Samson won his first victory over the Philistines by means of the jawbone of the ass on which Abraham had made his way to Mount Moriah. It had been preserved miraculously. After this victory a great wonder befell. Samson was at the point of perishing from thirst, when water began to flow from his own mouth as from a spring.

Besides physical prowess, Samson possessed also spiritual distinctions. He was unselfish to the last degree. He had been of exceeding great help to the Israelites, but he never asked the smallest service for himself. When Samson told Delilah that he was a "Nazarite unto God," she was certain that he had divulged the true secret of his strength. She knew his character too well to entertain the idea that he would couple the name of God with an untruth. There was a weak side to his character, too. He allowed sensual pleasures to dominate him. The consequences was that "he who went astray after his eyes, lost his eyes." Even this severe punishment produced no change of heart. He continued to lead his old life of profligacy in prison, and he was encouraged thereto by the Philistines, who set aside all considerations of family purity in the hope of descendants who should be the equals of Samson in giant strength and stature.

As throughout life Samson had given proofs of superhuman power, so in the moment of death. He entreated God to realize in him the blessing of Jacob, and endow him with Divine strength. He expired with these words upon his lips: "O Master of the world! Vouchsafe unto me in this life a recompense for the loss of one of my eyes. For the loss of the other I will wait to be rewarded in the world to come." Even after his death Samson was a shield unto the Israelites. Fear of him had so cowed the Philistines that for twenty years they did not dare attack the Israelites.

THE CRIME OF THE BENJAMITES

A part of the money which Delilah received from the Philistine lords as the price of Samson's secret, she gave to her son Micah, and he used it to make an idol for himself. This sin was the more unpardonable as Micah owed his life to a miracle performed by Moses. During the times of the Egyptian oppression, if the prescribed number of bricks was not furnished by the Israelites, their children were used as building material. Such would have been Micah's fate, if he had not been saved in a miraculous way. Moses wrote down the Name of God, and put the words on Micah's body. The dead boy came to life, and Moses drew him out of the wall of which he made a part. Micah did not show himself worthy of the wonder done for him. Even before the Israelites left Egypt, he made his idol, and it was he who fashioned the golden calf. At the time of Othniel the judge, he took up his abode at a distance of not more than three miles from the sanctuary at Shiloh, and won over the grandson of Moses to officiate as priest before his idol.

The sanctuary which Micah erected harbored various idols. He had three images of boys, and three of calves, one lion, an eagle, a dragon, and a dove. When a man came who wanted a wife, he was directed to appeal to the dove. If riches were his desire, he worshipped the eagle. For daughters both, to the calves; to the lion for strength, and to the dragon for long life. Sacrifices and incense alike were offered to these idols, and both had to be purchased with cash money from Micah, even didrachms for a sacrifice, and one for incense.

The rapid degeneration in the family of Moses may be accounted for by the fact that Moses had married the daughter of a priest who ministered to idols. Yet, the grandson of Moses was not an idolater of ordinary calibre. His sinful conduct was not without a semblance of morality. From his grandfather he had heard the rule that a man should do "Abodah Zarah" for hire rather than be dependent upon his fellow-creatures. The meaning of "Abodah Zarah" here naturally is "strange," in the sense of "unusual" work, but he took the term in its ordinary acceptation of "service of strange gods." So far from being a whole-souled idolater, he adopted methods calculated to harm the cause of idol worship. Whenever any one came leading an animal with the intention of sacrificing it, he would say: "What good can the idol do thee? It can neither see nor hear nor speak." But as he was concerned about his won livelihood, and did not want to offend the idolaters too grossly, he would continue: "If thou bringest a dish of flour and a few eggs, it will suffice." This offering he would himself eat.

Under David he filled the position of treasurer. David appointed him because he thought that a man who was willing to become priest to an idol only in order to earn his bread, must be worthy of confidence. However sincere his repentance may have been, he relapsed into his former life when he was removed from his office by Solomon, who filled all position with new incumbents at his accession to the throne. Finally he abandoned his idolatrous ways wholly, and became so pure a man that the was favored by God with the gift of prophecy. This happened on the day on which the man of God out of Judah came to Jeroboam, for the grandson of Moses is none other than the old prophet at Beth-el who invited the man of God out of Judah to come to his house.

The mischief done by Micah spread further and further. Especially the Benjamites distinguished themselves for their zeal in paying homage to his idols. God therefore resolved to visit the sins of Israel and Benjamin upon them. The opportunity did not delay to come. It was not long before the Benjamites committed the outrage of Gibeah. Before the house of Bethac, a venerable old man, they imitated the disgraceful conduct of the Sodomites before the house of Lot. When the other tribes exacted amends from the Benjamites, and were denied satisfaction, bloody combats ensued. At first the Benjamites prevailed, in spit of the fact that the Urim and Thummim questioned by Phinehas had encouraged the Israelites to take up the conflict, with the words: "Up to war, I shall deliver them into your hands." After the tribes had again and again suffered defeat, they recognized the intention of God, to betray them as a punishment for their sins. They therefore ordained a day of fasting and convocation before the holy Ark, and Phinehas the son of Eleazar entreated God in their behalf: "What means this, that Thou leadest us astray? Is the deed of the Benjamites right in Thine eyes? Then why didst Thou not command us to desist from the combat? But if what our brethren have done is evil in Thy sight, then why dost Thou cause us to fall before them in battle? O God of our fathers, hearken unto my voice. Make it known this day unto Thy servant whether the war waged with Benjamin is pleasing in Thine eyes, or whether thou desirest to punish Thy people for its sins. Then the sinners among us will amend their ways. I am mindful of what happened in the days of my youth, at the time of Moses. In the zeal of my soul I slew two for the sin of Zimri, and when his well-wishers sought to kill me, Thou didst send an angel, who cut off twenty-four thousand of them and delivered me. But now eleven of Thy tribes have gone forth to do Thy bidding, to avenge and slay, and, lo, they have themselves been slain, so that they are made to believe that Thy revelations are lying and deceitful. O Lord, God of our forefathers, naught is hidden before Thee. Make it manifest why this misfortune has overtaken us."

God replied to Phinehas at great length, setting forth why eleven tribes had suffered so heavily. The Lord had wanted to punished them for having permitted Micah and his mother Delilah to pursue their evil ways undisturbed, though they were zealous beyond measure in avenging the wrong done to the woman at Gibeah. As soon as all those had perished who were guilty of having aided and abetted Micah in his idolatrous practices, whether directly or indirectly, God was willing to help them in their conflicts with the Benjamites.

So it came. In the battle fought soon after, seventy-five thousand Benjamites fell slain. Only six hundred of the tribe survived. Fearing to remain in Palestine, the small band emigrated to Italy and Germany.

At the same time the punishment promised them by God overtook the two chief sinners. Micah lost his life by fire, and his mother rotted alive; worms crawled from her body.

In spite of the great mischief caused by Micah, he had one good quality, and God permitted it to plead for him when the angel stood up against him as his accusers. He was extremely hospitable. His house always stood wide open to the wanderer, and to his hospitality he owed it that he was granted a share in the future world. In hell Micah is the first in the sixth division, which is under the guidance of the angel Hadriel, and he is the only one in the division who is spared hell tortures. Micah's sons was Jeroboam, whose golden calves were sinful far beyond anything his father had done.

In those days God spake to Phinehas: "Thou art one hundred and twenty years old, thou hast reached the natural term of man's life. Go now, betake thyself to the mountain Danaben, and remain there many years. I will command the eagles to sustain thee with food, so that thou returnest not to men until the time when thou lockest fast the clouds and openest them again. Then I will carry thee to the place where those are who were before thee, and there thou wilt tarry until I visit the world, and bring thee thither to taste of death."

Chapter 3

III. SAMUEL AND SAUL

ELKANAH AND HANNAH

The period of the Judges is linked to the period of the Kingdom by the prophet Samuel, who anointed both Saul and David as kings. Not only was Samuel himself a prophet, but his forebears also has been prophets, and both his parents, Elkanah and Hannah, were endowed with the gift of prophecy. Aside from this gift, Elkanah possessed extraordinary virtue. He was a second Abraham, the only pious man of his generation, who saved the world from destruction when God, made wroth by the idolatry of Micah, was on the point of annihilating it utterly. His chief merit was that he stimulated the people by his example to go on pilgrimages to Shiloh, the spiritual centre of the nation. Accompanied by his whole household, including kinsmen, he was in the habit of making the three prescribed pilgrimages annually, and though he was a man of only moderate means, his retinue was equipped with great magnificence. In all the towns through which it passed, the procession caused commotion. The lookers-on invariably inquired into the reason of the rare spectacle, and Elkanah told them: "We are going to the house of the Lord at Shiloh, for thence come forth the law. Why should you not join us?" Such gentle, persuasive words did not fail of taking effect. In the first year five households undertook the pilgrimage, the next year ten, and so on until the whole town followed his example. Elkanah chose a new route every year. Thus he touched at many towns, and their inhabitants were led to do a pious deed.

In spite of his God-fearing ways, Elkanah's domestic life was not perfectly happy. He had been married ten years, and his union with Hannah had not been blessed with offspring. The love he bore his wife compensated him for his childlessness, but Hannah herself insisted upon his taking a second wife. Peninnah embraced every opportunity of vexing Hannah. In the morning her derisive greeting to Hannah would be: "Dost thou not mean to rise and wash thy children, and send them to school?" Such jeers were to keep Hannah mindful of her childlessness. Perhaps Peninnah's intentions were laudable: she may have wanted to bring Hannah to the point of praying to God for children. However it may have been forced from her, Hannah's petition for a son was fervent and devout. She entreats God: "Lord of the world! Hast Thou created aught in vain? Our eyes Thou hast destined for sight, our ears for hearing, our mouth for speech, our nose to smell therewith, our hands for work. Didst Thou not create these breasts above my heart to give suck to a babe? O grant me a son, that he may draw nourishment therefrom. Lord, Thou reignest over all beings, the mortal and the heavenly beings. The heavenly beings neither eat nor drink, they do not propagate themselves, nor do they die, but they live forever. Mortal man eats, drinks, propagates his kind and dies. If, now, I am of the heavenly beings, let me live forever. But if I belong to mortal mankind, let me do my part in establishing the race."

Eli the high priest, who at first misinterpreted Hannah's long prayer, dismissed her with the blessing: "May the son to be born unto thee acquire great knowledge in the law." Hannah left the sanctuary, and at once her grief-furrowed countenance changes. She felt beyond a doubt that the blessing of Eli would be fulfilled.

THE YOUTH OF SAMUEL

Hannah's prayer was heard. At the end of six months and a few days Samuel was born to her, in the nineteenth year of her married life, and the one hundred and thirtieth of her age. Samuel was of a frail constitution, and required tender care and nurture. For this reason he and his mother could not accompany Elkanah on his pilgrimages. Hannah withheld her boy from the sanctuary for some years. Before Samuel's birth a voice from heaven had proclaimed that in a short time a great man would be born, whose name would be Samuel. All men children of that time were accordingly named Samuel. As they grew up, the mothers were in the habit of getting together and telling of their children's doings, in order to determine which of them satisfied the expectations the prophecy had aroused. When the true Samuel was born, and by his wonderful deed excelled all his companions, it became plain to whom the word of God applied. His preeminence now being undisputed, Hannah was willing to part with him.

The following incident is an illustration of Samuel's unusual qualities manifested even in infancy. He was two years old when his mother brought him to Shiloh to leave him there permanently. An occasion at once presented itself for the display of his learning and acumen, which were so great as to arouse the astonishment of the high priest Eli himself. On entering the sanctuary Samuel noticed that they were seeking a priest to kill the sacrificial animal. Samuel instructed the attendants that a non-priest was permitted to kill the sacrifice. The high priest Eli appeared at the moment when, by Samuel's directions, the sacrifice was being killed by a non-priest. Angered by the child's boldness, he was about to have him executed, regardless of Hannah's prayer for his life. "Let him die," he said, "I shall pray for another in his place." Hannah replied: "I lent him to the Lord. Whatever betide, he belongs neither to thee nor to me, but to God." Only then, after Samuel's life was secure, Hannah offered up her prayer of thanksgiving. Beside the expression of her gratitude, it contains also many prophecies regarding Samuel's future achievements, and it recited the history of Israel from the beginning until the advent of Messiah. Her prayer incidentally brought relief to the Sons of Korah. Since the earth had swallowed them, they had been constantly sinking lower and lower. When Hannah uttered the words, "God bringeth down to Sheol, and bringeth up," they came to a standstill in their downward course.

Hannah was spared to witness, not only the greatness of her son, but also the undoing of her rival. Every time Hannah bore a child, Peninnah lost two of hers, until eight of her ten children had died, and she would have had to surrender all, had not Hannah interceded for her with prayer.

ELI AND HIS SONS

Shortly before Samuel entered upon his novitiate in the sanctuary, Eli succeeded to the three highest offices in the land: he was made high priest, president of the Sanhedrin, and ruler over the political affairs of Israel. Eli was a pious man, and devoted to the study of the Torah, wherefore he attained to a good old age and to high honors. In his office as high priest he was successor to no less a personage than Phinehas, who had lost his high-priestly dignity on account of his haughty bearing toward Jephthah. With Eli the line of Ithamar rose to power instead of the line of Eleazar. However, the iniquitous deed of his two sons brought dire misfortune upon Eli and upon his family, though the Scriptural account of their conduct may not be taken literally. The sons of Eli transgressed only in that they sometimes kept the women waiting who came to the sanctuary to bring the purification offerings, and so they retarded their return to their families. This was bad enough for priest of God. Their misdeeds recoiled upon their father, who was not strict enough in rebuking them. Eli's punishment was that he aged prematurely, and, besides, he had to give up his various offices.

During his lifetime, his youngest son Phinehas, the worthier of the two, officiated as high priest. The only reproach to which Phinehas laid himself open was that he made no attempt to mend his brother's ways.

The worst of God's decree against Eli he learned from Elkanah, the man of God who came unto Eli, and who announced that the high-priestly dignity would be wrested from his house, and once more conferred upon the family of Eleazar, and, furthermore, his descendant would all die in their prime. The latter doom can be averted by good deeds, devotion in prayer, and zealous study of the Torah. These means were often employed successfully. But against the loss of the high priest's office there is no specific. The house of Eli forfeited it irrevocably. Abiathar, the great-grandson of Eli's son Phinehas, the last of the high priest of the line of Ithamar, had to submit to the fate of seeing David transfer his dignity to Zadok, in whose family it remained forever.

The sons of Eli brought misfortune also upon the whole of Israel. To their sins and the ease with which the people condoned them was attributed the unhappy issue of the war with the Philistines. The holy Ark, the receptacle for the broken table of the law, which accompanied the people to the camp, did not have the expected effect of compelling victory for the Israelites. What Eli feared happened. He enjoined upon his sons not to appear before him if they should survive the capture of the Ark. But they did not survive it; they died upon the battlefield on which their nation had suffered bitter defeat. The Philistines, to be sure, had to pay dearly for their victory, especially those who had spoken contemptuous words when the holy Ark had appeared in the Israelitish camp: "The God of the Israelites had ten plagues, and those he expended upon the Egyptians. He no longer has it in His power to do harm." But God said: "Do ye but wait to see. I shall bring plague down upon you like of which hath never been." This new plague consisted in mice crawling forth out of the earth, and jerking the entrails out of the bodies of the Philistines while they eased nature. If the Philistines sought to protect themselves by using brass vessels, the vessels burst at the touch of the mice, and, as before, the Philistines were at their mercy. After some months of suffering, when they realized that their god Dagon was the victim instead of the victor, they resolved to send the Ark back to the Israelites. Many of the Philistines, however, were not yet convinced of God's power. The experiment with the milch kine on which there had come no yoke was to establish the matter for them. The result was conclusive. Scarcely had the cows begun to draw the cart containing the Ark when they raised their voices in song:

Arise thou, O Acacia! Soar aloft in the fulness of thy splendor,

Thou who art adorned with gold embroidery,

Thou who art reverenced within the Holiest of the palace,

Thou who art covered by the two Cherubim!

When the holy Ark was thus brought into the Israelitish domain, there was exceeding great rejoicing. Yet the people were lacking in due reverence. They unloaded the holy vessel while doing their usual work. God punished them severely. The seventy members of the Sanhedrin perished, and with them fifty thousand of the people. The punishment was meet for another reason. At first sight of the Ark some of the people had exclaimed: "Who vexed these that thou didst feel offended, and what had mollified thee now?"

THE ACTIVITIES OF SAMUEL

In the midst of the defeats and other calamities that overwhelmed the Israelites, Samuel's authority grew, and the respect for him increased, until he was acknowledged the helper of his people. His first efforts were directed toward counteracting the spiritual decay in Israel. When he assembled the people at Mizpah for prayer, he sought to distinguish between the faithful and the idolatrous, in order to mete out punishment to the disloyal. He had all the people drink water, whose effect was to prevent idolaters from opening their lips. The majority of the people repented of their sins, and Samuel turned to God in their behalf: "Lord of the world! Thou requirest naught of man but that he should repent of his sins. Israel is penitent, do Thou pardon him." The prayer was granted, and when, after his sacrifice, Samuel led an attack upon the Philistines, victory was not withheld from the Israelites. God terrified the enemy first by an earthquake, and then by thunder and lightning. Many were scattered and wandered about aimlessly; many were precipitated into the rents torn in the earth, the rest had their faces scorched, and in their terror and pain their weapons dropped from their hands.

In peace as in war Samuel was the type of a disinterested, incorruptible judge, who even refused compensation for the time, trouble, and pecuniary sacrifices entailed upon him by his office. His sons fell far short of resembling their father in these respects. Instead of continuing Samuel's plan of journeying from place to place to dispense judgment, they had the people come to them, and they surrounded themselves with a crew of officials who preyed upon the people for their maintenance. In a sense, therefore, the curse with which Eli threatened Samuel in his youth was accomplished: both he and Samuel had sons unworthy of their fathers. Samuel at least had the satisfaction of seeing his sons mend their ways. One of them is the prophet Joel, whose prophecy forms a book of the Bible.

Though, according to this account, the sons of Samuel were by no means so iniquitous as might be inferred from the severe expressions of the Scripture, still the demand for a king made by the leaders of the people was not unwarranted. All they desired was a king in the place of a judge. What enkindled the wrath of God and caused Samuel vexation, was the way in which the common people formulated the demand. "We want a king," they said, "that we may be like the other nations."

THE REIGN OF SAUL

There were several reasons for the choice of Saul as king. He had distinguished himself as a military hero in the unfortunate engagement of the Philistines with Israel under the leadership of the sons of Eli. Goliath captured the tables of the law. When Saul heard of this in Shiloh, he marched sixty miles to the camp, wrested the tables from the giant, and returned to Shiloh on the same day, bringing Eli the report of the Israelitish misfortune. Besides, Saul possessed unusual beauty, which explains why the maidens whom he asked about the seer in their city sought to engage him in a lengthy conversation. At the same time he was exceedingly modest. When he and his servant failed to find the asses they were looking for, he said, "My father will take thought of us," putting his servants on a level with himself, and when he was anointed king, he refused to accept the royal dignity until the Urim and Thummin were consulted. His chief virtue, however, was his innocence. He was as free from sin as "a one year old child." No wonder, then, he was held worthy of the prophetic gift. The prophecies he uttered concerned themselves with the war of Gog and Magog, the meting out of reward and punishment at the last judgment. Finally, his choice as king was due also to the merits of his ancestors, especially his grandfather Abiel, a man interested in the public welfare, who would have the streets lighted so that people might go to the houses of study after dark.

Saul's first act as king was his successful attack upon Nahash, king of the Ammonites, who had ordered the Gileadites to remove the injunction from the Torah barring the Ammonites from the congregation of Israel. In his next undertaking, the campaign against the Philistines, he displayed his piety. His son Jonathan had fallen under the severe ban pronounced by Saul against all who tasted food on a certain day, and Saul did not hesitate to deliver him up to death. Jonathan's trespass was made know by the stones in the breastplate of the high priest. All the stones were bright, only the one bearing the name Benjamin had lost its brilliancy. By lot it was determined that its dimmed lustre was due to the Benjamite Jonathan. Saul desisted from his purpose of executing Jonathan only when it appeared that he had transgressed his father's command by mistake. A burnt offering and his weight in gold paid to the sanctuary were considered an atonement for him. In the same war Saul had occasion to show his zeal for the scrupulous observance of the sacrificial ordinances. He reproached his warriors with eating the meat of the sacrifices before the blood was sprinkled on the altar, and he made it his task to see to it that the slaughtering knife was kept in the prescribed condition. As recompense, an angel brought him a sword, there being none beside Saul in the whole army to bear one.

Saul manifested a different spirit in the next campaign, the war with the Amalekites, whom, at the bidding of God, he was to exterminate. When the message of God's displeasure was conveyed to Saul by the prophet Samuel, he said: "If the Torah ordains that a heifer of the herd shall be beheaded in the valley as an atonement for the death of a single man, how great must be the atonement required for the slaughter of so many men? And granted they are sinners, what wrong have their cattle done to deserve annihilation? And granted that the adults are worthy of their fate, what have the children done?" Then a voice proclaimed from heaven, "Be not overjust." Later on, when Saul commissioned Doeg to cut down the priests at Nob, the same voice was heard to say, "Be not overwicked." It was this very Doeg, destined to play so baleful a part in his life, who induced Saul to spare Agag, the king of Amalekites. His argument was the law prohibits the slaying of an animal and its young on the same day. How much less permissible is it to destroy at one time old and young, men and children. As Saul had undertaken the war of extermination against Amalek only because forced into it, he was easily persuaded to let the people keep a part of the cattle alive. As far as he himself was concerned, he could have had no personal interest in the booty, for he was so affluent that he took a census of the army by giving a sheep to every one of his soldiers, distributing not less than two hundred thousand sheep.

Compared with David's sins, Saul's were not sufficiently grievous to account for the withdrawal of the royal dignity from him and his family. The real reason was Saul's too great mildness, a drawback in a ruler. Moreover, his family was of such immaculate nobility that his descendants might have become too haughty. When Saul disregarded the Divine command about the Amalekites, Samuel announced to him that his office would be bestowed upon another. The name of his successor was not mentioned on that occasion, but Samuel gave him a sign by which to recognize the future king: he who would cut off the corner of Saul's mantle, would reign in his stead. Later on, when David met Saul in the cave and cut off a piece of the king's skirt, Saul knew him for a certainty to be his destined successor.

So Saul lost his crown on account of Agag, and yet did not accomplish his purpose of saving the life of the Amalekite king, for Samuel inflicted a most cruel death upon Agag, and that not in accordance with Jewish, but with heathen, forms of justice. No witnesses of Agag's crime could be summoned before the court, nor could it be proved that Agag, as the law requires, had been warned when about to commit the crime. Though due punishment was meted out to Agag, in a sense it came too late. Had he been killed by Saul in the course of the battle, the Jews would have been spared the persecution devised by Haman, for, in the short span of time that elapsed between war and his execution, Agag became the ancestor of Haman.

The Amalekite war was the last of Saul's notable achievements. Shortly afterward he was seized by the evil spirit, and the rest of his days were passed mainly in persecuting David and his followers. Saul would have died immediately after the Amalekite war, if Samuel had not interceded for him. The prophet prayed to God that the life of the disobedient king be spared, at least so long as his own years had not come to their destined close: "Thou regardest me equal to Moses and Aaron. As Moses and Aaron did not have their handiwork destroyed before their eyes during their life, so may my handiwork not cease during my life." God said: "What shall I do? Samuel will not let me put an end to Saul's days, and if I let Samuel die in his prime, people will speak ill of him Meanwhile David's time is approaching, and one reign may not overlap the time assigned to another by his hairbreadth." God determined to let Samuel age suddenly, and when he died at fifty-two, the people were under the impression the days of an old man had come to an end. So long as he lived, Saul was secure. Scarcely was he dead, when the Philistines began to menace the Israelites and their king. Soon it appeared how well justified had been the mourning services for the departed prophet in all the Israelitish towns. It was not remarkable that the mourning for Samuel should have been universal. During his active administration as judge, he had been in the habit of journeying through every part of the country, and so he was known personally to all the people. This practice of his testifies not only to the zeal with which he devoted himself to his office, but also to his wealth, for the expenses entailed by these journeys were defrayed from his own purse. Only one person in all the land took no part in the demonstrations of grief. During the very week of mourning Nabal held feasts. "What!" God exclaimed, "all weep and lament over the death of the pious, and this reprobate engages in revelry!" Punishment was not withheld. Three days after the week of mourning for Samuel Nabal dies.

There was none that felt the death of Samuel more keenly than Saul. Left alone and isolated, he did not shrink from extreme measures to enter into communication with the departed prophet. With his two adjutants, Abner and Amasa, he betook himself to Abner's mother, the witch of En-dor. The king did not reveal his identity, but the witch had no difficulty in recognizing her visitor. In necromancy the peculiar rule holds good that, unless it is summoned by a king, a spirit raised from the dead appears head downward and feet in the air. Accordingly, when the figure of Samuel stood upright before them, the witch knew that the king was with her. Though the witch saw Samuel, she could not hear what he said, while Saul heard his words, but could not see his person another peculiar phenomenon in necromancy: the conjuror sees the spirit, and he for whom the spirit had been raised only hears it. Any other person present neither sees nor hears it.

The witch's excitement grew when she perceived a number of spirits arise by the side of Samuel. The dead prophet, when he was summoned back to earth, thought that the judgement day had arrived. He requested Moses to accompany him and testify to his always having executed the ordinances of the Torah as Moses had established them. With these two great leaders a number of the pious arose, all believing that the day of judgment was at hand. Samuel was apparelled in the "upper garment" his mother had made for him when she surrendered him to the sanctuary. This he had worn throughout his life, and in it he was buried. At the resurrection all the dead wear their grave clothes, and so it came about that Samuel stood before Saul in his well-known "upper garment."

Only fragments of the conversation between Samuel and Saul have been preserved in the Scriptures. Samuel reproached Saul with having disturbed him. "Was it not enough," he said, "for thee to enkindle the wrath of thy Creator by calling up the spirits of the dead, must thou need change me into an idol? For is it not said that like unto the worshippers so shall the worshipped be punished?" Samuel then consented to tell the king God's decree, that he had resolved to rend the kingdom out of his hand, and invest David with the royal dignity. Whereupon Saul: "These are not the words thou spakest to me before." "When we dwelt together," rejoined Samuel, "I was in the world of lies. Now I abide in the world of truth, and thou heardest lying words from me, for I feared thy wrath and thy revenge. Now I abide in the world of truth, and thou hearest words of truth from me. As to the thing the Lord hath done unto thee, thou hast deserved it, for thou didst not obey the voice of the Lord, nor execute his fierce wrath upon Amalek." Saul asked: "Can I still save myself by flight?" "Yes," replied Samuel, "if thou fleest, thou art safe. But if thou acceptest God's judgment, by to-morrow thou wilt be united with me in Paradise."

When Abner and Amasa questioned Saul about his interview with Samuel, he replied: "Samuel told me I should go into battle to-morrow, and come forth victorious. More than that, my sons will be given exalted positions in return for their military prowess." The next day his three sons went with him to the war, and all were stricken down. God summoned the angels and said to them: "Behold the being I have created in my world. A father as a rule refrains from taking his sons even to a banquet, lest he expose them to the evil eye. Saul goes to war knowing that he will lose his life, yet he takes his sons with him, and cheerfully accepts the punishment I ordain."

So perished the first Jewish king, as a hero and a saint. His latter days were occupied with regrets on account of the execution of the priest of Nob, and his remorse secured pardon for him. Indeed, in all respects his piety was so great that not even David was his equal: David had many wives and concubines; Saul had but on wife. David remained behind, fearing to lose his life in battle with his son Absalom; Saul went into the combat knowing he should not return alive. Mild and generous, Saul led the life of a saint in his own house, observing even the priestly laws of purity. Therefore God reproached David with having pronounced a curse upon Saul in his prayer. Also, David in his old age was punished for having cut off the corner of Saul's mantle, for no amount of clothing would keep him warm. Finally, when a great famine fell upon the land during the reign of David, God told him it had been inflicted upon him because Saul's remains had not been buried with the honor due to him, and at that moment a heavenly voice resounded calling Saul "the elect of God."

THE COURT OF SAUL

The most important figure at the court of Saul was his cousin Abner, the son of the witch of En-dor. He was a giant of extraordinary size. A wall measuring six ells in thickness could be moved more easily than one of Abner's feet. David once chanced to get between the feet of Abner as he lay asleep, and he was almost crushed to death, when fortunately Abner moved them, and David made his escape. Conscious of his vast strength he once cried out: "If only I could seize the earth at some point, I should be able to shake it." Even in the hour of death, wounded mortally by Joab, he grasped his murderer like a worsted ball. He was about to kill him, but the people crowded round them, and said to Abner: "If thou killest Joab, we shall be orphaned, and our wives and children will be prey to the Philistines." Abner replied: "What can I do? He was about to extinguish my light." The people consoled him: "Commit thy cause to the true Judge." Abner thereupon loosed his hold upon Joab, who remained unharmed, while Abner fell dead instantly. God had decided against him. The reason was that Joab was in a measure justified in seeking to avenge the death of his brother Asahel. Asahel, the supernaturally swift runner, so swift that he ran through a field without snapping the ears of wheat had been the attacking party. He had sough to take Abner's life, and Abner contended, that in killing Asahel he had but acted in self-defense. Before inflicting the fatal wound, Joab held a formal court of justice over Abner. He asked: "Why didst thou no render Asahel harmless by wounding him rather than kill him?" Abner replied that he could not have done it. "What," said Joab, incredulous, "if thou wast able to strike him under the fifth rib, dost thou mean to say thou couldst not have made him innocuous by a wound, and saved him alive?"

Although Abner was a saint, even a "lion in the law," he perpetrated many a deed that made his violent death appear just. It was in his favor that he had refused to obey Saul's command to do away with the priests of Nob. Yet a man of his stamp should not have rested content with passive resistance. He should have interposed actively, and kept Saul from executing his blood design. And granted that Abner could not have influenced the king's mind in this matter, at all events he is censurable for having frustrated a reconciliation between Saul and David. When David, holding in his hand the corner of the king's mantle which he had cut off, sought to convince Saul of his innocence, it was Abner who turned the king against the suppliant fugitive. "Concern not thyself about it," he said to Saul. "David found the rag on a thornbush in which thou didst catch the skirt of thy mantle as thou didst pass it." On the other hand, no blame attaches to Abner for having espoused the cause of Saul's son against David for two years and a half. He knew that God had designated David for the royal office, but, according to an old tradition, God had promised two kings to the tribe of Benjamin, and Abner considered it his duty to transmit his father's honor to the son of Saul the Benjamite.

Another figure of importance during Saul's reign, but a man of radically different character, was Doeg. Doeg, the friend of Saul from the days of his youth, died when he was thirty-four years old, yet at that early age he had been president of the Sanhedrin and the greatest scholar of his time. He was called Edomi, which means, not Edomite, but "he who causes the blush of shame," because by his keen mind and his learning he put to shame all who entered into argument with him. But his scholarship lay only on his lips, his heart was not concerned in it, and his one aim was to elicit admiration. Small wonder, then, that his end was disastrous. At the time of his death he had sunk so low that he forfeited all share in the life to come. Wounded vanity caused his hostility to David, who had got the better of him in a learned discussion. From that moment he bent all his energies to the task of ruining David. He tried to poison Saul's mind against David, by praising the latter inordinately, and so arousing Saul's jealousy. Again, he would harp on David's Moabite descent, and maintain that on account of it he could not be admitted into the congregation of Israel. Samuel and other prominent men had to bring to bear all the weight of their authority to shield David against the consequences of Doeg's sophistry.

Doeg's most grievous transgression, however, was his informing against the priests of Nob, whom he accused of high treason and executed as traitors. For all his iniquitous deeds he pressed the law into his service, and derived justification of his conduct from it. Abimelech, the high priest at Nob, admitted that he had consulted the Urim and Thummim for David. This served Doeg as the basis for the charge of treason, and he stated it as an unalterable Halakah that the Urim and Thummim may be consulted only for a king. In vain Abner and Amasa and all the other members of the Sanhedrin demonstrated that the Urim and Thummim may be consulted for any on whose undertaking concerns the general welfare. Doeg would not yield, and as no one could be found to execute the judgement, he himself officiated as hangman. When the motive of revenge actuated him, he held cheap alike the life and honor of his fellow-man. He succeeded in convincing Saul that David's marriage with the king's daughter Michal had lost its validity from the moment David was declared a rebel. As such, he said, David was as good as dead, since a rebel was outlawed. Hence his wife was no longer bound to him. Doeg's punishment accorded with his misdeeds. He who had made impious use of his knowledge of the law, completely forgot the law, and even his disciples rose up against him, and drove him from the house of study. In the end he died a leper.

Dreadful as this death was, it was not accounted an atonement for his sins. One angel burned his soul, and another scattered his ashes in all the house of study and prayer. The son of Doeg was Saul's armor-bearer, who was killed by David for daring to slay the king even though he longed for death.

Along with Abner and Doeg, Jonathan distinguished himself in the reign of his father. His military capacity was joined to deep scholarship. To the latter he owed his position as Ab Bet Din. Nevertheless he was one of the most modest men known in history. Abinadab was another one of Saul's sons who was worthy of his father, wherefore he was sometimes called Ishvi. As for Saul's grandson Mephibosheth. He, too, was reputed a great man. David himself did not scorn to sit at his feet, and he revered Mephibosheth as his teacher. The wrong done him by David in granting one-half his possessions to Ziba, the slave of Mephibosheth, did not go unavenged. When David ordered the division of the estate of Mephibosheth, a voice from heaven prophesied: "Jeroboam and Rehoboam shall divide the kingdom between themselves."

Chapter 4

IV. DAVID

DAVID'S BIRTH AND DESCENT

David, the "elect of God," was descended from a family which itself belonged to the elect of Israel. Those ancestors of his who are enumerated in the Bible by name are all of them men of distinguished excellence. Besides, David was a descendant of Miriam, the sister of Moses, and so the strain of royal aristocracy was reinforced by the priestly aristocracy. Nor was David the first of his family to occupy the throne of a ruler. His great-grandfather Boaz was one and the same person with Ibzan, the judge of Bethlehem. Othniel, too, the first judge in Israel after the death of Joshua, and Caleb, the brother of Othniel, were connected with David's family. As examples of piety and virtue, David had his grandfather and more particularly his father before him. His grandfather's whole life was a continuous service of God, whence his name Obed, "the servant," and his father Jesse was one of the greatest scholars of his time, and one of the four who died wholly untainted by sin. If God had not ordained death for all the descendants of our first parents after their fall, Jesse would have continued to live forever. As it was, he died at the age of four hundred, and then a violent death, by the hand of the Moabite king, in whose care David, trusting in the ties of kinship between the Moabites and the seed of Ruth, left his family when he was fleeing before Saul. Jesse's piety will not go unrewarded. In the Messianic time he will be one of the eight princes to rule over the world.

In spite of his piety, Jesse was not always proof against temptation. One of his slaves caught his fancy, and he would have entered into illicit relations with her, had his wife, Nazbat, the daughter of Adiel, not frustrated the plan. She disguised herself as the slave, and Jesse, deceived by the ruse, met his own wife. The child borne by Nazbat was given out as the son of the freed slave, so that the father might not discover the deception practiced upon him. This child was David.

In a measure David was indebted for his life to Adam. At first only three hours of existence had been allotted to him. When God caused all future generations to pass in review before Adam, he besought God to give David seventy of the thousand years destined for him. A deed of gift, signed by God and the angel Metatron, was drawn up. Seventy years were legally conveyed from Adam to David, and in accordance with Adam's wishes, beauty, dominion, and poetical gift went with them.

ANOINTED KING

Beauty and talent, Adam's gifts to David, did not shield their possessor against hardship. As the supposed son of a slave, he was banished from association with his brothers, and his days were passed in the desert tending his father's sheep. It was his shepherd life that prepared him for his later exalted position. With gentle consideration he led the flocks entrusted to him. The young lambs he guided to pastures of tender grass; the patches of less juicy herbs he reserved for the sheep; and the full-grown sturdy rams were given the tough weeds for food. Then God said: "David knows how to tend sheep, therefore he shall be the shepherd of my flock Israel."

In the solitude of the desert David had opportunities of displaying his extraordinary physical strength. One day he slew four lions and three bears, though he had no weapons. His most serious adventure was with the reem. David encountered the mammoth beast asleep, and taking it for a mountain, he began to ascend it. Suddenly the reem awoke, and David found himself high up in the air on its horns. He vowed, if he were rescued, to build a temple to God one hundred ells in height, as high as the horns of the reem. Thereupon God sent a lion. The king of beasts inspired even the reem with awe. The reem prostrated himself, and David could easily descend from his perch. At that moment a deer appeared. The lion pursued after him, and David was saved from the lion as well as the reem.

He continued to lead the life of a shepherd until, at the age of twenty-eight, he was anointed king by Samuel, who was taught by a special revelation that the despised youngest son of Jesse was to be king. Samuel's first charge had been to anoint one of the sons of Jesse, but he was not told which one. When he saw the oldest, Eliab, he thought him the king of God's choice. God had allowed him to be deceived, in order to punish Samuel for his excessive self-consciousness in calling himself the seer. It was thus proved to him that he could not foresee all things. However, Samuel's error was pardonable. God's first choice had rested upon Eliab. Only on account of his violent nature, his swiftness to anger against David, the position destined for him was transferred to his youngest brother. Eliab was in a sense compensated by seeing his daughter become the wife of Rehoboam. Thus he, too, enjoys the distinction of being among the ancestors of the Judaic kings, and Samuel's vision of Eliab as king was not wholly false.

The election of David was obvious from what happened with the holy oil with which he was anointed. When Samuel had tried to pour the oil on David's brothers, it had remained in the horn, but at David's approach it flowed of its own accord, and poured itself out over him. The drops on his garments changed into diamonds and pearls, and after the act of anointing him, the horn was as full as before.

The amazement was great that the son of a slave should be made king. Then the wife of Jesse revealed her secret, and declared herself the mother of David.

The anointing of David was for a time kept a secret, but its effect appeared in the gift of prophecy which manifested itself in David, and in his extraordinary spiritual development. His new accomplishments naturally earned envy for him. None was more bitterly jealous than Doeg, the greatest scholar of his time. When he heard that Saul was about to have David come to court as his attendant, Doeg began to praise David excessively, with the purpose of arousing the king's jealousy and making David hateful in his eyes. He succeeded, yet Saul did not relinquish his plan of having David at court. David had become known to Saul in his youth, and at that time the king had conceived great admiration for him. The occasion was one on which David had shown cleverness as well as love of justice. A rich woman had had to leave her home temporarily. She could not carry her fortune with her, nor did she wish to entrust it to any one. She adopted the device of hiding her gold in honey jars, and these she deposited with a neighbor. Accidentally he discovered what was in the jars, and he abstracted the gold. On her return the woman received her vessels, but the gold concealed in them was gone. She had no evidence to bring up against her faithless neighbor, and the court dismissed her complaint. She appealed to the king, but he was equally powerless to help. When the woman came out of the palace of the king, David was playing with his companions. Seeing her dejection, he demanded an audience of the king, that truth might prevail. The king authorized him to do as he saw fit. David ordered the honey jars to be broken, and two coins were found to adhere to the inner side of the vessels. The thief had overlooked them, and they proved his dishonesty.

ENCOUNTER WITH GOLIATH

David was not long permitted to enjoy the ease of life at court. The aggressive manner assumed by Goliath drove him to the front. It was a curious chance that designated David to be the slayer of Goliath, who was allied with him by the ties of blood. Goliath, it will be remembered, was the son of the Moabitess Orpah, the sister-in-law of David's ancestress Ruth, and her sister as well, both having been the daughters of the Moabite king Eglon. David and Goliath differed as widely as their grandams, for in contrast to Ruth, the pious, religious Jewess, Orpah had led a life of unspeakable infamy. Her son Goliath was jeered at as "the son of a hundred fathers and one mother." But God lets naught go unrewarded, even in the wicked. In return for the forty steps Orpah had accompanied her mother-in-law Naomi, Goliath the Philistine, her son, was permitted to display his strength and skill for forty days, and in return for the four tears Orpah had shed on parting from her mother-in-law, she was privileged to give birth to four giant sons.

Of the four, Goliath was the strongest and greatest. What the Scriptures tell about him is but a small fraction of what might have been told. The Scriptures refrain intentionally from expatiating upon the prowess of the miscreant. Nor do they tell how Goliath, impious as he was, dared challenge the God of Israel to combat with him, and how he tried by every means in his power to hinder the Israelites in their Divine worship. Morning and evening he would appear in the camp at the very time when the Israelites were preparing to say the Shema.

All the more cause, then, for David to hate Goliath and determine to annihilate him. His father encouraged him to oppose Goliath, for he considered it David's duty to protect Saul the Benjamite against the giant, as Judah, his ancestor, had in ancient days pledged himself for the safety of Benjamin, the ancestor of Saul. For Goliath was intent upon doing away with Saul. His grievance against him was that once, when, in a skirmish between the Philistines and the Israelites, Goliath had succeeded in capturing the holy tables of the law, Saul had wrested them from the giant. In consequence of his malady, Saul could not venture to cross swords with Goliath, and he accepted David's offer to enter into combat in his place. David put on Saul's armor, and when it appeared that the armor of the powerfully-built king fitted the erstwhile slender youth, Saul recognized that David had been predestined for the serious task he was about to undertake, but at the same time David's miraculous transformation did not fail to arouse his jealousy. David, for this reason, declined to array himself as a warrior for his contest with Goliath. He wanted to meet him as a simple shepherd. Five pebbles came to David of their own accord, and when he touched them, they all turned into one pebble. The five pebbles stood for God, the three Patriarchs, and Aaron. Hophni and Phinehas, the descendants of the last, had only a short time before been killed by Goliath.

Scarcely did David begin to move toward Goliath, when the giant became conscious of the magic power of the youth. The evil eye David cast on his opponent sufficed to afflict him with leprosy, and in the very same instant he was rooted to the ground, unable to move. Goliath was so confused by his impotence that he scarcely knew what he was saying, and he uttered the foolish threat that he would give David's flesh to the cattle of the field, as though cattle ate flesh. One can see, David said to himself, that he is crazy, and there can be no doubt he is doomed. Sure of victory, David retorted that he would cast the carcass of the Philistine to the fowls of the air. At the mention of fowls, Goliath raised his eyes skyward, to see whether there were any birds about. The upward motion of his head pushed his visor slightly away from his forehead, and in that instant the pebble aimed by David struck him on the exposed spot. An angel descended and cast him to the ground face downward, so that the mouth that had blasphemed God might be choked with earth. He fell in such wise that the image of Dagon which he wore on his breast touched the ground, and his head came to lie between the feet of David, who now had no difficulty in dispatching him.

Goliath was encased, from top to toe, in several suits of armor, and David did not know how to remove them and cut off the head of the giant. At this juncture Uriah the Hittite offered him his services, but under the condition that David secure him an Israelitish wife. David accepted the condition, and Uriah in turn showed him how the various suits of armor were fastened together at the heels of the giant's feet.

David's victory naturally added fuel to the fire of Saul's jealousy. Saul sent Abner, his general, to make inquiry whether David, who, he knew, was of the tribe of Judah, belonged to the clan of the Perez or to the clan of the Zerah. In the former case his suspicion that David was destined for kingship would be confirmed. Doeg, David's enemy from of old, observed that David, being the descendant of the Moabitess Ruth, did not even belong to the Jewish communion, and Saul need entertain no fears from that quarter. A lively discussion arose between Abner and Doeg, as to whether the law in Deuteronomy regarding Moabites affected women as well as men. Doeg, an expert dialectician, brilliantly refuted all of Abner's arguments in favor of the admission of Moabitish women. Samuel's authority had to be appealed to in order to establish for all times the correctness of Abner's view. Indeed, the dispute could be settled only by recourse to threats of violence. Ithra, the father of Amasa, in Arab fashion, for which reason he was sometimes called the Ishmaelite, threatened to hew down any one with his sword who refused to accept Samuel's interpretation of the law, that male Moabites and male Ammonites are forever excluded from the congregation of Israel, but not Moabite and Ammonite women.

PURSUED BY SAUL

As God stood by David in his duel with Goliath, so he stood by him in many other of his difficulties. Often when he thought all hope lost, the arm of God suddenly succored him, and in unexpected ways, not only bringing relief, but also conveying instruction on God's wise and just guidance of the world.

David once said to God: "The world is entirely beautiful and good, with the one exception of insanity. What use does the world derive from a lunatic, who runs hither and thither, tears his clothes, and is pursued by a mob of hooting children?" "Verily, a time will come," said God in reply, "when thou wilt supplicate me to afflict thee with madness." Now, it happened when David, on his flight before Saul, came to Achish, the king of the Philistines, who lived in Gath, that the brothers of Goliath formed the heathen king's body-guard, and they demanded that their brother's murderer be executed. Achish, though a heathen, was pious, for which reason he is called Abimelech in the Psalms, after the king of Gerar, who also was noted for piety. He therefore sought to pacify David's enemies. He called their attention to the fact that Goliath had been the one to challenge the Jews to combat, and it was meet, therefore, that he should be left to bear the consequences. The brothers rejoined, if that view prevailed, then Achish would have to give up his throne to David, for, according to the conditions of the combat, the victor was to have dominion over the vanquished as his servants. In his distress, David besought God to let him appear a madman in the eyes of Achish and his court. God granted his prayer. As the wife and daughter of the Philistine king were both bereft of reason, we can understand his exclamation: "Do I lack madmen, that ye have brought this fellow to play the madman in my presence?" Thus it was that David was rescued. Thereupon he composed the Psalm beginning with the words, "I will bless the Lord at all times," which includes even the time of lunacy.

On another occasion David expressed his doubt of God's wisdom in having formed such apparently useless creatures as spiders are. They do nothing but spin a web that has no value. He was to have striking proof that even a spider's web may serve an important purpose. On one occasion he had taken refuge in a cave, and Saul and his attendants, in pursuit of him, were about to enter and seek him there. But God sent a spider to weave its web across the opening, and Saul told his men to desist from fruitless search in the cave, for the spider's web was undeniable proof that no one had passed through its entrance.

Similarly, when David became indebted to one of them for his life, he was cured of his scorn for wasps. He had thought them good for nothing but to breed maggots. David once surprised Saul and his attendants while they were fast asleep in their camp, and he resolved to carry off, as proof of his magnanimity, the cruse that stood between the feet of the giant Abner, who like the rest was sleeping. Fortunately his knees were drawn up, so that David could carry out his intention unhindered. But as David was retiring with the cruse, Abner stretched out his feet, and pinned David down as with two solid pillars. His life would have been forfeit, if a wasp had not stung Abner, who mechanically, in his sleep, moved his feet, and released David.

There were still other miracles that happened to David in his flight. Once, when Saul and his men compassed David round about, an angel appeared and summoned him home, to repulse the raid of the Philistines upon the land. Saul gave up the pursuit of David, but only after a majority had so decided, for some had been of the opinion that the seizure of David was quite as important as the repulse of the Philistines. Again, in his battle with the Amalekites, David enjoyed direct intervention from above. Lightning in flashes and sheets illumined the dark night, so enabling him to carry on the struggle.

WARS

David's first thought after ascending the throne was to wrest Jerusalem, sacred since the days of Adam, Noah, and Abraham, from the grasp of the heathen. The plan was not easy of execution for various reasons. The Jebusites, the possessors of Jerusalem, were the posterity of those sons of Heth who had ceded the Cave of Machpelah to Abraham only on condition that their descendants should never be forcibly dispossessed of their capital city Jerusalem. In perpetuation of this agreement between Abraham and the sons of Heth, monuments of brass were erected, and when David approached Jerusalem with hostile intent, the Jebusites pointed to Abraham's promise engraven upon them and still plainly to be read. They maintained that before David could take the city, which they had surrounded with a high wall, he would have to destroy the monuments. Joab devised a plan of getting into Jerusalem. He set up a tall cypress tree near the wall, bent it downward, and standing on David's head, he grasped the very tip of the tree. When the tree rebounded, Joab sat high above the wall, and could jump down upon it. Once in the city, he destroyed the monuments, and possessed himself of Jerusalem. For David a miracle had happened; the wall had lowered itself before him so that he could walk into the city without difficulty. David, however, was not desirous of using forcible means. He therefore offered the Jebusites six hundred shekels, fifty shekels for each Israelitish tribe. The Jebusites accepted the money, and gave David a bill of sale.

Jerusalem having been acquired, David had to prepare for war with the Philistines, in which the king gave proof at once of his heroic courage and his unshakable trust in God. The latter quality he displayed signally in the battle that took place in the Valley of the Giants. God had commanded David not to attack the host of the Philistines until he heard "the sound of marching in the tops of the mulberry trees." God desired to pass judgment upon the tutelary angels of the heathen, before surrendering the heathen themselves to the pious, and the motion of the tops of the trees was to indicate that the battle could proceed. The enemy advanced until there were but four ells between them and the Israelites. The latter were about to throw themselves against the Philistines, but David restrained them, saying: "God forbade me to attack the Philistines before the tops of the trees begin to move. If we transgress God's command, we shall certainly die. If we delay, it is probable that we shall be killed by the Philistines, but, at least, we shall die as pious men that keep God's command. Above all, let us have confidence in God." Scarcely had he ended his speech when the tops of the trees rustled, and David made a successful assault upon the Philistines. Whereupon God said to the angels, who were constantly questioning him as to why he had taken the royal dignity from Saul and given it to David: "See the difference between Saul and David."

Of David's other campaigns, the most notable is his war with Shobach the Aramean, whom he conquered in spite of his gigantic size and strength. Shobach was very tall, as tall as a dove-cote, and one look at him sufficed to strike terror to the heart of the beholder. The Aramean general indulged in the belief that David would treat the Syrians gently on account of the monument, still in existence at that time, which Jacob and Laban had erected on the frontier between Palestine and Aram as a sign of their covenant that neither they nor their descendants should wage war with each other. But David destroyed the monument. Similarly, the Philistines had placed trust in a relic from Isaac, the bridle of a mule which the Patriarch had given to Abimelech, the king of the Philistines, as a pledge of the covenant between Israel and his people. David took it from them by force.

However, David was as just as he was bold. Disregard of the covenants made by the Patriarchs was far removed from his thoughts. Indeed, before departing for the wars with the Arameans and the Philistines, he had charged the Sanhedrin to investigate carefully the claims of the two nations. The claims of the Philistines were shown to be utterly unfounded. In no sense were they the descendants of those Philistines who had concluded a treaty with Isaac; they had immigrated from Cyprus at a much later date. The Arameans, on the other hand, had forfeited their claims upon considerate treatment, because under the "Aramean" Balaam, and later again, in the time of Othniel, under their king Cushan-rishathaim, they had attacked and made war upon the Israelites.

AHITHOPHEL

Among David's courtiers and attendants, a prominent place is occupied by his counsellor Ahithophel, with whom the king was connected by family ties, Bath-sheba being his granddaughter. Ahithophel's wisdom was supernatural, for his counsels always coincided with the oracles rendered by the Urim and Thummim, and great as was his wisdom, it was equalled by his scholarship. Therefore David did not hesitate to submit himself to his instruction, even though Ahithophel was a very young man, at the time of his death not more than thirty-three years old. The one thing lacking in him was sincere piety, and this it was that proved his undoing in the end, for it induced him to take part in Absalom's rebellion against David. Thus he forfeited even his share in the world to come.

To this dire course of action he was misled by astrologic and other signs, which he interpreted as prophecies of his own kingship, when in reality they pointed to the royal destiny of his granddaughter Bath-sheba. Possessed by his erroneous belief, he cunningly urged Absalom to commit an unheard-of crime. Thus Absalom would profit nothing by his rebellion, for, though he accomplished his father's ruin, he would yet be held to account and condemned to death for his violation of family purity, and the way to the throne would be clear for Ahithophel, the great sage in Israel.

The relation between David and Ahithophel had been somewhat strained even before Absalom's rebellion. Ahithophel's feelings had been hurt by his being passed over at the time when David, shortly after ascending the throne, invested, on a single day, no less than ninety thousand functionaries with positions.

On that day a remarkable incident occurred. When the Ark was to be brought up from Geba to Jerusalem, the priests who attempted to take hold of it were raised up in the air and thrown violently to the ground. In his despair the king turned for advice to Ahithophel, who retorted mockingly: "Ask thy wise men whom thou hast but now installed in office." It was only when David uttered a curse on him who knows a remedy and withholds it from the sufferer, that Ahithophel advised that a sacrifice should be offered at every step taken by the priests. Although the measure proved efficacious, and no further disaster occurred in connection with the Ark, yet Ahithophel's words had been insincere. He knew the real reason of the misadventure, and concealed it from the king. Instead of following the law of having the Ark carried on the shoulders of priests, David had had it put on a wagon, and so incurred the wrath of God.

Ahithophel's hostility toward David showed itself also on the following occasion. When David was digging the foundations of the Temple, a shard was found at a depth of fifteen hundred cubits. David was about to lift it, when the shard exclaimed: "Thou canst not do it." "Why not?" asked David. "Because I rest upon the abyss." "Since when?" "Since the hour in which the voice of God was heard to utter the words from Sinai, 'I am the Lord thy God,' causing the earth to quake and sink into the abyss. I lie here to cover up the abyss." Nevertheless David lifted the shard, and the waters of the abyss rose and threatened to flood the earth. Ahithophel was standing by, and he thought to himself: "Now David will meet with his death, and I shall be king." Just then David said: "Whoever knows how to stem the tide of waters, and fails to do it, will one day throttle himself." Thereupon Ahithophel had the Name of God inscribed upon the shard, and the shard thrown into the abyss. The waters at once commenced to subside, but they sank to so great a depth that David feared the earth might lose her moisture, and he began to sing the fifteen "Songs of Ascents," to bring the waters up again.

Nevertheless David's curse was realized. Ahithophel ended his days by hanging himself. His last will contained the following three rules of conduct: 1. Refrain from doing aught against a favorite of fortune. 2. Take heed not to rise up against the royal house of David. 3. If the Feast of Pentecost falls on a sunny day, then sow wheat.

Posterity has been favored with the knowledge of but a small part of Ahithophel's wisdom, and that little through two widely different sources, through Socrates, who was his disciple, and through a fortune-book written by him.

JOAB

Joab, the warrior, was a contrast to Ahithophel in every essential. He was David's right hand. It was said, if Joab had not been there to conduct his wars, David would not have had leisure to devote himself to the study of the Torah. He was the model of a true Jewish hero, distinguished at the same time for his learning, piety, and goodness. His house stood wide open for all comers, and the campaigns which he undertook redounded invariably to the benefit of the people. They were indebted to him for luxuries even, and more than that, he took thought for the welfare of scholars, he himself being the president of the Sanhedrin.

It interested Joab to analyze the character of men and their opinions. When he heard King David's words: "Like as a father pitieth his children, so the Lord pitieth them that fear him," he expressed his astonishment that the comparison should be made with the love of a father for a child, and not with the love of a mother; mother love as a rule is considered the stronger and the more self-sacrificing. He made up his mind to keep his eyes open, and observe whether David's idea was borne out by facts. On one of his journeys he happened into the house of a poor old man who had twelve children, all of whom the father supported, however meagrely, with the toil of his own hands. Joab proposed that he sell him one of the twelve children; he would thus be relieved of the care of one, and the selling-price could be applied to the better support of the rest. The good father rejected the proposition brusquely. Then Joab approached the mother, offering her a hundred gold denarii for one of the children. At first she resisted the temptation, but finally she yielded. When the father returned in the evening, he cut the bread, as was his wont, into fourteen pieces, for himself, his wife, and his twelve children. In allotting the portions he missed a child, and insisted upon being told its fate. The mother confessed what had happened during his absence. He neither ate nor drank, and next morning he set out, firmly resolved to return the money to Joab and to slay him if he should refuse to surrender the child. After much parleying, and after the father had threatened him with death, Joab yielded the child to the old man, with the exclamation: "Yes, David was right when he compared God's love for men to a father's love for his child. This poor fellow who has twelve children to support was prepared to fight me to the death for one of them, which the mother, who calmly stayed at home, had sold to me for a price."

Among all the heroic achievements of Joab, the most remarkable is the taking of the Amalekite capital. For six months the flower of the Israelitish army, twelve thousand in number, under the leadership of Joab, had been besieging the capital city of the Amalekites without result. The soldiers made representations to their general, that it would be well for them to return home to their wives and children. Joab urged that this not only would earn for them contempt and derision, but also would invite new danger. The heathen would be encouraged to unite against the Israelites. He proposed that they hurl him into the city by means of a sling, and then wait forty days. If at the end of this period they saw blood flow from the gates of the fortress, it should be a sign to them that he was still alive.

His plan was executed. Joab took with him one thousand pieces of money and his sword. When he was cast from the sling, he fell into the courtyard of a widow, whose daughter caught him up. In a little while he regained consciousness. He pretended to be an Amalekite taken prisoner by the Israelites, and thrown into the city by his captors, who thus wished to inflict death. As he was provided with money, which he dispensed lavishly among his entertainers, he was received kindly, and was given the Amalekite garb. So apparelled, he ventured, after ten days, on a tour of inspection through the city, which he found to be of enormous size.

His first errand was to an armorer, to have him mend his sword, which had been broken by his fall. When the artisan scanned Joab's weapon, he started back--he had never seen a sword like it. He forged a new one, which snapped in two almost at once when Joab grasped it firmly. So it happened with a second sword, and with a third. Finally he succeeded in fashioning one that was acceptable. Joab asked the smith whom he would like him to slay with the sword, and the reply was, "Joab, the general of the Israelitish king." "I am he," said Joab, and when the smith in astonishment turned to look at him, Joab ran him through so skillfully that the victim had no realization of what was happening. Thereupon he hewed down five hundred Amalekite warriors whom he met on his way, and not one escaped to betray him. The rumor arose that Asmodeus, the king of demons, was raging among the inhabitants of the city, and slaying them in large numbers.

After another period of ten days, which he spent in retirement with his hosts, Joab sallied forth a second time, and caused such bloodshed among the Amalekites that his gory weapon clave to his hand, and his right hand lost all power of independent motion, it could be made to move only in a piece with his arm. He hastened to his lodging place to apply hot water to his hand and free it from the sword. On his way thither the woman who had caught him up when he fell into the city called to him: "Thou eatest and drinkest with us, yet thou slayest our warriors." Seeing himself betrayed, he could not but kill the woman. Scarcely had his sword touched her, when it was separated from his hand, and his hand could move freely, for the dead woman had been with child, and the blood of the unborn babe loosed the sword.

After Joab had slain thousands, the Israelites without, at the very moment when they were beginning to mourn their general as dead, saw blood issue from the city, and joyfully they cried out with one accord: "Hear, O Israel, the Lord is our God, the Lord is One." Joab mounted a high tower, and in stentorian tones shouted: "The Lord will not forsake his people." Inspired with high and daring courage, the Israelites demanded permission to assault the city and capture it. As Joab turned to descend from the tower, he noticed that six verses of a Psalm were inscribed on his foot, the first verse running thus: "The Lord answers thee in the day of trouble, the name of the God of Jacob is thy defense." Later David added three verses and completed the Psalm. Thereupon the Israelites took the Amalekite capital, destroyed the heathen temples in the city, and slew all its inhabitants, except the king, whom, with his crown of pure gold on his head, they brought before David.

DAVID'S PIETY AND HIS SIN

Neither his great achievements in war nor his remarkable good fortune moved David from his pious ways, or in aught changed his mode of life. Even after he became king he sat at the feet of his teachers, Ira the Jairite and Mephibosheth. To the latter he always submitted his decisions on religious questions, to make sure that they were in accordance with law. Whatever leisure time his royal duties afforded him, he spent in study and prayer. He contented himself with "sixty breaths" of sleep. At midnight the strings of his harp, which were made of the gut of the ram sacrificed by Abraham on Mount Moriah, began to vibrate. The sound they emitted awakened David, and he would arise at once to devote himself to the study of the Torah.

Besides study, the composition of psalms naturally claimed a goodly portion of his time. Pride filled his heart when he had completed the Psalter, and he exclaimed: "O Lord of the world, is there another creature in the universe who like me proclaims thy praise?" A frog came up to the king, and said: "Be not so proud; I have composed more psalms than thou, and, besides, every psalm my mouth has uttered I have accompanied with three thousand parables." And, truly, if David indulged in conceit, it was only for a moment. As a rule he was the exemplar of modesty. The coins which were stamped by him bore a shepherd's crook and pouch on the obverse, and on the reverse the Tower of David. In other respects, too, his bearing was humble, as though he were still the shepherd and not the king.

His great piety invested his prayer with such efficacy that he could bring things in heaven down to earth. It is natural that so godly a king should have used the first respite granted by his wars to carry out his design of erecting a house of worship to God. But in the very night in which David conceived the plan of building the Temple, God said to Nathan the prophet: "Hasten to David. I know him to be a man with whom execution follows fast upon the heels of thought, and I should not like him to hire laborers for the Temple work, and then, disappointed, complain of me. I furthermore know him to be a man who obligates himself by vows to do good deeds, and I desire to spare him the embarrassment of having to apply to the Sanhedrin for absolution from his vow."

When David heard Nathan's message for him, he began to tremble, and he said: "Ah, verily, God hath found me unworthy to erect His sanctuary." But God replied with these words: "Nay, the blood shed by thee I consider as sacrificial blood, but I do not care to have thee build the Temple, because then it would be eternal and indestructible." "But that would be excellent," said David. Whereupon the reply was vouchsafed him: "I foresee that Israel will commit sins. I shall wreak My wrath upon the Temple, and Israel will be saved from annihilation. However, thy good intentions shall receive their due reward. The Temple, though it be built by Solomon, shall be called thine."

David's thinking and planning were wholly given to what is good and noble. He is one of the few pious men over whom the evil inclination had no power. By nature he was not disposed to commit such evil-doing as his relation to Bath-sheba involved. God Himself brought him to his crime, that He might say to other sinners: "Go to David and learn how to repent." Nor, indeed, may David be charged with gross murder and adultery. There were extenuating circumstances. In those days it was customary for warriors to give their wives bills of divorce, which were to have validity only if the soldier husbands did not return at the end of the campaign. Uriah having fallen in battle, Bath-sheba was a regularly divorced woman. As for the death of her husband, it cannot be laid entirely at David's door, for Uriah had incurred the death penalty by his refusal to take his ease in his own house, according to the king's bidding. Moreover, from the first, Bath-sheba had been destined by God for David, but by way of punishment for having lightly promised Uriah the Hittite an Israelitish woman to wife, in return for his aid in unfastening the armor of the prostrate Goliath, the king had to undergo bitter trials before he won her.

Furthermore, the Bath-sheba episode was a punishment for David's excessive self-consciousness. He had fairly besought God to lead him into temptation, that he might give proof of his constancy. It came about thus: He once complained to God: "O Lord of the world, why do people say God of Abraham, God of Isaac, God of Jacob, and why not God of David?" The answer came: "Abraham, Isaac, and Jacob were tried by me, but thou hast not yet been proved." David entreated: "Then examine me, O Lord, and try me." And God said: "I shall prove thee, and I shall even grant thee what I did not grant the Patriarchs. I shall tell thee beforehand that thou wilt fall into temptation through a woman."

Once Satan appeared to him in the shape of a bird. David threw a dart at him. Instead of striking Satan, it glanced off and broke a wicker screen which hid Bath-sheba combing her hair. The sight of her aroused passion in the king. David realized his transgression, and for twenty-two years he was a penitent. Daily he wept a whole hour and ate his "bread with ashes." But he had to undergo still heavier penance. For a half-year he suffered with leprosy, and even the Sanhedrin, which usually was in close personal attendance upon him, had to leave him. He lived not only in physical, but also in spiritual isolation, for the Shekinah departed from him during that time.

ABSALOM'S REBELLION

Of all the punishments, however, inflicted upon David, none was so severe as the rebellion of his own son.

Absalom was of such gigantic proportions that a man who was himself of extraordinary size, standing in the eye-socket of his skull, sank in down to his nose. As for his marvellous hair, the account of it in the Bible does not convey a notion of its abundance. Absalom had taken the vow of a Nazarite. As his vow was for life, and because the growth of his hair was particularly heavy, the law permitted him to clip it slightly every week. It was of this small quantity that the weight amounted to two hundred shekels.

Absalom arranged for his audacious rebellion with great cunning. He secured a letter from his royal father empowering him to select two elders for his suite in every town he visited. With this document he travelled through the whole of Palestine. In each town he went to the two most distinguished men, and invited them to accompany him, at the same time showing them what his father had written, and assuring them that they had been chosen by him because he had a particular affection for them. So he succeeded in gathering the presidents of two hundred courts about him. This having been accomplished, he arranged a large banquet, at which he seated one of his emissaries between every two of his guests, for the purpose of winning them over to his cause. The plan did not succeed wholly, for, though the elders of the towns stood by Absalom, in their hearts they hoped for David's victory.

The knowledge that a part of Absalom's following sided with him in secret,--that, though he was pursued by his son, his friends remained true to him,--somewhat consoled David in his distress. He thought that in these circumstances, if the worst came to the worst, Absalom would at least feel pity for him. At first, however, the despair of David knew no bounds. He was on the point of worshipping an idol, when his friend Hushai the Archite approached him, saying: "The people will wonder that such a king should serve idols." David replied: "Should a king such as I am be killed by his own son? It is better for me to serve idols than that God should be held responsible for my misfortune, and His Name thus be desecrated." Hushai reproached him: "Why didst thou marry a captive?" "There is no wrong in that," replied David, "it is permitted according to the law." Thereupon Hushai: "But thou didst disregard the connection between the passage permitting it and the one that follows almost immediately after it in the Scriptures, dealing with the disobedient and rebellious son, the natural issue of such a marriage."

Hushai was not the only faithful friend and adherent David had. Some came to his rescue unexpectedly, as, for instance, Shobi, the son of Nahash, who is identical with the Ammonite king Hanun, the enemy of David at first, and later his ally. Barzillai, another one of his friends in need, also surprised him by his loyalty, for on the whole his moral attitude was not the highest conceivable.

Absalom's end was beset with terrors. When he was caught in the branches of the oak-tree, he was about to sever his hair with a sword stroke, but suddenly he saw hell yawning beneath him, and he preferred to hang in the tree to throwing himself into the abyss alive. Absalom's crime was, indeed, of a nature to deserve the supreme torture, for which reason he is one of the few Jews who have no portion in the world to come. His abode is in hell, where he is charged with the control of ten heathen nations in the second division. Whenever the avenging angels sit in judgment on the nations, they desire to visit punishment on Absalom, too, but each time a heavenly voice is heard to call out: "Do not chastise him, do not burn him. He is an Israelite, the son of My servant David." Whereupon Absalom is set upon his throne, and is accorded the treatment due to a king. That the extreme penalties of hell were thus averted from him, was on account of David's eightfold repetition of his son's name in his lament over him. Besides, David's intercession had the effect of re-attaching Absalom's severed head to his body.

At his death Absalom was childless, for all his children, his three sons and his daughter, died before him, as a punishment for his having set fire to a field of grain belonging to Joab.

DAVID'S ATONEMENT

All these sufferings did not suffice to atone for David's sin. God once said to him: "How much longer shall this sin be hidden in thy hand and remain unatoned? On thy account the priestly city of Nob was destroyed, on thy account Doeg the Edomite was cast out of the communion of the pious, and on thy account Saul and his three sons were slain. What dost thou desire now--that thy house should perish, or that thou thyself shouldst be delivered into the hands of thine enemies?" David chose the latter doom.

It happened one day when he was hunting, Satan, in the guise of a deer, enticed him further and further, into the very territory of the Philistines, where he was recognized by Ishbi the giant, the brother of Goliath, his adversary. Desirous of avenging his brother, he seized David, and cast him into a winepress, where the king would have suffered a torturous end, if by a miracle the earth beneath him had not begun to sink, and so saved him from instantaneous death. His plight, however, remained desperate, and it required a second miracle to rescue him.

In that hour Abishai, the cousin of David, was preparing for the advent of the Sabbath, for the king's misfortune happened on Friday as the Sabbath was about to come in. When Abishai poured out water to wash himself, he suddenly caught sight of drops of blood in it. Then he was startled by a dove that came to him plucking out her plumes, and moaning and wailing. Abishai exclaimed: "The dove is the symbol of the people of Israel. It cannot be but that David, the king of Israel, is in distress." Not finding the king at home, he was confirmed in his fears, and he determined to go on a search for David on the swiftest animal at his command, the king's own saddle-beast. But first he had to obtain the permission of the sages to mount the animal ridden by the king, for the law forbids a subject to avail himself of things set aside for the personal use of a king. Only the impending danger could justify the exception made in this case.

Scarcely had Abishai mounted the king's animal, when he found himself in the land of the Philistines, for the earth had contracted miraculously. He met Orpah, the mother of the four giant sons. She was about to kill him, but he anticipated the blow and slew her. Ishbi, seeing that he now had two opponents, stuck his lance into the ground, and hurled David up in the air, in the expectation that when he fell he would be transfixed by the lance. At that moment Abishai appeared, and by pronouncing the Name of God he kept David suspended 'twixt heaven and earth.

Abishai questioned David how such evil plight had overtaken him, and David told him of his conversation with God, and how he himself had chosen to fall into the hands of the enemy, rather than permit the ruin of his house. Abishai replied: "Reverse thy prayer, plead for thyself, and not for thy descendants. Let thy children sell wax, and do thou not afflict thyself about their destiny." The two men joined their prayers, and pleaded with God to avert David's threatening doom. Abishai again uttered the Name of God, and David dropped to earth uninjured. Now both of them ran away swiftly, pursued by Ishbi. When the giant heard of his mother's death, his strength forsook him, and he was slain by David and Abishai.

VISITATIONS

Among the sorrows of David are the visitations that came upon Palestine during his reign, and he felt them all the more as he had incurred them through his own fault. There was first the famine, which was so desolating that it is counted among the ten severest that are to happen from the time of Adam to the time of the Messiah. During the first year that it prevailed, David had an investigation set on foot to discover whether idolatry was practiced in the land, and was keeping back the rain. His suspicion proved groundless. The second year he looked into the moral conditions of his realm, for lewdness can bring about the same punishment as idolatry. Again he was proved wrong. The third year, he turned his attention to the administration of charity. Perhaps the people had incurred guilt in this respect, for abuses in this department also were visited with the punishment of famine. Again his search was fruitless, and he turned to God to inquire of Him the cause of the public distress. God's reply was: "Was not Saul a king anointed with holy oil, did he not abolish idolatry, is he not the companion of Samuel in Paradise? Yet, while you all dwell in the land of Israel, he is 'outside of the land.'" David, accompanied by the scholars and the nobles of his kingdom, at once repaired to Jabesh-gilead, disinterred the remains of Saul and Jonathan, and in solemn procession bore them through the whole land of Israel to the inheritance of the tribe of Benjamin. There they were buried. The tributes of affection paid by the people of Israel to its dead king aroused the compassion of God, and the famine came to an end.

The sin against Saul was now absolved, but there still remained Saul's own guilt in his dealings with the Gibeonites, who charged him with having killed seven of their number. David asked God why He had punished His people on account of proselytes. God's answer to him was: "If thou dost not bring near them that are far off, thou wilt remove them that are near by." To satisfy their vengeful feelings, the Gibeonites demanded the life of seven members of Saul's family. David sought to mollify them, representing to them that they would derive no benefit from the death of their victims, and offering them silver and gold instead. But though David treated with each one of them individually, the Gibeonites were relentless. When he realized their hardness of heart, he cried out: "Three qualities God gave unto Israel; they are compassionate, chaste, and gracious in the service of their fellow-men. The first of these qualities the Gibeonites do not possess, and therefore they must be excluded from communion with Israel."

The seven descendants of Saul to be surrendered to the Gibeonites were determined by letting all his posterity pass by the Ark of the law. Those who were arrested before it were the designated victims. Mephibosheth would have been one of the unfortunates, had he not been permitted to pass by unchecked in answer to the prayer of David, to whom he was dear, not only as the son of his friend Jonathan, but also as the teacher who instructed him in the Torah.

The cruel fate that befell the descendants of Saul had a wholesome effect. All the heathen who saw and heard exclaimed: "There is no God like unto the God of Israel, there is no nation like unto the nation of Israel; the wrong inflicted upon wretched proselytes has been expiated by the sons of kings." So great was the enthusiasm among the heathen over this manifestation of the Jewish sense of justice that one hundred and fifty thousand of them were converted to Judaism.

As for David, his wrong in connection with the famine lay in his not having applied his private wealth to the amelioration of the people's suffering. When David returned victorious from the combat with Goliath, the women of Israel gave him their gold and silver ornaments. He put them aside for use in building the Temple, and even during the three years' famine this fund was not touched. God said: "Thou didst refrain from rescuing human beings from death, in order to save thy money for the Temple. Verily, the Temple shall not be built by thee, but by Solomon."

David is still more blameworthy on account of the census which he took of the Israelites in defiance of the law in the Pentateuch. When he was charged by the king with the task of numbering the people, Joab used every effort to turn him away from his intention. But in vain. Incensed, David said: "Either thou art king and I am the general, or I am king and thou art the general." Joab had no choice but to obey. He selected the tribe of Gad as the first to be counted, because he thought that the Gadites, independent and self-willed, would hinder the execution of the royal order, and David would be forced to give up his plan of taking a census. The Gadites disappointed the expectations of Joab, and he betook himself to the tribe of Dan, hoping that if God's punishment descended, it would strike the idolatrous Danites. Disliking his mission as he did, Joab spent nine months in executing it, though he might have dispatched it in a much shorter time. Nor did he carry out the king's orders to the letter. He himself warned the people of the census. If he saw the father of a family of five sons, he would bid him conceal a few of them. Following the example set by Moses, he omitted the Levites from the enumeration, likewise the tribe of Benjamin, because he entertained particularly grave apprehensions in behalf of this greatly decimated tribe. In the end, David was not informed of the actual number obtained. Joab made two lists, intending to give the king a partial list if he found that he had no suspicion of the ruse.

The prophet Gad came to David and gave him the choice of famine, oppression by enemies, or the plague, as the penalty for the heavy crime of popular census-taking. David was in the position of a sick man who is asked whether he prefers to be buried next to his father or next to his mother. The king considered: "If I choose the calamities of war, the people will say, 'He cares little, he has his warriors to look to.' If I choose famine, they will say, 'He cares little, he has his riches to look to.' I shall choose the plague, whose scourge strikes all alike." Although the plague raged but a very short time, it claimed a large number of victims. The most serious loss was the death of Abishai, whose piety and learning made him the counterpoise of a host of seventy-five thousand.

David raised his eyes on high, and he saw the sins of Israel heaped up from earth to heaven. In the same moment an angel descended, and slew his four sons, the prophet Gad, and the elders who accompanied him. David's terror at this sight, which was but increased when the angel wiped his dripping sword on the king's garments, settled in his limbs, and from that day on they never ceased to tremble.

THE DEATH OF DAVID

David once besought God to tell him when he would die. His petition was not granted, for God has ordained that no man shall foreknow his end. One thing, however, was revealed to David, that his death would occur at the age of seventy on the Sabbath day. David desired that he might be permitted to die on Friday. This wish, too, was denied him, because God said that He delighted more in one day passed by David in the study of the Torah, than in a thousand holocausts offered by Solomon in the Temple. Then David petitioned that life might be vouchsafed him until Sunday; this, too, was refused, because God said it would be an infringement of the rights of Solomon, for one reign may not overlap by a hairbreadth the time assigned to another. Thereafter David spent every Sabbath exclusively in the study of the Torah, in order to secure himself against the Angel of Death, who has no power to slay a man while he is occupied with the fulfillment of God's commandments. The Angel of Death had to resort to cunning to gain possession of David. One

Sabbath day, which happened to be also the Pentecost holiday, the king was absorbed in study, when he heard a sound in the garden. He rose and descended the stairway leading from his palace to the garden, to discover the cause of the noise. No sooner had he set foot on the steps than they tumbled in, and David was killed. The Angel of Death had caused the noise in order to utilize the moment when David should interrupt his study. The king's corpse could not be moved on the Sabbath, which was painful to those with him, as it was lying exposed to the rays of the sun. So Solomon summoned several eagles, and they stood guard over the body, shading it with their outstretched pinions.

DAVID IN PARADISE

The death of David did not mean the end of his glory and grandeur. It merely caused a change of scene. In the heavenly realm as on earth David ranks among the first. The crown upon his head outshines all others, and whenever he moves out of Paradise to present himself before God, suns, stars, angels, seraphim, and other holy beings run to meet him. In the heavenly court-room a throne of fire of gigantic dimensions is erected for him directly opposite to the throne of God. Seated on this throne and surrounded by the kings of the house of David and other Israelitish kings, he intones wondrously beautiful psalms. At the end he always cites the verse: "The Lord reigns forever and ever," to which the archangel Metatron and those with him reply: "Holy, holy, holy, is the Lord of hosts!" This is the signal for the holy Hayyot and heaven and earth to join in with praise. Finally the kings of the house of David sing the verse: "And the Lord shall be king over all; in that day shall the Lord be one, and His name one."

The greatest distinction to be accorded David is reserved for the judgment day, when God will prepare a great banquet in Paradise for all the righteous. At David's petition, God Himself will be present at the banquet, and will sit on His throne, opposite to which David's throne will be placed. At the end of the banquet, God will pass the wine cup over which grace is said, to Abraham, with the words: "Pronounce the blessing over the wine, thou who art the father of the pious of the world." Abraham will reply: "I am not worthy to pronounce the blessing, for I am the father also of the Ishmaelites, who kindle God's wrath." God will then turn to Isaac: "Say the blessing, for thou wert bound upon the altar as a sacrifice." "I am not worthy," he will reply, "for the children of my son Esau destroyed the Temple." Then to Jacob: "Do thou speak the blessing, thou whose children were blameless." Jacob also will decline the honor on the ground that he was married to two sisters at the same time, which later was strictly prohibited by the Torah. God will then turn to Moses: "Say the blessing, for thou didst receive the law and didst fulfil its precepts." Moses will answer: "I am not worthy to do it, seeing that I was not found worthy to enter the Holy Land." God will next offer the honor to Joshua, who both led Israel into the Holy Land, and fulfilled the commandments of the law. He, too, will refuse to pronounce the blessing, because he was not found worthy to bring forth a son. Finally God will turn to David with the words: "Take the cup and say the blessing, thou the sweetest singer in Israel and Israel's king. And David will reply: 'Yes, I will pronounce the blessing, for I am worthy of the honor.'" Then God will take the Torah and read various passages from it, and David will recite a psalm in which both the pious in Paradise and the wicked in hell will join with a loud Amen. Thereupon God will send his angels to lead the wicked from hell to Paradise.

THE FAMILY OF DAVID

David had six wives, including Michal, the daughter of Saul, who is called by the pet name Eglah, "Calfkin," in the list given in the Bible narrative. Michal was of entrancing beauty, and at the same time the model of a loving wife. Not only did she save David out of the hands of her father, but also, when Saul, as her father and her king, commanded her to marry another man, she acquiesced only apparently. She entered into a mock marriage in order not to arouse the anger of Saul, who had annulled her union with David on grounds which he thought legal. Michal was good as well as beautiful; she showed such extraordinary kindness to the orphan children of her sister Merab that the Bible speaks of the five sons of Michal "whom she bore to Adriel." Adriel, however, was her brother-in-law and not her husband, but she had raised his children, treating them as though they were her own. Michal was no less a model of piety. Although the law exempted her, as a woman, from the duty, still she executed the commandment of using phylacteries. In spite of all these virtues, she was severely punished by God for her scorn of David, whom she reproached with lack of dignity, when he had in mind only to do honor to God. Long she remained childless, and at last, when she was blessed with a child, she lost her own life in giving birth to it.

But the most important among the wives of David was Abigail, in whom beauty, wisdom, and prophetical gifts were joined. With Sarah, Rahab, and Esther, she forms the quartet of the most beautiful women in history. She was so bewitching that passion was aroused in men by the mere thought of her. Her cleverness showed itself during her first meeting with David, when, though anxious about the life of her husband Nabal, she still, with the utmost tranquility, put a ritual question to him in his rage. He refused to answer it, because, he said, it was a question to be investigated by day, not by night. Thereupon Abigail interposed, that sentence of death likewise may be passed upon a man only during the day. Even if David's judgment were right, the law required him to wait until daybreak to execute it upon Nabal. David's objection, that a rebel like Nabal had no claim upon due process of law, she overruled with the words: "Saul is still alive, and thou art not yet acknowledged king by the world."

Her charm would have made David her captive on this occasion, if her moral strength had not kept him in check. By means of the expression, "And this shall not be unto thee," she made him understand that the day had not yet arrived, but that it would come, when a woman, Bath-sheba, would play a disastrous part in his life. Thus she manifested her gift of prophecy.

Not even Abigail was free from the feminine weakness of coquetry. The words "remember thine handmaid" should never have been uttered by her. As a married woman, she should not have sought to direct the attention of a man to herself. In the women's Paradise she supervises the fifth of the seven divisions into which it is divided, and her domain adjoins that of the wives of the Patriarchs, Sarah, Rebekah, Rachel, and Leah.

Among the sons of David, Adonijah, the son of Haggith, must be mentioned particularly, the pretender to the throne. The fifty men whom he prepared to run before him had fitted themselves for the place of heralds by cutting out their spleen and the flesh of the soles of their feet. That Adonijah was not designated for the royal dignity, was made manifest by the fact that the crown of David did not fit him. This crown had the remarkable peculiarity of always fitting the legitimate king of the house of David.

Chileab was a son worthy of his mother Abigail. The meaning of his name is "like the father," which had been given him because of his striking resemblance to David in appearance, a circumstance that silenced the talk against David's all too hasty marriage with the widow of Nabal. Intellectually, too, Chileab testified to David's paternity. In fact, he excelled his father in learning, as he did even the teacher of David, Mephibosheth, the son of Jonathan. On account of his piety he is one of the few who have entered Paradise alive.

Tamar cannot be called one of the children of David, because she was born before her mother's conversion to Judaism. Consequently, her relation to Amnon is not quite of the grave nature it would have been, had they been sister and brother in the strict sense of the terms.

To the immediate household of David belonged four hundred young squires, the sons of women taken captive in battle. They wore their hair in heathen fashion, and, sitting in golden chariots, they formed the vanguard of the army, and terrified the enemy by their appearance.

HIS TOMB

When David was buried, Solomon put abundant treasures into his tomb. Thirteen hundred years later the high priest Hyrcanus took a thousand talents of the money secreted there to use it in preventing the siege of Jerusalem by the Greek king Antiochus. King Herod also abstracted great sums. But none of the marauders could penetrate to the resting-place of the kings,--next to David his successors were interred,--for it was sunk into the earth so skillfully that it could not be found.

Once on a time, a Moslem pasha visited the mausoleum, and as he was looking through the window in it, a weapon of his ornamented with diamonds and pearls dropped into the tomb. A Mohammedan was lowered through the window to fetch the weapon. When he was drawn up again, he was dead, and three other

Mohammedans who tried to enter in the same way met the fate of their comrade. At the instigation of the kadi, the pasha informed the Rabbi of Jerusalem that the Jews would be held responsible for the restoration of the weapon. The Rabbi ordered a three days' fast, to be spent in prayer. Then lots were cast to designate the messenger who was to be charged with the perilous errand. The lot fell upon the beadle of the synagogue, a pious and upright man. He secured the weapon, and returned it to the pasha, who manifested his gratitude by kindly treatment of the Jews thereafter. The beadle later told his adventures in the tomb to the Hakam Bashi. When he had descended, there suddenly appeared before him an old man of dignified appearance, and handed him what he was seeking.

Another miraculous tale concerning the tomb of David runs as follows: A poor but very pious Jewish washerwoman was once persuaded by the keeper of the tomb to enter it. Hardly was she within, when the man nailed up the entrance, and ran to the kadi to inform him that a Jewess had gone in. Incensed, the kadi hastened to the spot, with the intention of having the woman burnt for her presumptuousness. In her terror the poor creature had begun to weep and implore God for help. Suddenly a flood of light illumined the dark tomb, and a venerable old man took her by the hand, and led her downward under the earth until she reached the open. There he parted from her with the words: "Hasten homeward, and let none know that thou wert away from thy house." The kadi had the tomb and its surroundings thoroughly searched by his bailiffs, but not a trace of the woman could be discovered, although the keeper again and again swore by the Prophet that the woman had entered. Now the messengers whom the kadi had sent to the house of the woman returned, and reported they had found her washing busily, and greatly astonished at their question, whether she had been at the tomb of David. The kadi accordingly decided that for his false statements and his perjury, the keeper must die the very death intended for the innocent woman, and so he was burnt. The people of Jerusalem suspected a miracle, but the woman did not divulge her secret until a few hours before her death. She told her story, and then bequeathed her possessions to the congregation, under the condition that a scholar recite Kaddish for her on each anniversary of her death.

Chapter 5

V. SOLOMON

SOLOMON PUNISHES JOAB

At the youthful age of twelve Solomon succeeded his father David as king. His real name was Jedidiah, the "friend of God," but it was superseded by the name Solomon on account of the peace that prevailed throughout the realm during his reign. He bore three other names besides: Ben, Jakeh, and Ithiel. He was called Ben because he was the builder of the Temple; Jakeh, because he was the ruler of the whole world; and Ithiel, because God was with him.

The rebellion Adonijah intended to lead against the future king was suppressed during David's lifetime, by having Solomon anointed in public. On that occasion Solomon rode upon a remarkable she-mule, remarkable because she was not the product of cross-breeding, but of a special act of creation.

As soon as he ascended the throne, Solomon set about executing the instructions his father had given him on his death-bed. The first of them was the punishment of Joab.

Notwithstanding all his excellent qualities, which fitted him to be not only David's first general, but also the president of the Academy, Joab had committed great crimes, which had to be atoned for. Beside the murder of Abner and Amasa of which he was guilty, he had incurred wrong against David himself. The generals of the army suspected him of having had Uriah the Hittite put out of the way for purposes of his own, whereupon he showed them David's letter dooming Uriah. David might have forgiven Joab, but he wanted him to expiate his sins in this world, so that he might be exempt from punishment in the world to come.

When Joab perceived that Solomon intended to have him executed, he sought the protection of the Temple. He knew full well that he could not save his life in this way, for the arm of justice reaches beyond the doors of the sanctuary, to the altar of God. What he wished was to be accorded a regular trial, and not suffer death by the king's order. In the latter case he would lose fortune as well as life, and he was desirous of leaving his children well provided for. Thereupon Solomon sent word to him that he had no intention of confiscating his estates.

Though he was convinced of Joab's guilt, Solomon nevertheless granted him the privilege of defense. The king questioned him: "Why didst thou kill Abner?"

Joab: "I was the avenger of my brother Asahel, whom Abner had slain."

Solomon: "Why, it was Asahel who sought to kill Abner, and Abner acted in self-defense."

Joab: "Abner might have disabled Asahel without going to extremes."

Solomon: "That Abner could not do."

Joab: "What! Abner aimed directly at Asahel's fifth rib, and thou wouldst say he could not have managed to wound him lightly?"

Solomon: "Very well, then, we shall drop Abner's case. But why didst thou slay Amasa?"

Joab: "He acted rebelliously toward King David. He omitted to execute his order to gather an army within three days; for that offense he deserved to suffer the death penalty."

Solomon: "Amasa failed to obey the king's order, because he had been taught by our sages that even a king's injunctions may be set at defiance if they involve neglect of the study of the Torah, which was the case with the order given to Amasa. And, indeed," continued Solomon, "it was not Amasa but thou thyself who didst rebel against the king, for thou wert about to join Absalom, and if thou didst refrain, it was from fear of David's strong-fisted troops."

When Joab saw that death was inevitable, he said to Benaiah, who was charged with the execution of the king's order: "Tell Solomon he cannot inflict two punishments upon me. If he expects to take my life, he must remove the curse pronounced by David against me and my descendants on account of the slaying of Abner. If not, he cannot put me to death." Solomon realized the justness of the plea. By executing Joab, he transferred David's curse to his own posterity: Rehoboam, his son, was afflicted with an issue; Uzziah suffered with leprosy; Asa had to lean on a staff when he walked; the pious Josiah fell by the sword of Pharaoh, and Jeconiah lived off charity. So the imprecations of David were accomplished on his own family instead of Joab's.

THE MARRIAGE OF SOLOMON

The next to suffer Joab's fate was Shimei ben Gera, whose treatment of David had outraged every feeling of decency. His death was of evil portent for Solomon himself. So long as Shimei, who was Solomon's teacher, was alive, he did not venture to marry the daughter of Pharaoh. When, after Shimei's death, Solomon took her to wife, the archangel Gabriel descended from heaven, and inserted a reed in the sea. About this reed more and more earth was gradually deposited, and, on the day on which Jeroboam erected the golden calves, a little hut was built upon the island. This was the first of the dwelling-places of Rome.

Solomon's wedding-feast in celebration of his marriage with the Egyptian princess came on the same day as the consecration of the Temple. The rejoicing over the king's marriage was greater than over the completion of the Temple. As the proverb has it: "All pay flattery to a king." Then it was that God conceived the plan of destroying Jerusalem. It was as the prophet spoke: "This city hath been to me a provocation of mine anger and of my fury from the day that they built it even unto this day."

In the nuptial night Pharaoh's daughter had her attendants play upon a thousand different musical instruments, which she had brought with her from her home, and as each was used, the name of the idol to which it was dedicated was mentioned aloud. The better to hold the king under the spell of her charms, she spread above his bed a tapestry cover studded with diamonds and pearls, which gleamed and glittered like constellations in the sky. Whenever Solomon wanted to rise, he saw these stars, and thinking it was night still, he slept on until the fourth hour of the morning. The people were plunged in grief, for the daily sacrifice could not be brought on this very morning of the Temple dedication, because the Temple keys lay under Solomon's pillow, and none dared awaken him. Word was sent to Bath-sheba, who forthwith aroused her son, and rebuked him for his sloth. "Thy father," she said, "was known to all as a God-fearing man, and now people will say, 'Solomon is the son of Bath-sheba, it is his mother's fault if he goes wrong.' Whenever thy father's wives were pregnant, they offered vows and prayed that a son worthy to reign might be born unto them. But my prayer was for a learned son worthy of the gift of prophecy. Take care, 'give not thy strength unto women nor thy ways to them that destroy kings,' for licentiousness confounds the reason of man. Keep well in mind the things that are necessary in the life of a king. 'Not kings, Lemuel.' Have naught in common with kings who say: 'What need have we of a God?' It is not meet that thou shouldst do like the kings who drink wine and live in lewdness. Be not like unto them. He to whom the secrets of the world are revealed, should not intoxicate himself with wine."

Apart from having married a Gentile, whose conversion to Judaism was not dictated by pure motives, Solomon transgressed two other Biblical laws. He kept many horses, which a Jewish king ought not to do, and, what the law holds in equal abhorrence, he amassed much silver and gold. Under Solomon's rule silver and gold were so abundant among the people that their utensils were made of them instead of the baser metals. For all this he had to atone painfully later on.

HIS WISDOM

But Solomon's wealth and pomp were as naught in comparison with his wisdom. When God appeared to him in Gibeon, in a dream by night, and gave him leave to ask what he would, a grace accorded to none beside except King Ahaz of Judah, and promised only to the Messiah in time to come, Solomon chose wisdom, knowing that wisdom once in his possession, all else would come of itself. His wisdom, the Scriptures testify, was greater than the wisdom of Ethan the Ezrahite, and Heman, and Calcol, and Darda, the three sons of Mahol. This means that he was wiser than Abraham, Moses, Joseph, and the generation of the desert. He excelled even Adam. His proverbs which have come down to us are barely eight hundred in number. Nevertheless the Scripture counts them equal to three thousand, for the reason that each verse in his book admits of a double and a triple interpretation. In his wisdom he analyzed the laws revealed to Moses, and he assigned reasons for the ritual and ceremonial ordinances of the Torah, which without his explanation had seemed strange. The "forty-nine gates of wisdom" were open to Solomon as they had been to Moses, but the wise king sought to outdo even the wise legislator. He had such confidence in himself that he would have dispensed judgment without resort to witnesses, had he not been prevented by a heavenly voice.

The first proof of his wisdom was given in his verdict in the case of the child claimed by two mothers as their own. When the women presented their difficulty, the king said that God in His wisdom had foreseen that such a quarrel would arise, and therefore had created the organs of man in pairs, so that neither of the two parties to the dispute might be wronged. on hearing these words from the king, Solomon's counsellors lamented: "Woe to thee, O land, when thy king is a youth." In a little while they realized the wisdom of the king, and then they exclaimed: "Happy art thou, O land, when thy king is a free man." The quarrel had of set purpose been brought on by God to the end that Solomon's wisdom might be made known. In reality the two litigants were not women at all, but spirits. That all doubt about the fairness of the verdict might be dispelled, a heavenly voice proclaimed: "This is the mother of the child."

During the lifetime of David, when Solomon was still a lad, he had settled another difficult case in an equally brilliant way. A wealthy man had sent his son on a protracted business trip to Africa. On his return he found that his father had died in the meantime, and his treasures had passed into the possession of a crafty slave, who had succeeded in ridding himself of all the other slaves, or intimidating them. In vain the rightful heir urged his claim before King David. As he could not bring witnesses to testify for him, there was no way of dispossessing the slave, who likewise called himself the son of the deceased. The child Solomon heard the case, and he devised a method of arriving at the truth. He had the father's corpse exhumed, and he dyed one of the bones with the blood first of one of the claimants, and then of the other. The blood of the slave showed no affinity with the bone, while the blood of the true heir permeated it. So the real son secured his inheritance.

After his accession to the throne, a peculiar quarrel among heirs was brought before Solomon for adjudication. Asmodeus, the king of demons, once said to Solomon: "Thou art the wisest of men, yet I shall show thee something thou hast never seen." Thereupon Asmodeus stuck his finger in the ground, and up came a double-headed man. He was one of the Cainites, who live underground, and are altogether different in nature and habit from the denizens of the upper world. When the Cainite wanted to descend to his dwelling-place again, it appeared that he could not return thither. Not even Asmodeus could bring the thing about. So he remained on earth, took unto himself a wife, and begot seven sons, one of whom resembled his father in having two heads. When the Cainite died, a dispute broke out among his descendants as to how the property was to be divided. The double-headed son claimed two portions. Both Solomon and the Sanhedrin were at a loss; they could not discover a precedent to guide them. Then Solomon prayed to God: "O Lord of all, when Thou didst appear to me in Gibeon, and didst give me leave to ask a gift of Thee, I desired neither silver nor gold, but only wisdom, that I might be able to judge men in justice."

God heard his prayer. When the sons of the Cainite again came before Solomon, he poured hot water on one of the heads of the double-headed monster, whereupon both heads flinched, and both mouths cried out: "We are dying, we are dying! We are but one, not two." Solomon decided that the double-headed son was after all only a single being.

On another occasion Solomon invented a lawsuit in order to elicit the truth in an involved case. Three men appeared before him, each of whom accused the others of theft. They had been travelling together, and, when the Sabbath approached, they halted and prepared to rest and sought a safe hiding-place for their money, for it is not allowed to carry money on one's person on the Sabbath. They all three together secreted what they had in the same spot, and, when the Sabbath was over, they hastened thither, only to find that it had been stolen. It was clear one of the three must have been the thief, but which one?

Solomon said to them: "I know you to be experienced and thorough business men. I should like you to help me decide a suit which the king of Rome has submitted to me. In the Roman kingdom there lived a maiden and a youth, who promised each other under oath never to enter into a marriage without obtaining each other's permission. The parents of the girl betrothed their daughter to a man whom she loved, but she refused to become his wife until the companion of her youth gave his consent. She took much gold and silver, and sought him out to bribe him. Setting aside his own love for the girl, he offered her and her lover his congratulations, and refused to accept the slightest return for the permission granted. On their homeward way the happy couple were surprised by an old highwayman, who was about to rob the young man of his bride and his money. The girl told the brigand the story of her life, closing with these words: 'If a youth controlled his passion for me, how much more shouldst thou, an old man, be filled with fear of God, and let me go my way.' Her words took effect. The aged highwaymen laid hands neither on the girl nor on the money."

"Now," Solomon continued to the three litigants, "I was asked to decide which of the three persons concerned acted most nobly, the girl, the youth, or the highwayman, and I should like to have your views upon the question."

The first of the three said: "My praise is for the girl, who kept her oath so faithfully." The second: "I should award the palm to the youth, who kept himself in check, and did not permit his passion to prevail." The third said: "Commend me to the brigand, who kept his hands off the money, more especially as he would have been doing all that could be expected of him if he had surrendered the woman he might have taken the money."

The last answer sufficed to put Solomon on the right track. The man who was inspired with admiration of the virtues of the robber, probably was himself filled with greed of money. He had him cross-examined, and finally extorted a confession. He had committed the theft, and he designated the spot where he had hidden the money.

Even animals submitted their controversies to Solomon's wise judgment. A man with a jug of milk came upon a serpent wailing pitifully in a field. To the man's question, the serpent replied that it was tortured with thirst. "And what art thou carrying in the jug?" asked the serpent. When it heard what it was, it begged for the milk, and promised to reward the man by showing him a hidden treasure. The man gave the milk to the serpent, and was then led to a great rock. "Under this rock," said the serpent, "lies the treasure." The man rolled the rock aside, and was about to take the treasure, when suddenly the serpent made a lunge at him, and coiled itself about his neck. "What meanest thou by such conduct?" exclaimed the man. "I am going to kill thee," replied the serpent, "because thou art robbing me of all my money." The man proposed that they put their case to King Solomon, and obtain his decision as to who was in the wrong. So they did. Solomon asked the serpent to state what it demanded of the man. "I want to kill him," answered the serpent, "because the Scriptures command it, saying: 'Thou shalt bruise the heel of man.'" Solomon said: "First release thy hold upon the man's neck and descend; in court neither party to a lawsuit may enjoy an advantage over the other." The serpent glided to the floor, and Solomon repeated his question, and received the same answer as before from the serpent. Then Solomon turned to the man and said: "To thee God's command was to bruise the head of the serpent do it!" And the man crushed the serpent's head.

Sometimes Solomon's assertions and views, though they sprang from profound wisdom, seemed strange to the common run of men. In such cases, the wise king did not disdain to illustrate the correctness of his opinions. For instance, both the learned and the ignorant were stung into opposition by Solomon's saying: "One man among a thousand have I found; but a virtuous woman among all those have I not found." Solomon unhesitatingly pledged himself to prove that he was right. He had his attendants seek out a married couple enjoying a reputation for uprightness and virtue. The husband was cited before him, and Solomon told him that he had decided to appoint him to an exalted office. The king demanded only, as an earnest of his loyalty, that he murder his wife, so that he might be free to marry the king's daughter, a spouse comporting with the dignity of his new station. With a heavy heart the man went home. His despair grew at sight of his fair wife and his little children. Though determined to do the king's bidding, he still lacked courage to kill his wife while she was awake. He waited until she was tight asleep, but then the child enfolded in the mother's arms rekindled his parental and conjugal affection, and he replaced his sword in its sheath, saying to himself: "And if the king were to offer me his whole realm, I would not murder my wife." Thereupon he went to Solomon, and told him his final decision. A month later Solomon sent for the wife, and declared his love for her. He told her that their happiness could be consummated if she would but do away with her husband. Then she should be made the first wife in his harem. Solomon gave her a leaden sword which glittered as though fashioned of steel. The woman returned home resolved to put the sword to its appointed use. Not a quiver of her eyelids betrayed her sinister purpose. On the contrary, by caresses and tender words she sought to disarm any suspicion that might attack to her. In the night she arose, drew forth the sword, and proceeded to kill her husband. The leaden instrument naturally did no harm, except to awaken her husband, to whom she had to confess her evil intent. The next day both man and wife were summoned before the king, who thus convinced his counsellors of the truth of his conviction, that no dependence can be placed on woman.

The fame of Solomon's wisdom spread far and wide. Many entered the service of the king, in the hope of profiting by his wisdom. Three brothers had served under him for thirteen years, and, disappointed at not having learnt anything, they made up their minds to quit his service. Solomon gave them the alternative of receiving one hundred coins each, or being taught three wise saws. They decided to take the money. They had scarcely left the town when the youngest of the three, regardless of the protests of his two brothers, hastened back to Solomon and said to him: "My lord, I did not take service under thee to make money; I wanted to acquire wisdom. Pray, take back thy money, and teach me wisdom instead." Solomon thereupon imparted the following three rules of conduct to him: "When thou travellest abroad, set out on thy journey with the dawn and turn in for the night before darkness falls; do not cross a river that is swollen; and never betray a secret to a woman." The man quickly overtook his brothers, but he confided nothing to them of what he had learned from Solomon. They journeyed on together. At the approach of the ninth hour three hours after noon they reached a suitable spot in which to spend the night. The youngest brother, mindful of Solomon's advice, proposed that they stop there. The others taunted him with his stupidity, which, they said, he had begun to display when he carried his money back to Solomon. The two proceeded on their way, but the youngest arranged his quarters for the night. When darkness came on, and with it nipping cold, he was snug and comfortable, while his brothers were surprised by a snow storm, in which they perished. The following day he continued his journey, and on the road he found the dead bodies of his brothers. Having appropriated their money, he buried them, and went on. When he reached a river that was very much swollen, he bore Solomon's advice in mind, and delayed to cross until the flood subsided. While standing on the bank, he observed how some of the king's servants were attempting to ford the stream with beasts laden with gold, and how they were borne down by the flood. After the waters had abated, he crossed and appropriated the gold strapped to the drowned animals. When he returned home, wealthy and wise, he told nothing of what he had experienced even to his wife, who was very curious to find out where her husband had obtained his wealth. Finally, she plied him so closely with questions that Solomon's advice about confiding a secret to a woman was quite forgotten. Once, when his wife was quarrelling with him, she cried out: "Not enough that thou didst murder thy brothers, thou desirest to kill me, too." Thereupon he was charged with the murder of their husbands by his two sisters-in-law. He was tried, condemned to death, and escaped the hangman only when he told the king the story of his life, and was recognized as his former retainer. It was with reference to this man's adventures that Solomon said: "Acquire wisdom; she is better than gold and much fine gold."

Another of his disciples had a similar experience. Annually a man came from a great distance to pay a visit to the wise king, and when he departed Solomon was in the habit of bestowing a gift upon him. Once the guest refused the gift, and asked the king to teach him the language of the birds and the animals instead. The king was ready to grant his request, but he did not fail to warn him first of the great danger connected with such knowledge. "If thou tellest others a word of what thou hearest from an animal," he said, "thou wilt surely suffer death; thy destruction is inevitable." Nothing daunted, the visitor persisted in his wish, and the king instructed him in the secret art.

Returned home, he overheard a conversation between his ox and his ass. The ass said: "Brother, how farest thou with these people?"

The ox: "As thou livest, brother, I pass day and night in hard and painful toil."

The ass: "I can give thee relief, brother. If thou wilt follow my advice, thou shalt live in comfort, and shalt rid thyself of all hard work."

The ox: "O brother, may thy heart be inclined toward me, to take pity on me and help me. I promise not to depart from thy advice to the right or the left."

The ass: "God knows, I am speaking to thee in the uprightness of my heart and the purity of my thoughts. My advice to thee is not to eat either straw or fodder this night. When our master notices it, he will suppose that thou art sick. He will put no burdensome work upon thee, and thou canst take a good rest. That is the way I did to-day."

The ox followed the advice of his companion. He touched none of the food thrown to him. The master, suspecting a ruse on the part of the ass, arose during the night, went to the stable, and watched the ass eat his fill from the manger belonging to the ox. He could not help laughing out loud, which greatly amazed his wife, who, of course, had noticed nothing out of the way. The master evaded her questions. Something ludicrous had just occurred to him, he said by way of explanation.

For the sly trick played upon the ox, he determined to punish the ass. He ordered the servant to let the ox rest for the day, and make the ass do the work of both animals. At evening the ass trudged into the stable tired and exhausted. The ox greeted him with the words: "Brother, hast thou heard aught of what our heartless masters purpose?" "Yes," replied the ass, "I heard them speak of having thee slaughtered, if thou shouldst refuse to eat this night, too. They want to make sure of thy flesh at least." Scarcely had the ox heard the words of the ass when he threw himself upon his food like a ravenous lion upon his prey. Not a speck did he leave behind, and the master was suddenly moved to uproarious laughter. This time his wife insisted upon knowing the cause. In vain she entreated and supplicated. She swore not to live with him any more if he did not tell her why he laughed. The man loved her so devotedly that he was ready to sacrifice his life to satisfy her whim, but before taking leave of this world he desired to see his friends and relations once more, and he invited them all to his house.

Meantime his dog was made aware of the master's approaching end, and such sadness took possession of the faithful beast that he touched neither food nor drink. The cock, on the other hand, gaily appropriated the food intended for the dog, and he and his wives enjoyed a banquet. Outraged by such unfeeling behavior, the dog said to the cock: "How great is thy impudence, and how insignificant thy modesty! Thy master is but a step from the grave, and thou eatest and makest merry." The cock's reply was: "Is it my fault if our master is a fool and an idiot? I have ten wives, and I rule them as I will. Not one dares oppose me and my commands. Our master has a single wife, and this one he cannot control and manage." "What ought our master to do?" asked the dog. "Let him take a heavy stick and belabor his wife's back thoroughly," advised the cock, "and I warrant thee, she won't plague him any more to reveal his secrets."

The husband had overheard this conversation, too, and the cock's advice seemed good. He followed it, and death was averted.

On many occasions, Solomon brought his acumen and wisdom to bear upon foreign rulers who attempted to concoct mischief against him. Solomon needed help in building the Temple, and he wrote to Pharaoh, asking him to send artists to Jerusalem. Pharaoh complied with his request, but not honestly. He had his astrologers determine which of his men were destined to die within the year. These candidates for the grave he passed over to Solomon. The Jewish king was not slow to discover the trick played upon him. He immediately returned the men to Egypt, each provided with his grave clothes, and wrote: "To Pharaoh! I suppose thou hadst no shrouds for these people. Herewith I send thee the men, and what they were in need of."

Hiram, king of Tyre, the steadfast friend of the dynasty of David, who had done Solomon such valuable services in connection with the building of the Temple, was desirous of testing his wisdom. He was in the habit of sending catch-questions and riddles to Solomon with the request that he solve them and help him out of his embarrassment about them. Solomon, of course, succeeded in answering them all. Later on he made an agreement with Hiram, that they were to exchange conundrums and riddles, and a money fine was to be exacted from the one of them who failed to find the proper answer to a question propounded by the other. Naturally it was Hiram who was always the loser. The Tyrians maintain that finally Solomon found more than his match in one of Hiram's subjects, one Abdamon, who put many a riddle to Solomon that baffled his wit.

Of Solomon's subtlety in riddle guessing only a few instances have come down to us, all of them connected with riddles put to him by the Queen of Sheba. The story of this queen, of her relation to Solomon, and what induced her to leave her distant home and journey to the court at Jerusalem forms an interesting chapter in the eventful life of the wise king.

THE QUEEN OF SHEBA

Solomon, it must be remembered, bore rule not only over men, but also over the beasts of the field, the birds of the air, demons, spirits, and the spectres of the night. He knew the language of all of them and they understood his language.

When Solomon was of good cheer by reason of wine, he summoned the beasts of the field, the birds of the air, the creeping reptiles, the shades, the spectres, and the ghosts, to perform their dances before the kings, his neighbors, whom he invited to witness his power and greatness. The king's scribes called the animals and the spirits by name, one by one, and they all assembled of their own accord, without fetters or bonds, with no human hand to guide them.

On one occasion the hoopoe was missed from among the birds. He could not be found anywhere. The king, full of wrath, ordered him to be produced and chastised for his tardiness. The hoopoe appeared and said: "O lord, king of the world, incline thine ear and hearken to my words. Three months have gone by since I began to take counsel with myself and resolve upon a course of action. I have eaten no food and drunk no water, in order to fly about in the whole world and see whether there is a domain anywhere which is not subject to my lord the king. and I found a city, the city of Kitor, in the East. Dust is more valuable than gold there, and silver is like the mud of the streets. Its trees are from the beginning of all time, and they suck up water that flows from the Garden of Eden. The city is crowded with men. On their heads they wear garlands wreathed in Paradise. They know not how to fight, nor how to shoot with bow and arrow. Their ruler is a woman, she is called the Queen of Sheba. If, now, it please thee, O lord and king, I shall gird my loins like a hero, and journey to the city of Kitor in the land of Sheba. Its kings I shall fetter with chains and its rulers with iron bands, and bring them all before my lord the king."

The hoopoe's speech pleased the king. The clerks of his land were summoned, and they wrote a letter and bound it to the hoopoe's wing. The bird rose skyward, uttered his cry, and flew away, followed by all the other birds.

And they came to Kitor in the land of Sheba. It was morning, and the queen had gone forth to pay worship to the sun. Suddenly the birds darkened his light. The queen raised her hand, and rent her garment, and was sore astonished. Then the hoopoe alighted near her. Seeing that a letter was tied to his wing, she loosed it and read it. And what was written in the letter? "From me, King Solomon! Peace be with thee, peace with the nobles of thy realm! Know that God has appointed me king over the beasts of the field, the birds of the air, the demons, the spirits, and the spectres. All the kings of the East and the West come to bring me greetings. If thou wilt come and salute me, I shall show thee great honor, more than to any of the kings that attend me. But if thou wilt not pay homage to me, I shall send out kings, legions, and riders against thee. Thou askest, who are these kings, legions, and riders of King Solomon? The beasts of the field are my kings, the birds my riders, the demons, spirit, and shades of the night my legions. The demons will throttle you in your beds at night, while the beasts will slay you in the field, and the birds will consume your flesh."

When the Queen of Sheba had read the contents of the letter, she again rent her garment, and sent word to her elders and her princes: "Know you not what Solomon has written to me?" They answered: "We know nothing of King Solomon, and his dominion we regard as naught." But their words did not reassure the queen. She assembled all the ships of the sea, and loaded them with the finest kinds of wood, and with pearls and precious stones. Together with these she sent Solomon six thousand youths and maidens, born in the same year, in the same month, on the same day, in the same hour all of equal stature and size, all clothed in purple garments. They bore a letter to King Solomon as follows: "From the city of Kitor to the land of Israel is a journey of seven years. As it is thy wish and behest that I visit thee, I shall hasten and be in Jerusalem at the end of three years."

When the time of her arrival drew nigh, Solomon sent Benaiah the son of Jehoiada to meet her. Benaiah was like unto the flush in the eastern sky at break of day, like unto the evening star that outshines all other stars, like unto the lily growing by brooks of water. When the queen caught sight of him, she descended from her chariot to do him honor. Benaiah asked her why she left her chariot. "Art thou not King Solomon?" she questioned in turn. Benaiah replied: "Not King Solomon am I, only one of his servants that stand in his presence." Thereupon the queen turned to her nobles and said: "If you have not beheld the lion, at least you have seen his lair, and if you have not beheld King Solomon, at least you have seen the beauty of him that stands in his presence."

Benaiah conducted the queen to Solomon, who had gone to sit in a house of glass to receive her. The queen was deceived by an illusion. She thought the king was sitting in water, and as she stepped across to him she raised her garment to keep it dry. On her bared feet the king noticed hair, and he said to her: "Thy beauty is the beauty of a woman, but thy hair is masculine; hair is an ornament to a man, but it disfigures a woman."

Then the queen began and said: "I have heard of thee and thy wisdom; if now I inquire of thee concerning a matter, wilt thou answer me?" He replied: "The Lord giveth wisdom, out of His mouth cometh knowledge and understanding." She then said to him:

1. "Seven there are that issue and nine that enter; two yield the draught and one drinks." Said he to her: "Seven are the days of a woman's defilement, and nine the months of pregnancy; two are the breasts that yield the draught, and one the child that drinks it." Whereupon she said to him: "Thou art wise."

2. Then she questioned him further: "A woman said to her son, thy father is my father, and thy grandfather my husband; thou art my son, and I am thy sister." "Assuredly," said he, "it was the daughter of Lot who spake thus to her son."

3. She placed a number of males and females of the same stature and garb before him and said: "Distinguish between them." Forthwith he made a sign to the eunuchs, who brought him a quantity of nuts and roasted ears of corn. The males, who were not bashful, seized them with bare hands; the females took them, putting forth their gloved hands from beneath their garments. Whereupon he exclaimed: "Those are the males, these the females."

4. She brought a number of men to him, some circumcised and others uncircumcised, and asked him to distinguish between them. He immediately made a sign to the high priest, who opened the Ark of the covenant, whereupon those that were circumcised bowed their bodies to half their height, while their countenances were filled with the radiance of the Shekinah; the uncircumcised fell prone upon their faces. "Those," said he, "are circumcised, these uncircumcised." "Thou art wise, indeed," she exclaimed.

5. She put other questions to him, to all of which he gave replies. "Who is he who neither was born nor has died?" "It is the Lord of the world, blessed be He."

6. "What land is that which has but once seen the sun?" "The land upon which, after the creation, the waters were gathered, and the bed of the Red Sea on the day when it was divided."

7. "There is an enclosure with ten doors, when one is open, nine are shut; when nine are open, one is shut?" "That enclosure is the womb; the ten doors are the ten orifices of man his eyes, ears, nostrils, mouth, the apertures for the discharge of the excreta and the urine, and the navel; when the child is in the embryonic state, the navel is open and the other orifices are closed, but when it issues from the womb, the navel is closed and the others are opened."

8. "There is something which when living moves not, yet when its head is cut off it moves?" "It is the ship in the sea."

9. "Which are the three that neither ate, nor did they drink, nor did they have bread put into them, yet they saved lives from death?" "The signet, the cord, and the staff are those three."

10. "Three entered a cave and five came forth therefrom?" "Lot and his two daughters and their two children."

11. "The dead lived, the grave moved, and the dead prayed: what is that?" "The dead that lived and prayed, Jonah; and the fish, the moving grave."

12. "Who were the three that ate and drank on the earth, and yet were not born of male and female?" "The three angels who visited Abraham."

13. "Four entered a place of death and came forth alive, and two entered a place of life and came forth dead?" "The four were Daniel, Hananiah, Mishael, and Azariah, and the two were Nadab and Abihu."

14. "Who was he that was born and died not?" "Elijah and the Messiah."

15. "What was that which was not born, yet life was given to it?" "The golden calf."

16. "What is that which is produced from the ground, yet man produces it, while its food is the fruit of the ground?" "A wick."

17. "A woman was wedded to two, and bore two sons, yet these four had one father?" "Tamar."

18. "A house full of dead; no dead one came among them, nor did a living come forth from them?" "It is the story of Samson and the Philistines."

19. The queen next ordered the sawn trunk of a cedar tree to be brought, and she asked Solomon to point out at which end the root had been and at which the branches. He bade her cast it into the water, when one end sank and the other floated upon the surface of the water. That part which sank was the root, and that which remained uppermost was the branch end. Then she said to him: "Thou exceedest in wisdom and goodness the fame which I heard, blessed be thy God!"

The last three riddles which the Queen of Sheba put to Solomon were the following:

20. "What is this? A wooden well with iron buckets, which draw stones and pour out water." The king replied: "A rouge-tube."

21. "What is this? It comes as dust from the earth, its food is dust, it is poured out like water, and lights the house." "Naphtha."

22. "What is this? It walks ahead of all; it cries out loud and bitterly; its head is like the reed; it is the glory of the noble, the disgrace of the poor; the glory of the dead, the disgrace of the living; the delight of birds, the distress of fishes." He answered: "Flax."

SOLOMON MASTER OF THE DEMONS

Never has there lived a man privileged, like Solomon, to make the demons amenable to his will. God endowed him with the ability to turn the vicious power of demons into a power working to the advantage of men. He invented formulas of incantation by which diseases were alleviated, and others by which demons were exorcised so that they were banished forever. As his personal attendants he had spirits and demons whom he could send hither and thither on the instant. He could grow tropical plants in Palestine, because his ministering spirits secured water for him from India.

As the spirits were subservient to him, so also the animals. He had an eagle upon whose back he was transported to the desert and back again in one day, to build there the city called Tadmor in the Bible This city must not be confounded with the later Syrian city of Palmyra, also called Tadmor. It was situated near the "mountains of darkness," the trysting-place of the spirits and demons. Thither the eagle would carry Solomon in the twinkling of an eye, and Solomon would drop a paper inscribed with a verse among the spirits, to ward off evil from himself. Then the eagle would reconnoitre the mountains of darkness, until he had spied out the spot in which the fallen angels 'Azza and 'Azzael lie chained with iron fetters a spot which no one, not even a bird, may visit. When the eagle found the place, he would take Solomon under his left wing, and fly to the two angels. Through the power of the ring having the Holy Name graven upon it, which Solomon put into the eagle's mouth, 'Azza and 'Azzael were forced to reveal the heavenly mysteries to the king.

The demons were of greatest service to Solomon during the erection of the Temple. It came about in this wise: When Solomon began the building of the Temple, it once happened that a malicious spirit snatched away the money and the food of one of the king's favorite pages. This occurred several times, and Solomon was not able to lay hold on the malefactor. The king besought God fervently to deliver the wicked spirit into his hands. His prayer was granted. The archangel Michael appeared to him, and gave him a small ring having a seal consisting of an engraved stone, and he said to him: "Take, O Solomon, king, son of David, the gift which the Lord God, the highest Zebaot, hath sent unto thee. With it thou shalt lock up all the demons of the earth, male and female; and with their help thou shalt build up Jerusalem. But thou must wear this seal of God; and this engraving of the seal of the ring sent thee is a Pentalpha." Armed with it, Solomon called up all the demons before him, and he asked of each in turn his or her name, as well as the name of the star or constellation or zodiacal sign and of the particular angel to the influence of which each is subject. One after another the spirits were vanquished, and compelled by Solomon to aid in the construction of the Temple.

Ornias, the vampire spirit who had maltreated Solomon's servant, was the first demon to appear, and he was set to the task of cutting stones near the Temple. And Solomon bade Ornias come, and he gave him the seal, saying: "Away with thee, and bring me hither the prince of all the demons." Ornias took the finger-ring, and went to Beelzeboul, who has kingship over the demons. He said to him: "Hither! Solomon calls thee." But Beelzeboul, having heard, said to him: "Tell me, who is this Solomon of whom thou speakest to me?" Then Ornias threw the ring at the chest of Beelzeboul, saying: "Solomon the king calls thee." But Beelzeboul cried aloud with a mighty voice, and shot out a great, burning flame of fire; and he arose and followed Ornias, and came to Solomon. Brought before the king, he promised him to gather all the unclean spirits unto him. Beelzeboul proceeded to do so, beginning with Onoskelis, that had a very pretty shape and the skin of a fair-hued woman, and he was followed by Asmodeus; both giving an account of themselves.

Beelzeboul reappeared on the scene, and in his conversation with Solomon declared that he alone survived of the angels who had come down from heaven. He reigned over all who are in Tartarus, and had a child in the Red Sea, which on occasion comes up to Beelzeboul and reveals to him what he has done. Next the demon of the Ashes, Tephros, appeared, and after him a group of seven female spirits, who declared themselves to be of the thirty-six elements of the darkness. Solomon bade them dig the foundation of the temple, for the length of it was two hundred and fifty cubits. And he ordered them to be industrious, and with one united murmur of protest they began to perform the tasks enjoined.

Solomon bade another demon come before him. And there was brought to him a demon having all the limbs of a man, but without a head. The demon said to Solomon: "I am called Envy, for I delight to devour heads, being desirous to secure for myself a head; but I do not eat enough, and I am anxious to have such a head as thou hast." A hound-like spirit, whose name was Rabdos, followed, and he revealed to Solomon a green stone, useful for the adornment of the Temple. A number of other male and female demons appeared, among them the thirty-six world-rulers of the darkness, whom Solomon commanded to fetch water to the Temple. Some of these demons he condemned to do the heavy work on the construction of the Temple, others he shut up in prison, and others, again, he ordered to wrestle with fire in the making of gold and silver, sitting down by lead and spoon, and to make ready places for the other demons, in which they should be confined.

After Solomon with the help of the demons had completed the Temple, the rulers, among them the Queen of Sheba, who was a sorceress, came from far and near to admire the magnificence and art of the building, and no less the wisdom of its builder.

One day an old man appeared before Solomon to complain of his son, whom he accused of having been so impious as to raise his hand against his father and give him a blow. The young man denied the charge, but his father insisted that his life be held forfeit. Suddenly Solomon heard loud laughter. It was the demon Ornias, who was guilty of the disrespectful behavior. Rebuked by Solomon, the demon said: "I pray thee, O king, it was not because of thee I laughed, but because of this ill-starred old man and the wretched youth, his son. For after three days his son will die untimely, and, lo, the old man desires to make away with him foully." Solomon delayed his verdict for several days, and when after five days he summoned the old father to his presence, it appeared that Ornias had spoken the truth.

After some time, Solomon received a letter from Adares, the king of Arabia. He begged the Jewish king to deliver his land from an evil spirit, who was doing great mischief, and who could not be caught and made harmless, because he appeared in the form of wind. Solomon gave his magic ring and a leather bottle to one of his slaves, and sent him into Arabia. The messenger succeeded in confining the spirit in the bottle. A few days later, when Solomon entered the Temple, he was not a little astonished to see a bottle walk toward him, and bow down reverently before him; it was the bottle in which the spirit was shut up. This same spirit once did Solomon a great service. Assisted by demons, he raised a gigantic stone out of the Red Sea. Neither human beings nor demons could move it, but he carried it to the Temple, where it was used as a cornerstone.

Through his own fault Solomon forfeited the power to perform miraculous deed, which the Divine spirit had conferred upon him. He fell in love with the Jebusite woman Sonmanites. The priests of Moloch and Raphan, the false gods she worshiped, advised her to reject his suit, unless he paid homage to these gods. At first Solomon was firm, but, when the woman bade him take five locusts and crush them in his hands in the name of Moloch, he obeyed her. At once he was bereft of the Divine spirit, of his strength and his wisdom, and he sank so low that to please his beloved he built temples to Baal and Raphan.

THE BUILDING OF THE TEMPLE

Among the great achievements of Solomon first place must be assigned to the superb Temple built by him. He was long in doubt as to where he was to build it. A heavenly voice directed him to go to Mount Zion at night, to a field owned by two brothers jointly. One of the brothers was a bachelor and poor, the other was blessed both with wealth and a large family of children. It was harvesting time. Under cover of night, the poor brother kept adding to the other's heap of grain, for, although he was poor, he thought his brother needed more on account of his large family. The rich brother, in the same clandestine way, added to the poor brother's store, thinking that though he had a family to support, the other was without means. This field, Solomon concluded, which had called forth so remarkable a manifestation of brotherly love, was the best site for the Temple, and he bought it.

Every detail of the equipment and ornamentation of the Temple testifies to Solomon's rare wisdom. Next to the required furniture, he planted golden trees, which bore fruit all the time the building stood. When the enemy entered the Temple, the fruit dropped from the trees, but they will put forth blossoms again when it is rebuilt in the days of the Messiah.

Solomon was so assiduous that the erection of the Temple took but seven years, about half the time for the erection of the king's palace, in spite of the greater magnificence of the sanctuary. In this respect, he was the superior of his father David, who first built a house for himself, and then gave thought to a house for God to dwell in. Indeed, it was Solomon's meritorious work in connection with the Temple that saved him from being reckoned by the sages as one of the impious kings, among whom his later actions might properly have put him.

According to the measure of the zeal displayed by Solomon were the help and favor shown him by God. During the seven years it took to build the Temple, not a single workman died who was employed about it, nor even did a single one fall sick. And as the workmen were sound and robust from first to last, so the perfection of their tools remained unimpaired until the building stood complete. Thus the work suffered no sort of interruption. After the dedication of the Temple, however, the workmen died off, lest they build similar structures for the heathen and their gods. Their wages they were to receive from God in the world to come, and the master workman, Hiram, was rewarded by being permitted to reach Paradise alive.

The Temple was finished in the month of Bul, now called Marheshwan, but the edifice stood closed for nearly a whole year, because it was the will of God that the dedication take place in the month of Abraham's birth. Meantime the enemies of Solomon rejoiced maliciously. "Was it not the son of Bath-sheba," they said, "who built the Temple? How, then, could God permit His Shekinah to rest upon it?" When the consecration of the house took place, and "the fire came down from heaven," they recognized their mistake.

The importance of the Temple appeared at once, for the torrential rains which annually since the deluge had fallen for forty days beginning with the month of Marheshwan, for the first time failed to come, and thenceforward appeared no more.

The joy of the people over the sanctuary was so great that they held the consecration ceremonies on the Day of Atonement. It contributed not a little to their ease of mind that a heavenly voice was heard to proclaim: "You all shall have a share in the world to come."

The great house of prayer reflected honor not only on Solomon and the people, but also on King David. The following incident proves it: When the Ark was about to be brought into the Holy of Holies, the door of the sacred chamber locked itself, and it was impossible to open it. Solomon prayed fervently to God, but his entreaties had no effect until he pronounced the words: "Remember the good deeds of David thy servant."

The Holy of Holies then opened of itself, and the enemies of David had to admit that God had wholly forgiven his sin.

In the execution of the Temple work a wish cherished by David was fulfilled. He was averse to having the gold which he had taken as booty from the heathen places of worship during his campaigns used for the sanctuary at Jerusalem, because he feared that the heathen would boast, at the destruction of the Temple, that their gods were courageous, and were taking revenge by wrecking the house of the Israelitish God. Fortunately Solomon was so rich that there was no need to resort to the gold inherited from his father, and so David's wish was fulfilled.

THE THRONE OF SOLOMON

Next to the Temple in its magnificence, it is the throne of Solomon that perpetuates the name and fame of the wise king. None before him and none after him could produce a like work of art, and when the kings, his vassals, saw the magnificence of the throne they fell down and praised God. The throne was covered with fine gold from Ophir, studded with beryls, inlaid with marble, and jewelled with emeralds, and rubies, and pearls, and all manner of gems. On each of its six steps there were two golden lions and two golden eagles, a lion and an eagle to the left, and a lion and an eagle to the right, the pairs standing face to face, so that the right paw of the lion was opposite to the left wing of the eagle, and his left paw opposite to the right wing of the eagle. The royal seat was at the top, which was round.

On the first step leading to the seat crouched an ox, and opposite to him a lion; on the second, a wolf and a lamb; on the third, a leopard and a goat; on the fourth perched an eagle and a peacock; on the fifth a falcon and a cock; and on the sixth a hawk and a sparrow; all made of gold. At the very top rested a dove, her claws set upon a hawk, to betoken that the time would come when all peoples and nations shall be delivered into the hands of Israel. Over the seat hung a golden candlestick, with golden lamps, pomegranates, snuff dishes, censers, chains, and lilies. Seven branches extended from each side. On the arms to the right were the images of the seven patriarchs of the world, Adam, Noah, Shem, Job, Abraham, Isaac, and Jacob; and on the arms to the left, the images of the seven pious men of the world, Kohath, Amram, Moses, Aaron, Eldad, Medad, and the prophet Hur. Attached to the top of the candlestick was a golden bowl filled with the purest olive oil, to be used for the candlestick in the Temple, and below, a golden basin, also filled with the purest olive oil, for the candlestick over the throne. The basin bore the image of the high priest Eli; those of his sons Hophni and Phinehas were on the two faucets protruding from the basin, and those of Nadab and Abihu on the tubes connection the faucets with the basin.

On the upper part of the throne stood seventy golden chairs for the members of the Sanhedrin, and two more for the high priest and his vicar. When the high priest came to do homage to the king, the members of the Sanhedrin also appeared, to judge the people, and they took their seats to the right and to the left of the king. At the approach of the witnesses, the machinery of the throne rumbled the wheels turned, the ox lowed, the lion roared, the wolf howled, the lamb bleated, the leopard growled, the goat cried, the falcon screamed, the peacock gobbled, the cock crowed, the hawk screeched, the sparrow chirped all to terrify the witnesses and keep them from giving false testimony.

When Solomon set foot upon the first step to ascend to his seat, its machinery was put into motion. The golden ox arose and led him to the second step, and there passed him over to the care of the beasts guarding it, and so he was conducted from step to step up to the sixth, where the eagles received him and placed him upon his seat. As soon as he was seated, a great eagle set the royal crown upon his head. Thereupon a huge snake rolled itself up against the machinery, forcing the lions and eagles upward until they encircled the head of the king. A golden dove flew down from a pillar, took the sacred scroll out of a casket, and gave it to the king, so that he might obey the injunction of the Scriptures, to have the law with him and read therein all the days of his life. Above the throne twenty-four vines interlaced, forming a shady arbor over the head of the king, and sweet aromatic perfumes exhaled from two golden lions, while Solomon made the ascent to his seat upon the throne.

It was the task of seven heralds to keep Solomon reminded of his duties as king and judge. The first one of the heralds approached him when he set foot on the first step of the throne, and began to recite the law for kings, "He shall not multiply wives to himself." At the second step, the second herald reminded him, "He shall not multiply horses to himself"; at the third, the next one of the heralds said, "Neither shall he greatly multiply to himself silver and gold." At the fourth step, he was told by the fourth herald, "Thou shalt not wrest judgment"; at the fifth step, by the fifth herald, "Thou shalt not respect persons," and at the sixth, by the sixth herald, "Neither shalt thou take a gift." Finally, when he was about to seat himself upon the throne, the seventh herald cried out: "Know before whom thou standest."

The throne did not remain long in the possession of the Israelites. During the life of Rehoboam, the son of Solomon, it was carried to Egypt. Shishak, the father-in-law of Solomon, appropriated it as indemnity for claims which he urged against the Jewish state in behalf of his widowed daughter. When Sennacherib conquered Egypt, he carried the throne away with him, but, on his homeward march, during the overthrow of his army before the gates of Jerusalem, he had to part with it to Hezekiah. Now it remained in Palestine until the time of Jehoash, when it was once more carried to Egypt by Pharaoh Necho. His possession of the throne brought him little joy. Unacquainted with its wonderful mechanism, he was injured in the side by one of the lions the first time he attempted to mount it, and forever after he limped, wherefore he was given the surname Necho, the hobbler. Nebuchadnezzar was the next possessor of the throne. It fell to his lot at the conquest of Egypt, but when he attempted to use it in Babylonia, he fared no better than his predecessor in Egypt. The lion standing near the throne gave him so severe a blow that he never again dared ascend it. Through Darius the throne reached Elam, but, knowing what its other owners had suffered, he did not venture to seat himself on it, and his example was imitated by Ahasuerus. The latter tried to have his artificers fashion him a like artistic work, but, of course, they failed. The Median rulers parted with the throne to the Greek monarchs, and finally it was carried to Rome.

THE HIPPODROME

The throne was not the only remarkable sight at the court of the magnificent king. Solomon attracted visitors to his capital by means of games and shows. In every month of the year the official who was in charge for the month, was expected to arrange for a horse race, and once a year a race took place in which the competitors were ten thousand youths, mainly of the tribes of Gad and Naphtali, who lived at the court of the king year in, year out, and were maintained by him. For the scholars, their disciples, the priests, and the Levites, the races were held on the last of the month; on the first day of the month the residents of Jerusalem were the spectators, and, on the second day, strangers. The hippodrome occupied an area of three parasangs square, with an inner square measuring one parasang on each side, around which the races were run. Within were two grilles ornamented with all sorts of animals. Out of the jaws of four gilded lions, attached to pillars by twos, perfumes and spices flowed for the people. The spectators were divided into four parties distinguished by the color of their garb: the king and his attendants, the scholars and their disciples, and the priests and Levites were attired in light blue garments; all the rest from Jerusalem wore white; the sight-seers from the surrounding towns and villages wore red, and green marked the heathen hailing from afar, who came laden with tribute and presents. The four colors corresponded to the four seasons. In the autumn the sky is brilliantly blue; in winter the white snow falls; the color of spring is green like the ocean, because it is the season favorable to voyages, and red is the color of summer, when the fruits grow red and ripe.

As the public spectacles were executed with pomp and splendor, so the king's table was royally sumptuous. Regardless of season and climate, it was always laden with the delicacies of all parts of the globe. Game and poultry, even of such varieties as were unknown in Palestine, were not lacking, and daily there came a gorgeous bird from Barbary and settled down before the king's seat at the table. The Scriptures tell us of great quantities of food required by Solomon's household, and yet it was not all that was needed. What the Bible mentions, covers only the accessories, such as spices and the minor ingredients. The real needs were far greater, as may be judged from the custom that all of Solomon's thousand wives arranged a banquet daily, each in the hope of having the king dine with her.

LESSONS IN HUMILITY

Great and powerful as Solomon was, and wise and just, still occasions were not lacking to bring home to him the truth that the wisest and mightiest of mortals may not indulge in pride and arrogance.

Solomon had a precious piece of tapestry, sixty miles square, on which he flew through the air so swiftly that he could eat breakfast in Damascus and supper in Media. To carry out his orders he had at his beck and call Asaph ben Berechiah among men, Ramirat among demons, the lion among beasts, and the eagle among birds. Once it happened that pride possessed Solomon while he was sailing through the air on his carpet, and he said: "There is none like unto me in the world, upon whom God has bestowed sagacity, wisdom, intelligence, and knowledge, besides making me the ruler of the world." The same instant the air stirred, and forty thousand men dropped from the magic carpet. The king ordered the wind to cease from blowing, with the word: "Return!" Whereupon the wind: "If thou wilt return to God, and subdue thy pride, I, too, will return." The king realized his transgression.

On one occasion he strayed into the valley of the ants in the course of his wanderings. He heard one ant order all the others to withdraw, to avoid being crushed by the armies of Solomon. The king halted and summoned the ant that had spoken. She told him that she was the queen of the ants, and she gave her reasons for the order of withdrawal. Solomon wanted to put a question to the ant queen, but she refused to answer unless the king took her up and placed her on his hand. He acquiesced, and then he put his question: "Is there any one greater than I am in all the world?" "Yes," said the ant.

Solomon: "Who?"

Ant: "I am."

Solomon: "How is that possible?"

Ant: "Were I not greater than thou, God would not have led thee hither to put me on thy hand."

Exasperated, Solomon threw her to the ground, and said: "Thou knowest who I am? I am Solomon, the son of David."

Not at all intimidated, the ant reminded the king of his earthly origin, and admonished him to humility, and the king went off abashed.

Next he came to a magnificent building, into which he sought to enter in vain; he could find no door leading into it. After long search the demons came upon an eagle seven hundred years old, and he, unable to give them any information, sent him to his nine hundred years old brother, whose eyrie was higher than his own, and who would probably be in a position to advise them. But he in turn directed them to go to his still older brother. His age counted thirteen hundred years, and he had more knowledge than himself. This oldest one of the eagles reported that he remembered having heard his father say there was a door on the west side, but it was covered up by the dust of the ages that had passed since it was last used. So it turned out to be. They found an old iron door with the inscription: "We, the dwellers in this palace, for many years lived in comfort and luxury; then, forced by hunger, we ground pearls into flour instead of wheat but to no avail, and so, when we were about to die, we bequeathed this palace to the eagles." A second statement contained a detailed description of the wonderful palace, and mentioned where the keys for the different chambers were to be found. Following the directions on the door, Solomon inspected the remarkable building, whose apartments were made of pearls and precious stones. Inscribed on the doors he found the following three wise proverbs, dealing with the vanity of all earthly things, and admonishing men to be humble:

1. O son of man, let not time deceive thee; thou must wither away, and leave thy place, to rest in the bosom of the earth.

2. Haste thee not, move slowly, for the world is taken from one and bestowed upon another.

3. Furnish thyself with food for the journey, prepare thy meal while daylight lasts, for thou wilt not remain on earth forever, and thou knowest not the day of thy death.

In one of the chambers, Solomon saw a number of statues, among them one that looked as though alive. When he approached it, it called out in a loud voice: "Hither, ye satans, Solomon has come to undo you." Suddenly there arose great noise and tumult among the statues. Solomon pronounced the Name, and quiet was restored. The statues were overthrown, and the sons of the satans ran into the sea and were drowned. From the throat of the lifelike statue he drew a silver plate inscribed with characters which he could not decipher, but a youth from the desert told the king: "These letters are Greek, and the words mean: 'I, Shadad ben Ad, ruled over a thousand thousand provinces, rode on a thousand thousand horses, had a thousand thousand kings under me, and slew a thousand thousand heroes, and when the Angel of Death approached me, I was powerless.'"

ASMODEUS

When Solomon in his wealth and prosperity grew unmindful of his God, and, contrary to the injunctions laid down for kings in the Torah, multiplied wives unto himself, and craved the possession of many horses and much gold, the Book of Deuteronomy stepped before God and said: "Lo, O Lord of the world, Solomon is seeking to remove a Yod from out of me, for Thou didst write: 'The king shall not multiply horses unto himself, nor shall he multiply wives to himself, neither shall he greatly multiply to himself silver and gold'; but Solomon has acquired many horses, many wives, and much silver and gold." Hereupon God said: "As thou livest, Solomon and a hundred of his kind shall be annihilated ere a single one of thy letters shall be obliterated."

The charge made against Solomon was soon followed by consequences. He had to pay heavily for his sins. It came about in this way: While Solomon was occupied with the Temple, he had great difficulty in devising ways of fitting the stone from the quarry into the building, for the Torah explicitly prohibits the use of iron tools in erecting an altar. The scholars told him that Moses had used the shamir, the stone that splits rocks, to engrave the names of the tribes on the precious stones of the ephod worn by the high priest. Solomon's demons could give him no information as to where the shamir could be found. They surmised, however, that Asmodeus, king of demons, was in possession of the secret, and they told Solomon the name of the mountain on which Asmodeus dwelt, and described also his manner of life. On this mountain there was a well from which Asmodeus obtained his drinking water. He closed it up daily with a large rock, and sealed it before going to heaven, whither he went every day, to take part in the discussions in the heavenly academy. Thence he would descend again to earth in order to be present, though invisible, at the debates in the earthly houses of learning. Then, after investigating the seal on the well to ascertain if it had been tampered with, he drank of the water.

Solomon sent his chief man, Benaiah the son of Jehoiada, to capture Asmodeus. For this purpose he provided him with a chain, the ring on which the Name of God was engraved, a bundle of wool, and a skin of wine. Benaiah drew the water from the well through a hole bored from below, and, after having stopped up the hole with the wool, he filled the well with wine from above. When Asmodeus descended from heaven, to his astonishment he found wine instead of water in the well, although everything seemed untouched. At first he would not drink of it, and cited the Bible verses that inveigh against wine, to inspire himself with moral courage. At length Asmodeus succumbed to his consuming thirst, and drank till his senses were overpowered, and he fell into a deep sleep. Benaiah, watching him from a tree, then came, and drew the chain about Asmodeus' neck. The demon, on awakening, tried to free himself, but Benaiah called to him: "The Name of thy Lord is upon thee." Though Asmodeus now permitted himself to be led off unresistingly, he acted most peculiarly on the way to Solomon. He brushed against a palm-tree and uprooted it; he knocked against a house and overturned it; and when, at the request of a poor woman, he was turned aside from her hut, he broke a bone. He asked with grim humor: "Is it not written, 'A soft tongue breaketh the bone?'" A blind man going astray he set in the right path, and to a drunkard he did a similar kindness. He wept when a wedding party passed them, and laughed at a man who asked his shoemaker to make him shoes to last for seven years, and at a magician who was publicly showing his skill.

Having finally arrived at the end of the journey, Asmodeus, after several days of waiting, was led before Solomon, who questioned him about his strange conduct on the journey. Asmodeus answered that he judged persons and things according to their real character, and not according to their appearance in the eyes of human beings. He cried when he saw the wedding company, because he knew the bridegroom had not a month to live, and he laughed at him who wanted shoes to last seven years, because the man would not own them for seven days, also at the magician who pretended to disclose secrets, because he did not know that a buried treasure lay under his very feet; the blind man whom he set in the right path was one of the "perfect pious," and he wanted to be kind to him; on the other hand, the drunkard to whom he did a similar kindness was known in heaven as a very wicked man, but he happened to have done a good deed once, and he was rewarded accordingly.

Asmodeus told Solomon that the shamir was given by God to the Angel of the Sea, and that Angel entrusted none with the shamir except the moor-hen, which had taken an oath to watch the shamir carefully. The moor-hen takes the shamir with her to mountains which are not inhabited by men, splits them by means of the shamir, and injects seeds, which grow and cover the naked rocks, and then they can be inhabited. Solomon sent one of his servants to seek the nest of the bird and lay a piece of glass over it. When the moor-hen came and could not reach her young, she flew away and fetched the shamir and placed it on the glass. Then the man shouted, and so terrified the bird that she dropped the shamir and flew away. By this means the man obtained possession of the coveted shamir, and bore it to Solomon. But the moor-hen was so distressed at having broken her oath to the Angel of the Sea that she committed suicide.

Although Asmodeus was captured only for the purpose of getting the shamir, Solomon nevertheless kept him after the completion of the Temple. One day the king told Asmodeus that he did not understand wherein the greatness of the demons lay, if their king could be kept in bonds by a mortal. Asmodeus replied, that if Solomon would remove his chains and lend him the magic ring, he would prove his own greatness. Solomon agreed. The demon stood before him with one wing touching heaven and the other reaching to the earth. Snatching up Solomon, who had parted with his protecting ring, he flung him four hundred parasangs away from Jerusalem, and then palmed himself off as the king.

SOLOMON AS BEGGAR

Banished from his home, deprived of his realm, Solomon wandered about in far-off lands, among strangers, begging his daily bread. Nor did his humiliation end there; people thought him a lunatic, because he never tired of assuring them that he was Solomon, Judah's great and mighty king. Naturally that seemed a preposterous claim to the people. The lowest depth of despair he reached, however, when he met some one who recognized him. The recollections and associations that stirred within him then made his present misery almost unendurable.

It happened that once on his peregrinations he met an old acquaintance, a rich and well-considered man, who gave a sumptuous banquet in honor of Solomon. At the meal his host spoke to Solomon constantly of the magnificence and splendor he had once seen with his own eyes at the court of the king. These reminiscences moved the king to tears, and he wept so bitterly that, when he rose from the banquet, he was satiated, not with the rich food, but with salt tears. The following day it again happened that Solomon met an acquaintance of former days, this time a poor man, who nevertheless entreated Solomon to do him the honor and break bread under his roof. All that the poor man could offer his distinguished guest was a meagre dish of greens. But he tried in every way to assuage the grief that oppressed Solomon. He said: "O my lord and king, God hath sworn unto David He would never let the royal dignity depart from his house, but it is the way of God to reprove those He loves if they sin. Rest assured, He will restore thee in good time to thy kingdom." These words of his poor host were more grateful to Solomon's bruised heart than the banquet the rich man had prepared for him. It was to the contrast between the consolations of the two men that he applied the verse in Proverbs: "Better is a dinner of herbs where love is, than a stalled ox and hatred therewith."

For three long years Solomon journeyed about, begging his way from city to city, and from country to country, atoning for the three sins of his life by which he had set aside the commandment laid upon kings in Deuteronomy not to multiply horses, and wives, and silver and gold. At the end of that time, God took mercy upon him for the sake of his father David, and for the sake of the pious princess Naamah, the daughter of the Ammonite king, destined by God to be the ancestress of the Messiah. The time was approaching when she was to become the wife of Solomon and reign as queen in Jerusalem. God therefore led the royal wanderer to the capital city of Ammon. Solomon took service as an underling with the cook in the royal household, and he proved himself so proficient in the culinary art that the king of Ammon raised him to the post of chief cook. Thus he came under the notice of the king's daughter Naamah, who fell in love with her father's cook. In vain her parents endeavored to persuade her to choose a husband befitting her rank. Not even the king's threat to have her and her beloved executed availed to turn her thoughts away from Solomon. The Ammonite king had the lovers taken to a barren desert, in the hope that they would die of starvation there. Solomon and his wife wandered through the desert until they came to a city situated by the sea-shore. They purchased a fish to stave off death. When Naamah prepared the fish, she found in its belly the magic ring belonging to her husband, which he had given to Asmodeus, and which, thrown into the sea by the demon, had been swallowed by a fish. Solomon recognized his ring, put it on his finger, and in the twinkling of an eye he transported himself to Jerusalem. Asmodeus, who had been posing as King Solomon during the three years, he drove out, and himself ascended the throne again.

Later on he cited the king of Ammon before his tribunal, and called him to account for the disappearance of the cook and the cook's wife, accusing him of having killed them. The king of Ammon protested that he had not killed, but only banished them. Then Solomon had the queen appear, and to his great astonishment and still greater joy the king of Ammon recognized his daughter.

Solomon succeeded in regaining his throne only after undergoing many hardships. The people of Jerusalem considered him a lunatic, because he said that he was Solomon. After some time, the members of the Sanhedrin noticed his peculiar behavior, and they investigated the matter. They found that a long time had passed since Benaiah, the confidant of the king, had been permitted to enter the presence of the usurper. Furthermore the wives of Solomon and his mother Bath-sheba informed them that the behavior of the king had completely changed it was not befitting royalty and in no respect like Solomon's former manner. It was also very strange that the king never by any chance allowed his foot to be seen, for fear, of course, of betraying his demon origin. The Sanhedrin, therefore, gave the king's magic ring to the wandering beggar who called himself King Solomon, and had him appear before the pretender on the throne. As soon as Asmodeus caught sight of the true king protected by his magic ring, he flew away precipitately.

Solomon did not escape unscathed. The sight of Asmodeus in all his forbidding ugliness had so terrified him that henceforth he surrounded his couch at night with all the valiant heroes among the people.

THE COURT OF SOLOMON

As David had been surrounded by great scholars and heroes of repute, so the court of Solomon was the gathering-place of the great of his people. The most important of them all doubtless was Benaiah the son of Jehoiada, who had no peer for learning and piety either in the time of the first or the second Temple. In his capacity as the chancellor of Solomon, he was the object of the king's special favor. He was frequently invited to be the companion of the king in his games of chess. The wise king naturally was always the winner. One day Solomon left the chess-board for a moment, Benaiah used his absence to remove one of the king's chess-men, and the king lost the game. Solomon gave much thought to the occurrence. He came to the conclusion that his chancellor had dealt dishonestly with him, and he was determined to give him a lesson.

Some days later Solomon noticed two suspicious characters hanging about the palace. Acting at once upon an idea that occurred to him, he put on the clothes of one of his servants and joined the two suspects. The three of them, he proposed, should make the attempt to rob the royal palace, and he drew forth a key which would facilitate their entrance. While the thieves were occupied in gathering booty, the king roused his servants, and the malefactors were taken into custody. Next morning Solomon appeared before the Sanhedrin, which was presided over by Benaiah at the time, and he desired to know from the court what punishment was meted out to a thief. Benaiah, seeing no delinquents before him, and unwilling to believe that the king would concern himself about the apprehension of thieves, was convinced that Solomon was bent on punishing him for his dishonest play. He fell at the feet of the king, confessed his guilt, and begged his pardon. Solomon was pleased to have his supposition confirmed, and also to have Benaiah acknowledge his wrong-doing. he assured him he harbored no evil designs against him, and that when he asked this question of the Sanhedrin, he had had real thieves in mind, who had broken into the palace during the night.

Another interesting incident happened, in which Benaiah played a part. The king of Persia was very ill, and his physician told him he could be cured by nothing but the milk of a lioness. The king accordingly sent a deputation bearing rich presents to Solomon, the only being in the world who might in his wisdom discover means to obtain lion's milk. Solomon charged Benaiah to fulfil the Persian king's wish. Benaiah took a number of kids, and repaired to a lion's den. Daily he threw a kid to the lioness, and after some time the beasts became familiar with him, and finally he could approach the lioness close enough to draw milk from her udders.

On the way back to the Persian king the physician who had recommended the milk cure dreamed a dream. All the organs of his body, his hands, feet, eyes, mouth, and tongue, were quarrelling with one another, each claiming the greatest share of credit in procuring the remedy for the Persian monarch. When the tongue set forth its own contribution to the cause of the king's service, the other organs rejected its claim as totally unfounded. The physician did not forget the dream, and when he appeared before the king, he spoke: "Here is the dog's milk which we went to fetch for you." The king, enraged, ordered the physician to be hanged, because he had brought the milk of a bitch instead of the milk of a lion's dam. During the preliminaries to the execution, all the limbs and organs of the physician began to tremble, whereupon the tongue said: "Did I not tell you that you all are of no good? If you will acknowledge my superiority, I shall even now save you from death." They all made the admission it demanded, and the physician requested the executioner to take him to the king. Once in the presence of his master, he begged him as a special favor to drink of the milk he had brought. The king granted his wish, recovered from his sickness, and dismissed the physician in peace. So it came about that all the organs of the body acknowledge the supremacy of the tongue.

Besides Benaiah, Solomon's two scribes, Elihoreph and Ahijah, the sons of Shisha, deserve mention. They both met their death in a most peculiar way. Solomon once upon a time noticed a care-worn expression on the countenance of the Angel of Death. When he asked the reason, he received the answer, that he had been charged with the task of bringing the two scribes to the next world. Solomon was desirous of stealing a march upon the Angel of Death, as well as keeping his secretaries alive. He ordered the demons to carry Elihoreph and Ahijah to Luz, the only spot on earth in which the Angel of Death has no power. In a jiffy, the demons had done his bidding, but the two secretaries expired at the very moment of reaching the gates of Luz. Next day, the Angel of Death appeared before Solomon in very good humor, and said to him: "Thou didst transport those two men to the very spot in which I wanted them." The fate destined for them was to die at the gates of Luz, and the Angel of Death had been at a loss how to get them there.

A most interesting incident in Solomon's own family circle is connected with one of his daughters. She was of extraordinary beauty, and in the stars he read that she was to marry an extremely poor youth. To prevent the undesirable union, Solomon had a high tower erected in the sea, and to this he sent his daughter. Seventy eunuchs were to guard her, and a huge quantity of food was stored in the tower for her use.

The poor youth whom fate had appointed to be her husband was travelling one cold night. He did not know where to rest his head, when he espied the rent carcass of an ox lying in the field. In this he lay down to keep warm. When he was ensconced in it, there came a large bird, which took the carcass, bore it, together with the youth stretched out in it, to the roof of the tower in which the princess lived, and, settling down there, began to devour the flesh of the ox. In the morning, the princess, according to her wont, ascended to the roof to look out upon the sea, and she caught sight of the youth. She asked him who he was, and who had brought him thither? He told her that he was a Jew from Accho, and had been carried to the tower by a bird. She showed him to a chamber, where he could wash and anoint himself, and array himself in a fresh garb. Then it appeared that he possessed unusual beauty. Besides, he was a scholar of great attainments and of acute mind. So it came about that the princess fell in love with him. She asked him whether he would have her to wife, and he assented gladly. He opened one of his veins, and wrote the marriage contract with his own blood. Then he pronounced the formula of betrothal, taking God and the two archangels Michael and Gabriel as witnesses, and she became his wife, legally married to him.

After some time the eunuchs noticed that she was pregnant. Their questions elicited the suspected truth from the princess, and they sent for Solomon. His daughter admitted her marriage, and the king, though he recognized in her husband the poor man predicted in the constellations, yet he thanked God for his son-in-law, distinguished no less for learning than for his handsome person.

Chapter 6

VI. JUDAH AND ISRAEL

THE DIVISION OF THE KINGDOM

The division of the kingdom into Judah and Israel, which took place soon after the death of Solomon, had cast its shadow before. When Solomon, on the day after his marriage with the Egyptian princess, disturbed the regular course of the Temple service by sleeping late with his head on the pillow under which lay the key of the Temple, Jeroboam with eighty thousand Ephraimites approached the king and publicly called him to account for is negligence. God administered a reproof to Jeroboam; "Why dost thou reproach a prince of Israel? As thou livest, thou shalt have a taste of his rulership, and thou wilt see thou are not equal to its responsibilities."

On another occasion a clash occurred between Jeroboam and Solomon. The latter ordered his men to close the openings David had made in the city wall to facilitate the approach of the pilgrims to Jerusalem. This forced them all the walk through the gates and pay toll. The tax thus collected Solomon gave to his wife, the daughter of Pharaoh, as pin-money. Indignant at this, Jeroboam questioned the king about it in public. In other ways, too, he failed to pay Solomon the respect due to royal position, as his father before him, Sheba the son of Bichri, had rebelled against David, misled by signs and tokens which he had falsely interpreted as pointing to his own elevation to royal dignity, when in reality they concerned themselves with his son.

It was when Jeroboam was preparing to depart from Jerusalem forever, in order to escape the dangers to which Solomon's displeasure exposed him, that Ahijah of Shilo met him with the Divine tidings of his elevation to the kingship. The prophet Ahijah, of the tribe of Levi, was venerable, not only by reason of his hoary age, his birth occurred at least sixty years before the exodus from Egypt, but because his piety was so profound that a saint of the exalted standing of Simon ben Yohai associated Ahijah with himself. Simon once exclaimed: "My merits and Ahijah together suffice to atone for the iniquity of all sinners from the time of Abraham until the advent of the Messiah."

JEROBOAM

Jeroboam was the true disciple of this great prophet, His doctrine was as pure as the new garment Ahijah wore when he met Jeroboam near Jerusalem, and his learning exceeded that of all the scholars of his time except his own teacher Ahijah alone. The prophet was in the habit of discussing secret love with Jeroboam and subjects in the Torah whose existence was wholly unknown to others.

Had Jeroboam proved himself worthy of his high position, the length of his reign would have equalled David's. It was his pride that led him into destruction. He set up the golden calves as objects to be worshipped by the people, in order to wean them from their habit of going on pilgrimages to Jerusalem. He knew that in the Temple only members of the royal house of David were privileged to sit down. No exception would be made in favor of Jeroboam, and so he would have to stand while Rehoboam would be seated. Rather than appear in public as the subordinate of the Judean king, he introduced the worship of idols, which secured him full royal prerogatives.

In the execution of his plan he proceeded with great cunning, and his reputation as a profound scholar and pious saint stood him in good stead. This was his method: He seated an impious man next to a pious man, and then said to each couple: "Will you put your signature to anything I intend to do?" The two would give an affirmative answer. "Do you want me as king?" he would then ask, only to receive and affirmative answer again. "And you will do whatever I order?" he continued. "Yes," was the reply. "I am to infer, then, that you will even pay worship to idols if I command it?" said Jeroboam. "God forbid!" the pious member of the couple would exclaim, whereupon his impious companion, who was in league with the king, would turn upon him: "Canst thou really suppose for an instant that a man like Jeroboam would serve idols? He only wishes to put our loyalty to the test." Through such machinations he succeeded in obtaining the signatures of the most pious, even the signature of the prophet Ahijah. Now Jeroboam had the people is his power. He could exact the vilest deeds from them.

So entrenched, Jeroboam brought about the division between Judah and Israel, a consummation which his father, Sheba the son of Bichri, had not been able to compass under David, because God desired to have the Temple erected before the split occurred. Not yet satisfied, Jeroboam sought to involve the Ten Tribes in a war against Judah and Jerusalem. But the people of the northern kingdom refused to enter into hostilities with their brethren, and with the ruler of their brethren, a descendant of David. Jeroboam appealed to the elders of the Israelites, and they referred him to the Danites, the most efficient of their warriors; but they swore by the head of Dan, the ancestor of their tribe, that they would never consent to shed blood of their brethren. They were even on the point of rising against Jeroboam, and the clash between them and the followers of Jeroboam was prevented only because God prompted the Danites to leave Palestine.

Their first plan was to journey to Egypt and take possession of the land. They gave it up when their princes reminded them of the Biblical prohibition against dwelling in Egypt. Likewise they were restrained from attacking the Edomites, Ammonites, and Moabites, for the Torah commands considerate treatment of them. Finally they decided to go to Egypt, but not to stay there, only to pass through to Ethiopia. The Egyptians were in great terror of the Danites, and their hardiest warriors occupied the roads travelled by them. Arrived in Ethiopia, the Danites slew a part of the population, and exacted tribute from the rest.

The departure of the Danites relieved Judah from the apprehended invasion by Jeroboam, but danger arose from another quarter. Shishak, the ruler of Egypt, who was the father-in-law of Solomon, came to Jerusalem and demanded his daughter's jointure. He carried off the throne of Solomon, and also the treasure which the Israelites had taken from the Egyptians at the time of the exodus. So the Egyptian money returned to its source.

THE TWO ABIJAHS

Jeroboam did not entirely forego his plan of a campaign against Judah, but it was not executed until Abijah had succeeded his father Rehoboam on the throne of Jerusalem. The Judean king was victorious. However, he could not long enjoy the fruits of his victory. Shortly after occurred his death, brought on by his own crimes. In his war against Jeroboam he had indulged in excessive cruelty; he ordered the corpses of the enemy to be mutilated, and permitted them to be buried only after putrefaction had set in. Such savagery was all the more execrable as it prevented many widows from entering into a second marriage. Mutilating the corpses had made identification impossible, and so it was left doubtful whether their husbands were among the dead.

Moreover, Abijah used most disrespectful language about the prophet Abijah the Shilonite; he called him a "son of Belial" in his address to the people on Mount Zemaraim. That in itself merited severe punishment. Finally, his zeal for true worship of God, which Abijah had urged as the reason of the war between himself and Jeroboam, cooled quickly. When he obtained possession of Beth-el, he failed to do away with the golden calves.

In this respect his namesake, the Israelitish king Abijah, the son of Jeroboam, was by far his superior. By removing the guards stationed at the frontier, he bade defiance to the command of his father, who had decreed the death penalty for pilgrimages to Jerusalem. More than this, he himself ventured to go up to Jerusalem in fulfilment of his religious duty.

ASA

Asa, the son of Abijah of Judah, was a worthier and a more pious ruler than his father had been. He did away with the gross worship of Priapus, to which his mother was devoted. To reward him for his piety, God gave him the victory over Zerah, the king of the Ethiopians. As a result of this victory he came again into possession of the throne of Solomon and of the treasures Shishak had taken from his grandfather, which Zerah in turn had wrested form Shishak. Asa himself did not long keep them. Baasha, the king of Israel, together with Ben-hadad, the Aramean king, attacked Asa, who tried to propitiate Ben-hadad by giving him his lately re-acquired treasures. The prophet justly rebuked him for trusting in princes rather than in God, and that in spite of the fact that Divine help had been visible in his conflicts with the Ethiopians and the Lubim; for there had been no need for him to engage in battle with them; in response to his mere prayer God had slain the enemy. In general, Asa showed little confidence in God; he rather trusted his own skill. Accordingly, he made even the scholars of his realm enlist in the army sent out against Baasha. He was punished by being afflicted with gout, he of all men, who was distinguished on account of the strength residing in his feet. Furthermore, the division between Judah and Israel was made permanent, though God had at first intended to limit the exclusion of David's house from Israel to only thirty-six years. Had Asa shown himself deserving, he would have been accorded dominion over the whole of Israel. In point of fact, Asa, through his connection by marriage with the house of Omri, contributed to the stability of the Israelitish dynasty, for as a result of the support given by the southern ruler Omri succeeded in putting his rival Tibni out of the way. Then it was that God resolved that the descendants of Asa should perish simultaneously with the descendants of Omri. This doom was accomplished when Jehu killed the king of Judah on account of his friendship and kinship with Joram the king of Samaria.

JEHOSHAPHAT AND AHAB

The successors of Omri and Asa, each in his way, were worthy of their fathers. Jehoshaphat, the son of Asa, was very wealthy. The treasures which his father had sent to the Aramean ruler reverted to him in consequence of his victory over the Ammonites, themselves the conquerors of the Arameans, whom they had despoiled of their possessions. His power was exceedingly great; each division of his army counted no less than one hundred and sixty thousand warriors. Yet rich and powerful as he was, he was so modest that he refused to don his royal apparel when he went to the house of the prophet Elisha to consult him; he appeared before him in the attire of one of the people. Unlike his father, who had little consideration for scholars, Jehoshaphat was particularly gracious toward them. When a scholar appeared before him, he arose, hastened to meet him, and kissing and embracing him, greeted him with "Rabbi, Rabbi!"

Jehoshaphat concerned himself greatly about the purity and sanctification of the Temple. He was the author of the ordinance forbidding any one to ascend the Temple mount whose term of uncleanness had not expired, even though he had taken the ritual bath. His implicit trust in God made him a complete contrast to his skeptical father. He turned to God and implored His help when to human reason help seemed an utter impossibility. In the war with the Arameans, an enemy held his sword at Jehoshaphat's very throat, ready to deal the fatal blow, but the king entreated help of God, and it was granted.

In power and wealth, Ahab, king of Samaria, outstripped his friend Jehoshaphat, for Ahab is one of that small number of kings who have ruled over the whole world. No less than two hundred and fifty-two kingdoms acknowledged his dominion. As for his wealth, it was so abundant that each of his hundred and forty children possessed several ivory palaces, summer and winter residences. But what gives Ahab his prominence among the Jewish kings is neither his power nor his wealth, but his sinful conduct. For him the gravest transgressions committed by Jeroboam were slight peccadilloes. At his order the gates of Samaria bore the inscription: "Ahab denies the God of Israel." He was so devoted to idolatry, to which he was led astray by his wife Jezebel, that the fields of Palestine were full of idols. But he was not wholly wicked, he possessed some good qualities. He was liberal toward scholars, and he showed great reverence for the Torah, which he studied zealously. When Ben-hadad exacted all he possessed his wealth, his wives, his children he acceded to his demands regarding everything except the Torah; that he refused peremptorily to surrender. In the war that followed between himself and the Syrians, he was so indignant at the presumptuousness of the Aramean upstart that he himself saddled his warhorse for the battle. His zeal was rewarded by God; he gained a brilliant victory in a battle in which no less than a hundred thousand of the Syrians were slain, as the prophet

Micaiah had foretold to him. The same seer admonished him not to deal gently with Ben-hadad. God's word to him had been: "Know that I had to set many a pitfall and trap to deliver him into thy hand. If thou lettest him escape, thy life will be forfeit for his."

Nevertheless the disastrous end of Ahab is not to be ascribed to his disregard of the prophet's warning for he finally liberated Ben-hahad, but chiefly to the murder of his kinsman Naboth, whose execution on the charge of treason he had ordered, so that he might put himself in possession of Naboth's wealth. His victim was a pious man, and in the habit of going on pilgrimages to Jerusalem on the festivals. As he was a great singer, his presence in the Holy City attracted many other pilgrims thither. Once Naboth failed to go on his customary pilgrimage. Then it was that his false conviction took place a very severe punishment for the transgression, but not wholly unjustifiable. Under Jehoshaphat's influence and counsel, Ahab did penance for his crime, and the punishment God meted out to him was thereby mitigated to the extent that his dynasty was not cut off from the throne at this death. In the heavenly court of justice, at Ahab's trial, the accusing witnesses and his defenders exactly balanced each other in number and statements, until the spirit of Naboth appeared and turned the scale against Ahab. The spirit of Naboth it had been, too, that had let astray the prophets of Ahab, making them all use the very same words in prophesying a victory at Ramothgilead. This literal unanimity aroused Jehoshaphat's suspicion, and caused him to ask for "a prophet of the Lord," for the rule is: "The same thought is revealed to many prophets, but no two prophets express it in the same words." Jehoshaphat's mistrust was justified by the issue of war. Ahab was slain in a miraculous way by Naaman, at the time only a common soldier of the rank and file. God permitted Naaman's missile to penetrate Ahab's armor, though the latter was harder than the former.

The mourning for Ahab was so great that the memory of it reached posterity. The funeral procession was unusually impressive; no less than thirty-six thousand warriors, their shoulders bared, marched before his bier. Ahab is one of the few in Israel who have no portion in the world to come. He dwells in the fifth division of the nether world, which is under the supervision of the angel Oniel. However, he is exempt from the tortures inflicted upon his heathen associates.

JEZEBEL

Wicked as Ahab was, his wife Jezebel was incomparably worse. Indeed, she is in great part the cause of his suffering, and Ahab realized it. Once Rabbi Levi expounded the Scriptural verse in which the iniquity of Ahab and the influence of his wife over him are discussed, dwelling upon the first half for two months. Ahab visited him in a dream, and reproached him with expatiating on the first half of the verse to the exclusion of the latter half. Thereupon the Rabbi took the second half of the verse as the text of his lectures for the next two months, demonstrating all the time that Jezebel was the instigator of Ahab's sins. Her misdeed are told in the Scriptures. To those there recounted must be added her practice of attaching unchaste images to Ahab's chariot for the purpose of stimulating his carnal desires. Therefore those parts of his chariot were spattered with his blood when he fell at the hand of the enemy. She had her husband weighed every day, and the increase of his weight in gold she sacrificed to the idol. Jezebel was not only the daughter and the wife of a king, she was also co-regent with her husband, the only reigning queen in Jewish history except Athaliah.

Hardened sinner though Jezebel was, even she had good qualities. One of them was her capacity for sympathy with others in joy and sorrow. Whenever a funeral cortege passed the royal palace, Jezebel would descend and join the ranks of the mourners, and, also, when a marriage procession went by, she took part in the merry-making in honor of the bridal couple. By way of reward the limbs and organs with which she had executed these good deeds were left intact by the horses that trampled her to death in the portion of Jezreel.

JORAM OF ISRAEL

Of Joram, the son of Ahab, it can only be said that he had his father's faults without his father's virtues. Ahab was liberal, Joram miserly, nay, he even indulged in usurious practices. From Obadiah, the pious protector of the prophets in hiding, he exacted a high rate of interest on the money needed for their support. As a consequence, at his death he fell pierced between his arms, the arrow going out at his heart, for he had stretched out his arms to receive usury, and had hardened his heart against compassion. In his reign only one event deserves mention, his campaign against Moab, undertaken in alliance with the kings of Judah and Edom, and ending with a splendid victory won by the allied kings. Joram and his people, it need hardly be said, failed to derive the proper lesson from the war. Their disobedience to God's commands went on as before. The king of Moab, on the other hand, in his way sought to come nearer to God. He assembled his astrologers and inquired of them, why it was that the Moabites, successful in their warlike enterprises against other nations, could not measure up to the standard of the Israelites. They explained that God was gracious to Israel, because his ancestor Abraham had been ready to sacrifice Isaac at His bidding. Then the Moabite king reasoned, that if God set so high a value upon mere good intention, how much greater would be the reward for its actual execution, and he, who ordinarily was a sun worshipper, proceeded to sacrifice his son, the successor to the throne, to the God of Israel. God said: "The heathen do not know Me, and their wrong-doing arises from ignorance; but you, Israelites, know Me, and yet you act rebelliously toward Me."

As a result of the seven years' famine, conditions in Samaria were frightful during the great part of Joram's reign. In the first year everything stored in the houses was eaten up. In the second, the people supported themselves with what they could scrape together in the fields. The flesh of the clean animals sufficed for the third year; in the fourth the sufferers resorted to the unclean animals; in the fifth, the reptiles and insects; and in the sixth the monstrous thing happened that women crazed by hunger consumed their own children as food. But the acme of distress was reached in the seventh year, when men sought to gnaw the flesh from their own bones. To these occurrences the prophecies of Joel apply, for he lived in the awful days of the famine in Joram's reign.

Luckily, God revealed to Joel at the same time how Israel would be rescued from the famine. The winter following the seven years of dearth brought no relief, for the rain held back until the first day of the month of Nisan. When it began to fall, the prophet said to the people, "Go forth and sow seed!" But they remonstrated with him, "Shall one who hath saved a measure of wheat or two measures of barely not use his store for food and live, rather than for seed and die?" But the prophet urged them, "Nay, go forth and sow seed." And a miracle happened. In the ant hills and mouse holes, they found enough grain for seed, and they cast it upon the ground on the second, the third, and the fourth day of Nisan. On the fifth day of the month rain fell again. Eleven days later the grain was ripe, and the offering of the 'Omer could be brought at the appointed time, on the sixteenth of the month. Of this the Psalmist was thinking when he said, "They that sow in tears shall reap in joy."

Chapter 7

VII. ELIJAH

ELIJAH BEFORE HIS TRANSLATION

The Biblical account of the prophet Elijah, of his life and work during the reigns of Ahab and his son Joram, gives but a faint idea of a personage whose history begins with Israel's sojourn in Egypt, and will end only when Israel, under the leadership of the Messiah, shall have taken up his abode again in Palestine.

The Scripture tells us only the name of Elijah's home, but it must be added that he was a priest, identical with Phinehas, the priest zealous for the honor of God, who distinguished himself on the journey through the desert, and played a prominent role again in the time of the Judges.

Elijah's first appearance in the period of the Kings was his meeting with Ahab in the house of Hiel, the Beth-elite, the commander-in-chief of the Israelitish army, whom he was visiting to condole with him for the loss of his sons. God Himself had charged the prophet to offer sympathy to Hiel, whose position demanded that honor be paid him. Elijah at first refused to seek out the sinner who had violated the Divine injunction against rebuilding Jericho, for he said that the blasphemous talk of such evil-doers always called forth his rage. Thereupon God promised Elijah that fulfilment should attend whatever imprecation might in his wrath escape him against the godless for their unholy speech. As the prophet entered the general's house, he heard Hiel utter these words: "Blessed be the Lord God of the pious, who grants fulfilment to the words of the pious." Hiel thus acknowledged that he had been justly afflicted with Joshua's curse against him who should rebuild Jericho.

Ahab mockingly asked him: "Was not Moses greater than Joshua, and did he not say that God would let no rain descend upon the earth, if Israel served and worshipped idols? There is not an idol known to which I do not pay homage, yet we enjoy all that is goodly and desirable. Dost thou believe that if the words of Moses remain unfulfilled, the words of Joshua will come true?" Elijah rejoined: "Be it as thou sayest: 'As the Lord, the God of Israel liveth, before whom I stand, there shall not be dew nor rain these years, but according to my word.'" In pursuance of His promise, God could not but execute the words of Elijah, and neither dew nor rain watered the land.

A famine ensued, and Ahab sought to wreak his vengeance upon the prophet. To escape the king's persecutions, Elijah hid himself. He was sustained with food brought from the larder of the pious king Jehoshaphat by ravens, which at the same time would not approach near to the house of the iniquitous Ahab.

God, who has compassion even upon the impious, tried to induce the prophet to release Him from His promise. To influence him He made the brook run dry whence Elijah drew water for his thirst. As this failed to soften the inflexible prophet, God resorted to the expedient of causing him pain through the death of the son of the widow with whom Elijah was abiding, and by whom he had been received with great honor. When her son, who was later to be known as the prophet Jonah, died, she thought God had formerly been gracious to her on account of her great worthiness as compared with the merits of her neighbors and of the inhabitants of the city, and now He had abandoned her, because her virtues had become as naught in the presence of the great prophet. In his distress Elijah supplicated God to revive the child. Now God had the prophet in His power. He could give heed unto Elijah's prayer only provided the prophet released Him from the promise about a drought, for resuscitation from death is brought about by means of dew, and this remedy was precluded so long as Elijah kept God to His word withholding dew and rain from the earth. Elijah saw there was nothing for it but to yield. However, he first betook himself to Ahab with the purpose of overcoming the obduracy of the people, upon whom the famine had made no impression. Manifest wonders displayed before their eyes were to teach them wisdom. The combat between God and Baal took place on Carmel. The mount that had esteemed itself the proper place for the greatest event in Israelitish history, the revelation of the law, was compensated, by the many miracles now performed upon it, for its disappointment at Sinai's having been preferred to it.

The first wonder occurred in connection with the choice of the bullocks. According to Elijah's arrangement with Ahab, one was to be sacrificed to God, and then one to Baal. A pair to twins, raised together, were brought before the contestants, and it was decided by lot which belonged to God and which to Baal. Elijah had no difficulty with his offering; quickly he led it to his altar. But all the priests of Baal, eight hundred and fifty in number, could not make their victim stir a foot. When Elijah began to speak persuasively to the bullock of Baal, urging it to follow the idolatrous priests, it opened its mouth and said: "We two, yonder bullock and myself, came forth from the same womb, we took our food from the same manger, and now he has been destined for God, as an instrument for the glorification of the Divine Name, while I am to be used for Baal, as an instrument to enrage my Creator." Elijah urged: "Do thou but follow the priests of Baal that they may have no excuse, and then thou wilt have a share in that glorification of God for which my bullock will be used." The bullock: "So dost thou advise, but I swear I will not move from the spot, unless thou with thine own hands wilt deliver me up." Elijah thereupon led the bullock to the priests of Baal.

In spite of this miracle, the priests sought to deceive the people. They undermined the altar, and Hiel hid himself under it with the purpose of igniting a fire at the mention of the word Baal. But God sent a serpent to kill him. In vain the false priests cried and called, Baal! Baal! the expected flame did not shoot up. To add to the confusion of the idolaters, God had imposed silence upon the whole world. The powers of the upper and of the nether regions were dumb, the universe seemed deserted and desolate, as if without a living creature. If a single sound had made itself heard, the priests would have said, "It is the voice of Baal."

That all preparations might be completed in one day, the erection of the altar, the digging of the trench, and whatever else was necessary, Elijah commanded the sun to stand still. "For Joshua," he said, "thou didst stand still that Israel might conquer his enemies; now stand thou still, neither for my sake, nor for the sake of Israel, but that the Name of God may be exalted." And the sun obeyed his words.

Toward evening Elijah summoned his disciple Elisha, and bade him pour water over his hands. A miracle happened. Water flowed out from Elijah's fingers until the whole trench was filled. Then the prophet prayed to God to let fire descend, but in such wise that the people would know it to be a wonder from heaven, and not think it a magician's trick. He spoke: "Lord of the world, Thou wilt send me as a messenger 'at the end of time,' but if my words do not meet with fulfilment now, the Jews cannot be expected to believe me in the latter days." His pleading was heard on high, and fire fell from heaven upon the altar, a fire that not only consumed what it touched, but also licked up the water. Nor was that all; his prayer for rain was also granted. Scarcely had these words dropped from his lips, "Though we have no other merits, yet remember the sign of the covenant which the Israelites bear upon their bodies," when the rain fell to earth.

In spite of all these miracles, the people persisted in their idolatrous ways and thoughts. Even the seven thousand who had not bowed down unto Baal were unworthy sons of Israel, for they paid homage to the golden calves of Jeroboam.

The misdeeds of the people had swelled to such number that they could no longer reckon upon "the merits of the fathers" to intercede for them; they had overdrawn their account. When they sank to the point of degradation at which they gave up the sign of the covenant, Elijah could control his wrath no longer, and he accused Israel before God. In the cleft of the rock in which God had once aforetimes appeared to Moses, and revealed Himself as compassionate and long-suffering, He now met with Elijah, and conveyed to him, by various signs, that it had been better to defend Israel than accuse him. But Elijah in his zeal for God was inexorable. Then God commanded him to appoint Elisha as his successor, for He said: "I cannot do as thou wouldst have me." Furthermore God charged him: "Instead of accusing My children, journey to Damascus, where the Gentiles have an idol for each day of the year. Though Israel hath thrown down My altars and slain My prophets, what concern is it of thine?"

The four phenomena that God sent before His appearance wind, earthquake, fire, and a still small voice were to instruct Elijah about the destiny of man. God told Elijah that these four represent the worlds through which man must pass: the first stands for this world, fleeting as the wind; the earthquake is the day of death, which makes the human body to tremble and quake; fire is the tribunal in Gehenna, and the still small voice is the Last Judgment, when there will be none but God alone.

About three years later, Elijah was taken up into heaven, but not without first undergoing a struggle with the Angel of Death. He refused to let Elijah enter heaven at his translation, on the ground that he exercised jurisdiction over all mankind, Elijah not excepted. God maintained that at the creation of heaven and earth He had explicitly ordered the Angel of Death to grant entrance to the living prophet, but the Angel of Death insisted that by Elijah's translation God had given just cause for complaint to all other men, who could not escape the doom of death. Thereupon God: "Elijah is not like other men. He is able to banish thee from the world, only thou dost not recognize his strength." With the consent of God, a combat took place between Elijah and the Angel of Death. The prophet was victorious, and, if God had not restrained him, he would have annihilated his opponent. Holding his defeated enemy under his feet, Elijah ascended heavenward.

In heaven he goes on living for all time. There he sits recording the deeds of men and the chronicles of the world. He has another office besides. He is the Psychopomp, whose duty is to stand at the cross-ways in Paradise and guide the pious to their appointed places; who brings the souls of sinners up from Gehenna at the approach of the Sabbath, and leads them back again to their merited punishment when the day of rest is about to depart; and who conducts these same souls, after they have atoned for their sins, to the place of everlasting bliss.

Elijah's miraculous deeds will be better understood if we remember that he had been an angel from the very first, even before the end of his earthly career. When God was about to create man, Elijah said to Him:

"Master of the world! If it be pleasing in Thine eyes, I will descend to earth, and make myself serviceable to the sons of men." Then God changed his angel name, and later, under Ahab, He permitted him to abide among men on earth, that he might convert the world to the belief that "the Lord is God." His mission fulfilled, God took him again into heaven, and said to him: "Be thou the guardian spirit of My children forever, and spread the belief in Me abroad in the whole world."

His angel name is Sandalphon, one of the greatest and mightiest of the fiery angel host. As such it is his duty to wreathe garlands for God out of the prayers sent aloft by Israel. Besides, he must offer up sacrifices in the invisible sanctuary, for the Temple was destroyed only apparently; in reality, it went on existing, hidden from the sight of ordinary mortals.

AFTER HIS TRANSLATION

Elijah's removal from earth, so far being an interruption to his relations with men, rather marks the beginning of his real activity as a helper in time of need, as a teacher and as a guide. At first his intervention in sublunar affairs was not frequent. Seven years after his translation, he wrote a letter to the wicked king Jehoram, who reigned over Judah. The next occasion on which he took part in an earthly occurrence was at the time of Ahasuerus, when he did the Jews a good turn by assuming the guise of the courtier Harbonah, in a favorable moment inciting the king against Haman.

It was reserved for later days, however, for Talmudic times, the golden age of the great scholars, the Tannaim and the Amoraim, to enjoy Elijah's special vigilance as protector of the innocent, as a friend in need, who hovers over the just and the pious, ever present to guard them against evil or snatch them out of danger. With four strokes of his wings Elijah can traverse the world. Hence no spot on earth is too far removed for his help. As an angel he enjoys the power of assuming the most various appearances to accomplish his purposes. Sometimes he looks like an ordinary man, sometimes he takes the appearance of an Arab, sometimes of a horseman, now he is a Roman court-official, now he is a harlot.

Once upon a time it happened that when Nahum, the great and pious teacher, was journeying to Rome on a political mission, he was without knowledge robbed of the gift he bore to the Emperor as an offering from the Jews. When he handed the casket to the ruler, it was found to contain common earth, which the thieves had substituted for the jewels they had abstracted. The Emperor thought the Jews were mocking at him, and their representative, Nahum, was condemned to suffer death. In his piety the Rabbi did not lose confidence in God; he only said: "This too is for good." And so it turned out to be. Suddenly Elijah appeared, and, assuming the guise of a court-official, he said: "Perhaps the earth in this casket is like that used by Abraham for purposes of war. A handful will do the work of swords and bows." At his instance the virtues of the earth were tested in the attack upon a city that had long resisted Roman courage and strength. His supposition was verified. The contents of the casket proved more efficacious than all the weapons of the army, and the Romans were victorious. Nahum was dismissed, laden with honors and treasures, and the thieves, who had betrayed themselves by claiming the precious earth, were executed, for, naturally enough, Elijah works no wonder for evil-doers.

Another time, for the purpose of rescuing Rabbi Shila, Elijah pretended to be a Persian. An informer had announced the Rabbi with the Persian Government, accusing him of administering the law according to the Jewish code. Elijah appeared as witness for the Rabbi and against the informer, and Shila was honorably dismissed.

When the Roman bailiffs were pursuing Rabbi Meir, Elijah joined him in the guise of a harlot. The Roman emissaries desisted from their pursuit, for they could not believe that Rabbi Meir would choose such a companion.

A contemporary of Rabbi Meir, Rabbi Simon ben Yohai, who spent thirteen years in a cave to escape the vengeance of the Romans, was informed by Elijah of the death of the Jew-baiting emperor, so that he could leave his hiding-place.

Equally characteristic is the help Elijah afforded the worthy poor. Frequently he brought them great wealth. Rabbi Kahana was so needy that he had to support himself by peddling with household utensils. Once a lady of high standing endeavored to force him to commit an immoral act, and Kahana, preferring death to iniquity, threw himself from a loft. Though Elijah was at a distance of four hundred parasangs, he hastened to the post in time to catch the Rabbi before he touched the ground. Besides, he gave him means enough to enable him to abandon an occupation beset with perils.

Rabba bar Abbahu likewise was a victim of poverty. He admitted to Elijah that on account of his small means he had no time to devote to his studies. Thereupon Elijah led him into Paradise, bade him remove his mantle, and fill it with leaves grown in the regions of the blessed. When the Rabbi was about to quit Paradise, his garment full of leaves, a voice was heard to say: "Who desires to anticipate his share in the world to come during his earthly days, as Rabba bar Abbahu is doing?" The Rabbi quickly cast the leaves away; nevertheless he received twelve thousand denarii for his upper garment, because it retained the wondrous fragrance of the leaves of Paradise.

Elijah's help was not confined to poor teachers of the law; all who were in need, and were worthy of his assistance, had a claim upon him. A poor man, the father of a family, in his distress once prayed to God: "O Lord of the world, Thou knowest, there is none to whom I can tell my tale of woe, none who will have pity upon me. I have neither brother nor kinsman nor friend, and my starving little ones are crying with hunger. Then do Thou have mercy and be compassionate, or let death come and put an end to our suffering." His words found a hearing with God, for, as he finished, Elijah stood before the poor man, and sympathetically inquired why he was weeping. When the prophet had heard the tale of his troubles, he said: "Take me and sell me as a slave; the proceeds will suffice for thy needs." At first the poor man refused to accept the sacrifice, but finally yielded, and Elijah was sold to a prince for eighty denarii. This sum formed the nucleus of the fortune which the poor man amassed and enjoyed until the end of his days. The prince who had purchased Elijah intended to build a palace, and he rejoiced to hear that his new slave was an architect. He promised Elijah liberty if within six months he completed the edifice. After nightfall of the same day, Elijah offered a prayer, and instantaneously the palace stood in its place in complete perfection. Elijah disappeared. The next morning the prince was not a little astonished to see the palace finished. But when he sought his slave to reward him, and sought him in vain, he realized that he had had dealings with an angel. Elijah meantime repaired to the man who had sold him, and related his story to him, that he might know he had not cheated the purchaser out of his price; on the contrary, he had enriched him, since the palace was worth a hundred times more than the money paid for the pretended slave.

A similar thing happened to a well-to-do man who lost his fortune, and became so poor that he had to do manual labor in the field of another. Once, when he was at work, he was accosted by Elijah, who had assumed the appearance of an Arab: "Thou art destined to enjoy seven good years. When dost thou want them now, or as the closing years of thy life?" The man replied: "Thou art a wizard; go in peace, I have nothing for thee." Three times the same question was put, three times the same reply was given. Finally the man said: "I shall ask the advice of my wife." When Elijah came again, and repeated his question, the man, following the counsel of his wife, said: "See to it that seven good years come to us at once." Elijah replied: "Go home. Before thou crossest thy threshold, thy good fortune will have filled thy house." And so it was. His children had found a treasure in the ground, and, as he was about to enter his house, his wife met him and reported the lucky find. His wife was an estimable, pious woman, and she said to her husband: "We shall enjoy seven good years. Let us use this time to practice as much charity as possible; perhaps God will lengthen out our period of prosperity." After the lapse of seven years, during which man and wife used every opportunity of doing good, Elijah appeared again, and announced to the man that the time had come to take away what he had given him. The man responded: "When I accepted thy gift, it was after consultation with my wife. I should not like to return it without first acquainting her with what is about to happen." His wife charged him to say to the old man who had come to resume possession of his property: "If thou canst find any who will be more conscientious stewards of the pledges entrusted to us than we have been, I shall willingly yield them up to thee." God recognized that these people had made a proper use of their wealth, and He granted it to them as a perpetual possession.

If Elijah was not able to lighten the poverty of the pious, he at least sought to inspire them with hope and confidence. Rabbi Akiba, the great scholar, lived in dire poverty before he became the famous Rabbi. His rich father-in-law would have nothing to do with him or his wife, because the daughter had married Akiba against her father's will. On a bitter cold winter night, Akiba could offer his wife, who had been accustomed to the luxuries wealth can buy, nothing but straw as a bed to sleep upon, and he tried to comfort her with assurances of his love for the privations she was suffering. At that moment Elijah appeared before their hut, and cried out in supplicating tones: "O good people, give me, I pray you, a little bundle of straw. My wife has been delivered of a child, and I am so poor I haven't even enough straw to make a bed for her." Now Abika could console his wife with the fact that their own misery was not so great as it might have been, and thus Elijah had attained his end, to sustain the courage of the pious.

In the form of an Arab, he once appeared before a very poor man, whose piety equalled his poverty. He gave him two shekels. These two coins brought him such good fortune that he attained great wealth. But in his zeal to gather worldly treasures, he had no time for deeds of piety and charity. Elijah again appeared before him and took away the two shekels. In a short time the man was as poor as before. A third time Elijah came to him. He was crying bitterly and complaining of his misfortune, and the prophet said: "I shall make thee rich once more, if thou wilt promise me under oath thou wilt not let wealth ruin they character." He promised, the two shekels were restored to him, he regained his wealth, and he remained in possession of it for all time, because his piety was not curtailed by his riches.

Poverty was not the only form of distress Elijah relieved. He exercised the functions of a physician upon Rabbi Shimi bar Ashi, who had swallowed a noxious reptile. Elijah appeared to him as an awe-inspiring horseman, and forced him to apply the preventives against the disease to be expected in these circumstances.

He also cured Rabbi Judah ha-Nasi of long-continued toothache by laying his hand on the sufferer, and at the same time he brought about the reconciliation of Rabbi Judan with Rabbi Hayyah, whose form he had assumed. Rabbi Judah paid the highest respect to Rabbi Hayyah after he found out that Elijah had considered him worthy of taking his appearance.

On another occasion, Elijah re-established harmony between a husband and his wife. The woman had come home very late on Friday evening, having allowed herself to be detained by the sermon preached by Rabbi Meir. Her autocratic husband swore she should not enter the house until she had spat in the very face of the highly-esteemed Rabbi. Meantime Elijah went to Rabbi Meir, and told him a pious woman had fallen into a sore predicament on his account. To help the poor woman, the Rabbi restored to a ruse. He announced that he was looking for one who knew how to cast spells, which was done by spitting into the eye of the afflicted one. When he caught sight of the woman designated by Elijah, he asked her to try her power upon him. Thus she was able to comply with her husband's requirement without disrespect to the Rabbi; and through the instrumentality of Elijah conjugal happiness was restored to an innocent wife.

Elijah's versatility is shown in the following occurrence. A pious man bequeathed a spice-garden to his three sons. They took turns in guarding it against thieves. The first night the oldest son watched the garden. Elijah appeared to him and asked him: "My son, what wilt thou have knowledge of the Torah, or great wealth, or a beautiful wife?" He chose wealth, great wealth. Accordingly Elijah gave him a coin, and he became rich. The second son, to whom Elijah appeared the second night, chose knowledge of the Torah. Elijah gave him a book, and "he knew the whole Torah." The third son, on the third night, when Elijah put the same choice before him as before his brothers, wished for a beautiful wife. Elijah invited this third brother to go on a journey with him. Their first night was passed at the house of a notorious villain, who had a daughter. During the night Elijah overheard the chickens and the geese say to one another: "What a terrible sin that young may must have committed, that he should be destined to marry the daughter of so great a villain!" The two travellers journeyed on. The second night the experiences of the first were repeated. The third night they lodged with a man who had a very pretty daughter. During the night Elijah heard the chickens and the geese say to one another: "How great must be the virtues of this young man, if he is privileged to marry so beautiful and pious a wife." In the morning, when Elijah arose, he at once became a matchmaker, the young man married the pretty maiden, and husband and wife journeyed homeward in joy.

If it became necessary, Elijah was ready to do even the services of a sexton. When Rabbi Akiba died in prison, Elijah betook himself to the dead man's faithful disciple, Rabbi Joshua, and the two together went to the prison. There was none to forbid their entrance; a deep sleep had fallen upon the turnkeys and the prisoners alike. Elijah and Rabbi Joshua took the corpse with them, Elijah bearing it upon his shoulder. Rabbi Joshua in astonishment demanded how he, a priest, dared defile himself upon a corpse. The answer was: "God forbid! the pious can never cause defilement." All night the two walked on with their burden. At break of day they found themselves near Caesarea. A cave opened before their eyes, and within they saw a bed, a chair, a table, and a lamp. They deposited the corpse upon the bed, and left the cave, which closed up behind them. Only the light of the lamp, which had lit itself after they left, shone through the chinks. Whereupon Elijah said: "Hail, ye just, hail to you who devote yourselves to the study of the law. Hail to you, ye God-fearing men, for your places are set aside, and kept, and guarded, in Paradise, for the time to come. Hail to thee, Rabbi Akiba, that thy lifeless body found lodgment for a night in a lovely spot."

CENSOR AND AVENGER

Helpfulness and compassion do not paint the whole of the character of Elijah. He remained the stern and inexorable censor whom Ahab feared. The old zeal for the true and the good he never lost, as witness, he once struck a man dead because he failed to perform his devotions with due reverence.

There were two brothers, one of them rich and miserly, the other poor and kind-hearted. Elijah, in the garb of an old beggar, approached the rich man, and asked him for alms. Repulsed by him, he turned to the poor brother, who received him kindly, and shared his meagre supper with him. On bidding farewell to him and his equally hospitable wife, Elijah said: "May God reward you! The first thing you undertake shall be blessed, and shall take no end until you yourselves cry out Enough!" Presently the poor man began to count the few pennies he had, to convince himself that they sufficed to purchase bread for his next meal. But the few became many, and he counted and counted, and still their number increased. He counted a whole day, and the following night, until he was exhausted, and had to cry out Enough! And, indeed, it was enough, for he had become a very wealthy man. His brother was not a little astonished to see the fortunate change in his kinsman's circumstances, and when he heard how it had come about, he determined, if the opportunity should present itself again, to show his most amiable side to the old beggar with the miraculous power of blessing. He had not long to wait. A few days later he saw the old man pass by. He hastened to accost him, and, excusing himself for his unfriendliness at their former meeting, begged him to come into his house. All that the larder afforded was put before Elijah, who pretended to eat of the dainties. At his departure, he pronounced a blessing upon his hosts: "May the first thing you do have no end, until it is enough." The mistress of the house thereupon said to her husband: "That we may count gold upon gold undisturbed, let us first attend to our most urgent physical needs." So they did and they had to continue to do it until life was extinct.

The extreme of his rigor Elijah displayed toward teachers of the law. From them he demanded more than obedience to the mere letter of a commandment. For instance, he pronounced severe censure upon Rabbi Ishmael ben Jose because he was willing to act as bailiff in prosecuting Jewish thieves and criminals. He advised Rabbi Ishmael to follow the example of his father and leave the country.

His estrangement from his friend Rabbi Joshua ben Levi is characteristic. One who was sought by the officers of the law took refuge with Rabbi Joshua. His pursuers were informed of his place of concealment. Threatening to put all the inhabitants of the city to the sword if he was not delivered up, they demanded his surrender. The Rabbi urged the fugitive from justice to resign himself to his fate. Better for one individual to die, he said, than for a whole community to be exposed to peril. The fugitive yielded to the Rabbi's argument, and gave himself up to the bailiffs. Thereafter Elijah, who had been in the habit of visiting Rabbi Joshua frequently, stayed away from his house, and he was induced to come back only by the Rabbi's long fasts and earnest prayers. In reply to the Rabbi's question, why he had shunned him, he said: "Dost thou suppose I care to have intercourse with informers?" The Rabbi quoted a passage from the Mishnah to justify his conduct, but Elijah remained unconvinced. "Dost thou consider this a law for a pious man?" he said. "Other people might have been right in doing as thou didst; thou shouldst have done otherwise."

A number of instances are known which show how exalted a standard Elijah set up for those who would be considered worthy of intercourse with him. Of two pious brothers, one provided for his servants as for his own table, while the other permitted his servants to eat abundantly only of the first course; of the other courses they could have nothing but the remnants. Accordingly, with the second brother Elijah would have nothing to do, while he often honored the former with his visits.

A similar attitude Elijah maintained toward another pair of pious brothers. One of them was in the habit of providing for his servants after his own needs were satisfied, while the other of them attended to the needs of his servants first. To the latter it was that Elijah gave the preference.

He dissolved an intimacy of many years' standing, because his friend built a vestibule which was so constructed that the supplications of the poor could be heard but faintly by those within the house.

Rabbi Joshua ben Levi incurred the displeasure of Elijah a second time, because a man was torn in pieces by a lion in the vicinity of his house. In a measure Elijah held Rabbi responsible, because he did not pray for the prevention of such misfortunes.

The story told of Elijah and Rabbi Anan forms the most striking illustration of the severity of the prophet. Someone brought Rabbi Anan a mess of little fish as a present, and at the same time asked the Rabbi to act as judge in a lawsuit he was interested in. Anan refused in these circumstances to accept a gift from the litigant. To demonstrate his single-mindedness, the applicant urged the Rabbit to take the fish and assign the case to another judge. Anan acquiesced, and he requested one of his colleagues to act for him, because he was incapacitated from serving as a judge. His legal friend drew the inference, that the litigant introduced to him was a kinsman of Rabbi Anan's, and accordingly he showed himself particularly complaisant toward him. As a result, the other party to the suit was intimidated. He failed to present his side as convincingly as he might otherwise have done, and so lost the case. Elijah, who had been the friend of Anan and his teacher as well, thenceforth shunned his presence, because he considered that the injury done the second party to the suit was due to Anan's carelessness. Anan in his distress kept many fasts, and offered up many prayers, before Elijah would return to him. Even then the Rabbi could not endure the sight of him; he had to content himself with listening to Elijah's words without looking upon his face.

Sometimes Elijah considered it his duty to force people into abandoning a bad habit. A rich man was once going to a cattle sale, and he carried a snug sum of money to buy oxen. He was accosted by a stranger none other than Elijah who inquired the purpose of his journey. "I go to buy cattle," replied the would-be purchaser. "Say, it if please God," urged Elijah. "Fiddlesticks! I shall buy cattle whether it please God or not! I carry the money with me, and the business will be dispatched." "But not with good fortune," said the stranger, and went off. Arrived at the market, the cattle-buyer discovered the loss of his purse, and he had to return home to provide himself with other money. He again set forth on his journey, but this time he took another road to avoid the stranger of ill omen. To his amazement he met an old man with whom he had precisely the same adventure as with the first stranger. Again he had to return home to fetch money. By this time had learned his lesson. When a third stranger questioned him about the object of his journey, he answered: "If it please God, I intend to buy oxen." The stranger wished him success, and the wish was fulfilled. To the merchant's surprise, when a pair of fine cattle were offered him, and their price exceeded the sum of money he had about his person, he found the two purses he had lost on his first and second trips. Later he sold the same pair of oxen to the king for a considerable price, and he became very wealthy.

As Elijah coerced this merchant into humility toward God, so he carried home a lesson to the great Tanna Eliezer, the son of Rabbi Simon ben Yohai. This Rabbi stood in need of correction on account of his overweening conceit. Once, on returning from the academy, he took a walk on the sea-beach, his bosom swelling with pride at the thought of his attainments in the Torah. He met a hideously ugly man, who greeted him with the words: "Peace be with thee, Rabbi." Eliezer, instead of courteously acknowledging the greeting, said: "O thou wight, how ugly thou art! Is it possible that all the residents of thy town are as ugly as thou?" "I know not," was the reply, "but it is the Master Artificer who created me that thou shouldst have said: 'How ugly is this vessel which Thou hast fashioned.'" The Rabbi realized the wrong he had committed, and humbly begged pardon of the ugly man another of the protean forms adopted by Elijah. The latter continued to refer him to the Master Artificer of the ugly vessel. The inhabitants of the city, who had hastened to do honor to the great Rabbi, earnestly urged the offended man to grant pardon, and finally he declared himself appeased, provided the Rabbi promised never again to commit the same wrong.

The rigor practiced by Elijah toward his friends caused one of them, the Tanna Rabbi Jose, to accuse him of being passionate and irascible. As a consequence, Elijah would have nothing to do with him for a long time. When he reappeared, and confessed the cause of his withdrawal, Rabbi Jose said he felt justified, for his charge could not have received a more striking verification.

INTERCOURSE WITH THE SAGES

Elijah's purely human relations to the world revealed themselves in their fulness, neither in his deeds of charity, nor in his censorious rigor, but rather in his gentle and scholarly intercourse with the great in Israel, especially the learned Rabbis of the Talmudic time. He is at once their disciple and their teacher. To one he resorts for instruction on difficult points, to another he himself dispenses instruction. As a matter of course, his intimate knowledge of the supernatural world makes him appear more frequently in the role of giver than receiver. Many a bit of secret lore the Jewish teachers learnt from Elijah, and he it was who, with the swiftness of lightning, carried the teachings of one Rabbi to another sojourning hundreds of miles away.

Thus it was Elijah who taught Rabbi Jose the deep meaning hidden in the Scriptural passage in which woman is designated as the helpmeet of man. By means of examples he demonstrated to the Rabbi how indispensable woman is to man.

Rabbi Nehorai profited by his exposition of why God created useless, even noxious insects. The reason for their existence is that the sight of superfluous and harmful creatures prevents God from destroying His world at times when, on account of the wickedness and iniquity prevailing in it, it repents Him of having created it. If He preserves creatures that at their best are useless, and at their worst injurious, how much more should He preserve human beings with all their potentialities for good.

The same Rabbi Nehorai was told by Elijah, that God sends earthquakes and other destructive phenomena when He sees places of amusement prosperous and flourishing, while the Temple lies a heap of dust and ashes.

To Rabbi Judah he communicated the following three maxims: Let not anger master thee, and thou wilt not fall into sin; let not drink master thee, and thou wilt be spared pain; before thou settest out on a journey, take counsel with thy Creator.

In case of a difference of opinion among scholars, Elijah was usually questioned as to how the moot point was interpreted in the heavenly academy. Once, when the scholars were not unanimous in their views as to Esther's intentions when she invited Haman to her banquets with the king, Elijah, asked by Rabba bar Abbahu to tell him her real purpose, said that each and every one of the motives attributed to her by various scholars were true, for her invitations to Haman had many a purpose.

A similar answer he gave the Amora Abiathar, who disputed with his colleagues as to why the Ephraimite who cause the war against the tribe of Benjamin first cast off his concubine, and then became reconciled to her. Elijah informed Rabbi Abiathar that in heaven the cruel conduct of the Ephraimite was explained in two ways, according to Abiathar's conception and according to his opponent Jonathan's as well.

Regarding the great contest between Rabbi Eliezer ben Hyrcanus and the whole body of scholars, in which the majority maintained the validity of its opinion, though a heavenly voice pronounced Rabbi Eliezer's correct, Elijah told Rabbi Nathan, that God in His heaven had cried out: "My children have prevailed over Me!"

On one occasion Elijah fared badly for having betrayed celestial events to his scholars. He was a daily attendant at the academy of Rabbi Judah ha-Nasi. One day, it was the New Moon Day, he was late. The reason for his tardiness, he said, was that it was his daily duty to awaken the three Patriarchs, wash their hands for them, so that they might offer up their prayers, and after their devotions lead them back to their resting-places. On this day their prayers took very long, because they were increased by the Musaf service on account of the New Moon celebration, and hence he did not make his appearance at the academy in good time. Elijah did not end his narrative at this point, but went on to tell the Rabbi, that this occupation of his was rather tedious, for the three Patriarchs were not permitted to offer up their payers at the same time. Abraham prayed first, then came Isaac, and finally Jacob. If they all were to pray together, the united petitions of three such paragons of piety would be so efficacious as to force God to fulfil them, and He would be induced to bring the Messiah before his time. Then Rabbi Judah wanted to know whether there were any among the pious on earth whose prayer possessed equal efficacy. Elijah admitted that the same power resided in the prayers of Rabbi Hayyah and his two sons. Rabbi Judah lost no time in proclaiming a day of prayer and fasting and summoning Rabbi Hayyah and his sons to officiate as the leaders in prayer. They began to chant the Eighteen Benedictions. Then they uttered the word for wind, a storm arose; when they continued and made petition for rain, the rain descended at once. But as the readers approached the passage relating to the revival of the dead, great excitement arose in heaven, and when it became known that Elijah had revealed the secret of the marvellous power attaching to the prayers of the three men, he was punished with fiery blows. To thwart Rabbi Judah's purpose, Elijah assumed the form of a bear, and put the praying congregation to flight.

Contrariwise, Elijah was also in the habit of reporting earthly events in the celestial regions. He told Rabba bar Shila that the reason Rabbi Meir was never quoted in the academy on high was because he had had so wicked a teacher as Elisha ben Abuyah. Rabba explained Rabbi Meir's conduct by an apologue. "Rabbi Meir," he said, "found a pomegranate; he enjoyed the heart of the fruit, and cast the skin aside." Elijah was persuaded of the justness of this defense, and so were all the celestial powers. Thereupon one of Rabbi Meir's interpretations was quoted in the heavenly academy.

Elijah was no less interested in the persons of the learned than in their teachings, especially when scholars were to be provided with the means of devoting themselves to their studies. It was he who, when Rabbi Eliezer ben Hyrcanus, later a great celebrity, resolved to devote himself to the law, advised him to repair to Jerusalem and sit at the feet of Rabban Johanan ben Zakkai.

He once met a man who mocked at his exhortations to study, and he said that on the great day of reckoning he would excuse himself for his neglect of intellectual pursuits by the fact that he had been granted neither intelligence nor wisdom. Elijah asked him what his calling was. "I am a fisherman," was the reply. "Well, my son," questioned Elijah, "who taught thee to take flax and make nets and throw them into the sea to catch fish?" He replied: "For this heaven gave me intelligence and insight." Hereupon Elijah: "If thou possessest intelligence and insight to cast nets and catch fish, why should these qualities desert thee when thou dealest with the Torah, which, thou knowest, is very nigh unto man that he may do it?" The fisherman was touched, and he began to weep. Elijah pacified him by telling him that what he had said applied to many another beside him.

In another way Elijah conveyed the lesson of the great value residing in devotion to the study of the Torah. Disguised as a Rabbi, he was approached by a man who promised to relieve him of all material cares if he would but abide with him. Refusing to leave Jabneh, the centre of Jewish scholarship, he said to the tempter: "Wert thou to offer me a thousand million gold denarii, I would not quit the abode of the law, and dwell in a place in which there is no Torah."

By Torah, of course, is meant the law as conceived and interpreted by the sages and the scholars, for Elijah was particularly solicitous to establish the authority of the oral law, as he was solicitous to demonstrate the truth of Scriptural promises that appeared incredible at first sight. For instance, he once fulfilled Rabbi Joshua ben Levi's wish to see the precious stones which would take the place of the sun in illuminating Jerusalem in the Messianic time. A vessel in mid-ocean was nigh unto shipwreck. Among a large number of heathen passengers there was a single Jewish youth. To him Elijah appeared and said, he would rescue the vessel, provided the boy went to Rabbi Joshua ben Levi, and took him to a certain place far removed from the town and from human habitation, and showed him the gems. The boy doubted that so great a man would consent to follow a mere slip of a youth to a remote spot, but, reassured by Elijah, who told him of Rabbi Joshua's extraordinary modesty, he undertook the commission, and the vessel with its human freight was saved. The boy came to the Rabbi, besought him to go whither he would lead, and Joshua, who was really possessed of great modesty, followed the boy three miles without even inquiring the purpose of the expedition. When they finally reached the cave, the boy said: "See, here are the precious stones!" The Rabbi grasped them, and a flood of light spread as far as Lydda, the residence of Rabbi Joshua. Startled, he cast the precious stones away from him, and they disappeared.

This Rabbi was a particular favorite of Elijah, who even secured him an interview with the Messiah. The Rabbi found the Messiah among the crowd of afflicted poor gathered near the city gates of Rome, and he greeted him with the words: "Peace be with thee, my teacher and guide!" Whereunto the Messiah replied: "Peace be with thee, thou son of Levi!" The Rabbi then asked him when he would appear, and the Messiah said, "To-day." Elijah explained to the Rabbi later that what the Messiah meant by "to-day" was, that he for his part was ready to bring Israel redemption at any time. If Israel but showed himself worthy, he would instantly fufil his mission.

Elijah wanted to put Rabbi Joshua into communication with the departed Rabbi Simon ben Yohai also, but the later did not consider him of sufficient importance to honor him with his conversation. Rabbi Simon had addressed a question to him, and Rabbi Joshua in his modesty had made a reply not calculated to give one a high opinion of him. In reality Rabbi Joshua was the possessor of such sterling qualities, that when he entered Paradise Elijah walked before him calling out: "Make room for the son of Levi."

GOD'S JUSTICE VINDICATED

Among the many and various teachings dispensed by Elijah to his friends, there are none so important as his theodicy, the teachings vindicating God's justice in the administration of earthly affairs. He used many an opportunity to demonstrate it by precept and example. Once he granted his friend Rabbi Joshua ben Levi the fulfilment of any wish he might express, and all the Rabbi asked for was, that he might be permitted to accompany Elijah on his wanderings through the world. Elijah was prepared to gratify this wish. He only imposed the condition, that, however odd the Rabbi might think Elijah's actions, he was not to ask any explanation of them. If ever he demanded why, they would have to part company. So Elijah and the Rabbi fared forth together, and they journeyed on until they reached the house of a poor man, whose only earthly possession was a cow. The man and his wife were thoroughly good-hearted people, and they received the two wanderers with a cordial welcome. They invited the strangers into their house, set before them food and drink of the best they had, and made up a comfortable couch for them for the night. When Elijah and the Rabbi were ready to continue their journey on the following day, Elijah prayed that the cow belonging to his host might die. Before they left the house, the animal had expired. Rabbi Joshua was so shocked by the misfortune that had befallen the good people, he almost lost consciousness. He thought: "Is that to be the poor man's reward for all his kind services to us?" And he could not refrain from putting the question to Elijah. But Elijah reminded him of the condition imposed and accepted at the beginning of their journey, and they travelled on, the Rabbi's curiosity unappeased. That night they reached the house of a wealthy man, who did not pay his guest the courtesy of looking them in the face. Though they passed the night under his roof, he did not offer them food or drink. This rich man was desirous of having a wall repaired that had tumbled down. There was no need for him to take any steps to have it rebuilt, for, when Elijah left the house, he prayed that the wall might erect itself, and, lo! it stood upright. Rabbi Joshua was greatly amazed, but true to his promise he suppressed the question that rose to his lips. So the two travelled on again, until they reached an ornate synagogue, the seats in which were made of silver and gold. But the worshippers did not correspond in character to the magnificence of the building, for when it came to the point of satisfying the needs of the way-worn pilgrims, one of those present said: "There is not dearth of water and bread, and the strange travellers can stay in the synagogue, whither these refreshments can be brought to them." Early the next morning, when they were departing, Elijah wished those present in the synagogue in which they had lodged, that God might raise them all to be "heads." Rabbi Joshua again had to exercise great self-restraint, and not put into words the question that troubled him profoundly. In the next town, they were received with great affability, and served abundantly with all their tired bodies craved. On these kind hosts Elijah, on leaving, bestowed the wish that God might give them but a single head. Now the Rabbi could not hold himself in check any longer, and he demanded an explanation of Elijah's freakish actions. Elijah consented to clear up his conduct for Joshua before they separated from each other. He spoke as follows: "The poor man's cow was killed, because I knew that on the same day the death of his wife had been ordained in heaven, and I prayed to God to accept the loss of the poor man's property as a substitute for the poor man's wife. As for the rich man, there was a treasure hidden under the dilapidated wall, and, if he had rebuilt it, he would have found the gold; hence I set up the wall miraculously in order to deprive the curmudgeon of the valuable find. I wished that the inhospitable people assembled in the synagogue might have many heads, for a place of numerous leaders is bound to be ruined by reason of multiplicity of counsel and disputes. To the inhabitants of our last sojourning place, on the other hand, I wished a 'single head,' for the one to guide a town, success will attend all its undertakings. Know, then, that if thou seest an evil-doer prosper, it is not always unto his advantage, and if a righteous man suffers need and distress, think not God is unjust." After these words Elijah and Rabbi Joshua separated from each other, and each went his own way.

How difficult it is to form a true judgment with nothing but external appearances as a guide, Elijah proved to Rabbi Baroka. They were once waling in a crowded street, and the Rabbi requested Elijah to point out any in the throng destined to occupy places in Paradise. Elijah answered that there was none, only to contradict himself and point to a passer-by the very next minute. His appearance was such that in him least of all the Rabbi would have suspected a pious man. His garb did not even indicate that he was a Jew. Later Rabbi Baroka discovered by questioning him that he was a prison guard. In the fulfilment of his duties as such he was particularly careful that the virtue of chastity should not be violated in the prison, in which both men women were kept in detention. Also, his position often brought him into relations with the heathen authorities, and so he was enabled to keep the Jews informed of the disposition entertained toward them by the powers that be. The Rabbi was thus taught that no station in life precluded its occupant from doing good and acting nobly.

Another time Elijah designated two men to whom a great future was assigned in Paradise. Yet these men were nothing more than clowns! They made it their purpose in life to dispel discontent and sorrow by their jokes and their cheery humor, and they used the opportunities granted by their profession to adjust the difficulties and quarrels that disturb the harmony of people living in close contact with each other.

ELIJAH AND THE ANGEL OF DEATH

Among the many benevolent deeds of Elijah, special mention ought to be made of his rescue of those doomed by a heavenly decree to fall into the clutches of the Angel of Death. He brought these rescues about by warning the designated victims of their impending fate, and urging them to do good deeds, which would prove protection against death.

There was once a pious and rich man with a beautiful and saintly daughter. She had had the misfortune of losing three husbands in succession, each on the day after the wedding. These sorrows determined her never again to enter into the marriage state. A cousin of hers, the nephew of her father, induced by the poverty of his parents, journeyed from his distant home to apply for help to his rich uncle. Scarcely had he laid eyes upon his lovely cousin when he fell victim to her charms. In vain her father sought to dissuade his nephew from marrying his daughter. But the fate of his predecessors did not affright him, and the wedding took place. While he was standing under the wedding canopy, Elijah came to him in the guise of an old man, and said: "My son, I want to give thee a piece of advice. While thou are seated at the wedding dinner, thou wilt be approached by a ragged, dirty beggar, with hair like nails. As soon as thou catchest sight of him, hasten to seat him beside thee, set food and drink before him, and be ready to grant whatever he may ask of thee. Do as I say, and thou wilt be protected against harm. Now I shall leave thee and go my way." At the wedding feast, a stranger as described by Elijah appeared, and the bridegroom did according to Elijah's counsel. After the wedding the stranger revealed his identity, introducing himself as the messenger of the Lord sent to take the young husband's life. The supplications of the bridegroom failed to move him; he refused to grant a single day's respite. All he yielded was permission to the young husband to bid farewell to his newly-wed wife. When the bride saw that what she had feared was coming to pass, she repaired to the Angel of Death and argued with him: "The Torah distinctly exempts the newly-wed from all duties for a whole year. If thou deprivest my husband of life, thou wilt give the lie to the Torah." Thereupon God commanded the Angel of

Death to desist, and, when the relatives of the bride came to prepare the grave of the groom, they found him well and unharmed.

A similar thing befell the son of the great and extremely pious scholar Rabbi Reuben. To him came the Angel of Death and announced that his only son would have to die. The pious man was resigned: "We mortals can do nothing to oppose a Divine decree," he said, "but I pray there, give him thirty days' respite, that I may see him married." The Angel of Death acquiesced. The Rabbi told no one of this encounter, waited until the appointed time was drawing to a close, and, on the very last day, the thirtieth, he arranged his son's wedding feast. On that day, the bridegroom-to-be met Elijah, who told him of his approaching death. A worthy son of his father, he said: "Who may oppose God? And am I better than Abraham, Isaac, and Jacob? They, too, had to die." Elijah told him furthermore, that the Angel of Death would appear to him in the guise of a ragged, dirty beggar, and he advised him to receive him in the kindliest possible manner, and in particular he was to insist upon his taking food and drink from him. All happened as Elijah had predicted, and his advice, too, proved efficacious, for the heart of the Angel of Death, who finally revealed his identity with the beggar, was softened by the entreaties of the father, combined with the tears of the young wife, who resorted to the argument cited above, of the year of exemption from duty granted to the newly-married. The Angel of Death, disarmed by the amiable treatment accorded to him, himself went before the throne of God and presented the young wife's petition. The end was God added seventy years to the life of Rabbi Reuben's son.

TEACHER OF THE KABBALAH

The frequent meetings between Elijah and the teachers of the law of the Talmudic time were invested with personal interest only. Upon the development of the Torah they had no influence whatsoever. His relation to the mystic science was of quite other character. It is safe to say that what Moses was to the Torah, Elijah was to the Kabbalah.

His earliest relation to it was established through Rabbi Simon ben Yohai and his son Rabbi Eliezer. For thirteen years he visited them twice daily in their subterranean hiding-place, and imparted the secrets of the Torah to them. A thousand years later, Elijah again gave the impetus to the development of the Kabbalah, for it was he that revealed mysteries, first to the Nazarite Rabbi Jacob, then to his disciple of the latter, Abraham ben David. The mysteries in the books "Peliah" and "Kanah," the author Elkanah owed wholly to Elijah. He had appeared to him in the form of a venerable old man, and had imparted to him the secret lore taught in the heavenly academy. Besides, he led him to a fiery rock whereon mysterious characters were engraved, which were deciphered by Elkanah.

After his disciple had thus become thoroughly impregnated with mystical teachings, Elijah took him to the tomb of the Patriarchs, and thence to the heavenly academy. But the angels, little pleased by the intrusion of one "born of woman," inspired him with such terror that he besought Elijah to carry him back to earth. His mentor allayed his fears, and long continued to instruct him in the mystical science, according to the system his disciple has recorded in his two works.

The Kabbalists in general were possessed of the power to cite Elijah, to conjure him up by means of certain formulas. One of them, Rabbi Joseph della Reyna, once called upon Elijah in this way, but it proved his own undoing. He was a saintly scholar, and he had conceived no less a purpose than to bring about the redemption of man by the conquest of the angel Samael, the Prince of Evil. After many prayers and vigils and long indulgence in fasting, and other ascetic practices, Rabbi Joseph united himself with his five disciples for the purpose of conjuring up Elijah. When the prophet, obeying the summons, suddenly stood before him, Rabbi Joseph spoke as follows: "Peace be with thee, our master! True prophet, bearer of salvation, be not displeased with me that I have troubled thee to come hither. God knows, I have not done it for myself, and not for mine own honor. I am zealous for the name and the honor of God, and I know thy desire is the same as mine, for it is thy vocation to make the glory of God to prevail on earth. I pray thee, therefore, to grant my petition, tell me with what means I can conquer Satan." Elijah at first endeavored to dissuade the Rabbi from his enterprise. He described the great power of Satan, ever growing as it feeds upon the sins of mankind. But Rabbi Joseph could not be made to desist. Elijah then enumerated what measures and tactics he would have to observe in his combat with the fallen angel. He enumerated the pious, saintly deeds that would win the interest of the archangel Sandalphon in his undertaking, and from this angel he would learn the method of warfare to be pursued. The Rabbi followed out Elijah's directions carefully, and succeeded in summoning Sandalphon to his assistance. If he had continued to obey instructions implicitly, and had carried out all Sandalphon advised, the Rabbi would have triumphed over Satan and hastened the redemption of the world. Unfortunately, at one point the Rabbi committed an indiscretion, and he lost the great advantages he had gained over Satan, who used his restored power to bring ruin upon him and his disciples.

The radical transformation in the character of Kabbalistic teaching which is connected with the name of Rabbi Isaac Loria likewise is an evidence of Elijah's activity. Elijah sought out this "father of the Kabbalistic Renaissance," and revealed the mysteries of the universe to him. Indeed, he had shown his interest in him long before any one suspected the future greatness of Rabbi Isaac. Immediately after his birth, Elijah appeared to the father of the babe, and enjoined him not to have the rite of circumcision performed until he should be told by Elijah to proceed. The eighth day of the child's life arrived, the whole congregation was assembled at the synagogue to witness the solemn ceremonial, but to the great astonishment of his fellow-townsmen the father delayed it. The people naturally did not know he was waiting for Elijah to appear, and he was called upon once and again to have the ceremony take place. But he did not permit the impatience of the company to turn him from his purpose. Suddenly, Elijah, unseen, of course, by the others, appeared to him, and bade him have the ceremony performed. Those present were under the impression that the father was holding the child on his knees during the circumcision; in reality, however it was Elijah. After the rite was completed, Elijah handed the infant back to the father with the words: "Here is thy child. Take good care of it, for it will spread a brilliant light over the world."

It was also Elijah who in a similar way informed Rabbi Eliezer, the father of Rabbi Israel Baal Shem Tob, the father of him whose name is unrivalled in the annals of the Hasidic Kabbalah that a son would be born to him who should enlighten the eyes of Israel. This Rabbi Eliezer was justly reputed to be very hospitable. He was in the habit of stationing guards at the entrances to the village in which he lived, and they were charged to bring all strangers to his house. In heaven it was ordained that Rabbi Eliezer's hospitable instincts should be put to a test. Elijah was chosen for the experiment. On a Sabbath afternoon, arrayed in the garb of a beggar, he entered the village with knapsack and staff. Rabbi Eliezer, taking no notice of the fact that the beggar was desecrating the Sabbath, received him kindly, attended to his bodily wants, and the next morning, on parting with him, gave him some money besides. Touched by his kind-heartedness, Elijah revealed his identity and the purpose of his disguise, and told him that, as he had borne the trial so well, he would be rewarded by the birth of a son who should "enlighten the eyes of Israel."

FORERUNNER OF THE MESSIAH

Many-sided though Elijah's participation in the course of historical events is, it cannot be compared with what he is expected to do in the days of the Messiah. He is charged with the mission of ordering the coming time aright and restoring the tribes of Jacob. His Messianic activity thus is to be twofold: he is to be the forerunner of the Messiah, yet in part he will himself realize the promised scheme of salvation. His first task will be to induce Israel to repent when the Messiah is about to come, and to establish peace and harmony in the world. Hence he will have to settle all legal difficulties, and solve all legal problems, that have accumulated since days immemorial, and decide vexed questions of ritual concerning which authors entertain contradictory views. In short, all difference of opinion must be removed from the path of the Messiah. This office of expounder of the law Elijah will continue to occupy even after the reign of peace has been established on earth, and his relation to Moses will be the same Aaron once held.

Elijah's preparatory work will be begun three days before the advent of the Messiah. Then he will appear in Palestine, and will utter a lament over the devastation of the Holy Land, and his wail will be heard throughout the world. The last words of his elegy will be: "Now peace will come upon earth!" When the evil-doers hear this message, they will rejoice. On the second day, he will appear again and proclaim: "Good will come upon earth!" And on the third his promise will be heard: "Salvation will come upon earth." Then Michael will blow the trumpet, and once more Elijah will make his appearance, this time to introduce the Messiah. To make sure of the identity of the Messiah, the Jews will demand that he perform the miracle of resurrection before their eyes, reviving such of the dead as they had known personally. But the Messiah will do the following seven wonders: He will bring Moses and the generation of the desert to life; Korah and his band he will raise from out of the earth; he will revive the Ephraimitic Messiah, who was slain; he will show the three holy vessels of the Temple, the Ark, the flask of manna, and the cruse of sacred oil, all three of which disappeared mysteriously; he will wave the sceptre given him by God; he will grind the mountains of the Holy Land into powder like straw, and he will reveal the secret of redemption. Then the Jews will believe that Elijah is the Elijah promised to them, and the Messiah introduced by him is the true Messiah.

The Messiah will have Elijah blow the trumpet, and, at the first sound, the primal light, which shone before the week of Creation, will reappear; at the second sound the dead will arise, and with the swiftness of wind assemble around the Messiah from all corners of the earth; at the third sound, the Shekinah will become visible to all; the mountains will be razed at the fourth sound, and the Temple will stand in complete perfection as Ezekiel described it.

During the reign of peace, Elijah will be one of the eight princes forming the cabinet of the Messiah. Even the coming of the great judgment day will not end his activity. On that day the children of the wicked who had to die in infancy on account of the sins of their fathers will be found among the just, while their fathers will be ranged on the other side. The babes will implore their fathers to come to them, but God will not permit it. Then Elijah will go to the little ones, and teach them how to plead in behalf of their fathers. They will stand before God and say: "Is not the measure of good, the mercy of God, larger than the measure of chastisements? If, then, we died for the sins of our fathers, should they not now for our sakes be granted the good, and be permitted to join us in Paradise?" God will give assent to their pleadings, and Elijah will have fulfilled the word of the prophet Malachi; he will have brought back the fathers to the children.

The last act of Elijah's brilliant career will be the execution of God's command to slay Samael, and so banish evil forever.

Chapter 8

VIII. ELISHA AND JONAH

ELISHA THE DISCIPLE OF ELIJAH

The voices of the thousands of prophets of his time were stilled when Elijah was translated from earth to heaven. With him vanished the prophetical spirit of those who in former times had in no wise been his inferiors. Elisha was the only one among them whose prophetical powers were not diminished. On the contrary, they were strengthened, as a reward for the unhesitating readiness with which he obeyed Elijah's summons, and parted with the field he was ploughing, and with all else he possessed, in favor of the community. Thenceforward he remained Elijah's unwearying companion. When the angel descended from heaven to take Elijah from earth, he found the two so immersed in a learned discussion that he could not attract their attention, and he had to return, his errand unfulfilled.

Elijah's promise to bestow a double portion of his wondrous spirit upon his disciple was realized instantaneously. During his life Elisha performed sixteen miracles, and eight was all his master had performed. The first of them, the crossing of the Jordan, was more remarkable than the corresponding wonder done by Elijah, for Elisha traversed the river alone, and Elijah had been accompanied by Elisha. Two saints always have more power than one by himself.

His second miracle, the "healing" of the waters of Jericho, so that they became fit to drink, resulted in harm to himself, for the people who had earned their livelihood by the sale of wholesome water were very much incensed against the prophet for having spoiled their trade. Elisha, whose prophetic powers enabled him to read both the past and the future of these tradesmen, knew that they, their ancestors, and their posterity had "not even the aroma of good about them." Therefore he cursed them. Suddenly a forest sprang up and the bears that infested it devoured the murmuring traders. The wicked fellows were not undeserving of the punishment they received, yet Elisha was made to undergo a very serious sickness, by way of correction for having yielded to passion. In this he resembled his master Elijah; he allowed wrath and zeal to gain the mastery over him. God desired that the two great prophets might be purged of this fault. Accordingly, when Elisha rebuked King Jehoram of Israel, the spirit of prophecy forsook him, and he had to resort to artificial means to re-awaken it within himself.

Like his teacher, Elisha was always ready to help the poor and needy, as witness his sympathy with the widow of one of the sons of the prophets, and the effective aid he extended to her. Her husband had been none other than Obadiah, who, though a prophet, had at the same time been one of the highest officials at the court of the sinful king Ahab. By birth an Edomite, Obadiah had been inspired by God to utter the prophecy against Edom. In his own person he embodied the accusation against Esau, who had lived with his pious parents without following their example, while Obadiah, on the contrary, lived in constant intercourse with the iniquitous King Ahab and his still more iniquitous spouse Jezebel without yielding to the baneful influence they exercised. This same Obadiah not only used his own fortune, but went to the length of borrowing money on interest from the future king, in order to have the wherewithal to support the prophets who were in hiding. On his death, the king sought to hold the children responsible for the debt of the father. In her despair the pious wife of Obadiah went to the graveyard, and there she cried out: "O thou God-fearing man!" At once a heavenly voice was heard questioning her: "There are four God-fearing men, Abraham, Joseph, Job, and Obadiah. To which of them does thou desire to speak?" "To him of whom it is said, 'He feared the Lord greatly.'"

She was led to the grave of the prophet Obadiah, where she poured out the tale of her sorrow. Obadiah told her to take the small remnant of oil she still had to the prophet Elisha and request him to intercede for him with God, "for God," he said, "is my debtor, seeing that I provided a hundred prophets, not only with bread and water, but also with oil to illuminate their hiding-place, for do not the Scriptures say: 'He that hath pity upon the poor lendeth unto the Lord'?" Forthwith the woman carried out his behest. She went to Elisha, and he helped her by making her little cruse of oil fill vessels upon vessels without number, and when the vessels gave out, she fetched potsherds, saying, "May the will that made empty vessels full, make broken vessels perfect." So it was. The oil ceased to flow only when the supply of potsherds as well as vessels gave out. In her piety the woman wanted to pay her tithe-offering, but Elisha was of the opinion that, as the oil had been bestowed upon her miraculously, she could keep it wholly and entirely for her own use. Furthermore, Elisha reassured her as to the power of the royal princes to do her harm: "The God who will close the jaws of the lions set upon Daniel, and who did close the jaws of the dogs in Egypt, the same God will blind the eyes of the sons of Ahab, and deafen their ears, so that they can do thee no harm." Not only was the poor widow helped out of her difficulties, her descendants unto all times were provided for. The oil rose in price, and it yielded so much profit that they never suffered want.

THE SHUNAMMITE

The great woman of Shunem, the sister of Abishag and wife of the prophet Iddo, also had cause to be deeply grateful to Elisha. When Elisha came to Shunem on his journey through the land of Israel, his holiness made a profound impression upon the Shunammite. Indeed, the prophet's eye was so awe-inspiring that now woman could look him in the face and live. Contrary to the habit of most women, who are intent upon diminishing their expenses and their toil, the Shunammite took delight in the privilege of welcoming the prophet to her house as a guest. She observed that not even a fly dared approach close to the holy man, and a grateful fragrance exhaled from his person. "If he were not so great a saint," she said, "and the holiness of the Lord did not invest him, there were no such pleasant fragrance about him." That he might be undisturbed, she assigned the best chambers in the house to the prophet. He on his part, desiring to show his appreciation of her hospitality, knew no better return for her kindness than to promise that she should be blessed with a child within a year. The woman protested: "O, my husband is an old man, nor am I of an age to bear children; the promise cannot be fulfilled." Yet it happened as the prophet had foretold. Before a twelvemonth had passed, she was a mother.

A few years later her child died a sudden death. The mother repaired to the prophet, and lamented before him: "O that the vessel had remained empty, rather than it should be filled first, and then be left void." The prophet admitted that, though as a rule he was acquainted with all things that were to happen, God had left him in the dark about the misfortune that had befallen her. With trust in God, he gave his staff to his disciple Gehazi, and sent him to bring the boy back to life. But Gehazi was unworthy of his master. His conduct toward the Shunammite was not becoming a disciple of the prophet, and, above all, he had no faith in the possibility of accomplishing the mission entrusted to him. Instead of obeying the behest of Elisha, not to speak a word on his way to the child of the Shunammite, Gehazi made sport of the task laid upon him. To whatever man he met he addressed the questions: "Dost thou suppose this staff can bring the dead back to life?" The result was that he forfeited the power of executing the errand with which he had been charged. Elisha himself had to perform the miracle. The prophet uttered the prayer: "O Lord of the world! As Thou didst wonders through my master Elijah, and didst permit him to bring the dead to life, so, I pray Thee, do Thou perform a wonder through me, and let me restore life to this lad." The prayer was granted, and the child was revived. The act of the prophet proves the duty of gratitude in return for hospitality. Elisha did not attempt to resuscitate his own kith and kin who had been claimed by death; he invoked a miracle for the sake of the woman who had welcomed him kindly to her house.

GEHAZI

Gehazi, proved untrustworthy by his conduct on this occasion, again aroused the ire of the prophet when he disregarded the order not to accept money from Naaman, the Syrian captain. He did not succeed in deceiving the prophet. On his return from Naaman he found Elisha occupied with the study of the chapter in the Mishnah Shabbat which deals with the eight reptiles. The prophet Elisha greeted him with the rebuke: "Thou villain! the time has come for me to be rewarded for the study of the Mishnah about the eight reptiles. May my reward be that the disease of Naaman afflict thee and thy descendants for evermore." Scarcely had these words escaped his lips, when he saw the leprosy come out on Gehazi's face. Gehazi deserved the punishment on account of his base character. He was sensual and envious, and did not believe in the resurrection of the dead. His unworthy qualities were displayed in his conduct toward the Shunammite and toward the disciples of Elisha. When the pretty Shunammite came to the prophet in her grief over the death of her child, Gehazi took her passionately in his arms, under the pretext of forcing her away from the prophet, on whom she had laid hold in her supplications.

As for the other disciples of Elisha, he endeavored to keep them away from the house of the prophet. He was in the habit of standing without the door. This induced many to turn away and go home, for they reasoned that, if the house were not full to overflowing, Gehazi would not be standing outside. Only after Gehazi's dismissal did the disciples of Elisha increase marvellously. That Gehazi had no faith in the resurrection of the dead, is shown by his incredulity with regard to the child of the Shunammite.

In spite of all these faults, Elisha regretted that he had cast off his disciple, who was a great scholar in the law, especially as Gehazi abandoned himself to a sinful life after leaving the prophet. By means of magnetism he made the golden calves at Beth-el float in the air, and many were brought to believe in the divinity of these idols. Moreover, he engraved the great and awful Name of God in their mouth. Thus they were enabled to speak, and they gave forth the same words God had proclaimed from Sinai: "I am the Lord thy God Thou shalt have no other gods before Me." Elisha accordingly repaired to Damascus to lead Gehazi back to the paths of righteousness. But he remained impenitent, for he said: "From thyself I have learned that there is no return for him who not only sins himself, but also induces others to sin." So Gehazi died without having done aught to atone for his transgressions, which were so great that he is one of the few Jews who have no share in Paradise. His children inherited his leprosy. He and his three sons are the four leprous men who informed the king of Israel of the precipitate flight of the Syrian host.

Elisha's excessive severity toward his servant Gehazi and toward the mocking boys of Jericho did not go unpunished. He had to endure two periods of disease, and the third sickness that befell him cause his death. He is the first known to history who survived a sickness. Before him death had been the inevitable companion of disease.

A great miracle marked the end of a life rich in miraculous deeds: a dead man revived at the touch of Elisha's bier, and stood on his feet. It was a worthy character for whom the wonder was accomplished Shallum the son of Tikvah, the husband of Huldah the prophetess, a man of noble descent, who had led a life of lovingkindness. He was in the habit of going daily beyond the city bearing the pitcher of water, from which he gave every traveller to drink, a good deed that received a double reward. His wife became a prophetess, and when he died and his funeral, attended by a large concourse of people, was disturbed by the invasion of the Arameans, he was given new life by contact with the bones of Elisha. He lived to have a son, Hanamel by name.

The death of Elisha was a great misfortune for the Israelites. So long as he was alive, no Aramean troops entered Palestine. The first invasion by them happened on the day of his burial.

THE FLIGHT OF JONAH

Among the many thousands of disciples whom Elisha gathered about him during the sixty years and more of his activity, the most prominent was the prophet Jonah. While the master was still alive, Jonah was charged with the important mission of anointing Jehu king. The next task laid upon him was to proclaim their destruction to the inhabitants of Jerusalem. The doom did not come to pass, because they repented of their wrong-doing, and God had mercy upon them. Among the Israelites Jonah was, therefore, known as "the false prophet." When he was sent to Nineveh to prophesy the downfall of the city, he reflected: "I know to a certainly that the heathen will do penance, the threatened punishment will not be executed, and among the heathen, too, I shall gain the reputation of being a false prophet." To escape this disgrace, he determined to take up his abode on the sea, where there were none to whom prophecies never to be fulfilled would have to be delivered.

On his arrival at Joppa, there was no vessel in port. To try him, God cause a storm to arise, and it carried a vessel back to Joppa, which had made a two days' journey away from the harbor. The prophet interpreted this chance to mean that God approved his plan. He was so rejoiced at the favorable opportunity for leaving land that he paid the whole amount for the entire cargo in advance, no less a sum than four thousand gold denarii. After a day's sailing out from shore, a terrific storm broke loose. Wonderful to relate, it injured no vessel but Jonah's. Thus he was taught the lesson that God is Lord over heaven and earth and sea, and man can hide himself nowhere from His face.

On the same vessel were representatives of the seventy nations of the earth, each with his peculiar idols. They all resolved to entreat their gods for succor, and the god from whom help would come should be recognized and worshipped at the only one true God. But help came from none. Then it was that the captain of the vessel approached Jonah where he lay asleep, and said to him: "We are suspended 'twixt life and death, and thou liest here asleep. Pray, tell me, to what nation dost thou belong?" "I am a Hebrew," replied Jonah. "We have heard," said the captain, "that the God of the Hebrews is the most powerful. Cry to Him for help. Perhaps He will perform such miracles for us as He did in days of old for the Jews at the Red Sea."

Jonah confessed to the captain that he was to blame for the whole misfortune, and he besought him to cast him adrift, and appease the storm. The other passengers refused to consent to so cruel an act. Though the lot decided against Jonah, they first tried to save the vessel by throwing the cargo overboard. Their efforts were in vain. Then they placed Jonah at the side of the vessel and spoke: "O Lord of the world, reckon this not up against us as innocent blood, for we know not the case of this man, and he himself bids us throw him into the sea." Even then they could not make up their minds to let him drown. First they immersed him up to his knees in the water of the sea, and the storm ceased; they drew him back into the vessel, and forthwith the storm raged in its old fury. Two more trials they made. They lowered him into the water up to his navel, and raised him out of the depths when the storm was assuaged. Again, when the storm broke out anew, they lowered him to his neck, and a second time they took him back into the vessel when the wind subsided. But finally the renewed rage of the storm convinced them that their danger was due to Jonah's transgressions, and they abandoned him to his fate. He was thrown into the water, and on the instant the sea grew calm.

JONAH IN THE WHALE

At the creation of the world, God made a fish intended to harbor Jonah. He as so large that the prophet was as comfortable inside of him as in a spacious synagogue. The eyes of the fish served Jonah as windows, and, besides, there was a diamond, which shone as brilliantly as the sun at midday, so that Jonah could see all things in the sea down to its very bottom.

It is a law that when their time has come, all the fish of the sea must betake themselves to leviathan, and let the monster devour them. The life term of Jonah's fish was about to expire, and the fish warned Jonah of what was to happen. When he, with Jonah in his belly, came to leviathan, the prophet said to the monster: "For thy sake I came hither. It was meet that I should know thine abode, for it is my appointed task to capture thee in the life to come and slaughter thee for the table of the just and pious." When leviathan observed the sign of the covenant on Jonah's body, he fled affrighted, and Jonah and the fish were saved. To show his gratitude, the fish carried Jonah whithersoever there was a sight to be seen. He showed him the river from which the ocean flows, showed him the spot at which the Israelites crossed the Red Sea, showed him Gehenna and Sheol, and many other mysterious and wonderful place.

Three days Jonah had spent in the belly of the fish, and he still felt so comfortable that he did not think of imploring God to change his condition. But God sent a female fish big with three hundred and sixty-five thousand little fish to Jonah's host, to demand the surrender of the prophet, else she would swallow both him and the guest he harbored. The message was received with incredulity, and leviathan had to come and corroborate it; he himself had heard God dispatch the female fish on her errand. So it came about that Jonah was transferred to another abode. His new quarters, which he had to share with all the little fish, were far from comfortable, and from the bottom of his heart a prayer for deliverance arose to God on high. The last words of his long petition were, "I shall redeem my vow," whereupon God commanded the fish to spew Jonah out. At a distance of nine hundred and sixty-five parasangs from the fish he alighted on dry land. These miracles induced the ship's crew to abandon idolatry, and they all became pious proselytes in Jerusalem.

THE REPENTANCE OF NINEVEH

Jonah went straightway to Nineveh, the monster city covering forty square parasangs and containing a million and half of human beings. He lost no time in proclaiming their destruction to the inhabitants. The voice of the prophet was so sonorous that it reached to every corner of the great city, and all who heard his words resolved to turn aside from their ungodly ways. At the head of the penitents was King Osnappar of Assyria. He descended from his throne, removed his crown, strewed ashes on his head instead, took off his purple garments, and rolled about in the dust of the highways. In all the streets royal heralds proclaimed the king's decree bidding the inhabitants fast three days, wear sackcloth, and supplicate God with tears and prayers to avert the threatened doom. The people of Nineveh fairly compelled to God's mercy to descend upon them. They held their infants heavenward, and amid streaming tears they cried: "For the sake of these innocent babes, hear our prayers." The young of their stalled cattle they separated from the mother beasts, the young were left within the stable, the old were put without. So parted from one another, the young and the old began to bellow aloud. Then the Ninevites cried: "If Thou wilt not have mercy upon us, we will not have mercy upon these beasts."

The penance of the Ninevites did not stop at fasting and praying. Their deeds showed that they had determined to lead a better life. If a man had usurped another's property, he sought to make amends for his iniquity; some went so far as to destroy their palaces in order to be able to give back a single brick to the rightful owner. Of their own accord others appeared before the courts of justice, and confessed their secret crimes and sins, known to none beside themselves, and declared themselves ready to submit to well-merited punishment, though it be death that was decreed against them.

One incident that happened at the time will illustrate the contrition of the Ninevites. A man found a treasure in the building lot he had acquired from his neighbor. Both buyer and seller refused to assume possession of the treasure. The seller insisted that the sale of the lot carried with it the sale of all it contained. The buyer held that he had bought the ground, not the treasure hidden therein. Neither rested satisfied until the judge succeeded in finding out who had hidden the treasure and where were his heirs, and the joy of the two was great when they could deliver the treasure up to its legitimate owners.

Seeing that the Ninevites had undergone a real change of heart, God took mercy upon them, and pardoned them. Thereupon Jonah likewise felt encouraged to plead for himself with God, that He forgive him for his flight. God spoke to him: "Thou wast mindful of Mine honor," the prophet had not wanted to appear a liar, so that men's trust in God might not be shaken "and for this reason thou didst take to sea. Therefore did I deal mercifully with thee, and rescue thee from the bowels of Sheol."

His sojourn in the inside of the fish the prophet could not easily dismiss from his mind, nor did it remain without visible consequences. The intense heat in the belly of the fish had consumed his garments, and made his hair fall out, and he was sore plagued by swarms of insects. To afford Jonah protection, God caused the kikayon to grow up. When he opened his eyes one morning, he saw a plant with two hundred and seventy-five leaves, each leaf measuring more than a span, so that it afforded relief from the heat of the sun. But the sun smote the gourd that it withered, and Jonah was again annoyed by the insects. He began to weep and wish for death to release him from his troubles. But when God led him to the plant, and showed him what lesson he might derive from it, how, though he had not labored for the plant, he had pity on it, he realized his wrong in desiring God to be relentless toward Nineveh, the great city, with its many inhabitants, rather than have his reputation as a prophet suffer taint. He prostrated himself and said: "O God, guide the world according to Thy goodness."

God was gracious to the people of Nineveh so long as they continued worthy of His lovingkindness. But at the end of forty days they departed from the path of piety, and they became more sinful than ever. Then the punishment threatened by Jonah overtook them, and they were swallowed up by the earth.

Jonah's suffering in the watery abyss had been so severe that by way of compensation of God exempted him from death: living he was permitted to enter Paradise. Like Jonah, his wife was known far and wide for her piety. She had gained fame particularly through her pilgrimage to Jerusalem, a duty which, by reason of her sex, she was not obliged to fulfil. On one of these pilgrimages it was that the prophetical spirit first descended upon Jonah.

Chapter 9

IX. THE LATER KINGS OF JUDAH

JOASH

When the prophet Jonah, doing the behest of his master Elisha, anointed Jehu king over Israel, he poured the oil out of a pitcher, not out of a horn, to indicate that the dynasty of Jehu would not occupy the throne long. At first Jehu, though a somewhat foolish king, was at least pious, but he abandoned his God-fearing ways from the moment he saw the document bearing the signature of the prophet Ahijah of Shilo, which bound the signers to pay implicit obedience to Jeroboam. The king took this as evidence that the prophet had approved the worship of the golden calves. So it came to pass that Jehu, the destroyer of Baal worship, did nothing to oppose the idolatrous service established by Jeroboam at Beth-el. The successors of Jehu were not better; on the contrary, they were worse, and therefore in the fifth generation an end was put to the dynasty of Jehu by the hand of the assassin.

The kings of Judah differed in no essential particular from their colleagues in the north. Ahaziah, whom Jehu killed, was a shameless sinner; he had the Name of God expurged from every passage in which it occurred in the Holy Scriptures, and the names of idols inserted in its place.

Upon the death of Ahaziah followed the reign of terror under the queen Athaliah, when God exacted payment from the house of David for his trespass in connection with the extermination of the priest at Nob. As Abiathar had been the only male descendant of Abimelech to survive the persecution of Saul, so the sole representative of the house of David to remain after the sword of Athaliah had raged was Joash, the child kept in hiding, in the Holy of Holies in the Temple, by the high priest Jehoiada and his wife Jehosheba. Later

Jehoiada vindicated the right of Joash upon the throne, and installed him as king of Judah. The very crown worn by the rulers of the house of David testified to the legitimacy of the young prince, for it possessed the peculiarity of fitting none but the rightful successors to David.

At the instigation of Jehoiada, King Joash undertook the restoration of the Temple. The work was completed so expeditiously that one living at the time the Temple was erected by Solomon was permitted to see the new structure shortly before his death. This good fortune befell Jehoiada himself, the son of Benaiah, commander-in-chief of the army under Solomon. So long as Joash continued under the tutelage of Jehoiada, he was a pious king. When Jehoiada departed this life, the courtiers came to Joash and flattered him: "If thou wert not a god, thou hadst not been able to abide for six years in the Holy of Holies, a spot which even the high priest is permitted to enter but once a year." The king lent ear to their blandishments, and permitted the people to pay him Divine homage. But when the folly of the king went to the extreme of prompting him to set up an idol in the Temple, Zechariah, the son of Jehoiada, placed himself at the entrance, and barring the way said: "Thou shalt not do it so long as I live." High priest, prophet, and judge though Zechariah was, and son-in-law of Joash to boot, the king still did not shrink from having him killed for his presumptuous words, not was he deterred by the fact that it happened on a Day of Atonement which fell on the Sabbath. The innocent blood crimsoning the hall of the priests did not remain unavenged. For two hundred and fifty-two years it did not leave off seething and pulsating, until, finally, Nebuzaradan, captain of Nebuchadnezzar's guard, ordered a great carnage among the Judeans, to avenge the death of Zechariah.

Joash himself, the murderer of Zechariah, met with an evil end. He fell into the hands of the Syrians, and they abused him in their barbarous, immoral way. Before he could recover from the suffering inflicted upon him, his servants slew him.

Amaziah, the son and successor of Joash, in many respects resembled his father. At the beginning of his reign he was God-fearing, but when, through the aid of God, he had gained a brilliant victory over the Edomites, he knew no better way of manifesting his gratitude than to establish in Jerusalem the cult of the idol worshipped by his conquered enemies. To compass his chastisement, God inspired Amaziah with the idea of provoking a war with Joash, the ruler of the northern kingdom. Amaziah demanded that Joash should either recognize the suzerainty of the southern realm voluntarily, or let the fate of battle decide the question. At first Joash sought to turn Amaziah aside from his purpose by a parable reminding him of the fate of Shechem, which the sons of Jacob had visited upon him for having done violence to their sister Dinah. Amaziah refused to be warned. He persisted in his challenge, and a war ensued. The fortune of battle decided against Amaziah. He suffered defeat, and later he was tortured to death by his own subjects.

THREE GREAT PROPHETS

The reign of Uzziah, who for a little while occupied the throne during his father Amaziah's lifetime, is notable particularly because it marks the beginning of the activity of three of the prophets, Hosea, Amos, and Isaiah. The oldest of the three was Hosea, the son of the prophet and prince Beeri, the Beeri who later was carried away captive by Tiglath-pileser, the king of Assyria. Of Beeri's prophecies we have but two verses, preserved for us by Isaiah.

The peculiar marriage contracted by Hosea at the command of God Himself was not without a good reason. When God spoke to the prophet about the sins of Israel, expecting him to defend or excuse his people, Hosea said severely: "O Lord of the world! Thine is the universe. In place of Israel choose another as Thy peculiar people from among the nations of the earth." To make the true relation between God and Israel known to the prophet, he was commanded to take to wife a woman with a dubious past. After she had borne him several children, God suddenly put the question to him: "Why followest thou not the example of thy teacher Moses, who denied himself the joys of family life after his call to prophecy?" Hosea replied: "I can neither send my wife away nor divorce her, for she has borne me children." "If, now," said God to him, "thou who hast a wife of whose honesty thou art so uncertain that thou canst not even be sure that her children are thine, and yet thou canst not separate from her, how, then can I separate Myself from Israel, from My children, the children of My elect, Abraham, Isaac, and Jacob!" Hosea entreated God to pardon him. But God said: "Better were it that thou shouldst pray for the welfare of Israel, for thou art the cause that I issued three fateful decrees against them." Hosea prayed as he was bidden, and his prayer averted the impending threefold doom.

Hosea died at Babylon at a time in which a journey thence to Palestine was beset with many perils. Desirous of having his earthly remains rest in sacred ground, he requested before his death that his bier be loaded upon a camel, and the animal permitted to make its way as it would. Wherever it stopped, there his body was to be buried. As he commanded, so it was done. Without a single mishap the camel arrived at Safed. In the Jewish cemetery of the town it stood still, and there Hosea was buried in the presence of a large concourse.

The prophetical activity of Amos commenced after Hosea's had closed, and before Isaiah's began. Though he had an impediment in his speech, he obeyed the call of God, and betook himself to Beth-el to proclaim to the sinful inhabitants thereof the Divine message with which he had been charged. The denunciation of the priest Amaziah, of Beth-el, who informed against the prophet before King Jeroboam of Israel, did him no harm, for the king, idolater though he was, entertained profound respect for Amos. He said to himself: "God forbid I should think the prophet guilty of cherishing traitorous plans, and if he were, it would surely be at the bidding of God." For this pious disposition Jeroboam was rewarded; never had the northern kingdom attained to such power as under him.

However, the fearlessness of Amos finally caused his death. King Uzziah inflicted a mortal blow upon his forehead with a red-hot iron.

Two years after Amos ceased to prophesy, Isaiah was favored with his first Divine communication. It was the day on which King Uzziah, blinded by success and prosperity, arrogated to himself the privileges of the priesthood. He tried to offer sacrifices upon the altar, and when the high priest Azariah ventured to restrain him, he threatened to slay him and any priest sympathizing with him unless they kept silent. Suddenly the earth quaked so violently that a great breach was torn in the Temple, through which a brilliant ray of sunlight pierced, falling upon the forehead of the king and causing leprosy to break forth upon him. Nor was that all the damage done by the earthquake. On the west side of Jerusalem, half of the mountain was split off and hurled to the east, into a road, at a distance of four stadia. And not heaven and earth alone were outraged by Uzziah's atrocity and sought to annihilate him; even the angels of fire, the seraphim, were on the point of descending and consuming him, when a voice from on high proclaimed, that the punishment appointed for Uzziah was unlike that meted out to Korah and his company despite the similarity of their crimes.

When Isaiah beheld the august throne of God on this memorable day, he was sorely affrighted, for he reproached himself with not having tried to turn the king away from his impious desire. Enthralled he hearkened to the hymns of praise sung by the angels, and lost in admiration he failed to join his voice with theirs. "Woe is me," he cried out, "that I was silent! Woe is me that I did not join the chorus of the angels praising God! Had I done it, I, too, like the angels, would have become immortal, seeing I was permitted to look upon sights to behold which had brought death to other men." Then he began to excuse himself: "I am a man of unclean lips, and I dwell in the midst of people of unclean lips." At once resounded the voice of God in rebuke: "Of thyself thou art the master, and of thyself thou mayest say what thou choosest, but who gave thee the right to calumniate My children of Israel and call them 'a people of unclean lips'?" And Isaiah heard God bid one of the seraphim touch his lips with a live coal as a punishment for having slandered Israel. Though the coal was so hot that the seraph needed tongs to hold the tongs with which he had taken the coal from the altar, the prophet yet escaped unscathed, but he learned the lesson, that it was his duty to defend Israel, not traduce him. Thenceforth the championship of his people was the mainspring of the prophet's activity, and he was rewarded by having more revelations concerning Israel and the other nations vouchsafed him than any other prophet before or after him. Moreover God designated Isaiah to be "the prophet of consolation." Thus it happened that the very Isaiah whose early prophecies foretold the exile and the destruction of the Temple, later described and proclaimed, in plainer terms than any other prophet, the brilliant destiny in store for Israel.

THE TWO KINGDOMS CHASTISED

Afflicted with leprosy, Uzziah was unfit to reign as king, and Jotham administered the affairs of Judah for twenty-five years before the death of his father. Jotham possessed so much piety that his virtues added to those of two other very pious men suffice to atone for all the sins of the whole of mankind committed from the hour of creation until the end of all time.

Ahaz, the son of Jotham; was very unlike him. "From first to last he was a sinner." He abolished the true worship of God, forbade the study of the Torah, set up an idol in the upper room of the Temple, and disregarded the Jewish laws of marriage. His transgressions are the less pardonable, because he sinned against God knowing His grandeur and power, as appears from his reply to the prophet. Isaiah said to him: "Ask a sign of God, as, for instance, that the dead should arise, Korah come up from Sheol, or Elijah descend from heaven." The king's answer was: "I know thou hast the power to do any of these, but I do not wish the Name of God to be glorified through me."

The only good quality possessed by Ahaz was respect for Isaiah. To avoid his reproaches, Ahaz would disguise himself when he went abroad, so that the prophet might not recognize him. Only to this circumstance, joined to the fact he was the father of a pious son and the son of an equally pious father, is it to be ascribed that, in spite of his wickedness, Ahaz is not one of those who have forfeited their portion in the world to come. But he did not escape punishment; on the contrary, his chastisement was severe, not only as king but also as man. In the ill-starred war against Pekah, the king of the northern kingdom, he lost his first-born son, a great hero.

Pekah, however, was not permitted to enjoy the fruits of his victory, for the king of Assyria invaded his empire, captured the golden calf at Dan, and led the tribes on the east side of Jordan away into exile. The dismemberment of the Israelitish kingdom went on apace for some years. Then the Assyrians, in the reign of Hoshea, carried off the second golden calf together with the tribes of Asher, Issachar, Zebulon, and Naphtali, leaving but one-eighth of the Israelites in their own land. The larger portion of the exiles was taken to Damascus. After that Israel's doom overtook it with giant strides, and the last ruler of Israel actually hastened the end of his kingdom by a pious deed. After the golden calves were removed by the Assyrians, Hoshea, the king of the north, abolished the institution of stationing the guards on the frontier between Judah and Israel to prevent pilgrimages to Jerusalem. But the people made no use of the liberty granted them. They persisted in their idolatrous cult, and this quickened their punishment. So long as their kings had put obstacles in their path, they could excuse themselves before God for not worshipping Him in the true way. The action taken by their king Hoshea left them no defense. When the Assyrians made their third incursion into Israel, the kingdom of the north was destroyed forever, and the people, one and all, were carried away into exile.

The heathen nations settled in Samaria by the Assyrians instead of the deported Ten Tribes were forced by God to accept the true religion of the Jews. Nevertheless they continued to worship their olden idols: the Babylonians paid devotion to a hen, the people of Cuthah to a cock, those of Hamath to a ram, the dog and the ass were the gods of the Avvites, and the mule and the horse the gods of the Sepharvites.

HEZEKIAH

While the northern kingdom was rapidly descending into the pit of destruction, a mighty upward impulse was given to Judah, both spiritually and materially, by its king Hezekiah. In his infancy the king had been destined as a sacrifice to Moloch. His mother had saved him from death only by rubbing him with the blood of a salamander, which made him fire-proof. In every respect he was the opposite of his father. As the latter is counted among the worst of sinners, so Hezekiah is counted among the most pious of Israel. His first act as king is evidence that he held the honor of God to be his chief concern, important beyond all else. He refused to accord his father regal obsequies; his remains were buried as though he had been poor and of plebeian rank. Impious as he was, Ahaz deserved nothing more dignified. God had Himself made it known to Hezekiah, by a sign, that his father was to have no consideration paid him. On the day of the dead king's funeral daylight lasted but two hours, and his body had to be interred when the earth was enveloped in darkness.

Throughout his reign, Hezekiah devoted himself mainly to the task of dispelling the ignorance of the Torah which his father had caused. While Ahaz had forbidden the study of the law, Hezekiah's orders read: "Who does not occupy himself with the Torah, renders himself subject to the death penalty." The academies closed under Ahaz were kept open day and night under Hezekiah. The king himself supplied the oil needed for illuminating purposes. Gradually, under this system, a generation grew up so well trained that one could search the land from Dan even to Beer-sheba and not find a single ignoramus. The very women and the children, both boys and girls, knew the laws of "clean and unclean." By way of rewarding his piety, God granted Hezekiah a brilliant victory over Sennacherib.

This Assyrian king, who had conquered the whole world, equipped an army against Hezekiah like unto which there is none, unless it be the army of the four kings whom Abraham routed, or the army to be raised by Gog and Magog in the Messianic time. Sennacherib's army consisted of more than two millions and a half of horsemen, among them forty-five thousand princes sitting in chariots and surrounded by their paramours, by eighty thousand armor-clad soldiers, and sixty thousand swordsmen. The camp extended over a space of four hundred parasangs, and the saddle-beasts standing neck to neck formed a line forty parasangs long. The host was divided into four divisions. After the first of them had passed the Jordan, it was well nigh dry, for the soldiers had all slaked their thirst with water of the river. The second division found nothing to quench their thirst except the water gathered under the hoofs of the horses. The third division was forced to dig wells, and when the fourth division crossed the Jordan, they kicked up great clouds of dust.

With this vast army Sennacherib hastened onward, in accordance with the disclosures of the astrologers, who warned him that he would fail in his object of capturing Jerusalem, if he arrived there later than the day set by them. His journey having lasted but one day instead of ten, as he had expected, he rested at Nob. A raised platform was there erected for Sennacherib, whence he could view Jerusalem. On first beholding the Judean capital, the Assyrian king exclaimed: "What! Is this Jerusalem, the city for whose sake I gathered together my whole army, for whose sake I first conquered all other lands? Is it not smaller and weaker than all the cities of the nations I subdued with my strong hand?" He stretched himself and shook his head, and waved his hand contemptuously toward the Temple mount and the sanctuary crowning it. When his warriors urged him to make his attack upon Jerusalem, he bade them take their ease for one night, and be prepared to storm the city the next day. It seemed no great undertaking. Each warrior would but have to pick up as much mortar from the wall as is needed to seal a letter and the whole city would disappear. But Sennacherib made the mistake of not proceeding directly to the attack upon the city. If he had made the assault at once, it would have been successful, for the sin of Saul against the priest at Nob had not yet been wholly expiated; on that very day it was fully atoned for. In the following night, which was the Passover night, when Hezekiah and the people began to sing the Hallel Psalms, the giant host was annihilated. The archangel Gabriel sent by God to ripen the fruits of the field, was charged to address himself to the task of making away with the Assyrians, and he fulfilled his mission so well that of all the millions of the army, Sennacherib alone was saved with his two sons, his son-in-law Nebuchadnezzar, and Nebuzaradan. The death of the Assyrians happened when the angel permitted them to hear the "song of the celestials." Their souls were burnt, though their garments remained intact. Such an end was too good for Sennacherib. To him a disgraceful death was apportioned. On his flight away from Jerusalem, he met a Divine apparition in the guise of an old man. He questioned Sennacherib as to what he would say to the kings allied with him, in reply to their inquiry about the fate of their sons at Jerusalem. Sennacherib confessed his dread of a meeting with those kings. The old man advised him to have his hair cut off, which would change his appearance beyond recognition. Sennacherib assented, and his advisor sent him to a house in the vicinity to fetch a pair of shears. Here he found some people angels in disguise busying themselves with a hand-mill. They promised to give him the shears, provided he ground a measure of grain for them. So it grew late and dark by the time Sennacherib returned to the old man, and he had to procure a light before his hair could be cut. As he fanned the fire into a flame, a spark flew into his beard and singed it, and he had to sacrifice his beard as well as his hair. On his return to Assyria, Sennacherib found a plank, which he worshipped as an idol, because it was part of the ark which had saved Noah from the deluge. He vowed that he would sacrifice his sons to this idol if he prospered in his next ventures. But his sons heard his vows, and they killed their father, and fled to Kardu where they released the Jewish captives confined there in great numbers. With these they marched to Jerusalem, and became proselytes there. The famous scholars Shemaiah and Abtalion were the descendants of these two sons of Sennacherib.

MIRACLES WROUGHT FOR HEZEKIAH

The destruction of the Assyrian host delivered Hezekiah from an inner as well as an outer enemy, for he had opponents in Jerusalem, among them the high priest Shebnah. Shebnah had a more numerous following in the city than the king himself, and they and their leader had favored peace with Sennacherib. Supported by Joah, another influential personage, Shebnah had fastened a letter to a dart, and shot the dart into the Assyrian camp. The contents of the letter were: "We and the whole people of Israel wish to conclude peace with thee, but Hezekiah and Isaiah will not permit it." Shebnah's influence was so powerful that Hezekiah began to show signs of yielding. Had it not been for the prophet Isaiah, the king would have submitted to Sennacherib's demands.

Shebnah's treachery and his other sins did not go unpunished. When he and his band of adherents left Jerusalem to join the Assyrians, the angel Gabriel closed the gate as soon as Shebnah had passed beyond it, and so he was separated from his followers. To the inquiry of Sennacherib about the many sympathizers he had written of, he could give no reply but that they had changed their mind. The Assyrian king thought Shebnah had made sport of him. He, therefore, ordered his attendants to bore a hole through his heels, tie him to the tail of a horse by them, and spur the horse on to run until Shebnah was dragged to death.

The unexpected victory won by Hezekiah over the Assyrians, to whom the kingdom of Samaria had fallen a prey but a short time before, showed how wrong they had been who had mocked at Hezekiah for his frugal ways. A king whose meal consisted of a handful of vegetables could hardly be called a dignified ruler, they had said. These critics would gladly have seen his kingdom pass into the hands of Pekah, the king of Samaria, whose dessert, to speak of nothing else, consisted of forty seim of young pigeons.

In view of all the wonders God had done for him, it was unpardonable that Hezekiah did not feel himself prompted at least to sing a song of praise to God. Indeed, when the prophet Isaiah urged him to it, he refused, saying that the study of the Torah, to which he devoted himself with assiduous zeal, was a substitute for direct expressions of gratitude. Besides, he thought God's miracles would become known to the world without action on his part, in such ways as these: After the destruction of the Assyrian army, when the Jews searched the abandoned camps, they found Pharaoh the king of Egypt and the Ethiopian king Tirhakah. These kings had hastened to the aid of Hezekiah, and the Assyrians had taken them captive and clapped them in irons, in which they were languishing when the Jews came upon them. Liberated by Hezekiah, the two rulers returned to their respective realms, spreading the report of the greatness of God everywhere. And again, all the vassal troops in Sennacherib's army, set free by Hezekiah, accepted the Jewish faith, and on their way home they proclaimed the kingdom of God in Egypt and in many other lands.

By failing in gratitude Hezekiah lost a great opportunity. The Divine plan had been to make Hezekiah the Messiah, and Sennacherib was to be Gog and Magog. Justice opposed this plan, addressing God thus: "O Lord of the world! David, king of Israel, who sang so many songs and hymns of praise to Thee, him Thou didst not make the Messiah, and now Thou wouldst confer the distinction upon Hezekiah, who has no word of praise for Thee in spite of the manifold wonders Thou hast wrought for him?" Then the earth appeared before God, and said: "Lord of the world! I will song Thee a song in place of this righteous man; make him to be the Messiah," and the earth forthwith intoned a song of praise. Likewise spake the Prince of the World: "Lord of the world! Do the will of this righteous man." But a voice from heaven announced: "This is my secret, this is my secret." And again, when the prophet exclaimed sorrowfully, "Woe is me! How long, O Lord, how long!" the voice replied: "The time of the Messiah will arrive when the 'treacherous dealers and the treacherous dealers' shall have come."

The sin committed by Hezekiah asleep, he had to atone for awake. If he refused to devote a song of praise to God for his escape from the Assyrian peril, he could not refrain from doing it after his recovery from the dangerous sickness that befell him. This sickness was a punishment for another sin beside ingratitude. He had "peeled off" the gold from the Temple, and sent it to the king of the Assyrians; therefore the disease that afflicted him caused his skin to "peel off." Moreover, this malady of Hezekiah's was brought upon him by God, to afford an opportunity for the king and the prophet Isaiah to come close to each other. The two had had a dispute on a point of etiquette. The king adduced as a precedent the action of Elijah, who "went to show himself unto Ahab," and demanded that Isaiah, too, should appear before him. The prophet, on the other hand, modelled his conduct after Elisha's, who permitted the kings of Israel, and Judah, and Edom, to come to him. But God settled the dispute by afflicting Hezekiah with sickness, and then He bade Isaiah go to the king and pay the visit due to the sick. The prophet did the bidding of God. When he appeared in the presence of the ailing king, he said: "Set thine house in order, for thou wilt die in this world and not live in the next" a fate which Hezekiah incurred because he had failed to take unto himself a wife and bring forth posterity. The king's defense, that he had preferred a celibate's life because he had seen in the holy spirit that he was destined to have impious children, the prophet did not consider valid. He rebutted it with the words: "Why does thou concern thyself with the secrets of the All-Merciful? Thou hast but to do thy duty. God will do whatsoever it pleases Him." Thereupon Hezekiah asked the daughter of the prophet in marriage, saying: "Perchance my merits joined to thine will cause my children to be virtuous." But Isaiah rejected the proposal of marriage, because he knew that the decree of God ordaining the king's death was unalterable. Whereupon the king: "Thou son of thus has it been transmitted to me from the house of my ancestor: Even if a sharp sword rests at the very throat of a man, he may yet not refrain from uttering a prayer for mercy."

And the king was right. Though death had been decreed against him, his prayer averted it. In his prayer he supplicated God to keep him alive for the sake of the merits of his ancestors, who had built the Temple and brought many proselytes into the Jewish fold, and for the sake of his own merits, for, he said, "I searched out all the two hundred and forty-eight members of my body which Thou didst give me, and I found none which I had used in a manner contrary to Thy will."

His prayer was heard. God added fifteen years to his life, but He made him understand very clearly, that he owed the mercy solely to the merits of David, not at all to his own, as Hezekiah fondly believed. Before Isaiah left the court of the palace, God instructed him to return to the king, and announce his recovery to him. Isaiah feared lest Hezekiah should place little trust in his words, as he had but a short while before predicted his swiftly approaching end. But God reassured the prophet. In his modesty and piety, the king would harbor no doubt derogatory to the prophet's trustworthiness. The remedy employed by Isaiah, a cake of figs applied to the boil, increased the wonder of Hezekiah's recovery, for it was apt to aggravate the malady rather than alleviate it.

A number of miracles besides were connected with the recovery of Hezekiah. In itself it was remarkable, as being the first case of a recovery on record. Previously illness had been inevitably followed by death. Before he had fallen sick, Hezekiah himself had implored God to change this order of nature. He held that sickness followed by restoration to health would induce men to do penance. God had replied: "Thou art right, and the new order shall be begun with thee." Furthermore, the day of Hezekiah's recovery was marked by the great miracle that the sun shone ten hours longer than its wonted time. The remotest lands were amazed thereat, and Baladan, the ruler of Babylon, was prompted by it to send an embassy to Hezekiah, which was to carry his felicitations to the Jewish king upon his recovery. Baladan, it should be said by the way, was not the real king of Babylon. The throne was occupied by his father, whose face had changed into that of a dog. Therefore the son had to administer the affairs of state, and he was known by his father's name as well as his own. This Baladan was in the habit of dining at noon, and then he took a nap until three o'clock of the afternoon. On the day of Hezekiah's recovery, when he awoke from his sleep, and saw the sun overhead, he was on the point of having his guards executed, because he thought they had permitted him to sleep a whole afternoon and the night following it. He desisted only when he was informed of Hezekiah's miraculous recovery, and realised that the God of Hezekiah was greater than his own god, the sun. He at once set about sending greetings to the Jewish king. His letter read as follows: "Peace be with Hezekiah, peace with his great God, and peace with Jerusalem." After the letter was dispatched, it occurred to Baladan that it had not been composed properly. Mention of Hezekiah had been made before mention of God. He had the messengers called back, and ordered another letter to be written, in which the oversight was made good. As a reward for his punctiliousness, three of his descendants, Nebuchadnezzar, Evil-merodach, and Belshazzar, were appointed by God to be world monarchs. God said: "Thou didst arise from thy throne, and didst take three steps to do Me honor, by having thy letter re-written, therefore will I grant thee three descendants who shall be known from one end of the world to the other."

The embassy sent by the Babylonian monarch was an act of homage to God for his miracle-working power. Hezekiah, however, took it to be an act of homage toward himself, and it had the effect of making him arrogant. Not only did he eat and drink with the heathen who made up the embassy, but also, in his haughtiness of mind, he displayed before them all the treasures which he had captured from Sennacherib, and many other curiosities besides, among them magnetic iron, a peculiar sort of ivory, and honey as solid as stone.

What was worse, he had his wife partake of the meal in honor of the embassy, and, most heinous crime of all, he opened the holy Ark, and pointing to the tables of law within it, said to the heathen: "With the help of these we undertake wars and win victories." God sent Isaiah to reproach Hezekiah for these acts. The king, instead of confessing his wrong at once, answered the prophet haughtily. Then Isaiah announced to him that the treasures taken from Sennacherib would revert to Babylon some time in the future, and his descendants, Daniel and the three companions of Daniel, would serve the Babylonia ruler as eunuchs.

Despite his pride in this case, Hezekiah was one of the most pious kings of Judah. Especially he is deserving of praise for his efforts to have Hebrew literature put into writing, for it was Hezekiah who had copies made of the books of Isaiah, Ecclesiastes, Song of Songs, and Proverbs. On the other hand, he had concealed the books containing medical remedies.

Great was the mourning over him at his death. No less than thirty-six thousand men with bared shoulders marched before his bier, and, rarer distinction still, a scroll of the law was laid upon his bier, for it was said: "He who rests in this bier, has fulfilled all ordained in this book." He was buried next to David and Solomon.

MANASSEH

Hezekiah had finally yielded to the admonitions of Isaiah, and had taken a wife unto himself, the daughter of the prophet. But he entered upon marriage with a heavy heart. His prophetic spirit foretold to him that the impiousness of the sons he would beget would make their death to be preferable to their life. These fears were confirmed all too soon. His two sons, Rabshakeh and Manasseh, showed their complete unlikeness to their parents in early childhood. Once, when Hezekiah was carrying his two little ones on his shoulders to the Bet ha-Midrash, he overheard their conversation. The one said: "Our father's bald head might do for frying fish." The other rejoined: "It would do well for offering sacrifices to idols." Enraged by these words, Hezekiah let his sons slip from his shoulders. Rabshakeh was killed by the fall, but Manasseh escaped unhurt. Better had it been if Manasseh had shared his brother's untimely fate. He was spared for naught but murder, idolatry, and other abominable atrocities.

After Hezekiah had departed this life, Manasseh ceased to serve the God of his father. He did whatever his evil imagination prompted. The altar was destroyed, and in the inner space of the Temple he set up an idol with four faces, copied from the four figures on the throne of God. It was so placed that from whatever direction one entered the Temple, a face of the idol confronted him.

As Manasseh was sacrilegious toward God, he was malevolent toward his fellows. He had fashioned an image so large that it required a thousand men to carry it. Daily a new force was employed on this task, because Manasseh had each set of porters killed off at the end of the day's work. All his acts were calculated to cast contempt upon Judaism and its tenets. It did not satisfy his evil desire to obliterate the name of God from the Holy Scriptures; he went so far as to deliver public lectures whose burden was to ridicule the Torah. Isaiah and the other prophets, Micah, Joel, and Habakkuk, left Jerusalem and repaired to a mountain in the desert, that they might be spared the sight of the abominations practiced by the king. Their abiding-place was disclosed to the king. A Samaritan, a descendant of the false prophet Zedekiah, had taken refuge in Jerusalem after the destruction of the Temple. But he did not remain there long; charges were made against him before the pious king Hezekiah, and he withdrew to Bethlehem, where he gathered hangers-on about him. This Samaritan it was who traced the prophets to their retreat, and lodged accusations against them before Manasseh. The impious king sat in judgment on Isaiah, and condemned him to death. The indictment against him was that his prophecies contained teachings in contradiction with the law of Moses. God said unto Moses: "Thou canst not see My face; for man shall not see Me and live"; while Isaiah said: "I saw the Lord sitting upon a throne, high and lifted up." Again, Isaiah compared the princes of Israel and the people with the impious inhabitants of Sodom and Gomorrah, and he prophesied the downfall of Jerusalem and the destruction of the Temple. The prophet offered no explanation. He was convinced of the uselessness of defending himself, and he preferred Manasseh should act from ignorance rather than from wickedness. However, he fled for safety. When he heard the royal bailiffs in pursuit of him, he pronounced the Name of God, and a cedar-tree swallowed him up. The king ordered the tree to be sawn in pieces. When the saw was applied to the portion of the bark under which the mouth of Isaiah lay concealed, he died. His mouth was the only vulnerable part of his body, because at the time when he was called to his prophetical mission, it had made use of the contemptuous words "a people of unclean lips," regarding Israel. Isaiah died at the age of one hundred and twenty years, by the hands of his own grandchild.

God is long-suffering, but in the end Manasseh received the deserved punishment for his sins and crimes. In the twenty-second year of his rulership, the Assyrians came and carried him off to Babylon in fetters, him together with the old Danite idol, Micah's image. In Babylonia, the king was put into an oven which was heated from below. Finding himself in this extremity, Manasseh began to call upon god after god to help him out of his straits. As this proved inefficacious, he resorted to other means. "I remember," he said, "my father taught me the verse: 'When thou art in tribulation, if in the latter days thou shalt return to the Lord thy God, and hearken unto His voice, He will not fail thee.' Now I cry to God. If He inclines His ear unto me, well and good; if not, then all kinds of god are alike." The angels stopped up the windows of heaven, that the prayer of Manasseh might not ascend to God, and they said: "Lord of the world! Art Thou willing to give gracious hearing to one who has paid worship to idols, and set up an idol in the Temple?" "If I did not accept the penance of this man," replied God, "I should be closing the door in the face of all repentant sinners." God made a small opening under the Throne of His Glory, and received the prayer of Manasseh through it. Suddenly a wind arose, and carried Manasseh back to Jerusalem. His return to God not only helped him in his distress, but also brought him pardon for all his sins, so that not even his share in the future world was withdrawn from him.

The people of this time were attracted to idolatry with so irresistible a force that the vast learning of Manasseh, who knew fifty-two different interpretations of the Book of Leviticus, did not give him enough moral strength to withstand its influence. Rab Ashi, the famous compiler of the Talmud, once announced a lecture on Manasseh with the words: "To-morrow I shall speak about our colleague Manasseh." At night the king appeared to Ashi in a dreams, and put a ritual question to him, which the Rabbi could not answer. Manasseh told him the solution, and Ashi, in amazement at the king's scholarship, asked why one so erudite had served idols. Manasseh's reply was: "Hadst thou lived at my time, thou wouldst have caught hold of the hem of my garment and run after me."

Amon, the son of Manasseh, surpassed his father in wickedness. He was in the habit of saying: "My father was a sinner from early childhood, and in his old age he did penance. I shall do the same. First I shall satisfy the desires of my heart, and afterward I shall return to God." Indeed, he was guilty of more grievous sins than his predecessor; he burned the Torah; under him the place of the altar was covered with spiderwebs; and, as though of purpose to set at naught the Jewish religion, he committed the worst sort of incest, a degree more heinous than his father's crime of a similar nature. Thus he executed the first half of his maxim literally. For repentance, however, he was given no time; death cut him off in the fulness of his sinful ways.

JOSIAH AND HIS SUCCESSORS

That the full measure of punishment was not meted out to Amon his evil deeds were such that he should have forfeited his share in the world to come was due to the circumstance that he had a pious and righteous son. Josiah offers a shining model of true, sincere repentance. Though at first he followed in the footsteps of his father Amon, he soon gave up the ways of wickedness, and became one of the most pious kings of Israel, whose chief undertaking was the effort to bring the whole people back to the true faith. It dates from the time when a copy of the Torah was found in the Temple, a copy that had escaped the holocaust kindled by his father and predecessor Amon for the purpose of exterminating the Holy Scriptures. When he opened the Scriptures, the first verse to strike his eye was the one in Deuteronomy: "The Lord shall bring thee and thy king into exile, unto a nation which thou hast not known." Josiah feared this doom of exile was impending, and he sought to conciliate God through the reform of his people.

His first step was to enlist the intercession of the prophets in his behalf. He addressed his request, not to Jeremiah, but to the prophetess Huldah, knowing that women are more easily moved to compassion. As Jeremiah was a kinsman of the prophetess their common ancestors were Joshua and Rahab the king felt no apprehension that the prophet take his preference for Huldah amiss. The proud, dignified answer of the prophetess was, that the misfortune could not be averted from Israel, but the destruction of the Temple, she continued consolingly, would not happen until after the death of Josiah. In view of the imminent destruction of the Temple, Josiah hid the holy Ark and all its appurtenances, in order to guard them against desecration at the hands of the enemy.

The efforts of the king in behalf of God and His law found no echo with the great majority of the people. Though the king was successful in preventing the worship of idols in public, his subjects knew how to deceive him. Josiah sent out his pious sympathizers to inspect the houses of the people, and he was satisfied with their report, that they had found no idols, not suspecting that the recreant people has fastened half an image on each wing of the doors, so that the inmates faced their household idols as they closed the door upon Josiah's inspectors.

This godless generation contemporaneous with Josiah was to blame for his death. When King Pharaoh, in his campaign against the Assyrians, wanted to travel through Palestine, Jeremiah advised the king not to deny the Egyptians the passage through his land. He cited a prophecy by his teacher Isaiah, who had foreseen the war between Assyria and Egypt. But Josiah retorted: "Moses, thy teacher's teacher, spake: 'I will give peace in the land, and no sword shall go through your land,' not even the sword that is not raised against Israel with hostile intent." The king, innocent of the deception practiced by the people, knew not that they were idol worshippers, to whom the promises of the Torah have no application. In the engagement that ensued between the Jews and the Egyptians, no less than three hundred darts struck the king. In his death agony he uttered no word of complaint; he only said: "The Lord is righteous, for I have rebelled against His commandment," thus admitting his guilt in not having heeded the advice of the prophet.

So ended the days of this just king after a brilliant career, the only king since Solomon to rule over both Judah and Israel, for Jeremiah had brought back to Palestine the ten exiled tribes of the north, and made them subject to Josiah. The mourning for him was profound. Even Jeremiah perpetuated his memory in his Lamentations.

Pharaoh of Egypt was not permitted to enjoy the results of his victory to the full, for it was soon after this that, in attempting to ascend the wondrous throne of Solomon, he was stuck down by the lions and rendered lame by the blow.

The people put Jehoahaz on the throne of Judah to succeed Josiah, though his brother Jehoiakim was the older by two years. To silence the legitimate claims of Jehoiakim, the new king underwent the ceremony of anointing. But his reign was very brief. At the end of three months Pharaoh carried him off into exile in Egypt, and Jehoiakim ruled in his stead.

Jehoiakim was another of the sinful monarchs of the Jews, uncharitable toward men and disobedient to God and the laws of God. His garments were of two kinds of stuff mingled together, his body was tattooed with the names of idols, and in order that he might appear as a non-Jew, he performed the operation of an epipost upon himself. Various forms of incest were committed by him, and, besides, he was in the habit of putting men to death that he might violate their wives, and confiscate their possessions. Blasphemous as he was, he spoke: "My predecessors did not know how to provoke the wrath of God. As for me, I say frankly, we have no need whatsoever of Him; the very light He gives us we can dispense with, for the gold of Parvaim can well replace it."

Seeing such abominations, God desired to resolve the world into its original chaos. If He desisted from His purpose, it was only because the people led a God-fearing life during the time of Jehoiakim. After he had reigned eleven years, Nebuchadnezzar put an end to his dominion. Advancing with his army, the Babylonian king halted at Daphne, a suburb of Antioch. Here he was met by the Sanhedrin of Jerusalem, who desired to know whether he was coming with the purpose of destroying the Temple. Nebuchadnezzar assured them, that all he wanted was the surrender of Jehoiakim, who had rebelled against his authority. Returned to Jerusalem, the Sanhedrin informed Jehoiakim of Nebuchadnezzar's intention. The king asked the elders, whether it was ethical to purchase their lives by sacrificing his. For answer they referred him to the story of the way Joab dealt with the city of Abel of Beth-maacah, which had saved itself by surrendering the rebel Sheba, the son of Bichri. The king's objections did not deter the Sanhedrin from following the example of Joab acting under the direction of David. They made Jehoiakim glide down from the city walls of Jerusalem by a chain. Below, the Babylonians stood ready to receive him. Nebuchadnezzar took Jehoiakim in fetters to all the cities of Judah, then he slew him, and, his rage still unabated, threw his corpse to the dogs after having stuck it into the carcass of an ass. The dogs left nothing of Jehoiakim's body over except his skull, on which were written the words: "This and something besides." Many centuries later it was found by a Rabbi near the gates of Jerusalem. He tried in vain to give it burial; the earth refused to retain it, and the Rabbi concluded therefrom that it belonged to the corpse of Jehoiakim. He wrapped the skull in a cloth, and laid it in a closet. One day the wife of the Rabbi discovered it there, and she burnt it, thinking the skull belonged to a former wife of her husband, so dear to him even after her death that he could not separate himself from this relic.

When Nebuchadnezzar returned to Babylonia from his Palestinian expedition, the people received him with great pomp and solemnity. He announced to them that in place of Jehoiakim, whom he had slain, he had installed Mattaniah, the rebel's son, called Jehoiachin, as king over Judah, and the people uttered the warning: "One cannot educate a well-behaved puppy whose dam was ill-conditioned; let alone an ill-conditioned puppy whose dam was ill-conditioned."

Nebuchadnezzar returned to Daphne, and informed the Sanhedrin, who hastened from Jerusalem to meet him, that he desired the surrender of Jehoiachin. If they refused to satisfy his demand, he would destroy the Temple. When the Jewish king was told the threat of his Babylonian adversary, he mounted upon the roof of the Temple, and, holding all the keys of its chambers in his hand, he spoke thus to God: "Until now Thou didst consider us worthy of confidence, and Thou didst entrust Thy keys to us. Since Thou no longer dost esteem us trustworthy, here, take back Thy keys." He was held to his word: a hand was stretched forth from heaven, and it received the keys.

Jehoiachin, good and pious, did not desire the city of Jerusalem to be exposed to peril for his sake. So he delivered himself to the Babylonian leaders, after they swore that neither city nor people should suffer harm. But the Babylonians did not keep their oath. A short while thereafter they carried into exile, not only the king, but also his mother, and ten thousand of the Jewish nobility and of the great scholars. This was the second attempt made by Nebuchadnezzar to deport the Jews. On taking the former king Jehoiakim captive, he had exiled three hundred of the noblest of the people, among them the prophet Ezekiel.

The king Jehoiachin was incarcerated for life, a solitary prisoner, separated from his wife and his family. The Sanhedrin, who were among those deported with the king, feared that the house of David die out. They therefore besought Nebuchadnezzar not to separate Jehoiachin from his wife. They succeeded in enlisting the sympathy of the queen's hairdresser, and through her of the queen herself, Semiramis, the wife of Nebuchadnezzar, who in turn prevailed upon the king to accord mild treatment to the unfortunate prince exiled from Judea. Suffering had completely changed the once sinful king, so that, in spite of his great joy over his reunion with his wife, he still paid regard to the prescriptions of the Jewish law regulating conjugal life. He was prepared to deny himself every indulgence, when the purchase price was an infringement of the word of God. Such steadfastness pleaded with God to pardon the king for his sins, and the heavenly Sanhedrin absolved God from His oath, to crush Jehoiachin and deprive his house of sovereignty. By way of reward for his continence he was blessed with distinguished posterity. Not only was Zerubbabel, the first governor of Palestine after the destruction of the Temple, a grandson of Jehoiachin's, but also the Messiah himself will be a descendant of his.

Chapter 10

ZEDEKIAH

The execution of one king and the deportation of another were but preludes to the great national catastrophe in the time of Zedekiah, the destruction of the Temple and the exile of the whole people. After Nebuchadnezzar had led Jehoiachin and a portion of the people into banishment, his commiseration was aroused for the Jews, and he inquired, whether any other sons of Josiah were still living. Only Mattaniah was left. He was re-named Zedekiah, in the hope that he would be the father of pious sons. In reality the name became the omen of the disasters to happen in the time of this king.

Nebuchadnezzar, who invested Zedekiah with the royal office, demanded that he swear fealty to him. Zedekiah was about to swear by his own soul, but the Babylonian king, not satisfied, brought a scroll of the law, and made his Jewish vassal take the oath upon that. Nevertheless he did not keep faith with Nebuchadnezzar for long. Nor was this his only treachery toward his suzerain. He had once surprised Nebuchadnezzar in the act of cutting a piece from a living hare and eating it, as is the habit of barbarians. Nebuchadnezzar was painfully embarrassed, and he begged the Jewish king to promise under oath not to mention what he had seen. Though Nebuchadnezzar treated him with great friendliness, even making him sovereign lord over five vassal kings, he did not justify the trust reposed in him. To flatter Zedekiah, the five kings once said: "If all were as it should be, thou wouldst occupy the throne of Nebuchadnezzar." Zedekiah could not refrain from exclaiming: "O yes, Nebuchadnezzar, whom I once saw eating a live hare!"

The five kings at once repaired to Nebuchadnezzar, and reported what Zedekiah had said. Thereupon the king of Babylonia marched to Daphne, near Antioch, with the purpose of chastising Zedekiah. At Daphne he found the Sanhedrin of Jerusalem, who had hastened thither to receive him. Nebuchadnezzar met the Sanhedrin courteously, ordered his attendants to bring state chairs for all the members, and requested them to read the Torah to him and explain it. When they reached the passage in the Book of Numbers dealing with the remission of vows, the king put the question: "If a man desires to be released from a vow, what steps must he take?" The Sanhedrin replied: "He must repair to a scholar, and he will absolve him from his vow." Whereupon Nebuchadnezzar exclaimed: "I verily believe it was you who released Zedekiah from the vow he took concerning me." And he ordered the members of the Sanhedrin to leave their state chairs and sit on the ground. They were forced to admit, that they had not acted in accordance with the law, for Zedekiah's vow affected another beside himself, and without the acquiescence of the other party, namely, Nebuchadnezzar, the Sanhedrin had no authority to annul the vow.

Zedekiah was duly punished for the grievous crime of perjury. When Jerusalem was captured, he tried to escape through a cave extending from his house to Jericho. God sent a deer into the camp of the Chaldeans, and in their pursuit of this game, the Babylonian soldiers reached the farther opening of the cave at the very moment when Zedekiah was leaving it. The Jewish king together with his ten sons was brought before Nebuchadnezzar, who addressed Zedekiah thus: "Were I to judge thee according to the law of thy God, thou wouldst deserve the death penalty, for thou didst swear a false oath by the Name of God; no less wouldst thou deserve death, if I were to judge thee according to the law of the state, for thou didst fail in thy sworn duty to thy overlord."

Zedekiah requested the grace that his execution take place before his children's, and he be spared the sight of their blood. His children, on the other hand, besought Nebuchadnezzar to slay them before he slew their father, that they might be spared the disgrace of seeing their father executed. In his heartlessness Nebuchadnezzar had resolved worse things than Zedekiah anticipated. In the sight of their father, the children of Zedekiah were killed, and then Zedekiah himself was deprived of sight; his eyes were blinded. He had been endowed with eyes of superhuman strength, they were the eyes of Adam, and the iron lances forced into them were powerless to destroy his sight. Vision left him only because of the tears he shed over the fate of his children. Now he realized how true Jeremiah had spoken when he had prophesied his exile to Babylonia. Though he should live there until his death, he would never behold the land with his eyes. On account of its seeming contradictoriness, Zedekiah had thought the prophecy untrue. For this reason he had not heeded Jeremiah's advice to make peace with Nebuchadnezzar. Now it had all been verified; he was carried to Babylonia a captive, yet, blind as he was, he did not see the land of his exile.

JEREMIAH

Though Zedekiah besmirched his career by perjury, he was nevertheless so good and just a king that for his sake God relinquished his purpose of returning the world to its original chaos, as a punishment for the evil-doing of a wicked generation. In this depraved time, it was first and foremost Jeremiah to whom was delegated the task of proclaiming the word of God. He was a descendant of Joshua and Rahab, and his father was the prophet Hilkiah. He was born while his father was fleeing from the persecution of Jezebel, the murderess of prophets. At his very birth he showed signs that he was destined to play a great part. He was born circumcised, and scarcely had he left his mother's womb when he broke into wailing, and his voice was the voice, not of a babe, but of a youth. He cried: "My bowels, my bowels tremble, the walls of my heart they are disquieted, my limbs quake, destruction upon destruction I bring upon earth." In this strain he continued to moan and groan, complaining of the faithlessness of his mother, and when she expressed her amazement at the unseemly speech of her new-born son, Jeremiah said: "Not thee do I mean, my mother, not to thee doth my prophecy refer; I speak of Zion, and against Jerusalem are my words directed. She adorns her daughters, arrays them in purple, and puts golden crowns upon their heads. Robbers will come and strip them of their ornaments."

As a lad he received the call to be a prophet. But he refused to obey, saying: "O Lord, I cannot go as a prophet to Israel, for when lived there a prophet whom Israel did not desire to kill? Moses and Aaron they sought to stone with stones; Elijah the Tishbite they mocked at because his hair was grown long; and they called after Elisha, 'Go up, thou bald head' no, I cannot go to Israel, for I am still naught but a lad." God replied: "I love youth, for it is innocent. When I carried Israel out of Egypt, I called him a lad, and when I think of Israel lovingly, I speak of him as a lad. Say not, therefore, thou art only a lad, but thou shalt go on whatsoever errand I shall send thee. Now, then," God, continued, "take the 'cup of wrath,' and let the nations drink of it." Jeremiah put the question which land was to drink first from the "cup of wrath," and the answer of God was: "First Jerusalem is to drink, the head of all earthly nations, and then the cities of Judah." When the prophet heard this, he began to curse the day of his birth. "I am like the high priest," he said, "who has to administer the 'water of bitterness' to a woman who is held under the suspicion of adultery, and when he approaches the woman with the cup, lo, he beholds his own mother. And I, O Mother Zion, thought, when I was called to prophesy, that I was appointed to proclaim prosperity and salvation to thee, but now I see that my message forebodes thee evil."

Jeremiah's first appearance in public was during the reign of Josiah, when he announced to the people in the streets: "If ye will give up your wicked doings, God will raise you above all nations; if not, He will deliver His house into the hands of the enemies, and they will deal with it as seemeth best to them."

The prophets contemporary with Jeremiah in his early years were Zechariah and Huldah. The province of the latter was among women, while Zechariah was active in the synagogue. Later, under Jehoiakim, Jeremiah was supported by the prophets of his relative Uriah of Kiriathjearim, a friend of the prophet Isaiah. But Uriah was put to death by the ungodly king, the same who had the first chapter of Lamentations burnt after obliterating the Name of God wherever it occurs in the whole book. But Jeremiah added four chapters.

The prophet fell upon evil times under Zedekiah. He had both the people and the court against him. Nor was that surprising in a day when not even the high priests in the Temple bore the sign of the covenant upon their bodies. Jeremiah had called forth general hostility by condemning the alliance with Egypt against Babylonia, and favoring peace with Nebuchadnezzar; and this though to all appearances the help of the Egyptians would prove of good effect for the Jews. The hosts of Pharaoh Necho had actually set forth from Egypt to join the Jews against Babylon. But when they were on the high seas, God commanded the waters to cover themselves with corpses. Astonished, the Egyptians asked each other, whence the dead bodies. Presently the answer occurred to them: they were the bodies of their ancestors drowned in the Red Sea on account of the Jews, who had shaken off Egyptian rule. "What," said the Egyptians thereupon, "shall we bring help to those who drowned our fathers?" So they returned to their own country, justifying the warning of Jeremiah, that no dependence could be put upon Egyptian promises.

A little while after this occurrence, when Jeremiah wanted to leave Jerusalem to go to Anathoth and partake of his priestly portion there, the watchman at the gate accused him of desiring to desert to the enemy. He was delivered to his adversaries at court, and they confined him in prison. The watchman knew full well that it was a trumped up charge he was bringing against Jeremiah, and the intention attributed to him was as far as possible from the mind of the prophet, but he took this opportunity to vent an old family grudge. For this gateman was a grandson of the false prophet Hananiah, the enemy of Jeremiah, the one who had prophesied complete victory over Nebuchadnezzar within two years. It were proper to say, he calculated the victory rather than prophesied it. He reasoned: "If unto Elam, which is a mere ally of the Babylonians against the Jews, destruction has been appointed by God through Jeremiah, so much the more will the extreme penalty fall upon the Babylonians themselves, who have inflicted vast evil upon the Jews." Jeremiah's prophecy had been the reverse: so far from holding forth any hope that a victory would be won over Nebuchadnezzar, the Jewish state, he said, would suffer annihilation. Hananiah demanded a sign betokening the truth of Jeremiah's prophecy. But Jeremiah contended there could be no sign for such a prophecy as his, since the Divine determination to do evil can be annulled. On the other hand, it was the duty of Hananiah to give a sign, for he was prophesying pleasant things, and the Divine resolution for good is executed without. Finally, Jeremiah advanced the clinching argument: "I, a priest, may be well content with the prophecy; it is to my interest that the Temple should continue to stand. As for thee, thou art a Gibeonite, thou wilt have to do a slave's service in it so long as there is a Temple. But instead of troubling thy mind with the future in store for others, thou shouldst rather have thought of thine own future, for this very year thou wilt die." Hananiah, in very truth, died on the last day of the year set as his term of life, but before his death he ordered that it should be kept secret for two days, so to give the lie to Jeremiah's prophecy. With his last words, addressed to his son Shelemiah, he charged him to seek every possible way of taking revenge upon Jeremiah, to whose curse his death was to be ascribed. Shelemiah had no opportunity of fulfilling his father's last behest, but it did not pass from his mind, and when he, in turn, lay upon his death-bed, he impressed the duty of revenge upon his son Jeriah. It was the grandson of Hananiah who, when he saw Jeremiah leaving the city, hastened to take the opportunity of accusing the prophet of treason. His purpose prospered. The aristocratic enemies of Jeremiah, enraged against him, welcomed the chance to put him behind prison bars, and gave him in charge of a jailer, Jonathan, who had been a friend of the false prophet Hananiah. Jonathan pleased himself by mocking at his prisoner: "See," he would say, "see what honor thy friend does thee, to put thee in so fine a prison as this; verily, it is a royal palace."

Despite his suffering, Jeremiah did not hold back the truth. When the king inquired of him, whether he had a revelation from God, he replied: "Yes, the king of Babylonia will carry thee off into exile." To avoid irritating the king, he went into no further detail. He only prayed the king to liberate him from prison, saying: "Even wicked men like Hananiah and his descendants at least cast about for a pretext when they desire to take revenge, and their example ought not to be lost upon thee who art called Zedekiah, 'just man.'" The king granted his petition, but Jeremiah did not enjoy liberty for long. Hardly out of prison, he again advised the people to surrender, and the nobility seized him and cast him into a lime pit filled with water, where they hoped he would drown. But a miracle happened. The water sank to the bottom, and the mud rose to the surface, and supported the prophet above the water. Help came to him from Ebed-melech, a "white raven," the only pious man at court. Ebed-melech hastened to the king and spoke: "Know, if Jeremiah perishes in the lime pit, Jerusalem will surely be captured." With the permission of the king, Ebed-melech went to the pit, and cried out aloud several times, "O my lord Jeremiah," but no answer came. Jeremiah feared the words were spoken by his former jailer Jonathan, who had not given up his practice of mocking at the prophet. He would come to the edge of the pit and call down jeeringly: "Do not rest thy head on the mud, and take a little sleep, Jeremiah." To such sneers Jeremiah made no reply, and hence it was that Ebed-melech was left unanswered. Thinking the prophet dead, he began to lament and tear his clothes. Then Jeremiah, realizing that it was a friend, and not Jonathan, asked: "Who is it that is calling my name and weeps therewith?" and he received the assurance that Ebed-melech had come to rescue him from his perilous position.

NEBUCHADNEZZAR

The suffering to which Jeremiah was exposed was finally ended by the capture of Jerusalem by Nebuchadnezzar. This Babylonian king was a son of King Solomon and the Queen of Sheba. His first contact with the Jews happened in the time of his father-in-law Sennacherib, whom he accompanied on his campaign against Hezekiah. The destruction of the Assyrian army before the walls of Jerusalem, the great catastrophe from which only Nebuchadnezzar and four others escaped with their life, inspired him with fear of God. Later, in his capacity as secretary to the Babylonian king Merodach-baladan, it was he who called his master's notice to the mention of the Jewish king's name before the Name of God. "Thou callest Him 'the great God,' yet thou dost name Him after the king," he said. Nebuchadnezzar himself hastened after the messenger to bring back the letter and have it changed. He had advanced scarce three steps when he was restrained by the angel Gabriel, for even the few paces he had walked for the glory of God earned him his great power over Israel. A further step would have extended his ability to inflict harm immeasurably.

For eighteen years daily a heavenly voice resounded in the palace of Nebuchadnezzar, saying: "O thou wicked slave, go and destroy the house of thy Lord, for His children hearken not unto Him." But Nebuchadnezzar was beset with fears lest God prepare a fate for him similar to that of his ancestor Sennacherib. He practiced belomancy and consulted other auguries, to assure himself that he was against Jerusalem would result favorably. When he shook up the arrows, and questioned whether he was to go to Rome or Alexandria, not one arrow sprang up, but when he questioned about Jerusalem, one sprang up. He sowed seeds and set out planets; for Rome or Alexandria nothing came up; for Jerusalem everything sprouted and grew. He lighted candles and lanterns; for Rome or Alexandria they refused to burn, for Jerusalem they shed their light. He floated vessels on the Euphrates; for Rome or Alexandria they did not move, for Jerusalem they swam.

Still the fears of Nebuchadnezzar were not allayed. His determination to attack the Holy City ripened only after God Himself had shown him how He had bound the hands of the archangel Michael, the patron of the Jews, behind his back, in order to render him powerless to bring to his wards. So the campaign against Jerusalem was undertaken.

THE CAPTURE OF JERUSALEM

If the Babylonians thought that the conquest of Jerusalem was an easy task, they were greatly mistaken. For three years God endured the inhabitants with strength to withstand the onslaughts of the enemy, in the hope that the Jews would amend their evil ways and abandon their godless conduct, so that the threatened punishment might be annulled.

Among the many heroes in the beleaguered city that was bidding defiance to the Babylonians, one by the name of Akiba was particularly distinguished. The stones were hurled at the walls of the city from the catapults wielded by the enemy without, he was wont to catch on his feet, and throw them back upon the besiegers. Once it happened that a stone was so cast as to drop, not upon the wall, but in front of it. In his swift race toward it, Akiba was precipitated into the space between the inner and the outer wall. He quickly reassured his friends in the city, that his fall had in no wise harmed him. He was only a little shaken up and weak; as soon as he had his accustomed daily meal, a roasted ox, he would be able to scale the wall and resume the struggle with the Babylonians. But human strength and artifice avail naught against God. A gust of wind arose, and Akiba was thrown from the wall, and he died. Thereupon the Chaldeans made a breach in the wall, and penetrated into the city.

Equally fruitless were the endeavors of Hanamel, the uncle of Jeremiah, to save the city. He conjured the angels up, armed them, and had them occupy the walls. The Chaldeans retreated in terror at the sight of the heavenly host. But God changed the names of the angels, and brought them back to heaven. Hanamel's exorcisms availed naught. When he called the Angel of the Water, for instance, the response would come from the Angel of Fire, who bore the former name of his companion. Then Hanamel resorted to the extreme measure of summoning the Prince of the World, who raised Jerusalem high up in the air. But God thrust the city down again, and the enemy entered unhindered.

Nevertheless, the capture of the city could not have been accomplished if Jeremiah had been present. His deeds were as a firm pillar for the city, and his prayers as a stony wall. Therefore God sent the prophet on an errand out of the city. He was made to go to his native place, Anathoth, to take possession of a field, his by right of inheritance. Jeremiah rejoiced; he took this as a sign that God would be gracious to Judah, else He would not have commanded him to take possession of a piece of land. Scarcely had the prophet left Jerusalem when an angel descended upon the wall of the city and caused a breach to appear, at the same time crying out: "Let the enemy come and enter the house, for the Master of the house is no longer therein. The enemy has leave to despoil it and destroy it. Go ye into the vineyard and snap the vines asunder, for the Watchman hath gone away and abandoned it. But let no man boast and say, he and his have vanquished the city. Nay, a conquered city have ye conquered, a dead people have ye killed."

The enemy rushed in and ascended the Temple mount, and on the spot whereon King Solomon had been in the habit of sitting when he took counsel with the elders, the Chaldeans plotted how to reduce the Temple to ashes. During their sinister deliberations, they beheld four angels, each with a flaming torch in his hand, descending and setting fire to the four corners of the Temple. The high priest, seeing the flames shoot up, cast the keys of the Temple heavenward, saying: "Here are the keys of Thy house; it seems I am an untrustworthy custodian," and, as he turned, he was seized by the enemy and slaughtered in the very place on which he had been wont to offer the daily sacrifice. With him perished his daughter, her blood mingling with her father's. The priests and the Levites threw themselves into the flames with their harps and trumpets, and, to escape the violence feared from the licentious Chaldeans, the virgins who wove the curtains for the sanctuary followed their example. Still more horrible was the carnage caused among the people by Nebuzaradan, spurred on as he was by the sight of the blood of the murdered prophet Zechariah seething on the floor of the Temple. At first the Jews sought to conceal the true story connected with the blood. At length they had to confess, that it was the blood of a prophet who had prophesied the destruction of the Temple, and for his candor had been slain by the people. Nebuzaradan, to appease the prophet, ordered the scholars of the kingdom to be executed first on the bloody spot, then the school children, and at last the young priests, more than a million souls in all. But the blood of the prophet went on seething and reeking, until Nebuzaradan exclaimed: "Zechariah, Zechariah, the good in Israel I have slaughtered. Dost thou desire the destruction of the whole people?" Then the blood ceased to seethe.

Nebuzaradan was startled by the thought, if the Jews, who had a single life upon their conscience, were made to atone so cruelly, what would be his own fate! He left Nebuchadnezzar and became a proselyte.

THE GREAT LAMENT

On his return from Anathoth, Jeremiah saw, at a distance, smoke curling upward from the Temple mount, and his spirit was joyful. He thought the Jews had repented of their sins, and were bringing incense offerings. Once within the city walls, he knew the truth, that the Temple had fallen a prey to the incendiary. Overwhelmed by grief, he cried out: "O Lord, Thou didst entice me, and I permitted myself to be enticed; Thou didst send me forth out of Thy house that Thou mightest destroy it."

God Himself was deeply moved by the destruction of the Temple, which He had abandoned that the enemy might enter and destroy it. Accompanied by the angels, He visited the ruins, and gave vent to His sorrow: "Woe is Me on account of My house. Where are My children, where My priests, where My beloved? But what could I do for you? Did I not warn you? Yet you would not mend your ways." "To-day," God said to Jeremiah, "I am like a man who has an only son. He prepares the marriage canopy for him, and his only beloved dies under it. Thou doest seem to feel but little sympathy with Me and with My children. Go, summon Abraham, Isaac, Jacob, and Moses from their graces. They know how to mourn." "Lord of the world," replied Jeremiah, "I know not where Moses is buried." "Stand on the banks of the Jordan," said God, "and cry: 'Thou son of Amram, son of Amram, arise, see how wolves have devoured thy sheep.'"

Jeremiah repaired to the Double Cave, and spake to the Patriarchs: "Arise, ye are summoned to appear before God." When they asked him the reason of the summons, he feigned ignorance, for he feared to tell them the true reason; they might have cast reproaches upon him that so great a disaster had overtaken Israel in his time. Then Jeremiah journeyed on to the banks of the Jordan, and there he called as he had been bidden: "Thou son of Amram, son of Amram, arise, thou are cited to appear before God." "What has happened this day, that God calls me unto Him?" asked Moses. "I know not," replied Jeremiah again. Moses thereupon went to the angels, and from them he learned that the Temple had been destroyed, and Israel banished from his land. Weeping and mourning, Moses joined the Patriarchs, and together, rending their garments and wringing their hands, they betook themselves to the ruins of the Temple. Here their wailing was augmented by the loud lamentations of the angels: "How desolate are the highways to Jerusalem, the highways destined for travel without end! How deserted are the streets that once were thronged at the seasons of the pilgrimages! O Lord of the world, with Abraham the father of Thy people, who taught the world to know Thee as the ruler of the universe, Thou didst make a covenant, that through him and his descendants the earth should be filled with people, and now Thou hast dissolved Thy covenant with him. O Lord of the world! Thou hast scorned Zion and Jerusalem, once Thy chosen habitation. Thou hast dealt more harshly with Israel than with the generation of Enosh, the first idolaters."

God thereupon said to the angels: "Why do ye array yourselves against Me with your complaints?" "Lord do the world," they replied, "on account of Abraham, Thy beloved, who has come into Thy house wailing and weeping, yet Thou payest no heed unto him." Thereupon God: "Since My beloved ended his earthly career, he has not been in My house. 'What hath My beloved to do in My house'?"

Now Abraham entered into the conversation: "Why, O Lord of the world, hast Thou exiled my children, delivered them into the hands of the nations, who torture them with all tortures, and who have rendered desolate the sanctuary, where I was ready to bring Thee my son Isaac as a sacrifice?" "Thy children have sinned," said God, "they have transgressed the whole Torah, they have offended against every letter of it." Abraham: "Who is there that will testify against Israel, that he has transgressed the Torah?" God: "Let the Torah herself appear and testify." The Torah came, and Abraham addressed her: "O my daughter, dost thou indeed come to testify against Israel, to say that he violated thy commandments? Dost thou feel no shame? Remember the day on which God offered thee to all the peoples, all the nations of the earth, and they all rejected thee with disdain. Then my children came to Sinai, they accepted thee, and they honored thee. And now, on the day of their distress, thou standest up against them?" Hearing this, the Torah stepped aside, and did not testify. "Let the twenty-two letters of the Hebrew alphabet in which Torah is written come and testify against Israel," said God. They appeared without delay, and Alef, the first letter, was about to testify against Israel, when Abraham interrupted it with the words: "Thou chief of all letters, thou comest to testify against Israel in the time of his distress? Be mindful of the day on which God revealed Himself on Mount Sinai, beginning His words with thee: 'Anoki the Lord thy God.' No people, no nation accepted thee, only my children, and now thou comest to testify against them!" Alef stepped aside and was silent. The same happened with the second letter Bet, and with the third, Gimel, and with all the rest all of them retired abashed, and opened not their mouth. Now Abraham turned to God and said: "O Lord of the world! When I was a hundred years old, Thou didst give me a son, and when he was in the flower of his age, thirty-seven years old, Thou didst command me to sacrifice him to Thee, and I, like a monster, without compassion, I bound him upon the altar with mine own hands. Let that plead with Thee, and have Thou pity on my children."

Then Isaac raised his voice and spake: "O Lord of the world, when my father told me, 'God will provide Himself the lamb for a burnt offering, my son,' I did not resist Thy word. Willingly I let myself be tied to the altar, my throat was raised to meet the knife. Let that plead with Thee, and have Thou pity on my children."

Then Jacob raised his voice and spake: "O Lord of the world, for twenty years I dwelt in the house of Laban, and when I left it, I met with Esau, who sought to murder my children, and I risked my life for theirs. And now they are delivered into the hands of their enemies, like sheep led to the shambles, after I coddled them like fledglings breaking forth from their shells, after I suffered anguish for their sake all the days of my life. Let that plead with Thee, and have Thou pity on my children."

And at last Moses raised his voice and spake: "O Lord of the world, was I not a faithful shepherd unto Israel for forty long years? Like a steed I ran ahead of him in the desert, and when the time came for him to enter the Promised Land, Thou didst command: 'Here in the desert shall thy bones drop!' And now that the children of Israel are exiled, Thou hast sent for me to mourn and lament over them. That is what the people mean when they say: The good fortune of the master is none for the slave, but the master's woe is his woe." And turning to Jeremiah, he continued: "Walk before me, I will lead them back; let us see who will venture to raise a hand against them." Jeremiah replied: "The roads cannot be passed, they are blocked with corpses." But Moses was not to be deterred, and the two, Moses following Jeremiah, reached the rivers of Babylon. When the Jews saw Moses, they said: "The son of Amram has ascended from his grave to redeem us from our enemies." At that moment a heavenly voice was heard to cry out: "It is decreed!" And Moses said: "O my children, I cannot redeem you, the decree is unalterable may God redeem you speedily," and he departed from them.

The children of Israel raised their voices in sore lamentations, and the sound of their grief pierced to the very heavens. Meantime Moses returned to the Fathers, and reported to them to what dire suffering the exiled Jews were exposed, and they all broke out into woe-begone plaints. In his bitter grief, Moses exclaimed: "Be cursed, O sun, why was not thy light extinguished in the hour in which the enemy invaded the sanctuary?" The sun replied: "O faithful shepherd, I sware by the life, I could not grow dark. The heavenly powers would not permit it. Sixty fiery scourges they dealt me, and they said, 'Go and let thy light shine forth,'" Another last complaint Moses uttered: "O Lord of the world, Thou hast written it in Thy Torah: 'And whether it be cow or ewe, ye shall not kill it and her young both in one day.' How many mothers have they slaughtered with their children and Thou art silent!"

Then, with the suddenness of a flash, Rachel, our mother, stood before the Holy One, blessed be He: "Lord of the world," she said, "Thou knowest how overwhelming was Jacob's love for me, and when I observed that my father thought to put Leah in my place, I gave Jacob secret signs, that the plan of my father might be set at naught. But then I repented me of what I had done, and to spare my sister mortification, I disclosed the signs to her. More than this, I myself was in the bridal chamber, and when Jacob spake with Leah, I made reply, lest her voice betray her. I, a woman, a creature of flesh and blood, of dust and ashes, was not jealous of my rival. Thou, O God, everlasting King, Thou eternal and merciful Father, why wast Thou jealous of the idols, empty vanities? Why hast Thou driven out my children, slain them with swords, left them at the mercy of their enemies?" Then the compassion of the Supreme God was awakened, and He said: "For thy sake, O Rachel, I will lead the children of Israel back to their land."

JEREMIAH'S JOURNEY TO BABYLON

When Nebuchadnezzar dispatched his general Nebuzaradan to the capture of Jerusalem, he gave him three instructions regarding the mild treatment of Jeremiah: "Take him, and look well to him, and do him no harm; but do unto him even as he shall say unto thee." At the same time he enjoined him to use pitiless cruelty toward the rest of the people. But the prophet desired to share the fate of his suffering brethren, and when he saw a company of youths in the pillory, he put his own head into it. Nebuzaradan would always withdraw him again. Thereafter if Jeremiah saw a company of old men clapped in chains, he would join them and share their ignominy, until Nebuzaradan released him. Finally, Nebuzaradan said to Jeremiah: "Lo, thou art one of three things; either thou are a prophesier of false things, or thou art a despiser of suffering, or thou art a shedder of blood. A prophesier of false things for since many a year hast thou been prophesying the downfall of this city, and now, when thy prophecy has come true, thou sorrowest and mournest. Or a despiser of suffering for I seek to do thee naught harmful, and thou thyself pursuest what is harmful to thee, as thou to say, 'I am indifferent to pain.' Or a shedder of blood for the king has charged me to have a care of thee, and let no harm come upon thee, but as thou insistest upon seeking evil for thyself, it must be that the king may hear of thy misfortune, and put me to death."

At first Jeremiah refused Nebuzaradan's offer to let him remain in Palestine. He joined the march of the captives going to Babylon, along the highways streaming with blood and strewn with corpses. When they arrived at the borders of the Holy Land, they all, prophet and people, broke out into loud wails, and Jeremiah said: "Yes, brethren and countrymen, all this hath befallen you, because ye did not hearken unto the words of my prophecy." Jeremiah journeyed with them until they came to the banks of the Euphrates. Then God spoke to the prophet: "Jeremiah, if thou remainest here, I shall go with them, and if thou goest with them, I shall remain here." Jeremiah replied: "Lord of the world, if I go with them, what doth it avail them? Only if their King, their Creator accompanies them, will it bestead them."

When the captives saw Jeremiah make preparations to return to Palestine, they began to weep and cry: "O Father Jeremiah, wilt thou, too, abandon us?" "I call heaven and earth to witness," said the prophet, "had you wept but once in Zion, ye had not been driven out."

Beset with terrors was the return journey for the prophet. Corpses lay everywhere, and Jeremiah gathered up all the fingers that lay about; he strained them to his heart, fondled them, kissed them, and wrapped them in his mantle, saying sadly: "Did I not tell you, my children, did I not say to you, 'Give glory to the Lord your God, before He cause darkness, and before your feet stumble upon the dark mountains'?"

Dejected, oppressed by his grief, Jeremiah saw the fulfilment of his prophecy against the coquettish maidens of Jerusalem, who had pursued but the pleasures and enjoyments of the world. How often had the prophet admonished them to do penance and lead a God-fearing life! In vain; whenever he threatened them with the destruction of Jerusalem, they said: "Why should we concern ourselves about it?" "A prince will take me unto wife," said one, the other, "A prefect will marry me." And at first it seemed the expectations of Jerusalem's fair daughters would be realized, for the most aristocratic of the victorious Chaldeans were charmed by the beauty of the women of Jerusalem, and offered them their hand and their rank. But God sent disfiguring and repulsive diseases upon the women, and the Babylonians cast them off, threw them violently out of their chariots, and ruthlessly drove them over the prostrate bodies.

TRANSPORTATION OF THE CAPTIVES

Nebuchadnezzar's orders were to hurry the captives along the road to Babylon without stop or stay. He feared the Jews might else find opportunity to supplicate the mercy of God, and He, compassionate as He is, would release them instantly they did penance. Accordingly, there was no pause in the forward march, until the Euphrates was reached. There they were within the borders of the empire of Nebuchadnezzar, and he thought he had nothing more to fear.

Many of the Jews died as soon as they drank of the Euphrates. In their native land they had been accustomed to the water drawn from springs and wells. Mourning over their dead and over the others that had fallen by the way, they sat on the banks of the river, while Nebuchadnezzar and his princes on their vessels celebrated their victory amid song and music. The king noticed that the princes of Judah, though they were in chains, bore no load upon their shoulders, and he called to his servants: "Have you no load for these?" They took the parchment scrolls of the law, tore them in pieces, made sacks of them, and filled them with sand; these they loaded upon the backs of the Jewish princes. At sight of this disgrace, all Israel broke out into loud weeping. The voice of their sorrow pierced the very heavens, and God determined to turn the world once more into chaos, for He told Himself, that after all the world was created but for the sake of Israel. The angels hastened thither, and they spake before God: "O Lord of the world, the universe is Thine. Is it not enough that Thou hast dismembered Thy earthly house, the Temple? Wilt Thou destroy Thy heavenly house, too?" God restraining them said: "Do ye think I am a creature of flesh and blood, and stand in need of consolation? Do I not know beginning and end of all things? Go rather and remove their burdens from the princes of Judah." Aided by God the angels descended, and they carried the loads put upon the Jewish captives until they reached Babylon.

On their way, they passed the city of Bari. The inhabitants thereof were not a little astonished at the cruelty of Nebuchadnezzar, who made the captives march naked. The people of Bari stripped their slaves of their clothes, and presented the slaves to Nebuchadnezzar. When the king expressed his astonishment thereat, they said: "We thought thou wert particularly pleased with naked men." The king at once ordered the Jews to be arrayed in their garments. The reward accorded the Bariites was that God endowed them forever with beauty and irresistible grace.

The compassionate Bariites did not find many imitators. The very opposite quality was displayed by the Ammonites, Moabites, Edomites, and Arabs. Despite their close kinship with Israel, their conduct toward the Jews was dictated by cruelty. The two first-mentioned, the Ammonites and the Moabites, when they heard the prophet foretell the destruction of Jerusalem, hastened without a moment's delay to report it to Nebuchadnezzar, and urge him to attack Jerusalem. The scruples of the Babylonian king, who feared God, and all the reasons he advanced against a combat with Israel, they refuted, and finally they induced him to act as they wished. At the capture of the city, while all the strange nations were seeking booty, the Ammonites and the Moabites threw themselves into the Temple to seize the scroll of the law, because it contained the clause against their entering into the "assembly of the Lord even to the tenth generation." To disgrace the faith of Israel, they plucked the Cherubim from the Holy of Holies and dragged them through the streets of Jerusalem, crying aloud at the same time: "Behold these sacred things that belong to the Israelites, who say ever they have no idols."

The Edomites were still more hostile in the hour of Israel's need. They went to Jerusalem with Nebuchadnezzar, but they kept themselves at a distance from the city, there to await the outcome of the battle between the Jews and the Babylonians. If the Jews had been victorious, they would have pretended they had come to bring them aid. When Nebuchadnezzar's victory became known, they showed their true feelings. Those who escaped the sword of the Babylonians, were hewn down by the hand of the Edomites.

But in fiendish cunning these nations were surpassed by the Ishmaelites. Eighty thousand young priests, each with a golden shield upon his breast, succeeded in making their way through the ranks of Nebuchadnezzar and in reaching the Ishmaelites. They asked for water to drink. The reply of the Ishmaelites was: "First eat, and then you may drink," at the same time handing them salt food. Their thirst was increased, and the Ishmaelites gave them leather bags filled with nothing but air instead of water. When they raised them to their mouths, the air entered their bodies, and they fell dead.

Other Arabic tribes showed their hostility openly; as the Palmyrenes, who put eighty thousand archers at the disposal of Nebuchadnezzar in his war against Israel.

THE SONS OF MOSES

If Nebuchadnezzar thought, that once he had the Jews in the regions of the Euphrates they were in his power forever, he was greatly mistaken. It was on the very banks of the great river that he suffered the loss of a number of his captives. When the first stop was made by the Euphrates, the Jews could no longer contain their grief, and they broke out into tears and bitter lamentations. Nebuchadnezzar bade them be silent, and as though to render obedience to his orders the harder, he called upon the Levites, the minstrels of the Temple to sing the songs of Zion for the entertainment of his guests at the banquet he had arranged. The Levites consulted with one another. "Not enough that the Temple lies in ashes because of our sins, should we add to our transgressions by coaxing music from the strings of our holy harps in honor of these 'dwarfs'?" they said, and they determined to offer resistance. The murderous Babylonians mowed them down in heaps, yet they met death with high courage, for it saved their sacred instruments from the desecration of being used before idols and for the sake of idolaters.

The Levites who survived the carnage the Sons of Moses they were bit their own fingers off, and when they were asked to play, they showed their tyrants mutilated hands, with which it was impossible to manipulate their harps. At the fall of night a cloud descended and enveloped the Sons of Moses and all who belonged to them. They were hidden from their enemies, while their own way was illuminated by a pillar of fire. The cloud and the pillar vanished at break of day, and before the Sons of Moses lay a tract of land bordered by the sea on three sides. For their complete protection God made the river Sambation to flow on the fourth side. This river is full of sand and stones, and on the six working days of the week, they tumble over each other with such vehemence that the crash and the roar are heard far and wide. But on the Sabbath the tumultuous river subsides into quiet. As a guard against trespassers on that day, a column of cloud stretches along the whole length of the river, and none can approach the Sambation within three miles. Hedged in as they are, the Sons of Moses yet communicate with their brethren of the tribes of Naphtali, Gad, and Asher, who dwell near the banks of the Sambation. Carrier pigeons bear letters hither and thither.

In the land of the Sons of Moses there are none but clean animals, and in every respect the inhabitants lead a holy and pure life, worthy of their ancestor Moses. They never use an oath, and, if perchance an oath escapes the lips of one of them, he is at once reminded of the Divine punishment connected with his act his children will die at a tender age.

The Sons of Moses live peaceably and enjoy prosperity as equals through their common Jewish faith. They have need of neither prince nor judge, for they know not strife and litigation. Each works for the welfare of the community, and each takes from the common store only what will satisfy his needs. Their houses are built of equal height, that no one may deem himself above his neighbor, and that that the fresh air may not be hindered from playing freely about all alike. Even at night their doors stand wide open, for they have naught to fear from thieves, nor are wild animals known in their land. They all attain a good old age. The son never dies before the father. When a death occurs, there is rejoicing, because the departed is known to have entered into life everlasting in loyalty to his faith. The birth of a child, on the other hand, calls forth mourning, for who can tell whether the being ushered into the world will be pious and faithful? The dead are buried near the doors of their own houses, in order that their survivors, in all their comings and goings, may be reminded of their own end. Disease is unknown among them, for they never sin, and sickness is sent only to purify from sins.

EBED-MELECH

The Sons of Moses were not the only ones to escape from under the heavy hand of Nebuchadnezzar. Still more miraculous was the deliverance of the pious Ethiopian Ebed-melech from the hands of the Babylonians. He was saved as a reward for rescuing Jeremiah when the prophet's life was jeopardized. On the day before the destruction of the Temple, shortly before the enemy forced his way into the city, the Ethiopian was sent, by the prophet Jeremiah acting under Divine instruction, to a certain place in front of the gates of the city, to dole out refreshments to the poor from a little basket of figs he was to carry with him. Ebed-melech reached the spot, but the heat was so intense that he fell asleep under a tree, and there he slept for sixty-six years. When he woke up, the figs were still fresh and juicy, but all the surroundings had so changed, he could not make out where he was. His confusion increased when he entered the city to seek Jeremiah, and found nothing as it had been. He accosted an old man, and asked him the name of the place. When he was told it was Jerusalem, Ebed-melech cried out in amazement: "Where is Jeremiah, where is Baruch, and where are all the people?" The old man was not a little astonished at these questions. How was it possible that one who had known Jeremiah and Jerusalem should be ignorant of the events that had passed sixty years before? In brief words he told Ebed-melech of the destruction of the Temple and of the captivity of the people, but what he said found no credence with his auditor. Finally Ebed-melech realized that God had performed a great miracle for him, so that he had been spared the sight of Israel's misfortune.

While he was pouring out his heart in gratitude to God, an eagle descended and led him to Baruch, who lived not far from the city. Thereupon Baruch received the command from God to write to Jeremiah that the people should remove the strangers from the midst of them, and then God would lead them back to Jerusalem. The letter written by Baruch and some of the figs that had retained their freshness for sixty-six years were carried to Babylonia by an eagle, who had told Baruch that he had been sent to serve him as a messenger. The eagle set out on his journey. His first halting-place was a dreary waste spot to which he knew Jeremiah and the people would come it was the burial-place of the Jews which Nebuchadnezzar had given the prophet at his solicitation. When the eagle saw Jeremiah and the people approach with a funeral train, he cried out: "I have a message for thee, Jeremiah. Let all the people draw nigh to receive the good tidings." As a sign that his mission was true, the eagle touched the corpse, and it came to life. Amidst tears all the people cried unto Jeremiah: "Save us! What must we do to return to our land?"

The eagle brought Jeremiah's answer to Baruch, and after the prophet had sent the Babylonian women away, he returned to Jerusalem with the people. Those who would not submit to the orders of Jeremiah relative to the heathen women, were not permitted by the prophet to enter the holy city, and as they likewise were not permitted to return to Babylonia, they founded the city of Samaria near Jerusalem.

THE TEMPLE VESSELS

The task laid upon Jeremiah had been twofold. Besides giving him charge over the people in the land of their exile, God had entrusted to him the care of the sanctuary and all it contained. The holy Ark, the altar of incense, and the holy tent were carried by an angel to the mount whence Moses before his death had viewed the land divinely assigned to Israel. There Jeremiah found a spacious place, in which he concealed these sacred utensils. Some of his companions had gone with him to note the way to the cave, but yet they could not find it. When Jeremiah heard of their purpose, he censured them, for it was the wish of God that the place of hiding should remain a secret until the redemption, and then God Himself will make the hidden things visible.

Even the Temple vessels not concealed by Jeremiah were prevented from falling into the hands of the enemy; the gates of the Temple sank into the earth, and other parts and utensils were hidden in a tower at Bagdad by the Levite Shimur and his friends. Among these utensils was the seven-branched candlestick of pure gold, every branch set with twenty-six pearls, and beside the pearls two hundred stones of inestimable worth. Furthermore, the tower at Bagdad was the hiding-place for seventy-seven golden tables, and for the gold with which the walls of the Temple had been clothed within and without. The tables had been taken from Paradise by Solomon, and in brilliance they outshone the sun and the moon, while the gold from the walls excelled in amount and worth all the gold that had existed from the creation of the world until the destruction of the Temple. The jewels, pearls, gold, and silver, and precious gems, which David and Solomon had intended for the Temple were discovered by the scribe Hilkiah, and he delivered them to the angel Shamshiel, who in turn deposited the treasure in Borsippa. The sacred musical instruments were taken charge of and hidden by Baruch and Zedekiah until the advent of the Messiah, who will reveal all treasures. In his time a stream will break forth from under the place of the Holy of Holies, and flow through the lands to the Euphrates, and, as it flows, it will uncover all the treasures buried in the earth.

BARUCH

At the time of the destruction of the Temple, one of the prominent figures was Baruch, the faithful attendant of Jeremiah. God commanded him to leave the city one day before the enemy was to enter it, in order that his presence might not render it impregnable. On the following day, he and all other pious men having abandoned Jerusalem, he saw from a distance how the angels descended, set fire to the city walls, and concealed the sacred vessels of the Temple. At first his mourning over the misfortunes of Jerusalem and the people knew no bounds. But he was in a measure consoled at the end of a seven days' fast, when God made known to him that the day of reckoning would come for the heathen, too. Other Divine visions were vouchsafed him. The whole future of mankind was unrolled before his eyes, especially the history of Israel, and he learned that the coming of the Messiah would put an end to all sorrow and misery, and usher in the reign of peace and joy among men. As for him, he would be removed from the earth, he was told, but not through death, and only in order to be kept safe against the coming of the end of all time.

Thus consoled, Baruch addressed an admonition to the people left in Palestine, and wrote two letters of the same tenor to the exiles, one to the nine tribes and a half, the other to the two tribes and a half. The letter to the nine tribes and a half of the captivity was carried to them by an eagle.

Five years after the great catastrophe, he composed a book in Babylon, which contained penitential prayers and hymns of consolation, exhorting Israel and urging the people to return to God and His law. This book Baruch read to King Jeconiah and the whole people on a day of prayer and penitence. On the same occasion a collection was taken up among the people, and the funds thus secured, together with the silver Temple vessels made by order of Zedekiah after Jeconiah had been carried away captive, were sent to Jerusalem, with the request that the high priest Joakim and the people should apply the money to the sacrificial service and to prayers for the life of King Nebuchadnezzar and his son Belshazzar. Thus they might ensure peace and happiness under Babylonian rule. Above all, they were to supplicate God to turn away His wrath from His people.

Baruch sent his book also to the residents of Jerusalem, and they read it in the Temple on distinguished days, and recited the prayers it contains.

Baruch is one of the few mortals who have been privileged to visit Paradise and know its secrets. An angel of the Lord appeared to him while he was lamenting over the destruction of Jerusalem and took him to the seven heavens, to the place of judgment where the doom of the godless is pronounced, and to the abodes of the blessed.

He was still among the living at the time in which Cyrus permitted the Jews to return to Palestine, but on account of his advanced age he could not avail himself of the permission. So long as he was alive, his disciple Ezra remained with him in Babylonia, for "the study of the law is more important than the building of the Temple." It was only after the death of Baruch that he decided to gather together the exiles who desired to return to the Holy Land and rebuild the Temple in Jerusalem.

THE TOMBS OF BARUCH AND EZEKIEL

The piety of Baruch and the great favor he enjoyed with God were made known to later generations many years after his death, through the marvellous occurrences connected with his tomb. Once a Babylonian prince commanded a Jew, Rabbi Solomon by name, to show him the grave of Ezekiel, concerning which he had heard many remarkable tales. The Jew advised the prince first to enter the tomb of Baruch, which adjoined that of Ezekiel. Having succeeded in this, he might attempt the same with the tomb of Ezekiel, the teacher of Baruch. In the presence of his grandees and his people the prince tried to open the grave of Baruch, but his efforts were fruitless. Whosoever touched it, was at once stricken dead. An old Arab advised the prince to call upon the Jews to gain entrance for him, seeing that Baruch had been a Jew, and his books were still being studied by Jews. The Jews prepared themselves by fasts, prayers, penitence, and almsgiving, and they succeeded in opening the grave without a mishap. Baruch was found lying on marble bier, and the appearance of the corpse was as though he had only then passed away. The prince ordered the bier to be brought to the city, and the body to be entombed there. He thought it was not seemly that Ezekiel and Baruch should rest in the same grave. But the bearers found it impossible to remove the bier more than two thousands ells from the original grave; not even with the help of numerous draught-animals could it be urged a single step further. Following the advice of Rabbi Solomon, the prince resolved to enter the bier on the spot they had reached and also to erect an academy there. These miraculous happenings induced the prince to go to Mecca. There he became convinced of the falseness of Mohammedanism, of which he had hitherto been an adherent, and he converted to Judaism, he and his whole court.

Near the grave of Baruch there grows a species of grass whose leaves are covered with gold dust. As the sheen of the gold is not readily noticeable by day, the people seek out the place at night, mark the very spot on which the grass grows, and return by day and gather it.

Not less famous is the tomb of Ezekiel, at a distance of two thousand ells from Baruch's. It is overarched by a beautiful mausoleum erected by King Jeconiah after Evil-merodach had released him from captivity. The mausoleum existed down to the middle ages, and it bore on its walls the names of the thirty-five thousand Jews who assisted Jeconiah in erecting the monument. It was the scene of many miracles. When great crowds of people journeyed thither to pay reverence to the memory of the prophet, the little low gate in the wall surrounding the grave enlarged in width and height to admit all who desired to enter. Once a prince vowed to give a colt to the grave of the prophet, if but his mare which had been sterile would bear one. When his wish was fulfilled, however, he did not keep his promise. But the filly ran a distance equal to a four days' journey to the tomb, and his owner could not recover it until he deposited his value in silver upon the grace. When people went on long journeys, they were in the habit of carrying their treasures to the grave of the prophet, and beseeching him to let none but the rightful heirs remove them thence. The prophet always granted their petition. Once when an attempt was made to take some books from the grave of Ezekiel, the ravager suddenly became sick and blind. For a time a pillar of fire, visible at a great distance, rose above the grave of the prophet, but it disappeared in consequence of the unseemly conduct of the pilgrims who resorted thither.

Not far from the grave of Ezekiel was the grave of Barozak, who once appeared to a rich Jew in a dream. He spoke: "I am Barozak, one of the princes who were led into captivity with Jeremiah. I am one of the just. If thou wilt erect a handsome mausoleum for me, thou wilt be blessed with progeny." The Jew did as he had been bidden, and he who had been childless, shortly after became a father.

DANIEL

The most distinguished member of the Babylonian Diaspora was Daniel. Though not a prophet, he was surpassed by none in wisdom, piety, and good deeds. His firm adherence to Judaism he displayed from his early youth, when, a page at the royal court, he refused to partake of the bread, wine, and oil of the heathen, even though the enjoyment of them was not prohibited by the law. In general, his prominent position at the court was maintained at the cost of many a hardship, for he and his companions, Hananiah, Mishael, and Azariah, were envied their distinctions by numerous enemies, who sought to compass their ruin.

Once they were accused before King Nebuchadnezzar of leading an unchaste life. The king resolved to order their execution. But Daniel and his friends mutilated certain parts of their bodies, and so demonstrated how unfounded were the charges against them.

As a youth Daniel gave evidence of his wisdom, when he convicted two old sinners of having testified falsely against Susanna, as beautiful as she was good. Misled by the perjured witnesses, the court had condemned Susanna to death. Then Daniel, impelled by a higher power, appeared among the people, proclaimed that wrong had been done, and demanded that the case be re-opened. And so it was. Daniel himself cross-questioned the witnesses one after the other. The same questions were addressed to both, and as the replies did not agree with each other, the false witnesses stood condemned, and they were made to suffer the penalty they would have had the court inflict upon their victim.

Daniel's high position in the state dates from the time when he interpreted Nebuchadnezzar's dream. The king said to the astrologers and magicians: "I know my dream, but I do not want to tell you what it was, else you will invent anything at all, and pretend it is the interpretation of the dream. But if you tell me the dream, then I shall have confidence in your interpretation of it."

After much talk between Nebuchadnezzar and his wise men, they confessed that the king's wish might have been fulfilled, if but the Temple had still existed. The high priest at Jerusalem might have revealed the secret by consulting the Urim and Thummim. At this point the king became wrathful against his wise men, who had advised him to destroy the Temple, though they must have known how useful it might become to the king and the state. He ordered them all to execution. Their life was saved by Daniel, who recited the king's dream, and gave its interpretation. The king was so filled with admiration of Daniel's wisdom that he paid him Divine honors. Daniel, however, refused such extravagant treatment he did not desire to be the object of idolatrous veneration. He left Nebuchadnezzar in order to escape the marks of honor thrust upon him, and repaired to Tiberias, where he build a canal. Besides, he was charged by the king with commissions, to bring fodder for cattle to Babylonia and also swine from Alexandria.

THE THREE MEN IN THE FURNACE

During Daniel's absence Nebuchadnezzar set up an idol, and its worship was exacted from all his subject under penalty of death by fire. The image could not stand on account of the disproportion between its height and its thickness. The whole of the gold and silver captured by the Babylonians in Jerusalem was needed to give it steadiness.

All the nations owning the rule of Nebuchadnezzar, including even Israel, obeyed the royal command to worship the image. Only the three pious companions of Daniel, Hananiah, Mishael, and Azariah, resisted the order. In vain Nebuchadnezzar urged upon them, as an argument in favor if idolatry, that the Jews had been so devoted to heathen practices before the destruction of Jerusalem that they had gone to Babylonia for the purpose of imitating the idols there and bringing the copies they made to Jerusalem. The three saints would not hearken to these seductions of the king, nor when he referred them to such authorities as Moses and Jeremiah, in order to prove to them that they were under obligation to do the royal bidding. They said to him: "Thou art our king in all that concerns service, taxes, poll-money, and tribute, but with respect to thy present command thou art only Nebuchadnezzar. Therein thou and the dog are alike unto us. Bark like a dog, inflate thyself like a water-bottle, and chirp like a cricket."

Now Nebuchadnezzar's wrath transcended all bound, and he ordered the three to be cast into a red hot furnace, so hot that the flames of its fire darted to the height of forty-nine ells beyond the oven, and consumed the heathen standing about it. No less than four nations were thus exterminated. While the three saints were being thrust into the furnace, they addressed a fervent prayer to God, supplicating His grace toward them, and entreating Him to put their adversaries to shame. The angels desired to descend and rescue the three men in the furnace. But God forbade it: "Did the three men act thus for your sakes? Nay, they did it for Me; and I will save them with Mine own hands." God also rejected the good offices of Yurkami, the angel of hail who offered to extinguish the fire in the furnace. The angel Gabriel justly pointed out that such a miracle would not be sufficiently striking to arrest attention. His own proposition was accepted. He, the angel of fire, was deputed to snatch the three men from the red hot furnace. He executed his mission by cooling off the fire inside of the oven, while on the outside the heat continued to increase to such a degree that the heathen standing around the furnace were consumed. The three youths thereupon raised their voices together in a hymn of praise to God, thanking Him for His miraculous help. The Chaldeans observed the three men pacing up and down quietly in the furnace, followed by a fourth the angel Gabriel as by an attendant. Nebuchadnezzar, who hastened thither to see the wonder, was stunned with fright, for he recognized Gabriel to be the angel who in the guise of a column of fire had blasted the army of Sennacherib. Six other miracles happened, all of them driving terror to the heart of the king: the fiery furnace which had been sunk in the ground raised itself into the air; it was broken; the bottom dropped out; the image erected by Nebuchadnezzar fell prostrate; four nations were wasted by fire; and Ezekiel revived the dead in the valley of Dura.

Of the last, Nebuchadnezzar was apprised in a peculiar way. He had a drinking vessel made of the bones of a slain Jew. When he was about to use it, life began to stir in the bones, and a blow was planted in the king's face, while a voice announced: "A friend of this man is at this moment reviving the dead!" Nebuchadnezzar now offered praise to God for the miracles performed, and if an angel had not quickly struck him a blow on his mouth, and forced him into silence, his psalms of praise would have excelled the Psalter of David.

The deliverance of the three pious young men was a brilliant vindication of their ways, but at the same time it caused great mortification to the masses of the Jewish people, who had complied with the order of Nebuchadnezzar to worship his idol. Accordingly, when the three men left the furnace which they did not do until Nebuchadnezzar invited them to leave the heathen struck all the Jews they met in the face, deriding them at the same time: "You who have so marvellous a God pay homage to an idol!" The three men thereupon left Babylonia and went to Palestine, where they joined their friend, the high priest Joshua.

Their readiness to sacrifice their lives for the honor of God had been all the more admirable as they had been advised by the prophet Ezekiel that no miracle would be done for their sakes. When the king's command to bow down before the idol was published, and the three men were appointed to act as the representatives of the people, Hananiah and his companions resorted to Daniel for his advice. He referred them to the prophet Ezekiel, who counselled flight, citing his teacher Isaiah as his authority. The three men rejected his advice, and declared themselves ready to suffer the death of martyrs. Ezekiel bade them tarry until he inquired of God, whether a miracle would be done for them. The words of God were: "I shall not manifest Myself as their savior. They caused My house to be destroyed, My palace to be burnt, My children to be dispersed among the heathen, and now they appeal for My help. As I live, I will not be found of them."

Instead of discouraging the three men, this answer but infused new spirit and resolution in them, and they declared with more decided emphasis than before, that they were ready to meet death. God consoled the weeping prophet by revealing to him, that He would save the three saintly heroes. He had sought to restrain them from martyrdom only to let their piety and steadfastness appear the brighter.

On account of their piety it became customary to swear by the Name of Him who supports the world on three pillars, the pillars being the saints Hananiah, Mishael, and Azariah. Their deliverance from death by fire worked a great effect upon the disposition of the heathen. They were convinced of the uselessness of their idols, and with their own hands they destroyed them.

EZEKIEL REVIVES THE DEAD

Among the dead whom Ezekiel restored to life at the same time when the three men were redeemed from the fiery furnace were different classes of persons. Some were the Ephraimites that had perished in the attempt to escape from Egypt before Moses led the whole nation out of the land of bondage. Some were the godless among the Jews that had polluted the Temple at Jerusalem with heathen rites, and those still more godless who in life had not believed in the resurrection of the dead. Others of those revived by Ezekiel were the youths among the Jews carried away captive to Babylonia by Nebuchadnezzar whose beauty was so radiant that it darkened the very splendor of the sun. The Babylonian women were seized with a great passion for them, and at the solicitation of their husbands, Nebuchadnezzar ordered a bloody massacre of the handsome youths. But the Babylonian women were not yet cured of their unlawful passion; the beauty of the young Hebrews haunted them until their corpses lay crushed before them, their graceful bodies mutilated. These were the youths recalled to life by the prophet Ezekiel. Lastly, he revived some that had perished only a short time before. When Hananiah, Mishael, and Azariah were saved from death, Nebuchadnezzar thus addressed the other Jews, those who had yielded obedience to his command concerning the worship of the idol: "You know that your God can help and save, nevertheless you paid worship to an idol which is incapable of doing anything. This proves that, as you have destroyed your own land by your wicked deeds, so you are now trying to destroy my land with your iniquity." Forthwith he commanded that they all be executed, sixty thousand in number. Twenty years passed, and Ezekiel was vouchsafed the vision in which God bade him repair to the Valley of Dura, where Nebuchadnezzar had set up his idol, and had massacred the host of the Jews. Here God showed him the dry bones of the slain with the question: "Can I revive these bones?" Ezekiel's answer was evasive, and as a punishment for his little faith, he had to end his days in Babylon, and was not granted even burial in the soil of Palestine. God then dropped the dew of heaven upon the dry bones, and "sinews were upon them, and flesh came up, and skin covered them above." At the same time God sent forth winds to the four corners of the earth, which unlocked the treasure houses of souls, and brought its own soul to each body. All came to life except one man, who, as God explained to the prophet, was excluded from the resurrection because he was a usurer.

In spite of the marvellous miracle performed from them, the men thus restored to life wept, because they feared they would have no share at the end of time in the resurrection of the whole of Israel. But the prophet assured them, in the name of God, that their portion in all that had been promised Israel should in no wise be diminished.

NEBUCHADNEZZAR A BEAST

Nebuchadnezzar, the ruler of the whole world, to whom even the wild animals paid obedience, his pet was a lion with a snake coiled about its neck, did not escape punishment for his sins. He was chastised as none before him. He whom fear of God had at first held back from a war against Jerusalem, and who had to be dragged forcibly, as he sat on his horse, to the Holy of Holies by the archangel Michael, he later became so arrogant that he thought himself a god, and cherished the plan of enveloping himself in a cloud, so that he might live apart from men. A heavenly voice resounded: "O thou wicked man, son of a wicked man, and descendant of Nimrod the wicked, who incited the world to rebel against God! Behold, the days of the years of a man are threescore years and ten, or perhaps by reason of strength fourscore years. It takes five hundred years to traverse the distance of the earth from the first heaven, and as long a time to penetrate from the bottom to the top of the first heaven, and not less are the distances from one of the seven heavens to the next. How, then, canst thou speak of ascending like unto the Most High 'above the heights of the clouds'?" For this transgression of deeming himself more than a man, he was punished by being made to live for some time as a beast among beasts, treated by them as though he were one of them. For forty days he led this life. As far down as his navel he had the appearance of an ox, and the lower part of his body resembled that of a lion. Like an ox he ate grass, and like a lion he attacked a curious crowd, but Daniel spent his time in prayer, entreating that the seven years of this brutish life allotted to Nebuchadnezzar might be reduced to seven months. His prayer was granted. At the end of forty days reason returned to the king, the next forty days he passed in weeping bitterly over his sins, and in the interval that remained to complete the seven months he again lived the life of a beast.

HIRAM

Hiram, the king of Tyre, was a contemporary of Nebuchadnezzar, and in many respects resembled him. He, too, esteemed himself a god, and sought to make men believe in his divinity by the artificial heavens he fashioned for himself. In the sea he erected four iron pillars, on which he build up seven heavens, each five hundred ells larger than the one below. The first was a plate of glass of five hundred square ells, and the second a plate of iron of a thousand square ells. The third, of lead, and separated from the second by canals, contained huge round boulders, which produced the sound of thunder on the iron. The fourth heaven was of brass, the fifth of copper, the sixth of silver, and the seventh of gold, all separated from each other by canals. In the seventh, thirty-five hundred ells in extent, he had diamonds and pearls, which he manipulated so as to produce the effect of flashes and sheets of lightening, while the stones below imitated the growling of the thunder.

As Hiram was thus floating above the earth, in his vain imagination deeming himself superior to the rest of men, he suddenly perceived the prophet Ezekiel next to himself. He had been waved thither by a wind. Frightened and amazed, Hiram asked the prophet how he had risen to his heights. The answer was: "God brought me here, and He bade me ask thee why thou art so proud, thou born of woman?" The king of Tyre replied defiantly: "I am not one born of woman; I live forever, and as God resides on the sea, so my abode is on the sea, and as He inhabits seven heavens, so do I. See how many kings I have survived! Twenty-one of the House of David, and as many of the Kingdom of the Ten Tribes, and no less than fifty prophets and ten high priests have I buried." Thereupon God said: "I will destroy My house, that henceforth Hiram may have no reason for self-glorification, because all his pride comes only from the circumstance that he furnished the cedar-trees for the building of the Temple." The end of this proud king was that he was conquered by Nebuchadnezzar, deprived of this throne, and made to suffer a cruel death. Though the Babylonian king was the step-son of Hiram, he had no mercy with him. Daily he cut off a bit of the flesh of his body, and forced the Tyrian king to eat it, until the finally perished. Hiram's palace was swallowed by the earth, and in the bowels of the earth it will remain until it shall emerge in the future world as the habitation of the pious.

THE FALSE PROPHETS

Not only among the heathen, but also among the Jews there were very sinful people in those days. The most notorious Jewish sinners were the two false prophets Ahab and Zedekiah. Ahab came to the daughter of Nebuchadnezzar and said: "Yield thyself to Zedekiah," telling her this in the form of a Divine message. The same was done by Zedekiah, who only varied the message by substituting the name of Ahab. The princess could not accept such messages as Divine, and she told her father what had occurred. Though Nebuchadnezzar was so addicted to immoral practices that he was in the habit of making his captive kings drunk, and then satisfying his unnatural lusts upon them, and a miracle had to interpose to shield the pious of Judah against this disgrace, yet he well knew that the God of the Jews hates immorality. He therefore questioned Hananiah, Mishael, and Azariah about it, and they emphatically denied the possibility that such a message could have come from God. The prophets of lies refused to recall their statements, and Nebuchadnezzar decided to subject them to the same fiery test as he had decreed for the three pious companions of Daniel. To be fair toward them, the king permitted them to choose a third fellow-sufferer, some pious man to share their lot. Seeing no escape, Ahab and Zedekiah asked for Joshua, later the high priest, as their companion in the furnace, in the hope that his distinguished merits would suffice to save all three of them. They were mistaken. Joshua emerged unhurt, only his garments were seared, but the false prophets were consumed. Joshua explained the singeing of his garments by the fact that he was directly exposed to the full fury of the flames. But the truth was that he had to expiate the sins of his sons, who had contracted marriages unworthy of their dignity and descent. Therefore their father escaped death only after the fire had burnt his garments.

DANIEL'S PIETY

No greater contrast to Hiram and the false prophets Ahab and Zedekiah can be imagined than is presented by the character of the pious Daniel. When Nebuchadnezzar offered him Divine honors, he refused what Hiram sought to obtain by every means in his power. The Babylonian king felt so ardent an admiration for Daniel that he sent him from the country when the time arrived to worship the idol he had erected in Dura, for he knew very well that Daniel would prefer death in the flames to disregard of the commands of God, and he could not well have cast the man into the fire to whom he had paid Divine homage. Moreover, it was the wish of God that Daniel should not pass through the fiery ordeal at the same time as his three friends, in order that their deliverance might not be ascribed to him.

In spite of all this, Nebuchadnezzar endeavored to persuade Daniel by gentle means to worship an idol. He had the golden diadem of the high priest inserted in the mouth of an idol, and by reason of the wondrous power that resides in the Holy Name inscribed on the diadem, the idol gained the ability to speak, and it said the words: "I am thy God." Thus were many seduced to worship the image. But Daniel could not be misled so easily. He secured permission from the king to kiss the idol. Laying his mouth upon the idol's, he adjured the diadem in the following words: "I am but flesh and blood, yet at the same time a messenger of God. I therefore admonish thee, take heed that the Name of the Holy One, blessed be He, may not be desecrated, and I order thee to follow me." So it happened. When the heathen came with music and song to give honor to the idol, it emitted no sound, but a storm broke loose and overturned it.

On still another occasion Nebuchadnezzar tried to persuade Daniel to worship an idol, this time a dragon that devoured all who approached it, and therefore was adored as a god by the Babylonians. Daniel had straw mixed with nails fed to him, and the dragon ate and perished almost immediately.

All this did not prevent Daniel from keeping the welfare of the king in mind continually. Hence it was that when Nebuchadnezzar was engaged in setting his house in order, he desired to mention 'Daniel in his will as one of his heirs. But the Jew refused with the words: "Far be it from me to leave the inheritance of my fathers for that of the uncircumcised."

Nebuchadnezzar died after having reigned forty years, as long as King David. The death of the tyrant brought hope and joy to many a heart, for his severity had been such that during his lifetime none dared laugh, and when he descended to Sheol, its inhabitants trembled, fearing he had come to reign over them, too. However, a heavenly voice called to him: "Go down, and be thou laid down with the uncircumcised."

The interment of this great king was anything but what one might have expected, and for this reason: During the seven years spent by Nebuchadnezzar among the beast, his son Evil-merodach ruled in his stead. Nebuchadnezzar reappeared after his period of penance, and incarcerated his son for life. When the death of Nebuchadnezzar actually did occur, Evil-merodach refused to accept the homage the nobles brought him as the new king, because he feared that his father was not dead, but had only disappeared as once before, and would return again. To convince him of the groundlessness of his apprehension, the corpse of Nebuchadnezzar, badly mutilated by his enemies, was dragged through the streets.

Shortly afterward occurred the death of Zedekiah, the dethroned king of Judah. His burial took place amid great demonstrations of sympathy and mourning. The elegy over him ran thus: "Alas that King Zedekiah had to die, he who quaffed the lees which all the generations before him accumulated."

Zedekiah reached a good old age, for though it was in his reign that the destruction of Jerusalem took place, yet it was the guilt of the nation, not of the king, that had brought about the catastrophe.

Chapter 11

XI. THE RETURN OF THE CAPTIVITY

BELSHAZZAR'S FEAST

When God resolved to take revenge upon Babylon for all the sufferings it had inflicted on Israel, He chose Darius and Cyrus as the agents of vengeance. Cyrus, the king of Persia, and his father-in-law Darius, the king of Media, together went up against Belshazzar, the ruler of the Chaldeans. The war lasted a considerable time, and fortune favored first one side, then the other, until finally the Chaldeans won a decisive victory. To celebrate the event, Belshazzar arranged a great banquet, which was served from the vessels taken out of the Temple at Jerusalem by his father. While the king and his guests were feasting, the angel sent by God put the "Mene, Mene, Tekel, Upharsin" on the wall, Aramaic words in Hebrew characters, written with red ink. The angel was seen by none but the king. His grandees and the princes of the realm who were present at the orgy perceived nothing. The king himself did not see the form of the angel, only his awesome fingers as they traced the words were visible to him.

The interpretation given to the enigmatical words by Daniel put an end to the merry-making of the feasters. They scattered in dread and fear, leaving none behind except the king and his attendants. In the same night the king was murdered by an old servant, who knew Daniel from the time of Nebuchadnezzar, and doubted not that his sinister prophecy would be fulfilled. With the head of King Belshazzar he betook himself to Darius and Cyrus, and told them how his master had desecrated the sacred vessels, told them of the wonderful writing on the wall, and of the way it had been interpreted by Daniel. The two kings were moved by his recital to vow solemnly that they would permit the Jews to return to Palestine, and would grant them the use of the Temple vessels.

They resumed the war against Babylonia with more energy, and God vouchsafed them victory. They conquered the whole of Belshazzar's realm, and took possession of the city of Babylon, whose inhabitants, young and old, were made to suffer death. The subjugated lands were divided between Cyrus and Darius, the latter receiving Babylon and Media, the former Chaldea, Persia, and Assyria.

But this is not the whole story of the fall of Babylon. The wicked king Belshazzar arranged the banquet at which the holy vessels were desecrated in the fifth year of his reign, because he thought it wholly certain then that all danger was past of the realization of Jeremiah's prophecy, foretelling the return of the Jews to Palestine at the end of seventy years of Babylonian rule over them. Nebuchadnezzar had governed twenty-five years, and Evil-merodach twenty-three, leaving five years in the reign of Belshazzar for the fulfilment of the appointed time. Not enough that the king scoffed at God by using the Temple vessels, he needs must have the pastry for the banquet, which was given on the second day of the Passover festival, made of wheaten flour finer than that used on this day for the `Omer in the Temple.

Punishment followed hard upon the heels of the atrocity. Cyrus and Darius served as door-keepers of the royal palace on the evening of the banquet. They had received orders from Belshazzar to admit none, though he should say he was the king himself. Belshazzar was forced to leave his apartments for a short time, and he went out unnoticed by the two door-keepers. On his return, when he asked to be admitted, they felled him dead, even while he was asseverating that he was the king.

DANIEL UNDER THE PERSIAN KINGS

Daniel left Belshazzar and fled to Shushtar, where he was kindly received by Cyrus, who promised him to have the Temple vessels taken back to Jerusalem, provided Daniel would pray to God to grant him success in his war with the king of Mosul. God gave Daniel's prayer a favorable hearing, and Cyrus was true to his promise.

Daniel now received the Divine charge to urge Cyrus to rebuild the Temple. To this end he was to introduce Ezra and Zerubbabel to the king. Ezra then went from place to place and called upon the people to return to Palestine. Sad to say, only a tribe and a half obeyed his summons. Indeed, the majority of the people were so wroth against Ezra that they sought to slay him. He escaped the peril to his life only by a Divine miracle.

Daniel, too, was exposed to much suffering at this time. King Cyrus cast him into a den of lions, because he refused to bow down before the idol of the king. For seven days Daniel lay among the wild beasts, and not a hair of his head was touched. When the king at the end of the week found Daniel alive, he could not but acknowledge the sovereign grandeur of God. Cyrus released Daniel, and instead had his calumniators thrown to the lions. In an instant they were rent in pieces.

In general Cyrus fell far short of coming up to the expectations set in him for piety and justice. Though he granted permission to the Jews to rebuild the Temple, they were to use no material but wood, so that it might easily be destroyed if the Jews should take it into their head to rebel against him. Even in point of morals, the Persian king was not above reproach.

Another time Cyrus pressingly urged Daniel to pay homage to the idol Bel. As proof of the divinity of the idol the king advanced the fact that it ate the dishes set before it, a report spread by the priests of Bel, who entered the Temple of the idol at night, through subterranean passages, themselves ate up the dishes, and then attributed their disappearance to the appetite of the god. But Daniel was too shrewd to be misled by a fabricated story. He had the ashes strewn upon the floor of the Temple, and the foot-prints visible the next morning convinced the king of the deceit practiced by the priests.

Pleasant relations did not continue to subsist forever between Cyrus and Darius. A war broke out between them, in which Cyrus lost life and lands. Fearing Darius, Daniel fled to Persia. But an angel of God appeared to him with the message: "Fear not the king, not unto him will I surrender thee." Shortly afterward he received a letter from Darius reading as follows: "Come to me, Daniel! Fear naught, I shall be even kinder to thee than Cyrus was." Accordingly Daniel returned to Shushtar, and was received with great consideration by Darius.

One day the king chanced to remember the sacred garments brought by Nebuchadnezzar out of the Temple at Jerusalem to Babylon. They had vanished, and no trace of them could be discovered. The king suspected Daniel of having had something to do with their disappearance. It booted little that he protested his innocence, he was cast into prison. God sent an angel who was to blind Darius, telling him at the same time that he was deprived of the light of his eyes because he was keeping the pious Daniel in durance, and sight would be restored to him only if Daniel interceded for him. The king at once released Daniel, and the two together journeyed to Jerusalem to pray on the holy place for the restoration of the king. An angel appeared to Daniel, and announced to him that his prayer had been heard. The king had but to wash his eyes, and vision would return to them. So it happened. Darius gave thanks to God, and in his gratitude assigned the tithe of his grain to the priests and the Levites. Besides, he testified his appreciation to Daniel by loading him down with gifts, and both returned to Shushtar. The recovery of the king convinced many of his subjects of the omnipotence of God, and they converted to Judaism.

Following the advice of Daniel, Darius appointed a triumvirate to take charge of the administration of his realm, and Daniel was made the chief of the council of three. His high dignity he was second to none but the king himself exposed him to envy and hostility on all sides. His enemies plotted his ruin. With cunning they induced the king to sign an order attaching the penalty of death to prayers addressed to any god or any man other than Darius. Though the order did not require Daniel to commit a sin, he preferred to give his life for the honor of the one God rather than omit his devotions to Him. When his jealous enemies surprised him during his prayers, he did not interrupt himself. He was dragged before the king, who refused to give credence to the charge against Daniel. Meanwhile the hour for the afternoon prayer arrived, and in the presence of the king and his princes Daniel began to perform his devotions. This naturally rendered unavailing all efforts made by the king to save his friend from death. Daniel was cast into a pit full of lions. The entrance to the pit was closed up with a rock, which had all of its own accord rolled from Palestine to protect him against any harm contemplated by his enemies. The ferocious beasts welcomed the pious Daniel like dogs fawning upon their master on his return home, licking his hands and wagging their tails.

While this was passing in Babylon, an angel appeared to the prophet Habakkuk in Judea. He ordered the prophet to bring Daniel the food he was about to carry to his laborers in the field. Astonished, Habakkuk asked the angel how he could carry it to so great a distance, whereupon he was seized by his hair, and in a moment set down before Daniel. They dined together, and then the angel transported Habakkuk back to his place in Palestine. Early in the morning Darius went to the pit of the lions to discover the fate of Daniel. The king called his name, but he received no answer, because Daniel was reciting the Shema at that moment, after having spent the night in giving praise and adoration to God. Seeing that he was still alive, the king summoned the enemies of Daniel to the pit. It was their opinion that the lions had not been hungry, and therefore Daniel was still unhurt. The king commanded them to put the beasts to the test with their own persons. The result was that the hundred and twenty-two enemies of Daniel, together with their wives and children numbering two hundred and forty-four persons, were torn in shreds by fourteen hundred and sixty-four lions.

The miraculous escape of Daniel brought him more distinguished consideration and greater honors than before. The king published the wonders done by God in all parts of his land, and called upon the people to betake themselves to Jerusalem and help in the erection of the Temple.

Daniel entreated the king to relieve him of the duties of his position, for the performance of which he no longer felt himself fit, on account of his advanced age. The king consented on condition that Daniel designate a successor worthy of him. His choice fell upon Zerubbabel. Loaded with rich presents and amid public demonstrations designed to honor him, Daniel retired from public life. He settled in the city of Shushan, where he abode until his end. Though he was no prophet, God vouchsafed to him a knowledge of the "end of time" not granted his friends, the prophets Haggai, Zechariah, and Malachi, but even he, in the fulness of his years, lost all memory of the revelation with which he had been favored.

THE GRAVE OF DANIEL

Daniel was buried in Shushan, on account of which a sore quarrel was enkindled among the inhabitants of the city. Shushan is divided in two parts by a river. The side containing the grave of Daniel was occupied by the wealthy inhabitants, and the poor citizens lived on the other side of the river. The latter maintained that they, too, would be rich if the grave of Daniel were in their quarter. The frequent disputes and conflicts were finally adjusted by a compromise; one year the bier of Daniel reposed on one side of the river, the next year on the other. When the Persian king Sanjar came to Shushan, he put a stop to the practice of dragging the bier hither and thither. He resorted to another device for guarding the peace of the city. He had the bier suspended from chains precisely in the middle of the bridge spanning the river. In the same spot he erected a house of prayer for all confessions, and out of respect to Daniel he prohibited fishing in the river for a distance of a mile on either side of the memorial building. The sacredness of the spot appeared when the godless tried to pass by. They were drowned, while the pious remained unscathed. Furthermore, the fish that swam near it had heads glittering like gold.

Beside the house of Daniel lay a stone, under which he had concealed the holy Temple vessels. Once an attempt was made to roll the stone from its place, but whoever ventured to touch it, fell dead. The same fate overtook all who later tried to make excavations near the spot; a storm broke out and mowed them down.

ZERUBBABEL

The successor to Daniel in the service of the king, Zerubbabel, enjoyed equally as much royal consideration and affection. He occupied a higher position than all the other servants and officials, and he and two others constituted the body-guard of the king. Once when the king lay wrapped in deep slumber, his guards resolved to write down what each of them considered the mightiest thing in the world, and he who wrote the sagest saying should be given rich presents and rewards by the king. What they wrote they laid under the pillow on which the head of the king rested, that he might not delay to make a decision after he awoke. The first one wrote: "Wine is the mightiest thing there is"; the second wrote: "The king is the mightiest on earth," and the third, Zerubbabel, wrote: "Women are the mightiest in the world, but truth prevails over all else." When the king awoke, and he perused the document, he summoned the grandees of his realm and the three youths as well. Each of the three was called upon to justify his saying. In eloquent words the first described the potency of wine. When it takes possession of the senses of a man, he forgets grief and sorrow. Still more beautiful and convincing were the words of the second speaker, when his turn came to establish the truth of his saying, that the king was the mightiest on earth. Finally Zerubbabel depicted in glowing words the power of woman, who rules even over kings. "But," he continued, "truth is supreme over all; the whole earth asks for truth, the heavens sing the praises of truth, all creation quakes and trembles before truth, naught of wrong can be found in truth. Unto truth belongeth the might, the dominion, the power, and the glory of all times. Blessed be the God of truth." When Zerubbabel ceased from speaking, the assembly broke out into the words: "Great is truth, it is mightier than all else!" The king was so charmed with the wisdom of Zerubbabel that he said to him: "Ask for aught thou wishest, it shall be granted thee." Zerubbabel required nothing for himself, he only sought permission of the king to restore Jerusalem, rebuild the sanctuary, and return the holy Temple vessels to the place whence they had been carried off. Not only did Darius grant what Zerubbabel wished for, not only did he give him letters of safe-conduct, but he also conferred numerous privileges upon the Jews who accompanied Zerubbabel to Palestine, and he sent abundant presents to the Temple and its officers.

As unto his predecessor Daniel, so unto Zerubbabel, God vouchsafed a knowledge of the secrets of the future. Especially the archangel Metatron dealt kindly with him. Besides revealing to him the time at which the Messiah would appear, he brought about an interview between the Messiah and Zerubbabel.

In reality, Zerubbabel was none other than Nehemiah, who was given this second name because he was born in Babylon. Richly endowed as Zerubbabel-Nehemiah was with admirable qualities, he yet did not lack faults. He was excessively self-complacent, and he did not hesitate to fasten a stigma publicly upon his predecessors in the office of governor in the land of Judah, among whom was so excellent a man as Daniel. To punish him for these transgressions, the Book of Ezra does not bear the name of its real author Nehemiah.

When Darius felt his end approach, he appointed his son-in-law Cyrus, who had hitherto reigned only over Persia, to be the ruler over his kingdom as well. His wish was honored by the princes of Media and Persia. After Darius had departed this life, Cyrus was proclaimed king.

In the very first year of his reign, Cyrus summoned the most distinguished of the Jews to appear before him, and he gave them permission to return to Palestine and rebuild the Temple at Jerusalem. More than this, he pledged himself to contribute to the Temple service in proportion to his means, and pay honor to the God who had invested him with strength to subdue the Chaldeans. These actions of Cyrus partly flowed from his own pious inclinations, and partly were due to his desire to accomplish the dying behests of Darius, who had admonished him to give the Jews the opportunity of rebuilding the Temple.

When the first sacrifice was to be brought by the company of Jews who returned to Jerusalem under the leadership of Ezra, and set about restoring the Temple, they missed the celestial fire which had dropped from heaven on the altar in the time of Moses, and had not been extinguished so long as the Temple stood. They turned in supplication to God to be instructed by Him. The celestial fire had been hidden by Jeremiah at the time of the destruction of the Holy City, and the law did not permit them to bring "strange fire" upon the altar of God. An old man suddenly remembered the spot in which Jeremiah had buried the holy fire, and he led the elders thither. They rolled away the stone covering the spot, and from under it appeared a spring flowing not with water, but with a sort of oil. Ezra ordered this fluid to be sprinkled upon the altar, and forthwith an all-consuming flame shot up. The priests themselves scattered in fright. But after the Temple and its vessels were purified by the flame, it confined itself to the altar never more to leave it, for the priest guarded it so that it might not be extinguished.

Among the band of returned exiles were the prophets Haggai, Zechariah, and Malachi. Each one of them had a place of the greatest importance to fill in the rebuilding of the Temple. By the first the people were shown the plan of the altar, which was larger than the one that had stood in Solomon's Temple. The second informed them of the exact location of the altar, and the third taught them that the sacrifices might be brought on the holy place even before the completion of the Temple. On the authority of one of the prophets, the Jews, on their return from Babylonia, gave up their original Hebrew characters, and re-wrote the Torah in the "Assyrian" characters still in use at this day.

While the Temple work was in progress, the builders found the skull of Araunah, the owner of the Temple site in the time of David. The priests, unlearned as they were, could not decide to what extent the corpse lying there had defiled the holy place. It was for this that Haggai poured out his reproaches upon them.

EZRA

The complete resettlement of Palestine took place under the direction of Ezra, or, as the Scriptures sometimes call him, Malachi. He had not been present at the earlier attempts to restore the sanctuary, because he could not leave his old teacher Baruch, who was too advanced in years to venture upon the difficult journey to the Holy Land.

In spite of Ezra's persuasive efforts, it was but a comparatively small portion of the people that joined the procession winding its way westward to Palestine. For this reason the prophetical spirit did not show itself during the existence of the Second Temple. Haggai, Zechariah, and Malachi were the last representatives of prophecy. Nothing was more surprising than the apathy of the Levites. They manifested no desire to return to Palestine. Their punishment was the loss of the tithes, which were later given to the priest, though the Levites had the first claim upon them.

In restoring the Jewish state in Palestine, Ezra cherished two hopes, to preserve the purity of the Jewish race, and to spread the study of the Torah until it should become the common property of the people at large. To help on his first purpose, he inveighed against marriages between the Jews and the nations round about. He himself had carefully worked out his own pedigree before he consented to leave Babylonia, and in order to perpetuate the purity of the families and groups remaining in the East, he took all the "unfit" with him to Palestine.

In the realization of his second hope, the spread of the Torah, Ezra was so zealous and efficient that it was justly said of him: "If Moses had not anticipated him, Ezra would have received the Torah." In a sense he was, indeed, a second Moses. The Torah had fallen into neglect and oblivion in his day, and he restored and re-established it in the minds of his people. It is due to him chiefly that it was divided up into portions, to be read annually, Sabbath after Sabbath, in the synagogues, and he it was, likewise, who originated the idea of re-writing the Pentateuch in "Assyrian" characters. To further his purpose still more, he ordered additional schools for children to be established everywhere, though the old ones sufficed to satisfy the demand. He thought the rivalry between the old and the new institutions would redound to the benefit of the pupils.

Ezra is the originator of institutions known as "the ten regulations of Ezra." They are the following: 1. Readings from the Torah on Sabbath afternoons. 2. Readings from the Torah on Mondays and Thursdays. 3. Sessions of the court on Mondays and Thursdays. 4. To do laundry work on Thursdays, not Fridays. 5. To eat garlic on Friday on account of its salutary action. 6. To bake bread early in the morning that it may be ready for the poor whenever they ask for some. 7. Women are to cover the lower parts of their bodies with a garment called Sinar. 8. Before taking a ritual bath, the hair is to be combed. 9. The ritual bath prescribed for the unclean is to cover the case of one who desires to offer prayer or study the law. 10. Permission to peddlers to sell cosmetics to women in the towns.

Ezra was not only a great teacher of his people and their wise leader, he was also their advocate with the celestials, to whom his relation was of a peculiarly intimate character. Once he addressed a prayer to God, in which he complained of the misfortune of Israel and the prosperity of the heathen nations. Thereupon the angel Uriel appeared to him, and instructed him how that evil has its appointed time in which to run its course, as the dead have their appointed time to sojourn in the nether world. Ezra could not rest satisfied with this explanation, and in response to his further question, seven prophetic visions were vouchsafed him, and interpreted by the angel for him. They typified the whole course of history up to his day, and disclosed the future to his eyes. In the seventh vision he heard a voice from a thorn-bush, like Moses aforetimes, and it admonished him to guard in his heart the secrets revealed to him. The same voice had given Moses a similar injunction: "These words shalt thou publish, those shalt thou keep secret." Then his early translation from earth was announced to him. He besought God to let the holy spirit descend upon him before he died, so that he might record all that had happened since the creation of the world as it was set down in the Torah, and guide men upon the path that leads to God.

Hereupon God bade him take the five experienced scribes, Sarga, Dabria, Seleucia, Ethan, and Aziel, with him into retirement, and dictate to them for forty days. After one day spent with these writers in isolation, remote from the city and from men, a voice admonished him: "Ezra, open thy mouth, and drink whereof I give thee to drink." He opened his mouth, and a chalice was handed to him, filled to the brim with a liquid that flowed like water, but in color resembled fire. His mouth opened to drink, and for forty days it was not closed. During all that time, the five scribes put down, "in signs they did not understand," they were the newly adopted Hebrew characters, all that Ezra dictated to them, and it made ninety-four books. At the end of the forty days' period, God spoke to Ezra thus: "The twenty-four books of the Holy Scriptures thou shalt publish, for the worthy and the unworthy alike to read; but the last seventy books thou shalt withhold from the populace, for the perusal of the wise of thy people." On account of his literary activity, he is called "the Scribe of the science of the Supreme Being unto all eternity."

Having finished his task, Ezra was removed from this mundane world, and he entered the life everlasting. But his death did not occur in the Holy Land. It overtook him at Khuzistan, in Persia, on his journey to King Artachshashta.

At Raccia, in Mesopotamia, there stood, as late as the twelfth century, the synagogue founded by Ezra when he was journeying from Babylonia to Palestine.

At his grave, over which columns of fire are often seen to hover at night, a miracle once happened. A shepherd fell asleep by the side of it. Ezra appeared to him and bade him tell the Jews that they were to transport his bier to another spot. If the master of the new place refused assent, he was to be warned to yield permission, else all the inhabitants of his place would perish. At first the master refused to allow the necessary excavations to be made. Only after a large number of the non-Jewish inhabitants of the place had been stricken down suddenly, he consented to have the corpse transported thither. As soon as the grave was opened, the plague ceased.

Shortly before the death of Ezra, the city of Babylon was totally destroyed by the Persians. There remained but a portion of the wall which was impregnable by human strength. All the prophecies hurled against the city by the prophets were accomplished. To this day there is a spot on its site which no animal can pass unless some of the earth of the place is strewn upon it.

THE MEN OF THE GREAT ASSEMBLY

At the same time with Ezra, or, to speak more accurately, under his direction, the Great Assembly carried on its beneficent activities, which laid the foundations of Rabbinical Judaism, and constituted the binding link between the Jewish Prophet and the Jewish Sage. The great men who belonged to this august assembly once succeeded, through the efficacy of their prayers, in laying hands upon the seducers unto sin, and confining them, to prevent them from doing more mischief. Thus they banished from the world "the desire unto idolatry." They tried to do the same to "the desire unto lustfulness." This evil adversary warned them against making away with him, for the world would cease to exist without him. For three days they kept him a prisoner, but then they had to dismiss him and let him go free. They found that not even an egg was to be had, for sexual appetite had vanished from the world. However, he did not escape altogether unscathed. They plastered up his eyes, and from that time on he gave up inflaming the passions of men against their blood relations.

Among the decrees and ordinances of the Great Assembly, the most prominent is the fixation of the prayer of the Eighteen Benedictions. The several benedictions composing this prayer date back to remote ancient times. The Patriarchs were their authors, and the work of the Great Assembly was to put them together in the order in which we now have them. We know how each of the benedictions originated: 1. When Abraham was saved from the furnace angels spoke: "Blessed art Thou, O Lord, the Shield of Abraham," which is the essence of the first of the Eighteen. 2. When Isaac lay stunned by fright on Mount Moriah, God sent His dew to revive him, whereupon the angels spoke: "Blessed art Thou, O Lord, who quickenest the dead." 3. When Jacob arrived at the gates of heaven and proclaimed the holiness of God, the angels spoke: "Blessed art Thou, O Lord, Thou holy God." 4. When Pharaoh was about to make Joseph the ruler over Egypt, and it appeared that he was unacquainted with the seventy tongues which an Egyptian sovereign must know, the angel Gabriel came and taught him those languages, whereupon the angels spoke: "Blessed art Thou, O Lord, who graciously bestowest knowledge." 5. When Reuben committed the trespass against his father, sentence of death was pronounced upon him in the heavens. But when he repented, he was permitted to continue to live, and the angels spoke: "Blessed art Thou, O Lord, who hast delight in repentance." 6. When Judah had committed a trespass against Tamar, and confessing his guilt obtained forgiveness, the angels spoke: "Blessed art Thou, O Lord, who pardonest greatly." 7. When Israel was sore oppressed by Mizraim, and God proclaimed his redemption, the angels spoke: "Blessed art Thou, O Lord, who redeemest Israel." 8. When the angel Raphael came to Abraham to soothe the pain of his circumcision, the angels spoke: "Blessed art Thou,

O Lord, who healest the sick." 9. When Israel's sowing in the land of the Philistines bore an abundant harvest, the angels spoke: "Blessed art Thou, O Lord, who blessest the years." 10. When Jacob was reunited with Joseph and Simon in Egypt, the angels spoke: "Blessed art Thou, O Lord, who gatherest the dispersed of Thy people Israel." 11. When the Torah was revealed and God communicated the code of laws to Moses, the angels spoke: "Blessed art Thou, O Lord, who lovest righteousness and justice." 12. When the Egyptians were drowned in the Red Sea, the angels spoke: "Blessed art Thou, O Lord, who shatterest the enemy and humiliatest the presumptuous." 13. When Joseph laid his hands on the eyes of his father Jacob, the angels spoke: "Blessed art Thou, O Lord, who are the stay and the support of the pious." 14. When Solomon built the Temple, the angels spoke: "Blessed art Thou, O Lord, who buildest Jerusalem." 15. When the children of Israel singing hymns of praise unto God passed through the Red Sea, the angels spoke: "Blessed art Thou, O Lord, who causest the hour of salvation to sprout forth." 16. When God lent a gracious ear to the prayer of the suffering Israelites in Egypt, the angels spoke: "Blessed art Thou, O Lord, who hearest our prayer." 17. When the Shekinah descended between the Cherubim in the Tabernacle, the angels spoke: "Blessed art Thou, O Lord, who wilt restore Thy Divine Presence to Jerusalem." 18. When Solomon dedicated his Temple, the angels spoke: "Blessed art Thou, O Lord, whose Name is worthy of praise." 19. When Israel entered the Holy Land, the angels spoke: "Blessed art Thou, O Lord, who establishest peace."

Chapter 12

XII. ESTHER

THE FEAST FOR THE GRANDEES

The Book of Esther is the last of the Scriptural writings. The subsequent history of Israel and all his suffering we know only through oral tradition. For this reason the heroine of the last canonical book was named Esther, that is, Venus, the morning-star, which sheds its light after all the other stars have ceased to shine, and while the sun still delays to rise. Thus the deeds of Queen Esther cast a ray of light forward into Israel's history at its darkest.

The Jews at the time of Ahasuerus were like the dove about to enter her nest wherein a snake lies coiled. Yet she cannot withdraw, because a falcon bides without to swoop down upon her. In Shushan the Jews were in the clutches of Haman, and in other lands they were at the mercy of many murderous enemies to their race, ready to do the bidding of Haman to destroy and to slay them, and cause them to perish.

But the rescue of the Jews from the hand of their adversaries is only a part of this wonderful chapter in the history of Israel. No less important is the exalted station to which they rose in the realm of Ahasuerus after the fall of Haman, especially the power and dignity to which Esther herself attained. On this account the magnificent feast prepared by Ahasuerus for his subjects belongs to the history of Esther.

The splendor of his feast is the gauge whereby to measure the wealth and power she later enjoyed.

Ahasuerus was not the king of Persia by right of birth. He owed his position to his vast wealth, with which he purchased dominion over the whole world.

He had various reasons for giving a gorgeous feast. The third year of his reign was the seventieth since the beginning of Nebuchadnezzar's rule, and Ahasuerus thought it quite certain that the time had passed for the fulfilment of the prophecy of Jeremiah foretelling the return of Israel to the Holy Land. The Temple was still in ruins, and Ahasuerus was convinced that the Jewish kingdom would never again be restored. Needless to say, it was not Jeremiah who erred. Not with the accession of King Nebuchadnezzar had the prophet's term of years begun, but with the destruction of Jerusalem. Reckoned in this way, the seventy years of desolation were at an end exactly at the time when Darius, the son of Ahasuerus, permitted the rebuilding of the Temple.

Beside this mistaken cause for a celebration, there were reasons personal to Ahasuerus why he desired to give expression to joy. A short time before, he had crushed a rebellion against himself, and this victory he wanted to celebrate with pomp and ceremony. The first part of the celebration was given over to the hundred and twenty-seven rulers of the hundred and twenty-seven provinces of his empire. His purpose was to win the devotion of those of them with whom otherwise he did not come in direct contact. But can it be said with certainty that this was a good policy? If he had not first made sure of the loyalty of his capital, was it not dangerous to have these rulers near him in case of an insurrection?

For six whole months he celebrated the feast for the grandees the nobles and the high officials, the latter of whom, according to the constitution, were all required to be Medians under the Persian king Ahasuerus, as they would have had to be Persians under a Median king.

This was the program of the feast: In the first month Ahasuerus showed his treasures to his guests; in the second, the delegates of the king's royal vassals saw them; in the third the presents were exposed to view; in the fourth the guests were invited to admire his literary possessions, among them the sacred scroll; in the fifth his pearl and diamond-studded ornaments of gold were put on exhibition; and in the sixth he displayed the treasures which had been given him as tribute. All this vast wealth, however, appertained to the crown, it was not his personal property. When Nebuchadnezzar felt his end draw nigh, he resolved to sink his immense treasures in the Euphrates rather than let them ascend to his son Evil-merodach, so great was his miserliness. But, again, when Cyrus gave the Jews permission to build the Temple, his divinely appointed reward was that he discovered the spot in the river at which the treasures were sunk, and he was permitted to take possession of them. These were the treasures of which Ahasuerus availed himself to glorify his feast. So prodigious were they that during the six months of the feast he unlocked six treasure-chambers daily to display their contents to his guests.

When Ahasuerus boasted of his wealth, which he had no right to do, as his treasures had come from the Temple, God said: "Verily, has the creature of flesh and blood any possessions of his own? I alone possess treasures, for 'the silver is mind, and the gold is mine.'"

Among the treasures displayed were the Temple vessels, which Ahasuerus had desecrated in his drinking bouts. When the noble Jews who had been invited to the capital saw these, they began to weep, and they refused to take further part in the festivities. Thereupon the king commanded that a separate place be assigned to the Jews, so that their eyes might be spared the painful sight.

This was not the only incident that aroused poignant memories in them, for Ahasuerus arrayed himself in the robes of state once belonging to the high priests at Jerusalem, and this, too, made the Jews smart uncomfortably. The Persian king had wanted to mount the throne of Solomon besides, but herein he was thwarted, because its ingenious construction was an enigma to him. Egyptian artificers tried to fashion a throne after the model of Solomon's, but in vain. After two years' work they managed to produce a weak imitation of it, and upon this Ahasuerus sat during his splendid feast.

THE FESTIVITIES IN SHUSHAN

At the expiration of the hundred and eighty days allotted to the feast for the nobles, Ahasuerus arranged a great celebration for the residents of Shushan, the capital city of Elam. From the creation of the world until after the deluge the unwritten law had been in force, that the first-born son of the patriarchs was to be the ruler of the world. Thus, Seth was the successor to Adam, and he was followed in turn by Enosh, and so the succession went on, from first-born son to first-born son, down to Noah and his oldest son Shem. Now, the first-born son of Shem was Elam, and, according to custom, he should have been given the universal dominion which was his heritage. Shem, being a prophet, knew that Abraham and his posterity, the Israelites, would not spring from the family of Elam, but from that of Arpachshad. Therefore he named Arpachshad as his successor, and through him rulership descended to Abraham, and so to Isaac, Jacob, and Judah, and to David and his posterity, down to the last Judean king Zedekiah, who was deprived of his sovereignty by Nebuchadnezzar.

Then it was that God spake thus: "So long as the government rested in the hands of My children, I was prepared to exercise patience. The misdeeds of the one were made good by the other. If one of them was wicked, the other was pious. But now that the dominions has been wrested from My children, it shall at least revert to its original possessors. Elam was the first-born son of Shem, and his seed shall be given the rule." So it happened that Shushan, the capital city of Elam, became the seat of government.

That there were any celebrations in Shushan was due to Haman, who even in those early days was devising intrigues against the Jews. He appeared before Ahasuerus, and said: "O king, this people is a peculiar people. May it please thee to destroy it." Ahasuerus replied: "I fear the God of this people; He is very mighty, and I bear in mind what befell Pharaoh for his wicked treatment of the Israelites." "Their God," said Haman, "hates an unchaste life. Do thou, therefore, prepare feasts for them, and order them to take part in the merry-makings. Have them eat and drink and act as their heart desireth, so that their God may become wrathful against them."

When Mordecai heard of the feasts that were planned, he advised the Jews not to join in them. All the prominent men of his people and many of the lower classes took his advice to heart. They fled from Shushan, to avoid being compelled to take part in the festivities. The rest remained in the city and yielded to force; they participated in the celebrations, and even permitted themselves to eat of food prepared by the heathen, though the king had taken care not to offend the religious conscience of the Jews in such details. He had been so punctilious that there was no need for them to drink wine touched by the hand of an idolater, let alone eat forbidden food. The arrangements for the feast were entirely in the charge of Haman and Mordecai, so that neither Jew nor Gentile might absent himself for religious reasons.

It was the aim of the king to let every guest follow the inclination of his heart. When Ahasuerus issued the order, that the officers of his house were to "do according to every man's pleasure," God became wroth with him. "Thou villain," He said, "canst thou do every man's pleasure? Suppose two men love the same woman, can both marry her? Two vessels sail forth together from a port, the one desires a south wind, the other a north wind. Canst thou produce a wind to satisfy the two? On the morrow Haman and Mordecai will appear before thee. Wilt thou be able to side with both?"

The scene of the festivities was in the royal gardens. The upper branches of the high trees were made to interlace with each other, so as to form vaulted arches, and the smaller trees with aromatic foliage were taken up out of the ground, and placed in artfully constructed tents. From tree to tree stretched curtains of byssus, white and sapphire blue, and vivid green and royal purple, fastened to their supports by ropes depending from round silver beams, these in turn resting on pillars of red, green, yellow, white, and glittering blue marble. The couches were made of delicate draperies, their frames stood on silver feet, and the rods attached to them were of gold. The floor was tiled with crystal and marble, outlined with precious stones, whose brilliance illuminated the scene far and wide.

The wine and the other beverages were drunk only from golden vessels, yet Ahasuerus was so rich that no drinking cup was used more than a single time. But magnificent as these utensils of his were, when the holy vessels of the Temple were brought in, the golden splendor of the others was dimmed; it turned dull as lead. The wine was in each case older than its drinker. To prevent intoxication from unaccustomed drinks, every guest was served with the wine indigenous to his native place. In general, Ahasuerus followed the Jewish rather than the Persian manner. It was a banquet rather than a drinking bout. In Persia a custom prevailed that every participant in a banquet of wine had to drain a huge beaker far exceeding the drinking capacity of any human being, and do it he must, though he lost reason and life. The office butler accordingly was very lucrative, because the guests at such wassails were in the habit of bribing him to purchase the liberty of drinking as little as they pleased or dared. This Persian habit of compelling excess in drinking was ignored at Ahasuerus's banquet; every guest did as he chose.

The royal bounty did not show itself in food and drink alone. The king's guests could also indulge in the pleasures of the dance if they were so minded. Dancers were provided, who charmed the company with their artistic figures displayed upon the purple-covered floor. That the enjoyment of the participants might in no wise be marred, as by separation from their families, all were permitted to bring their households with them, and merchants were released from the taxes imposed upon them.

So sure was Ahasuerus of his success as a host that he dared say to his Jewish guests: "Will your God be able to match this banquet in the future world?" Whereunto the Jews replied: "The banquet God will prepare for the righteous in the world to come is that of which it is written, 'No eye hath seen it but God's; He will accomplish it for them that wait upon Him.' If God were to offer us a banquet like unto thine, O king, we should say, Such as this we ate at the table of Ahasuerus."

VASTHI'S BANQUET

The banquet given by Queen Vashti to the women differed but slightly from Ahasuerus's. She sought to emulate her husband's example even in the point of exhibiting treasures. Six store-chambers she displayed daily to the women she had bidden as guests; aye, she did not even shrink from arraying herself in the high-priestly garments. The meats and dishes, as at Ahasuerus's table, were Palestinian, only instead of wine, liqueurs were served, and sweets.

As the weak sex is subject to sudden attacks of indisposition, the banquet was given in the halls of the palace, so that the guests might at need withdraw to the adjoining chambers. The gorgeously ornamented apartments of the palace, besides, were more attractive to the feminine taste than the natural beauties of the royal gardens, "for a woman would rather reside in beautiful chambers and possess beautiful clothes than eat fatted calves." Nothing interested the women more than to become acquainted with the arrangement of the interior of the palace, "for women are curious to know all things." Vashti gratified their desire. She showed them all there was to be seen, describing every place as she came to it: This is the dining-hall, this the wine-room, this the bed-chamber.

Vashti, too, was actuated by a political motive when she determined to give her banquet. By inviting the wives of hostages in case the men rose in insurrection against the king. For Vashti knew the ways of statecraft. She not only was the wife of a king, but also the daughter of a king, of Belshazzar. The night of Belshazzar's murder in his own palace, Vashti, alarmed by the confusion that ensued, and not knowing of the death of her father, fled to the apartments in which he was in the habit of sitting. The Median Darius had already ascended the throne of Belshazzar, and so it happened that Vashti, instead of finding the hoped-for refuge with her father, ran straight into the hands of his successor. But he had compassion with her, and gave her to his son Ahasuerus for wife.

THE FATE OF VASHTI

Though Ahasuerus had taken every precaution to prevent intemperate indulgence in wine, his banquet revealed the essential difference between Jewish and pagan festivities. When Jews are gathered about a festal board, they discuss a Halakah, or a Haggadah, or, at the least, a simple verse from the Scriptures. Ahasuerus and his boon companions rounded out the banquet with prurient talk. The Persians lauded the charms of the women of their people, while the Medians admitted none superior to the Median women. Then "the fool" Ahasuerus up and spake: "My wife is neither a Persian nor a Median, but a Chaldean, yet she excels all in beauty. Would you convince yourselves of the truth of my words?" "Yes," shouted the company, who were deep in their cups, "but that we may properly judge of her natural charms, let her appear before us unadorned, yes, without any apparel whatsoever," and Ahasuerus agreed to the shameless condition.

The thing was from God, that so insensate a demand should be made of Vashti by the king. A whole week Mordecai had spent in fasting and praying, supplicating God to mete out punishment to Ahasuerus for his desecration of the Temple utensils. On the seventh day of the week, on the Sabbath, when Mordecai after his long fast took food, because fasting is forbidden on the Sabbath day, God heard his prayer and the prayer of the Sanhedrin. He sent down seven Angels of Confusion to put an end to Ahasuerus's pleasure. They were named: Mehuman, Confusion; Biztha, Destruction of the House; Harbonah, Annihilation; Bigtha and Abagtha, the Pressers of the Winepress, for God had resolved to crush the court of Ahasuerus as one presses the juice from grapes in a press; Zetha, Observer of Immorality; and Carcas, Knocker.

There was a particular reason why this interruption of the feast took place on the Sabbath. Vashti was in the habit of forcing Jewish maidens to spin and weave on the Sabbath day, and to add to her cruelty, she would deprive them of all their clothes. It was on the Sabbath, therefore, that her punishment overtook her, and for the same reason it was put into the king's heart to have her appear in public stripped of all clothing.

Vashti recoiled from the king's revolting order. But it must not be supposed that she shrank from carrying it out because it offended her moral sense. She was not a whit better than her husband. She fairly revelled in the opportunity his command gave her to indulge in carnal pleasures once again, for it was exactly a week since she had been delivered of a child. But God sent the angel Gabriel to her to disfigure her countenance. Suddenly signs of leprosy appeared on her forehead, and the marks of other diseases on her person. In this state it was impossible for her to show herself to the king. She made a virtue of necessity, and worded her refusal to appear before him arrogantly: "Say to Ahasuerus: 'O thou fool and madman! Hast thou lost thy reason by too much drinking? I am Vashti, the daughter of Belshazzar, who was a son of Nebuchadnezzar, the Nebuchadnezzar who scoffed at kings and unto whom princes were a derision, and even thou wouldst not have been deemed worthy to run before my father's chariot as a courier. Had he lived, I should never have been given unto thee for wife. Not even those who suffered the death penalty during the reign of my forefather Nebuchadnezzar were stripped bare of their clothing, and thou demandest that I appear naked in public! Why, it is for thine own sake that I refuse to heed they order. Either the people will decide that I do not come up to thy description of me, and will proclaim thee a liar, or, bewitched by my beauty, they will kill thee in order to gain possession of me, saying, Shall this fool be the master of so much beauty?'"

The first lady of the Persian aristocracy encouraged Vashti to adhere to her resolution. "Better," her adviser said, when Ahasuerus's second summons was delivered to Vashti, together with his threat to kill her unless she obeyed, "better the king should kill thee and annihilate thy beauty, than that thy person should be admired by other eyes than thy husband's, and thus thy name be disgraced, and the name of thy ancestors."

When Vashti refused to obey the repeated command to appear before the king and the hundred and twenty-seven crowned princes of the realm, Ahasuerus turned to the Jewish sages, and requested them to pass sentence upon his queen. Their thoughts ran in this wise: If we condemn the queen to death, we shall suffer for it as soon as Ahasuerus becomes sober, and hears it was at our advice that she was executed. But if we admonish him unto clemency now, while he is intoxicated, he will accuse us of not paying due deference to the majesty of the king. They therefore resolved upon neutrality. "Since the destruction of the Temple," they said to the king, "since we have not dwelt in our land, we have lost the power to give sage advice, particularly in matters of life and death. Better seek counsel with the wise men of Ammon and Moab, who have ever dwelt at ease in their land, like wine that hath settled on its lees, and hath not been emptied from vessel to vessel.

Thereupon Ahasuerus put his charge against Vashti before the seven princes of Persia, Carshena, Shethar, Admatha, Tarshish, Meres, Marsena, and Memucan, who came from Africa, India, Edom, Tarsus, Mursa, Resen, and Jerusalem, respectively. The names of these seven officials, each representing his country, were indicative of their office. Carshena had the care of the animals, Shethar of the wine, Admatha of the land, Tarshish of the palace, Meres of the poultry, Marsena of the bakery, and Memucan provided for the needs of all in the palace, his wife acting as housekeeper.

This Memucan, a native of Jerusalem, was none other than Daniel, called Memucan, "the appointed one," because he was designated by God to perform miracles and bring about the death of Vashti.

When the king applied for advice to these seven nobles, Memucan was the first to speak up, though in rank he was inferior to the other six, as appears from the place his name occupies in the list. However, it is customary, as well among Persians as among Jews, in passing death sentence, to begin taking the vote with the youngest of the judges on the bench, to prevent the juniors and the less prominent from being overawed by the opinion of the more influential.

It was Memucan's advice to the king to make an example of Vashti, so that in future no woman should dare refuse obedience to her husband. Daniel-Memucan had had unpleasant experiences in his conjugal life. He had married a wealthy Persian lady, who insisted upon speaking to him in her own language exclusively. Besides, personal antipathy existed between Daniel and Vashti. He had in a measure been the cause of her refusal to appear before the king and his princes. Vashti hated Daniel, because it was he who had prophesied his death to her father, and the extinction of his dynasty. She could not endure his sight, wherefore she would not show herself to the court in his presence. Also, it was Daniel who, by pronouncing the Name of God, had caused the beauty of Vashti to vanish, and her face to be marred. In consequence of all this, Daniel advised, not only that Vashti should be cast off, but that she should be made harmless forever by the hangman's hand. His advice was endorsed by his colleagues, and approved by the king. That the king might not delay execution of the death sentence, and Daniel himself thus incur danger to his own life, he made Ahasuerus swear the most solemn oath known to the Persians, that it would be carried out forthwith. At the same time a royal edict was promulgated, making it the duty of wives to obey their husbands. With special reference to Daniel's domestic difficulties, it was specified that the wife must speak the language of her lord and master.

The execution of Vashti brought most disastrous consequences in its train. His whole empire, which is tantamount to saying the whole world, rose against Ahasuerus. The widespread rebellion was put down only after his marriage with Esther, but not before it had inflicted upon him the loss of one hundred and twenty-seven provinces, the half of his kingdom. Such was his punishment for refusing permission to rebuild the Temple. It was only after the fall of Haman, when Mordecai had been made the chancellor of the empire, that Ahasuerus succeeded in reducing the revolted provinces to submission.

The death of Vashti was not undeserved punishment, for it had been she who had prevented the king from giving his consent to the rebuilding of the Temple. "Wilt thou rebuild the Temple," said she, reproachfully, "which my ancestors destroyed?"

THE FOLLIES OF AHASUERUS

Ahasuerus is the prototype of the unstable, foolish ruler. He sacrificed his wife Vashti to his friend Haman-Memucan, and later on again his friend Haman to his wife Esther. Folly possessed him, too, when he arranged extravagant festivities for guests from afar, before he had won, by means of kindly treatment, the friendship of his surroundings, of the inhabitants of his capital. Ridiculous is the word that describes his edict bidding wives obey their husbands. Every one who read it exclaimed: "To be sure, a man is master in his own house!" However, the silly decree served its purpose. It revealed his true character to the subjects of Ahasuerus, and thenceforward they attached little importance to his edicts. This was the reason why the decree of annihilation directed against the Jews failed of the effect expected by Haman and Ahasuerus. The people regarded it as but another of the king's foolish pranks, and therefore were ready to acquiesce in the revocation of the edict when it came.

The king's true character appeared when he grew sober after the episode with Vashti. Learning that he had had her executed, he burst out furiously against his seven counsellors, and in turn ordered them to death.

Foolish, too, is the only word to describe the manner in which he set about discovering the most beautiful woman in his dominion. King David on a similar occasion wisely sent out messengers who were to bring to him the most beautiful maiden in the land, and there was none who was not eager to enjoy the honor of giving a daughter of his to the king. Ahasuerus's method was to have his servants gather together a multitude of beautiful maidens and women from all parts, and among them he proposed to make choice. The result of this system was that the women concealed themselves to avoid being taken into the harem of the king, when it was not certain that they would be found worthy of becoming his queen.

With his stupidity Ahasuerus combined wantonness. He ordered force to be used in taking the maidens from their parents and the wives from their husbands, and then he confined them in his harem. On the other hand, the moral sense of the heathen was so degraded that many maidens displayed their charms to public view, so that they might be sure to attract the admiring attention of the royal emissaries.

As for Esther, for four years Mordecai kept her concealed in a chamber, so that the king's scouts could not discover her. But her beauty had long been known to fame, and when they returned to Shushan, they had to confess to the king, that the most superbly beautiful woman in the land eluded their search. Thereupon Ahasuerus issued a decree ordaining the death penalty for the woman who should secrete herself before his emissaries. There was nothing left for Mordecai to do but fetch Esther from her hiding-place, and immediately she was espied and carried to the palace of the king.

MORDECAI

The descent of Mordecai and of his niece Esther is disposed of in a few words in the Scripture. But he could trace it all the way back to the Patriarch Jacob, from whom he was forty-five degrees removed. Beside the father of Mordecai, the only ancestor of his who is mentioned by name is Shimei, and he is mentioned for a specific reason. This Shimei is none other then the notorious son of Gera, the rebel who had so scoffed and mocked at David fleeing before Absalom that he would have been killed by Abishai, if David had not generously interfered in his favor. David's prophetic eye discerned in Shimei the ancestor of Israel's savior in the time of Ahasuerus. For this reason he dealt leniently with him, and on his death-bed he bade his son Solomon reserve vengeance until Shimei should have reached old age and could beget no more children. Thus Mordecai deserves both appellations, the Benjamite and the Judean, for he owed his existence not only to his actual Benjamite forebears on his father's side, but also to the Judean David, who kept his ancestor Shimei alive.

Shimei's distinction as the ancestor of Israel's redeemer was due to the merits of his wife. When Jonathan and Ahimaaz, David's spies in his war against his son, fled before the myrmidons of Absalom, they found the gate of Shimei's house open. Entering, they concealed themselves in the well. That they escaped detection was due to the ruse of Shimei's pious wife. She quickly transformed the well into a lady's chamber. When Absalom's men came and looked about, they desisted from searching the place, because they reasoned, that men as saintly as Jonathan and Ahimaaz would not have taken refuge in the private apartment of a woman. God determined, that for having rescued two pious men He would reward her with two pious descendants, who should in turn avert the ruin of Israel.

On his mother's side, Mordecai was, in very deed, a member of the tribe of Judah. In any event, he was a son of Judah in the true sense of the word; he publicly acknowledged himself a Jew, and he refused to touch of the forbidden food which Ahasuerus set before his guest at his banquet.

His other appellatives likewise point to his piety and his excellencies. His name Mordecai, for instance, consists of Mor, meaning "myrrh," and Decai, "pure," for he was as refined and noble as pure myrrh. Again, he is called Ben Jair, because he "illumined the eyes of Israel"; and Ben Kish, because when he knocked at the gates of the Divine mercy, they were opened unto him, which is likewise the origin of his name Ben Shimei, for he was heard by God when he offered up prayer. Still another of Mordecai's epithets was Bilshan, "master of languages." Being a member of the great Sanhedrin he understood all the seventy languages spoken in the world. More than that, he knew the language of the deaf mutes. It once happened that no new grain could be obtained at Passover time. A deaf mute came and pointed with one hand to the roof and with the other to the cottage. Mordecai understood that these signs meant a locality by the name of Gagot-Zerifim, Cottage-Roofs, and, lo, new grain was found there for the 'Omer offering. On another occasion a deaf mute pointed with one hand to his eye and with the other to the staple of the bolt on the door. Mordecai understood that he meant a place called En-Soker, "dry well," for eye and spring are the same word, En, in Aramaic, and Sikra also has a double meaning, staple and exhaustion.

Mordecai belonged to the highest aristocracy of Jerusalem, he was of royal blood, and he was deported to Babylonian together with King Jeconiah, by Nebuchadnezzar, who at that time exiled only the great of the land. Later he returned to Palestine, but remained only for a time. He preferred to live in the Diaspora, and watch over the education of Esther. When Cyrus and Darius captured Babylon, Mordecai, Daniel, and the Jewish community of the conquered city accompanied King Cyrus to Shushan, where Mordecai established his academy.

ESTHER'S BEAUTY AND PIETY

The birth of Esther caused the death of her mother. Her father had died a little while before, so she was entirely orphaned. Mordecai and his wife interested themselves in the poor babe. His wife became her nurse, and he himself did not hesitate, when there was need for it, to do services for the child that are usually performed only by women.

Both her names, Esther as well as Hadassah, are descriptive of her virtues. Hadassah, or Myrtle, she is called, because her good deeds spread her fame abroad, as the sweet fragrance of the myrtle pervades the air in which it grows. In general, the myrtle is symbolic of the pious, because, as the myrtle is ever green, summer and winter alike, so the saints never suffer dishonor, either in this world or in the world to come. In another way Esther resembled the myrtle, which, in spite of its pleasant scent, has a bitter taste. Esther was pleasant to the Jews, but bitterness itself to Haman and all who belonged to him.

The name Esther is equally significant. In Hebrew it means "she who conceals," a fitting name for the niece of Mordecai, the woman who well knew how to guard a secret, and long hid her descent and faith from the king and the court. She herself had been kept concealed for years in the house of her uncle, withdrawn from the searching eyes of the king's spies. Above all she was the hidden light that suddenly shone upon Israel in his rayless darkness.

In build, Esther was neither tall nor short, she was exactly of average height, another reason for calling her Myrtle, a plant which likewise is neither large nor small. In point of fact, Esther was not a beauty in the real sense of the word. The beholder was bewitched by her grace and her charm, and that in spite of her somewhat sallow, myrtle-like complexion. More than this, her enchanting grace was not the grace of youth, for she was seventy-five years old when she came to court, and captivated the hearts of all who saw her, from king to eunuch. This was in fulfilment of the prophecy which God made to Abraham when he was leaving the home of his father: "Thou art leaving the house of thy father at the age of seventy-five. As thou livest, the deliverer of thy children in Media also shall be seventy-five years old."

Another historical event pointed forward to Esther's achievement. When the Jews, after the destruction of Jerusalem, broke out into the wail, "We are orphans and fatherless," God said: "in very sooth, the redeemer whom I shall send unto you in Media shall also be an orphan fatherless and motherless."

Ahasuerus put Esther between two groups of beauties, Median beauties to right of her, and Persian beauties to left of her. Yet Esther's comeliness outshone them all. Not even Joseph could vie with the Jewish queen in grace. Grace was suspended above him, but Esther was fairly laden down with it. Whoever saw her, pronounced her the ideal of beauty of his nation. The general exclamation was: "This one is worthy of being queen." In vain Ahasuerus had sought a wife for four years, in vain fathers had spent time and money bringing their daughters to him, in the hope that one or the other would appeal to his fancy. None among the maidens, none among the women, pleased Ahasuerus. But scarcely had he set eyes upon Esther when he thrilled with the feeling, that he had at last found what he had long yearned for.

All these years the portrait of Vashti had hung in his chamber. He had not forgotten his rejected queen. But once he beheld Esther, Vashti's picture was replaced by hers. Maiden grace and womanly charm were in her united.

The change in her worldly position wrought no change in Esther's ways and manners. As she retained her beauty until old age, so the queen remained as pure in mind and soul as ever the simple maiden had been. All the other women who entered the gates of the royal palace made exaggerated demands, Esther's demeanor continued modest and unassuming. The others insisted that the seven girl pages assigned to them should have certain peculiar qualities, as, that they should not differ, each from her mistress, in complexion and height. Esther uttered no wish whatsoever.

But her unpretending ways were far from pleasing to Hegai, chief of the eunuchs of the harem. He feared lest the king discover that Esther did nothing to preserve her beauty, and would put the blame for it upon him, an accusation that might bring him to the gallows. To avoid such a fate, he loaded Esther down with resplendent jewels, distinguishing her beyond all the other women gathered in the palace, as Joseph, by means of costly gifts lavished upon him, had singled out her ancestor Benjamin from among his brethren.

Hegai paid particular attention to what Esther ate. For her he brought dishes from the royal table, which, however, she refused obstinately to ouch. Only such things passed her lips as were permitted to Jews. She lived entirely on vegetable food, as Hananiah, Mishael, and Azariah had aforetimes done at the court of Nebuchadnezzar. The forbidden tidbits she passed over to the non-Jewish servants. Her personal attendants were seven Jewish maidens as consistently pious as herself, whose devotion to the ritual law Esther could depend upon.

Otherwise Esther was cut off from all intercourse with Jews, and she was in danger of forgetting when the Sabbath bath came around. She therefore adopted the device of giving her seven attendants peculiar names, to keep her in mind of the passage of time. The first one was called Hulta, "Workaday," and she was in attendance upon Esther on Sundays. On Mondays, she was served by Rok`ita, to remind her of Rek`ia, "the Firmament," which was created on the second day of the world. Tuesday's maid was called Genunita, "Garden," the third day of creation having produced the world of plants. On Wednesday, she was reminded by Nehorita's name, "the Luminous," that it was the day on which God had made the great luminaries, to shed their light in the sky; on Thursday by Ruhshita, "Movement," for on the fifth day the first animated beings were created; on Friday, the day on which the beasts came into being, by Hurfita, "little Ewelamb"; and on the Sabbath her bidding was done by Rego`ita, "Rest." Thus she was sure to remember the Sabbath day week after week.

Mordecai's daily visits to the gate of the palace had a similar purpose. Thus Esther was afforded the opportunity of obtaining instruction from him on all ritual doubts that might assail her. This lively interest displayed by Mordecai in Esther's physical and spiritual welfare is not wholly attributable to an uncle's and guardian's solicitude in behalf of an orphaned niece. A much closer bond, the bond between husband and wife, united them, for when Esther had grown to maidenhood, Mordecai had espoused her. Naturally, Esther would have been ready to defend her conjugal honor with her life. She would gladly have suffered death at the hands of the king's bailiffs rather than yield herself to a man not her husband. Luckily, there was no need for this sacrifice, for her marriage with Ahasuerus was but a feigned union. God has sent down a female spirit in the guise of Esther to take her place with the king. Esther herself never lived with Ahasuerus as his wife.

At the advice of her uncle, Esther kept her descent and her faith a secret. Mordecai's injunction was dictated by several motives. First of all it was his modesty that suggested secrecy. He thought the king, if he heard from Esther that she had been raised by him, might offer to install him in some high office. In point of fact, Mordecai was right in his conjecture; Ahasuerus had pledged himself to make lords, princes, and kings of Esther's friends and kinspeople, if she would but name them.

Another reason for keeping Esther's Jewish affiliations a secret was Mordecai's apprehension, that the fate of Vashti overtake Esther, too. If such were in store for her, he desired at least to guard against the Jews' becoming her fellowsuffers. Besides, Mordecai knew only too well the inimical feelings entertained by the heathen toward the Jews, ever since their exile from the Holy Land, and he feared that the Jew-haters, to gratify their hostility against the Jews, might bring about the ruin of Esther and her house.

Mindful of the perils to which Esther was exposed, Mordecai allowed no day to pass without assuring himself of her well-being. His compensation therefore came from God: "Thou makest the well-being of a single soul they intimate concern. As thou livest, the well-being and good of thy whole nation Israel shall be entrusted to thee as thy task." And to reward him for his modesty, God said: "Thou withdrawest thyself from greatness; as thou livest, I will honor thee more than all men on earth."

Vain were the efforts made by Ahasuerus to draw her secret from Esther. He arranged great festivities for the purpose, but she guarded it well. She had an answer ready for his most insistent questions: "I know neither my people nor my family, for I lost my parents in my earliest infancy." But as the king desired greatly to show himself gracious to the nation to which the queen belonged, he released all the peoples under his dominion from the payment of taxes and imposts. In this way, he thought, her nation was bound to be benefited.

When the king saw that kindness and generosity left her untouched, he sought to wrest the secret from her by threats. Once when she parried his inquiries in the customary way, saying, "I am an orphan, and God, the

Father of the fatherless, in His mercy, has brought me up," he retorted: I shall gather virgins together the second time." His purpose was to provoke the jealousy of Esther, "for a woman is jealous of nothing so much as a rival."

When Mordecai noticed that women were being brought to court anew, he was overcome with anxiety for his niece. Thinking that the fate of Vashti might have befallen her, he was impelled to make inquires about her.

As for Esther herself, she was but following the example of her race. She could keep silent in all modesty, as Rachel, the mother of Benjamin, had kept a modest silence when her father gave her sister Leah to Jacob for wife instead of herself, and as Saul the Benjamite was modestly reserved when, questioned by his uncle, he told about the finding of his she-asses, but nothing about his elevation to the kingship. Rachel and Saul were recompensed for their self-abnegation by being given a descendant like Esther.

THE CONSPIRACY

Once the following conversation took place between Ahasuerus and Esther. The king asked Esther: "Whose daughter art thou?"

Esther: "And whose son art thou?"

Ahasuerus: "I am a king, and the son of a king."

Esther: "And I am a queen, the daughter of kings, a descendant of the royal family of Saul. If thou art, indeed, a real prince, how couldst thou put Vashti to death?"

Ahasuerus: "It was not to gratify my own wish, but at the advice of the great princes of Persia and Media."

Esther: "Thy predecessors took no advice from ordinary intelligences; they were guided by prophetical counsel. Arioch brought Daniel to Nebuchadnezzar, king of Babylon, and Belshazzar, too, summoned Daniel before him."

Ahasuerus: "Is there aught left of those toothsome morsels? Are there still prophets abroad?

Esther: "Seek and thou wilt find."

The result was that Mordecai was given the position at court once occupied by the chamberlains Bigthan and Teresh. Indignant that a place once filled by senators should be given to a barbarian, the ousted officials resolved to be revenged upon the king and take his life. Their purpose was to administer poison, which seemed easy of accomplishment, as they were the royal butlers, and could find many occasions to drop poison into a cup of water before handing it to the king. The plan successfully carried out would have satisfied their vengeful feelings, not only as to the king, but as to Mordecai as well. It would have made it appear that the death of Ahasuerus was attributable to the circumstance, that he had entrusted his person to the care of the Jew, as his life had been secure under Bigthan and Teresh. They discussed their plans in the presence of Mordecai, acting upon the unwarranted assumption, that he would not understand the language they spoke, the Tarsian, their native tongue. They were ignorant of the fact, that Mordecai was a member of the Sanhedrin, and as such knew all the seventy languages of the world. Thus their own tongue betrayed them to ruin.

However, Mordecai had no need to make use of his great knowledge of languages; he obtained his information about the plot of the two chamberlains through prophetical channels. Accordingly, he appeared one night in the palace. By a miracle the guards at the gates had not seen him, and he could enter unrestrained. Thus he overheard the conversation between the two conspirators.

Mordecai had more than a single reason for preventing the death of Ahasuerus. In the first place, he desired to secure the king's friendship for the Jews, and more especially his permission for the rebuilding of the Temple. Then he feared, if the king were murdered immediately after his rise to a high place in the state, the heathen would assign as the cause of the disaster his connection with the Jews his marriage with Esther and the appointment of Mordecai to office.

Esther's confidence in Mordecai's piety was so great that she unhesitatingly gave credence to the message she received from him concerning the mischievous plot hatched against the king. She believed that God would execute the wishes of Mordecai. Albeit Bigthan and Teresh had no plans of the sort attributed to them by her uncle, they would conceive then now in order to make Mordecai's words true. That Esther's confidence was justified appeared at once. The conspirators got wind of their betrayal to the king, and in good time they removed the poison they had already placed in Ahasuerus's cup. But that the lie might not be given to Mordecai, God caused poison to appear where none had been, and the conspirators were convicted of their crime. The king had the water analyzed which he was given to drink, and it was made manifest that it contained poison. Other evidence besides existed against the two plotters. It was established that both had at the same time busied themselves about the person of the king, though the regulations of the palace assigned definite hours of service to the one different from those assigned to the other. This made it clear that they intended to perpetrate a dark deed in common.

The two conspirators sought to escape the legitimate punishment for their dastardly deed by ending their own life. But their intention was frustrated, and they were nailed to the cross.

HAMAN THE JEW-BAITER

The conspiracy of Bigthan and Teresh determined the king never again to have two chamberlains guard his person. Henceforward he would entrust his safety to a single individual, and he appointed Haman to the place. This was an act of ingratitude toward Mordecai, who, as the king's savior, had the most cogent claims upon the post. But Haman possessed one important advantage, he was the owner of great wealth. With the exception of Korah he was the richest man that had ever lived, for he had appropriated to himself the treasures of the Judean kings and of the Temple.

Ahasuerus had an additional reason for distinguishing Haman. He was well aware of Mordecai's ardent desire to see the Temple restored, and he instinctively felt he could not deny the wish of the man who had snatched him from untimely death. Yet he was not prepared to grant it. To escape from the dilemma he endeavored to make Haman act as a counterpoise against Mordecai, that "what the one built up, the other might pull down."

Ahasuerus had long been acquainted with Haman's feeling against the Jews. When the quarrel about the rebuilding of the Temple broke out between the Jews and their heathen adversaries, and the sons of Haman denounced the Jews before Ahasuerus, the two parties at odds agreed to send each a representative to the king, to advocate his case. Mordecai was appointed the Jewish delegate, and no more rabid Jew-hater could be found than Haman, to plead the cause of the antagonists of the Temple builders.

As for his character, that, too, King Ahasuerus had had occasion to see in its true light, because Haman is but another name for Memucan, the prince who is chargeable in the last resort with the death of Vashti. At the time of the king's wrath against the queen, Memucan was still lowest in the rank among the seven princes of Persia, yet, arrogant as he was, he was the first to speak up when the king put his question about the punishment due to Vashti an illustration of the popular adage: "The common man rushes to the front." Haman's hostility toward Vashti dated from her banquet, to which the queen had failed to bid his wife as guest. Moreover, she had once insulted him by striking him a blow in the face. Besides, Haman calculated, if only Vashti's repudiation could be brought about, he might succeed in marrying his own daughter to the king. He was not the only disappointed man at court. In part the conspiracy of Bigthan and Teresh was a measure of revenge against Ahasuerus for having made choice of Esther instead of a kinswoman of theirs.

Esther once married to the king, however, Haman made the best of a bad bargain. He tried by every means in his power to win the friendship of the queen. Whether she was Jewess or heathen, he desired to claim kinship with her as a Jewess through the fraternal bond between Esau and Jacob, as a heathen easily enough, "for all the heathen area akin to one another."

MORDECAI'S PRIDE

When Ahasuerus raised Haman to his high office, he at the same time issued the order, that all who saw him were to prostrate themselves before him and pay him Divine honors. To make it manifest that the homage due to him had an idolatrous character, Haman had the image of an idol fastened to his clothes, so that whoever bowed down before him, worshipped an idol at the same time. Mordecai alone of all at court refused to obey the royal order. The highest officials, even the most exalted judges, showed Haman the reverence bidden by the king. The Jews themselves entreated Mordecai not to call forth the fury of Haman, and cause the ruin of Israel thereby. Mordecai, however, remained steadfast; no persuasions could move him to pay to a mortal the tribute due to Divinity.

Also the servants of the king who sat at the gate of the royal palace said to Mordecai: "Wherein art thou better than we, that we should pay reverence to Haman and prostrate ourselves, and thou doest naught of all commanded us in the matter?" Mordecai answered, saying "O ye fools without understanding! Hear ye my words and make meet reply thereunto. Who is man that he should act proudly and arrogantly man born of woman and few in days? At his birth there is weeping and travailing, in his youth pain and groans, all his days are 'full of trouble,' and in the end he returns unto dust. Before such an one I should prostrate myself? I bend the knee before God alone, the only living One in heaven, He who is the fire consuming all other fires; who holds the earth in His arms; who stretches out the heavens in His might; who darkens the sun when it pleases Him, and illumines the darkness; who commanded the sand to set bounds unto the seas; who made the waters of the sea salt, and caused its waves to spread an aroma as of wine; who chained the sea as with manacles, and held it fast in the depths of the abyss that it might not overflow the land; it rages, yet it cannot pass its limits. With His word He created the firmament, which He stretched out like a cloud in the air; He cast it over the world like a dark vault, like a tent it is spread over the earth. In His strength He upholds all there is above and below. The sun, the moon, and the Pleiades run before Him, the stars and the planets are not idle for a single moment; they rest not, they speed before Him as His messengers, going to the right and to the left, to do the will of Him who created them. To Him praise is due, before Him we must prostrate ourselves."

The court officials spake and said: "Yet we know well that thy ancestor Jacob prostrated himself before Haman's ancestor Esau!"

Whereunto Mordecai made reply: "I am a descendant of Benjamin, who was not yet born when his father Jacob and his brothers cast themselves upon the earth before Esau. My ancestor never showed such honor to a mortal. Therefore was Benjamin's allotment of land in Palestine privileged to contain the Temple. The spot whereon Israel and all the peoples of the earth prostrated themselves before God belonged to him who had never prostrated himself before mortal man. Therefore I will not bend my knee before this sinner Haman, nor cast myself to earth before him."

Haman at first tried to propitiate Mordecai by a show of modesty. As though he had not noticed the behavior of Mordecai, he approached him, and saluted him with the words: "Peace be with thee, my lord!" But Mordecai bluntly replied: "There is no peace, saith my God, to the wicked."

The hatred of Mordecai cherished by Haman was due to more than the hereditary enmity between the descendants of Saul and Agag. Not even Mordecai's public refusal to pay the homage due to Haman suffices to explain its virulence. Mordecai was aware of a certain incident in the past of Haman. If he had divulged it, the betrayal would have been most painful to the latter. This accounts for the intensity of his feeling.

It once happened that a city in India rebelled against Ahasuerus. In great haste troops were dispatched thither under the command of Mordecai and Haman. It was estimated that the campaign would require three years, and all preparations were made accordingly. By the end of the first year Haman had squandered the provisions laid in to supply the part of the army commanded by him, for the whole term of the campaign. Greatly embarrassed, he requested Mordecai to give him aid. Mordecai, however, refused him succor; they both had been granted the same amount of provisions for an equal number of men. Haman then offered to borrow from Mordecai and pay him interest. This, too, Mordecai refused to do, and for two reasons. If

Mordecai had supplied Haman's men with provisions, his own would have to suffer, and as for interest, the law prohibits it, saying "Unto thy brother thou shalt not lend upon usury," and Jacob and Esau, the respective ancestors of Mordecai and Haman, had been brothers.

When starvation stared them in the face, the troops commanded by Haman threatened him with death unless he gave them their rations. Haman again resorted to Mordecai, and promised to pay him as much as ten per cent interest. The Jewish general continued to refuse the offer. But he professed himself willing to help him out of his embarrassment on one condition, that Haman sell himself to Mordecai as his slave. Driven into a corner, he acquiesced, and the contract was written upon Mordecai's knee-cap, because there was no paper to be found in the camp.

The bill of sale ran thus: "I, Haman, the son of Hammedatha of the family of Agag, was sent out by King Ahasuerus to make war upon an Indian city, with an army of sixty thousand soldiers, furnished with the necessary provisions. Precisely the same commission was given by the king to Mordecai, the son of Shimei of the tribe of Benjamin. But I squandered the provisions entrusted to me by the king, so that I had no rations to give to my troops. I desired to borrow from Mordecai on interest, but, having regard to the fact that Jacob and Esau were brothers, he refused to lend me upon usury, and I was forced to sell myself as slave to him. If, now, I should at any time decline to serve him as a slave, or deny that I am his slave, or if my children and children's children unto the end of all time should refuse to do him service, if only a single day of the week; or if I should act inimically toward him on account of this contract, as Esau did toward Jacob after selling him his birthright; in all these cases, a beam of wood is to be plucked out of the house of the recalcitrant, and he is to be hanged upon it. I, Haman, the son of Hammedatha of the family of Agag, being under no restraint, do hereby consent with my own will, and bind myself to be slave in perpetuity to Mordecai, in accordance with the contents of this document."

Later, when Haman attained to high rank in the state, Mordecai, whenever he met him, was in the habit of stretching out his knee toward him, so that he might see the bill of sale. This so enraged him against Mordecai and against the Jews that he resolved to extirpate the Jewish people.

CASTING THE LOTS

Haman's hatred, first directed against Mordecai alone, grew apace until it included Mordecai's colleagues, all the scholars, whom he sought to destroy, and not satisfied with even this, he plotted the annihilation of the whole of Mordecai's people, the Jews.

Before beginning to lay out his plans, he desired to determine the most favorable moment for his undertaking, which he did by casting lots.

First of all he wanted to decide on the day of the week. The scribe Shimshai began to cast lots. Sunday appeared inappropriate, being the day on which God created heaven and earth, whose continuance depends on Israel's existence. Were it not for God's covenant with Israel, there would be neither day nor night, neither heaven nor earth. Monday showed itself equally unpropitious for Haman's devices, for it was the day on which God effected the separation between the celestial and the terrestrial waters, symbolic of the separation between Israel and the heathen. Tuesday, the day on which the vegetable world was created, refused to give its aid in bringing about the ruin of Israel, who worships God with branches of palm trees. Wednesday, too, protested against the annihilation of Israel, saying: "On me the celestial luminaries were created, and like unto them Israel is appointed to illumine the whole world. First destroy me, and then Thou mayest destroy Israel." Thursday said: "O Lord, on me the birds were created, which are used for sin offerings. When Israel shall be no more, who will bring offerings? First destroy me, and then Thou mayest destroy Israel." Friday was unfavorable to Haman's lots, because it was the day of the creation of man, and the Lord God said to Israel, "Ye are men." Least of all was the Sabbath day inclined to make itself subservient to Haman's wicked plans. It said: "The Sabbath is a sign between Israel and God. First destroy me, and then Thou mayest destroy Israel!"

Baffled, Haman gave up all idea of settling upon a favorable day of the week. He applied himself to the task of searching out the suitable month for his sinister undertaking. As it appeared to him, Adar was the only one of the twelve owning naught that might be interpreted in favor of the Jews. The rest of them seemed to be enlisted on their side. In Nisan Israel was redeemed from Egypt; in Iyar Amlek was overcome; In Siwan the Ethiopian Zerah was smitten in the war with Asa; in Tammuz the Amorite kings were subjugated; in Ab the Jews won a victory over Arad, the Canaanite; in Tishri the Jewish kingdom was firmly established by the dedication of Solomon's Temple, while in Heshwan the building of the Temple at Jerusalem was completed; Kislew and Tebet were the months during which Sihon and Og were conquered by the Israelites, and in Shebat occurred the sanguinary campaign of the eleven tribes against the godless children of Benjamin. Not alone was Adar a month without favorable significance in Jewish history, but actually a month of misfortune, the month in which Moses died. What Haman did not know was, that Adar was the month in which occurred also the birth of Moses.

Then Haman investigated the twelve signs of the zodiac in relation to Israel, and again it appeared that Adar was the most unfavorable month for the Jews. The first constellation, the Ram, said to Haman, "'Israel is a scattered sheep,' and how canst thou expect a father to offer his son for slaughter?"

The Bull said: "Israel's ancestor was 'the firstling bullock.'"

The Twins: "As we are twins, so Tamar bore twins to Judah."

The Crab: "As I am called Saratan, the scratcher, so it is said of Israel, 'All that oppress him, he shall scratch sorely.'"

The Lion: "God is called the lion, and is it likely the lion will permit the fox to bite his children?"

The Virgin: "As I am a virgin, so Israel is compared unto a virgin."

The Balance: "Israel obeys the law against unjust balances in the Torah, and must therefore be protected by the Balance."

The Scorpion: "Israel is like unto me, for he, too, is called scorpion."

The Archer: "The sons of Judah are masters of the bow, and the bows of mighty men directed against them will be broken."

The Goat: "It was a goat that brought blessing unto Jacob, the ancestor of Israel, and it stands to reason that the blessing of the ancestor cannot cause misfortune to the descendant."

The Water-bearer: "His dominion is likened unto a bucket, and therefore the Water-bearer cannot but bring him good."

The Fishes were the only constellation which, at least according to Haman's interpretation, made unfavorable prognostications as to the fate of the Jews. It said that the Jews would be swallowed like fishes. God however spake: "O thou villain! Fishes are sometimes swallowed, but sometimes they swallow, and thou shalt be swallowed by the swallowers." And when Haman began to cast lots, God said: "O thou villain, son of a villain! What thy lots have shown thee is thine own lot, that thou wilt be hanged."

THE DENUNCIATION OF THE JEWS

His resolve to ruin the Jews taken, Haman appeared before Ahasuerus with his accusation against them. "There is a certain people," he said, "the Jews, scattered abroad and dispersed among the peoples in all the provinces of the kingdom. They are proud and presumptuous. In Tebet, in the depth of winter, they bathe in warm water, and they sit in cold water in summer. Their religion is diverse from the religion of every other people, and their laws from the laws of every other land. To our laws they pay no heed, our religion finds no favor with them, and the decrees of the king they do not execute. When their eye falls upon us, they spit out before us, and they consider us as unclean vessels. When we levy them for the king's service, they either jump upon the wall, and hide within the chambers, or they break through the walls and escape. If we hasten to arrest them, they turn upon us, glare at us with their eyes, grind their teeth, stamp their feet, and so intimidate us that we cannot hold them fast. They do not give us their daughters unto wives, nor do they take our daughters unto wives. If one of them has to do the king's service, he idles all the day long. If they want to buy aught of us, they say, 'This is a day for doing business.' But if we want to buy aught of them, they say, 'We may do no business to-day,' and thus we can buy nothing from them on their market-days.

"Their time they pass in this wise: The first hour of the day, they say, they need for reciting the Shema; the second for praying; the third for eating; the fourth for saying grace, to give thanks to God for the food and drink He has granted them; the fifth hour they devote to their business affairs; in the sixth they already feel the need of rest; in the seventh their wives call for them, saying, 'come home, ye weary ones, who are so exhausted by the king's service!'

"The seventh day they celebrate as their Sabbath; they go to the synagogues on that day, read out of their books, translate pieces from their Prophets, curse our king, and execrate our government, saying: 'This is the day whereon the great God rested; so may He grant us rest from the heathen.'

"The women pollute the waters with their ritual baths, which they take after the seven days of their defilement. On the eighth day after the birth of sons, they circumcise them mercilessly, saying, 'This shall distinguish us from all other nations.' At the end of thirty days, and sometimes twenty-nine, they celebrate the beginning of the month. In the month of Nisan they observe eight days of Passover, beginning the celebration by kindling a fire of brushwood to burn up the leaven. They put all the leaven in their homes out of sight before they use the unleavened bread, saying, 'This is the day whereon our fathers were redeemed from Egypt.' Such is the festival they call Pesah. They go to their synagogues, read out of their books, and translate from the writings of the Prophets, saying: 'As the leaven has been removed out of our houses, so may this wicked dominion be removed from over us.'

"Again, in Siwan, they celebrate two days, on which they go to their synagogues, recite the Shema, and offer up prayers, read out of the Torah, and translate from the books of their Prophets, curse our king, and execrate our government. This is the holiday which they call Azarta, the closing festival. They ascend to the roofs of their synagogues, and throw down apples, which are picked up by those below, with the words, 'As these apples are gathered up, so may we be gathered together from our dispersion among the heathen.' They say they observe this festival, because on these days the Torah was revealed to their ancestors on Mount Sinai.

"On the first of Tishri they celebrate the New Year again they go to their synagogues, read out of their books, translate pieces from the writings of their Prophets, curse our king, execrate our government, and blow the trumpets, saying: 'On this Day of Memorial may we be remembered unto good, and our enemies unto evil.'

"On the ninth day of the same month they slaughter cattle, geese, and poultry, they eat and drink and indulge in dainties, they and their wives, their sons and their daughters. But the tenth day of the same month they call the Great Fast, and all of them fast, they together with their wives, their sons, and their daughters, yea, they even torture their little children without mercy, forcing them to abstain from food. They say: 'On this day our sins are pardoned, and are added to the sum of the sins committed by our enemies.' They go to their synagogues, read from their books, translate from the writings of their Prophets, curse our king, and execrate our government, saying: 'May this empire be wiped off from the face of the earth like unto our sins.' They supplicate and pray that the king may die, and his rule be made to cease.

"On the fifteenth of the same month they celebrate the Feast of Tabernacles. They cover the roofs of their houses with foliage, they resort to our parks, where they cut down palm branches for their festal wreaths, pluck the fruit of the Etrog, and cause havoc among the willows of the brook, by breaking down the hedges in their quest after Hosha'not, saying: 'As does the king in the triumphal procession, so do we.' Then they repair to their synagogues to pray, and read out of their books, and make circuits with their Hosha'not, all the while jumping and skipping like goats, so that there is no telling whether they curse us or bless us. This is Sukkot, as they call it, and while it lasts, they do none of the king's service, for, they maintain, all work is forbidden them on these days.

"In this way they waste the whole year with tomfoolery and fiddle-faddle, only in order to avoid doing the king's service. At the expiration of every period of fifty years they have a jubilee year, and every seventh year is a year of release, during which the land lies fallow, for they neither sow nor reap therein, and sell us neither fruits nor other products of the field, so that those of us who live among them die of hunger. At the end of every period of twelve months, they observe the New Year, at the end of every thirty days the New Moon, and every seventh day is the Sabbath, the day on which, as they say, the Lord of the world rested."

After Haman had finished his arraignment of the Jews, God said: "Thou didst well enumerate the holidays of the Jews, yet thou didst omit the two Purim and Shushan-Purim which the Jews will celebrate to commemorate thy fall."

Clever though Haman's charge was, the vindication of the Jews was no whit less clever. For they found a defender in the archangel Michael. While Haman was delivering his indictment, he spoke thus to God: "O Lord of the world! Thou knowest well that the Jews are not accused of idolatry, nor of immoral conduct, nor of shedding blood; they are accused only of observing Thy Torah." God pacified him: "As thou livest, I have not abandoned them, I will not abandon them."

Haman's denunciations of the Jewish people found a ready echo in the heart of the king. He replied: "I, too, desire the annihilation of the Jews, but I fear their God, for He is mighty beyond compare, and He loves His people with a great love. Whoever rises up against them, He crushes under their feet. Just think of Pharaoh! Should his example not be a warning to us? He ruled the whole world, yet, because he oppressed the Jews, he was visited with frightful plagues. God delivered them from the Egyptians, and cleft the sea for them, a miracle never done for any other nation, and when Pharaoh pursued them with an army of six hundred thousand warriors, he and his host together were drowned in the sea. Thy ancestor Amalek, O Haman, attacked them with four hundred thousand heroes, and all of them God delivered into the hands of Joshua, who slew them. Sisera had forty thousand generals under him, each one commander of a hundred thousand men, yet they all were annihilated. The God of the Jews ordered the stars to consume the warriors of Sisera, and then He caused the great general to fall into the power of a woman, to become a by-word and a reproach forever. Many and valorous rulers have risen up against them, they all were cast down by their God and crushed unto their everlasting disgrace. Now, then, can we venture aught against them?"

Haman, however, persisted. Day after day he urged the king to consent to his plan. Ahasuerus thereupon called together a council of the wise men of all nations and tongues. To them he submitted the question, whether the Jews ought not to be destroyed, seeing they differed from all other peoples. The sage councillors inquired: "Who is it that desires to induce thee to take so fatal a step? If the Jewish nation is destroyed, the world itself will cease to be, for the world exists only for the sake of the Torah studied by Israel. Yea, the very sun and moon shed their light only for the sake of Israel, and were it not for him, there were neither day nor night, and neither dew nor rain would moisten the earth. More than this, all other nations beside Israel are designated as 'strangers' by God, but Israel He called in His love 'a people near to Him,' and His 'children.' If men do not suffer their children and kinsmen to be attacked with impunity, how much less will God sit by quiet when Israel is assailed God the Ruler over all things, over the powers in heaven above and on earth beneath, over the spirits and the souls God with whom it lies to exalt and to degrade, to slay and to revive."

Haman was ready with a reply to these words of the wise: "The God who drowned Pharaoh in the sea, and who did all the wonders and signs ye have recounted, that God is now in His dotage, He can neither see nor protect. For did not Nebuchadnezzar destroy His house, burn His palace, and scatter His people to all corners of the earth, and He was not able to do one thing against it? If He had had power and strength, would he not have displayed them? This is the best proof that He was waxed old and feeble."

When the heathen sages heard these arguments advance by Haman, they agreed to his plan, and put their signature to an edict decreeing the persecution of the Jews.

THE DECREE OF ANNIHILATION

This is the text of the decree which Haman issued to the heads of all the nations regarding the annihilation of the Jews: "This herein is written by me, the great officer of the king, his second in rank, the first among the grandees, and one of the seven princes, and the most distinguished among the nobles of the realm. I, in agreement with the rulers of the provinces, the princes of the king, the chiefs and the lords, the Eastern kings and the satraps, all being of the same language, write you at the order of King Ahasuerus this writing sealed with his signet, so that it may not be sent back, concerning the great eagle Israel. The great eagle had stretched out his pinions over the whole world; neither bird nor beast could withstand him. But there came the great lion Nebuchadnezzar, and dealt the great eagle a stinging blow. His pinions snapped, his feathers were plucked out, and his feet were hacked off. The whole world has enjoyed rest, cheer, and tranquillity since the moment the eagle was chased from his eyrie until this day. Now we notice that he is using all efforts to secure wings. He is permitting his feathers to grow, with the intention of covering us and the whole world, as he did unto our forefathers. At the instance of King Ahasuerus, all the magnates of the king of Media and Persia are assembled, and we are writing you our joint advice, as follows: 'Set snares for the eagle, and capture him before he renews his strength, and soars back to his eyrie.' We advise you to tear out his plumage, break his wings, give his flesh to the fowl of heaven, split the eggs lying in his nest, and crush his young, so that his memorial may vanish from the world. Our counsel is not like unto Pharaoh's; he sought to destroy only the men of Israel; to the women he did no harm. It is not like unto the plan of Esau, who wanted to slay his brother Jacob and keep his children as slaves. It is not like unto the tactics of Amalek, who pursued Israel and smote the hindmost and feeble, but left the strong unscathed. It is not like unto the policy of Nebuchadnezzar, who carried them away into exile, and settled them near his own throne. And it is not like unto the way of Sennacherib, who assigned a land unto the Jews as fair as their own had been. We, recognizing clearly what the situation is, have resolved to slay the Jews, annihilate them, young and old, so that their name and their memorial may be no more, and their posterity may be cut off forever."

The edict issued by Ahasuerus against the Jews ran thus: "To all the peoples, nations, and races: Peace be with you! This is to acquaint you that one came to us who is not of our nation and of our land, an Amalekite, the son of great ancestors, and his name is Haman. He made a trifling request of me, saying: 'Among us there dwells a people, the most despicable of all, who are a stumbling-block in every time. They are exceeding presumptuous, and they know our weakness and our shortcomings. They curse the king in these words, which are constantly in their mouths: "God is the King of the world forever and ever: He will make the heathen to perish out of His land: He will execute vengeance and punishments upon the peoples." From the beginning of all time they have been ungrateful, as witness their behavior toward Pharaoh. With kindness he received them, their wives, and their children, at the time of a famine. He gave up to them the best of his land. He provided them with food and all they needed. Then Pharaoh desired to build a palace, and he requested the Jews to do it for him. They began the work grudgingly, amid murmurings, and it is not completed unto this day. In the midst of it, they approached Pharaoh with these words: "We wish to offer sacrifices to our God in a place that is a three days' journey from here, and we petition thee to lend us silver and gold vessels, and clothes, and apparel." So much did they borrow, that each one bore ninety ass-loads off with him, and Egypt was emptied out. When, the three days having elapsed, they did not return, Pharaoh pursued them in order to recover the stolen treasures. What did the Jews? They had among them a man by the name of Moses, the son of Amram, an arch-wizard, who had been bred in the house of Pharaoh. When they reached the sea, this man raised his staff, and cleft the waters, and led the Jews through them dryshod, while Pharaoh and his host were drowned.

"'Their God helps them as long as they observe His law, so that none can prevail against them. Balaam, the only prophet we heathens ever had, they slew with the sword, as they did unto Sihon and Og, the powerful kings of Canaan, whose land they took after killing them. Likewise they brought ruin upon Amalek, the great and glorious ruler they, and Saul their king, and Samuel their prophet. Later they had an unmerciful king, David by name, who smote the Philistines, the Ammonites, and the Moabites, and not one of them could discomfit him. Solomon, the son of this king, being wise and sagacious, built them a house of worship in Jerusalem, that they might not scatter to all parts of the world. But after they had been guilty of many crimes against their God, He delivered them into the hand of King Nebuchadnezzar, who deported them to Babylonia.

"'To this day they are among us, and though they are under our hand, we are of none account in their eyes. Their religion and their laws are different from the religion and he laws of all the other nations. Their sons do not marry with our daughters, our gods they do not worship, they have no regard for our honor, and they refuse to bend the knee before us. Calling themselves freemen, they will not do our service, and our commands they heed not.'

"Therefore the grandees, the princes, and the satraps have been assembled before us, we have taken counsel together, and we have resolved an irrevocable resolution, according to the laws of the Medes and Persians, to extirpate the Jews from among the inhabitants of the earth. We have sent the edict to the hundred and twenty-seven provinces of my empire, to slay them, their sons, their wives, and their little children, on the thirteenth day of the month of Adar none is to escape. As they did to our forefathers, and desired to do unto us, so shall be done unto them, and their possessions are to be given over to the spoilers. Thus shall ye do, that ye may find grace before me. This is the writing of the letter which I send to you, Ahasuerus king of Media and Persia."

The price Haman offered the king for the Jews was ten thousand hundredweights of silver. He took the number of the Jews at their exodus from Egypt, six hundred thousand, as the basis of his calculation, and offered a half-shekel for every soul of them, the sum each Israelite had to pay yearly for the maintenance of the sanctuary. Though the sum was so vast that Haman could not find coin enough to pay it, but promised to deliver it in the form of silver bars, Ahasuerus refused the ransom. When Haman made the offer, he said: "Let us cast lots. If thou drawest Israel and I draw money, then the sale stands as a valid transaction. If the reverse, it is not valid." Because of the sins of the Jews, the sale was confirmed by the lots. But Haman was not too greatly pleased with his own success. He disliked to give up so large a sum of money. Observing his ill humor, Ahasuerus said: "Keep the money; I do not care either to make or to lose money on account of the Jews."

For the Jews it was fortunate that the king did not accept money for them, else his subjects would not have obeyed his second edict, the one favorable to the Jews. They would have been able to advance the argument, that the king, by accepting a sum of money for them, had resigned his rights over the Jews in favor of Haman, who, therefore, could deal with them as he pleased.

The agreement between Ahasuerus and Haman was concluded at a carouse, by way of punishment for the crime of the sons of Jacob, who had unmercifully sold their brother Joseph into slavery to the Ishmaelites while eating and drinking.

The joy of this Jew-hating couple for Ahasuerus hated the Jews with no less fierce a hatred than Haman did was shared by none. The capital city of Shushan was in mourning and sorely perplexed. Scarcely had the edict of annihilation been promulgated against the Jews, when all sorts of misfortunes began to happen in the city. Women who were hanging up their wash to dry on the roofs of the houses dropped dead; men who went to draw water fell into the wells, and lost their lives. While Ahasuerus and Haman were making merry in the palace, the city was thrown into consternation and mourning.

SATAN INDICTS THE JEWS

The position of the Jews after the royal edict became known beggars description. If a Jew ventured abroad on the street to make a purchase, he was almost throttled by the Persians, who taunted him with these words: "Never mind, to-morrow will soon be here, and then I shall kill thee, and take thy money away from thee." If a Jew offered to sell himself as a slave, he was rejected; not even the sacrifice of his liberty could protect him against the loss of his life.

Mordecai, however, did not despair; he trusted in the Divine help. On his way from the court, after Haman and his ilk had informed him with malicious joy of the king's pleasure concerning the Jews, he met Jewish children coming from school. He asked the first child what verse from the Scriptures he had studied in school that day, and the reply was: "Be not afraid of sudden fear, neither of the desolation of the wicked when it cometh." The verse committed to memory by the second was: "Let them take counsel together, but it shall be brought to naught; let them speak the word, but it shall not stand; for God is with us." And the verse which the third had learnt was: "And even to old age I am He, and even to hoar hairs I will carry you: I have made and will bear; yea, I will carry and will deliver."

When Mordecai heard these verses, he broke out into jubilation, astonishing Haman not a little. Mordecai told him, "I rejoice at the good tidings announced to me by the school children." Haman thereupon fell into such a rage that he exclaimed: "In sooth, they shall be the first to feel the weight of my hand."

What gave Mordecai the greatest concern, was the certainty that the danger had been invited by the Jews themselves, through their sinful conduct in connection with the banquets given by Ahasuerus. Eighteen thousand five hundred Jews had taken part in them; they had eaten and drunk, intoxicated themselves and committed immoralities, as Haman had foreseen, the very reason, indeed, he had advised the king to hold the banquets.

Thereupon Satan had indicted the Jews. The accusations which he produced against them were of such a nature that God at once ordered writing materials to be brought to Him for the decree of annihilation, and it was written and sealed.

When the Torah heard that Satan's designs against the Jews had succeeded, she broke out into bitter weeping before God, and her lamentations awakened the angels, who likewise began to wail, saying: "If Israel is to be destroyed, of what avail is the whole world?"

The sun and the moon heard the lamentations of the angels, and they donned their mourning garb and also wept bitterly and wailed, saying: "Is Israel to be destroyed, Israel who wanders from town to town, and from land to land, only for the sake of the study of the Torah; who suffers grievously under the hand of the heathen, only because he observes the Torah and the sign of the covenant?"

In great haste the prophet Elijah ran to the Patriarchs and to the other prophets, and to the saints in Israel, and addressed these words to them: "O ye fathers of the world! Angels, and the sun and the moon, and heaven and earth, and all the celestial hosts are weeping bitterly. The whole world is seized with throes as of a woman in travail, by reason of your children, who have forfeited their life on account of their sins, and ye sit quiet and tranquil." Thereupon Moses said to Elijah: "Knowest thou any saints in the present generation of Israel?" Elijah named Mordecai, and Moses sent the prophet to him, with the charge that he, the "saint of the living generation," should unite his prayers with the prayers of the saints among the dead, and perhaps the doom might be averted from Israel. But Elijah hesitated. "O faithful shepherd," he said, "the edict of annihilation issued by God is written and sealed." Moses, however, did not desist; he urged the Patriarchs: "If the edict is sealed with wax, your prayers will be heard; if with blood, then all is vain."

Elijah hastened to Mordecai, who, when first he heard what God had resolved upon, tore his garments and was possessed by a great fear, though before he had confidently hoped that help would come form God. He gathered together all the school children, and had them fast, so that their hunger should drive them to moan and groan. Then it was that Israel spoke to God: "O Lord of the world! When the heathen rage against me, they do not desire my silver and gold, they desire only that I should be exterminated from off the face of the earth. Such was the design of Nebuchadnezzar when he wanted to compel Israel to worship the idol. Had it not been for Hananiah, Mishael, and Azariah, I had disappeared from the world. Now it is Haman who desires to uproot the whole vine."

Then Mordecai addressed all the people thus: "O people of Israel, that art so dear and precious in the sight of thy Heavenly Father! Knowest thou not what has happened? Hast thou not heard that the king and Haman have resolved to remove us off the face of the earth, to destroy us from beneath the sun? We have no king on whom we can depend, and no prophet to intercede for us with prayers. There is no place whither we can flee, no land wherein we can find safety. We are like sheep without a shepherd, like a ship upon the sea without a pilot. We are like an orphan born after the death of his father, and death robs him of his mother, too, when he has scarce begun to draw nourishment from her breast."

After this address a great prayer-meeting was called outside of Shushan. The Ark containing the scroll of the law, covered with sackcloth and strewn with ashes, was brought thither. The scroll was unrolled, and the following verses read from it: "When thou art in tribulation, and all these things are come upon thee, in the latter days thou shalt return to the Lord thy God, and hearken unto His voice, for the Lord thy God is a merciful God: He will not fail thee, neither destroy thee, nor forget the covenant of they fathers which He swore unto them."

Thereunto Mordecai added words of admonition: "O people of Israel, thou art dear and precious to thy Father in heaven, let us follow the example of the inhabitants of Nineveh, doing as they did when the prophet Jonah came to them to announce the destruction of the city. The king arose from his throne, laid his crown from him, covered himself with sackcloth, and sat in ashes, and he made proclamation, and published through Nineveh by the decree of the king and his nobles, saying, 'Let neither man nor beast, herd nor flock, taste anything; let them not feed, nor drink water, but let them be covered with sackcloth, both man and beast, and let them cry mightily unto God; yea, let them turn every one from his evil way, and from the violence that is in their hands.' Then God repented Him of the evil He had designed to bring upon them, and He did it not. Now, then, let us follow their example, let us hold a fast, mayhap God will have mercy upon us."

Furthermore spake Mordecai: "O Lord of the world! Didst Thou not swear unto our fathers to make us as many as the stars in the heavens? And now we are as sheep in the shambles. What has become of Thine oath?" He cried aloud, though he knew God hears the softest whisper, for he said: "O Father of Israel, what hast Thou done unto me? One single cry of anguish uttered by Esau Thou didst repay with the blessing of his father Isaac, 'By thy sword shall thou live,' and now we ourselves are abandoned to the mercy of the sword." What Mordecai was not aware of, was that he, the descendant of Jacob, was brought unto weeping and wailing by Haman, the descendant of Esau, as a punishment, because Jacob himself had brought Esau unto weeping and wailing.

THE DREAM OF MORDECAI FULFILLED

Esther, who knew naught of what was happening at court, was greatly alarmed when her attendants told her that Mordecai had appeared in the precincts of the palace clothed in sackcloth and ashes. She was so overcome by fright that she was deprived of the joys of motherhood to which she had been looking forward with happy expectancy. She sent clothes to Mordecai, who, however, refused to lay aside his garb of mourning until God permitted miracles to come to pass for Israel, wherein he followed the example of such great men in Israel as Jacob, David, and Ahab, and of the Gentile inhabitants of Nineveh at the time of Jonah. By no means would he array himself in court attire so long as his people was exposed to sure suffering. The queen sent for Daniel, called also Hathach in the Scriptures, and charged him to learn from Mordecai wherefore he was mourning.

To escape all danger from spying ears, Hathach and Mordecai had their conversation in the open, like Jacob when he consulted with his wives Leah and Rachel about leaving their father Laban. By Hathach Mordecai sent word to the queen, that Haman was an Amalekite, who like his ancestor sought to destroy Israel. He requested her to appear before the king and plead for the Jews, reminding her at the same time of a dream he had once had and told her about.

Once, when Mordecai had spent a long time weeping and lamenting over the misery of the Jews in the Dispersion, and prayed fervently to God to redeem Israel and rebuild the Temple, he fell asleep, and in his sleep a dream visited him. He dreamed he was transported to a desert place he had never seen before. Many nations lived there jumbled together, only one small and despised nation kept apart at a short distance. Suddenly a snake shot up from the midst of the nations, rising higher and higher, and growing stronger and larger in proportion as it rose. It darted in the direction of the spot in which they tiny nation stood, and tried to project itself upon it. Impenetrable clouds and darkness enveloped the little nation, and when the snake was on the point of seizing it, a hurricane arose from the four corners of the world, covering the snake as clothes cover a man, and blew it to bits. The fragments scattered hither and thither like chaff before the wind, until not a speck of the monster was to be found anywhere. Then the cloud and the darkness vanished from above the little nation, the splendor of the sun again enveloped it.

This dream Mordecai recorded in a book, and when the storm began to rage against the Jews, he thought of it, and demanded that Esther go to the king as the advocate of her people. At first she did not feel inclined to accede to the wishes of Mordecai. By her messenger she recalled to his mind, that he himself had insisted upon her keeping her Jewish descent a secret. Besides, she had always tried to refrain from appearing before the king at her own initiative, in order that she might not be instrumental in bringing down sin upon her soul, for she well remembered Mordecai's teaching, that "a Jewish woman, captive among the heathen, who of her own accord goes to them, loses her portion in the Jewish nation." She had been rejoicing that her petitions had been granted, and the king had not come nigh unto her this last month. Was she now voluntarily to present herself before him? Furthermore, she had her messenger inform Mordecai, that Haman had introduced a new palace regulation. Any one who appeared before the king without having been summoned by Haman, would suffer the death penalty. Therefore, she could not, if she would, go to the king to advocate the cause of the Jews.

Esther urged her uncle to refrain from incensing Haman and furnishing him with a pretext for wreaking the hatred of Esau to Jacob upon Mordecai and his nation. Mordecai, however, was firmly convinced that Esther was destined by God to save Israel. How could her miraculous history be explained otherwise? At the very moment Esther was taken to court, he had thought: "Is it conceivable that God would force so pious a woman to wed with a heathen, were it not that she is appointed to save Israel from menacing dangers?"

Firm as Mordecai was in his determination to make Esther take a hand in affairs, he yet did not find it a simple matter to communicate with her. For Hathach was killed by Haman as soon as it was discovered that he was acting as mediator between Mordecai and Esther. There was none to replace him, unto God dispatched the archangels Michael and Gabriel to carry messages from one to the other and back again.

Mordecai sent word to her, if she let the opportunity to help Israel slip by, she would have to give account for the omission before the heavenly court. To Israel in distress, however, help would come from other quarters. Never had God forsaken His people in time of need. Moreover, he admonished her, that, as the descendant of Saul, it was her duty to make reparation for her ancestor's sin in not having put Agag to death. Had he done as he was bidden, the Jews would not now have to fear the machinations of Haman, the offspring of Agag. He bade her supplicate her Heavenly Father to deal with the present enemies of Israel as He had dealt with his enemies in former ages. To give her encouragement, Mordecai continued: "Is Haman so surpassing great that his plan against the Jews must succeed? Dost though mean to say that he is superior to his own ancestor Amalek, whom God crushed when he precipitated himself upon Israel? Is he mightier than the thirty-one kings who fought against Israel and whom Joshua slew 'with the word of God'? Is he stronger than Sisera, who went out against Israel with nine hundred iron chariots, and yet met his death at the hands of a mere woman, the punishment for having withdrawn the use of the water-springs from the Israelites and prevented their wives from taking the prescribed ritual baths and thus from fulfilling their conjugal duty? Is he more powerful than Goliath, who reviled the warriors of Israel, and was slain by David? Or is he more invincible than the sons of Orpah, who waged wars with Israel, and were killed by David and his men? Therefore, do not refrain thy mouth from prayer, and thy lips from supplication, for on account of the merits of our fathers, Israel has ever and ever been snatched out of the jaws of death. He who has at all times done wonders for Israel, will deliver the enemy into our hands now, for us to do with him as seemeth best to us."

What he endeavored to impress upon Esther particularly, was that God would bring help to Israel without her intermediation, but it was to her interest to use the opportunity, for which alone she had reached her exalted place, to make up for the transgressions committed by her house, Saul and his descendants.

Yielding at last to the arguments of Mordecai, Esther was prepared to risk life in this world, in order to secure life in the world to come. She made only one request of her uncle. He was to have the Jews spend three days in prayer and fasting in her behalf, that she might find favor in the eyes of the king. At first Mordecai was opposed to the proclamation of a fast, because it was Passover time, and the law prohibits fasting on the holidays. But he finally assented to Esther's reasoning: "Of what avail are the holidays, if there is no Israel to celebrate them, and without Israel, there would not be even a Torah. Therefore it is advisable to transgress on law, that God may have mercy upon us."

THE PRAYER OF ESTHER

Accordingly Mordecai made arrangements for a fast and a prayer-meeting. On the very day of the festival, he had himself ferried across the water to the other side of Shushan, where all the Jews of the city could observe the fast together. It was important that the Jewish residents of Shushan beyond all other Jews should do penance and seek pardon from God, because they had committed the sin of partaking of Ahasuerus's banquet. Twelve thousand priests marched in the procession, trumpets in their right hands, and the holy scrolls of the law in their left, weeping and mourning, and exclaiming against God: "Here is the Torah Thou gavest us. Thy beloved people is about to be destroyed. When that comes to pass, who will be left to read the Torah and make mention of Thy name? The sun and the moon will refuse to shed their light abroad, for they were created only for the sake of Israel." Then they fell upon their faces, and said: "Answer us, our Father, answer us, our King." The whole people joined in their cry, and the celestials wept with them, and the Fathers came forth from their graves.

After a three days' fast, Esther arose from the earth and dust, and made preparations to betake herself to the king. She arrayed herself in a silken garment, embroidered with gold from Ophir and spangled with diamonds and pearls sent her from Africa; a golden crown was on her head, and on her feet shoes of gold.

After she had completed her attire, she pronounced the following prayer: "Thou art the great God, the God of Abraham, Isaac, and Jacob, and the God of my father Benjamin. Not because I consider myself without blemish, do I dare appear before the foolish king, but that the people of Israel may not be cut off from the world. Is it not for the sake of Israel alone that the whole world was created, and if Israel should cease to exist, who will come and exclaim 'Holy, holy, holy' thrice daily before Thee? As Thou didst save Hananiah, Mishael, and Azariah out of the burning furnace, and Daniel out of the den of lions, so save me out of the hand of this foolish king, and make me to appear charming and graceful in his eyes. I entreat Thee to give ear to my prayer in this time of exile and banishment from our land. By reason of our sins the threatening words of the Holy Scriptures are accomplished upon us: 'Ye shall sell yourselves unto your enemies for bondmen and for bondwomen, and no man shall buy you.' The decree to kill us has been issued. We are delivered up unto the sword for destruction, root and branch. The children of Abraham covered themselves with sackcloth and ashes, but though the elders sinned, what wrongs have the children committed, and though the children committed wrongs, what have the sucklings done? The nobles of Jerusalem came forth from their graves, for their children were given up to the sword.

"How quickly have the days of our joy flown by! The wicked Haman has surrendered us to our enemies for slaughter.

"I will recount before Thee the deeds of Thy friends, and with Abraham will I begin. Thou didst try him with all temptations, yet didst Thou find him faithful. O that Thou wouldst support his beloved children for his sake, and aid them, so that Thou wouldst bear them as an unbreakable seal upon Thy right hand. Call Haman to account for the wrong he would do us, and be revenged upon the son of Hammedatha. Demand requital of Haman and not of Thy people, for he sought to annihilate us all at one stroke, he, the enemy and afflicter of Thy people, whom he endeavors to hem in on all sides.

"With an eternal bond Thou didst bind us unto Thee. O that Thou wouldst uphold us for the sake of Isaac, who was bound. Haman offered the king ten thousand talents of silver for us. Raise Thou our voice, and answer us, and bring us forth out of the narrow place into enlargement. Thou who breakest the mightiest, crush Haman, so that he may never again rise from his fall. I am ready to appear before the king, to entreat grace for my inheritance. Send Thou an angel of compassion with me on mine errand, and let grace and favor be my companions. May the righteousness of Abraham go before me, the binding of Isaac raise me, the charm of Jacob be put into my mouth, and the grace of Joseph upon my tongue. Happy the man who putteth his trust in God; he is not confounded. He will lend me His right hand and His left hand, with which He created the whole world. Ye, all ye of Israel, pray for me as I pray in your behalf. For whatsoever a man may ask of God in the time of his distress, is granted unto him. Let us look upon the deeds of our fathers and do like unto them, and He will answer our supplications. The left hand of Abraham held Isaac by the throat, and his right hand grasped the knife. He willingly did Thy bidding, nor did he delay to execute Thy command. Heaven opened its windows to give space to the angels, who cried bitterly, and said: 'Woe to the world, if this thing should come to pass!' I also call upon Thee! O answer me, for Thou givest ear unto all who are afflicted and oppressed. Thou art called the Merciful and the Gracious; Thou art slow to anger and great in lovingkindness and truth. Hear our voice and answer us, and lead us out of distress into enlargement. For three days have I fasted in accordance with the number of days Abraham journey to bind his son upon the altar before Thee. Thou didst make a covenant with him, and didst promise him: 'Whenever thy children shall be in distress, I will remember the binding of Isaac favorably unto them, and deliver them out of their troubles.' Again, I fasted three days corresponding to the three classes Israel, priests, Levites, and Israelites, who stood at the foot of Sinai, and said: 'All the Lord hath spoken will we do, and be obedient.'"

Esther concluded her prayer and said: "O God, Lord of hosts! Thou that searchest the heart and the reins, in this hour do Thou remember the merits of Abraham, Isaac, and Jacob, that my petition to Thee may not be turned aside, nor my request be left unfulfilled.'

ESTHER INTERCEDES

After finishing her prayer, Esther betook herself to the king, accompanied by three attendants, one walking to the right of her, the second on the other side, and the third bearing her train, heavy with the precious stones with which it was studded. Her chief adornment was the holy spirit that was poured out over her. But scarcely did she enter the chamber containing the idols, when the holy spirit departed from her, and she cried out in great distress: "Eli, Eli, lamah azabtani! Shall I be chastised for acts that I do against my will, and only in obedience to the promptings of sore need? Why should my fate be different from that of the Mother? When Pharaoh only attempted to approach Sarah, plagues came upon him and his house, but I have been compelled for years to live with this heathen, and Thou dost not deliver me out of his hand. O Lord of the world! Have I not paid scrupulous heed to the three commands Thou didst specially ordain for women?"

To reach the king, Esther had to pass through seven apartments, each measuring ten ells in length. The first three she traversed unhindered; they were too far off for the king to observe her progress through them. But barely had she crossed the threshold of the fourth chamber, when Ahasuerus caught sight of her, and, overcome by rage, he exclaimed: "O for the departed, their like is not found again on earth! How I urged and entreated Vashti to appear before me, but she refused, and I had her killed therefor. This Esther come hither without invitation, like unto a public prostitute."

In consternation and despair Esther stood rooted to the centre of the fourth chamber. Having once allowed her to pass through the doors under their charge, the guards of the first four rooms had forfeited their authority over her; and to the guards in the other three rooms, she had not yet given cause for interfering with her. Yet the courtiers were so confident that Esther was about to suffer the death penalty, that the sons of Haman were already busy dividing her jewels among themselves, and casting lots for her royal purple. Esther herself was keenly aware of her dangerous position. In her need, she besought God: "Eli, Eli, lamah azabtani," and prayed to Him the words which have found their place in the Psalter composed by King David. Because she put her confidence in God, He answered her petition, and sent her three angels to help her: the one enveloped her countenance with "the threads of grace," the second raised her head, and the third drew out the sceptre of Ahasuerus until it touched her. The king turned his head round, to avoid seeing Esther, but the angels forced him to look her way, and be conquered by her seductive charm.

By reason of her long fast, Esther was so weak that she was unable to extend her hand toward the sceptre of the king. The archangel Michael had to draw her near it. Ahasuerus then said: "I see, thou must have a most important request to prefer, else thou hadst not risked thy life deliberately. I am ready to give it thee, even to the half of the kingdom. There is but one petition I cannot grant, and that is the restoration of the Temple. I gave my oath to Geshem the Arabian, Sanballat the Horonite, and Tobiah the Ammonite, not to allow it to be rebuilt, from fear of the Jews, lest they rise up against me."

For the moment, Esther refrained from uttering her petition. All she asked was, that the king and Haman would come to a banquet she proposed to give. She had good reasons for this peculiar course of conduct. She desired to disarm Haman's suspicions regarding her Jewish descent, and to lead her fellow-Jews to fix their hope upon God and not upon her. At the same time, it was her plan to arouse jealousy of Haman in both the king and the princes. She was quite ready to sacrifice her own life, if her stratagems would but involve the life of Haman, too. At the banquet she therefore favored Haman in such manner that Ahasuerus could not but be jealous. She moved her chair close to Haman's, and when Ahasuerus handed her his wine-cup, to let her drink of it first, she passed it on to his minister.

After the banquet, the king repeated his question, and again made the asseveration, that he would fulfill all her wishes at whatever cost, barring only the restoration of the Temple. Esther, however, was not yet ready; she preferred to wait another day before taking up the conflict with Haman. She had before her eyes the example of Moses, who also craved a day's preparation before going out against Amalek, the ancestor of Haman.

Deceived by the attention and distinction accorded him by Esther, Haman felt secure in his position, priding himself not only on the love of the king, but also on the respect of the queen. He felt himself to be the most privileged being in all the wide realm governed by Ahasuerus.

Filled with arrogant self-sufficiency, he passed by Mordecai, who not only refused to give him the honors decreed in his behalf, but, besides, pointed to his knee, inscribed with the bill of sale whereby Haman had become the slave of Mordecai. Doubly and triply enraged, he resolved to make an example of the Jew. But he was not satisfied with inflicting death by a simple kick.

On reaching his home he was disappointed not to find his wife Zeresh, the daughter of the Persian satrap Tattenai. As always when Haman was at court, she had gone to her paramours. He sent for her and his three hundred and sixty-five advisers, and with them he took counsel as to what was to be done to Mordecai. Pointing to a representation of his treasure chamber, which he wore on his bosom, he said: "And all this is worthless in my sight when I look upon Mordecai, the Jew. What I eat and drink loses its savor, if I but think of him."

Among his advisers and sons, of whom there were two hundred and eight, none was so clever as Zeresh his wife. She spoke thus: "If the man thou tellest of is a Jew, thou wilt not be able to do aught to him except by sagacity. If thou castest him into the fire, it will have no effect upon him, for Hananiah, Mishael, and Azariah escaped from the burning furnace unhurt; Joseph went free from prison; Manasseh prayed to God, and He heard him, and saved him from the iron furnace; to drive him out in the wilderness is useless, thou knowest the desert did no evil to the Israelites that passed through it; putting out his eyes avails naught, for Samson blind did more mischief than ever Samson seeing. Therefore hang him, for no Jew has ever escaped death by hanging."

Haman was well pleased with the words of his wife. She fetched artificers in wood and iron, the former to erect the cross, the latter to make the nails. Their children danced around in high glee while Zeresh played upon the cithern, and Haman in his pleasurable excitement said: "To the wood workers I shall give abundant pay, and the iron workers I shall invite to a banquet."

When the cross was finished, Haman himself tested it, to see that all was in working order. A heavenly voice was heard: "It is good for Haman the villain, and for the son of Hammedatha it is fitting."

THE DISTURBED NIGHT

The night during which Haman erected the cross for Mordecai was the first night of Passover, the very night in which miracles without number had ever been done for the Fathers and for Israel. But this time the night of joy was changed into a night of mourning and a night of fears. Wherever there were Jews, they passed the night in weeping and lamenting. The greatest terrors it held for Mordecai, because his own people accused him of having provoked their misfortunes by his haughty behavior toward Haman.

Excitement and consternation reigned in heaven as well as on earth. When Haman had satisfied himself that the cross intended for his enemy was properly constructed, he repaired to the Bet ha-Midrash, where he found Mordecai and all the Jewish school children, twenty-two thousand in number, in tears and sorrow. He ordered them to be put in chains, saying: "First I shall kill off these, and then I shall hang Mordecai." The mothers hastened thither with bread and water, and coaxed their children to take something before they had to encounter death. The children, however, laid their hands upon their books, and said: "As our teacher Mordecai liveth, we will neither eat nor drink, but we will perish exhausted with fasting." They rolled up their sacred scrolls, and handed them to their teachers with the words: "For our devotion to the study of the Torah, we had hoped to be rewarded with long life, according to the promised held out in the Holy Scriptures. As we are not worthy thereof, remove the books!" The out-cries of the children and of the teachers in the Bet ha-Midrash, and the weeping of the mothers without, united with the supplications of the Fathers, reached unto heaven in the third hour of the night, and God said: "I hear the voice of tender lambs and sheep!" Moses arose and addressed God thus: "Thou knowest well that the voices are not of lambs and sheep, but of the young of Israel, who for three days have been fasting and languishing in fetters, only to be slaughtered on the morrow to the delight of the arch-enemy."

Then God felt compassion with Israel, for the sake of his innocent little ones. He broke the seal with which the heavenly decree of annihilation had been fastened, and the decree itself he tore in pieces. From this moment on Ahasuerus became restless, and sleep was made to flee his eyes, for the purpose that the redemption of Israel might be brought to pass. God sent down Michael, the leader of the hosts of Israel, who was to keep sleep from the king, and the archangel Gabriel descended, and threw the king out of his bed on the floor, no less than three hundred and sixty-five times, continually whispering in his ear: "O thou ingrate, reward him who deserves to be rewarded."

To account for his sleeplessness, Ahasuerus thought he might have been poisoned, and he was about to order the execution of those charged with the preparation of his food. But they succeeded in convincing him of their innocence, by calling to his attention that Esther and Haman had shared his evening meal with him, yet they felt no unpleasant effects. Then suspicions against his wife and his friend began to arise in his mind. He accused them inwardly of having conspired together to put him out of the way. He sought to banish this thought with the reflection, that if a conspiracy had existed against him, his friends would have warned him of it. But the reflection brought others in its train: Did he have any friends? Was it not possible that by leaving valuable services unrewarded, he had forfeited the friendly feelings toward him? He therefore commanded that the chronicles of the kings of Persia be read to him. He would compare his own acts with what his predecessors had done, and try to find out whether he might count upon friends.

What was read to him, did not restore his tranquility of mind, for he saw a poor man before him none other than the angel Michael who called to him continually: "Haman wants to kill thee, and become king in thy stead. Let this serve thee as proof that I am telling thee the truth: Early in the morning he will appear before thee and request permission of thee to kill him who saved thy life. And when thou inquirest of him what honor should be done to him whom the king delighteth to honor, he will ask to be given the apparel, the crown, and the horse of the king as signs of distinction."

Ahasuerus's excitement was soothed only when the passage in the chronicles was reached describing the loyalty of Mordecai. Had the wishes of the reader been consulted, Ahasuerus had never heard this entry, for it was a son of Haman who was filling the office of reader, and he was desirous of passing the incident over in silence. But a miracle occurred the words were heard though they were not uttered!

The names of Mordecai and Israel had a quieting influence upon the king, and he dropped asleep. He dreamed that Haman, sword in hand, was approaching him with evil intent, and when, early in the morning, Haman suddenly, without being announced, entered the antechamber and awakened the king, Ahasuerus was persuaded of the truth of his dream. The king was still further set against Haman by the reply he gave to the question, how honor was to be shown to the man whom the king delighteth to honor. Believing himself to be the object of the king's good-will, he advised Ahasuerus to have his favorite arrayed in the king's coronation garments, and the crown royal put upon his head. Before him one of the grandees of the kingdom was to run, doing herald's service, proclaiming that whosoever did not prostrate himself and bow down before him whom the king delighteth to honor, would have his head cut off, and his house given over to pillage.

Haman was quick to notice that he had made a mistake, for he saw the king's countenance change color at the mention of the word crown. He therefore took good care not to refer to it again. In spite of this precaution, Ahasuerus saw in the words of Haman a striking verification of his vision, and he was confident that Haman cherished designs against his life and his throne.

THE FALL OF HAMAN

Haman was soon to find out that he had gone far afield in supposing himself to be the man whom the king delighted to honor. The king's command ran: "Hasten to the royal treasure chambers; fetch thence a cover of find purple, a raiment of delicate silk, furnished forth with golden bells and pomegranates and bestrewn with diamonds and pearls, and the large golden crown which was brought me from Macedonia upon the day I ascended the throne. Furthermore, fetch thence the sword and the coat of mail sent me from Ethiopia, and the two veils embroidered with pearls which were Africa's gift. Then repair to the royal stables, and lead forth the black horse whereon I sat at my coronation. With all these insignia of honor, seek out Mordecai!"

Haman: "Which Mordecai?"

Ahasuerus: "Mordecai the Jew."

Haman: "There be many Jews named Mordecai."

Ahasuerus: "The Jew Mordecai who sits at the king's gate."

Haman: "There be many royal gates; I know not which thou meanest."

Ahasuerus: "The gate that leads from the harem to the palace."

Haman: "This man is my enemy and the enemy of my house. Rather would I give him ten thousand talents of silver than do him this honor."

Ahasuerus: "Ten thousand talents of silver shall be given him, and he shall be made lord over thy house, but these honors must thou show unto him."

Haman: "I have ten sons. I would rather have them run before his horse than do him this honor."

Ahasuerus: "Thou, thy sons, and thy wife shall be slaves to Mordecai, but these honors must thou show unto him."

Haman: "O my lord and king, Mordecai is a common man. Appoint him to be ruler over a city, or, if thou wilt, even over a district, rather than I should do him this honor."

Ahasuerus: "I will appoint him ruler over cities and districts. All the kings on land and on water shall pay him obedience, but these honors must thou show unto him."

Haman: "Rather have coins struck bearing thy name together with his, instead of mine as hitherto, than I should do him this honor."

Ahasuerus: "The man who saved the life of the king deserves to have his name put on the coin of the realm. Nevertheless, these honors must thou show unto him."

Haman: "Edicts and writings have been issued to all parts of the kingdom, commanding that the nation to which Mordecai belongs shall be destroyed. Recall them rather than I should do him this honor."

Ahasuerus: "The edicts and writings shall be recalled, yet these honors must thou show unto Mordecai."

Seeing that all petitions and entreaties were ineffectual, and Ahasuerus insisted upon the execution of his order, Haman went to the royal treasure chambers, walking with his head bowed like a mourner's, his ears hanging down, his eyes dim, his mouth screwed up, his heart hardened, his bowels cut in pieces, his loins weakened, and his knees knocking against each other. He gathered together the royal insignia, and took them to Mordecai, accompanied on his way by Harbonah and Abzur, who, at the order of the king, were to take heed whether Haman carried out his wishes to the letter.

When Mordecai saw his enemy approach, he thought his last moment had come. He urged his pupils to flee, that they might not "burn themselves with his coals." But they refused, saying: "In life as in death we desire to be with thee." The few moments left him, as he thought, Mordecai spent in devotion. With words of prayer on his lips he desired to pass away. Haman, therefore, had to address himself to the pupils of Mordecai: "What was the last subject taught you by your teacher Mordecai?" They told him they had been discussing the law of the `Omer, the sacrifice brought on that very day so long as the Temple had stood. At his request, they described some of the details of the ceremony in the Temple connected with the offering. He exclaimed: "Happy are you that your ten farthings, with which you bought the wheat for the `Omer, produced a better effect than my ten thousand talents of silver, which I offered unto the king for the destruction of the Jews."

Meantime Mordecai had finished his prayer. Haman stepped up to him, and said: "Arise, thou pious son of Abraham, Isaac, and Jacob. Thy sackcloth and ashes availed more than my ten thousand talents of silver, which I promised unto the king. They were not accepted, but thy prayers were accepted by thy Father in heaven."

Mordecai, not yet disabused of the notion that Haman had come to take him to the cross, requested the grace of a few minutes for his last meal. Only Haman's repeated protests assured him. When Haman set about arraying him with the royal apparel, Mordecai refused to put it on until he had bathed, and had dressed his hair. Royal apparel agreed but ill with his condition after three days of sackcloth and ashes. As luck would have it, Esther had issued the command that the bathkeepers and barbers were not to ply their trades on that day, and there was nothing for Haman to do but perform the menial services Mordecai required. Haman tried to play upon the feelings of Mordecai. Fetching a deep sigh, he said: "The greatest in the king's realm is now acting as bathkeeper and barber!" Mordecai, however, did not permit himself to be imposed upon. He knew Haman's origin too well to be deceived; he remembered his father, who had been bathkeeper and barber in a village.

Haman's humiliation was not yet complete. Mordecai, exhausted by his three days' fast, was too weak to mount his horse unaided. Haman had to serve him as footstool, and Mordecai took the opportunity to give him a kick. Haman reminded him of the Scriptural verse: "Rejoice not when thine enemy falleth, and let not thine heart be glad when he is overthrown." Mordecai, however, refused to apply it to himself, for he was chastising, not a personal enemy, but the enemy of his people, and of such it is said in the Scriptures: "And thou shalt tread upon the high places of thine enemies."

Finally, Haman caused Mordecai to ride through the streets of the city, and proclaimed before him: "Thus shall it be done unto the man whom the king delighteth to honor." In front of them marched twenty-seven thousand youths detailed for this service from the court. In their right hands they bore golden cups, and golden beakers in their left hands, and they, too, proclaimed: "Thus shall be done unto the man whom the king delighteth to honor." The procession furthermore was swelled by the presence of Jews. They, however, made a proclamation of different tenor. "Thus shall be done," they cried out, "unto the man whose honor is desired by the King that hath created heaven and earth."

As he rode along, Mordecai gave praise to God: "I will extol Thee, O Lord; for Thou hast raised me up, and hast not made my foes to rejoice over me. O Lord my God, I cried unto Thee, and Thou hast healed me. O Lord, Thou hast brought up my soul from Sheol; Thou hast kept me alive, that I should not go down to the pit." Whereupon his pupils joined in with: "Sing praise unto the Lord, O ye saints of His, and give thanks to His holy name. For His anger is but for a moment; in His favor is life; weeping may tarry for the night, but joy cometh in the morning." Haman added the verse thereto: "As for me, I said in my prosperity, I shall never be moved. Thou, Lord, of Thy favor hadst made my mountain to stand strong. Thou didst hide Thy face; I was troubled." Queen Esther continued: "I cried to Thee, O Lord; and unto the Lord I made supplication. What profit is there in my blood, when I go down to the pit? Shall the dust praise Thee? Shall it declare Thy truth?" and the whole concourse of Jews present cried out: "Thou hast turned for me my mourning into dancing; Thou hast loosed my sackcloth, and girded me with gladness, to the end that my glory may sing praise to Thee, and not be silent. O Lord my God, I will give thanks unto Thee forever."

When this procession passed the house of Haman, his daughter was looking out of the window. She took the man on the horse to be her father, and the leader of it, Mordecai. Raising a vessel filled with offal, she emptied it out over the leader her own father. Scarce had the vessel left her hand, when she realized the truth, and she threw herself from the window, and lay crushed to death on the street below.

In spite of the sudden change in his fortunes, Mordecai ended the eventful day as he had begun it, in prayer and fasting. No sooner was the procession over than he put off the royal robes, and, again covering himself with sackcloth, he prayed until night fell.

Haman was plunged in mourning, partly on account of the deep disgrace to which he had been subjected, partly on account of the death of his daughter. Neither his wife nor his friends could advise him how to mend his sad fortunes. They could hold out only sorry consolation to him: "If this Mordecai is of the seed of the saints, thou wilt not be able to prevail against him. Thou wilt surely encounter the same fate as the kings in their battle with Abraham, and Abimelech in his quarrel with Isaac. As Jacob was victorious over the angel with whom he wrestled, and Moses and Aaron caused the drowning of Pharaoh and his host, so Mordecai will overcome thee in the end."

While they were yet talking, the king's chamberlains came, and hastily carried Haman off to the banquet Esther had prepared, to prevent him and his influential sons from plotting against the king. Ahasuerus repeated his promise, to give Esther whatever she desired, always expecting the restoration of the Temple. This time, casting her eyes heavenward, Esther replied: "If I have found favor in thy sight, O Supreme King, and if it please Thee, O King of the world, let my life be given me, and let my people be rescued out of the hands of its enemy." Ahasuerus, thinking these words were addressed to him, asked in irritation: "Who is he, and where is he, this presumptuous conspirator, who thought to do thus?" These were the first words the king had ever spoken to Esther herself. Hitherto he had always communicated with her through an interpreter. He had not been quite satisfied she was worthy enough to be addressed by the king. Now made cognizant of the fact that she was a Jewess, and of royal descent besides, he spoke to her directly, without the intervention of others.

Esther stretched forth her hand to indicate the man who had sought to take her life, as he had actually taken Vashti's, but in the excitement of the moment, she pointed to the king. Fortunately the king did not observe her error, because an angel guided her hand instantaneously in the direction of Haman, whom her words described: "This is the adversary and the enemy, he who desired to murder thee in thy sleeping-chamber during the night just passed; he who this very day desired to array himself in the royal apparel, ride upon thy horse, and wear they golden crown upon his head, to rise up against thee and deprive thee of thy sovereignty. But God set his undertaking at naught, and the honors he sought for himself, fell to the share of my uncle Mordecai, who this oppressor and enemy thought to hang."

The anger of the king already burnt so fiercely that he hinted to Esther, that whether Haman was the adversary she had in mind or not, she was to designate him as such. To infuriate him still more, God sent ten angels in the guise of Haman's ten sons, to fell down the trees in the royal park. When Ahasuerus turned his eyes toward the interior of the park, he saw the ruthless destruction of which they were guilty. In his rage he went out into the garden. This was the instant utilized by Haman to implore grace for himself from Esther. Gabriel intervened, and threw Haman upon the couch in a posture as though he were about to do violence to the queen. At that moment Ahasuerus reappeared. Enraged beyond description by what he saw, he cried out: "Haman attempts the honor of the queen in my very presence! Come, then, ye peoples, nations, and races, and pronounce judgment over him!"

When Harbonah, originally a friend of Haman and an adversary of Mordecai, heard the king's angry exclamation, he said to him: "Nor is this the only crime committed by Haman against thee, for he was an accomplice of the conspirators Bigthan and Teresh, and his enmity to Mordecai dates back to the time when Mordecai uncovered their foul plots. Out of revenge therefor, he has erected a cross for him." Harbonah's words illustrate the saying: "Once the ox has been cast to the ground, slaughtering knives can readily be found." Knowing that Haman had fallen from his high estate, Harbonah was intent upon winning the friendship of Mordecai. Harbonah was altogether right, for Ahasuerus at once ordered Haman to be hanged.

Mordecai was charged with the execution of the king's order, and Haman's tears and entreaties did not in the least move him. He insisted upon hanging him like the commonest of criminals, instead of executing him with the sword, the mode of punishment applied to men of rank guilty of serious misdemeanors.

The cross which Haman, at the advice of his wife Zeresh and of his friends, had erected for Mordecai, was now used for himself. It was made of wood from a thorn-bush. God called all the trees together and inquired which one would permit the cross for Haman to be made of it. The fig-tree said: "I am ready to serve, for I am symbolic of Israel, and, also, my fruits were brought to the Temple as firstfruits." The vine said: "I am ready to serve, for I am symbolic of Israel and, also, my wine is brought to the altar." The apple-tree said: "I am ready to serve, for I am symbolic of Israel." The nut-tree said: "I am ready to serve, for I am symbolic of Israel." The Etrog tree said: "I should have the privilege, for with my fruit Israel praises God on Sukkot." The willow of the brook said: "I desire to serve, for I am symbolic of Israel." The cedar-tree said: "I desire to serve, for I am symbolic of Israel." The palm-tree said: "I desire to serve, for I am symbolic of Israel." Finally the thorn-bush came and said: "I am fitted to do this service, for the ungodly are like pricking thorns." The offer of the thorn-bush was accepted, after God gave a blessing to each of the other trees for its willingness to serve.

A sufficiently long beam cut from a thorn-bush could be found only in the house of Haman, which had to be demolished in order to obtain it. The cross was tall enough for Haman and his ten sons to be hanged upon it. It was planted three cubits deep in the ground, each of the victims required three cubits space in length, one cubit space was left vacant between the feet of the one above and the head of the one below, and the youngest son, Vaizatha, had his feet four cubits from the ground as he hung.

Haman and his ten sons remained suspended a long time, to the vexation of those who considered it a violation of the Biblical prohibition in Deuteronomy, not to leave a human body hanging upon a tree overnight. Esther pointed to a precedent, the descendants of Saul, whom the Gibeonites left hanging half a year, whereby the name of God was sanctified, for whenever the pilgrims beheld them, they told the heathen, that the men had been hanged because their father Saul had laid hand on the Gibeonites. "How much more, then," continued Esther, "are we justified in permitting Haman and his family to hang, they who desired to destroy the house of Israel?"

Beside these ten sons, who had been governors in various provinces, Haman had twenty others, ten of whom died, and the other ten of whom were reduced to beggary. The vast fortune of which Haman died possessed was divided in three parts. The first part was given to Mordecai and Esther, the second to the students of the Torah, and the third was applied to the restoration of the Temple. Mordecai thus became a wealthy man. He was also set up as king of the Jews. As such he had coins struck, which bore the figure of Esther on the obverse, and his own figure on the reverse. However, in the measure in which Mordecai gained in worldly power and consideration, he lost spiritually, because the business connected with his high political station left him no time for the study of the Torah. Previously he had ranked sixth among the eminent scholars of Israel, he now dropped to the seventh place among them. Ahasuerus, on the other hand, was the gainer by the change. As soon as Mordecai entered upon the office of grand chancellor, he succeeded in subjecting to his sway the provinces that had revolted on account of Vashti's execution.

THE EDICT OF THE KING

The edict issued against the Jews was revoked by Ahasuerus in the following terms:

"King Ahasuerus sends this letter to all the inhabitants of water and earth, to all the rulers of districts, and to generals of the army, who dwell in every country; may your peace be great! I write this to you to inform you, that although I rule over many nations, over the inhabitants of land and sea, yet I am not proud of my power, but will rather walk in lowliness and meekness of spirit all my days, in order to provide for you great peace. Unto all who dwell under my dominion, unto all who seek to carry on business on land or on sea, unto all who desire to export goods from one nation to the other, from one people to the other unto them all, I am the same, from one end of the earth to the other, and none may seek to cause excitement on land or on sea, or enmities between one nation and another, between one people and another. I write this, because in spite of our sincerity and honesty with which we love all the nations, revere all the rulers, and do good to all the potentates, there are nevertheless people who were near to the king, and into whose hand the government was entrusted, who by their intrigues and falsehoods misled the king, and wrote letters which are not right before heaven, which are evil before men, and harmful for the empire. This was the petition they requested from the king: that righteous men should be killed, and most innocent blood be shed, of those who have not done any evil, nor were guilty of death such righteous people as Esther, celebrated for all virtues, and Mordecai, wise in every branch of wisdom, there is no blemish to be found in them nor in their nation. I thought that I was requested concerning another nation, and did not know it was concerning the Jews, who were called the Children of the Lord of All, who created heaven and earth, and who led them and their fathers through great and mighty empires. And now as he, Haman, the son of Hammedatha, from Judea, a descendant of Amalek, who came to us and enjoyed much kindness, praise, and dignity from us, whom we made great, and called 'father of the king,' and seated him at the right of the king, did not know how to appreciate the dignity, and how to conduct the affairs of state, but harbored thoughts to kill the king and take away his kingdom, therefore we ordered the son of Hammedatha to be hanged, and all that he desired we have brought upon his head; and the Creator of heaven and earth brought his machinations upon his head."

As a memorial of the wonderful deliverance from the hands of Haman, the Jews of Shushan celebrated the day their arch-enemy had appointed for their extermination, and their example was followed by the Jews of the other cities of the Persian empire, and by those of other countries. Yet the sages, when besought by Esther, refused at first to make it a festival for all times, lest the hatred of the heathen be excited against the Jews. They yielded only after Esther had pointed out to them that the events on which the holiday was based, were perpetuated in the annals of the kings of Persia and Media, and thus the outside world would not be able to misinterpret the joy of the Jews.

Esther addressed another petition to the sages. She begged that the book containing her history should be incorporated in the Holy Scriptures. Because they shrank from adding anything to the triple Canon, consisting of the Torah, the Prophets, and the Hagiographa, they again refused, and again they had to yield to Esther's argument. She quoted the words from Exodus, "Write this for a memorial in a book," spoken by Moses to Joshua, after the battle of Rephidim with the Amalekites. They saw that it was the will of God to immortalize the warfare waged with the Amalekite Haman. Nor is the Book of Esther an ordinary history. Without aid of the holy spirit, it could not have been composed, and therefore its canonization resolved upon "below" was endorsed "above." And as the Book of Esther became an integral and indestructible part of the Holy Scriptures, so the Feast of Purim will be celebrated forever, now and in the future world, and Esther herself by her pious deeds acquired a good name both in this world and in the world to come.